D1733166

SPINAL
Rehabilitation

Edited By
David E. Stude, MS, DC, DACBSP, DACBN, CNN, CSCS
Associate Professor
Wolfe-Harris Center for Clinical Studies
Northwestern College of Chiropractic
Bloomington, Minnesota

APPLETON & LANGE
Stamford, Connecticut

Notice: The authors and the publisher of this volume have taken care to make certain that the doses of drugs and schedules of treatment are correct and compatible with the standards generally accepted at the time of publication. Nevertheless, as new information becomes available, changes in treatment and in the use of drugs become necessary. The reader is advised to carefully consult the instruction and information material included in the package insert of each drug or therapeutic agent before administration. This advice is especially important when using, administering, or recommending new or infrequently used drugs. The authors and publisher disclaim all responsibility for any liability, loss, injury, or damage incurred as a consequence, directly or indirectly, of the use and application of any of the contents of this volume.

www.appletonlange.com

99 00 01 02 / 10 9 8 7 6 5 4 3 2 1

Prentice Hall International (UK) Limited, *London*
Prentice Hall of Australia Pty. Limited, *Sydney*
Prentice Hall Canada, Inc., *Toronto*
Prentice Hall Hispanoamericana, S.A., *Mexico*
Prentice Hall of India Private Limited, *New Delhi*
Prentice Hall of Japan, Inc., *Tokyo*
Simon & Schuster Asia Pte. Ltd., *Singapore*
Editora Prentice Hall do Brasil Ltda., *Rio de Janeiro*
Prentice Hall, *Upper Saddle River, New Jersey*

Library of Congress Cataloging-in-Publication Data
Spinal rehabilitation / edited by David E. Stude.
p. cm
Includes bibliographical references and index.
ISBN 0-8385-3685-9 (case : alk. paper)
1. Spine—Wounds and injuries—Exercise therapy—Handbooks, manuals, etc. 2. Spine—Abnormalities—Exercise therapy—Handbooks, manuals, etc. 3. Backache—Exercise therapy—Handbooks, manuals, etc. 4. Backache—Patients—Rehabilitation—Handbooks, manuals, etc. I. Stude, David E.
RD768.S6537 1999
617.5′6062—dc21 99-17146
CIP

Production Editor: Mary Ellen McCourt
Production Service: Andover Publishing Services
Interior Design: Rohani Design
Cover Designer: Janice Bielawa

ISBN 0-8385-3685-9

PRINTED IN THE UNITED STATES OF AMERICA

Contents

Contributors

Paul Allard, PhD, P.Eng
Director, Laboratoire D'Etude Mouvement
Research Center
Sainte-Justine Hospital
Montréal, Canada

Gunnar Andersson, MD, PhD
Chairman, Department of Orthopedics
Rush University Medical School
Chicago, Illinois

Suzan F. Ayers, MS
Exercise Physiologist
Director, Spinal Rehabilitation Certification Program
University of Florida
Gainesville, Florida

Douglas Barenburg, DC, CredMDT
Private Practice
Santa Monica, California

Thomas F. Bergmann, DC, FICC
Professor, Chiropractic Department
Faculty Clinician, Center for Clinical Studies
Northwestern College of Chiropractic
Bloomington, Minnesota

Jennifer E. Bolton, PhD
Senior Lecturer and Course Leader
Anglo-European College of Chiropractic
Bournemouth, England

James M. Cox, DC, DACBR
Director, Low Back Pain Clinic
Fort Wayne, Indiana
Postgraduate Faculty
National College of Chiropractic
Lombard, Illinois

Morris Duhaime, MD
Orthopaedic Surgery
Sainte-Justine Hospital
Chief, Orthopaedic Surgery
Shriner's Hospital
Montréal, Canada

Mark S. Edinger, DC
Yeomans Chiropractic Center
Ripon, Wisconsin

David Elton, DC
Director of Quality Management
American Chiropractic Network
Minnetonka, Minnesota

Jon D. Fagerness, DC, NREMT
Clinic Director
Spine and Sport Chiropractic Care Center
Cambridge, Minnesota

Nader Farahpour, MSC
Laboratoire D'Etude Mouvement
Research Center
Sainte-Justine Hospital
Montréal, Canada

Natalie I. Gluck, DC
Private Practice
Los Angeles, California
Postgraduate Lecturer
Los Angeles College of Chiropractic
Whittier, California

Jeff Gullickson, DC
Director, Sports and Industrial Rehabilitation Center
Edina, Minnesota

Steven Heffner, DC, DipMDT
Laurel Wellness Center
Blossburg, Pennsylvania

Steven M. Heifetz, MD
Staff Cardiologist
University of Minnesota Hospitals
Minnesota Heart Clinic
Minneapolis, Minnesota

Richard A. Hills, PT, DC
Director
Northwestern Sports and Spine Rehabilitation
Northwestern College of Chiropractic
Bloomington, Minnesota

Bruce Hoffmann, DC
Director, Sports and Industrial Rehabilitation Center
Apple Valley, Minnesota

Ann P. Hooke, MA
Independent Consultant for Senior Exercise
St. Paul, Minnesota

Gary Jacob, DC, Lac, DipMDT
Private Practice
Los Angeles, California

Andrew S. Klein, MS, DC, DACBSP
Practicing Clinician
Park Nicollet Health System Minnesota
Instructor
Northwestern College of Chiropractic
Bloomington, Minnesota

Hubert Labelle, MD
Chief, Orthopaedic Surgery
Sainte-Justine Hospital
Montréal, Canada

P. Michael Leahy, DC, CCSP
ART® Developer
Colorado Springs, Colorado

Craig S. Liebenson, DC
Private Practice
Los Angeles, California
Postgraduate Faculty
Los Angeles College of Chiropractic
Whittier, California

K. Lee Lundgren, ATC, CSCS
Rehabilitation Associate
Palmer Chiropractic Clinics
Davenport, Iowa

J. Clay McDonald, DC, DACRB, MBA, CSCS
Dean, Palmer Chiropractic Clinics
Davenport, Iowa

Cathy Maloney-Hills, PT
Physical Therapist
Courage Center
Golden Valley, Minnesota

Robert Medcalf, PT, DipMDT
Private Practice
Los Angeles, California

Timothy J. Mick, DC, DACBR
Associate Professor and Chair, Department of Radiology
Director, Radiological Consultation Service
Northwestern College of Chiropractic
Consulting Radiologist, St. Paul, Minnesota
Bloomington, Minnesota

Donald R. Murphy, DC
Director, Rhode Island Spine Center
Providence, Rhode Island

Michael J. Nehring, DC
Private Practice
Boulder, Colorado

Joe Pelino, DC, BSc, DACBSP
Credentialed ART® Instructor
Faculty of Physical Education and Health
University of Toronto
Toronto, Ontario, Canada

Michael L. Pollock, PhD†
Director, Center for Exercise Science
University of Florida
Gainesville, Florida

Michael Reed, DC, EMT, DACBSP
Coordinator, Sports Medicine Program
Post-Graduate Department
Los Angeles College of Chiropractic
Los Angeles, California

Charles-Hilaire Rivard, MD
Orthopaedic Surgery
Sainte-Justine Hospital
Montréal, Canada

Mary Sanders, MS
Exercise Physiologist
Speedo Corporation Associate
Reno, Nevada

Daryl Schapmire, MS
Exercise Physiologist
Director, Midwest Industrial Rehabilitation
Decatur, Illinois

Clayton D. Skaggs, DC
Director, Clayton Physical Medicine
St. Louis, Missouri
Instructor, Logan College of Chiropractic
Chesterfield, Missouri
Postgraduate Faculty
Los Angeles College of Chiropractic
Whittier, California

Pamela Snyder, PT
Private Practice
Eden Prairie, Minnesota

Suzan Starler, DC, CredMDT
Private Practice
Malibu, California

David E. Stude, MS, DC, DACBSP, DACBN, CCN, CSCS
Associate Professor
Wolfe-Harris Center for Clinical Studies
Northwestern College of Chiropractic
Bloomington, Minnesota

Steven G. Yeomans, DC, FACO
Director, Yeomans Chiropractic Center
Ripon, Wisconsin

†Deceased.

Foreword

It is a great pleasure to write a foreword for this very forward thinking book. It is unique in that it blends the two major physical approaches to spinal care—manual therapy and active exercise. For too long the respective disciplines represented in this book have focused on either one or the other of these approaches. Emerging evidence, however, points to the need for both. Certainly passive care offers a significant opportunity for pain relief, but it really cannot be assumed to change tissue structure very much when used alone. Active care in the form of progressive resistance exercises is the only maneuver short of surgery that can significantly influence tissue structure and function in the long run. Look at the rehabilitation program used for any injury to a professional athlete, and it is clear that both methods are used.

It is also very healthy to see this book emerging from a chiropractic perspective. Although many disciplines are represented among the chapters' authors, the major influence throughout this book is chiropractic. The breadth of the various chapters written by doctors of chiropractic clearly demonstrates the ongoing integation of chiropractic into comprehensive medical care.

It is clear that incorporating exercise with manual care allows measurement of function. To what degree the improving function is enhanced by manual methods versus active exercise is not that significant from the patient, employer, or funding agency standpoint, but certainly valuable from the clinician's viewpoint. If successful rehabilitation can be accomplished in a timely manner, with diminished likelihood for recurrence, all the interested parties will certainly be satisfied.

It is important that sections of this book are focused on motivation. Passive care requires minimal motivation for success. Patients always like to have things done to them, which makes them feel better. Active exercise, however, requires energy, time, and motivation. The patient not only has to want to feel better, but also must be motivated to take the necessary steps to get better.

Considerable discussion in this book is focused on methods to carry out the exercise programs, including choices between high-tech and low-tech, complex and simple, and low cost and expensive. The relative benefits of each are contrasted. The authors of each section naturally favor that which has worked in their experience. There is a place for all levels of complexity, with obvious tradeoffs related to costs and benefits.

As health care policy becomes progressively oriented towards rationing, definable evidence of effectiveness will become more highly prized. Treatment programs that offer only brief benefit and no opportunity to change the natural history of the problem will be less likely to be funded. Spinal problems are one of the major sources of medical costs. Efforts to control the costs of this seldom life-threatening ailment are already evident in the minimal amount of chiropractic and physical therapy care available from many HMOs. Treatment programs for soft tissue disorders that can document effectiveness in the least amount of time and with reduced recurrence will be the ones that will most likely be supported. The blend of skills in this book offers that opportunity. It is the way of the future. It is forward thinking at its best.

Vert Mooney, MD

Preface

The primary objective of *Spinal Rehabilitation* is to serve as a resource manual that addresses the role that active exercise plays in reducing the likelihood of spinal injury, in maintaining or enhancing spinal health, and in the outpatient rehabilitation of individuals with spinal dysfunction. All health care professionals who use an "active component" to manage spinal dysfunction—including doctors of chiropractic, doctors of medicine, doctors of osteopathy, physical therapists, occupational therapists, exercise physiologists, physical therapy assistants, and athletic trainers—will find this an invaluable reference resource.

The use of exercise to treat spinal dysfunction has recently gained popularity, sparked by research studies that suggest the effectiveness and relative low risk of exercise in the successful treatment of back pain patients. Because the etiology of low back pain is multi-factorial, however, the health care professional must be careful to avoid the "gold standard" approach to evaluating and treating patients who present with spinal dysfunction. This book presents the reader with principles that can be applied to a variety of patient presentations and which, it is hoped, increase the likelihood for successful treatment outcomes.

The authors of this work reflect an approach to merging selected information that will provide the reader with the best from experts of many disciplines. Well documented, literature-based support, combined with suggestions for practical application, makes this informative reading for a wide audience.

The text is organized into five sections. The first section provides background material that is essential for those involved in the day-to-day operation of a rehabilitation facility. Being prepared for an emergency, introducing principles for measuring treatment effectiveness, patient education recommendations and current research support for active exercise in managing spinal dysfunction are examples for those chapters included in this first section.

The second section is dedicated to presenting the reader with recommendations for evaluating an individual's candidacy for active exercise. It presents the reader with a fresh approach for the examination procedure. Rather than re-reviewing "standard" orthopedic tests and spinal range of motion protocols, essential principles in assessing patients with back pain are presented, from a structural, radiological approach, to a functional and psycho-social perspective. This well-rounded and comprehensive coverage of evaluation protocols prepares health care professionals to confront a wide spectrum of clinical presentations.

In this era of technological, computer-aided advancements, there has been an explosion of interest in the use of specialized instruments in assessing and rehabilitating patients with back pain and dysfunction. The third section presents four primary methods of objectively assessing spinal function: triaxial isoinertial dynamometry, isometric dynamometry, three-dimensional spinal kinematics using video motion monitors, and isokinetic dynamometry. Although there is no current "gold standard" for this kind of testing, research does suggest that there may be advantages when such tests are used to assist the clinician in the evaluation process. In addition to covering actual testing procedures, the authors discuss the advantages and disadvantages of each form of testing so that the reader can be in a better position to make a decision regarding which protocol would serve their needs best, either in terms of equipment purchase or in terms of patient referral requirements. Equipment reliability and validity, an essential topic in terms of data interpretation, is also covered.

A fourth section deals with manual therapy. It has been included since there are many health care providers that utilize manual therapy as a primary intervention when caring for patients with spinal pain and dysfunction. Also, many include manual therapy in their definition of rehabilitation. A recent Agency for Health Care Policy and Research (AHCPR) publication on the effectiveness of manual therapy in addressing acute back pain further supported our decision to include this section, even though an exhaustive presentation of this material is available elsewhere.

The fifth section is devoted to the principles of exercise methodology. There is not one book on the market that covers every possible exercise maneuver, since this is only limited by the imagination, and so this text does not attempt to compete with others in this fashion. The main objective of this section is to address the principles of exercise progression so that appropriate exercises can be designed on an individualized basis. Land- and water-based exercises are presented, as well as special recommendations for introducing exercise programs for the older adult.

Specifically, "low-tech" spinal stabilization principles are outlined, with photographs used to walk the reader through exercise progressions.

In this era of health care reform, health care providers are being monitored for therapeutic outcomes. In some states, legislative mandates have made the use of an "active component" a requirement for individuals involved in treating a work-related injury. In other states, databases are being used to exclude providers from participating contractually, if treatment "success" cannot be documented. In the end, we all have the professional obligation to provide patients with high-quality, cost-effective, and successful treatment intervention, which ultimately leads to increased patient self-sufficiency. This book is intended to serve as a guide for coming closer to achieving that objective. It is likely that if we as a society become more committed to appropriate, safe, and consistent exercise habits, we can refer to the back pain epidemic as a thing of the past.

David E. Stude, DC

Acknowledgments

First of all, this book is dedicated to my family.

- A special loving tribute to my wife, Mary Ann Stude, not only for supporting me with the added responsibility of this immense project, but for her willingness to expertly serve as the coordinator for the editorial portion of the textbook project.
- To my daughter Teryn Marie and my son Matthew David, for their love, laughter, and support, and for reminding me not to take things too seriously.
- To my parents, Edward Andrew and Dolores Jean Stude and Robert and Lorraine Stock, for their support and encouragement.
- Finally, and most importantly, to my Lord for the gifts and talents and love and direction needed to bring me to this stage in my life. Thank you.

The persistent dedication of many people from around the world is respectfully acknowledged for this manuscript, and specifically for the comprehensive and three-dimensional nature of the finished product. Only with numerous experts willing to contribute specialized information would this have been possible in the first place. The quality of this book is truly a reflection of the authors who dedicated their time and expertise to capturing current but timeless principles for each chapter presented, and to the editorial review board who painstakingly reviewed each chapter, sometimes many times, to make suggestions for positive change.

Arne Krogsveen and Emil Bainhardt were responsible for much of the artwork and photographs contained in the Exercise Methodology Section, specifically, the chapters addressing Spinal Stabilization and Aquatic Rehabilitation. Mr. Krogsveen runs the Audio-Visual department at Northwestern College of Chiropractic and Mr. Bainhardt is a Physical Therapist with a professional photography background. This is the first time some of these principles have been captured on film, especially spinal stabilization principles in an aquatic environment.

The administration, faculty, and staff at Northwestern College of Chiropractic are acknowledged for assisting and supporting me as founder and creator of a rehabilitation division on its campus several years ago.

Linda Marshall, our original editor at Appleton & Lange, was enthusiastically and intimately involved in all of the details of this project, and there are many details! For her constant, professional assistance, and encouragement I express my deepest gratitude. Thanks to Lin for helping me keep up on NBA statistics when time was such a valuable and short commodity, and thanks to her assistant Phil Gardiner and all of the staff at Appleton & Lange. Special thanks to Niels Buessem for coordinating the process of turning over 1400 pages of loose manuscript into a well-designed and organized reference textbook.

"The reward of a thing well done is to have done it,"[1] but the excitement of a project completed leaves open the possibility of just what might be possible if we believe in our inherent ability to grow.

[1]Ralph Waldo Emerson. *The New Dictionary of Thoughts: A Cyclopedia of Quotations*. Standard Book Company; Copyright 1964.

The doctor of the future will give no medicine, but will interest his patients in the care of the human frame, in diet, and in the cause and prevention of disease.

—*Thomas Edison*

SPINAL
Rehabilitation

SECTION I

Introduction: Foundation Principles

The highest function of a specialty is to prevent what it treats.
—*Jan Jirout*, M.D.
Acta Radiologica, *1956*

Science is the pursuit above all which impresses us with the capacity of man for intellectual and moral progress and awakens the human intellect to aspiration for higher condition of humanity.
—*Joseph Henry, first secretary of the Smithsonian Institution*
Inscription on the National Museum of American History
Washington, D.C.

CHAPTER 1

The Role of Active Exercise in the Management of Musculoskeletal Spinal Dysfunction

A Review of the Literature

J. Clay McDonald, DC, DACRB, MBA, CSCS
K. Lee Lundgren, ATC, CSCS

INTRODUCTION

At present, the efficacy of exercise in the management of spinal disorders and dysfunction remains debatable. Although the literature generally supports the role of active intervention in the successful management of back dysfunction, there are many varying approaches and opinions with regard to the type, frequency, intensity, and duration of those exercises. Historically, recommendations for back pain have ranged between immobilization and inactivity to high-intensity exercise therapy. Regimes ranging from 3 to 10 days of bed rest to high-intensity exercise involving stabilization, weight training, and/or aerobic exercise have been prescribed. Currently, there is a trend in managing musculoskeletal dysfunction toward active care, involving early motion, mobilization, and exercise, which is progressive in nature. This relatively recent emphasis on activity-based management of spinal dysfunction necessitates the development of basic guidelines for clinicians employing exercise as part of a total care package based on scientific evidence in support of its use. These guidelines should include recommended modes of exercise and the best frequency, intensity, and duration of that exercise for patients with spinal pain or recovering from spinal injury, and should be approached from a functional aspect that includes activities that parallel activities of daily living.

The term *exercise* is extremely general and may encompass a variety of modes or techniques. The modes of exercise most commonly used or prescribed include passive range of motion (PROM) exercises, active-assistive range of motion (AAROM) exercises, active range of motion (AROM) exercises, stretching or flexibility exercises, proprioceptive and kinesthetic awareness development activities, isometric exercises, progressive resistance exercises (isotonic, isokinetic, and isoinertial), and aerobic or cardiovascular exercises. Because of the wide range of exercises used by health care providers, it is difficult to study the efficacy of all exercise, in a general sense, with regard to spinal management. Most of the research literature is specific not only to a single mode of exercise, but also to individual injuries, disorders, or dysfunctions of the spine. Many times, the exercise programs outlined in the literature were vague with regard to all parameters of the regime. In reviewing the literature, the authors found it necessary to extrapolate pertinent information, results, and conclusions in order to generalize about the role of active care and exercise in the care and management of patients with spinal dysfunction.

This review of the literature examines the use and efficacy of exercise and rehabilitation as a proactive management technique for spinal pain and dysfunction. A MEDLINE computerized database was used to search for relevant articles published from 1990 using the medical subject heading terms *active care, exercise, therapeutic exercise, spine, rehabilitation, back, musculoskeletal, mechanical low back pain*. The Manga report ("A Study to Examine the Effectiveness and Cost-Effectiveness of Chiropractic Management of Low-Back Pain"),[31] the Rand study ("The Appropriateness of Spinal Manipulation for Low-Back Pain"),[46] the Quebec study ("Scientific Monograph of the Quebec Task Force on Whiplash-Associated Disorders: Redefining "Whiplash" and Its Management"),[8] and the United States Department of Health and Human Services Clinical Practice Guidelines: *Acute Low Back Problems in Adults*[52] were reviewed and the bibliographies of those documents were drawn upon, since those documents are current and comprehensive regarding pertinent literature published prior to 1990.

Articles included in the review were selected because they contained data supporting, refuting, or incorporating the efficacy of exercise in the prevention or management of spinal disorders. Priority was given to those articles published in peer-reviewed journals, and case reports were excluded. As shown in Table 1–1, the literature is most prolific with respect to exercise and low back pain and dysfunction. There is a relative dearth of research on the efficacy and outcomes of exercise in treating the cervical spine and other spinal disorders such as scoliosis, osteoporosis, and arthritic conditions.

SPINAL DYSFUNCTION/BACK PAIN

HIGH-INTENSITY VERSUS LOW-INTENSITY EXERCISE

High-intensity exercise, as described by Manniche et al,[33] is high-load or heavy resistance exercise incorporating a high number of repetitions of a few exercises in which the patient does not stop exercising because of pain, discomfort, or inconvenience. Low-intensity exercise can be described as relatively low loads or mild, mobility-oriented exercise, using a low number of repetitions, in which the patient is allowed to discontinue exercise in the presence of pain, discomfort, or inconvenience.

TABLE 1–1: A Summary of the Literature Reviewed and Categorized by Clinical Presentation

REGION/DISORDER	NUMBER OF ARTICLES REVIEWED
Cervical spine	4
Lumbar spine	24
Spine (in general)	4
Scoliosis	5
Osteoporosis	5
Arthritis (general)	2
Exercise-specific	9

Three trials that specifically addressed the use of high-intensity exercise in the treatment of low back dysfunction in comparison to traditional low-intensity, mobility-oriented regimes were conducted by Manniche and his colleagues.[32–34] The results of these studies supported the use of intensive exercise with no adverse effects, no differences in pain, and no difference in objective measures between groups. The high-intensity groups experienced greater success with regard to improved objective measures and reduced disability levels.

In one study, a trend favoring intensive exercise could be seen after 1 year following first-time lumbar discectomy. The program for intensive exercise included a structured training routine without allowing pain to be a limiting factor. Although there was no difference in pain or physical impairment, the patients in the high-intensity group had reduced disability index scores and higher work capacity levels on follow-ups at 26 and 52 weeks.[31]

In a comparison of three intensive rehabilitation programs for chronic low back pain, Bendix et al[4] reported that functional restoration programs are superior to shorter active rehabilitative programs. At one follow-up, the subjects who participated in an intensive multidisciplinary program of 3 weeks' duration had better outcomes for readiness to work, disability, and low back pain, as well as maintenance of activity level and decreased dependence on analgesics, than those who participated in active exercise and back school or psychological pain management with physical activity.

When necessity of including hyperextension exercise in a high-intensity rehabilitation program for postsurgical lumbar disc patients was investigated, results regarding high-intensity exercise were similar to the previous study and hyperextension exercise had no significant additional benefit. It should be noted that "hyperextension" in the context of this report is defined by Manniche as "active extension of the lumbar spine to the greatest extension of the hips and spine."[32] This is not traumatic, injurious hyperextension of the lumbar spine, but rather an extension performed on a raised exercise mat to a position in which the trunk is beyond parallel to the floor. "Extension" as compared to "hyperextension" was defined by the researchers as trunk extension in an arc from 90° of trunk flexion to 0° of trunk flexion. This study further concluded that high-intensity training on the order of two to three months or more duration was necessary to significantly decrease subjective reports of back pain.

In an excellent review of current literature regarding exercise and low back pain, Chapman-Smith[9] concluded that "structured exercises are not necessary or proven effective in the first six weeks" of a low back pain episode. Conversely, he indicates that intensive exercise programs promote early return to activity for chronic cases of low back pain and dysfunction. This conclusion is consistent with our findings in the current literature.

In summary, the current literature supports the use of high-intensity exercise in the treatment of low back pain and postoperative disc lesions.

EXERCISE MODE

Very few studies address specific modes of exercise separately, specifically or comparatively. Most have used exercise programs which involve multiple forms of exercise in a relatively nonspecific manner. Of the articles reviewed, five either identified specific modes of exercise or clearly outlined the specific exercises used in the rehabilitation program used in the study.

In studying the effects of physical therapy on health outcomes in patients with spinal impairments, Jette and Jette[28] found improvements in most health scales and noted that endurance exercise was associated with better outcomes and that heat and cold modalities were associated with poorer outcomes.

Pollock et al[39] studied the effect of resistance training on lumbar extension strength using the MedX lumbar extension machine. The equipment was used to determine the effect of variable resistance training on lumbar extension strength development. This study showed that there were significant gains in lumbar extensor strength when subjects trained using variable resistance through a full range of motion. The investigators emphasize the importance of full range of motion training because of the assumption that strength gains, as a result of isometric training, occur in a range which is approximately only 20° to either side of the training angle. A more recent study challenges the necessity of training the lumbar spine through a full range of motion in order to gain strength in lumbar extension through that range.[18]

A type of therapeutic exercise training that is currently being used by some in the rehabilitation of patients with low back pain is limited range of motion resistance exercise for lumbar extension. Limited extension exercise between 0° and 36° of lumbar flexion produced increases in isometric trunk strength at 72° of flexion. This implies that there is a nonspecific training response in the lumbar spine through a wide range of motion. Although the subjects were not low back pain patients, a similar training response is currently assumed to occur in low back pain patients who train through a limited range of motion.[18]

In another study, flexion and extension exercises were compared to determine which group of exercises was most effective at reducing low back pain and enhancing spinal mobility in patients with chronic low back pain.[13] Conclusions drawn from the results of this study describe reductions in severity of low back pain in both groups of patients, regardless of whether they performed flexion exercises or extension exercises. There was no significant difference in the degree of pain reduction experienced between the groups. With regard to spinal mobility, both groups displayed no significant differences in coronal and transverse mobility, while the group that followed the flexion exercise regime significantly increased sagittal mobility. Based on this study it can be concluded that using either flexion or extension exercises can be an effective method of treating chronic mechanical low back pain, leading to a possible reduction in pain severity and an increase in spinal mobility.[13]

In a study comparing active ("high-tech" and "low-tech" exercise) and passive (physical agents and joint manipulation) care in the treatment of postsurgical chronic low back pain patients, low-tech active care or low-tech exercise produced significant improvements in low back pain, produced the longest periods of relief, was most cost-effective and, clinically, may be the method of choice for management of those patients.[48] In general, active care involving either low-tech exercise or high-tech exercise produced significant increases in force output, decreases in Oswestry scores, and improvement in objective measures of mobility and function. High-tech exercise has logistical and economic limitations, whereas low-tech exercise may have compliance limitations since many low-tech regimes involve some home programs. Otherwise, there were no statistically significant differences in outcomes between the active care groups (high-tech exercise and low-tech exercise). High-tech exercise, although considered costly, was shown to be more cost-effective than the passive care treatments because of its effectiveness. There were no significant changes in mobility, range of motion, force output, spinal function, and Oswestry scores among patients assigned to the other groups (physical agents, joint manipulation, and control), all of which were classified as passive care.

Saal and Saal,[45] in their outcome study of nonoperative treatments of herniated lumbar intervertebral discs with radiculopathy, showed favorable outcomes for a majority of the subjects when those subjects underwent an aggressive, nonoperative treatment program. The program included back school, exercise training for stabilization, dynamic posture maintenance, trunk and general body strengthening, and flexibility exercises. All patients were considered surgical candidates at the time of the study. Surgical indicators included positive straight leg raise, extruded disc, neurologic weakness, failure to improve with bedrest, traction, and therapeutic exercise. One group of patients (31%) had been advised by surgeons (second opinion) that surgery was "necessary" and 26% of the patients had extruded discs diagnosed by computerized tomography (CT).

Fifty of 52 nonoperative patients had "good" or "excellent" outcomes, with a 92% total return to work rate, 90% of whom returned to their previous occupations. The results of this study indicate that disc extrusion may not necessarily be an absolute indication for surgery. Only 6 patients of 64 in the study were "nonoperative failures." Four of these "failures" required subsequent surgery and showed significant stenosis at the time of surgery, one did not complete the program, and one had progressive weakness. The study suggests that aggressive nonoperative care may be the treatment of choice for patients presenting with intervertebral disc herniations with radiculopathy, and that if a patient fails with this care, it may be indicative of stenosis and the possibility of subsequent surgery.[45]

A comparison study of group hydrotherapy and group land-based therapy for low back pain suggests that group exercise, in general, is advantageous for those with chronic low back pain. There appears to be no significant difference in outcomes between patients treated with group hydotherapy and those treated with group land-based rehabilitation exercises. Both modes of treatment can significantly improve function and reduce pain.[47]

GENERAL EXERCISE FOR PATIENTS WITH LOW BACK PAIN

Jackson and Brown[26,27] have attempted to clarify the role of exercise as a treatment modality for patients with low back pain. Exercise has been prescribed for back patients for a variety of reasons, from decreasing pain and improving function to using it as a "last resort" method of treatment. The authors conclude that, although many of the clinical methods used are unsubstantiated in the literature, exercises that improve fitness, strength, and mobility have documented benefits in general; however, there is no data at this time to support the use of exercise to improve posture, reduce mechanical stress, or improve stability of spinal segments.

There is a dearth of definitive scientific evidence to support the benefits of return to work. Extrapolating and interpreting data from many studies that investigate the biomechanics of the low back, the effects of motion on injuries to the low back, educational programs for the treatment of low back pain including back schools, psychologic overlay in patients with low back pain, and the physiology of pain modulation suggests that early return to work is beneficial to low back pain patients.[34] Evidence suggests that there should be an emphasis on the part of the treating physician on early motion and progressive increases in activity that will lead to a return to work. This will increase the probability of proper healing of tissue and decrease the incidence of psychological factors that influence the course of recovery by prolonging the condition and potentially leading to chronic pain syndromes.

LeFort and Hannah[29] studied return to work rates following a program of water-based exercise and muscle strengthening in patients with low back injury. The program incorporated flexibility, aerobic conditioning, muscular strength, and endurance training. Subjects were grouped into return to work and non–return to work groups. Both groups showed an overall improvement in fitness at 8 weeks. Interestingly, patients in the return to work group showed significant lessening in pain, disability, and anxiety and enhanced vigor, whereas the non–return to work group reported no change in pain and disability and the psychological variables diminished with time. First-time experiences of low back pain seemed to be the variable that was the best predictor of returning to work, and deterioration of self-esteem significantly decreased the likelihood of returning to work. This study suggests that the positive psychological benefits of exercise (decreased mental stress and anxiety, decrease in perceived helplessness, improved self-image and self-esteem and increased vigor) may be as important in improving return to work rates as the physical benefits in patients experiencing low back pain, perhaps more so in those with repeat episodes or chronicity of low back pain. Different and additional intervention techniques should be examined to target those patients with recurrent episodic low back pain or chronic low back pain.

In a review of the literature related to trunk muscle performance, Beimborn and Morrissey[5] concluded that, in general, the greatest force is produced by the trunk extensors, followed in descending order by the trunk flexors, the lateral flexors of the trunk, and the rotators of the trunk. This was determined by combining data from several studies that assessed force outputs in the trunk, measured by various means. Isokinetic force outputs were measured using an isokinetic trunk dynamometer. Isotonic strength was measured through combinations of dynamometry, one-repetition maximum lifts, spring balance, and Elgin exercise units. Isometric testing was performed with strain gauge, load-cell dynamometry, pressductor force transducers, and cable tensiometers.

Exercise that is supervised with regular follow-ups can significantly decrease sick leave and absenteeism from work in patients with low back pain. Supervision and follow-up allow for regular monitoring of home exercise programs, allow the clinician to upgrade and vary the program, and provide valuable motivation and feedback for the patient. This in turn, appears to encourage patients to adhere to a regimen of regular exercise for low back pain and dysfunction.[30]

Rainville and colleagues[42] investigated the effect of compensation involvement on patient reports of pain and disability. Patients underwent aggressive low back exercises to improve flexibility, strength, endurance, and lifting capacity. Patients who were compensated for their complaint or dysfunction were compared to those who were not involved with any compensation. Treatment recommendations were the same for both groups and compliance was not affected by compensation or the lack thereof. Although both groups improved with respect to depression and disability, the group that was compensated reported more pain, depression, and disability than the uncompensated group. This study suggests that compensation involvement in cases of low back pain and rehabilitation may have deleterious effects on self-reported pain, disability, and depression.[42]

TREATMENT OF LOW BACK INJURY IN ATHLETES

In an article reviewing common nonoperative treatment protocols for low back injury, Chilton and Nisenfeld[11] examined the usefulness of various treatment regimes for treating athletes with low back injury. The authors address bedrest, medication, physical modalities, exercise, traction, education, and manipulation and their effectiveness in the management of low back injury.

Although bedrest is the most widely recognized mode of treatment for low back pain due to its effect on pain and paravertebral muscle spasm, there is no agreement upon protocol and much evidence that prolonged bedrest may have complicating residual effects of deconditioning and reduced bone density.[20] Many medications have been shown to be effective at relieving low back pain but have known side effects. Muscle relaxants have been ineffective, and there is no conclusive evidence that trigger point injections or epidural steroid injections have reliable efficacy.[10]

Heat and cold have been shown to provide palliative relief to athletes suffering from acute low back pain, and use of these modalities in conjunction with exercise may lead to earlier restoration of function. Ultrasound, shortwave diathermy, and massage, conversely, are not supported scientifically as having any added value in the treatment of these athletes.[15]

Exercise is supported in the literature since increased activity has many positive physiologic effects on the bones, joints, and soft tissues as well as decreasing the recurrence of low back pain.[50] Education with regard to posture, standing, sitting, and lifting has been effective in the prevention of low back injury and pain and chronic pain syndrome.[36]

There is not much evidence to support the use of traction in the treatment of acute low back pain. There is, however, suggestive evidence to support the use of traction in patients with disc herniation and sciatica. Studies on manipulation of patients with spinal pain show that this form of treatment may have short-term benefits, but studies on the long-term effects are inconclusive.[10]

Another article outlines a rehabilitation program for athletes following various injuries of the spine, both lumbar and cervical. General experience with the management of spine pain was used to develop rehabilitation programs for high-level athletes. No trials of comparison were conducted to determine the efficacy of the program. Rather, the clinical experience of the authors was drawn upon to develop the exercise program outlined. The rehabilitation described incorporates exercises to increase mobility, flexibility, strength, stability, and aerobic endurance in a progressive manner to restore function to the preinjury level.[24]

OUTPATIENT VERSUS INPATIENT MANAGEMENT OF LOW BACK PAIN

In an outcome study[7] comparing the inpatient and outpatient treatment for low back pain, patients receiving inpatient care for low back pain initially had greater decreases in pain, greater increases in activity, and greater decreases in medication usage than the outpatient group, but the outpatient group had significant improvements at long-term follow-up with regard to pain level, activity level, and medication, as well as return to work percentages. The authors conclude that it is difficult to predict which patients should be placed in inpatient programs and which should be placed in outpatient programs, because universal predictions with regard to outcome cannot be made without significant prediction information assessing a multitude a variables that may bias the course of treatment and the success of that treatment for individual patients with chronic low back pain.

Chase[10] outlines a specific treatment protocol that involves education, exercise, physical modalities, bracing, and manipulation. The author suggests that management plans emphasize rehabilitation and restoration of function and that patients who actively participate in the management process return more quickly to their normal activity levels with minimal negative effect on their lifestyles.

THE EFFECTS OF LIFESTYLE ON LOW BACK PAIN

People in a state of relative deconditoning may be predisposed to episodes of low back pain. Aspects of low back pain include pain, depression, and dysfunction, both physical and psychological. There is significant correlation between the level of physical fitness and physical dysfunction as well as between physical fitness and depression. The component of fitness found to be the best predictor of physical dysfunction is muscular strength. Patients who display greater degrees of strength show less physical dysfunction. There are weak correlations between aerobic capacity and physical dysfunction and flexibility and physical dysfunction. Strength values have been shown to be less in individuals suffering from depression, although these patients may be less motivated to perform well on strength tasks.[34]

There is no apparent relationship between physical fitness and intensity of pain. The McQuade et al[35] study did not investigate the cause and effect relationship between physical fitness and low back pain or the efficacy of fitness training in patients with low back pain. The study did, however, suggest that the more physically fit a person is, the less likely he or she is to be limited by low back pain.

In a follow-up study on physical measurements used to indicate the risk for low back trouble, Sorensen[49] attempted to identify physical indicators that could be used to develop a prognosis for the recurrence of low back trouble. Physical measurements of girth, elasticity, flexibility, strength, and endurance were investigated. The results of the study showed that isometric endurance of low back muscles may prevent initial episodes of low back pain and that persons with hypermobility of the lumbar spine were more likely to experience low back trouble. Reduced strength of trunk muscles and reduced flexibility of the back and hamstrings predisposed the patients to recurrence of low back trouble. Other measures that were considered risk factors for low back pain, because of their statistical significance after 1 year of retrospective observations, include leg length discrepancies, tallness, and heaviness.

Addison and Schultz[1] compared the trunk strengths of patients seeking hospitalization for chronic low back pain to those of healthy subjects and to those of subjects seeking treatment through outpatient care of medical orthopedists. The results showed that the patients seeking inpatient care had 50% of the trunk strength of the healthy individuals and had apparently suffered major long-term disabilities when compared to the outpatient group.

In their study examining the lifestyles of smoking and obesity and the subsequent effects of each on the prevalence of low back pain, Deyo and Bass[12] found that the incidence of low back pain was increased in both obese and smoking populations. The risk of low back pain increased linearly with overall exposure of smoking. Smoking preceded the onset of low back pain in most subjects, which indicates that the role of smoking in the development of low back pain is greatest for young adults, and is less for those individuals over the age of 45, who may have more variables influencing the etiology of low back pain. A linear relationship also was shown between increased incidence of back pain and increased body mass. Body mass index was a very strong indicator of back pain in more obese patients. There was a stronger correlation among obese men than obese women. Obesity can alter body mechanics and place increased loads on the lumbar spine, predisposing it to abnormal stress and pain due to injury.

CERVICAL SPINE DYSFUNCTION AND PAIN

KINESTHETIC CHANGES/PROPRIOCEPTIVE REHABILITATION

Patients with chronic cervical spine pain have a significantly decreased kinesthetic awareness when compared to healthy subjects. Revel et al[43] investigated neck pain patients with regard to head repositioning accuracy initially and 10 weeks following a proprioceptive rehabilitation program for the cervical spine.

Exercise programs that incorporate eye-head coordination significantly improve head relocation accuracy and decrease pain perception, indicating that proprioception can be improved in the cervical spine through specific rehabilitation techniques that address postural learning through head-eye coordination. Decreases in reported neck pain and increases in function were found to be significantly greater in the rehabilitation group than in the control group at 10 weeks. This suggests that cervical rehabilitation programs should incorporate eye-head coupling exercises to facilitate improvements in proprioception and kinesthesia. This type of rehabilitation is increasingly appropriate in cases of chronic neck pain as well as vertigo secondary to cervical trauma.[43]

EFFECT OF TRAINING ON STRENGTH AND RANGE OF MOTION

In an original study on the effects of clinical rehabilitation on isometric strength and range of motion in the cervical spine, Highland et al[23] found that improvements in strength, range of motion, and pain perception resulted from rehabilitating the necks of patients diagnosed with herniated discs, degenerative disc disease, and cervical strain. Patients were rehabilitated using a MedX cervical extension machine. The dynamic rehabilitation program was based on 80% of isometric strength curves defined by the initial testing. After the pretest, patients underwent 8 weeks of exercise and were then tested again. The results of the test showed significant gains in strength and range of motion across groups, in general. All groups increased cervical strength, but gains in range of motion were only seen in patients with degenerative discs and cervical strain. Interestingly, of the patients studied, those who did not return to work saw only an increase in range of motion, not strength. With regard to pain perception, all patients, in general, showed significant reductions in pain. Of the subgroups studied, only those who did not return to work did not show significant decreases in pain perception. In summary, the MedX cervical extension machine provides an effective and safe means to dynamically improve strength and range of motion as well as reduce pain perception in neck pain patients suffering from disc herniations, degeneration of the discs, or cervical strain.

Because of the importance of injury prevention in the cervical spine, resistance exercise regimes have been studied to determine what frequency and volume of exercise have the greatest positive effects on cervical extension strength. Using the MedX cervical extension machine, asymptomatic subjects were grouped according to various assigned training regimes, with one group who did not train serving as a control group. Training groups were as follows: once a week with one set of dynamic exercise, once a week with one set of dynamic exercise plus one set of maximal isometric exercise at eight different angles, twice a week with one set of dynamic exercise, and twice a week with one set of dynamic exercise plus one set of maximal isometric exercise at eight different angles. The training groups underwent a 10-week program after which a posttest was given. The results showed significant improvements in all groups for cervical extension strength, the greatest of which were seen in the group that exercised both dynamically and isometrically twice a week, although these results were not statistically significant. This study showed that, with regard to frequency of training, moderate strength gains can be attained by training one time per week, although the gains do not provide a full range of motion effect. Two training sessions per week proved to be an adequate training frequency to attain full range of motion gains in strength. When investigating training volume, one set provided only moderate improvements in strength through a limited range of motion, while two sets (one dynamic, one isometric) provided an enhanced training response and statistically significant increases in strength through a full range of motion.[23]

In summary, to effect significant full-range gains in cervical extension strength, training must incorporate multiple sets of exercise per training session. Also, training must occur at least two times per week to have significant results. Future studies should examine whether increasing training frequency and volume beyond two sets, two times per week will further enhance the training response.[23]

In reviewing the Quebec Task Force's study[8] on whiplash-associated disorders and the management of these conditions, exercise, limitation of inactivity, avoidance of dependency on cervical collars, and analgesics as a "prescription of function" were determined to be effective in improving range of motion, symptomatology, and function within 72 hours of a motor vehicle collision. This "prescription of function" was also shown to be as effective as physiotherapy and mobilization techniques in the short-term outcomes, and more effective than those modalities for long-term outcomes. As a general consensus regarding a wide range of treatment modalities, those treatments that promoted activity, including mobilization and manipulation, and active exercise were beneficial in managing whiplash-associated disorders. Rest, inactivity, and cervical collars most likely prolong restoration of function and disability. Specifics regarding mode, frequency, intensity, and duration of exercise activity or other suggested care were not outlined.

OSTEOPOROSIS AND RELATED DISORDERS

KYPHOSIS AND BACK STRENGTH

Itoi and Sinaki[25] conducted a study to evaluate the effectiveness of strengthening exercises in healthy estrogen-deficient women. The study was designed to evaluate changes in postural curvature (normal spinal lordosis and kyphosis), particularly with regard to thoracic kyphosis, as a result of back strengthening exercises. Baseline and 2-year follow-up measures included back extensor strength and lateral x-rays of the thoracic and lumbar spine for measurement of thoracic kyphosis, lumbar lordosis, and sacral inclination. Previous studies have linked exercise/activity with increased back extensor strength and decreased thoracic kyphosis in estrogen-deficient women.

At the follow-up examination, both the control and exercise groups had increased back extensor strength significantly from the initial exam, with a statistically significant improvement of the exercise group over the control group. It should be noted that those in the control group were allowed to maintain their level of activity over 2 years, although they were given no formal prescription for exercise. In general, individual improvements in back extensor strength (subjects from either group) were more indicative of the amount of exercise that was performed regularly by individual subjects.

Follow-up radiographs showed no significant changes with the exception of decreased lumbar lordosis in the exercise group only. Results also showed that exercise had a positive effect on posture for those with increased kyphosis. Subjects who initially had what was considered normal posture remained normal. Those subjects determined to be "hyperkyphotic" initially showed a significant decrease in thoracic kyphosis when back extensor strength was increased significantly. With regard to lumbar lordosis or sacral inclination, there were no significant changes in the kyphotic or hyperkyphotic group. This study justifies the efficacy of prescribed back extensor strengthening exercise for patients with hyperkyphotic posture.

BONE MASS, EXERCISE, OSTEOPOROSIS, AND POSTMENOPAUSAL WOMEN

In a study[22] to determine the effect of high-intensity trunk exercise on bone mineral density, postmenopausal women were divided into exercise and control groups. Strength tests and bone mineral density tests were conducted at baseline, 6 months, and 12 months. As with other studies, the control group maintained their normal daily activities while the exercise group was given progressive resistance exercises for the trunk. These exercises were performed three to four times per week in addition to normal daily activities. Exercises included sit-ups, double leg raises, and prone trunk extensions. Three sets of 10 repetitions were performed at 70% of the baseline maximal strength test, and resistance was increased by 2% to 5% each month.

The results of the study showed significant increases in overall trunk strength of the exercise group over a 1-year period. There were very few changes seen over the 12 months for the control group. As for bone mineral density at the lumbar spine and hip, there were no significant changes in either the exercise group or the control group over the 1-year study period.[22] Other studies have shown positive effects of exercise on bone mineral density. However, these other studies incorporated aerobic, weight-bearing exercise, suggesting that mode, as well as frequency, intensity, and duration of exercise, may be a significant factor in increasing bone mineral density.

The importance of aerobic exercise is recognized for the maintenance or improvement of bone mineral density in postmenopausal women. However, the intensity of the exercise also appears to be a significant factor. When subjects exercised above their anaerobic threshold three times per week for 30 minutes at a time for 7 months (high intensity), there was a statistically significant increase in bone mineral density when compared to controls. Moderate-intensity aerobic exercise (exercise below the anaerobic threshold) does not appear to cause statistically significant increases in bone mineral density, although moderate-intensity exercise effects less bone mineral density loss than no exercise at all. Evidence suggests that the optimal training intensity for maintaining bone mineral density in postmenopausal women is that which is above the anaerobic threshold.[22]

It should also be noted that in the Hatori et al 1993 study, urinary output of calcium was significantly decreased in both the high-intensity and moderate-intensity groups as compared to the control group. This study showed that in order to effect an increase in bone mineral density through exercise, the exercise must be performed at an intensity above the anaerobic threshold. Other studies have had similar results showing bone mineral density increases when aerobic exercise was performed at 70% to 90% of maximum oxygen uptake (VO_2max) or 80% of maximum heart rate. There are significant data to support the prescription of high-intensity aerobic exercise to postmenopausal women to maintain or increase bone mineral density.[22]

In a 4-year follow-up study[21] on a rehabilitation program for osteoporosis, encouraging, although not statistically significant, results were reported for improvement of fitness (VO_2max) on increasing bone mineral density and decreasing the incidence of fractures. Patients in the program received educational seminars, participated in social activities, and exercised aerobically for 30 minutes, as well as undergoing a strengthening regime for 20 minutes twice a week. Patients were encouraged to join and continue with supervised exercise classes. However, after an initial 2-month period, some patients carried out the exercise program at home. Results of the study were inconclusive because the analysis of data showed no statistically significant improvement in bone mineral density over a 4-year period. It should be noted that patients reported significant benefit from the exercise program because of decreased back pain, ability to perform more vigorous activity without pain, and improvement in confidence and morale.

EXERCISE AND SCOLIOSIS

Focarile et al[16] extrapolated data from 24 articles to be used for the planning of care and for planning future research regarding nonsurgical treatments for idiopathic scoliosis. Early treatment of scoliosis is strongly favored and outcomes are significantly better in patients with a Cobb angle less than 30° when compared to patients with Cobb angles equal to or greater than 30° at the onset of treatment. This finding is consistent across many studies. Treatments consist of bracing, lateral electrical surface stimulation, posture therapy, and bracing and exercise combined. There is no scientific literature available that describes the effects of exercise alone on idiopathic scoliosis. There is significant variance in outcomes, regardless of the therapy used. Thirty percent of patients, from pooled data, had an impairment at the end of the treatment. There appears to be a clear need for randomized controlled trials comparing the efficacy of specific treatments, including exercise, because of the high incidence of exercise prescription as a part of scoliosis management.

The Scroth Method of scoliosis management was evaluated to assess the effectiveness of this specific exercise regime on vital capacity and rib mobility in patients with idiopathic scoliosis.[54] The Scroth method of treatment is an in patient program in which patients exercised 6 to 8 hours per day to improve or correct scoliotic posture and breathing patterns. Trunk exercises are performed in conjunction with sensorimotor feedback mechanisms such as using a mirror to control proprioceptive and exteroceptive stimulation. This facilitates individual learning of postural correction and breathing pattern correction. At the end of the program the patient is able to maintain the corrected posture and corrected breathing pattern without the aid of mirrors, therapists, or external feedback mechanisms. This 4-year study showed an increase in vital capacity of approximately 11% for patients receiving repeat (not first-time) treatment, which is in accordance with other similar studies. As for patients who were being treated for the first time, increases in vital capacity were nearly double, about 19%.[54]

Patients participating in the inpatient Scroth method rehabilitation have had superior results in increasing vital capacity, an increase which lasts far beyond the course of treatment. In comparison, several weeks of physical conditioning effect increases in cardiopulmonary performance which are relatively short-lived. Increases in overall vital capacity are not shown to be present after several weeks of general physical conditioning. With regard to chest expansion, increases were found in almost every case, with a large number of cases increasing chest expansion by over 30% of baseline values. Although no direct correlation can be drawn between chest expansion and vital capacity, chest expansion is indicative of an improvement in rib mobility, which was noted even in patients with a rigid thorax.[54]

El-sayyad and Conine[14] investigated the effect of exercise, bracing, and electrical stimulation on idiopathic scoliosis. Thirty children with progressive idiopathic scoliosis were randomly assigned to 3 months of exercise only, exercise with bracing, or exercise with electrical surface stimulation. The results of this study showed significant decreases in the scoliotic curve (Cobb angle) of about 3% to 4% in all groups after 3 months. The bracing group had the greatest improvement, although it was not found to be significantly better than the other two treatments studied (exercise only and exercise with electrical surface stimulation). This study was limited by its small sample size and short duration. Future long-term studies with larger groups may more effectively demonstrate variability of outcomes between groups.

EXERCISE FOR ARTHRITIC CONDITIONS

A review of available data on osteoarthritis, rheumatoid arthritis, and ankylosing spondylitis examined the efficacy of therapeutic exercise in the treatment of these conditions. The data showed that, although exercise involving range of motion, aerobic conditioning, and strengthening is safe for patients with osteoarthritis, the therapeutic value cannot be determined. There appears to be no direct link between exercise and improvement of overall function, despite improved endurance for activity, improved cardiorespiratory fitness, and reduction in pain.[53]

There is more heartening evidence in support of strengthening and aerobic conditioning in the management of rheumatoid arthritis. Data indicate that improvements in cardiovascular conditioning and increases in muscle strength do improve physical function in these patients. However, it is postulated that the significant increases in conditioning, strength, and function may be due to higher degrees of deconditioning of these patients prior to beginning an exercise program.

With regard to ankylosing spondylitis, studies show that intense physical activity has significant short-term benefits derived through improvements in spinal and hip mobility. Improvements in cardiorespiratory function appear to be a direct result of conditioning responses to exercise rather than increases in thoracic cage mobility. In summary, it is recommended that exercise play an active role in the overall treatment of arthritic conditions because it is safe and may improve function. Exercise, however, should be individually tailored for each patient.[53]

Russell et al[44] studied the effect of exercise on ankylosing spondylitis specifically. This study differs from previous studies in that it evaluated the effects of physiotherapy on lumbar spine mobility solely, rather than combined mobility of the lumbar spine and the hip. Short- and long-term effects were examined separately. Patients were divided into exercise (formal exercise, 1.5 hours per session, one time per week) and nonexercise (no formal exercise session) groups. The exercise group was further subdivided into a moderate exercise group and a rigorous exercise group. Patients in both exercise groups were evaluated each week for 4 to 5 weeks to rule out individual weekly fluctuations in mobility. An average of these measures was used to determine maximum values for flexion, extension, and lateral bending.

Overall, a wide variability in the change of range of motion resulted over time between all patients, with no significant reduction in mobility over the 2 to 3 month interval. A significant loss of flexion and lateral bending was noted after 5 to 6 months in the vigorous exercise group only. When all groups were combined, a significant loss was seen in flexion and lateral bending. These findings lead to the conclusion that extension deteriorates less rapidly than flexion and lateral bending, whether the patients exercise vigorously, moderately, or not at all.[44]

Exercise is often painful and requires a degree of effort for patients with ankylosing spondylitis. Because of this, compliance rates are about 50% within the first 6 months of the exercise program. Self-help groups have been suggested to help patients maintain healthy behaviors, including exercise over an extended period of time.[3] Self-help groups, in general, have proven effective in encouraging people to adopt various lifestyle changes.

The inclusion of psychosocial variables in the examination of patients with ankylosing spondylitis and the incorporation of self-help groups into traditional management with active regular exercise were investigated for their efficacy in the treatment of ankylosing spondylitis.[3] Patients were divided into two groups: those who were members of a self-help group while they were treated with exercise and those who were treated with exercise alone. In comparing the groups, the self-help group showed less reliance on "powerful others" for control of their health, were more satisfied with social support, saw more value in exercise, and exercised more on a weekly basis. The self-help group also was significantly more likely to seek information about the disease. Physical mobility was found to improve over 6 months, and it is thought that through exercise, deterioration of mobility can be slowed and complete immobility is not always an inevitable outcome of the disease progression.[3]

Based on the findings of this study, it may be important, if not necessary, to incorporate a psychosocial profile into the examination of patients with ankylosing spondylitis. Self-help group membership, in addition to exercise, appears to be the most effective means by which clinicians can help patients manage this painful, progressive, and debilitating condition.

SUMMARY

Virtually all patients with spinal pain or dysfunction will derive some benefit from active exercise. Active exercise of relatively high intensity is tolerated well with better outcomes, in terms of both sustained symptom relief and early return to work, than low-intensity exercise and passive care. There is no conclusive evidence indicating that any specific type or mode of exercise is superior to another, which may be a suggestion for future comparative studies.

There is significant evidence supporting the notion that exercise is the treatment of choice for patients previously considered to be strong or absolute candidates for surgery for lumbar disc herniations. Studies have shown that improvements in overall fitness, strength, flexibility, and mobility and early return to work decrease pain and disability and that lifestyle factors of deconditioning, smoking, and obesity increase the risk of suffering low back pain or dysfunction. Improvements in proprioception, kinesthetic awareness, and coordination can effectively decrease reports of pain and improve function.

Regular, high-load exercise decreases pain and improves range of motion, strength, and function in cervical spine disorders, including whiplash-associated disorders. Regular, high-intensity, weight-bearing exercise produces positive outcomes for patients with osteoporosis, especially with regard to improved vigor, morale, confidence, and decreased incidence of reported back pain.

Active exercise should be considered an integral part of the management of spinal pain and dysfunction. There is abundant and conclusive evidence to support the role of exercise for a variety of spinal complaints and conditions. Increased emphasis on restoration of function and return to work dictates that health care practitioners investigate and consider all substantiated modalities of treatment, including active exercise, to best serve their patients, themselves, and the entire population of patients who suffer from spinal pain and dysfunction.

REFERENCES

1. Addison R, Schultz A. Trunk strengths in patients seeking hospitalization for chronic low back pain. *Spine*. 1980;5(6):539–544.
2. Andersson G, Ortengren R, Nachemson A. Intradiskal pressure, intra-abdominal pressure, and myoelectric back muscle activity related to posture loading. *Clinical Orthopedics and Related Research*. 1977;129:156–164.
3. Barlow J, Macey S, Struthers G. Health locus of control, self-help and treatment adherence in relation to ankylosing spondylitis patients. *Patient Education and Counseling*. 1993;20:153–166.
4. Bendix AF, Bendix T, Lund C, Kirkbak S, Ostenfeld S. Comparison of three intensive programs for chronic low back pain patients: A prospective, randomized, observer-blinded study with one-year follow-up. *Scandinavian Journal of Rehabilitation Medicine*. 1997;29(2):81–89.
5. Biemborn D, Morrissey M. A review of the literature related to trunk muscle performance. *Spine*. 1988;13(6):655–660.
6. Bruns J, Rehder U, Dahmen GP, Behrens P, Meiss L. Morbus de Anquin or spinous engagement syndrome. *European Spine Journal*. 1994;3:265–269.
7. Cairns D, Mooney V, Crane P. Spinal pain rehabilitation: Inpatient and outpatient treatment results and development of predictors for outcome. *Spine*. 1984;9(1):91–99.
8. Cassidy JD, Spitzer WO, Skovron ML, Duranceau J, Suissa S, Zeiss E. Scientific Monograph of the Quebec Task Force on Whiplash-Associated Disorders: Redefining "whiplash" and its management. *Spine*. 1995;20(8S):1S–70S.
9. Chapman-Smith D. Exercise programs—Do they really work? *The Chiropractic Report*. 1997;11(6):1–7.
10. Chase J. Outpatient management of low back pain. *Orthopaedic Nursing*. 1992;11(1):11–21.
11. Chilton MD, Nisenfeld FG. Nonoperative treatment of low back injuries in athletes. *Clinics in Sports Medicine*. 1993;12(3):547–555.
12. Deyo RA, Bass JE. Lifestyle and low back pain: The influence of smoking and obesity. *Spine*. 1989;14(5):501–506.
13. Elnaggar IM, Nordin M, Sheikhzadeh A, Parnianpour M, Kahanovitz N. Effects of spinal flexion and extension exercises on low-back pain and spinal mobility in chronic mechanical low-back pain patients. *Spine*. 1991;16(8):967–972.
14. El-sayyad M, Conine TA. Effect of exercise, bracing and electrical surface stimulation on idiopathic scoliosis: A preliminary study. *International Journal of Rehabilitation Research*. 1994;17:70–74.
15. Fast A. Low back disorders: Conservative management. *Archives of Physical and Medical Rehabilitation*. 1988;69:880–891.
16. Focarile FA, Bonaldi A, Giarolo MA, Ferrari U, Zilioli E, Ottoviani C. Effectiveness of nonsurgical treatment for idiopathic scoliosis: Overview of available evidence. *Spine*. 1991;16(4):395–401.
17. Frank C, Akeson WH, Woo SL-Y, Amiel D, Coutts RD. Physiology and therapeutic value of passive joint motion. *Clinical Orthopaedics and Related Research*. 1984;185: 113–125.
18. Graves JE, Pollock ML, Leggett SH, Carpenter DM, Fix CK, Fulton MN. Limited range-of-motion lumbar extension strength training. *Medicine and Science in Sports and Exercise*. 1992;24(1):128–133.
19. Halpern AA, Bleck EE. Sit-up exercises: An electromyographic study. *Clinical Orthopaedics and Related Research*. 1979;145:172–178.
20. Hanson TH, Roos BO, Nachemson A. Development of osteopenia in the fourth lumbar vertebra during prolonged bedrest after operation for scoliosis. *Acta Orthop Scand*. 1975;46:621.
21. Harrison JE, Chow R, Dornan J, Goodwin S, Strauss A, Mineral Group of the University of Toronto. Evaluation of a program for rehabilitation of osteoporotic patients (PRO): 4-year follow-up. *Osteoporosis International*. 1993;3:13–17.
22. Hatori M, Hasegawa A, Adachi H, Shinozaki A, Hayashi R, Okano H, Mizunuma H, Murata K. The effects of walking at the anaerobic threshold level on vertebral bone loss in postmenopausal women. *Calcified Tissue International*. 1993;52:411–414.

23. Highland TR, Dreisinger TE, Vie LL, Russell GS. Changes in isometric strength and range of motion of the isolated cervical spine after eight weeks of clinical rehabilitation. *Spine*. 1992;17(6):S77–S82.
24. Hopkins TJ, White AA. Rehabilitation of athletes following spine surgery. *Clinics in Sports Medicine*. 1993;12(3):603–619.
25. Itoi E, Sinaki M. Effect of back-strengthening exercise on posture in healthy women 49 to 65 years of age. *Mayo Clinic Proceedings*. 1994;69:1054–1059.
26. Jackson CP, Brown MD. Analysis of current approaches and a practical guide to prescription of exercise. *Clinical Orthopaedics and Related Research*. 1983;179:46–54.
27. Jackson CP, Brown MD. Is there a role for exercise in the treatment of patients with low back pain? *Clinical Orthopaedics and Related Research*. 1983;179:39–45.
28. Jette DU, Jette AM. Physical therapy and health outcomes in patients with spinal impairments. *Physical Therapy*. 1996;76(9):930–941; discussion 942–945.
29. LeFort SM, Hannah TE. Return to work following an aquafitness and muscle strengthening program for the low back injured. *Archives of Physical Medicine and Rehabilitation*. 1994;75:1247–1255.
30. Ljunggren AE, Weber H, Kogstad O, Thom E, Kirkesola G. Effect of exercise on sick leave due to low back pain. A randomized, comparative, long-term study. *Spine*. 1997;22(14):1610–1616.
31. Manga P, Angus DE, Papadopoulos C, Swan WR. A study to examine the effectiveness and cost-effectiveness of chiropractic management of low-back pain. Ottawa, Ontario: Pran Manga & Associates, 1993.
32. Manniche C, Asmussen K, Lauitsen B, Vinterberg H, Karbo H, Abildstrup S, Fischer-Nielsen K, Krebs R, Ibsen K. Intensive dynamic back exercises with or without hyperextension in chronic back pain after surgery for lumbar disc protrusion. *Spine*. 1993;18(5):560–567.
33. Manniche C, Bentzen L, Hesselsoe G, Christensen I, Lundberg E. Clinical trial of intensive muscle training for chronic low back pain. *The Lancet*. 1988;2:1473–1476.
34. Manniche C, Skall HF, Braendholt L, Christensen BH, Christophersen L, Ellegaard B, Heilbuth A, Ingerlev M, Jorgensen O, Larsen E, Lorentzen L, Nielsen C, Nielsen H, Windelin M. Clinical trial of postoperative dynamic back exercises after first lumbar discectomy. *Spine*. 1993;18(1):92–97.
35. McQuade KJ, Turner JA, Buchner DM. Physical fitness and chronic low back pain. *Clinical Orthopaedics and Related Research*. 1988;233:198–204.
36. Morris JM, Benner G, Lucas DB. An electromyographic study of the intrinsic muscle firing patterns of the back in man. *Journal of Anatomy*. 1962;96:509–520.
37. Nachemson AL. Advances in low back pain. *Clinical Orthopaedics*.1985;200:266–279.
38. Nachemson A. Work for all for those with low back pain as well. *Clinical Orthopaedics and Related Research*. 1983;179:77–85.
39. Pollock ML, Graves JE, Bamman MM, Leggett SH, Carpenter DM, Carr C, Cirulli J, Matkozich J, Fulton M. Frequency and volume of resistance training: Effect on cervical extension strength. *Archives of Physical Medicine and Rehabilitation*. 1993;74:1080–1086.
40. Pollock ML, Leggett SH, Graves JE, Jones A, Fulton M, Cirulli J. Effect of resistance training on lumbar extension strength. *American Journal of Sports Medicine*. 1989;17(5):624–629.
41. Poulsen E. Back muscle strength and weight limits in lifting burdens. *Spine*. 1981;6(1):73–75.
42. Rainville J, Sobel JB, Hartigan C, Wright A. The effect of compensation involvement on the reporting of pain and disability by patients referred for rehabilitation of chronic low back pain. *Spine*. 1997;22(17): 2016–2024.
43. Revel M, Minguet MD, Gregory P, Vaillant J, Manuel JL. Changes in cervicocephalic kinesthesia after a proprioceptive rehabilitation program in patients with neck pain: A randomized controlled study. *Archives of Physical Medicine and Rehabilitation*. 1994;75:895–899.
44. Russell P, Unsworth A, Haslock I. The effect of exercise on ankylosing spondylitis—A preliminary study. *British Journal of Rheumatology*. 1993;32:498–506.
45. Saal JA, Saal JS. Nonoperative treatment of herniated lumbar intervertebral disc with radiculopathy: An outcome study. *Spine*. 1989;14(4):431–437.
46. Shekelle PG, Adams AH, Chassin MR, Hurwitz EL, Phillips RB, Brook RH. The appropriateness of spinal manipulation for low-back pain: Project overview and literature review. Rand Corporation, 1991.
47. Sjogren T, Long N, Storay I, Smith J. Group hydrotherapy versus land-based treatment for chronic low back pain. *Physiotherapy Research International*. 1997;2(4):212–222.
48. Smidt GL, Lin S-Y, O'Dwyer KD, Blanpied PS. The effect of high-intensity trunk exercise on bone mineral density of postmenopausal women. *Spine*. 1992;17(3):280–285.
49. Sorensen FB. Physical measurements as risk indicators for low-back trouble over a one-year period. *Spine*. 1984;9(2):106–119.

50. Spratt KF, Weinstien JN, Lehmann TR, Woody J, Sayre H. Efficacy of flexion and extension treatments incorporating braces for low-back pain patients with retrodisplacement, spondylolisthesis, or normal sagittal translation. *Spine*. 1993;18(13):1839–1849.
51. Timm KE: A randomized-control study of active and passive treatments for chronic low back pain following L5 laminectomy. *Journal of Orthopaedic and Sports Physical Therapy*. 1994;20(6):276–286.
52. U.S. Department of Health and Human Services. Acute low back problems in adults. Clinical Practice Guideline, 1994.
53. Waddell G: A new clinical model for the treatment of low back pain. *Spine*. 1987;12:634–642.
54. Weiss HR. The effect of an exercise program on vital capacity and rib mobility in patients with idiopathic scoliosis. *Spine*. 1991;16(1):88–93.
55. Weiss HR: Influence of an in-patient program on scoliotic curve. *Italian Journal of Orthopaedics & Traumatology*. 1992;18(3):395–406.
56. Ytterberg SR, Mahowald ML, Krug HE: Exercise for arthritis. *Bailliere's Clinical Rheumatology*. 1994;8(1):161–189.

CHAPTER 2

Database and Outcome Management

David Elton, DC

INTRODUCTION

In today's competitive and rapidly evolving health care environment all parties involved in the delivery of health care are accountable for their performance. Considerable resources are devoted to the development of report cards, or profiles, that compare the performance of providers and health plans. These performance data are used to make judgments regarding the quality of care and, increasingly, as a decision-making resource by purchasers of health care attempting to obtain the most quality for their health care dollar. It is this concept of value, or the relationship between the level of quality being sought and the cost of acquiring that level of quality, that is driving many of the changes currently being experienced by health care providers. Consumers want high-quality, cost-efficient health care.

Health care quality can be described in the context of the organizational structure of the provider or health plan, the clinical and administrative processes and procedures utilized, and the outcomes of care. Historically, judgments regarding and attempts to improve health care quality relied on descriptions of the ideal structure and processes to be used in the delivery of health care services. Currently, purchasers of health care who are comparing providers and health plans are relying on performance data regarding the outcomes of care as the most important indicator of health care quality.

As principles of continuous quality improvement are incorporated into health care management, structure, process, and outcomes are linked in a cycle of measurement, monitoring, and improvement. The structural and procedural elements involved in the delivery of health care services are evaluated in the context of patient outcomes. Structure and processes are modified in an effort to continuously improve the outcomes of care and to reduce the resources used to achieve the outcome.

With the growth of managed care, the ability of individual health care providers to demonstrate and continuously improve the value of their services is becoming increasingly important. Clearly, the changes in health care are being fueled by the need to control rapidly escalating costs. Fanning the flame, however, is the evolution of computer technology. More data regarding the performance of individual providers and health care organizations can be captured, stored, analyzed, and reported faster, and at a lower cost, than ever before. The degree to which health care providers embrace technology, as a means of improving both the clinical effectiveness and administrative efficiency of delivering care and documenting the care process, may determine how well they are prepared to meet the challenges encountered in the evolving health care system.

The greatest difficulty in utilizing outcome data for comparing the performance of providers or health care organizations is related to two factors. First, the lack of standardization of data, quality, and outcomes definitions and the wide variety of measurement instruments available present a barrier both when attempting to share data between and when comparing the performance of individual providers and health care organizations. Multiple sources, including government bodies, payers, providers, academic institutions, accrediting organizations, business coalitions, and managed care organizations, are involved in the development and reporting of performance measures and in making quality judgments. The absence of a common methodology for capturing, storing, and reporting data makes valid comparisons of performance difficult.

The second factor impacting outcome measurement is the presence of a variety of confounding factors that have the potential to significantly influence the outcome data of providers or health plans. Confounding factors include patient-related factors such as the severity of conditions treated, provider-related factors such as technical and interpersonal skills, organization-related factors such as human, capital, and information resources, and community-related factors such as the structure of the local health care system.

Although the standardization of performance measures can theoretically be accomplished through extensive collaboration, confounding factors can only be controlled statistically.

The goal of this chapter is to present an overview of the knowledge and skills necessary for a provider to develop and implement an outcomes assessment system. The chapter begins with definitions of outcome measurement, data, and information. The attributes of useful outcome measurement instruments will be identified and a review of outcome measurement instruments relevant to patients with spinal complaints will be presented. Issues relating to database development and the creation of an outcome measurement information system will be reviewed. The chapter concludes with a presentation of the concepts of performance, quality, and value.

Throughout the remainder of this chapter important concepts will be illustrated using data from the American Chiropractic Network's® Partners in Quality (PIQ) program. The American Chiropractic Network (ACN) provides managed chiropractic, physical therapy, and occupational therapy programs to health plans around the country. The PIQ program was developed to accomplish the following objectives, all of which are relevant to this chapter:

- Implement a large-scale multidisciplinary outcomes assessment program
- Continuously improve provider performance through periodic distribution of report cards demonstrating how provider performance compares with regional and national peers
- Develop an information system that facilitates efficient data collection, storage, analysis, and reporting
- Reduce the administrative burden associated with a managed care environment

At the time this chapter was written approximately 250 chiropractors, 50 physical therapists, and 25 occupational therapists in 3 states had seen approximately 15,000 patients through the PIQ program. A comprehensive set of clinical, administrative, and claims data from these providers and patients had been captured using standardized forms.

DEFINITION OF OUTCOME ASSESSMENT

Outcome assessment is "a procedure or method of measuring change in patient status over time, primarily to evaluate the effect of treatment."[1] Outcome data are used both as a case management tool to assess and monitor the progress of individual patients and to evaluate and compare the outcomes of groups of patients with similar clinical conditions receiving the same or different types of treatment.

Outcome measurement must be distinguished from process measurement. The outcomes of care can be thought of as the benefits of care. In contrast, the processes of care can be thought of as "what is done to, for, or by patients as part of the delivery of care, such as the performance of a test or procedure."[2] Care processes are associated with the majority of the costs of care. Thus, the benefits of care, the outcomes, are typically evaluated in the context of the costs of care, or the processes of care. By linking the outcomes of care and the processes of care, a cycle of continuous measurement, monitoring, and improvement is established.

A diagnosis, in contrast to an outcome measure, is a label that leads to the development of a treatment plan. Although the history and physical examination enable the clinician to formulate a diagnosis, outcome assessment instruments help assess the severity of the condition and establish a baseline from which progress can be measured and outcomes of care documented.[3] Procedures used for outcome assessment are not necessarily used in the formulation of a diagnostic impression. For example, for patients with a diagnosis of a lumbar disc lesion, treatment may not necessarily change the diagnosis, whereas corresponding outcome measures may demonstrate that treatment leads to a reduction in impairment and improved function. However, if treatment is designed to eliminate the diagnosis, as in the case of a patient with a hypertonic iliopsoas group, the diagnosis, as documented through objective assessment, may also be the outcome measure.

The reason we collect data regarding patient outcomes is to generate information to help answer the question "Did our treatment make a difference?" This leads to the next section in which characteristics of data and information are explored.

DATA AND INFORMATION

When one contemplates implementing an outcome measurement system, initial thoughts typically involve the question "What data should we collect?" "In order to avoid the problems that often plague data collection efforts, it is important (1) to understand the difference between data and information and (2) to think carefully about the questions that one wishes to answer with the data."[4]

Understanding the difference between data and information, although seemingly subtle, is critical to developing and implementing an effective, sustainable outcomes management system. In simple terms, "Data are facts; information is the answer to a question."[5] Data are of little use until they have been analyzed statistically or through nonstatistical methods to transform them into information that will assist decision making.[6]

When we are struck by the urge to collect data, what we really want is information, or answers to questions. Many outcome assessment and quality management programs have resulted in frustration when, after data were diligently collected for weeks or months, answers to the questions that were the catalyst for the data collection effort are not forthcoming. Time spent refining the questions to be answered will pay dividends in more efficient data collection leading to the production of information that can actually be used. Before commencing with any data collection effort it is useful to proceed through the following thought process:[7]

What question am I trying to answer?
What specific data do I need to answer the question?
How do I intend to analyze the data and communicate it to others?
What type of data collection instruments can I use to get the data?

As illustrated in Figure 2–1, as information is generated in an attempt to answer a question, new questions emerge. This fuels further data collection, and a cycle of continuous measurement and improvement is underway.

The first step in collecting useful data is the creation of a specific question to be answered. Most of the questions that lead to data collection efforts arise from two sources. First, for example, some company may wonder how its performance compares with that of an external benchmark, or a competitor. Second, intuitive questions about an important process are formulated because of detailed knowledge of the process and the associated outcomes. Strong analytical skills and strong intuitive thinking are both important to generating useful information.[8]

The second important element of asking good questions is a knowledge of data collection methodology. This leads to the topic of the next section, measurement.

MEASUREMENT

Measurement is the process of quantifying people, objects, events, or their characteristics. It is the assignment of numerals or characters to these people, objects, or events according to rules.[9] When measurements are made using valid and reliable methodology, data are produced. Data are used to generate information that answers a question.

Measurements performed without using valid and reliable methods don't produce data, but piles of numbers. Analysis of numbers lacking validity and reliability produces misinformation that leads to errors in decision making. In today's competitive health care environment, few can afford to make many incorrect decisions.

"An instrument is a clinical tool that yields a measure."[10] All outcome measurement instruments that prove to be useful share some common traits. When considering whether or not to utilize a particular instrument, you should evaluate it in the context of the following five characteristics:

- Reliability
- Validity
- Responsiveness
- Practicality
- Clinical relevance

Any statistics text will provide the interested reader with a comprehensive review of these topics. A brief overview of concepts relevant to this chapter follows.

RELIABILITY

Reliability is the ability of an instrument to give the same value consistently upon repeat measurements of the same phenomenon. It may be defined as "the degree to which a

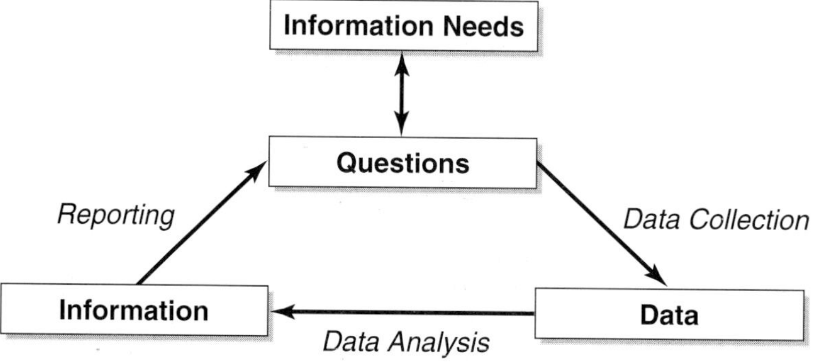

Figure 2–1. The relationship between questions, data, and information.

(Modified with permission, from Plsek, PE. Tutorial: Planning for data collection. Part 1: Asking the right question. Quality Management in Health Care. *1994;2(2):77.)*

measure is free from random error. The reliability of a measure is usually quantified in the terms of the degree to which it renders consistent or reproducible results when properly administered under similar circumstances."[11]

The reliability of outcome measurement instruments must be established in order to ensure that variation in a measurement over time reflects a true change in patient status, rather than a measurement variation.

"Reliability should not be seen as a property which a particular instrument does or does not possess; rather any measure will have a certain degree of reliability when applied to certain populations under certain conditions. The issue which must be addressed for each type of reliability is how much is good enough."[12] The type of data collected and type of reliability being evaluated will determine the statistic utilized to report the reliability of a test or instrument. Generally, the closer a reliability statistic is to +1.0, the more reliable is the test instrument. "If the reliability coefficient falls below +0.5 one should be cautious about the interpretation of the measurement results."[13]

Reliability can be thought of as consisting of two components: reliability of the measurement instrument itself and repeatability of the measurements obtained.[14] A brief description of three types of reliability follows.

Test-Retest Reliability

The stability of a measurement over time is an important aspect of all instruments used to measure the outcomes of care. Variation in repeat measurements may be due to true change in the phenomenon measured or due to an error variance in the tester or the instrument. Any change in a measurement over time must be evaluated in the context of the amount of variation experienced on repeated test administration in a stable state of the phenomenon measured.

Interrater Reliability

This type of reliability is the consistency of measurements obtained by two or more observers measuring the same phenomenon. If more than one observer will be recording outcome data, it is important that all observers use the test instrument, and interpret the results from the test, consistently.

Intrarater Reliability

The degree to which data obtained by an observer agree with the data obtained when the same observer readministers the same test at another time is the intrarater reliability. Depending on the specific measurement instrument, repeatability of measurements is more difficult to demonstrate and is influenced by both subject- and examiner-dependent factors.

"Emotional, psychologic, and personality factors inevitably play a part in the subject's response to measurement, be it self-rating questionnaires or physical performance tests. Such factors as pain tolerance, self-image, beliefs and attitudes about health and health providers, mood, and underlying motivation may all influence the participation of an individual in functional measurement."[15]

Examiner-dependent factors include such issues as equipment calibration and measurement protocol standardization. In addition, "The presence or absence of an examiner while the patient is completing various tests may influence their response."[16]

With regard to muscle performance testing, occasionally used as a type of outcome measurement, Sapega states, "The degree of attention and care that is necessary to conduct a well controlled test of muscular performance makes seemingly simple testing modalities as complex as some operative procedures. It is deceptively easy to measure something other than what one is actually attempting to measure, and it is surprisingly difficult to measure any parameter of muscular performance in a reproducible fashion. Obtaining valid and reliable results in a non-laboratory setting poses a considerable challenge to clinicians. Physicians must maintain strict quality control and consistent testing procedures if they conduct or supervise their own quantitative inhouse evaluation of muscular performance. When results of a test that have been conducted at outside therapy facilities, especially multiple tests over a period of time performed by different testers, are evaluated great caution should be exercised when clinical judgments are based on small (less than 15%) changes in performance. Outside facilities should have fully qualified staff and standardized test protocols that are available for review by physicians on request."[17]

Although this quotation was in reference to reliability issues involved in the high-tech evaluation of muscle performance, the same issues must be considered when evaluating the reliability of all outcome measurement instruments.

VALIDITY

The validity of a test is the ability of the test to accurately measure the specified function.[18] It can also be defined as "the extent to which measurements are useful for making decisions relevant to a given purpose."[19] In other words, validity can not be demonstrated solely for a device, but must be demonstrated for the specific inferential use of a measurement.[20]

As was the case with reliability, there are several types of validity.

Face Validity

This type of validity relates to the subject's acceptance of the measurement instrument. If a test does not make sense or does not relate to something the patient understands, resistance to the test may be encountered. Although face validity may be important in enhancing patient cooperation, there may be times when the purpose of a test should not be revealed in an effort to minimize any bias in the patient's response.

Construct Validity

All types of validity depend on construct validity, which is concerned with the questions "what does the score on this test mean or signify?, and what does the score tell us about the person, object, event or characteristic being measured?

Construct validity is particularly important when we are measuring concepts that cannot be examined directly but can only be inferred from behaviour."[21]

Content Validity

"Content validity raises the question: does this measure truly sample the behavior that I want to study? The scope of a given test should be proportional and comprehensive."[22]

Concurrent Validity

This form of validity is concerned with how well a measure correlates with some event or criterion occurring at the same time. Concurrent validity is often used to establish the validity of a new test by comparing performance on the test to performance on another test for which the validity is known. The establishment of concurrent validity is a preliminary step to establishing predictive validity.

Predictive Validity

This is the ability of a test or measure to predict future abilities and limitations.

Internal Validity

An outcome study is considered internally valid when the outcomes measured are accounted for by the treatment provided. Internal validity is maintained through adherence to strict controls in the research design. High internal validity is achieved when all factors that might influence the outcome are controlled except the variables under study.

External Validity

"External validity is concerned with generalization from the sample to the population; therefore, methods of sampling are crucial. The more externally valid the study, the more safely one can make predictive statements about the population on the basis of the results of the study."[23]

The high-technology assessment of muscular performance will be used to provide an illustration of the difference between the described and practical validity of a measurement instrument. Isokinetic, isodynamic, and isometric systems are described as providing valid and reliable data regarding muscle strength and endurance. Although these sophisticated systems have been shown to be intrinsically accurate in the measurement of force output, they are not necessarily valid as measures of muscle strength.

High-technology muscle performance assessment systems have been used to document improvements in patient force output in studies in which the intervention was purely psychological, without exercise participation. In one such study the author concluded, "Lumbar dynamometry should be regarded as an indicator of the level of performance at the time of testing, more as a psycho-physical test than as a valid measure of true muscle capacity. Performance (during lumbar dynamometry) was enhanced after therapy primarily because of factors other than increases in muscle strength and range of motion. These factors might be psychological or behavioral in nature."[24]

In this example, while the high-technology muscular performance assessment systems are valid as instruments capable of measuring force output, they are not necessarily valid as instruments used for measuring muscular strength and endurance.

CASE STUDY 2–1

VALIDITY/RELIABILITY

One deficiency present in the many large-scale outcome assessment programs is the reliance on claims data for obtaining the diagnosis of the patient's condition. Diagnostic data derived from the claims submitted by health care providers is notorious for being of poor quality. In ACN's PIQ program providers use a standardized format for describing the patient's clinical condition. The provider's diagnostic impression is submitted along with standardized history and examination reporting forms. The diagnostic impression and standardized history and examination findings submitted by the provider are reviewed by an ACN peer case manager who confirms the accuracy of the ICD-9 code. This step significantly improves the validity and reliability of the diagnostic data collected in the PIQ program and subsequently used when generating condition-specific outcome reports.

RESPONSIVENESS

Responsiveness is the ability of the measurement instrument to detect subtle, but clinically significant changes in patient status.[25] The responsiveness of an instrument is related to both the instrument's validity and its reliability.

Although the reliability, validity, and responsiveness of a measurement instrument are objective attributes that are demonstrated using research methodology, the last two characteristics of useful outcome measurement instruments—practicality and clinical relevance—are subjective in nature.

PRACTICALITY

Practicality is the feasibility of implementing an outcome measurement instrument and is related to issues such as cost, training requirements, patient acceptance, and time demands for providers, staff, and patients. An instrument may be valid, reliable, and responsive, but if it places a significant burden on patients, such as a long questionnaire, or is too expensive, such as a high-technology muscle performance assessment system, the instrument may not be practical to implement.

CLINICAL RELEVANCE

A useful outcome measurement instrument must in some way contribute to the case management of individual patients or contribute to the improvement of the quality of care provided to all patients. The relevance of a particular measurement instrument will vary considerably depending on the types of health conditions being treated and the ways in which the data produced by the instrument will be used.

LEVELS OF MEASUREMENT

There are four types, or levels, or measurement: nominal, ordinal, interval, and ratio. Interval and ratio measurements are occasionally combined and referred to as metric measurements. As was the case with the review of validity and reliability, any statistics text will thoroughly describe the characteristics of measurement scales. The following brief review of this topic is summarized from *The Validation of Clinical Practice* by Otto D. Payton[26] and "Pain and Disability Questionnaires in Chiropractic Rehabilitation" by Howard Vernon.[27]

The weakest level of measurement, in which data are placed into broad categories, uses a nominal scale. With a nominal scale, each person or characteristic should fit into only one of the categories and there should be a category for everyone or everything being measured. Examples of nominal data include patient handedness and gender, or questions answered with a yes-no response format. Letters, numbers, or any type of symbol could be used to represent each category. If numbers are used to indicate a category, there is no mathematical value assigned to the number. Summary statistics of nominal data are limited to frequency counts or percentage of the total sample in each category.

As with a nominal scale, with an ordinal scale data are distributed into independent, mutually exclusive and exhaustive categories. However, unlike a nominal scale, there is a qualitative relationship between categories. This means an ordinal scale is used to rank data. Although the categories of an ordinal scale indicate a greater-than, less-than relationship, there is not an objective measure of difference between adjacent categories on the scale. "On an ordinal scale, the number 2 represents a greater value than 1; however, the true intervals of such a scale are really unknown. In other words, whether 2 really represents twice as much of the value as 1, or, on a scale from 1 to 5, whether each interval really represents 25% of the total value is, at best, uncertain."[28] Examples of ordinal data include many activity of daily living (ADL) scales, questionnaires, and pain scales. As was the case with nominal data, summary statistics of ordinal data are limited to frequency counts or percentage of the total sample that falls in each category. Because the difference between adjacent categories cannot be objectively quantified, arithmetic operations such as addition, subtraction, multiplication, and division cannot be performed on data from an ordinal scale.

In interval and ratio scales, the distance between any two adjacent points on the scale is known and of equal size. These scales are used to measure characteristics such as length, height, weight, temperature, and time. The distinguishing feature separating interval and ratio scales is the presence or absence of an absolute zero point. With an interval scale, the zero point is arbitrary. An example is the measurement of temperature. With a ratio scale, there is an absolute zero point. An example is the measurement of length, in which the absence of length is recorded as zero. Numerical data from interval and ratio scales can be summarized using arithmetical procedures.

At this point, it would be easy to get discouraged. Implementing an outcome assessment program would appear to be analogous to conducting a randomized, double-blind, controlled clinical trial. Most providers are busy enough delivering care and documenting the care process that, even if they had the expertise to design a clinical trial, they simply do not have the time. However, providers are being asked to provide outcome data demonstrating the effectiveness of their treatment. Fortunately, implementing an effective outcome assessment program does not require the same level of rigor as conducting a clinical trial.

IMPROVEMENT, ACCOUNTABILITY, OR RESEARCH?

Most clinicians are trained in the scientific method and rely on research data when acquiring new knowledge regarding their discipline. This background can prove to be a barrier to the implementation of an effective outcome measurement system. Before selecting specific outcome measurement instruments and developing data collection processes, clinicians must determine why they are interested in collecting data. There are three basic purposes for implementing an outcome measurement program in a health care setting: improvement, accountability, and research.[29] Identifying the questions to be answered by an outcome measurement program and understanding the characteristics and requirements of each of the three purposes for implementing the program is important to the ultimate success of the data collection efforts. Successful outcome measurement programs are those with a methodology consistent with the intended purpose of the program.

Table 2–1 compares and contrasts measurements made for improvement, accountability, and research.

Data collection for research is slow, labor-intensive, and costly. Attempting to measure and control for all possible confounding factors results in complex data collection, analysis, and reporting. Insisting on applying rigorous research methodology to data analysis and reporting intended to fulfill improvement and/or accountability needs will at best lead to frustration, and at worst, abandoning data collection all together.

Most health care providers implement an outcome measurement program to collect and report improvement and accountability data. This necessitates a different approach to measurement than that used when measuring for research. Measuring for improvement or accountability requires a few valid and reliable measures that are relatively easy to collect. An awareness of potential confounding factors is important,

Table 2–1: Characteristics of Measurements Made for Improvement, Accountability, and Research

	IMPROVEMENT	ACCOUNTABILITY	RESEARCH
Audience (customers)	Providers and staff Administrators Quality improvement team	Patients Insurance companies Employers	Science community General public
Purpose	Understanding of processes Understanding of customers Motivation for change Evaluate changes	Comparison Basis for choice Motivation for change	New knowledge without regard for its applicability
Scope	Specific to an individual clinic or organization	Specific to an individual clinic or organization	Universal (though often limited generalizability)
Measures	Few Easy to collect Approximate	Very few Complex collection Precise and valid	Many Complex collection Very precise and valid
Confounders	Consider but rarely measure	Describe and try to measure	Measure or control
Measurers	Internal	External/internal	External
Sample size	Small	Large	Large
Collection process	Simple Minimal time, cost, and expertise Usually repeated	Complex Moderate effort and cost	Extremely complex Expensive

Modified with permission, from Solberg LI, Mosser G, McDonald S. The three faces of performance measurement: Improvement, accountability, and research. The Joint Commission Journal on Quality Improvement. *1977;23(3):141.*

but caution should be exercised to keep data analysis and reporting simple so that a continuous flow of useful information is produced in a timely manner.

RELEVANT OUTCOMES IN SPINAL REHABILITATION

Measurement instruments used for assessing the outcome of care in spinal rehabilitation have taken on a variety of forms ranging from simple numeric rating scales to sophisticated and expensive computerized muscle testing systems. The most appropriate measurement instruments for a specific provider will be determined by the patient population seen, treatment administered, and potential uses of the data collected.

Outcome measures in spinal rehabilitation can be placed into one of the four categories indicated in Table 2–2.

A description follows of examples of relevant outcome measures that fit into each of these categories.

IMPAIRMENT

Impairment is defined as "the loss of, or derangement of any body part, system or function."[30] It is seen as an adverse alteration in the physical and/or mental status of an individual resulting from anatomical, physiological, chemical, or psychiatric abnormalities.

Table 2–2: Categories of Outcome Measurement in Spinal Rehabilitation

OUTCOME MEASUREMENT	PARAMETERS
Impairment	Pain, range of motion, muscle strength
Disability	Functional status, work status
Cost	Direct, indirect
Patient satisfaction	Access, choice, communication, financial, interpersonal, outcomes, technical quality, time with provider

Impairment measures are most useful for evaluating the progress of individual patients during the course of treatment. They are of limited value as accountability measures, in which reports are generated that summarize the outcomes of groups of patients.

Many instruments used in the measurement of impairment are described as providing "objective" data. However, pain, motivation, and psychosocial factors influence the measurements produced by these instruments. Thus, the so-called "objective" measurements of range of motion and muscle performance often reflect subjective issues as much as the actual physical characteristic being measured.[31]

The following is not an all-inclusive list of all of the instruments available to measure impairment; rather, examples of different types of commonly utilized impairment measurement instruments are presented.

Pain

"In the acute stage pain is a symptom indicating that tissue damage has occurred. In the chronic state, pain may persist in the absence of detectable tissue trauma and become a disease in its own right. (In either case), it makes sense for practitioners to attempt to measure pain as a way of evaluating the success of their care."[32]

Of the dimensions of pain—severity, duration, frequency, quality, and location—severity is the dimension that is most commonly used as an outcome measure. Important design elements of pain measurement instruments have been extensively studied, and a variety of instruments have been developed to measure pain.[33] In a comparison of six methods of measuring pain it was found that the Visual Analog Scale (VAS) and the Numerical Rating Scale (NRS) were the most practical.[34] The NRS has been shown to be the more responsive than the VAS and has been recommended for use in most outcome studies.[35]

CASE STUDY 2–2

NUMERIC RATING SCALE

The standardized forms used by ACN PIQ providers include a numeric rating scale (NRS) that is completed by the patient. Patients grade the severity of their pain on a 0- to 10-point scale. Patients are asked to grade their pain at its best and at its worst during the previous week. This is used to obtain an objective measure of the patient's self-reported level of pain prior to beginning treatment. In the ACN PIQ program providers do not have patients repeat this measurement upon completion of treatment. In this capacity the NRS is used as an indicator of the severity of the patients' condition, as opposed to being used as an outcome measurement. This is consistent with its categorization as an impairment measurement. Figure 2–2 is a frequency distribution of the average NRS measurement from 6135 ACN PIQ patients.

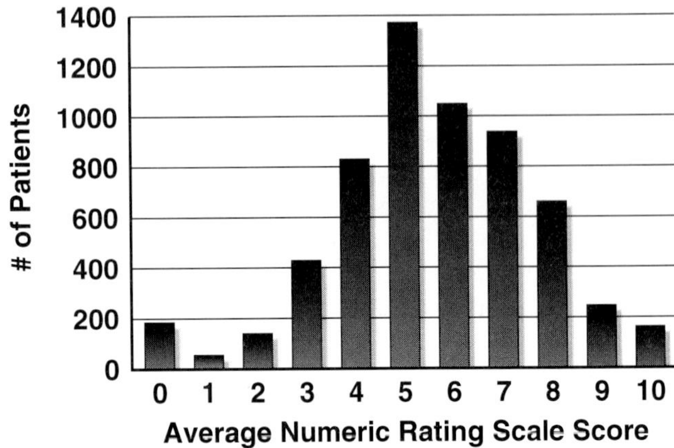

Figure 2–2. Distribution of average numeric rating scale measurements.

Range of Motion

Range of motion is routinely assessed during the examination of the patient and provides a measurement of the amount of impairment that exists in a specific plane of movement. A variety of instruments are used in the measurement of range of motion, with the two most common being goniometers and inclinometers.

As with any measurement instrument, in order to produce valid and reliable data from a range of motion assessment several examiner- and subject-dependent variables must be controlled through strict adherence to a standardized range of motion assessment protocol. These variables include equipment calibration, test instructions, patient positioning and stabilization, anatomical landmarks, learning effect, and patient warm-up, cooperation, and motivation.

The accuracy of the goniometer has been shown to be limited to a range of ± 10 to 15 degrees, while the accuracy of the inclinometer is ± 3 to 5 degrees.[36] In the case of the goniometer, in order to exceed the amount of measurement variation inherent in the instrument, range of motion would have to improve at least 15 degrees in order to indicate patient progress. The inclinometer is more responsive. With an inclinometer a 5-degree difference in range of motion indicates change.

Although the inclinometer is more responsive than a goniometer, and as a result would appear to be more useful, recall that relevance is another important characteristic of useful outcome measurement instruments. As an impairment measure, range of motion is most relevant in guiding the day-to-day case management of individual patients and is of limited value in reporting the outcomes of groups of patients. Thus, it is the provider's preference for one or the other that will determine which instrument is ideal for measuring range of motion.

Muscle Performance

With the development of various high-technology assessment instruments, the measurement of muscle performance has become popular and has been the subject of a great deal of research. Recently, these computerized measurement instruments have overshadowed traditional manual muscle testing methods in the quantification of muscle performance in the back pain patient. When viewed in the context of the characteristics of clinically useful outcome measurement instruments, neither method of measuring muscle performance is superior. The issue that prevents measurement of muscle function from assuming a more important role in outcome assessment is the fact that isolated measures of muscle function have not been shown to correlate with a patient's ability to perform functional activities.[37,38] Thus, as was the case with range of motion, the assessment of muscle performance is useful for guiding treatment, but has minimal relevance in reporting the outcomes of groups of patients.

The various computerized high-technology muscle performance measurement instruments, although intrinsically valid and reliable and capable of generating large quantities of data, suffer from additional limitations as outcome assessment instruments. In the majority of clinical settings, the cost of acquiring one of these systems simply is not practical. In those clinical settings in which patients are engaging in active treatment modalities, such as therapeutic exercise and work conditioning programs, the critical issues are applicability and clinical relevance. To what extent computerized muscle performance assessment instruments enhance treatment planning beyond simple low-tech assessment protocols remains unclear.

DISABILITY

Disability is defined as "the limiting, loss or absence of the capacity of an individual to meet personal, social or occupational demands, or to meet statutory or regulatory requirements."[39] It is an administrative finding that an individual is unable to engage in certain activities by reason of medical impairment and other nonmedical considerations. Because they provide an indication of how a patient is functioning in his or her daily activities, disability measures are referred to as functional measures.

It is the loss of functional status, or disability, that results in the greatest direct and indirect costs associated with a patient's condition. As a result, improvement in functional status is generally regarded as the most important outcome measure in the back pain patient

Functional Status

Because the task of attempting to directly observe and quantify a patient's functional abilities and limitations is nearly impossible, the measurement of a patient's functional status typically is done through the administration of a relevant questionnaire. The patient self-report of symptoms and behavior is occasionally labeled "subjective" and as a result is considered unreliable. However, pain, motivation, and psychosocial issues significantly influence data from many of the so-called "objective" measurement instruments. The important issue is reliability. Based on reliability, many functional status questionnaires are at least as reliable as so-called "objective" measurement instruments.

There are advantages to using questionnaires in the assessment of a patient's functional status. "Although a questionnaire is naturally biased by the vagaries of self-report, it offers certain advantages of assessing function. It can be a brief, practical and inexpensive way to quantify information. It may be the most consistent way of obtaining data to describe subjective features of disability. In this way, an appropriate questionnaire will help in acquiring information that is not easily obtained during the clinical interview. Using a standardized format also makes it possible simultaneously to gather information about many key activities that occur naturally in everyday life. This information can then be easily communicated among care givers and between clinician and patient as they seek to monitor progress."[40]

As with other types of outcome measurement instruments, reliability, validity, responsiveness, and practicality are critical issues in choosing and implementing a questionnaire. There are several references that provide comprehensive summaries of questionnaires relevant to the back pain patient.[41–44]

The Oswestry questionnaire[45] is an instrument widely used to obtain an objective measurement of a patient's self-reported level of disability due to low back pain. The popularity of this instrument is related to its practicality and responsiveness.

Although the Oswestry questionnaire is practical and responsive, it was originally developed for patients experiencing back pain. Most providers treating patients with spinal complaints also treat many patients with neck pain. Thus a questionnaire for patients with neck pain, with similar attributes as the Oswestry—validity, reliability, practicality, and responsiveness—was needed. The Neck Disability Index[46] (NDI) was developed in response to this need. The format of the NDI is identical to the Oswestry and, as a result, it shares many of the characteristics that have made the Oswestry popular.

The SF-12[47] was developed as a shorter, more practical version of the SF-36.[48] One strength of both instruments is that they are designed to measure the general health status of patients with any type of health condition. The SF-36 provides eight health indices and summary scales for physical and mental health. The SF-12 also measures the physical and mental health summary indices, and because of its shorter length it is more practical for most back pain patients.

The Roland Morris Scale[49] is another instrument that has been developed to measure the effect of low back pain on a patient's ability to perform daily activities. With 24 questions it is slightly longer than the Oswestry questionnaire; however, it remains a practical instrument. It has been shown to be valid, reliable, and responsive.[50]

Table 2–3: Summary of Attributes of Functional and General Health Status Questionnaires

QUESTIONNAIRE	VALIDITY/CLINICAL RELEVANCE	DESCRIPTION	PRACTICALITY (TIME TO COMPLETE)
Oswestry questionnaire	Measures disability due to low back pain	10 items—ordinal scale	<5 minutes
Neck Disability Index	Measures disability due to neck pain	10 items—ordinal scale	<5 minutes
SF-12	Measures general health status	12 items—variable format	<5 minutes
Roland Morris disability questionnaire	Measures disability due to low back pain	24 items—yes/no format	<5 minutes
Pain Disability Index	Measures effect of pain on daily activities	7 items—analog scale	<5 minutes

The Pain Disability Index[51] (PDI) was developed to measure the effect of pain on a patient's ability to perform daily activities. An advantage of the PDI is that it was designed for use with patients experiencing pain from any location.[52]

Table 2–3 contains a summary of the attributes of some of the many functional and general health status questionnaires relevant to back pain patients.

When selecting which of the valid, reliable, and responsive questionnaires to implement, the clinician should keep in mind that the important characteristics to evaluate are clinical relevance and practicality. With regard to clinical relevance, each of the NRS, NDI, and Oswestry were developed with an emphasis on a specific condition, or on a different aspect of functional status. There is no single questionnaire that is relevant for all conditions. The important issues regarding practicality are the length of the survey, ease of scoring, and whether completion of the questionnaire requires the involvement of the provider and/or the staff. Although brevity is desirable in order to minimize patient burden in completing the questionnaire, reliability and comprehensiveness can be compromised as questionnaire length decreases. An ideal questionnaire is not longer than one page in length and is easy to explain and interpret.[53] Questionnaires are either self-reporting or provider-administered. Provider-administered questionnaires offer the benefit of a trained observer assisting with questionnaire completion.

Clinicians have been encouraged to utilize available questionnaires as opposed to developing new questionnaires and "reinventing the wheel."[54,55] Although attempting to develop a new questionnaire is an admirable undertaking, there is, more than likely, an available, valid, and reliable questionnaire for the intended use. What is needed more than another questionnaire is additional information regarding utilization of available questionnaires.

CASE STUDY 2–3

OSWESTRY QUESTIONNAIRE AND NECK DISABILITY INDEX

The Oswestry and NDI were selected for use in the ACN PIQ program because of their relevance to the patient

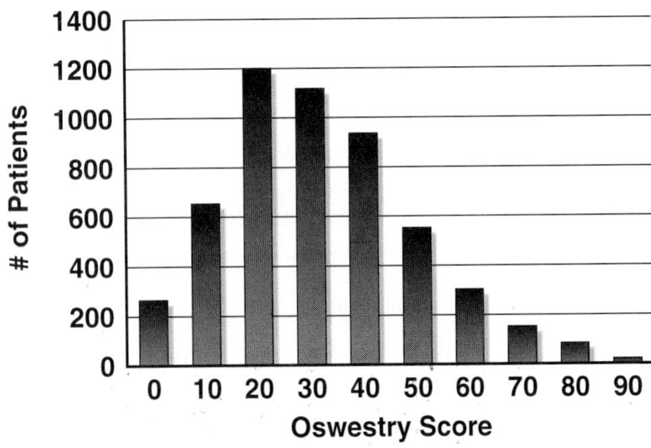

Figure 2–3. Distribution of Oswestry scores from the initial patient evaluation.

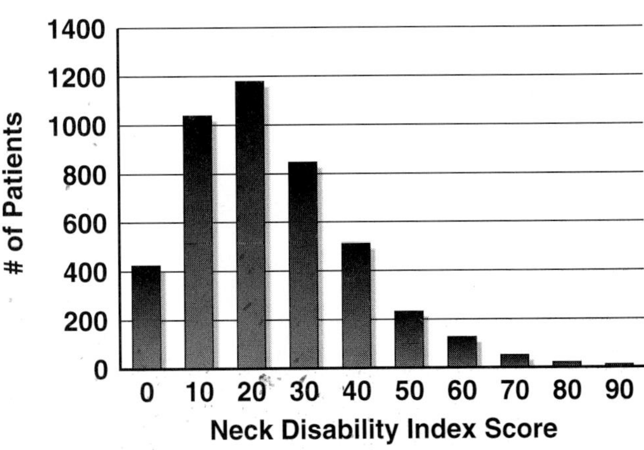

Figure 2–4. Distribution of Neck Disability Index scores from the initial patient evaluation.

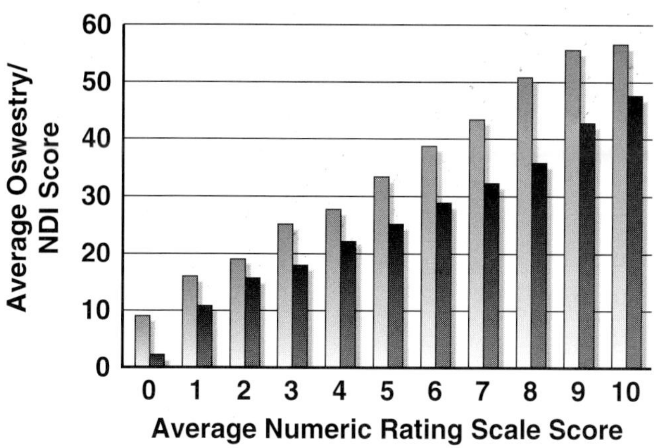

Figure 2–5. Relationship between numeric rating scale and Oswestry/Neck Disability Index measurements.

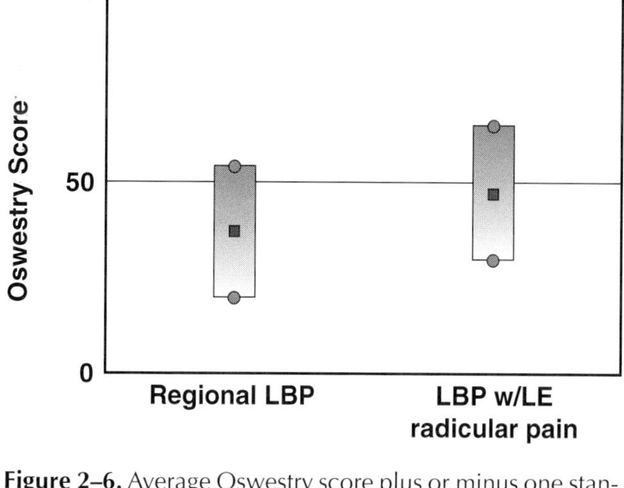

Figure 2–6. Average Oswestry score plus or minus one standard deviation for patients with regional low back pain and low back pain with lower extremity radicular pain.

population seen by PIQ provider, their practicality and ease of use, and their validity, reliability, and responsiveness. Depending on the patient's condition, one or both of the instruments are administered as part of the initial and final evaluations. Both instruments measure the effect of the patient's condition on his or her ability to perform daily activities. The Oswestry and NDI possess identical structures and scoring equations. Both instruments yield a score between 0 and 100 with 0 indicating no disability and 100 indicating complete disability. Figure 2–3 demonstrates the distribution of scores from 5262 ACN PIQ patients completing the Oswestry questionnaire at the time of the initial evaluation.

Figure 2–4 demonstrates the distribution of scores from 4399 ACN PIQ patients completing the NDI at the time of the initial evaluation. By comparing a patient's score on the Oswestry and/or NDI with the distribution of scores shown in Figures 2–3 and 2–4, the provider can gain perspective on the relative level of disability being reported by the patient.

Figure 2–5 demonstrates that there is a relationship between the patient's self-reported level of pain as measured by the NRS and the patient's self-reported level of disability as measured by the Oswestry and NDI. Higher levels of reported pain are associated with higher levels of reported disability.

In addition to categorizing the patient's diagnosis using an ICD code, the ACN peer case manager categorizes each patient according to a more general classification scheme. Table 2–4 illustrates the four categories used for low back patients.

4564 patients with a primary complaint of regional low back pain and 310 patients with a primary complaint of low back pain with lower extremity radicular pain have been seen by ACN PIQ providers. Figure 2–6 demonstrates the average Oswestry score, plus or minus one standard deviation, for these two categories of low back patients. As expected, the patients with low back pain accompanied by lower extremity radicular pain reported a higher level of disability than patients whose pain was confined to the low back.

Table 2–4: ACN PIQ Clinical Categories for Patients with Low Back Pain

CATEGORY	DESCRIPTION
Regional low back pain (LBP)	LBP without radicular pain
LBP with lower extremity (LE) radicular pain	Radicular pain confirmed by positive SLR producing pain to or below the knee
LBP with progressive LE neurological deficit	Progressive LE neurologic deficit as indicated by reflex and/or strength loss, muscle atrophy
Cauda equina syndrome	Saddle anesthesia, bowel and bladder incontinence, bilateral sciatica

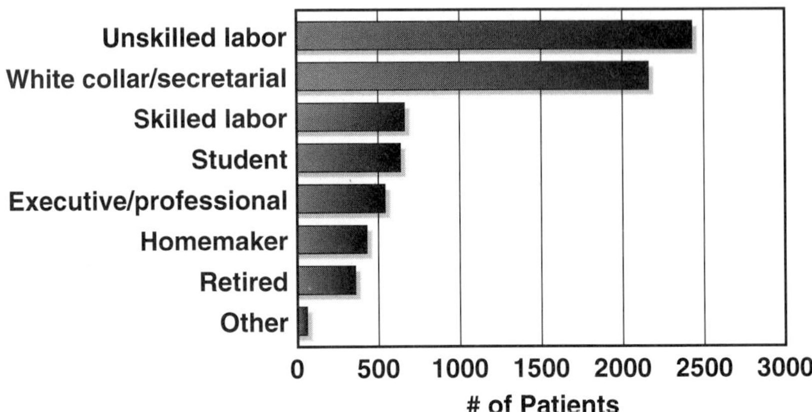

Figure 2–7. ACN PIQ patient occupation measurement scale.

Work Status

In those cases in which a patient's condition is associated with a partial or total inability to perform his or her work activities, one of the most important outcome measures is the degree to which treatment improved the patient's ability to work, ideally returning the patient to pre-onset work status. Returning a patient to work is a complex process involving many variables including, but not limited to, the length of time off work, the patient's job satisfaction and relationship with his or her supervisor and fellow employees, the employer's return to work policies, and the physical demands of the job. In order to place return to work outcomes in the proper context, this additional data must be captured and reported.

CASE STUDY 2–4
WORK STATUS

The standardized forms used by ACN PIQ providers include two questions directed at obtaining information regarding the patient's occupation, and whether the patient's condition has resulted in any change in his or her ability to perform occupational activities. Figures 2–7 and 2–8 illustrate the patient occupation and work status measurement scales and the distribution of patients into each category, respectively.

The fact that patients report that their conditions have a minimal impact on their ability to work means that for the population of patients seen as part of the ACN PIQ program measuring a change in work status is not a relevant outcome measurement. Of course, in other settings, such as a clinic that has a high proportion of patients with work injuries, a change in work status is not only relevant, but it may be the most important outcome measurement.

PATIENT STATUS AT THE END OF TREATMENT

One of the most important, yet often overlooked outcome measurements is the patient's status at the end of treatment.

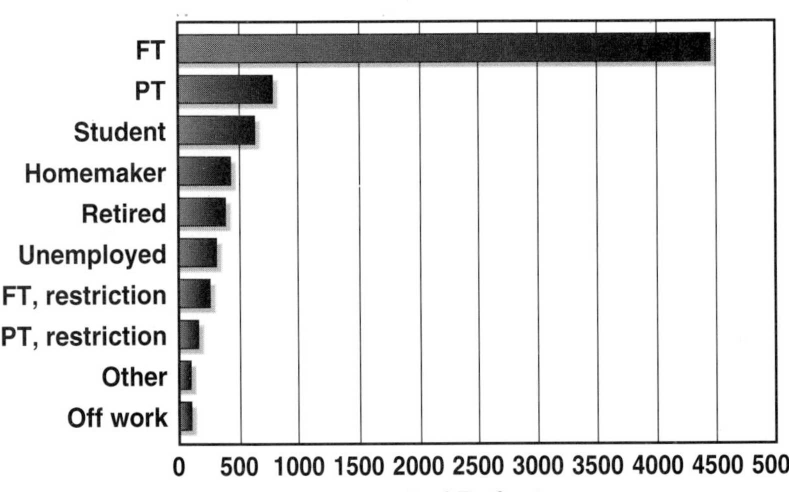

Figure 2–8. ACN PIQ patient work status measurement scale.

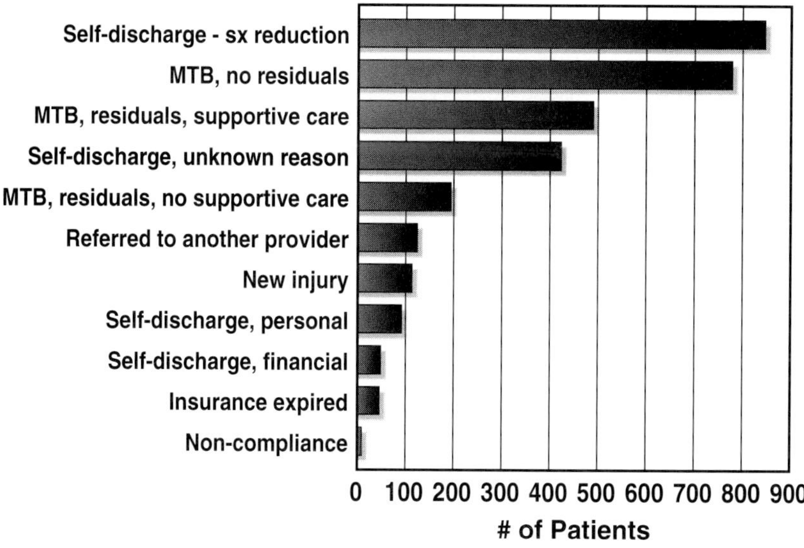

Figure 2–9. ACN PIQ patient final status measurement scale.

As the case study will illustrate, the patient's final status has a significant impact on the change observed in other outcome measurements.

CASE STUDY 2–5
PATIENT FINAL STATUS

Collecting data on the patients final, or discharge, status is critical to analyzing and reporting outcome data. In the ACN PIQ program, the treating provider assigns each patient 1 of 15 final status categories upon completion of treatment. Figure 2–9 illustrates 11 of the categories and the distribution of ACN PIQ patients into these categories. The ideal final status category is maximum therapeutic benefit (MTB) without residual complaints. The nature of chiropractic care is such that many patients self-discharge from care because of a reduction in symptoms. This is the most frequent final status category reported by ACN PIQ providers.

The essence of outcome measurement occurs when the various measurements used to assess the change in a patient's level of impairment or disability are viewed in the context of the patient's final status. Figures 2–10 and 2–11 demonstrate the initial and final Oswestry and NDI scores for patients reaching four of the previously described final status categories.

Patients who reach MTB without residual complaints show a large reduction in their level of disability as measured by both the Oswestry and NDI. Patients who reach MTB with residual complaints requiring supportive care demonstrate a reduction in disability, indicating treatment effectiveness. However, the residual complaints are associated with a higher level of disability, demonstrating the need for supportive care. As expected, patients who are referred to another health care provider or who sustain a new injury during the course of treatment show an increase in their level of disability.

COST/UTILIZATION

Recall that earlier in the chapter the outcomes of care were differentiated from the processes of care. Care processes, those services done to, for, or by the patient, were described

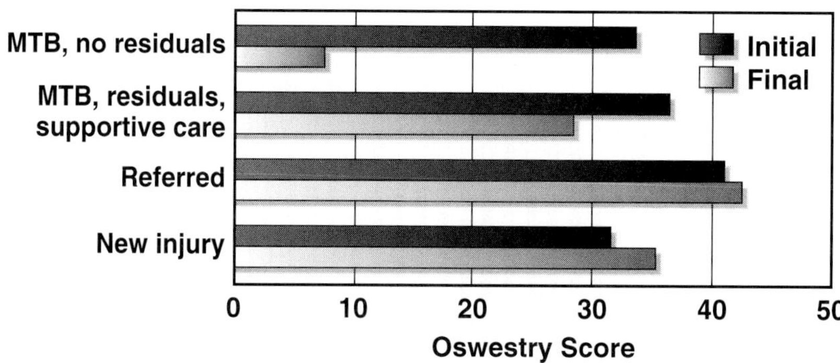

Figure 2–10. Initial and final Oswestry scores for patients reaching four final status categories.

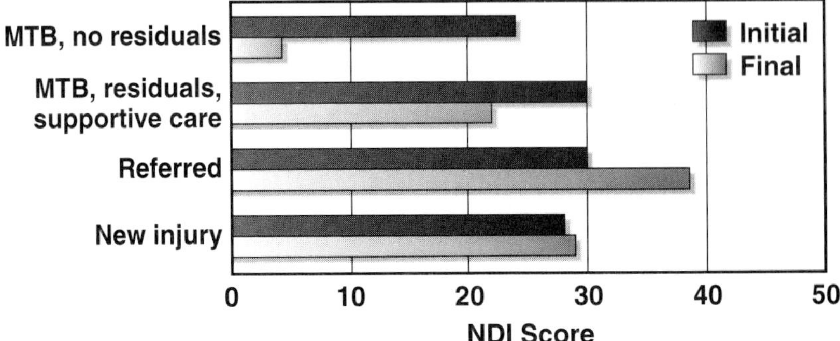

Figure 2–11. Initial and final Neck Disability Index scores for patients reaching four final status categories.

as accounting for the majority of the costs of care. Thus, although perhaps not a true outcome measure, the costs of care are invariably measured as part of any comprehensive outcome assessment program.

CASE STUDY 2–6
COST OF CARE

In the current health care environment the costs associated with treating both individuals and groups of patients is measured with great detail and monitored very closely. This is also the case in the ACN PIQ program. Figure 2–12 demonstrates the average cost of treating uncomplicated back pain patients for approximately 40 ACN PIQ providers all practicing in the same metropolitan area. The providers included in Figure 2–12 had treated a minimum of 30 uncomplicated back pain patients. The average number of uncomplicated back pain patients treated was 89. The costs associated with manipulative therapy, therapeutic modalities, examinations, and x-rays are added to arrive at the total cost indicated in the bar graph.

To control for potential differences in the benefit structure of a patient's insurance coverage and differences in provider fees, a relative-value-based approach was used in the cost equation. There was no difference between providers with respect to patient age, gender, and severity as measured by NRS, or disability as measured by Oswestry and NDI. Another point that cannot be overlooked in this analysis is that while these data were derived from a managed care environment, providers did not request authorization for, nor did ACN authorize, a specific number of visits. Providers simply treated according to their clinical judgement. Thus, the variation in total cost represents a valid indication of the variation that exists in the 40 providers.

In addition to the variation in total cost demonstrated in Figure 2–12, it is interesting to look at the differences in the number of individual services used to manage patients with similar conditions of similar severity. Some providers do not use passive therapeutic modalities or x-rays, whereas other providers use relatively high levels of these services.

Historically, a one-dimensional evaluation of provider or health care organization performance, based on cost, has been used when comparing providers or health care organizations. As outcome measurement has evolved, the outcomes of care are evaluated in the context of costs to

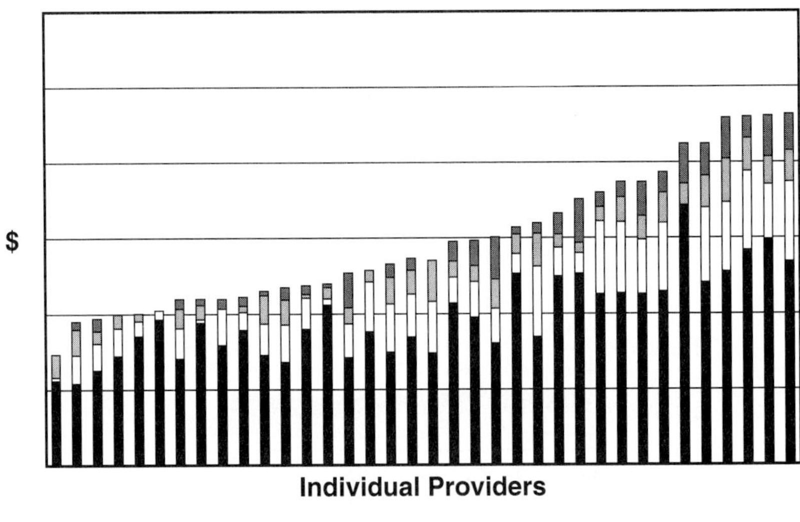

Figure 2–12. Average costs associated with the treatment of uncomplicated back pain patients by ACN PIQ providers.

provide a more comprehensive assessment of performance. A subsequent case study will demonstrate this principle.

PATIENT SATISFACTION

"There is an increasing acceptance that consumer satisfaction is an important indicator of the quality of health care."[56] Patient satisfaction is a complex phenomenon involving expectations, perceptions, and the relative importance to the patient of elements of both the care process and the outcomes of care. A patient may evaluate a particular element of the care process as poor, yet have high overall satisfaction if the performance expectation regarding that particular element of care is low.

There are two reasons for measuring patient satisfaction: the measurement of performance and the diagnosis of sources of dissatisfaction. Generally, when administering a patient satisfaction survey, it is not enough to simply find out if the patient is satisfied or not. To efficiently allocate human and financial resources to processes and procedures in need of improvement, those performing the survey should attempt to determine the sources of any dissatisfaction.[57]

Generally, there are eight attributes of health care that are assessed in a patient satisfaction survey:[58]

- Accessibility/availability of services/providers
- Choice and continuity of care
- Communication
- Financial arrangements
- Interpersonal aspects of care
- Outcomes of care
- Technical quality of care
- Time spent with providers

Patient satisfaction is typically measured using some type of survey instrument using either a mail-out, mail-back format or using a telephone interview. Developing a patient satisfaction survey would appear to be as easy as assembling a few questions regarding the patient's satisfaction with different elements of care. However, with such a complex phenomenon, developing a valid and reliable measurement instrument is beyond the capabilities of the majority of clinicians. Fortunately, several instruments are available. The visit-specific satisfaction questionnaire (VSQ)[59] is one widely used instrument that is applicable in most health care environments. As was the case with functional status measures, providers are encouraged to use one of the available, valid, and reliable instruments as opposed to attempting to develop their own survey.

CASE STUDY 2–7
PATIENT SATISFACTION

Every 2 years ACN administers a patient satisfaction survey to a random sample of all patients who had visited an ACN provider in the preceding 6 months. The survey is designed to provide both benchmarking and diagnostic data. Figure 2–13 provides an example of benchmarking data from this survey, in which we ask for feedback regarding the patients' evaluation of the time they spend waiting to see their health care provider. The average level of patient satisfaction, plus or minus one standard deviation, is reported.

Although the type of data presented in Figure 2–13 may be interesting, it does not provide any information that gives direction when attempting to improve patient satisfaction. Recall that the first step in data collection is refining the question to be answered. Patients are generally satisfied with their care. Thus, the question to be answered with a patient satisfaction survey is rarely "Are patients satisfied?" The real question to be answered is "How do we improve satisfaction?" The only way to answer this question is to construct the satisfaction survey so that diagnostic data are produced. As an example of diagnostic

Figure 2–13. Benchmarking data: patient satisfaction with time spent waiting to see provider.

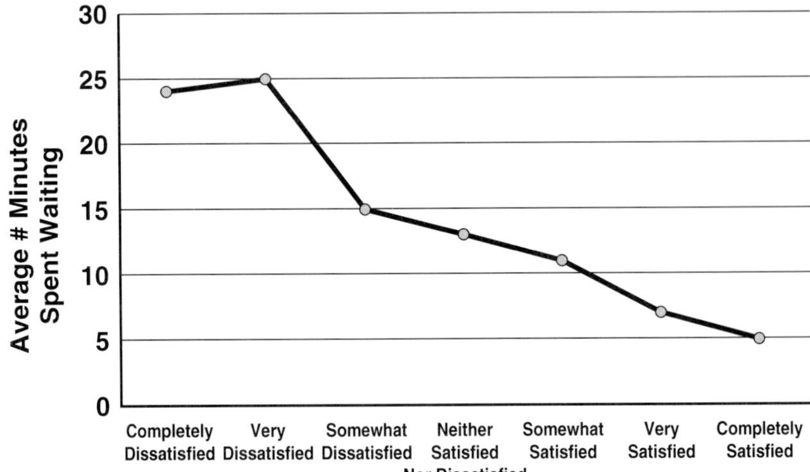

Figure 2–14. Diagnostic data: patient satisfaction with time spent waiting to see provider.

data, the ACN survey also asks patients how many minutes they wait, on average, to see their health care provider, after their scheduled appointment time. Figure 2–14 demonstrates the information produced when the benchmarking data are combined with the diagnostic data regarding patient wait time. As expected, patient satisfaction decreases as the time spent waiting increases. At wait times of greater than 10 minutes, patient satisfaction begins to become compromised. Using this type of information, providers can examine their office procedures to make certain patients are not kept waiting more than 10 minutes.

FACTORS THAT AFFECT OUTCOMES

There are many factors that could potentially affect the outcomes of care for an individual patient or for groups of patients. These are the structure and process issues previously described. When outcome data are used to compare the performance of individual providers or health care organizations, the influence of these factors must be considered. This necessitates collecting data regarding the following issues:[60]

1. Patient-related factors
   Biological variations among patients (e.g., those associated with sex and age)
   Severity of the patient's illness or condition
   The patient's other illnesses (e.g., comorbidities)
   The patient's preference (and consent) for a specific treatment intervention or lack of intervention
   Certain other patient-related factors (e.g., socioeconomic level, education, occupation, environment, home, family, payment source)
2. Clinician-related factors
   Clinician's level of knowledge (based on education and experience)
   Clinician's current technical and interpersonal skills, including empathy (based on personality, training, and experience)
   Clinician's judgement (based on education, training, and experience)
3. Provider organization–related factors
   The availability of the following and how they are managed:
   - Human resources (e.g., numbers and qualifications of staff, continuing education)
   - Capital resources (e.g., space, equipment)
   - Information resources (e.g., patient health records, library, ethics consultation)
   - Financial resources

   The organization's systems and processes for governance, management, clinical care, and support services
4. Community-related factors
   The structure of the community's health care system (e.g., whether it is integrated to provide continuity of care across provider organizations and clinicians, and through time)
   The amount and allocation of health care resources in the community (e.g., financial resources available for health care, allocation of resources between preventive and treatment services, shortages of nursing staff)
   Other factors that affect the population's health (e.g., environmental pollution, workplace safety, socioeconomic and education levels)

OUTCOME MEASUREMENT PROCESS

There are three points in the care process where most, if not all, outcome measurement activity occurs. (Data regarding the process of care, or the services that were performed when treating the patient, are captured throughout the course of treatment via the generation of claims.)

1. At the initial patient evaluation a comprehensive set of demographic, diagnostic, clinical, and baseline

outcome data are captured using both patient and provider forms and questionnaires.

2. At the final patient evaluation, impairment and functional status measurements are repeated using standardized protocols, scales, and questionnaires identical to those used during the initial evaluation. Comparing this data with the data captured as part of the initial evaluation demonstrates the degree to which a patient, or groups of patients, benefited from treatment. As part of the final evaluation the provider assigns the patient final status. As demonstrated in a previous case study, analyzing and reporting changes in the various outcome measures in the context of a patient's final status is the essence of outcome measurement.
3. Within 1 to 2 weeks of the final evaluation and discharge of a patient, a confidential patient satisfaction survey is administered. Typically, this will be performed using a mail-out, mail-back format. Inclusion of a stamped, self-addressed return envelope will maximize the return rate of the survey.

The payback for all the effort that goes into developing and implementing an outcome management program comes when data have been collected for a period of time and can begin to be queried to produce information that is used to improve clinical and administrative efficiency and effectiveness.

In order to be able to analyze data to produce information to answer a question, the data must be stored in an easily retrievable format. This will involve the use of computer hardware and software, the topic of the next section.

TECHNOLOGY AND DATABASE MANAGEMENT

A review of the important concepts to consider when implementing an outcome measurement program would not be complete without at least a brief consideration of technology and database management. The complexity of this topic is compounded by the fact that computer technology evolves at such a rapid pace.

"Information is one of an organization's four core resources: people, plant and equipment, capital and information. Like the organization's other core resources, information is costly to acquire and manage. While information is an asset, information management is a 'cost center.'"[61] To minimize the costs associated with capturing and storing data, an organization must develop efficient information management processes and procedures. Typically, this will involve the use of computer technology.

As a health care organization develops and implements an outcome measurement program, relevant data regarding patient demographics and outcomes of care will more than likely be stored in a database separate from the database used for claims submission. In addition, the three different points in the care process where data are collected will typically have separate, corresponding database tables and data entry screens. This results in the need for an internal linkage between the "clinical" database and the "claims" database, and between separate tables within each of the databases. Previous sections of this chapter have described the importance of collecting valid and reliable data and the characteristics of measurement instruments used to collect data. Just as important as the validity and reliability of data is the ability to link sources of data both within a clinic or organization and externally.

"Linkage between multiple types of data from multiple sources within a health care organization is possible only when the organization uses internally uniform data definitions, terminology, data capture methods, classification schemes, codes and coding practices, and standards for data transmission throughout the organization. The ability to link with external sources of data and to efficiently meet external demands for data requires the use of externally uniform definitions, terminology, classification, codes, and standards for data transmission. Therefore, health care organizations should use externally uniform codes and standards when developing their internal system architecture."[62] The electronic submission of claims data is one common way in which a clinic or health care organization is linked externally. Those involved in this process know the importance of having uniform data classification and codes.

In relational database architecture, uniformity in key data fields establishes the link between clinical and claims databases and between individual tables within databases. These key fields typically are patient and/or case identification numbers. The patient identification number issued by the patient's insurance company is typically used as a method of linking various databases and tables within databases.

The level of sophistication built into off-the-shelf database software from the major manufacturers places powerful data management capabilities within reach of the smallest clinic. The presence of extensive help menus means developing databases and corresponding data entry screens can be accomplished by anyone with basic computer skills. As the volume of data being collected grows, data entry processes can be shifted from manual, to scanning, to a paperless system using a computerized medical record. For large-scale outcome measurement programs, retaining the services of an information system professional to assist with the design of the databases and data entry processes will lead to cost savings associated with more efficient data collection and storage.

Whether computer-based medical records or manual processes are used for collecting and entering data, an important concept to consider is that data should be collected as a result of performing a process, not in addition to the process. Through careful design of measurement instruments, workflow, and data entry processes, duplication of effort can and should be avoided. A common example of collecting data as a result of performing a process is the inclusion of automatic date/time markers at critical points in the care delivery process.

When attempting to develop efficient data collection processes, it is useful to ask the following questions:[63]

1. Where in the care delivery process can we get the data we need to answer the questions we need answers to? Although it may be ideal to collect all data at one point in a process, reality typically dictates multiple data entry points. However, the number of points in a process at which data are collected and entered should be minimized to avoid the necessity of having to collect and enter redundant data.
2. Who in the process can provide us the data?
3. How can we collect the data from these people with minimum effort and minimum chance of error? In most settings, the people performing work as part of a care process will also be involved in capturing data. This creates an environment in which bias may adversely impact the utility of the data collected. In order to minimize bias, those collecting and entering data must receive comprehensive training regarding data collection methodologies and processes. Auditing the data collected is important for a period of time after implementing a new data collection process or after a new collector is introduced to the process. Forms, sheets, and data entry screens should be designed so that they are consistent with the workflow of the data collector and should be designed with consideration given to the ease with which the data can be collected.
4. What additional information might we want to capture to facilitate subsequent data analysis? While the underlying goal of data collection is to minimize the number of measures, as long as one is going to the trouble of collecting data it is important not to overlook capturing a couple of extra data elements that may prove to be very useful when the data are analyzed.

It bears repeating that the information management function of a clinic or health care organization is a cost center. The costs associated with acquiring new technology must be weighed against potential efficiency gains. Computer technology should be used as a means to enhancing the efficiency of data collection, storage, analysis, and reporting.

PERFORMANCE, QUALITY, AND VALUE

The terms *performance*, *quality*, and *value* have been used throughout this chapter. These related, yet distinct and sometimes confused concepts are often used when reporting the outcomes of care. These are the concepts driving many of the changes being experienced in health care. Therefore, it is important to have a clear understanding of what is meant by each term.

PERFORMANCE

"Performance, in contrast to quality, is something an organization does, as in processes, or achieves, as in outcomes."[64] Performance can be defined as "the way in which a health care organization carries out or accomplishes its important functions."[65]

An important characteristic of performance measurement is that "levels of performance, expressed as absolute numbers or as proportions, are neutral—neither good nor bad—in themselves."[66] For example, as an isolated performance measurement, a clinic that returns to full-time work 75% of patients who were off work because of their condition is neither good nor bad.

Performance measurement involves applying the previously described measurement methodologies to collect and report data regarding the processes and outcomes of a health care organization. The National Committee for Quality Assurance (NCQA), through its Health Employer Data and Information Set (HEDIS) project, is a leader in establishing standardized performance measurement systems for health care organizations. Its Report Care Pilot Project provides an example of comparing the performance of health care organizations for a variety of procedures and conditions ranging from preventive services such as childhood immunization rates, mammograms, and cholesterol screening to health plan utilization rates for coronary bypass, laminectomy, and cesarean sections.[67] Although much has been published regarding the evaluation and treatment of patients with back pain, relatively little work has gone into developing standardized performance measurements and quality indicators for those treating back pain patients.

Although performance measures are objective data reported without judgment, purchasers of health care use performance data as the basis for making subjective judgments regarding the quality of health care.

CASE STUDY 2–8
PERFORMANCE

All patients seen by ACN PIQ providers receive a confidential patient satisfaction survey upon completion of treatment. ACN analyzes, reports, and compares patient satisfaction with individual providers. As an example of a performance measure, Figure 2–15 illustrates average overall patient satisfaction, plus or minus one standard deviation, for one PIQ provider. Looking at this chart raises the question "How does this level of performance compare with other providers?" In asking this question, we are searching for a context by which to make judgments regarding quality of care.

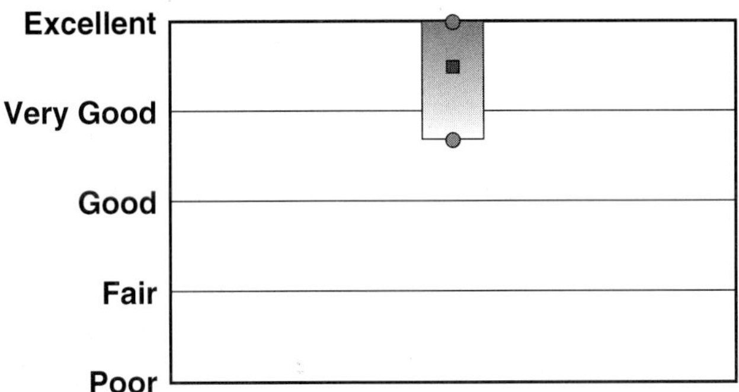

Figure 2–15. Overall patient satisfaction with an ACN PIQ provider.

QUALITY

The distinguishing feature between performance and quality is that performance measures are neutral, whereas quality involves a judgment regarding the level of performance. This judgment may be based on the comparison of performance data with a subjective internal standard, a published benchmark, or the performance of others. In other words, performance is objective whereas quality is subjective. "Quality of care is a judgment shaped by interests of the individual or group making the judgment."[68]

When a clinic with a return to work rate of 75% is compared with competing clinics with return to work rates of 89% and 90%, a health care consumer, such as an employer, will begin to make judgments regarding the relative quality of the three clinics.

Because of the subjective nature of quality and the different dimensions of performance, "Different parties may make different judgments about quality using the same performance data."[69]

With the proliferation of report cards, in which performance data is summarized for consumers, health care organizations are increasingly competing on the basis of quality judgments. Although health care organizations can attempt to shape the subjective criteria by which purchasers make their decisions, maintaining the validity, reliability, and standardization of the underlying performance measures is essential.

CASE STUDY 2–9

QUALITY

Building on the preceding case study, Figure 2–16 demonstrates the average overall patient satisfaction, plus or minus one standard deviation, for several PIQ providers from the same metropolitan region. From this chart judgments can be made regarding the relative quality of care of each of the providers. If you had this kind of information when making a decision regarding which health care provider to see, which side of the chart would you begin with when contacting a provider for an appointment?

VALUE

In today's cost-conscious health care environment performance data and quality judgments are evaluated in the context of the costs associated with a treatment or service. Value is the relationship between quality and cost. Figure 2–17 illustrates this relationship via the value matrix.

With a value matrix, the scales for quality judgments and the costs associated with a treatment or service are placed on opposing axes. Although the cost axis is fairly straightforward, depending on the consumer, the quality axis could include any number of measurements. Average levels of quality and cost are placed in the middle of each axis. The resulting matrix consists of four quadrants. Best practice is characterized by high-quality, cost-effective care. High-cost care possesses both above-average quality and above-average cost. Quality-deficient care is defined as low-cost care with below-average quality. Unsustainable value is poor-quality care with above-average cost. The arrows in the value matrix indicate the desired effect of improvement efforts. Areas of performance deficit are identified and improvement activities are directed at the related processes.

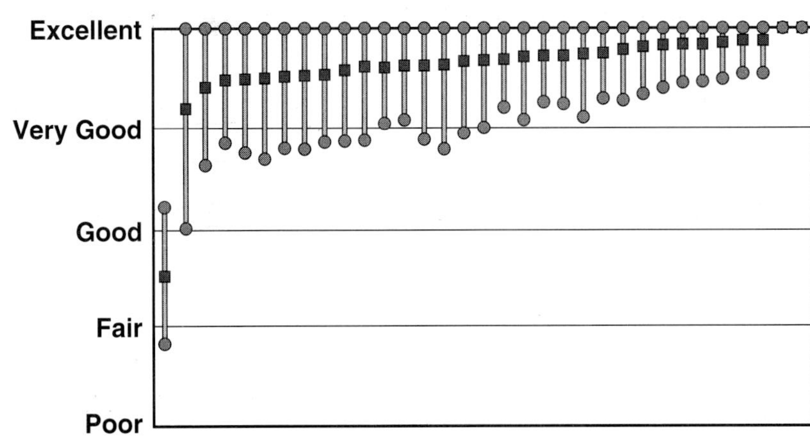

Figure 2–16. Overall patient satisfaction with several ACN PIQ providers.

Figure 2–17. Value matrix.

With subjective judgments regarding quality included as part of the value equation, different consumers may perceive different value from the same treatment or service. Additionally, different consumers may seek different levels of value in a transaction.

To continue the example of the three clinics with different return to work rates, the clinics with return to work rates of 89% and 90% may be viewed as of higher quality than the clinic with a return to work rate of 75%. However, if the clinic with the 89% rate has an average cost per case of $250, compared with an average case cost of $450 for the clinic with a rate of 90%, which would provide the most value? And if the clinic with the 75% rate had an average cost of $150, what is the answer? When judgements are made regarding value, there is rarely a clear answer. The desired level of value sought in a transaction is subjective and is dependent on many additional patient, provider, and community-related factors.

Purchasers of health care, such as insurance companies, managed care plans, and buyers' coalitions, have used a variety of methodologies to improve the value of treatments or services being purchased. Managed care evolved as a method of maximizing value to consumers by controlling costs through using information to limit treatment to those services shown to produce positive patient outcomes. In this environment providers have been challenged to maintain, and even improve, their level of quality and performance in the face of neutral or declining reimbursement. Areas of debate include whether managed care has been successful in controlling costs, and whether, while the focus has been on the cost axis of the value matrix, there has been deterioration in quality on the other side of the value equation.

Moving forward in this environment, a balance must be reached in which purchasers and providers find innovative, sustainable ways to continuously improve the value of health care services provided to the public. For all types of organizations, part of the solution to maintaining quality while controlling costs involves using technology to enhance administrative efficiency and produce information that improves clinical knowledge.

CASE STUDY 2–10
VALUE

Meaningful evaluations of health care quality require more than a one-dimensional measurement of structure, process, or cost. The concept of evaluating performance or quality in the context of cost results in the type of information consumers want, information regarding the value of a provider or health care organization.

Figure 2–18 demonstrates the relative value of 40 ACN PIQ providers from the same metropolitan region for the management of regional, uncomplicated back pain patients

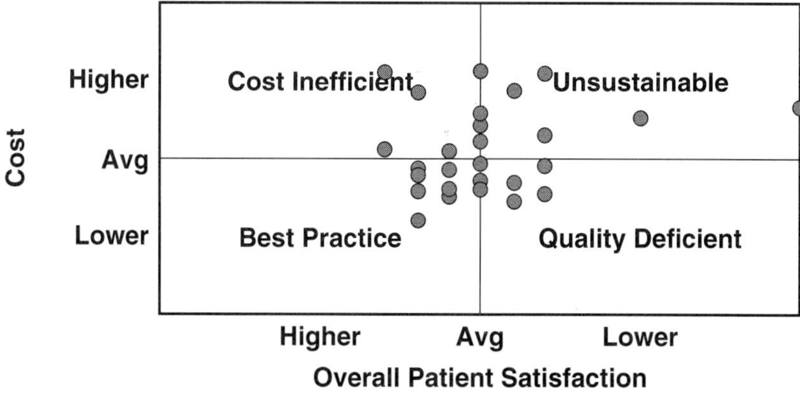

Figure 2–18. Relative value of ACN PIQ providers.

of similar age, gender, and severity. Cost and overall patient satisfaction data from previous case studies are combined in a value matrix. As a marker for overall quality, patient satisfaction is useful as the quality measure of the value matrix.

As expected, most providers are clustered around the intersection of the average performance gridlines. However, there are providers in each of the four quadrants. Particularly, for those outside the best practice quadrant, this type of comparison can be a powerful motivator to improve performance. When supplemented with a report card or profile containing specific data detailing clinical and administrative efficiency and effectiveness, not only is there motivation for improvement, but improvement efforts can be focused on areas of performance deficit.

SUMMARY

"Today more than ever, health care providers and organizations are driven to continuously improve their performance. Motivated in the past primarily by a professional desire to improve patients' health, improvement today is also motivated by the demands for public accountability and the desire to survive in a cost-cutting and competitive environment."[70]

The following recommendations are useful when beginning the process of implementing an outcome measurement system:[71]

1. Limit the number of measurements.
2. Pick measurements that are important to clinicians and patients.
3. Make the data collection easy enough to allow for trending of changes over time.
4. Do not try to have the same measures serve research purposes at the same time as improvement or accountability needs.
5. Build in baseline measures before implementing any changes.
6. Provide training, tools, and examples to those in clinical settings who are not used to data and this type of measurement.

Outcome management must not be viewed as a "research project" to be performed in addition to normal daily activities. Rather, as a key element of an organization's performance and quality improvement activities, outcome measurement processes and procedures will interface with all aspects of an organization's operations. As a result of the necessity to standardize processes and clinic procedures, implementing an outcome assessment system has the potential to be a unifying influence on a clinic or health care organization. The information produced by a well-designed outcome measurement program will prove to be an asset to both providers and health care organizations competing in today's health care environment.

REFERENCES

1. *Guidelines for Chiropractic Quality Assurance and Practice Parameters*. Gaithersburg, MD: Aspen Publishers, Inc., 1993.
2. *Using Clinical Practice Guidelines to Evaluate the Quality of Care: Volume 1: Issues*. Rockville, MD: U.S. Department of Health and Human Services, Agency for Health Care Policy and Research, March 1995.
3. *Guidelines for Chiropractic Quality Assurance and Practice Parameters*. Gaithersburg, MD: Aspen Publishers, Inc., 1993.

4–5. Plsek PE. Tutorial: Planning for data collection. Part I: Asking the right question. *Quality Management in Health Care*. 1994;2(2):76–81.

6. Schyve PM, Kamowski DB. Information management and quality improvement: The joint commission's perspective. *Quality Management in Health Care*. 1994;2(4):54–62.

7–8. Plsek PE. Tutorial: Planning for data collection. Part I: Asking the right question. *Quality Management in Health Care*. 1994;2(2):76–81.

9. Payton O. *Research: The Validation of Clinical Practice*. Edition 2. Philadelphia: F.A. Davis Company, 1988.
10. *Guidelines for Chiropractic Quality Assurance and Practice Parameters*. Gaithersburg, MD: Aspen Publishers, Inc., 1993.
11. Johnston VM, Keith RA, Hinderer SR. Measurement standards for interdisciplinary medical rehabilitation. *Archives of Physical Medicine and Rehabilitation*. 1992;73:S3–S23.
12. Streiner DL, Norman GR. *Health Measurement Scales: A Practical Guide to Their Development and Use*. New York: Oxford University Press, 1987.
13. Payton O. *Research: The Validation of Clinical Practice*. Edition 2. Philadelphia: F.A. Davis Company, 1988.
14. Dvir Z. Clinical applicability of isokinetics: A review. *Clinical Biomechanics*. 1991;6:133–144.

15–16. Vernon H. Pain and disability questionnaires in chiropractic rehabilitation. In: *Rehabilitation of the Spine. A Practitioners Manual*. Baltimore: Williams and Wilkins, 1996.

17. Sapega AA. Muscle performance evaluation in orthopaedic practice. *Journal of Bone and Joint Surgery Am.* 1990;72A:1562–1574.
18. Dvir Z. Clinical applicability of isokinetics: A review. *Clinical Biomechanics.* 1991;6:133–144.
19. Crocker LM. Validity of criterion measures for occupational therapists. *American Journal of Occupational Therapy.* 1976;30:229.
20. Rothstein JM, Lamb RL, Mayhew TP. Clinical uses of isokinetic measurements: Critical issues. *Physical Therapy.* 1987;67:1840–1844.
21–23. Payton O. *Research: The Validation of Clinical Practice.* Edition 2. Philadelphia: F.A. Davis Company, 1988.
24. Cooke D, Menard MR, Beach GN, et al. Serial lumbar dynamometry in low back pain. *Spine.* 1992;17:653–662.
25. Dvir Z. Clinical applicability of isokinetics: A review. *Clinical Biomechanics.* 1991;6:133–144.
26. Payton O. *Research: The Validation of Clinical Practice.* Edition 2. Philadelphia: F.A. Davis Company, 1988.
27–28. Vernon H. Pain and disability questionnaires in chiropractic rehabilitation. In: *Rehabilitation of the Spine. A Practitioners Manual.* Baltimore: Williams and Wilkins, 1996.
29. Solberg LI, Mosser G, McDonald S. The three faces of performance measurement: improvement, accountability and research. *Journal on Quality Improvement.* 1997;23(3):135–147.
30. *Guides to the Evaluation of Permanent Impairment*, Edition 3. Chicago: AMA, 1988.
31. Deyo RA. Measuring the functional status of patients with low back pain. *Archives of Physical Medicine and Rehabilitation.* 1988;69:1044–1053.
32. *Guidelines for Chiropractic Quality Assurance and Practice Parameters.* Gaithersburg, MD: Aspen Publishers, Inc., 1993.
33. Vernon H. Pain and disability questionnaires in chiropractic rehabilitation. In: *Rehabilitation of the Spine. A Practitioners Manual.* Baltimore: Williams and Wilkins, 1996.
34. Huskisson EC. Measurement of pain. *Journal of Rheumatology.* 1982;9:768–769.
35. Bolton JE, Wilkinson RC. Responsiveness of pain scales: A comparison of three pain intensity measures in chiropractic patients. *Journal of Manipulative and Physiological Therapeutics.* 1998;21(1):1–7.
36. *Guidelines for Chiropractic Quality Assurance and Practice Parameters.* Gaithersburg, MD: Aspen Publishers, Inc., 1993.
37. Newton M, Waddell G. Trunk strength testing with iso-machines: Part 1: Review of a decade of scientific evidence. *Spine.* 1994;18:801–811.
38. Rothstein JM, Lamb RL, Mayhew TP. Clinical uses of isokinetic measurements: Critical issues. *Physical Therapy.* 1987;67:1840–1844.
39. *Guides to the Evaluation of Permanent Impairment*, Edition 3. Chicago: AMA, 1988.
40. Millard RW, Jones RH. Construct validity of practical questionnaires for assessing disability of low back pain. *Spine.* 1991;16:835–838.
41. Deyo RA. Measuring the functional status of patients with low back pain. *Archives of Physical Medicine and Rehabilitation.* 1988;69:1044–1053.
42. McDowell I, Newell C. *Measuring Health: A Guide to Rating Scales and Questionnaires.* New York: Oxford University Press, 1987.
43. Cole B, Finch E, Gowland C, Mayo N. *Physical Rehabilitation Outcome Measures.* Toronto: Canadian Physiotherapy Association, 1994.
44. Vernon H. Pain and disability questionnaires in chiropractic rehabilitation. In: *Rehabilitation of the Spine. A Practitioners Manual.* Baltimore: Williams and Wilkins, 1996.
45. Fairbank JCT, Couper J, Davies JB, O'Brien JP. The Oswestry low back pain disability questionnaire. *Physiotherapy.* 1980;66:271.
46. Vernon HT, Mior S. The neck disability index: A study of reliability and validity. *Journal of Manipulative Physiological Therapeutics.* 1991;14:409–415.
47. Ware JE, Kosinski M, Keller SD. A 12-item short-form health survey: Construct of scales and preliminary tests of reliability and validity. *Medical Care.* 1996;34(3):220–223.
48. Ware JE, Sherbourne C. The MOS 36-item short-form health survey (SF-36): Conceptual framework and item selection. *Medical Care.* 1992;30(6):473–483.
49. Roland M, Morris R. Study of natural history of back pain. Part 1: Development of reliable and sensitive measure of disability. *Spine.* 1983;8:141–144.
50. Deyo RA. Comparative validity of the sickness impact profile and shorter scales for functional assessment in low back pain. *Spine.* 1986;11(9):951–954.

51. Tait RC, Pollard CA, Margolis RB, et al. Pain disability index: Psychometric and validity data. *Archives of Physical Medicine and Rehabilitation*. 1987;68:438–441.
52. Vernon H. Pain and disability questionnaires in chiropractic rehabilitation. In: *Rehabilitation of the Spine. A Practitioners Manual*. Baltimore: Williams and Wilkins, 1996.

53–54. Deyo RA. Measuring the functional status of patients with low back pain. *Archives of Physical Medicine and Rehabilitation*. 1988;69:1044–1053.

55. Millard RW, Jones RH. Construct validity of practical questionnaires for assessing disability of low back pain. *Spine*. 1991;16:835–838.
56. Coulter ID, Hays RD, Danielson CD. The chiropractic satisfaction questionnaire. *Topics in Clinical Chiropractic*. 1994;1(4):40–43.
57. Stratmann WC, Zastowny TR, et al. Patient satisfaction and multicollinearity. *Quality Management in Health Care*. 1994;2(2):1–12.

58–59. Davies AR, Ware JE. *GHAA's Consumer Satisfaction Survey and User's Manual*. Edition 2. Washington, D.C.: Group Health Association of America, Inc., May 1991.

60. *Using Clinical Practice Guidelines to Evaluate the Quality of Care: Volume 1: Issues*. Rockville, MD: U.S. Department of Health and Human Services, Agency for Health Care Policy and Research, March 1995.

61–62. Schyve PM, Kamowski DB. Information management and quality improvement: The joint commission's perspective. *Quality Management in Health Care*. 1994;2(4):54–62.

63. Plsek PE. Tutorial: Planning for data collection. Part II: Designing the study. *Quality Management in Health Care*. 1994;2(4):73–81.

64–66. Defining performance of organizations. *Journal on Quality Improvement*. 1993;19(7):215–221.

67. *Report Card Pilot Project*. Washington, D.C.: The National Committee for Quality Assurance, 1995.

68–69. Defining performance of organizations. *Journal on Quality Improvement*. 1993;19(7):215–221.

70. Schyve PM, Kamowski DB. Information management and quality improvement: The joint commission's perspective. *Quality Management in Health Care*. 1994;2(4):54–62.
71. Solberg LI, Mosser G, McDonald S. The three faces of performance measurement: improvement, accountability and research. *Journal on Quality Improvement*. 1997;23(3):135–147.

CHAPTER 3

The Integration of Passive and Active Care

Craig S. Liebenson, DC, Natalie I. Gluck, DC, & Clayton D. Skaggs, DC

INTRODUCTION

In this chapter, we discuss the current approach to combining both passive and active care in rehabilitating a patient to restore function. Historically, rehabilitation was applied to physically exceptional individuals, such as athletes or physically disabled individuals. However, with the development of clinical guidelines, the concept of incorporating rehabilitation techniques to restore function in individuals is becoming increasingly emphasized. Rehabilitation is now indicated for patients who are in the subacute phase of care, for chronic pain patients, for disabled patients, for deconditioned patients, and to prevent injury or symptom recurrence.

Qualified, licensed health care professionals are trained to assess each patient's ability to move—specifically, spinal range of motion, gait, and the quality and quantity of individual joint motion. Treatment is directed toward restoration of function, both at the individual joint level and more holistically for the entire body.

Passive treatment interventions serve an important role in patient care, but are limited in their ability to prevent the development of patient deconditioning or abnormal illness behavior sometimes associated with treatment dependency. Active care provides several beneficial advantages, including enhancing the patient's overall active or functional mobility, muscle strength, coordination, endurance, and posture and possibly reducing the likelihood of deconditioning or chronicity.

By combining passive with active care, we have the tools to treat not only the signs and symptoms of the patient's injury, but to increase the likelihood of correcting the underlying cause of the problem and preventing functional deficits from developing. Herring stated, "Signs and symptoms of injury abate, but these functional deficits persist . . . adaptive patterns develop secondary to the remaining deficits . . . rehabilitation . . . must therefore address more than the pain of an individual injury. The rehabilitation plans . . . must be oriented toward return to function, not just relief of symptoms."[1] These practical principles are summarized in Table 3–1.

Passive care, used independently, has its limitations. In order to shift from passive to active care, the practitioner must be able to assess the patient's current functional status and work demands. Through good communication skills and the use of appropriate tests (some of which will be outlined in Chapter 10, which deals with functional testing), the practitioner will establish patient baseline data and set rehabilitation goals that will restore the patient to the level of function necessary to meet his or her work demands (see Table 3–2). If an individual has a high work demand, greater functional goals will need to be established. Patients should be taught how to reduce mechanical stress, while simultaneously being trained to improve their functional status.

Table 3–1: Essential Components of Active Care

Goal: Restore Spinal Stability

1. Education
   a. Learn proper posture (i.e., sit, stand)
   b. Learn postural control in activities of daily living (ADLs) (e.g., lifting, walking)
2. Mobility/flexibility
   a. Specific joint adjustment/mobilization
   b. Muscle relaxation/stretch
   c. Connective tissue stretch
3. Coordination and skill
   a. Muscle inhibition and facilitation
   b. "Spinal stabilization" training
   c. Propriosensory retraining
4. Strength and endurance
   a. Cardiorespiratory
   b. Progressive resistance
   c. Work hardening

EMERGING CLINICAL GUIDELINES FOR CARE

Understanding the place for manipulation, bed rest, passive care modalities, active rehabilitation, and multidisciplinary management is important in order to achieve optimum results with long-term patient care. Studies show that a minimum of 60% to 80% of the general population will suffer lower back pain at some point during their lives.[2–7] Most will recover symptomatically within 6 weeks, but 5% to 15% are unresponsive and have continued disability.[8–11] This smaller group is expanding and accounts for up to 85% of the total cost associated with low back pain.[8,12–18] Even among those who resolve, there is a high recurrence rate.[19–21] Van de Hoogen et al recently showed three out of four patients with low back pain reporting to general practice will have a relapse within a year.[22] This evidence confirms previous speculation that the concept of low back pain as incidental and temporary is likely false. The majority of the costs, 60%, are due to indemnity, while only 40% are from treatment.[16] According to Waddell, "Conventional medical treatment for low back pain has failed, and the role of medicine in the present epidemic must be critically examined."[23] Unfortunately, it is often difficult, if not impossible, to predict which patients will fall into the 5% to 15% "unresponsive" category. Active care is a very important aspect of treatment to help reduce the likelihood of patients from entering the difficult to manage group of low back pain patients who develop costly, chronic, disabling pain.

The emerging clinical practice guidelines as proposed by the Mercy Conference,[24] Quebec Report,[25] and the Agency for Health Care Policy and Research (AHCPR) Clinical Practice Guidelines for Acute Low Back Problems in Adults[26] are helpful for practitioners to guide their clinical decision-making skills for patient care (see Table 3–3). The following recommended guidelines are drawn from the current literature and provide a basis for determining how to proceed: They will assist in determining whether a patient is a suitable candidate for continued care, the need for an outside referral, or whether a multidisciplinary team approach would be an appropriate option.

DIAGNOSTIC TRIAGE

Some individuals have back pain as the presenting symptom of a serious medical disease. "Red flags" such as infection, tumor, etc., may be identified by a thorough history and appropriate examination. Such individuals should be promptly referred to an appropriate health care specialist.

Nerve root compression should be identified. Leg symptoms below the knee and positive nerve root tension signs (positive straight leg raise) are valuable indicators. In addition, changes in autonomic nervous system functions, such as bowel or bladder changes or motor losses, are an important indicator of a possible cauda equina syndrome and possible surgical emergency. These patients should be referred for a surgical consultation.

The vast majority of patients present without "red flags" or nerve root signs and are categorized as nonspecific back pain patients. They typically have mechanical pain that is relieved by certain postures and aggravated by others.

Ever since Mixter and Barr's[27] work in 1934, the belief that back pain was due to structural pathology of traumatic origin was accepted as scientific fact. However, until very recently, the scientific literature did not support a strong relationship between pathoanatomy and clinical symptoms in the lumbar spine.

Table 3–2: Rehabilitation Case Management Objectives

- Restoration of function
- Return patient to preinjury activities of daily living (ADLs)
- Increase patient's trunk strength/endurance
- Identify and address psychosocial variables

Table 3–3: Emerging Clinical Guidelines

1. Diagnostic triage
2. Patient reassurance
3. Time-limited passive care
4. Active rehabilitation
5. Identify and address abnormal illness behavior

Overwhelming evidence has accumulated that shows only a weak correlation between structural pathology and low back pain. It is now accepted that for approximately 80% of chronic low back pain patients, an anatomic cause cannot be identified.[28,29] Numerous controlled studies have shown little relationship between radiologic signs of degeneration and clinical symptoms.[30–37]

Imaging techniques have been able to clearly demonstrate a structural cause in only 19% of the cases of chronic low back pain.[28] In a study of cadaveric specimens, no correlation was found between various lumbar spine pathologies (including facet osteoarthritis, osteophytosis, symmetrical disc degeneration, or end plate defect) and a previous history of low back pain.[38] CT and MRI advanced imaging have shown a significant number of false positive results in completely asymptomatic groups.[39–41] Myelograms and discograms have shown significant abnormalities in 30% to 50% of asymptomatic subjects.[42] Although most studies have been conducted on the lumbar spine, cervical spine studies show very similar findings.[43] Annular tears, often believed to produce pain by virtue of resultant nuclear leakage, were found in only14% of these asymptomatic individuals. According to Frymoyer, "Most commonly, diagnosis is speculative and unconfirmed by objective testing."[29] Studies by Jensel et al demonstrated that disc bulges are present in 52% of the asymptomatic population, and that disc protrusions are present in 27%; finding them in people with low back pain may be coincidental.

The Quebec Task Force on Spinal Disorders states, "Before we become mesmerized with the developing diagnostic imaging technology, such techniques must be adjudicated rigidly as to their scientific merits and analyzed as to their cost-benefit, risk-benefit, and cost-effectiveness ratios."[25] Since imaging modalities have been unable to correlate structural pathology with low back pain, most patients receive the label of benign or nonspecific back pain. It is no surprise that treatment based on inadequate diagnosis has been largely unsuccessful!

However, very recent evidence is beginning to show more promise for our ability to utilize advanced testing to accurately diagnose more than 20% of our patients, and thus avoid having to label them with nonspecific pain. A 1995 study of diagnostic blocks by Schwarzer et al demonstrated that sacroiliac joints are pain generators in 13% to 30% of a group of chronic low back pain patients.[44] Currently, no correlation with physical examination tests (provocation tests, motion palpation, range of motion, etc.) has emerged. Because of the expertise available in diagnosing and conservatively treating neuromusculoskeletal disorders, this is an area that holds tremendous potential for future chiropractic research. These efforts could seek to correlate physical signs with the "gold standard" diagnostic blocks. Evaluation of the functional changes associated with these pain generators could potentially complement medical research efforts that focus on identifying structural pathology.

Since the significance of structural pathology is controversial at this time, a focus on patients' functional status and directing treatment toward improving functional ability is considered prudent.

PATIENT REASSURANCE

Patients with nonspecific back pain or nerve root pain should be reassured of the excellent prognosis for their condition. Approximately 90% of these patients will improve within 6 weeks. Recommendations regarding activity alterations to minimize back irritation should be made. The patients should be encouraged to return to or maintain their normal level of activities. Low-stress aerobic exercises should also be recommended. If mechanical problems are present or if pain relief is required, spinal manipulation should be recommended. The goal of care should be clearly stated to be resumption of normal activities without debilitating pain. Recovery should not be equated only with pain relief. In addition, the patient should be prepared for the high likelihood of occasional recurrences in the years immediately following the back pain episode. Having the patient know the return of pain is "okay" and likely, versus catastrophic, is possibly the most vital treatment we can apply.

Overuse of bed rest has been associated with increasing the potential for disability. Allan and Waddell have noted, "Tragically, despite the best of intentions to relieve pain, our whole approach to backache has been associated with increasing low back disability. Despite a wide range of treatments, or perhaps because none of them provide a lasting cure, our whole strategy of management has been negative, based on rest. We have actually prescribed low back disability!"[45]

According to the Quebec Task Force on Spinal Disorders, "Bed rest is not necessary for low back pain without significant radiation. When prescribed, it should last no longer than two days. Prolonged bed rest may be counterproductive."[25] For nonradicular low back pain, 2 days of bed rest is the maximum supported by the literature;[25] for radicular complaints with nerve compression, rest up to 7 days is supported by the literature.[25]

TIME-LIMITED PASSIVE CARE (MANIPULATION)

Spinal manipulation has demonstrated a clear benefit for the acute/subacute population of low back pain sufferers. A recent meta-analysis reveals that manipulation is a proven, cost-effective treatment for acute/subacute low back pain without distal leg pain.[46] It provides up to 30% likelihood of improvement in the first month of care.[46] AHCPR guidelines state that spinal manipulative therapy should be the first choice for acute back pain.[26] Guidelines proposed by the Royal College of General Practitioners, London, also report manipulation resulted in a 30% reduction of low back pain in the first month.[47] Additonally, studies are surfacing with equal confidence for manipulative management of cervical spine disorders.[48] At present, approximately 96% of spinal manipulative therapies are performed by highly trained chiropractic physicians. By utilizing chiropractic manipulation to improve motion and decrease symptoms, practitioners can enhance the rate of recovery for most patients, and help prevent the onset of chronicity and/or disability. According to Troup, "The first attack is the ideal time for active and perhaps aggressive treatment, but if it is tacitly assumed that the vast majority of patients recover from back pain whether or not they are treated, then the opportunity may be missed."[47]

According to the care guidelines recommended by the Quebec Report, "Management strategies should be directed at maximizing the number of workers returning to work before one month, and minimizing the number whose spinal disorder keeps them idle for longer than six months."[25] Since manipulation has been shown to enhance the recovery process, it is clearly indicated as the treatment protocol of choice.

Even patients who have a demonstrable pathoanatomical lesion, such as a herniated disc, will often benefit from manipulation. Bush, after studying a group of patients with operable disc lesions, commented that "Even if patients have marked reduction of straight leg raising, positive neurologic signs, and a substantial intervertebral disc herniation (as opposed to a bulge) . . . if the pain can be controlled, nature can be allowed to run its course with the partial or complete resolution of the mechanical factors."[48]

A 1994 study by Erhard and Delitto demonstrated that patients who received manipulation and performed McKenzie exercises outperformed those receiving exercise alone.[51] Jette and Jette also reported that exercise and spinal manipulation were predictors of better outcomes for patients with spinal impairments.[52] The clinical significance of the literature is clear: Chiropractic physicians should perform two 2-week trials of chiropractic manipulative therapy for acute pain, unless complicating factors (such as severe pain or the presence of a structural lesion) are present, and one 2-week trial of manipulation for chronic pain. Triano concludes, "Judicious integration of manipulation into the rehabilitation treatment plan helps span the fear of movement and helps sustain the momentum of improvement when any symptomatic exacerbations occur."[53]

Physical agents are of equivocal value in the treatment of back pain or nerve root pain patients. According to the AHCPR guidelines, the use of physical agents or modalities is of "insufficiently proven benefit to justify their cost."[26] Home treatment with heat or cold is recommended. Since some patients appear to have temporary symptomatic relief, the decision to utilize physical agents should be at the doctor's discretion, but should involve cost considerations.

ACTIVE REHABILITATION

The primary goal of treatment for the back pain or sciatica pain patient is functional restoration. Passive care should not be limited as an end in itself, but should be used to facilitate active rehabilitation. Low-stress exercises can usually commence at the onset of care. Conditioning exercises usually can start by the second week (later in nerve root patients). By the end of the first month of care, some form of active rehabilitation is nearly always necessary in order to prevent both physical and psychological deconditioning. The goal is always to proceed to active rehabilitation as soon as possible.

By combining spinal manipulation with exercise and patient education, the practitioner has an extremely powerful and effective treatment protocol to restore a patient's ability to function. Feuerstein stated, "Active rehabilitation efforts, using a sports medicine model directed at rapid safe return to work, coupled with ergonomic intervention have replaced much of the traditional passive, i.e., modality-driven, approaches to rehabilitation of musculoskeletal injuries."[54] According to Mooney, "Prolonged rest and passive physical therapy modalities no longer have a place in the treatment of the chronic problem."[55] Waddell stated that the "modern theme of management must change from rest to rehabilitation and restoration of function."[23]

Acute Injuries

Patients presenting with acute injuries are most likely to make rapid progress when manipulation, physiologic therapeutics (such as cryotherapy), and active rehabilitation protocols are combined from the very earliest stages of treatment. Linton et al demonstrated that early aggressive treatment (comprised of patient education, exercises, and physical therapy modalities) was superior to traditional approaches (rest, analgesics, passive care). "Properly administered early active intervention may therefore decrease sick leave and prevent chronic problems, thus saving considerable resources."[56] The risk of developing chronic pain was eight times lower in the early active intervention group than in the traditional group.

According to Nordin, ". . . there is a very small window of time in low back pain care; we must act quickly within 4–6 weeks to bring patients into an active reconditioning program if we expect to return them to productive lives and prevent recurrence."[57]

Subacute Injuries

In those patients who present with injuries in the subacute stage, the combination of manipulation with active rehabilitation has been demonstrated to be very beneficial. Lindstrom et al looked at early treatment in subacute patients with active rehabilitation and compared this to passive treatment. Earlier return to work and decreased reinjury were reported.[58]

Mitchell and Carmen reported that "Active exercise to provide mobility, muscle strengthening, and work conditioning has shown superior results . . . substantial savings have been realized in the number of days absent from work and savings in the dollars expended for compensation benefits. There was an initial increase in health care costs resulting from the intensity of the treatment, but these costs were more than offset by savings in wage loss cost."[59]

Chronic Injuries

The chronic pain population has been extensively studied due to the disproportionate financial burden placed upon greater society by this subgroup. In the chronic, disabled population, functional restoration programs have demonstrated excellent results. A prospective study of chronic pain/disability sufferers (over a 2-year period) found that 87% were treated successfully with functional restoration and a behavioral support program.[60] Hazard et al studied chronic pain/disability sufferers (average of 19 months) and found that 81% were treated successfully with functional restoration and a behavioral support program.[61] The patients were followed for 1 year postrehabilitation to determine the long-term success of treatment.[61]

According to Sachs, ". . . appropriate treatment through a comprehensive spinal functional rehabilitation program based on objective physical capacity measurements is effective in enabling individuals to enhance ability to return to work."[62] Sachs's approach demonstrated that if we screen for abnormal illness behavior, we needn't utilize expensive, multidisciplinary functional restoration for every patient.

Alaranta et al found that a multidisciplinary functional restoration program was more effective than a program consisting of primarily passive physical therapy, light exercise, and no training guided by outcomes measurement. Improvement was noted in physical measures, pain, and disability, whereas no improvement was demonstrated in psychologic variables, sick leave, or retirement.[63] Burke et al demonstrated that surgical and nonsurgical patients both had higher return to work rates if involved in a functional restoration program.[64]

Herniated Discs

Many patients with "operable" herniated discs will respond very well to an aggressive rehabilitation program. It may be inappropriate to perform surgery prior to placing the patient through an aggressive rehabilitation program. According to Saal and Saal, who studied a group of patients referred for surgery with herniated disc and nerve root compression, "Failure of passive nonoperative treatment is not sufficient for the decision to operate."[65] Some patients may respond well enough to the rehabilitation program that surgery is no longer indicated. Those patients who do require surgery will benefit greatly from an aggressive postsurgical rehabilitation program to restore their functional status.

Saal and Saal have stated, "All patients had undergone an aggressive physical rehabilitation program consisting of back school and stabilization exercise training . . . 92 percent return to work rate."[65] They added that "Surgery should be reserved for those patients for whom function cannot be satisfactorily improved with a physical rehabilitation program."[65]

In a 1994 randomized control study by Timm of 250 chronic low back pain patients, 6 months after failed L5 laminectomy surgery, the effectiveness of low-tech and high-tech exercises was evaluated (in addition to other treatment modalities). The results found that low-tech and high-tech exercises were the only effective treatments, and that low-tech exercise (consisting of stabilization exercises and McKenzie protocols) was more cost-effective than the high-tech (Cybex) equipment.[66]

The clinical significance of the above literature is that active care should be started within 4 weeks of initiation of passive care. Most surgery is not advisable unless the active care trial has been attempted and has failed.

IDENTIFY AND ADDRESS ABNORMAL ILLNESS BEHAVIOR

Abnormal illness behavior must be identified to help predict which patients are prone to become disabled. Abnormal illness behavior was defined by Pilowsky as a patient's inappropriate or maladaptive response to a physical complaint.[67] Such behavior consists of the following characteristics: symptom magnification, pain avoidance behavior, psychological distress, catastrophizing as a coping strategy, anxiety, and treatment dependency.

Abnormal illness behavior is a complicating factor in low back pain. Frymoyer says, "There is increasing evidence from the general field of disability, and specifically low back disability, that a 'disability prone profile' can be identified and used to predict potential disability before the condition becomes truly chronic."[29] Besides abnormal illness behavior, Cats-Baril and Frymoyer found these predictors of disability: work status and job satisfaction, injury viewed as compensable, past hospitalization, and education level.[68]

Whereas acute pain is directly related to tissue injury or painful stimuli, chronic pain is more related to depression and inactivity[12]. According to Linton, inactivity or "avoidance of certain activities seems to be related more to anxiety and fear about pain, than to an actual pain-activity relationship."[69]

The experience or perception of pain has been shown to be affected by the amount of circulating endorphins. Psychological states have a clear and demonstrated effect on the production of endorphins.[70] Depression, anxiety, hypochondriasis, and hysteria are factors leading to unfavorable outcomes for chemonucleolysis and surgery.[71] Individuals who perceive their work to be emotionally stressful, anxiety-provoking, or demanding report more low back episodes.[4] Treatment programs that focus on activating patients according to behavioral models have proven to be beneficial.[69,72]

The natural history for most low back pain episodes is favorable for symptom resolution. Unfortunately, when disability is involved, social, legal, and economic factors become more important than nociceptive factors. Fear and anxiety, combined with failure of the treatment program to emphasize movement and activity, lead to prolonged inactivity. The resultant illness behavior is a potent factor in chronic symptomatology.

Those patients who are disability-prone (because of psychosocial complicating factors) should be identified early in the course of care. This will provide a more accurate prognosis and early referral to a multidisciplinary team. According to Frymoyer, if a patient is identified as being at high risk for disability early in the course of the low back pain episode, "early, aggressive rehabilitative efforts may be more successful and cost effective than permitting the patient to have a longer period of disability with its resultant economic, social and medical consequences."[29]

These patients will only respond if a biopsychosocial approach is taken. Focusing on functional outcomes, instead of pain, is key to this approach. According to Fordyce, the "social nonresponsiveness to pain behaviors" technique is one of the keys to this behavioral strategy.[73] Also, it is crucial to give exercise or work-related activities with end points set by quota, and not pain experience.[72] The doctor's role as helper, rather than healer, becomes paramount. Explaining the difference between *hurt* and *harm*, especially with respect to mobilizing stiff, deconditioned tissues, will relax an anxious patient who involuntarily remains very guarded. Individuals with abnormal illness behavior are much more likely to become disabled or develop chronic pain syndromes. Quickly shifting from passive (conservative) to active (rehabilitative) care in such individuals can prevent much disability. Additionally, many of these patients may require referral for multidisciplinary functional restoration, involving psychological support and biobehavioral reeducation.

The clinical significance is clear: Treat the patient, not the disease. Illness behavior is a normal response to chronic pain that is not dealt with in a functional manner. Overemphasizing structural pathology and not teaching patients what they can do (exercise and advice) promotes illness behavior.

SUMMARY

Guidelines for directing treatment protocols, based on scientific literature, are here to stay. Although sometimes perceived as a threat to practice independence, they can be an advantage for a quality-minded health care provider who emphasizes quality care procedures. When forming a prognosis for a patient or justifying the need for additional care to a third-party payor, it is important to address the following factors (obtained from the Mercy Guidelines), each of which may complicate and prolong recovery:[24]

1. Past history of more than four episodes of back pain.
2. Symptoms for more than 1 week, before presenting to doctor.
3. Severe pain intensity.
4. Preexisting structural pathology or skeletal anomaly (for example, spondylolisthesis) directly related to a new injury or condition.

For the majority of spinal disorders, the natural history predicts that symptoms will resolve within 6 to 8 weeks. The standard of care includes approximately 6 weeks of aggressive, conservative care. If after an initial 2-week trial of manipulative therapy no significant progress is documented, manipulative care may be continued for a second 2-week trial. Whether or not progress occurs between the second and the fourth weeks, passive care should be gradually deemphasized in favor of active care approaches. Recovery time may be increased by 1.5 to 2 times the natural history if any of the above complicating factors are present.[24] Additionally, if signs of nerve root pain are present, 6 to 16 weeks of care may also be necessary.[24]

FUNCTIONAL PATHOLOGY OF THE MOTOR SYSTEM

The sensorimotor system is comprised of bones, joints, muscles and their attachments, fascia, and the sensory and motor components of the central and peripheral nervous system. The term *functional pathology* is intended to describe alterations of the sensorimotor system in the absence of structural pathoanatomical lesions. In other words, functional pathology refers to imbalances of muscle activity, length and tone, joint motion, and altered sensorimotor performance. If these imbalances become chronic in nature, they may often be the precursor to pathoanatomical changes in the musculoskeletal system.

By assessing the various components of the sensorimotor system, the practitioner can evaluate the patient for the presence of functional pathology. Once pathology is identified, the practitioner can apply the principles of active care outlined later in this chapter to promote restoration of normal function.

In this section, we consider the role of muscle imbalance, aberrant joint motion, and faulty movement patterns. In addition, the evaluation of proprioception and selective tissue tensions are addressed since they are components of the sensorimotor system.

THE ETIOLOGY OF MUSCULAR IMBALANCE

Muscle imbalances gradually form due to sedentary lifestyle, stress, and pain (see Table 3–4). Postural (antigravity)

Table 3–4: Four Factors That Contribute to Muscle Imbalance

1. Sedentary lifestyle
2. Stress reactions
3. Adaptation to pain
4. Reciprocal inhibition

muscles tend to become tight or tense, whereas phasic muscles tend to become inhibited or weak. This muscular imbalance is perpetuated in a cycle described by Sherrington's Law of Reciprocal Inhibition: Once a muscle becomes tight, its antagonist is automatically inhibited.

Janda suggests that the basis for muscle imbalance comes from our predictable response to stressful environmental demands (such as constrained postures, repetitive tasks, gravity stress, and inactivity). He has found that postural muscles tend towards overuse and eventual shortening, whereas phasic muscles tend towards disuse and weakness (Table 3–5).[74,75] These muscles are often grouped as paired antagonists and appear to be affected by Sherrington's Law of Reciprocal Inhibition. Thus, if a postural muscle such as the iliopsoas becomes shortened from overuse, it will mechanically limit the range of motion of the gluteus maximus, its antagonist, *and* will neurologically inhibit its action. This combination of biomechanical and neurophysiological influences is a strong stimulus to the development and maintenance of muscle imbalance.

Stress contributes to muscle imbalance via the startle reflex. Engagement of the "fight or flight" response tenses the antigravity (postural) muscles. If emotions remain pent up, the muscles become gradually reprogrammed into a state of increased neuromuscular tension. The gamma system of motor neurons establishes the sensitivity of muscle spindles to stretch and thereby regulates muscle tonus. Under conditions of emotional stress or sleeplessness, the gamma system becomes hypersensitive.

Table 3–5: Categories of Postural and Phasic Muscles

POSTURAL MUSCLES	PHASIC MUSCLES
Type I: Tend to Hyperactivity	**Type II: Tend to Hypoactivity**
Triceps surae	Tibialis anterior
Hamstrings	Gluteus maximus
Adductors	Gluteus medius
Rectus femoris	Rectus abdominus
Tensor fascia latae (TFL)	Lower/middle trapezius
Psoas	Scaleni/longus colli
Erector spinae	Deltoids
Quadratus lumborum (QL)	Digastrics
Pectoralis	
Upper trapezius	
Sternocleidomastoid (SCM)	
Suboccipital	
Masticatories	

Adapted from Jull G, Janda V. Muscles and motor control in low back pain. In: Twommey LT, Taylor JR, eds. Physical Therapy for the Low Back. *New York: Churchill Livingstone, 1987.*

When muscles react to prevent physical injury, or to reduce pain, normal movement patterns may be altered. Certain muscles tend to become overactive while others become inhibited. Joint stress is altered and accelerated muscle fatigue usually follows. When such protective reactions are called for, the postural muscle groups are most easily activated, while the antagonist phasic muscles tend to be reciprocally inhibited.

According to Janda, EMG data demonstrate that during trunk flexion, a tight erector spinae will remain active and inhibit the action of its agonist, the abdominals. After stretching, the erector spinae muscle relaxes during trunk flexion, and a significant spontaneous facilitation effect is seen in the abdominal muscles.

Postural muscles keep humans upright while standing and walking. Much of normal gait is spent on one leg; therefore, special emphasis should be placed on the muscles involved in one-leg standing. Sedentary life in modern society overutilizes postural muscles, thus encouraging tightness to develop. Simultaneously, the phasic or dynamic muscles tend to become weak from disuse.

Postural and phasic muscles are made up of mixed fiber types. However, there is a predominance of "slow-twitch" fibers (Type S) in postural muscles and "fast-twitch" fibers (Type FF) in phasic muscles. The Type S muscles (Type I) have been shown histologically to hypertrophy in chronic lower back pain patients, whereas the Type FF (Type II) have been shown to atrophy.[77]

Muscle imbalances alter the performance of related movements (see Table 3–6). Repeated performance of abnormal movements may lead to tissue irritation, pain generation, and eventual injury. In the workplace, the combination of muscle imbalance and performing repetitive tasks in constrained postures has likely contributed to an epidemic of overuse syndromes.

Common types of muscular dysfunction like trigger points are best understood in the context of muscular imbalance. A short, tight postural muscle may house trigger points because of its increased metabolic demands and tension, which can produce ischemia and irritating metabolites.

Table 3–6: Possible Consequences of Muscular Imbalance

- Altered joint mechanics/uneven distribution of pressure
- Limited range of motion and compensatory hypermobility
- Change in proprioceptive input
- Impaired reciprocal inhibition
- Altered programming of movement patterns

Adapted from Janda V. Muscle spasm—A proposed procedure for differential diagnosis. J Man Med. *1991;6:136–139. Reprinted with permission from Liebenson CS. Integrating rehabilitation into chiropractic practice (blending active and passive care). In: Liebenson CS, ed.* Spinal Rehabilitation: A Manual of Active Care Procedures. *Baltimore: Williams and Wilkins, 1995.*

An inhibited phasic muscle may also form trigger points because of its increased fatigability, and thus its susceptibility to overload and mechanical failure. A trigger point in either muscle type cannot be successfully treated unless muscle balance is restored. The inhibited muscle must be activated and the short, tight muscle must be both relaxed and lengthened. Additionally, joint dysfunction, abnormal movement patterns, and poor posture must also be improved, or muscular imbalance and trigger points will likely recur.

Muscular imbalance is typically identified by postural analysis (two- and one-leg stance), gait analysis, muscle length tests, and key movement patterns. Postural analysis seeks to identify structural asymmetries (e.g., oblique pelvis, winged scapula), pelvic position (e.g., anterior pelvic tilt, rotated pelvis), hypertrophied muscles (e.g., thoracolumbar erector spinae, upper trapezius), and atrophic muscles (e.g., gluteus maximus, lumbosacral erector spinae). Postural analysis during one-leg standing seeks to identify gluteus medius weakness, pelvic obliquity, and other muscular compensations. Gait analysis is mostly concerned with hip ROM (decreased hip hyperextension), increased pelvic side shift (weakness of the gluteus medius), compensatory hyperlordosis, and lack of pelvic motion due to a sacroiliac lesion. Muscle length tests are specific tests to identify the presence of muscle shortening. Several basic movement patterns are tested to evaluate the muscle activation sequence or coordination during performance of hip, trunk, scapulothoracic, scapulohumeral, and cervical movements.

THE RELATIONSHIP BETWEEN MUSCLE AND JOINT DYSFUNCTION

Joints are a passive component of the musculoskeletal system. "Muscles move bones" is an old saying, but one that should not be forgotten. Muscles are the active part of the body and are responsible for carrying out willful actions, as well as performing reflex adaptations to any strain or threat of injury. Controlling the muscles and receiving feedback from all peripheral structures (muscles, joints, skin, ligaments, etc.) is the responsibility of the central nervous system. Specificially, the cerebellum is responsible for smoothing out movements and improving our stability and skill on a reflex, automatic basis.

When the body is injured, the passive structures (joints and ligaments) are most vulnerable. Sudden or repetitive overload leads to tissue strain and deformation when the muscles are too slow or weak to protect them. Joints, being richly innervated, quickly report their status to the dorsal horn. A feedback loop is immediately established, with muscles attempting to protect the injured tissues. Such protective mechanisms become "programmed" so that long after strained soft tissues have been injured, adaptive patterns may persist.

Muscles are the medium through which central motor commands or reflex spinal activity compensates for any disturbance such as an injury. Certain muscles will typically react when specific joints are injured or dysfunctional, and likewise joint movement will be altered to compensate for an injured muscle or other soft tissue injury. If a muscle is shortened or overactive, increased pressure and strain will develop in the joint capsule and tendoperiosteal junction. If a muscle is inhibited and weak, poorer stability for the related joints will likely result, including compensatory joint fixations or joint hypermobility. This may be due to the slow speed of activating inhibited muscles, which makes the joints more vulnerable.

As described above, Johannson et al have correlated nonnoxious joint afferent activity with increased reflex gamma motor neuron activity.[78] They hypothesize that long-lasting noxious stimulation may activate the flexion withdrawal reflex.[78] Similar reflex discharges from joints mediated by efferent sympathetic fibers were described by Schiable and Grubb.[79] Joint inflammation in the knee, for example, can lead to reflex muscle inhibition.[80–82] In the low back, Hides et al correlated segmental, reflex muscle atrophy with acute low back pain in patients in whom specific lumbar joint dysfunction was manually diagnosed.[83] Bullock-Saxton et al were able to show a correlation between poor ankle joint stability and inhibition of the gluteus maximus and medius muscles during gait.[84]

Functional assessment of associated muscles and joints, which are linked in functional chains, can reveal therapeutic shortcuts. Lewit identified specific joint dysfunctions that were linked to individual dysfunctional muscles (Table 3–7).[85,86]

THE CLINICAL IMPORTANCE OF ALTERED MOVEMENT PATTERNS

When pain, muscular imbalance, trigger points, or joint dysfunction are present, the patient's performance of certain stereotypical movement patterns will be altered, even though this may be subtle and difficult to identify for the untrained practitioner. The negative relationship between individual functional pathologies and abnormal performance of basic movement patterns is self-perpetuating. Altered or faulty movement patterns themselves place new strains on the locomotor system and lead to the spread of a local problem beyond a single region.

Such movement patterns were first recognized clinically by Janda when he noticed that the classic muscle testing of Kendall and Kendall did not differentiate between normal recruitment of muscles for an action and "trick" patterns of substitution during an action. So called "trick" movements are uneconomical and place unusual strain on the joints. They involve muscles in uneconomical ways, are uncoordinated, and are prone to fatigue. On a Kendall test of prone hip extension, it is difficult to identify overactivity of the lumbar erector spinae or hamstrings as substitutes for an inhibited gluteus maximus. Janda's tests seem to be more sensitive, in that they allow us to identify these clinically pertinent muscle imbalances and faulty movement patterns

Table 3–7: Lewit's Muscle and Joint Functional Chains

JOINT	MUSCLE
C0/1	Suboccipitals, SCM, upper trapezius (masticatories, submandibular)
C1/2	SCM, levator scapulae, upper trapezius
C2/3	SCM, levator scapulae, upper trapezius
C3/6	Upper trapezius, cervical erector spinae (supinator, wrist extensor, biceps)
C6/T3	SCM, upper or middle trapezius, scaleni (subscapularis)
T3/T10	Pectoralis, thoracic erector spinae, serratus anterior (subscapularis)
T10/L2	Quadratus lumborum, psoas, abdominals, thoracolumbar erector spinae
L2/L3	Gluteus medius
L3/L4	Rectus femoris, lumbar erector spinae, adductors
L4/L5	Piriformis, hamstrings, lumbar erector spinae, adductors
L5/S1	Iliacus, hamstrings, lumbar erector spinae, adductors
SI	Gluteus maximus, piriformis, iliacus, hamstrings, adductors, contralateral gluteus medius
Coccyx	Levator ani, gluteus maximus, piriformis (iliacus)
Hip	Adductors

Reprinted with permission from Liebenson CS. Integrating rehabilitation into chiropractic practice (blending active and passive care). In: Liebenson CS, ed. Spinal Rehabilitation: A Manual of Active Care Procedures. *Baltimore: Williams and Wilkins, 1995.*

by observing abnormal substitution during our muscle testing protocols.

When a movement pattern is altered, the activation sequence or firing order of muscles involved in a specific movement is disturbed. The prime mover may be slow to activate, while synergists or stabilizers substitute and become overactive. When this is the case, new joint stresses will be encountered. Sometimes the timing sequence is normal, but the overall range may be limited due to joint stiffness or antagonist muscle shortening.

A classic example of muscular imbalance, causing an impaired movement pattern, is the presence of tight hip flexors combined with a weak or inhibited gluteus maximus, causing an uncoordinated hip extension movement pattern. The gluteus maximus may be inhibited and activate poorly during the movement, leading to overactivity of the erector spinae muscles, which are stabilizers of the lumbar spine. Although such an altered pattern may have formed as a result of hip flexor compensation for a low back strain, hyperpronation problem, leg length inequality, etc., it may eventually perpetuate instability by overstressing the lumbar joints. In this case, the following functional pathologies will all be interconnected: shortening of the psoas, inhibition/weakness/trigger points of the gluteus maximus, overactivity/trigger points of the lumbar erector spinae, lumbar spine joint dysfunction, and altered coordination/endurance of hip extension, particularly during gait.

Testing individual muscles for strength, without evaluating the speed of activation or relaxation, or the activation sequence of agonist, synergists, and stabilizers, reflects an incomplete examination and will likely result in the examiner missing critical details that are necessary for establishing a successful case management plan. According to Korr, "The brain thinks in terms of whole motions, not individual muscles."[87] Muscles may have anatomical individuality, but they function interdependently to create smooth, well-orchestrated movements.

Examples of typical pairs of overactive and weak muscles and the altered movement patterns are listed in Table 3–8. These pairs are used as a screening evaluation to correlate joint overstress, trigger points, tight muscles, and inhibited or weak muscles. Other key functional demands such as squatting, lunging, reaching, etc., can also be looked at for muscle imbalances, incoordination, and other dysfunctions.

The cerebellum can memorize pain motor programs, poor postural habits, or altered movement patterns. Motor programs may be beneficial (such as for athletes and musicians) or detrimental (such as poor posture). Once learned, inefficient or uneconomical movement patterns will likely perpetuate the muscular imbalance and joint dysfunction that may have caused them. Treatment aimed at peripheral functional pathology, such as tight muscles, trigger points, or joint dysfunction, may fail if altered movement patterns are not identified and reeducated.

Janda promoted the concept that the central nervous system's control of movement can be reeducated. His theory has recently been tested in a study by Bullock-Saxton et al in which propriosensory stimulation exercises were given to individuals in an attempt to improve the speed of recruitment of the gluteus maximus and gluteus medius muscles during gait.[84] Individuals performed balance exercises for 15 minutes per day for 1 week. These exercises led to significant increases in the speed of activation of the gait

Table 3–8: The Relationship Between Agonist, Antagonist, and Synergist Muscles and Movement

WEAK AGONIST	OVERACTIVE ANTAGONIST	OVERACTIVE SYNERGIST	MOVEMENT PATTERN
Gluteus maximus	Psoas, rectus femoris	Erector spinae, hamstrings	Hip extension
Gluteus medius	Adductors	QL, TFL, piriformis	Hip abduction
Abdominals	Erector spinae	Psoas	Trunk flexion
Serratus anterior	Pectoralis major/minor	Upper trapezius, levator scapulae, rhomboids	Trunk lowering from a push-up (scapular fixation)
Deep neck flexors	Suboccipitals	SCM	Neck flexion
Lower and middle trapezius		Upper trapezius, levator scapulae, rhomboids	Shoulder abduction, or flexion, (scapular fixation)
Diaphragm		Scalenes, pectoralis major	Respiration

muscles. Such propriosensory retraining improved gluteal activity "automatically and subconsciously, and not as a voluntary muscle contraction."[84]

THE CLINICAL CLASSIFICATION OF TIGHT OR TENSE MUSCLES

The presence of tight or tense muscles may be due to several etiologies, which can be classified as either neuromuscular in origin or caused by connective tissue alterations (see Table 3–9). According to the neurophysiologist Paillard, "Muscle tone, once widely used as a basic semilogical dimension of clinical neurology, is now almost ignored by neurophysiology. It certainly deserves new consideration as a potent contextual dimension of motor performance."[88]

Neuromuscular Etiologies for Muscle Tightness

There are several neuromuscular causes of tight/tense muscles that fall under this category, including reflex spasm, interneuron facilitation, trigger points, and the limbic system.

Reflex spasm

The cause of the reflex spasm is nociceptive. Abnormal EMG activity is present in these cases. Examples include spinal cord injury, reflex spasm such as appendicitis, or acute lumbar antalgia with loss of flexion relaxation response.[89] Long-lasting noxious stimulation has been shown to activate the flexion withdrawal reflex.[90] Treatment is directed at addressing the cause of the nociceptive activity (see Table 3–10).

Interneuron facilitation

The cause is mechanoreceptor facilitation due to joint dysfunction. Travell and Simons consider this to be the most important complicating factor of myofascial pain. Low-intensity stimulation of joint afferents in the knee has been shown to influence stretch sensitivity.[78,91,92] Schiable and Grubb have implicated reflex discharges from joints mediated by efferent sympathetic fibers in the production of

Table 3–9: Etiologies of Tight or Tense Muscles

A. Neuromuscular

1. Reflex spasm
2. Interneuron facilitation
3. Trigger point
4. Limbic system

B. Connective Tissue

1. Muscle stiffness
2. Fibrosis

Modified from Liebenson CS. Manual resistance techniques. In: Liebenson CS, ed. Spinal Rehabilitation: A Manual of Active Care Procedures. *Baltimore: Williams and Wilkins, 1995.*

Table 3–10: Treatment of Muscle Tension/Tightness Types

1. Reflex spasm: Treat the nociceptive cause
2. Interneuron facilitation: Joint manipulation
3. Trigger point: Postisometric relaxation or hold-relax muscle techniques
4. Limbic system: Yoga, meditation, counseling
5. Muscle tightness: Postfacilitatory stretch (PFS) or eccentric muscle relaxation techniques (MRTs); cross-fiber massage

Modified from Liebenson CS. Manual resistance techniques. In: Liebenson CS, ed. Spinal Rehabilitation: A Manual of Active Care Procedures. *Baltimore: Williams and Wilkins, 1995.*

neuromuscular tension.[79] Treatment is joint manipulation to correct joint dysfunction.

Partial "spasm": trigger points

In these cases, the involved muscle fails to relax properly. Muscles that house trigger points have been shown to have dramatically elevated levels of EMG activity. Hubbard and Berkoff demonstrated EMG hyperexcitability in the nidus of the trigger point in a taut band that had a characteristic pattern of reproducible referred pain.[93] Treatment is by utilizing modalities such as ice and stretch, hold-relax, or postisometric relaxation (PIR) muscle energy techniques.

Limbic system

The limbic system, under the influence of stress or poor sleep patterns, can alter the stretch sensitivity of the intrafusal muscle spindles. An elevated gamma discharge from the reticular formation will sensitize the intrafusal spindles so that they will fire at decreased lengths. This leads to extrafusal contractions within the formerly resting length of the muscle. Treatment is directed at stress management, and may include meditation, counseling, exercise for stress relief, and other approaches.

Viscoelastic or Connective Tissue

As a result of overuse or secondary to injury, muscle stiffness or fibrosis can occur. These alterations in the quality of muscle tissue result in the presence of muscle stiffness.

Muscle stiffness

Muscle stiffness is a viscoelastic phenomena described by Walsh[94] as due to altered fluid mechanics and tissue viscosity secondary to trauma. According to Hagbarth, muscle fibers adapt themselves to imposed length changes. "After stretching or passive shortening, it may take 15 minutes or more before muscle fibers spontaneously return to their initial resting length."[95] Muscle plasticity depends on the formation and disruption of cross-bridges between actin and myosin filaments. This plasticity is called muscle *thixotropy*. Thixotropic liquids have high viscosity at rest, but become fluid when shaken or stirred; both extrafusal and intrafusal muscle fibers have thixotropic properties.

Fibrosis

Overuse can gradually lead to increased neuromuscular tension. Any of the types of tension described above (reflex, interneuron, trigger point, or limbic) can alter stretch sensitivity and reprogram the regulation of muscle tone. Travell explains that "when injured, most tissues heal, but skeletal muscles learn; they readily develop habits of guarding that limit movement and impair circulation." Increased sensitivity to stretch is also a factor under conditions of local ischemia.[96] This can occur from the prolonged muscle overload that can occur in sustained static postures, such as typing.

Fibrotic changes have been shown to occur posttrauma. They involve the connective tissues surrounding the muscle, too. Lehto et al found that fibroblasts proliferate in injured tissue during the inflammatory phase.[97] If the inflammatory phase is prolonged, then a connective tissue scar will form since the fibroblasts are not reabsorbed.

CLINICAL AND SCIENTIFIC EVIDENCE FOR MUSCLE IMBALANCES

Several studies have demonstrated the clinical significance of muscle imbalances that lead to a variety of pathologies. Watson and Trott identified the presence of forward head posture and decreased isometric strength and endurance of neck flexors as two key findings that differentiated headache from nonheadache sufferers. They utilized a strain gauge to quantify neck flexor isometric strength.[98]

In a study by Treleaven et al, three distinguishable factors were found in postconcussional headache patients: upper cervical joint dysfunction, weak neck flexors, and tight suboccipitals.[99] In addition, Janda's neck flexor test (described below) was validated versus the strain gauge test, and shown to be reliable! The scientific literature supports the view that muscle groups react to injury, inflammation, and pain by demonstrating inhibition or facilitation (see Table 3–11).[77,80–84,89,100,101]

Table 3–11: Scientific Evidence for the Etiology of Muscle Imbalance

A. Increased tension or tightness

1. Relative Type I muscle fiber hypertrophy on the symptomatic side in patients with chronic low back pain has been demonstrated.[77,101]
2. Prolonged nociceptive bombardment produces excessive contraction of skeletal muscles in the vicinity of the nociceptors, leading to the flexion reflex.[69,103]
3. Fibroblasts proliferate in injured tissues during the post-inflammatory stage of healing.[99]

B. Muscle inhibition, weakness, or atrophy

1. Reflex inhibition of the vastus medius lateralis is present after knee inflammation/injury.[80–82]
2. Unilateral, segmental Type II muscle fiber atrophy occurs after acute onset of low back pain.[83]
3. Bilateral Type II muscle fiber atrophy is prevalent in chronic low back pain patients.[77,101]
4. Patients with herniated discs demonstrate atrophy of Type II muscle fibers in the multifidus muscle group.[103–105]
5. Decreased endurance of the trunk extensors has not only been shown to correlate with pain, but to predict recurrences and first time onset in healthy individuals.[107,108]
6. Increased ratio of rectus abdominus to transverse abdominus/oblique abdominals is correlated with low back pain.[109]
7. Increased levels of muscle coactivation may constitute an objective indicator of the dysfunction in the passive stabilization system of the spine.[110]

Muscle Inhibition/Weakness

Case studies suggest that trigger points in one muscle are related to inhibition of other functionally related muscles.[84,98] Simons showed that the deltoid muscle can be inhibited when there are infraspinatus trigger points.[100] Headley has shown that lower trapezius inhibition is associated with trigger points in the upper trapezius.[102] Reflex inhibition of the vastus medialis after knee joint inflammation or ligamentous injury is well documented.[80–82] Correcting the cause of inhibition will quickly restore muscle strength.

Muscle Atrophy

Hides et al found unilateral, segmental wasting of the multifidus in acute back pain patients.[83] This occurred rapidly, thus ruling out the possibility of disuse atrophy. In chronic back pain patients, generalized atrophy was found, but a relative increase in the cross-sectional analysis (CSA) was found on the symptomatic side.[101] In other words, although generalized atrophy was present in these patients, there was relatively less atrophy on the symptomatic side, which rules out the likelihood of disuse atrophy. Type 1 fiber hypertrophy on the symptomatic side and Type II fiber atrophy bilaterally have been documented in chronic back pain patients.[77]

EVALUATION AND TREATMENT OF MUSCLE IMBALANCES

Evaluation of the motor system includes assessment of passive (joint) and active (muscle) tissues. It also includes evaluation of postural and motor function, controlled by the central nervous system (cerebellum). A functional evaluation leading to a rehabilitation prescription evaluates the specific tasks that patients perform. Assessing the stability of the spine during performance of typical tasks is an essential starting point. This leads to specific tests of muscle and joint function. Posture, gait, muscle length, joint mobility, selective tissue tension, pain provocation, movement patterns, and strength/endurance tests are all part of this comprehensive assessment of the stability of the locomotor system.

POSTURE AND GAIT ANALYSIS

Postural analysis looks at hypo- and hypertrophic changes and effects on body topography and symmetry. For example, a hypotrophic serratus anterior leads to winging of the scapula. (See Figure 3–1.) The presence of a hypertrophic upper trapezius leads to the appearance of "Gothic shoulders." (See Figure 3–2).

Gait analysis can reveal many muscle imbalances and areas of joint overstress. For instance, failure to toe off is a sign of decreased hip hyperextension. This will typically be accompanied by lumbar overstress due to compensatory hypermobility. Other examples are the presence of Trendelenburg gait, which is a sign of gluteus medius weakness, and hip hiking, which is a sign of an overactive quadratus lumborum (QL).

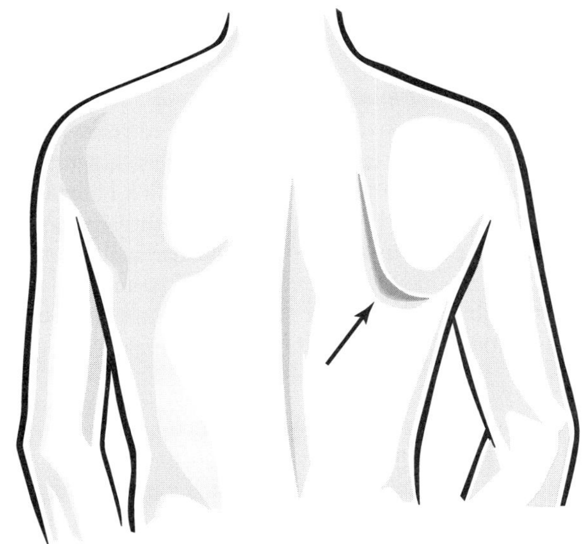

Figure 3–1. Abduction and winging of the right scapula. *(Reprinted from Tunnell P., 1996.[124])*

Table 3–12 provides a checklist of signs found in gait and postural analysis, and their clinical interpretation.

MOBILITY (INCLINOMETRY) AND MUSCLE LENGTH EVALUATION

Quantification

Inclinometers can be used reliably to evaluate range of motion of trunk flexion/extension, side bending, cervical spine motion, hip extension, internal and external hip rotation,

Figure 3–2. "Gothic" shoulders: angulation at neck-shoulder angle with straightening or slight upward convexity of the shoulder contour. *(Reprinted from Tunnell P., 1996.[124])*

Table 3–12: Gait and Postural Analysis

INFORMATION SIGN	FUNCTIONAL PATHOLOGY
Gait	**Gait**
Hyperpronation	Rearfoot instability
Failure to toe off	Hip flexor tightness
Lumbar hyperlordosis	Overactivity of lumbar erector spinae/hip flexor tightness
Posture	**Posture**
A to P	***A to P***
Flat feet	Hypermobile subtalar joint
Hypertrophied sternocleidomastoid	Overactive sternocleidomastoid
Arms internally rotated	Shortened pectorals
P to A	***P to A***
Sagging buttock	Weak glutei
Hypertrophied thoracolumbar erector spinae	Overactive erector spinae
Winging of the scapulae	Weak serratus anterior
Elevated shoulder girdle	Shortened upper trapezius or levator scapulae
Lateral	***Lateral***
Protruding abdomen	Weak rectus abdominus
Head forward	Weak deep neck flexors/tight suboccipitals
Rounded shoulders	Shortened pectoralis major

Modified from Liebenson CS. Muscular imbalances and myofascial pain. J Myofasc Ther. *1995.*

straight leg raise, and knee flexion ROM. The length of the erector spinae, iliopsoas, rectus femoris, hamstrings, gastrocnemius, and soleus can also be quantified. Other important muscles, such as the hip adductors, tensor fascia latae (TFL), quadratus lumborum (QL), and piriformis are harder to quantify; thus, "softer" tests must be used.

Length Tests

These length tests are designed to evalute the muscle and its associated fascia. In performing the following series of length tests, it is important to be consistent and thorough in positioning the patient in order to obtain repeatable and thus reliable measurements.

Hamstrings

Hamstring tightness is evaluated by the straight leg raise (SLR) test. To avoid the influence of a tight iliopsoas on the position of the pelvis and thus on the range of hip flexion, the non-tested hip should be in flexion. Under these circumstances, the normal range of motion is 80 degrees.

Hip flexors

Hip flexors (iliopsoas, rectus femoris) are tested in a modified Thomas position. (See Figure 3–3.) The patient is supine at an oblique angle, with the torso resting on the table and the tested thigh hanging off the side of the table. The nontested leg is maximally flexed to stabilize the pelvis and flatten the lumbar spine. The following components should be evaluated while the patient is in this position.

HIP EXTENSION. Less than 10 to 15 degrees of hip extension is a positive test, indicating a shortened iliopsoas. The presence of a simultaneous flexion of the knee joint indicates a shortened rectus femoris.

KNEE FLEXION. Less than 100 to 105 degrees of knee flexion is a positive test, indicating a shortened rectus femoris. The tendency for compensatory hip flexion should occur during the test.

HIP ADDUCTION. Less than 15 to 20 degrees of hip adduction is a positive test, indicating a shortened tensor fasciae latae and iliotibial band. There will be an associated deepening of the groove on the outside of the thigh.

HIP ABDUCTION. Less than 15 to 20 degrees of hip abduction is a positive test, indicating shortened hip adductors. The tendency to compensatory hip flexion should be controlled during the test. A false positive is possible due to hip capsule tightness.

Adductors

There are several muscles that perform hip adduction of which some are one-joint muscles (crossing the hip joint) and others are two-joint muscles (crossing the hip and

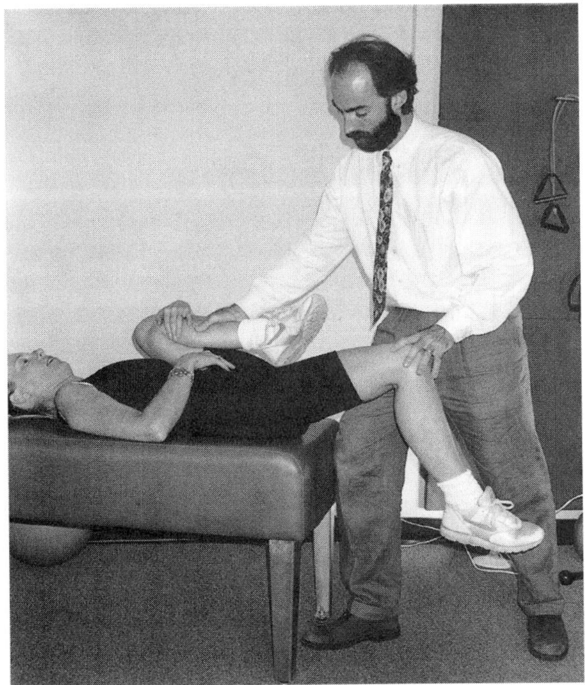
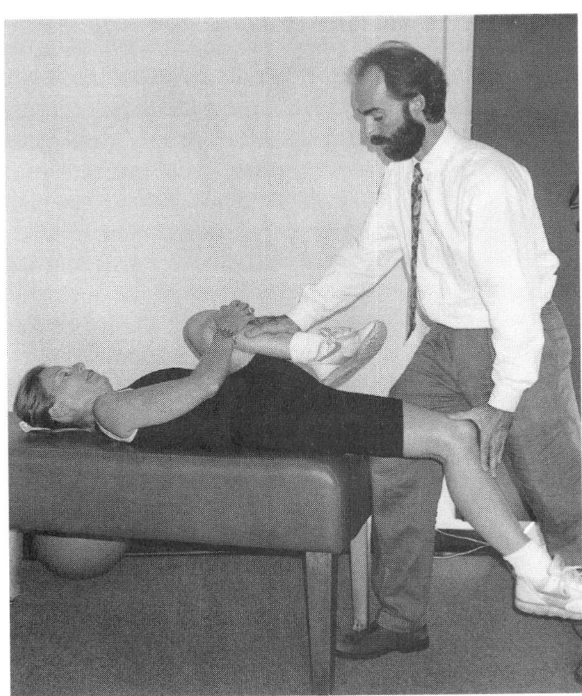

Figure 3–3. Modified Thomas test.

knee joints). In evaluating the adductors, the clinician must take care to distinguish between shortened one-joint and shortened two-joint adductors. (See Figure 3–4.)

ONE-JOINT. These are the pectineus, adductor magnus, adductor brevis, and adductor longus.

TWO-JOINT. These are the gracilis, semimembranosus, and semitendinosis.

Thigh adductors are tested supine. Passive abduction in the hip joint should be at least 40 degrees. If there is no increase in abduction with the knee bent, then the one-joint adductors are shortened. A false positive may occur due to tight hamstrings.

Erector spinae

Erector spinae are difficult to examine. As a screening test, forward bending in a short sit (sitting with knees flexed at table's edge and legs dangling off the table) is performed, and reversal of the lumbar lordosis is observed. If the lumbar spine does not reverse its curve, it is a positive test for shortened erector spinae. Inclinometric evaluation or the Schober's test is more reliable.

Quadratus lumborum

The quadratus lumborum is difficult to examine since too many spinal segments are involved. Passive trunk side-bending in a sidelying position may be used as a screening test. The reference point is the level of the inferior angle of the scapula, which should be raised from the floor by approximately 2 inches. In standing side-bending, inclinometers may be used or the clinician may observe failure to achieve a smooth, contralateral convexity of the lumbar curve. Straightening of the curve below T12 is a positive test.

Piriformis

The piriformis is tested in a supine position. The tested leg is placed with the hip joint in less than 60 degrees of flexion, and in maximal adduction. The pelvis is stabilized by placing pressure over the knee of the tested leg, along the long axis of the femur. After prepositioning is complete, internal rotation of the hip is performed. The muscle may be "wound up" in a different sequence so long as pelvic stabilization is not sacrificed. Normally there is a soft, gradually increasing resistance at the end of the range of motion. If the muscle is tight, the end feeling is hard and may be associated with pain deep in the buttock.

Gastrocnemius and soleus

The gastrocnemius and soleus may be tested by passively dorsiflexing the foot. Inability to dorsiflex the foot to 90 degrees is a positive test. With knee extension the gastrocnemius is tested, whereas with knee flexion the soleus is tested (the soleus is a one-joint muscle crossing only the ankle, whereas the gastrocnemius crosses both the knee and ankle joints).

Upper trapezius and levator scapulae

The upper trapezius is tested in the supine position. The patient's head is passively flexed forward and inclined to the ipsilateral side. From this position, the patient's head is held still, and the shoulder girdle is pushed distally. Nor-

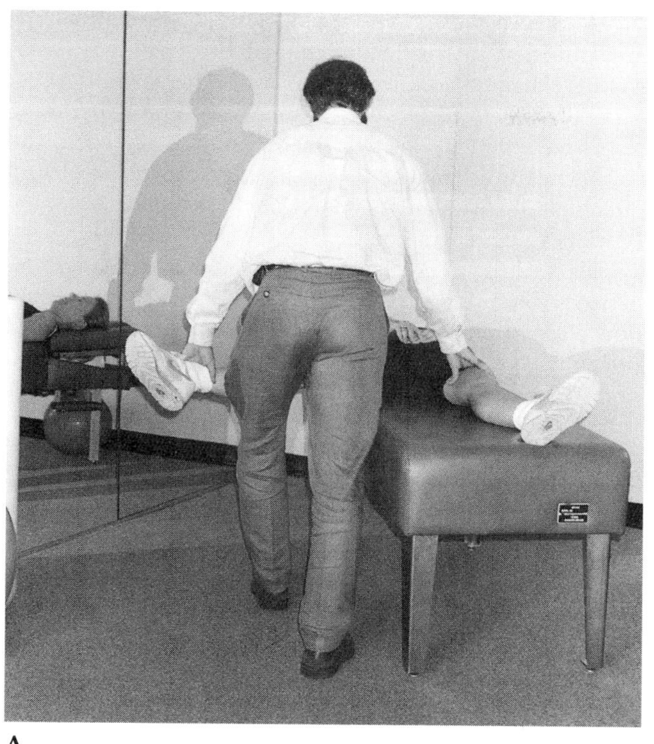
A

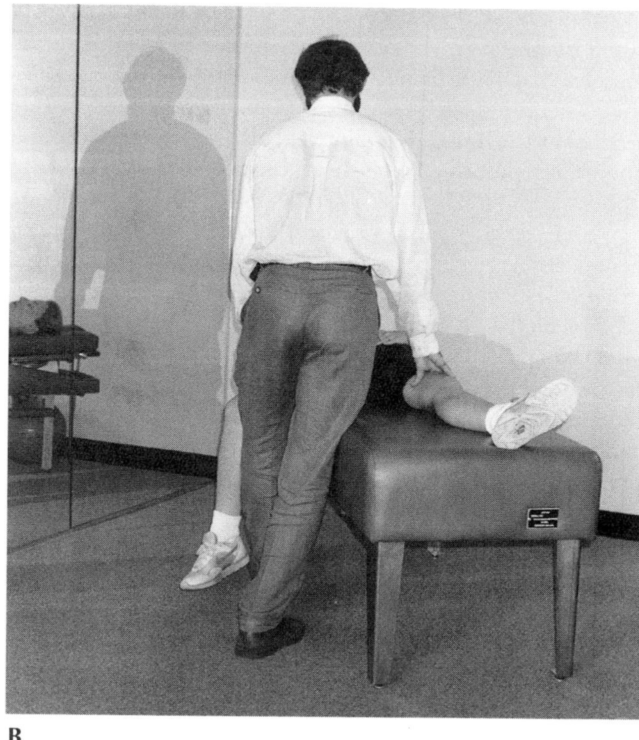
B

Figure 3–4. A. Two-joint adductor test. **B.** One-joint adductor test.

mally at the end of the push there is a soft barrier; when the movement is restricted, there is a hard end feeling. The levator scapulae is examined in a similar manner, only the head is rotated to the contralateral side, away from the shoulder to be depressed.

Pectoralis major

The pectoralis major is tested in the supine position. The patient's trunk is stabilized with one hand, and then the patient's arm is moved passively into abduction. The trunk has to be stabilized before the arm is placed into abduction since a possible twist of the trunk might give a false negative result. The various portions of the pectoralis major are tested by altering the position of the arm. For the sternal portion, the patient's arm is abducted approximately 90 degrees away from the trunk; the arm should be horizontal to the table. If it is less than horizontal, this is a positive test. For the clavicular portion, the patient's arm is abducted only approximately 30 degrees away from the trunk; the arm should be a minimum of 20 degrees below table level. Only gentle overpressure is applied (to avoid injuring the glenohumeral joint). Normally, only a slight soft barrier is felt.

Summary of muscle length testing

The muscle length testing above highlights several of the most commonly involved muscles in postural imbalances. The subject of muscle length testing has been dealt with very effectively by several authors including Janda and Evjenth. For more detailed explanations and corresponding pictures, please refer to the appropriate reference texts.

SELECTIVE AND PROVOCATIVE TISSUE TENSION TESTS AND PROVOCATIVE MANEUVERS

The literature on selective tissue tension tests is increasingly sophisticated and emphasizes the necessity of evaluating skin, fascia, muscle, and nerve tissue, in addition to joints, as potential sources of pain and pathology.

Cyriax developed a screen for differentially assessing "contractile" and "noncontractile" or "inert" structures.[106] He described specific active ROM, passive end feel, and active resistance tests. When inert structures are dysfunctional or inflamed, active and passive movements are painful in the same direction. Typically, contractile tissues become provoked by active and resisted movements, although passive movements that stretch the tissue may also be provocative. Stretching, pinching, or compression will lead to pain provocation of inert structures. Stretching or contracting has a tendency to provoke symptoms in contractile tissues. Generally, active movements (i.e., resisted isometric movements) are most valuable for testing contractile tissues, and passive movements (end feel) for testing inert structures.

Active ROM tests usually take place at the beginning of a screening examination. They are followed by passive overpressure at the end point or passive ROM tests. Resisted isometric movements are then used to isolate specific muscles that are inflamed. With the related joints placed in their "neutral position," strong isometric contractions are resisted at the muscle's midrange. False positives do occur if a joint is inflamed as a result of joint compression or shear forces.

Elvy developed a provocative test to evaluate for neural tissue tension in the upper extremity. Just as the straight leg raise test identifies adverse tension and/or irritability of the sciatic nerve for the lower extremity, Elvy used the upper limb tension test to identify adverse tension or decreased extensibility of nerves emerging from the brachial plexus.[111] The upper limb tension test (ULTT) can be performed by sequentially combining scapular depression, shoulder abduction and external rotation, forearm supination, wrist and finger extension, and finally elbow extension. The angle of elbow extension is a reliable measure of nerve tension during the ULTT. This version of the ULTT has an ulnar nerve bias.

Butler built upon Elvy's work to develop a series of selective tissue tests to evaluate for the presence of adverse neural tissue tensions in the trunk and extremities.[112] Butler's tests utilize a specific sequence of movements to apply stress to the upper limb's neural structures. In these procedures, the end point is achieved when pain provocation occurs and tension within the tissues prevents further movement. Another ULTT (radial nerve bias) involves sequential scapular depression, elbow extension, shoulder internal rotation, forearm pronation, wrist and finger flexion or extension, and lastly shoulder abduction. Contralateral cervical lateral flexion may also be added. The shoulder abduction may be measured as a quantifiable measure of the test. Butler has also developed a mobilization technique to treat peripheral nerve entrapments.[112]

A recent study by Yaxley and Jull suggests that Butler's neural tension tests can be used to identify the presence of decreased neural tissue extensibility. In addition, they suggest a correlation between the presence of decreased nerve extensibility and the pain that is present in chronic repetitive stress injuries such as lateral epicondylitis.[113] In a 1994 study by Wright et al, it was shown that the presence of mechanical hyperalgesia in patients with tennis elbow is due to secondary hyperalgesia ("reduced mechanical pain threshold, no change in heat pain threshold.").[114] This suggests that "neuronal changes within the spinal cord may be more important than peripheral nociceptor sensitization in the development of chronic musculoskeletal disorders such as tennis elbow."[114] In other words, the presence of decreased neural tissue extensibility may lead to spinal cord changes resulting in increased peripheral nociception.

In cases of lateral epicondylitis, the ULTT should be compared to tests of forearm and wrist flexibility. The muscles are tested on their own following standard procedures and then compared with the results following scapular depression, shoulder internal rotation, and shoulder abduction.

McKenzie uses provocative tests to determine the type and direction of treatment required by a patient's symptoms.[115] His tests seek to determine whether there is a postural, dysfunction, or derangement syndrome by using repetitive endrange loading. In McKenzie's approach, the pain-generating tissue is not sought. Instead, the type and direction of treatment is adjudicated by the reduction or centralization of symptoms.

According to McKenzie's clinical reasoning system, patients with a postural syndrome will report pain provocation after sustained static loading (commonly, prolonged sitting in a slumped position). This information is derived from the patient history since no examination procedures will provoke or alleviate the symptoms in the postural syndrome patient.

Patients with a dysfunction syndrome will demonstrate pain provocation with endrange loading of the adaptively shortened structures, and no improvement is noted with any repetitive endrange activities. All other positions are painless, and there is no pain in the midrange of motion.

Patients with a derangement syndrome will demonstrate pain provocation in the midrange of certain repeated movements and will obtain immediate pain relief or centralization of symptoms by performing other repeated nonpainful movements to end point.

Adhesions between the skin and underlying fascia, particularly in postsurgical patients, can often be generators of pain. Lewit describes the presence of hyperalgesic zones in which skin stretch and mobility are decreased.[85] At times, the hyperalgesic zone may be the pain generator responsible for the patient's discomfort. To evaluate for the presence of skin-fascial adhesions, the therapist first runs fingers lightly over the skin and notes areas where there is increased friction. The skin may also be rolled in various directions between the therapist's fingers. Areas of skin tightness, hyperalgesia, and decreased mobility may be addressed by treating with skin rolling or skin stretching over the area until greater mobility of the skin is achieved.[85]

EVALUATION OF ALTERED MOVEMENT PATTERNS

Several movement patterns have been identified by Jull and Janda that can be used to evaluate the presence of muscle imbalance and aberrant firing patterns.[74] The following summarizes these identified patterns, with suggested evaluation protocols.

Hip Extension Coordination[85] (See Figure 3–5.)

Purpose

To identify incoordination of hip extension.

To determine if the gluteal maximus is weak or inhibited.

To determine if the erector spinae are overactive.

To determine if the hamstring is overactive.

To determine if the hip joint has reduced extension mobility, or if the psoas is shortened.

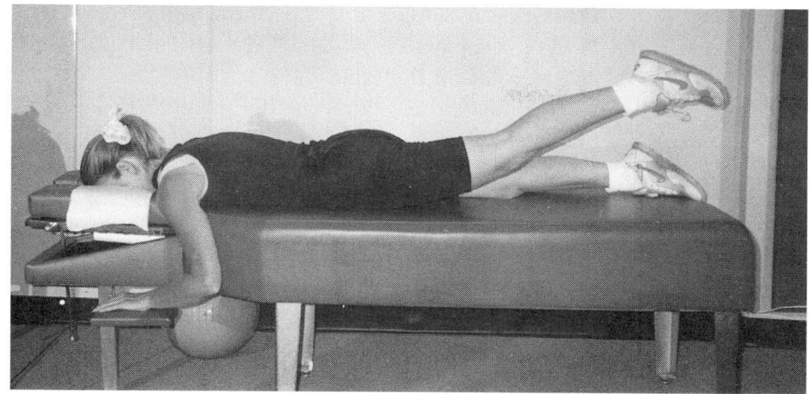

Figure 3–5. Hip extension test.

Patient positioning and test performance
Patient lies prone.
Patient attempts to raise leg into extension with knee held in extended position.
Positive test, if erector spinae musculature contracts before gluteus maximus.
Doctor should observe the activation sequence of hamstrings (1), gluteus maximus (2), contralateral lumbar erector spinae (3), and ipsilateral erector spinae (4).
Grade 1: contralateral erector spinae fire before the gluteus maximus.
Grade 2: contralateral and ipsilateral erector spinae fire before the gluteus maximus.
Light palpation should be used only to confirm the results.
Prognosis is better for grade 1 versus grade 2.

Quantification
With dynamic EMG.

Qualification
Pass/fail.
Fail if erector spinae contract before gluteal maximus.
Record activation sequence or firing order of gluteal maximus, hamstrings, lumbar erector spinae, and thoracolumbar erector spinae (ipsilateral and contralateral).
Note if contralateral shoulder/neck musculature contracts (overrecruitment).

Hip Abduction Coordination Test (Gluteus Medius, TFL, QL, Piriformis).[85] (See Figure 3–6.)

Purpose
To identify coordination of hip abduction.
To identify tightness/overactivity of quadratus lumborum (hip hiking), tensor fascia latae (hip flexion and external rotation), thigh adductors (limited abduction range, piriformis (external rotation), psoas (hip flexion).
To identify poor hip joint mobility (decreased extension).
To identify weakness of the gluteus medius.

Patient positioning and test performance
Patient side lying with lower knee flexed and upper leg extended.
Pelvis is placed in a slightly untucked position.

Concentric test
Upper leg is raised into abduction and held for 2 seconds.
Positive test if any pelvic movement occurs:
- Hip hiking (QL).
- Posterior rotation of the ilium (psoas).

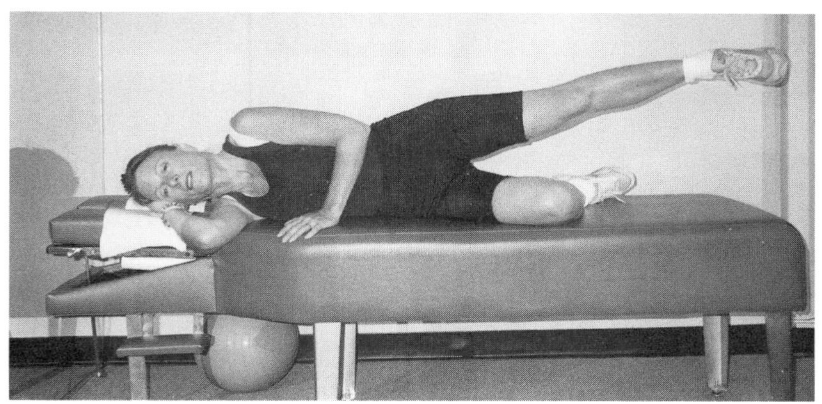

Figure 3–6. Hip abduction coordination test.

Positive test if external rotation of the hip occurs (piriformis).
Positive test if hip flexion and/or external rotation occurs (psoas, TFL).

Note
If patient can raise leg.
Shaking or twisting.
Any hip flexion or hip external rotation.
Excessive hip hiking.
Posterior rotation of upper ilium.

Quantification
Only with dynamic EMG.

Qualification
Pass/fail.
Fail if patient cannot abduct leg without hip flexion, if foot raises less than 6 inches, and if hip externally rotates, pelvis rotates, or hip hiking occurs.

Isometric test

Preposition leg in abduction without flexion and ask patient to hold leg for 5 seconds.
Support may be suddenly removed to increase the difficulty.

Note
If shaking occurs.
Hip flexion, external rotation, pelvic rotation, or hip hiking (positive test).

Quantification
None.

Qualification
Pass/fail.

Trunk Flexion Coordination Test.[85,116] (See Figure 3–7.)

Purpose
Quantify rectus abdominus strength/endurance and coordination.

Patient positioning and test performance
Patient is supine with knees bent, arms across chest, and feet flat on the table.
Doctor may either contact under patient's heels or place under small of the back.
Patient is instructed to perform posterior pelvic tilt and raise trunk up until scapulae are off the table, and then hold for 2 seconds.
Patient should hold the pelvic tilt while lowering back to the table.
Patient is asked to perform 10 repetitions.
Last repetition is held for 30 seconds.
Positive test if heels rise up (psoas recruitment) or if patient loses posterior pelvic tilt.
Fewer false negatives (more sensitive) if doctor places hands under patient's heels than if doctor merely watches for feet to lift up.

Note
If heels rise off table (positive test).
If posterior pelvic tilt cannot be maintained (positive test).
If excessive shaking occurs.
If head is markedly forward of trunk.
If curl-up is performed segmentally or as mass movement at the hip joint.

Quantification
With dynamic EMG.

Qualification
Pass/fail.
Fail if heels rise up or if lumbar spine arches before 10 repetitions and a 30-second hold can be accomplished.

Shoulder Abduction Coordination Test.[85] (See Figure 3–8.)

Purpose
Identify loss of normal glenohumeral rhythm due to overactivity of the upper trapezius and/or levator scapulae muscles.

Figure 3–7. Trunk flexion coordination test.

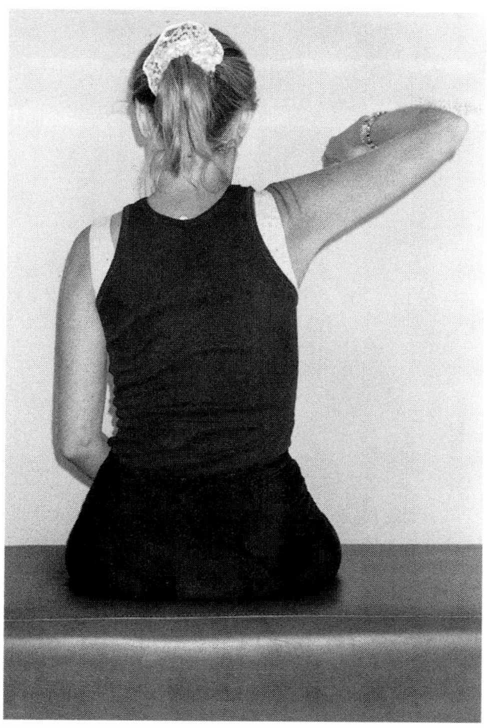

Figure 3–8. Shoulder abduction coordination test.

Patient positioning and test performance
Patient is seated with elbow flexed to 90 degrees to limit unwanted rotation.
Patient is instructed to slowly abduct arm.

Quantification
Only possible with dynamic EMG.

Qualification
Pass/fail.
Positive test if scapular elevation or rotation (laterally) occurs in first 30 to 60 degrees.
False positive can occur if scapula is already elevated and laterally rotated with arms still at side.

Trunk Lowering from a Push-Up.[117] *(See Figure 3–9.)*

Purpose
To evaluate the patient for serratus anterior weakness and/or overactive upper trapezius and levator scapulae.

Patient positioning and test performance
Patient is positioned in push-up position, preferably with legs extended.
Patient is instructed to slowly lower self from push-up position (i.e., bend elbows).
Patient is instructed to do a push-up.
Patient is asked to raise thorax and protract scapulae.

Qualification
Pass/fail.
Positive test if winging of scapulae occurs (serratus anterior weakness) or if there is cephalad shift of scapulae (overactive upper trapsezius and/or levator scapulae).
Identify scapular retraction or winging.

Head/Neck Flexion Coordination Test.[85,98,99] *(See Figure 3–10.)*

Purpose
To identify if neck flexor weakness or incoordination is present.
In particular to identify if deep neck flexors are weak and the S.C.M. is tight or overactive.

Patient positioning and test performance
Patient is supine and is instructed to bring chin to chest.
Overpressure may be added at end point.
More sensitive test (fewer false negatives) if patient's neck is prepositioned in a chin tuck and raised 1 centimeter off table, and patient holds position isometrically.

Note
If chin juts forward during movement.
If there is shaking during movement.

Figure 3–9. Push-up test.

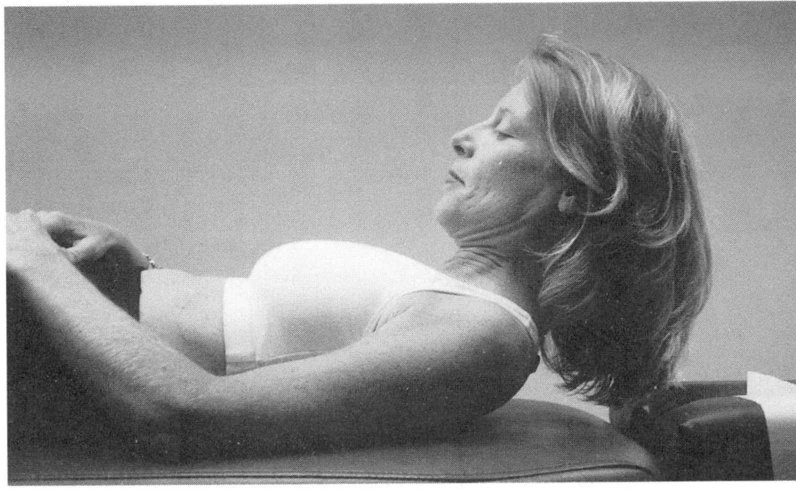

Figure 3–10. Head/neck flexion coordination test.

If there is chin jutting or shaking with overpressure added.
If head elevates from 1 centimeter position (this indicates a change in the center of mass of the head, as an attempt to compensate for neck flexor weakness).

Quantification
With strain gauge.

Qualification
Pass/fail.
Fail if chin juts forward during movement.

Respiration Coordination Test[85]

Purpose
To identify if paradoxical breathing (chest breathing predominates over diaphragm) is present.

Patient positioning and test performance
Patient lies supine.
Patient is asked to take a deep breath in.

Note
Excessive chest breathing.
Lateral chest excursion.
If scalene muscles are visibly active during respiration.

Quantification
None.

Qualification
Pass/fail.
Fail if chest raises more than the abdomen.

ADDITIONAL FUNCTIONAL TESTS

One-Leg Standing Test.[42,118] *(See Figure 3–11.)*

Purpose
Identify need for propriosensory reeducation.
Screening test for gluteus medius weakness.

Patient positioning and test performance
Patient stands on one foot with eyes open.
Foot on the raised leg is at knee level.
Arms are relaxed at the side.
Patient fixes gaze on a point on the wall.
Patient then closes eyes and attempts to maintain balance for 10 seconds.

Quantification
Record the number of seconds until:
- Patient loses balance.
- Reaches out for stability.
- Touches foot to floor.
- Slides supporting foot.

With force platform.[118]

Qualification
Watch for excessive lateral pelvic shift within first 20 seconds.
Positive test if any of the above shifts occur.

Stand to Kneel (Lunge Coordination) Test[119]

Purpose
Qualifiable test for balance, coordination, hip extension mobility, and quadriceps strength.

Patient positioning and test performance
Patient stands with feet about shoulder width apart.
Patient is instructed to perform a lunge to the kneeling position.
One foot steps forward with knee flexing to 90 degrees and back knee just touches the floor.
Back should remain straight (lumbar lordosis is preserved) with arms at the side.

Quantification
None, except with Chattanooga lumbar motion monitor.

Qualification
Pass/fail.
Positive test if patient flexes trunk while performing test.

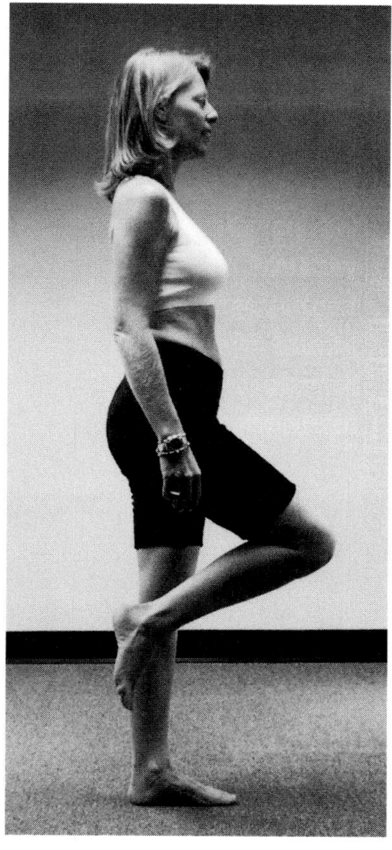
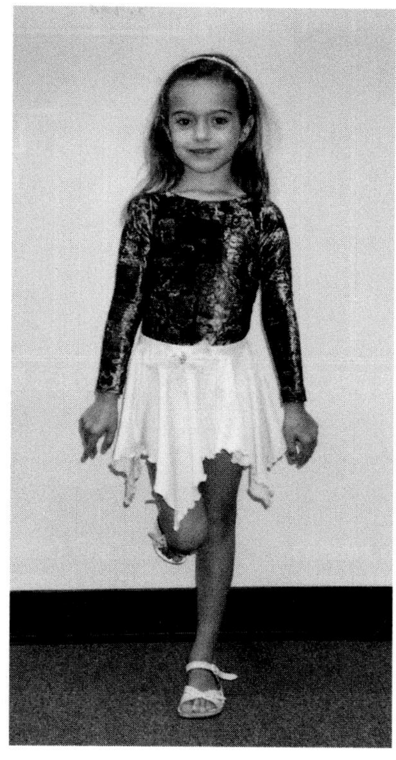

Figure 3–11. One-leg standing test.

Note
Balance of forward foot.
Strength of quadriceps.
Mobility of hip joint and flexibility of hip flexors of back leg.
If patient shifts from side to side while performing lunge, indicates lateral instability (gluteus medius weakness).

Squat Coordination Test.[120] *(See Figure 3–12.)*

Purpose
Qualifiable test for balance, coordination, quadriceps strength, soleus flexibility.

Patient positioning and test performance
Patient stands with feet about shoulder width apart and is instructed to perform a squat.
Patient performs a deep knee bend to about 90 degrees of knee flexion, without losing lumbar lordosis.

Quantification
None.

Qualification
Pass/fail.
Positive test if patient flexed trunk or cannot reach 90 degrees of knee flexion.

Note
If heels raise off floor (soleus tightness).

Sit to Stand Test.[121] *(See Figure 3–13.)*

Purpose
To evaluate the patient for weak or inhibited neck flexors, abdominals, quadriceps, and other related muscle groups.

Patient positioning and test performance
Patient sits with feet flat on floor.
Patient stands up.

Quantification
None, except photographically.

Qualification
Pass/fail.
Fail if head moves forward and chin pokes.
Fail if trunk slumps forward.
Fail if hands push off thighs.
Fail if low back hyperextends.

STRENGTH AND ENDURANCE TESTS

Sorensen Test (Static Back Extensor Endurance)[122]

Purpose
To evaluate lumbar erector spinae static endurance.

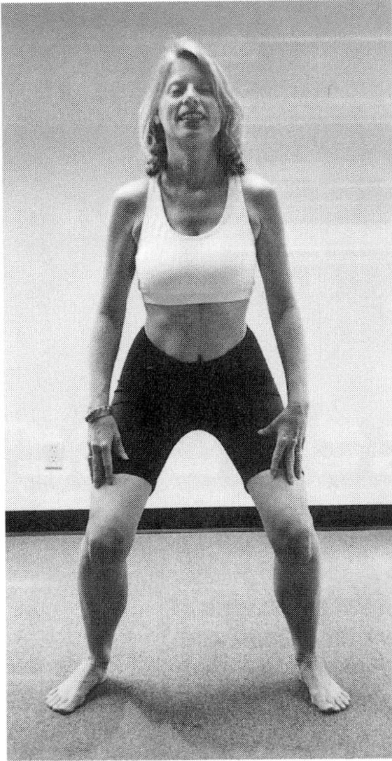
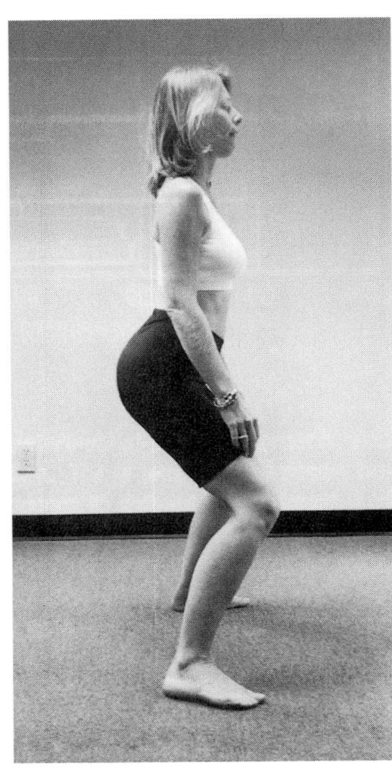

Figure 3–12. Squat coordination test.

Patient positioning and test performance
Patient prone with waist at edge of table and arms at side.
With legs supported, patient is asked to lift torso up to a horizontal position.
Patient should be able to hold position for 4 minutes.

Quantification
Number of seconds subject can hold horizontal position is recorded.

The next three tests are repetitive tests. The rate of repetition is one repetition per 2 to 3 seconds. The movements are repeated at a constant pace and stopped when 50 repetitions have been accomplished.

Repetitive Arch-Up Test (Dynamic Back Extensor Endurance)[123]

Purpose
To evaluate lumbar erector spinae dynamic strength and endurance.

Patient positioning and test performance
Patient prone with waist at edge of table and trunk flexed 45 degrees.
Patient's arms at sides.
With legs supported, patient is asked to lift torso up to horizontal.

Quantification
Number of repetitions performed.

Repetitive Sit-Up Test[123]

Purpose
To evaluate abdominal dynamic strength and endurance.

Patient positioning and test performance
Patient supine with the knees flexed 90 degrees.
Patient's feet are fixed at the ankle by the examiner.
Patient curls up and touches kneecaps with thenar region.

Quantification
Number of repetitions performed.

Repetitive Squatting Test[123]

Purpose
To evaluate quadriceps and gluteal dynamic strength and endurance.

Patient positioning and test performance
Patient stands with feet 15 centimeters apart.
Patient squats until the thighs are horizontal and then returns to upright.

Quantification
Number of repetitions performed.

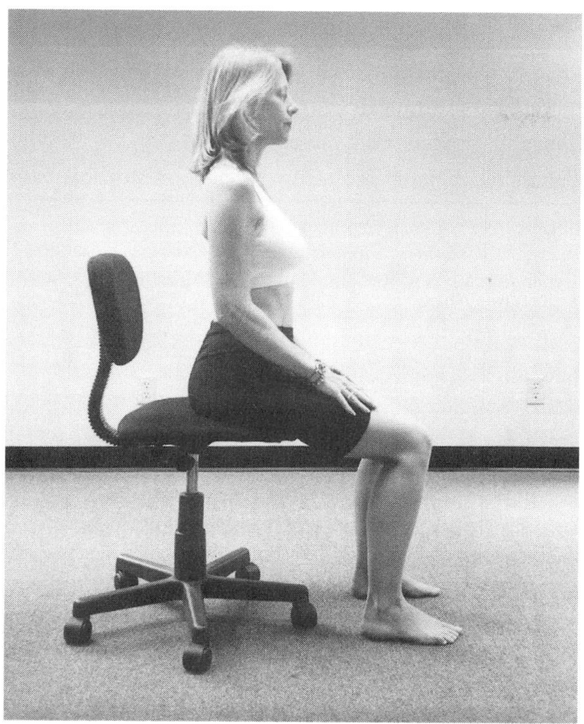

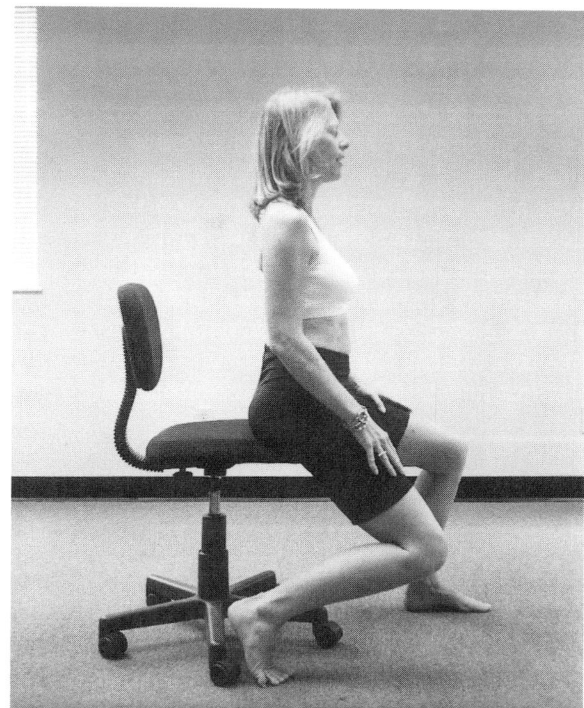

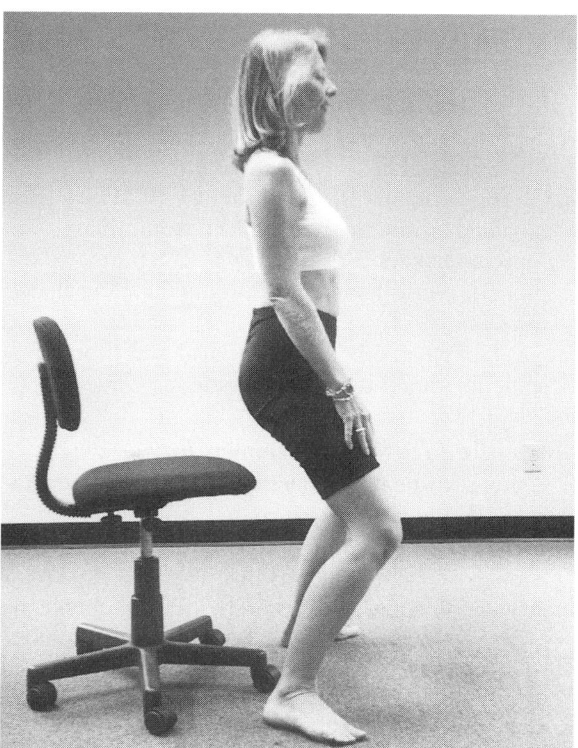

Figure 3–13. Sit to stand test.

FINDING THE KEY FUNCTIONAL PATHOLOGY

Once a functional evaluation has been performed, it is essential to attempt to sort out the key functional pathologies from the ones that are secondary. First, we must tap the patient's history for all relevant information.Then provocative testing, especially of trigger points, can help find the area of overstress. The key is to look for the faulty movement pattern that is the cause of the trigger point. Always look for the kinetic chain dysfunction in the motor system which has led to the symptoms.

CHAIN REACTIONS IN THE MOTOR SYSTEM

Along with identifying pain-provoking movements and tissues, there are other biomechanical and neurophysiological principles that can assist in identifying primary functional pathologies. First, it is important to understand that nearly any tissue can be a pain generator. Therefore, we should focus on identifying the primary dysfunctions, not the secondary compensations or adaptations that inevitably surround the area of pain. This is not intended as a lofty goal, but it is clinically necessary if we are to be successful in achieving long-term rehabilitation (alleviation of chronic pain and prevention of recurrent pain) outcome success.

Biomechanical functional chains have been previously described. In human beings, the lower extremity functions as a closed kinetic chain. Any dysfunction in the foot, such as poor ankle dorsiflexion, will inevitably lead to a chain reaction involving the knee, hip, and lumbar spine. A stiff hip joint may develop as a result of hip flexor tightness and this may lead to compensatory lumbar hypermobility and paraspinal trigger points. This could result in low back or buttock pain, or even a lumbosacral nerve root compression.

In the case of back or buttock pain, conservative treatments involving manipulative (joint or soft tissue) therapy will likely improve the situation. However, a more comprehensive approach will typically be required to prevent recurrences. Treatment aimed at relaxing a tight psoas and strengthening a weak gluteus maximus may be the primary treatment for lumbosacral facet pain or paraspinal myofascial pain. The key pathology, if addressed successfully, will result in improved whole-person coordination and stability (see Table 3–13).

Table 3–13: Treatment for Altered Movement Patterns

- Relax/stretch overactive/tight muscles
- Mobilize/adjust stiff joints
- Facilitate/strengthen weak muscles
- Reeducate movement patterns on a reflex, subcortical basis

Reprinted with permission from Liebenson CS. Integrating rehabilitation into chiropractic practice (blending active and passive care). In: Liebenson CS. ed. Spinal Rehabilitation: A Manual of Active Care Procedures. *Baltimore: Williams and Wilkins, 1995.*

LEVELS OF TREATMENT

Treatment of the patient involves three types of intervention: manipulation, patient education on biomechanics and ergonomics, and exercise protocols.

Muscles are often reactive tissues and thus may compensate for dysfunction. If the dysfunction remains present for a prolonged period of time, structural changes will occur (such as creep and hysteresis) in the connective tissues. Similarly, neuroumuscular changes in the form of "reprogramming" may occur at the cerebellar level. Additionally, hyperalgesia can become established via dorsal horn "sensitization" from a sustained nociceptive bombardment. Such hyperalgesia may result in impaired coordination (muscular imbalance), pain in midrange positions (joint pain), and expanded receptor fields (trigger point referred pain).

Several examples of treatment follow (in approximate order of increasing complexity or level of intervention).

Examples of Manual Therapy Interventions

i. Trigger point therapy to suboccipitals for cervicogenic headache.
ii. Chiropractic manipulative therapy (CMT) to thoracolumbar junction for reduced trunk rotation.
iii. Muscle relaxation techniques (MRTs) directed at psoas or rectus femoris for inhibited gluteus maximus.
iv. CMT of wrist, elbow, and cervical and thoracic spine for carpal tunnel syndrome.

Examples of educational interventions:

i. Using a keyboard wrist rest for a data entry operator suffering from carpal tunnel syndrome.
ii. Ice massage, elevation, and ace bandage wrap for acute pain from ankle inversion sprain.
iii. Advice on appropriate stretches for the dental hygienist with posturally shortened pectoralis minor, upper trapezius, scalene, and suboccipital musculature.
iv. Ergonomic workstation modification for the chronic cervicogenic headache patient.

Examples of exercise interventions:

i. Strengthening neck flexors for improved head and neck posture.
ii. Reducing muscle imbalance between upper trapezius, pectoralis minor/middle and lower trapezius and serratus anterior for midback and upper back pain.

iii. Propriosensory retraining for chronic ankle inversion sprains.
iv. Swiss gym ball exercises for scapulohumeral strengthening.
v. Eccentric resisted exercises of wrist extensors for tennis elbow.

LUMBOPELVIC STABILIZATION EXERCISE TRACKS

Stabilization training as described here deals with a progressive program of exercises designed to reverse the effects of deconditioning or to maximize performance potential while stabilizing the spine. Exercises are organized into various "tracks." Each track challenges the patient's ability to stabilize his or her spine in a different way.

Within each track, the exercises are ordered so that they progress from simple movements to more complex ones. Each track is, in effect, a progress chart of a patient's spinal stability. The patient who can successfully perform only the first few exercises in a specific track is more deconditioned than the patient who can execute all exercises in a track.

To design the appropriate exercise protocol, the practitioner will work in each track to find the exercise that the patient has difficulty performing. Once this is done, the practitioner will "peel back" the patient to the level of difficulty that the patient can control. Finding the patient's limit and then peeling him or her back is the art of spinal stabilization.

Progressing through a stabilization program does not require mastering one track before moving on to the next. When difficulty or weakness is encountered in one track, then switching to another is often a catalyst to progress.

One of the primary goals of stabilization exercises is to help the patient to form new, functional motor engrams that utilize good posture and coordinated muscle activity. There are four stages of motor control that a patient must pass through to achieve a new engram formation. These stages are outlined in Table 3–14.

To facilitate the patient in developing kinesthetic awareness of an inhibited muscle, and to aid in the training of coordinated movements, various facilitation techniques are available. These techniques are outlined in Table 3–15, and include using hand contacts, verbal cues, and passively or actively prepositioning the patient to make the exercise easier to perform. These techniques are derived from proprioceptive neuromuscular facilitation, which offers a complex series of facilitation methods for practitioners to use to achieve these treatment goals.

Table 3–14: Stages of Motor Control

1. Conscious perception (kinesthetic awareness)
2. Volition (willful, conscious activation)
3. Coordinated activity (requires attention; not automatized)
4. Engram formation (new habit; subcortical or automatized)

Table 3–15: Facilitation Techniques

1. Prepositioning the patient (positioning can be performed passively by the doctor, or actively by the patient)
2. Hand contacts (help to increase the patient's awareness of direction of movement)
3. Tissue stimulation (skin brushing, resistance, goading)
4. Verbal cues or commands

Modified from Liebenson CS. Integrating rehabilitation into chiropractic practice (blending active and passive care). In Liebenson CS, ed. Spinal Rehabilitation: A Manual of Active Care Procedures. *Baltimore: Williams and Wilkins, 1995.*

FLOOR STABILIZATION EXERCISES

Exploring the Patient's Lumbopelvic Functional Range

When a patient has difficulty performing pelvic tilts in the supine position, it is often the result of poor neuromuscular control. Giving the patient appropriate verbal commands, utilizing facilitory cues, passive prepositioning, and appropriately directed resistance are all helpful in aiding the patient to perform these basic movements.

The lumbopelvic functional range is defined as the pain-free range in which the patient is able to perform anterior and posterior pelvic tilts. Adjustment or mobilization of the lumbar spine in either flexion or extension (depending on the patient's needs) is often helpful in improving lumbopelvic motion. Relaxation of overactive erector spinae muscles, by stretching them, may also be helpful.

If the patient continues to have difficulty performing a pelvic tilt in the supine position, try the quadruped position. (See Figure 3–14.)

Figure 3–14. Quadruped position with pelvic tilt.

Abdominal Hollowing/Bracing (Transverse Abdominus, Multifidus)

Once the patient has obtained kinesthetic awareness through pelvic tilts, it is easier to implement hollowing/bracing of the lower abdominal musculature and spinal intrinsics (transverse abdominus and multifidus). The patient is instructed to bring the umbilicus toward the spine or to "suck it in." This should not involve posterior tilting of the pelvis since the objective is spinal neutrality.

"Dead-Bug" Track (Rectus Abdominus, Multifidus, Transverse Abdominus) (See Figure 3–15.)

This track is called the "dead-bug" because of the appearance of the patient lying supine on the floor with arms and legs in the air. For each exercise in this track be sure to monitor that the patient maintains the abdominal hollowing/bracing or posterior pelvic tilt not only at the beginning of the movement, but all the way until the end of the exercise.

Difficulty with the dead-bug track is usually associated with poor neuromuscular control or weak abdominals. Shortened psoas (hip flexors) or lumbosacral erector spinae may also be a factor, and can be addressed with stretching techniques.

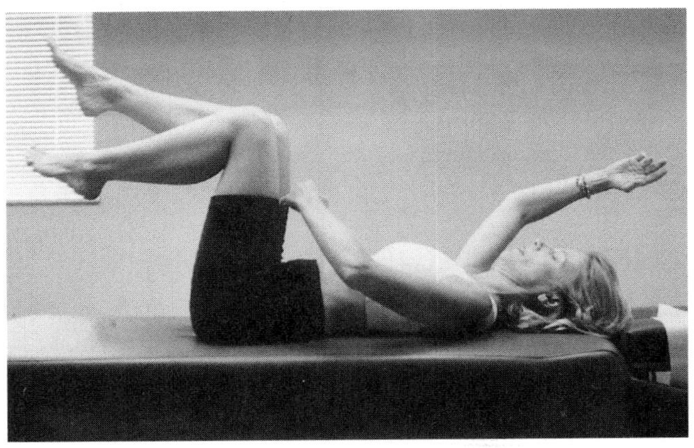

Figure 3–15. "Dead bug" track.

Bridge Track (Gluteals, Quadriceps) (See Figure 3–16.)

In the bridge position the patient is supine, with knees in approximately 90 degrees of flexion, feet flat on the ground, and the pelvis actively lifted off the ground. Difficulty with the bridge track is often associated with a shortened psoas

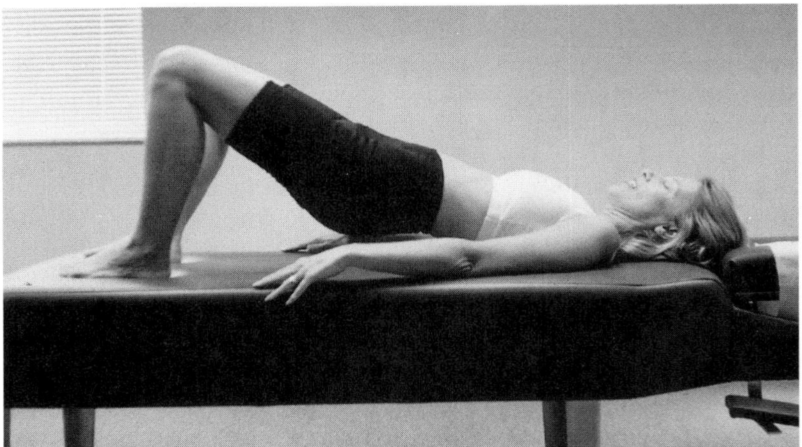

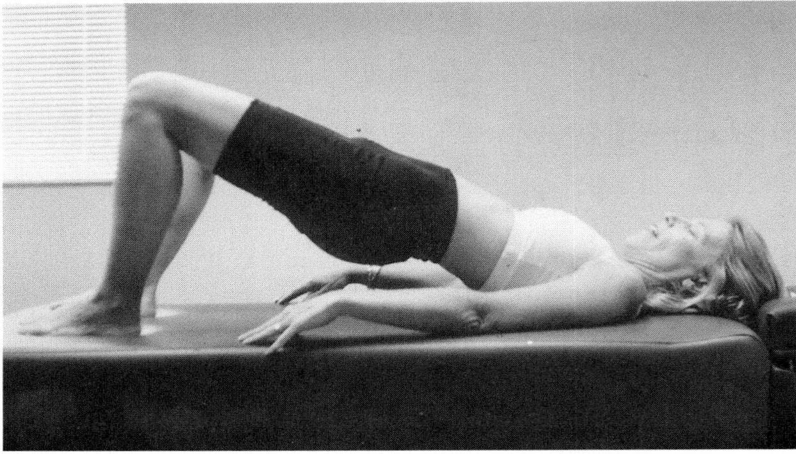

Figure 3–16. Bridge track.

Figure 3–17. Quadruped position with one arm raised.

muscle or overactivity in the lumbar erector spinae muscles. Bridging exercises begin with both feet on the ground and progress in difficulty to one-leg bridging exercises, which utilize the gluteus medius in addition to the gluteus maximus. Difficulty in performing one-leg bridging may be associated with QL, TFL, piriformis, or thigh adductor tightness/overactivity. In addition, lumbar segments may have decreased flexion motion. Sacroiliac and thoracolumbar joint dysfunction should be evaluated.

Prone Track (Gluteus Maximus)

In this track, the patient lies prone and performs arm and leg extension exercises. Difficulty often arises due to decreased spinal and hip extensibility. A tight psoas (hip flexor) or hip capsule may be involved. Decreased lumbar spine mobility in extension (fixed kyphosis) is also a factor. Stretching tight muscles and adjusting restricted joints will often facilitate patient function.

Quadruped Track (Gluteal Maximus, Medius, Scapular Stabilizers) (See Figure 3–17.)

Difficulty with the quadruped track is encountered when the prone track is not successfully mastered. Gluteus medius weakness/inhibition on the support leg side may be present because of adductor, piriformis, TFL, or quadratus lumborum hyperactivity/tightness. Inhibition or weakness of the scapular stabilizers (middle and lower trapezius, serratus anterior) may be due to a tight/hyperactive upper trapezius and/or pectoralis minor.

Kneeling Track (Quadriceps, Gluteal Maximus) (See Figure 3–18.)

Kneeling may be difficult because of knee problems or tightness in the erector spinae or biceps femoris. Erector spinae shortening or decreased lumbar flexion motion is also a factor.

Abdominals

Difficulty is often encountered when the erector spinae or hip flexors are overactive/tight. Lumbar spine joint dysfunction may also be present.

Lunge (Quadriceps)

When performing lunges, the patient should maintain a slight lumbar lordosis throughout the lunge (front knee at 90 degrees flexion). A slight posterior pelvic tilt may be needed near completion of the descent to prevent lumbar hyperextension. The stride should be long enough so that the knee is directly over the ankle to avoid excess stress on the knee and ankle joints. Difficulty may be encountered when hip flexors (back leg) or hamstrings (front leg) are tight. Observe balance errors (lateral instability is due to gluteus medius weakness/inhibition), inappropriate neck/shoulder movements (i.e., chin poke, shoulder shrug), and small jerky transitional movements.

Squats

With feet shoulder width apart, the patient is actively prepositioned in a partial anterior pelvic tilt and performs partial squats (no more than 90 degrees knee flexion). Difficulty may be encountered if hamstrings or adductors are shortened. Heels will lift up if the soleus is tight.

Other Exercises

A variety of other equipment may be used, including styrofoam rolls, medicine balls, stick exercises, exercise tubing stabilization exercises, gymnastic ball exercises, pulleys, and stationary bicycles.

To use the checklists, understand the concept of the pain-free functional range and peel back the patient!

OFFICE BASICS AND CASE MANAGEMENT

STAGES OF TREATMENT

In blending passive plus active care, case management generally has four stages of treatment: acute intervention, remobilization, rehabilitation and reconditioning, and lifestyle adaptations. Tables 3–16 and 3–17 outline the manner in which active care can be incorporated into patient care from the early stages of treatment.

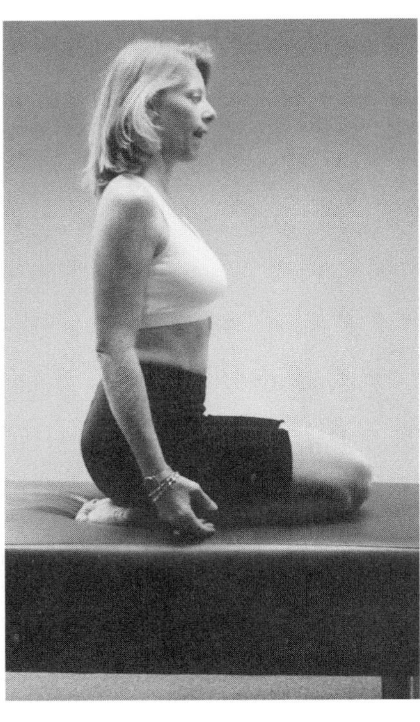
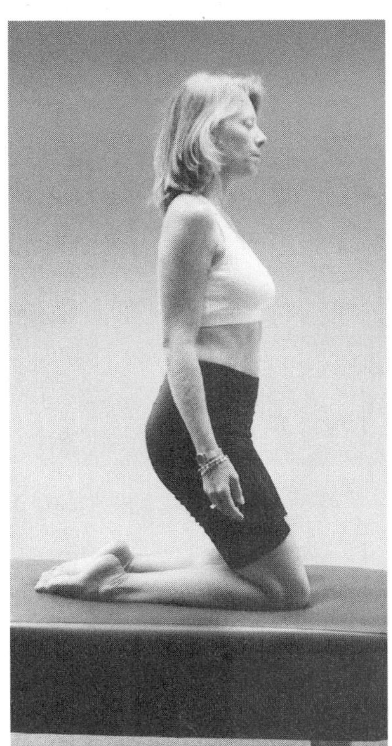
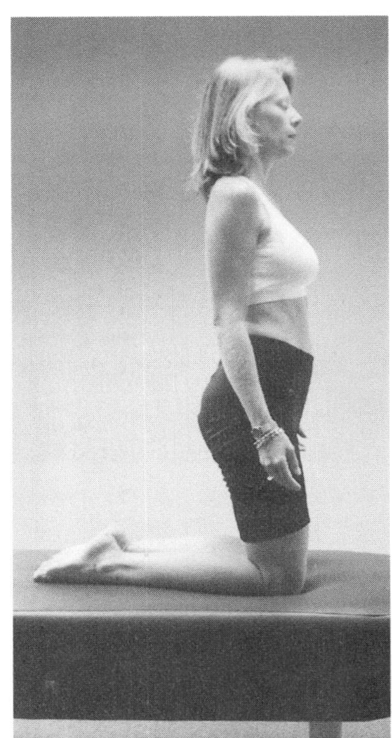

Figure 3–18. Kneeling track.

Table 3–16: Stages of Treatment

ACUTE INTERVENTION	REMOBILIZATION	REHABILITATION AND RECONDITIONING	LIFESTYLE ADAPTATIONS
Reduce inflammation	Increase pain-free mobility	Increase muscle strength/endurance	Improve ergonomic factors
Pain relief	Minimize deconditioning	Improve coordination	Address psychosocial factors
		Increase flexibility	
		Increase aerobic capacity	

Modified from Liebenson CS. Integrating rehabilitation into chiropractic practice (blending active and passive care). In Liebenson CS, ed. Spinal Rehabilitation: A Manual of Active Care Procedures. *Baltimore: Williams and Wilkins, 1995.*

Table 3–17: Sports Medicine Model of Treatment

ACUTE INTERVENTION	REMOBILIZATION	REHABILITATION AND RECONDITIONING FACTORS	PREVENTION AND LIFESTYLES
Rest/ice	Chiropractic manipulation	Strengthening	Stress management
Supports/braces	Soft tissue manipulation	Stretching	Ergonomics
Gentle stretching	Physical therapy	Cardiovascular fitness	Biomechanics: "lifting/bending"
McKenzie protocols			
Physical therapy	Postural correction	Balance and coordination	Diet/nutrition
Anti-inflammatories		Functional exercise	

Modified from Liebenson CS. Integrating rehabilitation into chiropractic practice (blending active and passive care). In Liebenson CS, ed. Spinal Rehabilitation: A Manual of Active Care Procedures. *Baltimore: Williams and Wilkins, 1995.*

Table 3–18: Case Management Protocols

1. **Initial evaluation**
   - Rule out red flags and refer if necessary
   - Diagnose nerve root compression
   - Identify abnormal illness behavior or other complicating factors
2. **Aggressive, conservative care for 4 to 6 weeks**
   - Patient education and reassurance
   - Two-week trial of manipulation
   - If progressing, continue
   - If not, another 2-week trial of different type of manipulation
   - Begin active care within first 4 weeks
3. **Establish objective baselines for outcomes assessment**
   - Lifestyle factors, pain measures, and functional assessment
4. **Biopsychosocial assessment of nonresponders**
   - Imaging and laboratory work
   - Psychosocial questionnaires and assessment
   - Possible referral or multidisciplinary management

CASE MANAGEMENT

Case management involves three parts: evaluation, treatment, and reimbursement. Table 3–18 outlines case management procedures for subacute, recurrent, or chronic pain syndromes.

Evaluation

This includes history, physical examination including orthopedic and neurologic tests, and functional evaluation. The functional evaluation includes postural assessment, gait analysis, one-leg standing, muscle length tests, ranges of motion, movement patterns, and other functional tests.

Treatment

This includes chiropractic manipulation, physiological therapeutics, muscle relaxation and strengthening techniques, propriosensory retraining, lumbopelvic stabilization exercises, cardiovascular training, ergonomic retraining, and work hardening.

Reimbursement

In order to improve the likelihood of reimbursement, the practitioner should utilize outcomes measures, follow standards of care, and address complicating factors.

SUMMARY

For musculoskeletal problems, it is essential to objectively assess deficits in biomechanical function. This includes range of motion, muscle strength/endurance, and cardiovascular fitness. Questionnaires, algometry, and other tools also make it possible to quantify disability and the subjective experience of pain. By utilizing functional outcome assessment tools to evaluate an injured patient's progress, we shift the emphasis from subjective factors of pain to more realistic functional measures.

In most soft tissue injuries, functional changes are the only objective findings upon which to base treatment and judge progress. Unfortunately, most orthopedic examinations rely on tests that search for structural lesions (such as nerve root compression or dural tension). These conditions account for only about 20% of the patients, yet the search to diagnose structural pathology leads to overutilization of expensive diagnostic tests (such as magnetic resonance imaging.)[1]

The remaining 80% of patients have no diagnosable structural pathology; they require treatment based on an evaluation of functional deficits. Outcomes assessment that utilizes objective functional testing gives third-party payors, the patient, and the doctor a way to measure progress over time and therefore establish the credibility of a specific treatment approach. A functional approach does not provide a diagnosis; rather, it offers realistic goals or end points of care. If the patient's functional capacity is improving, then the treatment is successful. If not, then treatment needs to be redirected. This allows a rewarding corroboration between doctor and patient, one that is understandable, credible, and easily visible for payors and additional providers.

Functional restoration addresses the deconditioning syndrome, the subacute phase of care, and the patients with recurrent or chronic pain. It usually does not require specialized testing or training equipment. Small practitioners in private practice can begin to train patients with customized exercise programs, using very simple equipment. This approach provides measurable functional outcomes, which are of growing importance for both patient motivation and reimbursement. Focusing patients on improving their functional status, rather than on pain relief, is essential to success with this approach.

REFERENCES

1. Herring SA. Rehabilitation of muscle injuries. *Med Sci Sports Exer.* 1990;22:453,456.
2. Hult L. The Munkfors investigation. *Acta Orthop Scand.* 1954;16 (Suppl).
3. Cassidy JD, Wedge JH. The epidemiology and natural history of low back pain and spinal degeneration. In: WH Kirkaldy-Willis, ed. *Managing Low Back Pain.* New York: Churchill Livingstone, 1988;3–15.
4. Frymoyer JW, Pope MH, Costanza MC, et al. Epidemiologic studies of low-back pain. *Spine.* 1980;5:419–423.
5. Svensson HO, Andersson GBJ. Low back pain in forty to forty-seven year old men. I. Frequency of occurrence and impact on medical services. *Scand J Rehabil Med.* 1982;14:47–53.
6. Valkenburg HA, Haanen HCM. The epidemiology of low back pain. *Clin Orthop.* 1983;179:9–22.
7. Biering-Sorensen F. A prospective study of low back pain in a general population. I. Occurrence, recurrence and aetiology. *Scand J Rehabil Med.* 1983;15:71–79.
8. Benn RT, Wood PH. Pain in the back: An attempt to estimate the size of the problem. *Rheumatol Rehabil.* 1975;14:121–128.
9. Horal J. The clinical appearance of low back pain disorders in the city of Gothenburg, Sweden. *Acta Orthop Scand.* 1969;18:1–109 (Suppl).
10. Rowe ML. Low back pain in industry. *J Occup Med.* 1969;11:161–169.
11. Berquist-Ullman M, Larsson U. Acute low back pain in industry. *Acta Orthop Scand.* 1977;170:1–117 (Suppl).
12. Pheasant HC. The problem back. *Curr Pract Orthop Surg.* 1977;7:89–115.
13. Snook SH. Low back pain in industry. In: White AA, Gordon SL, eds. *Symposium on Idiopathic Low Back Pain.* St. Louis: C.V. Mosby, 1982.
14. Spengler DM, Bigos SJ, Martin NA, et al. Back injuries in industry: A retrospective study. I. Overview and cost analysis. *Spine.* 1986;11:241–245.
15. Frymoyer JW, Pope MH, Clements JH, et al. Risk factors in low-back pain: An epidemiological study. *J Bone Joint Surg.* 1983;65A:213–218.
16. Andersson GBJ, Pope MH, Frymoyer JW. Epidemiology. In: Pope MH, Frymoyer JW, Andersson G, eds. *Occupational Low Back Pain.* New York: Praeger, 1984;101–114.
17. Morris A. Identifying workers at risk to back injury is not guesswork. *Occup Health Safety.* 1985;55:16–20.
18. Frymoyer JW. Epidemiology. In: Frymoyer JW, Gordon SL, eds. *Symposium on New Perspectives on Low Back Pain.* Park Ridge, IL: American Academy of Orthopaedic Surgeons, 1989;19–33.
19. Rossignol M, Suissa S, Abenheim L. Working disability due to occupational back pain: Three-year follow-up of 2,300 compensated workers in Quebec. *J Occup Med.* 1988;502–506.
20. Abenheim L, Suissa S, Rossignol M. Risk of recurrence of occupational back pain over a three year follow up. *Br J Ind Med.* 1988;45:829–833.
21. Frymoyer JW, Rosen JC, Clements J, et al. Psychologic factors in low-back-pain disability. *Clin Orthop.* 1985;195:178–184.
22. Van de Hoogen H, Koes B, Eijk J, Buoter L, Deville W. On the course of low back pain in general practice: A one year follow up study. *Ann Rheum Dis.* 1998;57:13–19.
23. Waddell G. A new clinical model for the treatment of low-back pain. *Spine.* 1987;12:634–644.
24. Haldeman S, Chapman-Smith D, Petersen DM. Frequency and duration of care. In: *Guidelines for Chiropractic Quality Assurance and Practice Parameters.* Gaithersburg, MD: Aspen, 1993;115,130.
25. Spitzer WO, Le Blanc FE, Dupuis M, et al. Scientific approach to the assessment and management of activity-related spinal disorders: A monograph for clinicians. Report of the Quebec Task Force on Spinal Disorders. *Spine.* 1987;12(Suppl 7):S1–S59.
26. Bigos S, Bowyer O, Braen G, et al. *Acute Low Back Problems in Adults.* Clinical Practice Guideline No. 14. AHCPR Publication No. 95-0642. Rockville, MD: Agency for Health Care Policy and Research, Public Health Service, U.S. Department of Health and Human Services, December 1994.
27. Mixter WJ, Barr JS. Rupture of the intervertebral disc with involvement of the spinal canal. *New Eng J Med.* 1934;211:210–215.
28. Nachemson AL. Newest knowledge of low back pain. *Clin Orthop.* 1992;279:8–20.
29. Frymoyer JW. Predicting disability from low back pain. *Clin Orthop.* 1992;279:103.
30. Frymoyer JW, Newberg A, Pope MH, et al. Spine radiographs in patients with low-back pain: An epidemiological study in men. *J Bone Joint Surg.* 1984:66A:1048–1055.
31. Fullenlove TM, Williams AJ. Comparative roentgen findings in symptomatic and asymptomatic backs. *JAMA.* 1957;168:572–574.

32. LaRocca H, Macnab IA. Value of pre-employment radiographic assessment of the lumbar spine. *Can Med Assoc J*. 1969;101:383–388.
33. Magora A, Schwartz A. Relation between the low back pain syndrome and X-ray findings. *Scand J Rehabil Med*. 1976;8:115–125.
34. Mensor MC, Duvall G. Absence of motion at the fourth and fifth lumbar interspaces. *J Bone Joint Surg*. 1959;41A:1047–1054.
35. Splithoff CA. Lumbosacral junction: Roentgenographic comparison of patients with and without back ache. *JAMA*. 1953;152:1610–1613.
36. Torgeson WR, Dotler WE. Comparative roentgenographic study of the asymptomatic and symptomatic lumbar spine. *J Bone Joint Surg*. 1976;58A:850–853.
37. Dabbs VM, Dabbs LG. Correlation between disc height narrowing and low-back pain. *Spine*. 1990;15: 1366–1399.
38. Videman T, Nurminen M, Troup JDG. Lumbar spinal pathology in cadaveric material in relation to history of back pain, occupation, and physical loading. *Spine*. 1990;15:728–738.
39. Wiesel SE, Tsourmans N, Feffer HL, et al. A study of computer-assisted tomography: I. The incidence of positive CAT scans in an asymptomatic group of patients. *Spine*. 1984;9:549–551.
40. Rothman RH, et al. A study of computer-assisted tomography. *Spine*. 1984;9:548–556.
41. Boden SD, Davis DO, Dina TS, et al. Abnormal magnetic-resonance scans of the lumbar spine in asymptomatic subjects. *J Bone Joint Surg*. 1990;72-A:403–408.
42. Hitselberger WE, Witten RM. Abnormal myelograms in asymptomatic patients. *J Neurosurg*. 1968;28: 204–206.
43. Matsumoto M, Fujumura Y, et al. MRI of cervical intervertebral discs in asymptomatic subjects. *J Bone Joint Surg*. 1998;80:19–24
44. Schwarzer AC, April CN, Bogduk N. The sacroiliac joint in chronic low back pain. *Spine*. 1995;20:31–37.
45. Allan DB, Waddell G. An historical perspective on low back pain and disability. *Acta Ortho Scan*. 1989;60:1–22 (Suppl).
46. Shekelle PG, Adams AH, Chassin MR, et al. Spinal manipulation for low-back pain. *Ann Int Med*. 1992;117:590–598.
47. Troup JDG. The perception of musculoskeletal pain and incapacity for work: Prevention and early treatment. *Physiotherapy*. 1988;74:435–439.
48. Bush K, Cowan N, Katz DE, Gishen P. The natural history of sciatica associated with disc pathology: A prospective study with clinical and independent radiologic follow-up. *Spine*. 1992;17(10):1205–1212.
49. Waddell G, Feder G, McIntosh A, Lewis M, Hutchinson A. *Low Back Evidence Review*. London: Royal College of General Practitioners, 1996.
50. Jordan A, Bendix T, Nielsen H, et al. Intensive training, physiotherapy, or manipulation for patients with chronic neck pain. *Spine*. 1998;23(3):311–319.
51. Erhard RE, Delitto A. Relative effectiveness of an extension program and a combined program of manipulation and flexion and extension exercises in patients with acute low back syndrome. *Phys Ther*. 1994;74:1093–1100.
52. Jette AM, Jette DU. Physical therapy and health outcomes in patients with spinal impairments. *Phys Ther*. 1996;76:930–941.
53. Triano J. Use of chiropractic manipulation in lumbar rehabilitation. *J Rehabil Res Dev*. 1997;34(4): 394–404.
54. Feuerstein M. A multidisciplinary approach to the prevention, evaluation, and management of work disability. *J Occup Rehab*. 1991:1;11.
55. Mooney V. Where is the pain coming from? *Spine*. 1987;12:754–759.
56. Linton SJ, Hellsing AL, Andersson D. A controlled study of the effects of an early intervention on acute musculoskeletal pain problems. *Pain*. 1993;54:353–359.
57. Nordin M. Letter. *Spine*. 1994;2:5.
58. Lindstrom A, Ohlund C, Eek C, et al. Activation of subacute low back patients. *Phys Ther*. 1992;293.
59. Mitchell RI, Carmen GM. Results of a multicenter trial using an intensive active exercise program for the treatment of acute soft tissue and back injuries. *Spine*. 1990;15:514–521.
60. Mayer TG, Gatchel RJ, Mayer H, et al. A prospective two-year study of functional restoration in industrial low back injury. *JAMA*, 1987;258:1763–1767.
61. Hazard RG, Fenwick JW, Kalisch SM, et al. Functional restoration with behavioral support. *Spine*. 1989;14:157–161.
62. Sachs BL, David JF, Olimpio D, et al. Spinal rehabilitation by work tolerance based on objective physical capacity assessment of dysfunction. *Spine*. 1990;15:1325–1332.

63. Alaranta H, Rytokoski U, Rissanen A, et al. Intensive physical and psychosocial training program for patients with chronic low back pain. *Spine*. 1994;12:1339–1349.
64. Burke SA, Harms-Constas CK, Aden PS. Return to work/work retention outcomes of a functional restoration program. *Spine*. 1994;17:1880–1886.
65. Saal JA, Saal JS. Nonoperative treatment of herniated lumbar intervertebral disc with radiculopathy. *Spine*. 1989;14:431–437.
66. Timm KE. A randomized-control study of active and passive treatments for chronic low back pain following L5 laminectomy. *JOSPT*. 1994;20:6:276–286.
67. Pilowsky I. A general classification of abnormal illness behavior. *Brit J Med Psychiat*. 1979;51:131–137.
68. Cats-Baril WI, Frymoyer JW. Identifying patients at risk of becoming disabled because of low-back pain. *Spine*. 1991;16:605–607.
69. Linton SJ. The relationship between activity and chronic pain. *Pain*. 1985;21:289–294.
70. Fordyce WE, McMahon R, Rainwater G, et al. Pain complaint—exercise performance relationship in chronic pain. *Pain*. 1981;10:311–321.
71. Wifling FG, Klonoff H, Kokan P. Psychological, demographic and orthopaedic factors associated with prediction of outcome of spinal fusion. *Clin Orthop*. 1973;90:153.
72. Fordyce WE, Brockway JA, Bergman JA, Spengler D. Acute back pain: A control group comparison of behavioural vs. traditional management methods. *J Behav Med*. 1986;9:127–140.
73. Fordyce WE. Pain history musings. *APS*. 1994; 3(2):140–141.
74. Jull G, Janda V. Muscles and motor control in low back pain. In: Twomney LT, Taylor JR, eds. *Physical Therapy for the Low Back, Clinics in Physical Therapy*. New York: Churchill Livingstone, 1987.
75. Janda V. Some Aspects of Extracranial Causes of Facial Pain. *J Prosthet Dent*. 1986;56:484.
76. Sahrmann SA. Posture and muscle imbalance: Faulty lumbar pelvic alignments. *Phys Ther*. 1987;67: 1840–1844.
77. Fitzmaurice R, Cooper RG, Freemont AJ. A histo-morphometric comparison of muscle biopsies from normal subjects and patients with ankylosing spondylitis and severe mechanical low back pain. *J Pathol*. 1992;163:182.
78. Johansson H, Sjolander P, Sojka P. Receptors in the knee joint ligaments and their role in the biomechanics of the joint. *Crit Rev Biomed Eng*. 1991;18:341–368.
79. Schiable HG, Grubb BD. Afferent and spinal mechanisms of joint pain. *Pain*. 1993;55:5–54.
80. DeAndrade JR, Grant C, and Dixon AJ. Joint distension and reflex muscle inhibition in the knee. *J Bone Joint Surg*. 1965;47:313–322.
81. Brucini M, Duranti R, Galleti R, Pantaleo T, and Zucchi PL. Pain thresholds and electromyographic features of periarticular muscles in patients with osteoarthritis of the knee. *Pain*. 1981;10:57–66.
82. Spencer JD, Hayes KC, and Alexander IJ. Knee joint effusion and quadriceps reflex inhibition in man. *Arch Phys Med Rehab*. 1984;65:171–177.
83. Hides JA, Stokes MJ, Saide M, et al. Evidence of lumbar multifidus muscles wasting ipsilateral to symptoms in patients with acute/subacute low back pain. *Spine*. 1994;19:165–172.
84. Bullock-Saxton JE, Janda V, Bullock MI. Reflex activation of gluteal muscles in walking. *Spine*. 1993;18:704–708.
85. Lewit K. *Manipulative Therapy in Rehabilitation of the Motor System*. 2nd Edition. London: Butterworths, 1991.
86. Lewit K. Chain reactions in disturbed function of the motor system. *Man Med*. 1987;3:27–29.
87. Korr I. The spinal cord as organizer of disease processes: Some preliminary perspectives. *J Am Osteopath Assoc*. 1976;76:35–45.
88. Paillard J. Posture and locomotion: Old problems and new concepts. In: Amblard B, Berthoz A, Clarac F, eds. *Posture and Gait: Development, Adaptation and Modulation*. Amsterdam, Elsevier Science Publishers, 1988;V–XII.
89. Triano J, Schultz AB. Correlation of objective measure of trunk motion and muscle function with low-back disability ratings. *Spine*. 1987;12:561.
90. Dahl JB, Erichsen CJ, Fuglsang-Frederiksen A, Kehlet H. Pain sensation and nociceptive reflex excitability in surgical patients and human volunteers. *Br J Anesth*. 1992;69:117–121.
91. Johansson H, Sjolander P, Sojka P. Fusimotor reflexes in triceps surae muscle elicited by natural and electrical stimulation of joint afferents. *Neuro-Orthop*. 1988;6:67–80.
92. Johansson H, Sjolander P, Sojka P, Wadell I. Reflex actions on the gamma-muscle spindle systems acting at the knee joint elicited by the stretch of the posterior cruciate ligament. *Neuro-Orthop*. 1989;8: 9–21.
93. Hubbard DR, Berkoff GM. Myofascial trigger points show spontaneous needle EMG activity. *Spine*. 1993;18:1803–1807.

94. Walsh EG. *Muscles, Masses and Motion. The Physiology of Normality, Hypotonicity, Spasticity, and Rigidity.* Oxford: MacKeith Press, Blackwell Scientific Publication Ltd., 1992.
95. Hagbarth KE. Evaluation of and methods to change muscle tone. *Scand J Rehab Med.* 1994:30(Suppl);19–32.
96. Mense S. Nociception from skeletal muscle in relation to clinical muscle pain. *Pain.* 1993;54:241–290.
97. Lehto M, Jarvinen M, Nelimarkka O. Scar formation after skeletal muscle injury. *Arch Orthop Trauma Surg.* 1986;104:366–370.
98. Watson DH, Trott PH. Cervical headache: An investigation of natural head posture and upper cervical flexor muscle performance. *Cephalgia.* 1993:13;272–284.
99. Treleaven J, Jull G, Atkinson L. Cervical musculoskeletal dysfunction in post-concussional headache. *Cephalgia.* 1994:14;273–279.
100. Simons DG. Referred phenomena of myofascial trigger points. In: Vecchiet L, Albe-Fessard D, Lindlom U. *New Trends in Referred Pain and Hyperalgesia.* Amsterdam: Elsevier, 1993.
101. Stokes MJ, Cooper RG, Jayson MIV. Selective changes in multifidus dimensions in patients with chronic low back pain. *Eur Spine J.* 1992;1:38–42.
102. Headley BJ. Muscle inhibition. Physical Therapy Forum, 24—November 1, 1993.
103. Matilla H, Hurme M, Alaranta H, et al. The multifidus muscle in patients with lumbar disc herniation. *Spine.* 1986;11:732.
104. Lehto M, Hurme M, Alaranta H, et al. Connective tissue changes in the multifidus muscle in patients with lumbar disc herniation: An immunohistologic study of collagen types I and II and fibronectin. *Spine.* 1989;14:302.
105. Zhu XZ, Parniapour M, Nordin M, Kahanovitz N. Histochemistry and morphology of erector spinae muscle in lumbar disc herniation. *Spine.* 1989;14:394.
106. Cyriax J. *Textbook of Orthopaedic Medicine, Vol. 1: Diagnosis of Soft Tissue Lesions.* 8th Edition. London: Bailliere Tindall, 1982.
107. Biering-Sorensen F. Physical measurements as risk indicators for low back trouble over a one year period. *Spine.* 1984;9:106–119.
108. Luuto S, Heliovaara M, Hurri H, Alaranta H. Static back endurance and the risk of low back pain. *Clin Biomech.* 1995;10:323–324.
109. O'Sullivan P, Twomey L, Allison G, et al. Altered patterns of abdominal muscle activation in patients with chronic low back pain. *Aust J Physio.* 1997;43:91–98.
110. Cholewicki J, Panjabi MM, Khachatryan A. Stabilizing of the trunk flexor-extensor muscles around a neutral spine posture. *Spine.* 22:19:2207–2212.
111. Elvey RL. The need to test the brachial plexus in painful shoulder and upper quarter conditions. Proceedings of Neck and Shoulder Symposium, MTAA Conference, Brisbane, pp. 39–52.
112. Butler D. *Mobilisation of the Nervous System.* Melbourne: Churchill Livingstone, 1991.
113. Yaxley GA, Jull GA. Adverse tension in the neural system. A preliminary study of tennis elbow. *Aust Physio.* 1993;39(1);15–22.
114. Wright A, Thurnwald P, et al. Hyperalgesia in tennis elbow patients. *J Musculoskeletal Pain.* 1994;2(4):83–97.
115. McKenzie R. *The Lumbar Spine: Mechanical Diagnosis and Therapy.* Waikanae, New Zealand: Spinal Publications, 1981.
116. Nelson RM. *NIOSH Low Back Atlas of Standardized Tests/Measures.* U.S. Department of Health and Human Services, National Institute for Occupational Safety and Health, December 1988.
117. Janda V. *Muscle Function Testing.* London: Butterworths, 1983.
118. Inamura K. Re-assessment of the method of analysis of electrogravitiograph and the one foot test. *Aggressologie.*
119. Hyman J. Seminar, Los Angeles College of Chiropractic, 1994.
120. Morgan D. Seminar, Los Angeles College of Chiropractic, 1992.
121. Murphy D. Seminar, Los Angeles College of Chiropractic, 1995.
122. Biering-Sorensen F. Physical measurements as risk indicators for low-back trouble over a one-year period. *Spine.* 1984;9:106–119.
123. Alaranta H, Hurri H, Heliovaara M, et al. Non-dynametric trunk performance tests: Reliability and normative data base. *Scand J Rehab Med.* 1994;26:211–215.
124. Tunnell P. Protocol for visual assessment. *J Bodywork Movement Ther.* 1996;1(1):21–27.

CHAPTER 4

High Versus Low Technology

David E. Stude, MS, DC & Gunnar Andersson, MD, PhD

INTRODUCTION

Recently, there has been a focused interest in developing objective instrumentation for evaluating human performance, and in particular, for spinal functional performance. Back pain is an epidemic in American society,[1] and statistics indicate the majority of the population will have at least one disabling episode of back pain in their lifetime.[2–6] Furthermore, although many of these episodes seem to resolve symptomatically with no intervention following a previously described natural history, approximately 20% tend to become chronic and possibly 50% or more of the patients experience recurrent back pain complaints.[7–10] It is this group of chronic low back pain sufferers that account for the significant costs associated with evaluating and treating back pain.[11–17] This is one of the reasons for renewed interest in more accurately evaluating spinal function and having better opportunities for predicting and preventing the increasing incidence of chronic back pain. The purpose of this chapter is to examine the differences between computer-aided machine-based testing and rehabilitation and non-machine-based testing and functional training.

Even though there have been many specialized, high-technology evaluation protocols developed that seem to offer reliable examination information for the clinician in evaluating and making case management recommendations, there is a current tendency to assume that there are also increased benefits associated with exercise performed on machines. Computer-assisted machines seem to be thought of as more technologically advanced and so more beneficial in terms of physical outcome measures. This assumption has not yet been supported in the literature, and, on the contrary, the reverse may actually be true. Also, computer-aided instrumentation that is available commercially does not typically measure functional parameters, varies with regard to subject testing position(s), and varies considerably in cost (Table 4–1).

The practical differences between machine and nonmachine testing and training are important for the following reasons:

1. Some investigators suggest that poor strength may be a risk factor for those who are required to perform labor-intensive tasks.
2. Strength training of some sort is typically included as part of an integrated approach to treating spinal dysfunction.
3. One of the preventive approaches to preventing back injuries is teaching workers to perform their jobs properly, and this implies that rehabilitation programs should emphasize functional maneuvers that reflect activities of daily living (ADLs) so that there is significant overlap between the types of exercises they perform in a rehabilitation setting and those they will be expected to perform on the job or in their home.

SPINAL BIOMECHANICS

In order to properly enhance spinal biomechanical function, whether it be through the use of active exercise, stretching, or manipulative therapy, it is necessary to first of all know how the spine functions when in an optimal

Table 4–1: Comparison of Several Computer-Aided Instruments That Can Be Used for Testing and Rehabilitation

INSTRUMENT	PTM[a]	PTP[b]	PLANES TESTED[c]	COST[d]
Biodex	K	SE	S	45
Cybex	K	SE	SCT-3	160
Dynatronics-2000	M	ST or SE	ISOM	20
ISO-B-200	I	ST or SE	SCT-1	80
Isotechnologies Lift-Task	I	ST	DYNA	70
Loredan Lido-Back	K	SE	S	60
Med-X	M	SE	EXT	65
Promotron-3000	M	ST	ISOM + S	25

[a]PTM = Principal testing mode; I = isoinertial; K = isokinetic; M = isometric.
[b]PTP = Patient testing position; SE = seated; ST = standing.
[c]Planes tested; SCT-1 = one machine tests functional parameters simultaneously in the sagittal, coronal, and transverse planes; SCT-3 = a separate machine is available for testing trunk performance parameters in each of the primary planes of motion; S = sagittal plane; EXT = extension plane; ISOM = isometric whole-body lift-task measurements based on NIOSH guidelines; DYNA = multiple-plane whole-body lift-task measurements.
[d]Appropriate cost is expressed in U.S. dollars × 1000 per machine.

state. One frame of reference that is gaining acceptance is use of the right-handed Cartesian orthogonal coordinate system.[18] Research evaluating spinal motion demonstrates that movement is not uniplanar.[19–21] In other words, motion of the spine occurs in complex, coupled patterns, and these patterns differ from region to region. Also, there is evidence to suggest that there are characteristic centers of rotation that can be used to describe segmental motion.[22,23]

The use of machine-based exercise (MBE) for the back would appear to restrict the ability of the spine to move about three-dimensionally. This premise is important from a practical point of view for many reasons. First, it seems intuitive that people who perform work-related tasks do so without the use of restrictive devices that are characteristic of machines. It would seem prudent, therefore, to train these people to perform activities that actually reflect the work they characteristically perform. This makes logical sense for the labor-intensive worker, the athlete, or the homemaker. Since comparison studies have not been properly addressed through controlled clinical trials, the increased expense associated with high-technology exercise devices currently appears unsubstantiated.

The body works as a whole integrated unit rather than as independent regional entities.[24–28] MBE is typically associated with some degree of isolation, usually exercising one primary muscle group at a time. Based on objective descriptions of whole-body movements, the MBE approach seems potentially to prevent the development of three-dimensional, neuromotor skills necessary for the normal and safe accomplishment of daily tasks (Figures 4–1 and 4–2).

In defense of MBE, it may be necessary initially to train some individuals in a more isolated fashion, if the injury they sustained was severe and if whole-body movements are not possible. This then could be used in some cases as an initial training recommendation, with more complex tasks being introduced as tolerated. Also, MBE may be appropriate if it is only a portion of the entire exercise program, in order to target specific outcomes based on identified deficiencies (Figure 4–3).

MBE cannot provide or promote the kind of multiple-joint motions that are typically associated with three-dimensional, nonrestrained activities. Furthermore, because most machines have a fixed cam or fulcrum, they may actually retard these complex joint motions. This may result in asymmetrical joint stressors that could promote long-term segmental dysfunction.

NEUROMOTOR SKILL ACQUISITION

The sequence of events that occurs when an Olympic weight lifter performs a clean and jerk, although of short duration, is very complex. Similarly, when an individual is lifting boxes

Figure 4–1. Lifting against a preset resistance, in this case above shoulder height, can increase the strength of the muscles involved in performing this activity. However, the handles are fixed in terms of the direction they can be moved so there is no demand placed on the lifter to have to balance the weight in an appropriate arc. Using machine-based exercise (MBE) as the sole method for training could potentially detrain the system responsible for doing real work in a three-dimensional environment. The SAID principle, an acronym for "specific adaptation to imposed demands," suggests that in order to gain three-dimensional balance skills typical in performing activities of daily living (ADLs), a balance demand must be introduced as part of a functional training program.

Figure 4–2. Exercising with free weights, as demonstrated in this example, demands that the weights be balanced in all directions so that they can be safely moved within the desired plane of motion. In this case there are increased physical demands placed on the exerciser, primarily secondary stabilizer muscles in the trunk and upper extremities. Since there is no such thing as prescribing the "perfect" exercise routine for a rehabilitation patient, the program should be prescribed to slightly overaddress associated on-the-job demands, instead of a program with less demand that might make the patient slightly underprepared to safely perform job-related tasks long term.

all day long, proper body mechanics are essential to reduce the likelihood of injury and muscular fatigue. Even though strength is considered essential to include in a rehabilitation program for spinal dysfunction, strength deficiencies do not have predictive value in determining the likelihood for future back injuries. Strength gains are also relatively easy to achieve in an appropriate setting, but strength alone does not ensure that one will be less prone to injury than one who does not undergo specific strength training. The ability to use strength gains in an appropriate fashion may be more important than strength itself. This ability to activate appropriate musculature in order to more safely control whole-body movements and activities is termed *neuromotor skill* (NMS).

The body's ability to function in an integrated fashion relies in part on the communication between the musculoskeletal system and proprioceptive system. This system provides feedback about joint position, location, movement position and velocity, temperature alterations, and pain (Figures 4–4 to 4–6).

One reason that it may be difficult for some individuals to learn relatively complex skills initially is that there is a lot that the person must remember and process cognitively, rather than being able to rely on learned reflex skills. Once an individual practices a skill repetitively, movement and position pattern habits begin to replace the need for continuous conscious control of all activities.

MBE will, theoretically, alter proprioceptive feedback compared to nonmachine training and consequently may reduce or eliminate the development of NMS that is necessary to safely perform complex tasks. Again, as mentioned above, the development of NMS may be a more important priority than strength for enhancing spinal functional performance. This also suggests that there is an important mind-body connection required for performance of ADLs, and there is no evidence at this time to suggest that MBE enhances this relationship. On the contrary, there is evidence to suggest that MBE can prevent normal NMS development. Parkhurst and Burnett[29] evaluated the relationship between low back injury and lumbopelvic proprioception in 88 working male firefighters. They found that there was a significant increase in the number of low back injuries in which proprioceptive deficits were identified even though they did both show normal strength indices. Age was the factor that most strongly influenced proprioceptive status. Although more work is necessary in this area, it may be that age was an influential factor because there are less opportunities to maintain NMS with increasing chronological age, possibly because of reduced physical activity in general or general deconditioning, or both.

Figure 4–3. Although it is prudent to enhance patient self-sufficiency as soon as possible, severe injuries and disability can prevent an individual initially from safely handling demanding, whole-person, three-dimensional activities. In these cases, isolated, partial range of motion, machine-based maneuvers can be used to begin to prepare individuals for more demanding activities. It may also be helpful to use this approach as part of a comprehensive functional training program if identified deficiencies suggest that certain exercise maneuvers be of primary focus. Early activation is well supported in the literature, even if the activities that can be tolerated at first do not necessarily reflect actual ADLs.

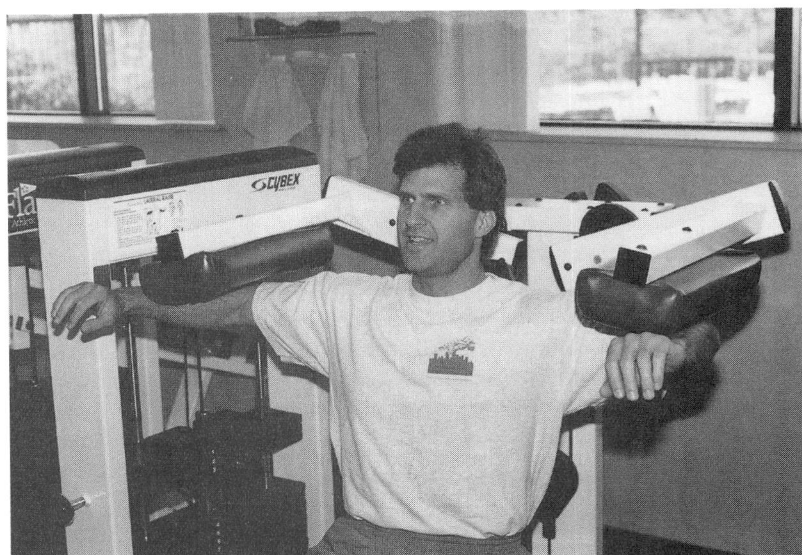

Figure 4–4. This figure shows exercising the deltoid (and some rotator cuff) muscles in a relatively restrained manner. The patient does not have to balance the weight but merely push the weight upward.

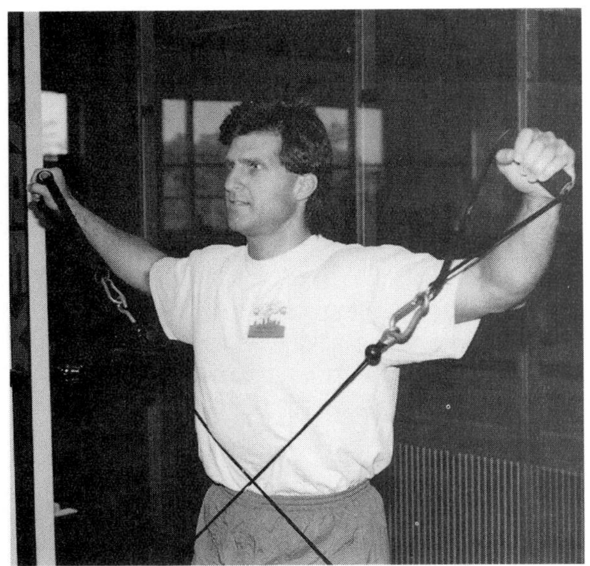

Figure 4–5. This cable exercise still involves the shoulder abductors (deltoid and some rotator cuff muscles), but it is less restrained than the exercise depicted in Figure 4–4. Here the patient has to exercise by consciously controlling the movement arc, instead of merely pushing upward. This is an example of progressive exercise platforms (PEPs), used as a method of helping to determine which level of exercise is most appropriate for an individual, and how to advance a patient safely to more challenging levels.

Figure 4–6. This depicts the performance of shoulder abduction maneuvers in a much less restrained way compared with Figures 4–4 and 4–5. This is a more advanced PEP and since there is more demanded physically of the patients when performing a less restrained activity, they have to be screened to be certain they can safely tolerate the challenge and that the likelihood for latent pain symptoms is unlikely. Remember, when activities become more complex in terms of being less restrained, and more whole-person in terms of involving more than just an isolated muscle group(s), there is a greater tendency for spinal musculature to be recruited, as reflected in normal whole-person ADLs.

Lander et al[30] evaluated differences between performing a bench press maneuver with a free-weight barbell and using an isokinetic dynamometer. Their conclusions, supported by others,[31,32] suggest that measured differences were due to the "the balancing and stabilizing efforts required in the free-weight condition, the muscle elastic property effects, and the differing baseline forces associated with the two activities" (Figures 4–7 to 4–9).

Lord and Castell[33] evaluated the effects of a physical activity program for 44 people ranging from 50 to 75 years of age and demonstrated that it was responsible for improving sensorimotor skills that contribute to stability. The program included non-machine-based exercise activities for 10 weeks' duration, and the control group, although not involved in the exercise component, was measured for the same physical outcomes. The exercise group was the only one to show improvements in balance, strength, reaction time, and body sway on a firm surface with the eyes closed and on a compliant surface with the eyes open and closed (Figures 4–10 to 4–12).

Figure 4–7A. In this example, the supine bench press (also known as the chest press) is being performed with a wide base of support (i.e., the feet firmly planted on the floor and relatively wide) and with an Olympic-style, free-weight barbell (7 feet long and 45 pounds). There are many trunk muscles that are recruited to perform this maneuver safely. The barbell must be balanced in all directions so that it can be controlled along the arc it is to travel, and initially this requires conscious control of the muscles responsible for this maneuver. Since this exercise is not restrained, as it would be, for example, in Figure 4–7B (seated chest press), the proprioceptive system must be made available to successfully control the position of the barbell throughout its movement arc.

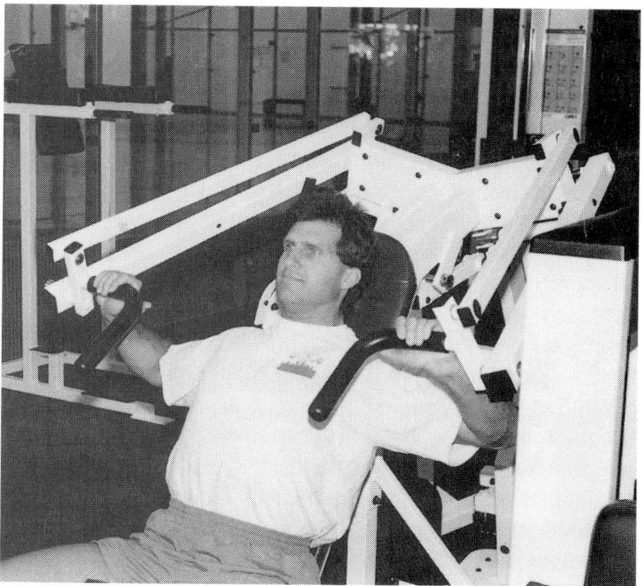

Figure 4–7B. Performing the seated chest press in a relatively restrained environment will be easier since the demand for stability is relatively reduced, compared to the maneuver depicted in Figure 4–7A. Here the proprioceptive demands are relatively less and the need for trunk muscle recruitment is also proportionately less. This may be an advantage for patients involved in an initial program, especially for increased patient compliance, since it may assist deconditioned patients in becoming accustomed to exercise and better prepare them psychologically and physically to better handle more demanding exercise requirements.

NMS development involves not only complex vertebral movement patterns, but also rotation about a joint or region. Although MBE can be useful for isolated strength development, it could be considered an incomplete training method because machines are fixed, stable devices that do not allow these rotational movement patterns to occur through their full range of motion. Compensatory lifting maneuvers could promote improper lifting habits when training on machines, and this could be potentially harmful since an exercise supervisor would be unable to see asymmetries clearly. Traditionally, machines do not exercise the right and left sides of an extremity or of the trunk independently. This makes it easier for an individual to twist and strain without asymmetrical deficiencies being apparent (Figures 4–13 to 4–15).

DESIGN CONSIDERATIONS

Since exercise machines are designed to fit the "average" person, it is impossible to accurately fit the force-position curves for movements throughout their full range of motion for most people using them. If machines were custom-

Figure 4–8. Performing the supine, free-weight bench press maneuver this way involves a narrower base of support (i.e., feet together and on top of the bench platform) so this exercise will more strongly recruit the proprioceptive system, when compared to the exercise demands in Figure 4–7A. More trunk muscles will be recruited in this example since there will be less assistance available from the muscles of the lower extremity.

Figure 4–9. This example of the supine, free-weight bench press is a more advanced PEP than Figure 4–8 since the base of support is smaller (i.e., feet are elevated and not in contact with any surface). This maneuver will require much more of the trunk musculature than a more isolated and restricted form of exercise. The demand on the proprioceptive system will be proportionately increased in this example since the relative degree of stability is reduced.

Figure 4–10. This example of supine bench press exercises primary chest and shoulder musculature, but trunk muscles act as stabilizers for this maneuver, being more active with lessening stability. The barbell is unrestrained so the exerciser has to use all available senses to balance the barbell three-dimensionally as it is moved along its movement path. The proprioceptive system is much more strongly recruited here compared to performing a chest press maneuver on a relatively restrained machine with fixed cams.

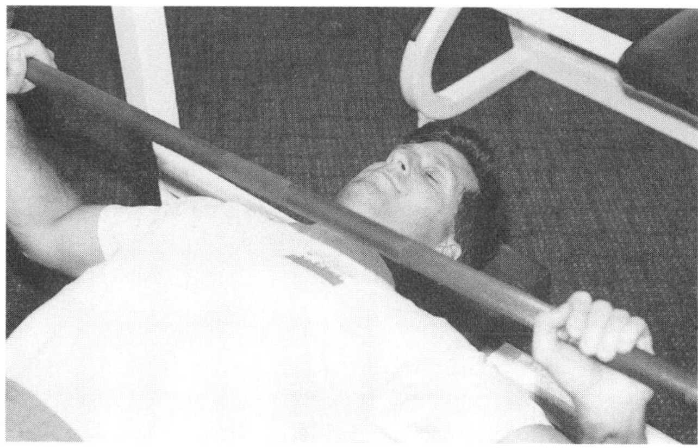

Figure 4–11. To really activate the proprioceptive system, shown to be so important in the safe and appropriate performance of ADLs, patients may have to perform some exercises without the use of visual acuity (i.e., with the eyes closed). Trunk muscles and mechanoreceptors are strongly recruited when visual information is removed, and this may be a highly desirable demand for functional training programs if safely tolerated by patients.

Figure 4–12. An advanced system for improving proprioceptive awareness, for those individuals with labor-demanding requirements or for elite-level athletes, may be introducing demanding activities without the availability of visual information *and* with both extremities having to work more independently. This is another example of an advanced PEP, and patients/athletes must be carefully screened to be sure they can safely tolerate these demands. This system should be used to prepare an individual for daily work-related tasks, as a proactive intervention for reducing the likelihood for injury, deconditioning, or progressively addressing NMS dysfunction.

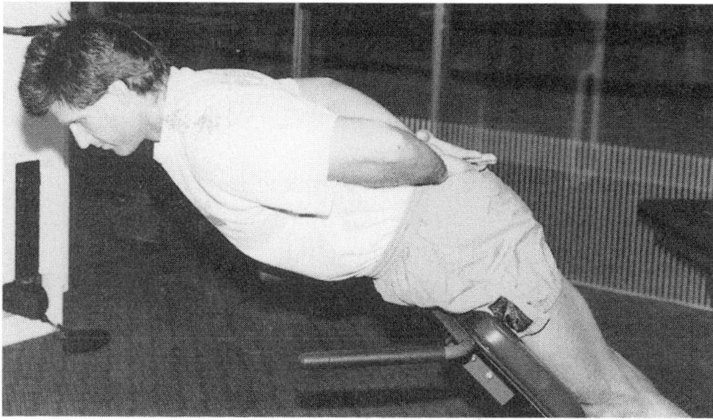

Figure 4–13. Exercising the posterior trunk musculature and the gluteal and hamstring muscles on a relatively inexpensive device will allow patients to move dynamically and in a coupled, unrestrained fashion. Patients may have to be taught how to activate the appropriate muscles in the appropriate chronological sequence; otherwise, compensations may be present and NMS may be abnormally ingrained subconsciously. In some instances, isolation of identified weak trunk muscles may have to be addressed successfully before more complex, three-dimensional movements are introduced.

Figure 4–14. Another advanced method for increasing the relative demand on the trunk musculature is to progressively move the upper limbs further away from the body's center of gravity (approximately 6 inches anterior to the first sacral tubercle). This increased demand on the trunk muscles should only be introduced if the patient has already mastered the initial demand and only if chronological sequencing can be performed successfully.

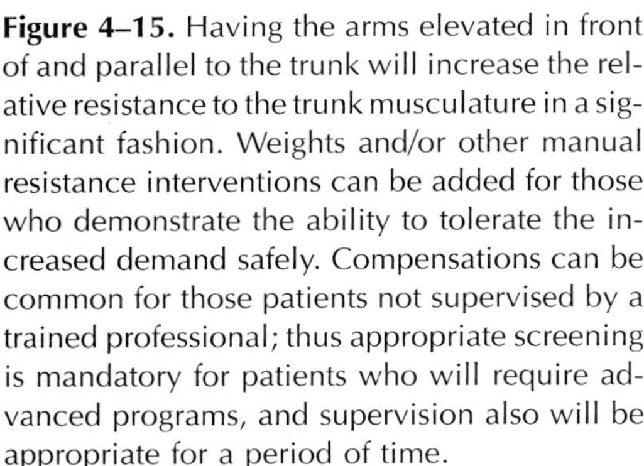

Figure 4–15. Having the arms elevated in front of and parallel to the trunk will increase the relative resistance to the trunk musculature in a significant fashion. Weights and/or other manual resistance interventions can be added for those who demonstrate the ability to tolerate the increased demand safely. Compensations can be common for those patients not supervised by a trained professional; thus appropriate screening is mandatory for patients who will require advanced programs, and supervision also will be appropriate for a period of time.

made for each person in an exercise program, they might more closely approximate true force-position curves, but there is no current evidence that suggests this has been accomplished. Theoretically, an individual who is significantly larger or smaller than "average" may be at a significant disadvantage in terms of joint stress at certain ranges of motion.

CONCEPTUAL ADVANTAGES AND DISADVANTAGES FOR NON-MBE AND MBE

Conceptual advantages for non-MBE include:

1. Relative low cost and maintenance.
2. Opportunity for infinite exercise method variability.
3. Asymmetrical training patterns can be recommended, if appropriate.
4. Asymmetrical training patterns can be more easily detected by a supervisor and corrected, if appropriate.
5. Whole-person movement patterns can be incorporated with associated proprioceptive demands.
6. It more closely parallels ADLs so the potential carryover effect is greater.
7. Variations in movement velocity are greater.
8. Increased opportunity to promote patient self-sufficiency, since this method can be more easily performed at home.
9. Coupled, vertebral spinal movement patterns can occur in the absence of machine-based restraints.
10. It does not require a lot of specialized, expensive equipment and so is more accessible to the general public at large.

Conceptual disadvantages for non-MBE include:

1. Since it largely involves whole-person, three-dimensional movements, it presents a higher potential risk for injury. This emphasizes the need for professional supervision.
2. If an individual presents with severe dysfunction, restrained and limited movements may be necessary during the early phases of a rehabilitation program.
3. Automatic adjustment to maintain constant velocity, thereby reducing the potential for injury, is difficult, if not impossible (i.e., isokinetics training mode).
4. Uniform resistance throughout the full range of motion is more difficult to achieve, and so addressing the "weak link" may be more challenging.
5. Small, subtle, but very critical alterations in the performance of an exercise maneuver could produce latent pain symptoms and subsequently further damage and delay in achieving a positive outcome. This may be less likely in a restrained, and therefore more controlled environment.

Conceptual advantages for MBE include:

1. The machines are large and heavy so security is not a problem.
2. Machines restrain movement activity and so may be beneficial for patients with severe spinal dysfunction and in need of restricted activity during the early phases of their program.
3. Since machines promote restrained activities, they are potentially safer by eliminating movements that could produce injury. However, there is the potential to promote subtle damage over the long term by preventing normal complex joint movements, and thereby introducing aberrant joint stressors.

4. Less supervision is typically required of machines.
5. Using machines to assist a clinician in the evaluation process may prove to be a reliable way for gathering specific information regarding the presence or absence of physical deficiencies, providing an objective method for reevaluation of these identified elements.

Conceptual disadvantages for MBE include:

1. Most exercise machines are built to accommodate the "average" body type. This implies that at least one-third of the individuals who use them do not fit them properly.
2. Most machines are fixed instruments that restrain a person's activity and therefore restrict the multiplanar movements that are associated with ADLs.
3. Since there are individual machines required that each promote limited movement potential, many of them are necessary to address all major muscle groups adequately. Therefore, the costs associated with purchase and maintenance are considerable relative to non-MBE.
4. Most machines have weight increments from 2.5 to 10 pounds, and this may be too much of an increase for some people.
5. Most machines do not allow individuals to train opposite sides independently. Therefore, training may be incomplete. Also, an individual could recruit more effort from the "good" side and an imbalance could be created. A supervisor would also have more difficulty detecting asymmetrical differences.
6. There are very few machines that are easily accessible to the general public that adequately address the trunk musculature.
7. Most machines require that individuals exercise in a recumbent or seated posture, and most ADLs are performed while standing.
8. There is significantly less training variability available with a program that is dedicated only to an MBE environment.
9. Because MBE is more restricted and therefore controlled, the potential benefits associated with intensive exercise are proportionately reduced (i.e., it may be safer since the potential risk for injury with MBE is relatively less).

There has been one study conducted[34] that evaluated the differences between passive and active treatment interventions in a chronic low back pain population. Also, comparisons were made between two different forms of active exercise, specifically the MBE versus the non-MBE approach.

The patients participating in this study (N = 250) were all employed for an automobile manufacturing plant and were working for at least 6 months prior to the initiation of the study. Each individual complained of chronic low back pain (68 females, 182 males) following an L5 laminectomy performed at least 1 year prior to the initiation of the study. Table 4–2 summarizes the characteristics of the subjects included in the study.

Table 4–2: Description of Subjects Included in the Study

N = 250
Age range = 34–51 years
Males enrolled = 182
Females enrolled = 68
Surgical history = L5 laminectomy:
133 (53.2%) = right-sided laminectomy
117 (46.8%) = left-sided laminectomy
Lower extremity pain = yes (but not below the knee)
Passive SLR testing = negative

Subjects were divided into five experimental groups (Table 4–3) and the treatment sessions were scheduled for 8 weeks at a frequency of three times per week. The relative costs associated with various treatment interventions are summarized in Table 4–4 (not including objective baseline and comparison measurements for the high-technology group).

The results of the study suggest the following:

1. Active approaches to managing chronic low back pain are more effective than passive interventions. However, the fact that passive modalities were not used in combination with other interventions may have influenced the results. Also, the choice for spinal manipulation techniques may not have been the most effective choice for this form of mechanical dysfunction.
2. Although both the MBE and non-MBE approaches used in this study for managing chronic low back pain were statistically superior to passive interventions, the non-MBE approach provided the longest period of pain relief and was the most cost-effective.

Table 4–3: A Summary Description of the Five Experimental Groups Who Participated in the Study

GROUP	NUMBER OF SUBJECTS (TOTAL)	AGE RANGE
Physical agents	50	36–47
Joint manipulation	50	35–50
Low-tech exercise	50	37–51
High-tech exercise	50	34–49
Control	50	34–51
Overall	250	34–51

Table 4–4: A Summary of Treatment Interventions and Their Relative Costs

TREATMENT GROUP	RELATIVE COSTS[a]
Physical agents: hydrocollation, ultrasound, TENS	$1,842.00/subject $76.75/session
Joint manipulation: manual therapy procedures (short-amplitude, high-velocity mobilization)	$1,260.00/subject $52.50/session
Low-tech exercise: McKenzie-based spinal loading procedures and spinal stabilization exercises (supervised and nonsupervised)	$1,392.00/subject $58.00/session
High-tech exercise: Supervised program of cardiovascular, isotonic, and isokinetic exercise	$1,716.00/subject $71.50/session

[a]Costs described do not include all of the evaluation protocols that were required of all subjects.

SUMMARY

The first line of defense to protect a joint complex is the muscles that surround it. If this muscle system is functioning properly, assuming neurological communication is intact and normal, it should reflexively adjust to the variety of stressors that are being placed upon it. By doing so, it can potentially prevent or retard harmful load-bearing patterns from promoting destructive joint changes. There is evidence to suggest that one's ability to properly compensate load-bearing stressors becomes increasingly difficult with increasing muscular fatigue.[35–37] Therefore, subsequent increases in aberrant spinal loading, especially if prolonged, could increase the likelihood for injury.

Training patients to protect themselves involves teaching them to perform movements that recruit muscles that they will be using for extended periods of time. They will need to learn to use muscles of the trunk and limbs in a coordinated, sequential, and synergistic fashion, and they may need to do so for relatively extended periods of time. This principle of dynamic stabilization training has not been shown to be possible with machine-based exercise alone.

The muscles associated with trunk performance function by acting as prime movers and stabilizers[38–40] and therefore act as a first line of defense for load-bearing stress to the spine.[41] This is made possible only by the muscles of the trunk being constantly influenced by nervous system afferent pathways that communicate information to them from the environment. This afferent information is processed and transmitted to efferent communication channels, which directly influences motor function. When training a patient with a spinal injury to safely perform ADLs, the clinician must expose this person to environmental information (positional stress, alterations in gravitational forces, variations in resistance, etc.) that will promote neuromotor learning to retard nondestructive load-bearing patterns. MBE, if used alone and providing some measure of restraint, may prevent the appropriate acquisition of these neuromotor skills.

A functional rehabilitation program cannot be completed without influencing the nervous system. The afferent pathways that come from environmental influences are responsible for prescribing the action of the muscles they innervate. If the body is used to perceiving outside environmental information appropriately, then there is the potential for successful adaptation to aberrant loading. Even though spinal muscle strength may be present, lack of neuromotor control of the performance of unstrained activities might be one potential cause for aberrant spinal loading stress and subsequent injury. Trunk muscle endurance may also play a pivotal role in spinal stabilization, and so should be one considered ingredient when recommending spinal rehabilitative exercise.[42–46] There is also a strong role for proprioception in spinal stabilization exercise methods in young and in older patients,[47–50] and there is evidence that these spinal stabilization methods can be successfully targeted at specific conditions, including vertebral spondylolisthesis.[51] Clinicians do not have to choose between machine-based or non-machine-base exercise, but rather should focus on clinical case management objectives and establish target goals that reflect identified deficiencies. In the end, for programs that have progressed beyond initial training demands, it appears that the evidence currently favors exercise performed primarily in a non-machine-based functional fashion that reflects the demands of daily living.

REFERENCES

1. Frymoyer JW. Epidemiology. In: Frymoyer JW, Gordon SL, eds. *Symposium on New Perspectives on Low Back Pain*. Park Ridge: IL: American Academy of Orthopaedic Surgeons, 1989:19–33.
2. Cassidy JD, Wedge JH. The epidemiology and natural history of low back pain and spinal degeneration. In: Kirkaldy-Willis WH, ed. *Managing Low Back Pain*. New York: Churchill-Livingstone, 1988:3–15.
3. Frymoyer JW, Pope MH, Costanza MC, et al. Epidemiologic studies of low back pain. *Spine*. 1980;5:419–423.
4. Svensson HO, Andersson GBJ. Low back pain in 40–47-year-old men. I. Frequency occurrence and impact on medical services. *Scand J Rehabil Med*. 1982;14:47–53.

5. Valdenburg HA, Haanen HCM. The epidemiology of low back pain. *Clin Orthop.* 1983;179:9–22.
6. Biering-Sorenson FA. Prospective study of low back pain in a general population. I. Occurrence, recurrence and aetiology. *Scand J Rehabil Med.* 1983;15:71–79.
7. Berquiest-Ullman M, Larsson U. Acute low back pain in industry. *Acta Orthop Scan.* 1977;170(Suppl):1–117.
8. Rowe ML. Low back pain in industry. *J Occup Med.* 1969;11:161–169.
9. Horal J. The clinical appearance of low back pain disorders in the city of Gotenburg, Sweden. *Acta Orthop Scand.* 1969;18(Suppl):1–109.
10. Benn RT, Wood PH. Pain in the back: An attempt to estimate the size of the problem. *Rheumatol Rehabil.* 1975;14:121–128.
11. Frymoyer JW, Rosen JC, Clemonts J, et al. Psychologic factors in low back pain disability. *Clin Orthop.* 1985;195:178–184.
12. Pheasant HC. The problem back. *Curr Pract Orthop Surg.* 1977;7:89–115.
13. Snook SH. Low back pain in industry. In: White AA, Gordon SL, eds. *Symposium in Idiopathic Low Back Pain.* St. Louis: CV Mosby, 1982.
14. Spengler DM, Bigos SJ, Martin NA, et al. Back injuries in industry: A restrospective study. I. Overview and cost analysis. *Spine.* 1986;11:241–245.
15. Frymoyer JW, Pope MH, Clemonts JH, et al. Risk factors in low back pain: An epidemiological study. *J Bone Joint Surg.* 1983;65A:213–218.
16. Andersson GBJ, Pope MH, Frymoyer JW. Epidemiology. In: Pope MH, Frymoyer JW, Andersson G, eds. *Occupational Low Back Pain.* New York: Praeger, 1984:101–114.
17. Morris A. Identifying workers at risk to back injury is not guesswork. *Occup Health Saf.* 1985;55:16–20.
18. Smith TJ, Fernie GR. Functional Biomechanics of the Spine. Symposium on Biomechanical Testing, September 1987, Vancouver, British Columbia, Canada.
19. Koreska J, Robertson D, Hills R, Gibson D, Albisser A. Biomechanics of the lumbar spine and its clinical signficance. *Orthop Clin North Am.* 1977;8(1).
20. McGill S, Norman R. Dynamically and statically determined low back moments during lifting. *J Biomech.* 1985;18:877–885.
21. Panjabi MM. Error in kinematic parameters of planar joint. *J Biomech.* 1982;15:537.
22. Gertzbein S. Determination of a locus of instantaneous centres of rotation of the lumbar disk by moire fringes. *Spine.* 1984;9:409.
23. Woltring HJ. Finite centroid and helical axis estimation. *J Biomech.* 1985;18:379.
24. Nemeth G, Ekholm J, Arborelius UP. Hip load moments and muscular activity during lifting. *Scand J Rehabil Med.* 1984;16:103–111.
25. Nouwen A, Van Akkerveeken PF, Versloot JM. Patterns of muscular activity during movements in patients with chronic low back pain. *Spine.* 1987;12:777–782.
26. Thorstensson A, Oddsson L, Carlson H. Motor control of voluntary trunk movements in standing. *Acta Physiol Scand.* 1985;125:309–321.
27. Paquet N, Malouin F, Richards C. Hip-spine movement interaction and muscle activation patterns during sagittal trunk movements in low back pain patients. *Spine.* 1994;19(5):596–603.
28. Reynolds H. Stereoradiographic measurement and analysis of three-dimensional body movement. *Concepts and mechanisms of neuromuscular functions.* 1984;42–46.
29. Parkhurst T, Burnett C. Injury and proprioception in the lower back. *JOSPT.* 1994;19(5):282–293.
30. Lander J, Bates B, Sawhill J, Hamill J. A comparison between free-weight and isokinetic bench pressing. Biomechanics/Sports Medicine Laboratory, University of Oregon, 1984;344–352.
31. Andrews JG, Hay JG, Vaughn CL. Knee shear forces during a squat exercise using a barbell and a weight machine. In: Masui HJ, Kobayashi K, eds. *Biomechanics VIII-B.* Champaign, IL: Human Kinetics, 1983:923–927.
32. Hay JG, Andrews JG, Vaughn CL, Ueya K. Load, speed, and equipment affects in strength-training exercises. In: Masui HJ, Kobayashi K, eds. *Biomechanics VIII-B.* Champaign, IL: Human Kinetics, 1983:939–950.
33. Lord S, Castell S. Physical activity program for older persons: Effect on balance, strength, neuromuscular control, and reaction time. *Arch Phys Med Rehabil.* 1994;75:648–652.
34. Timm K. A randomized-control study of active and passive treatments for chronic low back pain following L5 laminectomy. *JOSPT.* 1994;20(6):276–285.
35. Bigland-Ritchie B. Muscle fatigue and the influence of changing neural drive. Symposium on exercise: Physiology and clinical application. *Clin Chest Med.* 1984;5:21.
36. Farfan HF. Muscular mechanism of the lumbar spine and the position of power efficiency. *Orthop Clin North Am.* 1975;6:135.

37. Donisch EW, Basmajian JV. Electromyography of deep back muscles in man. *Am J Anat*. 1972;133:25.
38. Morris JM, Lucas DB, Bresler B. The role of the trunk in the stability of the spine. *J Bone Joint Surg*. 1961;43A:327.
39. Nordin M, Frankel VH. Biomechanics of tendons and ligaments. In: Frankel VH, Nordin M. *Basic Biomechanics of the Skeletal System*. Philadelphia: Lea and Febiger, 1989:59–60.
40. Schultz A, Anderson GBJ, Ortengren R, et al. Analysis and quantitative myoelectric measurements of loads of the lumbar spine when holding weights in standing postures. *Spine*. 1982;7:390.
41. Ortengren R, Anderson GBJ. Electromyographic studies of trunk muscles with special reference to the functional anatomy of the spine. *Spine*. 1977;2:44.
42. Mayer T, Kondraske G, Mooney V, Carmichael T, Butsch R. Lumbar myoelectric spectral analysis for endurance assessment. A comparison of normals with deconditioned patients. *Spine*. 1989;14:986–990.
43. Roy S, De Luca C, Casavant D. Lumbar muscle fatigue and chronic lower back pain. *Spine*. 1989;14:992–1001.
44. Nordin M, Kahanovitz N, Verderame R, Parnianpour M, Yabut S, Viola K, Greenidge N, Mulvihill M. Normal trunk strength and endurance in women and the effect of exercises and electrical stimulation: Part 1—Normal endurance and trunk muscle strength in 101 women. *Spine*. 1987;12:105–111.
45. Kahanovitz N, Nordin M, Verderame R, Yabut S, Parnianpour M, Viola K, Mulvihill M. Normal trunk strength and endurance in women and the effect of exercises and electrical stimulation: Part 2—Comphrehensive analysis of electrical stimulation and exercises to increase trunk strength and endurance. *Spine*. 1987;12:112–118.
46. De Luca C. Myoelectrical manifestations of localized muscular fatigue in humans. *Crit Rev Biomed Eng*. 1984;11:251–279.
47. Lephart S, Pincivero D, Giraldo L, Fu F. The role of proprioception in the management and rehabilitation of athletic injuries. *Am J Sports Med*. 1997;25(1):130–137.
48. Anonymous. Balance exercises. Staying on your feet. *Mayo Clin Health Letter*. 1998;16(2):4–5.
49. Buchner DM, Cress ME, deLateur BJ, Esselman PC, Margherita AJ, Price R, Wagner EH. A comparison of the effects of three types of endurance training on balance and other fall risk factors in older adults. *Aging*. 1997;9(1–2):112–119.
50. Chandler JM, Duncan PW, Kochersberger G, Studenski S. Is lower extremity strength gain associated with improvement in physical performance and disability in frail, community-dwelling elders? *Arch Phys Med Rehab*. 1998;79(1):24–30.
51. Sullivan P, Phyty G, Twomey L, Allison G. Evaluation of specific stabilizing exercise in the treatment of chronic low back pain with radiologic diagnosis of spondylolysis or spondylolisthesis. *Spine*. 1997;22(24):2959–2967.

CHAPTER 5

Patient Education and Activation

BRUCE HOFFMANN, DC

INTRODUCTION

Much has been learned about spinal-related pain and its multiple associated factors, particularly over the past decade. This is probably in response to the growing statistics regarding spinal injuries, the frequency of which and their costs continue to rise. Most alarming is the disproportionate rise in the cost compared to the frequency of back injuries. This has been described as the low back pain epidemic in America.[1]

Despite the latest in diagnostic equipment, the most advanced rehabilitation equipment, and the most multidisciplinary and comprehensive treatment centers, the epidemic continues. With support from the literature, most leading experts have agreed that there is little diagnostic certainty when assessing patients, and few treatment methods have demonstrated superiority to others. With this in mind, it may be prudent to reevaluate patient case management protocols.

BACK SCHOOLS

The back school has been mentioned in the literature as a common treatment approach for low back pain. Others have suggested that it be used as an adjunctive tool in a comprehensive goal-orientated treatment plan, because as a sole treatment modality it has less impact.[2] A typical back school consists primarily of education and/or exercise, yet great variance exists with contents, intensity and duration, patient selection, and outcomes.[3–7] Recent attempts to validate the efficacy of this treatment method have been fraught with error as well as lacking in a clear definition of what a back school is.[8] It was pointed out that a great diversity exists in the definition of and the components included in back schools. Furthermore, several flaws in study designs and outcome measures were identified, making valid interpretations difficult. Low back pain has many etiological elements, and this must be taken into account when designing clinical trials. Specifically, in regard to back schools, the following variables need to be controlled and/or accounted for: age and sex of patients, compensation and reimbursement issues, pain or diagnostic classification, treatment and class size, content, comprehension, and visit frequency.

With this in mind, a closer examination of the basic tenets of back school, education and activation, will be reviewed. This will be done to improve the likelihood of selecting the optimal treatment approaches for back pain patients, and thus improving the potential for a successful treatment outcome track record.

A BETTER UNDERSTANDING OF THE PATIENT

The premise of adequate care is best summarized by Waddell[9]: We must approach the patient as a whole person. Fordyce et al state similarly that results from treatment often fail because of reliance on too narrow a conceptual model of pain.[10] Thus it appears essential to consider the physical, psychological, and social aspects of each patient. It is all three of these components that modulate the patient's pain experience and, ultimately, the treatment outcome. This is the basis for the *biophysical model.*

To apply this model to case management elements, a clear understanding of disease, illness, and disability is appropriate. A patient's pathology or injury is viewed as the disease or physical insult that causes a nociceptive stimulus. Illness on the other hand, is the patient's interpretation of this nociceptive stimulus. This interpretation is influenced by the actual physical stimulus, psychological factors, and emotional factors. Illness is outwardly manifested by verbal symptoms given by the patient and objective signs of observable physical changes or actions. In short, Waddell defines illness as "observable and potentially measurable actions and conduct which express and communicate the individual's own perception of the disease." Ultimately, the illness behavior is represented in functional loss and is defined as disability. The problem arises when the physical problem persists, ultimately causing distress. This distress leads to increased illness behavior, and if reinforced will lead to the adoption of the sick role and ultimate permanent disability.

Lethem et al[11] have built on Waddell's approach in describing patients coping response to disease as being either avoidance or confrontation. Patients who assume the avoidance role, also called fear avoidance, avoid physical and social activities that cause or are associated with causing pain, which leads to physical and psychological consequences. All too often the patient's perception of physically painful activities is just that, a perception that often correlates poorly with biomechanical evidence. This can be reinforced by the clinician or therapist who says, "If it hurts then don't do it," which likely reinforces illness behavior and disability.

Following the acute episode and based on coping strategies, patients may adopt an avoidance routine. This includes avoidance of physical and social activities and will likely lead to physical changes such as decreased flexibility, strength, endurance, etc.; an overall deconditioning process will evolve if the avoidance strategy is prolonged. On the psychological side, an exaggerated pain perception develops as limited exposure to painful stimuli and fewer opportunities to calibrate pain sensation with pain experience are available.

The patients' subjective pain experience can often become out of proportion with the objective findings for pain or disease. In short, the patients' illness behavior, the expressed pain and functional loss report, is greater than that supported by the disease process. It appears likely that the psychological and emotional aspects are just as strong as the physical disease process in creating disability. Waddell further points out that illness behavior is often proportional to disease in the early and acute stage. As time and pain progress, illness behaviors often become out of proportion with the disease and lead to permanent disability; it is this disability that is escalating in the United States and not the physical disease process.

This model is in stark contrast to the traditional medical model. The medical model's approach to disease depends on the illness associated to a physical pathology, with symptoms and disability being directly related to and proportional to that physical pathology. Clinical recognition and diagnosis of the underlying pathology were used to provide the basis for rational physical treatment of the illness. This concept is too narrowly focused, and may account for or add to the poor outcome of low back pain patients.

The disability process is better understood and defined in the context of the biophysical and pain avoidance models. In doing so, pain and its associated components of illness can be better treated in their acute stage to improve outcomes and help prevent the development of chronic pain, the latter being considerably more costly to successfully resolve.

Although back schools have not been shown to be consistently effective in the management of low back pain, the basic tenets of back school, education and activation, continue to deserve special attention by the clinician. This is particularly true when patients are viewed in the context of the biopsychosocial model. Each patient presents with his or her own unique set of beliefs about low back pain and coping mechanisms. It is the clinician's role to understand these issues and base patient education and activation accordingly to that patient's unique needs. This cannot be done effectively in a group setting. What follows are suggestions for evaluating and developing patient education and activation plans.

THE CONSULTATION

The initial evaluation and management of a patient may set the stage for whether a successful resolution of the chief complaint is achieved, or for the migration of the patient's condition into the chronic category.[12] In order to manage and effectively direct the patient's care, the trust and reassurance of the patient must be gained by the doctor. The first opportunity for this to be established is during the history and physical. Many chronic pain patients have described their first encounter with the designated company doctor as very brief and rather unprofessional.[11] How can trust and control be maintained with this type of relationship?

The importance of a proper history is well supported. When forming a clinical picture, most of the information necessary can be gathered from the history.[13] Common historical factors are presented in Table 5–1. In addition to those listed, and possibly more important, are factors such as perception of fault, anger, anxiety, perception of severity, pain descriptions, and family, social, and work history. These factors, as we will see, may be the most crucial for predicting outcome and thus determining the degree of therapeutic intervention required.

More importance needs to be placed on the injured person's perceptions, particularly when work issues are involved. Matheson writes "The greatest limitations on the functioning of workers with painful low back injuries are psychophysical; that is, they are based on the worker's perception of ability and as such are accentuated by pain and fear." As well, low back pain patients may have preconceived notions about their condition, from family or friends' experiences, that may be misguided. For these reasons, an

Table 5–1: Common Historical Components

1. Present complaint
   a. History of trauma
   b. Description of complaint
   c. Quality/character
   d. Intensity
   e. Frequency
   f. Location and radiation
   g. Onset
   h. Duration
   i. Palliative factors
   j. Provocative factors
2. Family history
3. Past health history
4. Psychosocial history
5. Social history
6. Review of systems

adequate consultation with patients is necessary to become aware of such issues. This must be followed up with appropriate education, frequent reassurance, and close monitoring and guidance to ensure a positive outcome.[14]

In a large review of 3020 injuries of aircraft employees, Bigos et al studied factors affecting the reporting of back injuries.[15] They found that other than a previous history, workers perceptions had the highest predictive capacity. They concluded that a job that is perceived to be a burden, not enjoyable, and not fulfilling, and that provides few assets influences the report of low back injuries. Although this study deals with primary predictors of low back pain, it helps demonstrate the role of perception. One would likely conclude that work perceptions that affected the report of injury would likely play a role in a patient's return to work following an injury. Furthermore, they may affect the patient's initial presentation and treatment progress.

Historical components will likely provide further insight into the emotional aspects of pain perception as defined in the biophysical model. Lethem et al[11] developed and validated four subgroupings that greatly affect this emotional reactionary response.[7]. These include: stressful life events, personal pain history, personal coping strategies, and personality issues. Previous stressful life events preceding the initial spell of acute pain may alter the ability to cope or manage pain. It may allow for an escape from these stresses or may be a better option in the patient's mind. Past pain history, such as previous low back pain, and the number and intensity of the episodes may greatly reduce coping ability. This gives further support to the poor long-term prognosis in unmanaged low back pain and the natural history. In terms of individual coping strategies, these are often modeled from peers and reflections of personal experiences or determined and encouraged by health care providers. The latter source should encourage all health care professionals to take a more active care approach with patients. Passive care signals to the patient that movement is bad and the condition is serious and fosters more fear-avoidance routines, ultimately leading to prolonged disability. Finally, personality factors, associated with the so-called neurotic triad, affect the patient's presentation. These consist of hysteria, depression, and hypochondriasis.

PHYSICAL EXAMINATION

Findings during the physical examination may be helpful in more fully understanding the patient's presentation, more than purely for diagnostic purposes. Keefe reported on common pain behaviors demonstrated by patients during the physical examination.[16] Most common were guarding, bracing, rubbing, grimacing, and sighing. These are easily measurable during the examination and the clinician should look for consistency and/or exaggeration of these behaviors. It was found that these pain behaviors did not correlate well with the severity of examination findings. For example, evidence of nerve root irritation did not necessarily result in more pain behaviors. In other words, a patient's presentation and report are influenced both by sensory and emotional stimuli. The amount of pain reported or demonstrated for a given examination finding does not necessarily correlate with the severity of physical insult. Most importantly, Keefe describes that patients prone to displaying pain behaviors are likely to elicit solicitous responses from family or friends that may serve to maintain or promote these pain behavior patterns long after underlying tissue pathology has healed. Physicians must recognize such behaviors and help extinguish them.

Behaviors observed during the examination are associated with the patient's interpretation of the pain/sensory component and his or her ability to tolerate pain.[17] Those patients with a lower pain threshold will likely present with more restricted spinal mobility, greater flexor/extensor muscular strength imbalance, and lower angle of straight leg raise. In other words, patients self-regulated their range of motion based on perceived bodily harm, physical vulnerability, and/or willingness to endure pain.

The nonorganic physical findings, also known as Waddell nonorganic signs, may yield additional information regarding the patient's illness behavior. These five nonorganic examination findings are not considered physiologically consistent with low back pain complaints. Reference to the original text should be made for specific techniques and protocols,[18] and these consist of superficial tenderness, axial loading, distractions, rotation, and nonanatomical pain distribution. When three or more of these findings are present, patients may be exhibiting excessive illness behavior. According to Waddell's original research, those with scores higher that 3 typically scored high on several Minnesota Multiphasic Personality Inventory (MMPI) scales and demonstrated exaggerated pain drawings.

RATIONALE FOR INCLUSION OF ACTIVE CARE

Fordyce et al[19] compared two approaches to the care of acute low back pain. Group A received medication as needed, undertook activities within pain tolerance, and exercised using pain as a guide. Group B had no medication refills, activity was prescribed by the doctor, and exercise was prescribed at a specific time with reps and sets preset. They found at follow-up that group A had a higher pain report and impairment than group B. In short, group A's treatment and progress were dependent on the patient's pain report. Group B's treatment was a time-contingent program which was based on and progressed with healing physiology. They concluded that the behavioral perspective on pain is defined on the premise that pain experience and behaviors are not necessarily an indicator of nociceptive input. Further, physicians who rely solely on a patient's report of pain and illness are likely to promote chronicity. In a similar study, this behavioral approach was found equally as successful in a large patient population of subacute low back pain sufferers.[20] They found that not only did these patients return to work significantly faster than control subjects, but the patients had less sick leave for 1 year following the program.

There is an abundance of support in the literature for the use of early active care in treating the acute injury.[9–11,21–32] Waddell[9] points out that active care makes the patient a more active participant in the care process, which ultimately decreases doctor dependence and feelings of helplessness. Fordyce et al[10] demonstrated that increased exercise performance correlated with decreased observable pain behaviors such as statements, gestures, and audible gasps. Troup[32] concluded that active care is the only valid treatment approach in chronic pain patients. It may be prudent for this active care element to be included as soon as possible to reduce the likelihood of conditions becoming chronic. Mitchell and Carmen[33] pointed out from their work that early activation with exercise care greatly reduced lost work time and costs: The later this treatment process begins, the less likely is a positive outcome. Bigos[28] reported after an extensive search of the literature that the application of three principles, education with early return to work, judicious use of surgery, and early use of exercise and cardiovascular endurance, was *proven* to prevent chronic low back pain and disability.

There is substantial support for the use of early active care with behavior support, but how does this fit into the model presented earlier? How does active care control nociception, illness behavior, and the ultimate expression as disability? Several studies have demonstrated the positive physical effects of exercise activities for spinal pain patients.[34] Promotion of bone and muscle strength,[9,35] improved disc and cartilage nutrition, and decreased pain through endorphin release are a few of the more commonly reported physical effects.[36] Further documentation shows reduced psychological stress and fewer pain complaints with a reversal of the consequences of inactivity, primarily depression and lower self-esteem.[32] Early activation helps decrease the likelihood of the patient assuming the sick role and developing doctor dependence. Furthermore, exercise helps reinforce in the patient's mind that activity is not harmful and that he or she can continue to safely perform activities of daily living. Overall, exercise has a positive effect on both the physical and psychological aspects of patient recovery and thus fits well into this model.

There continues to be strong support among practitioners for the natural history process and the self-limiting aspect of low back pain. The natural history has been interpreted by some to be a treatment process. In reviewing some of the commonly reported sources for natural history data, Deyo estimates that 75% to 95% of acute low back pain patients will improve symptomatically in 1 month.[37] Nachemson writes that 90% of acute low back pain patients are asymptomatic within 2 months.[36] Von Korff et al reviewed other sources stating that 40% of acute low back pain patients continued to experience pain after 6 months.[38] Another source found that after 4 weeks, 47% were somewhat improved, 25% were unchanged or worse, and 28% were pain-free.[39] Rolland[40] found that after 1 week approximately 27% of patients reported increasing pain and at 4 weeks 22% reported continued increasing pain. This group was shown to have a poorer prognosis. Other reports have shown even a more prolonged natural history for acute sciatica.[41]

There exists some discrepancy in the exactness of the self-limiting nature of back pain, with the picture becoming more complicated when recurrent episodes are considered. Berquist-Ullman and Larsson found that 62% of acute low back pain patients had one or more relapses during a 1-year follow-up.[31] Troup[32] points out that after the initial episode of back pain, a patient is four times more likely to experience a recurrence within the next 2 to 3 years. He sets the scenario, following a recurrence, that individuals are likely to restrict activities and are at risk for becoming progressively weaker and stiffer. From this point on the patient does a little bit less, even though the injury may be stabilized. This vicious cycle of repeated pain exposure with alteration in function and overall deconditioning will likely lead to illness behavior and disability.

Von Korff et al[38] further report that this repeated pain exposure challenges a person's adaptive capacities and forces them into an avoidance or chronic pain cycle. They also found that the more days spent in pain, the poorer the outcome. In reviewing this, the natural history would appear to be a poor treatment option as it is suggested that the longer a patient is in pain, the more likely he or she is to develop chronic pain. More recent epidemiological studies are showing a less promising outcome. Cherkin et al reported that only 17% of patients presenting to family physicians reported no symptoms after 1 week, 35% at 3 weeks, 46% at 7 weeks, and 52% at 1 year.[42] Similar results were reported by Von Korff et al demonstrating that after 1 year 30% of patients had a poor outcome.[43] Additionally, 69% of the patients reported having some low back pain in the previous month when they were questioned 1 year after initial onset. In summary, the high recurrence rate is alarming. What once may have started as purely mechanical low back pain may, after repeated pain exposures, unnecessarily become a statistic in the rapidly rising disabling low back pain population.

Active care is often scrutinized by some who misunderstand the benefits afforded, both physically and psychologically. This is further compounded by the physician basing the treatment progress on the patient's report of pain, rather than on the healing process. Waddell[9] states the need to avoid emphasis on pain as the single most important aspect of illness. Fordyce et al,[44] in supporting this, have shown that the report of pain is influenced by many factors independent of the pathology. Further studies have shown that people with low back pain can tolerate the majority of activities of daily living without increased pain.[45]

The study of biomechanics should also help us in understanding the stress, or lack of, during exercise performance. Bigos[28] reported in a comprehensive review that the vast majority of patients can tolerate walking or standing quite well. Walking or mild activities of daily living do not increase the risk of worsening one's condition, not even with disc herniations. Furthermore, it has been found that intradiscal pressures are higher with sitting than jogging in place and jumping up and down. The ability to tolerate exercise is best summarized in a report by Saal and Saal.[22] A large patient population was presented, and all individuals were diagnosed with herniated lumbar disc with associated radiculopathy. This was confirmed with CT, MRI, and/or electromyography. Typically, these patients are considered surgical candidates and at best functionally debilitated. Yet, following participation in a comprehensive education and exercise program, they experienced good to excellent results. In conclusion, there should be ways to keep patients active to decrease deconditioning and prevent worsening of illness behaviors, without aggravating or worsening their symptoms.

WHO NEEDS EXERCISE AND HOW MUCH?

The majority of low back pain patients should receive some form of exercise-based treatment, whether home-based or supervised. Considering the high reoccurrence rate of low back pain compounded by the detrimental effect of repeated pain exposure, some form of instruction on the only suggested effective secondary preventor of low back pain, exercise, should be considered a primary element within a case management plan.

In terms of strict criteria for the degree of exercise intensity, very little literature data exist. Options range from home exercise, to health clubs, to structured supervised rehabilitation programs. The program should be based on the individual patient and be goal-orientated. If the use of rehabilitation is based on treatment goals, there is some supporting evidence for the degree of intensity necessary to reach these goals.

Berwick et al conducted a randomized study with 222 low back patients to assess the effectiveness of a back school in an HMO setting.[4] This back school consisted of a single, 4-hour session, which attempted to educate the patient on anatomy, ergonomics, exercises, natural history, and psychological issues. A subset of this group received reinforcement by telephone and mail for 12 months. A control group received an educational pamphlet. They concluded that there were no positive effects on the short-term or long-term outcomes as compared to the natural history. Home exercises may have an early positive effect, but it seems rather short-lived. This would seem logical since most home exercises are rather basic and are considered entry-level-type exercises. Personal reinforcement and guidance may be important for compliance.

A more recent review performed by Faas et al concluded that exercise therapy for patients with acute low back pain has no advantage over the usual care provided by a general medical practitioner.[46] Further insight into exercise methodology demonstrated the use of mostly entry-level-type flexion exercises that were performed twice a week for 5 weeks. It can be concluded from this information that the use of simple home exercises has at best a short-term benefit of activating the patient early, but in terms of producing long-term physical changes, home exercises are not suited for improving the likelihood for positive long-term recovery.

Mellin performed a long-term follow up on 476 patients who reported to a clinic with low back pain.[47] Patients were randomly allocated into two groups: (1) physiotherapy and home exercise or (2) physiotherapy and moderate physical exercise in a structured rehabilitation setting. At the 3-month follow-up, the moderate exercise group demonstrated a greater improvement in physical measures. Yet at the 1.5- and 2.5-year follow-ups, there were minimal differences between the two groups in physical measures. Mellin concluded that a single rehabilitation period could not bring about sufficient exercise after treatment to reach or maintain long-term physical improvement. Guidance after treatment such as refresher programs, follow-up visits, and access to facilities will most likely enhance motivation to exercise more regularly.

Donchin evaluated the effectiveness of exercise as secondary prevention of low back pain for subacute patients. Two hundred and seventy-seven subjects with low back pain were randomized into three groups: (1) aggressive exercise for 45 minutes biweekly, (2) four back school sessions of 90 minutes each that emphasized home exercise, and (3) the control group. The aggressive exercise group demonstrated greater improvement in physical measures and had fewer reported reoccurrences over a 1-year follow-up than the other two groups.

In summary, home exercises are best suited for entry-level rehabilitation programs. This would typically occur during the pain reduction and recovery treatment stages. These types of exercises have not proven to be effective in developing long-term physical outcomes, but may serve most importantly in initiating patient activation. Continued education and guidance into more aggressive regimens is typically indicated.

In terms of the need for more aggressive or structured rehabilitation, the following are some guidelines for patient selection: a patient who progresses slower than the natural history or as expected, historical and physical findings suggesting a predilection for chronicity, increasing illness behavior, illness behavior that is disproportionate to that which would be expected, difficulty with return to work issues, difficulty with returning to functional status, and previous episodes of low back pain with recurrent patterns developing.

PATIENT EDUCATION

Deyo and Diehl[48] write that the single most reported factor for dissatisfaction with traditional medical care for back pain was lack of a proper explanation of the condition. A proper explanation of the patient's condition should always be given; furthermore, patients must understand that treatment will be aimed at the restoration of function and not orientated exclusively on pain relief. Pain relief will occur naturally as treatment progresses and function is returned.[34] Berquist-Ullman and Larsson[31] found that teaching patients about their backs, what to expect, and how to control symptoms led to the most effective results. If these issues are not adequately addressed, ongoing pain can produce great anxiety and ultimately distrust in the doctor, with self-removal from the treatment program. This was evident in a study by Hansen et al,[27] which experienced a high dropout rate in an exercise group because of reported increase in pain. No evidence of behavior support or education was discussed, and that may have contributed to the high dropout rate.

The early management and education of the patient can hinder or support the development of chronic pain. Furthermore, the patient may receive anecdotal information from well-meaning laypeople that may help develop attitudes and expectations that become fixed in a negative way.[31] Because of this, physicians must often act as deprogrammers. Unfortunately and inadvertently, a patient's notion that his or her pain is serious, debilitating, and permanent can be reinforced through the patient-doctor relationship.

An important issue in patient education, according to Hall, is to create greater awareness of the patient's condition, which will ultimately lead to greater active participation in the recovery process.[49] This is based on the premise that greater understanding of the physical injury on the part of the patient will lead to greater self-control of the problem, and this could be considered a cornerstone in the back school philosophy. Although little data are available to support this, Hall summarizes through his experience that in terms of patient education of the condition, the more they learned, the better the outcome. Close attention to educational methods is of growing concern. It has been shown that back school participants often misunderstand the medical terms used, retention rates are questionable, and prior notions are typically not influenced by the session.[50] This places continued importance on understanding the patients' perceptions of the condition and appropriately addressing misconceptions.

A thorough explanation of the diagnosis is therefore necessary, but caution should be used in its presentation. Firstly, an inadequate explanation of findings and how they relate to the patients' complaints may foster suspicion, insecurity, anxiety, and other emotional reactions. On the other hand, Deyo reports on the danger of labeling.[48] This consists of assigning a patient to a diagnostic label, which has been shown to increase sick role behavior. Similar adverse affects may result from descriptors as torn muscle or ligament, slipped or ruptured disc, bones out of place, and degenerative spinal changes. These may to some individuals conjure alarming mental images, imply permanent structural damage, create unnecessary disability, and add to emotional stresses. Less alarming and equally descriptive are sprains or strains, disc derangement, or segmental dysfunction. Often at this point, patients with previous histories and treatment may have misguided or misconceived ideas concerning diagnostic philosophies, for which some form of well-guided reeducation is needed.

The use of imaging techniques is an excellent example of misinformation and/or incomplete patient education. Quite often there is little association of radiographic findings and onset of injury, severity, or outcome, with the exception of instability, pathology, or fractures.[51] Pointing out to the patient every bit of spinal degeneration, structural anomaly, etc., only reinforces the severity of the condition in the patient's mind, yet typically adds little to the clinical picture. The use of CT and MRI and their interpretation as presented to the patient is important. Recent research has indicated that with a variety of conservative care treatments, previously documented disc herniations have decreased or diminished all together.[52,53] It has also been found that in a large percentage of the population, disc abnormalities can be documented with advanced imaging, yet they experience no back symptoms.[54,55] All too often, findings of this sort become the primary factor in determining treatment or the focal point in the patient's diagnosis without proper clinical correlation. The psychological consequences of this may be great patient anxiety, leading to prolonged illness behavior, and ultimately undue and prolonged disability.

Beyond the diagnosis the patient needs to know what to expect in terms of treatment and prognosis. Physicians need to place themselves in a position of guide and facilitator. Emphasis should be placed on the patient's role in returning to function rather than the doctor's role. Treatment explanation should be based on what the patient needs to do to get better, rather than what the doctor is going to do to get rid of the pain. It has been shown that patients who attribute treatment gains to their treatment environment, rather than to their own initiative and skills acquisition, tend to have a poorer prognosis.[56] Health care providers need to put emphasis on the patient's role during periods in which conjunctive therapy is provided.

Explanation of the treatment process and duration is necessary. Of course, all patients are different, as will be their progress. Yet, patients almost invariably ask, "How long will it take?" Giving a patient an exact or estimated length of care is often unfair to the patient, unless it is based on the natural history. This in itself allows for great variance but at least provides a window for comparison of treatment outcome. Possibly more effective would be educating the patient on treatment expectations. For example, when undergoing a trial of spinal manipulative therapy (SMT), a clinician typically would expect a significant amount of improvement within the first 2 weeks. Patients should be educated that treatment progress will be based on the healing process. Patients need to know ahead of time that even though some pain may persist, more aggressive treatment approaches will be taken as progress is made from the acute pain reduction phase of care to remobilization and rehabilitation phases. Even though some pain may continue, activity will not produce increased harm. Patients need to understand that as function returns, the pain will progressively decrease, instead of thinking that as the pain decreases, function will subsequently resume. This is the basis for time-contingent treatment, rather than pain-contingent care.

More specific to chronic low back pain patients and those with chronic reoccurring back pain, physicians may find it helpful to explain why patients need to embrace active care through presenting a deconditioning model. This is particularly true in patients who have adapted an avoidance role. Through prolonged decreased and modified activity levels, muscular weakness and tightening occur about the back and associated regions. This renders the muscles and low back more irritable and subject to overload, causing recurrent pain. This increase in pain may force the patient into more avoidance or be misinterpreted as a new injury requiring more rest or acute care interventions. This cycle becomes a vicious downward spiral that can most effectively be broken by providing time-contingent pain relief and progressive activation. This example helps patients see the need to change from a passive care model to one that embraces active care.

Including the patients in the consultation, allowing them to ask questions and actively participate in the consultation, has been shown to be beneficial. Physician-dominated consultations with little mention of psychosocial topics lead to poor patient satisfaction and outcome.[57] Patients who are participants during the consultation and who have active role perceptions report more satisfactory relationships with physicians, an increased sense of self-control and ability to tolerate pain, and an overall better outcome.[58,59]

Table 5–2: Improving Patient Compliance

1. Give patients realistic treatment expectations and prognosis
2. Provide suggestions for self-care
3. Give expected results and how to achieve those results
4. Involve the patient
5. Set functional goals that are attractive to the patient
6. Give positive feedback on treatment progress

Education about proper body mechanics to decrease physical stress and help continue activity should be stressed. As previously discussed, maintenance of activity is paramount to preventing continuing illness behavior and ultimately, chronic disability. Nowhere is this more important than in the workplace. Using ergonomics and biomechanics to the injured workers' advantage, modification of the workplace may allow for a more expedient and successful return to work. Typically, the injured worker is the best source of information because no one is as familiar with his or her workstation, and worker perceptions can then be more accurately identified and successfully addressed.

There is an abundance of material available that addresses the ergonomic topics of back school. In teaching proper body mechanics, the clinician is best advised to perform them "hands on" with immediate feedback. This allows for customization to individual patient needs. Typically, it is best to use common activities of daily living or common workplace situations specific to that patient. Most commonly, techniques such as spinal stabilization (see Chapter 22 by Stude et al) or those outlined by McKenzie (see Chapter 8 by Jacob et al) are utilized.

EDUCATION, ACTIVATION, AND PATIENT COMPLIANCE

Poor patient compliance can often be related to poor treatment outcomes. Is there anything one can do to promote compliance? Pioneering work in this emerging field would suggest yes.[60] Quite simply, the use of education and activation for patients with low back pain should improve compliance with appropriate treatment regimes. Table 5–2 summarizes several elements that relate to improved patient compliance.

SUMMARY

Back schools have been a commonly used treatment modality for many years. Current literature reviews provide conflicting results on their success. Low back pain and subsequent disability are multifactorial and unique for each patient. Each patient's unique needs cannot be met in a group setting. When the primary components of back

Table 5–3: Patient Orientation Checklist for Chronic Neck/Low Back Pain

TOPIC	✔
Plausible diagnosis	
Issues of deconditioning	
Issues of fear avoidance	
Past diagnostics and treatment	
Psychological distress/depression	
Pain experience, both physical and psychological	
Passive treatment/coping	
Transition to active care	
Active patient participation	
Time frame for treatment and frequency	
Functional goals	

Table 5–4: Patient Orientation Checklist for Acute Neck/Low Back Pain

TOPIC	✔
Clear mechanism of pain	
Simple diagnostic descriptor	
Treatment expectations	
Give home care	
Give preventative care	
Short-term vs. long-term prognosis	
Invite patient participation	
Compliance Issues	
Set functional goals	
Short-term attractive goals	
Use objective tools to provide feedback	
Hurt not equal to harm/good days and bad days	
Long-term outcome	
Short-term outcome	
Patient misconceptions about prognosis	
Work is a vital component to treatment	
Address patient questions	

school are evaluated, namely, education and exercise, indications for their use can be supported. These components become increasingly important in the context of the biophysical model, in which many unique aspects affect the patient's presentation and progress. Thus, the case management approach must be tailored to address all of the involved components.

Improving patient outcomes based on the biopsychosocial model should be initiated with the initial patient contact. This consists of taking into consideration factors other than typical historical ingredients and classically recorded physical examination findings. Although these may be important in forming the clinical picture, there is increasing support for other factors being more directly related to outcome. Two educational templates are shown in Tables 5–3 and 5–4 that include components that have been shown to have the greatest impact in educating patients with low back pain.

Patients need to be educated on the probable cause or mechanism of their back pain, how to get better, and more importantly, their role in that process. Education should not foster doctor dependence or create helplessness in patients, but rather focus on how patients get better with emphasis on their own role. Patients should be educated to get better, not to become better patients.

Activation through activities of daily living, exercise, and work is important for the patient's physical, psychological, and long-term outcome. Activation should occur in a time-contingent manner, and be based on healing physiology. Furthermore, treatment goals should be aimed at the restoration of function rather than pain reduction, while reassuring the patient that pain with activation does not typically imply physical harm.

Ameis[30] summarizes this active care principle well by stating, "Most effective seem to be those that incorporate reassurance without creating dependency, provide perspective and insight, and maintain steady pressure on the patients to maximize the recovery by actively and aggressively responding to and managing the pain, impairments, and secondary inactivity and deconditioning."

REFERENCES

1. Vernon H. Chiropractic: A model of incorporating the illness behavior model in the management of low back pain patients. *J Manipulative Physical Ther.* 1991;14:379–389.
2. Nordin M, et al. Back schools in prevention of chronicity. *Baillieres Clin Rheumatol.* 1992;6:685–703.

3. Stankovic R, Johnell O. Conservative treatment of acute low back pain, a prospective randomized trial: McKenzie method of treatment versus patient education in Mini back school. *Spine.* 1990;15:120–123.
4. Berwick DM, Budman S, Feldstein M. No clinical effect of back schools in an HMO setting. *Spine.* 1989;14:338–343.
5. Moffett JK, et al. A controlled prospective study to evaluate the effectiveness of a back school in the relief of low back pain. *Spine.* 1986;11:120–122.
6. Brown KC, et al. Cost effectiveness of a back school intervention for municipal employees. *Spine.* 1992;17:1224–1228.
7. Lindstrom I, et al. The effect of graded activity on patients with subacute low back pain: A randomized prospective study with an operant-conditioning behavioral approach. *Phys Ther.* 1992;72:279–290.
8. Linton SJ, Kamwendo K. Low back schools: A critical review. *Practice.* 1987;67:1375–1383.
9. Waddell G. A new clinical model for the treatment of low back pain. *Spine.* 1987;12:632–644.
10. Fordyce W, et al. Pain complaint—Exercise performance relationship in chronic pain. *Pain.* 1981; 10:311–322.
11. Lethem J, et al. Outline of a fear avoidance model of exaggerated pain perception. *Behav Res Ther.* 1983;21:401–408.
12. Doleys DM, Gouchneaur KS. Behavioral Management. In: Tollison D, Kriegel M. *Interdisciplinary Rehab of Low Back Pain.* Baltimore: Williams and Wilkins, 1989:205–214.
13. Cutler P. *Problem Solving Clinical Medicine: From Data to Diagnosis.* 2nd ed. Baltimore: Williams and Wilkins, 1985:13.
14. Matheson LN. Work hardening for patients with back pain. *J Musculoskel Med.* 1993;10:53–63.
15. Bigos SJ, et al. A prospective study of work perceptions and psychosocial factors affecting the report of back injury. *Spine.* 1991;16:1–6.
16. Keefe F, Wilkins R, Cook W. Direct observation of pain behavior in low back pain patients during physical examination. *Pain.* 1984;20:59–68.
17. Pope MH, et al. The relation between biomechanical and psychological factors in patients with low back pain. *Spine.* 1980;5:173–177.
18. Waddell G, et al. Chronic low back pain, psychologic distress and illness behavior. *Spine.* 1984;9:209–213.
19. Fordyce W, et al. Acute pain: Behavioral vs. traditional treatment. *J Behav Med.* 1986;9:127–140.
20. Lindstrom I, et al. The effect of graded activity on patients with subacute low back pain: A randomized prospective clinical study with an operant-conditioning behavioral approach. *Phys Ther.* 1992;72:279–290.
21. Troup JD. Perception of musculoskeletal pain and incapacity for work: Prevention and early treatment. *Physiotherapy.* 1988;74:435–439.
22. Saal JA, Saal JS. Nonoperative treatment of herniated lumbar intervertebral disc with radiculopathy. *Spine.* 1989;14:431–437.
23. Mitchell R, Carmen GM. Results of a multicenter trial using an intensive active exercise program for the treatment of acute soft tissue and back injuries. *Spine.* 1990;15:514–521.
24. Oland G, Tveiten G. A trial of modern rehabilitation for chronic low back pain and disability. *Spine.* 1991;16:457–459.
25. Fitzier S, Berger R. Attitudinal change: The Chelsea back program. *Occup Health Saf.* 1982;Feb.:24–26.
26. Von Korff M, et al. Back pain in primary care. *Spine.* 1993;18:855–862.
27. Hansen FR, et al. Intensive, dynamic back muscle exercises, conventional physiotherapy, or placebo control of low back pain. *Spine.* 1993;18:98–108.
28. Bigos S, Battie M. Acute care to prevent back disability. *Clin Orthop.* 1987;221:121–130.
29. Fenelson G. Early mobilization of acute whiplash injuries. *BMJ.* 1986;292:656–657.
30. Ameis A. Cervical whiplash: Considerations in the rehabilitation of cervical myofascial injury. *Can Fam Physician.* 1986;32:1871–1876.
31. Berquist-Ullman M, Larsson V. Acute low back pain in industry. *Acta Orthop Scand.* 1977;(Suppl):170.
32. Troup JD. Perception of musculoskeletal pain and incapacity for work: Prevention and early treatment. *Physiotherapy.* 1988;74:435–439.
33. Mitchell R, Carmen GM. Results of a multicenter trial using an intensive active exercise program for the treatment of acute soft tissue and back injuries. *Spine.* 1990;15:514–521.
34. Jackson C, Brown M. Is there a role for exercise in the treatment of patients with low back pain? *Clin Orthop.* 1983;179:39–45.
35. Bortz WM. The disuse syndrome. *West J Med.* 1984;141:691–694.
36. Nachemsom A. Work for all. *Clin Orthop.* 1983;179:77–85.

37. Deyo RA. The role of the primary care physician in reducing work absenteeism and costs due to back pain. In: Deyo RA. *Occupational Low Back Pain*. Philadelphia: Hanley and Belfus, 1987:17–30.
38. Von Korff M, et al. Back pain in primary care. *Spine*. 1993;18:855–862.
39. Philips HC, Grant L. Acute back pain: A psychological analysis. *Behav Res Ther*. 1991;29:429–434.
40. Rolland M, Morris R. A study of the natural history of low back pain: Part II. *Spine*. 1983;8:145–150.
41. Weber H, Holme I, Amlie E. The natural course of acute sciatica with nerve root symptoms in a double blind placebo-controlled trial evaluating the effect of piroxicam. *Spine*. 1993;18:1433–1438.
42. Cherkin D, et al. Predicting poor outcome for back pain seen in primary care using patients' own criteria. *Spine*. 1996;24:2900–2907.
43. Von Korff M, et al. Back pain in primary care. *Spine*. 1993;18:855–862.
44. Fordyce W, et al. Operant conditioning in the treatment of chronic pain. *Arch Phys Med*. 1973;54:399–408.
45. Berkson M, et al. Voluntary strength in male adults with acute low back pain. *Clin Orthop*. 1977;129:84–95.
46. Faas A, et al. A randomized, placebo-controlled trial of exercise therapy in patients with acute low back pain. *Spine*. 1993;1388–1395.
47. Mellin G. A controlled study of the outcome of inpatient and outpatient treatment of low back pain: Long term effects on physical measures. *Scan J Rehab Med*. 1990;22:189–194.
48. Deyo R, Diehl A. Patient satisfaction with medical care for low back pain. *Spine*. 1986;11:28–30.
49. Hall H. Back school. In: Tollison D, Kriegel M. *Interdisciplinary Rehab of Low Back Pain*. Baltimore: Williams and Wilkins, 1989:291–304.
50. Cedraschi C, et al. The role of prior knowledge on back pain education. *J Spinal Disord*. 1992;5:267–276.
51. Witt I, et al. A comparative analysis of x-ray findings of the lumbar spine in patients without lumbar pain. *Spine*. 1984;9:298–300.
52. Delauche-Cavallier MC, et al. Lumbar disc herniation. Computed tomography scan changes after conservative treatment of nerve root compression. *Spine*. 1992;17:927–933.
53. Bozzao A, et al. Lumbar disk herniation: MR imaging assessment of natural history in patients treated without surgery. *Radiology*. 1992;185:135–141.
54. Boden SD, et al. Abnormal magnetic resonance scans of the cervical spine in asymptomatic subjects. *J Bone Joint Surg*. 1984;66a:1048–1055.
55. Boden SD, et al. Abnormal magnetic resonance scans of the lumbar spine in asymptomatic subjects. *J Bone Joint Surg*. 1990;72A:403–408.
56. Dolces JJ. Self efficacy and disability beliefs in behavioral treatment of pain. *Behav Res Ther*. 1987;25:289–299.
57. Bertakis K, Roter D, Putnam S. The relationship of the physician medical interview style to patient satisfaction. *J Fam Prac*. 1991;32:175–181.
58. Greenfield S, Kaplan S, Ware J. Expanding patient involvement in care. *Ann Intern Med*. 1985;102:520–528.
59. Brody D, et al. Patient perceptions of involvement in medical care. *J Gen Intern Med*. 1989;4:506–511.
60. Lutz RW, et al. Treatment outcome and compliance with therapeutic regimes. *Pain*. 1983;17:301–308.

CHAPTER 6

Emergency Principles and Applications for the Outpatient Rehabilitation Facility

Michael Reed, DC, DACBSP, CSCS & Jon D. Fagerness, DC, NREMT

INTRODUCTION

Emergencies are rare in health, fitness, and rehabilitation facilities, but they do occur. Physical activity alone increases the chances of musculoskeletal injury and life-threatening cardiovascular illnesses.[1] Studies on exercise report an acute event rate of 1 per 187,500 person-hours of exercise by apparently healthy adults.[2] One of the primary concerns of the health care professional should be in providing a safe environment for both the staff and the patients. To accomplish this, legal and ethical issues must be addressed, body substance isolation practices must be in place, an effective emergency action plan must be developed and practiced, and emergency care skills must be reviewed. This chapter is specifically focused to address each of these items, limited to the events that could take place within the confines of an outpatient rehabilitation facility. Clinical applications are provided to assist the health care professional in implementation and review of the primary emergency care skills presented in this chapter. The majority of the presented information is based on national standards; local protocols may vary slightly. This text in no way is designed to replace formal training and certification. Always adhere to the local protocols set forth by your medical director.

LEGAL AND ETHICAL ISSUES

OVERVIEW

The primary legal and ethical issues involve the actual events of an injury or illness and protection from possible liability. Proper risk assessment of the facility and attending patients will serve as the basis for the prevention of dangerous events, whereas documentation will provide protection for the facility and staff in the event an injury or illness actually occurs.

RISK MANAGEMENT

The emphasis of risk management involves the prevention of injuries or illnesses that a patient could sustain while under care and within a facility. The remainder of risk management covers how one responds to unpreventable injuries or illnesses.

The avoidance of risk takes two paths. First is the proper screening of patients, and the second is proper care and maintenance of your facility. There is always the threat of different medical emergencies including, for example, myocardial infarction, angina, shock, cardiac arrest, diabetic attacks, and seizures. To decrease the risk of medical emergencies, the patient should be screened according to the guidelines set forth by the American College of Sports Medicine (ACSM).[3] The potential for various types of traumatic injuries does exist and may depend, for example, on the type of equipment being utilized and the condition in which it is maintained. It is necessary to instruct patients in the proper use of the equipment they will use and to monitor the patients to ensure that equipment and exercise protocols are used properly. Furthermore, it is important to have a preventive maintenance schedule for exercise apparatus to remove the likelihood for injuries due to unexpected failure. Failures of equipment can cause crushing injuries, or the patient being struck with the equipment. If your equipment is well maintained, traumatic injuries should be infrequent. There is also the possibility of accidents such as trips and falls and your facility should be screened carefully for potential risks. Finally, you should always be aware of the possibility of environmental emergencies, such as earthquakes, storms, floods, etc., and have a plan to deal with their effects so as to protect both staff and clients.

DOCUMENTATION

Documentation should be the same for emergencies and training as it is for routine patient care. This makes the staff accustomed to completing paperwork in an appropriate fashion. Remember if a patient is injured, you must receive informed consent before you can render appropriate care. If the patient refuses care, this needs to be documented and the documentation signed by the patient.

Two of the most important pieces of documentation that need to be in the patient's chart are an **Assumption of Risk** form and an **Informed Consent for Participation in an Exercise Program** form.[4]

All documentation should include the following information: date of the incident, patient's name, address, and phone number, the location of the accident, and an evaluation of the situation. What happened to the patient? For example, was there a specific traumatic injury or is it a medical emergency? If there is a traumatic injury, determine what happened. If it is a medical emergency, determine the factors leading to the emergency. Was the patient exercising? If so, how intense was the level of exercise? Has the patient had this type of problem before? Be sure to document the specific time of the injury, the amount of time the patient was down, and when the emergency medical services (EMS) system was activated. Document the action that was taken.

Document the name of the team leader, all communication, the scribe, other staff present, and what job duties they performed. Additionally, make a note of all nonstaff who were present. It is very important to establish a baseline by continuing to monitor the vitals and by keeping track of the vital signs at appropriate time intervals. There need to be two copies of this information so that one copy may be given to the EMS personnel and one copy retained for facility records.

Indicate the arrival time of EMS personnel, the time the patient was turned over to the ambulance, and the hospital they were taken to. If the patient does not leave your facility by ambulance, indicate how he or she left. For example, did the patient leave under his or her own power, or was the patient turned over to the care of a family member or friend. Indicate if the patient was transported to a hospital, or to an urgent care center. Additional documentation should include the restocking of medical supply kits and bloodborne pathogens kits and periodic inspections for time-dated materials. It should be noted if the incident involved blood, and if the U.S. Occupational Health and Safety Administration (OSHA) and the U.S. Centers for Disease Control (CDC) guidelines were met. Following the departure of the patient or the end of the training session, there should be discussion and evaluation of the incident.

THE EMERGENCY ACTION PLAN

Your facility must have an **emergency action plan**[5] (Figure 6–1). The plan must be written with specific goals in mind and be workable. The following issues must be addressed in your emergency action plan:

- How the staff and patients will be able to exit from the facility in the event of an emergency must be decided.
- Designate who will secure, use, and replace emergency supplies and how the facility will interact with community resources, 911, fire rescue, ambulance company, hospital, or urgent care center.
- The specific duties and positions of the staff must be addressed. Determine who will treat the patient, who will assist treatment, who will deal with communications, and who will be the scribe so there is complete documentation (Table 6–1).

Once the goals are established and the plan is written, it is necessary to make sure it is functional. The facility staff must periodically practice the emergency plan. Routine practice will ensure that the staff is adequately prepared. The plan should be periodically reevaluated and revised as needed. Drills should be performed two times per year and all staff should be present. The drills should address numerous typical health/rehabilitation facility scenarios to cover a broad range of potential emergencies that may occur.

The staffing of facilities will vary greatly depending on the size and type of facility. You can expect to have various types of doctors (DC, MD, DO, PhD), physical therapists (RPT), physical therapy assistants (PTA), athletic trainers (ATC), rehabilitation nurses, physicians assistants (PA-C), certified strength and conditioning specialists (CSCS), exercise physiologists, and noncertified personnel. All members of the staff should be certified in cardiopulmonary resuscitation (CPR), and it should be at the health care provider level. In this chapter, CPR is defined by the American Heart Association (AHA) standards.[6] It is very disheartening to teach a recertification class to various types of health care providers, including physicians, nurses, and EMTs, who cannot demonstrate proficiency in CPR performance. With this in mind, fol-

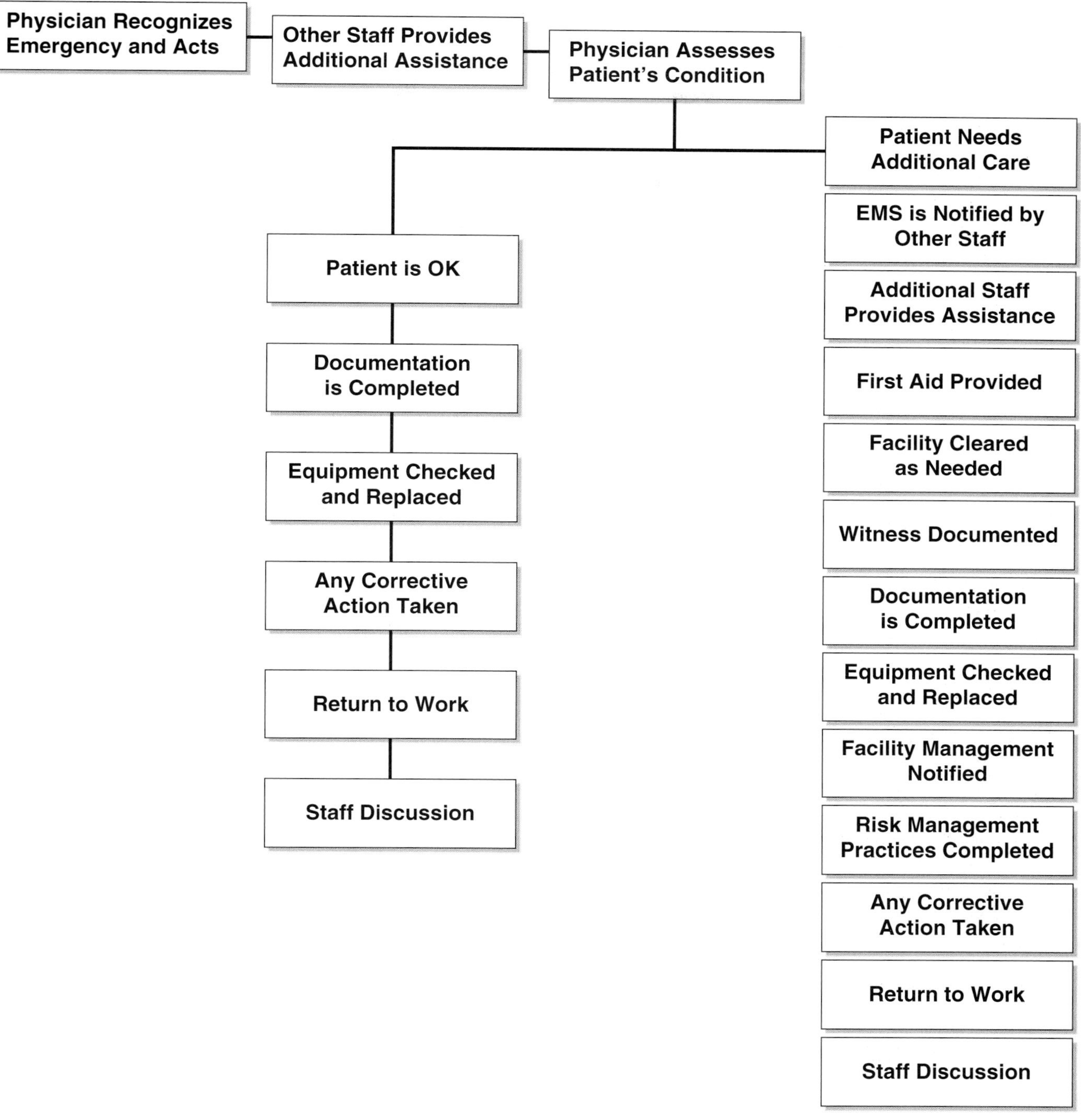

Figure 6–1. Example emergency action plan flow chart.

lowing the USDOT's recommendations for annual recertification in CPR is extremely important. Additionally, it is highly recommended that members of the staff be trained in first aid.

In some facilities, it may be necessary for members of the staff to perform multiple jobs. It is imperative that the staff realizes that one person must be in charge when an emergency arises. This must be established before an incident occurs so that everyone works together efficiently. Too many people giving orders and talking to the patient will cause confusion in an already difficult situation. It is also important to realize that if blood or body fluids are involved, treatment will require a minimum of two people. To avoid cross-contamination of the medical kit, one person treats the patient while someone else removes the necessary equipment or supplies from the kit.

Table 6–1: The Emergency Action Plan

- Provision for emergency exit or evacuation from the facility
- Provision for securing and using supplies
- Provision for interaction with predetermined community resources
- Provision for specific duties and positions of staff
- Provision for exposure to biohazardous materials
- Provision for staff communication
- Provision for documentation

BODY SUBSTANCE ISOLATION PRACTICES

INCIDENTS INVOLVING EXPOSURE TO BODY SUBSTANCES

In response to the threats facing health care workers, OSHA announced it's Final Rule on Protecting Health Care Workers from Occupational Exposure to Blood Borne Pathogens (Title 29 CFR 1910.1030) in March 1992. The rule requires employers to provide employees with "appropriate" protective clothing when the threat of bloodborne pathogen exposure exists so as to minimize the exposure to possible biohazardous materials (Table 6–2). The OSHA standard points out that protective clothing, including gloves, gowns, laboratory coats, face shields, masks, and other items should offer protection consistent with the circumstances selected for potential exposure. Well-stocked first aid kits should have items consistent with the types of illnesses and injuries one can expect in the specific environment, as well as some unexpected incidents (Table 6–3). When purchasing examination gloves, be sure they meet National Fire Protection Association (NFPA) 1999 requirements and that they are registered with the Food and Drug Administration (FDA) as Class I medical devices. This will assure you are buying a glove offering the highest level of protection, and one that has been thoroughly tested by independent groups capable of verifying manufacturer compliance and marketing claims.[7]

Table 6–2: Minimization of Exposure to Biohazardous Materials

- Establish criteria for the initiation of care
- Take care of the situation in a timely, organized fashion
- Prevent the exposure with a written plan, proper training, and work practice controls
- Provide protection through proper equipment for hands, clothing, mouth, nose, and eyes
- Contain any biohazardous waste
- Minimize damage to the patient
- Minimize exposure to nonstaff personnel

Table 6–3: Recommended Medical Supply List

• Latex gloves	• Bag valve mask
• Scissors/trauma shears	• Wound cleanser
• Bandages	• Antibacterial cream
• Sterile gauze pads (4 × 4)	• Portable suction unit
• Abdominal pads	• Alcohol swabs
• Mass trauma dressing	• Betadine swabs
• Adhesive tape	• BP cuff
• Ziploc bags	• Stethoscope
• Splints in a variety of types and sizes	• Kling (gauze wrap)
	• Normal saline/sterile water
• Pocket mask with oxygen inlet	• Note pad and pen
	• Eye and face protection
• Household bleach or bacterial/virucidal agent	• Liquidproof gowns
• Biohazard disposal bags with labels	

Anyone who, in the course of their daily activity or occupation, may be potentially exposed to blood and/or other body fluids should be protected from exposure and possible infection from bloodborne pathogens such as hepatitis B, tuberculosis, and HIV. The best way to decide if you or your employees are at risk is to answer this question: "Are you expected to give first aid, or are you expected to handle bleeding individuals or material contaminated with blood or body fluids as part of your job?" It is important to identify the type and degree of anticipated exposure incidents likely to be encountered by you and your staff.

EXPOSURE CONTROL PLAN

The development of body substance isolation precautions and exposure control plans is a step the health care provider must take in order to ensure personal protection from airborne droplet infection, blood to blood contact, and body fluid contact with mucous membranes or open wounds. The following is an example of steps that should be taken to establish an exposure control plan:

1. Identify the type and degree of anticipated exposure incidents likely to be encountered by you and your staff.
2. Latex gloves must be worn when touching open skin, blood, body fluids, or mucous membranes or performing venapuncture.
3. Wash hands with soap and warm water immediately after exposure to blood or body fluids, even if gloves were used. If there has been contact with blood or other infectious materials, hands should be washed before eating, drinking, smoking, applying cosmetics, and touching contact lenses and after using the lavatory facilities.

4. Clean any surface that has had contact with blood with an EPA-approved germicide.
5. Dispose of sharp objects, scalpels, hypodermic needles, suture needles, etc., in an approved sharps receptacle.
6. Dispose of any infectious or body fluid waste in approved biohazardous waste bags. Biohazardous waste must be disposed of through an approved agency.
7. Make sure that anyone treating patients has any wounds covered prior to treatment and all dressings have no fluid seepage.
8. If you or a staff member has an open wound, especially on the hands, avoid providing first aid for injuries involving blood and body fluids until the wound is healed.
9. Wear gloves when cleaning up body fluids after first aid has been provided.
10. Do not contaminate the first aid kit with bloody gloves; have someone hand the first aid provider everything from the kit.
11. Refill the biohazardous waste kit after use.
12. Uniforms and clothing contaminated with blood should be removed and put into a red biohazard bag until washed with detergent at 71°C or greater for 25 minutes.
13. Pocket masks or resuscitation bags must be available for emergency mouth-to-mouth resuscitation.
14. All personal protective equipment must be removed before leaving the area of exposure and if overtly contaminated, placed in an appropriate area for storage, washing, or disposal.
15. In work areas where there is a reasonable likelihood of exposure to blood or other potentially infectious materials, no one is to eat, drink, apply cosmetics or lip balm, smoke, or handle contact lenses.
16. Equipment that has become contaminated with blood or other potentially infectious materials shall be decontaminated prior to reuse. Examples of such equipment include blankets, stethoscopes and blood pressure cuffs, tape scissors, tweezers, treatment tables, and rehabilitation equipment.

IN THE EVENT OF A SPILL

Materials and equipment that have been exposed to biohazards should be washed and disinfected according to USDOT and OSHA (Title 29 CFR 1910.1030) guidelines. The following is a suggested plan of action in the event of a biohazardous spill:

1. Wear gloves *first*.
2. Use a paper towel or commercial blood absorbent to absorb the spill. Always wipe toward the center of the spill.
3. Wipe the spill site with a generous amount of bleach solution or other bacterial/virucidal agent. Disinfect beyond the apparent limits of contamination.
4. If the 1 part bleach to 10 parts water solution is used, allow it to stay in contact with the contaminated area for 20 minutes. If another bacterial/virucidal agent is used, follow manufacturer's instructions for cleaning spills.
5. Wipe the site with clean, dry paper towels or gauze pads.
6. Place all contaminated items in a biohazard bag.
7. Dispose of the bag according to local laws (contact your state's DOT for more information).

EMERGENCY CARE SKILLS

PATIENT ASSESSMENT—PART I

Overview

The elements of patient assessment are comprised of five vital components: scene size-up, initial assessment, physical examination, ongoing assessment, and patient hand-off (Figure 6–2). Performance of the scene size-up and the initial assessment will enable the caregiver to form a general impression of the patient, to assess the patient's mental status, to identify and treat any life-threatening conditions the patient may have regarding airway, breathing, and/or circulation problems, and to prioritize the patient.

Patients suffering injury or illness can be placed into one of the four following categories: trauma/responsive, trauma/unresponsive, medical/responsive, and medical/unresponsive. Trauma patients are the result of blunt forces that do physical bodily harm. All other patients can be categorized as medical. This categorization is important because

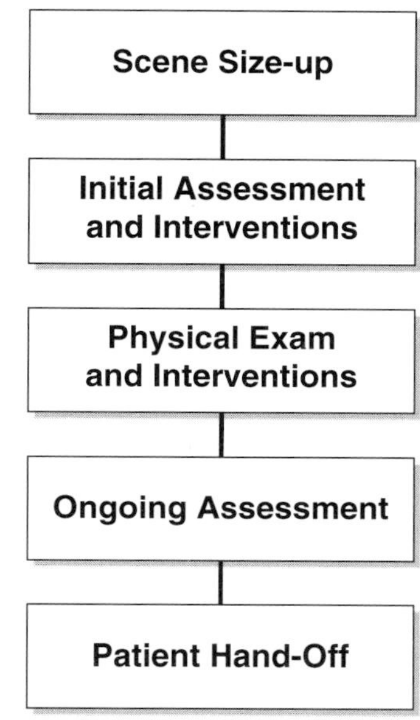

Figure 6–2. Patient assessment flow chart.

it will determine the assessment that is provided for the patient. Regardless of the patient's chief complaint or mental status, the scene size-up and the initial assessment will remain relatively the same.

Scene Size-Up

Setting the foundation for the rest of the patient assessment process, the scene size-up's importance cannot be underestimated. Information regarding scene safety, the mechanism of the injury, the nature of the illness, the number of patients involved, the additional resources needed to manage the incident, and the form of immediate interventions are all vital components that will determine the care rendered to the patient. **H5I** is an acronym that can be used to assist the caregiver in remembering the elements of the scene size-up (Table 6–4). Each element is summarized below.

Hands and eyes covered. Body substance isolation precautions should be taken prior to engaging in a situation that could potentially result in contact with biohazardous materials.

Hazards. Scene safety is an important issue that will protect the caregiver from potential harm and attempt to minimize or contain further injuries to the patient. Hazards such as broken equipment should be assessed for their ability to cause further harm prior to initiating patient care. Accommodations should be made for personal safety, patient safety, and bystander safety.

How or what happened. Determining the mechanism of injury or the nature of the illness will assist in deciding the interventions and procedures that the caregiver will utilize during the initial assessment and detailed or focused assessment.

How many people involved. The number of people that require care in the event of an incident will proportionally require additional help. The utilization of additional resources may be necessary.

How much additional help. The type of hazards present at the scene, the type of injury or illness that exists, and the number of people involved will determine the additional help and resources needed. You may chose to activate the emergency medical services (EMS) at this point based on the severity of the situation.

Immediate interventions. Finally, are there any immediate interventions to be made such as stabilizing or removing objects that may have caused the patient harm? Is it necessary to perform an emergency move of the patient because of falling objects or an unsafe scene? Does the scene need to be cleared to allow adequate access to the patient?

Table 6–4: The Elements of the Scene Size-Up (H5I)

- Hands and eyes covered
- Hazards
- How or what happened
- How many people involved
- How much help
- Immediate interventions

Initial Assessment

Emergency patient care always begins with the initial assessment. The purpose is to identify and treat immediately life-threatening conditions and to prioritize additional assessment and treatment of potentially life-threatening conditions. One of the first things that must be done in the care of an individual with an emergency is to assess if there is a life-threatening condition.[8] The mnemonic **SSHHARPPSSS-NCD** will serve to prompt the caregiver to assess the following points of interest (Table 6–5):

Safety, supplies, scan, and statement. Scene safety is a constant concern and should be a top priority even after entering the scene. The necessary supplies needed should be within reach, such as oxygen equipment and first aid supplies. A general impression should be formulated regarding the patient's condition in the form of a mental statement.

Stabilize. If there is sufficient evidence to support the possibility of a head or spine injury, stabilization of the cervical spine should be performed and maintained throughout the care process. Remember, if you are not sure, stabilize anyway.

Hey! Are you OK? A key indicator regarding the severity of the patient's condition is the patient's mental status, which is graded on a four-part scale

Table 6–5: The Elements of the Initial Assessment (SSHHARPPSSS-NCD)

- Safety, supplies, scan, statement
- Stabilize
- Hey! Are you OK?—AVPU (Alert, Verbal, Pain, Unresponsive)
- Helpers delegated
- Airway—opened and maintained
- Respirations—assessed, corrected, and maintained
- Pulse—carotid
- Pulse—radial
- Skin assessment
- Severe bleeding sweep
- Shock management
- Neck
- Chest
- Decision

following the mnemonic **AVPU.** The stimulus used and the patient's response to that stimulus should be noted in the documentation.

- A: Alert. The patient is awake and answers all questions appropriately.
- V: Verbal. The patient is responsive only when spoken to.
- P: Pain. The patient is responsive only when a painful stimulus is applied such as a sternal rub or pinching of the upper trapezius.
- U: Unresponsive. The patient fails to respond to any and all stimuli.

Helpers delegated. Other team members need to be instructed as to what to do. If the patient has an altered mental status or is unresponsive, you should activate the EMS at this point.

Airway. The airway should be opened utilizing either the head-tilt chin-lift method, the modified jaw thrust method, or a combination of the two methods known as the triple airway maneuver. In an unresponsive patient, it is appropriate to select either an oropharyngeal or a nasopharyngeal airway adjunct so as to maintain an open airway and to allow the rescuer to free his or her hands to continue the rest of the patient assessment process. Remember, if there is the possibility of a head or spine injury, the only appropriate method for opening an airway is the modified jaw thrust method.

Respirations. Breathing needs to be assessed with regard to adequate chest rise and estimated rate of respiration (too fast, too slow, or within normal limits). Additionally, if the respirations are not adequate, interventions need to be made to correct and maintain adequate cardiopulmonary perfusion through the use of artificial ventilation and oxygen.

Pulse (carotid and radial). The carotid pulse is palpated, assessed regarding an estimated rate (too fast, too slow, or within normal limits), and compared to the radial pulse in quality. If the carotid pulse is absent, initiate CPR. Remember, absence of a radial pulse when the carotid pulse is present indicates a systolic blood pressure of less than 90 mmHg. This is a basic sign of advanced hypoperfusion and warrants immediate intervention.

Skin condition. Observe the patient's skin condition including color, temperature, moisture, and capillary refill.

Severe bleeding sweep. Perform a quick check for severe bleeding, especially bleeding that may be hidden underneath the patient or residing within the patient's clothing.

Shock management. Interventions include patient position (flat or Trendelenburg's position with feet higher than the heart), patient warmth (multiple layers underneath as well as covering the patient), airway maintenance (use of airway adjuncts as needed), and the use of supplemental oxygen according to indications. Because of the importance of the cardiopulmonary structures, assessment of the regions that these structures lie within is extremely important.

Neck. The neck contains the superior portion of the cardiopulmonary structures and should be exposed and assessed for tracheal deviation, distended jugular veins, the use of accessory muscles for breathing (retractive breathing), **DOTS** (**D**eformity, **O**pen injuries, **T**enderness, and **S**welling), and medical alert tags.

Chest. Contained within the walls of the chest lies most of the cardiopulmonary system. The chest should be exposed and the following items assessed: breath sounds auscultated for presence and quality in at least four quadrants, the point of maximal impulse (PMI) auscultated, and paradoxical breathing, retractive breathing and **DOTS** assessed.

Decision. Finally, the patient needs to be prioritized with regard to the information obtained during the initial assessment. A **high-priority** patient is one with some alteration either in mental status or ABCs or one in a marked amount of distress. The **low-priority** patient is one with normal mental status and ABCs and one in moderate to low distress.

Remember that a change in the patient's level of responsiveness at any given point demands that the assessment process be started over from the beginning. Assessing and evaluating the respiratory and cardiovascular systems are vital during the initial evaluation of any patient in respiratory distress.[9]

AIRWAY AND BREATHING MANAGEMENT

Overview

The first priority when providing emergency intervention is to establish and maintain a **patent airway.** Airway management is the most basic of all medical skills. Managing the airway and the proper delivery of supplemental oxygen are crucial to patient survival. Without mastery of proper airway management, treatment on behalf of the patient can be ineffective. Without oxygen to meet the metabolic needs of the cells, other lifesaving techniques are futile. The airway may be compromised without dramatic outward sign; therefore, it must be dealt with in a quick and efficient manner. Airway management can take many different forms depending upon the patient's level of consciousness and injuries, training of the care provider, and equipment available. The management skills used will depend on the situation and the skills of the care provider. The provider must know the techniques, indications, and most importantly, the contraindications of airway management.

Airway Management

When approaching a potentially unresponsive patient, perform a scene size-up. Note anything that may cause you harm or may cause the patient further harm. Determine the patient's level of responsiveness by tapping and gently shaking the person while shouting, "Hey, are you OK?" If this does not elicit a response, provide a painful stimulus such as a sternal rub, pressure on the nailbeds, or pinching of the trapezius muscle. Avoid the use of ammonia inhalants if there is the possibility of head or spinal trauma. You do not want the patient to react suddenly by withdrawing the head, causing further trauma to the spine. If the patient does not respond, activate your facility's emergency action plan. Before proceeding any further, make sure to take appropriate body substance isolation precautions. Assess the patient's breathing by looking for chest rise, listening for breath sounds, and feeling for the movement of air for about 5 seconds. If you are unable to determine whether or not the patient is breathing, place the patient on his or her back while supporting the head and neck and open the airway. This can be achieved by performing the head-tilt chin-lift method, the modified jaw thrust method, or the triple airway method.

The **head-tilt chin-lift method is** used for an uninjured, unresponsive patient. It is essential to rule out a mechanism of injury that suggests trauma or injury to the head or spine. To perform the maneuver, place one hand on the forehead, applying firm pressure to tilt the head backward. Complete the maneuver by placing two fingers of the other hand under the jaw, lifting the chin upward (Figure 6–3).

The **modified jaw thrust technique** for opening an airway is used for suspected head or spinal trauma, and is considered the safest approach to opening the airway when a cervical spine injury is suspected. It is performed in the same manner as the triple airway maneuver with the exception of cervical extension. To perform this maneuver, place your hands on either side of the patient's head with your thumbs resting on the cheek bones. Using your fingers, take hold of the posterior portion of the angles of the lower jaw. Press down with your thumbs and up with your fingers to slide the lower jaw open and forward (Figure 6–4).

The last recommended method of opening an airway is called the **triple airway maneuver.** This combines the backward tilt of the head with anterior displacement of the mandible while opening the mouth. Patients with a suspected injury to the head or spine should not have this procedure performed on them. To perform this maneuver, tilt the head back into extension. The fingers of both hands are used to grasp the ascending rami of the mandible so as to displace them anteriorly. This maneuver is very useful when a pocket mask is used for resuscitation. The mask is held firmly in place with the thumbs to form a good seal (Figure 6–5).

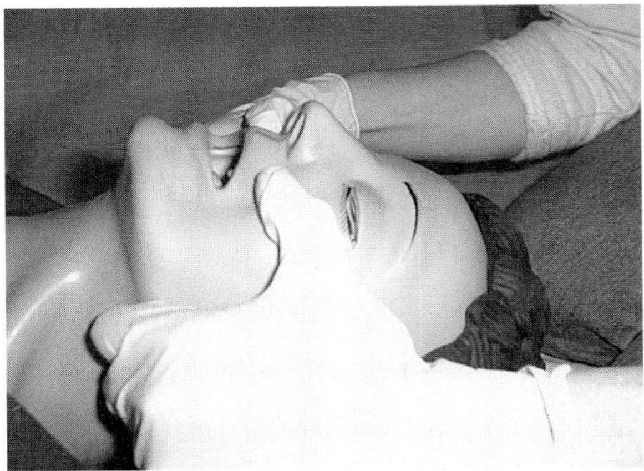

Figure 6–4. The modified jaw thrust technique for opening the airway.

Keeping an airway open using just your hands can be tiresome and limit the amount of emergency interventions that can be provided in a basic first-response situation. Therefore, mechanical airway devices are utilized to aid in maintaining the airway of an unresponsive patient.

Mechanical adjuncts to airway management

The most commonly used artificial airway is the **oral pharyngeal airway (OPA).**[10] The oral pharyngeal airway aids in ventilation by maintaining the airway of an unrespon-

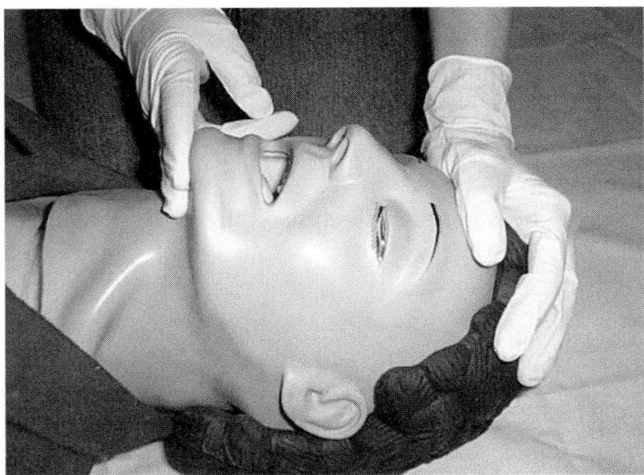

Figure 6–3. Head-tilt chin-lift method for opening the airway.

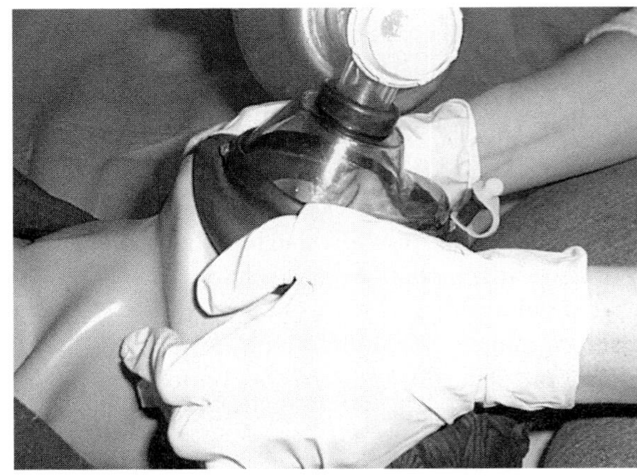

Figure 6–5. The triple airway maneuver for opening the airway (shown with the use of a pocket mask).

sive patient with no gag reflex. The OPA works by holding the tongue away from the back of the throat and the epiglottis and tracheal opening. The following is a description of its use (Figure 6–6).

To select the proper size OPA, measure from the corner of the patient's mouth to the tip of the ear lobe or angle of the mandible. Open the patient's mouth utilizing the crossfinger technique. Insert the OPA with the convex side toward the roof of the mouth (or upside down). As the tip reaches the back of the pharynx, rotate the OPA 180 degrees. Stop insertion when the flange rests on the lips or teeth. Reassess the patient to ensure the airway is open. Remove the OPA if the patient gags during insertion, or if the gag reflex returns later on, by pulling it directly out of the mouth.

The **nasopharyngeal airway (NPA)** is a soft rubber (latex) device that is inserted through one of the nares and then along the curvature of the posterior wall of the na-

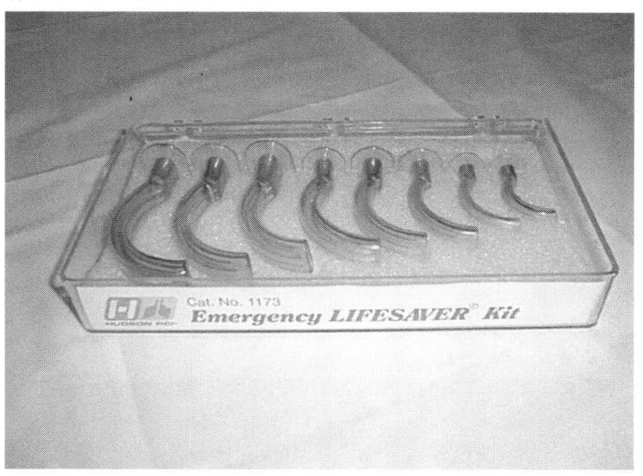

A

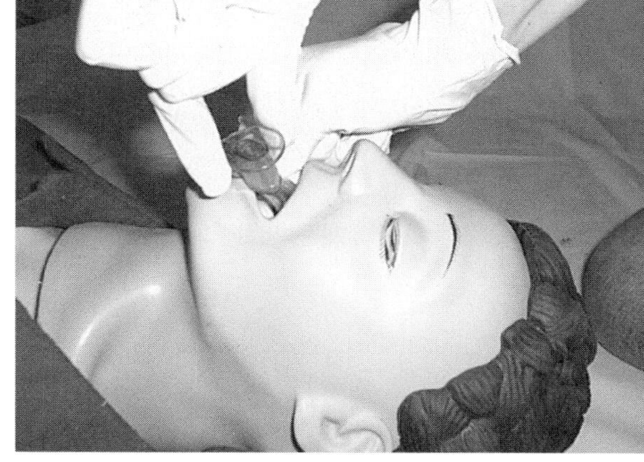

D

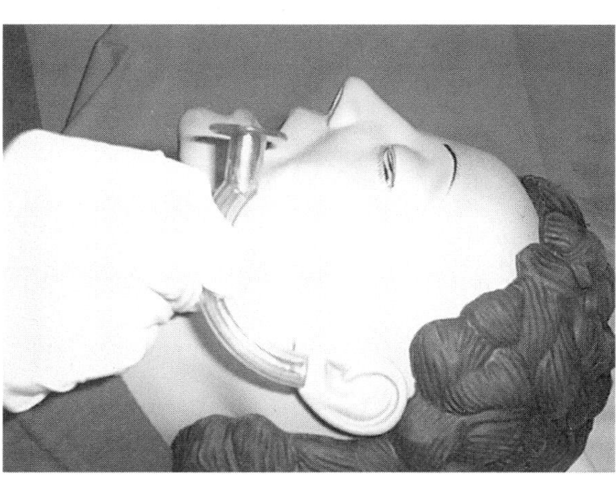

B

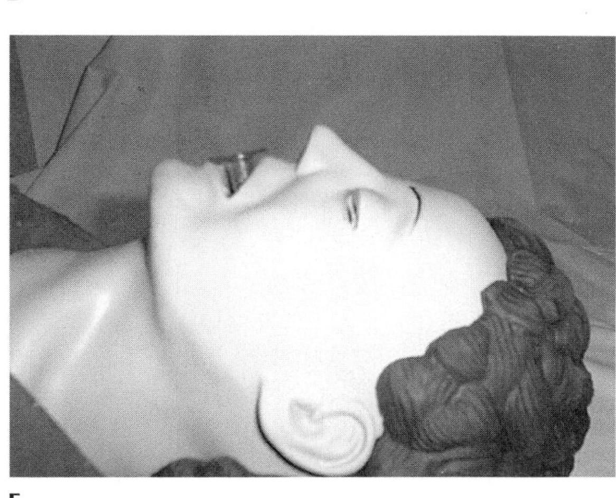

E

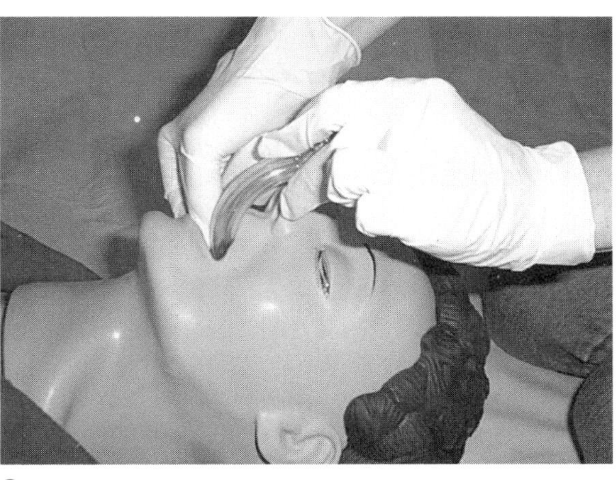

C

Figure 6–6. Oral pharyngeal airway utilization. **A.** Oral pharyngeal airways. **B.** Measure the OPA for correct size. **C.** Insert the airway with the convex portion toward the roof of the mouth. **D.** Rotate the OPA 180 degrees as the tip enters the back of the throat. **E.** A correctly placed OPA should rest with the flange on the patient's lips.

sopharynx and oropharynx.[11] The purpose of the nasopharyngeal airway is to open and maintain the airway. Patients with a present gag reflex will not tolerate an oral airway, but often have no problem with the nasal airway. The nasopharyngeal airway is an excellent device for use with a seizing patient or one with a gag reflex, or in a case in which a gag reflex would cause more damage, such as increasing intracranial pressure due to a head injury. It can be utilized on a semi-conscious patient. Contraindications to use of the nasopharyngeal airway are patients with severe maxillofacial trauma or the possibility of injury to the cribriform plate. The following is a description of its use (Figure 6–7).

The NPA is measured from the tip of the patient's nose to the tragus or tip of the earlobe. The diameter of the NPA should be small enough to fit inside the nostril (about the same size as the diameter of the patient's little finger). Lubricate the outside of the airway with K-Y jelly to allow it to slide easily. Insert in either nostril along the floor of

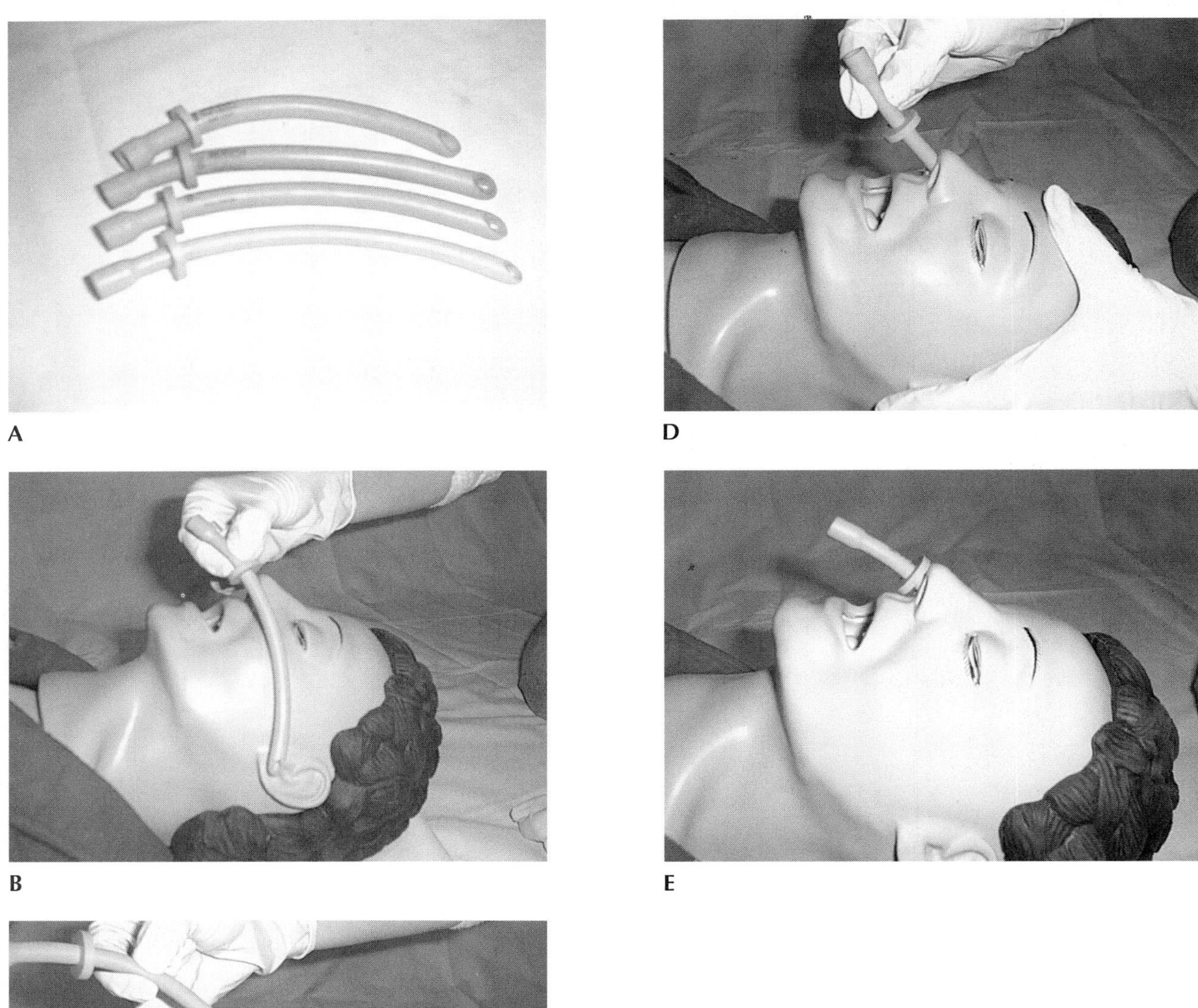

Figure 6–7. Nasopharyngeal airway utilization. **A.** Nasopharyngeal airways. **B.** Measure for the proper size and lubricate the airway. **C.** Insert the NPA with the bevel facing upward. **D.** Rotate the bevel toward the nasal septum as the NPA reaches the back of the throat. **E.** A correctly placed NPA should rest with the flange on the patient's nose.

the nasal cavity, parallel to the hard palate, with the bevel facing upward. If excessive resistance is encountered, you should stop and attempt insertion in the opposite nostril. When the NPA hits the nasopharynx, turn the bevel so that it faces the nasal septum and advance it further into the pharynx; it may help to lift the jaw to allow the airway to pass behind the tongue. If the nasal airway is too long, it may enter the esophagus, thus directing any ventilation efforts into the stomach. If it is too short, the patient's tongue will occlude the tip of the airway, preventing airway patency.

Breathing Management

Once you have opened the airway, you need to assess breathing. **Look** for the chest to rise and fall. **Listen** for breathing. **Feel** for breath passing in and out of the nose and mouth on the side of your face. Quickly assess the respirations for estimated rate, rhythm, depth, and effort. Are they rapid, slow, or about right? Are they regular or irregular in rhythm? Are they full or shallow in depth? Patients who are breathing less than 10 breaths per minute or who are breathing shallowly and at a rate greater than 24 breaths per minute are not adequately breathing and require positive pressure ventilation with 100% oxygen. Remember, irregular rhythms are dangerous and should be watched carefully. A patient who is breathing full and regularly and within the limits of normal may still be in respiratory distress as indicated by the level of effort needed for the patient to breathe (such as a cyanotic patient or one utilizing accessory muscles to breathe). If the patient is breathing adequately, maintain an open airway and continue the initial assessment.

If ventilation is unsuccessful, readjust the airway and reattempt ventilation. If you are still unsuccessful, assume the airway is blocked and then position yourself for manual abdominal thrusts. Straddle the victim's thighs, place the heel of one hand slightly above the umbilicus and well below the xiphoid process. Place the second hand on top of the first. Deliver five quick thrusts from anterior to posterior and inferior to superior. These are followed by a finger sweep of the mouth (this is only performed on an unresponsive, adult patient). Again, attempt ventilation of the patient. If ventilation is unsuccessful, readjust the airway and reattempt ventilation. Continued unsuccessful attempts at ventilation will require repetition of the above sequence until ventilation is successful or more advanced help arrives.

Upon successful ventilation, deliver two slow breaths and then check the carotid pulse for 5 to 10 seconds. If the pulse is present, perform rescue breathing by providing one breath every 5 seconds. Reassess the patient after the first minute and every few minutes thereafter.

There are several techniques of ventilation. The recommended technique is mouth-to-mask ventilation.[12,13] Pocket mouth-to-mouth resuscitation masks, designed to isolate emergency response personnel from contact with the victim's blood and blood-saliva, respiratory secretions, and vomitus, should be provided to all personnel who provide or will potentially provide emergency treatment.

Mouth-to-mask breathing, as performed with a **simple pocket mask,** is the common method of choice for providing artificial ventilation to the unresponsive, nonbreathing patient. There are many pocket masks in today's market. It is important to select a pocket mask that can be enriched with oxygen. A pocket mask with no supplemental oxygen delivers about 16% oxygen, whereas a pocket mask with a supplemental oxygen source at 15 liters per minute delivers approximately 50% oxygen.[14] After opening the airway and checking for breathing, position the mask so as to make a seal using the nose as a guide to place the mask. Begin ventilations with two slow breaths through the one-way valve. Remember, the addition of supplemental oxygen to the mask only enhances your ventilation of the patient. You must keep breathing for the patient.

The **bag valve mask** (BVM) is the most common forced-air technique used for ventilation of the nonbreathing or shallow-breathing patient (Figure 6–8). The BVM is self-inflating and can be enriched with oxygen to 100%. This device eliminates the need for mouth-to-mouth ventilation. It is designed to deliver 1200 to 1500 cubic centimeters of air, but only delivers approximately an average of 500 cubic centimeters of air if used by one person. It has been shown that mouth-to-mask ventilation with oxygen enhancement is often more effective than one-rescuer BVM ventilation because the provider needs to maintain the airway, form a good seal with the mask, and deliver the oxygen. It has been demonstrated that BVM ventilation requires extensive experience and special training. BVM ventilation should be performed by two rescuers: one person managing the airway and mask seal and the other compressing the bag, delivering oxygen.[15]

Essentially, whenever a patient is unable to clear secretions blocking the airway, **suctioning** is needed.[16] Suction is available in portable battery-operated and manual pump devices. The purpose of a suction device is to remove fluid from the patient's mouth and upper airway. Proper utilization should, if possible, involve preoxygenation of the patient for 3 to 5 minutes. Open the patient's mouth using the cross-finger technique, and then sweep out any foreign material. Be aware that suctioning may interfere with the patient's oxygen supply; you should apply oxygen to the pa-

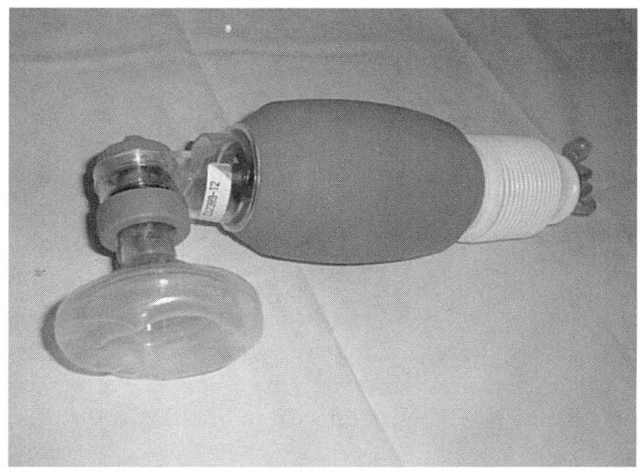

Figure 6–8. The bag valve mask.

Clinical Application 6–1

You are called to respond to an incident involving a middle-aged male patient. You find a co-worker rescue breathing for an unresponsive patient of unknown problem using the **mouth-to-mouth technique.**

(A) With regard to the previous scenario, place the following actions in order of importance:

- Assisting with immediate interventions
- Providing BSI precautions for your co-worker and yourself if needed
- Assuring EMS is enroute
- Determining what happened

(B) Upon completion of the scene size-up, you are told the patient is suffering from chronic lung disease and became unresponsive during an acute onset of difficult breathing. Of the following items, what should your next step be?

- Start CPR
- Begin an initial assessment
- Take a set of vital signs
- Do not do anything until EMS personnel arrive

Clinical Application 6–1 Answers

(A)
Keep in mind the chronological order of the scene size-up (Table 6–4)

1. Provide BSI precautions (hands and eyes covered)
2. Determine what happened
3. Assure EMS is en route
4. Assist with immediate interventions

(B)
After completing a scene size-up, begin an initial assessment. Verify that what the first care-giver found is what you find also.

tient immediately after suctioning. To avoid insertion of the device too far into the pharynx, measure the tip of the suction catheter from the corner of the mouth to the ear lobe. Place your fingers on the catheter to mark the distance so as to assure insertion only to the proper depth. Suction only as you are removing the catheter, making certain not to suction for longer than 15 seconds at a time. Then reoxygenate the patient. Remember, if the patient vomits, clear the airway manually first by removing the large chunks of debris with a gloved finger. Utilize suctioning to clear the remainder of the vomitus.

FYI—OXYGEN THERAPY

Overview

It is important to remember that oxygen is a medication and one must be sure to use it carefully. Use oxygen only if you are trained and equipped to do so. The purpose of oxygen is to treat hypoxia, which may arise from a variety of causes. These causes include but are not limited to airway obstruction, unconsciousness, seizures, cardiac arrest, respiratory arrest, shock, hypotension defined as a systolic BP less than 90 mmHg, suspected cerebral vascular accident, and trauma (Table 6–6). Administration of oxygen may prevent death or may even prevent the patient's condition from worsening. It is important to identify patients who need oxygen. The following patients require the use of high-flow oxygen (defined as a nonrebreather oxygen mask supplied with 15 liters per minute of supplemental oxygen): all patients breathing inadequately (as defined previously), all patients classified as high-priority patients (as defined previously), all patients suffering from but not limited to shortness of breath, chest pain, altered mental status, and shock (Table 6–7). Patients suffering from chronic lung diseases such as emphysema, chronic bronchitis, and elderly asthma regulate breathing based on the amount of oxygen in their blood (hypoxic drive) because of the chronically

Table 6–6: Criteria for Initiating Oxygen Therapy

- Cardiac or respiratory arrest
- Hypotension: systolic BP less than 100 mmHg
- Hypoxemia from any cause
- Metabolic acidosis
- Respiratory distress

Table 6–7: Patients Who Need Oxygen

• Any patient at risk of airway obstruction
• Any patient who is unresponsive
• Any patient having seizures
• Any patient requiring artificial ventilation
• Any patient in cardiac arrest
• Any patient suffering from shock
• Any patient complaining of shortness of breath
• Any patient with signs of respiratory distress, tachypnea, hyperpnea, gasping, or accessory muscle usage
• Any patient complaining of chest pain
• Any patient with a suspected stroke

trapped amount of carbon dioxide in their lungs. Therefore, delivering high-concentration oxygen could stop their breathing, although this would be rare. If a patient is in respiratory distress, however, administer high-flow oxygen. Never withhold oxygen from a patient who needs it.

Oxygen Equipment

The **oxygen cylinder** is a seamless steel or alloy tank filled with oxygen under pressure and usually painted green (Figure 6–9). Carrying 2000 to 2200 pounds per square inch when full, the oxygen cylinder should not be emptied completely because damage can result to the inside of the cylinder. It should be labeled "OXYGEN U.S.P." and be not more than 5 years old. Oxygen cylinders come in various sizes, the most common being the "D" tank, which holds 350 liters of oxygen, and the "E" tank, which holds 625 liters of oxygen. Safety must be observed because oxygen acts as an accelerant in the presence of open flames or combustible materials. When using an oxygen cylinder, always use oxygen regulators and tubing, nonferrous oxygen tank wrenches, and gaskets in excellent condition. Be careful never to drop a tank, leave an unsecured tank standing upright, allow smoking in the area of use, or use flammable petroleum products such as adhesive tape near the oxygen cylinders. Additionally, the oxygen cylinder should be stored in a cool, well-ventilated area.

The **oxygen pressure regulator** controls the flow of oxygen from the tank to the patient (Figure 6–10). For portable oxygen tanks, the pressure regulator is usually a pin-yoke assembly type designed to ensure its use only on medical oxygen cylinders. The regulator contains a flowmeter that will control the flow of oxygen in liters per minute and possibly a **restricted flow demand valve** used for positive pressure ventilation on adults only. The most popular type of flowmeter currently used is the constant flow selector valve that allows for flow adjustments in stepped increments.

The delivery of oxygen to patients who are breathing and have adequate ventilation is accomplished with the use of two devices: the **nasal cannula,** which can deliver between 24% and 44% oxygen (Figure 6–11), and the **nonrebreathing oxygen mask,** capable of delivering up to 90% oxygen (Figure 6–12). Current USDOT standards are recommending the use of the nonrebreathing mask in any case in which it is felt oxygen is needed.[17] Use of the nonrebreathing mask requires high-flow oxygen at 15 liters per minute. Any patient who develops a feeling of suffocation can utilize the nasal cannula, which only should be supplied with no more than 6 liters per minute. Higher flows become uncomfortable and will excessively dry the mucous membranes of the nose. Remember, patients in respiratory arrest should be provided with artificial ventilations utilizing supplemental oxygen at 15 liters per minute or more by way of the simple pocket mask or BVM.

Procedure for Delivery of Oxygen

To administer supplemental oxygen (Figure 6–13), first check to see that the tank is labeled "Oxygen U.S.P." and/or has the yellow oxygen placard. The tank should

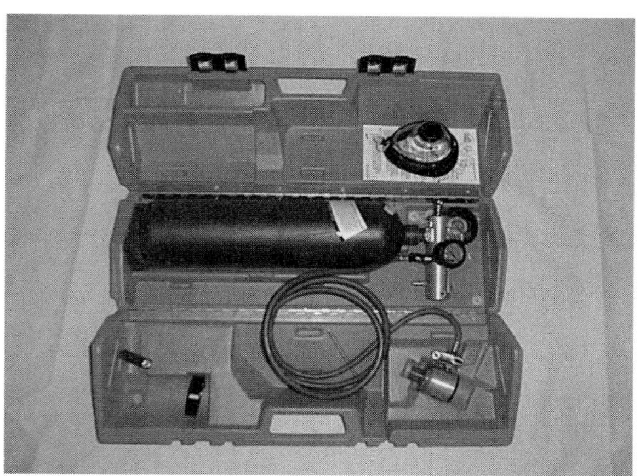

Figure 6–9. The oxygen tank, case, and regulator.

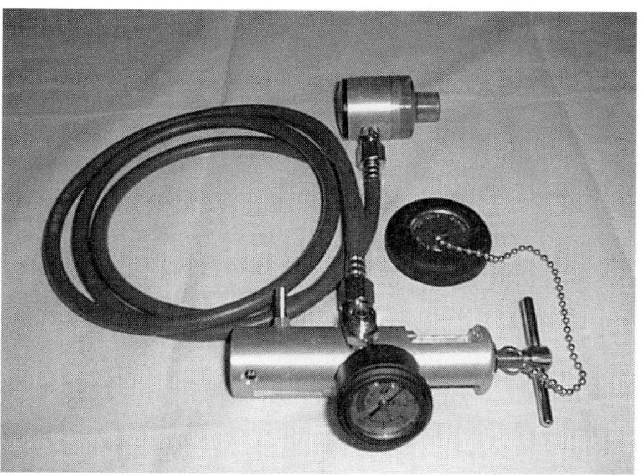

Figure 6–10. The oxygen regulator (shown with the demand valve attachment).

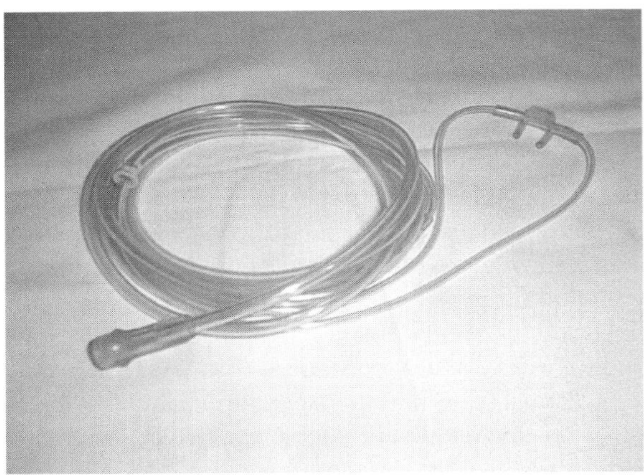

Figure 6–11. The nasal cannula.

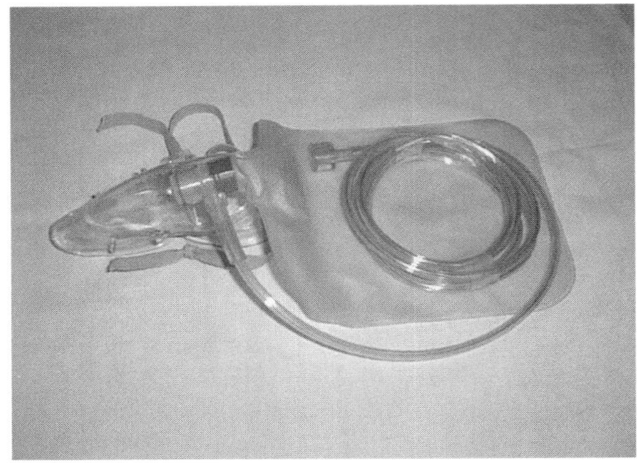

Figure 6–12. The nonrebreathing oxygen mask.

A

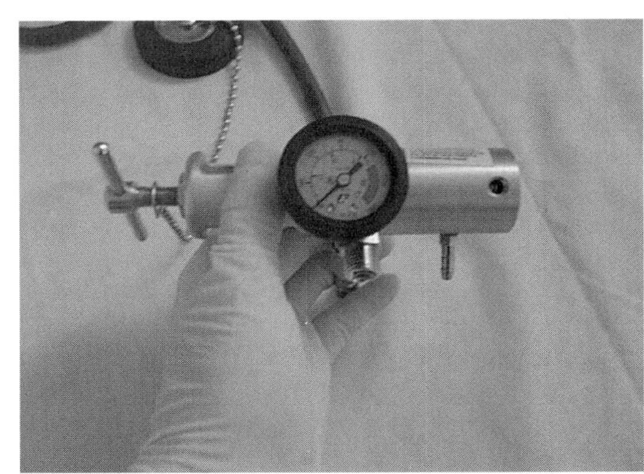

C

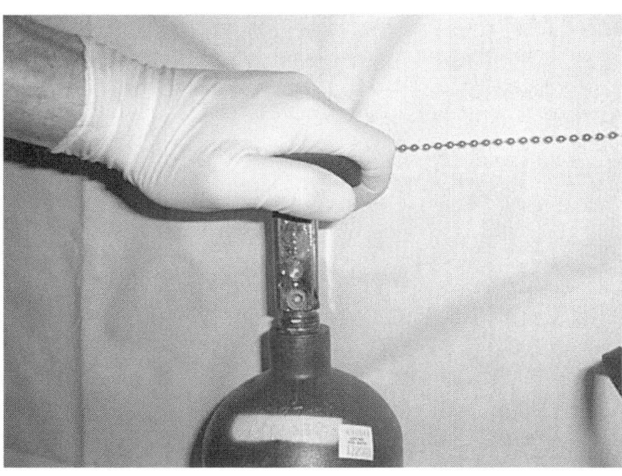

B

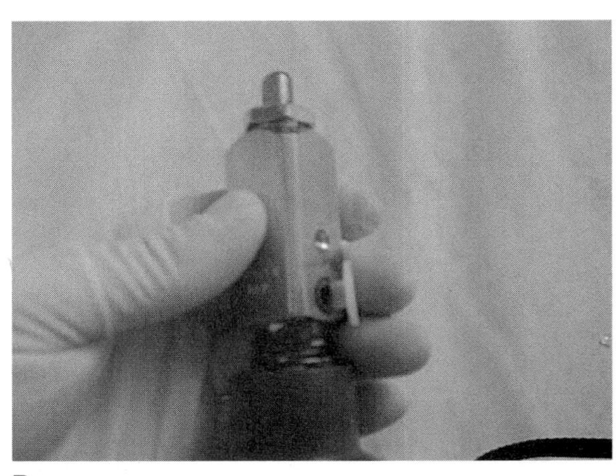

D

Figure 6–13. Procedure for delivery of oxygen. **A.** Make sure the cylinder is marked oxygen. **B.** Clear the valve. **C.** Make sure you are using an oxygen pressure regulator. **D.** Make sure there is an O-ring either on the tank's valve or on the regulator.

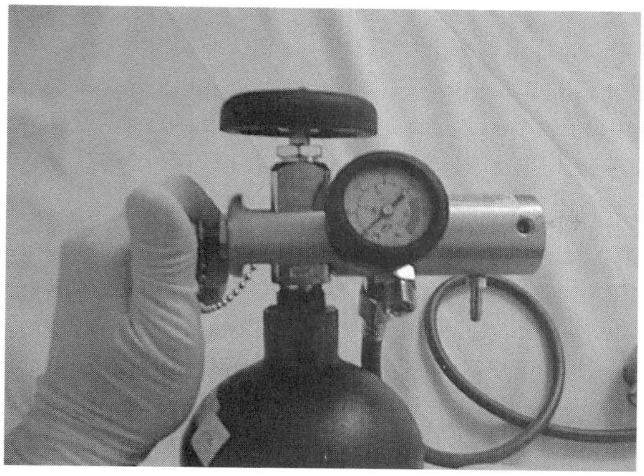

E

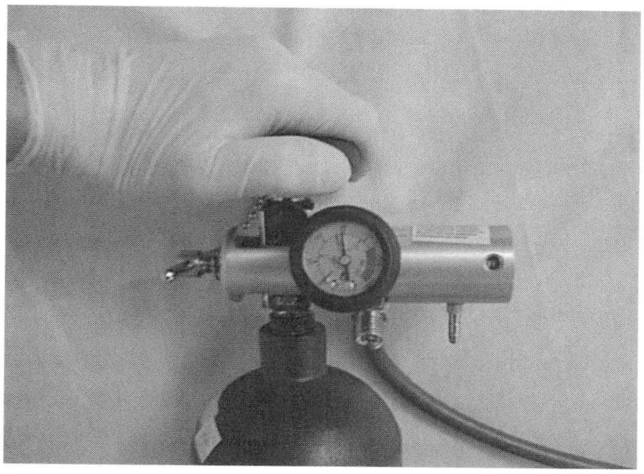

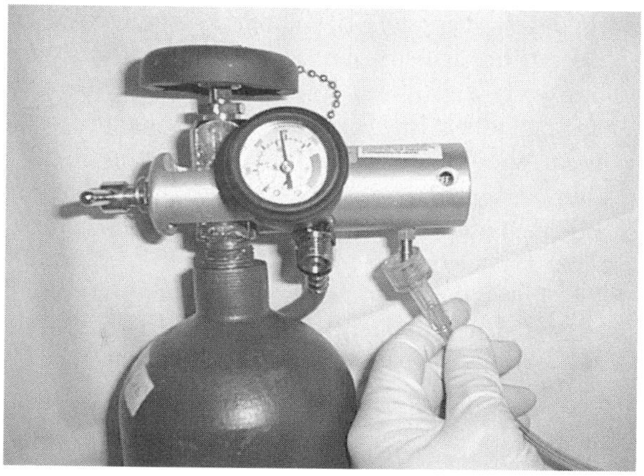

H

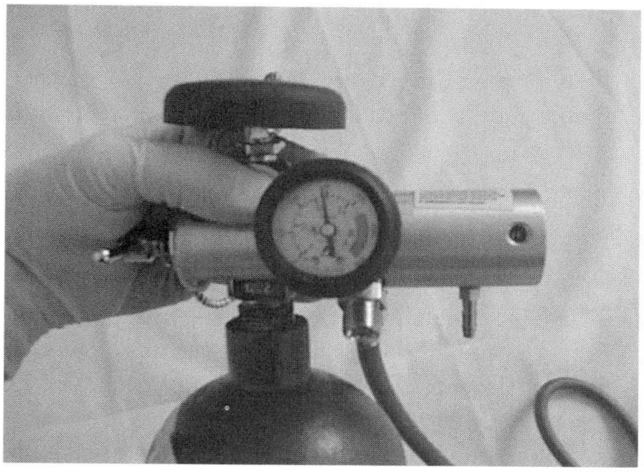

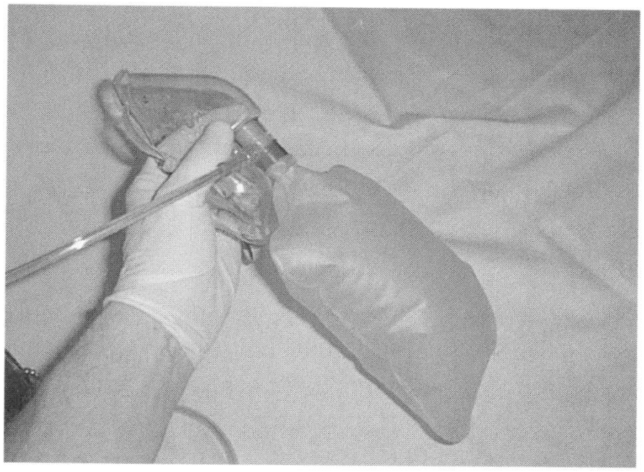

F

I

G

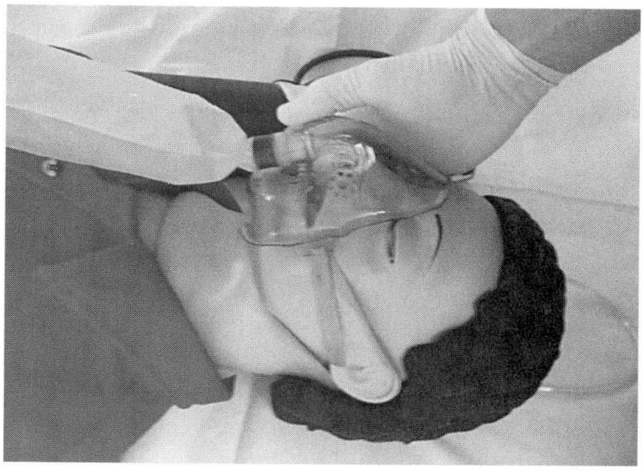

J

Figure 6–13. (continued) E. Attach the regulator to the tank, making sure to seat the two prongs into their proper places on the tank. Hand tighten the T-screw until snug. **F.** Open the oxygen cylinder **one full turn. G.** Check the pressure gauge. **H.** Attach the delivery device and adjust the flowmeter. **I.** Ensure that the oxygen is flowing to the device. **J.** Place the delivery device on the patient.

be secured in a position that will prevent it from being tipped over. "Crack" the main valve to clear it of dust and debris. Also, make sure that the regulator is an oxygen regulator. There should be an O-ring within the regulator oxygen port to prevent the leakage of oxygen during use. Attach the regulator to the tank, seating the pins correctly. Hand-tighten the T-screw until snug. Open the oxygen cylinder by turning the oxygen cylinder wrench one full turn and check for leaks. Check the pressure gauge to ensure adequate pressure. Attach the delivery device via oxygen tubing and adjust the flow rate. Check the delivery device to make certain oxygen is flowing to it. Finally, place the delivery device on the patient. Remember, high-priority patients requiring high-flow oxygen should be reassessed every 5 minutes.

When oxygen is no longer needed, close the main valve on the tank and check to make certain there is no longer any pressure on the regulator. Then close the flow regulator valve to prevent dust from entering the regulator. An oxygen kit not frequently used should be stored with the regulator off the tank.

CIRCULATION AND CPR

Overview

Assessment of the cardiovascular system is essential in the treatment and prevention of life-threatening injuries. Ultimately, all critical care conditions lead to inadequate circulation or loss of circulation. Therefore, it's important to recognize the signs of advanced pathological processes involving the heart and blood vessels. Circulatory assessment includes a simultaneous pulse check of both the carotid and radial pulses and a dermal assessment consisting of distal capillary refill, color, moisture, and temperature.

Cardiogenic shock as it relates to myocardial infarction occurs when the heart loses its ability to function as a pump. Failure of the body to adequately circulate oxygenated blood can result in irreversible damage to the myocardial and peripheral tissues within a relatively short amount of time.[18] Early recognition and treatment are essential in diverting deadly complications such as cardiac arrest. The most important factors surrounding the survival of a patient in cardiac arrest are early access into the EMS system, early CPR, early cardiac defibrillation, and early advanced cardiac life support (ACLS).

The Single Health Care Professional and Adult CPR

When approaching a potentially unresponsive patient, perform a scene size-up. Note anything that may cause you harm or may cause the patient further harm. Determine the patient's level of responsiveness by tapping and gently shaking the person while shouting, "Hey, are you OK?" If that does not elicit a response, provide a painful stimulus such as a sternal rub or pressure on nailbeds. Avoid the use of ammonia inhalants if there is the possibility of head or spinal trauma. You do not want the patient to react suddenly by withdrawing the head, causing further trauma to the spine. If the patient does not respond, activate your facility's emergency action plan. Before proceeding any farther, make sure to take appropriate body substance isolation precautions. Assess the patient's breathing by looking for chest rise, listening for breath sounds, and feeling for the movement of air for about 5 seconds. If you are unable to determine whether or not the patient is breathing, place the patient on his or her back while supporting the head and neck. Open the airway and reassess breathing for about 5 seconds. If the patient is not breathing at this point, give two slow breaths and then check the carotid pulse for 5 to 10 seconds. An absent pulse requires the initiation of cardiac compressions. Find your hand position by locating the sternal notch. Place the heel of one hand two fingers' width above the sternal notch along the midline of the sternum. Place the second hand on top of the first hand, being careful to keep your fingers off the patient's chest wall. Deliver fifteen cardiac compressions compressing to a depth of approximately $1\frac{1}{2}$ to 2 inches. Again, open the airway and give two slow breaths. Repeat the cycles of compressions and breaths for 1 minute, and then reassess the patient's carotid pulse and breathing for 5 to 10 seconds. Repeat the cycles as needed, stopping to reassess the patient every few minutes. Be careful not to interrupt CPR for more than 30 seconds.

Entry of a Second Health Care Professional and Adult CPR

When CPR is already in progress and a second person who is medically trained becomes available, the second person should:

- Identify himself or herself
- Determine if advanced medical personnel have been summoned
- Briefly question the first professional on scene as to the events of the incident. It is important to note if the condition resulted from trauma or a medically related condition such as heart disease. The use of an automated external defibrillation device (AED) is contraindicated on the trauma patient in cardiac arrest.
- Verify the absence of a carotid pulse
- Complete the initial assessment (severe bleeding sweep)
- Provide advanced interventions based on training and equipment (such as the use of supplemental oxygen or an AED device).

When the second person becomes available to help with CPR, he or she should begin by getting into position to start chest compressions. The first professional will finish with two slow breaths and call to stop CPR to verify the absence of a carotid pulse. Upon verification that the carotid pulse is absent, CPR can resume with the delivery of **five** chest compressions to every one ventilation. The patient is then reassessed every few minutes.

FYI—DEFIBRILLATION

Over 500,000 Americans die each year as the result of coronary artery disease. Of the patients that experience cardiac death caused by coronary artery disease, it is estimated that up to 90% could benefit from early defibrillation. Again, early access, early CPR, early defibrillation, and early ACLS are the keys to survival for the patient in cardiac arrest caused by heart disease. The introduction of

Clinical Application 6–2

You are called to respond to an unresponsive 59-year-old male patient in your rehabilitation center. Other co-workers have already begun two-person CPR observing BSI precautions.

(A) Place the following items in order of importance regarding the previous scenario:

- Begin advanced interventions
- Verify the absence of a carotid pulse
- Verify that EMS has been notified
- Complete the initial assessment

(B) The patient begins to vomit. Place the following items in the order in which you would perform them:

- Continue CPR
- Verify the absence of a carotid pulse and breathing
- Roll the patient on the side and clear the airway

Clinical Application 6–2 Answers

(A)

1. Verify that EMS has been notified
2. Verify the absence of a carotid pulse
3. Complete the initial assessment
4. Begin advanced interventions

(B)

1. Roll the patient on the side and clear the airway
2. Verify the absence of a carotid pulse and breathing
3. Continue CPR

the fully automated external defibrillation (AED) device has enabled first responders to provide the next vital link in the chain of survival. The single most important intervention for the patient in ventricular fibrillation is defibrillation by AED. Health care professionals who are required to perform basic CPR should be trained in the operation of AEDs.[19] The use of AEDs is restricted to those persons who are properly trained and equipped. Always follow your formal training and local protocols.

SHOCK AND BLEEDING CONTROL

Shock or hypoperfusion is defined as the inability to adequately circulate oxygenated blood to the body's vital organs, tissues, and cells. It can result from a problem with either the heart, the blood vessels, or the blood. The early stages of myocardial infarction result in cardiogenic shock. A problem with the lungs such as an acute asthma attack can lead to respiratory shock. A poorly managed diabetic condition can alter the normal composition of the blood, leading an individual into metabolic shock. No matter what the problem, shock becomes apparent when the body is no longer able to cope with traumatic injury or pathologic illness. Failure of the body to cope with injury or illness becomes apparent when the following signs and symptoms begin to appear:

- Restlessness and anxiety
- Rapid, weak pulse
- Rapid, shallow respirations
- Mental status changes
- Extreme thirst
- Cyanosis
- Pale, cool, and damp skin

A patient showing signs and symptoms of shock is classified as a high-priority patient and is in need of immediate advanced medical attention. Basic treatment for shock involves the following steps:

- Maintain the patient's ABCs
- Provide high-flow oxygen if you are equipped and trained to do so
- Prevent further blood loss
- Place the patient in Trendelenberg's position (also known as the shock position—lying down with legs elevated about 12 inches) if possible
- Prevent the patient from becoming chilled or overheated
- Provide care for other injuries
- Reassess the patient

Clinically, shock can be classified into the categories of hypovolemic, distributive, and cardiac, with end-organ cellular metabolism failure as a result of all three. The most common cause for hypovolemic shock is trauma resulting in either internal or external hemorrhage.

Severe hemorrhage, either internal or external, needs to be dealt with promptly even when dealing with a patient in cardiac arrest. Performing CPR on a patient in cardiac arrest with severe hemorrhage can be a no-win situation unless measures are taken to attempt control of the hemorrhage.

Management of external hemorrhage includes the following steps in order of importance:

- Follow BSI precautions
- Apply direct pressure
- Elevate the body part if possible
- Reassess the wound if bleeding does not stop
- Apply a pressure bandage
- Use pressure points (brachial, femoral, or temporal)

In addition to the signs and symptoms of shock, internal hemorrhage may also be indicated by discoloration of the skin in the injured area or by the local soft tissues being tender, swollen, or firm. Examples of internal hemorrhage would include ecchymosis around the eyes (racoon's eyes) potentially indicating a fracture of the cranial vault or rigidity, tenderness, and edema of the abdomen somewhat localized in the left upper quadrant potentially indicating intraabdominal hemorrhage from a ruptured spleen.

PATIENT ASSESSMENT—PART II

Overview

The **focused assessment** is the second part of patient assessment, and is instrumental in discovering and treating **potentially life-threatening injuries.** This part of the assessment process includes taking a focused history, performing a physical examination, and taking vital signs. Each of these components will yield further information regarding the status of the patient. For the purpose of specificity, the focus of this section will be on the medical patient. Once the focused assessment is completed, the performance of an ongoing assessment is critical to maintain the patient's status. Upon the arrival of EMS services, it will be necessary to give a report on the patient's status to EMS personnel in order to provide for a smooth transition of patient care.

Focused History

The purpose of the focused history and physical exam is to gather important information regarding the nature of the in-

Clinical Application 6–3

You are asked to provide care for a patient exhibiting signs of restlessness, altered mental status, and somewhat shallow, rapid breathing. You have completed a scene size-up and activated EMS. During your initial assessment you find that the patient also has a rapid, weak radial pulse and is showing signs of cyanosis.

(A) Based on the information previously given regarding the patient, list the interventions you would make during the *initial assessment* to treat this patient.

(B) Would you classify this patient as high-priority or low-priority? Why?

Clinical Application 6–3 Answers

(A)
Treat for shock:

- Maintain the patient's ABCs
- Provide high-flow oxygen if you are equipped and trained to do so
- Add supplemental oxygen delivered at a rate of 15 liters per minute by nonrebreather mask
- Prevent further blood loss
- Place the patient in Trendelenberg's position (the shock position—lying down with legs elevated about 12 inches) if possible
- Prevent the patient from becoming chilled or overheated
- Provide care for other injuries
- Reassess the patient

(B)
This patient is a *high*-priority patient because of the presence of distress, altered mental status, and signs of shock.

Table 6–8: The Elements of the Focused History (CSAMPLED-OPQRSTI)

- Chief complaint
- Signs and symptoms **(OPQRSTI)**
  - Onset
  - Provocation
  - Quality
  - Region and radiation
  - Severity
  - Timing
  - Interventions
- Allergies
- Medications
- Pertinent past medical history
- Last . . .
- Events prior
- Document

jury or illness and to identify any potentially life-threatening conditions that the patient may have. It is important to note that the focused history is primarily applicable to a responsive patient. However, friends, family members, and even bystanders can fill in the information if the patient cannot. An easy mnemonic used to remember the elements of the focused history (Table 6–8) is **CSAMPLED** which will serve to prompt the caregiver to elicit the following information:

Chief complaint. Note the patient's primary complaint, such as difficulty breathing, chest pain, or an altered mental status.

Signs and symptoms. The caregiver needs a description of the patient's condition such as sounds of noisy breathing, seeing blood, or a description of the pain experienced by the patient. The acronym **OPQRSTI** can provide the groundwork for efficient questioning regarding the patient's current condition (Table 6–8).

- Onset. When did the present condition first start?
- Provocation. What brings on the pain or makes it worse?
- Quality. Can you describe the pain? Is it dull, sharp, or throbbing?
- Region and radiation. Where is the pain located? Does it feel like it moves or spreads?
- Severity. On a scale of 1 to 10, how would you grade your pain?
- Timing. How often do you get this pain? How long have you had this pain?
- Interventions. What have other people or the patient done for the illness so far?

Allergies. Any allergies to medications, foods, or the environment need to be known since these may be the cause of the current condition.

Medications. Patients are often taking at least a few types of medication. This can be an important clue as to the patient's present condition or can be a factor in treatment.

Pertinent past history. A patient's medical history involves prior conditions, events, and related treatment such as surgery.

Last . . . The amount of previously ingested food or drink is important in allergy and drug-related conditions (such as how quickly drugs will take effect). The last time medications were taken may be vital information as well.

Events leading to the illness or injury. The patient's description of the incident that lead to his or her current condition can give more insight into the mechanism of the injury or the cause of the current condition.

Documentation. Remember, if the information gained from the focused history is not written down, all of your work is in vain.

Physical Examination

Especially important in an unresponsive patient, the physical examination will direct the treatment of the patient. Therefore, it should be specific for the type of patient and focused toward the illness or injuries present. A complete head-to-toe examination (rapid assessment) is warranted to identify additional problems in an unresponsive patient. However, a responsive patient can limit the area of focus to only those problems that pertain to the injury or illness. For example, a person complaining of chest pain with a known history of angina pectoris may only warrant examination of the head, neck, chest, and extremities (focused examination).

Each region of the physical examination should cover region-specific items, as well as deformities, open wounds, tenderness, and swelling **(DOTS)**. During a rapid assessment, each region will be screened but may not be examined in great detail. The acronym **HNSCASPER** can help guide your approach (Table 6–9).

Table 6–9: The Elements of the Physical Examination (HNSCASPER)

- Head
- Neck—anterior portion
- Spine—cervical
- Chest
- Abdomen
- Spine—lumbar
- Pelvis
- Extremities
- Reverse (back)

Head. Assess for DOTS. Examine the scalp and face. Look in the eyes, ears, nose, and mouth for leaking fluids such as blood or cerebrospinal fluid. Also, check for subdermal hemorrhage around the eyes and behind the ears (intracranial fracture signs). Look for broken or missing teeth, foreign objects, or dentures in the mouth that could lead to obstruction of the airway. Make certain that the pupillary reflexes are intact.
Neck. Assess the anterior portion of the neck for DOTS, jugular vein distention (JVD), tracheal deviation, accessory muscle usage, retractive breathing, or soft tissue abnormalities. (Because of the importance of this step, it is also performed during the initial assessment.)
Spine—cervical. Assess the posterior portion of the neck for DOTS and gross instability.
Chest. Assess for DOTS, paradoxical breathing, and retractive breathing. Auscultate breath sounds for presence and quality in at least four quadrants and the point of maximal impulse (PMI). (Because of the importance of this step, it is also performed during the initial assessment.)
Abdomen. Assess for DOTS. Palpate the abdomen in at least four quadrants looking for rigidity, tenderness, skin discoloration, and distention.
Spine—lumbar. Assess the lower, posterior portion of the trunk for DOTS and gross instability.
Pelvis. Assess for DOTS, gross instability, and priapism.
Extremities. Assess each of the extremities for DOTS and neurovascular integrity. Neurovascular integrity can be assessed utilizing the acronym **CMS:**

- Circulation. Check the distal pulse and skin condition, including capillary refill.
- Motor. Check gross motor movement.
- Sensory. Check the sensation of light touch.

Reverse (back). Assess the entire posterior portion of the thorax for the presence of DOTS. This may demand the performance of a log roll to view the patient's back.

Vital Signs

The final part of the focused assessment involves taking vital signs. They are key indicators that reveal how the patient's body is reacting to the injury or illness. A complete set of vital signs includes the following:

- Level of responsiveness (AVPU)
- Pupil assessment (equality, reactivity, size, and shape)
- Airway status
- Breathing rate (rate, rhythm, and quality) and lung fields (at least four quadrants)
- Circulation—pulse rate (rate, rhythm, and quality), skin condition, and blood pressure
- Document the above including the time, the position of the patient, and the patient arm used

Ongoing Assessment

Following completion of the patient's assessment and interventions made on the patient's behalf, a reassessment of the patient is warranted to verify that the interventions made are appropriate and that the patient's status is not changing. The following are important aspects of the ongoing assessment:

- Repeating the initial assessment
- Reassessing and recording the vital signs
- Repeating the focused assessment
- Checking the interventions made

The time interval at which you will be performing the ongoing assessment will depend on the priority level of the patient. A high-priority or unstable patient should be reassessed every 5 minutes. The low-priority patient, one with no immediately life-threatening injuries or illnesses, should be reassessed every 15 minutes to maintain the patient's status.

Patient Hand-Off

Including the patient report, the transfer of care, and assistance in moving the patient, the patient hand-off is the final step in ensuring the best care possible for the patient. Upon the arrival of EMS personnel, a patient report should be given in order to provide information regarding the patient, to introduce new caregivers, and to facilitate the transfer of care. The patient report should include the patient's identifying data, the chief complaint, the priority level, the level of responsiveness, the airway, breathing, and circulation status, the results of the focused assessment, all interventions made, the patient's response to those interventions, and the current status of the patient. Once the patient report has been given, the transfer of care will take place when the EMS personnel begin management of the situation. At this point, the caregiver may be asked to assist in the extrication, packaging, and transport of the patient.

EMERGENCY CARE APPLICATIONS

OVERVIEW

This section is designed to test your skills in providing emergency care specifically related to the types of medical emergencies that any given health care provider could encounter in a general rehabilitation facility (nonmedical). The emergency supplies on hand will be limited to a basic first aid kit and a basic airway and oxygen kit. Try to apply an emergency action plan to the following scenarios.

DIFFICULTY BREATHING

Because of the body's need for oxygen, difficulty breathing is a concern that needs to be addressed seriously. Signs

Clinical Application 6–4

You are working with a female patient in your examination room who begins to have unusual trouble breathing. She is an elderly person in obvious distress whom you have not seen previously. She is pale, seated in a tripod position, and breathing rapidly. The patient, in short sentences, tells you that she has chronic lung disease and that she does not have her oxygen unit with her today.

(A) What is it about this situation that should alert you to a serious problem that could be life-threatening?

(B) After recognizing that a serious problem exists, you should start providing emergency care by performing a __________.

(C) List the elements of the scene size-up that are applicable in this case.

(D) When would you need to activate EMS?

(E) What sort of immediate interventions would be appropriate for this patient?

(F) Your general impression of the patient is that she is in respiratory distress accompanied by signs of hypoperfusion. Place the following emergency steps of the initial assessment in chronological order:

- Assess airway and breathing
- Determine responsiveness
- Consider stabilizing the cervical spine
- Determine apparent life threats
- Delegate helpers

(G) After completing the above emergency steps, you find the following: The patient is alert and appropriately responsive, the airway status is patent, and respirations are 22 beats per minute and shallow. What would appropriate airway and breathing management consist of utilizing supplemental oxygen?

(H) You continue your initial assessment by assessing circulation. Place the following emergency steps in chronological order:

- Assess for severe bleeding
- Provide shock management
- Assess carotid and radial pulses
- Assess the skin

(I) After completing the above emergency steps, you find the following: The pulse is 110 beats per minute and weak, the skin is pale, cool, and clammy with signs of diminished capillary refill, and you find no evidence of severe blood loss. Based on this information, what additional interventions would you make at this time to treat the presence of shock?

(J) What two items still need to be rapidly assessed before you prioritize the patient?

(K) Identify the priority of this patient (high or low). Explain why.

(L) List the elements of the focused history as they pertain to the patient's present illness.

(M) You find out that the patient has suffered from chronic lung disease for the past 10 years, and that she began having difficulty breathing 3 days previously after a day-long rain storm. Today, she had problems catching her breath. She did not sleep much the previous night due to constant coughing. There is no history of allergies. She does have medically prescribed oxygen and an inhaler that she does not have with her at this time nor does she know the name of the prescription medication. There have been no other recent interventions made for this problem. The next two steps of the focused assessment are to perform a __________ and obtain baseline __________.

(N) The focused physical examination should which parts of the body?

(O) List the things that you would include when taking the patient through baseline vital signs.

(P) You find diminished breath sounds bilaterally in the lower lung fields as well as the presence of crackles and rales. There exists evidence of retractive

continued

Clinical Application 6–4 Continued

breathing as well. The patient is alert, but has difficulty responding due to her rapid respirations. Her pupils are equal and reactive bilaterally with both consensual and accommodative reflexes intact. The skin is showing signs of cyanosis and diminished capillary refill. Respirations are 24 breaths per minute, shallow and regular. Pulse is 118 beats per minute, weak and regular. Blood pressure is 100/70. At this time, you should check your ____________ and make any additional ____________ needed.

(Q) Since she is a high-priority patient, you should perform the ongoing assessment every ____________ minutes.

(R) List the elements of the ongoing assessment.

Clinical Application 6–4 Answers

(A)
In addition to difficulty breathing, the patient is showing signs of hypoperfusion or shock.

(B)
scene size-up

(C)

- Hands and eyes covered: You should be prepared if the patient should stop breathing.
- Hazards: Is the scene safe?
- How or what happened: Determine the nature of the illness.
- How many people involved: Information needed by EMS dispatch.
- How much help is needed: Decision to activate EMS.
- Immediate Interventions: Initiation of oxygen therapy.

(D)
With evidence that hypoperfusion is already taking place, EMS should be activated during the scene size-up. Waiting for the person to stop breathing is too late. You can always call EMS back and cancel the transport. Never take on something you are not sure of. Remember, always "pass the buck" if you are unsure of the situation.

(E)

- Initiate low-flow oxygen therapy (supplemental oxygen delivered at 4 to 6 liters per minute by nasal cannula). Remember, the patient suffering from chronic lung disease should have oxygen therapy started conservatively.
- Allow the patient to stay seated if she is capable of maintaining that position. Be prepared if she becomes unresponsive.
- Follow the patient's lead. If she feels she needs to lay down (due to advanced hypoperfusion), allow her to do so. Patients usually know what their body needs.

(F)
(Refer to Table 6–5 for help with the chronological order.)

1. Determine apparent life threats
2. Consider stabilizing the cervical spine
3. Determine responsiveness
4. Delegate helpers
5. Assess airway and breathing

(G)
The patient is alert and the airway is patent. At this point, stay with the low-flow supplemental oxygen delivered at 4 to 6 liters per minute by nasal cannula.

(H)
(Refer to Table 6–5 for help with the chronological order.)

1. Assess carotid and radial pulses
2. Assess the skin
3. Assess for severe bleeding
4. Provide shock management

(I)
The patient is not responding the way we would like to see. Therefore, change to high-flow supplemental oxygen delivered at 15 liters per minute by nonrebreather mask.

(J)
Rapid assessment of the neck and the chest.

continued

Clinical Application 6–4 Continued

(K)
This is a high-priority patient because of the advancing signs of hypoperfusion or shock, alteration in normal vital signs, and continued difficulty breathing.

(L)
Refer to Table 6–8 for the elements of the focused history.

(M)
focused exam vital signs

(N)
The focused examination should include the neck, chest, and peripheral circulation.

(O)

- Level of responsiveness (AVPU)
- Pupil assessment (equality, reactivity, size, and shape)
- Airway status
- Breathing rate (rate, rhythm, and quality) and lung fields (at least four quadrants)
- Circulation—pulse rate (rate, rhythm, and quality), skin condition, and blood pressure
- Document the above including the time, the position of the patient, and the patient arm used

(P)
interventions interventions

(Q)
5

(R)

- Repeat the initial assessment
- Reassess and record the vital signs
- Repeat the focused assessment
- Check the interventions made

and symptoms may include air hunger, labored or noisy breathing, rapid, slow, or irregular breathing, use of accessory muscles for inspiration, or signs and symptoms of shock. Patients who exhibit gasping respirations, unusually slow breathing (less than 10 beats per minute), extreme fatigue, and inability to speak or who are unable to maintain an upright position may suddenly stop breathing. Difficulty breathing can have pulmonary or cardiovascular causes. Ultimately, however, the body is not able to intake enough oxygen, hence the term *respiratory shock*. Successful management of patients with difficulty breathing depends upon early recognition, early activation of EMS, aggressive interventions including high-flow oxygen, and continual reassessment.

CHEST PAIN

Chest pain can be caused by a variety of things including injuries to the chest wall, cardiopulmonary infections and injuries, heartburn, abdominal problems, and cardiac pathologies. Time is the most important factor related to the survival of the patient suffering from myocardial infarction. Chest pain resulting from myocardial infarction may also be accompanied by radiating pain to the shoulder, neck, jaw, or abdomen, profuse sweating, heart palpitations, the feeling of impending doom, and signs and symptoms of shock. Patient care priorities for the patient suffering from chest pain are early recognition, early activation of EMS, maintenance of the patient's ABCs including administration of high-flow oxygen, and continual reassessment. There always exists the potential for sudden cardiac arrest. The keys to survival for the patient in cardiac arrest are early access into the EMS system, early CPR, early defibrillation, and early ACLS intervention.

ALTERED MENTAL STATUS

Patients suffering from an altered mental status are challenging because of the number of possible causes and because they cannot communicate what they are experiencing. An alteration in mental status can be anything from confusion to complete unresponsiveness. The mnemonic

Clinical Application 6–5

Your next patient is a 45-year-old male who is being treated in your facility for low back pain. You begin your session with him by having him perform a brief warm-up. You notice that he has a distressed look on his face and that his skin is very pale. You ask him if he is OK and he responds by telling you that he has had a touch of indigestion all morning and that it seems to be getting worse. You allow him to rest for a few minutes and his subjective complaints begin to worsen. He states he feels nauseated and weak.

(A) What is it about this situation that should alert you as to a serious problem that could be life-threatening?

(B) After completing a scene size-up and activating EMS, you should begin an ___________.

(C) Place the following steps of the initial assessment in chronological order:

- Assess the airway, breathing, and circulation
- Consider stabilization of the cervical spine
- Determine the chief complaint or apparent life threats
- Form a general impression
- Determine responsiveness

(D) You find the patient is alert and appropriately responsive with no prior mechanism of injury to suggest a head or neck trauma. You find the airway is patent, respirations are 18 breaths per minute, full and regular, the pulse is 100 beats per minute, weak at the wrist and regular, and the skin is cool, pale, and clammy with diminished capillary refill. There is no evidence of severe bleeding. The next step is to prevent/manage ___________.

(E) List the interventions you would make at this point.

(F) Rapid assessment of the ___________ and ___________ follows.

(G) This is a ___________ priority patient in need of immediate transport to a medical facility.

(H) After performing a focused history, you find the patient was awakened early this morning by a sudden onset of chest pain. The pain is located in the center of his chest, radiates to the jaw and arms, and is currently the worst pain the patient has ever experienced. The pain is constant and getting worse. There is no prior history of allergies, use of over-the-counter or prescription medications, or heart disease or cardiac problems. The patient does has a family history of heart disease and high blood pressure. The next step is perform a focused exam of what areas of the body?

(I) After taking baseline vital signs, you find the patient is alert and appropriately responsive, his pupils are equal, symmetric, and reactive bilaterally with both accommodative and consensual reflexes intact, the airway is patent, respirations are 22 breaths per minute, full and regular, the pulse is 120 beats per minute, weak at the wrist and regular, and the blood pressure is 144/90. What should you do next?

(J) After checking and making additional interventions as needed, you should begin the ___________ performed at ___________ minute intervals.

Clinical Application 6–5 Answers

(A)
Chest pain accompanied by signs of shock.

(B)
initial assessment

(C)
(Refer to Table 6–5 for help.)

1. Form a general impression
2. Consider stabilization of the cervical spine
3. Determine the chief complaint or apparent life threats
4. Determine responsiveness
5. Assess the airway, breathing, and circulation

(D)
shock or hypoperfusion

Clinical Application 6–5 Continued

Clinical Application 6–5 Answers

(E)
Provide high-flow oxygen delivered at 15 liters per minute by nonrebreather mask. Provide additional treatment for shock as indicated.

(F)
neck chest

(G)
high

(H)
The focused exam should include the neck, chest, and peripheral circulation.

(I)
Check and make additional interventions as needed, such as obtaining medical direction.

(J)
ongoing assessment 5

Clinical Application 6–6

You are working with a 43-year-old female patient on a padded floor who is performing gymnastic ball exercises. While watching her, you suddenly see her roll off the ball onto the floor and begin convulsing. She appears unresponsive. She has no known history of seizures or epilepsy.

(A) Don't panic! Your first course of action is to begin with a ___________.

(B) Would you activate EMS immediately? Explain.

(C) What immediate interventions would you provide?

(D) After the convulsions stop, the patient remains unresponsive. Your watch tells you that the convulsions lasted approximately 1½ minutes in duration. Your next step is to begin an ___________.

(E) While assessing the patient's airway and breathing, you find noisy respirations that sound like snoring. What would you do to correct this and attempt to ensure a patent airway?

(F) The patient's respirations are 12 breaths per minute and full. Is she breathing adequately?

(G) Assessing the patient's circulation would include . . . ?

(H) The patient's pulse is 84, regular and strong. Her skin is red, warm, and wet with sweat. No evidence of severe bleeding exists. Rapid assessment of the neck and chest are unremarkable. List your interventions and prioritize the patient.

(I) Next, you perform a ___________, attempt to take a ___________, and obtain baseline ___________.

continued

Clinical Application 6–6 Continued

(J) The head-to-toe rapid assessment is unremarkable, but you are able to gain some information from the patient's medical history. The patient has a known allergy to penicillin and has a 5-year history of high blood pressure with associated prescription medication. The patient is unresponsive; her pupils are symmetric, equal, and reactive bilaterally. The patient's respirations are 12, full and regular, pulse is 80, strong and regular, and blood pressure is 128/74. Her skin is flushed, but cool and clammy. Would you change any of your previous interventions?

(K) EMS personnel arrive and begin to ask questions regarding the incident. Give a patient report.

Clinical Application 6–6 Answers

(A)
scene size-up

(B)
Yes. Activation is warranted because there is no known prior history of seizures. Medical examination is needed to determine the cause of the seizure and to prevent/limit future episodes.

(C)

- Clear the area of obstacles
- Make sure EMS is en route

(D)
initial assessment

(E)
Utilization of an oropharyngeal airway would be warranted at this point. If one is not available and you do not suspect a spinal injury, place the patient on her side (recovery position) and attempt to maintain an open airway for her by utilizing the modified jaw thrust technique. A lateral recumbent position will use gravity to help keep the tongue from blocking the back of the throat. Be careful with trying to open the mouth since you can actually cause more of an airway obstruction when the mouth is opened by the chin being pulled down.

(F)
Yes and no. Adequate respirations are defined for an adult as respirations between 12 and 20 that are full <u>with no associated signs of distress.</u> However, in this situation the presence of seizure activity would be a form of patient distress. Therefore, high-flow oxygen delivered at 15 liters per minute by nonrebreather mask is indicated.

(G)

- Assessing pulse
- Assessing skin
- Assessing/controlling severe bleeding

(H)

- Use of an oropharyngeal airway
- Use of high-flow oxygen
- Cooling the patient as indicated

This is a high-priority patient.

(I)
rapid assessment focused history vital signs

Because the patient is unresponsive, a full head-to-toe rapid assessment is needed because the area of focus cannot be limited by patient response.

(J)
No.

(K)
Make sure to include the following information in your patient report:

- Patient's identifying data
- Chief complaint
- Priority level
- Level of responsiveness
- Airway, breathing, and circulation status
- Results of the focused assessment
- All interventions made, the patient's response to those interventions, and the current status of the patient

continued

Clinical Application 6–6 Continued

Example Transfer of Patient Care Report

This is Mrs. Jan Smith. She is a 43-year-old female with an altered mental status due to a sudden seizure that lasted about a minute and a half. Jan is a high-priority patient. She is unresponsive to any stimuli. Following the seizure, she had snoring respirations that were corrected by the use of an OPA. Respirations are 12, full and regular, pulse is 80, strong and regular, and blood pressure is 128/74. Her skin is flushed, but cool and clammy. The rapid assessment was unremarkable. She has a known allergy to penicillin and has a 5-year history of high blood pressure with associated unknown prescription medication. The seizure took place approximately 10 minutes ago. Currently, we have an oropharyngeal airway in place, high-flow supplemental oxygen, and are trying to cool the patient. She remains unresponsive.

AEIOU-TIPS can be useful in remembering the possible causes:

- **A**lcohol
- **E**pilepsy
- **I**nsulin (diabetic emergency)
- **O**verdose of a drug
- **U**nderdose of a drug
- **T**rauma
- **I**nfections
- **P**sychiatric problems
- **S**hock or stroke

Seizures are one of the most common causes for a patient to suffer from an altered mental status. They can be the result of toxic reactions, brain tumors, congenital brain defects, infection, irregular body chemistry, or trauma. Convulsive seizures may be seen with epilepsy, stroke, childhood diseases, hypoglycemia, eclampsia, or hypoxia. Patient care priorities for the patient suffering from an altered mental status are early activation of EMS, aggressive intervention and maintenance of the ABCs, continual reassessment, and an accurate focused assessment. Seizures usually last no more than 1 to 3 minutes in duration. Seizures that last longer than this or multiple seizures that take place without the patient regaining full consciousness are danger signs and need immediate ALS intervention.

SUMMARY

Adequate preparation should be taken in order to reduce facility liability and to provide a safe environment for the performance of rehabilitation. All health care providers including clinicians, therapists, and assistants should maintain current CPR and first aid certifications. Providing BSI precautions is a must in the health care industry, regardless of the type of facility. Being able to implement predetermined plans of action will serve to significantly lower the risk of liability in the event that an incident does occur. Ensuring adequate supervision of the patients is key in the prevention of injuries due to improper use of exercise equipment.

This chapter was designed to provide the clinician/therapist with a brief review of important emergency skills and considerations that may need to be implemented in the event of injury or illness. It is not intended to replace formal training and certification.

Remember that the best risk management is quality supervision of patients and staff. Make every attempt to try to anticipate problems before they occur, and be able to react to them in an appropriate manner if and when they do.

REFERENCES

1. Kenney WL, et al (editors). *ACSM's Guidelines for Exercise Testing and Prescription*, Fifth Edition. Williams and Wilkins, 1995:8.
2. Gibbons LW, Blair SN, Kohl HW, Cooper KH. The safety of maximal exercise testing. *Circulation*. 1989;80:846–852.

3. Kenney WL, et al (editors). ACSM's *Guidelines for Exercise Testing and Prescription*, Fifth Edition. Williams and Wilkins, 1995:12.
4. Kenney WL, et al (editors), ACSM's *Guidelines for Exercise Testing and Prescription*, Fifth Edition. Williams and Wilkins, 1995:41–43.
5. Kenney WL, et al (editors). ACSM's *Guidelines for Exercise Testing and Prescription*, Fifth Edition. Williams and Wilkins, 1995:253.
6. American Heart Association.
7. Garnham P. OSHA: Trials of compliance. *Emergency*. 1994:26(11).
8. *NAEMT Pre-Hospital Trauma Life Support: Basic and Advanced*, Third Edition. Mosby-Lifeline, 1994.
9. Ruple JA. Inspiring confidence in oxygen therapy. *Journal of Emergency Medical Services*. 1990; Nov.
10. *NAEMT Pre-Hospital Trauma Life Support: Basic and Advanced*, Third Edition. Mosby-Lifeline, 1994.
11. *NAEMT Pre-Hospital Trauma Life Support: Basic and Advanced*, Third Edition. Mosby-Lifeline, 1994.
12. Stoy W. *EMT—Basic Curriculum Update Kit*. Mosby, 1995.
13. Occupational Exposure to Bloodborne Pathogens, U.S. Dept of Labor, Occupational Safety and Health Administration, OSHA 3127, 1992.
14. Forgues M. Airway: Step one. *Emergency*. 1990;22(2).
15. Forgues M. Airway: Step one. *Emergency*. 1990;22(2).
16. Smith S. Suctioning the airway. *Emergency*. 1993;25(3).
17. Stoy W. *EMT—Basic Curriculum Update Kit*. Mosby, 1995.
18. Bongard S, Sue DY. *Current Critical Care Diagnosis and Treatment*. Appleton and Lange, 1994:32.
19. Effron DM, ed. *Cardiopulmonary Resuscitation CPR*, Fourth Edition. CPR Publishers, 1993.

SECTION

II

Evaluation Principles and Applications

A wise man should consider that health is the greatest of human blessings, and learn how by his own thought to derive benefit from his illness.

—*Hippocrates (460-377* B.C.*)*

The trouble is not in science but in the uses men make of it. Doctor and layman alike must learn wisdom in their employment of science.

—*Wilder Penfield*

CHAPTER 7

Advanced Issues Associated with the Focused Orthopedic Evaluation

Michael J. Nehring, DC

INTRODUCTION

Over the past two decades the number and variety of diagnostic tests for patients with back and neck pain have grown significantly, with associated rises in health care costs. There are legitimate questions being raised about the necessity of many of these tests considering diagnostic sensitivity and specificity. The diagnostic accuracy of history taking, physical examination, and erythrocyte sedimentation rate in general practice settings remains unclear to a substantial extent when using single clinical parameters.[1] The impact of managed care and the increased understanding of the natural course of nonpathological spinal pain conditions have lead to close evaluation of diagnostic protocols. Advanced anatomic and physiologic tests within the first month should be reserved for patients with red flags for serious pathologic conditions on clinical examination. Guidelines for the testing of patients with chronic back and neck pain have yet to be developed, and stronger emphasis on psychosocial issues and assurance that pathologic progression has not been missed without the use of repetitive testing form the mainstay of diagnostic protocols for these patients.[2]

In the past the majority of patients needing evaluation for physical rehabilitation were those for whom health care had essentially failed, often in spite of extensive diagnostic workup and treatment interventions. Now however, patients who remain significantly symptomatically expressive and/or functionally impaired must be considered the exception rather than the rule. Of patients with low back pain 10% consume approximately 80% of the health care dollars in workers compensation claims.[3–5] The University of Florida Center for Exercise Science and the University of California Spine and Joint Conditioning Center have reported that current epidemiological literature on the natural history of soft tissue injuries indicates that nearly 90% will resolve spontaneously within 90 days regardless of the type of intervention (including none). Other longitudinal studies have suggested that back and neck pain are typically recurrent conditions and that chronic phases of pain of variable presentation occur more often than previously believed.[6–7]

It is well known that undifferentiated cells often promote soft tissue injury repair, particularly if the injury is localized and these cells may contribute to the expected natural course of resolution. Some of the more gradual degenerative processes, the overall reduced physical fitness associated with aging, and recurrent episodes of aggravation experienced by many people may at least partially explain recurrent acute and/or chronic pain complaints. Applications for permanent disability benefits are now at record highs, although there are no data suggesting that the incidence of disabling injuries or conditions has increased. It appears that current societal woes should be confronted in order to address the needs of increasingly disabled persons.

The orthopedic evaluation of spinal pain must take place in the context of current understandings of pain. Different individuals' pain perception for the same injury may range from mild to extreme and disabling. Obviously, a patient's pain experience is highly personalized and subjective. Orthopedic evaluation therefore must begin with a thorough review of medical documentation, detailed case history, consideration of the psychosocial milieu, and overall physical assessment of the patient.

PAIN COMPLEXITY

Pain is a subjective experience with two complementary aspects: One is a localized sensation in a particular body part, and the other is an unpleasant quality of varying severity commonly associated with behaviors directed at relieving or terminating the experience.[8] The way in which a patient experiences and manifests pain is dependent on a complex conglomeration of physiologic, psychologic, social, and cultural variables, prior painful experiences, and previous interactions with health care professionals. Moreover, certain personality characteristics appear to predispose a patient to experience prolonged pain.

For approximately the first 3 months physiologic factors dominate the experience of pain. Tissue damage initiates a cascade of cellular and humoral reactions that may sustain and amplify pain. Sensitization hyperactivity of the sympathetic nervous system, muscle contraction, and self-sustaining painful processes are all part of the physiology of pain.[9] Beyond 3 months, however, psychosocial factors associated with pain often complicate the patient's recovery. Social and psychologic stress can manifest itself in the first weeks of work disability and the onset of financial hardship.[10] Melzack and Wall have identified several important psychologic factors in the subjective sensation of pain: (1) cultural factors; (2) previous experience of pain; (3) the meaning of the context in which pain is experienced; (4) the degree of attention, anxiety, or distraction given to the pain; (5) the impression of control over the pain; and (6) the autosuggestion and placebo effect from outside influences.

In physical rehabilitation programs a high percentage of patients attribute their injuries to work, motor vehicle accidents, or other incidents. Weintraub reported that psychogenic pain was present in 63% of patients with chronic posttraumatic pain. Many of these patients are involved in litigation. Furthermore, statistical analysis has revealed that patients involved in litigation for longer periods of time are more likely to have pain of psychogenic origins.[11]

Gildenberg and DeVaul recommended that efforts should be made to identify nonphysical barriers to recovery, e.g., compensation and disability payments or lawsuits. In their opinion such considerations can sometimes compromise a patient's willingness to participate fully in rehabilitation and result in prolonged reporting of elevated levels of subjective pain and disability. Tarola suggested that the "process of litigation" might in itself be detrimental, particularly for those patients who enter the medicolegal arena shortly after injury or for those who are predisposed to litigation by premorbid personality.[12] Increased anxiety associated with psychosocial, economic, and behavioral pattern changes may all contribute to the development of chronic pain.

Because of the subjective nature of pain, there has been a movement toward functional assessment that can be more objectively measured. For additional psychosocial considerations please refer to Chapter 11. At the time of reevaluation, it is helpful if the therapist reviews with the patient the original complaints and then compares that level of function to the level reported and observed during rehabilitation. Reminding patients of their initial status and the progress that they made during rehabilitation increases their accuracy on reported pain rating scales, low back/neck disability indexes, functional assessment questionnaires, and the like. Although none of this is orthopedic evaluation, it is helpful to obtain such data initially and during the course of rehabilitation so that the assessment and case management decisions are appropriate.

DIAGNOSTIC DILEMMA AND RED FLAGS

In most cases of back pain, the exact source of the pain may be difficult, if not impossible, to confirm.[13] Diagnostic inaccuracy is estimated to be as high as 80% in patients with low back pain, depending on the interpretation of radiographic degenerative changes.[14] Other studies have suggested that a definitive diagnosis is impossible in up to 85% of patients because of weak associations among symptoms, pathologic changes, and imaging results.[15–16]

In primary care, only about 4% of patients with back pain prove to have compression fractures, 3% have spondylolisthesis, and less than 1% have spinal malignant neoplasms (primary or metastatic).[17,18] Even fewer have ankylosing spondylitis (approximately 0.3%) or spinal infections (0.01%).[19–22] A previous history of cancer has such high specificity that such patients should be considered to have cancer until proven otherwise.[23] However, only one-third of patients with an underlying malignant neoplasm have this history. Unexplained weight loss, pain duration greater than 1 month, and failure to improve with conservative therapy are moderately specific findings.[24] Most patients with back pain due to cancer report that pain is unrelieved by bed rest (sensitivity > 0.90), but the finding is nonspecific. In a study of nearly 2000 patients with back pain, no cancer was identified in any patient under age 50 years without a history of cancer, unexplained weight loss, or a failure of conservative therapy (combined sensitivity 1.00).[25] Spinal infections usually are bloodborne from other sites, including urinary tract infections, indwelling urinary catheters, skin infections, and injection sites for illicit intravenous drugs. In IV drug abusers an intravenous injection site is identified in approximately 40% of patients with spinal infections.[26] Patients with generalized osteoporosis are prone to compression fracture, even without apparent trauma. A person with back pain with a history of long-term corticosteroid therapy must be considered to have a compression fracture until proven otherwise (specificity 0.99). African-American and Mexican-American women have only one-fourth as many compression fractures as white women.[27]

Although plain film radiography is considered a reasonable evaluation of degenerative and inflammatory joint disease, fracture, infection, and neoplasm, there is unreliable correlation between patient complaints of mechanical pain and objective findings on plain film studies.[28–30] Imaging of a strain/sprain injury is invariably normal, for example. Moreover, even when radiographic findings are abnormal in the patient with low back pain, it is necessary to investigate further to determine the clinical significance.

A prospective investigation into the incidence of abnormal magnetic resonance scans of the lumbar spine in asymptomatic people revealed that approximately one-third of the test subjects had a substantial abnormality. Of those subjects less than 60 years of age, 20% had a herniated nucleus pulposus and one had spinal stenosis. In the group that was 60 years or older, abnormal findings were present on 57% of the scans; 36% of the subjects had a herniated nucleus pulposus, and 21% had spinal stenosis. At least one disc was degenerating or bulging on at least one level in 35% of the subjects between 20 and 39 years of age and in all but one of the 60- to 80-year old subjects.[31] Other studies of special imaging have reported anatomic evidence of herniated disc(s) in 20% to 30% of imaging tests [myelography, computed tomography (CT) and magnetic resonance imaging (MRI)] among asymptomatic persons. A normal imaging study does not rule out involvement of nociceptive structures. Imaging findings of potential significance must be confirmed by correlation with the patient's age, presentation, and clinical signs/symptoms.

The case history gives the examiner an understanding of the nature of the patient's complaint that will lead to preliminary diagnostic considerations. Various authors have reported that data obtained strictly from case history have provided clinically significant information, with relatively high diagnostic accuracy.[32–34] Taking the time to investigate further the patient's report of nighttime pain may generally differentiate between a potentially serious pathologic condition and a simply painful mechanical condition.

As part of the history of a back problem, certain critical factors must be carefully evaluated. The relationship of the pain to a "traumatic event" must be carefully assessed and documented because of the potential medicolegal significance. Suspicion of a substantial skeletal or visceral injury may predispose the evaluating physician to obtain certain diagnostic tests. On the other hand, a pattern of pain that is unrelenting, unresponsive to rest, is present primarily at night, or is related to other systemic manifestations (e.g., fever, weakness, unexplained weight loss, lassitude) may alert the physician to back pain of neoplastic, metabolic, infectious, or inflammatory etiology. These are the red flags that we all must be cognizant of. Furthermore, it is important to investigate the possibility of significant neurologic complaints that are affecting motor and sensory function in the extremities or bowel/bladder function, as well as any correlation of pain to posture.[35] For back pain, Cox noted several findings that differentiate disc pathology from tumor (Table 7–1).

The correlation of sciatic neuralgia with lumbar intervertebral disc herniation is so high (0.95) that its absence makes a clinically significant herniation unlikely when there is only localized back pain.[36] Sciatica is often intensified by coughing, sneezing, or straining with bowel movements (Dejerine's triad). The most common cause of sciatica is disc herniation, but other causes of spinal nerve root entrapment may include degenerative changes contributing to bony or ligamentous hypertrophy, congenital or developmental spinal stenosis, intramedullary or extramedullary tumors, and spinal or paraspinal infections. Hypertonicity of the piriformis muscle has been attributed to sciatic neuralgia. According to McCullough[37] the criteria for the diagnosis of sciatic neuralgia caused by intervertebral disc herniation are as follows:

1. Leg pain rather than back pain is the dominant symptom. It affects one leg only and follows a typical sciatic (or femoral) nerve distribution.
2. Paresthesias are localized to a dermatomal distribution.
3. Straight leg raising is reduced by 50% of normal, pain crosses over to the symptomatic leg when the unaffected leg is elevated, and/or pain radiates proximally or distally with digital pressure on the tibial nerve in the popliteal fossa.

Table 7–1: Differential Diagnostic Findings of Neoplasm and Disc Protrusion

	NEOPLASM	DISC PROTRUSION
Sitting and standing	No change	Aggravation
Bilateral	Often	Seldom
Night pain	Yes	Less
Character of pain	Unrelenting	Intermittent
Cauda equina	More	Less
Onset of first leg or back pain	Back usually	Either

From Cox JM. Low Back Pain Mechanism: Diagnosis and Treatment, 4th ed. Baltimore: Williams & Wilkins, 1985.

4. Two of four neurologic signs (e.g., wasting, motor weakness, diminished sensory appreciation, and diminution of muscle stretch reflex activity) are present.
5. A contrast study is abnormal and corresponds to the clinical level. (Current imaging protocol would more likely involve MRI for disc-related consideration.)

Referred pain may result from chemical or mechanical irritation of deep spinal and paraspinal tissues other than the nerve root. Kellgren's classic studies performed in the 1930s showed that injecting a hypertonic sodium chloride solution into the paravertebral musculature and into the deeper structures, including the apophyseal joints and spinal ligaments, and scratching the periosteum with a needle elicited local and referred pain in every instance.[35] When irritated, these structures contributed to diffuse pain patterns distant from the original site of irritation. Feinstein and associates found when injected with sodium solution, patients felt pain primarily in the reflexogenic hypertonic muscles. Autonomic symptoms (e.g., paleness, excessive sweating, fainting, nausea, and lowered blood pressure) were also observed in this study. Hockaday and Whitty performed similar clinical studies with similar findings as follows[38]: The superficial fascia of the back, the spinous processes, and the supraspinous ligaments induce local pain upon stimulation, whereas stimulation of the superficial portions of the interspinous ligaments and the superficial muscles results in a diffused type of pain. The deep muscles, ligaments, and periosteum of the apophyseal joints, as well as the joints themselves, can cause referred pain according to the segmental innervation when sufficiently stimulated. Kellgren also reported that the various structures containing nociceptive fibers (e.g., muscles, ligaments, and fascia) could be palpated. Thus, specific localization of the patient's pain complaint and differential palpation techniques help to isolate the involved structures, leading to more effective treatment interventions.

Mayer and Gatchel recommended that the initial rehabilitation examination be focused on assessing a few critical parameters[39]:

- Objective evidence corroborating pain complaints (e.g., spasm, deformity, immobility)
- Evidence confirming need for possible invasive treatment (e.g., neurological deficits, facet signs)
- Evidence of systemic illness (e.g., local tenderness, general debility, fever, adenopathy)
- Evidence of symptom magnification (i.e., nonorganic signs).

PREAMBLE TO THE EXAMINATION

Although the orthopedic evaluation has been of primary importance in years past, in the current context of physical medicine, classic orthopedic tests play a less crucial role. Nonetheless, provocative orthopedic testing lends observational and diagnostic data that can sometimes further substantiate a diagnosis. Preparing the patient for examination with specific instructions may contribute to or detract from diagnostic accuracy. The instructions given to the patient, the sincerity of the patient's response, the manner in which the patient's responses to specific orthopedic tests are recorded, and the assessment of the observer are all important in establishing a reliable diagnosis. Griner and associates reported that a diagnosis is likely to be more specific when based on a combination of test results rather than a single isolated result.[40] Therefore, the performance of orthopedic evaluation for any given patient tends to take on the character of the patient, as one test leads to the performance of another or perhaps leads the examiner to proceed in a different approach to the examination.

Many orthopedic tests provoke complaints of pain or discomfort in the healthy human population. These tests are called "provocative" tests. Placing certain pain-sensitive tissues under stress should cause a reaction in a person. However, the significance of this discomfort is the key to identifying a clinically significant patient response versus a subclinical or normal response to a given test. Therefore, the patients being examined should be given instructions that they are going to be subject to numerous tests, some of which will involve movement in different directions and compression or distractive forces and that they will feel this. They should report any discomfort that they feel is significant or different when compared side by side. Furthermore, the patient should provide detailed information about the exact location of the area of complaint by pointing to it if possible and describing the nature of the complaint, i.e., sharp pain, pulling, etc. If there is just a normal amount of compression or tension that they would normally expect to experience with the test being performed, this also should be documented. Simply recording a test as "+" or "positive" does not allow another health care provider to adequately interpret the patient's response to a given test. Therefore, the examiner is expected to record detailed patient responses to the various orthopedic tests. Such information will increase diagnostic sensitivity and specificity, but will detract if inadequately documented. Also, a "+/positive" response on one date looks no different than a "+/positive" response on a later date. Case monitoring is obviously compromised by such limited documentation and I believe demonstrates a careless attitude on the behalf of the examiner.

EXAMINATION

After taking a thorough case history, the examiner should include attention to the following.

1. Observation
2. Vitals
   a. Age
   b. Height/weight

   c. Blood pressure, pulse, respiration rate
   d. CV risk profile
3. Postural assessment
4. Localization of chief complaint(s)
5. Range of motion
6. Palpation
   a. Static
   b. Dynamic/functional
   c. Area of complaint
   d. Soft tissue
   e. Bony/articular
7. Provocative testing
8. Neurological examination

OBSERVATION

The orthopedic evaluation actually begins before the patient is aware that he or she is being observed. Noting the manner in which the patient sits, arises from the seated position, ambulates, and moves in general may provide useful information. Evidence of painful movements may include grimacing, muscular splinting, or dysrhythmic movement patterns. Grimacing or verbalization of pain should be associated with protective reactions, such as limp, withdrawal reaction, or muscular guarding; verbalization of pain without associated physical reactions suggests that the examiner should pay closer attention to nonphysical signs of pain. Consistency between these initial observations and responses to similar movements and activities performed during the formal examination is indicative of anatomic/physiologic pain reaction.

Gait analysis should begin with observing the patient walk from the reception area to the office or examination room. Once in the examination room, the patient's ability to untie shoes and remove a jacket and other garments gives additional functional indicators.

The patient's general appearance and general health of the skin should be observed. The presence of a hairy tuft in the lumbosacral region is thought to be indicative of spina bifida or possibly diastematomyelia. Café au lait spots often accompany neurofibromas. An expanding neurofibroma may cause structural bony alteration, as well as contribute to neurological compression or tension.

VITALS

Baseline measures of blood pressure, pulse, and respiration, as well as a cardiovascular risk profile should be obtained. Certainly, patients with cardiovascular risk must be screened prior to suggestion of any form of vigorous activity. At-risk patients require additional evaluation that is beyond the scope of this chapter.

POSTURE

The examiner should observe the patient's posture from the anterior, posterior, and lateral aspects. Forward head carriage with cervicothoracic prominence and anterior pelvic tilt may contribute to myofascial or facet joint discomfort. From the anteroposterior view the head should appear in the midline, with level ears. The sternum should be directly above the umbilicus, with symmetric rib cage. Viewed posteriorly, the shoulders, scapula, and iliac crests should be level. There is commonly a right midthoracic convexity, which is a generally a normal variant. Idiopathic scoliosis, a lateral curvature of unknown cause, is by far the most common spinal curvature abnormality of childhood.[41] Unusual or atypical signs or symptoms associated with scoliosis include (1) Pain in younger patients, (2) Paresthesias or weakness, and (3) rapid curve progression.[42] A striking association of progressive left thoracic or thoracolumbar convexity with hydrosyringomyelia has been reported.[43] In uncomplicated scoliosis plain radiography is sufficient. Atypical presentation, however, warrants MRI study of the axial spinal column.

The identification of postural or fatigue-related aggravating factors of spinal complaints necessitates more detailed postural assessment. Muscles produce and control motion throughout the body. The trunk and pelvic muscles serve as dynamic stabilizers of the spine. In muscle, there are primary afferent nociceptors that respond to pressure, muscle contraction, and irritating chemicals.[44–46] Muscle contraction under conditions of ischemia, such as static prolonged posture or activity, is an especially potent stimulus for some of these nociceptors.[47] When injury occurs or joint integrity is compromised, pain is produced, and function may be affected.[48] Tissue injury initiates a host of chemical and humoral changes that result in pain-producing chemicals activating or sensitizing primary afferent nociceptors.[49–52] All of the pain-producing chemicals are found in increased concentrations in regions of inflammation as well as pain.

Once a joint loses normal range of motion, the surrounding muscles may attempt to minimize stress by increasing postural muscle tone in the area. Such muscle tension can result in muscular fatigue, pain, and imbalance. Less gross muscular activity occurs, leading to deconditioning. The ongoing reinforcement of atypical motor patterns appears to bring about central nervous system learning, and the motor pathology becomes functional. Janda has suggested that postural muscles tend to shorten and become hypertonic, whereas phasic muscles are inhibited and weaken. The weak and protruded abdomen is often associated with hypertonic paralumbar muscles and tight hamstrings, with corresponding posterior torso carriage and/or hyperlordosis. Janda[52] suggests the following muscular characteristics:

Postural muscles (tend toward shortening and hyperactivity)	Phasic muscles (tend toward weakening and hypoactivity or inhibition)
1. Gastrocnemius/soleus	1. Peronei
2. Tibialis posterior	2. Tibialis anterior
3. Short hip adductors	3. Vastus medialis, vastus lateralis

4. Hamstrings	4. Gluteus maximus
5. Iliopsoas	5. Gluteus medius and minimus
6. Tensor fascia lata	6. Rectus abdominus
7. Pectoralis major	7. Rhomboids

Imrie and Barbuto[53] have developed a concise series of simple back power tests that have been suggested as a useful evaluation to determine muscular deconditioning and contracture. These simple tests include:

1. The flexed hip/knee sit-up: Performed as a standard sit-up with feet flat on the floor without support to ensure recruitment of the lower rectus abdominus. Tests for spinal flexibility and lower abdominal strength.
2. The double straight leg raise test: Requires sustained elevation of 6 inches with both legs while lumbar spine is kept pressed flat to the floor. Evaluates abdominal muscle strength.
3. The knee-chest test: With leg bent, knee is brought ipsilaterally to chest. The other leg remains flat on the floor. Tests flexibility of hip flexors.
4. The lateral torso lift test: In a side-lying position, both legs are stabilized at the ankles by the examiner. Patient lifts trunk off the floor. Performed bilaterally. Tests strength of lateral trunk and hip muscles.

LOCALIZATION OF CHIEF COMPLAINT(S)

It is now the examiner's task to attempt to identify where the patient's pain complaint stems from and the source of pain. Therefore, it is important that the patient be asked to specifically point to the area(s) of complaint. Many patients will report experiencing shoulder pain or hip pains, but in fact they are experiencing pain in the trapezius or gluteal muscles. The examiner should perform a detailed palpation of the area of complaint, trying to identify what tissue/structure may be involved. Muscular or tendon pain should be reproduced upon muscular contraction, with or without joint motion. Direct pressure on the palpation of the injured tissue should cause much greater pain than palpation of the surrounding tissues. Henninger has discussed the importance of differentiating between a contractile (muscle or tendon) versus noncontractile tissue (ligament, fascia, capsule, bursae, dura mater, and nerve roots).[54] In order to make this distinction the examiner uses isometric testing, together with passive and active range of motion examination. If isometric resistance provokes pain, the contractile tissue is likely involved. It is important to note at what point in motion pain develops. Pain before the stressing of the ligaments at end range indicates the involvement of a muscle or tendon, rather than a ligament.

In the cervical spine joints between C2 and C3 are referred to as the "headache joints", whereas joints below C4 contribute to shoulder and upper extremity symptoms. Disc herniations in the cervical spine are most common at the C5/C6 level and occur in both symptomatic and asymptomatic patients.[55–58] In the thoracic spine pain results most often from joint dysfunction involving the costovertebral or facet articulations. Thoracic intervertebral disc herniation is rare, accounting for perhaps 1 in 200 protruded discs.[59] In the lumbar spine, the L4/5 and L5/S1 levels account for 98% of all lumbar disc syndromes.[60] This is probably because biomechanical stress is increased at these levels.

PALPATION

At the end of active range of motion is a subtle passive motion that is essential for joint health and neuromusculoskeletal coordination. This motion is called joint play. The integrity of joint motion and the concept of joint play are a useful assessment for somatic dysfunction. Kisner and Colby[61] have developed a convenient seven-point grading system of joint stability as follows:

0 = No movement at all: ankylosis
1 = Hypomobile: moderate to severe limitation of movement
2 = Hypomobile: mild to slight limitation of movement
3 = Normal
4 = Hypermobile: mild to slight increase in movement
5 = Hypermobile: moderate to severe increase in movement
6 = Complete instability

Joint play can also be described in terms of the nature of joint passive motion. Utilizing overpressure palpation to stress the capsular and ligamentous status in multiple planes of motion may yield additional clinical findings that are not identifiable in linear range of motion or traditional joint stress testing. Such data are helpful in confirming the involved nociceptive tissue(s) and site of involvement. However, subclinical areas of tenderness and dysfunction do exist, and unless there is clinical correlation of the area of findings to the patient's area(s) of complaint, palpatory findings would be considered to be subclinical and secondary information.

Secondary to rule-out considerations, detailed palpation examination may elicit tenderness about the apophyseal joint or peripheral joints, often with associated reflexogenic soft tissue changes, which leads to the diagnosis of joint dysfunction.[62–63] The common soft tissue findings of tenderness and altered tonus in conjunction with joint dysfunction lead Sutter, based upon empirical and clinical observations, to coin the term "spondylogenic reflex syndrome."[64] Because of the altered position of a given spinal articulation, there is repetitive suprathreshold stimulation of the mechano- and nociceptive receptors, primarily of the joint capsules and spinal ligamentous structures.[65] Such CNS-mediated activity contributes to long-standing soft tissue alteration that may contribute to tender points or trigger points. Such joint dysfunction and soft tissue findings are palpable. Joint dysfunction of this nature leads to reversible, objectively demonstrable impairments of mobility in the appropriate skeletal segment.[66]

During examination of joint play, pressure should be applied using small oscillatory movements in multiple directions (lateral flexion, flexion, extension, rotation, and distraction in some joints) into the paraphysiological joint range. It is at this level that one appreciates the "joint play" of the paraphysiological range of motion. This motion is normally associated with a springy end feel. Going beyond this joint motion usually results in joint cavitation, and accesses the paraphysiological joint range, the end of which is the anatomical integrity of the joint capsule and ligaments. Therefore, there are actually four ranges of joint motion: (1) active, (2) passive, (3) paraphysiological zone, and (4) pathological zone of movement (beyond the anatomical integrity of the capsule and ligaments).[67,68]

Henninger[54] has described paraphysiological end play as follows:

> *Normal soft tissue resistance:* No further joint motion possible due to engagement of end range of soft tissue extensibility. This is associated with a soft, springy type of feel, with increasing tension as greater force is applied.
> *Bone against bone:* Abrupt cessation of joint motion. This may be normal, such as at the end range of elbow extension, or aberrant if it occurs prematurely, e.g., in the cervical spine of a patient with advanced degenerative joint disease with bony ankylosis or near ankylosis.
> *Spring block:* Mechanical blockage associated with intraarticular joint derangement, e.g., menisci that contribute to premature blockage of motion. The joint play feeling is similar to normal tissue stretch, but occurs prematurely.
> *Capsular:* Similar to normal tissue stretch, but occurs much earlier and is associated with significant decrease of range of motion. There are two subtypes to this category: (1) the soft capsular type, which is seen most often in acute conditions due to swelling that causes joint stiffness that presents early in the ROM and intensifies with greater motion, and (2) the hard capsular type that is generally of a more chronic nature due to capsular hypertrophy, adhesions, and/or muscle shortening.
> *Myospasm:* Often painful, with abrupt or hard end feel. It may occur during initial ROM, when it is often associated with an acute and inflamed condition, or later in motion, associated with a protective spasm compensating for joint instability.
> *Empty feeling:* Movement associated with significant pain. Partial ligament damage will contribute to softer than normal end feel. A lack of normal resistance, with inability to progress further into ROM due to pain suggests conditions such as acute bursitis, extraarticular abscess, or neoplasm.
> *Early hard end feel:* Typical of joint dysfunction and often associated with the "catch" described by patients. It is characterized by premature restriction of motion, similar to bone on bone but not as abrupt, and is often uncomfortable, but rarely extremely painful.

Mennell has reported pain and impairment associated with loss of joint play. Mennell also reports that joint dysfunction cannot be radiographically identified, and that it is necessary for normal efficient motion in anything that moves, including the human body.[69] The majority of researchers assessing the significance of passive intersegmental joint mobility value this examination procedure in the overall assessment of painful conditions.[70–73] Boline and associates found good to excellent interexaminer reliability of palpation for pain, both osseous and soft tissue.[73a] McCombe and associates reported that bony tenderness was more reliable than soft tissue tenderness in a study of the reproducibility of physical signs of lower back pain.[74]

The articular neuroanatomy and interactions between proprioceptive aberrations contributing to articular nociception are one of the theoretical models that appear to explain why spinal manipulation reduces back or neck pain for some people. Kirkaldy-Willis and Tchang suggested that pain relief as a result of manipulation directed to a specific joint is diagnostic evidence of dysfunction of that joint.[75] Beal also suggested that a positive response to manipulation contributes to the differential diagnosis of joint dysfunction.[76] Without the necessary palpatory or other premanipulative evaluations, however, the appropriate patient candidate will be passed over for manipulative care.

Based upon White and Panjabi's spinal biomechanical studies[77] Dvorik and Dvorik have proposed various procedures of functional spinal evaluation.[78] The cervical spine functional evaluation includes rotation from the neutral position, rotation from the flexed position, forced rotation of the axis with lateral flexion (lateral bending), and examination of axis rotation. In rotation from the neutral position it is noted that this movement occurs throughout the entire cervical spine and extends inferior to the first four thoracic vertebrae. Movement should be equal and symmetric from side to side (Figure 7–1).

Rotation from the flexed position precludes contribution from the lower cervical segments since they are locked in position via the flexion posture. Therefore, additional rotation from this flexed position primarily occurs as a result of atlantoaxial rotation and normally measures 45 degrees side to side (Figure 7–2). A reduction of motion, especially if noted unilaterally, may be reflective of joint dysfunction, with hypomobility of the atlantoaxial articulation. Movement in excess of this usually is due to inadequate flexion, and rarely to disruption of the alar ligament. However, this consideration certainly needs to be ruled out if suspected.

Forced rotation of the axis with lateral flexion results from coupling motions. Functional palpation examination

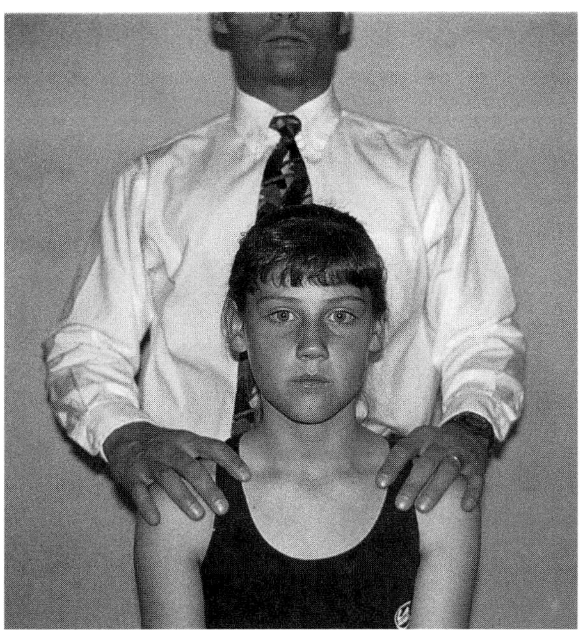

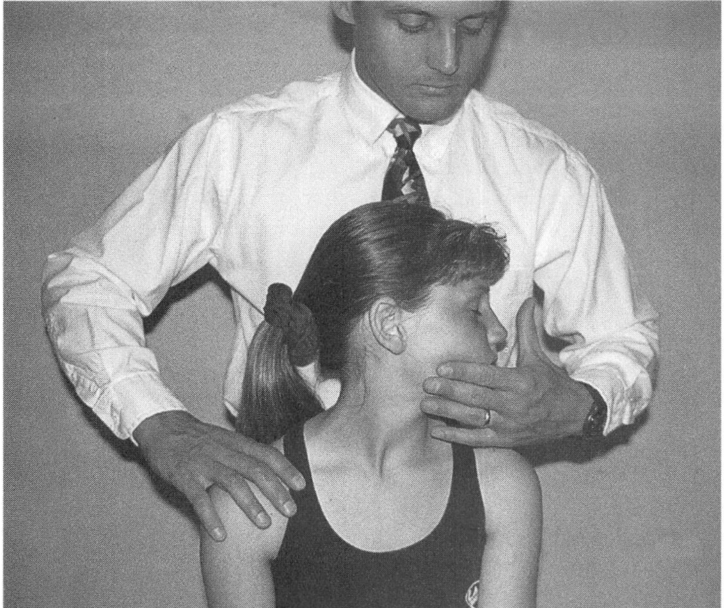

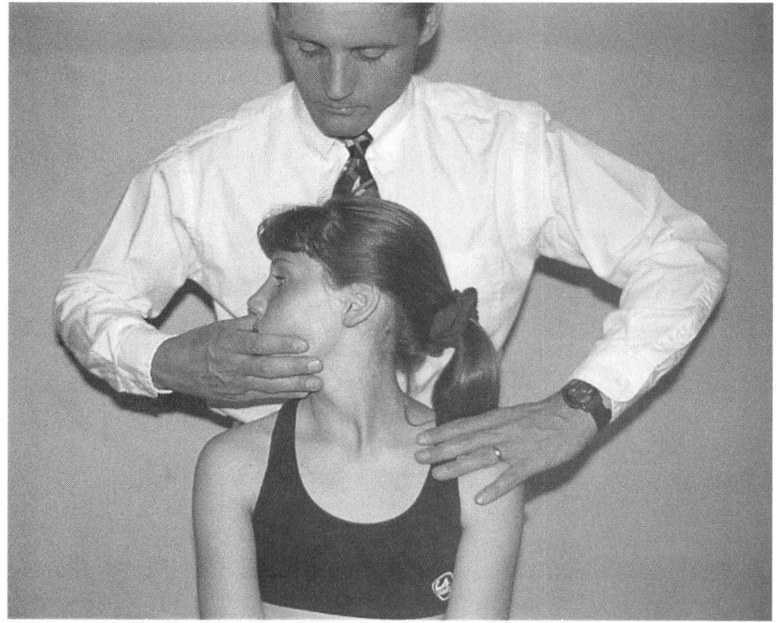

Figure 7–1. The patient's neutral upright head posture is observed. The patient is asked to fully rotate his or her neck to end range to the left and then to the right side. Observation is made not only comparing end range of motion, but also the speed and quality of movement. The point at which or during which pain is felt should be recorded.

of the lower cervical spine includes evaluation of the coupling patterns of lateral flexion and rotation. The patient must be seated upright. When the head is laterally flexed, the spinous processes normally move in the direction of the convexity. Placing the patient's head/neck in a position of extension effectively locks the occipital, atlantal, and axial joint complex, thereby allowing rotation to occur essentially exclusively in the lower cervical segments (Figure 7–3). Rotation from the extended position should again be symmetric, with normal end range reported as 60 degrees.[79,80]

Rotation of the head normally begins at the atlantoaxial level, and rotation of the lower cervical segments occurs secondary to end range atlantoaxial rotation. To examine axis rotation, the clinician palpates the axis spinous process and manually rotates the patient's head. Palpation of the spinous processes of the cervical spine should find the spinous processes rotating to the side of rotation of the head. The coupling patterns and intersegmental ranges of motion are greater and more easily detectable in the upper cervical spine (C1/C3) than in the lower cervical spine. Normally, rotation of the axis is not appreciable until approximately 25 to 30 degrees of head/cervical rotation have occurred. Premature axis rotation is indicative of hypomobility in the occipital, atlantal, and axial complex.

Lewit suggested that the thoracic functional spinal evaluation is best performed with the patient seated.[81]

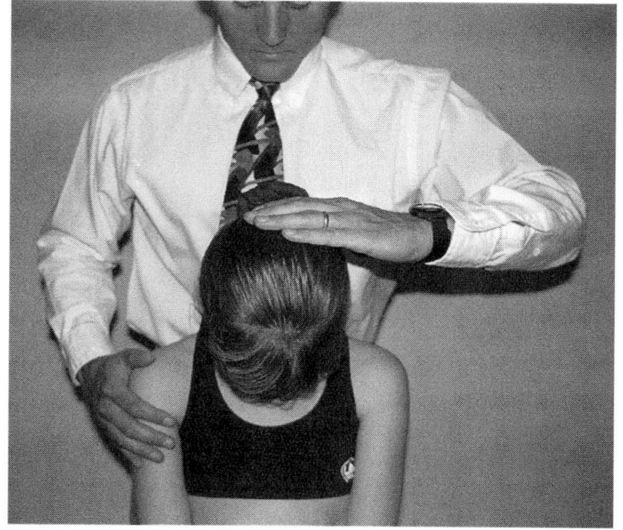

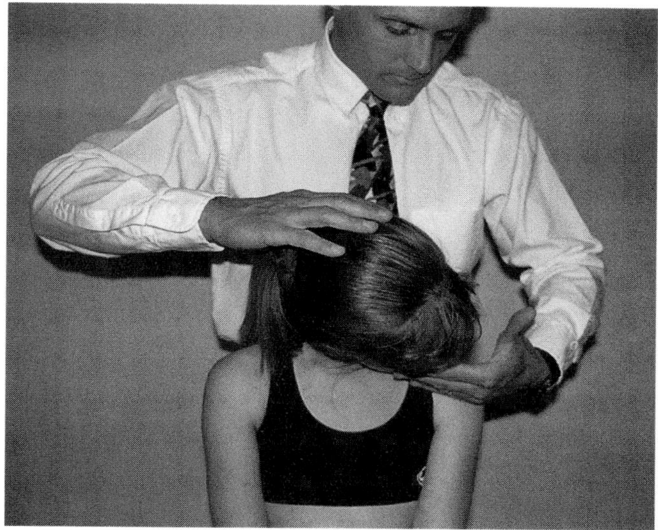

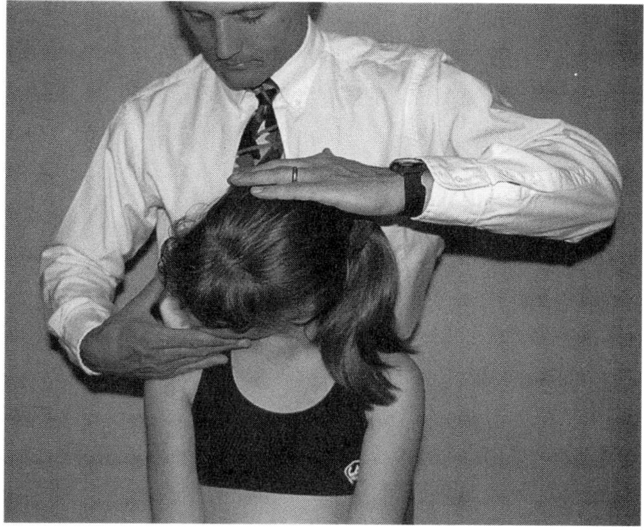

Figure 7–2. From a fully flexed neck posture the patient is asked to actively rotate his or her neck to the end range, which is performed bilaterally. Documenting this functional movement should include the degree of rotation as well as specific findings in terms of quality of movement and patient complaints.

Testing of flexion/extension, lateral bending, and rotation and inspection and palpation of the intercostal spaces are components of the examination. The patient is seated, with the hands clasped behind the head. The examiner grasps the patient's elbows and conducts passive flexion/extension of the trunk while palpating the spinous processes for excursion. The interspinous space should open and close upon flexion and extension, respectively.

During lateral bending, the examiner is behind the patient and places the guiding arm beneath the patient's axilla, across the chest to the opposite shoulder. In this manner the examiner has control of the patient and can induce lateral bending while palpating the spinous processes. The spinous processes should move toward the convexity during side bending. In the same position as just referenced, the patient is passively rotated from the waist. End range rotation is performed while the examiner with the free hand palpates the spinous processes, again assessing and comparing the excursion of motion. Finally, the intercostal spaces should be observed and palpated in the prone and supine positions. Examination of joint play of the costovertebral and costosternal articulations can be performed as well. While the patient is sitting, the patient's arm on the side being examined can be lifted, thus allowing the examiner to palpate the intercostal spaces during the raising and lowering of the arm and thereby the torso. Any asymmetries can be assessed in this manner.

Functional examination of the lumbar spine tests the three axes of motion. In flexion/extension the intersegmental motion is greatest at the lumbosacral junction, with diminishing motion going up the lumbar spine. Rotation is also greatest at the lumbosacral junction because of the facet articulation orientation.[82] Lateral bending is the least at the lumbosacral junction, and increases incrementally as you ascend. Palpation of the spinous processes and interspinous spaces is performed while side-lying for flexion/extension. The patient is asked to bring the knees towards the chest. The examiner can grasp the knees and flex and

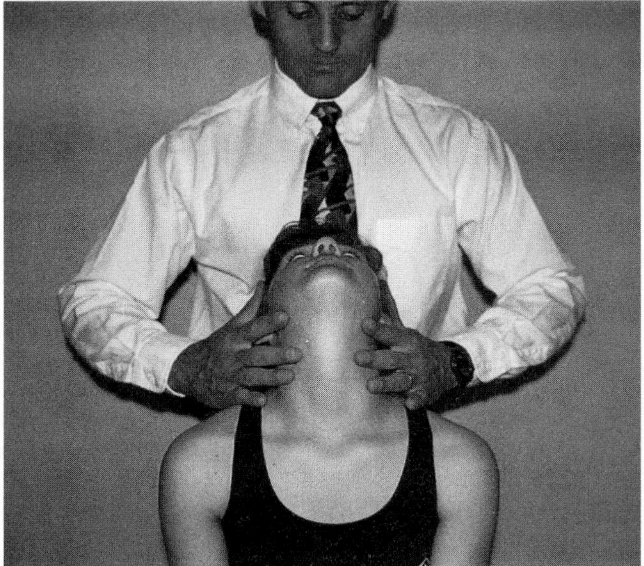

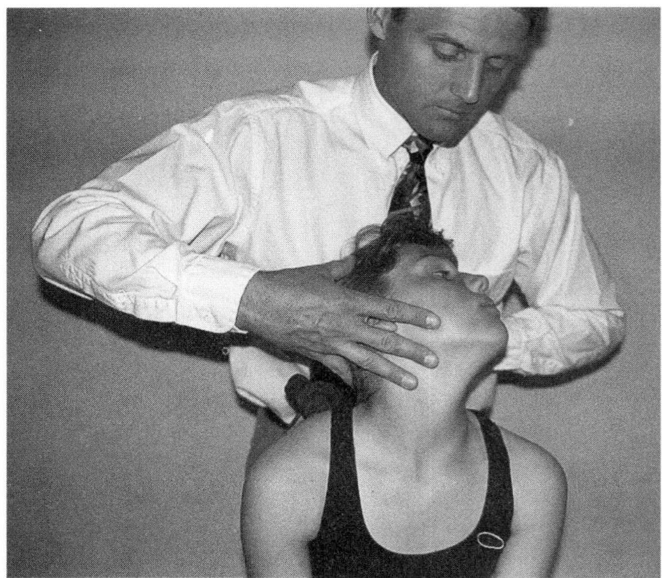

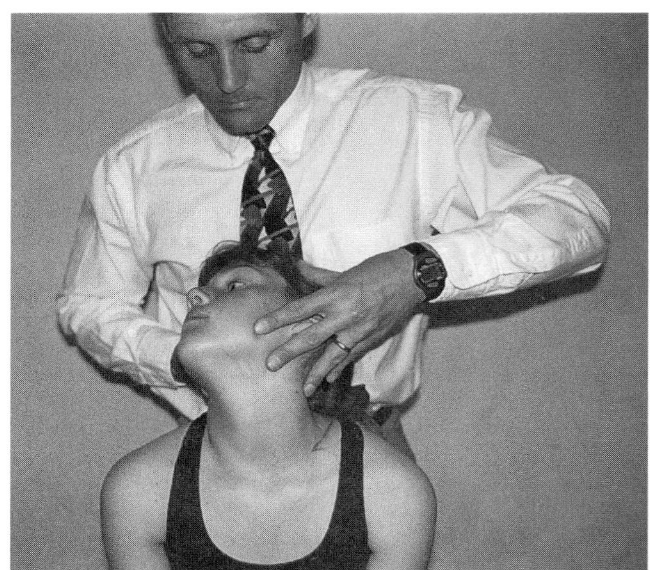

Figure 7–3. The patient is asked to fully extend the neck and then to rotate to end range to the left and to the right. The examiner notes the degree of rotation as well as quality of movement and any associated subjective complaints. Because of the possibility of vertebral artery compromise, the examiner must be in position to observe the patient's facial expressions as well as eye movements. If there is any indication of vertebral artery compromise, the patient should be immediately repositioned to neutral and monitored closely as appropriate. *Do not repeat this test if vertebral artery deficiencies are suspected.*

extend the patient's pelvis and lumbar spine by flexing the patient's trunk via the flexed hips/knees. Lateral bending can be palpated in the same manner by raising the knees as high as possible.

These same motions can also be assessed while the patient is seated, with the examiner standing behind the patient. The guiding hand/arm is placed across the anterior upper torso, with the palpating hand over the spinous processes and interspinous spaces. Counterpressure from the guiding arm/hand and the palpating hand can be applied in flexion/extension, as well as lateral bending to assess these motions. Likewise, with the patient seated in an upright manner, the examiner can guide the patient through rotation. However, rotation of the lower back region is quite minimal, and can only be reliably appreciated at the lumbosacral junction. During rotation the examiner palpates the L5 spinous process and the first sacral median crest. Upon rotation the distance between these structures should increase, although intersegmental rotation is limited to only 5 to 6 degrees at this level, and even less in the higher lumbar segments.

Pelvic or sacroiliac joint examination can be performed with the patient standing and the examiner kneeling behind the patient. The examiner places one thumb on the posterior superior iliac spine (PSIS) of the side being examined, with the other thumb on the superior sacral median crest. The patient is asked to raise the leg on the side of PSIS palpation (march in place). This is done slowly. Normal motion is for the PSIS to move inferiorly and laterally. If the sacroiliac (SI) joint nutation motion is restricted, the PSIS may move superiorly due to pelvic hiking on the contralateral side. The mechanics of this test are consistent with those described by Gillet. This is the most commonly utilized test to check for SI joint mobility.[83] Herzog et al found this test to be reliable.[84]

PROVOCATIVE (ORTHOPEDIC) TESTING

Subjecting an area of joint dysfunction to compressive or distractive forces is likely to trigger nociceptive and mechanoreceptive input. However, there is no one orthopedic test that is pathognomonic for joint dysfunction. It is secondary to close localization of the patient's area of complaint, detailed palpation of the bony, articular and soft tissue structures, and then keen interpretation of the results of provocative testing that one reasonably concludes the presence of joint dysfunction, or some other etiological consideration. The majority of orthopedic tests were developed secondary to consideration of a specific diagnostic condition. However, very few orthopedic tests have been adequately studied in terms of the specificity and sensitivity of the test for the specific presumed condition. Therefore, it is via the sum total consideration of information available that diagnostic accuracy is enhanced.

Cervical, midback and upper back evaluation

Cervical compression testing is most commonly provocative for articular somatic dysfunction with associated nociceptive stimulation via the positioning and compressive forces of these tests. The patient should be evaluated in multiple positions via compression testing. However, it is important to initially simply place the patient in the various positions of testing before applying any manual compressive forces over the vertex of the cranium. Active range of motion examination is often predictive of the patient's response to cervical compressive loading. Observing for pain or patient verbalization of pain simply caused by the positioning should preclude any significant further compressive testing. Assuming the patient is able to tolerate active cervical ranges of motion, one can proceed further with this part of the examination.

Compression testing should be performed in maximal flexion, extension, lateral flexion left/right (Figures 7–4 and 7–5) and rotation on both sides in order to screen for somatic dysfunction and/or radicular signs and symptoms. It is important to lightly grade the amount of force applied, and to forewarn the patient of what you will be doing during this series of tests. These tests will most often elicit complaints localized to the cervical facet column, occasionally with referral of a sclerotogenous nature into the cervicothoracic region. Only rarely are these tests truly positive in general practice for radiculoneuralgia syndromes. Once again, specific recording of the patient's response to the test will improve the diagnostic yield.

The classic positive response to shoulder depression is the replication of radiculoneuralgia symptoms. However,

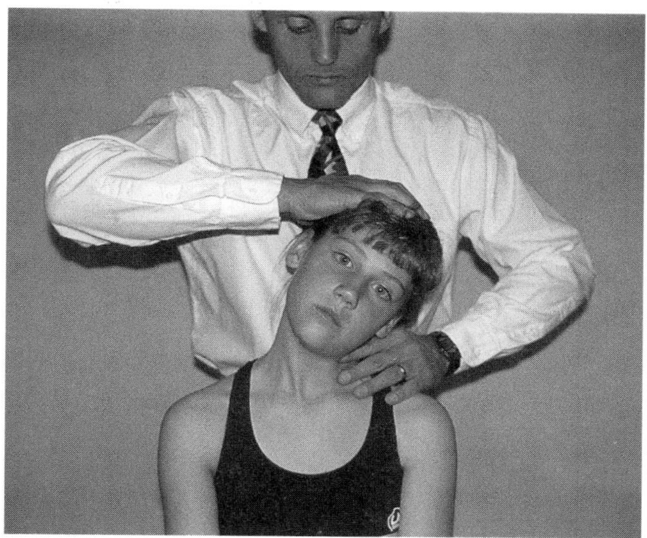

Figure 7–4. Compression testing can be performed initially in a laterally flexed posture as depicted. Before applying pressure, tell the patient exactly what to expect. Pressure should be slowly applied downward within patient tolerance. The patient should report any onset of pain which would terminate the procedure. To further compromise the lateral foramina, the patient's neck can be circumducted, and then vertical compressive forces can be progressively applied by the examiner.

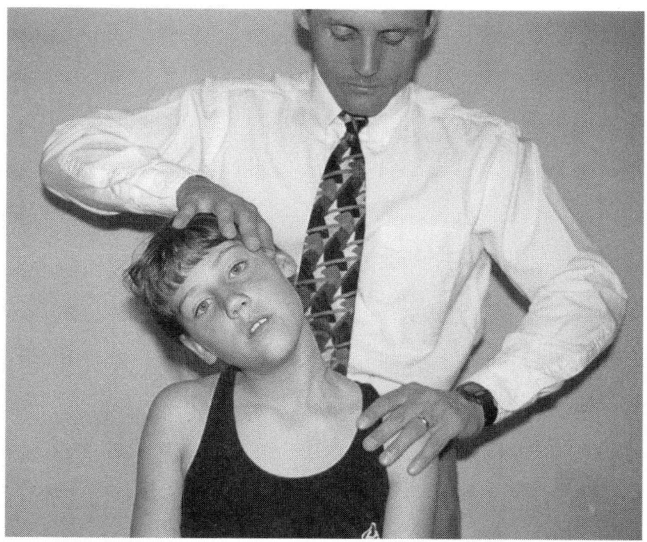

Figure 7–5. The patient's neck should be positioned in end-range lateral flexion. Then, the examiner applies downward pressure over the shoulder, contributing to a tractioning effect of the cervicobrachial plexus and cervicothoracic anatomy in general. It is important to identify simple soft tissue strain from any true radicular signs/symptoms.

most often this is a nonspecific test in which the patient is asked to side-tilt the head; the examiner maintains the patient's head and neck side tilt as he or she depresses the shoulder on the side opposite of head tilt. This test typically causes strain-type complaints on the side of shoulder depression or aggravation of the cervical facet column on the contralateral side. For the Soto Hall maneuver (Figure 7–6) the examiner supports the patient's head with one hand while stabilizing the patient's chest with the other (Figure 7–6A). The examiner then passively flexes the patient's chin to the chest (Figure 7–6B). Such movement pulls the posterior spinal musculature and ligaments, provoking pain when the area of injury is reached. This is a nonspecific test for the detection of subluxation, exostoses, disc lesion, sprain, strain, or fracture of the cervical to upper thoracic vertebrae. Both of these tests have a high response rate from healthy subjects and must be considered in the overall scheme of patient presentation.

In the febrile patient with nuchal rigidity the Soto Hall procedure may elicit reflexive hip and knee flexion, suggestive of meningeal irritation or inflammation.[85] In this instance, the orthopedic sign would be considered a Kernig or Brudzinski sign (Figure 7–7).

Thoracic orthopedic evaluation of the patient with spinal dysfunction is quite limited. Soto Hall's test is performed with the same considerations as noted above. Trunk lateral flexion, as well as circumduction to either side, may elicit complaints localized to the spinal column, possibly costovertebral, apophyseal, or discogenic in nature. Adams' sign is a screening for postural considerations. The examiner stands behind the patient. The patient flexes forward with fingertips approximating the floor. The fingertips of each hand should be equally close to the floor. The lumbar lordosis should be reversed, with a smooth C-curve evident throughout the thoracolumbar spinal column. When scoliosis caused by bony and ligamentous alteration is present, any associated rib cage distortion will remain while the patient is flexed. Upon returning upright there should be a smooth coordinated muscular effort of the hamstring and the gluteal and paraspinal muscles, with resumption of

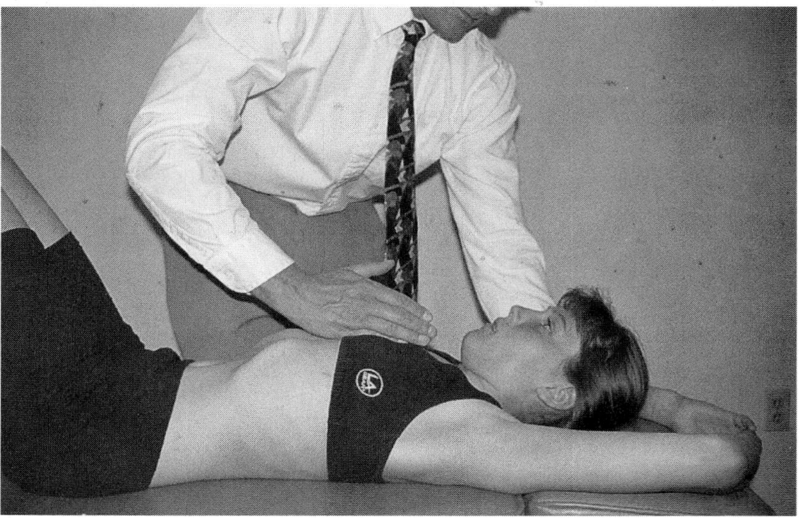

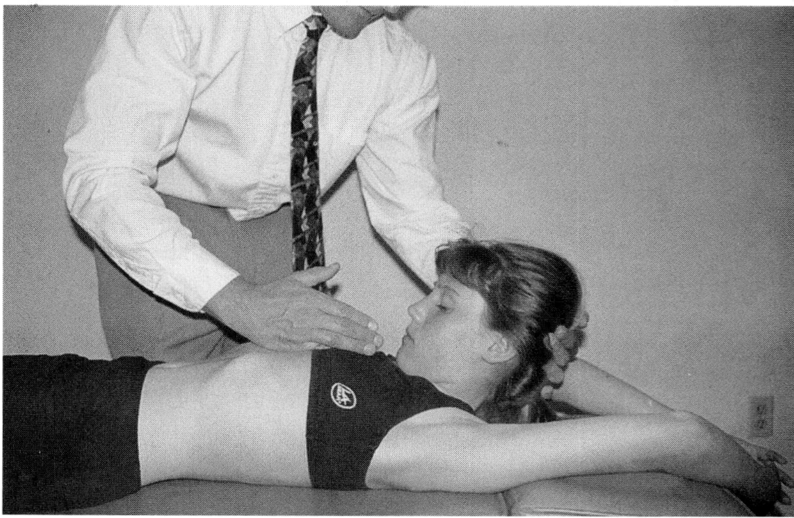

Figure 7–6. In the real application of this test the patient's arms should be along the torso and not overhead. The examiner raises the patient's head from the table top, monitoring the patient for onset of any discomfort.

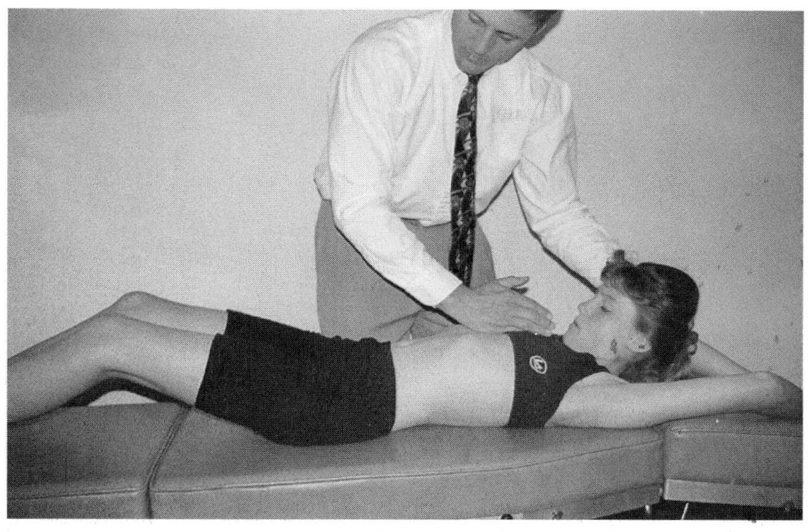

Figure 7–7. The examiner listens to the patient for any verbalization of complaints, and also observes for physical signs, such as hip/knee flexion, suggestive of meningeal irritation.

lumbar lordosis. Muscular or somatic dysfunction may result in pain or dysrhythmic movements during this test. Likewise, disc herniation of the thoracic or the lumbar region may preclude flexion, and may be associated with reactive protective spasm.

LOWER BACK EVALUATION

The classic lumbar nerve root tension test is the supine straight leg raise (SLR). This test simply involves cupping the heel in one hand and raising the leg while keeping the knee straight (Figure 7–8A). This movement contributes to a tractioning of the spinal cord and nerve roots, potentially causing a tractioning of the nerve root over a herniated or inflamed disc. Pain provocation at or below 30 degrees during supine straight leg raising has been found to be a reliable indicator for the presence of disc herniation. A finding above 60 degrees of hip flexion is of questionable clinical significance and is likely clinically insignificant in terms of radicular symptoms.[86] Localized or referred pain proximal to the knees may, however, be elicited upon SLR testing. It is the nature of the patient's complaint that is telling in terms of the specific diagnostic yield. Beyond 70 degrees of hip flexion there is negligible further nerve root movement at the lateral recess,[87] and therefore other biomechanical sources of pain must be considered. The well leg raise test is less sensitive than SLR, but has been found to be highly specific for discal involvement.[88] Additional tests that are often performed in tandem with SLR include cervical flexion (Figurer 7–8B), ankle dorsiflexion, and internal hip rotation. All of these movements contribute to greater spinal cord and nerve root tension.

The SLR test can also be performed with the patient in the seated position, although there are different loads and biomechanical considerations when performed in this position. Observation of a seated patient who helps bear his or her weight by placing the hands on the table top to reduce lower back pain is a nonspecific finding, termed the *tripod sign*. This suggests that loading of the disc is painful. For patients with pain that seems to be higher in the lumbar spine, perhaps with associated anterior hip or thigh paresthesia, the prone hip extension (femoral stretch) test should be performed. Keeping the patient's knee straight and stabilizing the pelvis with the hand, the examiner raises the leg (hip extension). Reproduction of the patient's complaints utilizing the femoral stretch test has been found to be potentially reliable for upper lumbar radiculitis (Figure 7–9).[89]

Examination of the sacroiliac joints (SIJ) is performed by various orthopedic maneuvers. However, most tests designed to identify SI motion aberration have not been validated, and the clinician must be cautious in the interpretation of such tests. Dreyfuss et al identified a 20% false positive rate secondary to screening 101 asymptomatic subjects using standing flexion, seated flexion, and Gillet's test in the study of sacroiliac joint dysfunction.[90] However, Herzog et al found Gillet's test to be reliable.[91] Laslett and Williams studied the interexaminer reliability of 13 tests for sacroiliac dysfunction and found that in only 2 of these tests did the examiner agreement exceed 70%—the distraction (Figure 7–10) and compression (Figure 7–11) provocation tests.[92] In the distraction test the examiner applies manual pressure in the anterior–posterior (AP) and lateral directions over the bilateral anterior superior iliac spines in order to stress the anterior SIJ ligaments. In the compression test the patient is side-lying while the examiner places his or her hands one on top of the other over the superior aspect of the iliac crest and pushes downward, toward the opposite iliac crest. Localization of SIJ pain is indicative of SIJ dysfunction.

The sacroiliac articulation in particular is best assessed by numerous stress tests. Additional tests to consider performing include extension of the hip while the other hip is flexed to the torso (Lewin-Gaenslen's test, Figure 7–12), as well as prone hip extension with knee flexion (Nachlas'

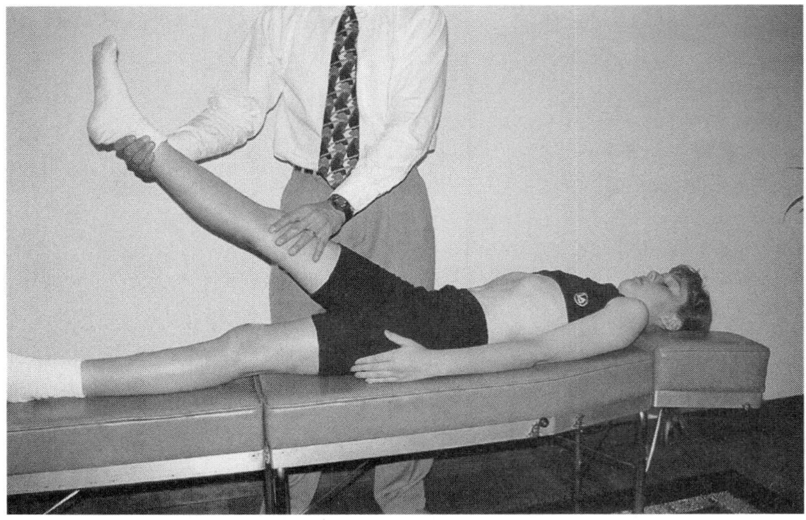

A

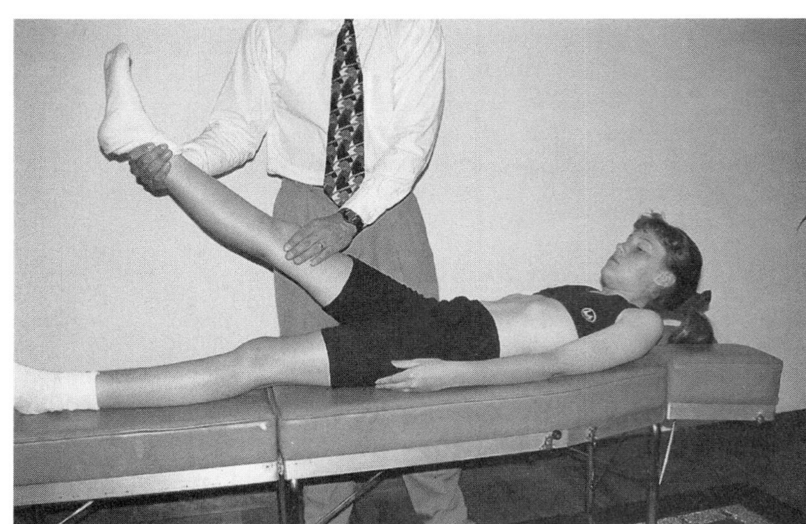

B

Figure 7–8. The patient is instructed to report onset of discomfort, as soon as it appears, if symptoms are provoked. The patient should be completely relaxed as the examiner raises the straight leg. To add additional nerve root tension, the patient's neck may be flexed such as in **B**. Additional nerve root tension is obtained via internal hip rotation and/or ankle dorsiflexion. Knee flexion should relieve nerve root tension signs.

test, Figure 7–13) and prone knee flexion with hip hyperextension (Yeoman's test). The repetitive reproduction of SIJ complaints lends more credence to positive findings on these tests. Via the mechanical compression of the lumbosacral and secondarily the lumbar facet articulations because of increasing extension of the lower back region secondary to hip extension and knee flexion, these tests commonly elicit complaints in the articulations of the lower back and lumbosacral regions that are suggestive of segmental dysfunction.

Piriformis syndrome is identified in the patient who has pain over the buttock, with only rare back pain. Pain referral along the distribution of the sciatic nerve, although usually only to the knee, is common. Entrapment of the sciatic nerve beneath the piriformis muscle is thought to contribute to this condition. Sciatic neuralgia may be provoked via resisted external rotation of the hip (piriformis contraction), as well as possibly SLR, especially if enhanced by internal hip rotation. Having the patient side-lying with the top hip and knee flexed exposes this area to easy palpation. Bilateral comparison is essential, as this area is often tender in healthy individuals. Having the patient lie in the supine position and observing for external rotation of one foot is another indicator of this condition caused by hypertonicity of the piriformis muscle. Given the neuromuscular reflex activity associated with somatic dysfunction involving disc lesion, there is a propensity for piriformis syndrome to be present in conjunction with disc lesion.[93]

While standing or sitting, the patient is asked to sidebend and then rotate and extend to the same side (Kemp's test). Localized lower back pain is likely due to mechanical facet or soft tissue irritation. In the patient with lower extremity pain referral of an apparent radicular nature, pain that is intensified by this test is assumed to arise from a subrhizal or lateral disc lesion. If the lower extremity pain is relieved or not further provoked, then it is assumed that the lesion is a more centrally located, possibly internal disc disruption.

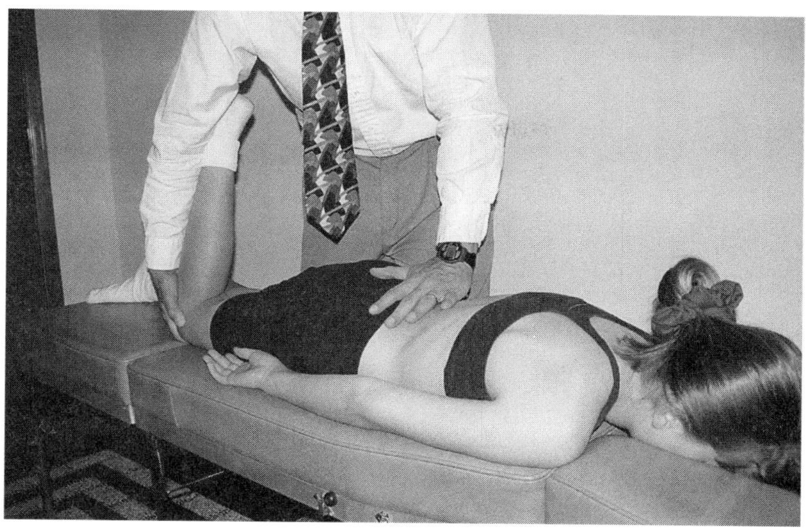

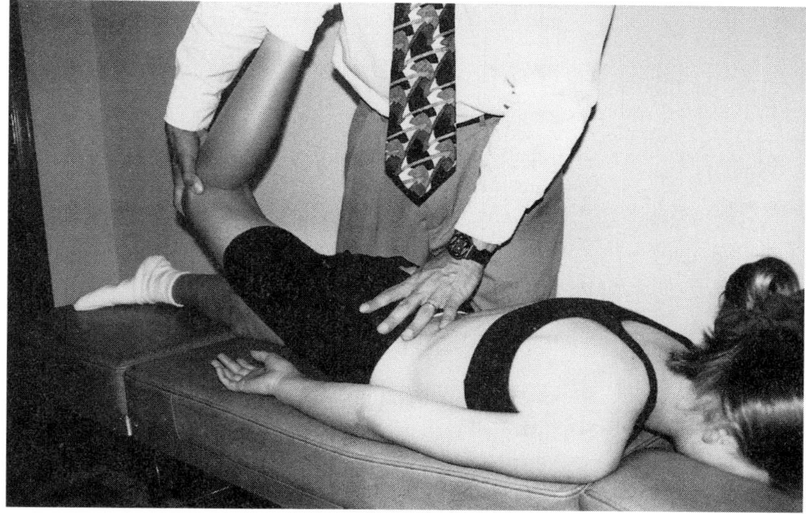

Figure 7–9. The patient is relaxed as the examiner brings the knee to 90 degrees and stabilizes the lumbosacral/sacroiliac region with the opposite hand. The examiner then raises the leg, resulting in extension of the hip, SI joint, and finally the LS/lumbar regions.

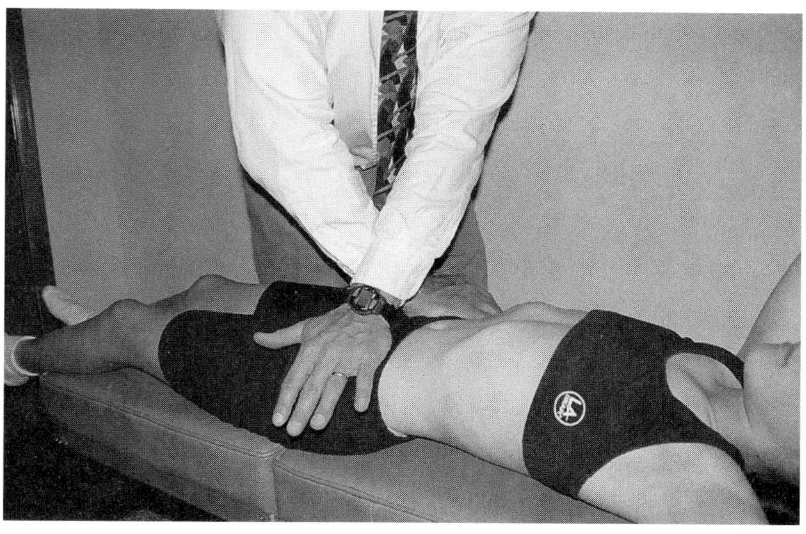

Figure 7–10. In order to apply distractive forces, the examiner must lean out over the patient's body to apply a downward force over the bilateral anterior superior iliac spines.

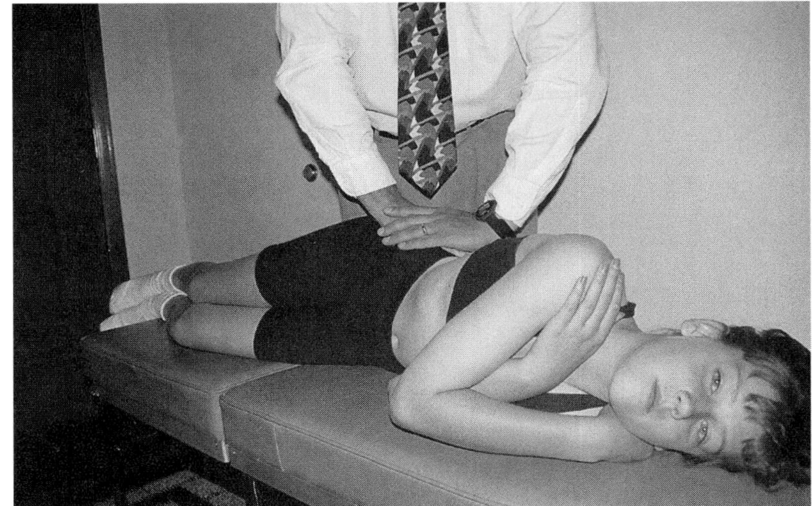

Figure 7–11. The patient needs to be perpendicular to the table surface, with slight hip and knee flexion in order to stabilize and relax the torso. Again, the examiner needs to lean forward to get his or her shoulders over the top of the iliac crest to deliver a compressive force to the sacroiliac articulation.

NEUROLOGIC EXAMINATION

For a detailed neurologic examination the reader is referred to neurology texts. The following is an abbreviated neurologic screening.[94]

Upon presentation the patient's affect and orientation can be quickly assessed. Any evidence of cognitive deficits should be documented. Notations as to the following neurologic observations/tests should be included in the patient's work-up.

1. Alertness and orientation to time, place, and person.
2. Mood (i.e., pleasant), demeanor (i.e., cooperative), emotional status (i.e., withdrawn, depressed, etc.), and thought process (i.e., good historian).
3. Cerebral function signs
   - *Aphasia:* Inability to communicate through spoken or written language because of a cortical lesion, rather than by mental defects, disturbances in sense organs, or paralysis of speech muscles. The patient is unable to understand you when you speak or speak to you in a coherent fashion.
   - *Agnosia:* The patient is unable to recognize objects through the five special senses (smell, taste, touch, sound, and sight).
   - *Apraxia:* The patient is unable to perform purposeful skilled or unskilled movements (coordination).

   Aphasia and agnosia are present when there is a lesion affecting cortical sensory integration, whereas apraxia is present when there is a lesion affecting cortical motor integration.
4. Tests for cerebellar function
   - *Dysmetria (past pointing—finger to nose):* A disturbance of ability to measure distance or orientation in space. This test is primarily performed with eyes closed.
   - *Dyssynergia (rapid repetitive movements—tapping):* Loss of coordination in performance of skilled or unskilled movements of arms or legs.
   - *Dysdiadochokinesia (rapid alternating movements):* Difficulty in performing rapid alternating movements of hands—supination and pronation.
   - *Dysarthria (scanning speech):* Difficulty in articulation; speech becomes garbled at the end of a sentence.
   - *Nystagmus:* To and fro involuntary oscillating of the eyeball either back and forth, up and down, or rotating movement. True: fast and slow component, eye shoots out and comes back slowly. False: same speed with the oscillating component. *Note:* Nystagmus in vestibular lesions is always accompanied with vertigo.
   - *Ataxia:* Inability to coordinate muscle action by demonstrating a reeling, unsteady gait with wide base. Patient may have a tendency to fall toward side of lesion. The cerebellum is important in the patient's ability to perform normal gait and heel-to-toe tandem gait.
   - *Heel-to-Shin Test:* The patient places one heel on the opposite knee and then moves the heel along the shin.

   The patient's gait and balance may be affected by a lesion in the cerebellum and/or possibly the vestibular apparatus of the inner ear and/or the posterior columns, which transmit proprioceptive afferent stimuli. *Note:* Disturbances of alternating movements, ataxia, and tremor are the most common findings in cerebellar disease.
5. Cranial nerve examination
6. Peripheral nerve examination
   - *Deep tendon reflexes* (stretch reflex): Wexler Scale (0 to 5+).

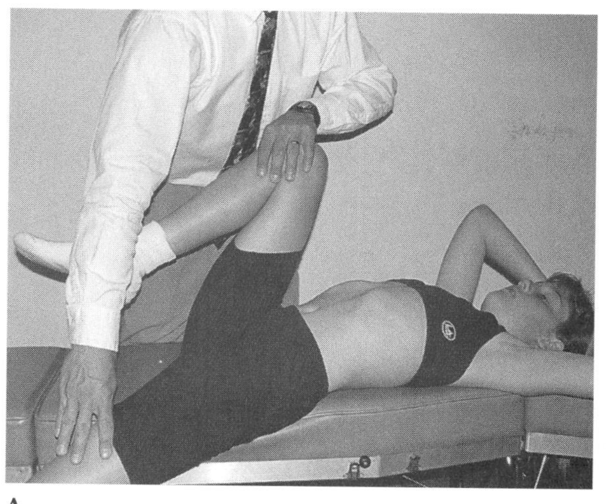
A

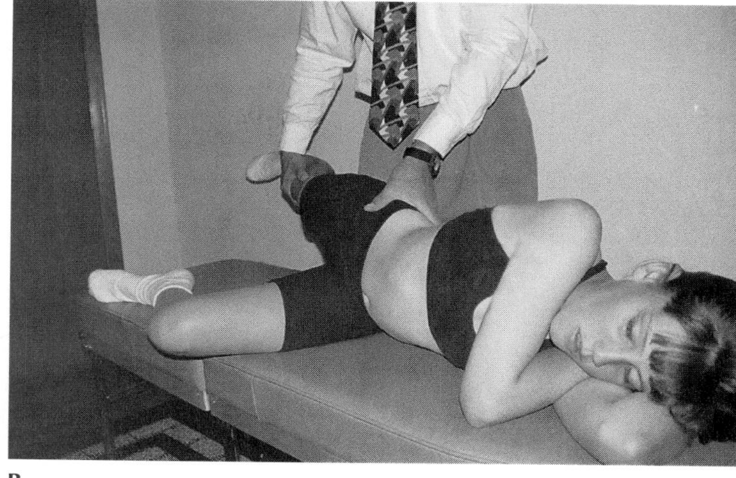
B

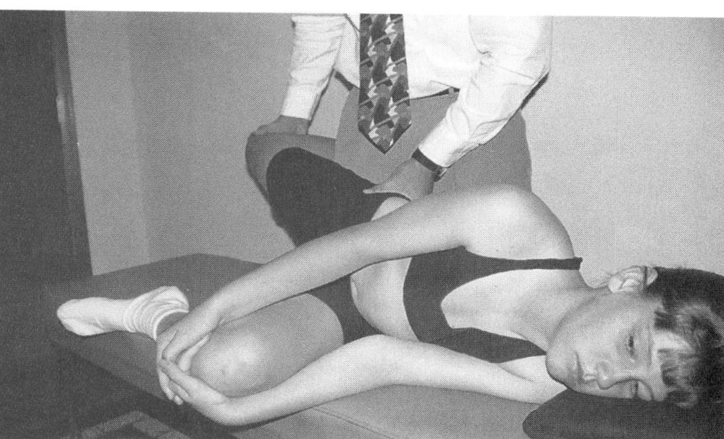
C

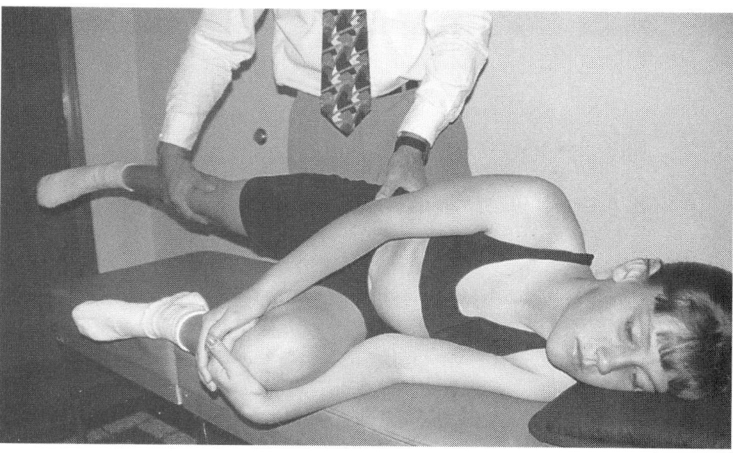
D

Figure 7–12. Stress to the sacroiliac joint can be applied to the patient in a supine position (**A**) or while side lying (**B–D**). In both patient positions one knee is raised by the patient toward the torso and held in place as the opposite hip is extended via examiner over pressure. While side lying, the patient's knee should be flexed to elongate the quadriceps, contributing to further pelvic anterior rotation and thus sacroiliac stress.

Lower motor neuron lesion: grade 0 and grade 1+.
Upper motor neuron lesion: grade 3+ to grade 5+ providing other signs are present as well.
Jaw (CN V), Biceps (C5/C6), Radial (C5/C6), Wrist (C7/C8), Triceps (C7/C8), Ulnar (C8/T1).

- *Pathological reflexes:* Babinski, Hoffman.
- *Manual strength testing:* Kendell and Kendell scale (0 = No ROM, no palpable contraction; 5 = normal strength against gravity with full resistance). *Note:* In some cases it may be necessary to fatigue an involved muscle group to reveal subclinical evidence of nerve root damage (radiculopathy).

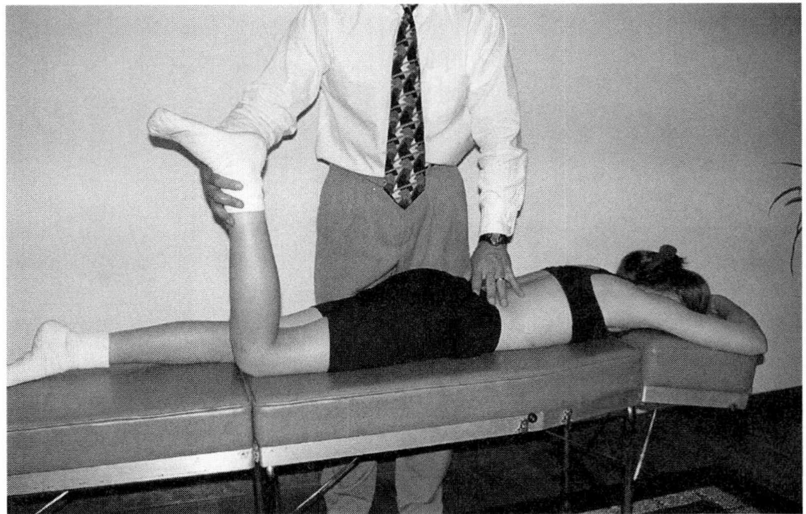

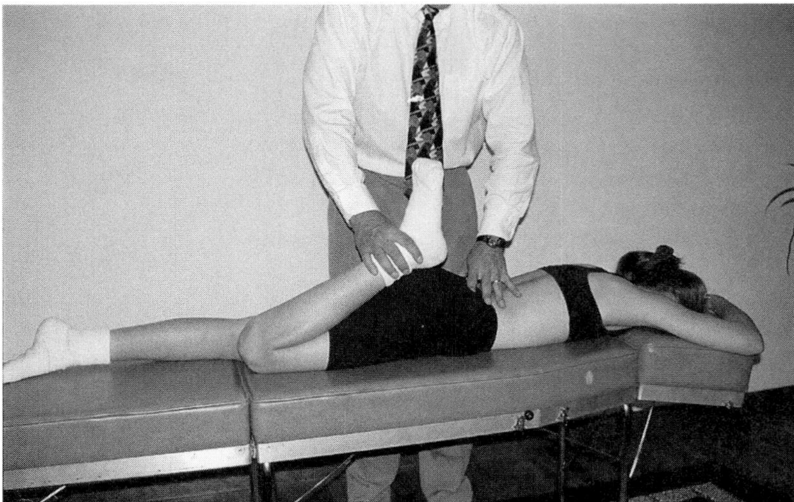

Figure 7–13. The patient is relaxed in a prone position as the examiner stabilizes the lumbosacral/ sacroiliac region with one hand and with the opposite hand grasps the ankle and flexes the patient's knee. Tightness of the quadriceps or hip flexors may inhibit knee flexion. This motion will also translate to stress of the sacroiliac and lumbosacral or lower lumbar facet articulations. Exact localization and the nature of the patient's complaint improve the diagnostic information of this and all tests.

Therefore, in some cases repetitive strength testing may be performed.

- *Sensory examination*
  - Superficial Sensations
    - Pain and temperature (pin prick, hot/cold)—lateral spinal thalamic
    - Light touch (cotton ball)—ventral spinal thalamic
    - Two-point discrimination (epicritic sense)—dorsal columns
    - Thermal (warm/cool)—dorsal columns
  - Deep Sensations
    - Vibration (C-128 tuning fork)—dorsal columns
    - Deep pressure (squeeze the part)—dorsal columns
  - Proprioception
    - Joint sense (position)—dorsal columns

Note: If you examine for light touch (VST) and pinprick (LST), you essentially rule out radicular/peripheral involvement. Thermal or vibratory sensations (dorsal columns) don't need to be checked unless you are considering CNS involvement.

Key: Abnormalities of any of these sensations may indicate an upper motor neuron lesion (central nervous system pathology) requiring a neurologic consult. The exception is with abnormal sensation to pin, pinwheel, or light touch, which may indicate a lower motor neuron lesion, e.g., radiculopathy or peripheral neuropathy.

7. Muscle Tone and Bulk
   - *Hypertonicity:* Spasm/hypertonicity; postural tension.
   - *Hypotonicity:* hypotonia.
   - *Fasciculation*
   - *Atrophy:* disuse/deconditioning; neurogenic.

SUMMARY

In general practice the first priority in patient examination is to rule out pathologic considerations. Recent guidelines suggest a conservative approach for patients devoid of history of pathology, unexplainable weight loss, nighttime pain, fever, and malaise. For those patients who present with neurologic compromise, further diagnostic work-up may be in order. Patients with nonspecific back and neck pain presented for physical rehabilitation are a large component of the clinically difficult cases. These patients are complex in their pain experience, which requires multiple considerations in the final assessment of the patient. The orthopedic examination is one component of many that contribute to solidifying an accurate diagnosis, which will lend to more appropriate treatment and case management decisions. The treatment direction can be made secondary to identifying movement patterns that are painful, nonpainful, or perhaps alleviating in effect. It is important that patients whose conditions remain markedly painful, with guarded movement patterns, not be put into a reconditioning program without first being calmed down. Interprofessional discussion to facilitate a transition from passive to active care is mandatory. To take these patients lightly will contribute to repetitive, nontherapeutic, nonrehabilitative health care services that are a tremendous burden on society, not to mention the lost time, lower quality of life, and diminished productivity of the patient.

REFERENCES

1. van den Hoogen H. On the accuracy of history, physical examination, and erythrocyte sedimentation rate in diagnosing low back pain in general practice. *Spine*. 1995;20(3):318–327.
2. Haldeman S. Diagnostic tests for the evaluation of back and neck pain. *Neurol Clin*. 1996:14(1): 103–117.
3. Bigos S, Spengler D, Martin N, Zeh J, Fisher L, Nachemson A, Wang M. Back injuries in industry: A retrospective study II. Employee-related factors. *Spine*. 1986;11:246–251.
4. Bigos et al. Back injuries in industry: A retrospective study II. Employee-related factors. *Spine*. 1986;11:252–256.
5. Spengler D, Bigos S, Martin N, Zeh J, Fisher L, Nachemson A. Back injuries in industry: A retrospective study I. Overview and cost analysis. *Spine*. 1986;11:241–245.
6. Von Korff M. Studying the natural history of back pain. *Spine*. 1994;19:2041S.
7. Bovim G, Schrader H, Sand R. Neck pain in the general population. *Spine*. 1994;19(12):1307–1309.
8. Institute of Medicine. *Pain and Disability*. Washington, DC: National Academy Press, 1987:123.
9. Institute of Medicine. *Pain and Disability*. Washington, DC: National Academy Press, 1987:12–13.
10. Institute of Medicine. *Pain and Disability*. Washington, DC: National Academy Press, 1987:123–142.
11. Weintraub MI. Medicolegal perspectives, litigation—chronic pain syndrome—A distinct entity: Analysis of 210 cases. *Am J Pain Mngt*. 1992;2(4).
12. Tarola G. Whiplash: General considerations in assessment, treatment, management and prognosis. *ACA J of Chiropractic*. 1993;Jan:63–70.
13. Deyo RA, Tsui-Wa JY. Descriptive epidemiology of low-back pain and its related medical care in the United States. *Spine*. 1987;12:264–268.
14. Report of the Quebec Task Force on Spinal Disorders. Scientific approach to the assessment and management of activity-related spinal disorders. *Spine*. 1987;12:S33.
15. Cypress BK. Characteristics of physician visits for back symptoms: A national perspective. *Am J Public Health*. 1983;73:389–395.
16. Deyo RA, et al. Designing studies of diagnostic tests for low back pain or radiculopathy. *Spine*. 1994;19:2058S.
17. White AA III, Gordon SL. Synopsis: Workshop on idiopathic low back pain. *Spine*. 1982;7:141–149.
18. Liang M, Komaroff AL. Roentgenograms in primary care patients with acute low back pain: A cost-effectiveness analysis. *Arch Intern Med*. 1982;142:1108–1112.
19. Baker AS, Ojemann RG, Swartz MN, et al. Spinal epidural abscess. *N Engl J Med*. 1975;293:468.
20. Liang M, Komaroff AL. Roentgenograms in primary care patients with acute low back pain: A cost-effectiveness analysis. *Arch Intern Med*. 1982;142:1108–1112.
21. Carter ET, McKenna CH, Brian DD, Kurland LT. Epidemiology of ankylosing spondylitis in Rochester, Minnesota, 1935–1978. *Arthritis Rheum*. 1979;22:365–370.
22. Hawkins BR, Dawkins RL, Christiansen FT, Zilko PJ. Use of the B27 test in the diagnosis of ankylosing spondylitis: A statistical evaluation. *Arthritis Rheum*. 1981;24:743–746.
23. Deyo RA, Diehl AK. Cancer as a cause of back pain: Frequency, clinical presentation, and diagnostic strategies. *J Gen Intern Med*. 1988;3:230–238.

24. Deyo RA, Rainville J, Kent DL. What can the history and physical examination tell us about low back pain? *JAMA*. 1992;268:760–761.
25. Deyo RA, Diehl AK. Cancer as a cause of back pain: Frequency, clinical presentation, and diagnostic strategies. *J Gen Intern Med*. 1988;3:230–238.
26. Waldvogel FA, Vasey H. Osteomyelitis: The past decade. *N Engl J Med*. 1980;303:360–370.
27. Bauer RL, Deyo RA. Low risk of vertebral fracture in Mexican American women. *Arch Intern Med*. 1987;147:1487–1489.
28. Hanssen et al. The lumbar lordosis in acute and chronic low back pain. *Spine*. 1985;10:154–155.
29. Deyo R, McNiesh L, Cone R. Observer variability in the interpretation of lumbar spine radiographs. *Arthritis Rheum*. 1985;128(9):1066–1070.
30. Frymoyer J. Spine radiographs in patients with low-back pain. *J Bone Joint Surg*. 1984;66A(7):1048–1055.
31. Boden et al. Abnormal magnetic-resonance scans of the lumbar spine in asymptomatic subjects. *J Bone Joint Surg*. 1990;72A,(3):403–408.
32. Sandler G. The importance of the history in the medical clinic and the cost of unnecessary tests. *Am Heart J*. 1980;100–928.
33. Cutler P. Problem Solving in Clinical Medicine: From Data to Diagnosis. 2nd ed. Baltimore: Williams and Wilkins, 1985:13.
34. Barrows HS, Norman GR, Neufeld GR, Neufeld VR, Feightner JW: The clinical reasoning of randomly selected physicians in general medical practice. *Clin Invest Med*. 1982;5:49.
35. Kellgren, JH. Observation of referred pain arising from muscles. *Clin Sci*. 1938;3:175.
36. Alpers RJ. The neurological aspects of sciatica. *Med Clin North Am*. 1953;87:503–510.
37. McCullough JA. Chemonucleolysis. *J Bone Joint Surg*. 1977;159B:45–52.
38. Hockaday JM, Whitty CWM. Patterns of referred pain in normal subject. *Brain*. 1967;90:481.
39. Mayer TG, Gatchel RJ. *Functional Restoration for Spinal Disorders: The Sports Medicine Approach*. Philadelphia: Lea & Febiger; 1988;78.
40. Griner PF, Mayewsky RJ, Mashlin AL, et al. Selection and interpretation of diagnostic tests and procedures: Principles and application. *Ann Intern Med*. 1981;94:559–563.
41. Robin GC. *The Aetiology of Idiopathic Scoliosis: A Review of a Century of Research*. Boca Raton, FL: CRC Press, 1990; and Wopert S, Bernes P. *MRI in Pediatric Neuroradiology*. St Louis:Mosby-Year Book, 1992;398–401.
42. Gillespie R. Juvenile and adolescent idiopathic scoliosis. In: Bradford DS, Hensinger PM, eds. *The Pediatric Spine*. New York: Thieme, 1985:233–350; and Winter RB. Spinal problems in pediatric orthopedics. In: Morrissy R, ed. *Lovell and Winter's Pediatric Orthopaedics*. 3rd ed. New York: Lippincott, 1990:636–655.
43. Barnes PD, et al. Atypical idiopathic scoliosis: MR imaging evaluation. *Radiology*. 1993;186:247–253.
44. Kumazawa T, Mizumura K. Thin fibre receptors responding to mechanical, chemical and thermal stimulation in the skeletal muscle of the dog. *J Physiol*. 1977;273:179–194.
45. Mense S, Meyer H. Different types of slowly conducting afferent units in cat skeletal muscle and tendon. *J Physiol*. 1985;363:403–417.
46. Mense S, Stahnke M. Responses in muscle afferent fibres of slow conduction velocity to contractions and ischaemia in cat. *J Physiol*. 1983;342:383–397.
47. Institute of Medicine. *Pain and Disability*. Washington, DC: National Academy Press, 1987;125–126.
48. Janda V. Muscles and motor control in low back pain: Assessment and management. In: Twomey T, ed. *Physical Therapy of the Low Back*. New York: Churchill Livingstone, 1987.
49. Bisgaard H, Kristensen JK. Leukotriene B4 produces hyperalgesia in humans. *Prostaglandins*. 1985;30: 791–797.
50. Juan H, Lembeck F. Action of peptides and other algesic agents on paravascular pain receptors of the isolated perfused rabbit ear. *Naunyn-Schmiedebergs Arch Pharm*. 1974;283:151–164.
51. Keele CA. Measurement of responses to chemically induced pain. In: *Touch Heat and Pain*. Boston: Little, Brown, 1966.
52. Janda V. Pain in the locomotor system—a broad approach. In: Glasgow E, Twomey L, Scull ER, Kleynhans AM, Idczak RM, eds. *Aspects of Manipulative Therapy*. New York: Churchhill Livingstone, 1985.
53. Imrie D, Barbuto L. *The Back Power Program*. New York: Wiley, 1990.
54. Henninger R. Back to basics . . . Evaluation of soft tissue pain. *Top Clin Chiro*. 1994;1(2):1–7.
55. Boden SD, McCowin PR, Davis DO, Dina TS, Mark AS, Wiesel S. Abnormal magnetic resonance scans of the cervical spine in asymptomatic subjects. *J Bone Joint Surg Am*. 1990;72:1178–1184.
56. Henderson CM, et al. Posterior-lateral foraminotomy as an exclusive operative technique for cervical radiculopathy: A review of 846 consecutively operated cases. *Neurosurgery*. 1983;13:504–572.
57. Lunsford L, Bissonette D. Anterior surgery for surgical disc disease. *J Neurosurg*. 1980;53:1.

58. Rodriguez JE. *Rehabilitation of the Spine—Science and Practice*. St. Louis: Mosby, 1993:27–33.
59. Kelsey JL, Golden AL, Mundt DJ. Low back pain/prolapsed lumbar intervertebral disc. *Rheum Dis Clin North Am*. 1990;16:699–712.
60. Spangfort EV. Lumbar disc herniation: A computer aided analysis of 2504 operations. *Acta Orthop Scand*. 1972;(Suppl 142):1–93.
61. Kisner C, Colby L. *Therapeutic Exercise—Foundations and Techniques*. 2nd ed. Philadelphia: F. A. Davis, 1990.
62. Jones LM. Spontaneous release by positioning. *Doctor of Osteopathy*. 1964;4:109.
63. Kellgren JH. Observation of referred pain arising from muscles. *Clin Sci*. 1938;3:175.
64. Sutter M. Wesen, Klinik and Bedeutung spondylogener Reflexsyndrome. *Schweiz Rundsch Med Praxis*. 1975;64:42.
65. Wyke BD, Polacek P. Articular neurology—the present position. *J Bone Joint Surg*. 1975;57B: 401.
66. Dvorak J, Dvorak V. *Manual Medicine*. New York:Thieme-Stratton, 1984;43.
67. Cassidy JD, Kirkaldy-Willis WH. *Managing Low Back Pain*. 2nd ed., New York: Churchill Livingstone, 1988;287–288.
68. Sandoz R. Some physical mechanisms and effects of spinal adjustments. *Ann Swiss Chiro Assoc*. 1976;6:91.
69. Mennell J. The Validation of the diagnosis "joint dysfunction" in the synovial joints of the cervical spine. *J Manipulative Physiol Ther*. 1990;13(1):7–12.
70. Grieve GP. *Common Vertebral Joint Problems*. Edinburgh: Churchill Livingstone, 1981;320.
71. Maitland GD. *Vertebral Manipulation*. 4th ed. London: Butterworths, 1977;31,316.
72. Mennell J. *The Science and Art of Joint Manipulation*. Vol 2. London: J and A Churchill, 1952;50.
73. Stoddard A. *Manual of Osteopathic Technique*. 3rd ed. London: Hutchinson Medical, 1981.
73a. Boline PD. Interexaminer reliability of eight evaluative dimensions of lumbar segmental abnormality: Part 2. *J Manip Physiol Ther*. 1993;16(6):363–374.
74. McCombe PF, et al. Reproducibility of physical signs of low-back pain. *Spine*. 1989;14(9):908–918.
75. Kirkaldy-Willis WK. *Managing Low Back Pain*. 2nd ed. New York: Churchill Livingstone, 1988.
76. Beal MC. Incidence of spinal palpatory findings: A review. *J Am Osteopath Assoc*. 1989;89(8):1027–1035.
77. White AA, Panjabi MM. *Clinical Biomechanics of the Spine*. Philadelphia: J. B. Lippincott, 1978.
78. Dvorik J, Dvorik V. *Manual Medicine Diagnostics*. New York: Thieme-Stratton, 1984.
79. Caviezel H. Klinische Diagnostik der Funktionsstörung an den Kopfgelenken. *Schweiz Rundsch Med Praxis*. 1976;65:1037.
80. Lewit K. Blockierung von Atlas-Axis und Atlas-Occiput im Ro-Bild und Klinik. *Z Orthop*. 1970;108:43.
81. Lewit K. *Manuelle Medizin im Rahmen der medizinischen Rehabilitation*. Munich: Urban & Schwarzenberg, 1977.
82. Lumsden RM, Morris JM. An in vivo study of axial rotation and immobilization at the lumbosacral joint. *J Bone Joint Surg*. 1968;50A:1591.
83. McCarthy KA. Improving the clinician's use of orthopedic testing: An application to low back pain. *Top Clin Chiro*. 1994;1(1):42–50.
84. Herzog W, Read LJ, Conway JW, Shaw LD, McEwen C. Reliability of motion palpation procedures to detect sacroiliac joint fixations. *J Manip Physiol Ther*. 1989;12:86–92.
85. Evans RC. *Illustrated Essentials in Orthopedic Physical Assessment*. St Louis: Mosby, 1994;58–59.
86. Kosteljanetz M, Flemming B, Schmidt-Olsen S. The clinical significance of straight-leg raising in the diagnosis of prolapsed lumbar disc. *Spine*. 1988;13:393–395.
87. Brieg A, Troup JDG. Biomechanical considerations in the straight-leg-raising test: Cadaveric and clinical studies of medial hip rotation. *Spine*. 1979;4:242–250.
88. Deyo RA, Rainville J, Daniel KL. What can the history and physical examination tell us about low back pain? *JAMA*. 1992;268:760–765.
89. McCombe PF, Fairbank JCT, Cockersole BC, Pynsent PB. Reproducibility of physical signs in low-back pain. *Spine*. 1989;14:908–918.
90. Dreyfuss P, Dreyer S, Griffin J, Hoffman J, Walsh N. Positive sacroiliac screening tests in asymptomatic adults. *Spine*. 1994;19(10):1138–1143.
91. Herzog W, Read LJ, Conway JW, Shaw LD, McEwen C. Reliability of motion palpation procedures to detect sacroiliac joint fixations. *J Manip Physiol Ther*. 1989;12:86–92.
92. Laslett M, Williams M. The reliability of selected pain provocation tests for sacroiliac joint pathology. The First Interdisciplinary World Congress on Low Back Pain and its Relation to the Sacroiliac Joint. Rotterdam, the Netherlands, ECO, 1992;425–431.
93. Steiner C, Staubs C, Ganon M, Buhlinger C. Piriformis syndrome: Pathogenesis, diagnosis and treatment. *J Am Osteopath Assoc*. 1987:318–323.
94. Conwell T: *Neurological Examination from Documenting Patient Progress*, SOAP note; Clinical Advancement Plus Seminars.

CHAPTER 8

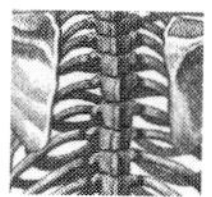

Evaluating the Patient Using the McKenzie Approach

GARY JACOB, DC, LAc, DIP.MDT, STEVEN HEFFNER, DC, DIP.MDT, ROBERT MEDCALF, PT, DIP.MDT, DOUGLAS BARENBURG, DC, CRED.MDT, & SUZAN STARLER, DC, CRED.MDT

INTRODUCTION

The main purpose of this chapter is to explore the clinical reasoning resulting from McKenzie's paradigm regarding the nature and solution of common activity-related spinal complaints. Clinical competency in the McKenzie approach is greatly aided by study of McKenzie's original texts[13,14] and supervised clinical training. Supervised clinical training is particularly important in order to develop the skills to best manage the fears faced by patients and clinicians when therapy involves promoting movement of patients' painful spines. Our primary purpose is to communicate the conceptual structure of the McKenzie paradigm.

Many approaches exist for patients with common spinal complaints. Each approach is based upon certain criteria. By choosing a particular evaluation or treatment approach, the practitioner (consciously or not) chooses certain criteria or paradigms upon which evaluation or treatment is predicated. The spinal evaluation and treatment paradigms employed often inculcate patients with belief systems regarding the nature of and solution to their spinal problems.

Rehabilitation philosophies argue passive therapies turn patients into passive receptacles of care. Intrinsic to the clinical reasoning, problem solving and goal setting of a rehabilitation program is the emphasis on motivating patients to participate actively in their own care. This is generally done through a conditioning program targeting posture, balance, cardiovascular, flexibility, and/or strength status.

The McKenzie paradigm distinguishes itself among rehabilitation approaches by means of the criteria upon which it predicates evaluation and treatment methods. The McKenzie paradigm accounts for common spinal complaints by classifying the mechanical and symptomatic responses to spinal loading (forces applied by means of movement and positioning). A McKenzie evaluation requires the clinician to look and listen for clues regarding patterns of mechanical and symptomatic responses to loading. Patients report movements and positionings of their spines affect them in a variable manner. Provocative spinal loading strategically performed in the clinical setting reveals different reactions to different loading strategies. The McKenzie approach explores activity-related solutions to activity-related complaints, employing the criteria of mechanical and symptomatic responses to loading to evaluate, treat, and provide prophylaxis.

McKenzie protocols permit the employment of a *rehabilitation* approach in the acute phase. Rehabilitation employs activity therapies to achieve restoration, self-sufficiency, and independent functioning skills. The clinician's responsibility is to introduce activity therapy as soon as possible and to identify cases where activity therapy is ineffective or inappropriate as soon as possible. The patient's responsibility is to participate actively in exploring the potential benefits of self-generated movements.

A PRIORI NOTIONS THAT LIMIT THERAPEUTIC POSSIBILITIES

Certain paradigms of spinal evaluation and treatment are based on preconceived notions regarding the cause of common spinal complaints. Two of the most common preconceived notions are those of *inflammation* and *pain of muscular origin*. Many passive therapies are employed for the purpose of reducing inflammation and/or pain of muscular origin. Promotion of rest and use of medication are often the preferred strategies to treat inflammation or pain of muscular origin. Exercise is considered contraindicated. Treatment predicated on such *a priori* notions prevents the exploration of the potential benefits of activity therapies.

INFLAMMATION

Relief by means of NSAIDs does not confirm the presence of inflammation. NSAIDs have analgesic as well as antiinflammatory properties and may suppress pain in the absence of inflammation. With joint complex inflammation (e.g., inflammatory arthritis), relief cannot be found by means of movement or positioning. Inflammation is thought of as a chemical event that would not be relieved greatly by mechanical factors. Contrary to this, acute and chronic spinal complaints commonly include a history of certain activities, movements, or positionings that relieve complaints, suggesting that the role of inflammation may not be significant. Prolonged rest used to treat purported *inflammation* promotes disability.[2]

MUSCLE SPASM

Most commonly, pain purported to be of muscular origin is ascribed to muscle spasm. This notion leads to inactivity as the strategy to *relax* the spasm. Thermal agents, electrical stimulation, massage, or other passive procedures are employed to this end. A diagnosis of "chronic spasm" condemns patients to prolonged inactivity, i.e., disability.

Medically, spasm is understood to be a violent, involuntary contraction of a muscle, something not seen commonly. What is commonly referred to as spasm in the clinical setting is curious:

1. When patients present with antalgia contralateral to the symptomatic side, it is often ascribed to muscle spasm even though the side of symptoms (spasm) would be expected to cause *ipsilateral* antalgia.
2. The ascription of kyphotic antalgia to spasm of posterior paraspinal muscles is not clear thinking, as paraspinal muscles are *extensors*, not *flexors*.
3. Most patients with spinal complaints are worse when sitting, during which time spinal muscles are recruited less, contrary to what would be expected from muscle spasm.
4. Expert physicians cannot reliably identify muscle spasm by means of palpation.[2]
5. A survey of the literature concluded that muscles are not the primary cause of spinal complaints.[3]

SPINAL MANIPULATION AS EVIDENCE OF THE EFFICACY OF MOVEMENT

The efficacy of spinal manipulation casts doubt on the wisdom of universally applying the models of inflammation, spasm, immobility, and rest to common, activity-related spinal complaints.

Chiropractic has successfully employed manipulation for the past 100 years, in spite of periods of aggressive medical opposition to manipulative therapies. Medicine accused those who "adjusted" the spine of adding insult to injury and prematurely introducing aggressive movement when rest, immobility, and inactivity were needed. Medical objections were predicated on the criteria that inflammation and spasm were the culpable physiologic processes, especially for the acute spine. Inflammation and spasm would be expected to respond poorly to movement, especially the aggressive end range loading movements of manipulation.

Current wisdom views manipulation as an efficacious approach worthy of consideration for acute, activity-related spinal complaints.[4,23,24] The same cannot be said for passive nonmovement modalities that target inflammation and/or spasm.

The efficacy of spinal manipulation for acute conditions suggests:

> Movement is of potential benefit for the acute spine.
> Aggressive movement is of potential benefit for the acute spine.
> Aggressive movement to end range is of potential benefit for the acute spine.

Manipulation, as in exercise, is a movement therapy. Both have been classified as forms of "activation."[24]

DETERMINING WHETHER LOADING STRATEGIES ARE APPROPRIATE

McKenzie protocols determine, early in the course of care, who are the *responders* and *nonresponders* to mechanical therapies. Mechanical therapies include postural training, all prescriptive exercises, mobilizations, manipulations, and advice concerning activities of daily living. If self-generated loading and/or clinical mobilizations in all movement plane directions fail to provide relief, manipulation or other mechanical therapies are less likely to be of benefit. If self-generated loading and/or clinical mobilizations in all movement plane directions appear to be to the patient's detriment, "red flags" go up raising suspicions of pernicious processes not amenable to mechanical therapies. If patient-generated end range loading or positioning is of benefit, these conditions are less likely. For those identified as being amenable to mechanical therapies, the clinician's task is to determine the preferred loading strategy, to institute activity therapies immediately, and to avoid passive care and rest. This entails determining which loading tactics to avoid, which to pursue, and when it is safe to introduce previously avoided loading tactics.

SPINAL MANIPULATION, REHABILITATION AND McKENZIE PROTOCOLS

Spinal manipulation and spinal rehabilitation are activity therapies that complement each other. Spinal manipulation involves passive movement. Rehabilitation involves active movement. The success of spinal manipulation for "acutes" suggests self-generated movements may benefit acute patients, something not entertained commonly. McKenzie employs a system of prescriptive exercises based on principles similar to that of spinal manipulation, i.e., end range loading. McKenzie protocols explore the mechanical and symptomatic responses to end range loading prior to introducing manipulative forces.

The McKenzie protocols employ manipulation when patient self-generated movement to end range is demonstrated to be of some, but not complete, benefit. If complete recovery is realized from self-generated end range loading, manual therapies are not needed. If a partial response is realized, the practitioner has a good understanding of which movement plane directions to manipulate. To "test the waters," the clinician would provide mobilization to end range to ensure the correct movement plane direction was being explored. If mobilization resolves complaints, there is no need to proceed to manipulation. If a full response is not realized, the progression of forces then considers manipulation. Premanipulative end range mobilization testing, whether performed by the patient or the clinician, *heralds* the mechanical and symptomatic responses one can expect from end range manipulation. These herald responses are evoked by means of progressive forces, from patient-generated to clinician mobilization to clinician manipulation.

McKENZIE EVALUATION PROTOCOLS

BASELINE MOTION MEASUREMENTS

Movement is first assessed without regard to symptomatic response or to how one movement may affect another, after which these responses are evaluated closely. Movements employed that differ from those conducted during usual range of motion examinations will be illustrated.

Baseline measurements are taken in the following order for the respective spinal areas:

Cervical Spine

- Protrusion (Figure 8–1)
- Flexion

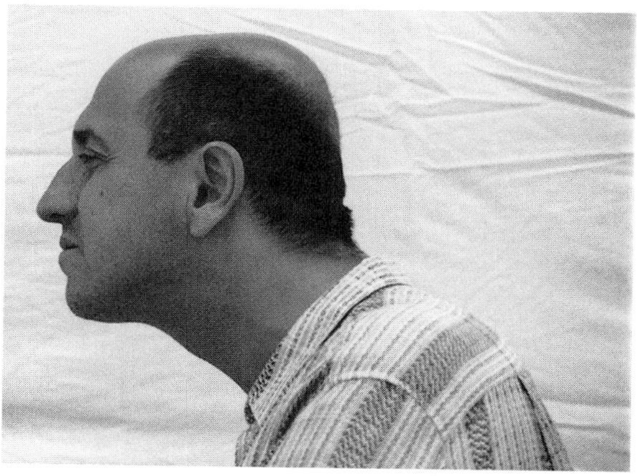

Figure 8–1. Cervical protrusion.

- Retraction (Figure 8–2)
- Extension
- Side bending right
- Side bending left
- Rotation right
- Rotation left

Protrusion and flexion are best evaluated from the slouched sitting posture. Evaluating protrusion or flexion from an erect sitting posture adds the undesired component of retraction (upper cervical flexion and lower cervical extension). All other cervical motions are best evaluated when sitting erect (Figure 8–3) or standing.

Retraction, extension, side bending, or rotation evaluated from a slouched sitting posture with protruded head adds the undesired component of upper cervical extension and lower cervical flexion.

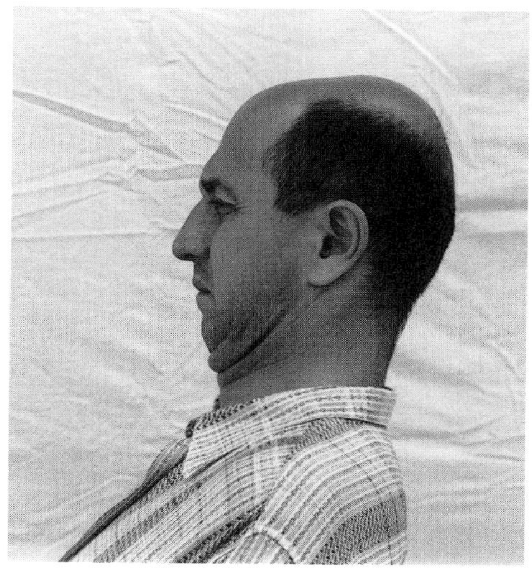

Figure 8–2. Cervical retraction.

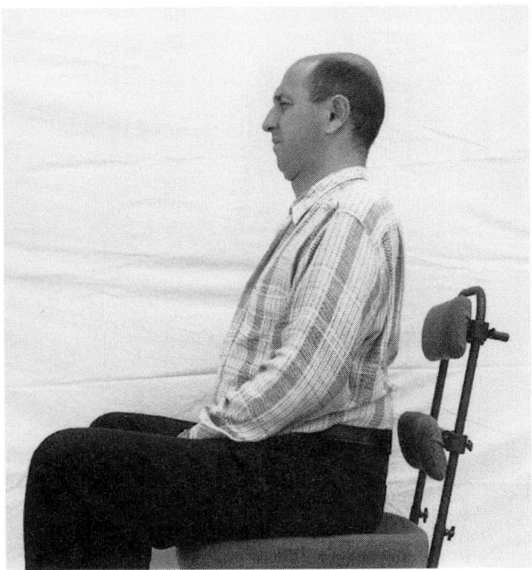

Figure 8–3. Sitting erect.

Lumbar Spine

- Flexion
- Extension
- Side gliding right (Figure 8–4)
- Side gliding left

For the lumbar spine, lateral flexions and rotations are not employed. Instead, side gliding (which combines these two movements) is utilized. Side gliding involves a translational movement in the coronal plane, whereby the pelvis and trunk are moved in opposite directions while attempting to keep the shoulders and iliac crests level.

Patients do not present with lateral flexion or rotation antalgias, but do present with antalgias resulting from side gliding. These antalgias or lists are known within McKenzie protocols, for the low back, as *lateral shifts* and indicate the relevance of considering side gliding as a potentially therapeutic movement to explore.

DYNAMIC AND STATIC EVALUATIONS

Subsequent to obtaining baseline motion measurements, the mechanical and symptomatic responses to loading are explored. McKenzie protocols have a preference for exploring dynamic (repetitive movement) loading within the sagittal plane first. If dynamic loading in the sagittal plane is of benefit, loading strategies are *not* explored in the coronal or transverse planes. If dynamic loading within the sagittal plane does not appear to be of any benefit, coronal and then transverse planes are explored. If dynamic loading fails to demonstrate benefit, static loading is then explored.

All cervical spine loading procedures except for flexion and protrusion are performed from the retracted position in order to promote maximum end range loading. Evaluations are performed in the following order for the respective spinal areas:

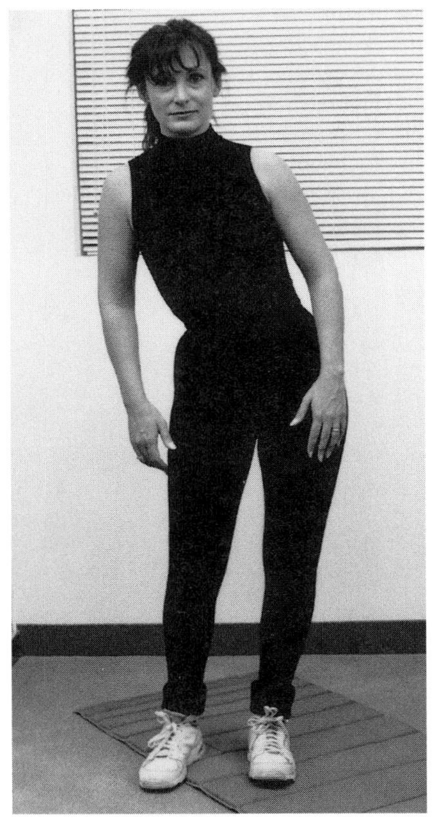

Figure 8–4. Side gliding right.

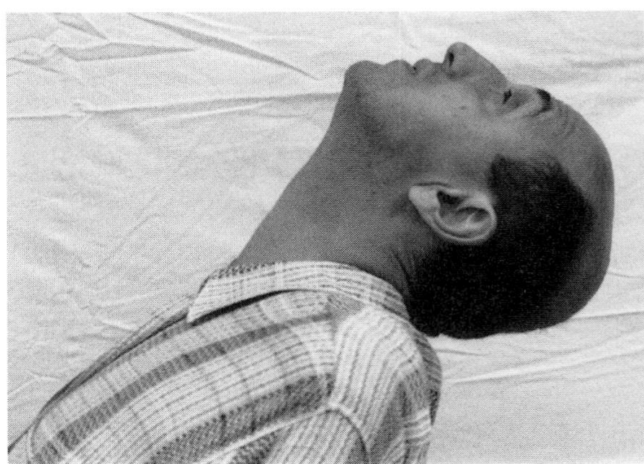

Figure 8–5. Cervical extension (from retraction).

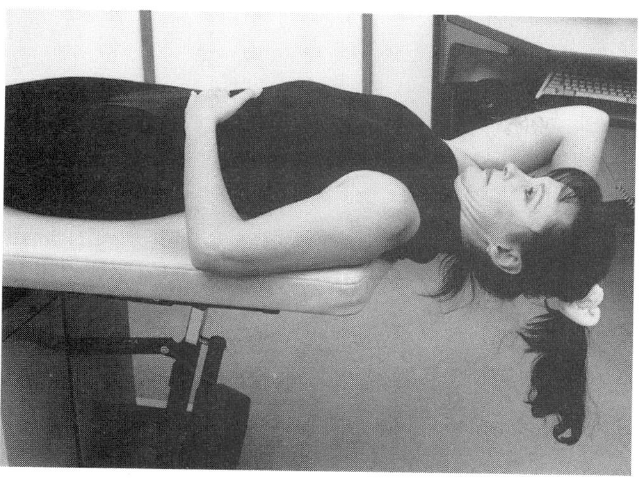

Figure 8–6. Cervical retraction lying.

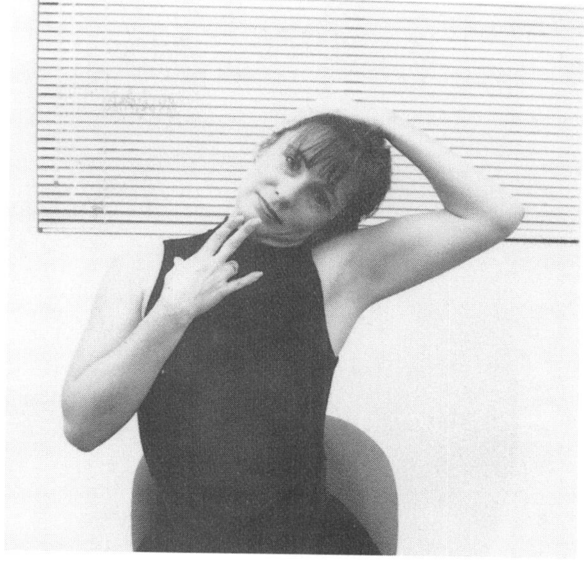

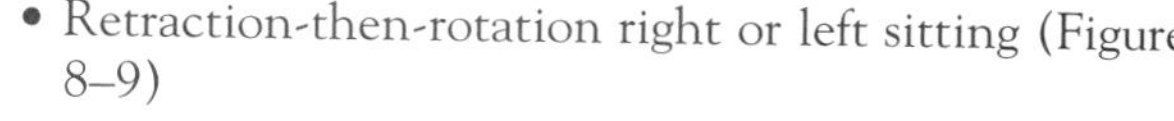

Figure 8–8. Cervical side bending (from retraction).

Cervical Spine Dynamic Tests

- Flexion sitting
- Retraction sitting (Figure 8–2)
- Retraction-then-extension sitting (Figures 8–2 and 8–5)
- Retraction lying (head off the edge of treatment table) (Figure 8–6)
- Retraction-then-extension lying (head off edge of treatment table) (Figures 8–6 and 8–7)

Other Cervical Spine Dynamic Tests (if required)

- Protrusion sitting (Figure 8–1)
- Retraction-then-side bending right or left sitting (Figure 8–8)
- Retraction-then-rotation right or left sitting (Figure 8–9)

Cervical Spine Static Tests

- Protrusion (Figure 8–1)
- Flexion
- Retraction (sitting or supine) (Figures 8–2 and 8–6)
- Retraction-then-extension (sitting, prone) (Figures 8–2 and 8–7)
- Retraction-then-side bending right or left (Figure 8–8)
- Retraction-then-rotation right or left (Figure 8–9)

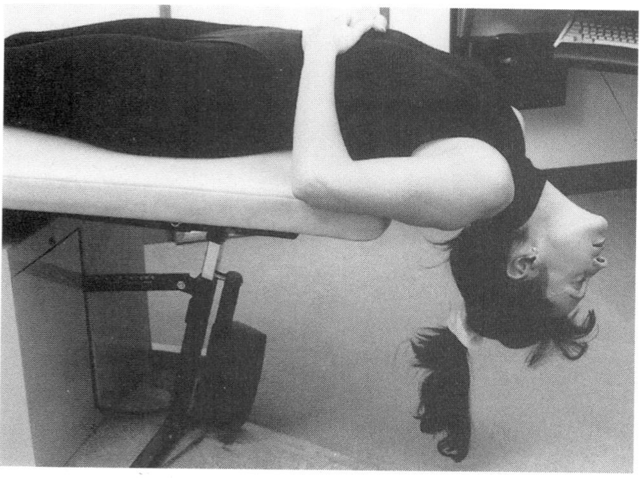

Figure 8–7. Cervical extension lying (from retraction).

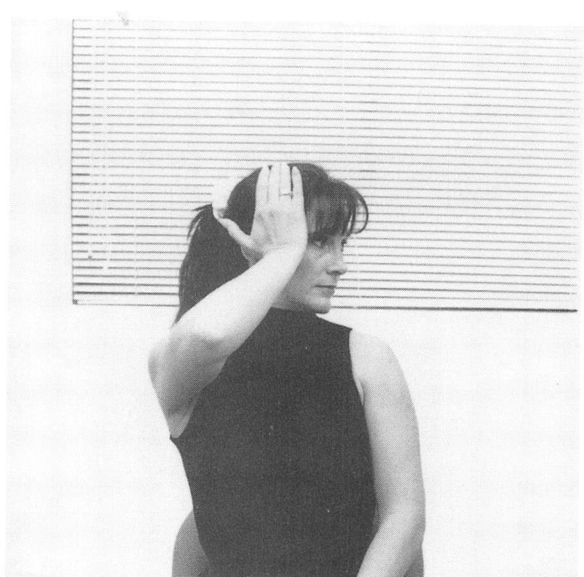

Figure 8–9. Cervical rotation (from retraction).

Figure 8–10. Lumbar extension standing.

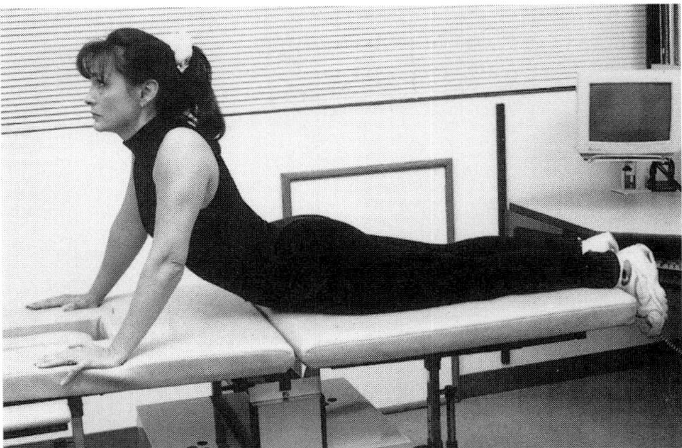

Figure 8–12. Lumbar extension in lying (McKenzie "press-up").

Lumbar Spine Dynamic Tests

- Flexion standing
- Extension standing (Figure 8–10)
- Flexion in lying (supine knee to chest) (Figure 8–11)
- Extension in lying (prone McKenzie press-up(Figure 8–12)

Other Lumbar Spine Dynamic Tests (if required)

- Side gliding right or left standing (Figure 8–4)
- Extension from prone right or left lateral shift position (Figure 8–13)

Lumbar Spine Static Tests

- Sitting slouched (Figure 8–1)
- Sitting erect (Figure 8–3)
- Standing slouched
- Standing erect
- Lying on elbows (Figure 8–14)

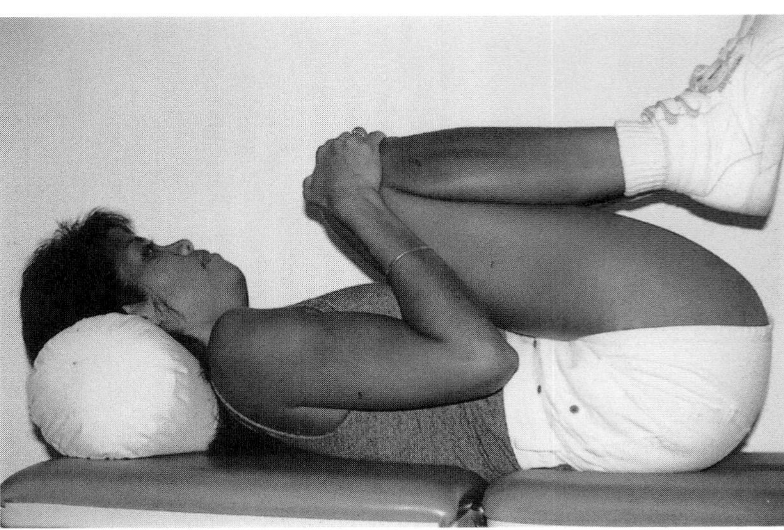

Figure 8–11. Lumbar flexion in lying.

- Long sitting
- Lateral shift right or left (Figure 8–4)
- Rotation in flexion (Figure 8–15)

THE USE OF OVERPRESSURE FOR EVALUATION AND TREATMENT

Overpressure represents strategies that may be employed by the patient or the clinician in order to realize further end range positioning. Chiropractors may think of overpressure as strategies that "take the slack out."

Overpressure may be used to obtain diagnostic information or as part of a therapeutic progression. Typically, overpressure exaggerates the mechanical and symptomatic responses of the joint complex it is applied to. The concept of overpressure is intimately connected to the McKenzie philosophy of introducing forces in a progressive manner. Patients may exert overpressure on joint complexes by strategic movements of their own. Patients must be encouraged to achieve as much end range as possible. If the therapist passively moves a joint to end range, this may be construed as *mobilization*. The next and final progression of overpressure forces toward end range would be *manipulation*.

Some examples of overpressure follow: Prone extensions offer more overpressure to the low back than do standing

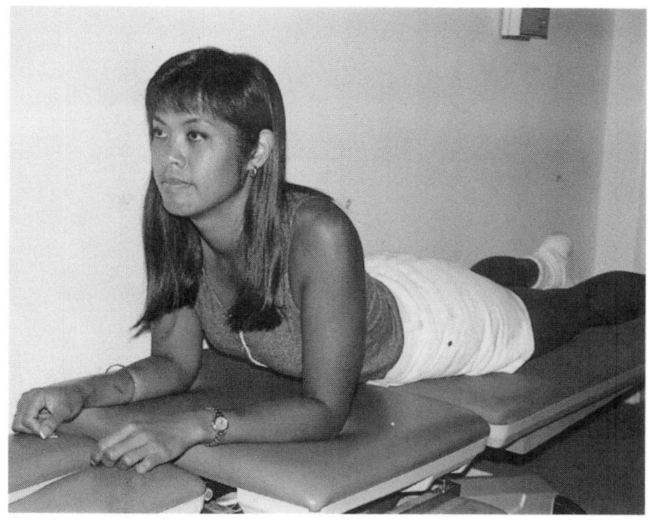

Figure 8–14. Lying on elbows ("lying prone in extension").

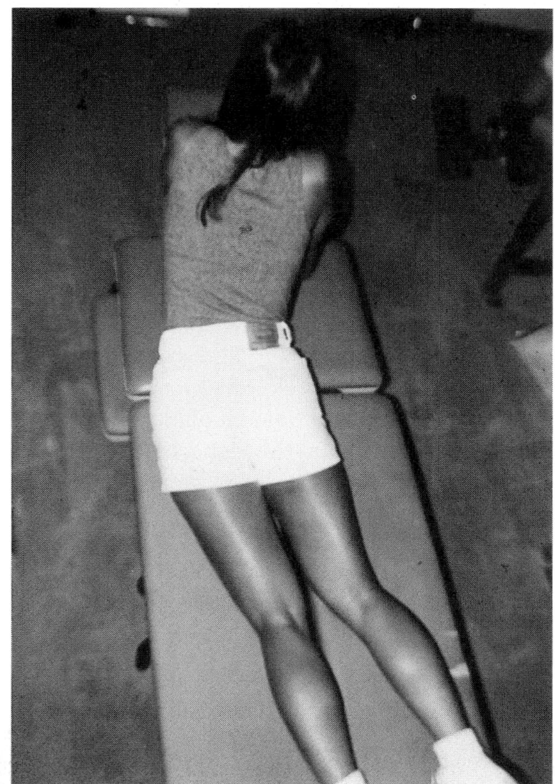

Figure 8–13. Lumbar prone extension (from right lateral shift).

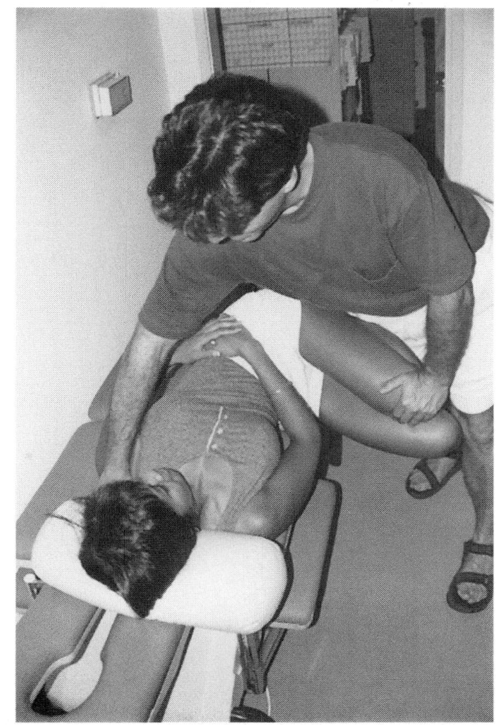

Figure 8–15. Lumbar rotation in flexion.

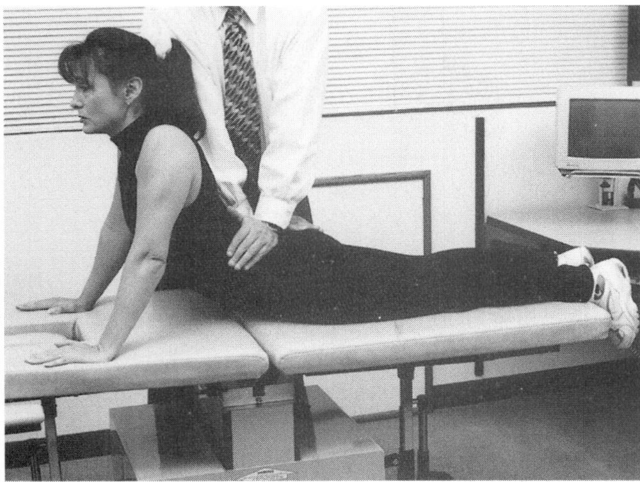

Figure 8–16. Therapist overpressure: prone extension.

extensions. A prone extension performed while the clinician's hands hold the patient's hips down, creates greater overpressure (Figure 8–16). For example, therapist overpressure is commonly employed to assist lumbar side gliding (in the direction opposite the presenting lateral shift) (Figure 8–17) and cervical retraction (Figure 8–18) and for cervical traction, retraction-then-extension when supine (Figure 8–19).

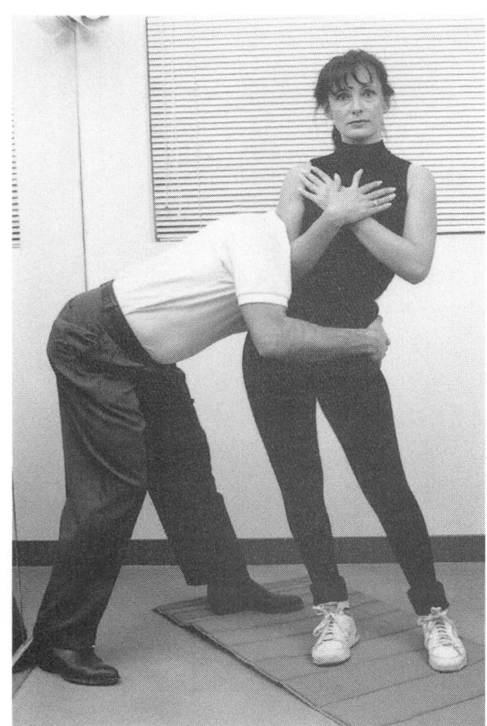

Figure 8–17. Therapist overpressure: left side gliding (to reverse right lateral shift).

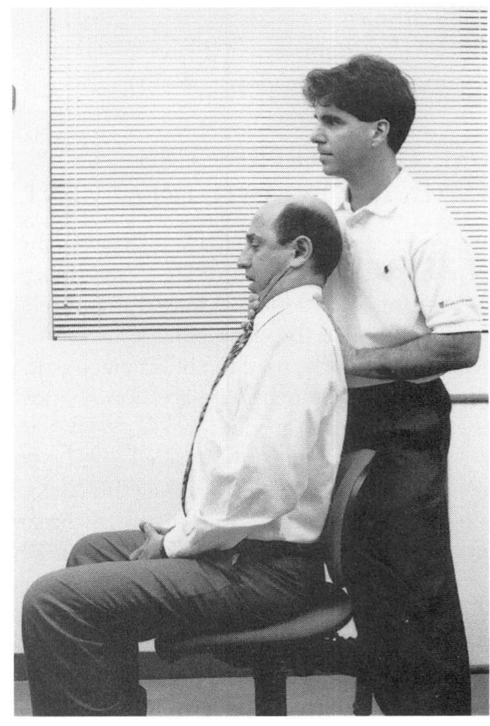

Figure 8–18. Therapist overpressure: cervical retraction.

McKENZIE'S SYNDROMES

McKenzie organizes mechanical and symptomatic responses to loading into three "syndrome patterns" that classify the manner in which mechanical and symptomatic responses occur in tandem. McKenzie protocols recognize the loading in one movement plane direction may affect the mechanical responses in that direction, the opposite movement plane direction, or an entirely different movement plane. The mechanical responses are range of motion and the ability to accomplish the movement in the intended movement plane without deviation. McKenzie protocols recognize the ability of loading in one movement plane direction to affect symptomatic responses in the same or other movement planes. Symptoms include the topography and severity of symptoms, the various "-esthesia," and subjectively perceived disabilities. The three syndromes are:

- Postural syndrome
- Dysfunction syndrome
- Derangement syndrome

The names given to the syndromes serve as functional, operational, and metaphorical definitions. Syndrome names are similes or "as if" identifications of what mechanical and symptomatic response patterns to loading behave "like."

The postural syndrome behaves *as if* postural stresses on normal tissue are culpable. Treatment is postural reedu-

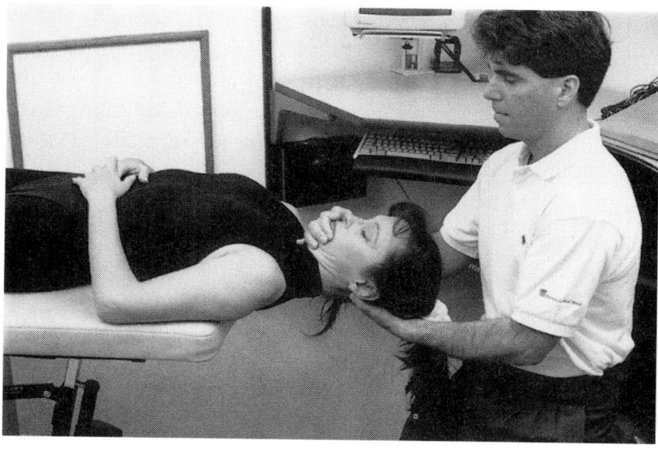
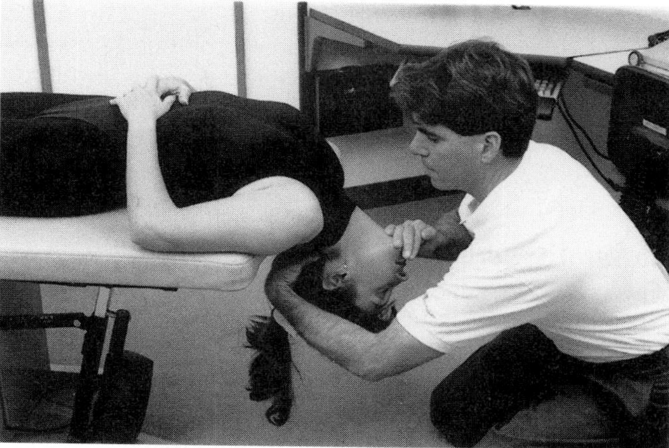

Figure 8–19. Therapist overpressure: cervical traction, retraction-then-extension (supine).

cation to reduce tissue tension. The dysfunction syndrome behaves *as if* tissue is shortened. Treatment remodels tissue by tensioning to make it more elastic. The derangement syndrome behaves *as if* disc material has been displaced. Treatment compresses the space displaced disc material occupies in order to reduce the derangement.

The treatment strategies for the three syndromes have been memorialized by McKenzie as the "three Rs"[14].

- Reeducate (postural)
- Remodel (dysfunction)
- Reduce (derangement)

SITTING AND THE SYNDROMES

The McKenzie perspective finds spinal flexion to be the most common (but not only) causative and complicating factor of spinal complaints. In this regard, sitting is viewed as the greatest culprit. Slouched sitting flexes the lumbar, thoracic, and lower cervical spine. If one is looking down while sitting, the upper cervical spine flexes in suit. However, if one is looking forward, protrusion of the head and neck occurs causing extension of the upper cervical spine. These sustained postures are thought to be key causative and perpetuating factors for a good deal of what is classified in all three syndromes, as will be discussed below.

POSTURAL SYNDROME

Postural syndrome mechanical and symptomatic responses to loading behave *as if* abnormal stresses are being placed on normal joint structures. For postural syndrome patients, sustained end range positioning of "normal" joint complexes causes symptoms proportional to the amount of the load and the time over which loading occurs. When a normal joint is held at end range, noncontractile structures such as ligaments and joint capsules are "stretch" stressed. The reader is invited to use one hand to hyperextend a finger of the other hand to end range to experience this discomfort. Hyperextend the finger just short of the symptomatic end range and discomfort will develop within the quarter hour. Spinal joints behave in the same manner. No *pathology* need exist for the symptoms to occur.

Postural syndrome patients do not evidence mechanical responses to loading (limited motion or deviation from the intended movement plane direction). They present with normal (or better than normal) ranges of motion, no symptoms during motion, and no symptoms at end range, unless end range is sustained for a prolonged period of time. Symptoms do not persist once the abnormal stretch stress ceases. There are no referred symptoms.

Postural syndrome complaints resulting from poor sitting posture often include the cervical, thoracic, and lumbosacral areas simultaneously. Postural syndrome patients are sometimes characterized as hypermobile or psychosomatic because they present with multiple areas of complaints in spite of normal range of motion. Complaints are not due to the sequelae of "better than normal range of motion," but to remaining motionless at end range. Complaints are intermittent because they only occur when sustained loading at end range occurs. When postural syndrome patients are "up and about," symptomatic sustained end range loading is avoided. Complaints are intermittent.

Postural syndrome is best treated with education in body mechanics. *Pain avoidance* is the strategy for this syndrome. Sustained loading at the culpable end range must be avoided. It takes vigilant conscious effort to accomplish the task. Muscle strengthening does not correct posture. One must choose correct posture by strengthening awareness of the positioning of one's body in space. The goal is to *reeducate* the patient. If the patient avoids the symptomatic end range posture, syndrome resolution should occur within a week or two. At that point in time, sustained end range loading should then be able to be accomplished without discomfort, although perpetuation of this habit could cause the syndrome to return.

Postural Syndrome and Sitting

Due to common poor sitting posture, the upper cervical spine extends and the rest of the spine slouches into flexion. A *sustained extension postural syndrome* develops at the upper cervical spine. A *sustained flexion postural syndrome* develops anywhere from the lower cervical spine to the lumbosacral junction.

Postural Syndrome and Spinal Manipulation

The postural syndrome represents abnormal stress placed on normal tissue. Range of motion is equal to or greater than normal in the postural syndrome. Complaints are only experienced when end range loading is performed for a protracted period of time. Spinal manipulation is not an appropriate consideration for the postural syndrome because there is no motion to restore. Only postural correction resolves the syndrome.

DYSFUNCTION SYNDROME

Dysfunction syndrome mechanical and symptomatic responses to loading behave *as if* adaptive shortening, loss of elasticity, scar tissue formation, etc., are restricting spinal movements. For dysfunction syndrome patients, symptom-free movement is accomplished until the end range of a shortened structure is realized, at which point there is prohibition of further movement, often accompanied by symptoms. Within the course of an initial examination, no matter how many repetitions of the limited motion are pursued, a mechanical impedance occurs at the same point in the movement arc. Responses are *as if* a shortened structure is present that cannot be lengthened during the course of the initial visit. It may take weeks or months of vigilant loading for this to be accomplished.

Like the postural syndrome, the dysfunction syndrome displays intermittent complaints. In the postural syndrome, complaints *develop over time* with sustained loading at end range. In the dysfunction syndrome, complaints are experienced *immediately* when the mechanically impeded, limited end range is realized and shortened tissue is challenged to lengthen. For both the postural and dysfunction syndromes, discomfort ceases once loading at the culpable end range ceases.

Postural syndrome patients do not present with symptom referral phenomena. Dysfunction syndrome patients experience localized symptoms except for the case of the *adherent nerve root*. The adherent nerve root is the only instance in which a dysfunction syndrome refers symptoms. This has been referred to as *adverse neural tension*,[3] and may be due to postsurgical scarring or scar formation resulting from natural healing processes without surgical intervention.

Like all dysfunction syndromes, adherent nerve root phenomena conform to a typical pattern. Adherent nerve root signs and symptoms are reproduced or intensified by increasing the "tension" on the adherent root. Nerve root tension is increased by means of spinal flexion combined with strategic movements of the involved extremity. Cervicothoracic adherent nerve root signs and symptoms are reproduced or intensified by cervical flexion, combined with cervical contralateral lateral flexion and abduction of the ipsilateral shoulder with extended elbow. Lumbosacral adherent nerve root signs and symptoms are reproduced or intensified by lumbosacral flexion, with ipsilateral hip flexion and knee extended. As with all dysfunction syndromes, the mechanical and symptomatic responses of an adherent nerve root occur at the limited end range of the "adherence." This is the point at which the adherence prevents any further movement as it anchors the root to resist the action of further spinal flexion. Mechanical and symptomatic responses occur immediately as the end range of the adherence is challenged. Responses fade once end range tensioning is terminated.

Unilateral dysfunctions may cause deviation from the intended movement plane direction as the body "accommodates" by deviating toward the side of dysfunction to continue a semblance of the intended movement. If a lumbosacral joint or nerve root is suffering dysfunction on the right of the spine, attempted flexion may be accompanied by movement toward the right without which further flexion would not be possible. Deviation to the right represents an attempt to "slacken" the adherence, thus permitting further flexion movement.

In the postural syndrome discomfort results from normal tissue being subjected to abnormal (sustained end range) forces whereas in the dysfunction syndrome abnormal (shortened) tissue causes discomfort when subjected to normal forces (movement within normal range of motion). For the postural syndrome, avoiding end range discomfort is the remedy; for the dysfunction syndrome, it perpetuates the problem. *Pain pursual* is the preferred strategy for the dysfunction syndrome. The loading strategy for the dysfunction syndrome is to challenge shortened tissue frequently. Dysfunction patients are required to elicit discomfort at the mechanically impeded limited end range over the course of the day. Dysfunction syndrome resolution employs the "use it or lose it" principle. Treatment behavior is conducted *as if* one were trying to *remodel* shortened tissue.

Dysfunction syndrome nomenclature employs the name of the movement plane direction limited by shortened tissue. If extension is limited due to adaptively shortened tissue, this would be referred to as an *extension dysfunction*.

Dysfunction Syndrome and Sitting

Dysfunction (adaptive shortening of tissue) is thought to develop as a result of habitual positionings absent movement or positioning in opposite directions. Poor sitting posture results in habitual upper cervical extension and lower cervical, thoracic, and lumbosacral flexion. This promotes the development of flexion dysfunctions of the upper cervical spine and extension dysfunctions of the lower cervical, thoracic, and lumbosacral spinal regions.

Spinal Manipulation and Dysfunction Syndrome

The dysfunction syndrome requires frequent end range loading during the course of the day in order to remodel shortened tissue. Tissue that is "too short" may not respond favorably to manipulation. If shortened tissue is overstretched, it will become inflamed and change the clinical picture from intermittent mechanical pain to constant chemical pain. After patient-generated and/or clinician-assisted mobilizations partially remodel shortened tissue, dynamic manipulative loading is less of a risk and may, in fact, be of further benefit to remodel the joint complex. Manipulation is appropriate in the later stages of dysfunction remodeling in order to stretch tissue beyond the range of the patient's own capabilities. Manipulation, without the performance of frequent patient-generated end range loading, cannot resolve this syndrome.

DERANGEMENT SYNDROME

Derangement syndrome mechanical and symptomatic responses behave *as if* there has been displacement, accumulation, migration, or directional pressure changes of intradiscal materials. In postural and dysfunction syndromes, loading in one movement plane direction does not affect mechanical and symptomatic responses in other movement plane directions. In the derangement syndrome, loading in one movement plane direction may affect mechanical and symptomatic responses in the opposite movement plane direction or in a totally different movement plane. If repetitive flexion forces disc material to derange posteriorly, this results in a symptomatic obstruction to extension due to the amount of disc material "in the way." If flexion and extension both cause lateral derangement of disc material (sagittal compressive forces causing coronal spread), a symptomatic mechanical obstruction to coronal movements will develop.

Derangement symptoms may be intermittent or constant. Intermittent symptoms occur as movements and positionings cause disc materially to cyclically derange and reduce. Constant symptoms occur if the derangement is too formidable to be reduced by movements and positionings.

Derangement syndrome patients must avoid spinal loadings that result in mechanical and symptomatic responses *as if* disc material is deranging further. When symptoms move distal to the spine or into the extremities, this is referred to as *peripheralization* and is regarded as evidence of further derangement of disc material. The *peripheralization* of derangement may be constant, and contrary to the peripheralization of dysfunction, does not occur at end range spinal movements only. Derangement peripheralization can occur during any point of the movement plane and may remain after the culpable loading action ceases, contrary to adherent nerve root dysfunction peripheralization, which "is gone" once flexion end range loading ceases.

Consider the following regarding the low back. If flexion in standing (bilateral hip flexion with extended knee) causes lower extremity symptoms that do not resolve once end range flexion loading ceases, the behavior pattern is one of a derangement. Supine knee-to-chest exercises (bilateral hip and knee flexion) should not tension an adherent nerve root dysfunction. Adherent nerve root dysfunction causes lower extremity complaints at end range when performing standing in flexion, not when performing supine knee-to-chest exercise. If supine knee-to-chest exercises peripheralize low back symptoms to the lower extremity, this is derangement behavior, not dysfunction behavior.

When peripheral symptoms resolve and/or "move toward the center" of the spine, this is referred to as *centralization*. This is regarded as evidence of the reduction of disc derangement. The "movement of symptoms" toward the center of the spine may be accompanied by increased intensity of central discomfort. The phenomenom of increased central symptoms accompanying the resolution of peripheral complaints is considered the "good pain" (hurt, not harm) of intradiscal derangement reduction to a "more central location." This centralization phenomenon indicates the therapeutic movement is being pursued. Any increase of central symptom intensity is usually short-lived.

For the postural syndrome, symptoms are realized at a sustained normal end range. In the dysfunction syndrome, symptoms are realized at the "limited" end range because of shortened tissue. For the postural and dysfunction syndromes, there are no mechanical or symptomatic responses during midrange. Derangement syndromes exhibit mechanical (deviation from the intended movement plane direction) and symptomatic responses during motion that are never evidenced by postural and dysfunction syndromes. Responses to loading may not cease once the precipitating loading tactic ceases, contrary to the postural and dysfunction syndromes in which symptoms resolve once end range loading is terminated.

For the postural syndrome patient, avoidance of symptoms resolves the syndrome. For the dysfunction patient, pursual of symptom resolves the syndrome. For the derangement syndrome, it is important to both avoid symptoms (as in the postural syndrome) and to pursue symptoms (as in the dysfunction syndrome). A preferred loading strategy is devised to pursue symptoms representing the *reduction* of deranged disc material. The remedy rule for the postural syndrome is to *avoid stretching* in a certain movement plane direction. The remedy rule for the dysfunction syndrome *is stretching*. The remedy rule for the derangement syndrome is *compressing* disc material to be driven in the direction *opposite* the compressive forces.

The strategy for the derangement syndrome, as for the dysfunction syndrome, is loading at a symptomatic, mechanically impeded end range. For the derangement syndrome, movement is not restricted by shortened tissue "holding the joint back" but by displaced disc material which is "in the way," or obstructing movement. Dysfunction syndrome patients respond *as if* whatever is holding movement back can be stretched. Derangement syndrome patients respond *as if* "something in the way" can be "compressed" or "pushed out of the way."

Overpressure is a useful tool to differentiate between dysfunction and derangement. Overpressure in the therapeutically correct direction *reveals dysfunction and reduces derangement*. That is, overpressure would increase the discomfort of dysfunction or reduce the derangement (which may be accompanied by the discomfort of a centralization). Overpressure, by promoting further end range loading, amplifies or accelerates the mechanical and/or symptomatic responses. Overpressure in the therapeutically incorrect direction would have no effect on dysfunction but has the potential of making derangement worse.

Derangement syndrome patients may have multiple obstructed movement plane directions. The goal is to find the *key* obstruction to reduce by compressive loading forces, so as to resolve the syndrome in the most time-efficient manner. Mechanical and symptomatic (especially centralization) responses are monitored to determine this.

Derangement syndrome nomenclature indicates the direction of disc displacement. Derangement syndromes are named according to the direction in which the *disc* has moved, whereas dysfunction syndromes are named by the direction in which the *patient* cannot move and postural syndromes are named according to the direction the *patient* doesn't move from.

A *posterior derangement* behaves as if disc material has deranged in a posterior direction. The patient may have loss of lordosis or, if severe, fixed kyphosis. Extension is obstructed. Flexion may be limited by symptoms but is not limited by mechanical obstruction. Sustained or repetitive flexion peripheralizes complaints and may cause greater obstruction to extension. Extension loading strategies return lordosis and cause centralization of complaints. Considering the amount of flexion performed in industrial societies, posterior derangement is common.

An *anterior derangement* behaves as if disc material has deranged in an anterior direction. The patient typically has a fixed lordosis in the lumbar spine and may or may not have fixed lordosis in the cervical spine. Anterior derangements are rare in the thoracic spine. Flexion is obstructed. Extension may be limited by symptoms but not by mechanical obstruction. Sustained or repetitive extension peripheralizes complaints and may cause greater obstruction to flexion. Flexion loading strategies resolve the fixed lordosis and cause centralization. Because of the frequency of flexion in industrial societies, anterior derangements are less common.

A *lateral derangement* may cause central or unilateral symptoms. Lateral derangements may, nonetheless, be reduced by loading strategies in the sagittal plane (flexion or extension). If sagittal loading tactics resolve unilateral complaints, those complaints are not considered to be caused by a *relevant* lateral component (i.e., one requiring coronal or transverse loading strategies). The extreme case of a lateral derangement is the fixed deformity of acute lumbar scoliosis or cervical torticollis. In general, when patients present with a fixed lateral deformity, McKenzie protocols do not require a full range of motion analysis, as the "writing is on the wall." Loading strategies are employed to reduce the fixed deformity in the coronal plane while monitoring for centralization versus peripheralization.

McKenzie also classifies derangements numerically, organized according to symptom topography and the presence or absence of fixed deformities. Derangements one through six are posterior derangements, whereas all anterior derangements are classified as "derangement seven." The numerical classification of derangements is as follows.

Derangement One

- Central or symmetrical symptoms about the spine
- Rarely, shoulder/arm or buttocks/thigh symptoms
- No deformity

Derangement Two

- Central or symmetrical symptoms about the spine
- With or without shoulder/arm or buttocks/thigh symptoms
- With deformity of kyphosis

Derangement Three

- Unilateral or asymmetrical symptoms about the spine
- With or without shoulder/arm or buttocks/thigh symptoms
- No deformity

Derangement Four

- Unilateral or asymmetrical symptoms about the spine
- With or without shoulder/arm or buttocks/thigh symptoms
- With deformity of torticollis or lumbar scoliosis

Derangement Five

- Unilateral or asymmetrical symptoms about the spine
- With or without shoulder/arm or buttocks/thigh symptoms
- With symptoms extending below the elbow or knee
- No deformity

Derangement Six

- Unilateral or asymmetrical symptoms about the spine
- With or without shoulder/arm or buttocks/thigh symptoms
- With symptoms extending below the elbow or knee
- With deformity of acute kyphosis, torticollis, or lumbar scoliosis

Derangement Seven

- Symmetrical or asymmetrical symptoms about the spine
- With or without shoulder/arm or buttocks/thigh symptoms
- Deformity of accentuated lordosis may or may not be present

For derangements one through six (posterior derangements), the even-numbered derangements have the same symptoms as the preceding odd-numbered derangements with the addition of a fixed deformity. A mnemonic device to remember the numerical classification of derangements employed by the senior author is the "deranged" poem:

One is central
Two is kyphotic
Three is unilateral
Four is scoliotic
Five is the arm or leg
Six is all the worst
Seven to two is the reverse

Derangement Syndrome and Sitting

The McKenzie paradigm perceives posterior derangements as more common because of the frequent, sustained, and repetitive spinal flexions of daily life. For the same reason, anterior derangements are considered less common.

A scenario for the genesis of posterior derangement is as follows: Sustained and repetitive flexion and the lack of extension movements during daily activities eventually leads to loss of extension. An extension dysfunction may develop. Sustained and repetitive spinal flexions, over time, compress the anterior disc space, promoting migration of disc material to the posterior disc space. The absence of compressive forces on the posterior disc space and the increased tension on posterior annular structures, over time, further increase susceptibility to posterior derangement.

Most posterior derangement patients are worse with sitting. Sitting represents spinal flexion. Spinal flexion would be expected to make posterior derangements worse. In general, anterior derangements feel better when sitting because the flexion reduces the anterior migration of disc material. Exceptions to these generalities are considered in the section below entitled "Clinical Reasoning Scenarios."

A

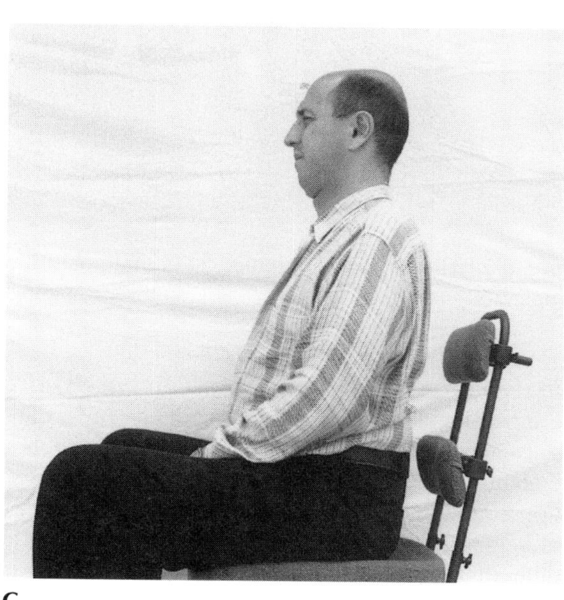

C

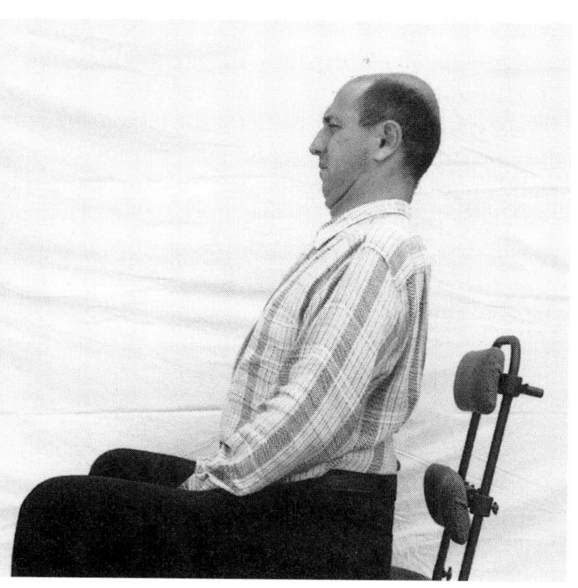

B

Figure 8–20. A. Sitting relaxed. **B.** Sitting "overcorrected". **C.** Relaxing 10% from overcorrected to "normal" erect sitting posture.

Figure 8–21. Teaching to maintain "standing posture when sitting".

Spinal Manipulation and Derangement Syndrome

The most dramatic responses to manipulation occur with derangement syndrome patients. McKenzie protocols advocate manipulation for derangement syndrome patients after self-generated movements demonstrate partial or short-lived benefits. Full recovery from self-generated end range loading obviates the need for manipulation.

Responses to patient-generated end range loading *herald* the responses to be expected if the patient were to be positioned, moved, or manipulated at that same end range. If self-generated end range loading in a particular movement plane direction is beneficial, manipulation to the same end range will most likely be as, if not more, beneficial. If self-generated end range loading, in a particular movement plane direction, is detrimental, manipulation to the same end range will most likely be as, if not more, detrimental.

THERAPEUTIC PROGRESSIONS AND RESPONSIBILITIES

The same movements employed to evaluate mechanical and symptomatic responses are employed for therapeutic purposes. Responses dictate which movements and positions are to be pursued or avoided.

Postural Syndrome

The goal is to reeducate the patient to avoid the culpable end range. When a patient frequently stresses the culpable end range, symptoms are provoked sooner and more often. When the culpable end range is avoided, symptoms are avoided.

Postural syndrome patients are not aware they are suffering the effects of sustained end range loading. Postural syndromes typically result from the poor, slouched sitting posture. Instruction in the body mechanics of sitting is essential. Vigilance is required on the part of the patient to avoid sustained loading at the culpable end range. The postural patient may have difficulty believing the solution is "so simple." It is the responsibility of the practitioner to educate the patient concerning the need to avoid end range discomfort. It is the patient's responsibility to avoid sustained end range loading long enough for the condition to resolve. This usually takes 1 or 2 weeks.

Proper sitting posture is taught as follows: The patient is asked to assume an "over corrected" sitting posture (fully retracted head and lordotic lumbar spine) and then to relax 10% to "normal" erect sitting posture (Figure 8–20). The benefit of assuming the overcorrected posture is twofold:

1. The patient develops kinesthetic awareness.
2. Over correction is so awkward that normal sitting posture does not seem so strange, something that keeps patients from "sitting up."

If a patient's spinal complaints are reduced by standing or walking, it is helpful to request that he or she sit in a posture identical to that of standing "from the buttocks up." The patient is asked to stand in front of the chair. The clinician places one hand on the manubrium and the other hand within the hollow of the back. The patient is asked to maintain the "relationship of the two hands" while sitting or making transitions to or from sitting (Figure 8–21). In addition to education in proper sitting posture, a lumbar support will enhance compliance.

Dysfunction Syndrome

The goal is to remodel shortened tissue by frequently provoking the discomfort of loading at the restricted end range. Dysfunction syndrome patients tend to avoid their discomforts at end range, perpetuating the condition. Complaints will persist unless the symptomatic, mechanically impeded end range is frequently pursued. It is the responsibility of the practitioner to educate the patient concerning the need to frequently pursue end range discomforts throughout the day. It is the responsibility of the patient to do so. Dysfunction syndrome patients are a challenge to motivate, as they are being asked to cause themselves frequent discomfort without rapid results. The clinician offers no "quick fix." The patient improves as the tissue becomes more elastic, a process that can take months.

Derangement Syndromes

The goal is to reduce displacement of disc material by loading the key obstructed end range. Symptoms of peripheralization are avoided. Symptoms of centralization are pursued. Derangement syndrome patients often avoid movements and positionings accompanied by the symptoms of centralization. The centralization response occurs as the obstruction to end range is reduced (relocated). It is the responsibility of the practitioner to educate the patient that increased central complaints are beneficial, especially when accompanied by diminished peripheral complaints. It is the practitioner's responsibility to make clear which movements and positionings are to be pursued and which are to be avoided. It is the patient's responsibility to comply. The successful resolution of a derangement syndrome requires:

- Reduction of the deranged disc material
- Maintenance of the reduction
- Reintroduction of movements previously considered to promote derangement (recovery of function)
- Prophylaxis by periodically pursuing loading strategies that reduce the derangement

CLINICAL REASONING SCENARIOS

The following "scenarios" explore clinical reasoning according to McKenzie protocols. How the patient experiences sitting and standing serves as posture examples for these clinical reasoning scenarios. The following scenarios demonstrate the importance of basing McKenzie diagnoses and treatments upon mechanical and symptomatic responses to repetitive movements and sustained positioning.

"SITTING MAKES IT WORSE"

Consider a patient presenting with spinal complaints made worse with sitting. This symptom alone does not tell you which syndrome is involved.

Could It Be a Postural Syndrome?

Typical poor sitting posture extends the upper cervical spine and flexes lower spinal levels. Sustained end range loading causes symptoms in one or more of these areas. Examination of the patient provokes no symptoms with end range dynamic loading, no symptoms during motion, no symptom referrals and no mechanical responses. Considering the way most individuals sit, resulting upper cervical complaints would be the result of a sustained extension postural syndrome, whereas all lower levels of spinal complaints would be manifestations of a sustained flexion postural syndrome.

Could It Be a Dysfunction Syndrome?

Poor sitting posture typically extends the upper cervical spine and flexes lower levels, promoting the development of upper cervical flexion dysfunction and extension dysfunctions of lower spinal levels. Dysfunctions typically develop in movement plane directions opposite that of the habitual poor posturing. There would be symptoms at an early limited end range. There are no symptoms during motion. The patient is essentially no better or worse as a result of provocative testing or therapeutic movement. Repetition of movement does not result in further gain of range of motion until weeks have transpired.

Could It Be a Derangement Syndrome?

Considering typical poor sitting posture, loading the upper cervical spine at sustained end range extension and lower spinal levels at sustained end range flexion, causes one to consider the possibility of anterior derangement of the upper cervical spine or posterior derangement at lower spinal levels. Dynamic or static loading in the direction that promotes the derangement may result in peripheralization of complaints that remain worse after loading ceases. There may be symptoms during motion. Dynamic or static loading at the key obstructed end range would be accompanied by centralization, improved mechanics, and maintained benefit.

However, the derangement syndrome patient's complaint of being "worse when sitting" may not be due to *promotion* of derangement. It may, in fact, be due to inadequate *reduction* of derangement. Recall centralization can be quite uncomfortable. When spinal loading begins to challenge the obstruction resulting from derangement but is not applied with enough intensity to reduce it, centralization-like discomforts may be experienced without any net benefit. Therefore, the patient who is worse with sitting may, in fact, have a posterior derangement of the upper cervical spine, or anterior derangement of lower spinal levels, for which sitting symptoms represent discomforts that should not be avoided and, in fact, should be pursued more vigorously.

Anterior derangements require flexion, and posterior derangements require extension. Treatment predicates on one symptom along with failure to perform careful analysis of the mechanical and symptomatic responses to dynamic and static loading may lead to a loading strategy opposite that which is required.

"STANDING MAKES IT WORSE"

Could It be a Postural Syndrome?

Postural syndromes are due to sustained end range loading of normal spinal joints. A variety of standing postures can be responsible (e.g., protruded head, hyperkyphotic thorax, hyperlordotic lumbars, standing with one's weight on one leg). The diagnosis is confirmed when dynamic loading is without mechanical or symptomatic responses and complaints are reproduced with sustained end range loading only.

Could It be a Dysfunction Syndrome?

Relative to sitting, standing involves retraction (flexion) of the upper cervical spine and relative extension of all lower spinal levels. Typically, a patient who is asymptomatic when sitting but experiences dysfunction symptoms when standing is suffering from upper cervical flexion (retraction) dysfunction. These conclusions, of course, would be reached after exploring the effects of mechanical and symptomatic responses to loading.

Could It be a Derangement Syndrome?

Relative to sitting, standing involves retraction (flexion of the upper cervical spine) and relative extension of all lower spinal levels, causing one to consider the possibilities of posterior derangement of the upper cervical spine or anterior derangement at lower spinal levels.

Lower cervical and low back derangement symptoms that worsen with standing most often are due to an anterior, not a posterior, derangement. Dynamic and static loading responses are the key to whether or not this is true for a particular patient. However, the derangement syndrome patient's complaint "worse when standing" may not be due to promotion of derangement. It may be due to the discomfort of centralization accompanying inadequate reduction of derangement. The patient avoids the centralization discomfort, not realizing its potential benefit. Therefore, the patient who is worse with standing may, in fact, have an anterior derangement of the upper cervical spine or posterior derangement of lower spinal levels, for which standing symptoms represent discomfort that should not be avoided and, in fact, should be pursued more vigorously.

MIXED SYNDROME SCENARIOS

It is possible for syndromes to coexist. We have considered how habitually flexed lumbosacral posture can at first result in postural syndrome symptoms and then lead to extension dysfunction and posterior migration (derangement) of disc material. Accordingly, the individual experiences all three of these syndromes simultaneously. Consider the following regarding mixed syndrome scenarios.

Mixed Syndrome Scenario 1

The patient presents complaining of low back symptoms after sitting slouched for 15 minutes. Examination reveals no symptoms during motion. All ranges of motion are full and unrestricted except for extension, which is limited by one-third. When the patient reaches two-thirds normal extension, discomfort is experienced immediately but resolves upon returning to neutral posture. No matter how many extension movements are performed during the initial exam, the range of motion or symptoms do not change appreciably. There are no symptoms during motion.

What McKenzie syndrome best accounts for presenting complaints?

The patient obviously suffers from an extension dysfunction. However, an extension dysfunction does not account for the presenting complaint of pain with slouched sitting. The pain with slouched sitting is best explained by the postural syndrome. The dysfunction syndrome should be addressed; however, it is not responsible for the complaint that brought the patient in. In order to treat the presenting complaint, postural syndrome protocols are required.

Mixed Syndrome Scenario 2

A patient presents complaining of low back symptoms that begin after sitting for 15 minutes. After sitting 30 minutes symptoms peripheralize to the buttock and right lower extremity. Standing, walking, and lying down are not problematic. Flexion in standing or supine knee-to-chest movements peripheralize complaints to the lower extremity. All ranges of motion are full and unrestricted except for extension, which is two-thirds normal. When the patient reaches two-thirds normal extension, discomfort is experienced immediately that resolves upon returning to neutral posture. Centralization does not occur with extension. No matter how many extension movements are performed, symptoms and range of motion do not change.

What McKenzie syndromes best account for presenting complaints?

The patient exhibits mechanical and symptomatic responses evidencing derangement peripheralization behavior. However, centralization responses are not achieved. The patient has an extension dysfunction syndrome in which the limited end range occurs before and prevents loading from "reaching" the obstructed end range of the derangement. It is not until the dysfunction is "worked through" that loading can be expected to reduce the derangement.

McKENZIE PROTOCOLS' IMPACT ON PATIENT BEHAVIOR

Consistent with the rehabilitation philosophies, McKenzie protocols promote self-sufficiency and independent functioning. The potentials of self-treatment are explored on the initial visit, even if the patient is acute. Patient responsibilities include the pursuit and/or avoidance of specific positions and exercises. The emphasis is placed on control of symptoms rather than actively avoiding symptoms. Fear of activity, symptom magnification, and practitioner dependence are discouraged.

A significant goal of component of treatment is to affect the mind set of the patient. If patients are taught to participate in their own care, the chance of recovery is greater and the chance of recurrence is less. In McKenzie's own words:

> "If there is the slightest chance that a patient can be educated in a method of treatment that enables him to reduce his own pain and disability using his own understanding and resources, he should receive that education. Every patient is entitled to this information, and every therapist should be obliged to provide it."[14]

Clinical Application 8–1

SUBJECTIVE HISTORY

A 40-year-old truck driver (Patient ID 10) presents with low back and left lower extremity pain to the midcalf (see Figure 8–22A). His postures and stresses are prolonged sitting while driving at work, and at home his activities include watching television, yardwork, and cutting wood.

The pain has been present for 3 weeks and is worsening. He has been off work for 1 week because of the symptoms. The pain commenced for no apparent reason and began in the lumbar region. He has intermittent low back pain, but constant thigh and leg pain.

Sitting and forward bending are guaranteed to increase his peripheral symptoms. Lying supine is guaranteed to decrease the leg symptoms, but it does not last. Rising from sitting is positive, and standing and walking make the back worse at times. He is better when awaking and gets worse as the day progresses. Walking makes the leg better at times, and he feels better on the move and worse when still.

His sleep is disturbed. He sleeps on his sides and back and on a firm mattress. Coughing and sneezing is positive for leg pain, but bowel, bladder, and gait are normal.

He has had back pain many times in the past, but a chiropractic manipulation or two provided symptomatic relief. The leg pain is now present for the first time, and it won't resolve.

Previous treatments for this episode included prescription pharmaceuticals, rest, and passive physical therapy (heat and exercises, including flexion and extension). None of the treatment interventions have had any lasting effect.

Diagnostic testing involved an (MRI) that revealed a left paracentral herniated nucleus pulposis of the L5 lumbar disc. His general health is good. He is currently taking antiinflammatory and analgesic medicine. He denies any recent or major surgery, accidents, or unexplained weight loss.

CLINICAL EVALUATION

His sitting posture is poor, standing posture is fair, lordosis is reduced, and he has a right lateral shift present (Figure 8–22B).

Movement loss is as follows:

Flexion: moderate to major loss with right deviation in flexion
Extension: moderate loss
Side gliding (R): nil
Side gliding (L): minimal to moderate loss

Pretest pain in standing was low back and left thigh pain. Flexion in standing (FIS) produced pain during movement (PDM) and end range pain (ERP). Repeated FIS increased thigh pain and produced leg pain and remained worse. Extension in standing (EIS) produced ERP, and repeated EIS increased leg and back pain but it did not remain worse.

Pretest pain in lying supine increased thigh and leg pain. Flexion in lying (FIL) produced PDM and ERP with repeated FIL increasing thigh and leg pain, and it remained worse. Extension in lying (EIL) produced ERP, and repeated EIL increased his low back pain but decreased his thigh and leg symptoms. They remained better. Both side gliding movements had no effect on the symptoms.

Static tests of sitting slouched increased and worsened the leg pain but had no effect on his low back pain. Sitting erect decreased the leg pain and increased his back pain. Lying prone abolished his low back pain and decreased his leg symptoms. Lying prone in extension only decreased his leg symptoms.

Neurological testing was all within normal limits (WNL), as was testing of the hip joints and SI joints.

Review Questions for Clinical Application 8–1*

1. Based on the subjective history, what is your working hypothesis as to his condition and why?
2. What would be the first clinical test you would perform? Why?
3. What is your working diagnosis? Why?
4. What would you recommend this patient do at home? How often? When would you see him for follow-up and what would you look for in the second-day assessment? What are the reasons for your answers?

*Answers appear in Appendix at end of chapter.

The McKenzie Institute Lumbar Spine Assessment

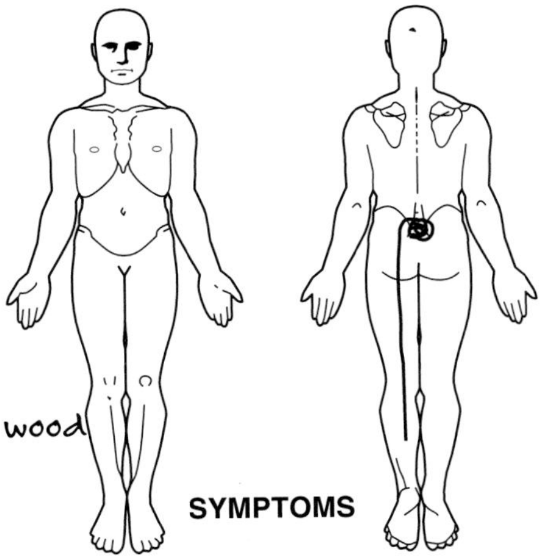

Date ___/___/___

Name Patient I.D. #10 40 yr old

Address

Date of Birth Sex: (M) / F

Occupation Truck Driver

Postures / Stresses Sit/Drive (work); TV/yard work, cut wood

Telephone

Referral: *GP / Orth / Self / Other*

Off work because of current episode? *(Yes) / No* Since Week

SYMPTOMS

Symptoms this episode to be marked on body diagram

HISTORY

Describe relevant symptoms LBP → (L) Calf Radiation pain/numbness

Present since ___/___/ 3 weeks *Improving / unchanging / (worsening)*

Commenced as a result of: (or no apparent reason)

Symptoms at onset *(back) / thigh / leg*

Constant Symptoms: *back / (thigh) / (leg)*

Intermittent Symptoms: *back / thigh / leg*

Worse: *(bending)* leg *(sitting) / (rising)* leg *standing* leg *walking* back *lying*

am / as day progresses / pm leg *(when still) / on the move*

other guaranteed produce, pain - sit/bend - leg

Better: *bending* *sitting / rising* *standing* *walking* leg *(lying)*

(am) / as day progresses / pm *when still / on the move*

other guaranteed decrease pain - Lie down; stay out of truck

Disturbed sleep? *(Yes) / No* Sleeping postures: *prone / (sup / side (R / L))* Surface: *(firm) / soft / sag / w. bed*

(Cough) / (sneeze) / strain: (+ve) / –ve Bladder: *(normal) / abnormal* Gait: *(normal) / abnormal*

Previous Episodes: *0 1–5 (6–10) 11+* Year of first episode: 19

Previous history: LBP epidsodic - manipulation or 2 & go away

This time leg pain a first, not going away

Previous treatments: P.M.D. - meds, rest; P.T. exercises, flx/ext - no better

X-rays: *(Yes) / No* MRI - L Paracentral HNP L5

Gen. Health: *(Good) / Fair / Poor*

Medications: *Nil / (NSAID) / (Analg) / Steroids / Anticong / Other*

Recent or major surgery: *Yes / (No)*

Accidents: *Yes / (No)* Unexplained weight loss: *Yes / (No)*

Figure 8–22A. Patient ID 10.

EXAMINATION

POSTURE
Sitting: Good / Fair / (Poor) Standing: Good / (Fair) / Poor Lordosis: (Red) / Add / Normal Lateral Shift: (Right) / Left / Nil
Other Observations: ________

MOVEMENT LOSS	maj	mod	min	nil
Flexion	X			
Extension		X		
Side Gliding (R)				X
Side Gliding (L)		X		

Deviation in Flexion: (Right) / Left / Nil
Deviation in Extension: Right / Left / (Nil)

TEST MOVEMENTS: Describe effects on present pain - produces, abolishes, increases, decreases, centralizes, peripheralises, better, worse, no better, no worse, no effect

		PDM	ERP
Describe pretest pain standing	(L) Thigh/LBP		
FIS		X	X
Rep FIS	↑ Thigh, Produce leg pain - worse	X	X
EIS			X
Rep EIS	↑ No worse leg, ↑ LBP - No worse		X
Describe pretest pain lying	↑ Thigh / leg		
FIL		X	X
Rep FIL	↑ Thigh / leg, worse	X	X
EIL			X
Rep EIL	↑ LBP - No worse, ↓ Thigh, abolished leg, better		X
If required SGIS (R)			
Rep SGIS (R)	No effect		
SGIS (L)			
Rep SGIS (L)	No worse		X

STATIC TESTS If required
Sitting Slouched ↑ Worsens leg.
Sitting erect ↓ Leg, produces back
Standing Slouched ↑ Thigh / leg.
Standing erect No effect
Lying prone in extension ↓ Thigh / leg LBP
Prone ↓ Thigh / leg, abolish LBP
Long sitting ________

NEUROLOGICAL
Motor Deficit: WNL
Reflexes: WNL
Sensory Deficit: WNL
Dural signs: Negative

OTHER
Hip Joints: ________
SI Joints: ________

CONCLUSION
Posture Dysfunction Derangement No. 5 Trauma
Other ________

PRINCIPLE OF TREATMENT
Posture Correction c̄ Roll
Extension EIL → day, Lie prone or prone in extension
Flexion Limit
Lateral ________
Other ________

BY PERMISSION OF THE McKENZIE INSTITUTE INTERNATIONAL
ORTHOPEDIC PHYSICAL THERAPY PRODUCTS, PO BOX 17009, MINNEAPOLIS, MN 55447 (612) 553-0452

Figure 8–22B. Patient ID 10.

Clinical Application 8–2

SUBJECTIVE HISTORY

This patient is a 20-year-old secretary (Patient ID 20) who sits most of the day in front of a computer and performs clerical duties. At home she is very active, which includes walking and riding a bicycle daily (see Figure 8–23A).

Her pain pattern is central low back pain present for no apparent reason and of 3 or 4 months' duration. It is gradually worsening and is described as an uncomfortable ache, and she has lost no time from work or stopped activities because of it. The onset was central low back pain, and it is of intermittent frequency.

The worse/better section revealed that what would guarantee to produce the pain was to sit for long periods. She has no pain or stiffness when rising from a sitting position. It worsens as the day progresses and when she is still. Guaranteed to decrease the pain is to get up and move around. She is better bending, walking, when waking up, when getting home from work, and when she is on the move.

She has had no disturbed sleep. Dejerine's triad is negative and her bladder and bowel function, as well as her gait patterns, are all normal.

She had no previous episodes of low back pain, and her previous history was unremarkable. She sought no treatment for this until now and had no diagnostic testing done.

Her general health is good. She uses no medicine, and denies previous surgeries or accidents. She denies the presence of unexplained weight loss.

CLINICAL EVALUATION

Sitting posture is poor, standing posture good, lordosis normal, and she has no lateral shift present (Figure 8–23B).

Movement loss is as follows:

Flexion: no loss
Extension: no loss
Side gliding (R): no loss
Side gliding (L): no loss

There was no pretest pain while standing. The following movements were tested: FIS, EIS, FIL, EIL, side gliding in standing right [SGIS(R)], and side gliding in standing left [SGIS(L)]. None of the movements had any PDM or ERP. All of the movements done repetitively had no effect on her condition.

Static tests performed included sitting slouched, sitting erect, standing slouched, standing erect, lying prone, lying prone in extension, and long sitting. The only positions that had any effect on her condition were sitting slouched, which reproduced her low back pain, and sitting erect, which decreased her low back pain.

Neurological testing was not performed because there were no radicular symptoms. Hip and SI joint testing was unremarkable.

Review Questions for Clinical Application 8–2

1. What is your working hypothesis? What may this be? What are the reasons to support your hypotheses? If any of the three syndromes are ruled out, why?
2. What will be the first clinical test you perform and why?
3. After reviewing the results of the movement loss section, what syndromes are ruled out? If you picked dysfunction, why?
4. What is your provisional diagnosis? Why?
5. Why would you rarely see patients with this type of syndrome in your office?

The McKenzie Institute Lumbar Spine Assessment

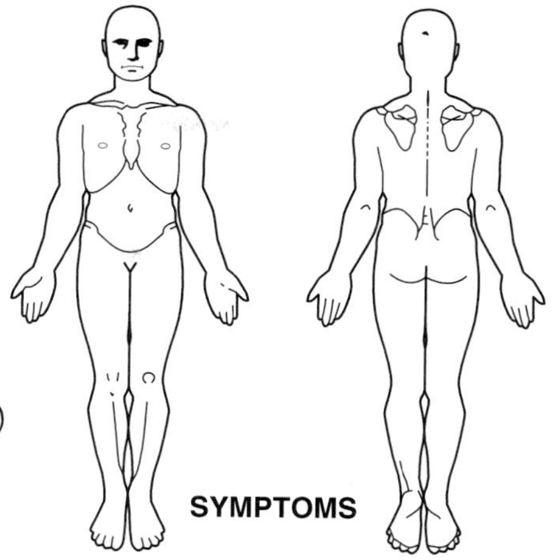

Date ____/____/____ 20 yrs

Name Patient I.D. #20

Address

Date of Birth ____ Sex: M / (F)

Occupation Secretarial

Postures / Stresses Sit computer., paperwork (work)

Telephone ____ walk, ride bike (home)

Referral: GP / Orth / Self / Other

Off work because of current episode? Yes / (No) Since

SYMPTOMS

Symptoms this episode to be marked on body diagram

HISTORY

Describe relevant symptoms general ache LBP

Present since __/3-4 mos/ Improving / unchanging / (worsening) gradual

Commenced as a result of: ____ (or no apparent reason)

Symptoms at onset: (back) / thigh / leg

Constant Symptoms: back / thigh / leg

Intermittent Symptoms: (back) / thigh / leg

Worse: bending (sitting) / ~~rising~~ standing walking lying

am / (as day progresses) / pm (when still) / on the move

other guaranteed to produce pain - sit long periods

Better: (bending) sitting / rising ~~standing~~ (walking) ~~lying~~

(am) / as day progresses / (pm) when still / (on the move)

other guaranteed to decrease pain - get up - move around

Disturbed sleep? Yes / (No) Sleeping postures: prone / sup / side (R / L) Surface: firm / soft / sag / w. bed

Cough / sneeze / strain: +ve / (-ve) Bladder: (normal) / abnormal Gait: (normal) / abnormal

Previous Episodes: 0 1–5 6–10 11+ Year of first episode: 19

Previous history: Unremarkable

Previous treatments:

X-rays: Yes / (No)

Gen. Health: (Good) / Fair / Poor

Medications: (Nil) / NSAID / Analg / Steroids / Anticong / Other

Recent or major surgery: Yes / (No)

Accidents: Yes / (No) Unexplained weight loss: Yes / (No)

BY PERMISSION OF THE McKENZIE INSTITUTE INTERNATIONAL

Figure 8–23A. Patient ID 20.

EXAMINATION

POSTURE
Sitting: Good / Fair / (Poor) Standing: (Good) / Fair / Poor Lordosis: Red / Add / (Normal) Lateral Shift: Right / Left / (Nil)

Other Observations: ______

MOVEMENT LOSS	maj	mod	min	nil
Flexion				X
Extension				X
Side Gliding (R)				X
Side Gliding (L)				X

Deviation in Flexion: Right / Left / Nil
Deviation in Extension: Right / Left / Nil

TEST MOVEMENTS: Describe effects on present pain - produces, abolishes, increases, decreases, centralizes, peripheralises, better, worse, no better, no worse, no effect

		PDM	ERP
Describe pretest pain standing	None		
FIS			
Rep FIS	No effect		
EIS			
Rep EIS	No effect		
Describe pretest pain lying	None		
FIL			
Rep FIL	No effect		
EIL			
Rep EIL	No effect		
If required SGIS (R)			
Rep SGIS (R)	No effect		
SGIS (L)			
Rep SGIS (L)	No effect		

STATIC TESTS If required
Sitting Slouched Produces LBP, then mid back, neck
Sitting erect ↓ all six
Standing Slouched No effect
Standing erect No effect
Lying prone in extension No effect
Long sitting No effect

NEUROLOGICAL
Motor Deficit: WNL
Reflexes: WNL
Sensory Deficit: WNL
Dural signs: Negative

OTHER
Hip Joints: WNL
SI Joints: WNL

CONCLUSION
(Posture) Dysfunction Derangement No. Trauma
Other ______

PRINCIPLE OF TREATMENT
Posture Correction With roll, slouch/overcorrect.
Extension ______
Flexion ______
Lateral ______
Other return 1 week - ✓ posture sit/ slouch-overcorrect

BY PERMISSION OF THE McKENZIE INSTITUTE INTERNATIONAL
ORTHOPEDIC PHYSICAL THERAPY PRODUCTS, PO BOX 17009, MINNEAPOLIS, MN 55447 (612) 553-0452

Figure 8–23B. Patient ID 20.

Clinical Application 8–3

SUBJECTIVE HISTORY

This 35-year-old laborer (Patient ID 30) sits and assembles parts all day. At home he watches television and likes to ride his four-wheeler. He has central low back pain that began 8 weeks ago when he fell off a chair at work. He originally missed 5 weeks of work and was virtually in bed during this time with short periods of sitting as tolerated. The condition has been unchanging for the past 2 weeks and is of intermittent frequency (see Figure 8–24A).

The better/worse section is unremarkable except that bending forward will reproduce the pain. Guaranteed to produce the pain is to bend forward and guaranteed to reduce the pain is to avoid bending forward.

He has no disturbed sleep. His bladder, bowel, and gait are normal. Dejerine's triad is negative. Previous history reveals a few bouts of low back pain over the past several years but each episode in the past self-resolved.

Previous treatments during this episode included no bending, twisting, lifting, or walking for 5 weeks. This resulted in the low back pain gradually decreasing, and it remained better. He then returned to restricted duty at work that was mentioned above. He was treated by the company doctor with prescription medication and rest. He had passive physical therapy (moist heat and electrical stimulation) performed with no relief.

Diagnostic tests included x-rays that were unremarkable. His general health is good. He continues taking antiinflammatory medicine. He has had no recent or major surgery, no accidents, and no unexplained weight loss.

CLINICAL EVALUATION

Sitting posture is poor. Standing is good. He has a normal lordosis and no lateral shift (see Figure 8–24B).

Movement loss is as follows:

Flexion: Moderate loss, no deviation
Extension: no loss
Side gliding (R): no loss
Side gliding (L): no loss

Pretest pain on standing was absent. FIS produced ERP but no worse. Repeated FIS produced ERP, but was no worse after. EIS had no effect. Repeated EIS had no effect.

Pretest pain in lying was absent. FIL produced ERP. Repeated FIL produced ERP but did not remain worse. EIL had no effect. Repeated EIL had no effect. Side gliding right and left had no effect, as did repeated movements of both.

Static testing had no effect for sitting slouched/erect, standing slouch/erect, lying prone in extension, and long sitting.

No neurological testing was performed because of the absence of radicular symptoms. Hip and SI joint testing was normal.

Review Questions for Clinical Application 8–3

1. With the better/worse section being so unremarkable, what additional questions could you have asked to further clarify the section, including but not limited to the bending movement?
2. What are your hypotheses of this condition? Why?
3. With the movement loss data available, what syndrome is ruled out? Why?
4. Can this be a posterior derangement? Defend your answer.
5. What is your working diagnosis? What are two repeated test movement clues that would initially indicate only one of the three syndromes based on the McKenzie system?

The McKenzie Institute Lumbar Spine Assessment

35 yrs.

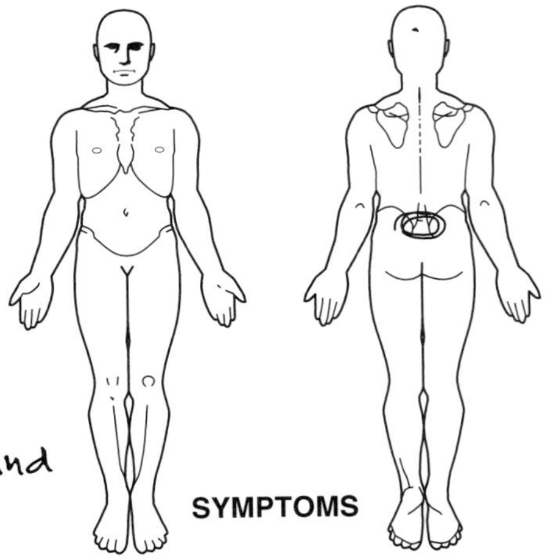

Date ____/____/____

Name Patient I.D. #30

Address

Date of Birth ____________ Sex: M / F

Occupation Laborer

Postures / Stresses Sits - assy parts - (work)

Telephone Home - watch TV, drive around

Referral: GP / Orth / Self / Other

Off work because of current episode? Yes / (No) Since ____ was for 5 weeks rest no bend, no lift

SYMPTOMS

Symptoms this episode to be marked on body diagram

HISTORY

Describe relevant symptoms Central LBP

Present since 8 weeks Improving / (unchanging) / worsening

Commenced as a result of: fell off chair @ work hurt back or no apparent reason

Symptoms at onset (back) / thigh / leg

Constant Symptoms: back / thigh / leg Intermittent Symptoms: (back) / thigh / leg

Worse: bending ~~sitting~~ / ~~rising~~ ~~standing~~ ~~walking~~ ~~lying~~

~~am~~ / as day ~~progresses~~ / ~~pm~~ ~~when~~ still / on ~~the move~~

other guaranteed to produce pain - bend over

Better: bending sitting / rising standing walking lying

am / as day progresses / pm when still / on the move

other guaranteed to decrease pain - don't bend over

Disturbed sleep? Yes / (No) Sleeping postures: prone / sup / side (R / L) Surface: firm / soft / sag / w. bed

Cough / sneeze / strain: +ve / (-ve) Bladder: (normal) / abnormal Gait: (normal) / abnormal

Previous Episodes: 0 (1–5) 6–10 11+ Year of first episode: 19

Previous history: LBP off/on yrs. Self limited. Was off work 5 weeks - rest - no bending, twist, lift, pain ↓, Better. returned to restricted work (No bend, lift); sit down job

Previous treatments: P.M.D. - Meds, P.T. - Heat, ultrasound, chiro manipulation

X-rays: (Yes) / No Unremarkable

Gen. Health (Good) / Fair / Poor

Medications: Nil / (NSAID) / Analg / Steroids / Anticong / Other

Recent or major surgery: Yes / (No)

Accidents: Yes / (No) Recently Unexplained weight loss: Yes / (No)

Figure 8–24A. Patient ID 30.

EXAMINATION

POSTURE

Sitting: Good / (Fair) / Poor Standing: (Good) / Fair / Poor Lordosis: Red / Add / (Normal) Lateral Shift: Right / Left / (Nil)

Other Observations: ____

MOVEMENT LOSS	maj	mod	min	nil
Flexion		X		
Extension				X
Side Gliding (R)				X
Side Gliding (L)				X

Deviation in Flexion: Right / Left / Nil

Deviation in Extension: Right / Left / Nil

TEST MOVEMENTS: Describe effects on present pain - produces, abolishes, increases, decreases, centralizes, peripheralises, better, worse, no better, no worse, no effect

		PDM	ERP
Describe pretest pain standing	None		
FIS			X
Rep FIS	No worse		X
EIS			
Rep EIS	No effect		
Describe pretest pain lying	None		
FIL			
Rep FIL	No worse		X
EIL			X
Rep EIL	No effect		
If required SGIS (R)			
Rep SGIS (R)	No effect		
SGIS (L)			
Rep SGIS (L)	No effect		

STATIC TESTS If required

Sitting Slouched: No effect

Sitting erect: No effect

Standing Slouched: ____

Standing erect: ____

Lying prone in extension: ____

Long sitting: ____

NEUROLOGICAL

Motor Deficit: WNL

Reflexes: WNL

Sensory Deficit: WNL

Dural signs: Negative

OTHER

Hip Joints: ____

SI Joints: ____

CONCLUSION

Posture ((Flexion) Dysfunction) Derangement No. Trauma

Other ____

PRINCIPLE OF TREATMENT

Posture Correction: Sit with roll

Extension: ____

Flexion: Flexion to end range pain x 10-15/ 2 hrs

Lateral: ____

Other: return 24 hrs to re-eval.

BY PERMISSION OF THE McKENZIE INSTITUTE INTERNATIONAL

ORTHOPEDIC PHYSICAL THERAPY PRODUCTS, PO BOX 17009, MINNEAPOLIS, MN 55447 (612) 553-0452

Figure 8–24B. Patient ID 30.

Clinical Application 8–4

SUBJECTIVE HISTORY

This 50-year-old male general contractor (Patient ID 40) assumes work-related postures/stresses that involve bending, lifting, walking, standing, and twisting throughout the day. At home he plays softball and basketball and watches the same on television (see Figure 8–25A).

His pain diagram shows central low back pain radiating to the posterior right midthigh. The pain has been present for 2 weeks and is worsening. Because he is self-employed, he has missed no work but believes the pain is bad enough at times that if he was not self-employed he would take some sick leave. The pain began 2 weeks ago while he was lifting a square of shingles and felt a sharp low back pain that gradually radiated down the buttock into the thigh. He states the back and thigh pain are constant but certain things do increase and decrease the pain.

The better/worse section illustrates that bending, sitting, rising from sitting, and walking make the condition worse and it lasts. He is worse as the day progresses and when still. Standing at times is painful. The things guaranteed to increase the pain are bending, lifting, and walking. He gets better lying on his right side and while on the move. When he wakes up he feels better and also before he goes to bed. Lying down on his right side is guaranteed to decrease his pain and it lasts until he does one of the worse movements.

His sleep is disturbed. He sleeps on his right side to start but ends up on his back or left side.

Cough, sneeze, and strain are negative. His bowel, bladder, and gait are all normal. He has a previous history of many episodes of low back pain. In fact, he states he has had it one or two times per year and it usually self-limits.

He has been treated by his family doctor with anti-inflammatory medicine and by his doctor of chiropractic with manipulation and heat. His symptoms have decreased but have not remained better.

He has had x-rays but they were nonrevealing. His general health is good. He denies any recent or major surgery. He denies any accidents or unexplained weight loss.

CLINICAL EVALUATION

His sitting posture is poor. His standing posture is fair. He has a reduced lordosis and a left lateral shift (see Figure 8–25B).

Movement loss is as follows:

Flexion: major loss with no deviation
Extension: minimal loss with no deviation
Side gliding (R): major loss
Side gliding (L): no loss

Pretest pain while standing is low back pain with pain to right midthigh pain. Pretest pain in lying decreases the symptoms but does not last. All sagittal standing and lying movements produce PDM and ERP. All sagittal repeated movements increase and worsen the symptoms. The frontal plane movement of SGIS(L) also produces PDM and ERP, and repeated movements increase the thigh pain and it remains worse. SGIS(R) has ERP, and repeated movements abolish the thigh pain and it remains better. But the low back pain increases and worsens.

Static tests reveal that sitting slouched increases and worsens the thigh. Erect sitting increases the thigh pain, but it is no worse after. Standing slouched increases and worsens both symptoms. Standing erect increases the thigh pain, but it is no worse after.

Neurological testing was done because he had thigh pain that was worsening. But all the tests were negative including dural tension tests. The SI and hip joints were normal.

Review Questions for Clinical Application 8–4

1. Which syndrome can be ruled out based on the pain drawing or assessment sheet for this clinical application? Why?
2. What other syndrome is ruled out now because of what was described in the paragraph beginning with the sentence "The pain has been present for 2 weeks and is worsening."? Give three reasons why that syndrome is now not possible?
3. At this time what syndrome are you strongly supporting? Provide three reasons.
4. What are your hypotheses regarding his condition?
5. With regard to the lateral shift, what question can you ask the patient to determine if this obvious shift is relevant?
6. If SGIS(R) is the preferred loading strategy for this to be a derangement, then after repeated SGIS(R) movements the reevaluation of the movement loss baselines should show what? Why?
7. What is your conclusion? If you suspected derangement, could you disprove your hypotheses with the clinical testing?
8. If you suspected derangement, was a lateral component present? Was it a relevant lateral component or irrelevant? Explain.

The McKenzie Institute Lumbar Spine Assessment

50 yrs. old

Date ___/___/___

Name Patient I.D. #40

Address

Date of Birth ______ Sex: (M) / F

Occupation general contractor

Postures / Stresses Bend/lift/walk/stand/twist

Telephone

Referral: GP / Orth / Self / Other

Off work because of current episode? Yes / (No) Since

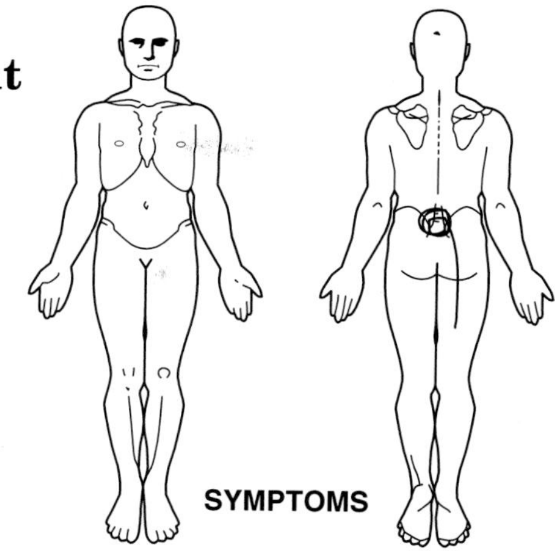

SYMPTOMS

Symptoms this episode to be marked on body diagram

HISTORY

Describe relevant symptoms LBP → (R) mid thigh pain

Present since 2 wks. — Improving / unchanging / (worsening)

Commenced as a result of: Bent to lift square of shingles felt LBP — or no apparent reason

Symptoms at onset (back) / thigh / leg

Constant Symptoms: (back) / (thigh) / leg — Intermittent Symptoms: back / thigh / leg

Worse: (bending) — (sitting) / (rising) — standing — (walking) — lying

am / (as day progresses) / pm — (when still) / on the move

other guaranteed to produce pain - bend/lift/walk.

Better: bending — sitting / rising — standing — walking — lying

(am) / as day progresses / (pm) — when still / (on the move)

other guaranteed to decrease pain - lie down

Disturbed sleep? (Yes) / No — Sleeping postures: prone / (sup) / (side (R) / (L)) — Surface: (firm) / soft / sag / w. bed

Cough / sneeze / strain: +ve / (−ve) — Bladder: (normal) / abnormal — Gait: (normal) / abnormal

Previous Episodes: 0 1–5 (6–10) 11+ — Year of first episode: 19

Previous history: Central back pain 1-2 times/yr. - Self limits

Previous treatments: P.M.D. - Meds, chiropractor - heat, manipulation - ↓, no better

X-rays: (Yes) / No Unremarkable

Gen. Health: (Good) / Fair / Poor

Medications: Nil / (NSAID) / (Analg) / Steroids / Anticong / Other

Recent or major surgery: Yes / (No)

Accidents: Yes / (No) — Unexplained weight loss: Yes / (No)

BY PERMISSION OF THE McKENZIE INSTITUTE INTERNATIONAL

ORTHOPEDIC PHYSICAL THERAPY PRODUCTS, PO BOX 17009, MINNEAPOLIS, MN 55447 (612) 553-0452 ©1993, OPTP, Inc.

Figure 8–25A. Patient ID 40

EXAMINATION

POSTURE

Sitting: Good / Fair / Poor Standing: Good / Fair / Poor Lordosis: Red / Add / Normal Lateral Shift: Right / (Left) / Nil

Other Observations: ______

MOVEMENT LOSS

	maj	mod	min	nil
Flexion	X			
Extension			X	
Side Gliding (R)	X			
Side Gliding (L)				X

Deviation in Flexion: Right / Left / Nil

Deviation in Extension: Right / Left / Nil

TEST MOVEMENTS: Describe effects on present pain - produces, abolishes, increases, decreases, centralizes, peripheralises, better, worse, no better, no worse, no effect

		PDM	ERP
Describe pretest pain standing	LBP → (R) mid thigh pain		
FIS		X	X
Rep FIS	↑, Worsens LBP, thigh	X	X
EIS		X	X
Rep EIS	↑, Worsens LBP, thigh	X	X
Describe pretest pain lying	↓ - No better		
FIL			
Rep FIL	↑, Worsens LBP, thigh	X	X
EIL		X	X
Rep EIL	↑, Worsens LBP, thigh	X	X
If required SGIS (R)		X	X
Rep SGIS (R)	Abolishes ~~(better)~~ thigh, ↑LBP, worse		X
SGIS (L)			
Rep SGIS (L)	Produces thigh, worse		

STATIC TESTS If required

Sitting Slouched: ↑, Worse thigh

Standing Slouched: ↑, Worse all

Lying prone in extension: " "

Sitting erect: ↑, Thigh, no worse

Standing erect: " "

Long sitting: ______

NEUROLOGICAL

Motor Deficit: WNL

Sensory Deficit: WNL

Reflexes: WNL

Dural signs: Negative

OTHER

Hip Joints: WNL

SI Joints: WNL

CONCLUSION

Posture Dysfunction Derangement No. 3 Trauma

Other: With a relevant lateral component

PRINCIPLE OF TREATMENT

Posture Correction: With roll - long period sit - avoid - try sit with side bude (L)

Extension: Avoid 1st 24 hrs

Flexion: Limits

Lateral: SGIS (R) Repeatedly → Day, Lie with (L) side down - to unload

Other: Return 24-48 hrs. - If centralizing - try get into extension

BY PERMISSION OF THE McKENZIE INSTITUTE INTERNATIONAL

Figure 8–25B. Patient ID 40

SUMMARY

The following is a summary of the literature support for the theoretical and practical aspects of the McKenzie approach. The McKenzie approach, as noted in the 1981 text *The Lumbar Spine*,[13] pays particular attention to symptom topography. In 1987, The Quebec Task Force on Activity Related Spinal Disorders concluded that the majority of patients with nonspecific spinal symptoms should be classified based on symptom topography.[23] The McKenzie approach is somewhat more sophisticated in subdividing these patients based upon the presence or absence of relevant spinal deformity and most importantly on the mechanical and symptomatic responses to dynamic and static end-range loading. Spratt et al recommended the use of the patient's response to repetitive test movements based upon documented reliability.[25]

Kilby et al[9] found good intertester reliability in documenting symptom response to McKenzie's repeated test movements but fair to poor intertester reliability in documenting the presence or absence of spinal deformity. Riddle and Rothstein[18] found less than acceptable intertester reliability in reaching a mechanical diagnosis based upon the McKenzie assessment process. It should be noted that none of the therapists in the study had undergone more than basic instruction in the McKenzie approach.

A common occurrence noted by practitioners of the McKenzie approach is that of centralization of symptoms. The frequency of centralization in common practice has ranged from 47% to 87%.[6,12] A two-part randomized, prospective study demonstrated that the referred pain of 58% of low back pain subjects could be centralized with a single direction of repeated test movements. It also demonstrated superior treatment outcomes in patients whose symptoms can be centralized compared to noncentralizers.

The mechanism responsible for centralization of symptoms is not fully understood currently. McKenzie has attributed this response to nuclear movement. Specifically he proposes that displacement of nuclear and/or annular material within the intervertebral disc causes a progressive increase in the intensity and distribution of symptoms. Conversely, in response to other movements and positions the nuclear/annular displacement is reversed, thereby causing the symptoms to reduce in distribution and intensity. This could occur only if the hydrostatic mechanism of the painful disc is intact and functional. If the symptoms could only be peripheralized but not centralized, the theoretical model would propose that the disc was responsible for the symptoms but that the painful disc is not intact and, therefore, the hydrostatic mechanism is no longer functional. Symptoms that cannot be centralized or peripheralized would be considered nondiscogenic in origin.

If the above proposal is accurate, then the following must be proven: (1) The disc would have to be implicated as the symptom generator in patients whose symptoms can be centralized or peripheralized only. (2) Nuclear movement would have to be demonstrated in vitro and in vivo. (3) A correlation between centralization and simultaneous nuclear movement would have to be demonstrated. The following will address the scientific evidence to support the theoretical model.

A recent study by Medcalf et al[15] found that examiners utilizing the McKenzie assessment process displayed a high level of accuracy in predicting the outcome of discography, including the symptomatic level, annular containment, and internal disc fissure pattern. A strong relationship between the occurrence of centralization and a positive discogram with a contained functional annulus was shown. During the McKenzie assessment, the referred symptoms of 50% centralized with 74% having positive discograms, of which 91% had an intact annulus. The conclusion from this study is that the McKenzie assessment process reliably differentiates discogenic from nondiscogenic symptoms ($p<.001$) and a competent from an incompetent annulus ($p<.042$).

Nuclear movement has been documented in vitro in several studies.[11,20–22] Schnebel et al[19] documented nuclear movement in vivo in normal discs. No clear pattern of nuclear movement was documented in discographically abnormal discs. Centralization was not monitored during repeated movements in the study by Schnebel. Currently, research is underway to assess the presence or absence of nuclear movement in discographically abnormal discs during the centralization process.

From a practical standpoint several studies have demonstrated the superiority of the McKenzie approach as compared to other treatments. Nwuga and Nwuga[16] and Ponte et al[17] found the McKenzie approach to be superior to the Williams approach to back treatment. However both studies do suffer from methodological flaws.

Recently, Stankovic and Johnell[26,27] found the McKenzie approach to be superior in terms of rapid resolution of symptoms and long-term recurrence rate to a "mini back school" at 1- and 5-year follow-ups. Kopp et al[10] and Alexander et al[1] found the McKenzie assessment process identified patients with surgical disc pathology. Patients with nonsurgical disc pathology were treated successfully with the McKenzie approach, and at 5-year follow-up 91% were maintaining a good to excellent treatment outcome. Several studies are currently underway around the world to assess the clinical and theoretical aspects of the McKenzie approach.

REFERENCES

1. Alexander AH, Jones AM, Rosenbaum DH Jr. Nonoperative management of herniated nucleus pulposus: Patient selection by the extension sign long-term follow-up. Presented at North American Spine Society Annual Meeting, Monterey, California, August 8–11, 1990.
2. Allan, DB, Waddell G: An historical perspective on low back pain and disability. *Acta Orthop Scand.* 1989;60(Suppl 234).
3. Andersson GBJ. Evaluation of muscle function. In: Frymoyer JW, et al, eds. *The Adult Spine, Principles and Practice*. New York: Raven Press, 1991;269.
4. Bigos S, Bowyer O, Braen G, et al. Acute low back problems in adults. Clinical Practice Guideline No. 14. AHCPR Publication No. 95-0642. Rockville, MD: Agency for Healthcare Policy and Research, Public Health Service, U.S. Department of Health and Human Services, December 1994.
5. Butler D. *Mobilization of the Nervous System*. Melbourne: Churchill Livingstone, 1991.
6. Donelson R, Murphy K, Silva G. The centralization phenomenon: Its usefulness in evaluating and treating referred pain. *Spine*. 1990;15:211–215.
7. Donelson R, Grant W, Kamps C, Medcalf R. Pain response to sagittal end-range spinal motion: A prospective randomized multicentered trial. *Spine*. 1991;16:S206–S212.
8. Donelson R, Grant W, Kamps C, Medcalf R. Pain response to end-range spinal motion in the frontal plane: A multi-centered, prospective trial. Presented at International Society for the Study of the Lumbar Spine, Heidelberg, Germany, May 1991.
9. Kilby J, Stignani M, Roberts A. The reliability of back pain assessment by physiotherapists, using a McKenzie algorithm. *Physiotherapy*. 1990;76(9):379–383.
10. Kopp JR, Alexander AH, Torocy RH, Levrini MG, Lichtman DM. The use of lumbar extension in the evaluation and treatment of patients with acute herniated nucleus pulposus. A preliminary report. *Clin Orthop*. 1986;202:211–218.
11. Krag MH, Seroussi RE, Wilder DG, et al. Internal displacements from vitro loading of human spinal motion segments. *Spine*. 1987;12(10):1001–1007.
12. Long AL. The centralization phenomenon: Its usefulness as a predictor of outcome in conservative treatment of chronic low back pain (a pilot study). *Spine*. 1995;20:2513–2521.
13. McKenzie RA. *The Lumbar Spine. Mechanical Diagnosis and Therapy*, 1st ed. Lower Hutt, New Zealand: Spinal Publications, 1981.
14. McKenzie RA. *The Cervical and Thoracic Spine. Mechanical Diagnosis and Therapy*, 1st ed. Walkanae, New Zealand: Spinal Publications, 1990.
15. Medcalf R, Aprill CA, Donelson R, Grant WA, Incorvaia K. Discographic outcomes predicted by pain centralization and "directional preference": A prospective, blinded study. Presented at Annual Meeting of the North American Spine Society, Washington, DC, October 1995.
16. Nwuga G, Nwuga V. Relative therapeutic efficacy of the Williams and McKenzie protocols in back pain management. *Physiother Pract*. 1985;1:99–105.
17. Ponte DJ, Jensen GJ, Kent BE. A preliminary report on the use of the McKenzie protocol versus Williams protocol in the treatment of low back pain. *J Orth Sports Phys Ther*. 1984;6(2):130–139.
18. Riddle DL, Rothstein JM. Intertester reliability of McKenzie's classifications of the syndrome types present in patients with low-back pain. *Spine*. 1994;21:1333–1344.
19. Schnebel BE, Simmons JW, Chowning J, et al. A digitizing technique for the study of movement of intradiscal dye in response to flexion and extension of the lumbar spine. *Spine*. 1988;13(3):309–312.
20. Seroussi RE, Krag MH, Muller DL, et al. Internal deformations of intact and denucleated human lumbar discs subjected to compression, flexion and extension loads. *J Orthop Res*. 1989;7(1):122–123.
21. Shah JS, Hampson WGJ, Jayson MIV. Distribution of surface strain in the cadaveric lumbar spine. *J Bone Joint Surg*. 1978;60B:246–251.
22. Sheppard J. Patterns of internal disc dynamics, cadaver motion studies. Abstract. The International Society for the Study of the Lumbar Spine, Boston, June 1990.
23. Spitzer WO, LeBlanc FE, Dupuis M, et al. Scientific approach to the assessment and management of activity-related spinal disorders (The Quebec Task Force). *Spine*. 1987;12(7S):22–30.
24. Spitzer WO, et al. Scientific monograph of the Quebec Task Force on whiplash-associated disorders (WAD); Redefining "whiplash" and its management. *Spine*. 1995;Suppl 20:8S.
25. Spratt KF, Lehmann TR, Weinstein JN, Sayze HA. A new approach to the low back physical examination: Behavioral assessment of mechanical signs. *Spine*. 1990;15:96–102.

26. Stankovic R, Johnell O. Conservative treatment of acute low-back pain. A perspective randomized trial: McKenzie method of treatment versus patient education in "Mini Back School." *Spine*. 1990;15:2.
27. Stankovic R, Johnell O. Conservative treatment of acute low back pain: A 5-year follow-up study of two methods of treatment. *Spine*. 1985;20(4):469–477.
28. Waddell G, et al. Normality and reliability in the clinical assessment of backache. *Br Med J* 1984;284:1519–1523.

Additional References Of Interest

Belanger AY, Depres MC, Goulet H, Troftier F. The McKenzie approach: How many clinical trials support its effectiveness? Proceedings of the World Confederation for Physical Therapy 11th International Congress, London, July 28–August 2, 1991.

DiMaggio A, Mooney V. Conservative care for low back pain: What works? *J Musculoskel Med*. 1987;4(9):27–34.

DiMaggio A, Mooney V. The McKenzie program: Exercise effective against back pain. *J Musculoskel Med*. 1987;4(12):63–74.

Donelson R. The McKenzie approach to evaluating and treating low back. *Orthop Rev*. 1990;XIX(5).

Donelson RG. Identifying appropriate exercises for your low back pain patient. *J Musculoskel Med*. 1991;8:14–29.

Donelson RG, McKenzie R. Mechanical assessment and treatment of spinal pain. In: Frymoyer JW, ed. *The Adult Spine: Principles and Practice*. New York: Raven Press, 1991;1627–1639.

Donelson R, McKenzie R. Letter to the Editor. *Spine*. 1992;17(10):1267.

Elnaggar IM, Nordin M, Shikhzadeh A, Parnianpour M, Kahanovitz N. Effects of spinal flexion and extension exercises on low-back pain and spinal mobility in chronic mechanical low-back pain patients. *Spine*. 1991;16(8):967–972.

Fredrickson BE, Murphy K, Donelson R, Yuan H. McKenzie Treatment of Low Back Pain: A correlation of significant factors in determining prognosis. Annual Meeting of International Society for the Study of the Lumbar Spine, Dallas, 1986.

Jacob G. Specific application of movement and positioning technique to the lumbar spine, considering theoretical formulation and therapeutic application. *Today's Chiro*. 1989–1990;Part I 18(6)/Part II 19(1).

Jacob G. The McKenzie protocol and the demand of rehabilitation. *Calif Chiro Assn J*. 1991;16:10.

Kay MA, Helowa A. The effects of Maitland and McKenzie techniques in the musculoskeletal management of low back pain: A pilot study. Abstract. *Phys Ther*. 1994;74:5 (Suppl) FS59.

Kuslich, SD, Ulstrom CL, Michael CJ. The tissue origin of low back pain and sciatica: A report of pain response to tissue stimulation during operations on the lumbar spine using local anesthesia. *Orthop Clin North Am*. 1991;22(2):181–187.

McKenzie RA. Manual correction of sciatic scoliosis. *NZ Med J*. 1972;76(484):194–199.

McKenzie RA. Prophylaxis in recurrent low back pain. *NZ Med J*. 1979;89(627):22–23.

McKenzie RA. *Treat Your Own Back*. Lower Hutt, New Zealand: Spinal Publications, 1981.

McKenzie RA. *The Lumbar Spine. Mechanical Diagnosis and Therapy*, 1st ed. Lower Hutt, New Zealand: Spinal Publications, 1981.

McKenzie RA. *Treat Your Own Neck*. Lower Hutt, New Zealand: Spinal Publications, 1983.

McKenzie RA. Mechanical diagnosis and therapy for low back pain: Toward a better understanding. In: Twomey LT, Taylor JR eds. *Clinics in Physical Therapy. Physical Therapy of the Low Back*. New York: Churchill Livingstone, 1987:157.

McKenzie RA. Early mobilization and outcome in acute sprains of the neck. *Br Med J*. 1989;299:1005.

McKenzie RA. Perspective on manipulative therapy. *Physiotherapy*. 1989;75(8):440–444.

McKenzie RA. *The Cervical and Thoracic Spine. Mechanical Diagnosis and Therapy*, 1st ed. Walkanae, New Zealand: Spinal Publications, 1990.

McKenzie RA. Mechanical diagnosis and therapy for low back pain: Toward a better understanding. In: Weinstein JN, Weisel SW, eds. *The Lumbar Spine. The International Society for the Study of the Lumbar Spine*. Philadelphia: WB Saunders, 1990:792–805.

McKenzie RA. A physical therapy perspective on acute spinal disorders. In: Mayer TG, Mooney V, Gatchel RJ, eds. *Contemporary Conservative Case for Painful Spinal Disorders: Concepts, Diagnosis and Treatment*. Malvera, PA: Lea & Febiger, 1991:211–220.

McKenzie RA. Mechanical diagnosis and therapy for disorders of the lower back. In: Twomey LT, Taylor JR, eds. *Clinics in Physical Therapy. Physical Therapy of the Low Back*. 2nd ed. New York: Churchill Livingstone (In Press).

McKenzie RA. Spinal assessment and therapy based on the behavior of pain and mechanical response to dynamic and static loading. In: Ernst E, ed. *Proceedings of Advances in Idiopathic Low Back Pain Symposium*. Vienna, November 27–28, 1992.

McKenzie RA. REPEX in acute and subacute low back pain. In: Ernst E, ed. *Proceedings of Advances in Idiopathic Low Back Pain Symposium*. Vienna, November 27–28, 1992.

McKinney LA, Doman JO, Ryan M. The role of physiotherapy in the management of acute neck sprains following road-traffic accidents. *Arch Emerg Med*. 1989;6:27–33.

McKinney MB. Treatment of dislocations of the cervical vertebrae in so-called whiplash injuries. Altnagelvin Hospital, Londonberry, Northern Ireland. *Orthopade*. 1994;23(4):287–290.

Poulter DC, McKenzie RA. The management of work related back pain. In: *Patient Management*. Auckland: Adio International Medical Publishers (In Press).

Rath WW, Rath JND, Duffy CG. A comparison of pain location and duration with treatment outcome and frequency. Presented at First International McKenzie Conference, Newport Beach, CA, July 1989.

Riddle DL, Rothstein JM. Intertester reliability of McKenzie's classifications of the syndrome types present in patients with low back pain. *Spine*. 1993;18(10):1333.

Schnebel BE, Watkins RG, Dillin W. The role of spinal flexion and extension in changing nerve root compression in disc herniations. *Spine*. 1989;14(8):835–837.

Spratt RF, Weinstein JN, Lehmann TK, Woody J, Bayne H. Efficacy of flexion and extension treatments incorporating braces for low-back pain patients with retrodisplacement, spondylolisthesis, or normal sagittal translation. *Spine*. 1993;18(13):1839–1849.

Stankovic R, Johnell O. Conservative treatment of acute low-back pain. A 5 year follow-up study of two methods of treatment. *Spine*. 1995;20:4.

Stevens BJ, McKenzie RA. Mechanical diagnosis and self treatment of the cervical spine, vol 17. In: Grant R, ed. *Clinics in Physical Therapy, Physical Therapy of the Cervical and Thoracic Spine*. New York: Churchill Livingstone, 1988.

Van Wijmen PM. Lumbar pain syndromes. In: Grieve GP, ed. *Modern Manual Therapy of the Vertebral Column*. New York: Churchill Livingstone, 1986:442–462.

Van Wijmen PM. The management of recurrent low back pain. In: Grieve GP, ed. *Modern Manual Therapy of the Vertebral Column*. New York: Churchill Livingstone, 1986:756–776.

Vanharanta H, Videman T, Mooney V. Comparison of McKenzie exercises back trac and back school in lumbar syndrome preliminary results. Annual Meeting of International Society for the Study of the Lumbar Spine, Dallas, 1986.

Williams M, Grant R. Effects of a McKenzie spinal therapy and rehabilitation program: Preliminary findings. Abstract. Presented at Society for Back Pain Research Annual Scientific Meeting, London, October 30, 1992.

Williams MM, Grant RN. A comparison of low-back and referred pain responses to end-range lumbar movement and position. Conference Proceedings at International Society for the Study of the Lumbar Spine, Chicago, May 20–24, 1992.

Williams MM, Hawley JA, McKenzie RA, Van Wijmen PM. A comparison of the effects of two sitting postures on back and referred pain. *Spine*. 1991;16(10):1185–1191.

Williams MM, Wright DGR, Mugglestone AA, Lynch GB, Spekreijse SA. Psychological distress in chronically disabled workers attending a Mckenzie spinal therapy and rehabilitation program. Abstract. Conference Proceedings at New Zealand Pain Society Annual Scientific Meeting, 1993.

APPENDIX

Answers to Review Questions for Clinical Applications

CLINICAL APPLICATION 8–1

1. Posterior derangement and I don't know. Posterior derangement because it is the only syndrome remaining. It cannot be a postural syndrome because the pain is radiating and he has pain affected by movement. It cannot be a dysfunction syndrome because there are constant symptoms and most importantly the condition has only been present for 3 weeks. You need a minimum of 6 weeks for the healing to conclude. I don't know is a hypothesis because it could always be something you never saw before.
2. See what effect sitting unsupported on the exam table has on his symptoms. Then have him sit erect and see if any change takes place. You do this now because: (1) It is a natural progression because he has already been sitting slouched through the subjective history. (2) It is a great time for postural correction education because all syndromes involve posture correction.
3. Posterior derangement versus I don't know. Derangement because he worsens with flexion movements and positions and centralizes with EIL. Derangement is the only syndrome that can centralize. The I don't know hypothesis could still be it until you cannot disprove posterior derangement over the next few days.
4. EIL, as often as he agrees to perform the exercise. Discuss when good times may be to perform these exercises, regularly 10 to 15 every 2 to 3 hours or when he feels the pain increase. If you can get him to decide when and how many, then he is in charge. Remember it is self-treatment, and he should be in charge.

   See him back in 24 hours if possible to recheck all baselines and see if centralization is taking place. If it is, you should see an abolishment of the most distal symptoms and an increase in the mobility of any or all the movement loss, especially extension. If extension is the preferred loading strategy, then attempt to get him doing EIS because it is much easier to do and more functional.

CLINICAL APPLICATION 8–2

1. Postural syndrome, derangement syndrome, and I don't know because derangement can be almost anything and is hard to disprove. At present she does fit all the categories of postural syndrome. It cannot be a dysfunction syndrome because it is worsening and she gets symptoms from the gradual onset of sitting. A dysfunction has no pain except at end range stretch when the pain is immediate and no worse after.
2. Check to see if any movement loss is present. If not, then it is not a derangement. Flex with intent to help rule out derangement because a posterior derangement will increase and worsen with flexion.
3. Dysfunction, because there is *no* movement loss in that section. There *must* be movement loss for a dysfunction syndrome to be present.
4. Postural syndrome versus I don't know. Postural syndrome because derangement is ruled out since there is no movement loss and no effect with any repetitive test movements. Also, it indicates postural syndrome because only static positions produce the symptoms and she is better whenever she is not in those positions.
5. You rarely see this type of person because the pain is not severe, it comes on gradually, it is so easily decreased or prevented, and they have not had to stop any activities of daily living because of the condition. Also, when at home they can avoid the prognosticator and generally have no symptoms.

CLINICAL APPLICATION 8–3

1. If the guarantee to produce the pain is bending over, is it *every* time? Does it *last?* Is the pain at the same point every time?
2. Dysfunction syndrome, derangement syndrome, postural syndrome, or I don't know.

   Dysfunction because the pain is intermittent, over 6 weeks present, unchanging, only produced through one movement, and no other movements or positions affect the symptoms.

   Derangement because it can be almost anything. It has many characteristics and resembles many conditions.

   It probably is not a postural syndrome because he states there is movement loss but keep it in mind until verifying in the objective evaluation.

   I don't know because it could always be something you never saw before.
3. Postural syndrome it is ruled out because there is movement loss present; postural syndrome has no movement loss.
4. It can be but probably not. Most postural derangements will increase and worsen with flexion. This did not, but it could be a healing derangement or a small enough one that the test flexion movements were not of the

quantity to affect it yet. To confirm, you can try one of two methods over a 24 to 48-hour treatment process: (1) Flex with intent to see if the condition (symptom or movements) changes; if it does change, then it is *not* a dysfunction. (2) Treat with postural correction and extensions exercises to see if the condition changes (symptoms or movements). If it does change, then it is not a dysfunction. (This is a safer method because the extension movements usually will not worsen the condition if it is a derangement, but will improve it.)

5. Flexion dysfunction. The FIS and FIL movements produced ERP, no worse.

CLINICAL APPLICATION 8–4

1. Postural syndrome because the symptoms radiate.
2. Dysfunction syndrome because the condition is of less than 6 weeks' duration, it is worsening, and the symptoms are constant.
3. Posterior derangement. You can use the same answers to question 2 to support this syndrome as to disprove dysfunction. Also, certain repetitive movements make the condition worse and it lasts; certain positions decrease the symptoms and it lasts.
4. Posterior derangement or I don't know.
5. How long has this shift been present? If it came during this episode, then it is relevant.
6. After repeated SGIS(R), if there is a derangement, then the mechanics should improve through increased mobility of the FF, SGIS(R), or both. For a condition to be a derangement, there must be both mechanics and pain.
7. Posterior derangement. No, because certain movements increased and worsened the condition and others decreased the symptoms and they remained better. He had a preferred loading strategy, and centralization did take place. These must be present for a derangement to be the syndrome. Remember derangement is the only syndrome in which centralization is possible during the mechanical evaluation.
8. Yes. Relevant because the condition only responded (preferred loading strategy) to frontal plane movements, in this instance SGIS(R). If sagittal movements would have decreased the symptoms and they remained better, then it would still be a lateral component but irrelevant because then it could have been treated the same as a straight posterior derangement.

NOTE: The references for the criteria for the above answers are *The Lumbar Spine* and *The Cervical and Thoracic Spine,* both by Robin McKenzie.[13,14]

CHAPTER 9

The Functional Capacity Evaluation

Foundation Principles and Applications

BRUCE HOFFMANN, D.C. & JEFF GULLICKSON, D.C.

INTRODUCTION

Low back injuries are of rising concern and cost in the American workplace. Incidence, cost, and disability are continuing to rise.[1]Lifting incidents have been associated with low back injuries up to 65% of the time.[2] Furthermore, injury rates up to eight times higher have been reported for individuals required to lift heavy objects regularly.[3] These statistics have lead to the development of lifting tests to be used as a preventative tool. They were used to compare a job applicant's physical ability to the physical requirements of the job and sometimes to a normative database. Later, these testing methods were used for assessing an injured worker's capacity for return to work.

This has lead to a rise in testing methodologies, manufacturing of specialized instrumentation, and facilities for performing functional capacity assessments. With this in mind, a review of the purpose, importance, proper methods, and applications concerning functional capacity assessments follows. Special attention is given to lift assessment methods. Issues regarding functional capacity evaluations (FCEs), return to work outcomes, and cost-effectiveness are discussed.

PURPOSE OF THE FCE

The definition of the functional capacity evaluation has been presented by numerous authors with a fair amount of consistency. Tramposh[4] describes a systematic, comprehensive, and objective measurement of an individual's maximum work abilities. Matheson[5] defines it as a systematic process of measuring and developing an individual's capacity to dependably sustain performance in response to broadly defined work demands. Isernhagen[6] describes the process through its basic makeup:

1. Function: purposeful activity that by its result can be measured
2. Capacity: maximum ability
3. Evaluation: an outcome statement that is explanatory and objective in measurement of activity

From these definitions, there appears to be some consensus regarding what an FCE is and its purpose, but this is where the similarities end. The specific evaluation protocols can differ greatly from provider to provider and from clinic to clinic. It is not the purpose of this chapter to discuss and compare each FCE system or approach, but instead provide guidelines for proper test selection, implementation, and data interpretation.

On the most fundamental level, functional testing helps substantiate impairment, disability, and when compared with job demands, a job handicap. These comparisons to job demands may demonstrate an ability to return to work fully, or suggest that placement in restricted duty is appropriate. On the other hand, it may be suggested that return to work is inappropriate, and work hardening or work conditioning may be necessary. In these situations, the FCE may serve as an objective functional database to guide specific rehabilitation goals and objectively monitor functional gains or lack thereof. This is a critical element and tool in the functional rehabilitation of low back pain patients.[7] In summary, reasons for performing an FCE may include:

1. Substantiate impairment
2. Determine level of disability
3. Determine specific job handicap
4. Establish return to work recommendations
5. Establish work restrictions
6. Demonstrate indications for rehabilitation with specific goals
7. Objectively monitor physical capacity improvement or lack thereof
8. Litigation
9. Social security

COMPONENTS OF AN FCE

When asked to determine an individual's capacity to work, some doctors continue to rely on personal experience and opinion, or solely on the patient's report of ability. This continues even though new technologies and advancements in human performance measures have evolved with both high- and low-tech methodologies. On the other hand, many new technologies lack credibility and are based on unsubstantiated manufacturer claims. It is the clinician's responsibility to choose appropriate methods for testing.

When evaluating functional abilities, one must understand that there are many facets that affect human performance and thus no gold standard is available.[8] Instead, a functional capacity test needs to consist of a battery of tests to evaluate all the necessary or applicable aspects of functional abilities. As Waddell[9] points out, low back pain disability is an intertwining of physical impairment, psychological reactions, and illness behavior. Therefore, the test battery may evaluate common physical measures, such as range of motion, various strength and functional values, and cardiovascular fitness, as well as psychosocial and psychophysical values.

A template for performing FCEs is founded in the hierarchical view of disease, impairment, disability, and handicap.[10] Disease refers to disruption of normal health, whether physical or psychological in nature. Impairment is defined as the change in function caused by the disease. If an impairment prevents a person from performing a functional task at a given level, then a disability is present. It is possible to have an impairment yet not demonstrate a disability. As stated in the *Guide to the Evaluation of Permanent Impairment*, impairment gives rise to disability only when the condition limits the individual's capacity to meet demands that pertain to activities.[11] And finally, a handicap is present when disabilities are severe enough to alter social role performance.

This hierarchical view gives rise to an evaluation system that first identifies pathology, typically during an examination, and records the presence of any impairment of function that rises from the presence of this pathology. The effect of any impairment on functional activities is assessed during the testing portion of the functional capacity evaluation. If an individual's impairment has caused difficulty or inability to perform a given task, this is now defined as a disability. This hierarchical view puts the evaluation findings into a simple context, as follows: An individual is unable to lift a 5-lb bundle of towels out of the tub due to decreased lumbar flexion from a previous lumbar fusion. In this example, we have listed the disability in relation to the impairment and pathology. In another example, an individual is unable to lift more than 15 lb from floor to waist at a frequent rate because of decreased strength and cardiovascular fitness, measured by lumbar strength dynamometry and sub-maximal VO_2 bicycle ergometry.

A common problem confronted when using this ideology is seen in the individual who presents with no remarkable objective findings yet is functionally impaired. This is commonly seen and supports the literature's assertion that much of occupational disability is rooted in pyschosocial issues. This underscores the importance of including a pyschosocial assessment as part of the test battery. Does a subjective report of pain alone substantiate an impairment or disability?

Although this model presents a systematic template of evaluating and presenting data that will reflect human performance, there are no reported standards of test components or common functional components described in the literature at this time. Fishbain et al have reported on their use of a standardization of testing components based on the *Dictionary of Occupational Titles*.[12] These components are listed in Table 9–1. This serves as an excellent baseline,

Table 9–1: Testing Components

Standing
Walking
Sitting
Lifting
Carrying
Pushing
Pulling
Climbing
Balance
Stooping
Kneeling
Crouching
Crawling
Reaching
Handling
Fingering
Feeling

yet should be defined by each patient and be job-specific, if possible. A second review presented in the literature compared results from a variety of functional testing techniques to conclude a concurrent validity between the methods reviewed.[13]

Although there are many tasks that commonly need evaluating, there is traditionally an emphasis placed on lifting capacity. The prevalence of low back injuries and their relationship to lifting mechanics have propagated this emphasis.

GUIDELINES FOR TEST SELECTION

Proper test selection and execution are critical in providing objective values for the clinician. Standardized criteria are made available by which testing methods should be judged. This pursuit of objectivity may be the most important aspect of testing. This is especially true when applying test results in medical-legal arenas or when making return to work recommendations that ultimately can affect an individual's earning capacity. Keyserling et al suggest criteria necessary for human performance measurements, including:[3]

1. Safety: Risk of injury should be of primary concern.
2. Relationship to job requirements: Recent laws make such requirements mandatory (Americans with Disabilities Act).
3. Reliability: The repeatability of a test to measure its designated outcome over time on subsequent test.
4. Predictive ability: Does the test provide you with what the user says it does?

For individuals with medical conditions, Hart suggests the following criteria:[14]

1. Safety: The procedure should not be expected to cause injury.
2. Reliability: The data produced should be dependable across evaluators, evaluees, and the date or time performed.
3. Validity: The data and its interpretation should be able to predict or reflect the evaluee's performance.
4. Practicality: The evaluation of cost, time, and usefulness of the information gained.
5. Utility: The usefulness to the assessment in terms of meeting the needs of the parties involved.

If our goal is to provide objective data for our given purpose of performing the FCE, then the above criteria act as an additional guide for test selection. A more comprehensive list of standards for such tests and physical measurements is available, and provides an excellent resource for protocol establishment.[15]

LIFT ASSESSMENT TECHNIQUES

The methods for lift assessment can be broken down primarily into two categories, dynamic and static.

DYNAMIC ASSESSMENT

Dynamic testing includes isokinetic and isoinertial/pyschophysical methods, which are described in the following sections.

Isokinetic Testing

Isokinetic testing consists of an external variable force designed or programmed to maintain a constant and predetermined speed. This technique of performance measure was initially popularized in the sports medicine arena and had primarily been utilized for extremity strength measures. Trunk testing and lifting assessment protocols followed later. Cost has made isokinetic methods less accessible and helped to prevent their acceptance and usage.

Mayer and Gatchel popularized the use of isokinetic dynamometry with lumbar flexion/extension and rotational machines.[16,17] These tools were used to evaluate strength at varying speeds with comparisons made to a normative database. They found this to be an excellent tool in their multidisciplinary program for making pre- and postprogram comparisons and monitoring improvement. Beyond this, there is minimal support for the use of single-plane testing in determining, limiting, or predicting functional performance.[18] They do however, allow one to evaluate for a specific weak link when lifting or functional deficits are present. Furthermore, functional status has been shown to improve when isolated strength deficits are addressed.[19]

Isokinetic lifting was introduced as one type of dynamic assessment because it was thought to more closely reflect actual lifting activities. Theoretically and biomechanically, this is somewhat the case, yet one must recall that isokinetic testing is performed at a constant velocity. Reviewing biomechanical data on lifting assessment demonstrates that lifting velocity changes between lifts as well as within a single lift. Isokinetic lifting techniques eliminate these variables of acceleration and deceleration and thus do not fully duplicate actual lifting. In terms of safety, very little has been reported on injuries that have occurred while performing isokinetic lift testing.

Newton performed a lengthy review of the literature on isokinetic methods[20] She concluded that they typically provide reliable measures of torque and force production. There is a strong learning effect, and two separate testing sessions may be warranted. In terms of normative data, the lift task provides sufficient normative data for comparisons. More important, there is little evidence that currently supports its ability to predict workplace performance.

Psychophysical Testing

Another form of dynamic lifting commonly utilized is the pyschophysical lifting test. Typically this encompasses lifting a box through a predetermined range, with self-adjustment of weight.

Snook and co-workers popularized this concept in determining safe manual material handling limits.[21] The protocol is based on pyschophysical principles for which an individual's perception of fatigue, pain, and/or exertion is used as an end point, as well as heart rate monitoring and examiner observation of control and postural safety. This technique is built on the premise that the individual is best suited to interpret physiological responses to different loading situations and determine the extremes of them.

The initial use of this branch of psychology was in the prevention of industry-related lifting injuries. Snook et al published large databases utilizing pyschophysical lifting protocols. They included many variables such as lifting posture, frequency of lift, and box size. They concluded that jobs requiring physical exertion greater than that acceptable through pyschophysical testing to 75% of the male or female population were at a threefold increased risk of injury.[22] The science of pyschophysical estimation gains further support from reports demonstrating a higher injury rate in workers who believe their jobs to be more physically demanding.[23]

Instructions for pyschophysical testing are fairly consistent between studies, with only slight variation. A recent article by Ciriello et al provides a good reference for standard instructions.[24] Generally, a candidate is asked to lift a box at a given frequency. Weight adjustments are made throughout the test period to achieve a weight that could be handled for an 8-hour day without straining oneself or becoming unusually tired, weakened, overheated, or out of breath. Typically, the amount of weight is concealed from the individual, forcing the individual to monitor his or her own physiologic indicators while avoiding any preconceived or self-determined arbitrary limits. Common test postures include floor to knuckle, knuckle to shoulder, shoulder to overhead, carry, and push/pull maneuvers.

Pyschophysical tests offer a moderate advantage over other tests. First, this branch of testing allows for an extremely high ability to recreate specific job requirements and their many variables. The importance of such job specific modifications is made more apparent when reviewing the new National Institute of Occupational Safety and Health (NIOSH) equation for the design and evaluation of manual lifting tasks.[25] Specifically, the researchers found it necessary to account for deviations in horizontal distance of the load from the body, any asymmetry of the load, and frequency of performance. All these variables are found to change an individual's lifting ability, and if not accounted for, may greatly overestimate an individual's capacity for that given situation. Secondly, this method is very cost-effective since there are minimal equipment costs. Third, safety is rarely an issue unless one is presented with an overachiever or if a poor candidate selection process is utilized.

No other form of lift assessment has undergone as many clinical investigations or trials or been reported on more in the literature than pyschophysical lifting. Studies have reported on utility and reliability in uninjured and injured patient populations, along with comparisons to other lift assessment techniques.

The utility of pyschophysical lifting has been best demonstrated by Snook et al.[26] They found that lifting injuries increased three times when work requirements were above acceptable levels of 75% of the population as determined by pyschophysical testing. If one accepts the basic premise that the individual is best suited to judge his physical limitations, then this is an excellent source. No other testing method comes as close to duplicating true lifting as it occurs in the work place.

The reliability issue with the pyschophysical protocol lies in the test's inherent subjectivity; the test is primarily based on the patient's subjective report of pain or exertion. Can a motivated individual discriminate a safe end point, and if so, can it be performed repeatedly? Can the same be said when applied to an injured population?

In a study by Legg and Myles, repeated testing over 5 days on a healthy population found that an individual's maximum acceptable lift did not vary greatly over repeated efforts.[27] Furthermore, there was no subjective, cardiovascular, or physiologic evidence of fatigue when their selected weights were lifted for an 8-hour day. Subjects were tested and worked at a frequency of five lifts every 2 minutes. This study sample was found to be working at 21% V_{O_2} max, which is well below the NIOSH recommended upper limit of 33% V_{O_2} max. Differences were also reported between experienced and nonexperienced material handlers. Experienced material handlers chose higher maximal acceptable lifts when compared to inexperienced material handlers and showed less variability on test-retest scores. This occurred even though both groups had similar isometric strengths.

Alpert reported on a variation of this pyschophysical technique for determining safe occasional lifts.[28] She used healthy individuals for the study. On single test-retest series, for which the retest was performed an average of 8 days later, good reliability was found.

In a similar study, Mital had shown a 35% decrease in psychophysically determined values for high-frequency lifts performed for 8 hours as estimated by a 25-minute pyschophysical testing session.[29] Fernandez et al showed a similar change with an average decrease of 15% for high-frequency lifts performed for 8 hours (lift frequency ranged from two to eight lifts per minute).[30] In this same study, a second group was not allowed to alter their chosen weights for the 8-hour shift. Nine of the twelve withdrew because of soreness. The authors concluded that pyschophysical lifting estimates are valid for low- or medium-frequency lifts, but tend to overestimate high-frequency lifts greater than eight per minute.

Other investigators have evaluated and compared pyschophysical reports of stress with estimates of stress through biomechanical models. Walker found an inverse relationship between the two.[31] Subjectively more stress was reported in the low back with the above-waist lifts, as compared to below-waist lifts. On the other hand, biomechanical estimates demonstrated more stress to the low back with the below-waist lifts than the above-waist lifts. This study points out the importance of subjective reports and perceptions, yet also raises questions regarding the ability of an individual to interpret these physiologic signals in an unbiased fashion. This is particularly significant if the person being tested has just been injured recently or is recovering from an injury.

STATIC ASSESSMENT

Isometric Testing

Isometric strength testing was popularized in part by the work of Chaffin and co-workers as well as from its inclusion in NIOSH publications.[32–34]

The early use of isometric testing was in the area of prevention of material handling injuries by matching workers to jobs based on strength. Keyserling et al found that individuals with work requirements above their static strength had an injury occurrence nearly three times higher than those who's strength was greater than job requirements.[3] This was further supported by Chaffin in his evaluation of 500 individuals.[33] He found when a worker's job requirements exceeded his or her isometric lifting strength, injury rates significantly increased. Based on this information, protocols were developed in which safe lifting limits for occasional, frequent, and constant rates were extrapolated as a percentage of the maximal isometric strength.

The early benefits offered by this form of testing included standardized posturing and setup and objectification of force production. Variance of force production over repeated efforts allows for more objective estimations of effort. It was also felt that in the lifting sequence, the most stressful aspect occurred at the initiation of the lift, the force needed to overcome inertia. This is ultimately a static contraction. Furthermore, lifting is considered most stressful at the postural endranges; this is the basis for the NIOSH standardized postures.

Test-retest reliability of isometric testing is very high.[35] Issues of safety have arisen particularly when using the NIOSH torso lift, although no reports in the literature of the injury incidence rate are available.[36] Biomechanically, this posture would seem to lend itself to producing moderate loading of the lumbar spine. We have personally chosen to eliminate this from our battery of test postures, yet this safety factor could seemingly be better addressed if pyschophysical protocols were used instead of maximum contraction instructions.

Some caution needs to be used when making safe lifting recommendations from static strength values. As pointed out by Chaffin, assumptions are made that lifting is smooth and unrestrictive, objects are only of moderate width, and ideal environmental factors are present such as handles, flooring, lighting, and temperature.[37]

The use of static lifting assessments has come under much scrutiny, primarily because of the many variables involved in dynamic lifting that are not accounted for in static testing. Numerous reports have documented the discrepancy between dynamic and static testing results in similar populations.[38–40]

COMPARISONS BETWEEN STATIC AND DYNAMIC ASSESSMENT

Much has been made of the debate between static and dynamic lifting evaluations. Much of the difficulty in evaluating the literature in which these comparisons have been made lies in the diverse methodologies employed and instructions used.

Khalil confirmed a poor correlation between lifting results from pyschophysical protocols and maximal contraction isometric protocols.[41] A much closer correlation was found between static and dynamic testing when both used pyschophysical protocols of maximum acceptable lift. Similar reports and confirmations were given by Forman,[42] Khalil,[43] and Matheson.[44]

In a comprehensive review of the literature concerning muscular strength and it's evaluation, Sapega reports isometric lift assessment bears a stronger relationship to human functional capacity than previously believed.[35]

TESTING IN AN INJURED POPULATION

Although much of the standardization and validation of the various tests were performed on a healthy population, one must question the validity of these tests when applied to an injured population. In terms of dynamic testing with injured populations, very little has been published in the literature. Griffin found that pyschophysical lifting assessment of individuals who reported back injuries selected much lower weights than those who had no injury, and more importantly were less reproducible on repeated efforts.[45] In a subsequent report by Troup, he summarized by stating that the experience of low back pain may lead to an exaggerated perception of pain or discomfort and may affect performance on psychophysically based assessments.[46] Mayer et al popularized the progressive isoinertial lifting evaluation (PILE) technique, which is similarly based on a pyschophysical approach.[2,47] They found this technique useful in a chronic low back pain population for monitoring improvement in a functional restoration program.

Kishino reported on the use of both static and dynamic/isokinetic lift assessment on an injured and uninjured population.[36] Both demonstrated the ability to discriminate between injured and uninjured persons, and both were able to document improvement in performance after participation in a functional restoration program.

Static lift assessment with an injured population is also not reported much in the literature. Khailil et al has shown static lift assessment using pyschophysical instructions for back pain patients to be highly reliable with a good test-retest reliability.[43] Furthermore, they found this to be an excellent tool to evaluate functional changes in chronic low back pain patients from treatment in a very quantitative manner. Harber supported this finding in his report.[48] He found a good coefficient of variation on repeated exertions in an injured population using a pyschophysical approach to static strength measurements.

THE INFLUENCE OF TESTER INSTRUCTION ON SUBJECT PERFORMANCE

A key component in maintaining test-retest and intertester reliability is standardization of instructions. Instruction sets have been shown to greatly affect effort and force production. The choice of instructions is critical in achieving maximal voluntary effort. Voluntary muscular control is achieved through an integration of a variety of bodily systems, and any inhibition placed on these coordinated events, whether it be physiological, neural, or behavioral, will affect performance. For example, it has been specifically cited that fear of injury may act as an inhibitory mechanism.[49] This same study evaluated the effect of simple instructions such as "Contract as hard as you can," or "Contract as fast as you can," compared to instructions that were more complex like "Contract as fast and as hard as you can." Each instruction group produced different results in terms of the magnitude and force-time recordings. They concluded that substantial consideration must be given to instruction sets, especially when accurate values are required for comparison between muscle groups or against normative data.

Matheson evaluated the effect of two different sets of instructions on isokinetic lifting and strength.[50] He compared a high-demand set of instructions ("put forth high effort") with another set of instructions ("put forth a consistent effort"). He found that different instructions greatly affect the reliability, variability, and magnitude of results from these isokinetic measures. In general, high-demand instructions were more effective.

Caldwell similarly reports on the effect of instructional sets and their effect on values recorded during isometric testing.[51] He concluded that instructions should be explicit in order to prevent subjects from developing their own strategies, based on their diverse interpretations of the task. Gamerale also reported on a reduction of reliable data when inconsistent instructions were given during pyschophysical lifting evaluations.[52]

VALIDATION PROCESS

Validity of effort is the cornerstone of an objective FCE, yet detecting submaximal effort has, to this point, been challenging. The definitions of force and effort are sometimes used interchangeably, and this needs to be clarified since they are both involved in evaluation procedures. Force is the amount of resistance given by the individual being tested. Effort is the amount of force given as a percentage of an individual's maximum ability for that given task. Are we measuring force or effort during a given task?

A common method for quantifying effort in lifting assessment is through the statistical outcome of coefficient of variation. It has been estimated that repeated trials of force production that show minimal variation are consistent with maximal effort. This measurement of consistency is defined as a coefficient of variation, and is typically recorded as a percentage. Most values that are below 15% are considered valid. This does not universally signify maximal effort, but is more indicative of a valid maximal acceptable effort.[47] This can differ greatly from maximal physical capacity, and more research will be helpful in clarifying this relationship.

Others have suggested that observation of the individual while looking for postural changes or cues can help in indicating maximal effort. Smith has shown that intertester evaluations using preset safety end point definitions to judge safe lifting end points have good agreement.[53] The basis for this methodology is that as an individual approaches or exceeds a safe maximal lift, body mechanics will deteriorate and reflect a biomechanical end point. This change was also noted in uninjured individuals while performing pyschophysical lift assessment in a study outlined by Alpert.[28] Postural changes were noted as individual's approached their maximum lifting capacity. These include changing from a leg lift (using the legs with maintenance of lordosis) to a back lift (knee extension preceding back extension). It was also noted that individuals began rising onto their toes and/or shrugging their shoulders as they approached their maximum for above-shoulder lifts. Although the basis of this method is posturally/biomechanically oriented, there is currently no well-accepted ideal lifting posture.

Hazard has provided some in-depth looks at verifying patient effort during lifting assessments. In one report, he evaluated test-retest variation of several indices commonly used that reflect patient effort.[54] The study used an uninjured, supposedly well-motivated population. It concluded heart rate was a poor indicator of effort during isometric testing, but better for isoinertial or isokinetic tests. In a second study, Hazard studied several indices of effort in an uninjured and well-motivated population.[55] Of special interest was the finding that peak force variance may not be as good an indicator of maximal effort in isokinetic or isometric testing. He suggests that a trained observer is better able to distinguish maximal from submaximal efforts than the most accurate physiologic indicators.

When evaluating patient effort, one must consider the many facets of human function and complicating factors that affect its production. Hirsch has listed them as nonorganic causes of poor motor performance: misunderstanding of instructions to perform maximal effort, test anxiety, depression, nociception, fear of pain, unconscious symptom magnification, and symptom magnification.[56] This becomes even more evident when the information presented by Menard, Cook, and Hirsch is reviewed. Menard found that in a large patient population that only differed in Waddell disability scores, those with higher Waddell scores consistently as a group performed statistically significantly lower on dynamometry tests.[57] Similarly, Cooke performed lumbar dynamometry on chronic low back pain patients before and after a rehabilitation program. Once again, patients were classified according to Waddell scores. Patients with higher Waddell scores produced significantly lower strength values than controls or those with low Waddell scores. Secondly, a retest performed after completion of a work conditioning program demonstrated increases in performance greater than that expected from any therapeutic or physiologic intervention on the group with high Waddell scores. The researchers concluded that dynamometry and performance testing does not reflect true musculoskeletal impairment alone, nor can it be assumed to reflect true maximal physical capacity in patients who are complaining of low back pain.[58] Hirsh, finding similar outcomes, concluded that dynamometry and functional testing for low back pain patients should be considered a pyschophysical test, and underscores the many facets affecting human performance in the population.[56]

There is inherent subjectivity in many of the testing methods utilized during functional assessment. One key to improving the quality of this type of evaluation lies in better objectifying protocols that will accurately and more reliably measure patient effort.

CLINICAL APPLICATIONS

In this chapter we have discussed the various principles of FCEs, including the purpose of FCEs, testing methodologies, and guidelines. In this next section we present two clinical cases which we have applied the FCE principles.

Clinical Application 9–1

HISTORY

The patient is a 32 year old male who experienced a work-related injury 3½ months ago. He initially experienced left-sided low back and leg pain, with pain extending to the left foot. The patient received conservative care, which included spinal manipulative therapy as the primary intervention, and he also recently completed a work conditioning program. Currently, he experiences left-sided low back pain with a mild amount of pain radiating into the left gluteal region. He is employed as a driver for a freight company and is required to lift/carry up to between 75 and 150 lb. He is required to make deliveries to rural areas; functionally, this requires prolonged sitting/driving, lifting, carrying, and repetitive bending and squatting. He has been unable to work for 2 months and has been under work restrictions for the past month. He is currently working 3 days a week, and is limited to 4-hour work shifts each day. He is under a restriction of lifting 25 lb. This patient was referred for an FCE to help determine his safe candidacy for increasing work-related demands.

PHYSICAL EXAMINATION

The lumbar range of motion test resulted in flexion 90 degrees, extension 20 degrees, left lateral flexion 35 degrees, and right lateral flexion 25 degrees with mild pain. Palpable tenderness was generalized throughout the lumbosacral spine. Hamstring flexibility was 70 degrees on the left and 60 degrees on the right. Nerve tension signs were unremarkable. Prone lumber extension was mildly limited by pain centrally.

He ranked his pain at a 3/10, on a scale of 0 to 10 with 10 being unbearable (visual analog scale). He scored a 10/50 on an Oswestry questionnaire, which places him at 20% for perceived functional disability.

Computer tomography of the lumbar spine revealed multilevel degenerative disc disease of the lumbar spine with a small partially calcified, right-sided disc herniation at the L5-S1 level, moderate bony lateral spinal stenosis with mild impingement on the left L5 nerve root, and a small, broad-based central bulging of the L4-5 disc annulus with mild subarticular impingement of the transversing left L5 nerve root.

continued

Clinical Application 9–1 Continued

FUNCTIONAL CAPACITY EVALUATION

A series of lift tasks were presented to the patient to assess safe occasional lifting recommendations. The patient was oriented with the goal and purpose of the FCE. He was encouraged to perform at maximum ability on each test. He was also instructed that each test could be terminated at any point. This procedure typically consists of six trials of lifts, with the weight increased with each trial of lifts.

1. Preferred floor to knuckle lift (Figure 9–1): The patient performed six trials and terminated the test on the sixth trial, stating that the weight was too much; in addition postural changes were noted during the final series of lifts. The patient was able to consistently lift 85 lb; above 85lb the patient stated that he had reached his maximum and the doctor also observed postural changes.

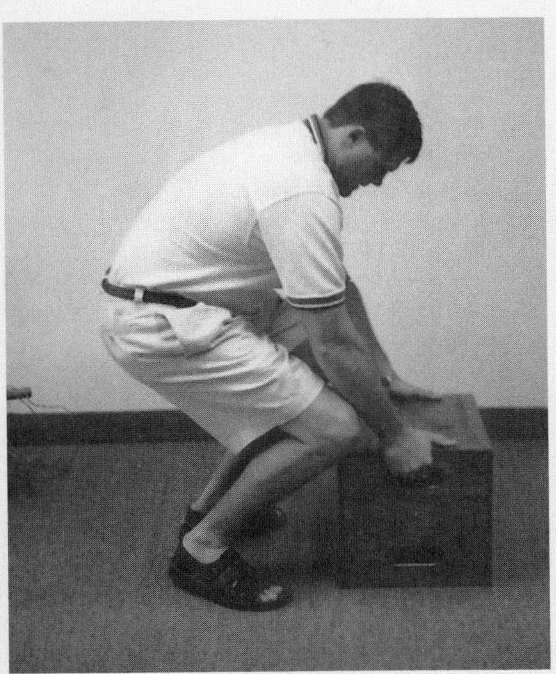

Figure 9–1. Subject performing a preferred floor to knuckle lift.

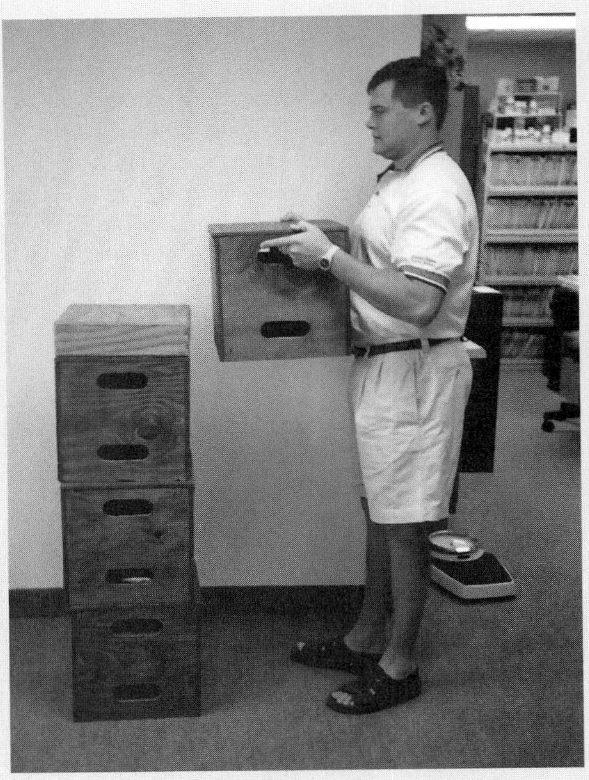

Figure 9–2. Knuckle to shoulder lift.

2. Knuckle to shoulder lift (Figure 9–2): The patient performed five trials of lifts, with the final trial being terminated by the doctor due to poor lifting mechanics. It would have been unsafe for the patient to continue the test. The patient was able to effectively lift 77.5 lb.
3. Shoulder to overhead lift (Figure 9–3): The patient self-terminated the testing procedure during the fifth trial, subjectively reporting that he had reached his maximum. The doctor also noted postural changes during the fifth lifting series. The patient was able to lift 64 lb. consistently.
4. Carry 8.5 m test (Figure 9–4): This test was terminated by the doctor after four trials of carries because of postural changes of increased lordosis, shortened stride, and carrying

Clinical Application 9–1 Continued

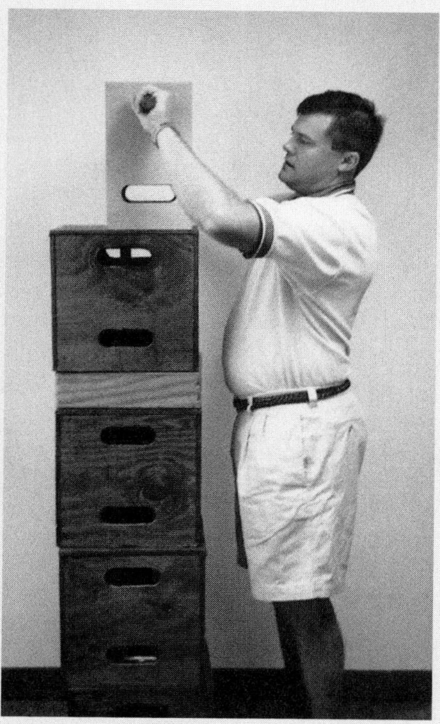

Figure 9–3. Subject performing shoulder to overhead lift.

Figure 9–4. Carry test.

the weight on his thighs. The patient was able to carry 70 lbs without discomfort.

The patient was tested with a series of repetitive flexion bendings to a 12-inch height, with the patient instructed to touch his palms on top of a box. The patient was able bend 25 times without discomfort. Additionally, the patient was asked to repetitively squat to a 12-inch height and touch his palms to the top of a box; he was able to perform this task without discomfort.

VALIDITY OF EFFORT

Several areas of this FCE demonstrate the validity of effort from this patient, and no gross pain behaviors or pyschosocial indicators were noted. The patient demonstrated excellent effort on the lifting tasks; in addition, postural cues suggest excellent effort.

Results: This patient demonstrated the ability to do the following tasks on an occasional basis:

Floor lift: 85 lb
Knuckle to shoulder lift: 77.5 lb
Shoulder to overhead lift: 64 lb
Carry: 70 lb

Other tasks critical to this patient's job include bending and squatting. He demonstrated good ability to tolerate repetitive bending and squatting.

continued

Clinical Application 9–1 Continued

CONCLUSIONS

This patient demonstrated the capacity to increase his work ability from the previous 25-lb restriction to the weight listed above. This patient should be able to continue to increase his work ability as his condition improves. This patient has demonstrated excellent effort in performing the tests and has not shown any pain behaviors, supporting the validity of the results.

Review Questions for Clinical Application 9.1*

1. Is this patient a good candidate for an FCE? Why?
2. Why was a dynamic lifting assessment performed?
3. Why would a lift trial be terminated if the patient showed postural cues of increased lordosis, shortened stride, and carrying a weight on his thighs?
4. Would an isokinetic lift assessment provide sufficient information to determine workplace performance, as compared to the dynamic lift assessment performed in this situation?
5. Is further testing appropriate for this patient?

*Answers appear in Appendix at end of chapter.

Clinical Application 9–2

HISTORY

The patient is a 34-year-old, right-handed male who experienced a work-related accident 7 months ago. He continues to experience considerable low back pain. He works as a baggage handler at a local airport. He has been returned to work on several occasions with work restrictions. On each of these occasions he has experienced flare-ups and has requested to be off duty. He has not been able to return to work for the past 2 months. He reports that he does not do many activities because of increased low back pain.

He reports that he feels a lot of anger toward his employer and the insurance company for returning him to work before he felt physically capable of doing so.

PHYSICAL EXAMINATION

The patient's movements were slow and guarded. Lumbar range of motion is limited and painful; with flexion 50 degrees, extension 5 degrees, left lateral flexion 20 degrees, and right lateral flexion 25 degrees, increased pain was felt in all ranges. Palpable tenderness was severe and generalized throughout the entire lumbar spine. Palpation revealed mild muscle hypertonicity of the lumbar paraspinal muscles. Cervical compression increased low back pain, as did straight leg raise, sitting root, and Kemp's tests. Waddell's tests of axial compression, truck rotation, and superficial tenderness were positive, for a score of 3/5. He scored an 37/50 on his Oswestry questionnaire, and ranked his pain at 8/10. He states that his pain will get worse with activity but rarely ever is better than an 8/10. A pain diagram showed multiple pain descriptors, i.e., descriptive words to describe the pain quality, arrows to the area of pain, etc.

Clinical Application 9–2 Continued

Because of the possibility of pyschosocial issues being involved, as revealed in the patient's history and pain questionnaires, grip testing was performed to look for testing inconsistencies. This test utilized a Jamar dynamometer to measure grip strength in a variety of grip positions, repetitive grip trials in position 2, and grip test in the five positions from position 1 through position 5. In the grip test position 2 test for the right hand was scored as 45, 40, and 42 lb, respectively. Five-position testing for the right hand revealed values of 20, 30, 40, 40, and 45 for positions 1 through 5.

FUNCTIONAL CAPACITY EVALUATION

Initially the patient was orientated with the goal and purpose of the FCE,; he was encouraged to perform at a maximum ability on each test. He was informed that any test could be terminated at any point if there was too much pain, if maximum effort was reached, or at the doctor's discretion. He appeared to understand the instructions and the purpose of the FCE.

The patient was initially tested on a static strength machine, during a series of isometric lifts (three repetitions). A Promatron 3000 lift task evaluation system was utilized for this procedure; this device was used to document static strength and record the coefficient of variation to document the effort of the subject. A coefficient of variation greater than 15% suggests that the subject may have not understood the directions, did not produce maximal effort, or is limited by pain.

1. High far lift (Figure 9–5): The patient lifted an average of 46 lb with coefficient of variation of 2.2%.
2. High near lift (Figure 9–6): The patient lifted an average of 59 lb with coefficient of variation of 1.0%.
3. Arm lift (Figure 9–7): The patient lifted an average of 49 lbs with a coefficient of variation of 1.2%.
4. Leg lift (Figure 9–8): The patient lifted an average of 35 lb with a coefficient of variation of 30.1%.
5. Floor lift (Figure 9–9): The patient lifted an average of 29 lb with a coefficient of variation of 18.2%.

Figure 9–5. High far lift performed on a Promatron 3000.

The patient was asked to perform a series of repetitive flexion bending from the waist to a height of 12 inches from the floor, and to place palms on top of a box 12 inches high. This required the patient to utilize 90 degrees of lumbar flexion. He was able to perform six repetitions before self-terminating the test, reporting increased pain.

Dynamic lifting: A series of lifts were presented to the patient to assess safe occasional lifting recommendations. He was instructed that each test could be terminated at any point. This procedure typically consists of six trials of lifts, with the weight increased with each lift trial.

continued

Clinical Application 9–2 Continued

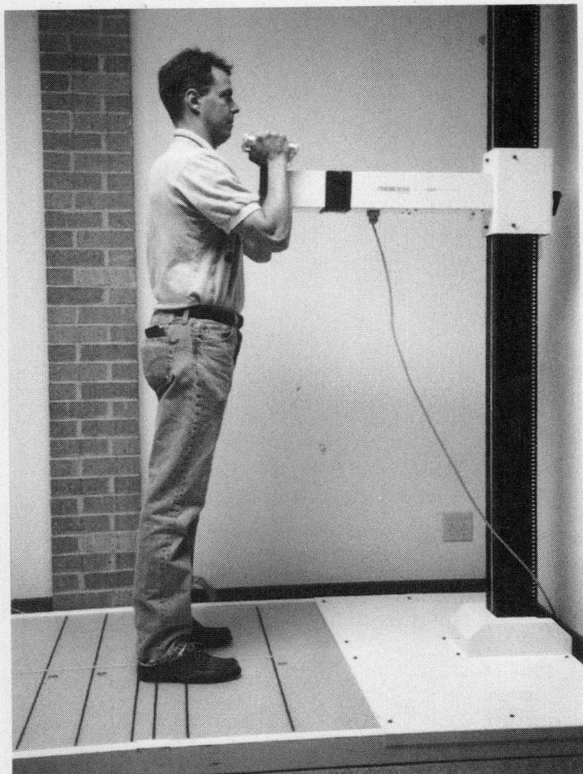

Figure 9–6. High near lift.

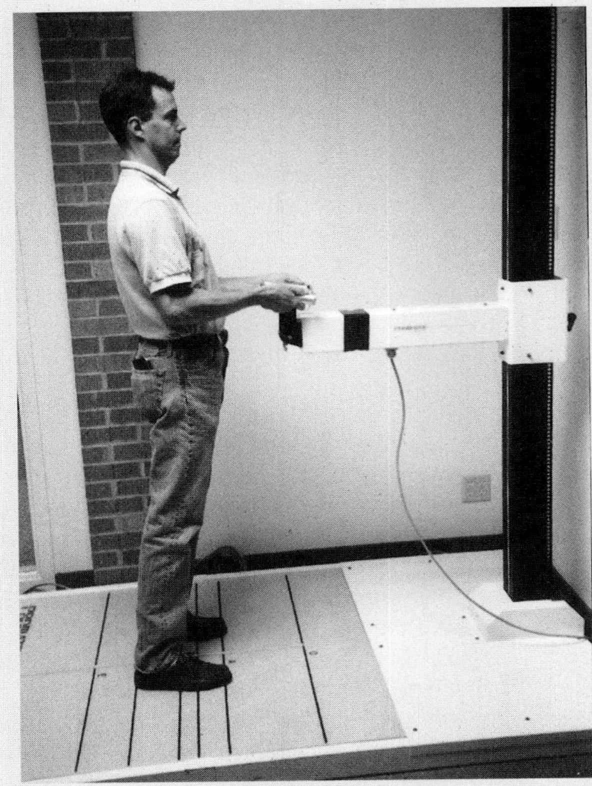

Figure 9–7. Subject demonstrating the arm lift.

1. Floor to knuckle lift (see Figure 9–1): The test was terminated at 25 lb because of increased pain after the patient performed three repetitions.
2. Knuckle to shoulder lift (see Figure 9–2): patient was able to lift 25 lb. and terminated the test due to increased pain.
3. Shoulder to overhead lift (see Figure 9–3): patient was able to lift 25 lb. and terminated the test due to increased pain.
4. Carry (see Figure 9–4): patient was able to carry 45 lb., the patient stated that he had reached his maximum effort. No postural observations were noted to suggest that the patient was near his physical maximal effort.

VALIDITY OF EFFORT

Several areas of the history, physical examination, and the FCE reveal the possibility of pyschosocial issues in this patient's case. These include the patient's positive Waddell's findings, positive orthopedic tests, grip strength tests, pain questionnaire, rating, and diagram results.

His static strength results also revealed discrepancies in his effort, with his coefficient of variation scores being greater than 15%. A coefficient of variation greater than 15% is considered invalid; this can result from not understanding the directions, failure to produce maximal effort, or being limited by pain.

Clinical Application 9–2 Continued

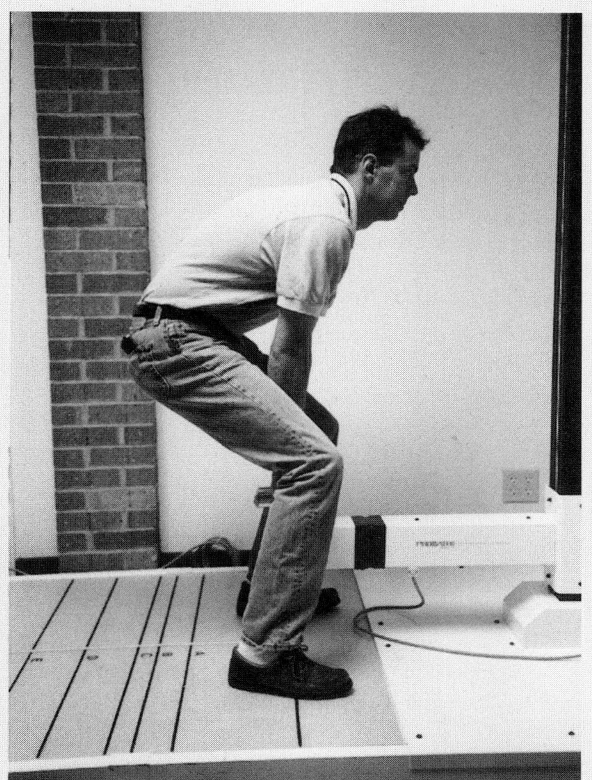

Figure 9–8. Leg lift.

Figure 9–9. Floor lift.

The dynamic lifting tests were terminated by the patient due to increased low back pain; there were no postural suggestions that the patient was near his maximal effort.

Comparing scores from the static and the dynamic lifting tests reveals the patient's scores were not consistent with comparable lifts. Grip strength testing for the five position test is considered valid when the scores follow a bell-shaped curve when plotted.

CONCLUSIONS

This patient has demonstrated numerous inconsistencies with his functional capacity evaluation. He has demonstrated the likelihood of pyschosocial issues being involved in his injury. The presence of these issues does not rule out the presence of an organic injury being present. These pyschosocial issues need to be addressed by the appropriate referral.

Review Questions for Clinical Application 9.2

1. Is this patient a good candidate for an FCE? Why?
2. Why would a grip strength test be performed on a patient with a low back complaint?
3. What would be considered as multiple descriptors on a pain diagram?
4. Does the presence of pyschosocial issues suggest that there is not an injury?
5. What are some the options available for clinicians managing a case of this nature?

REFERENCES

1. Frymoyer J, Cats-Baril W. An overview of the incidence and cost of low back pain. *Orthop Clin North Am.* 1991;22:263–271.
2. Mayer T, et al. Progressive isoinertial lifting evaluation. A standardized protocol and normative data. *Spine.* 1988;13:993–997.
3. Keyserling M, et al. Isometric strength testing as a means of controlling medical incidents on strenuous jobs. *J Occ Med* 1980;22:332–336.
4. Tramposh A. The functional capacity evaluation: Measuring maximal work abilities. *Spine.* 1991;5: 437–448.
5. Matheson L. Work hardening. In: Tollison D, Kriegel M, *Interdisciplinary Rehab Low Back Pain.* Baltimore: Williams and Wilkins; 1989:325–342.
6. Isernhagen S. *Work Injury: Management and Prevention.* Gaithersburg, MD: Aspen Publishers, 1988.
7. Mayer T, Gatchel R. Functional Restoration of Spinal Disorders: The Sports Medicine Approach. Philadelphia: Lea and Febiger, 1988.
8. Hoffmann B. Assessment of functional abilities following low back injury. In: Stude DE. *Clinicians Guide to Spinal Rehabilitation.* Gaithersburg, MD: Aspen Publishers, in press.
9. Waddell G. A new clinical model for the treatment of low back pain. *Spine.* 1987;10:632–644.
10. Menard M, Hoens A. Objective evaluation of functional capacity: Medical, occupational, and legal settings. *J. Orthop Sports Phys Ther.* 1994;19:249–260.
11. American Medical Association. *Guide to the Evaluation of Permanent Impairment.* Chicago: AMA, 1988.
12. Fishbain D, et al. Measuring residual functional capacity in chronic low back pain patients based on the *Dictionary of Occupational Titles. Spine.* 1994;19:872–880.
13. Dusik L, et al. Concurrent validity of the ERGOS work simulator versus conventional functional capacity evaluation techniques in a workers compensation population. *J Occ Med.* 1993;35:759–767.
14. Hart D, et al. Guidelines for functional capacity evaluation of people with medical conditions. *J Orthop Sports Phys Ther.* 1993;18:682–686.
15. Task force on standards for measurement in physical therapy. Standards for tests and measurements in physical therapy practice. *Phys Ther.* 1991;71:589–622.
16. Mayer R, et al. Objective assessment of spine function following industrial injury. *Spine.* 1985;10:482–493.
17. Mayer R, et al. Quantifying postoperative deficits of physical function following spinal surgery. *Clin Orthop.* 1989;224:147–157.
18. Newton M, Waddell G. Trunk strength testing with isomachines. *Spine.* 1993;18:801–811.
19. Brady S, Mayer T. Physical progress and residual impairment quantification after functional restoration: Part III isokinetic trunk strength. *Spine.* 1994;19:395–400.
20. Newton M, Waddell G. Trunk strength testing with isomachines. *Spine.* 1993;18:801–811.
21. Snook S, Ciriello V. The design of manual handling tasks: Revised tables of maximum acceptable weights and forces. *Ergonomics* 1991;34:1197–1213.
22. Snook S. The design of manual handling tasks. *Ergonomics.* 1978;21:963–985.
23. Snook S. Pyschophysical acceptability as a constraint in manual working capacity. *Ergonomics.* 1985;28:331–335.
24. Ciriello V, et al. Further studies of psychophysically determined maximum acceptable weights and forces. *Ergonomics.* 1993;35:175–186.
25. Waters T, et al. Revised NIOSH equation for the design and evaluation of manual lifting tasks. *Ergonomics.* 1993;36:749–776.
26. Snook S, Campanelli R. A study of three preventative approaches to low back injury. *J Occ Med.* 1978;20:478–481.
27. Legg S, Myles W. Metabolic and cardiovascular cost, and perceived effort over an 8 hour day when lifting loads selected by the pyschophysical method. *Ergonomics.* 1985;28:337–343.
28. Alpert J, et al. The reliability and validity of two new tests of maximum lifting capacity. *J Occup Rehabil.* 1991;1:13–29.
29. Mital A. The pyschophysical approach in manual lifting: A verification study. *Hum Factors.* 1983;25: 485–491.
30. Fernandez J, et al. Pyschophysical lifting capacity over extended periods. *Ergonomics.* 1991;34:23–32.
31. Walker A, et al. Evaluating lifting tasks using subjective and biomechanical estimates of stress at the lower back. *Ergonomics* 1991;34:33–47.

32. Chaffin D. Human strength capability and low back pain. *J Occ Med*. 1974;16:248–254.
33. Chaffin D, Park K. A longitudinal study of low back pain as associated with occupational weight lifting factors. *Am Ind Hyg Assoc J*. 1973;34:513–525.
34. Chaffin D, et al. Pre-employment strength testing: An updated position. *J Occ Med*. 1978;20:403–408.
35. Sapega A. Muscle performance evaluation in orthopedic practice. *J Bone Joint Surg*. 1990;72-A:1562–1574.
36. Kishino N, et al. Quantification of lumbar function: Part 4, isometric and isokinetic lifting simulation in normal subjects and low back dysfunction patients. *Spine*. 1985;10:921–927.
37. Chaffin D, Anderson G. *Occupational Biomechanics*. New York: John Wiley and Sons, 1984.
38. Pytel J, Kamon, E. Dynamic strength test as a predictor for maximal and acceptable lifting. *Ergonomics*. 1981;24:663–672.
39. Kumar S, et al. Isometric and isokinetic back and arm lifting strengths: Device and measurement. *J Biomech*. 1988;21:35–44.
40. Kumar S, Garand D. Static and dynamic lifting strength at different reach distances in symmetrical and asymmetrical planes. *Ergonomics*. 1992;35:861–880.
41. Khalil T, et al. Determination of lifting abilities: A comparison study of four techniques. *Am Ind Hyg Assoc J*. 1987;48:951–956.
42. Foreman T, et al. Ratings of acceptable load and maximal isometric lifting strengths: The effect of repetition. *Ergonomics*. 1984;27:1283–1288.
43. Khalil T, et al. Acceptable maximum effort. A pyschophysical measure of strength in back pain patients. *Spine*. 1987;12:372–376.
44. Matheson L, et al. Effect of computerized instructions on measurement of lift capacity: Safety, reliability, validity. *J Occup Rehabil*. 1993;3:65–81.
45. Griffin A, et al. Tests of lifting and handling capacity, and their repeatability and relationship to back symptoms. *Ergonomics*. 1984;27:305–320.
46. Troup J, et al. The perception of back pain and the role of pyschophysical test of lifting capacity. *Spine*. 1987;12:645–657.
47. Mayer T, et al. Progressive isoinertial lifting evaluation. Comparison with isokinetic lifting in a disabled chronic low back pain industrial population. *Spine*. 1988;13:998–1002.
48. Harber P, SooHoo K. Static ergonomic strength testing in evaluating occupational back pain. *J Occ Med*. 1984;26:877–884.
49. Christ C, et al. The effect of test protocol instructions on the measurement of muscle function in adult women. *J Orthop Sports Phys Ther*. 1993;18:502–510.
50. Matheson L, et al. Effect of instructions on isokinetic trunk strength testing variability, reliability, absolute value, and predictive value. *Spine*. 1992;17:914–921.
51. Caldwell L, et al. A proposed standard procedure for static muscle strength testing. *Am Ind Hyg Assoc J*. 1974;35:201–206.
52. Gamerale F. Maximum acceptable work loads for repetitive lift tasks. *Scan J Work Environ Health*. 1988;14:85–87.
53. Smith R. Therapists' ability to identify safe maximum lifting in low back pain patients during functional capacity evaluation. *J Orthop Sports Phys Ther*. 1994;19:277–281.
54. Hazard R, et al. Test-retest variation in lifting capacity and indices of subject effort. *Clin Biomech*. 1993;8:20–24.
55. Hazard R, et al. Lifting capacity, indices of subject effort. *Spine*. 1992;17:1065–1070.
56. Hirsch G, et al. Relationship between performance on lumbar dynamometry and Waddell score in a population with low back pain. *Spine*. 1991;16:1039–1043.
57. Menard M, et al. Pattern of performance in workers with low back pain during a comprehensive motor performance evaluation. *Spine*. 1194;19:1359–1366.
58. Cooke C, et al. Serial lumbar dynamometry in low back pain. *Spine*. 1992;17:653–662

APPENDIX

Answers to Review Questions for Clinical Applications

CLINICAL APPLICATION 9–1

1. Yes, this patient is a good candidate for an FCE for several reasons: to determine current work restrictions, the patient has been off work for over 3 months, and he has heavy occupational work demands. As previously discussed in the text of the chapter, the longer an individual is off work the worse are the chances for him or her to return to work in the same capacity.
2. A dynamic lift assessment was utilized based upon the patient's job demands as driver for a freight company. These job demands include lifting from a variety of positions, along with repetitive bending and squatting. A dynamic lift assessment will present a variety of lifting postures and can closely duplicate the job requirements.
3. This trial should be terminated by the doctor because the patient has shown that he has reached his near-maximal lifting capacity. To allow the patient to continue would put the patient at risk of injuring himself.
4. No, as mentioned previously in this chapter, there is little evidence to support the premise that isokinetic lifting can determine workplace performance.
5. This patient has continued to show improvement with care and his lifting ability has increased; however, his work requirements require him to lift between 75 and 150 lb. As his improvement progresses, it may be necessary to retest him to remove the work restrictions.

CLINICAL APPLICATION 9–2

1. Yes, this patient is a good candidate for an FCE because of the length of time missed from work, occupational demands, and the possibility of pyschosocial issues.
2. A grip strength test was performed to look for testing inconsistencies that would suggest the presence of other issues being involved with his low back injury.
3. These descriptors can include descriptive words, arrows drawn to the area of injury, or other forms to make sure that you are aware of the patient's injured areas, e.g., stars, multiple circles, bold drawings.
4. No, the patient may have an injury; however, other issues have now affected the outcome. These issues can be from a vareity of sources, such as animosity towards the employer, presence of litigation, or a lack of job satisfaction.
5. A trial period of active care would be warranted in this case. If the active care did not produce satisfactory results, a referral to a pain behavior specialist would be appropriate.

CHAPTER 10

Advanced Issues of Functional Testing and Patient Outcomes Assessment

STEVEN G. YEOMANS, DC, FACO, CRAIG S. LIEBENSON, DC, & MARK S. EDINGER, DC

INTRODUCTION

Interest in outcomes assessment (OA) and functional testing is growing because physicians, insurance companies, medicolegal reviewers, and managed care organizations are demanding a way to objectify patient status and document patient progress during the course of treatment.[1] OA represents a method used to measure a change in a patient's current or future health status that can be attributed to antecedent health care.[2] OA instruments are also emerging as the tools for measuring treatment effectiveness regardless of the methods utilized.[3] In fact, OA is a key fundamental pillar of quality care and cost containment. The discrepancy between the inflation rate (3% to 5%) and the rate of increase of health care costs (17%) is another reason why a means to monitor the effectiveness of the treatment plan is needed.[4] This was pointed out by Wennberg of Dartmouth Medical School, who found a wide geographic variation in practice style and associated costs, without corresponding differences in health outcomes.[5]

Outcomes assessments are most concerned with objectifying patient status and showing patient progress over time. Therefore, it is imperative that outcomes assessment be included in the patient evaluation along with diagnosis, therapeutic planning, and goals. The value of an OA test to a treating doctor truly comes to the fore when the doctor is called upon to document patient status in order to receive reimbursement or to motivate a patient towards a specific goal. Documenting patient status for these reasons may be accomplished with the following:

1. Validating a patient's subjective complaint and improvement (e.g., pain diagram, VAS)
2. Documenting functional loss and progress (e.g., inclinometer, dynamometer)
3. Documenting changes in ADLs (e.g., Oswestry, NDI)
4. Documenting psychosocial status (e.g., Beck, FABQ)
5. Documenting time off work (e.g., days off work)

There are four main issues that must be confronted when establishing an effective clinical treatment plan today:

1. *Ergonomic:* the evaluation of the workplace and job requirements
2. *Clinical:* the history and orthopedic/neurologic evaluation
3. *Functional:* strength, flexibility, lifting, cardiovascular, and motor control issues
4. *Biopsychosocial:* questionnaires, which may lead to a psychological referral

These issues are evaluated through the use of:

1. Provocative tests
2. Functional testing
3. Outcomes assessment tools

Provocative tests are valuable in acute presentations when function cannot be reliably and safely ascertained. OAs help establish objective baselines and show progress. Functional tests are concerned with isolating "key" functional pathologies, which in turn drive therapeutic planning and clinical decision making. Based on a literature review, there are five issues which must be addressed in the selection and use of any functional test in a patient population.[6] These issues, presented in hierarchical order, are:

1. *Safety:* Given the known characteristics of the patient, the procedure should not be expected to lead to injury.
2. *Reliability:* The test score should be dependable across the evaluators, patients, and the date or time of administration.
3. *Validity:* The interpretation of the test score should be able to predict or reflect the patient's performance in a target work setting.
4. *Practicality:* The cost of the test procedure should be reasonable and customary. Cost is measured in terms of the direct expense of the test procedure, plus the amount of time required of the patient, plus the delay in providing the information derived from the procedure to the referral source.
5. *Utility:* The usefulness of the procedure is the degree to which it meets the needs of the patient, referrer, and payor.

The importance of applying these criteria to the methods of evaluating the rehabilitation patient cannot be overemphasized.

Functional capacity evaluations can be divided into two camps. The first can be described as the "high-tech" method, in which precision dynametric, computerized instrumentation measures and reports the result of a test. This approach generally necessitates an expensive piece of equipment and is, therefore, often not very practical for the majority of health care providers. Criticism has also been expressed with regard to correlating unnatural movements often used in the high-tech testing approach to the more natural movements utilized in normal activities of daily living (ADLs).

The second method can be called a "low-tech" approach, in which the test is conducted by a provider with generally inexpensive instruments or tests still yields reliable and valid results. In addition, many of the low-tech methods test movements that are common in normal ADLs and hence may address functional pathologies more directly than high-tech methods. Since the low-tech methods may be more accessible and practical in a clinical setting, various instruments and testing methods will be discussed to the exclusion of the high-tech approaches.

When applying these criteria to the method of evaluating the rehabilitation patient, the following issues are of great importance.

QUESTIONNAIRES

Outcomes assessment instruments include a wide variety of questionnaires that are becoming standard protocol in the clinical setting for many good reasons. First, they are generally easy to administer and score and do not take up a significant amount of provider or staff time yet yield valid, useful information to assess outcomes. Second, they can provide the practitioner with very useful information that can be repeated in series or at later dates, thus providing a means that may affect clinical decision making (changing treatment approach, ordering of test(s), or referral to an allied health care provider for further assessment).

There has been a great influx of new instruments reported in many referenced journals claiming to be able to assess various problems or conditions. Many of the reported outcomes assessment tools appear to be valid and reliable. Because of the increasing number of instruments being introduced, it is practical to categorize these by variety or assessment goal. When instruments from several categories are grouped together, interpretation of the valid information obtained will facilitate case management of a patient and appropriate goals can then be addressed. Many of these groupings, or outcomes management systems, also take in data including demographics, diagnosis, lifestyle risk factors, co-morbidity issues, prognosis issues, and treatment. Categories may include: (1) general health, (2) pain perception, (3) condition-specific, (4) psychometrics, (5) patient satisfaction, (6) job dissatisfaction, and (7) disability.

GENERAL HEALTH QUESTIONNAIRES

The general health category includes several different instruments. These instruments include the SF-36,[7] HSQ 2.0,[8] Rand-36, Dartmouth COOP charts,[7,9] the Sickness Index Profile (SIP),[10] and the Quality of Well-Being Scale.[11]

The *SF-36* is similar to the HSQ without the last three questions regarding mental health assessment and is scored slightly differently. This is also a derivative of an earlier version, the *RAND 36-Item Health Survey*. The SF-36 has a large database and therefore may be preferred over the HSQ by some.

The *Health Status Questionnaire* (HSQ)2.0[8] was derived from the SF-36 but includes a three-item screener for major depression and dysthymia.[7] The advantages of both the HSQ, SF-36 and the Rand-36 include:

- 10 minute self-administered instrument
- *Not* condition-specific
- Includes a three-item screener for major depression and dysthymia (HSQ only)
- Is quantifiable and reliable and has been used as an outcomes assessment tool in many studies

Disadvantages include:

- Not specific enough to be used alone (use a specific-disorder questionnaire or TyPE in addition to SF-36, HSQ, or the Rand-36)
- Tedious to score

The *Dartmouth COOP charts*[7,9] are less sensitive and specific than the SF-36 but are much easier to complete for the patient (they take only 2 to 3 minutes) and score for the health care staff. Validity and reliability criteria have been met, making this a very user-friendly OA instrument.[12]

Lastly, the *Sickness Index Profile* (SIP)[10] and the *Quality of Well-Being Scale*,[11] though valid and reliable, are complex and lengthy and therefore are used primarily in research settings.

PAIN PERCEPTION QUESTIONNAIRES

The Mercy document regarding quality assurance considers severe pain intensity as one of the four factors that can be used to document that the patient is complicated and case management may be appropriate for 12 to 16 weeks rather than 6 to 8 weeks.[13] Subsequently, this category may function as an important factor in assessing the prognosis of a case. The Visual Analogue Scale (VAS),[14–17] Numerical Pain Scale (NPS),[14] the McGill/Melzack Pain Questionnaire,[20] and *pain drawing* are examples of OA instruments in this category.

The VAS instrument can be divided into three scores:[17]

- Pain level right now
- Average pain grade
- Worst pain grade

For the chronic patient, the clinician requests his or her pain level as it relates to the last 6 months (when describing the average pain grade). The average of the three ratings is then multiplied by 10 to yield a 0 to 100 score.[17] The final score can then be categorized as "low intensity" (pain <50) or "high intensity" (pain >50). The VAS, like other measures of a patient's progress, should be performed every 2 weeks since a patient's failure to progress over a 2-week period may indicate a need for a change in management approaches.[13]

The *NPS*[14] contains 11 boxes for numbers from 0 to 10 (where the patients check the appropriate box to represent their pain level). Most studies find the VAS and NPS instruments comparable,[18] whereas one found NPS superior.[19]

The *McGill/Melzack Pain Questionnaire*[20] is another option in the pain perception category. This instrument was designed to measure three items:[21]

- Sensory discrimination
- Motivational evaluation
- Cognitive evaluation

The popular *pain drawing* though used primarily as a qualitative tool,[22] has recently been reviewed as a scoring method and found to correlate reliably with the Hy and Hs scales of the Minnesota Multiphasic Personality Index (MMPI) (0.62 and .6, respectively).[23] The researchers concluded that this could screen out 93% of patients with "poor psychometrics," thus prompting an appropriate psychological referral.

CONDITION-SPECIFIC QUESTIONNAIRES

These questionnaires, also known as disease-specific questionnaires, are available for many conditions. To assess low back pain (LBP), the Oswestry Low Back Pain Questionnaire,[24] the Low Back Outcome Score,[29] the Quebec Back Pain Disability Scale,[30] the Roland-Morris Disability Questionnaire,[31] and the Low Back Pain TyPEs (Technology of Patient Experience specification,[33] the Neck Disability Index,[35] and the Headache Questionnaire[36] are only a few of the many instruments available.

The *Oswestry Low Back Pain Questionnaire*[24] is very popular and often used as a "gold standard" in studies comparing other low back questionnaires.[25,29,30] A "revised" version measures both impairment (function) and disability (limited ADLs).[26,27] Erhard and Delitto reported a score of 11% was necessary for discharge and return to work (RTW).[28]

The *Low Back Outcome Score* was recently introduced by Ruta et al, who utilized a rather stringent reliability and validity screen.[29] This article also contains a good literature review and includes several of the previously mentioned instruments.

Similarly, the *Quebec Back Pain Disability Scale* was also recently introduced and found a test-retest reliability of 0.92 and Cronbach's alpha coefficient of 0.96.[30] This instrument was compared to the Roland-Morris, Oswestry, and SF-36 scales and found reliable and valid. It was recommended to be used to monitor a patient's progress in treatment or rehabilitation programs.

The *Roland-Morris Disability Questionnaire*[31] was originally derived from the SIP[10] and modified for the low back. There are 24 items to check off for the patients to describe their condition as it feels *today*. Scores range from 0 to 24 (none to extreme disability), and this instrument is often used with the VAS. Reliability has been established when compared to the SIP and its major subscales.[32]

Low Back Pain TyPEs[33] was not designed to result in a single score. Rather, each question is sufficiently important to stand alone and serve as a baseline for future comparative assessment.[34] In essence, this instrument serves as an excellent history form specifically designed for LBP patients.

The *Neck Disability Index*[35] was designed to determine the disability issues associated with conditions of the cervical spine. This instrument was patterned after the Oswestry Low Back Pain Questionnaire, validated, and found reliable.

The *Headache Questionnaire*[36] consists of 85 questions and was used by Whittingham et al in testing the treatment efficacy of manipulation for headaches. No scoring method was received (personal correspondence), and therefore this serves as an excellent history gathering device void of a numerical score (qualitative).

In addition to the Low Back TyPEs, the Health Outcomes Institute has developed many other condition-specific questionnaires called "TyPEs". These include the following: (1) CTS, (2) asthma, (3) COPD, (4) depression, (5) hypertension/lipid disorders, (6) osteoarthritis, (7) rheumatoid arthritis, (8) allergic rhinitis, and (9) smoking cessation.[8]

PSYCHOMETRIC QUESTIONNAIRES

Psychometrics represents an outcomes assessment category that includes questionnaires that gather outcomes scores on issues such as depression, anxiety, and coping strategies. Psychosocial factors are a major complicating factor in patient management and must be flushed out early. Patients with significant problems in this area may require multidisciplinary care (at least the addition of a psychologist to the management team). Patients in this category often have:

- Job dissatisfaction
- Previous disability
- High anxiety
- Depression
- Symptom magnification
- Pain avoidance behavior
- Catastrophizing coping strategy
- Drug or alcohol dependency
- Family problems

The choice of psychometric questionnaire or test should take place after a thorough history. Just like ordering the right laboratory test requires a working hypothesis about whether we are looking for a metabolic, inflammatory, or carcinogenic disorder, the ordering of the correct psychosocial questionnaire similarly requires an idea about whether anxiety, depression, fear avoidance, etc., are the problem.

The choice of instruments in this category includes: HSQ (last three questions, nos. 37 through 39),[8] Waddell's Non-Organic LBP Signs,*[37,38] Somatic Amplification Rating Scale (SARS),*[39] Modified Zung Depression Index,[40] Modified Somatic Perception Questionnaire,[41] SCL-90R,[42] Distress and Risk Assessment Method (DRAM),[43] Beck,[44] Back Pain Classification Scale,[45] and FABQ.[46]

Of those listed above, *Waddell's Non-Organic LBP Signs* and *SARS* are physical examination procedures. The former has been utilized, well accepted, and used as a "gold standard" in many studies. The latter is basically a seven-item scale compared to the five-category/eight-item scale of Waddell. The SARS expands the scoring process by providing a rating of anatomic consistency, degree of disturbance, and amount of body involvement for each of the first three of the four components: (1) sensory findings, (2) motor findings, (3) tenderness findings, and (4) simulation tests. Also, the three simulation tests can be scored separately. The examiner is to use a four-point scale (0 to 3) to quantify the degree of somatic amplification sign that was noted during the examination. Thus, a total score of 21 is possible (3 times 7).

Though the two instruments are similar, the SARS dropped the simulation tests (axial compression and pelvic rotation) due to poor interrater reliability (R=0.69 and R=0.57, respectively) as well as the "overreaction" category because of very low interrater reliability (R=0.44). By doing so, the interrater reliability of the seven-item SARS improved significantly (R=0.93). Waddell also comments that neck pain and nerve root tension may be provoked by the two simulation tests (axial compression and pelvic rotation, respectively), and that care must be practiced to avoid a "false positive" Waddell sign when using these tests. The scoring differences between the five-category Waddell instrument (yes/no) and the seven-item SARS allows for better discrimination among patients with slight, moderate, and marked somatic amplification than does the yes/no approach (a total possible score of 5 for the Waddell versus a possible 21 for the SARS). The SARS was next compared to three of the SCL-90 scales (somatization, depression, and anxiety) of which only the somatization scale was associated with high SARS scores.[39]

PATIENT SATISFACTION QUESTIONNAIRES

Patient satisfaction is becoming an important issue, especially with managed care companies and with quality control assessment.[47] These instruments yield important information about the quality of the health care service by assessing the following:

1. Acceptance of care
2. Perception of the technical competence of a health care provider
3. The setting where care was provided
4. The effectiveness of the health care provider

This type of instrument was used in a study comparing MDs and DCs with regard to the "report of findings" given to the patient[48] by the health care provider and with overall patient satisfaction.[49] There are several varieties which can be used in a clinical setting. These include:

- Patient satisfaction questionnaire[50]
- Visit-specific questionnaire[49,51]
- Chiropractic satisfaction questionnaire[52]

*Obtained through physical examination procedures, *not* by questionnaires.

JOB DISSATISFACTION QUESTIONNAIRES

The next category measures job dissatisfaction. One method of assessing outcomes is the APGAR,[53] which resulted from working with 3020 aircraft employees to identify job dissatisfaction risk factors for reporting acute back pain at work. Factors identified in the MMPI (psychosocial responses) and certain work perceptions resulted in the following observations:

1. Those who "hardly ever" enjoyed their job tasks were 2.5 times more likely to report a low back injury (P=0.0001) than subjects who "almost always" enjoyed their work.
2. Subjects scoring highest on scale 3 (Hy) of the MMPI were 2.0 times more likely than subjects with the lowest score (P=0.0001).
3. These findings and others prompted the formation of the Modified Work APGAR (Table10–1).

Remember when considering the use of the work APGAR that some patients may not be happy about filling out this form for fear of employer retribution (per communication with Erhard).

DISABILITY PREDICTION QUESTIONNAIRES

Disability prediction represents an important category of outcome tools that may be predictive of chronicity as well as gathering outcomes information. The goal of these types of instruments is to attempt to determine who is at risk for becoming permanently disabled from chronic pain. The *Vermont Disability Prediction Questionnaire*[54] was compared to the ability of a group of physicians to predict disability. The model had a predictive value of 89% and was better in predicting disability than the physician group across all samples. The study indicated two potential uses for this type of predictive model. The first is to stratify patients into three groups:

1. Those who are going to return to work (RTW) with certainty, almost regardless of the treatment type received (very low disability scores).
2. Those who will be resistant to treatment and may not RTW "no matter what" (very high scores).
3. Those who are likely to RTW if treated effectively.

The second use is to alert health care providers to the critical risk factors associated with a poor prognosis in an attempt to prompt early recognition and institute appropriate management. The original "long" version contains 28 factors organized into eight categories (a total of 83 questions) covering job, psychosocial, injury, diagnostic, demographic, medical history, health behaviors, and anthropometric characteristics and was administered as a 15-minute written questionnaire.

A follow-up to the longer version resulted in a more refined, user-friendly short version of the Vermont Disability Prediction Questionnaire.[55] The short version has a total of 11 questions extracted from the original instrument that takes approximately 3 to 5 minutes to complete. Four of the questions emphasize past back problems; the remainder discuss occupational and psychosocial factors and the individual's perceptions of pain and disability. Hazard et al[55] studied 166 people within 15 days of a work-related back injury. From the original 83-question instrument, 11 questions were found to be most important with difficult LBP cases. When these 11 questions were combined, a significant association with RTW by the third month follow-

Table 10–1: Modified Work APGAR.[a]

	ALMOST ALWAYS	SOME OF THE TIME	HARDLY EVER
1. I am satisfied that I can turn to a fellow worker for help when something is troubling me.			
2. I am satisfied with the way my fellow workers talk things over with me and share problems with me.			
3. I am satisfied with the way my fellow workers accept and support my new ideas and thoughts.			
4. I am satisfied with the way my fellow workers respond to my emotions, such as anger, sorrow, or laughter.			
5. I am satisfied with the way my fellow workers and I share time together.			
6. I enjoyed the tasks involved in my job.			
7. Please check the column that indicates how well you get along with your closest or immediate supervisor.			

[a]The Work APGAR was modified with the addition of items 6 and 7.

Table 10–2: Partial List of Various Categories of Outcomes Assessment Instruments and Their Respective Goals[a]

ASSESSMENT GOALS	INSTRUMENT(S)
1. General health	**COOP charts, HSQ, SF-36**
2. Pain perception	**NPS, VAS,** McGill
3. Condition-specific	
• LBP	• **Oswestry, Roland-Morris,** Dallas, LB TyPE[b]
• Neck	• **NDI,** Headache Q[b]
• TyPE (from Health Outcomes Institute)[7]	• Asthma, **CTS,** COPD, Depression, **LBP,** Hypertension/lipid disorders, osteoarthritis of the knee, rheumatoid arthritis, allergic rhinitis, smoking cessation, and others[b]
4. Psychometrics	**HSQ** (ques. 37–39),[c7] SF-36,[c] **Waddell's signs,**[d] **SARS,**[d] mod. Zung, modified somatic perception Q, MMPI, Beck's Depression Scale
5. Patient satisfaction	**Chiropractic Satisfaction Q,** visit-specific Q
6. Job dissatisfaction	APGAR
7. Disability	Vermont Q, FASQ, FABQ

[a]Those in bold print have been used by the author and found quantifiable, easy to administer, and reliable.
[b]Cannot be scored (not quantitative, only qualitative).
[c]Only parts of the questionnaire relate to the categories.
[d]These are physical examination, not questionnaire tests.

ing injury was noted. Based on their regression coefficients, differential weighting was applied to the questions allowing for different values to be assigned to each question. For example, for the question asking how many times a medical doctor had been visited in the past for back problems, a score of 0 was assigned to the responses "never" and "1 to 5 times," but a score of 4 was assigned to the responses "6 to 10 times," "11 to 20 times," and "more than 20 times." For other questions, such as "How many times have you been married?," lower scores of 0 or 1 were assigned. The authors provide a scoring system and list a variety of cutoff scores yielding different specificities and sensitivities that can then be used for different purposes.

The *Functional Assessment Screening Questionnaire* (FASQ)[56] may also be used to gather information in this category of OA tools. This is a 15-item checklist designed for the primary care population for evaluating disability associated with chronic pain. A third scale, *Fear Avoidance Beliefs Questionnaire* (FABQ) is also available.[57]

The *PACT Spinal Function Sort* (authored and developed by Leonard N. Matheson, PhD, and Mary L. Matheson, MS, copyright 1991) is an instrument in which the patients score, on a 1 = able to 5 = unable scale, their perception of their capacity to complete the tasks shown on 50 different pictured activities of daily living that represent the positions defined in the *Dictionary of Occupational Titles* (DOT). A score is calculated from their rating of perceived capacity (RPC) of the various tasks and reliability checks that are made to determine internal consistency and effort. The patient's score is then compared to normative data of both healthy/employed as well as disabled/unemployed males or females. The score is then compared to a chart listing the physical demand characteristics of work developed by the U.S. Department of Labor.

GOALS OF OUTCOME ASSESSMENT INSTRUMENTS

The first issue is to determine which instrument(s) you would like to utilize in assessing outcomes. As you can see, many different OA instruments are available. Table 10–2 offers a summary of the outcomes assessment tools' goal(s) and several (the list is not all-inclusive) instruments one may choose from. Once an instrument is chosen, it should be utilized through the remainder of that particular patient's care because the instruments are not interchangeable. Care should be exercised in avoiding duplication of instruments and goals.

The second issue is, when do I use each instrument? To answer this question, case management may be broken down into the following stages:

1. Initial/base line
2. Follow-up/reexamination
3. At times of exacerbation
4. At the conclusion or discharge of the case

Table 10–3 summarizes the various instruments and when they can be applied.

CLINICAL EXAMINATION

The clinical examination is comprised of a focused assessment of a condition driven by the complaints described in

Table 10–3: Summary of the Various Instruments and When They May Be Applied

TEST	FIRST VISIT	DAILY VISITS	RTW AND/OR 2 WEEKS	REEXAMINATION 2–4 WEEKS	EXACER-BATIONS	END OF CARE
1. **General health**	X			X	X	X
• HSQ	a			a	a	a
• COOP	b			b	b	b
2. **Pain Qs**	X	X	X	X	X	X
• VAS	a	a	a	a	a	a
• NPS	b	b	b	b	b	b
3. **Pain Drawing**	X		X	X	X	X
4. **Condition-specific**	X		X	X	X	X
• LBP	a		a	a	a	a
• Neck Dis. Index	b		b	b	b	b
• Headache Q	c		c	c	c	c
• Other TyPEs	d+		d+	d+	d+	d+
5. **Psychometric**	X		X	X	X	X
• Waddell's	a		a	a	a	a
• SARS	b		b	b	b	b
• Beck's	c		c	c	c	c
6. **Patient satisfaction**			Possibly	X	X	X
• Chiropractic satisfaction Q			a	a	a	a
• Visit-specific Q	b		b	b	b	b
• Patient satisfaction Q			c	c	c	c
7. **Job dissatisfaction**	X		X	X	X	X
8. **Disability Q**	X		X	X	X	X
• Vermont Q			a	a	a	a
• FASQ			b	b	b	b
• FABQ			c	c	c	c
TOTALS	7	1	6	8	8	8

X indicates when the numbered general instrument category could be used during case management.
a–d represent different options for the numbered general category. It is *not* appropriate to administer all of the options (duplication issue). Stay with your same choice for all follow-up evaluations because the instruments are not interchangeable.

the history. The examination generally follows a particular outline which usually includes:[13]

1. Vital signs
2. Observation
3. Palpation
4. Auscultation
5. Range of motion assessment
6. Orthopedic provocative testing
7. Neurological testing

PALPATION

Palpation is one of the most relied-upon examination tools used by the chiropractic profession when assessing structural complaints. It is also a common "provocative test" used to describe areas of pain and is considered an important part of patient assessment. However, because palpatory pain has been criticized as being "subjective," the use of instrumentation to more objectively assess and quantify a pain response has been introduced. Pressure algometry is a test used in the diagnostic evaluation of soft tissue injuries and has been found reliable.[58] Normative data exists,[59–62] reliability coefficients range from 0.71 to 0.97,[62] and pressure pain threshold levels are sensitive to a variety of treatment interventions.[63,64] This can be performed pre- and posttreatment and therefore can be used as an outcomes measuring tool.

Qualifiable assessment of soft tissue tenderness is also possible,[65] using 4 kg of digital pressure (enough pressure to blanch the tip of your thumbnail if you pressed with the palmar surface of your thumb against a rigid surface). The grading scheme shown in Table 10–4 was adapted from Hubbard et al[66] and Wolfe et al.[65] This method of rating tenderness is physician-driven, *not* patient-driven (like the VAS or NPS).

A second pain rating scale utilizing palpation was recently reported with valid inter- and intra-examiner reliability results (0.88 and 0.85, respectively).[67] In this study, palpation of the cervical musculature was assessed using ". . . relatively firm palpation, with the 2nd and 3rd fingers performing small rotation movements and pressure throughout the bulk of the muscle." The scale in Table 10–5 was adapted.

Palpation of tenderness can also be quantified by adding the sum of tenderness scores (0 to 4 scale) at the 18 fibromyalgia sites to reach a score between 0 and 72.[68] This has been shown to correlate better with a clinical change in pain severity over time than does dolorimetry.[69] It is also of value to note the presence or absence of referred pain (expanded receptor field) upon soft tissue palpation of an area of tenderness.[70] Documenting areas of soft tissue tenderness along with their potential referred pain patterns serves a number of purposes. First, it helps to establish a baseline level of soft tissue tenderness or sensitivity. Secondly, it helps identify trigger points (taut bands with a twitch response and reproduction of characteristic referred pain). And third, it helps to identify signs of neuropathic pain (hypalgesia to non-noxious stimuli and an expanded receptor field caused by sensitization of dorsal horn neurons).

Thus, palpation can be used as an outcomes assessment tool by provoking the patient's pain experience throughout the course of treatment to monitor improvement.

Table 10–4: Soft Tissue Tenderness Grading Scheme[66]

GRADE	DEFINITION
0	No tenderness
I	Tenderness to palpation without grimace or flinch
II	Tenderness with grimace and/or flinch to palpation
III	Tenderness with withdrawal (+jump sign)
IV	Withdrawal (+jump sign) to non-noxious stimuli (i.e., superficial palpation, pin prick, gentle percussion)[a]

[a]In noninjured tissue, this is a sign of neuropathic pain.

Table 10–5: Total Tenderness Score System

GRADE	DEFINITION
0	No visible reaction and denial of tenderness
1	No visible reaction but verbal report of discomfort or mild pain on questioning
2	Spontaneous verbal report of painful tenderness before questioning, possibly with facial expression of discomfort
3	Marked grimacing and withdrawal; verbal report of marked painful tenderness and pain

PROVOCATIVE TESTS

Provocative tests are important in assessing the acute case when it is too early to properly or safely evaluate function. They provide ideal pre-and posttreatment checks so that the patient can see that a manipulation or exercise is actually making a positive change. Pain reduction is a powerful educational tool for the patient.

Provocative tests such as range of motion (ROM), muscle functions, and orthopedic/neurologic tests lead us into a discussion regarding "hard" versus "soft" tests. "Hard" tests are those that yield a reliable and valid outcome when utilized, whereas "soft" tests lack consistent results with respect to their proposed goal. Soft tests may often be helpful in clinical decision making without being ideal OA tests (i.e., motion palpation). McCombe et al[71] studied the reliability of certain tests commonly used in practice (Table 10–6). In conclusion, the following observations were made:

1. *Pain pattern:* The more distal, the more agreement. Disagreement occurred when differentiating back from buttock pain and illustrates the importance for careful pain localization.
2. *Tenderness:* The most unreliable signs were paravertebral and buttock (soft tissue tenderness), whereas bony tenderness was "potentially reliable" or "reliable."
3. *Root tension signs:* SLR and femoral stretch were more reliable than bowstring in general. Specifically, the bowstring test for leg pain and the femoral stretch for LBP were the most reliable for these two tests.
4. *Root compression signs:* There was good agreement between surgeon-surgeon but not between surgeon-physical therapist (PT). The PT found more positive signs, and a difference in training may be a reason. Root compression tests must be applied carefully to improve reliability.
5. *Inappropriate signs:* From Waddell's Non-Organic LBP Signs,[38] no clear pattern emerged. The two unreliable signs (superficial tenderness and abnormal regional sensory or motor disturbance) appear

Table 10–6: The Validity of Provocative Tests as Determined By an Orthopedic Surgeon and a Physical Therapist

SCANOGRAM QUADRANT	A	B	C	D
TEST	**MOST RELIABLE**	**POTENTIALLY RELIABLE**	**POTENTIALLY RELIABLE**	**POOR RELIABILITY**
1. Pain pattern	Thigh, leg	NA	Buttock, foot pain	Back
2. Posture	Measure lordosis (cm)	NA	NA	Spinal list measure (cm)
3. Movement	Flexion (Schober; pain on flexion; lateral bend	Extension, rotation	NA	Extension "catch"; Lateral bend (cm)
4. Tenderness	NA	Midline	SI, iliac crest	Paravertebral, buttock
5. SI and piriformis	Hip flexion (y/n)	NA	Pain w/ER	Maitland's t.; SI compres.; SI distraction
6. Root tension signs	SLR (onset P, max., LBP, leg P - y/n)	SLR sciatic stretch test, SLR repro. symptoms	Crossed SLR	NA
7. Root compression signs	Leg numbness (y/n)	NA	Atrophy and weakness: Quads, calf, tib.ant., peroneal L./B., knee ext.; Achilles DTR	Heel/toe strength, buttock atrophy, patellar DTR
8. Inappropriate signs	NA	Simulation, Over-reaction	Distraction	Tenderness, regional motor/sensory disturbance

DTR = deep tendon reflex; P = pain; SI = sacroiliac; SLR = straight leg raise; LBP = low back pain.

to require more subjective judgment than pain with simulation or distraction. (*Note:* This conflicts with Korbon et al,[39] who found sensory, motor, tenderness, and SLR distraction tests or "flip sign" *most* reliable.)

McCarthy discussed improving the clinician's use of orthopedic testing for LBP in a recent study.[72] A goal of this study was to assess the validity and reliability of commonly used orthopedic/neurologic tests.

McKenzie, using repetitive full ROM tests, also gathers important information about identifying specific patient classifications.[73] The classic intervertebral disc-deranged patient presents with pain referred distally into an extremity, which centralizes after repetitive end range motions in one direction (i.e., trunk extension) and peripheralizes with repetitive motion in the opposite direction (i.e., trunk flexion). This is termed the *derangement syndrome* and is most likely due to a disc problem.

Delitto and Erhard[74,75] have adapted some of McKenzie's work, proposing the use of single and sustained movements through a full range, in addition to repetitive movements. With these tests they have been able to show prescriptive validity for arranging patients into distinct treatment groups.

The key is to test various movements and ask the patients whether they feel their symptoms are:

- Status quo (no change)
- Better (with or without centralization)
- Worse (with or without peripheralization)

Different movements that can be tested include the following:

Standing:
1. Extension
2. Flexion
3. Repeated pelvic translation L (10×)
4. Repeated pelvic translation R (10×)

Prone:
5. Extension (press-up)
6. Repeated extension (10×)

Supine:
7. Flexion in supine
8. Repeated flexion (10×)
9. Sustained flexion (10 seconds)

According to Delitto et al,[75] if a patient's symptoms improve with at least two extension movements and worsen with at least one flexion movement, the patient is an extension classification patient. The tests had previously been shown to have proven reliability.[74] Sacroiliac tests were also performed on these patients. These included:

- Posterior Superior Iliac Spine (PSIS) height in the seated position
- Sitting flexion test
- Supine to long-sitting test
- Prone knee flexion test

Previous work had demonstrated the reliability of these SI tests.[76] Patients with this classification of extension "bias" and SI dysfunction were treated with extension exercises and SI manipulation. This patient group was then compared to a control treatment involving Williams flexion exercises. The study showed that a priori classification of patients and appropriate treatment gave superior results. In their 1994 study,[28] Erhard et al showed that the manipulation was a crucial component of the exercise program and that a group treated with exercise alone that had this classification faired poorer than the combined treatment group.

McKenzie's diagnostic classification system is summarized below:

1. *McKenzie dysfunction syndrome:* Repetitive end range active movements in one or a selected few directions increase pain most.
2. *McKenzie derangement syndrome (a more acute syndrome):* Repetitive midrange and end range active movements in a variety of directions increase pain.
3. *McKenzie postural syndrome (i.e., static loading disorder):* No repetitive end range active or passive movements can increase pain.

Selective tissue tension tests have a long history in the assessment of sciatic nerve compression. Recently, Elvey developed similar tests for the cervicobrachial plexus.[77] These have been shown to have good reliability for differentiating upper limb nerve tension from muscle tightness.[78] They have also been able to identify a cervical component in chronic tennis elbow patients with high reliability.[79] These tests differentiate between inert (nerve) and soft tissue (muscle, fascia) sources of mechanical restriction or irritation.

Many orthopedic tests involve altering patient positioning to stress specific nerve, ligament, or joint structures. Gaenslen's test selectively stresses the sacroiliac (SI) joint; therefore if pain is provoked, it indicates an SI problem. This test has been shown to have good reliability.[80]

Cyriax described resistance tests for inflamed muscles (i.e., tendinitis).[81,82] These tests are quite useful in assessing sports or occupational injuries involving repetitive strain. Resistance tests are performed usually on extremity muscles. The muscle is placed in a midrange position and an isometric contraction of gradually increasing intensity is resisted. A false positive can occur if there is an acute joint inflammation.[83]

Such pain provocation helps identify the mechanical etiology and sensitized tissues. It also provides an ideal baseline to which the patient and doctor can refer when looking for objective signs of progress. These are the important tests that show us that our clinical judgements and interventions are correct. Similarly, if we want to motivate patients to do self-treatment, we need to be able to prove to them that progress occurs when they do their exercises. In our attempt to find the key functional pathologies, we will frequently perform postintervention checks of our pain provocative maneuvers to see if a beneficial effect has been accomplished by a specific manipulation, therapy, or exercise.

Nerve tension signs are perhaps the most studied of the provocative tests. When present, the prognosis carries greater seriousness (when compared to conditions not harboring nerve tension) because it implies traction on a nerve root, such as a sciatic nerve condition. The occurrence of sciatic leg pain is high in patients with a disc lesion (999 in 1000).[84] The straight leg raise (SLR) is usually between 15 and 30 degrees with nerve root tension reproduced. When greater than 60 degrees (+/−10), the SLR is unreliable.[85] The well leg raise (WLR) is highly specific but less sensitive.[84] The SLR, WLR, and bowstring test were found to be "potentially reliable."[71] The greatest majority (98%) are L4 or 5 discs (L5, S1 nerve roots).[86] The reliability of neurologic tests is as follows[71]:

Potentially reliable:
1. Muscle wasting and weakness
2. Achilles DTR
3. Sensory deficit tests

Unreliable
1. Buttock wasting
2. Toe standing*
3. Heel stand
4. Patellar DTR

Femoral nerve stretch was found to be "potentially reliable."[71] Note that in higher lumbar disc lesions (<2%), symptoms may include LBP, anterior hip or thigh numbness (which is more prominent than calf symptoms), patellar DTR reduction, weakness of the hip flexors (psoas muscle) and/or quadriceps, and anterior and lateral upper leg and medial foot sensory losses.

The overall accuracy of neurologic tests for disc lesions is "moderate." When found in combination (such as decreased ankle DTR and weak foot plantar flexion), however, reliability increases with approximately a 90% sensitivity in patients with surgically proven disc herniations.[84] Similarly, a positive SLR and neurologic findings increase reliability (surgically confirmed).[88]

---

* This author has found that unilateral heel raising (tip-toe position) repeated five times can often reveal an early weakness (S1 nerve root). This procedure is carried out by having the patient stand on one foot and raise and lower the heel five times while holding onto the wall. Weakness is usually perceived by the third to fifth repetition and is usually observable by the physician when an early or mild weakness exists. Similarly, repeating this in the opposite manner (repetitive forefoot raising five times) can facilitate assessment of an early L4,5 (tibialis anterior) weakness. Ankle dorsiflexion rarely occurs alone and is often found with extensor hallucis longus (EHL) weakness and or sensory deficits.[87]

The SLR test correlated with the severity of symptoms in lumbar disc herniation[88] where there was almost a linear correlation existing between a positive SLR and pain at rest, pain at night, pain with coughing, and reduction of walking capacity. It was also noted that regular analgesic use was correlated to more significantly reduced SLRs (< 30 degrees). In addition, a positive SLR early postoperatively correlated with inferior outcome of the surgical procedure (Table 10–7).

Peripheral entrapment of the sciatic nerve in the piriformis muscle can occur clinically and mimic a nerve root lesion; a careful history and examination must be performed. When considering the historical findings in this syndrome, there is usually little if any LBP, and buttock pain is the primary complaint. Physical examination reveals a positive SLR, hip internal rotation during the SLR resulting in pain that occurs at a lower angle, and resisted hip ER, the latter of which was found "potentially reliable."[71] The neurologic functions are negative. Palpation typically reveals a trigger point (TP) over the piriformis, but caution is advised as Intervertebral Disk Syndrome (IVDS) and piriformis syndrome are frequently concurrent disorders.[89]

When differentiating conditions that create leg pain, spinal stenosis must be included. The history usually reveals a >55-year-old, chronic history of LBP, and neurogenic claudication. Examination findings reveals no pulse change with walking, and a longer time period is required for reduction of symptoms compared to vascular claudication. The cycling or walking test is preferred and reduced pain and increased time of walking or cycling is noted when lumbar forward flexion is maintained. This test, however, was not found reliable in differentiating vascular from neurogenic claudication using a small patient sample of 19.[90] Neurogenic claudication, when present, has a 60% sensitivity for diagnosis of spinal stenosis, but specificity is probably higher.

Low back provocative tests that do not include nerve tension may relate to a condition often described as "mechanical low back pain." Included in this group of tests are those which reproduce LBP arising from the facet joint. Studies of direct injections into the joint under flouroscopy have yielded mixed results. Facet joint saline injection reproduced LBP, buttock, and leg extending at times to the calf with reduction of deep tendon reflexes.[91] When low

Table 10–7: The SLR Test and Its Correlation with Pre- and Postsurgical Findings

Results of the SLR test as a percentage of each category preoperatively and at 4 months and 1 year postoperatively

		POSTOPERATIVELY	
+ SLR Test	**Preoperatively**	**4 Months**	**1 Year**
0–30	42	1	0
30–60	26	6	9
60–90	18	15	9
Negative	14	78	82

Percentage incidence of pain related to result from SLR test preoperatively

	POSITIVE SLR			NEGATIVE SLR
	0–30	**30–60**	**60–90**	
Pain at rest	95	79	77	71
Pain at night	89	74	50	47
Pain on coughing	82	68	58	62

Percentage incidence of pain related to result from SLR test preoperatively

	POSITIVE SLR			NEGATIVE SLR
	0–30	**30–60**	**60–90**	
Pain at rest	100	67	41	13
Pain at night	100	67	50	14
Pain on coughing	100	56	41	16

back and leg pain are present without radiculopathy (no nerve root signs), consider facet syndrome. It has been reported that an "extension catch" has "poor reliability."[71] Lippitt[92] found 66% of a patient population responded to facet injection when the following five criteria were met:

1. LBP
2. Hip and buttock pain
3. Cramping leg pain above the knee
4. Low back stiffness especially in the morning
5. Absence of dysesthesia in the legs

A scoring system[92] was then introduced assigning points for various clinical findings as follows:

1. 30 points: LBP with groin or thigh pain
2. 20 points: Well-localized paraspinal tenderness
3. 30 points: LBP reproduced with extension-rotation (Kemp's test)
4. 20 points: Corresponding radiographic changes (osteoarthritis)
5. −10 points: Pain below the knee

The study utilized a 22-patient sample and results indicate that scores of 60 or greater required prolonged treatment. Seven of nine patients with scores of 40 or more responded favorably, but four patients with scores <40 points also responded to the injection therapy. In conclusion, none of the studies reviewed revealed any one clinical finding that alone was discriminatory. Therefore, the diagnosis is best made when more than one test is positive.

Other provocative tests that are designed to reproduce LBP of a mechanical variety include those specific for the sacroiliac joint (controversial diagnostic category). Bernard and Kirkaldy-Willis diagnosed this in 23% of LBP patients over a 12-year period.[93] Clinical presentation may include a history of LBP with or without lower extremity pain. When present, a nondermatomal groin and/or lower extremity pain pattern with PSIS and/or buttock palpable pain and hip and knee referred pain with walking (differentiate this from a hip condition) may occur. It has been shown that women are affected more frequently than men (especially during pregnancy).[94] Other clinical findings may include palpable unilateral low back muscle spasm and gluteal trigger points; SLR may be positive with or without hamstring tension but no nerve tension or neurologic losses (in spite of LE paresthesia complaints at times).[94]

Provocative orthopedic tests for sacroiliac joint assessment may include a positive Gaenslen's test, Patrick-Fabre test, and hip extension test (Yeoman's test). When two of three are positive, a diagnosis may be considered.[94] The sacroiliac stretch and iliac compression tests revealed moderate intertester reliability.[95] In another study, the sacroiliac stretch test, iliac compression or pelvic rock test, and pelvic torsion (Gaenslen's test) resulted in moderate reliability.[80,96] Mobility testing called the Gillet or step test was described as the most common.[97] Erhard and Dellito utilized four SIJ provocative tests to place patients into a manipulation and flexion/extension ("hand-heel rock") exercise treatment category.[28] When three of the four tests are positive, this was indicative of "sacroiliac regional pain" and manipulation was indicated.[76] The four tests are as follows:

1. Sitting PSIS level test: Test the heights of the PSISs in a sitting position (+ = unlevel).
2. Standing flexion PSIS level test: Test the PSIS heights in standing versus sitting (+ = PSIS height changes).
3. Supine to long sitting: Check the medial malleoli leg length change when changing positions from supine to a sit-up (long-sitting) position (+ = a change in the leg length).
4. Prone knee flexion test: + = a change in leg length from knees straight to flexed positions.

Laslett and Williams[80] review seven orthopedic tests, finding five of the seven to be interexaminer reliable and also met Kappa significance (effectively discounting the proportion of agreement that is expected by chance). These tests include the following:

1. Distraction
2. Compression
3. Thigh thrust
4. Pelvic torsion right (essentially Gaenslen's test)
5. Pelvic torsion left

The two tests not meeting good agreement ($K > 0.60$) were the sacral thrust and cranial shear for a pair of therapists who examined 43% ($n = 32$ of the total 51) of the sampled patients (28 women and 23 men, mean age of 39.5 years +/− 13.4 years, with symptoms ranging from 1 day to 17.5 years, a median of 60 days; 23 had LBP and buttock pain only, 12 had radiating pain to the knee, and 16 had pain radiating below the knee). The authors indicate that the other four pairs of therapists who examined the other 29 patients did report good agreement with these two tests, stating that the direct pressure on the sacrum ". . . may have confused the therapist or patient when determining whether symptoms were produced or aggravated by the test. This confusion may come about because local sacral tenderness is common in low back pain syndromes." Laslett and Williams go on to state that their findings confirm reliability of the compression and distraction tests as reported by Potter and Rothstein[95] and discuss the poor reliability results of McCombe et al.[71] They indicate the poor reliability may have been due to examination technique differences of the orthopedic surgeon and the therapist, which were ". . . minimized in our study through employment of several training sessions."

Provocative tests regarding the soft tissues are also reported. Typically, a history of overuse, overload, or overstretch of muscle creates localized or radiating pain (myotomal distribution). On physical examination, palpation as well as active range of motion (AROM) will often reproduce pain, passive ROM (PROM) will typically reduce pain, and resisted ROM will usually worsen pain in muscle injuries. Buttock and paravertebral muscle pain has been found "unreliable," but improved specificity when reporting the exact structures palpated increases reliability.[72] Trigger points (TPs) reportedly found in an estimated 12% to 30% of the general population[98] are typically localized in the muscle belly, with or without referred pain and jump sign, and may respond to spray and stretch and other forms of myofascial release techniques. Muscle pain is often concurrent with other conditions such as disc lesions. The absence of fatigue, no pain at the muscle-tendon, and localized pain help to differentiate a muscle injury from fibromyalgia.[98]

A classification for fibromyalgia was established in 1990 by the American College of Rheumatology.[99] This system includes three categories:

1. Bilateral symptoms, above and below the waist
2. Pain in the axial spine
3. Digital palpatory pain at 11 of 18 prescribed tender point sites

The incidence rate of fibromyalgia is 5% to 20% in rheumatology clinics and 3% to 5% in general medical clinics.[98] Symptoms are usually chronic (>3 months), with diffuse areas of tenderness, fatigue, stiffness, and sleep disturbances. Research indicates a relationship exists between fibromyalgia and chronic fatigue syndrome in which 70% of patients with CFS met the criteria for fibromyalgia.[98]

Table 10–8 offers a list of various provocative tests (left vertical column), low back conditions (top row), and various test responses when used during the physical examination for several different causes of low back pain. The key at the bottom of the table addresses the issue of validity. Opinions from several authors[71,76,96,100,101] as well as this author's experience are offered. Please note conflicting in-

Table 10–8: Provocative Orthopedic Tests and Published Reliabilities

	IVDS: NERVE TENSION	PIRIFORMIS SYNDROME	SPINAL STENOSIS	FACET SYNDROME	SACROILIAC SYNDROME	MUSCLE PAIN	HIP PAIN
			Nerve Root Entrapment Tests				
Straight Leg Raise	+ (20–30 degrees) 1*(A)	(+) 5*	usually – 5*	(+) >50–60 degrees 5*	(+) >50 degrees 5*	(+) > 50 5*	(+) 5*
Well Leg Raise (Crosssed Sciatic Sign)	+ (specif>sensit.) 1* (C)			5*; if acute +	+ Low sensitivity 5*		
Bow String	+ 5* if acute						
Patellar Dtr	+ 1* (D); + 1A, + 1C		(+) 5*				
Achilles Dtr	+ 1* (C); + 1A, +1C		(+) 5*				
Muscle Weakness	+ –1A; + 1C		(+) 5*				
Muscle Atrophy	+ 1* (C: Quads, TA, peron.); 5*: Low sens/Hi specificity	+ 1* (D buttock)					
Heel-Toe Strength	+ 1* (D)						
Sensory Deficit	+ 1* (A)		(+) 5*				
Pain Pattern	+ 1* (A: thigh & leg); (C: butt/foot); (D: foot pain)						
Femoral Nerve Stretch	+ 1* (B) (upper lumbar)		(+) 5*				(+) 5*

(continued)

Table 10–8: (*Continued*)

	IVDS: NERVE TENSION	PIRIFORMIS SYNDROME	SPINAL STENOSIS	FACET SYNDROME	SACROILIAC SYNDROME	MUSCLE PAIN	HIP PAIN
Hip Joint Tests							
Hip IR W/Resistance	(+) 5*	+ 5*			(+) 5*		+ 5*
W/O Resistance	(+) 5*	+ 5*			(+) 5*		+ 5*
Hip ER W/Resistance		+ 1* (C)			(+) 5*		+ 5*
ER W/O Resistance		+ 5* less sens.			+ 1* (C)		+ 5*
Patrick Fabre	(+) 5*	+ 5*			+ 4* (1)		+ 4* (1)
Short Hip Extensions							+ 6*
Short Hip Flexors							+ 6*
Rectus Femoris							+ 6*
Hip External Rotator							+ 6*
Hip Internal Rotators							+ 6*
Knee Flexors							+ 6*
Sacroiliac Tests							
Hip Flexion Test		+ 1* (A)			+ 1* (A)		
Sitting PSIS Height					+ 3*		
Standing Flexion PSIS	+ 5*				+ 3*		
Supine To Long Sitting	+ 5*				+ 3*		
Prone Knee Flexion					+ 3*		
Thigh Thrust	+ 5*				+ 2*		
Iliac (SI) Compression					**+ [1* (D)] 2* (reliable)**		(+) 5*
SI Stretch (Distraction) Test					**+ [1* (D)] 2* (reliable)**		(+) 5*
Gaenslen (Pelvic Torsion Test)	+ 5*			(+) 5*	+ 2* (reliable)		+ 5*
Yeoman's	may centralize			+ 5*	+ 5*		+ 5*
Maitland's	pn				+ 1* (D)		

formation exists for some of the tests where one study determined a test to be valid and another did not. In addition, this author offers an opinion, based on experience using these tests, regarding outcome. It becomes apparent that crossover exists for many tests in that one test can provoke pain arising from several different types of injured tissue. For example, an SLR test can provoke pain arising from the entraped nerve root (0 to 30 degrees on either the homolateral or contralateral side of the entrapment), from the facet joint or SIJ (greater than 50 degrees), or from a degenerative hip, synovitis of the hip, peripheral nerve entrapment at the piriformis, or even a low back muscle injury. It therefore becomes apparent that the following issues must be documented in the patient's file when using provocative orthopedic tests:

1. *Location* of the provoked pain.
2. *Type* and *intensity* of pain provoked (e.g., "sharp pain rated at 3/4 on a 0 to 4 pain scale").
3. *Pain response* (whether the pain *peripheralized*, *centralized*, or *remained unchanged*).
4. *Estimated point of pain onset* (or, at what point in the test's range of motion did the pain provocation occur. For example, ". . . pain was provoked in the first 10% of the movement").

The importance for this becomes apparent when a third-party payor reviews the file seeking information that proves improvement over time is occurring, when a fellow practitioner who is resuming care of the patient reviews the file, and/or if the case is being reviewed for medicolegal reasons

Table 10–8: (*Continued*)

	IVDS: NERVE TENSION	PIRIFORMIS SYNDROME	SPINAL STENOSIS	FACET SYNDROME	SACROILIAC SYNDROME	MUSCLE PAIN	HIP PAIN
Miscellaneous Tests							
Palpation Tests		+ 1* (D) paravertebral −1C		midline 1* (B) 2* (unreliable) + 1C	+ 1* (C: SI & iliac crest pain) 2* (unreliable)	+ 1* (D) paravert. − 1C	
Kemp's Test	(+) 5*			+ 5*	(+) 5*		
Gillet/Step Test					+ (4*: unreliable) − 1C		+ 5*
LBP	+ 5*		+ 5*	+ 5*	May be combined syndrome	+ 5*	Referred pain at x
LBP < Leg Pain	+ 5*	+ 5*	+ w/ walking		+ 5*		+ 5*
LBP > Leg Pain			+ at rest	+ 5*	Localized SI pain	+ 5*	
Leg Pain (AK)	(+) 5*	(+) 5*	(+) 5*		(+) 5*		+ 5*
Leg Pain (BK)	+ 5*	(+) 5*	+ 5*		(+) 5*		Less common
Sclerotomal Leg Pain				+ 5*	+ 5*		+ 5*
Dermatomal Leg Pain	+ 5*		Usually not; pain global				
Myotomal Pain		(+) 5*				(+) 5*	
Flexion Reduces Pain			+ 5*	+ 5*	(+) 5*		(+) 5*
Flexion Induced Pain	+ 5*	(+) 5*				(+) 5*	(+) 5*
Extension Pain			+ 5*	+ 5*	(+) 5*		(+) 5*
Extension Reduces Leg Pain	+ 5*	(+) 5*					
Fatigue/Sleep Disturbances	+ 5*			(+) 5*	(+) 5*	+ 5*	(+) 5*
Trigger Points 11/18						+ 5* (99)	
Jump Sign						+ 5*	

AK = Above knee; BK = below knee

1* Reliability reported in McCombe et al[71] study; Rating Scale: A= Most reliable; B & C= Potentially reliable; D= Poor reliability

2* Found reliable in Laslett and Williams[96] study

3* Found reliable in Cibulka et al[76] study (+ if 3 out of 4 tests are positive)

4* Reliability reported in Souza's study[100]; Rating Scale: +1A=Good sensitivity; +1B=Good specificity; +1C=Good inter- or intraexaminer reliability; 1=No testing but based on scientific investigation (cadaveric or surgical); −1A=Poor sensitivity; −1B=Poor specificity; −1C=Poor inter-/intraexaminer reliability;

5* Found positive in author's experience

6* Found reliable in Bullock-Saxton et al[119] study (only reported normative data using healthy subjects measuring muscle length. No mention was made regarding pain or the significance of pain).

(+) = less common or "possible"

NOTE: Shaded area represent conflict in reported validity (see text for discussion).

or is the subject of a malpractice suit. As a result, the document used in recording the results of these tests must contain ample room for entering these data.

FUNCTIONAL CAPACITY EVALUATION

FUNCTIONAL CAPACITY EVALUATION AS AN OUTCOMES ASSESSMENT INSTRUMENT

Terminology related to functional capacity evaluation (FCE) and work capacity evaluation (WCE) is often used interchangeably, which to say the least, is quite confusing. A functional capacity evaluation consists of a collection of functional or physical performance tests that are either quantitative or qualitative. When *quantitative*, the tests serve as outcome assessment tools because they are capable of measuring change over time. Functional tests that are *qualitative* are typically kinesiological or biomechanical tests that are important to direct treatment decision making.

The chief purpose of the quantitative FCE (QFCE) is to *objectively* demonstrate an individual's level of impairment through the use of physical performance tests. Such impairment is related to both pain and disability.[102,103] This evaluation provides the health care provider with objective information so that treatment can be rationally prescribed and the results of treatment monitored. It also gives patients objective feedback of how their injury and/or pain is affecting their ability to perform normal activities, as well as giving them an objective way to see how they are progressing. Finally, the QFCE provides the third-party payor with quantifiable evidence of impairment caused by injury and provides objective support for the patient's subjective complaint(s). The QFCE is invaluable for the doctor and third-party payor in potentially contentious situations.

The work capacity evaluation, on the other hand, refers to whole-body or "real-world" movements such as crawling, reaching, climbing, stooping, etc. This evaluation attempts to simulate the workplace, and the results of the assessment will then allow the recipient of the information to better understand the capacities of the worker. The objective of the WCE is to identify the threshold of failure of the various tests in order to design a return to work plan that will prevent the worker from becoming reinjured.

The FCE identifies intrinsic impairments in the individual. Often, the extrinsic demands of the work environment are the overloading or injurious factor. A work capacity evaluation and/or job analysis may be required to identify such potential sources of repetitive overload or injury. Ergonomic principles may need to be applied to such work environments as computer workstations or loading bays. Training in sitting, lifting, or other repetitive tasks may be necessary.[104,105]

The WCE and the FCE should not be performed in the acute stage postinjury. According to Mooney, an FCE is recommended 2 weeks postinjury in order to identify the "weak functional link."[106] Mooney and Matheson instruct a 4-week time passage prior to the use of their California Functional Capacity Protocol (Cal-FCP).[107] The Cal-FCP may be used anytime after 4 weeks so long as the evaluation tasks are not likely to harm the evaluee. A screening examination prior to participation is appropriate if a problem has not stabilized. Through personal communication, Triano suggests 4 weeks as an appropriate time to begin testing. Hart, Isernhagen, and Matheson recently wrote that the indications for functional testing include.[108]:

1. Plateau of treatment progress.
2. Discrepancy between subjective and objective findings.
3. Difficulty returning to gainful employment.
4. Vocational planning or medicolegal case settlement.

It is also prudent and appropriate to monitor the patient's pain responses during the FCE. A numerical pain scale (NPS) that mirrors the VAS (0 to 10 scheme) has been utilized because of its ease and less cumbersome attributes compared to the VAS.[109] Though the VAS has traditionally been considered more reliable,[110] recent studies revealed that the NPS was more responsive than the VAS.[109] If pain levels prohibit continuation of the FCE, it is most ethical to discontinue and repeat the examination at a later date. Blankenship states that a VAS or numerical pain scale greater than 3 may warrant postponement of the FCE.[110] Further, he states that subjects that express high pain levels and yet agree to participate in an FCE may be exaggerating their symptoms. He states that symptom exaggeration is present when an injured person consents to participate in the FCE with:

1. Numerical pain rating of 6 or greater (0 to 10).
2. Visual Analogue pain rating of 6 or greater.
3. McGill Pain Questionnaire score of 30 or greater.

When functional outcomes are not addressed, incomplete healing, chronic pain, and overtreatment often result.[111,112] When utilized however, treatment is directed that will in turn confront incomplete healing and chronic pain issues, thus promoting cost containment.

The "sports medicine" approach, which measures functional impairment and uses active exercise to rehabilitate injured tissues, is recognized as the "standard of care" for soft tissue injuries.[103,113,114] This active approach is better suited to alleviating pain, completing soft tissue healing, and preventing reoccurrence.

The FCE should be mandatory for any patient still suffering pain after 6 or 7 weeks.[106] The FCE is composed of measurable functional tests and questionnaires. The functional tests measure flexibility, strength, coordination, endurance, aerobic capacity, posture, and balance. The questionnaires measure pain intensity and distribution, lifestyle changes (activities of daily living modifications), depression, and coping capacity.

Functional capacity evaluation should focus on relevant functions that can be safely and reliably measured. Where normative databases exist this is most helpful. Whenever possible, quantification is the ideal. The most valid tests are those that most closely resemble the actual way we use our bodies. If an effort factor can be measured, this will help unmask a malingerer. A low-technology approach is practical with the use of a tape measure, inclinometer, watch, strain gauge, and calipers. Simple grading schemes can be used that allow highly functional movements to be assessed that cannot be easily, inexpensively, or accurately quantified.

Tests should be chosen that are safe, reliable, valid, and cost-effective. They must not take too much time or require very expensive equipment. Tests should tell us something about the individual's ability to perform a real-life task. Validity is often ignored. According to Matheson ". . .the interpretation of the test score should be able to predict or reflect the evaluee's performance in a target task."[115]

As soon as a patient emerges from the acute stages of an injury, objective measurement of functional outcomes is necessary. This gives the doctor, patient, and third-party payor a means of communicating what the patient status is and what the goals of care are. This does not require great expense of time or money because it can be accomplished with questionnaires and low-tech instruments.

HIGH-TECH VERSUS LOW-TECH

A low-tech approach can be utilized with minimal expenditure and about 30 minutes of office time. This evaluation should be performed on subacute patients (when inflammation and excessive guarding reactions are minimized) and chronic patients. Positive tests can be used as a "barometer" of improvement with posttreatment or bimonthly reevaluations being carried out.

High-tech dynametric assessment of low back function has become the "gold standard" of lumbar spine functional assessment. However, a recent study by Grabiner et al demonstrated that normal strength measurements alone do not necessarily correlate with normal function.[116] Utilizing electromyography (EMG) evaluation during isometric trunk extension, they showed that decoupling or asymmetric lumbar paraspinal muscular activity was present in low back pain subjects who had been considered normal on dynamometry testing. This decoupling was also able to differentiate between pain and nonpain subjects.

Grabiner's study points out that musculoskeletal function involves not only strength but also coordination between muscles involved in a specific task. Simply because a patient passes a battery of high-tech functional strength tests does not necessarily mean that his or her spinal function is normal. The EMG test not only points out the limitations of high-tech dynamometry testing of muscle strength and endurance, but suggests that overly harsh criticism of lower-technology evaluations of coordination may be unjustified.

High-tech quantification of functional deficits can cost from $10,000 to $100,000. Dynatronics, Lido, Cybex, MedX, etc., isolate very specific movements and are highly repeatable and reliable. Costs make these units prohibitive for most small private practitioners. EMG units are also cost-prohibitive for the average field practitioner. However, in medical legal practices or research settings such equipment can be beneficial.

Based on the previous points the quality of high-tech tests has not been demonstrated sufficiently to lead to the abandonment of lower-tech qualitative tests of spinal function. Many reliable low-tech ways to identify functional pathology have been identified.[117–133] Moreover, because of the high costs associated with high-tech assessment instruments, the criteria of practicality, as discussed earlier in the chapter, has not been met. In addition, the inability of high-tech testing to be easily related to the demands of employment favors the low-tech tests such as the repetitive squat, back endurance, and repetitive arch-up tests.

Newton and Waddell said, "There is no convincing evidence that isokinetic or any other isomeasure has greater clinical utility in the patient with LBP than either clinical evaluation of physical impairment, isometric strength, simple isoinertial lifting or psychophysical testing."[134] As Lewit puts it, ". . . in many fields of medicine the importance of changes in function is now well recognized, whereas in the motor system, where function is paramount, this fundamental aspect is rarely considered. However, the functioning of the locomotor system is extremely complex, . . . and diagnosis of disturbed function is a highly sophisticated proceeding carried out, as it were in a clinical no man's land."[135]

LaRocca in his Presidential Address to the Cervical Spine Research Society Annual Meeting in December of 1991 criticized his colleagues for jumping to a psychological diagnosis when they cannot find a structural cause for a patient's persistent pain by stating, ". . . the error here is the automatic leap to psychology. It assumes that all organic factors have been considered, when in reality the clinician's appreciation of the complexity of such factors is often severely limited."[136]

PHYSICAL PERFORMANCE TESTS

Although quantification of functional deficits is the goal, it should be realized that this attempt is only in its infancy. Most physiological parameters of the musculoskeletal system cannot be realistically measured in a quantifiable way. Intersegmental accessory motion between articulations is regularly palpated, but interexaminer reliability is poor and no quantification is possible. Palpation of areas of tenderness by an algometer does not resemble manual palpation although it is quantifiable. Visual inspection of patients' posture, gait, and movement skills is part of a *qualitative* examination that is clinically invaluable. Manual palpation and visual inspection although not quantifiable, do utilize our most sensitive instruments—our eyes and hands. Although we should strive toward objective quantification and measurement, we should not limit ourselves to quantification alone.

Other low-tech tests that have been found reliable in assessing function include speed and endurance in walking, stair climbing, standing up from a chair, sit-ups, and arm endurance.[137]

Low Back Pain

Most LBP patients are treated without adequate subclassifications. In a recent study, 23 of 53 NIOSH LBP tests successfully discriminated between subjects with LBP and those without it. The seven strongest tests together had a sensitivity of 87% and specificity of 93%. Tests regarding symmetry, strength, passive mobility, and dynamic mobility, were found to be important.[138]

Symmetry

1. Iliac crest height from standing position (level table)
   - Observe PSIS levels
   - Common error: not observing iliac heights from the eye level (use of a bubble level may improve reliability)
2. Posterior superior iliac spine levels
   - Observe PSIS heights from the posterior

Strength

3. Upper abdominal muscle strength
   - Patient position: supine, hips straight or slightly flexed; Patient raises the head and shoulders, "curling" the trunk
   - Grading scheme: A: scapulae off table with hands locked behind head (best); B: scapulae off table with arms across chest; C: scapulae off table with arms at sides; D: cannot complete the procedure (worst)

Passive Mobility

4. Hip Joint ROM (gravity goniometer): Prone total internal/external rotation (IR/ER)
   - Patient position: Prone, testing knee is flexed 90°; Inclinometer is placed on the distal lateral lower leg (frontal plane); Inclinometer is set at 0
   - Passive IR (ankle moves outward) and record measurement at end point *prior to pelvis rotation* (common error; perform bilaterally)
   - Passive ER (ankle moves inward) and record measurement at end point *prior to pelvis rotation* (common error; perform bilaterally)
5. Straight leg raise
   - Supine patient's single leg is raised to the point of hamstring resistance when knee starts to flex on either the testing side or opposite side

Dynamic Mobility

6. Lumbar flexion (dual inclinometers); see Chapter 14 for technique
7. Presence of pain in prone press-up position (at initiation of movement)

Hip Function

The "functional" length of muscles around the hip has been studied in 11 normal 20- to 26-year-old, healthy subjects with reliability.[101] Each subject was evaluated in the 10-hour time period after midday because the least circadian rhythm affects body flexibility at this time of day.[139] For all muscle length measurements, an assistant helped in either moving or stabilizing a limb. To facilitate in reducing error, the following procedure was followed:

1. Skill in handling and maintaining a consistent speed of limb movement was coordinated between the assistant and researcher.
2. For each subject, the series of tests were repeated 10 times, and each test series was separated by a 2-minute rest period.
3. Landmarks were marked on the skin 10 cm proximal to the lateral femoral condyle (for thigh movement) or the lateral malleolus of the ankle (for lower leg movement assessment) to ensure accurate positioning of the inclinometer from test to test.
4. An instruction for full patient relaxation during each test to ensure accuracy of the angle measured was emphasized.
5. Care was exercised as to where the lower extremity was grasped in order to avoid neurologic facilitation of the tested muscle by the manual contact.

Six movements of the hip were studied for muscle length assessment using the following procedures:

1. Short hip extensors:
Patient position: Supine, fully relaxed.
Assistant position: Moved hip into flexion with knee flexed.
Researcher position: Palpated PSIS on the moving side.
Method: Electronic inclinometer strapped to femur 10 cm above lateral condyle of knee. Measurement read at the moment the PSIS was felt to move.
2. Short hip flexors:
Patient position: Supine, fully relaxed in the modified Thomas position.
Assistant position: Provided a force through the nontested flexed hip/knee while monitoring the pressure of the flattened lumbar spine against the bed with a pressure biofeedback unit.
Researcher position: Slowly lowered the thigh, supporting it from the posterior (to avoid facilitation of the hip flexor muscles). The motion was measured at a

point just prior to loss of contact of the lumbar spine on the table (decreased pressure on the biofeedback unit).
Method: Electronic inclinometer strapped to femur 10 cm above lateral condyle of knee. Measurement read at the point just short of lumbar spine loss of contact with the table/pressure gauge.
3. Rectus femoris:
Patient position: Supine, fully relaxed in the modified Thomas position.
Assistant position: Provided a force through the nontested flexed hip/knee while monitoring the pressure of the flattened lumbar spine against the bed with a pressure biofeedback unit.
Researcher position: Slowly lowered the thigh, supporting it from the posterior (to avoid facilitation of the hip flexor muscles). The motion was stopped when the thigh became parallel with the floor (to provide a controlled position of the hip). The knee was then passively flexed until resistance to the motion was first palpated and the angle of the lower leg measured against the horizontal.
Method: Electronic inclinometer strapped to lower leg 10 cm above the lateral malleolus of ankle. Measurement read at the first point of motion resistance.
4. External rotators of the hip:
Patient position: Prone, fully relaxed.
Assistant position: Moved knee into flexion at 90 degrees, thigh positioned neutral (avoid abduction or adduction). While researcher maintains the monitering at the pelvis, the assistant moves the thigh into ER.
Researcher position: Palpates PSIS on the opposite side, watching the pelvis.
Method: Electronic inclinometer strapped to anterior lower leg 10 cm above lateral malleolus of the ankle. Measurement read at the moment just short of pelvis movement.
5. Internal rotators of the hip:
Patient position: Prone, fully relaxed.
Assistant position: Moved knee into flexion at 90 degrees, thigh positioned neutral (avoid abduction or adduction). While researcher maintains the monitoring at the pelvis, the assistant moves the thigh into IR.
Researcher position: Palpates PSIS on the opposite side, watching the pelvis.
Method: Electronic inclinometer strapped to anterior lower leg 10 cm above lateral malleolus of the ankle. Measurement read at the moment just short of pelvis movement.
6. Knee flexors:
Patient position: Supine, fully relaxed.
Assistant position: Moves hip to 90 degrees of flexion with the knee flexed grasping thigh on lateral and medial borders to avoid hamstring muscle facilitation.
Researcher position: Moves the knee into extension to point of resistance where the pelvis rotates backwards or the thigh deviates downward (extends).
Method: Electronic inclinometer strapped to lateral lower leg 10 cm above lateral malleolus of the ankle. Measurement read at the moment just short of movement.

Table 10–9 shows normative data regarding the above hip function study.

The Quantitative Functional Capacity Evaluation

In 1995 the Quantitative Functional Capacity Evaluation (QFCE) was developed with the objective of creating a valid and reliable method of evaluating functional capacity of a patient which is low in cost and time-efficient.[140] Objective baselines of physical performance are provided by the QFCE, which can track outcomes during the course of active rehabilitation programs and/or at the conclusion of the rehabilitation program.

Several low-tech tests have been studied, revealing good to excellent reliability, and they appeared to correlate better with pain and disability than did the isokinetic tests.[141] In summary, ". . . non-dynamometric tests are still

Table 10–9: Normative Data Regarding the Functional Length of Muscle Derived from 11 Normal 20- to 26-Year-Old Subjects

MEASUREMENT	MEAN (SD)	CV	VARIANCE	ICC	PRECISION	LSD
Short hip extensors	66.4	10.2	48.7	0.87	0.45	6.12
Short hip flexors	0.9	1.7	2.3	0.98	2.08	1.33
Knee extensors	59.7	2.6	2.4	0.99	2.04	1.36
Knee flexors	48.2	4.0	3.6	0.99	1.70	3.31
Hip internal rotation	53.0	7.1	14.2	0.99	0.64	4.29
Hip external rotation	42.4	11.5	23.9	0.96	0.65	6.11

SD = standard deviation; CV = coefficient of variation; ICC = Intraclass correlation coefficient; LSD = least difference necessary for significance.

Table 10–10: A Quantifiable Approach to the Assessment of the Repetitive Squatting Test Segregated by Age, Gender, and Working Class (Blue Collar versus White Collar)[a]

AGE	MALES (N=242)						FEMALES (N=233)					
	Blue Collar		White Collar		All		Blue Collar		White Collar		All	
	x	SD	x	SD	x	SD	x	SD	x	SD	x	SD
35–39	39	13	46	8	42	12	24	11	27	12	26	12
40–44	34	14	45	9	38	13	22	13	18	8	20	12
45–49	30	12	40	11	33	13	19	12	26	13	22	13
50–54	28	14	41	11	33	14	13	10	18	14	14	11
35–54	33	14	43	10	37	13	20	12	23	12	21	12

[a]x = mean values and SD = standard deviations of the repetitive squatting test.

useful in clinical practice in spite of the development of more accurate muscle strength evaluation methods." Alaranta et al published normative data using a study sample of over 500 subjects, segregated by age and sex for the following low-tech tests[142]:

- Repetitive squatting
- Repetitive sit-ups
- Repetitive arch-ups
- Static back endurance tests

The low-tech tests are described as follows:

1. Repetitive Squatting:
Patient position: Standing with the feet 15 cm apart.
Technique: Patient squats until thighs are horizontal and returns to upright position. Each repetition rate is one repetition every 2 to 3 seconds. Repeat to maximum.
Observe: Count number of repetitions (maximum 50).
Normals: See Table 10–10.

2. Repetitive Sit-ups:
Patient position: Supine, knees flexed 90 degrees, ankles fixed.
Technique: Patient sits up until touching the thenar-hand to the patella, and curls back down to the supine position.
Observe: Count number of repetitions (maximum 50).
Normals: See Table 10–11.

3. Repetitive Arch-ups:
Doctor position: At table side holding patient's ankles (a strap is less work).
Patient position: Prone with the inguinal region at end of a table; arms at sides, ankles fixed, holding 45° trunk flexion angle.
Technique: Patient raises to horizontal position and back down to 45° angle.
Observe: Count number of repetitions (maximum 50).
Normals: See Table 10–12.

4. Static Back Endurance tests:
Doctor position: At table side holding patient's ankles (a strap is ideal).

Table 10–11: A Quantifiable Approach to the Assessment of the Repetitive Sit-up Test Segregated by Age, Gender, and Working Class (Blue Collar versus White Collar)[a]

AGE	MALES (N=242)						FEMALES (N=233)					
	Blue Collar		White Collar		All		Blue Collar		White Collar		All	
	x	SD	x	SD	x	SD	x	SD	x	SD	x	SD
35–39	29	13	35	13	32	13	24	12	30	16	27	14
40–44	22	11	34	12	27	13	18	12	19	13	19	12
45–49	19	11	33	15	24	14	17	14	22	15	19	14
50–54	17	13	36	16	23	16	9	10	20	13	11	11
35–54	23	13	35	13	27	14	17	13	24	15	19	14

[a]x = mean values and SD = standard deviations of the repetitive sit-up test.

Table 10–12: A Quantifiable Approach to the Assessment of the Repetitive Arch-up Test Segregated by Age, Gender, and Working Class (Blue Collar versus White Collar)[a]

AGE	MALES (N=242)						FEMALES (N=233)					
	Blue Collar		White Collar		All		Blue Collar		White Collar		All	
	x	SD	x	SD	x	SD	x	SD	x	SD	x	SD
35–39	26	11	34	14	29	13	28	13	27	11	27	12
40–44	23	12	36	14	28	14	25	14	20	11	23	13
45–49	24	13	34	16	28	15	25	15	31	16	27	15
50–54	21	11	35	17	26	15	18	14	26	14	19	14
35–54	24	12	35	15	28	14	24	14	26	13	24	14

[a]x = mean values and SD = standard deviations of the repetitive arch-up test.

Patient position: Prone with the inguinal region at end of a table; arms at sides, ankles fixed, holding horizontal position.
Technique: Patient maintains the horizontal position as long as possible.
Observe: Time the duration the position can be held (maximum 240 seconds).
Normals: See Table 10–13.

The last of the four strength and endurance tests described above was first introduced in 1984 and is often utilized in the assessment of trunk strength.[143] The introduction of the normative data, especially with the breakdown by age, sex, and occupation, can easily be applied to a patient population and, in this application, in a rehabilitation setting.

Another low-tech approach that can be utilized in the assessment of functional capacities is the measurement of movement. Spinal ROM can be assessed in many different ways. A tape measure, visual assessment, and inclinometry are commonly utilized to assess ROM. Recently, Mayer et al studied normative data in 160 male railroad workers and published the following data[144]:

1. ROM (lumbar):
Doctor position: Standing or sitting behind or to side of patient.
Patient position: Standing with feet shoulder width apart.
Inclinometer placement: Sagittal plane (flexion/extension) at T12 and S2, with the base of the inclinometer placed vertically, perpendicular to the spine in the midline. Frontal plane (lateral flexion) at T12 and S2 with the base of the inclinometer placed horizontal; the needle must hang freely in both planes.
Method: The end points of movement are recorded at both the T12 and S2 and the difference is calculated using the equation T12−S2=__________ degrees. If the average of three consecutive readings falls within 5 degrees or 10% of the average, the highest of the three

Table 10–13: A Quantifiable Approach to the Assessment of the Static Back Endurance Test Segregated by Age, Gender, and Working Class (Blue Collar versus White Collar)[a]

AGE	MALES (N=242)						FEMALES (N=233)					
	Blue Collar		White Collar		All		Blue Collar		White Collar		All	
	x	SD	x	SD	x	SD	x	SD	x	SD	x	SD
35–39	87	38	113	47	97	43	91	61	95	48	93	55
40–44	83	51	129	57	101	57	89	57	67	51	80	55
45–49	81	45	131	64	99	58	90	55	122	73	102	64
50–54	73	47	121	56	89	55	62	55	99	78	69	60
35–54	82	45	123	55	97	53	82	58	94	62	87	59

[a]x = mean values and SD = standard deviations of the static back endurance test.

Table 10–14: Lumbar Range of Motion Normative Data[a]

LUMBAR MOTION	MEAN AND SD	PERCENT OF NORMAL
True flexion	58 +/− 9.6	89.2 (65°)
True extension	22 +/− 9.7	72.7 (30°)
Pelvic flexion	60 +/− 13.8	109.1 (55°)
Straight leg raise		
Right	77 +/− 12.5	102.9 (75°)
Left	77 +/− 12.0	102.9 (75°)
Right lateral flexion	24 +/− 7.4	96.9 (25°)
Left lateral flexion	25 +/− 8.2	100.6 (25°)

[a]Taken of 160 male railroad workers: Average age 35 years (+/− 8); height 70 inches (+/− 3); weight 187 lb (+/− 29).[124]

readings is recorded (may repeat a maximum of six times to try to achieve this).
Normals: See Table 10–14
2. ROM (cervical):
Patient position: Sitting upright.
Inclinometer placement: Sagittal plane (flexion/extension) at T1 and occiput, with the base of the inclinometer placed vertically perpendicular to the spine/skull in the midline. Frontal plane (lateral flexion) at T2 and occiput with the base of the inclinometer placed horizontal; needle must hang freely in both planes.
Method: The end points of movement are recorded at both the T1 and occiput and the difference is calculated using the equation: T1−Occiput=____________ degrees. If the average of three consecutive readings fall within 5 degrees or 10% of the average, the highest of the three readings is recorded (may repeat a maximum of six times to try to achieve this).
Normal: See Table 10–15.

A pain scale developed by the McKenzie Institute has been utilized and seems very appropriate to use in the context of a rehabilitation FCE. The benefit of this scale over a 0 to 4 or a 0 to 10 VAS or numerical pain scale is the allowance of pain change, i.e., reduction and/or centralization as well as an increase in pain and/or peripheralization. This scale has been utilized in the past with validity[28,73,145,146] and an abbreviated approach is offered and defined as follows (+1, 0, −1):

- +1 = the pain worsened with movement and/or peripheralization occurred.
- 0 = no change in pain.
- −1 = the pain improved and/or centralized.

Other tests that can be quantified and thus function well in a low-tech FCE include various joint movement measurements. For example, measuring ankle dorsiflexion, first with the knee straight to test for gastrocnemius tension, and secondly, with the knee flexed to test for soleus tension, has been found reliable.[147,148] Ekstrand et al describe the technique as follows:

1. Gastrocnemius/ankle dorsiflexion test (knee straight)

Patient position: Standing upright, feet parallel.

Table 10–15: Cervical Range of Motion Normative Data[a]

CERVICAL MOTION	MEAN AND SD	PERCENT OF NORMAL
Flexion	53 +/− 12.1	105.6 (50°)
Extension	71 +/− 14.1	112.6 (63°)
Right lateral flexion	49 +/− 7.2	109.6 (45°)
Left lateral flexion	50 +/− 7.8	112.0 (45°)
Right rotation	88 +/− 10.6	103.3 (85°)
Left rotation	90 +/− 9.6	105.5 (85°)

[a]Taken of 160 male railroad workers: Average age 35 years (+/− 7.5); height 64.9 inches (+/− 2.6); weight 187 lb (+/− 28.6).[124]

Technique: Knee straight: lean forward against a wall, heel down to point of maximum ankle dorsiflexion (DF).
Observe: Fix (with Velcro) the inclinometer above the lateral malleolus and at 0 in upright standing position. Read at maximum ankle DF (patient leans forward to maximum ankle DF keeping heel down).
Normals: 22.5 degrees; SD 0.7, Intraassay CV 2.2%;,Interassay CV 2.5%.[147]

2. Soleus/ankle dorsiflexion test (knee flexed)
Patient position: Standing one leg on floor and testing foot on a bench.[147]
Technique: Knee flexed: maintain heel to bench contact at maximum ankle DF (kneeling position).
Normals: 24.9 degrees, SD 0.8, Intraassay CV 2.2%, Interassay CV 2.6%.[146]

Another quantifiable ROM test is the modified Thomas test, or hip extension test. This test has been shown to have validity in several studies.[147,149–151] This test is described as follows:

3. Modified Thomas test/hip extension test
Patient position: First, position the patient fully on the bench and obtain 0 reading. Second, move the patient to the end of bench (use a piece of plywood over the examination table secured by straps) with the contralateral knee/hip flexed to chest (to eliminate lumbar lordosis). The testing hip is then passively flexed to 90 degrees; the inclinometer is rezeroed, and then the hip is *maximally* extended followed by relaxation, hanging passively towards the floor (relaxed).
Technique: Place the inclinometer on the lateral thigh 5 cm above patella (may use Velcro strap) and adjust to 0 while the patient is laying supine, knee extended fully, and hip in neutral position (prior to positioning the patient at end of table). Move the patient to the end of the bench, drop the leg off while the contralateral leg is flexed to the chest. Remove all lumbar lordosis and test by placing a plastic ruler under L-spine (should be pinched between spine and table). The tested hip is then passively flexed to 90 degrees and the inclinometer reset to 0.
Observe: Record the angle when the homolateral leg is fully relaxed, hip extended, and L-lordosis is removed.
Normals: 83.5 degrees, SD 1.1. Intrassay CV 0.7%, Interassay CV 1.2%.[147]

The next ROM test that has been studied with published reliability is the straight leg raise (SLR) test, hamstring flexibility test, or the hip flexion test.[147,148,151,152] This test is described as follows:

4. SLR (hamstring flexibility) test
Doctor position: Standing to side of patient.
Patient position: Supine.
Technique: Perform SLR with doctor supporting lower extremity (with the crook of the elbow) while holding zeroed inclinometer on midtibia, or strap or Velcro to the lateral thigh (5 cm above patella) while indifferent hand stabilizes the pelvis. Raise leg to first point of knee flexion (leg being tested) and/or the pelvis begins to rock or the opposite knee flexes.
Quantification: Record hip flexion angle (normal = 70 to 90 degrees).[147]

The next quantifiable test is the knee flexion test (Nachlas test). Again, a simple measurement of maximum knee flexion can easily and reliably be performed as follows[147–151]:

5. Knee flexion test/Nachlas test
Doctor position: To side of patient.
Patient position: Prone.
Technique: Place the inclinometer on lower leg and adjust to 0. Strap the pelvis down. Passively flex the knee.
Observe: Record the angle at the moment hip flexion starts.
Normals: See Table 10–16.

Hip rotation has also been studied and found reliable by several sources[153–156] and is described as follows:

6. Hip Rotation ROM (IR and ER: internal and external rotation)
Doctor position: To the side of the patient. Hold inclinometer fixed to medial or lateral side of the distal third of lower leg; indifferent hand stabilizes pelvis (the use of a stabilizing strap is best).
Patient position: Prone, knee flexed 90 degrees.
Technique: Place the inclinometer on anterior lower leg and adjust to 0 with the knee flexed 90 degrees.
Observe: Record the angle at maximum IR and ER of the hip.
Normals: See Table 10–17.

Table 10–16: Knee Flexion Normative Data

	AVERAGE	SD	INTRAASSAY CV (%)	INTERASSAY CV (%)
Knee flexion	147.9	1.6	0.5	1.1

Table 10–17: Hip Rotation Normative Data as Reported by Four Authors

	AMA GUIDES	CHESWORTH	HOPPENFELD	KENDALL
Internal rotation	>20	41–45	35	45
External rotation	>30	41–43	45	45

The next set of tests that could be utilized in a "low-tech" FCE are the Waddell Non-Organic Low Back Pain Signs (WNLBPS).[38] Since these tests have been used as "gold standards" in many studies, the reliability of these tests seems to be well accepted. Only until recently have some of the tests that make up this group been challenged.[39,71,157] If care is utilized as recommended in the original article,[38] these tests appear to be reliable and important in the differentiation of organic versus nonorganic low back pain. There are five categories with a total of eight tests that make up the WNLBPS and they are as follows:

Note: the Waddell nonorganic pain tests, are *non-provocative tests;* i.e., they *do not* try to provoke a pain response as is the case when performing standard orthopedic provocative tests. Therefore, if a pain response occurs, this constitutes a positive (+) nonorganic response, but a "normal" or "organic" response is a report of no pain. Determine if there is a physiologic explanation for the response, and repeat the test as many times as needed in order to ensure evaluator objectivity.

1. Superficial and deep pain/tenderness (Waddell No. 1)

Doctor position: Standing or sitting behind the patient.
Patient position: Sitting, standing, or lying.
Technique: Superficial: lightly pinch over the lumbar skin. Deep: a nonanatomical, wide area of pain not localized to one structure.
Observe: Disproportionate/exaggerated response (jump sign, verbal response, etc.).
Differential diagnosis: Fibromyalgia

2. Simulation (Waddell No. 2)

Doctor position: Standing behind the patient.
Patient position: Standing.
Technique: Axial Loading: LBP is created by downward pressure on the skull. Rotation: LBP with passive pelvic/shoulder rotation (ignore if root pain is present).
Observe: LBP produced with minimal downward pressure or rotation (exaggerated response). Neck pain may occur with axial loading (look for an LBP, not neck pain response). Trunk rotation can reproduce root pain physiologically, thus representing a false-positive response; watch out for this!

3. Sitting SLR/distraction (Waddell No. 3).

Patient position: Sitting compared to supine straight leg raise (SLR).
Technique: Perform sitting SLR while distracting the patient by the performance of a plantar superficial reflex with rapid extension of the knee.
Observe: Positive if pain in a sitting SLR is less than the nondistracted supine SLR test (+ flip test). Note: if positive nerve tension signs exist, be cautious as to the speed at which the sitting SLR is performed. A disproportionate response may occur (tremor, outcry, collapse) during one of the two SLR movements (usually supine nondistracted SLR). Note: Only report as positive if there is a significant difference between the two SLR tests.

4. Regional neurology (Waddell No. 4)

Doctor position: Perform a standard neurologic exam (DTRs, muscle strength, sensory).
Patient position: Sitting, standing, or lying.
Observe: Motor: many muscle groups weak (a cogwheel or "giving way"); Sensory: a nondermatomal dysesthesia (differentiate from sclerotomal pain); i.e., inconsistent, nonanatomical neurologic findings constitutes a positive test.

5. Exaggeration/overreaction (Waddell No. 5)

Patient position: Sitting, standing, or lying; noted at any time during the consultation or examination.
Observe: Disproportionate responses which may include tremor, outcry, collapse, i.e., exaggerated characteristics.

A scoring method exists in which each positive sign is scored as 1 point. The group of tests (five in number) are then reported as 0 to +5 (e.g., +3/5). The following scoring scale has been defined[38]:

0–2/5 = within normal physiological ("organic") limits
3–5/5 = considered abnormal, or a positive test

Another low-tech FCE test is that of grip strength. Normative data segregating age, sex, and occupation factors have been reported.[153,158] This test is described as follows.

Grip Strength Dynamometry

Patient position: Sitting or standing, elbow at 90 degrees (try to obtain a pain-free position so as to avoid pain induced weakness).
Technique: The published normative data reflect tests using a Jamar hand dynamometer usually in the second or third position (dependent on size of hand); three readings are averaged.

Observe: Three tests taken at different intervals during the examination are considered reliable if there is <20% variation in three readings (screen for full effort).[153] Compare normal to abnormal (no significant difference in dominant side strength is considered). If bilateral, compare to charts in Table 10–18[153,158]:

For measuring both peripheral joint and spinal movements, the inclinometer is a very simple tool that can provide a great deal of practical information. Often a patient's musculoskeletal function cannot be quantified. However, qualitative tests may be performed that give insight into muscle imbalances, joint stiffness, postural dysfunction, and lack of movement coordination. They also can be used as secondary outcomes assessment methods.

First, the testing approaches described above provide a baseline level of functional capacity. Second, they identify targets for functional restoration. The baseline functional deficits are objective, quantifiable, and measurable. Thus, they are ideal outcomes assessment tools. However, they do not seek to find what dysfunction in the motor system is causally related to the patient's symptoms. That is the job of a rigorous search for key functional pathologies that are biomechanically or kinesiologically related to the symptomatic area. These tests are often "soft" and only *qualifiable*. Since functional restoration is our goal, assessment of functions such as coordination or joint end feel, even though qualifiable rather than quantifiable, is essential to successful rehabilitation of the motor system. We should not limit our functional evaluation to just that which is measurable. Function is paramount, and if there are key aspects of function that are hard to measure, we should not hesitate to pursue "softer" tests in an attempt to find the "key" functional pathology.

Other cost-effective methods exist to quantify trunk strength, lifting capacity, and cardiovascular fitness that can be utilized in an FCE and/or WCE. More expensive, but still low-tech approaches can be used to establish trunk flexor/extensor ratios, lifting capacity, and cardiovascular fitness. These include the following:

- A simple low-cost protocol exists for quantifiably measuring isometric trunk flexion and extension strength that can be accomplished by the use of a strain gauge. A ratio of 1.3/1.0 extension/flexion is normal for this test.[159–161] However, reliability is questionable.
- When assessing lifting, a strain gauge test for isometric lifting strength can be utilized. A simple low-cost protocol following the NIOSH guidelines exists for quantifiably measuring lifting strength.[122]

Table 10–18: Grip Strength and Pinch Strength. Normative Data Segregated by Age, Sex, and Occupation Factors

GRIP STRENGTH (KG)	MALES		FEMALES	
Occupation	**Major hand**	**Minor hand**	**Major hand**	**Minor hand**
Skilled	47.0	45.4	26.8	24.4
Sedentary	47.2	44.1	23.1	21.1
Manual	48.5	44.6	24.2	22.0
Average	47.6	45.0	24.6	22.4
GRIP STRENGTH (KG)	**MALES**		**FEMALES**	
Age Group	**Major hand**	**Minor hand**	**Major hand**	**Minor hand**
<20	45.2	42.6	23.8	22.8
20–29	48.5	46.2	24.6	22.7
30–39	49.2	44.5	30.8	28.0
40–49	49.0	47.3	23.4	21.5
50–59	45.9	43.5	22.3	18.2
PINCH STRENGTH (KG)	**MALES**		**FEMALES**	
Occupation	**Major hand**	**Minor hand**	**Major hand**	**Minor hand**
Skilled	6.6	6.4	4.4	4.3
Sedentary	6.3	6.1	4.1	3.9
Manual	8.5	7.7	6.0	5.5
Average	7.5	7.1	4.9	4.7

- Mayer has developed the PILE test and Matheson has more recently developed the EPIC test to test isotonic lifting strength. Both are low-cost and quantifiable methods.[123,124] They offer standardized protocols with normative databases established.
- Simple protocols exist for measuring cardiovascular fitness and aerobic capacity using treadmills, bicycles and other ergometric instruments.[162,163]
- Mooney and Matheson developed static position tolerance tests that measure the anthropometric range of motion or use the patient's own stature as a frame of reference.[6] This test is performed first by explaining the purpose of the test to the patient and the method utilized, in which the patient stands in front of a wall at a distance with arms outstretched, lightly touching the wall with the feet held at shoulder width apart. Instructions are then given to the patient requesting him or her to hold both hands at various heights while standing, stooping, crouching or kneeling, and reaching to various levels of either the shoulder, eye, or knee level. Each posture is held for 15 seconds with a countdown from 15 backward, while the patient's quality of posture is observed. A score of 1 = able, and 5 = unable, with 2 through 4 being slightly to very restricted, is scored based on the patient's complaints of symptoms or pain or discontinuing the test prior to the 15-second time allotted for the test. Up to 1 minute of time is allowed between postures for rest. A score of 1 or 2 (able or slightly restricted) is given if the patient can maintain the position for the full 15 seconds with only minimal complaints or noted quality of posture control impairment. A score of 3 is given when the patient cannot maintain the position for 15 seconds but can for greater than 5 seconds; a score of 4, or very restricted, is assigned to those who cannot hold the position for 5 seconds. If they cannot assume the position at all, an unable score is given.

APPLICATIONS OF QFCE AND DOT WITH RETURN TO WORK ISSUES

When return to work (RTW) issues need to be addressed, the QFCE results can be utilized and correlated with the *Dictionary of Occupational Titles* (DOT) information.[164,165] Many of the DOT tests necessitate either muscle strength, length, and/or joint motion to carry out each task. Activities such as balancing, crouching, and stooping are complex movements requiring many of the functions assessed by the QFCE. The last four (special senses) are assessed by cranial nerve neurologic physical examination procedures (Table 10–19).

The DOT has been adopted as a standard for describing the physical demands of a specific job task, which are referred to as "job factors."[12,166–168] There are 20 job factors described by the DOT, which include: (1) standing, (2) walking, (3) sitting, (4) lifting, (5) carrying, (6) pushing, (7) pulling, (8) climbing, (9) balancing, (10) stooping,

Table 10–19: DOT Specific Job Tasks Cross-Referenced with Related QFCE Tests

QFCE / DOT	REP. SQUAT	L-ROM	GASTRIC	SOLEUS	C-ROM	MODIFIED THOMAS	SLR	REPETITIVE SIT-UP	KNEE FLEXION	REPETITIVE ARCH-UP	HIP-ROM	STATIC BACK ENDURANCE	GRIP STRENGTH
Standing			Y	Y		Y			Y			Y	
Walking			Y	Y		Y	Y		Y		Y	Y	
Sitting							Y	Y		Y	Y	Y	
Lifting	Y	Y	Y	Y		Y	Y		Y	Y	Y	Y	Y
Carrying			Y	Y		Y	Y		Y		Y	Y	Y
Pushing	Y		Y	Y		Y	Y	Y	Y	Y	Y	Y	
Pulling	Y		Y	Y		Y	Y		Y	Y	Y	Y	Y
Climbing	Y		Y	Y		Y	Y		Y		Y		
Balancing	Y	Y	Y	Y	Y	Y	Y	Y	Y	Y	Y	Y	
Stooping	Y	Y	Y	Y		Y	Y		Y	Y	Y	Y	
Kneeling	Y		Y	Y		Y		Y		Y	Y		
Crouching	Y	Y			Y	Y	Y				Y	Y	
Crawling						Y	Y		Y		Y		
Reaching		Y											
Handling													Y
Fingering													Y

The following DOT tests are evaluated by standard neurological examination tests: Feeling, Talking, Hearing, and Seeing.
Source: Yeomans SG, Liebenson C. Functional capacity evaluation and chiropractic case management. Top Clin Chiro. *1996;3(3):23.*

Table 10–20: Physical Demand Characteristics of Work

PHYSICAL DEMAND LEVEL	OCCASIONAL (0–33% OF THE WORKDAY)	FREQUENT (34–66% OF THE WORKDAY)	CONSTANT (67–100% OF THE WORKDAY)	TYPICAL ENERGY REQUIRED
Sedentary	10 lbs	Negligible	Negligible	1.5–2.1 METS
Light	20 lbs	10 lbs and/or walk/stand/push/pull of arm/leg controls	Negligible and/or push/pull of arm/leg controls while seated	2.2–3.5 METS
Medium	50 lbs	20 lbs	10 lbs	3.6–6.3 METS
Heavy	100 lbs	50 lbs	20 lbs	6.4–7.5 METS
Very heavy	Over 100 lbs	Over 50 lbs	Over 20 lbs	Over 7.5 METS

This chart is based on the United States Department of Labor system for classifying the general strength demands of the occupations described in the *Dictionary of Occupational Titles* (1977 and supplements). The "Typical Energy Required" data are estimates of the metabolic demand (in terms of oxygen consumption) of the predominant job tasks at each PDC level.

(11) kneeling, (12) crouching, (13) crawling, (14) reaching, (15) handling (seizing, holding, grasping, turning), (16) fingering (picking, pinching), (17) feeling (size, shape, temperature, texture), (18) talking, (19) hearing, and (20) seeing (acuity, depth perception, field vision, accommodation, color vision). The DOT has made the attempt at defining the majority of jobs in the United States according to these job factors and recommended that a worker possess at least the equivalent of the physical demands of the job task. Hence, the phrase "demand minimum functional capacity" describes the minimum functional capacity needed to successfully and safely remain working at a particular job. Matheson and Mooney have devised a job demands questionnaire, which gathers the evaluee's perception of his or her job and thus, can be compared against the performance test measures.[108] Questions such as the length of time one must kneel or crawl, squat or remain bent or twisted at the hips, operate a foot pedal, lift and carry certain weights, etc., address the DOT job tasks. This information may help identify specific job traits and can play an important role in the detection of injury causation.

However, it is highly recommended that a lift/carry task assessment (such as PILE or EPIC) be performed in order to provide specific information on the physical demands characteristic of the category (Table 10–20) in which the patient can safely work.[123,107] Also, a job demands questionnaire identifies patients' current work requirements and proves useful when comparing their WCE lifting and carrying capacities (Table 10–21) to that demanded at their current job. A DOT test battery is part of the WCE. Such testing is necessary when reemployment issues are present.

SUMMARY

In conclusion, don't rely solely on self-administered questionnaires or one or two provocative orthopedic or neurologic tests in the assessment of a condition. Always correlate subjective/historical information with the objective/examination findings. The self-administered instruments provide a means by which patient performance of ADLs and treatment response can be assessed. They can also give clues regarding depression, general health, pain, satisfaction with care, job satisfaction, and disability issues. Utilizing OA tools that help identify those at risk for chronicity will help steer the patient to the appropriate form of treatment.

Table 10–21: The *Dictionary of Occupational Titles* (DOT) Maximum Lift and Maximum Carry Definitions

ABBREVIATION	TERM	MAXIMUM LIFTING (LB)	MAXIMUM CARRYING (LB)
S	Sedentary	10	5
L	Light	20	10
M	Medium	50	25
H	Heavy	100	50
V	Very Heavy	Over 100	Over 50

In the determination of low-tech versus high-tech, functional capacity evaluations measure actual whole-body functions such as the DOT items and not isolated functional limitations. Unfortunately, the FCEs that are indicated for patients with total work disability or limitations of ADLs are usually time-consuming and costly. Cost containment efforts have driven the need for low-cost functional tests that are valid, reliable, practical, safe, and of good utility. Hence, the QFCE appears to fulfill these criteria as well as facilitate the need for objective data which, when coupled with subjective outcomes assessment instruments, can provide the health care provider with the necessary information to make informed clinical decisions based on outcomes assessment. For these criteria to be met, care must be taken to perform the tests exactly the same as described to maintain reliability and validity. In the authors' opinion it is these attributes that give the QFCE and subjective outcomes assessment tools the edge in practicality of low-tech over high-tech instrumentation.

REFERENCES

1. Relman A. Assessment and accountability: The third revolution in health care. *N Engl J Med.* 1988;319:1221–1222.
2. Donabedian A. The quality of medical care. In: Graham NO, ed. *Quality Assurance in Hospitals.* Rockville, MD: Aspen Publishers, 1982.
3. Whitton M. Outcomes assessment: Its relationship to chiropractic and managed health care. *Journal of the American Chiropractic Association.* July 1994:37–40.
4. Chiropractic and managed care. *ACA/FYI.* 1992;June/July:29–31.
5. Wennberg JE, Freeman JL, Culp WJ. Are hospital services rationed in New Haven or overutilized in Boston? *Lancet.* 1987;1:1185–1189.
6. Mooney V, Matheson LN. Objective measurement of soft tissue injury: Feasibility study. *Examiner's manual.* 1994; October:4.
7. Goertz CMH. Measuring functional health status in the chiropractic office using self-report questionnaires. *Top Clin Chiro.* 1994;1(1):51–59.
8. Available from Health Outcomes Institute, 2001 Killebrew Drive, Suite 122, Bloomington, MN 55425; 612-858-9188 (O); 612-858-9189 (Fax) (HSQ, designed:4–1–93).
9. Available from Deborah Johnson; Dartmouth COOP Project; Dartmouth Medical School; Hanover, NH 03755-3862; 603/650-1974. (Copyright 1989).
10. Bergner M, Bobbitt RA, Carter WB, Gilson BS. The Sickness Index Profile: Development and final revision of a health status measure. *Med Care.* 1981;19:787–809.
11. Kaplan RM, Anderson JP. A general health policy model: Update and applications. *Health Serv Res.* 1982;23:203–235.
12. Nelson EC, Landgraf JM, Hays RD, Wasson JH, Kirk JW. The functional status of patients: How can it be measured in physicians' offices? *Med Care.* 1990;28(12):1111–1126.
13. Haldeman S, Chapman-Smith D, Peterson DM, Jr. *Guidelines for Chiropractic Quality Assurance and Practice Parameters.* Rockville, MD:Aspen Publishers, 1993.
14. Chapman-Smith D. Measuring results—The new importance of patient questionnaires. *Chiro Rep.*1992;7 (1):1–6.
15. Von Korff M, Deyo RA, Cherkin D, Barlow SF. Back pain in primary care: Outcomes at 1 year. *Spine.* 1993;18:855–862.
16. Dworkin SF, Von Korff M, Whitney WC, et al. Measurement of characteristic pain intensity in field research. *Pain.*1990;5(suppl):S290.
17. Von Korff M, Ormel J, Keefe F, Dworkin SF. Grading the severity of chronic pain. *Pain.* 1992;50:133–149.
18. McDowell I, Newell C. *Measuring Health: A Guide to Rating Scales and Questionnaires.* New York: Oxford University Press, 1987.
19. Downie WW, Leatham PA, Rhind VA, et al. Studies with pain rating scales. *Ann Rheum Dis.* 1978;37:378–381.
20. Melzack P. *Pain Measurement and Assessment.* New York: Raven Press, 1982.
21. Melzack R. The McGill Pain Questionnaire: Major properties and scoring methods. *Pain.* 1975;1: 277–279.
22. Kirkaldy-Willis WH. *Managing Low Back Pain.* New York: Churchill Livingstone, 1983.
23. Parker H, Wood PLR, Main CJ. The use of the pain drawing as a screening measure to predict psychological distress in chronic low back pain. *Spine.* 1995;20:236–243.

24. Fairbank J, Davies J, et al. The Oswestry Low Back Pain Disability Questionnaire. *Physiotherapy*. 1980;66(18):271–273.
25. Haas M, Jacobs GE, Raphail R, Petzing K. Low back pain outcome measurement assessment in chiropractic teaching clinics: Responsiveness and applicability of two functional disability questionnaires. *J Manipulative Physiol Ther*. 1995;18:79–87.
26. Roland M, Morris R. A study of the natural history of low back pain, Part II. *Spine*. 1983;8(2):141–144.
27. Hudson-Cook N, Tomes-Nicholson K. *The Revised Oswestry Low Back Pain Disability Questionnaire*. Bournemouth, England: Anglo-European College of Chiropractic;1988. Thesis.
28. Erhard RE, Delitto A, Cibulka MT. Relative effectiveness of an extension program and a combined program of manipulation and flexion and extension exercises in patients with acute low back syndrome. *Phys Ther*. 1994;74:1093–1100.
29. Ruta DA, Garratt AM, Wardlaw D, Russell IT. Developing a valid and reliable measure of health outcome for patients with low back pain. *Spine*. 1994;19:1887–1896.
30. Kopec JA, Esdaile JM, Abrahamowicz M, et al. The Quebec back pain disability scale: Measurement properties. *Spine*. 1995;20:341–352.
31. Roland M, Morris R. A study of the natural history of low back pain, Part II. *Spine*. 1983;8(2):145–150.
32. Deyo RA, Cherkin DC, Franklin G, Nichols JC. Low Back Pain (forms 6.1 to 6.4), Health Outcomes Institute, 10-12-92 (see ref. 8).
33. Deyo RA. Comparative validity of the Sickness Impact Profile Short Scales for functional assessment in low back pain. *Spine*. 1986;11(9):951–954.
34. Personal correspondence: (No scoring method intended) reply letter 2-10-95.
35. Vernon H, Mior S. The Neck Disability Index: A study of reliability and validity. *J Manipulative Physiol Ther*. 1991;14(7):409.
36. Whittingham W, Ellis WB, Molyneux TP. The effects of manipulation (toggle recoil technique) for headaches with upper cervical joint dysfunction: A pilot study. *J Manipulative Physiol Ther*. 1994;17: 369–375.
37. Waddell G, Main CJ. Normality and reliability in clinical assessment of backache. *Br Med J*. 1983;284:1519–1523.
38. Waddell G, McCulloch JA, Kimmel E, Venner RM. Nonorganic physical signs in low back pain. *Spine*. 1980;5:117–125.
39. Korbon GA, DeGood E, Schroeder ME, et al. The development of a somatic amplification rating scale for low-back pain. *Spine*.1987;12(8):787–791.
40. Zung WWK. A self-rating depression scale. *Arch Gen Psychiatry*. 1965;32:63–70.
41. Main CJ. 1983 Modified Somatic Perception Questionnaire. *J Psychosom Res*. 1983;27:503–514.
42. Bernstein IH, Jaremko ME, Hinkley BS. On the utility of the SCL-90-R with low-back pain patients. *Spine*. 1994;19:42–48.
43. Main CJ, Wood PL, Hollis S, et al. The distress and risk assessment method: A simple patient classification to identify distress and evaluate the risk of poor outcome. *Spine*. 1992;7:42.
44. Beck A. *Depression: Clinical, Experimental and Theoretical Aspects*. New York: Harper & Row, 1967.
45. Leavitt F, Garron DC, Whisler WW, D'Angleso CM. A comparison of patients treated by chymopapain and laminectomy for low back pain using a multidimensional pain scale. *Clin Orthop*. 1980;146:136.
46. Waddell G, Newton M, Henderson I, et al. A fear-avoidance beliefs questionnaire (FABQ) and the role of fear-avoidance beliefs in chronic low back pain and disability. *Pain*. 1993;52:157–168.
47. Donabedian A. Evaluating the quality of medical care. *Milbank Memorial Fund Q*. 1966;44:166–203.
48. Deyo RA, Diehl AK. Patient satisfaction with medical care for low back pain. *Spine*. 1986;11:28–30.
49. Cherkin D, MacCormack F. Patient evaluations of low-back pain are from family physicians and chiropractors. *West J Med*. 1989;150:351–355.
50. Ware J, Davies AR. Defining and measuring patient satisfaction with medical care. *Eval Program Plan*. 1983:6:247–263.
51. Ware JE, Davies-Avery A, Stewart AL. The measuring and meaning of patient satisfaction. *Health Med Care Services Rev*. 1978;1:1–15.
52. Coulter ID, Hays RD, Danielson CD. The chiropractic satisfaction questionnaire. *Top Clin Chiro*. 1994;1(4):40–43.
53. Bigos JS, Battie MC, Spenglere DM, et al. A prospective study of work perceptions and psychosocial factors affecting the report of back injury. *Spine*. 1991;16:1–6.
54. Cats-Baril WL, Frymoyer JW. Identifying patients at risk of becoming disabled because of low-back pain: The Vermont rehabilitation engineering center predictive model. *Spine*. 1991;16:605–607.

55. Hazard RG, Gaugh LD, Reid S, Preble JB, MacDonald L. Early prediction of chronic disability after occupational low back injury. *Spine*. 1996;21:945–951
56. Millard RW. The functional assessment screening questionnaire: Application for evaluating pain-related disability. *Arch Phys Med Rehabil*. 1989;70:303–307.
57. Waddell G, Newton M, Henderson I, et al:. A fear-avoidance beliefs questionnaire (FABQ) and the role of fear-avoidance beliefs in chronic low back pain and disability. *Pain*. 1993;52:157–168.
58. Waldorf T, Devlin L, Nansel DD. The comparative assessment of paraspinal tissue compliance in asymptomatic female and male subjects in both prone and standing positions. *J Manipulative Physiol Ther*. 1991;14:457–461.
59. Fisher AA. Pressure threshold meter: Its use for quantification of tender spots. *Arch Phys Med Rehabil*. 1986;67(11):836–838.
60. Fisher AA. Pressure algometry over normal muscles: Standard values, validity and reproducibility of pressure threshold. *Pain*. 1989;1:115–126.
61. Lee K-H, Lee M-H, Kim H-S, et al. Pressure pain thresholds [PPT] of head and neck muscles in a normal population. *J Musculoskel Pain*. 1994;2:67.
62. Reeves JL, Jaeger B, Graff-Radford SB. Reliability of the pressure algometer as a measure of myofascial trigger point sensitivity. *Pain*. 1986;24:313–321.
63. Vernon H. Applying research-based assessments of pain and loss of function to the issue of developing standards of care in chiropractic. *Chiro Technique*. 1990;2(3):121–126.
64. Vernon H, Aker P, Burns S, Viljakanen S, Short L. Pressure pain threshold evaluation of the effect of a spinal manipulation in the treatment of chronic neck pain. *J Manipulative Physiol Ther*. 1990,13(1):13.
65. Wolfe F, Smythe HA, Yunnus MB, et al. The American College of Rheumatology 1990 Criteria for Classification of Fibromyalgia. *Arthritis Rheum*. 1990;33:160–172.
66. Hubbard DR, Berkoff GM. Myofascial trigger points show spontaneous needle EMG activity. *Spine*. 1993;18:1803–1807.
67. Nilsson N. Measuring cervical muscle tenderness: A study of reliability. *J Manipulative Physiol Ther*. 1995;18:88–90.
68. Russell IJ, Vipraio GA, Morgan WW, Bowden CL. Is there a metabolic basis for the fibrositis syndrome? *Am J Med*. 1986;81:50–56
69. Russell IJ, Fletcher EM, Michalek JE, et al. Treatment of primary fibrositis/fibromyalgia syndrome with ibuprofen and alprazolam. A double-blind, placebo-controlled study. *Arthritis Rheum*. 1991;34: 552–560.
70. Travell JG, Simons DG. *Myofascial Pain and Dysfunction. The Trigger Point Manual, Part Two*. Baltimore: Williams & Wilkins, 1991.
71. McCombe PF, Fairbank CT, Cockersole BC, Pynsent PB. Reproducibility of physical signs in low-back pain. *Spine*. 1989;14:908–918.
72. McCarthy KA. Improving the clinician's use of orthopedic testing: An application to low back pain. *Top Clin Chiro*. 1994;1:42–50.
73. McKenzie RA. Mechanical diagnosis and therapy of the lumbar spine. Waikanae, New Zealand: Spinal Publications, 1981.
74. Delitto A, Shulman AD, Rose SL, et al. Reliability of a clinical examination to classify patients with low back syndrome. *Phys Ther Practice*. 1992;1:1–9.
75. Delitto A, Cibulka MT, Erhard RE, et al. Evidence for use of an extension-mobilization category in acute low back syndrome: A prescriptive validation pilot study. *Phys Ther*. 1993;73:216–228.
76. Cibulka MT, Delitto A, Koldehoff R. Changes in innominate tilt after manipulation of the sacroiliac joint in patients with low back pain: An experimental study. *Phys Ther*. 1988;68:1359–1363.
77. Elvey R. The investigation of arm pain. In: Grieve G, ed. *Modern Manual Therapy of the Vertebral Column*. Edinburgh: Churchill Livingstone, 1986;530–535.
78. Edgar D, Jull G, Sutton S. The relationship between upper trapezius muscle length and upper quadrant neural tissue extensibility. *Aust J Physiother*. 1994;40:99–103.
79. Yaxley GA, Jull G. Adverse tension in the neural system. A preliminary study of tennis elbow. *Aust J Physiother*. 1993;39:15–22.
80. Laslett M, Williams M. The reliability of selected pain provocation tests for sacroiliac joint pathology. *Spine*. 1994;19:1243–1249.
81. Cyriax J. *Textbook of Orthopedic Medicine Diagnosis of Soft Tissue Lesions*, 5th ed. Baltimore: Williams & Wilkins, 1970:1:217–274.
82. Magee DJ. *Orthopedic Physical Assessment*, 2nd ed. New York: Churchill Livingstone, 1994.

83. Bowling RW, Rockar PA, Erhard R. Examination of the shoulder complex. *Phys Ther*. 1986;66:1866–1877.
84. Deyo RA, Rainville J, Daniel KL. What can the history and physical examination tell us about low back pain? *JAMA*. 1992;16:699–712.
85. Kosteljanetz M, Flemming B, Schmidt-Olsen S. The clinical significance of straight-leg raising in the diagnosis of prolapsed lumbar disc. *Spine*. 1988;13:393–395.
86. Kelsey JL, Golden AL, Mundt DJ. Low back pain/prolapsed lumbar intervertebral disc. *Rheum Dis Clin North Am*. 1990;16:699–712.
87. Blower PW. Neurologic patterns in unilateral sciatica. *Spine*. 1989;14:908–918.
88. Jonsson B, Stromqvist B. The straight leg raise test and the severity of symptoms in lumbar disk herniation. *Spine*. 1995;20:27–30.
89. Steiner C, Staubs C, Ganon M, Buhlinger C. Piriformis syndrome: Pathogenesis, diagnosis and treatment. *J Am Osteopath Assoc*. 1987;4:318–323.
90. Dong GX, Porter RW. Walking and cycling tests in neurogenic and intermittent claudication. *Spine*. 1989;14:965–969.
91. Mooney V. Facet syndrome. In: Winstein J, Wiesel S, eds. *The Lumbar Spine*. Philadelphia: WB Saunders, 1990.
92. Lippitt AB. The facet joint and its role in spinal pain: Management with facet joint injections. *Spine*. 1984;9:746–750.
93. Bernard TN, Kirkaldy-Willis WH. Non-specific low back pain. *Clin Orthop*. 1987;217:266–272.
94. Cassidy JD, Mierau DR. Pathophysiology of the sacroiliac joint. In: Haldeman S, ed. *Principles and Practice of Chiropractic*. East Norwalk, CT: Appleton & Lange, 1992.
95. Potter NA, Rothstein JM. Intertester reliability for selected clinical tests of the sacroiliac joint. *Phys Ther*.1985;65:1671–1675.
96. Laslett M, Williams M. The reliability of selected pain provocation tests for sacroiliac joint pathology. In: Vleeming A, Mooney V, Snijders C, Dorman T, eds. *First Interdisciplinary World Congress on Low Back Pain and Its Relationship to the Sacroiliac Joint*, San Diego, CA. Rotterdam: ECO, 1992.
97. Herzog W, Read LJ, Conway JW, et al. Reliability of motion palpation procedures to detect sacroiliac joint fixations. *J Manipulative Physiol Ther*. 1989;12:86–92.
98. Goldenberg DL. Fibromyalgia, chronic fatigue syndrome, and myofascial pain syndrome. *Curr Opin Rheumatol*. 1991;3:247–258.
99. Wolfe F, Smythe HA, Yunus MB, et al. The American College of Rheumatology 1990 criteria for the classification of fibromyalgia. *Arthritis Rheum*. 1990;33:160–172.
100. Souza T. In: Lawrence DJ, ed. *Advances in Chiropractic*. Chicago: Mosby-Year Book, 1994:101–141.
101. Bullock-Saxon JE, Bullock MI. Repeatability of muscle length measures around the hip. *Physiother*. Canada. 1994;46:105–109.
102. Waddell G, Main CJ. Assessment of severity in low-back disorders. *Spine*. 1984;9:204–208.
103. Waddell G. A new clinical model for the treatment of low-back pain. *Spine*. 1987;12:634–644.
104. Videman T, Rauhala S, Asp K, et al. Patient-handling skill, back injuries, and back pain. *Spine*. 1989;14:148–156.
105. Gundewall B, Liljeqvist M, Hansson T. Primary prevention of back symptoms and absence from work. *Spine*. 1993;18:587–594.
106. Mooney V. The place of active care in disability prevention. In: Liebenson CL, ed. *Rehabilitation of the Spine: A Practitioner's Manual*. Baltimore: Williams & Wilkins, 1994.
107. Mooney V, Matheson LN. Objective measurement of soft tissue injury: Feasibility study. *Examiner's manual*. 1994;October:4.
108. Hart DL, Isernhagen SJ, Matheson LN. Guidelines for functional capacity evaluation of people with medical conditions. *J Orthop Sports Phys Ther*. 1993;18:682–686.
109. Bolton JE, Wilkenson RC. Responsiveness of pain scales: A comparison of three pain intensity measures in chiropractic patients. *J Manipulative Physiol Ther*. 1998;21:1–7.
110. Blankenship KL. *The Blankenship System: Functional Capacity Evaluation: FCE Test Booklet*. Macon, GA: The Blankenship Corp, 1991.
111. Mitchell RI, Carmen GM. Results of a multicenter trial using an intensive active exercise program for the treatment of acute soft tissue and back injuries. *Spine*. 1990;15:514–521.
112. Andersson GBJ, Pope MH, Frymoyer JW. Epidemiology. In: Pope MH, Frymoyer JW, Andersson G, eds. *Occupational Low Back Pain*. New York: Praeger, 1984:101–114.
113. Frymoyer JW. Epidemiology. In: Frymoyer JW, Gordon SL, eds. *Symposium on New Perspectives on Low Back Pain*. Park Ridge, IL: American Academy of Orthopaedic Surgeons, 1989:19–33.

114. Mayer TG, Gatchel RJ, Mayer H, et al. A prospective two-year study of functional restoration in industrial low back injury. *JAMA*. 1987;258:1763–1767.
115. Matheson LN. Basic requirements for utility in the assessment of physical disability. *APS*. 1994;3: 193–199.
116. Grabiner MD, Koh TJ, Ghazawi AE. Decoupling of bilateral paraspinal excitation in subjects with low back pain. *Spine*. 1992;17:1219–1223.
117. Mayer T, Gatchel R, Kishino N, et al. Objective assessment of spine function following industrial injury: A prospective study with comparison group and one-year follow-up. *Spine*. 1985;10:482–493.
118. Troup JDG, Martin JW, Lloyd DCEF. Back pain in industry: A prospective study. *Spine*. 1981;6:61–69.
119. Vernon H, Aker P, Aramenko M, et al. Evaluation of neck muscle strength with a modified sphygmomanometer dynamometer: Reliability and validity. *J Manipulative Physiol Ther*. 1992;15:343–349.
120. Cassidy JD, Lopes AA, Yong-Hing K. The immediate effect of manipulation versus mobilization on pain and range of motion in the cervical spine: A randomized controlled trial. *J Manipulative Physiol Ther*. 1992;15:570–575.
121. Toppenberg RM, Bullock MI. The interrelation of spinal curves, pelvic tilt and muscle lengths in the adolescent female. *Aust J Physiother*. 1986;32:6–12.
122. Konz S. NIOSH lifting guidelines. *Am Ind Hyg Assoc J*. 1982;43:931–933.
123. Mayer T, Barnes D, Kishino N, et al. Progressive isoinertial lifting evaluation. I. A standardized protocol and normative database. *Spine*. 1988;13:993–997.
124. Matheson L. An introduction to lift capacity testing as a component of functional capacity evaluation. *IRG*. Summer 1991.
125. Nansel D, Jansen R, Cremata E, et al. Effects of cervical adjustments on lateral-flexion passive end-range asymmetry and on blood pressure, heart rate and plasma catecholamine levels. *J Manipulative Physiol Ther*. 1991;14: 450–454.
126. Reid DC, Burnham RS, Saboe LA, Kushner SF: Lower extremity flexibility patterns in classical ballet dancers and their correlation to lateral hip and knee injuries. *Am J Sports Med*. 1987;15:347–352.
127. Inamura K. Re-assessment of the method of analysis of electrogravitiograph and the one foot test. *Aggressologie*. 1983;24:107–108.
128. Nelson RM. *NIOSH Low Back Atlas of Standardized Tests/Measures*. *Scand J Work Environ Health*. 1988;14 Suppl 10:82–84.
129. Hirasawa Y. Left foot to support human standing and walking. *Sci Amer (Japan)*. 1981;6:33–44.
130. Mayer T, Brady S, Bovasso E, et al. Noninvasive measurement of cervical tri-planar motion in normal subjects. *Spine*. 1994;18:2191–2195.
131. Youdas J, Carey J, Garret T. Reliability of measurements of cervical spine range of motion—Comparison of three methods. *Phys Ther*. 1991;71:98–106.
132. Gajdosik RL, Rieck MA, Sullivan DK, et al. Comparison of four clinical tests for assessing hamstring muscle length. *J Orthop Sports Phys Ther*. 1993;18:614–618.
133. Grice A. Lumbar exercises for kinesiological harmony and stability. *Canadian Chiropractic Assoc*. 1976;December.
134. Newton M, Waddell G. Trunk strength testing with iso-machines, Part 1: Review of a decade of scientific evidence. *Spine*. 1993;18:801–811.
135. Lewit K. *Manipulative Therapy in Rehabilitation of the Motor System*. 2nd ed. London: Butterworths, 1991.
136. LaRocca H. A taxonomy of chronic pain syndromes:1991 Presidential Address, Cervical Spine Research Society Annual Meeting, December 5, 1991. *Spine*. 1992;10S:S344–S355.
137. Harding VR, Williams AC. The development of a battery of measures for assessing physical functioning of chronic pain patients. *Pain*. 1994;58:367–375.
138. Moffroid MT. Distinguishable groups of musculoskeletal LBP patients and asymptomatic control subjects based on physical measures of the NIOSH low back atlas. *Spine*. 1994;12;1350–1358.
139. Gilford LS. Circadian variability in human flexibility and grip strength. *Aust J Phys Ther*. 1987;33:3–9.
140. Yeomans S, Liebenson C. Quantitative functional capacity evaluation: The missing link to outcomes assessment. *Top Clin Chiro*. 1996;3A(1):32–43.
141. Rissanen A, Alaranta H. Isokinetic and non-dynamometric tests in low back pain patients related to pain and disability index. *Spine*. 1994;19:1963–1967.
142. Alaranta H, et al. Non-dynamometric trunk performance tests: Reliability and normative data. *Scand J Rehab Med*. 1994;26:211–215.
143. Biering-Sorensen F. Physical measurements as risk indicators for low-back trouble over a one-year period. *Spine*. 1984;9:106–119.

144. Mayer T, Gatchel RJ, Keeley J, Mayer H, Richling D. A male incumbent worker industrial database. *Spine*. 1994;19:762–764.
145. Donaldson R, Silva G, Murphy K. Centralization phenomenon: Its usefulness in evaluating and treating referred pain. *Spine*. 1990;15:211–213.
146. Donaldson R, Grant W, Kamps C, et al. Pain response to sagittal end-range spinal motion: A prospective, randomized, multicentered trial. *Spine*. 1991;16(Suppl):S206–S212.
147. Ekstrand J, Wiktorsson M, Oberg B, Gillquist J. Lower extremity goniometric measurements: A study to determine their reliability. *Arch Phys Med Rehabil*. 1982;63:171–175.
148. Wang S, Whitney SL, Burdett RG, et al. Lower extremity muscular flexibility in long distance runners. *J Orthop Sports Phys Ther*. 1993;2:102–107.
149. Janda V. Muskelfunktionsdiagnostik: muskeltest, untersuchung verkurzter muskeln, untersuchung der hypermobilitat. Leuven/Belgien: Verlag Acco, 1979.
150. Kendall HO, Kendall FP, Wadsworth GE. Muscles, Testing and Function. 2nd ed. Baltimore: Williams & Wilkins, 1971.
151. Hyytiainen K, Salminen JJ, Suvitie T, et al. Reproducibility of nine tests to measure spinal mobility and trunk muscle strength. *Scand J Rehabil Med*. 1991;23:3–10.
152. Ekstrand J, Gillquist J. The frequency of muscle tightness and injuries in soccer players. *Am J Sports Med*. 1982;10:75–78.
153. American Medical Association. Guides to the Evaluation of Permanent Impairment. Chicago: AMA, 1993;78.
154. Ellison JB, Rose SJ, Sahrmann SA. Patterns of hip rotation range of motion: A comparison between healthy subjects and patients with low back pain. *Phys Ther*. 1990;70:537–541.
155. Chesworth BM, Padfield BJ, Helewa A, Stitt LW. A comparison of hip mobility in patients with low back pain and matched healthy subjects. *Physiother Canada*. 1994;46:267–274.
156. Hoppenfeld S. *Physical Examination of the Spine and Extremities*. New York: Appleton-Century-Crofts, 1976.
157. Fishbain DA, Goldberg M, Rosomoff RS, et al. Chronic pain patients and the nonorganic physical sign of nondermatomal sensory abnormalities (NDSA). *Psychosomatics*. 1991;32:294–302.
158. Swanson AB, Matev IB, de Groot Swanson G. The strength of the hand. *Bull Prosthet Res*. Fall 1970;145–153.
159. Triano JJ, Skogsbergh DR, Kowalski MH. The use of instrumentation and laboratory examination procedures by the chiropractor. In: Haldeman S, ed. *Principles and Practice of Chiropractic*, 2nd ed. Norwalk, CT: Appleton & Lange, 1992.
160. Sinaki M, Grubbs N. Back strengthening exercises: Quantitative evaluation of their efficacy for women aged 40–65 years. *Arch Phys Med Rehabil*. 1989;70:16–20.
161. Beimborn DS, Morrissey MC. A review of the literature related to trunk muscle performance. *Spine*. 1988;13:655.
162. Parker DL. A new submaximal treadmill for predicting VO_2max: Rationale and validation. Submitted for publication to *Annals of Sports Medicine*.
163. Astrand P-O, Rodahl K. *Textbook of Work Physiology*, 3rd ed. New York: McGraw-Hill, 1986.
164. U.S. Department of Labor, Employment and Training Administration. *Dictionary of Occupational Titles*, 4th ed. Supplement. Washington, DC: U.S. Government Printing Office, 1986.
165. U.S. Department of Labor, Employment and Training Administration. *Selected Characteristics of Occupations Defined in the Dictionary of Occupational Titles*. Washington, DC: U.S. Government Printing Office, 1981.
166. Smith RL. Therapists' ability to identify safe maximum lifting in low back pain patients during functional capacity evaluation. *J Orthop Sports Phys Ther*. 1994;19:277–281.
167. Moffroid MT, Haugh LD, Henry SM, Short B. Distinguishable groups of musculoskeletal low back pain patients and asymptomatic control subjects based on physical measures of the NIOSH low back atlas. *Spine*. 1994;12:1350–1358.
168. Putz-Anderson V, ed. *Cumulative Trauma Disorders. A Manual for Musculoskeletal Diseases of the Upper Limbs*. Philadelphia: Taylor and Francis, 1988:7.

CHAPTER 11

The Psychosocial Profile of the Chronic Back Patient

Jennifer E. Bolton, Ph.D.

INTRODUCTION

This chapter is concerned with **chronic disability** in the back pain patient and the **psychosocial factors** that influence its development. The **biopsychosocial model** to explain back disability was born from a need to explain the overt discrepancy between pain and physical impairment and the level of disability exhibited by the patient. This chapter attempts to describe the model and ways in which the **psychosocial profile** of the patient can be assessed in the routine clinical setting.

It is generally accepted that low back pain is a common complaint that is extraordinarily costly to our society. This is predominantly due to work loss and productivity, social security payments, and the cost of the treatment itself. Moreover, there is a human cost in terms of the pain, suffering, and disability to both the patient and his or her family. Although the statistics of the financial cost of back pain are plentiful, the economic consequences are still not fully realized. Studies suggest that the total cost in the United States in 1990 was in excess of $50 billion,[1] whereas in the United Kingdom in 1992/1993 the cost to the NHS alone was somewhere around £350 million.[2] Costs today not only remain high, but continue to climb. Even more astounding than the cost per se is that, given the natural history of back pain, it appears to spontaneously resolve in the majority of cases, so that most patients return to work within 6 weeks[3–5]; Thus a small minority of all back pain cases account for most of the costs. Hence, about 7% of those affected will have back pain that persists for more than 6 months[6]; Frymoyer[7] reported that approximately 5% of workers with back pain account for 85% of the costs borne by Workers' Compensation in the United States. It is hardly surprising therefore, that disabling low back pain has shot to the top of the health agenda on both sides of the Atlantic in an attempt to curtail social and economic calamity.

Back pain is a difficult condition to both diagnose and treat, factors undoubtedly responsible for its notoriety. Back pain, in the main, is not a disease but a symptom; only in a small minority of cases is it associated with serious spinal pathologies or nerve root and neurological problems. Considerable difficulty occurs in diagnosing a condition in which the etiology is essentially unresolved. Moreover, conventional medical treatment more often than not fails to alleviate the problem. This results in a patient who becomes increasingly confused, frustrated, demoralized, and angry, so that what may have started as an acute complaint resolves itself as a chronic disabling condition. Although chronic back pain is often thought of as a progression of acute back pain over time, this may not be the case. Instead, chronic back pain may arguably be a distinct condition not preceded by the acute phase.

Disability associated with back pain has been described as a distinctly twentieth-century phenomenon.[8] Waddell[9,10] portrays back pain disability as an epidemic sweeping the Western world in the last 40 years that shows no signs of abating and that cannot be explained by an increase in either low back pain or injury. It is apparent that back pain and disability must be distinguished. Although they are both linked to the underlying physical disorder or impairment, there is considerable variation in disability in patients with comparable physical findings in the back.[11] With time, disability becomes increasingly dissociated from the original physical disorder and increasingly associated with the adoption of a "sick role."[9,10]

In the light of increasing disability costs, it is the transition from acute disorder to chronic disability that requires particular attention. The relevant questions would appear to be: (1) Why do only some back pain patients become chronically disabled, (2) what is the process of developing chronic disability and how is this influenced, and (3) can susceptible patients be identified at an early enough stage to prevent this from occurring? Leading the field in resolving such issues is the **psychosocial model.** This model has gained considerable momentum over recent years as clinicians and research workers alike have realized the impact that **psychological** and **social factors** make in the transition from acute complaint to high-cost chronic disability. This is reinforced by current shifts from disease to illness and treatment to care models, all of which emphasize the whole patient and multidimensional approaches in active care.[12]

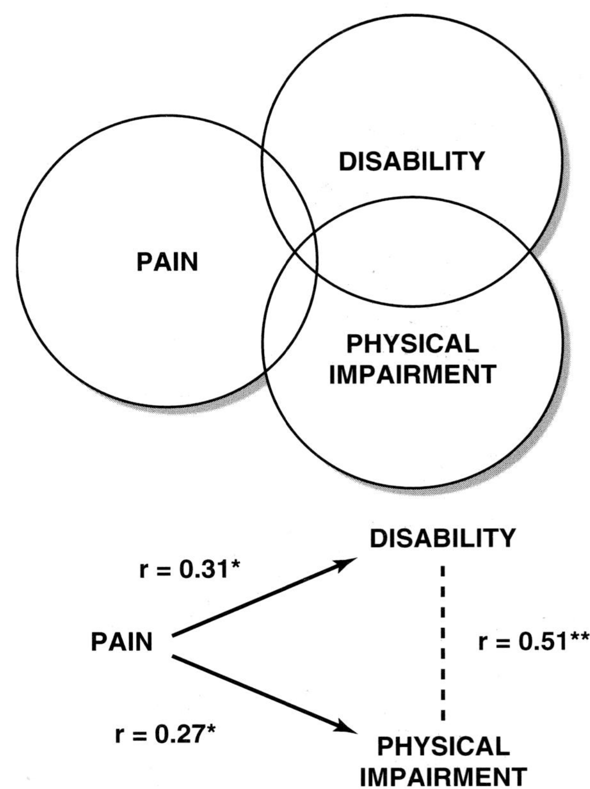

Figure 11–1. The relationship between pain, physical impairment and disability showing Pearson's product-moment correlation coefficient (r). *p<0.01 and **p<0.001.

Reprinted from Waddell[108] by permission of the publisher WB Saunders.

BACK PAIN, PHYSICAL IMPAIRMENT, AND DISABILITY

Back pain, physical impairment, and **disability** are all assumed to arise from the underlying physical disorder. **Pain** is a multidimensional entity that is now generally recognized to comprise both **biological, psychological,** and **social** dimensions.[13] This comprehensive concept of pain arises from the gate-control theory of pain[14] and includes sensory, affective, and cognitive-behavioral dimensions. Consequently, pain should not only be dealt with in terms of the sensation resulting from physical damage and injury (i.e., sensory), but also in terms of the emotive and cognitive components. Moreover, since pain is a subjective experience, it can only be realistically assessed in terms of the patient's verbal report (see Reference 15) or pain behavior.[16] Reflecting these concepts, outcome measures in back pain efficacy trials are now increasingly multidimensional, covering all aspects of the back pain experience.[12]

Physical impairment is normally defined as loss of normal bodily ability, usually anatomical abnormality, physiological loss, or limitation of function. It is normally assessed using clinical objective tests such as lumbar mobility and straight leg raise.[17] The objective nature of this testing means that it is often used to assess the patient for legal or social support reasons, although the objectivity of such testing is currently being challenged.[18] *Disability*, on the other hand, is defined as restriction in activity (either day-to-day living activities or work activity) resulting from physical impairment. However, we now know that disability appears to have little relationship to the underlying physical cause, thus calling into question the above definition. Like pain, disability is normally based on the patient's self-report[15,19] and is, therefore, once again subjective. This reliance on subjective measures in the assessment of back pain is, almost certainly, one of the principal contributory factors to the back pain epidemic.

When pain, physical impairment, and disability are investigated in back pain patients, it is found, perhaps not surprisingly, that the relationship between them is weak[17] (see Figure 11–1). Thus pain severity has been shown to account for only 10% of the variance in physical impairment and disability.[20] From these results, it is evident that there is some other parameter that can account for, or explain, these characteristics in back pain patients. Over the last 10 years or so, interest in psychosocial factors to explain back pain characteristics has gained considerable momentum. Consequently, models have been constructed to explain, at least in part, the demeanor of the back pain patient in terms of psychosocial considerations.

THE PSYCHOSOCIAL MODEL

The need for a model to explain back pain characteristics emerged from results showing that there was very little relationship between pain and disability. As a result, the Glasgow Illness Model was put forward to explain the role of the affective dimension of pain and social influences on disability[11,21]; this has been revised to take into account the cognitive-behavioral aspects of pain as well.[20] The model reflects the *biopsychosocial* aspect of the clinical presentation of back pain at any one point in time (see Figure 11–2).

Starting at the level of the **biological** or **physical disorder,** this gives rise to pain sensation via nociception, although in chronic pain there may well no longer be any physical damage.[17] Characteristics of sensory pain that influence disability are **intensity, distribution,** and **duration.**

Pain intensity is the common factor in back pain and consequently the parameter measured most consistently in back pain research. The widely used Visual Analogue Scale (VAS)[22] is a measure of sensory pain severity or intensity. Other measures of pain intensity are commonly used and have been investigated for their psychometric properties.[23] As has been already stated, however, the relationship between pain severity and disability is disappointingly weak; severity of pain has been shown to account for only 14% of the variance in day-to-day living activities and 5% of the variance in disability in the workplace (i.e., work loss).[20] It is apparent, therefore, that there are other factors besides pain that account for the reported level of disability.

Pain distribution is measured by the pain drawing,[24] which has been shown to be a useful diagnostic indicator in back pain[25] as well as an indicator of psychological distress.[24] Analysis of pain drawings suggests that acute pain tends to be localized and to follow specific radicular pathways, whereas chronic pain tends to be diffuse and widespread. Back pain distribution patterns have been shown to significantly influence the level of self-reported back disability.[26] Moreover, correlations have been found between the extent of the body surface in pain, as indicated on the pain drawing, and both psychological distress and disability, although again the relationship is weak.[27]

In contrast to pain intensity and distribution, **pain duration** is a strong predictor of disability. Certainly the longer the pain and/or disability has continued, the likelihood of return to work rapidly diminishes. Frymoyer[8] suggested that if a patient is disabled more than 6 months, the probability of return to work is 50%; by 1 year this falls to 20% and by 2 years the probability is essentially zero. However, using the biopsychosocial model to explain back pain characteristics, rehabilitation of most chronic back pain would appear possible given the correct evaluation and treatment.

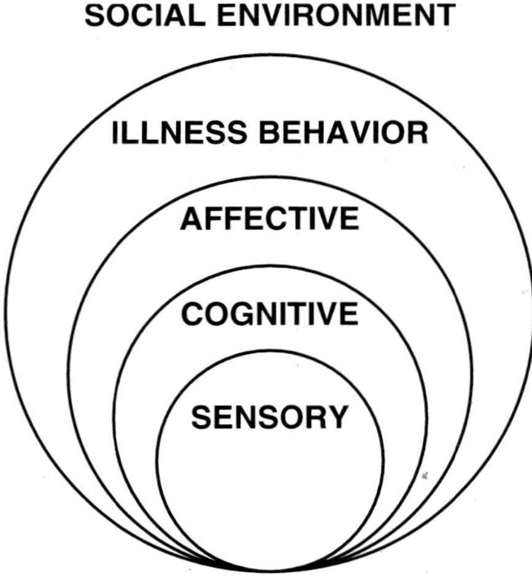

Figure 11–2. A cross-sectional analysis of the clinical presentation and assessment of low back pain and disability at one point in time.

Reprinted from Waddell[108] by permission of the publisher WB Saunders.

PSYCHOLOGICAL FACTORS

In addition to the sensory aspects of pain, the **biopsychosocial** model compels consideration of **psychological factors,** namely the **affective** and **cognitive-behavioral** dimensions of pain. Taking these in turn, the **affective** (or emotional) component of pain presents clinically as reactive psychological distress, whereas the **cognitive-behavioral** component presents clinically as attitudes and beliefs about pain, together with pain coping strategies.

Affective

Psychological distress is not diagnostic of psychiatric illness. Instead, it is the form in which the emotional (affective) aspect of back pain is manifested. It presents as **anxiety,** usually in the form of an increased somatic awareness, and **depression;** these are both emotional reactions to back pain. **Personality** has often been confused with psychological distress in the literature. Personality is a psychological factor, but is defined as a set of relatively stable and enduring traits, as opposed to reactive stress. There has been an ardent search for a personality trait that predisposes a person to become chronically disabled. By far the most widely used personality tests are the Minnesota Multiphasic Personality Inventory (MMPI)[28] and the Eynsenck Personality Questionnaire.[29] However, the search has all but been abandoned since it has been shown that the person's reaction (i.e., distress level) is much more important than personality in explaining chronic disability in back pain patients.[30] This may, however, be oversimplifying the situation since after all, reactive distress is determined in part by personality. It probably is the case, however, that reactive distress is easier to measure, more relevant to outcome, and easier to modify than is personality trait. Main and co-workers[31] reported a method of measuring psychological distress in back pain patients. However, psychological distress again only appears to be weakly related to disability in back pain patients, although interestingly the association is much stronger in women compared to men.[32]

Cognitive-Behavioral

Turning to **cognitive** (thought) dimensions of pain, these can be discussed in three main categories: (1) **attitudes** (feelings about a subject) and **beliefs** (perceived knowledge about a subject), (2) **locus of control** (belief of who bears the responsibility for the pain) and (3) **behavioral and coping strategies** (behavioral patterns of dealing with the pain). Although beliefs about illness and cognitive coping exist before the pain occurs, they are developed at the onset of back pain and may provide valuable information on the development of chronicity.

Jensen and co-workers[33] have reviewed the vast amount of literature on **coping responses** in chronic pain patients. There is now a growing recognition that particular types of coping attempts are important in determining the psychological and physical outcome of chronic pain; positive attempts to overcome pain are associated with good outcome. Certainly, there does appear to be a relationship between coping strategies and disability, although once again the relationship appears weak. However, a particularly strong relationship is displayed in emotionally distressed patients in whom coping strategies have been shown to be an important mediator between pain and depression,[34] and hence back disability. The negative coping strategy of catastrophizing (i.e.. imagining the worst) is particularly associated with depression. Rosenstiel and Keefe[35] showed that chronic low back pain patients often exhibit passive coping strategies (e.g., praying or hoping), whereas active attempts to reinterpret pain were rarely used. From this work, it has been postulated that cognitive therapy and the use of active coping techniques may improve outcome in chronic pain patients.

Pain behaviors refer to any physical or verbal attempt by the patient to communicate his or her pain. Nonverbal behaviors include grimacing, bracing, and holding or rubbing the affected body part, as well as lying down, using pain medication, and visiting doctors. Such behaviors can be videotaped and rated according to a set of pain behavior categories by trained observers.[16,36] Pain behaviors in the acute and chronic stages can be similar. However, whereas pain behavior in the acute stage may be entirely appropriate, in the chronic stage it may only be indicative of the patient's adoption of a sick role. Hence, Waddell and co-workers[21] have identified a set of behavioral responses to physical examination in the chronic back pain patient that are inappropriate and hence indicative of psychological distress. They termed these responses: (1) **inappropriate symptoms** (verbal report) and (2) **inappropriate signs** (response to physical examination). Patients demonstrating inappropriate signs and symptoms are described as exhibiting magnified illness behavior; again this was shown to be only weakly associated with disability.

Locus of control is defined as the place in which patients believe the control over their pain resides. Control can either be internalized (i.e., patients believe they have ownership and responsibility for their back pain) or externalized to either the clinician or fate. A common finding is that outcome is more positive in people who believe strongly in internal control over their illness. Harkapaa and co-workers[37] showed that back pain patients with stronger internal beliefs gained more from their treatment and had a more successful outcome. Encouraging the patient to take more responsibility for his or her pain is therefore seen as a positive approach to rehabilitation of the patient and forms the rationale for the shifts to active patient care seen today.

Although cognitive factors have been shown to be related to disability, the relationship remains weak[38] and too general to adequately explain back disability. Other cognitive factors have also been investigated, most notably patients' **beliefs and attitudes** about their pain.[39–41] This work has demonstrated a relationship between beliefs and back disability. Waddell and co-workers[20] expanded this work and measured patients' attitudes and beliefs about their pain, particularly **fear-avoidance beliefs.** In contrast to other cognitive factors, fear-avoidance beliefs were able to predict a substantial proportion of the variance in disability in activities of daily living (23%) and work loss (26%). It may be that the parameter of fear-avoidance beliefs, about work in particular, is one of the cognitive factors most strongly associated with back pain. On the basis of this work, Waddell et al[20] added a cognitive dimension to their Illness Model (Figure 11–2) and suggested that it may be the patients' beliefs about their pain that finally govern their disability and behavior, rather than the physical disorder and pain.

SOCIAL FACTORS

Social factors that affect the course of back pain are those variables that occur outside of the patient. There is considerable blurring between psychological and social factors since the patient's psychological makeup often influences the patient's report of social events.

Stressful life events, such as illness of a relative, bereavement, divorce, and redundancy, have been investigated for their effect on back pain. Craufurd and co-workers[42] showed that patients without a specific cause for their back pain had more adverse life events than patients with a specific diagnosis, although these patients had a higher rate of life events after onset but before seeking treatment. More long-term studies are required to determine the predictive value of life events on back pain. The role of the **family** in the progression of back pain also remains to be seen. It is interesting to note that those patients who have supportive spouses have more pain and exhibit greater pain behavior than patients whose spouses are not supportive.[43] Paradoxically, therefore, family support may not be in the best interests of the patient.

According to the biopsychosocial model, the **doctor-patient relationship** would appear to play an essential role in predicting the progress of the condition; the complaint should be treated as an illness rather than a physical disorder. Waddell[9] suggested that clinical management of a poorly understood complaint such as back pain is determined to a much greater extent than most clinicians realize by factors other than the actual physical disorder. **Patient satisfaction** with treatment has been shown to play an essential role in recovery.[44] As a result, Vernon[45] posed the question as to whether back pain treatment such as chiropractic is successful because the clinician, wittingly or unwittingly, provides care, not only for the physical disorder, but also of the illness component of back pain.

Work-related factors, particularly work satisfaction and work stress, have been widely investigated for their effect on the progress of back pain. Several studies attest to the relationship between work satisfaction/stress and back complaints.[1,46] Certainly, workers who enjoy their work or who have low work-related stress report less back pain than others.

Compensation status has often been associated with a poor outcome in back pain patients.[47,48] Patients with outstanding claims have lower success rates in rehabilitative programs compared with those who do not.[1,49] Guest and Drummond[50] showed that compensation recipients exhibited more emotional distress and greater difficulty in coping with pain. However, even after settlement, there was still clear evidence of emotional distress and the distinct probability of adoption of a sick role.

SUMMARY

1. Back pain disability has reached epidemic proportions. However, there is very little association between the physical disorder, pain sensation, and disability. Accordingly, treatment of the physical disorder alone has failed to alleviate the disability problem.
2. Psychosocial factors are leading contenders to explain, at least in part, back disability levels. These include the affective and cognitive-behavioral aspects of pain and external factors such as relationships with the family and the treating clinician, and those related to the work environment. Individually, however, psychosocial factors show only weak association with disability, suggesting they should be considered comprehensively and not in isolation.
3. Those factors that have been shown to have a relatively strong association with disability include the duration of pain, fear-avoidance beliefs, work-related factors, and the doctor-patient relationship.
4. Early intervention is required to identify those patients at risk of developing chronic disability symptoms. This is best done by evaluating the psychosocial profile of the patient at the acute stage.

EVALUATING THE PSYCHOSOCIAL PROFILE

Although there is still a long way to go, present research indicates that psychosocial factors contribute significantly to back disability. Between the extremes of the disability process (i.e., from acute presentation to the adoption of a sick role), the development of chronicity is a dynamic process. It may well be that in the acute phase reactive psychological distress predominates, whereas as the chronicity progresses, magnified illness behavior and feelings of helplessness and hopelessness emerge. The stage at which the psychosocial profile is assessed is therefore critical. It remains the case, however, that at whatever stage assessment and treatment is begun, patients should be involved in the choice and take responsibility for their treatment. This is the basis of the current trends in active care and rehabilitation seen today.

The fact that most people who suffer from nonspecific back pain either do not seek medical treatment or resolve spontaneously within a period of 6 weeks means that to assess all back pain patients for psychosocial factors is not only far too time-consuming and costly, but also unnecessary. However, if the patient exceeds this recovery period, or has recurrent back pain without known cause, then psychosocial assessment is not only indicated but critical to the prognosis of the condition. Many patients refuse to believe that their pain is anything but entirely somatic. For this reason, the subject of psychosocial testing should be introduced cautiously.

There are now many tools available for screening the back pain patient, and the most widely reported of these in the literature are given in Tables 11–1 to 11–4. Although the specific battery of tests should be tailored to meet the patient's specific situation, some standardization is useful.

The patient's **back pain history** should include close scrutiny of the duration of the current as well as previous episodes of back pain, and whether the pain is constant or recurrent. **Inappropriate signs and symptoms,** first described by Waddell and co-investigators,[11] remain a widely used screening tool in the detection of psychological overlay. The **level of pain** (sensory) should be noted by asking the patient to mark a pain visual analogue scale (VAS) or numerical pain rating scale (NRS) (Table 11–1). **Disability,** both in day-to-day living activities and work, can be assessed using any one of the large number of available disability questionnaires; the Oswestry, in particular the revised Oswestry, and StThomas' disability questionnaires are recommended (Table 11–2).

Considering the **psychological measures,** one of the main reasons hampering both research into, and routine clinical assessment of, psychological aspects of back pain is the cumbersome nature of many of the psychological tests and the expertise required both to administer and interpret them. Although this is still true to some extent, measures such as the DRAM for psychological distress, the CSQ for coping strategies, the PLC for pain locus of control, the

Table 11–1: Pain Measures

CHARACTERISTIC	MEASURES	REFERENCES
Intensity (sensory)	Visual Analogue Scale (VAS)	Huskisson[22]
		Scott and Huskisson[58]
		Price et al[59]
		Jensen et al[60]
		McCormack et al[61]
	Numerical Rating Scale (NRS)	Downie et al[62]
		Jensen et al[60]
		Price et al[63]
		Bolton and Wilkinson[23]
	Verbal Rating Scale (VRS)	Heft et al[64]
		Jensen et al[60]
Unpleasantness (affective)	Visual Analogue Scale (VAS)	Price et al[65]
All dimensions (Sensory, affective, and cognitive)	McGill Pain Questionnaire (MPQ)	Melzack[66]
		Melzack[67]
Pain distribution	Pain drawing (Spatial distribution and psychological)	Ransford et al[24]
	(Pain extent)	Margolis et al[68]

FABQ for fear-avoidance beliefs and inappropriate signs and symptoms are suitable for routine clinical assessment. These instruments are listed in Table 11–3.

Information concerning **social factors** such as family support, financial support including disability payments, work-related factors such as stress/satisfaction, and compensation status should also be obtained. As has already been described, the patient's satisfaction with treatment is also a useful indicator of chronicity. Evaluative methods of social influences are given in Table 11–4.

The relatively straightforward psychosocial measures described here can be used in the routine clinical setting for those patients with back pain that has not resolved within the expected recovery period. Interpretation of questionnaire scores is, however, not always straightforward, and the clinician is advised to refer to the original reports for guidance in this matter. Atypical scores should alert the clinician to possible problems, and patients at risk should be counselled and treatment started if appropriate. Waddell[9,10] has argued passionately for the abolition of bed

Table 11–2: Disability Measures

CHARACTERISTICS	MEASURES	REFERENCES
Daily activities	Oswestry Disability Questionnaire (ODQ)	Fairbank et al[69]
	Roland Disability Questionnaire (RDQ) (StThomas')	Roland and Morris[70]
	Waddell Disability Index (WDI)	Waddell and Main[71]
	Revised Oswestry Disability Questionnaire (RODQ)	Hudson-Cook et al[72]
	Aberdeen Low Back Pain Scale	Ruta et al[73]
	Quebec Back Pain Disability Scale	Kopec et al[74]
	North American Spine Society	Daltroy et al[75]
	Lumbar Spine Outcome Assessment Instrument (NASS)	
Daily activities (including work)	Sickness Impact Profile (SIP) (generic-multidimensional)	Bergner et al[76]
	Short-Form 36 (SF-36) (generic-multidimensional)	Brazier et al[77]
	Pain Disability Index (PDI)	Pollard[78]
		Tait et al[79]
	Low Back Outcome Scale	Greenough and Fraser[80]

Table 11–3: Psychological Measures

CHARACTERISTIC	MEASURES	REFERENCES
Distress		
Personality	Minnesota Multiphasic Personality Inventory (MMPI)	Dahlstrom and Welsh[28]
	Eynsenck Personality Questionnaire	Eynsenck and Eynsenck[29]
Anxiety	State-Trait Anxiety Inventory (STAI)	Spielberg et al[81]
	Cognitive Somatic Anxiety Questionnaire	Schwartz et al[82]
	Modified Somatic Perception Questionnaire (MSPQ)	Main[83]
	Pain Anxiety Symptom Scale (PASS)	McCracken et al[84]
Depression	Beck Depression Inventory (BDI)	Beck et al[85]
	Zung Depression Scale (ZDS)	Zung[86]
Distress	Distress and Risk Assessment Method (DRAM)	Main et al[31]
Cognitive-Behavioral		
Beliefs and attitudes	Cognitive Errors Questionnaire (CEQ)	Lefebvre[87]
	Survey of Pain Attitudes (SOPA)	Jensen and Karoly[88]
	Pain and Impairment Relationship Scale (PAIRS)	Riley et al[40]
	Cognitive Evaluative Questionnaire (CEQ)	Phillips[89]
	Pain Beliefs and Perceptions Inventory (PBPI)	Williams and Thorne[90]
	Pain Beliefs Questionnaire (PBQ)	Edwards et al[91]
	Fear-Avoidance Beliefs Questionnaire (FABQ)	Waddell et al[20]
	Pain-Related Control Scale (PRCS)	Flor et al[92]
	Pain-Related Self Statements Scale (PRSS)	
Coping	Coping Strategies Questionnaire (CSQ)	Rosenstiel and Keefe[35]
	Chronic Pain Coping Inventory	Jensen et al[93]
	Pain Management Inventory (PMI)	Brown and Nicassio[94]
	Ways of Coping Checklist (WCCL)	Regan et al[95]
Locus of control	Multidimensional Health Locus of Control Scale (MHLC)	Wallston et al[96]
	Beliefs about Pain Control Questionnaire (BPCQ)	Skevington[97]
	Pain Locus of Control (PLC)	Toomey et al[98]
Behavioral	Illness Behavior Questionnaire (IBQ)	Pilowsky and Spence[99]
	Behavioral Observation Test	Keefe and Block[16]
	Inappropriate signs and symptoms	Waddell et al[11]
		Waddell and Richardson[100]

Table 11–4: Social Measures

CHARACTERISTICS	MEASURES	REFERENCES
Life events	Life Events and Differences Scale	Craufurd et al[42]
Stress	Behavioral Support Scale (BSS)	Block et al[101]
	Stress Symptoms Score (SSS)	Leino[102]
	Personal/family/employment and stress factors	Lancourt and Kettelhut[103]
Work Satisfaction	Job Satisfaction Scale	Price and Mueller[104]
Patient satisfaction	Medical Interview Satisfaction Scale (MISS)	Wolf et al[105]
	Patient Satisfaction Scale (PSS)	Linder-Pelz and Struening[106]
	Visit-Specific Satisfaction Questionnaire (VSQ)	Ware and Hays[107]
	Patient Satisfaction Scale	Cherkin et al[44]

rest as a treatment for back pain. Patients should be encouraged to be as active as possible and, most importantly, to return to work if at all possible.

Inevitably, some patients will progress to overt chronic disability. Certainly, if the patient shows no signs of improvement after routine psychological intervention, then he or she should be referred to a psychologist. Normally, patients are not referred in this way until well into the chronic stage, by which time it is usually too late. All the research data indicating the enormity of the psychosocial impact on back disability suggest that we should be moving rapidly to a multidisciplinary approach to the treatment of back pain so that patients can get the help they need quickly enough to influence the prognosis. Figure 11–3 indicates suitable points at which to assess these psychosocial characteristics.

TREATMENT

Various psychological treatments have been advocated for the chronic back pain patient.[51] They are usually given as part of a multidisciplinary approach that includes medical management, exercise, and physical therapy. These rehabilitative programs are often aimed at rehabilitation of the patient rather than cure. Back schools are now used throughout Europe and North America; these formalized programs are mainly aimed at educating the patient in back biomechanics and correct posture, ergonomic advice as well as exercises.[52] They are mainly concerned with prevention. In contrast, pain management and active care and rehabilitation programs are directed more at the behavioral component of back pain and more suited to the chronic back pain patient. Psychological evaluation and counselling is increasingly being incorporated into such programs.[53]

Relaxation therapy consists of a variety of techniques from meditation to simple breathing exercises. They may be effective because they diminish fear and also provide a sense of control that may be lacking in the chronic back pain patient. They also allow the patient to become more receptive to other psychosocial approaches. Cognitive therapy is another branch of the psychosocial therapeutic approach that has come about as a result of the evidence that the patient's cognitions about his or her pain are related to disability. Cognitive therapy attempts to modify negative thoughts and to replace old beliefs with new ones. Creative imagery is another cognitive technique that enables patients to think of peaceful scenes that can be used as a distraction tool and a method of coping with their pain. All these therapeutic techniques are described by Borysenko.[54] Operant therapy, as an approach to rehabilitation of the patient, is described by Fordyce and co-workers.[55] This is essentially the reward and reinforcement of behavior incompatible with overt pain behavior. A number of functional restoration clinics operate very successfully

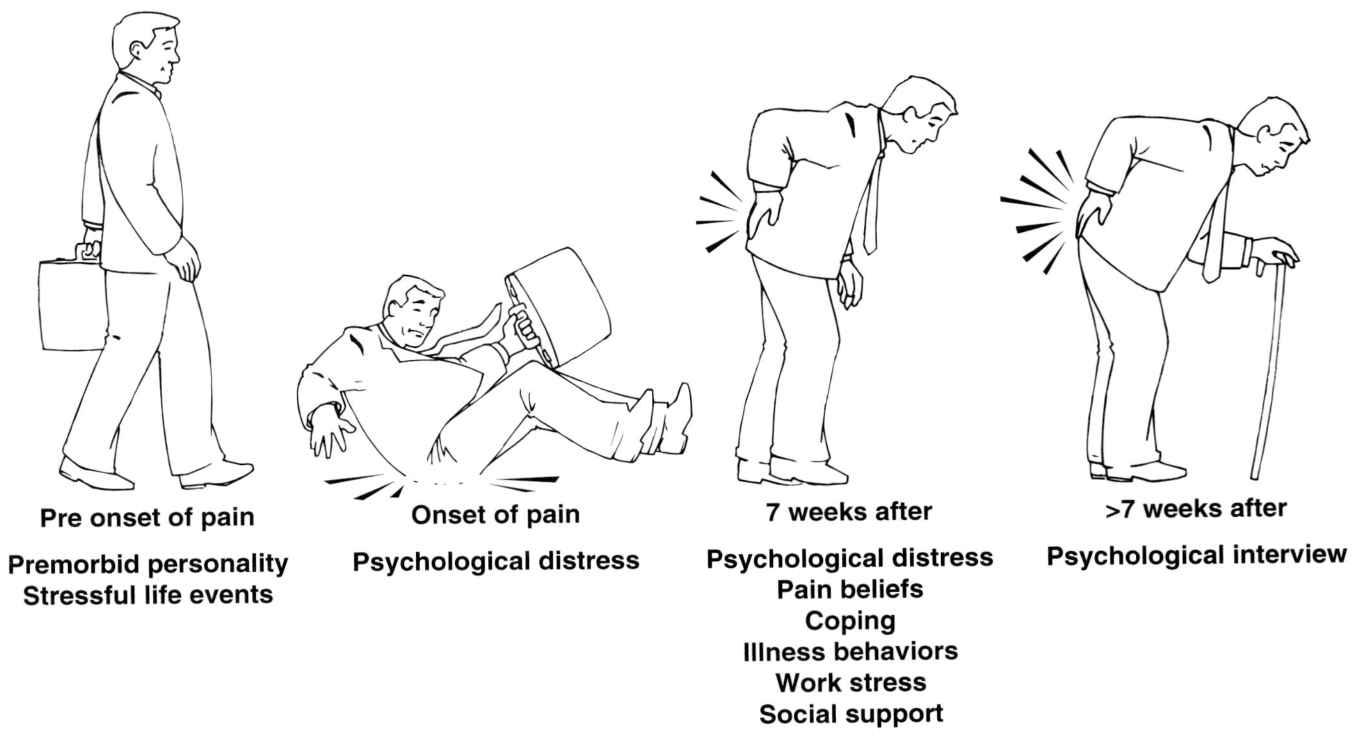

Figure 11–3. Optimal points at which to assess psychosocial characteristics of low back pain.
Reprinted from Weiser and Cedraschi[51] by permission of the publisher WB Saunders.

on this theory. Moreover, reduction of stress, including workplace stress, and psychotherapy itself are interventions shown to be beneficial in the management of the psychosocially disturbed patient. Finally, active rehabilitation programs adopting a multidisciplinary approach are increasingly being shown to be effective in the management of patients with musculoskeletal disorders.[56,57]

SUMMARY

The reason for the current interest in the psychosocial characteristics of back pain is twofold: (1) an epidemic of back disability resulting in a financially crippling burden on society and (2) the failure of modern treatment to help the vast majority of patients with chronic, nonorganic back pain. Fortunately, most patients with nonspecific back pain resolve within approximately 6 weeks, irrespective of administration of treatment or the type of treatment.

Returning to the three questions originally posed in the introduction to this chapter, it is possible to attempt to answer them using the biopsychosocial model:

1. People may have preexisting susceptibilities or vulnerabilities (congenital or learned) that place them at risk of developing chronic pain disability. These exist in the affective (e.g., personality trait) and cognitive-behavioral (e.g., negative thoughts about pain and always lying down when in pain) domains. This may be the reason, at least in part, why not all back pain patients end up chronically disabled.
2. Back pain, when it occurs, may persist and become increasingly associated with disability, inappropriate pain behavior, and adoption of a sick role. The influences on this progression may be of several types including affective (i.e., psychological distress) and cognitive-behavioral (i.e., beliefs and attitudes about pain and coping strategies) psychological dimensions and social factors (i.e., stressful events, family and doctor-patient relationships, financial considerations, work-related factors, and compensation status). The biopsychosocial model proposes that there are interactions between all these dimensions and that they are all, to a greater or lesser extent, responsible for the development of chronic back disability.
3. Patients at risk of developing chronic back disability can be identified at the subacute phase using psychosocial screening procedures in the routine clinical setting. A comprehensive assessment of psychological distress and cognitive (locus of control, coping strategies, and fear-avoidance beliefs) and social factors may well be powerful predictors of chronic disability.

On the basis of psychosocial screening, patients should be counselled with the express intent of rehabilitation as quickly as possible. In many cases treatment of the illness, rather than just the physical disorder, may be sufficient to prevent progress of the condition. It remains the case, however, that in many instances this sequence of events will fail to resolve the problem and patients should be referred for expert psychological evaluation. The recommendations outlined in this chapter are in no way meant as a substitution for trained psychological expertise but rather as a cost-effective way of assessing quickly and effectively patients at risk. The solution to the problem surely lies in a multidisciplinary approach to the treatment of back pain whereby the patients can be referred quickly and easily for the treatment they require, based on calculated and informed assessment. This would go some way toward increasing the chances of successfully rehabilitating the chronic back pain patient.

REFERENCES

1. Cats-Baril WL, Frymoyer JW. Identifying patients at risk of becoming disabled because of low back pain. The Vermont Rehabilitation Engineering Centre Predictive Model. *Spine*. 1991;16:605–607.
2. Klaber Moffett JA, Richardson G, Maynard A. *Back pain: What is its impact on society?* Centre for Health Economics, internal publication. University of York, UK, 1993.
3. Berquist-Ullman M, Larsson U. Acute back pain in industry. *Acta Orthopaedica Scandinavica*.1977;170: 1–117.
4. Troup JDG, Martin JW, Lloyd DCEF. Back pain in industry: A prospective study. *Spine*.1981;6:61–69.
5. Croft PR, MacFarlane GJ, Papageorgiou AC, Thomas E, Silman AJ. Outcome of low back pain in general practice: A prospective study. *British Medical Journal*. 1998;316:1356–1359.
6. Spitzer WO. Quebec Task Force on Spinal Disorders. Chapter 3. Diagnosis of the problem. *Spine*. 1987;12:S16–S21.
7. Frymoyer JW. Back pain and sciatica. *New England Journal of Medicine*. 1988;318:291–300.
8. Frymoyer JW. Predicting disability from low back pain. *Clinical Orthopaedics and Related Research*. 1992;279:101–109.
9. Waddell G. A new clinical model for the treatment of low back pain. *Spine*. 1987;12:632–644.

10. Waddell G. Low back pain: A twentieth century health care enigma. *Spine*. 1996;21:2820–2825.
11. Waddell G, Bircher M, Finlayson D, Main CJ. Symptoms and signs: Physical disease or illness behavior? *British Medical Journal*. 1984;289:739–741.
12. Bolton JE. Future directions for outcomes research in back pain. *European Journal of Chiropractic*. 1997;45:57–64.
13. Adams N. Psychosocial factors affecting pain. In: *The Psychophysiology of Low Back Pain*. London: Churchill Livingstone. 1997:Chapter 5, 55–67.
14. Melzack R, Wall PD. Pain mechanisms: A new theory. *Science*. 1965;150:971–979.
15. Bolton JE. Methods of assessing low back pain and related psychological factors. *European Journal of Chiropractic*. 1993;41:31–38.
16. Keefe FJ, Block AR.Development of an observation method for assessing pain behavior in chronic low back pain patients. *Behavior Research and Therapy*.1982;13:363–375.
17. Waddell G, Somerville D, Henderson I, Newton M. Objective clinical evaluation of physical impairment in chronic low back pain. *Spine*. 1992;17:617–628.
18. Bolton JE. Evaluation of treatment in back pain patients: Clinical outcome measures. *European Journal of Chiropractic*.1994;42:29–40.
19. Tait RC. Psychological factors in the assessment of disability among patients with chronic pain. *Journal of Back and Musculoskeletal Rehabilitation*. 1993;3:20–47.
20. Waddell G, Newton M, Henderson I, Somerville D, Main CJ. A Fear-Avoidance Beliefs Questionnaire (FABQ) and the role of fear-avoidance beliefs in chronic low back pain and disability. *Pain*. 1993; 52:157–168.
21. Waddell G, Main CJ, Morris EW, Di Paola M, Gray ICM. Chronic low back pain, psychological distress and illness behavior. *Spine*. 1984;9:209–213.
22. Huskisson EC. Measurement of pain. *Lancet*. 1974;2:1127–1131.
23. Bolton JE, Wilkinson RC. Responsiveness of pain scales: A comparison of three pain intensity measures in chiropractic patients. *Journal of Manipulative and Physiological Therapeutics*. 1998;21:1–7.
24. Ransford AO, Cairns D, Mooney V. The pain drawing as an aid to the psychological evaluation of patients with low back pain. *Spine*. 1976;1:127–134.
25. Uden A, Landin LA. Pain drawing and myelography in sciatic pain. *Clinical Orthopaedics and Related Research*. 1987;216:55–61.
26. Bolton JE, Christensen MNK. Back pain distribution patterns: Relationship to subjective measures of pain severity and disability. *Journal of Manipulative and Physiological Therapeutics*. 1994;17:211–218.
27. Tait RC, Chibnall JT, Margolis RB. Pain extent: Relations with psychological state, pain severity, pain history and disability. *Pain*. 1990;41:295–301.
28. Dahlstrom WG, Welsh GS. *An MMPI Handbook*. Minneapolis: University of Minnesota Press, 1960.
29. Eynsenck HJ, Eynsenck SBG. *Manual of the Eynsenck Personality Questionnaire*. Sevenoaks, Kent, UK: Hodder & Stoughton, 1975.
30. Main CJ, Waddell G. Personality assessment in the management of low back pain. *Clinical Rehabilitation*. 1987;1:139–142.
31. Main CJ, Wood PLR, Hollis S, Spanswick CC, Waddell G. The Distress and Risk Assessment Method. A simple patient classification to identify distress and evaluate the risk of poor outcome. *Spine*. 1992; 17:42–52.
32. Bolton JE. Psychological distress and disability in back pain patients: Evidence of sex differences. *Journal of Psychosomatic Research*. 1994;38:849–858.
33. Jensen MP, Turner JA, Romano JM, Karoly P. Coping with chronic pain: A critical review of the literature. *Pain*. 1991;47:249–283.
34. Rudy TE, Kerns RD, Turk DC. Chronic pain and depression: Toward a cognitive-behavioral meditation model. *Pain*. 1998;35:129–140.
35. Rosensteil AK, Keefe FJ. The use of coping strategies in chronic low back pain: Relationships to patient characteristics and current adjustment. *Pain*. 1983;17:33–44.
36. Keefe FJ, Williams DA. Assessment of pain behaviors. In: Turk DC, Melzack R, eds. *Handbook of Pain*. New York: Guilford, 1992:277–292.
37. Harkapaa K, Jarvikoski A, Mellin G, Hurri H, Luoma J. Health locus of control beliefs and psychological distress as predictors for treatment outcome in low back pain patients: Results of a 3 month follow-up of a controlled intervention study. *Pain*. 1991;46:35–41.
38. Waddell G, Main CJ. A comparison of cognitive measures in low back pain: Statistical structure and clinical validity at initial assessment. *Pain*. 1991;46:287–298.

39. Jensen MP, Karoly P, Huger R. The development and preliminary validation of an instrument to assess patients' attitudes towards pain. *Journal of Psychosomatic Research*. 1987;31:393–400.
40. Riley JF, Ahern DK, Follick MJ. Chronic pain and functional impairment: Assessing beliefs about their relationship. *Archives of Physical Medicine and Rehabilitation*. 1988;69:579–582.
41. Slater MA, Hall HF, Atkinson JH, Garfin SR. Pain and impairment beliefs in chronic low back pain: Validation of the Pain and Impairment Relationship Scale (PAIRS). *Pain*. 1991;44:51–56.
42. Craufurd DIO, Creed F, Jayson MIV. Life events and psychological disturbance in patients with low back pain. *Spine*. 1990;15:490–494.
43. Flor H, Kerns RD, Turk DC. The role of spouse reinforcement, perceived pain and activity levels in chronic pain patients. *Journal of Psychosomatic Research*. 1987;31:251–259.
44. Cherkin D, Deyo RA, Berg AO. Evaluation of a physician education intervention to improve primary care for low back pain. II. Impact on patients. *Spine*. 1991;16:1173–1178.
45. Vernon H. Chiropractic: A model incorporating the illness behavior model in the management of low back pain patients. *Journal of Manipulative and Physiological Therapeutics*. 1991;14:379–389.
46. Bigos SJ, Battie MC, Spengler DM, Fisher LD, Fordyce WE, Hansson TH, Nachemson AL, Wortley MD. A prospective study of work perceptions and psychological factors affecting the report of back injury. *Spine*. 1991;16:1–6.
47. Tollison CD. Comprehensive status as a predictor of outcome in non-surgically treated low back injury. *Southern Medical Journal*. 1993;86:1206–1209.
48. Cassisi JE, Sypert GW, Lagana L, Friedman EM. Pain, disability and psychological functioning in chronic back pain subgroups: Myofascial versus herniated disc syndrome. *Neurosurgery*. 1993;3:379–385.
49. Sander RA, Meyers JE. The relationship of disability to compensation status in railway workers. *Spine*. 1986;11:141–143.
50. Guest GH, Drummond PD. Effect of compensation on emotional state and disability in chronic back pain. *Pain*. 1992;48:125–130.
51. Weiser S, Cedraschi C. Psychosocial issues in the prevention of chronic low back pain—a literature review. *Bailliere's Clinical Rheumatology*. 1992;6:657–684.
52. Klaber Moffet JA. Exercises for back pain. In: Roland MO, Jenner JR, eds. *Back Pain. New Approaches to Rehabilitation and Education*. Manchester, UK: Manchester University Press. 1989:Chapter 3, 50–62.
53. Main CJ, Parker H. The evaluation and outcome of pain management programmes for chronic low back pain. In: Roland MO, Jenner JR, eds. *Back Pain. New Approaches to Rehabilitation and Education*. Manchester, UK: Manchester University Press. 1989: Chapter 9, 129–156.
54. Borysenko J. *Minding the Body, Mending the Mind*. New York: Bantam Books, 1988.
55. Fordyce WE, Fowler RS, Lehman JF, De Lateur BJ. Operant conditioning in the treatment of chronic pain. *Archives of Physical Medicine and Rehabilitation*. 1973;54:399–408.
56. Liebenson C, ed. *Rehabilitation of the Spine: A Practitioner's Manual*. Baltimore: Williams and Wilkins, 1995.
57. Jordan A, Ostergaard K. Rehabilitation of neck/shoulder patients in primary health care clinics. *Journal of Manipulative and Physiological Therapeutics*. 1996;19:32–35.
58. Scott J, Huskisson EC. Graphic representation of pain. *Pain*. 1976;2:175–184.
59. Price DD, McGrath PA, Rafii A, Buckingham B. The validation of visual analogue scales as ratio scale measures for chronic and experimental pain. *Pain*. 1983;17:45–56.
60. Jensen MP, Karoly P, Braver S. The measurement of clinical pain intensity: A comparison of six methods. *Pain*. 1986;27:117–126.
61. McCormack HM, Horne DJdeL, Sheather S. Clinical applications of visual analogue scales: A critical review. *Psychological Medicine*. 1988;18:1007–1019.
62. Downie WW, Leatham PA, Rhind VM, Wright V, Branco JA, Anderson JA. Studies with pain rating scales. *Annals of Rheumatic Diseases*. 1978;37:378–381.
63. Price DD, Bush FM, Long S, Harkins SW. A comparison of pain measurement characteristics of mechanical visual analogue and simple numerical rating scales. *Pain*. 1994;56:217–226.
64. Heft MW, Gracely RH, Dubner R, McGrath PA. A validation model for verbal descriptor scaling of human clinical pain. *Pain*. 1980;9:363–373.
65. Price DD, Harkins SW, Baker C. Sensory-affective relationships among different types of clinical and experimental pain. *Pain*. 1987;28:291–299.
66. Melzack R. The McGill pain questionnaire: Major properties and scoring method. *Pain*. 1975;1:277–299.
67. Melzack R. The short form McGill pain questionnaire. *Pain*. 1987;30:191–197.
68. Margolis RB, Tait RC, Krause SJ. A rating system for use with patient pain drawings. *Pain*. 1986; 24:57–65.

69. Fairbank JCT, Couper J, Davies JB, O'Brien JP. The Oswestry low back disability index. *Physiotherapy*. 1980;66:271–273.
70. Roland M, Morris R. A study of the natural history of back pain. Part I. Development of a reliable and sensitive measure of disability in low-back pain. *Spine*. 1983;8:141–144.
71. Waddell G, Main CJ. Assessment of severity in low back disorders. *Spine*. 1984;9:204–208.
72. Hudson-Cook N, Tomes-Nicholson K, Breen A. A revised Oswestry disability questionnaire. In: Roland M, Jenner JR, eds. *Back Pain. New Approaches to Rehabilitation and Education*. Manchester, UK, Manchester University Press. 1989:Chapter 13,187–204.
73. Ruta DA, Garratt AM, Wardlaw D, Russell IT. Developing a valid and reliable measure of health outcome for patients with low back pain. *Spine*. 1994;19:1887–1896.
74. Kopec JA, Esdaile JM, Abrahamowicz M, Abenhaim L, Wood-Dauphinee S, Lamping DL, Williams JI. The Quebec back disability scale. *Spine*. 1995;20:341–352.
75. Daltroy LH, Cats-Baril WL, Katz JN, Fossel AH, Liang MH. *Spine*. 1996;6:741–749.
76. Bergner M, Bobbitt RA, Carter WB, Gibson BS. Sickness Impact Profile: Development and final revision of health status measure. *Medical Care*. 1981;19:787–805.
77. Brazier JE, Harper R, Jones NMB, O'Cathain A, Thomas KJ, Usherwood T, Westlake L. Validating the SF-36 health survey questionaire: New outcome measure for primary care. *British Medical Journal*. 1992;305:160–164.
78. Pollard CA. Preliminary validity study of the Pain Disability Index. *Perceptual and Motor Skills*. 1984;59:974.
79. Tait RC, Chibnall JT, Krause S. The pain disability index: Psychometric properties. *Pain*. 1990;40:171–182.
80. Greenough CG, Fraser RD. Assessment of outcome in patients with low back pain. *Spine*. 1992;17:36–41.
81. Spielberg CD, Gorsuch RL, Lushere RE . *Manual for the State-Trait Anxiety Inventory*. Palo Alto, CA: Consulting Psychologist Press, 1970.
82. Schwartz GE, Davidson RJ, Goleman DJ. Patterning of cognitive and somatic processes in the self-regulation of anxiety: Effects of meditation versus exercise. *Journal of Psychosomatic Medicine*. 1978;40:321–328.
83. Main CJ. The modified somatic perception questionnaire. *Journal of Psychosomatic Research*. 1983;27: 503–514.
84. McCraken LM, Zayfert C, Gross RT. The Pain Anxiety Symptoms Scale: Development and validation of a scale to measure fear of pain. *Pain*. 1992;50:67–74.
85. Beck AT, Ward CH, Mendelson M, Mock J, Erbaugh J. An inventory for measuring depression. *Archives of General Psychiatry*. 1961;4:561–571.
86. Zung WWK. A self-rated depression scale. *Archives of General Psychiatry*. 1965;32:63–70.
87. Lefebvre MF. Cognitive distortion and cognitive errors in depressed psychiatric and low back patients. *Journal of Consulting and Clinical Psychology*. 1981;49:517–525.
88. Jensen MP, Karoly P. *Notes on the Survey of Pain Attitudes (SOPA): Original (24-item) and Revised (35-item) versions*. Tempe, AZ: Arizona State University, 1987.
89. Phillips HC. Thoughts provoked by pain. *Behavior Research and Therapy*. 1989;27:469–473.
90. Williams DA, Thorne BE. An empirical assessment of pain beliefs. *Pain*. 1989;36:351–358.
91. Edwards LC, Pearce SA, Turner-Stokes L, Jones A. The Pain Beliefs Questionnaire: An investigation of beliefs in the causes and consequences of pain. *Pain*. 1992;51:267–272.
92. Flor H, Behle DJ, Birbaumer N. Assessment of pain-related cognitions in chronic pain patients. *Behavior Research and Therapy*. 1993;31:63–73.
93. Jensen MP, Turner JA, Romano JM, Strom SE. The chronic pain coping inventory: Development and primary validation. *Pain*. 1995;60:203–216.
94. Brown GK, Nicassio PM. The development of a questionnaire for the assessment of active and passive coping strategies in chronic pain patients. *Pain*. 1987;31:53–65.
95. Regan CA, Lorig K, Thoresen CE. Arthritis appraisal and ways of coping: Scale development. *Arthritis Care and Research*. 1988;3:139–150.
96. Wallston BS, Wallston KA, Kaplan GD, Maides SA. Development and validation of the Health Locus of Control (HLC) scale. *Journal of Consulting and Clinical Psychology*. 1976;44:580–585.
97. Skevington SM. A standardised scale to measure beliefs about controlling pain (B.P.C.Q.): A preliminary study. *Psychology and Health*. 1990;4:221–232.
98. Toomey TC, Seville JL, Mann JD. The pain locus of control scale: Relationship to pain description, self-control skills and psychological symptoms. *The Pain Clinic*. 1995;8:315–322.
99. Pilowsky I, Spence ND. Patterns of illness behavior in patients with intractable pain. *Journal of Psychosomatic Research*. 1975;19:279–287.

100. Waddell G, Richardson J. Observation of overt pain behavior by physicians during routine clinical examination of patients with low back pain. *Journal of Psychosomatic Research*. 1992;36:77–87.
101. Block AR, Kremer EF, Gaylor M. Behavioral treatment of chronic pain: The spouse as a discriminative cue for pain behavior. *Pain*. 1980;9:243–252.
102. Leino P. Symptoms of stress predict musculoskeletal disorders. *Journal of Epidemiology and Community Health*. 1989;43:293–300.
103. Lancourt J, Kettelhut M. Predicting return to work for lower back pain patients receiving workers' compensation. *Spine*. 1992;17:629–639.
104. Price J, Mueller C. *Professional Turnover*. Jamaica, NY: Spectrum Publications, 1981.
105. Wolf MH, Putnam SM, James SA, Stiles WB. The Medical Interview Satisfaction Scale: Development of a scale to measure patient perceptions of physician behavior. *Journal of Behavioral Medicine*. 1978;1:391–401.
106. Linder-Pelz S, Struening EL. The multidimensionality of patient satisfaction with a clinic visit. *Journal of Epidemiology and Community Health*. 1985;10:42–54.
107. Ware JE, Hays RD. Methods for measuring patient satisfaction with specific medical encounters. *Medical Care*. 1988;26:393–402.
108. Waddell G. Biopsychosocial analysis of low back pain. *Bailliere's Clinical Rheumatology*. 1992;6:523–527.

CHAPTER 12

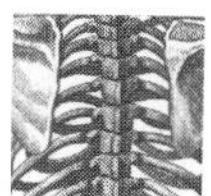

Applications of Radiological Findings for Exercise Prescription

Timothy J. Mick, DC

INTRODUCTION

Diagnostic imaging is frequently indicated in the evaluation of patients with musculoskeletal complaints, many of which may be the result of altered structure or function in the spine and bony pelvis. Plain film radiographs have been used since the end of the 19th century and more recently advanced imaging procedures such as computed tomography (CT) and magnetic resonance imaging (MRI) have done much to enhance our understanding of the various abnormalities that may affect the axial skeleton. This chapter will address the way in which diagnostic imaging modalities may be utilized in the area of active exercise programs. While other works have done an adequate job of describing the diagnosis of various pathologies using these imaging procedures, they have not described the way in which this information may be incorporated into protocols for conservative management of these conditions, particularly in the area of active exercise.

The chapter will begin with a discussion of spinal instability, outlining the methods for radiological diagnosis and describing the correlation between radiological and clinical signs of this entity. Obviously, spinal instability is a concern in individuals being considered for an active exercise program. Following this will be a discussion of transitional segments at the lumbosacral junction, as well as other congenital anomalies which may affect spinal biomechanics, potentially influencing the application of active exercise. The implications of developmental (congenital) and acquired spinal stenosis will also be addressed.

Spondylolisthesis of the lumbar spine is a massive topic and will not be exhaustively covered. However, there will be a discussion of unique motion patterns and static alignment seen with lytic spondylolisthesis of L5 as well as a discussion of degenerative spondylolisthesis of L4. The even more extensive topic of scoliosis will receive brief consideration relative to active exercise, as will several common arthritides of the axial skeleton which may affect the application of exercise. Finally, osteopenic and osteomalacic conditions that may contraindicate active exercise programs will be discussed and the role of advanced diagnostic imaging (including bone densitometry for osteoporosis) will be briefly considered.

SPINAL INSTABILITY

Individuals with instability of the cervical or lumbar spine may not be able to participate in certain exercise programs, especially those in which stresses are concentrated in the unstable spinal region. The diagnosis of spinal instability may be difficult or impossible on the basis of clinical findings alone. In fact, even the definition of spinal instability may be somewhat nebulous, as there is no universally accepted definition of either clinical or radiological instability. Furthermore, the distinctions between physiologic hypermobility, non-physiologic hypermobility and instability may be equally unclear. One must begin by deciding upon an operational definition for radiological instability, recognizing that disagreement exists regarding which is the best definition and recognizing that there may not be a clear relationship between radiological and clinical instability in a given case. The definition must be liberal enough to include those patients in whom traumatic or degenerative lesions have diminished the integrity of one or more motion segments to the extent that active exercise would likely result in harm to the patient. On the other hand, the definition must exclude physiologic hypermobility and normal physiologic motions frequently mistaken for instability on functional spine radiographs.

CERVICAL SPINE

It is widely recognized that instability of the upper cervical spine and particularly atlanto-axial instability (AAI) may occur as a result of deficiency of the transverse component of the cruciate ligament, commonly known as the transverse ligament of C1 (Table 12–1). This ligament may be agenetic or hypoplastic as is commonly seen in Down's syndrome or

Table 12–1: Frequent Causes of Atlanto-axial Subluxation/Instability

I. Congenital/Developmental

A. Down syndrome (approximately 20% of cases)
B. Anomalies involving the odontoid process of C2
C. Dysplasias, including Morquio's syndrome and spondyloepiphyseal dysplasia (SED)

II. Arthritides and Connective Tissue Diseases

A. Rheumatoid arthritis (in 20–25% of advanced cases)
B. Seronegative spondyloarthropathies (especially psoriatic spondylitis, in which there is an incidence of 45%)
C. Juvenile chronic arthritis (JCA)

III. Trauma

A relatively uncommon cause of AAI/AAS, since dens fracture typically occurs before ligamentous rupture

IV. Infection

Rare today, but formerly due to retropharyngeal abscess, as in tuberculosis

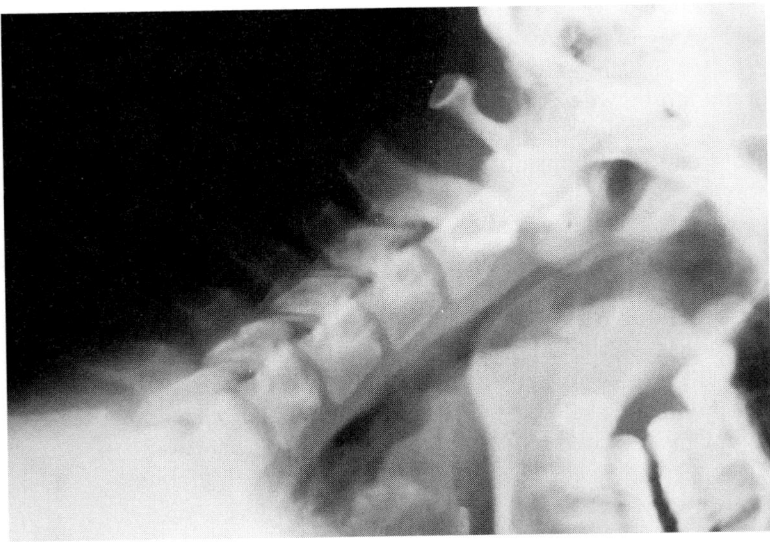

A

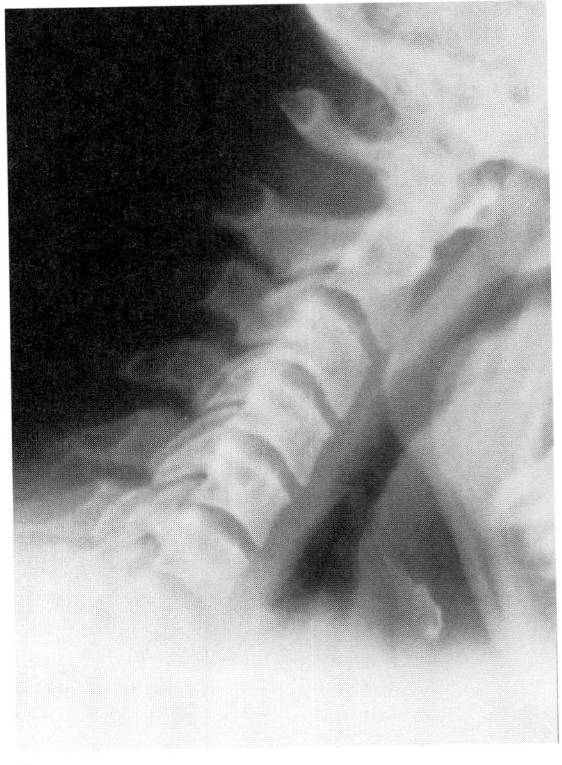

B

Figure 12–1. A. Increased ADI in an adult, measuring 4.0mm on flexion lateral view taken following a motor vehicle accident. This indicates minimal atlanto-axial instability/subluxation. **B.** Physiologic "V"-shaped ADI in a young adult, a normal variant often mistaken for atlanto-axial instability (AAI/AAS). Note normal alignment of the spinolaminar junction lines of C1 and C2. This helps to exclude true AAI/AAS despite the fact that this may appear more abnormal than the first case **(A)**.

with congenital osseous anomalies of the craniovertebral junction.[1] It may also be stretched or torn as a result of flexion trauma,[2–4] or ruptured due to inflammatory joint disease, especially rheumatoid arthritis.[5,6] For this reason, a flexion lateral cervical radiograph should be obtained in cases in which active exercise is being considered for patients with an underlying condition likely to produce AAI and/or atlanto-axial subluxation (AAS). Typically, if spinal manipulative therapy (SMT) is being utilized in the course of treatment of patients at risk for AAI/AAS, this film has already been obtained, since AAI/AAS would contraindicate many manipulative procedures in the upper cervical region. An atlantodental interspace (ADI) measuring greater than 3.0 mm is consistent with AAI.[3] The measurement should be made at the inferior aspect of the ADI to eliminate false positive results related to the common physiologic "V"-shaped atlantodental interspace. This is often mistaken for AAI, especially in children and young adults[7] (Figure 12–1).

While the diagnosis of AAI is relatively simple on a well positioned flexion lateral cervical radiograph, the diagnosis of instability is more complex in the lower cervical spine. This is, in part, related to the varying definitions of clinical and radiological instability appearing previously in the literature. Typically, lower cervical instability may be secondary to identifiable trauma, disease (commonly, degenerative joint disease), surgery or a combination of these.[8] Some traumatic lesions, such as bilateral facet dislocations are by definition unstable, but these are infrequently seen as acute lesions in an ambulatory care setting.[9–11] Traumatic lesions more likely to be seen include unilateral facet subluxations or dislocations and milder fractures such as minimal vertebral body compression fractures and spinous process fractures, all of which may be seen as either acute or chronic lesions. The majority of these will be stable and may not contraindicate active exercise programs. However, some of these seemingly milder lesions may be unstable and associated with neurologic damage or enough ligamentous disruption to place the cord or nerve roots at risk with active exercise.[12,13] It may be rather disturbing to the clinician to know that there is apparently poor correlation between radiographic findings and the presence of or potential for cord or nerve root injury. An injury may result in serious neurologic deficit or even death, yet may be associated with essentially normal plain film radiographs.[14–17]

Given the apparent limitations of plain film radiographs to predict the presence of clinical instability which may contraindicate active exercise, one may question the role for functional radiographs in this setting. Still, White, et al, believe that there is value in attempting to identify instability on flexion-extension lateral views of the cervical spine.[8] Based upon in vitro studies, they have outlined three radiographic criteria, along with several clinical indicators that suggest instability. Radiographic findings suggesting instability include:

1. evidence on flexion, extension or resting lateral x-rays of a relative sagittal plane anteroposterior translation of greater than 3.5 mm,
2. relative sagittal plane rotation greater than 11 degrees greater than at the two adjacent disc levels
3. an interspinous distance 1.5 times greater than the interspinous distances at the immediately adjacent levels, both above and below. Or,
4. complete destruction or functional disability of all the anterior or posterior elements.[8,18]

Recognizing their limitations, the use of these criteria is still recommended as a means for detecting at least some cases of instability due to trauma or arthritis or in assessing the integrity of surgical fusion prior to embarking on an active exercise program (Figure 12–2).

LUMBAR SPINE

As in the cervical spine, lumbar instability may be due to trauma, arthritis, failed spinal fusion or other less common causes. Also, as for the cervical spine, there are no universally accepted definitions for clinical and radiological instability. The challenge, then, is to arrive at a definition for instability that will be meaningful in screening for contraindications to active exercise of the low back. Traditionally, flexion-extension lateral radiographs of the lumbar spine have been obtained in order to observe for abnormal anteroposterior translation which, as in the cervical spine, may suggest instability. Both the cervical and lumbar spine normally demonstrate some small amount of sagittal plane translation as a normal component of coupled motion. This physiologic motion is frequently mistaken for instability, but this tends to be more of a pitfall in the cervical spine, particularly in children and young adults.[19–21] (Figure 12–3). Table 12–2 outlines differences between true instability and physiologic anteroposterior translation.

When one has accounted for variation in physiologic motion, there remains considerable disparity in previously reported criteria for diagnosing lumbar instability on plain films and serious questions have been raised as to the efficacy of detecting lumbar instability radiographically.[22–24] Nachemson concluded that instability is present when there is more than 3.0mm of anteroposterior translation or flexion-extension motion that was increased more than 10 degrees at a given level from L1-2 to L4-5. Figures of 4.0mm and 20 degrees were used at L5-S1.[25,26] Behrsin and Andrews stated that normal anteroposterior translation should not exceed 2.0mm at L4-5, but used figures of 6.0mm of translation and 18 degrees of flexion-extension as criteria for instability.[27] Hayes et al reported normal flexion-extension motion at individual spinal levels ranging from 2-27 degrees and up to 7.0mm of anteroposterior translation in healthy, asymptomatic subjects with no other radiographic evidence of lumbar spine abnormality.[28] Soini et al found no correlation between discographic evidence of disc degeneration and radiographic findings and concluded that disc degeneration seldom results in abnormal anteroposterior translation suggesting lumbar instability.[29] This raises the question of the efficacy of functional radiographs in the evaluation of instability secondary to degenerative disc disease.

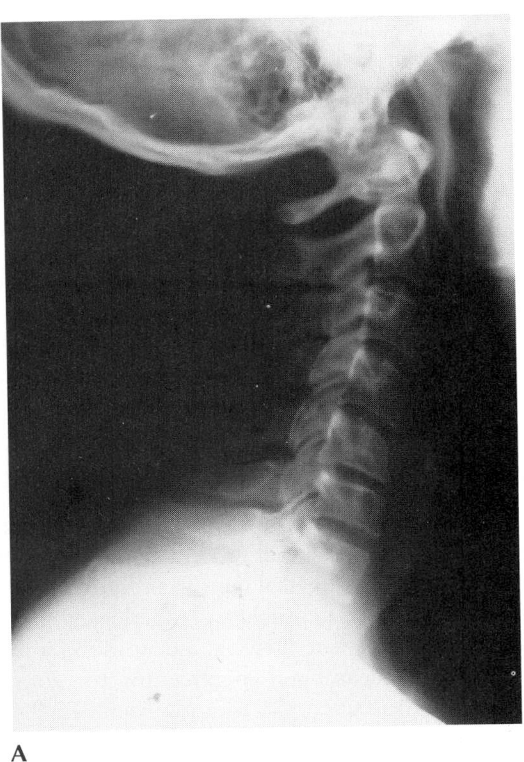

A

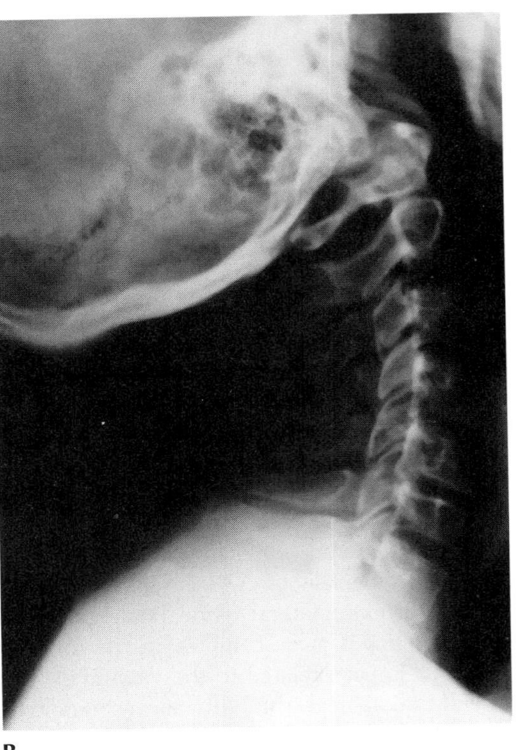

B

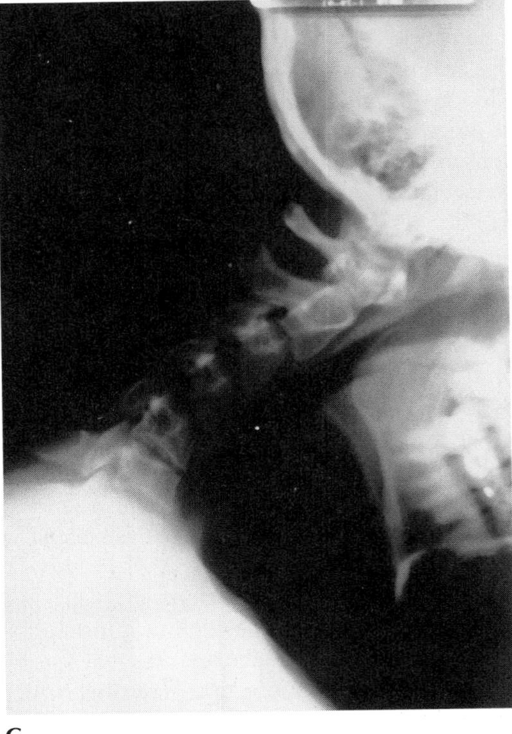

C

Figure 12–2. Cervical spine instability detected with neutral **(A),** extension **(B)** and flexion **(C)** lateral radiographs. Note increased anteroposterior translation measuring 3.5mm and excessive sagittal plane rotation of C5. Severe degenerative disc disease at C5-6 and flexion subluxation of C4 in a 22-year-old female with history of previous motor vehicle accident. These types of post-traumatic changes may exclude a patient from active exercise programs, but this should be based upon careful clinical correlation, since the associated clinical findings vary widely.

The utility of flexion-extension or standing versus recumbent radiographs in detecting instability secondary to spondylolytic spondylolisthesis has also been called into question. Friberg and Kalebo et al have employed traction-compression radiographs rather than flexion-extension films to identify instability in spondylolisthesis.[30,31] This technique demonstrated a sensitivity for detecting instability of spondylolisthesis of over 70% in one study, compared to 33% for standing versus recumbent views and only 20% for flexion-extension views.[32] However, this technique may not be readily accessible, since it does require some modification of the radiographic suite and technical factors related to positioning for these views must be considered.

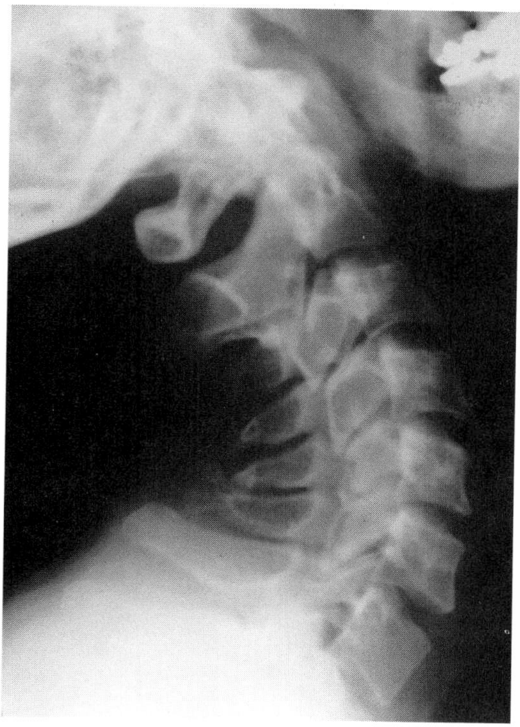

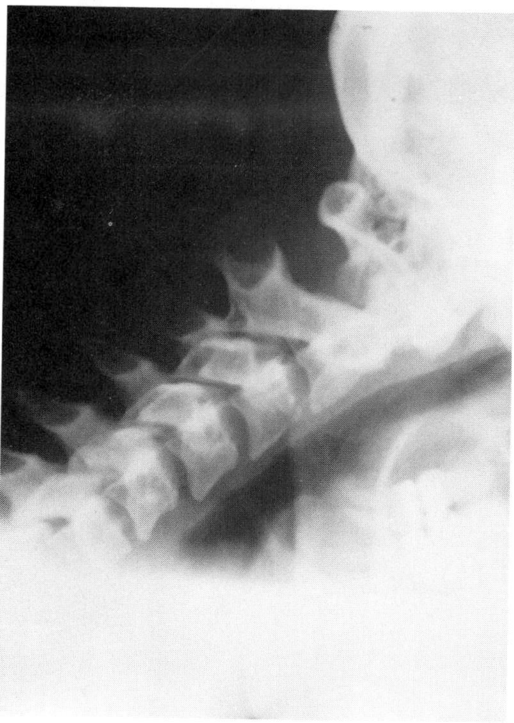

Figure 12–3. Physiologic anteroposterior (A-P) translation in the cervical spine, a normal coupled motion often mistaken for instability. The lesser magnitude of A-P translation and multilevel nature of this finding help to distinguish from true instability, as seen in Figure 12–2.

Given the apparent limitations of functional radiographs in documenting instability of the lumbar spine and the lack of consensus on the criteria for diagnosing instability, the routine use of flexion-extension lateral views of the lumbar spine to rule out instability prior to prescribing an active exercise program is questioned. It is recommended that the patient's early response to the exercise program be used as a guide for continuance or cessation of the program, especially when instability is not thought to be present clinically. In cases in which instability is thought to be likely based upon clinical findings, greater caution is obviously warranted in employing an active exercise program and functional radiographs may be indicated if there is a high clinical suspicion for instability. Clinical findings suggesting instability may include marked increase in severity of pain with specific movements, radicular symptoms with movement, a feeling of a "catch," "click," or "clunk" on certain movements, and a report by the patient of a sensation that the neck or back "gives out" with certain movements.

Table 12–2: Physiologic A-P Translation Versus Instability on Flexion-Extension Films

PHYSIOLOGIC A-P TRANSLATION	TRUE INSTABILITY
Several consecutive levels	Usually a single level
Translation of <3–3.5mm	Translation of 3–3.5mm or more
No other evidence of instability	Other signs of instability
Most prominent in children and young adults, esp. females with generally lax ligaments	May be seen at any age
	Typically associated with pathology such as spondylolisthesis, degenerative joint disease or iatrogenic (post-surgical)

SPINAL STENOSIS

It is important to begin a discussion of spinal stenosis and its significance in the context of active exercise programs with a discussion of terminology used. With a variety of confusing classification systems appearing in the literature, it is wise to keep things simple, while still being complete. Spinal stenosis may be described as "central" when it affects primarily the central spinal canal and its contents. When the stenosis is located laterally in the regions for passage of cervical or lumbar nerve roots, it is said to involve the "nerve root canals." In the lumbar spine, the terms "subarticular recesses" or "lateral recesses" may be substituted for "nerve root canals."

Theoretically, both central and lateral stenosis may be either developmental (i.e. congenital), acquired (as in lumbar lateral recess stenosis due to facet arthrosis) or due to a

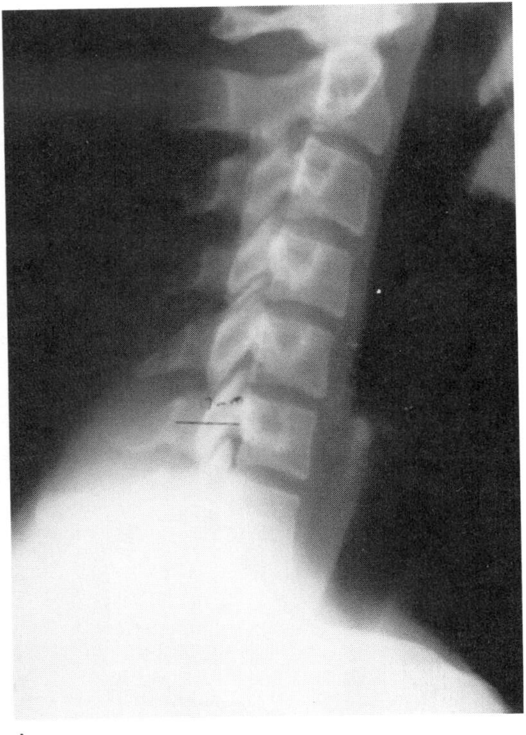

A

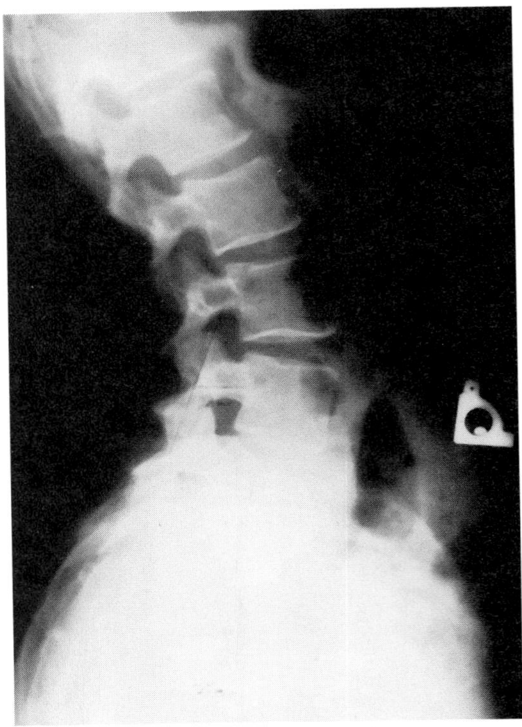

B

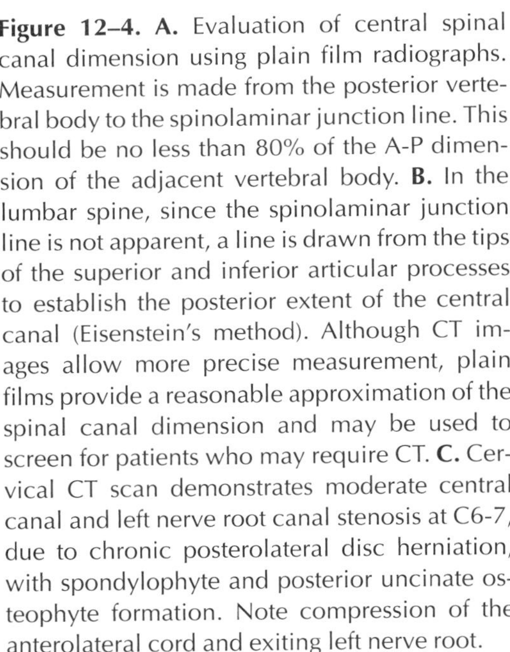

Figure 12–4. A. Evaluation of central spinal canal dimension using plain film radiographs. Measurement is made from the posterior vertebral body to the spinolaminar junction line. This should be no less than 80% of the A-P dimension of the adjacent vertebral body. **B.** In the lumbar spine, since the spinolaminar junction line is not apparent, a line is drawn from the tips of the superior and inferior articular processes to establish the posterior extent of the central canal (Eisenstein's method). Although CT images allow more precise measurement, plain films provide a reasonable approximation of the spinal canal dimension and may be used to screen for patients who may require CT. **C.** Cervical CT scan demonstrates moderate central canal and left nerve root canal stenosis at C6-7, due to chronic posterolateral disc herniation, with spondylophyte and posterior uncinate osteophyte formation. Note compression of the anterolateral cord and exiting left nerve root.

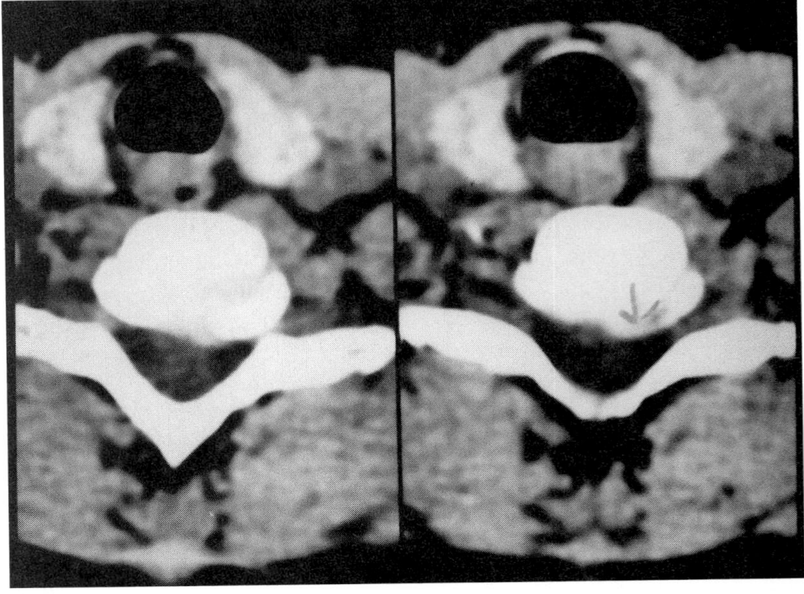

C

combination of developmental and acquired factors. However, lateral recess or nerve root canal stenosis is most often acquired, rather than congenital. Note that the term "intervertebral foraminal (IVF) stenosis" is often incorrectly used for the type of acquired stenosis affecting the nerve root canals or subarticular recesses, typically secondary to degenerative spondylophytes and uncinate and facet osteophytes. Some divide the nerve root canal into entrance zone, mid zone and exit zone. The exit zone, which is the equivalent of the IVF, is the least common site for nerve root compression.

CENTRAL CANAL STENOSIS

There is considerable age- and race-related variability in the central canal dimension.[33–35] In the cervical spine, the central canal is measured on a 72" lateral cervical neutral film from the spinolaminar junction line to the nearest osseous structure at the posterior vertebral body margin.[36] This point may be at the tip of a posterior spondylophyte or posterior uncinate osteophyte when degenerative disc disease is present, which would represent an example of acquired stenosis. Generally, the sagittal central canal dimension should be at least 13mm, and the ratio of the central canal to the anteroposterior dimension of the adjacent vertebral body should be no less than 80%. A measurement of 11-13mm indicates at least borderline stenosis and cord compression is likely at 10mm.[35,37] Because of variation in vertebral size, the method of assessing stenosis via a ratio is considered to be more reliable. Of course, many structures that may contribute to central canal stenosis such as thickened ligamentum flava and central disc herniations are not visible on plain films and are assessed with advanced diagnostic imaging, typically computed tomography (CT) or magnetic resonance imaging (MRI).[38]

Both central and lateral stenosis are uncommon in the thoracic spine.[39] In the lumbar spine, central stenosis is common and, as in the cervical spine, may be present congenitally or may be acquired secondary to arthritis, trauma, infection, neoplasm and metabolic disorders. Also, as in the cervical spine, symptoms and signs from central stenosis are more likely to occur when there is a combination of developmental and acquired factors producing the stenosis. Radiographic signs associated with lumbar central stenosis include narrowed interpediculate distance on frontal radiographs, vertically oriented laminae and decreased interlaminar spaces.[40] Degenerative spondylolisthesis or retrolisthesis commonly contributes to narrowing of the central canal.

The most popular method of measuring the central canal on a lateral lumbar view is one described by Eisenstein.[41] A line is drawn from the tip of the superior articular process to the tip of the inferior articular process, which will correspond approximately to the spinolaminar junction. A distinct radiopaque line is not present here as in the cervical spine, so that this landmark must be indirectly established. As in the cervical spine, measurement is made from this line to the posterior margin of the vertebral body or to the nearest osseous landmark, when posterior spondylosis is present. The average measurement varies with age and race, as well as lumbar level. In general, however, the midsagittal dimension should be no less than 15mm. The interpediculate distance should typically be at least 20mm on frontal films. A central canal measuring 12mm or less sagittally is generally considered to be definitely stenotic.[42]

Plain films represent no more than a somewhat helpful screen for spinal stenosis and, as in the cervical spine, many structures not visible on plain films may contribute to central stenosis. CT is significantly more accurate than plain films in quantifying the degree of stenosis and typically will demonstrate the "trefoil" configuration classically associated with central stenosis.[43] A sagittal measurement on CT of less than 11.5mm, a coronal (interpediculate) measurement of less than 16mm or a cross-sectional area for the central canal of less than 1.45 square centimeters would be considered at least mildly stenotic.[44] One must be cautious not to apply these measurements too strictly and to keep in mind other factors including the amount of epidural fat and the size of the spinal cord or thecal sac.[45]

Ultimately, the detection and assessment of the significance of central spinal canal stenosis rests heavily on clinical evaluation. Diagnostic imaging findings suggesting central stenosis must be considered in light of the history and physical examination. There are no clearly established guidelines to determine which individuals with central stenosis may benefit from active exercise programs and whether some may even be harmed by them. While individuals with a cauda equina syndrome from lumbar cervical stenosis should obviously be excluded from such programs, the question remains as to the appropriateness of active exercise programs for individuals with clinically silent or mildly symptomatic central stenosis (Figure 12–4).

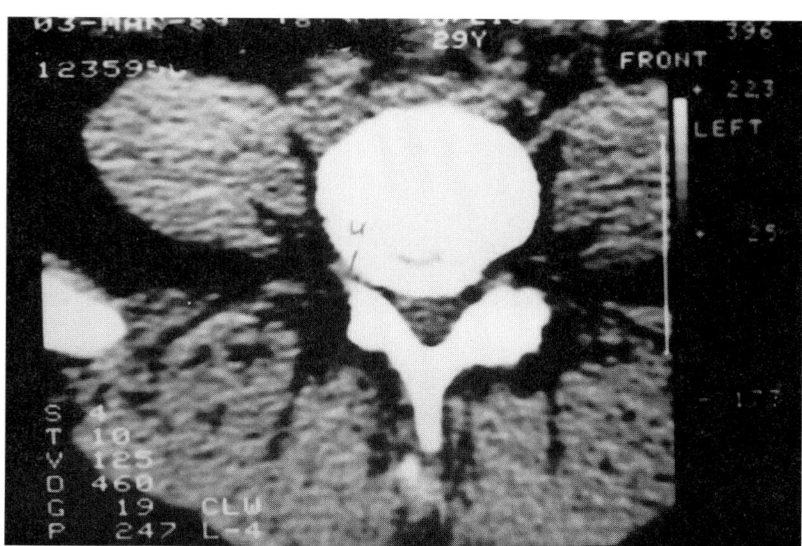

Figure 12–5. Stenosis involving the lumbar lateral recess and IVF. This may cause nerve root compression that could exclude patients from an active exercise program.

NERVE ROOT CANAL AND LATERAL (SUBARTICULAR) RECESS STENOSIS

For the sake of this discussion, the terms "nerve root canals" and "lateral recesses" will be used for the channels providing passage of the traversing cervical and lumbar nerve roots, respectively, from their point of departure from the cord or thecal sac centrally to the intervertebral foramina (IVF's) laterally. Admittedly, a variety of other terms have been used for these channels or "gutters," but these are considered to be the most accurate and descriptive terms.

No guidelines have been established for the normal size of the cervical IVF's on oblique plain films, nor for the nerve root canals medial to the IVF's, which may be readily visualized on CT and MRI scans. Still, cervical oblique views are commonly used to semiquantitatively assess the cervical IVF's, evaluating for significant bony stenosis caused by uncinate or facet osteophytes, which may result in nerve root compression (Figure 12–5). In addition to IVF compromise, an important, but not widely recognized compression of the vertebral artery at the intertransverse foramen may result from large facet or uncinate osteophytes projecting anteriorly to lie under these foramina. This may contraindicate many active exercises involving extension and rotation of the head and neck.

In the lumbar spine, the lateral recesses cannot be visualized on plain films, and bony compromise of the IVF's is less common. Therefore, plain films of the lumbar spine are largely useless for directly assessing stenosis which may affect the exiting nerve roots. The best that plain films may do is to demonstrate significant posterior spondylophyte formation or facet arthrosis and the degenerative retro- or spondylolisthesis, which so commonly accompany these and which tend to narrow the lateral recesses.

If one wishes to quantitatively assess the lateral recesses, a CT scan is required. The subarticular recess lies ventral to the superior articular process and pars interarticularis and is bordered laterally by the medial cortical margin of the pedicle. The posterior aspect of the vertebral body at the discovertebral junction forms the anterior border.[46] While many oppose the concept of measuring the nerve root canals, an anteroposterior dimension of less than 3mm has been said to indicate stenosis and a measurement of 3-5mm at least borderline for stenosis.[47] The measurement should be made at the superior margin of the pedicle, corresponding to the region of the tip of the supe-

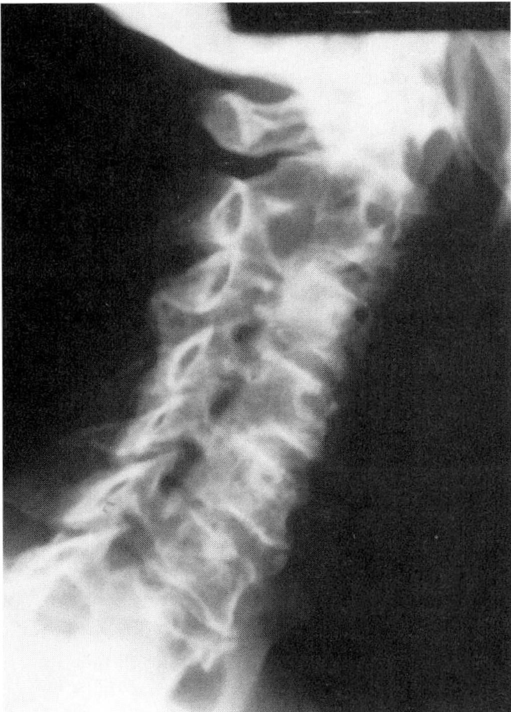

A

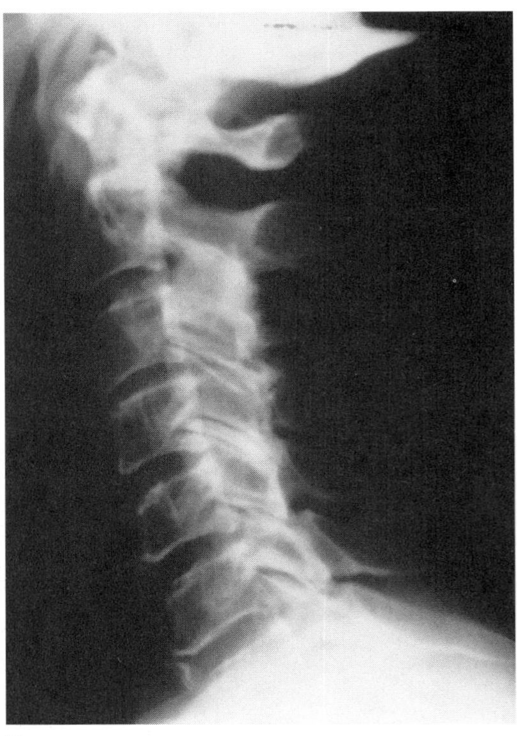

B

Figure 12–6. The same facet osteophytes that may project posteromedially to affect the cervical IVFs **(A)** and central canal may project anteriosuperiorly to lie near the intertransverse foramina **(B).** These large osteophytes may then compress the vertebral artery as it courses through the foramina. The same is true of large uncinate osteophytes. Note the proximity of the facet osteophytes to the gutter-shaped transverse processes on the LCN view, especially at C3 and C4. The foramina are not directly visualized due to their horizontal orientation.

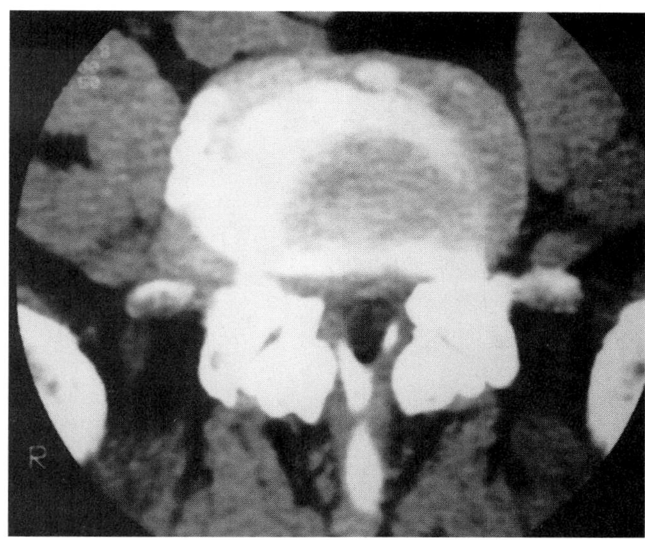

Figure 12–7. Central and lateral recess stenosis at L4-5 due to severe degenerative disc disease and facet arthrosis. There is also a far lateral right-sided disc herniation, which may affect the dorsal root ganglion in the IVF.

rior articular process. This is the site at which the lateral recess is narrowest physiologically and is most vulnerable to encroachment by facet osteophytes in the presence of significant facet arthrosis (osteoarthritis or degenerative joint disease)[48–50] (Figure 12–6).

CT or MRI may also be useful in evaluating for the less common lumbar IVF stenosis which may result from lateral disc herniation, lateral spondylosis, tumors, etc. Sagittally reformatted images are particularly useful for assessing stenosis of the IVF's, which may occur in either an anteroposterior ("front-back") or cephalocaudal ("up-down") dimension [51,52] (Figure 12–7).

LUMBOSACRAL TRANSITIONAL SEGMENTS

Transitional segments at the lumbosacral junction are seen in 15-27% of the general population.[53] They represent a spectrum of variations in segmentation, sometimes given rather meaningless and confusing terms such as "lumbarization" or "sacralization." It is more desirable to use descriptive terms for these transitional segments, terms that assist the clinician in understanding the way in which these transitional segments may alter spinal biomechanics and may affect the application of active exercise programs.

The variety of radiographic presentations may lead to some difficulty in identifying all lumbosacral transitional segments. For instance, slight hyperplasia of the L5 transverse processes technically represents a manifestation of minimal transitional characteristics, but should not necessarily imply that the L5 vertebrae is truly a transitional segment. Southworth and Bersack have suggested 19 mm as a minimum cephalocaudal measurement for the L5 transverse process indicating truly transitional morphology.[54] The transitional transverse processes may be fused to or separate from the sacral alae, either unilaterally or bilaterally. If separate, there may be an accessory articulation with the sacral alae. The body of the transitional segment typically demonstrates a trapezoidal configuration which is intermediate between the more accentuated trapezoidal shape of a true sacral segment and the generally more squared appearance of a true L5 segment. The transitional disc is typically thin and often calcified. This rudimentary disc is often misdiagnosed as evidence of degenerative disc disease.[53,55]

Once a lumbosacral transitional segment has been identified, the clinical relevance and implications relative to an active exercise program must be understood. The idea that even the slightest variation from a spine in which there are five true lumbar segments and no identifiable transitional characteristics alters the function of the lumbar spine and pelvis should be put to rest. On the other hand, it is not justifiable to pass off transitional segments as incidental findings having no clinical relevance, as some have done.[25] Approximately 15-27% of patients seeking treatment for lumbar disc herniation will have a transitional lumbosacral segment.[53]

Disc herniations, a common clinical problem, occur most often in the general population at L4-5 and L5-S1. The rate for herniation at L5-S1, relative to the rest of the lumbar spine has been reported to be in the range of 39-43%.[56,57] Disc herniation at the level of a transitional segment has been found to be rare[53,56] However, there appears to be a markedly increased incidence of herniation at both the transitional disc (17% in one series) and the adjacent disc level (nearly 85% in the same series) when the transitional segment has either bilateral accessory articulations with the sacral alae or a unilateral accessory articulation and opposite typical lumbar-type transverse without accessory joint.[58] This may be related to abnormal torque moments created at levels above the transitional segment.[59] Why these same torque moments would not be created by other types of transitional segments is unclear. It does not appear to be possible to accurately predict the amount and pattern of motion present at a transitional segment based upon radiographic appearance. Surgical findings providing evidence of motion at a transitional level often refute radiographic findings suggesting congenital fusion across the disc and no potential for significant motion.[60] The implications relative to implementation of an active exercise program seem obvious.

The incidence of structural pathology (other than herniated nucleus pulposus) detected on advanced diagnostic imaging is no higher in spines with transitional segments than in those without. However, the distribution of this pathology is significantly different. Specifically, degenerative disc disease, facet arthrosis, central canal and subarticular recess stenosis occur with significantly greater frequency at the level immediately above the transitional segment.[61] There is also a much greater incidence of conjoined nerve roots (two nerve roots exiting the thecal sac in the same dural sleeve) and other mild nerve root anomalies in patients with transitional segments than in the general population. These isolated nerve root anomalies may not be symptom producing, but may be associated with symptoms in the presence of milder disc lesions that would cause no significant problem in patients without underlying nerve root anomaly. Additionally, a well-defined syndrome, commonly referred to as "Bertolotti's syndrome," has been described in which there is low back pain, antalgic scoliosis, and sciatica ipsilateral to a transitional accessory joint.[62,63]

OTHER SPINAL ANOMALIES AND NORMAL VARIANTS

CERVICAL SPINE

Several congenital anomalies and normal variants of the cervical spine should be considered in the context of developing protocols for active exercise programs. Some of these may contraindicate certain movements of the head and neck, while others may represent normal physiologic findings mimicking abnormality which may needlessly exclude individuals from such programs.

Perhaps the most common normal finding or normal variant to be mistaken for abnormality is the physiologic anteroposterior translation occurring as a physiologic coupled motion on flexion-extension radiographs of the cervical spine. This phenomenon, which has been described as "pseudosubluxation" or "physiologic subluxation," was initially described and tends to be most pronounced at C2, and is particularly common in children. However, many young adults with generally lax ligaments and joints, especially thin females, demonstrate this same finding, often at several adjacent levels (typically, C2 through C5). This normal physiologic coupled monition may be distinguished from true subluxation or instability by careful consideration of patient age and overall joint mobility as well as noticing that the anteroposterior translation is approximately equal at the consecutive levels involved, does not exceed 2-2.5mm, and is not accompanied by other signs of cervical instability. Additionally, although there is appearance of exaggerated anteroposterior translation based upon assessment of George's line, the spinolaminar junction lines maintain normal alignment, indicating that much of the apparent anteroposterior translation is actually related to accentuated flexion motion rather than to true sagittal plane translation. The spinolaminar junction line of C2 may lie as much as 1-2mm anterior or posterior to that of C1 and C3 in the neutral posture as a normal variant, especially in children.[19,64,65]

Another commonly encountered normal variant mentioned earlier in the chapter which is often mistaken for abnormality, is the physiologic "V"-shaped atlantodental interspace (ADI). There has been debate relative to its precise etiology and as to whether this phenomenon is truly developmental or may in fact be related to selective weakening or stretching of the superior aspect of the transverse ligament of C1, possibly due to previous trauma. There does, however, appear to be consensus that this finding, though mimicking true atlantoaxial subluxation/instability, is clinically insignificant. This is not considered to represent a contraindication to exercise programs involving active flexion. The ADI should be measured at its inferior margin to prevent falsely increased measurement in the presence of a "V"-shaped ADI.[7]

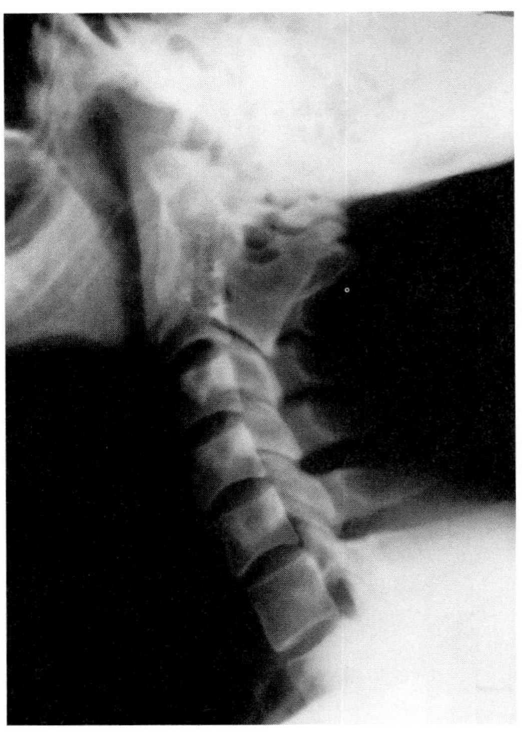

Figure 12–8. Partial bony assimilation ("occipitalization") and spina bifida occulta of C1, along with atypical upper cervical block vertebra ("congenital non-segmentation"). Craniovertebral junction and cervical spine anomalies such as this may alter spinal biomechanics and may predispose to compensatory hypermobility or instability at adjacent normal levels. Additionally, approximately 25% of cases may have associated Arnold-Chiari Type I malformation, which would require an MRI scan for diagnosis.

There is a wide variety of bony anomalies of the cervical spine, seen on a regular basis in a busy practice. Obviously, potentially unstable anomalies such as the os odontoideum, when seen on neutral plain films, warrant functional radiographs prior to implementing an active exercise program. The clinical significance and implications in the administration of active exercise programs of other anomalies, such as assimilation of C1 to occiput ("occipitalization"), occipital vertebrae, paracondylar processes, or congenital non-segmentation ("block vertebrae") are less clearly understood. Anecdotal reports of altered biomechanics related to these anomalies abound, but there is little or no information based upon clinical trials to determine whether these types of anomalies should be considered as contraindications to active exercise programs. Perhaps the most that may be said is that congenital non-segmentation at a given motion unit tends to result in compensatory hypermobility at adjacent levels, which may, in turn, lead to early, advanced degenerative disc disease and osteoarthritis at these hypermobile levels. A similar phenomenon occurs following surgical fusion of the cervical or lumbar spine, described as a "transitional syndrome." The hypermobility and risk for early, advanced degenerative disc disease, disc herniation, etc. may contraindicate active exercise programs in these patients.

Compensatory hypermobility at C1-2 due to congenital assimilation of C1 to occiput may produce brainstem or upper cord compression. Either of these may contraindicate active exercise programs.[66,67] One must also recall bony anomalies of the central nervous system and other organ systems, which may, likewise, contraindicate active exercise programs[68–70] (Figure 12–8)

The posterior ponticle is a far more common normal variant appearing on approximately 15% of lateral cervical neutral radiographs. This represents calcification or ossification of the arcuate ligament of C1, which serves as a foramen (the "arcuate foramen") for passage of the vertebral artery and the first cervical nerve. The posterior ponticle may be associated with vertebrobasilar insufficiency, especially with marked rotation and extension of the head and neck. This association is infrequent, but it should be screened for through appropriate tests for vertebrobasilar insufficiency, prior to implementation of an active exercise program that might include these types of motions.[71] The author has been involved in two cases in which young adult females involved in ballet or gymnastics experienced syncope when the head was turned markedly toward one side. No organic cause for such symptoms was discovered and there was no problem with marked rotation to the opposite side. Both patients had posterior ponticles, and a causative relationship was hypothesized, although not proven. These patients refused angiographic studies, and noninvasive techniques such as magnetic resonance angiography (MRA) were not available at the time. Several colleagues have also anecdotally noted a similar relationship in several of their patients (Figure 12–9).

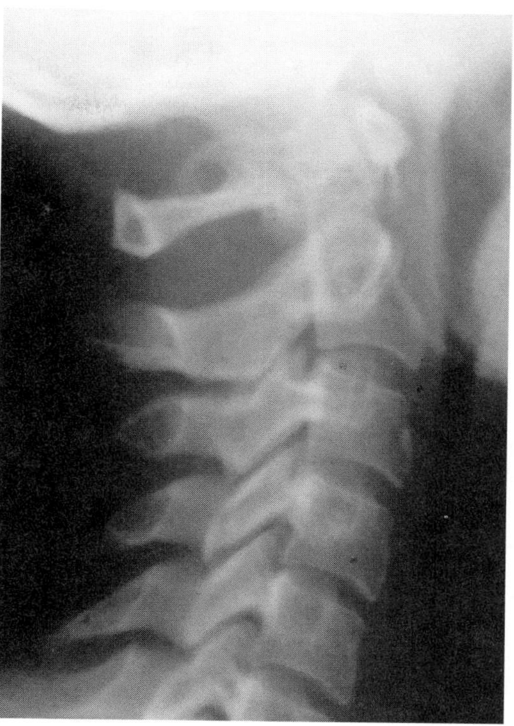

Figure 12–9. While the posterior ponticle of C1 is most often of no clinical significance, there are anecdotal reports of patients with no other known organic abnormality who may experience symptoms of vertebrobasilar insufficiency with extension and rotation of the head and neck. Although the posterior ponticle may be contributing to the signs and symptoms in these isolated cases, a predictable causative relationship has yet to be clearly established.

THORACIC SPINE

In the thoracic spine, the major anomalies that might preclude use of an active exercise program include dysraphic conditions such as diastematomyelia, in which a congenital osseous or fibrocartilaginous septum divides the central spinal canal and splits the spinal cord into two typically unequal parts. Diastematomyelia is seen in approximately 15% of all structural congenital scolioses.[72,73] The septum is visible on plain film radiographs in only about 50% of cases, but 80% of cases demonstrate superficial anomalies apparent clinically.[74,75] Additionally, plain film findings of a short-radius ("C"-shaped) scoliosis, increased interpediculate distance, spina bifida occulta, and multiple segmentation anomalies (i.e. hemivertebrae and other segmentation anomalies) suggest the diagnosis even when the spur is not readily visualized, allowing referral for appropriate advanced diagnostic imaging.[76–78] Although not clearly stated in the literature, it would appear that diastematomyelia and other forms of more significant spinal dysraphism and anomalies associated with tethering of the lower spinal cord should be considered to contraindicate most active exercise programs (Figure 12–10).

As in the cervical spine, other types of vertebral anomalies may occur either singly or as multiple segmentation anomalies. These include nonsegmentation, hemivertebrae, and "butterfly" vertebrae. Little has been written regarding the effects of these anomalies on spinal biomechanics, outside of the obvious association with scoliosis and altered sagittal curves. Compensatory hypermobility at levels adjacent to a non-segmentation would likely be less significant

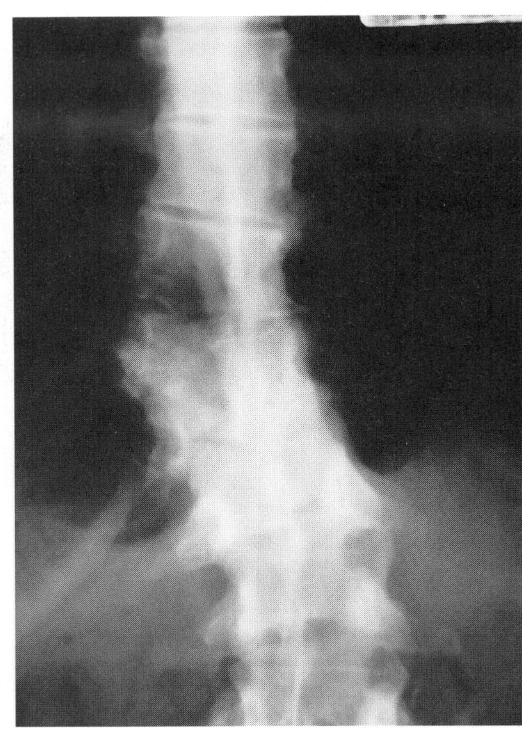

A

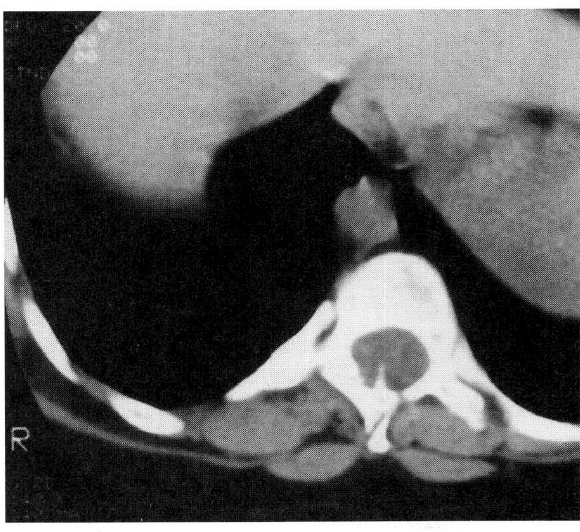

B

Figure 12–10. Prior to being diagnosed as having diastematomyelia, this patient had received spinal manipulation from a medical doctor in the region of the anomaly, with no change in symptoms. Although the spur traversing the cord was not visible on plain films **(A),** the characteristic findings of multiple segmentation anomalies, spina bifida, and a short-radius scoliosis should have suggested the diagnosis and prompted earlier referral for MRI or CT **(B).**

than in the cervical spine due to the general stabilizing effect of the thoracic cage. However, severe alterations of spinal curves may contraindicate active exercise programs. Due to uncertain correlation between radiographic and physical findings, clinical exclusion criteria should be developed.

Anomalies of the ribs, including anomalies of the cervicothoracic junction, may significantly affect biomechanics of the thoracic and lower cervical region. A variety of rib bifurcations, synostoses and foramina appear commonly in clinical practice. While most of these are probably of no clinical significance, one in particular seems to be associated with altered function and may affect active exercise. Srb's anomaly involves synostoses or accessory joint formation between either the first and second true thoracic ribs or, more often, between a cervical and first thoracic rib.[79] Anecdotal evidence and experience gained at this institution suggest that the presence of Srb's anomaly may necessitate modification of spinal manipulative therapy as well as active exercise programs (Figure 12–11).

Although not, strictly speaking, a congenital or developmental abnormality, Scheuermann's disease may be considered here, in the context of conditions associated with altered spinal curves. Typically classified with processes described as osteochondroses, Scheuermann's disease was initially called "kyphosis dorsalis juvenilis" and was thought to be closely related to avascular necrosis of the immature femoral head (Legg-Calvé-Perthes' disease).[80] The condition is now considered to be primarily related to cartilaginous (Schmorl's) node formation through relatively weakened, highly vascular, developing vertebral endplates. This results in multilevel endplate irregularity along with a variable degree of anterior vertebral body wedging and hyperkyphosis.[81,82] Because altered forces on the anterior vertebral body are thought to further prohibit growth of the body anteriorly and contribute to further increase in kyphosis, it is recommended that active exercise programs that minimize flexion forces be employed, especially when the patient is skeletally immature and the endplate abnormality and deformity may progress (Figure 12–12).

LUMBAR SPINE

Some of the anomalies of the lumbar spine and lumbosacral junction have already been covered either individually, as in the case of transitional segments, or in the context of cervical or thoracic anomalies such as hemivertebrae and congenital nonsegmentation. These same anomalies may also affect the lumbar spine. Additionally,

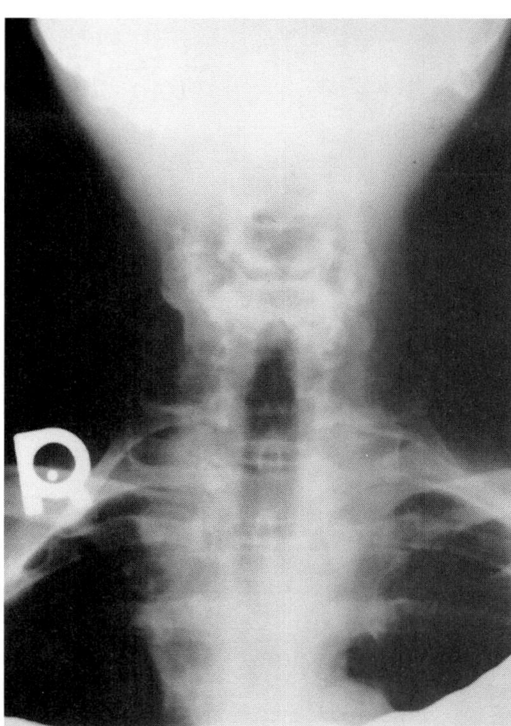

Figure 12–11. Srb's anomaly. The right side marker nearly overlies the accessory articulation between the right C7 rib and the first thoracic rib. Several variations of this anomaly may be encountered. These likely will necessitate alteration of adjustive technique in the cervicothoracic region and modification of active exercise programs. Motion of C7 on T1 will presumably be altered. In this case, the anomaly was not noted initially by the clinician, and the patient developed right brachial plexus neuropraxia following a cervical adjustment. Severe right axillary pain gradually resolved. Note also severe facet arthrosis on the right at C5-6.

the same false impression of instability observed in the cervical spine and representing normal coupled anteroposterior translation on flexion-extension radiographs may be seen in the lumbar spine.

An additional normal variant that has engendered much controversy regarding its clinical significance is the finding of facet joint asymmetry ("tropism") at the lumbosacral junction. While facet tropism has been considered by some to represent a potential factor contributing to the development of degenerative disc disease and lateralization of disc herniations,[83–86] little or no supporting evidence has been forthcoming and several more recent studies refute such a relationship.[87–89] Furthermore, because the facet joint planes at the lumbosacral junction are curved, estimation of true facet joint orientation on plain film radiographs is not considered to be reliable. A recent study using CT discography failed to demonstrate a positive correlation between facet joint asymmetry and the presence of either low back pain or degenerative disc disease.[90] Based upon available evidence, it is concluded that facet tropism is not accurately diagnosed on plain films and is not considered to be a factor in the application of active exercise programs (Figure 12–13).

Developmental anomalies of the pars interarticulari of the lumbar spine have been implicated in the pathogenesis of spondylolysis and lytic spondylolisthesis (Figure 12–14). It is now accepted that pars defects are not congenital lesions, but represent stress fractures of the pars, typically developing in adolescence.[91–94] It is believed that several structural factors in the lumbosacral junction, either singly or in combination, may contribute to the development of these stress fractures. Specifically, developmentally thin pars regions and hypoplastic lumbosacral facet joints have been considered as potential contributing factors. Developmentally attenuated pars regions may be more vulnerable to fracture, while hypoplastic facet structures may concentrate forces abnormally upon the pars regions. The potential influence of these structural anomalies in the application of active exercise programs has not been investigated; but it seems prudent to suggest that children or young adult patients with developmentally thin pars and/or hypoplastic facet structures be enrolled in active exercise programs which minimize extension of the lumbar spine, since extension is particularly suspect in the production of stress fractures of the pars regions.[95,96]

LUMBAR SPONDYLOLISTHESIS

There are some unique biomechanical phenomena that tend to accompany lytic spondylolisthesis of L5 and that may influence the development of an active exercise program. Some of these have already been covered, such as the potential for accompanying instability and the necessity to exclude this prior to employing an exercise program. Perhaps less widely recognized is the common association between spondylolisthesis and accompanying alterations in both coronal and sagittal alignment.

A specific pattern of scoliosis has been described in cases of unilateral spondylolysis or bilateral spondylolysis with asymmetric slip. The asymmetric anterolisthesis results in focal rotation at the lumbosacral junction and produces a typically mild structural type of scoliosis described as an "olisthetic" scoliosis.[97] Spondylolisthesis of L5 is also associated with lumbar hyperlordosis.[98] The actual role of either secondary scoliosis or hyperlordosis in the production of low back pain in patients with spondylolisthesis has yet to be determined. Likewise, the influence of either "olisthetic" scoliosis or hyperlordosis on the application of active exercise programs has not been explored. Still, it seems prudent that such structural abnormalities be considered when contemplating an exercise regimen for a patient with spondylolisthesis.

As mentioned earlier, instability is a well-recognized complication of both lytic spondylolisthesis of L5 and degenerative spondylolisthesis of L4, resulting from advanced facet

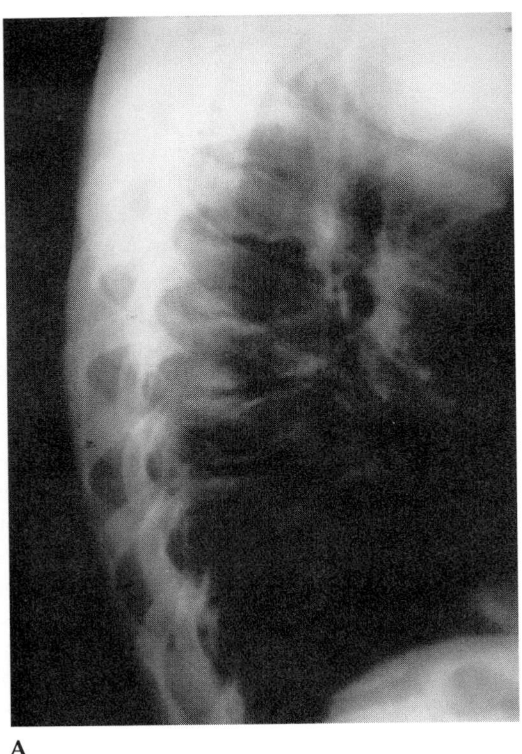

A

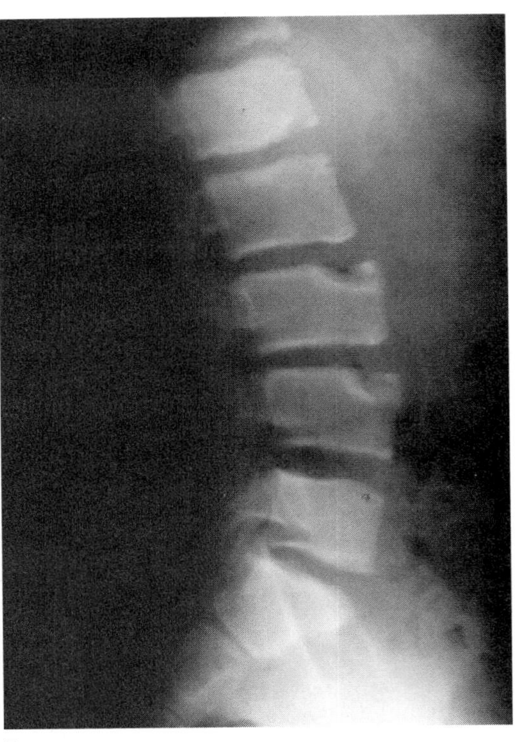

B

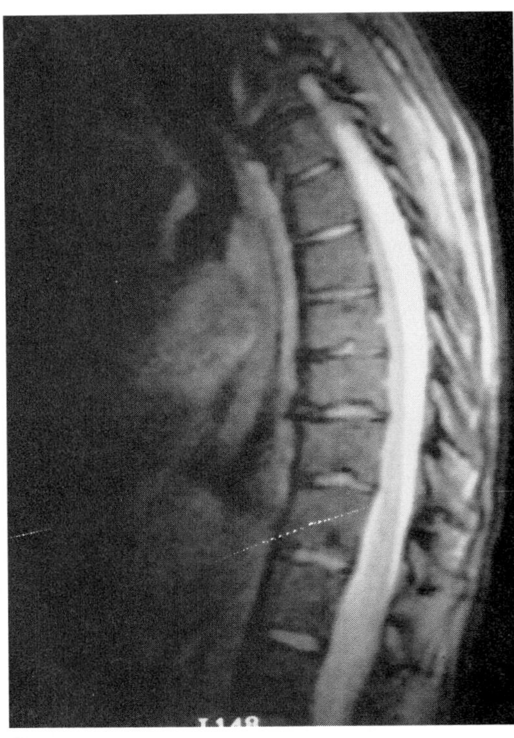

C

Figure 12–12. Plain films (**A** and **B**) and MRI (**C**) of two cases of classic Scheuermann's disease in a typical thoracic location, with characteristic hyperkyphosis secondary to multiple endplate irregularities and Schmorl's nodes associated with growth inhibition of the developing ring apophyses. Early, often advanced, degenerative disc disease is a common sequelae. Active exercise programs should generally limit flexion and encourage extension.

arthrosis at L4-5. Methods of assessing instability have already been described. It is recommended that patients with either lytic spondylolisthesis or L5 or degenerative spondylolisthesis of L4 being considered for active exercise programs undergo traction-compression or flexion-extension radiography in order to exclude patients with radiographically identifiable instability who are likely to respond unfavorably to the exercise. It should be recalled that negative findings on functional or traction-compression radiographs do not necessarily preclude a clinical diagnosis of instability, which may eliminate a patient from an exercise program despite the negative radiographs.

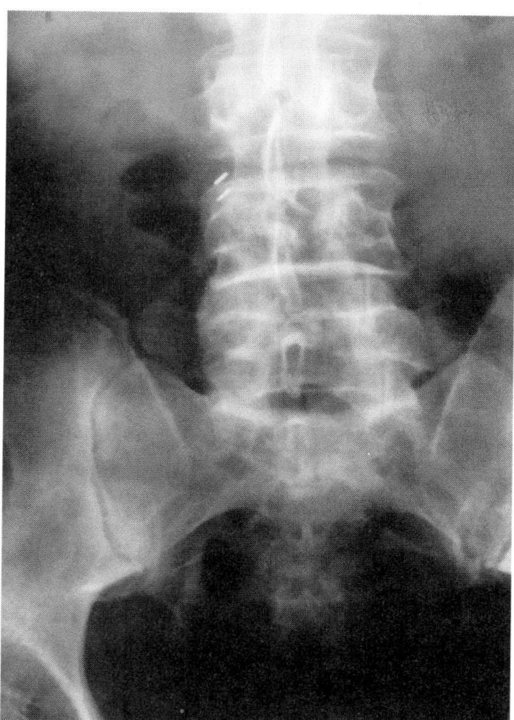

Figure 12–13. Apparent facet asymmetry ("tropism") on plain film may not be appreciated on CT. The converse may also be true. Plain films do not allow accurate and reliable estimation of facet joint planes, and the clinical relevance of tropism, even when proven via CT or MRI studies, is doubtful. In this case, rotation during positioning and facet arthrosis may contribute to the appearance of tropism. Tropism may generally be considered of no relevance in the formulation of active exercise programs.

SCOLIOSIS

There are no studies available to suggest that active exercise programs alter the natural history of idopathic scoliosis. On the other hand, there is certainly no evidence to indicate that patients with mild or even moderate scoliosis may not benefit from improved strength and function that may be attained through exercise, assuming significant congenital anomalies of the spine have been excluded. Some of these anomalies have been discussed previously. Plain films may be utilized to exclude these types of segmentation anomalies and spinal dysraphism. Functional radiographs may also be utilized to assess flexibility of curves, although their utility in the area of formulation of protocols for active exercise has not been explored.[99]

SPINAL ARTHRITIDES

There are a variety of spinal arthritides that must be considered in the development of protocols incorporating active exercise. Some of these involve active joint inflammation, which may be aggravated by movement. These same inflammatory arthritides, in a more advanced form, may sufficiently weaken or even rupture ligaments and tendons so as to make active exercise (and spinal manipulative therapy) dangerous and contraindicated. In other instances, bony ankylosis or heterotopic periarticular and intraspinal ossification may occur, which may, likewise, contraindicate various conservative therapeutic approaches.

It is widely recognized that rheumatoid arthritis may produce erosions of the odontoid process and transverse atlantoaxial ligament, leading to atlantoaxial subluxation and instability. This occurs in as many as 20-25% of advanced rheumatoid cases and obviously represents an absolute contraindication to manipulation of the upper cervical spine and to active exercise that may put the upper cervical cord at risk for compression.[5,6] As explained previously, atlantoaxial subluxation/instability may be identified with a flexion lateral radiograph of the cervical spine. Lateral, posterior, inferior or vertical subluxation ("cranial settling") are considerably less common, but must also be considered in long-standing rheumatoid arthritis of the cervical spine.[100,101] Subaxial involvement, predominantly of the synovial joints (facet articulations) may also occur and may produce subluxation and instability. This generally follows atlantoaxial involvement.[101–103]

Outside of the axial skeleton, rheumatoid arthritis affects synovial joints, especially small joints of the hands and feet. Bursae, bursal equivalents and tendon sheaths may also be affected, since synovial-type tissue is found at these sites. Enthesitis, or inflammation at ligament or tendon insertions on bone, is also common. Long-standing involvement of these structures may lead to tendon rupture and subsequent deformity, dysfunction, and instability, which may contraindicate active exercise. Although these peripheral tendon ruptures are typically best appreciated clinically, radiographs may demonstrate associated osseous erosions, along with joint destruction and deformity.[104–106] Prolonged corticosteroid use exacerbates the tendency toward tendon weakening and failure. This is a common clinical problem in patients with connective tissue disorders such as systemic lupus erthematosis (SLE)[107] (Figure 12–15).

The seronegative spondyloarthropathies (ankylosing spondylitis, enteropathic arthropathy, psoriatic arthritis, and Reiter's syndrome) may superficially resemble rheumatoid arthritis in peripheral joints and may produce similar bursal, tendinous and enthesopathic changes[108–113] (Figure 12–16). Of perhaps greater interest and clinical import is involvement of the axial skeleton, including sacroiliitis, discovertebral junction erosions, and syndesmophyte formation.[114–118] Ankylosis may result at the sacroiliac, intervertebral, and costotransverse joints. The latter may lead to diminished chest expansion, associated respiratory problems, and even chest pain that may mimic organic cardiopulmonary disease.[119]

The seronegative spondyloarthropathies have a broad spectrum of clinical and radiographic presentations, but obviously joint inflammation and loss of mobility due to ankylosis may exclude some of these patients from active

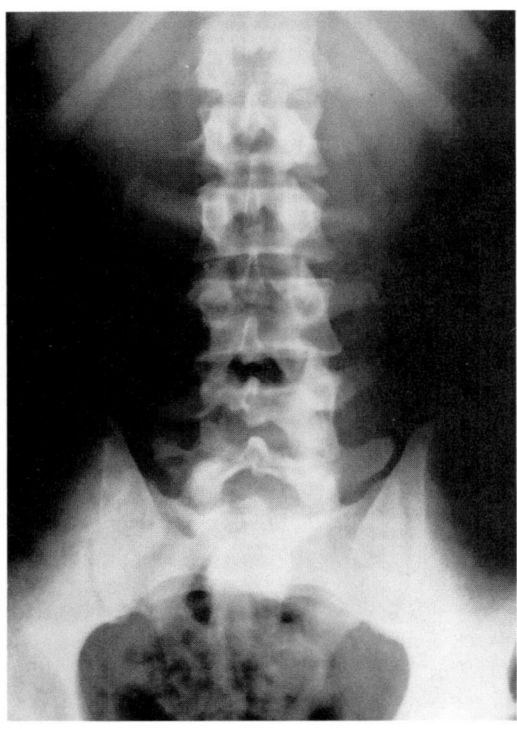

A

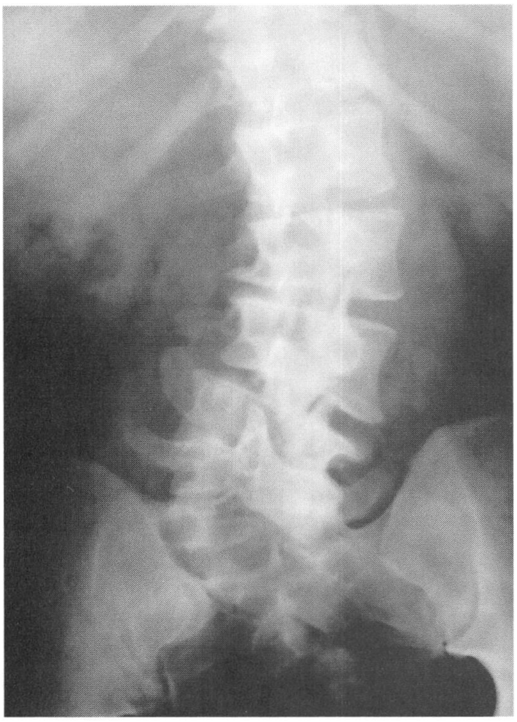

B

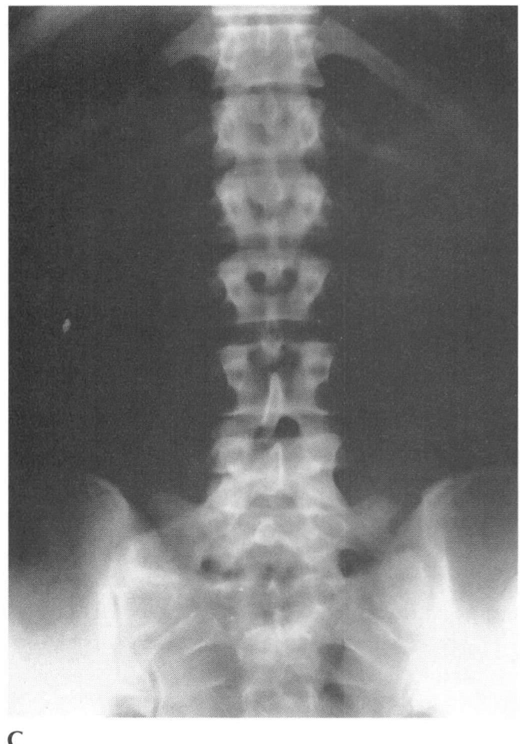

C

Figure 12–14. A. More significant facet anomaly on the right at L4-5, with agenesis of the right inferior articular process and marked dysplasia/hypoplasia of the right L4 pedicle. Although often described as pedicle "agenesis", true complete pedicle agenesis in the lumbar spine is very rare. Note sclerosis and hypertrophy of the left pedicle. Anomalies such as this may lead to altered biomechanics and instability, although documentation of this is scarce. **B.** Structural scoliosis due to lower lumbar segmentation anomalies, again with facet agenesis. **C.** Transitional lumbosacral segment (L5) with unilateral accessory articulation. There is an increased incidence of back pain and a particular increase in disc level (L4-5) with these types of asymmetric transitional segments. The same may not be true of other types of transitional segments.

exercise programs.[120] As in rheumatoid arthritis, spinal instability may occur, especially at the atlantoaxial joint. This is less common than in rheumatoid arthritis, but due to the potential for morbidity and mortality due to upper cervical cord or brainstem compression, this must be carefully screened for, using carefully obtained flexion lateral cervical x-rays.[121]

Another less common, but potentially serious complication of seronegative spondyloarthropathies, especially ankylosing spondylitis, is fracture of the ankylosed spine

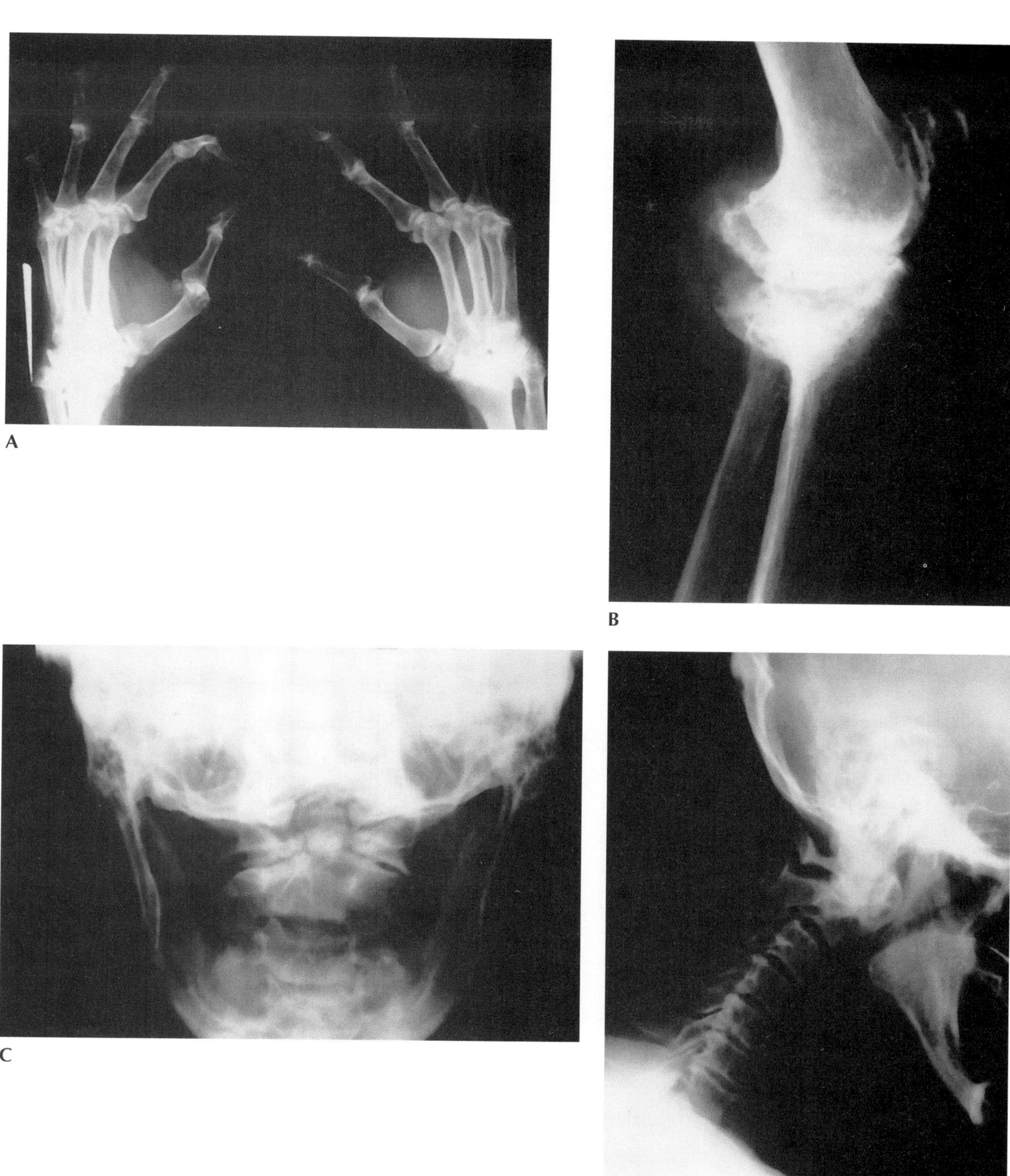

Figure 12–15. Inflammatory joint disease such as rheumatoid arthritis may produce both peripheral (**A** and **B**) and axial (**C** and **D**) subluxation as well as instability. This may exclude patients with these conditions from active exercise programs. Note the eroded dens on the APOM view and increased ADI indicating atlanto-axial subluxation/instability due to transverse ligament erosion.

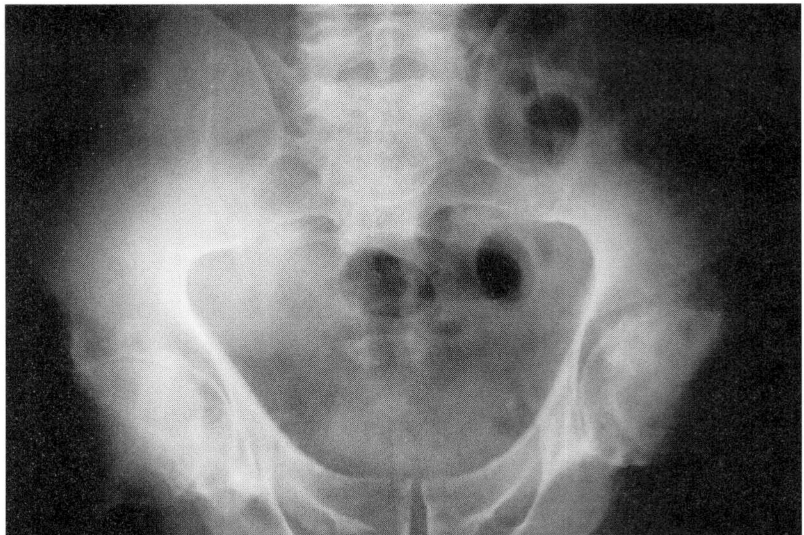

Figure 12–16. Advanced osteoarthritis of the hips. This degree of degenerative arthritis, especially in weight-bearing joints, may limit patients' ability to participate in active exercise programs.

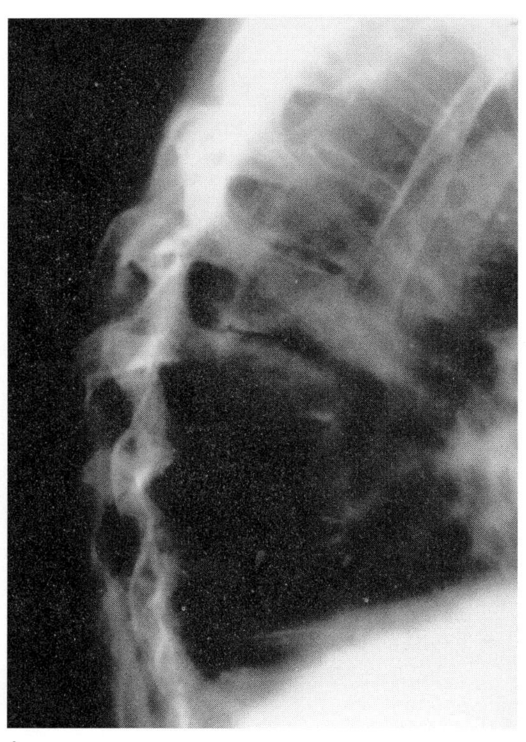

A

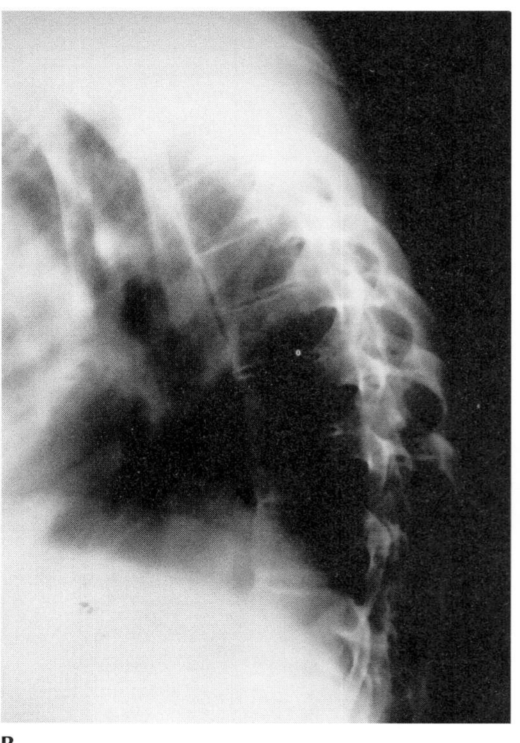

B

Figure 12–17. A. One of the most serious complications of ankylosing spondylitis is pathologic fracture through the ankylosed spine with development of a pseudoarthrosis (the "Andersson lesion"). This elderly male patient had fallen from a ladder 7 years earlier, and his Andersson lesion went undetected for an extended period of time, partially due to relative lack of symptoms and also to his aversion to doctors. Although he had no neurologic deficit, paresis, paralysis, or other deficits are commonly seen. **B.** 51-year old male with history of back stiffness, but no previous diagnosis of AS. There is a "carrot-stick" fracture through the T9 vertebral body, following a fall onto concrete at work.

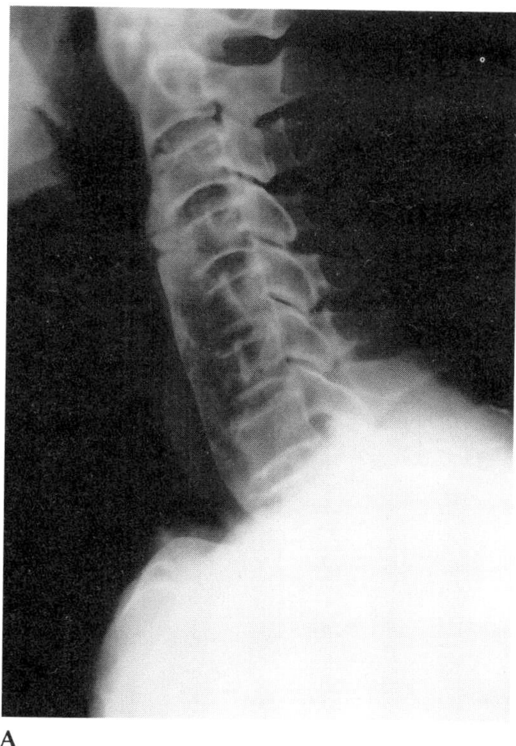

A

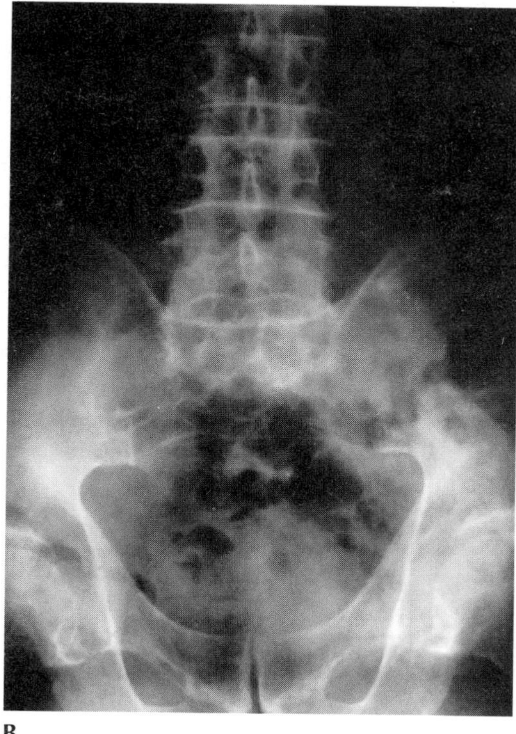

B

Figure 12–18. A. This 75-year old male has two end-stage spinal arthritides, with no less than four contraindications to active exercise programs. Diffuse idiopathic skeletal hyperostosis (DISH) has produced spinal ankylosis, as well as ossification of the posterior longitudinal ligament (OPLL). This is best visualized at C3-4. **B.** Ankylosing spondylitis (AS) has produced bony ankylosis of the sacroiliac joints, as well as erosion of the dens and slight atlanto-axial subluxation.

("carrot stick fracture") and formation of a pseudoarthrosis (the "Andersson lesion") (Figure 12–17). This may occur following normal activity or trivial trauma and may produce paresis, paralysis or even death.[122–126] Generalized connective tissue involvement may be seen in these conditions as well as in rheumatoid arthritis, typically in end-stage disease. This may lead to serious complications, such as aortitis, carditis and pericarditis, and pulmonary fibrosis.[127–129] Any of these would likely contraindicate active exercise programs.

While the most serious complications related to spinal arthritides are typically the result of inflammatory arthritis, there are several pathologies associated with degenerative arthritis that may also produce significant morbidity and possibly even mortality from the relatively minor traumas which may occur in active exercise programs. For example, it is widely recognized that posterior spondylophyte formation or uncovertebral arthrosis in the cervical spine may produce myelopathy and radiculopathy. Less widely recognized is potential compromise of the vertebral artery by large facet osteophytes projecting anteriorly to lie under the intertransverse foramina. With extension and rotation of the head and neck, the osteophytes may compress or injure the arteries as they pass through these foramina. This was alluded to earlier.

Another less commonly recognized abnormality associated with a degenerative arthritis is ossification of the posterior longitudinal ligament (OPLL). This is common in diffuse idiopathic skeletal hyperostosis (DISH), a bone-forming diathesis and degenerative enthesopathy typically beginning in late-middle age or older adulthood and leading to ankylosis or partial bridging of disc spaces in the spine. Patients with DISH should be carefully screened for OPLL, since it may produce serious myelopathy (Figure 12–18). This is a particular concern when the ossification is thicker than 7.0mm. The linear ossification paralleling the posterior vertebral body margins is present in approximately 50% of DISH patients and is most often visualized on the lateral cervical film. Unfortunately, the ossification is often too subtle to be detected on radiographs and may require a CT scan. On the other hand, in most cases in which there is a significant risk of myelopathy, the ossification will be thick enough to be seen on plain films. Interestingly, OPLL appears to be most common in people of Asian descent, in whom it was originally described and in whom it is typically present as an isolated abnormality, without associated DISH (Figure 12–19).

OSTEOPENIC AND OSTEOMALACIC CONDITIONS

Plain film radiographs are not generally considered to be useful in identifying early osteopenia ("bone poverty"), the radiographic description of osteoporosis. They are also generally no longer used in quantifying osteoporosis or in monitoring the effects of treatment. However, radiographs may be useful in excluding more moderate to severe osteoporosis, associated with a significant risk of morbidity due to pathologic fractures, either acute or insufficiency-type fractures. Patients with radiographically apparent osteopenia, particularly those with several risk factors for osteoporosis, may require more sophisticated bone mineral analysis prior to incorporation of an active exercise program. This is necessary to prevent the often debilitating or even life-threatening complications of osteoporotic fractures, especially of the proximal femur. Quantitative bone mineral analysis may be achieved in a variety of ways. Appendicular bone density measurements achieved through radiogrammetry, photodensitometry, or single-photon absorptiometry are typically not precise and accurate enough to be useful in predicting axial skeletal density. Dual photon absorptiometry (DPA), quantitative computed topography (QCT), and, more recently, dual energy x-ray absorptiometry (DEXA), have generally been favored for assessing axial bone density, for estimating fracture risk, and for assessing effects of treatment. These same techniques may be used in assessing osteoporosis or osteomalacia related to other conditions as well.[130,131]

In addition to the ubiquitous post-menopausal osteoporosis, other causes of osteopenia must be excluded in the clinical work-up of a patient being considered for an active exercise program. Some of these are listed in Table 12–3. This is not intended to be an exhaustive list, but should assist the clinician in considering the wide variety of conditions which may produce osteoporosis.

Not only are "brittle bones" a clinical concern, but conditions associated with bone softening must also be excluded. These include primary osteomalacia and osteomalacia secondary to hyperparathyroidism, which may, likewise, be primary (generally due to an active parathyroid tumor) or secondary (most often secondary to chronic renal failure) (Figure 12–20). Paget's disease is another condition associated with osteomalacia and is probably much more common than these other conditions in an otherwise relatively healthy, ambulatory patient. Paget's disease is characterized radiographically by initial marked osteoclastic activity which may produce geographic zones of osteopenia. This is gradually balanced by and sometimes dominated by reactive osteoblastic activity. This leads to a characteristic radiographic progression of Paget's disease from an initially predominantly lytic stage to a stage of mixed osteopenia and sclerosis and finally, a predominantly sclerotic stage. Along with the bone density changes, the trabeculae appear thickened and coarsened, which is associated with thickening of the cortex and generalized expansion of the affected bone. Pagetic bone is composed of a high percentage of poorly mineralized osteoid, similar to that seen in classic osteomalacia. For this reason, Pagetic bone is prone to fractures, insufficiency fractures and pseudofractures similar to those seen in osteomalacia. Paget's disease may also be associated with spinal canal stenosis due to expansion and thickening of bone in the posterior arch and, rarely, may degenerate into a malignancy such as osteosarcoma.[130,132–134] These factors must be considered in formulating protocols for active exercise programs (Figures 12–20 to 12–23).

Table 12–3: Causes of Generalized Osteoporosis

I. Blood-Related
- A. Hemolytic Anemia

II. Congenital
- A. Neuromuscular Disorders
- B. Osteogenesis Imperfecta
- C. Turner's Syndrome
- D. Other

III. Drug-Related
- A. Alcohol
- B. Corticosteroids
- C. Heparin

IV. Endocrine
- A. Acromegaly
- B. Addison's Disease
- C. Cushing's Syndrome
- D. Diabetes Mellitus
- E. Hyperthyroidism
- F. Hypogonadism
- G. Post-menopausal or Post-hysterectomy

V. Idiopathic

VI. Nutritional
- A. Malabsorption Syndromes
- B. Malnutrition
- C. Scurvy

VII. Tumor-Related
- A. Multiple Myeloma
- B. Metastasis

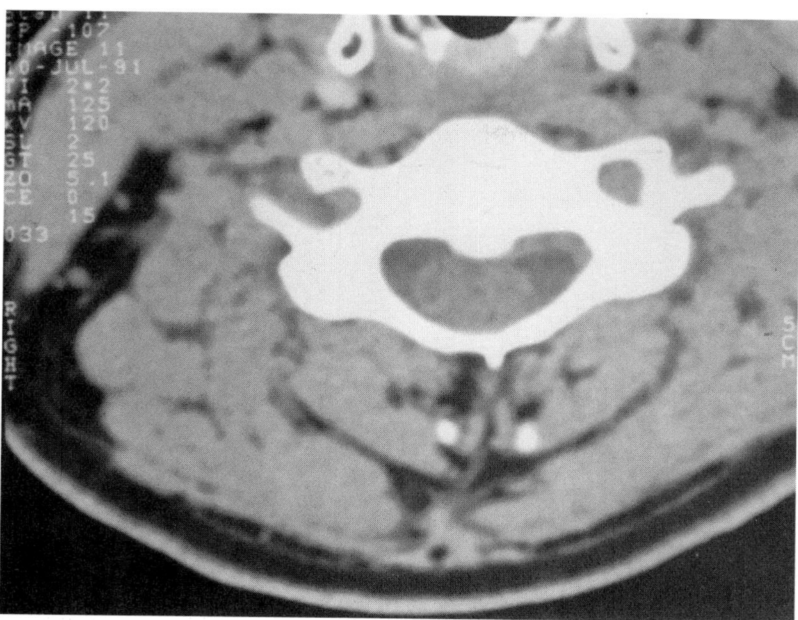

Figure 12–19. Isolated OPLL in a 37-year old Japanese American with neck pain following recent trauma. Note effacement of the cord anteriorly.

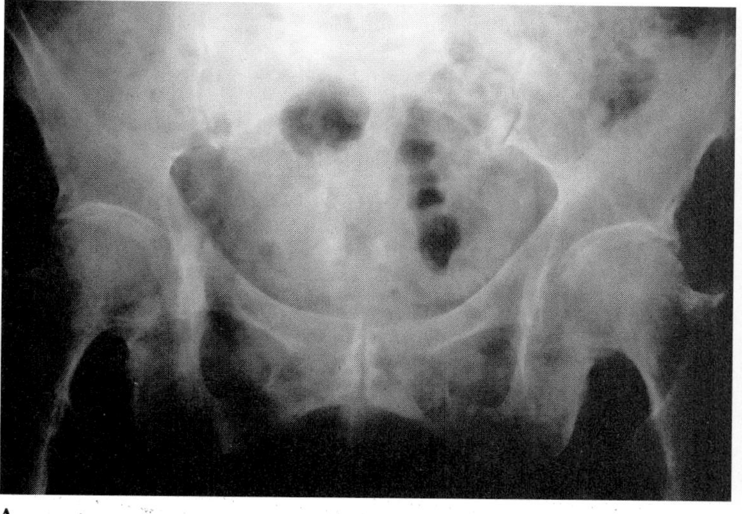

A

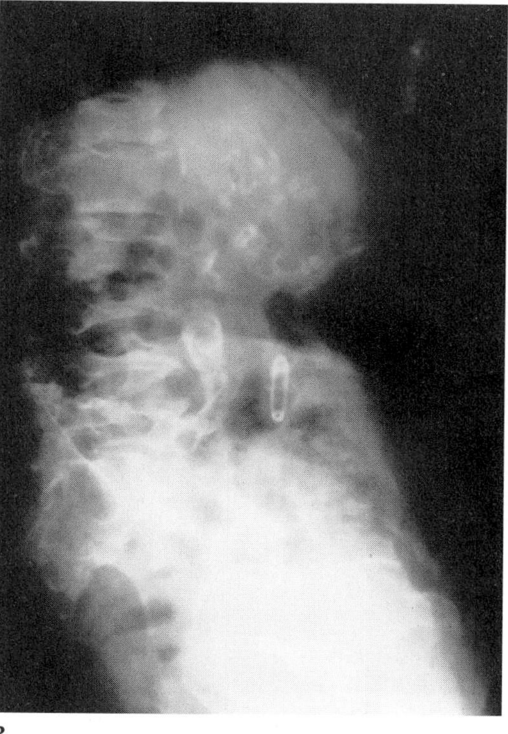

B

Figure 12–20. A. Elderly patient with osteomalacia and osteoporosis due to chronic renal failure and post-menopausal osteoporosis. Note insufficiency fractures of the left superior pubic ramus and ischiopubic junction. **B.** Severe post-menopausal osteoporosis with "vertebra plana" and "balloon discs". Patients with this degree of osteoporosis are at risk for fracture with even minimal activity and are obviously excluded from active exercise programs. Unfortunately, plain films are very poor for quantifying lesser degrees of osteopenia which may still be clinically relevant and a potential cause of morbidity related to active exercise.

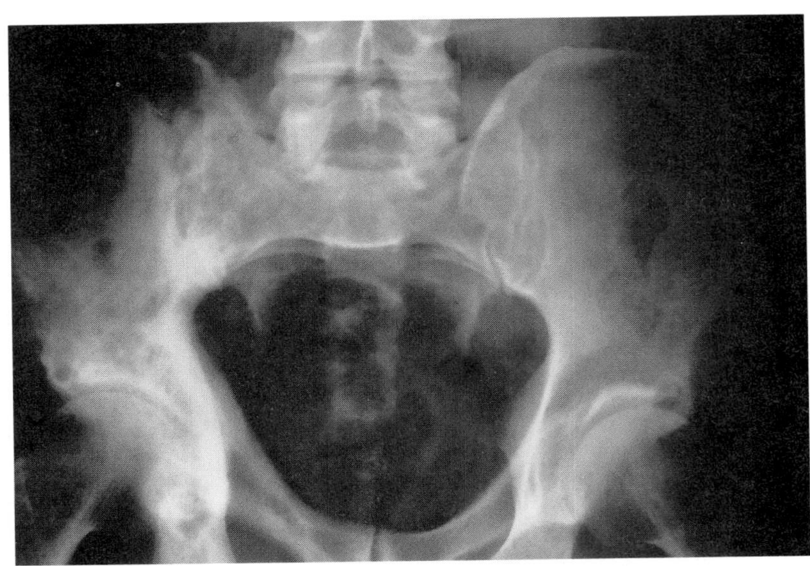

Figure 12–21. Endstage ("sclerotic") Paget's disease of bone in one of the most common patterns, involving an entire hemipelvis. Although Pagetic bone may appear dense and strong, it is osteomalacic and may be associated with pathologic fracture, insufficiency fracture, and pseudofracture. Active exercise protocols should be cautiously administered in the presence of this and other osteomalacic conditions and will vary with the degree of osteomalacia. Note advanced osteoarthritis of the left sacroiliac joint and earlier Pagetic change in the proximal femora.

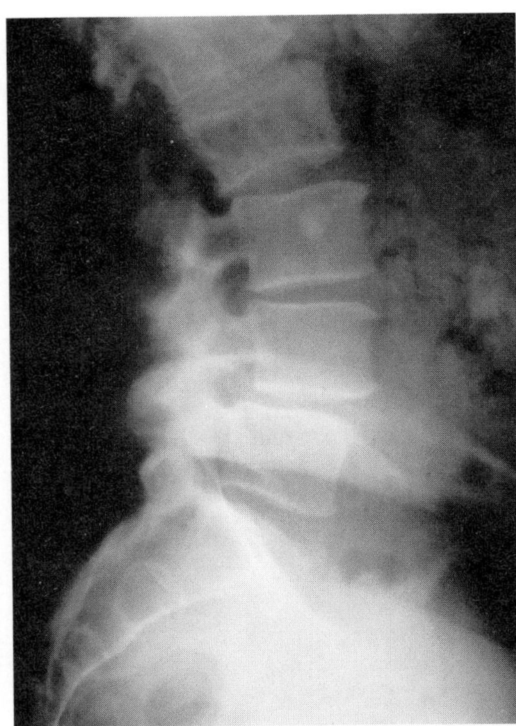

Figure 12–22. Elderly male with end-stage Paget's disease of L2, apparent osteoblastic focus of L3 and degenerative spondylolisthesis of L4, due to severe facet arthrosis. Note expansion of L2 and extension of Pagetic involvement into the posterior arch, which may lead to spinal stenosis and contraindicate active exercise programs. The L3 lesion was unchanged when compared to previous films from several years ago and was thus considered to represent a bone island.

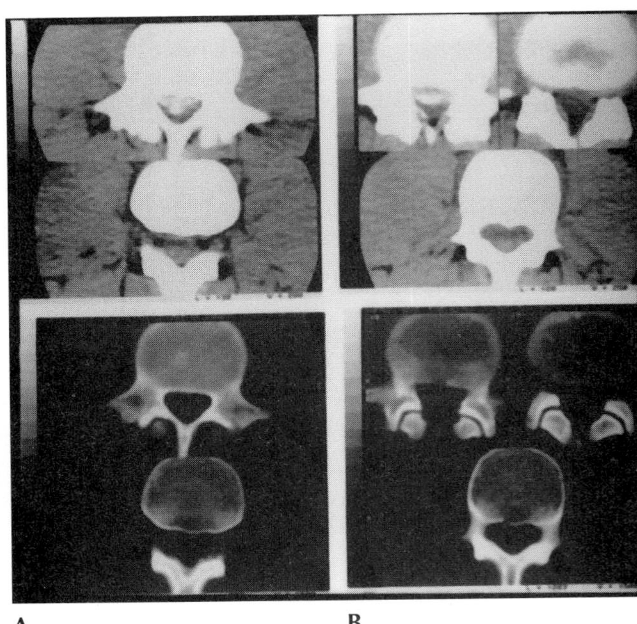

A **B**

Figure 12–23. CT scans of two young adult male patients active as power-lifters. **A.** Huge calcified central L5-S1 disc herniation and severe lateral recess stenosis. **B.** Large L4-5 disc herniation and posterior limbus bone (vertebral body edge separation or "slipped apophysis"), resulting in central and left lateral recess stenosis. Both patients had severe low back pain and varying radicular symptoms, but were managed conservatively with chiropractic. Surgery was averted and, in fact, both were able to return to their sport of power-lifting. These cases illustrate that findings on diagnostic imaging alone should not be used as exclusion criteria for active exercise programs.

SUMMARY

Prior to implementation of an active exercise program, a variety of questions must be answered relative to the patient's ability to tolerate specific stresses and regarding the likelihood of the patient deriving benefit from the exercise program. A variety of congenital/developmental, arthritic and traumatic conditions that may exclude patients from certain active exercise programs have been covered. This has not been an exhaustive discussion but has touched upon conditions most likely to be encountered in an ambulatory care setting. A summary checklist (Table 12–4) is provided for the physician or therapist as a guide in the process of ruling out those conditions which may contraindicate or necessitate modification of active exercise programs. This checklist is not exhaustive and includes some conditions not discussed in detail here. Its greatest value will likely be in prompting the clinician to consider categories of conditions rather than specific disease entities. Also, as several of the last cases illustrate, decisions regarding inclusion in or exclusion from active exercise programs must be primarily guided by clinical findings, especially where the correlation between imaging findings and clinical findings has not been well established.

Table 12–4: A Checklist of Radiographic Findings/Conditions That May Contraindicate Active Exercise Programs

I. Congenital/Developmental
- A. Segmentation Anomalies
- B. Transitional Segments
- C. Structural Scoliosis

II. Arthritides
- A. Degenerative (Includes DISH)
- B. Inflammatory (Esp, RA)
- C. Seronegative Spondyloarthropathies

III. Trauma
- A. Recent Fracture, Dislocation, or Severe Subluxation
- B. Spinal Instability

IV. Blood-Related Disorders
- A. Hemophilia
- B. Hemolytic Anemia

V. Infections

VI. Tumors
- A. Benign
- B. Malignant
- C. Tumor-like

VII. Endocrine-Metabolic
- A. Osteoporosis
- B. Rickets/Osteomalacia
- C. Paget's Disease

VIII. Soft-Tissue Abnormalities

RADIOLOGIC MEASUREMENT CONSIDERATIONS IN REHABILITATION

Tradition and common practice have provided at least anecdotal evidence that in the process of formulating a plan for rehabilitation of the spine and pelvis, there may be some value in considering certain lines and angles drawn on plain film radiographs. There have been studies testing the reliability or the ability to reproduce with consistency some of these measurements, by either the same observer repeating a given assessment (intra-examiner reliability) or by two or more observers making the same assessment (inter-examiner reliability). In general, these studies have shown reasonable reliability for at least the limited number of measurements that have been scrutinized. Unfortunately, there have been few studies attempting to determine the validity or clinical relevance of these measurements and such factors as to their predictive value or influence on clinical outcomes. While this is admittedly a substantial shortcoming of the use of roentgenometrics, a similar criticism may be made, to some extent, of most other assessment tools in clinical practice.

What the clinician is left with, unfortunately, is a rather confusing array of reports of the use of some measurements to direct clinical managment, the value of making and monitoring such measurements to determine clinical success, and the somewhat more completely studied use of certain of these measurements as contraindications for certain forms of therapy. It would be unwieldy to attempt a broad consideration of this topic area, but because of common practice alone, it would be negligent to completely disregard it. And in those areas, such as the assessment of central spinal canal stenosis, in which radiographic measurements have been more thoroughly studied, one would clearly be remiss in ignoring what is known. Therefore, the last part of this chapter will focus on some of the lines and measurements that hold at least some promise of utility in the area of assessment of patients for a rehabilitation program.

THE CRANIOVERTEBRAL JUNCTION AND UPPER CERVICAL COMPLEX

McGregor's Line

This line, drawn on a lateral skull film or lateral cervical neural (LCN) view, extends from the most inferior extent of the occiput to the hard palate, requiring a reasonably true lateral view without obliquity of the head. The odontoid process typically lies at or just below this line and not greater than 8-10 millimeters above this line, with the greater measurement used as a reference for females. An abnormal relationship may indicate basilar impression (basilar invagination), which may either be congenital, as in conjunction with assimilation (occipitalization) of C1 or acquired, due to some bone softening condition of the skull base. The latter includes osteomalacia, Paget's disease, or inflammatory arthritis affecting the upper cervical complex. This osseous abnormality of the skull base may exclude patients from certain types of rehabilitation placing stress on the craniovertebral junction, due to the risk of upper cervical cord, brainstem, or cerebellar compression, although this has not been thoroughly researched. Magnetic resonance imaging may be indicated to directly visualize associated soft tissue abnormality, especially in patients with plain film evidence of bony anomaly who may be experiencing intractable suboccipital headaches or other signs or symptoms of dural or neural compression or traction at the craniovertebral junction. A type I Chiari malformation, in which the cerebellar tonsils lie below the foramen magnum, may also be present and contribute to compressive myelopathy at the craniovertebral junction. This is also readily assessed with MRI[135,136] (Figure 12–24).

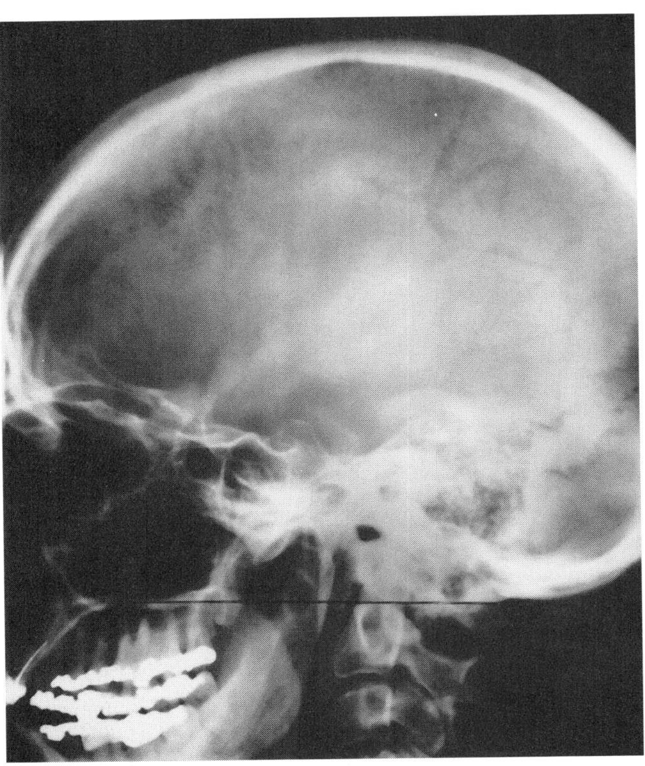

Figure 12–24. Abnormal relationship of the craniovertebral junction assessed via McGregor's line. This middle-aged female with headache and "giddiness" has an abbreviated form of assimilation of C1 to occiput ("occipitalization"), with associated congenital basilar impression. Note the tip of the dens lying more than one centimeter above McGregor's line.

Anterior Atlantodental Interspace (ADI)

Most clinicians familiar with the spine are familiar with this measurement and the upper limits of normal, typically listed as 3.0 millimeters for adults and 5.0 millimeters for children. Some sources allow 0.5 millimeters more for these measurements. Of perhaps the greatest importance is recalling in which situations the ADI is likely to be increased, indicating atlanto-axial subluxation/instability. Sometimes, the ADI may be normal on a neutral lateral view, and abnormality is discovered only on a flexion lateral view ordered by the astute clinician who recognizes the potential for an increased ADI related to some underlying condition. These conditions were discussed earlier and include congenital anomalies and inflammatory arthritides. The biomechanically vulnerable dens tends to fracture before the relatively strong transverse ligament ruptures from hyperflexion trauma, but trauma is still considered a potential cause of atlanto-axial instability (Figure 12–25).

As noted earlier, caution should be exercised in measuring the ADI at the midpoint or, more ideally, the inferior aspect, since a "V"-shaped ADI may be mistaken for an increased ADI, especially when the ADI is measured at its superior margin (Figure 12–26).

It should be emphasized that a flexion lateral view should be considered only as a screen for atlanto-axial subluxation/instability and is by no means 100% sensitive. It is likely to identify most cases of atlanto-axial subluxation/instability, which would presumably contraindicate rehabilitative procedures involving flexion stresses on the upper cervical complex.[7,137,138]

THE CERVICAL SPINE

Spinolaminar Junction Line

On a lateral film of the cervical spine, a distinct opaque vertical line is seen at the junction of the laminae and the base of the spinous process at each level from at least C2 through C7. This will sometimes be visible in the upper thoracic segments as well. This same "spinolaminar junction line" is present at C1 at the junction of the two halves of the posterior arch and the posterior tubercle, although technically there is no true spinous process at this level. Semantics aside, the spinolaminar junction line is a helpful means of assessing for anterolisthesis or retrolisthesis from C2 caudally, while at C1 it provides a second means of assessing for anterior atlanto-axial subluxation/instability or of demonstrating a

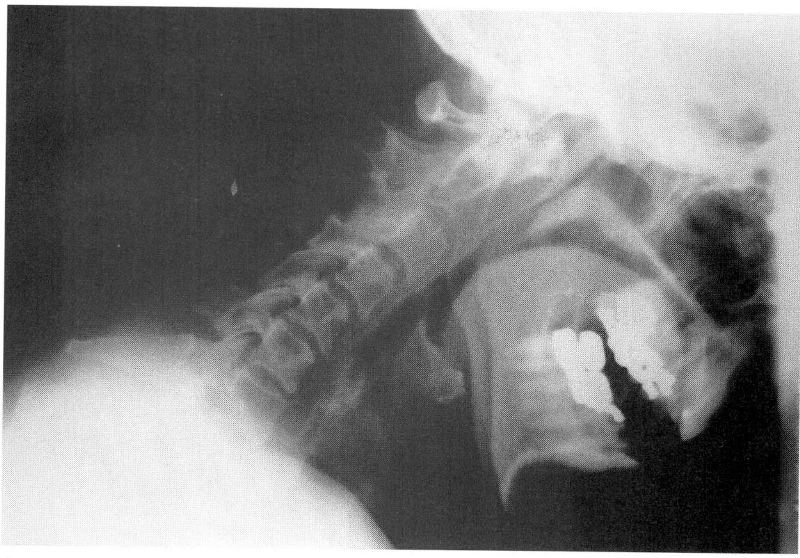

A

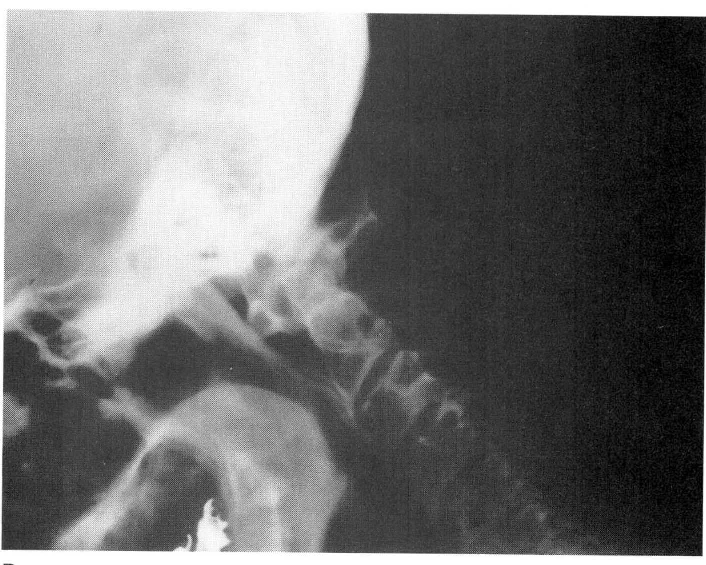

B

Figure 12–25. Increased atlanto-dental interspace (ADI) due to **(A)** trauma and **(B)** rheumatoid arthritis, resulting in laxity of the transverse portion of the cruciate ligament at C1-2.

posteriorly displaced or angulated dens fracture. Normally, the spinolaminar junction lines form a smooth contiguous arc from C1 through C7 and disruption of this arc indicates abnormality. In some instances, the spinolaminar junction line of C1 may lie anterior to that of C2, due to a developmentally slightly short posterior arch of C1. While this is typically asymptomatic and of doubtful clinical relevance, it may be mistaken for anterior atlanto-axial subluxation/instability. There is some question as to whether the corresponding slightly smaller central spinal canal dimension at C1-2 may make the upper cervical cord more vulnerable to compression in the presence of other factors that may produce atlanto-axial subluxation/instability, such as trauma, inflammatory arthritis, or Down's syndrome.

Minimally, caution and careful patient monitoring are recommended when there is a developmentally short posterior arch of C1 and, depending on the degree, this finding may preclude certain forms of rehabilitation. It should also be noted that there is a normal variant in children and some young adults in which the C2 spinolaminar junction line may lie 1-2 millimeters posterior to those of C1 and C3. This could also be mistaken for upper cervical malalignment[65] (Figure 12–27).

George's Line (Posterior Body Line)

George's line was originally described as a smooth, unbroken line drawn along the posterior vertebral body margins and used to assess for anterolisthesis or retrolisthesis from C2 caudally. Obviously, this line cannot be used at C1 since it has no body. Many today improperly draw a discontinuous line, interrupted at each cervical level, which exaggerates the appearance of slight offset of the vertebral margins at consecutive levels. Another common mistake involves attributing slight offset of the vertebral body mar-

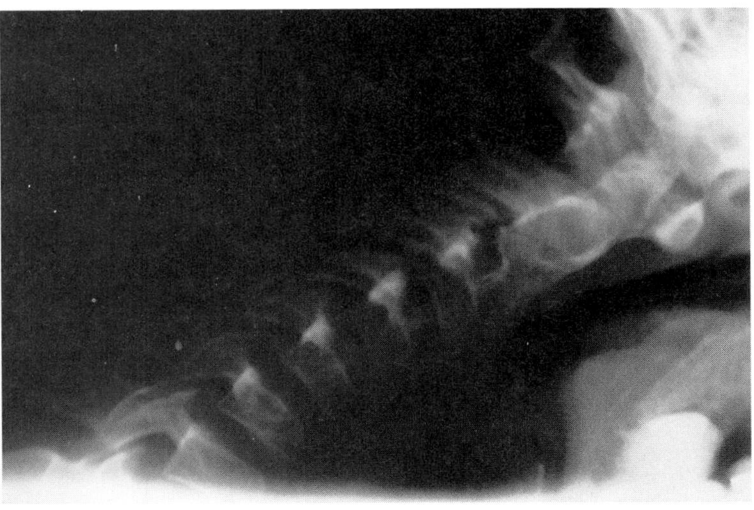

A

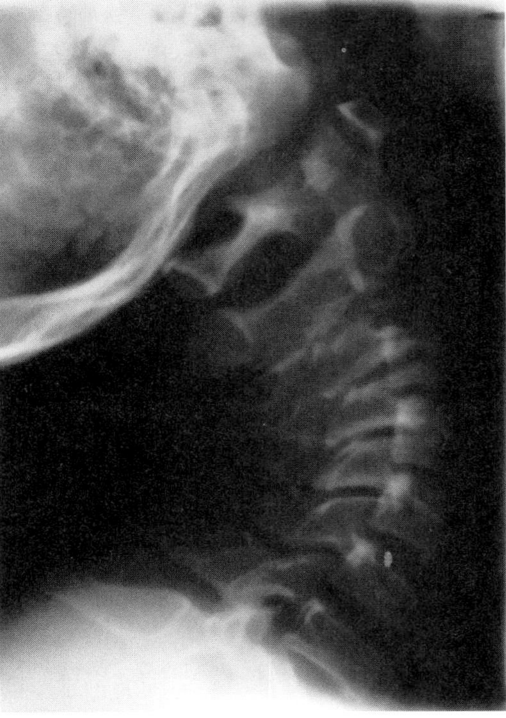

B

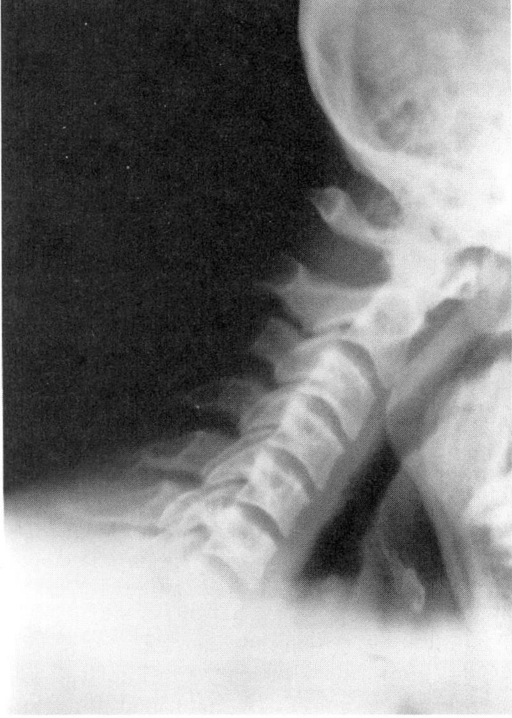

C

Figure 12–26. Physiologic "V′-shaped atlantodental interspace (ADI) in normal adolescent. **(A).** The ADI still measures within normal limits at its inferior margin. Note also the normal amount of physiologic anteroposterior translation between full flexion and **(B)** full extension. This is most prominent in children and young adults and is frequently mistaken for instability. This should not contraindicate spinal manipulation or active rehabilitation. A similar "V′-shaped ADI is seen in an adult **(C).**

gins to antero- or retrolisthesis, when the apparent slight offset is actually related to projectional phenomenon and obliquity of the cervical spine relative to the x-ray beam on the lateral cervical radiograph. In addition to true antero- or retrolisthesis, other causes of a true alteration of George's line include bursting type fractures of the vertebral body, disrupting the posterior vertebral body margin, posterior spondylophytes, and posterior uncinate osteophytes. A true disruption of George's line may, again, represent a contraindication to some rehabilitative procedures, although this has not been well studied[139] (Figure 12–28).

Central Spinal Canal Dimension

Below C1-2, the central spinal canal dimension is readily measured from the two distinct landmarks just mentioned, the spinolaminar junction line and the posterior vertebral body margin. Although more accurate measurement of both the sagittal and coronal central canal dimensions may be made on axial images from an advanced diagnostic imaging study (MRI or CT scan), this plain film assessment represents a reasonable screening measurement of the sagittal central spinal canal dimension. Normal and stenotic measurements have already been discussed. Because of considerable variation in the overall size of vertebral structures

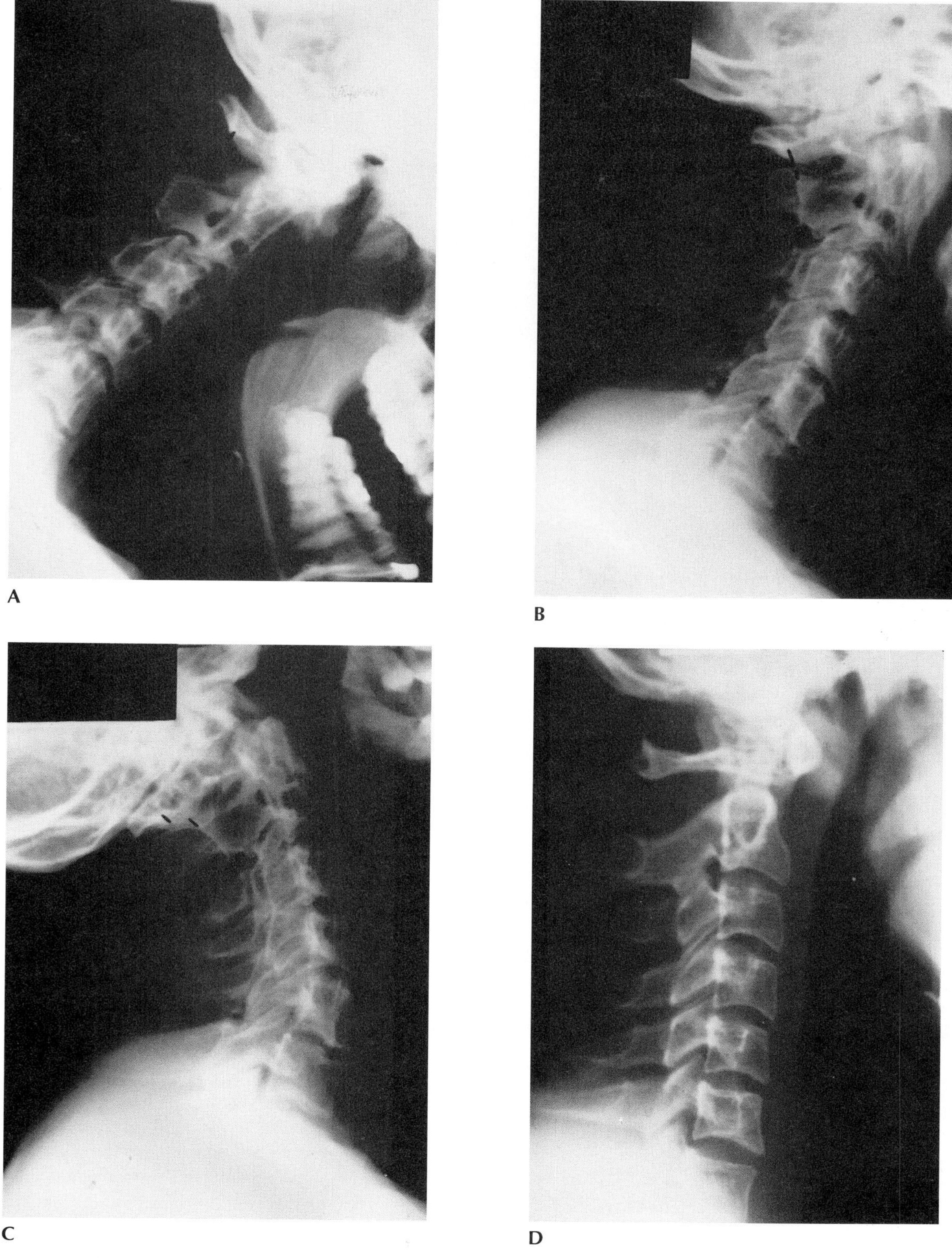

Figure 12–27. The spinolaminar junction line may be very helpful when the atlantodental interspace is not well visualized or when there is congenital anomaly or fracture of the dens. An os odontoideum above a congenital non-segmentation of C2-3 **(A-C)** and a very subtle dens fracture with slight anterior angulation **(D)** are associated with offset of the spinolaminar junction line of C1 relative to C2. The os odontoideum is radiographically unstable and the type II dens fracture, missed on emergency room radiographs is also presumably unstable, even without functional radiographs. Note the precervical soft tissue swelling at C1-2, another subtle sign of fracture.

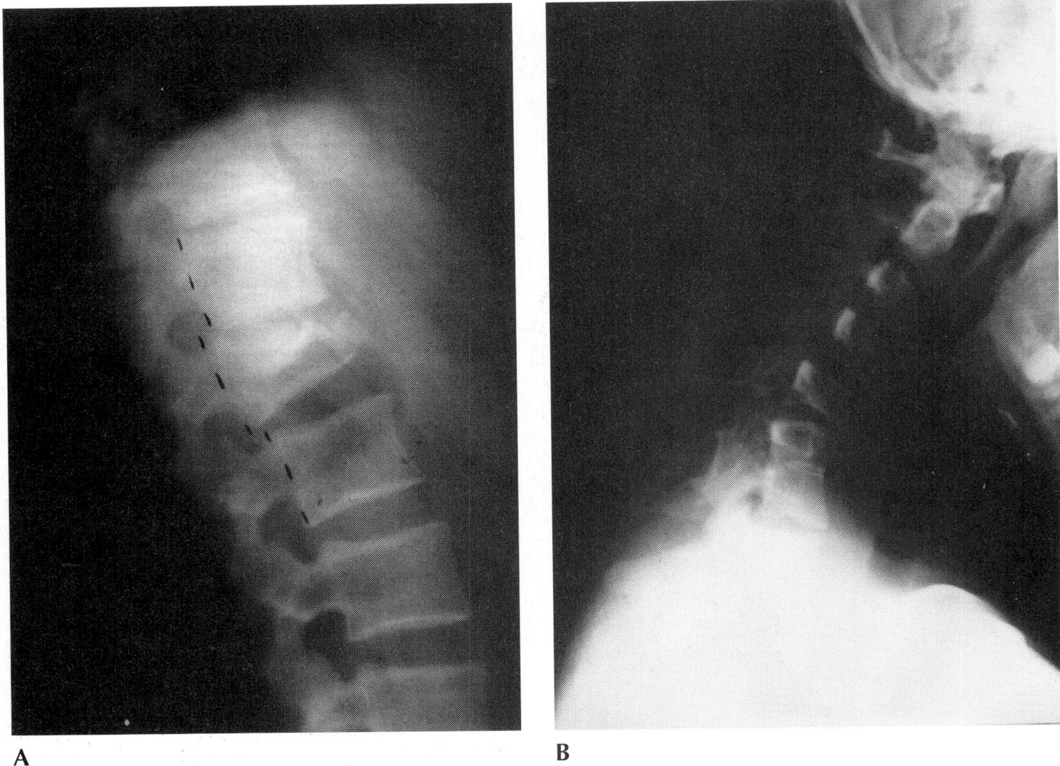

Figure 12–28. Note alterations of George's line due to trauma in an unstable burst fracture **(A)** and instability above a congenital non-segmentation **(B).**

with differing body habitus, it may be more favorable to assess the ratio of the sagittal canal dimension to the anteroposterior dimension of the adjacent vertebral body. This ratio should be greater than 80% (actually originally described as 0.82).

There may be some problems in applying this ratio in some individuals, such as large athletes with unusually large vertebral body mass. A ratio below the lower limits of normal may warrant follow-up advanced imaging, especially in patients with signs or symptoms of myelopathy or neuropathy secondary to spinal stenosis. MRI and CT are more sensitive and would allow direct visualization of neural structures, not visible on plain films. At C1-2, the sagittal central canal dimension may be measured from the posterior margin of the dens to the "spinolaminar junction line" of C2 and is typically about 20-22 millimeters. A measurement of less than 16-18 millimeters suggests stenosis, but again, follow-up with advanced imaging is typically indicated as a more accurate assessment for those patients who have a borderline or narrowed canal dimension on plain films. Patients with borderline or stenotic central canals may not be candidates for certain types of rehabilitation protocols that may increase the likelihood of cord compression, though this has not been well studied. It is known that the detrimental effects of trauma tend to be greater in patients with stenotic central canals than in those with average or larger than average canal dimensions, other factors being equal.[140,141]

Other Cervical Measurements, Lines and Angles

The extent to which alterations in other commonly assessed measurements, lines and angles may influence the application of rehabilitation protocols is not adequately studied. It would be purely speculative to ascribe significance to these assessments or to discount them as having relevance without information that is currently unavailable. The significance of alterations of such commonly assessed plain film findings such as the cervical lordosis, the cervical gravity line, and "lines of stress" drawn on cervical flexion and extension radiographs remains unknown. Likewise, the extent to which rehabilitative procedures may predictably alter such measurements has not been determined. The same is true in the lumbar spine for commonly made measurements, such as the lumbar lordosis, the sacral base angle, and the lumbosacral disc angle. So, while we may speculate that an anterior carriage of the head, as indicated by an anterior shift in the "cervical gravity line," or an anterior shift in weightbearing in the lumbar spine, as indicated by anterior shift in "Ferguson's gravity line," may place increased shearing stresses on the lower cervical and lower lumbar intervertebral discs, we have no data to support this. It would seem to be more appropriate to exclude patients from rehabilitative programs based upon a lack of response or adverse response to the program than to exclude patients from the program altogether based upon speculation regarding the potential clinical relevance of untested plain film assessments. This is assuming that there is a reasonable process of patient education and early careful monitoring of the patient's response to the program, with appropriate modification, as needed.

THE LUMBAR SPINE

Spondylolisthesis

Most clinicians familiar with the low back are familiar with the common methods of assessment of spondylolisthesis. Myerding's classification system divides the sacrum into four quadrants and grades the degree of anterolisthesis from 1 to 4 based upon which quadrant the posteroinferior margin of L5 lies within. Grade 5 is given when the L5 body has "slipped" entirely off the sacral base anteriorly, described as "spondyloptosis." This is infrequent. In fact, most spondylolistheses will not exceed grade 1 to 2. At other spinal levels, including the cervical or, rarely, the thoracic spine, the more inferior, normally positioned vertebra is used in place of the sacrum as the normal reference point and its superior endplate divided into four quadrants, in the same way as the sacrum was for L5. The same grading system is then used.

Most cases of spondylolytic spondylolisthesis (due to pars defects) will do most of their "slipping" within the first 18-24 months of the development of the spondylolysis. Rarely, there will be progressive slip later in adult life, most often involving the higher grade (3-5) spondylolistheses. Even these are most often remarkably stable over time. In cases in which clinical findings and/or serial radiographs suggest progressive and, by inference unstable, spondylolisthesis, functional (stress) radiographs may be used to document the degree of instability. A documented unstable spondylolisthesis may contraindicate some forms of rehabilitation stressing the lumbosacral junction and, if substantial, may necessitate a neurosurgical consultation. Formerly, flexion-extension lateral radiographs of the lumbar spine were primarily used to assess for unstable spondylolisthesis, but more recently, it has been suggested that traction-compression radiographs are more sensitive than flexion-extension views to demonstrate instability. This involves taking one lateral view with the patient hanging from a bar suspended over the grid cabinet, containing the x-ray cassette and film and a second view with the patient standing and carrying a heavy "rucksack" over the shoulders to provide compression. Assessment for instability in other forms of spondylolisthesis, such as degenerative spondylolisthesis of L4, may be achieved in the same way[30,142] (Figure 12–29).

Central Spinal Canal Dimension

Because the spinolaminar junction line is not visualized in the lumbar spine as in the cervical spine, assessment of the sagittal central spinal canal dimension in the lumbar spine on a lateral plain film radiograph entails artificially constructing a spinolaminar junction line through the use of "Eisenstein's method." Eisenstein used a line drawn between the tips of the superior and inferior articular processes for this purpose, with a horizontal line extended from there to the posterior vertebral body margin at the level of the pedicles to measure the sagittal canal (Figure 12–30).

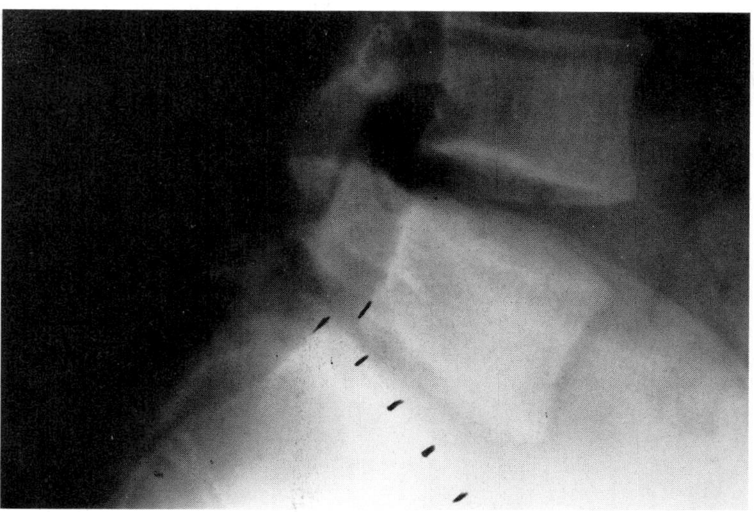

A

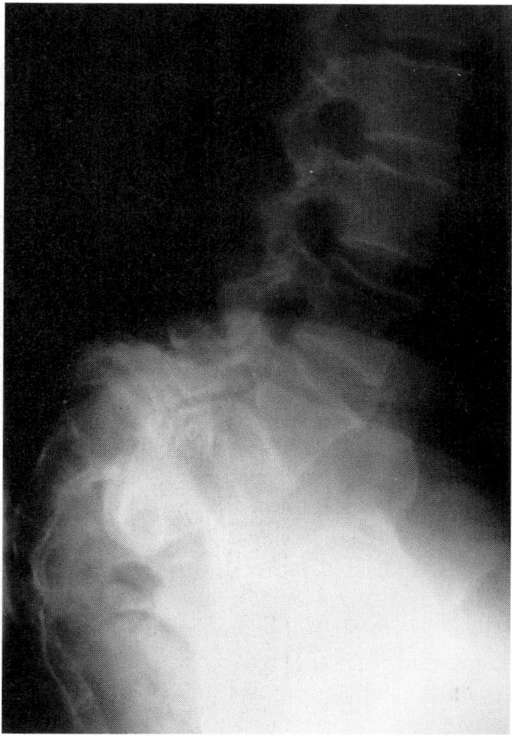

B

Figure 12–29. Grade 1 **(A)** and Grade 5 **(B)** spondylolisthesis. Note buttressing at the anterior lumbosacral disc margin with huge bridging spondylophyte in the grade 5 spondylolisthesis (spondyloptosis). L5 actually lies anterior to the S1 segment and has undergone autoankylosis. Remarkably, this may now be stable.

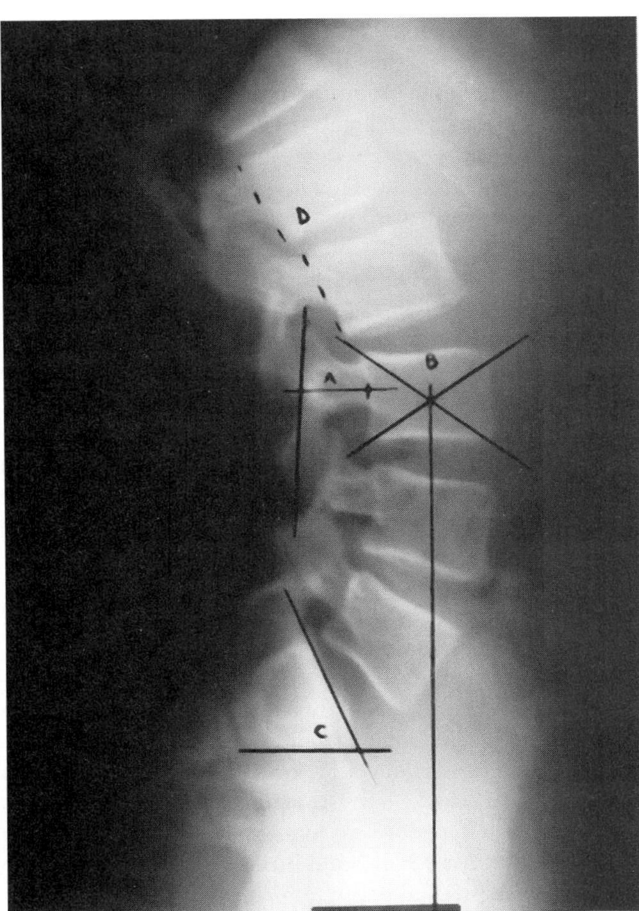

Figure 12–30. Eisenstein's method, demonstrating a normal sagittal central spinal canal dimension of 19 mm (A). Ferguson's gravity line, indicating slight anterior shift in weightbearing (B). Increased sacral base angle. The clinical relevance of this and the anterior shift in weightbearing, in the context of spinal rehabilitation is unknown (C). Slight alteration of George's line (D).

This has been found to correlate quite closely with the more precise measurement made on cross-sectional imaging. The coronal central canal dimension is readily measured directly on an A-P radiograph of the lumbar spine by measuring the interpediculate distance. Congenital coronal stenosis is not common, classically seen in achondroplasia. A rough screen for coronal stenosis involves observing a decrease in the interpediculate distance as one progresses in a cephalocaudal direction from L1 to L5. In normal individuals, this interpediculate distance increases in a cephalocaudal direction.[143]

As indicated earlier in the chapter, the anatomic sagittal central spinal canal dimension should typically be no less than 15mm. In the presence of posterior spondylophyte formation, measurement at the level of the disc, rather than the pedicles, to take into consideration the spondylophytes may be assumed to better assess for degenerative central canal stenosis. However, it cannot be detemined whether apparent posterior spondylophytes are central or posterolateral on the basis of plain films. This is significant, since posterolateral spondylophytes may narrow the nerve root canals without having any effect on the central spinal canal. Furthermore, substantial central canal stenosis may result from such common pathology as facet arthrosis and may not be detected at all on plain films.

The most important measurement may be the volume of the central canal rather than the sagittal and coronal dimensions, individually. It has also been shown recently that loading of the lumbar spine may be necessary to detect milder central canal stenosis in symptomatic patients with only borderline or low "normal" canal dimensions on conventional, recumbent CT or MRI studies. In summary, central canal stenosis may be screened for grossly on plain films, but more importantly, if there are clinical signs or symptoms suggesting stenosis or known underlying pathology that may result in stenosis, cross-sectional imaging must be relied upon to help exclude such patients from cer-

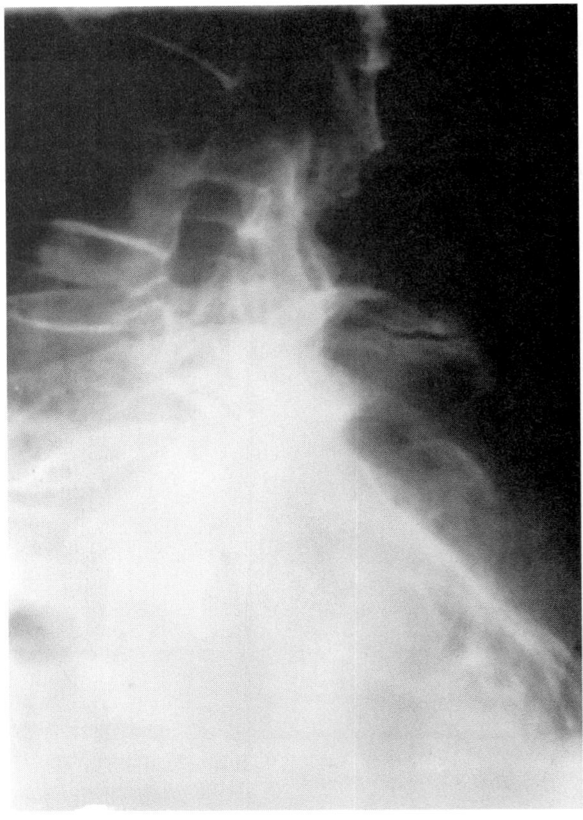

Figure 12–31. Baastrup's disease, with close approximation of the lower lumbar spinous processes, reactive sclerosis, irregularity, and hypertrophy, as well as vacuum phenomenon. This may be associated with symptoms, especially with extension of the low back, and is typically seen in the context of chronic postural faults such as hyperlordosis and swayback posture.

tain types of rehabilitation that may exacerbate the problem. Research has indicated that imaging a loaded spine may demonstrate a significantly greater number of patients with spinal stenosis, but because only recumbent studies are widely available in clinical settings, this is typically not possible. There may be false negative results in some patients with clinical evidence of central canal stenosis imaged with conventional recumbent protocols and clinical findings may need to be considered over imaging findings in decision-making.[144] In general, activities involving flexion minimize the effects of central stenosis, while extension maximally narrows the central canal. Therefore, patients with clinical, radiographic, or combined clinical and radiographic evidence of central spinal canal stenosis may benefit from programs incorporating flexion and should probably be excluded from activities involving extension. Other biomechanical abnormalities, including lumbar hyperlordosis, swayback posture and "Baastrup's disease" or "kissing spinouses" may, likewise, be relative contraindications to extension activities (Figure 12–31).

QUESTIONS

1. What is the role of plain film radiographs in assessment for spinal canal stenosis as an exclusion criterion for certain types of rehabilitation activities and exercises?

Answer: Plain films provide a rough screen for sagittal central canal stenosis and an even rougher screen for the coronal canal dimension. Assessment of bony cervical IVF compromise is possible, but correlates poorly with clinical findings of upper extremity radiculopathy. Plain films are poor for assessment of lumbar nerve root canal stenosis. Ultimately, if signs and symptoms warrant, advanced imaging is indicated to more optimally assess for central canal and/or nerve root canal stenosis.

2. What common normal variant is frequently mistaken for atlantoaxial subluxation/instability?

Answer: The "V"-shaped atlanto-dental interspace.

3. What soft tissue abnormality may be associated with alteration of McGregor's line due to congenital anomaly at the craniovertebral junction?

Answer: Chiari Type I malformation, with or without compression of the upper cervical cord or brainstem.

4. What is considered to be the most accurate assessment for instability in lumbar spondylolisthesis?

Answer: Traction-compression lateral radiographs.

5. What is the significance of alterations in the cervical and lumbar gravity lines in the application of rehabilitation exercises?

Answer: Unknown

REFERENCES

1. Berber BA. A new radiographic finding in mongolism. *Radiology*. 1966;86:332–335.
2. Fielding JW, Cochran GVB, Lawsing JF, Hohl M. Tears of the transverse ligament of the atlas: A clinical and biomechanical study. *J Bone Joint Surg*. 1974;56A:1683–1687.
3. Jackson H. Diagnosis of minimal atlantoaxial subluxation. *Brit J Radiol*. 1950;23:672–676.
4. Jackson H. Atlantoaxial subluxation. *Radiology*. 1983;148:864.
5. Conlon PW, Isdale IC, Rose BS. Rheumatoid arthritis of the cervical spine: An analysis of 333 cases. *Ann Rheum Dis*. 1966;25:120.
6. Mathews JA. Atlantoaxial subluxation in rheumatoid arthritis. *Ann Rheum Dis*. 1969;28:260.
7. Bohrer SP, Klein A, Martin W. "V"-shaped predens space. *Skeletal Radiol*. 1985;14:111–116.
8. White AA, Southwick WO, Panjabi MM. Clinical instability in the lower cervical spine: A review of past and current concepts. *Spine*. 1976;1:15–27.
9. Bedbrook GM. Are cervical spine fractures ever unstable? *J West Pac Orthop Assoc*. 1969;6:7–29.
10. Burke DC, Berryman D. The place of closed manipulation in the management of flexion-rotation dislocations of the cervical spine. *J Bone Joint Surg*. 1971;53B:165–182.
11. Cheshire DJE. The stability of the cervical spine following the conservative treatment of fractures and fracture dislocations. *Paraplegia*. 1969;7:193–203.
12. Beatson TR. Fractures and dislocations of the cervical spine. *Clin Orthop*. 1975;109:85–96.
13. Braakman R, Vinken PF. Unilateral facet interlocking in the lower cervical spine. *J Bone Joint Surg*. 1967;49B:249–257.
14. Barnes R. Paraplegia in cervical spine injuries. *J Bone Joint Surg*. 1948;30B:234–244.

15. Castellano V, Bocconi FL. Injuries of the cervical spine with spinal cord involvement (myelic fractures): Statistical considerations. *Bull Hosp Joint Dis*. 1970;31:188–194.
16. Horlyck E, Rahbek M. Cervical spine injuries. *Acta Orthop Scand*. 1974;45:845–853.
17. Schneider RC, Cherry G, Pantek H. The syndrome of acute central spinal cord injury. *J Neurosurg*. 1954;11:564–577.
18. White AA, Johnson RM, Panjabi MM, Southwick WO. Biomechanical analysis of clinical stability in the cervical spine. *Clin Orthop*. 1975;109:85–96.
19. Jacobson G, Beeckler HH. Pseudosubluxation of the axis in children. *Am J Roentgenol*. 1959;82:472.
20. Scher AT. Anterior subluxation: An unstable position. *Am J Roentgenol*. 1979;133:275.
21. Swischuk LE. The cervical spine in childhood. *Curr Probl Diagno Radiol*. 1984;13:10.
22. Pearcy M, Shepherd J. Is there instability in lumbar spondylolisthesis? *Spine*. 1985;10:175–177.
23. Saraste H, Brostrum LA, Aparisi T. Prognostic radiographic aspects of spondylolisthesis. *Acta Radiol Diagn*. 1984;25:427–432.
24. Stopkes IA, Frymoyer JW. Segmental motion and instability. *Spine*. 1987;12:688–691.
25. Nachemson A. Towards a better understanding of low back pain: A review of the mechanics of the lumbar disc. *Rheumatol Rehabil*. 1978;14:129–142.
26. Nachemson A. The role of spine fusion. *Spine*. 1981;6:306–307.
27. Behrsin JF, Andrews FJ. Lumbar segmental instability: Manual assessment findings supported by radiological measurement (A case study). *Australian Physiotherapy*. 1991;37:171–173.
28. Hayes MA, Howard TC, Cruel CR, Kopta JA. Roentgenographic evaluation of lumbar spine flexion-extension in normal individuals. Presented at the Federation of Spinal Association Meeting, New Orleans, February 19, 1986.
29. Soini J, Antti-Poika I, Tallroth K, Kontinnen HT, Honaken V, Santaverta S. Disc degeneration and angular movement of the lumbar spine: Comparative study using plain and flexion-extension radiography and discography. *J Spinal Disord*. 1991;4:183–187.
30. Friberg O. Lumbar instability: A dynamic approach by traction-compression radiography. *Spine*. 1987;12:119–129.
31. Kalebo P, Kadziolka R, Sward L. Compression-traction radiography of lumbar segmental instability. *Spine*. 1990;351–355.
32. Kalebo P, Kadziolka R, Sward L, Zachrisson BE. Stress views in the comparative assessment of spondylolytic spondylolisthesis. *Skeletal Radiol*. 1989;17:570–575.
33. Murone I. The importance of the sagittal diameters of the cervical spinal canal in relation to spondylosis and myelopathy. *J Bone Joint Surg*. 1974;56A:30.
34. Payne EE, Spillane JD. The cervical spine: An anatomicopathological study of seventy specimens (using a special technique) with particular reference to the problem of cervical spondylosis. *Brain*. 1957;80:571.
35. Wolf BS, Khilnani M, Malis L. The sagittal diameter of the bony cervical canal and its significance in cervical spondylosis. *J Mt Sinai Hosp*. 1956;23:283.
36. Hinck VC, Sachdev NS. Developmental stenosis of the cervical spinal canal. *Brain*. 1966;89:27.
37. Gupta SK, Roy RC, Srivastava A. Sagittal diameter of the cervical canal in normal Indian adults. *Clin Radiol*. 1982;33:681.
38. Omojola MF, Vas W, Banna M. Plain film assessment of spinal canal stenosis. *J Can Assoc Radiol*. 1981;32:95.
39. Govoni AF. Developmental stenosis of a thoracic vertebra resulting in narrowing of the spinal canal. *Am J Roentgenol*. 1971;112:401.
40. Chynn KY, Altman I, Shaw WI, Finby N. The roentgenographic manifestations and clinical features of lumbar spinal stenosis with special emphasis on the superior articular processes. *Neuroradiology*. 1978;16:378.
41. Eisenstein S. The morphometry and pathological anatomy of the lumbar spine in South African Negroes and Caucasoids with specific reference to spinal stenosis. J *Bone Joint Surg*. 1977;59B:173.
42. Grabias S. The treatment of spinal stenosis. *J Bone Joint Surg*. 1980;62A:308.
43. Eisenstein S. The trefoil configuration of the lumbar vertebral canal: A study of South African skeletal material. *J Bone Joint Surg*. 1980;62B:73.
44. Ullrich CG, Binet EF, Sanecki MG, Kieffer SA. Quantitative assessment of the lumbar spinal canal by computed tomography. *Radiology*. 1980;134:137.
45. Weisz GM, Lee P. Spinal canal stenosis. Concept of spinal reserve capacity: Radiologic measurement and clinical applications. *Clin Orthop Rel Res*. 1983;179:134.
46. Dorwart RH, Genant HK. Anatomy of the lumbosacral spine. *Radiol Clin North Am*. 1983;21:201.

47. Mikhael MA, Ciric I, Tarkington JA, Vick NA. Neuroradiological evaluation of lateral recess syndromes. *Radiology*. 1981;140:97.
48. Ciric I, Mikhael MA, Tarkington JA, Vick NA. The lateral recess syndrome: A variant of spinal stenosis. *J Neurosurg*. 1980;53:433.
49. Dorwart RH, Vogler JB, Helms CA. Computed tomography of spinal stenosis. *Radiol Clin North Am*. 1983;21:301.
50. Kirkaldy-Willis WH, Wedge JH, Yong-Hing K, Tchang S, DeKorompay V, Shannon R. Lumbar spinal nerve lateral entrapment. *Clin Orthop Rel Res*. 1982;169:171.
51. Risius B, Modic MT, Hardy RW Jr, Duchesneau PM, Weinstein MA. Sector computed tomographic spine scanning in the diagnosis of lumbar nerve root entrapment. *Radiology*. 1982;143:109.
52. Vanderlinden RG. Subarticular entrapment of the dorsal root ganglion as a cause of sciatic pain. *Spine*. 1984;9:19.
53. Wigh RE, Anthony HF Jr. Transitional lumbosacral discs: Probability of herniation. *Spine*. 1981;6:168–171.
54. Southworth JD, Bersack SR. Anomalies of the lumbosacral vertebrae in five hundred and fifty individuals without symptoms referable to the low back. *Am J Roentgenol*. 1950;64:624–634.
55. Wigh RE. The thoracolumbar and lumbosacral transitional junctions. *Spine*. 1980;5:215–222.
56. Gurdjian ES, Ostrowski AZ, Hardy WG, Lindner DW, Thomas LM. Results of operative treatment of protruded and ruptured lumbar discs. *J Neurosurg*. 1961;18:783–791.
57. Lansche WE, Ford LT. Correlation of the myelogram with clinical and operative findings in lumbar disc lesions. *J Bone Joint Surg*. 1960;42A:193–206.
58. Castellvi AE, Goldstein LA, Chan DPK. Lumbosacral transitional vertebrae and their relationship with lumbar extradural defects. *Spine*. 1984;9:493–495.
59. Kseim HA. Transitional lumbosacral vertebrae and Bertolotti's syndrome. Presented at the fifteenth annual meeting of the Scoliosis Research Society. Chicago, Sept, 1980.
60. Stinchfield FE, Sinton WA. Clinical significance of the transitional lumbosacral vertebrae: Relationship to back pain, disc disease and sciatica. *J Amer Med Assoc*. 1955;157:1107–1109.
61. Elster AD. Bertolotti's syndrome revisited: Transitional vertebrae of the lumbar spine. *Spine*. 1989;14:1373–1377.
62. Bertolotti M. Contributo alla conoscenza dei vizi di differenzazione regionale del rachide con speciale riguardo all assimilazione sacrale dell V. lombare. *Radiologigue Medica*. 1917;4113–4144.
63. Bertolotti M. Les syndromes lomboo-ischialgiques d'origine vertebrale: Leur entitee morphologique, radiographique et clinique. *Rev Nerol (Pans)*. 1922;38:1112–1125.
64. Harrison RB, et al. Pseudosubluxation of the axis in young adults. *J Can Assoc Radiol*. 1980;31:176.
65. Swischuk LE. Anterior displacement of C2 in children: Physiologic or pathologic. *Radiology*. 1977;122:759.
66. Lovell WW, Winter RB. *Pediatric Orthopedics*. Philadelphia: JB Lippincott, 1978.
67. Weisel SW, Rothman RH. Occipitoatlantal hypermobility. *Spine*. 1979;4:187.
68. Barne JC, Smith WL. The VATER association. *Radiology*. 1978;126:445.
69. Hensinger RN, Lang JE, MacEwen GD. Klippel-Feil syndrome. A constellation of associated anomalies. *J Bone Joint Surg*. 1974;56A:1246.
70. Quan L, Smith DW. The VATER association: Vertebral defects, anal atresia, tracheo-esophageal fistula with esophageal atresia, radial and renal dysplasia: A spectrum of associated defects. *J Pediatr*. 1973;82:104.
71. Buna M, Coghlan W, deGruchy M, et al. Ponticles of the atlas: A review and clinical perspective. *J Manip Physiol Therap*. 1984;7:261.
72. DeSmet AA. *Radiology of Spinal Curvature*. St. Louis: CV Mosby; 1985.
73. McMaster MJ. Occult intraspinal anomalies and congenital scoliosis. *J Bone Joint Surg*. 1984;66a:588.
74. Arredondo F, Haughton VM, Hemmny DC, Zelaya B, Williams AL. The computed tomographic appearance of the spinal cord in diastematomyelia. *Radiology*. 1980;13:685.
75. Hood RW, Riseborough EJ, Nehme AM, Micheli LJ, Strand RD, Neuhausere EBD. Diastematomyelia and structural spinal deformities. *J Bone Joint Surg*. 1980;62A:520.
76. Hilal SK, Marton D, Pollack E. Diastematomyelia in children. Radiographic study of 34 cases. *Radiology*. 1974;112:609.
77. Keim HA, Greene AF. Diastematomyelia and scoliosis. *J Bone Joint Surg*. 1973;55A:1425.
78. Kennedy PR. New data on diastematomyelia. *J Neurosurg*. 1979;51:355.
79. Kohler A, Zimmer EA. *Borderlands of the Normal and Early Pathologic in Skeletal Radiology*, 3rd ed. New York: Grune and Stratton, 1968.

80. Scheuermann HW. Kyphosis dorsalis juvenilis. *Z Orthop Chir.* 1921;41:305.
81. Alexander CJ. Scheuermann's disease. A traumatic spondylodystrophy? *Skel Radiol.* 1977;1:209.
82. Beadle O. The intervertebral disc. *Med Res Council Spec Rep Series.* 1931;161:1.
83. Brailsford JF. Deformities of the lumbosacral region of the spine. *Br J Surg.* 1928;16:562–626.
84. Cyron BM, Hutton WC. Articular tropism and stability of the lumbar spine. *Spine.* 1980;5:168–172.
85. Farfan HF, Sullivan JD. The relation of facet orientation to intervertebral disc failure. *Can J Surg.* 1967;10:179–185.
86. Farfan HF. Effects of torsion on the intervertebral joints. *Can J Surg.* 1969;12:335–341.
87. Ahmed AM, Duncan NA, Burke DL. The effect of facet geometry on the axial torque-rotation response of lumbar motion segments. *Spine.* 1990;15:391–401.
88. Cassidy JD, Loback D, Yong-Hing K, Tchang S. Lumbar facet joint asymmetry: Intervertebral disc herniation. *Spine.* 1992;17:570–574.
89. Hagg O, Wallner A. Facet joint asymmetry and protrusion of the intervertebral disc. *Spine.* 1990;15:356–359.
90. Vanharanta H, Floyd T, Ohnmeiss DD, Hochschuler SH, Guyer RD. The relationship of facet tropism to degenerative disc disease. *Spine.* 1993;18:1000–1005.
91. Cyron BM, Hutton WC. The fatigue strength of the lumbar neural arch in spondylolysis. *J Bone Joint Surg.* 1978; 60B:462.
92. Wiltse LL. Etiology of spondylolisthesis. *Clin Orthop.* 1957;10:48.
93. Wiltse LL. The etiology of spondylolisthesis. *J Bone Joint Surg.* 1962;44A:539.
94. Wiltse LL, Widell EH, Jackson DW. Fatigue fracture: The basic lesion in isthmic spondylolisthesis. *J Bone Joint Surg.* 1975;57A:17.
95. Laurent L, Emola S. Spondylolisthesis in children and adolescents. *Acta Orthop Scand.* 1961;31:45.
96. Rossi F. Spondylolysis, spondylolisthesis and sports. *Sports Med.* 1978;18:317.
97. Tojner H. Olisthetic scoliosis. *Acta Orthop Scand.* 1963:33:291.
98. Cassidy JD, Potter GE, Kirkaldy-Willis WH. Manipulative management of back pain in patients with spondylolisthesis. *J Can Chirop Assoc.* 1978;22:15.
99. Bradford DS, Lonstein JE, Ogilvie JW, Winter RB. *Moe'sTextbook of Scoliosis and Other Spinal Deformities*, 2nd ed. Philadelphia: WB Saunders; 1987.
100. Burry HC, Tweed JM, Robinson RG, Howes R. Lateral subluxation of the atlanto-axial joint in rheumatoid arthritis. *Ann Rheum Dis.* 1978;37:525.
101. Cabot A, Becker A. The cervical spine in rheumatoid arthritis. *Clin Orthop Rel Res.* 1978;131:130.
102. Crellin RQ, Maccabe JJ, Hamilton EBD. Severe subluxation of the cervical spine in rheumatoid arthritis. *J Bone Joint Surg.* 1970;52B:244.
103. Park WM, O'Neill M, McCall IW. The radiology of rheumatoid involvement of the cervical spine. *Skel Radiol.* 1979;4:1.
104. Lane PWF, Dyer NH, Hawkins CF. Synovial rupture of the shoulder joint. *Br Med J.* 1972;1:356.
105. Palmer DG. Tendon sheaths and bursae involved by rheumatoid disease at the foot and ankle. *Australas Radiol.* 1970;14:419.
106. Straub LR, Wilson EH Jr. Spontaneous rupture of extensor tendons in the hand associated with rheumatoid arthritis. *J Bone Joint Surg.* 1956;38A:1208.
107. Twinning RH, Marcus WY, Garey YJL. Tendon rupture in systemic lupus erthematosus. *JAMA.* 1964;189:377.
108. Ball J. Enthesopathy of rheumatoid and ankylosing spondylitis. *Am Rheum Dis.* 1971;30:213.
109. Csonka GW. The course of Reiter's syndrome. *Br Med J.* 1958;1:1088.
110. Gold RH, Bassett LW, Theros EG. Radiologic comparison of erosive polyarthritides with prominent interphalangeal involvement. *Skel Radiol.* 1982;8:89.
111. Lampman JH. Origin of enthesopathy. *J Rheumatol.* 1985;12:1030.
112. Peterson CC Jr, Silbiger ML. Reiter's syndrome and psoriatic arthritis. Their roentgen spectra and some interesting similarities. *Am J Roentgenol.* 1967;101:860.
113. Resnick D, Feingold ML, Curd J, Niwayama G, Goergen TG. Calcaneal abnormalities in articular disorders: Rheumatoid arthritis, ankylosing spondylitis and Reiter's syndrome. *Radiology.* 1977;125:355.
114. Bywaters EGL, Dixon AS. Paravertebral ossification in psoriatic arthritis. *Ann Rheum Dis.* 1965;23:313.
115. Jajic I. Radiological changes in the sacroiliac joints and spine of patients with psoriatic arthritis and psoriasis. *Ann Rheum Dis.* 1968;27:1.
116. Killebrew K, Gold RH, Sholkoff SD. Psoriatic spondylitis. *Radiology.* 1973;1089:9.

117. Mason RM, Murray RS, Oates JK, Young AC. A comparative radiological study of Reiter's disease, rheumatoid arthritis and ankylosing spondylitis. *J Bone Joint Surg.* 1959;41B:137.
118. McEwen C, Ditata D, Lingg C, Porini A, Good A, Rankin T. Ankylosing spondylitis and spondylitis accompanying ulcerative colitis, regional enteritis, psoriasis and Reiter's disease. *Arthritis Rheum.* 1971;14:291.
119. Good AE. The chest pain of ankylosing spondylitis. Its place in the differential diagnosis of heart pain. *Ann Intern Med.* 1963;58:926.
120. Resnick D, Dwosh IL, Goergen TG, Shapiro RF, Utsinger PD, Wiesner KB, Bryan BL. Clinical and radiographic abnormalities in ankylosing spondylitis: A comparison of men and women. *Radiology.* 1976;119:293.
121. Martel W. The occipital-atlanto-axial joints in rheumatoid and ankylosing spondylitis. *Am J Roentgenol.* 1961;86:223.
122. Dihlmann W, Delling G. Discovertebral destructive lesions (so-called Andersson lesions) associated with ankylosing spondylitis. *Skel Radiol.* 1978;3:10.
123. Gelman MI, Umber JS. Fractures of the thoracolumbar spine in ankylosing spondylitis. *Am J Roentgenol.* 1978;130:485.
124. Martel W. Spinal pseudoarthrosis: A complication of ankylosing spondylitis. *Arthritis Rheum.* 1978;21:485.
125. Rivelis M, Freiberger RH. Vertebral destruction at unfused segments in late ankylosing spondylitis. *Radiology.* 1969;93:251.
126. Woodruff FB, Dewing SB. Fracture of the cervical spine in patients with ankylosing spondylitis. *Radiology.* 1963;80:17.
127. Ansell BM, Bywaters EGL, Doniach I. The aortic lesion of ankylosing spondylitis. *Br Heart J.* 1958;20:507.
128. Rosenow EC, Strimlan CV, Muhm JR, Ferguson RH. Pleuropulmonary manifestations of ankylosing spondylitis. *Mayo Clin Proc.* 1977;52:641.
129. Sobin LH, Hagstrom JWC. Lesions of cardiac conduction tissue in rheumatoid arthritis. *JAMA.* 1962;180:1.
130. Resnick D, Niwayama G. *Diagnosis of Bone and Joint Disorders*, 2nd ed. Philadelphia: WB Saunders, 1988:1999–2018.
131. Richardson ML, Genant HK, Cann CE, et al. Assessment of metabolic bone disease by quantitative computed tomography. *Clin Orthop Rel Res.* 1985;195:224.
132. Feldman F, Seaman WB. The neurologic complications of Paget's disease in the cervical spine. *Am J Roentgenol.* 1969;105:375.
133. Hartman JT, Down JDF. Paget's disease of the spine with cord or nerve root compression. *J Bone Joint Surg.* 1966;48A:1079.
134. Poretta CA, Dahlin DC, Janes JM. Sarcoma in Paget's disease of bone. *J Bone Joint Surg.* 1957;39A:1314.
135. Hinck VC, Hopkins CE. Measurement of the atlanto-dental interval in the adult. *Am J Roentgenol.* 1960;84:945.
136. McGregor M. The significance of certain measurements of the skull in the diagnosis of basilar impression. *Br J Radiol.* 1948;21:171.
137. Hinck VC, Hopkins CE, Sasvara BS. Diagnostic criteria of basilar impression. *Radiology.* 1961;76:572.
138. Monu J, Bohrer SP, Howard G. Some upper cervical norms. *Spine.* 1987;12:515.
139. George AW. A method for more accurate study of injuries to the atlas and axis. *Boston Med Surg.* 1919;181:13.
140. Pavlov H, Torg JS, Robie B, et al. Cervical spinal stenosis: Determination with vertebral body ration method. *Radiology.* 1987;164:771.
141. Torg JS. Cervical spinal stenosis with cord neuropraxia and transient quadriplegia. *Current Opinions Orthop.* 1994;5:97.
142. Myerding HW. Spondylolisthesis. *Surg Gynecol Obstet.* 1932;54:371.
143. Eisenstein S. Measurements in the lumbar spinal canal in two racial groups. *Clin Orthop Rel Res.* 1976;115:42.
144. Willen J, Danielson B, Gaulitz A, et al. Dynamic effects on the lumbar spinal canal. *Spine.* 1997;22:2968.

CHAPTER 13

Cardiac Evaluation of the Spinal Rehabilitation Patient

STEVEN HEIFETZ, MD

INTRODUCTION

Cardiovascular diseases are the leading cause of death in the United States and, indeed, in most of the developed world. Because cardiovascular disease is so prominent in the general population, it is inevitable that the practitioner evaluating the spinal rehabilitation patient will also encounter patients with concomitant cardiovascular disease. Svensson et al[1] reported on a large cohort of middle-aged men with chronic diseases and low back pain. They noted a statistically significant increase in concomitant coronary artery disease in this population with 6% of the subjects reporting evidence of angina pectoris, 1.7% of patients having had prior myocardial infarction, and an additional 14% with hypertension. Although this has not been a universal observation,[2] several other studies have confirmed a significant increase in the incidence of hypertension and ischemic heart disease in their spinal cord population.[3–5]

Epidemiologic studies have suggested that the risk of acute myocardial infarction or cardiac arrest rises transiently shortly after the onset of heavy physical exertion. The relative risk of acute myocardial infarction within 1 hour of heavy physical exertion was reportedly 5.9 for the general population, but could range as high as 107 for those habitually sedentary.[6] The etiology for this acute risk is unclear but may be secondary to disruption of atherosclerotic plaque or the acute rise in catecholamines. Furthermore, it has been shown that platelet activation increases following strenuous exercise in sedentary subjects but not in physically active subjects.[7]

The importance of these data is quite germane to the health care practitioner who prescribes an extensive rehabilitation program since many patients fall in this high-risk group.

On occasion, the patient may present initially with symptoms suggestive of musculoskeletal disease or dysfunction when in fact the symptom is referred pain from a cardiovascular source. For these reasons, the practitioner has a moral, medical, and legal obligation to screen carefully any patient before he or she undergoes an extensive rehabilitation and exercise program.

The purpose of this chapter is to provide a working overview of the health risk profile and appraisal of the rehabilitation candidate. Special emphasis on the patient's historical data, physical examination, and supplementary diagnostic tests will be reviewed. Specific disease entities that should be included in the differential diagnosis will be reviewed in depth. A review of cardiovascular anatomy, physiology, and histology is beyond the scope of this chapter, and the reader is referred to the excellent reviews in the References section at the end of the chapter.[8,9]

HEALTH APPRAISAL

The cardiovascular status of the patient who presents for spinal rehabilitation may fall into one of four categories:

1. The patient has no underlying cardiovascular disease.
2. The patient has underlying cardiovascular disease but is not aware of it. Either it is a silent disease

such as coronary artery disease, or symptoms may be present but misinterpreted as being due to a noncardiovascular cause.
3. The patient has a known cardiovascular history.
4. The patient has a cardiovascular disease that is compounding his or her clinical presentation.

A health screening examination will be useful in categorizing such patients. This frequently starts with a self-administered health questionnaire, review of coronary artery disease (CAD) risk factors (Table 13–1), and physical examination. In certain high-risk individuals, referral to a specialist for diagnostic exercise testing or advanced cardiac testing may be necessary before granting medical clearance. The interview also provides key details regarding the severity of the underlying condition, any constraints the condition may pose regarding the planned rehabilitation program, and to rule out any possibility that the underlying symptom is primarily cardiovascular in nature.

HISTORY

The history begins with obtaining key information regarding the patient's primary complaint and any possible cardiovascular symptoms. A thorough description of the patient's pain is warranted. This includes evaluating the pain's location, duration, precipitating factors, intensity, and quality. One of the confounding variables that accounts for the confusion between cardiovascular symptoms and musculoskeletal symptoms is the concept of *referred pain*. Sensory impulses of visceral origin travel in somatic afferents in the spinal-thalamic tract. The radiation of these somatic afferents to a number of different spinal cord segments may explain the often diffuse or poorly characterized description of visceral origin pain. In addition, the visceral afferent fibers may travel up or down one or more segments of gray matter in the dorsal horn before synapsing onto the spinal-thalamic tract. Further complicating an assessment of the location or origin of the pain is the fact that the segments of the spinal cord that supply visceral structures are determined during their original location in the developing human embryo. As these organs migrate to their final location in the adult, the pain may be sensed far from the original input.

Table 13–1: Major Coronary Risk Factors

1. Hypertension (systolic blood pressure ≥ 160, or diastolic blood pressure ≥ 90 mmHg)
2. Serum cholesterol ≥ 200 mg/dL
3. Cigarette smoking
4. Diabetes mellitus
5. Family history of coronary artery disease in a first-degree relative prior to age 55
6. Sedentary life style

Generally, the pain of cardiac angina can be felt from the C8 to the T5 levels, whereas pericardial pain, which may irritate the diaphragmatic surface, presents in these same or higher levels. Pain of aortic dissection can span many levels depending on the area of disruption. The abdominal aorta ends at its bifurcation at the L4 level, and therefore abdominal aortic pain would not generally be felt below the lower abdomen unless blood flow to the iliac and femoral artery system is also compromised.

Key descriptions to elicit regarding the pain include:

Location: chest, neck, arm, back, abdomen
Quality: squeezing, tightness, heaviness, "indigestion," dullness
Intensity: slight, severe, crushing, "impending doom"
Duration: fleeting, minutes, chronic
Triggers/relief: body position, respiration, physical activity, emotional upset, food intake, antacids, rest

It is important to note that the patient may not describe the sensation as a pain, but rather as an ache. Associated symptoms (shortness of breath, diaphoresis, nausea, vomiting, dizziness, fatigue) should also be elicited.

PAST MEDICAL HISTORY

A known history of cardiovascular disease will generally alert the interviewer to a potentially high-risk cardiovascular patient. Past medical history is designed to elicit any of the allied conditions of atherosclerosis such as previous stroke, claudication, abdominal aneurysm, angina, or myocardial infarction. Also, inquiry into rheumatic fever, syncope, heart murmur, palpitations, hypertension, smoking history, diabetes, orthopnea/paroxysmal nocturnal dyspnea, or tachycardia can also lead one to be suspicious of significant underlying cardiovascular diseases.

FAMILY HISTORY

Atherosclerotic cardiovascular disease and peripheral vascular disease often have a strong genetic predisposition. Some cardiovascular diseases such as idiopathic hypertrophic subaortic stenosis (IHSS) and Marfan syndrome are also genetically transmitted, and such a history can be useful in evaluating the patient.

PHYSICAL EXAMINATION

A careful physical examination begins with simple observation of the patient. Immediately, one can gain insight into the overall nutritional status, development, and perhaps functional status of the patient. Assessment of skin changes and skin turgor can provide information regarding cardiovascular status, arterial or venous insufficiency, or hypoxia. Recording vital signs is imperative. This begins with assessing the blood pressure. An abnormal pulse pressure (systolic minus diastolic blood pressure) can alert one to valvular heart disease or reduced compliancy of the vascular tree. Heart rate, rhythm, respiratory rate, and temperature should be measured.

Auscultation of the lungs for rales or wheezing and percussion of the lung fields can be the first indication of pulmonary disease, left- and right-sided heart disease, or congestive heart failure. Visualization of the use of accessory respiratory muscles can also be a sign of both pulmonary or cardiac disease.

The cardiac examination should be quite thorough, including observation, palpation, and auscultation. An abnormal parasternal lift may signify right heart disease. Auscultation is difficult, but a careful examination can obviate the need for more expensive tests such as echocardiography. In addition to the normal first (S_1) and second (S_2) heart sounds ("lub-dub"), there can be a third (S_3) or fourth (S_4) heart sound. The third heart sound follows S_2 and is best heard with the bell of the stethoscope. Although this can be a normal finding, especially in younger patients, it is frequently a sign of a decompensated noncompliant left ventricle and congestive heart failure. The combination of S_1, S_2, and S_3 sounds like the word "Kentucky":

(Ken–tuck–y)
S_1 S_2 S_3

The fourth heart sound represents atrial emptying and occurs immediately before S_1. The S_4, S_1, and S_2 combination sounds like the word "Tennessee":

(Tenn–es–see)
S_4 S_1 S_2

An S_3, S_4 combination is called a *summation gallop*. It is frequently heard in decompensated congestive heart failure.

Heart murmurs may represent underlying pathologic valvular heart disease. All diastolic heart murmurs are pathologic, but not necessarily serious. A mild aortic insufficiency murmur can be quite striking on examination but have little clinical significance, whereas a loud diastolic rumble with presystolic accentuation may represent serious mitral valvular stenosis. Systolic murmurs, on the other hand, are quite variable and may often be benign. There are, however, several systolic murmurs that should alert the practitioner to a potentially serious underlying heart problem, which may be a contraindication to a rehabilitation program. The late-peaking, harsh systolic murmur heard at the base of the heart and radiating into the neck may represent critical aortic valve stenosis, which is an absolute contraindication to any extensive rehabilitation or exercise program. A similar but variable systolic murmur that is accentuated with a Valsalva maneuver or standing may represent IHSS. The holosystolic murmur of mitral insufficiency is often described as a blowing murmur heard at the apex of the heart. These murmurs are quite variable, and the intensity of the murmur does not necessarily correlate with the severity of the underlying valvular disease. A short systolic murmur heard following a systolic click represents mitral valve prolapse and can be quite benign, yet a soft holosystolic murmur accompanied by an S_3 may represent severe mitral insufficiency.

Additional sounds such as systolic clicks may represent a bicuspid aortic valve or a prolapsing mitral valve. An abnormally loud second heart sound (P_2—pulmonic valve closure) may alert the examiner to underlying pulmonary hypertension from any of a number of potential causes, and auscultation of a pericardial friction rub would immediately suggest a diagnosis of pericarditis.

Evaluation of the peripheral pulses is also part of a cardiac exam. Palpation of the carotid pulses and auscultation of bruits can alert one to severe carotid artery disease, a low-output cardiac state, or significant left ventricular outflow obstruction. Evaluation of the femoral, dorsal pedal, and posterior tibial pulses also should be performed. These may be the first signs that the condition being evaluated may actually be due to vascular insufficiency rather than spinal stenosis or other peripheral neuropathy. Similarly, auscultation and palpation of the abdominal aorta is important to rule out an abdominal aortic aneurysm. Comparison of the arterial pulses for symmetry will alert one to obstructive lesions or aortic dissection, whereas assessment of the jugular venous pulse in the neck can alert one to volume overload or tricuspid valve disease.

LABORATORY DATA

Certain minimal laboratory tests may be necessary before starting an extensive rehabilitation or exercise program. These include hemoglobin, potassium, and creatinine levels and in some cases drug levels for certain medications that the patient may be on such as digoxin or antiarrhythmics. In terms of overall assessment of the health risk profile, a lipid panel would be useful. Under circumstances in which inflammatory conditions such as infective endocarditis or pericarditis are a concern, a sedimentation rate and white blood cell count can be useful.

In addition to blood work, an electrocardiogram (EKG) is used to assess heart rhythm, evidence of previous myocardial infarction, ventricular hypertrophy, or conduction disturbance. A chest x-ray outlines the cardiac silhouette looking for chamber enlargement, evaluation of the mediastinum and pulmonary hila, and identifying underlying pathologic conditions such as dilated aorta, pulmonary hypertension, lung disease, or the venous redistribution of congestive heart failure.

DIAGNOSTIC CARDIAC TESTING

The American College of Sports Medicine recommends that apparently healthy men greater that 40 years of age and apparently healthy women greater than 50 have a medical examination and diagnostic exercise test before starting a vigorous exercise program. However, this may not be essential for those in a moderate-intensity exercise regimen or those undergoing a progressive rehabilitation program.[10]

The graded exercise stress test (GXT) is the most common screening test for coronary artery disease. It is a widely available test, simple and safe to perform. The risk of serious complication is rare when it is performed at a qualified center. A survey of 1375 centers reported a complication rate of 3.5 infarctions and 0.5 deaths per 10,000 patients.[11] Another study of nearly 10,000 patients demonstrated no mortality with near maximal testing.[12]

To understand how the exercise stress test can be used to diagnose underlying coronary disease, one must understand the concept of cardiac ischemia and supply and demand.

The myocardium uses approximately 8 to 10 cc of oxygen per hundred grams of muscle per minute at rest. With exercise, this oxygen consumption of the heart may increase threefold. Similarly with exercise, the heart rate and systolic pressure increase. Their product is called the rate-pressure product (RPP) and correlates roughly with myocardial oxygen uptake. There is a relatively linear association between the increase in myocardial oxygen consumption and coronary blood flow. Because of these linear associations, during exercise there is a roughly parallel increase in the work of the heart, afterload, cardiac output, coronary blood flow, and the heart rate. Therefore, one can use the noninvasive parameter RPP to make reasonable predictions about one parameter based on another.

SUPPLY AND DEMAND

Myocardial ischemia results when there is an overall imbalance between the oxygen demand of the myocardium and the available oxygen supply. The myocardial demand, represented noninvasively by the RPP, is dependent on the inotropic state and heart rate. On the supply side of the equation, factors include hemoglobin concentration, oxygen content, and the coronary blood flow. Coronary blood flow (CBF) is a complex value that is dependent on coronary artery diameter, coronary artery tone, perfusion pressure, coronary artery resistance, and collateral circulation.

When myocardial oxygen demand exceeds oxygen supply, the ischemic cascade is set in place (Figure 13–1). Flow heterogeneity in the various vascular beds is first noted. This leads first to diastolic dysfunction (failure of the myocardium to relax properly). Next, systolic dysfunction (failure of regional walls to contract normally) is noted. Eventually the characteristic ST segment depression is seen on the electrocardiogram and clinical angina may be noted.

The most common reason for an imbalance between oxygen supply and demand is reduced coronary perfusion caused by atherosclerotic narrowing of the coronary arteries. Although many parameters of cardiac ischemia can be

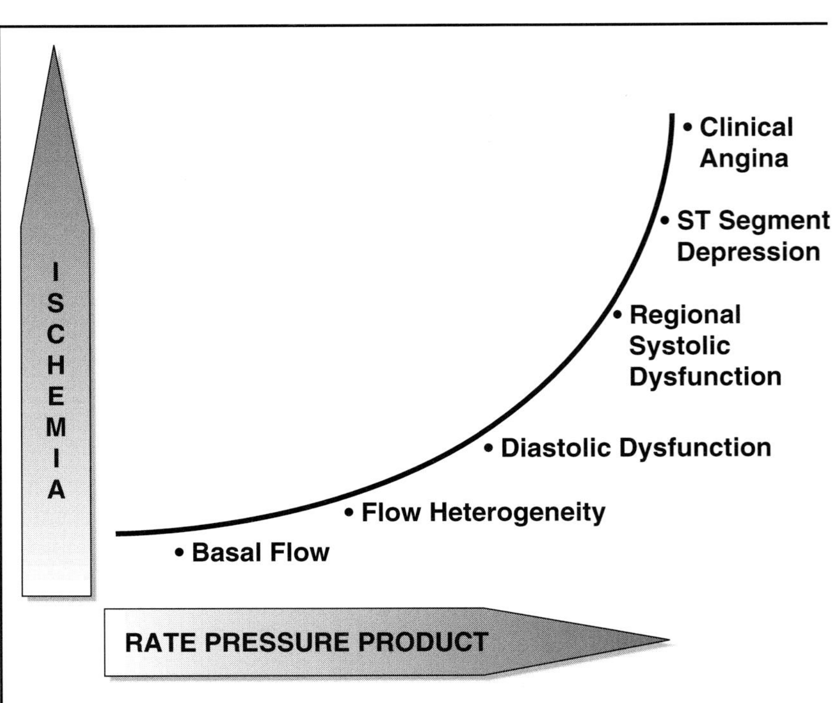

Figure 13–1. The ischemic cascade. With progressive exercise in the setting of a coronary stenosis, serial defects in blood flow and myocardial dysfunction occur prior to the patient's sensation of angina. Cardiac diagnostic tests may identify these earlier stages of ischemia.

gleaned from the exercise stress test, ST segment analysis has been the most useful. With significant degrees of ischemia, there is dysfunction of the cell membrane pumps, leading to a rapid loss of intracellular potassium, noted first along the endocardial surface. A dipole is established between the endocardium and epicardium, thus establishing a "current of injury" with the vector represented by ST segment depression. Because ST segment depression is an indirect reflection of ischemia and not an actual measure of blood flow or oxygen supply, there is an inherent error in its analysis for ischemia. At our institution, in order to strike a reasonable balance between a good sensitivity and specificity, we recognize at least 1.0 mm of horizontal to downsloping ST segment depression or a minimum of 1.5 mm of upsloping ST segment depression as the criteria for abnormality (Figure 13–2). Using this criteria, the test has a sensitivity of 50% to 75% for underlying coronary artery disease. Patients with a positive stress test can expect a 50% chance of cardiac events (progressive angina, myocardial infarction, death) over the next 5 years, where as the chance of such cardiac events with a negative stress test is less than 20% at 5 years.[13] The more severe the coronary stenosis or the more vascular territories involved, the more likely the test is to detect underlying coronary disease; however, smaller areas of ischemia may escape detection by this test.

INDICATIONS FOR STRESS TESTING

In general, indications for exercise testing include:

- Screening for latent coronary disease (silent ischemia)
- Evaluation of patients with chest pain of unknown origin
- Prognosis and severity of disease

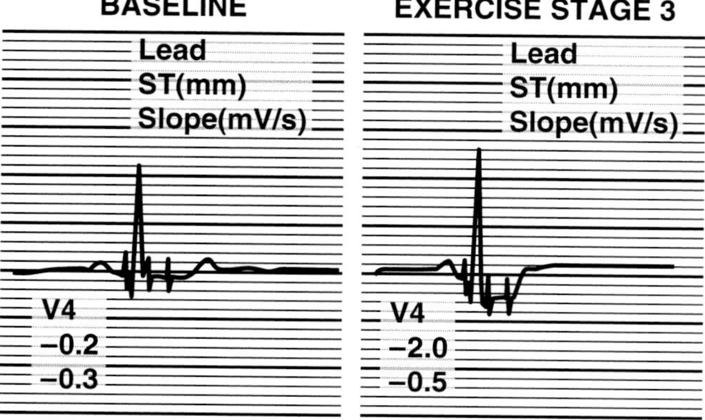

Figure 13–2. Lead V4—Abnormal stress test. Patient developed 2.0 mm of horizontal ST segment depression with exercise.

- Evaluation of therapeutic intervention
- Evaluation of syncope or an arrhythmia
- Evaluation of functional aerobic capacity

In the context of a spinal rehabilitation program, the stress test is used in combination with a generalized health screening to:

- Identify individuals with medical contraindications of the planned program
- Identify persons with clinically silent disease who may need to be referred to a cardiologist before enrolling in a rehabilitation program
- Identify a reasonable exercise prescription (rate-pressure product) at which exercise may be safely performed

RADIONUCLEOTIDE ANGIOGRAPHY

In an attempt to improve the sensitivity and specificity of the exercise test, a number of imaging modalities can be combined with the exercise stress test which take advantage of the earlier phases of the ischemic cascade (Figure 13–1). Radionucleotide tracers that track flow heterogeneity are frequently used to obtain this objective. Thallium 201 (Tl 201) is the most commonly used of the radionucleotide tracers. The thallium stress test is performed just as the graded exercise stress test is. Two minutes before exercise cessation, Tl 201 is injected intravenously and allowed to circulate. There are three phases to the thallium distribution. Immediately upon intravenous injection, 100% of the thallium activity lies within the blood pool. This is followed quickly by the early distribution phase in which the thallium activity in the blood pool quickly drops from 100% down to 2% as the thallium activity distributes according to the regional cardiac output. The heart, which initially has no thallium activity during the injection phase, acquires approximately 4% of the thallium activity during the early distribution phase. However, as areas of the myocardium subserved by stenotic arteries become ischemic during the exercise, there will be a variable regional distribution of thallium activity within the heart.[14] These areas of ischemia will have less thallium uptake and therefore present as "cold spots" on the nuclear image.

After several hours there is a delayed distribution phase during which there is an additional drop in the blood thallium pool from 2% down to 1% secondary to renal clearance of the tracer. There is, however, delayed redistribution in the heart itself due to wash-out of thallium from normally perfused cells to delayed accumulation of Tl 201 into the hypoperfused zone, such that now the heart shows uniform uptake of the tracer. By comparing the early distribution pictures to the delayed distribution pictures, "cold spots" that were seen initially and then "fill in" on the delayed pictures suggest an area of ischemic myocardium that is still viable. If the "cold spot" remains on both the early distribution and the delayed distribution pictures, this suggests nonviable myocardium (myocardial infarction zone) (Figure 13–3).

This test has the benefit of markedly improved sensitivity and specificity, generally well into the 85% to 95% range. However, a thallium test generally requires much more expertise, far more sophisticated equipment, and understandably higher costs. Newer myocardial perfusion imaging agents such as technetium 99-sestamibi and technetium 99-teboroxime take advantage of these agents' differing half-lives and distribution patterns. Technetium 99-sestamibi is a higher energy emitter, and may be less prone to false-positive results caused by impedance from overlaying soft tissue densities such as diaphragm or breast tissue.[15] Currently dual isotope studies using both Tl 201 and sestamibi are used at our institution.

STRESS ECHOCARDIOGRAPHY

Another new modality to test for coronary artery disease is the exercise stress echocardiogram. Exercise echocardiography offers several advantages over the radionucleotide studies. This technique is totally noninvasive, has no radiation exposure, permits global analysis of left ventricular function and valvular function, and allows for diagnosis of other structural heart disease.

In our laboratory, ultrasonically derived, digital image acquisition of the heart in four standard views is obtained during the resting phase. The patient then exercises using a standard treadmill protocol. Immediately post exercise the same four cardiac views are obtained and digitized. Side-by-side displays of the resting/exercise images are replayed in a continuous loop format. The images are interpreted qualitatively for the development of new regional wall motion abnormalities (systolic dysfunction—Figure 13–1). An area of the heart that had been contracting well before exercise but is no longer contracting postexercise suggests an area of cardiac ischemia subserved by a stenotic coronary artery (Figure 13–4). An area that is neither contracting during the resting phase nor post exercise suggests a fixed myocardial infarction. This testing format enjoys marked improvement in sensitivity and specificity over a standard nonimage stress test, with a sensitivity of 75% to 95% and specificity of 65% to 90%. The test also can generally be performed at lower costs and with less sophisticated equipment than the radionucleotide tests.

NONEXERCISE STRESS TESTING

A common problem that may be encountered in the spinal rehabilitation population is the patient unable to perform a graded exercise treadmill test because of his or her underlying back problem. When this is a clinical problem, there are still ways to analyze for cardiac ischemia with noninvasive tests. A variety of nonexercise "stress" modalities can be used:

– Pharmacologic Stress Testing
- Coronary vasodilators (dipyridamole, adenosine)
- Inotropic/chronotropic augmentation (dobutamine, isoproterenol)
- Coronary vasoconstrictors (ergonovine)

– Nonpharmacologic Stress Testing
- Atrial pacing
- Cold pressor test

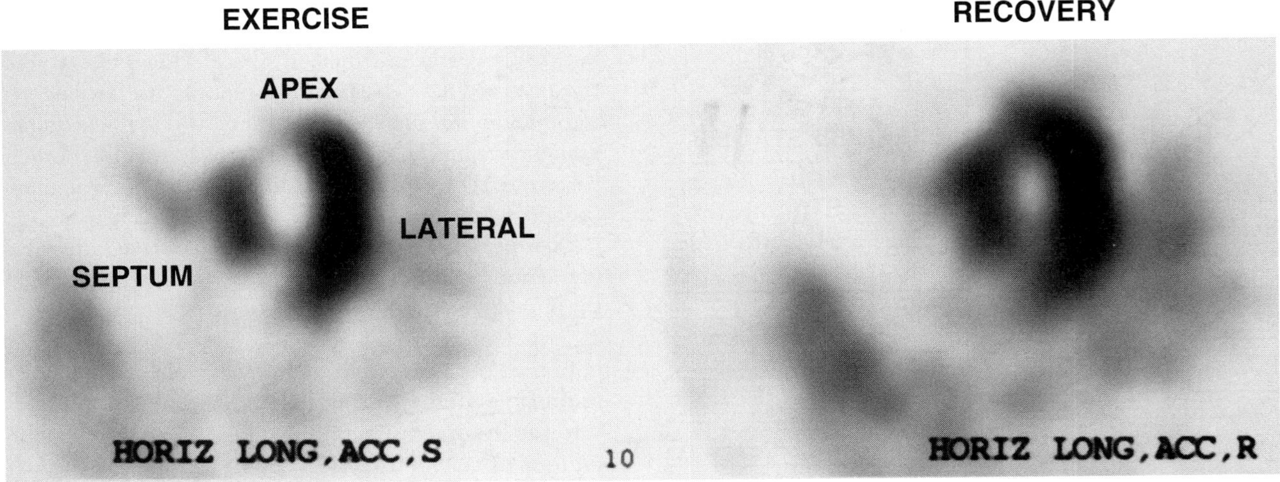

Figure 13–3 Exercise thallium radionucleotide angiogram. With exercise a "cold" spot is noted along the anterior septum and apex. During recovery (redistribution phase) the septum "fills in," but a persistent defect is seen in a small area of the apex. This study is consistent with a small apical myocardial infarction with a large area of septal ischemia.

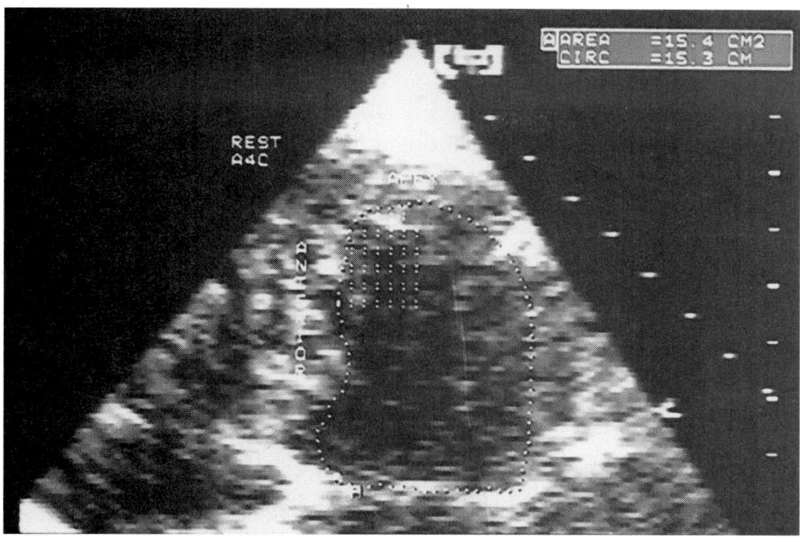

A

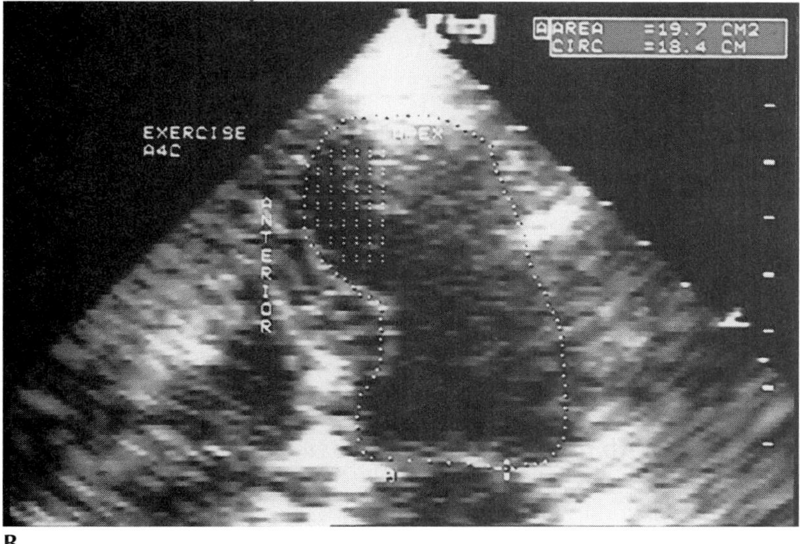

B

Figure 13–4 Stress echocardiogram. End systolic frames from the apical four-chamber (A4C) view, pre- and postexercise. Note the bulging (stippled area) of the anterior wall in the postexercise frame **(B)** compared to the preexercise frame **(A)**. This woman, who presented with neck and back pain, was found on angiography to have a 95% midleft anterior descending artery stenosis.

In our laboratory, pharmacologic stress testing using three standard agents—dipyridamole, adenosine, and dobutamine—is the favored technique.

Each of these agents has unique pharmacologic properties and there are specific clinical circumstances when one agent would be preferable over another. Adenosine and dipyridamole act via the A_2 receptor on the outer membrane of the endothelium and smooth muscle cell membrane. Stimulation of the receptor causes a coronary flow "steal" phenomenon by dilating normal segments of the artery and shunting blood away from stenotic segments. This pharmacologically induced flow heterogeneity is ideally suited for a radionucleotide coronary angiogram with thallium or technetium.

Caffeine and theophylline both competitively block the A_2 receptor, and therefore patients who have ingested large amounts of caffeine or patients on theophylline preparations should not have this form of pharmacologic stress test. In addition, these agents can precipitate bronchoconstriction; therefore, patients with asthma should not undergo this type of testing. Adenosine also acts on the A_1 receptor causing high-degree heart block. Therefore, adenosine is contraindicated in patients with preexisting high-degree heart block without a pacemaker.

Dobutamine acts as a positive inotropic agent via its effect on the $beta_1$ and $beta_2$ receptors. By increasing the RPP, dobutamine causes a true ischemia that mimics exercise, and this agent is ideally suited for imaging systolic wall dysfunction by stress echocardiography. Use of dobutamine would be contraindicated in patients on a beta-blocker because beta-blockade negates the positive inotropic effects of the dobutamine. Furthermore, there is a high incidence of arrhythmia with dobutamine, and therefore patients with high-grade ectopy (high-grade PVCs, ventricular couplets, uncontrolled atrial fibrillation, or supraventricular tachycardia) should not undergo dobutamine stress testing.

ADDITIONAL DIAGNOSTIC TESTING

ECHOCARDIOGRAPHY

When there is a clinical suspicion of underlying structural heart disease, an echocardiogram with Doppler study is quite useful. The echocardiogram is an ultrasonic image of the heart visualizing all the chambers, walls, and valves. Additionally, with Doppler study, cardiac hemodynamics can be noninvasively interpreted. However, this study does not allow direct imaging of the coronary arteries.

Echocardiography can be useful in diagnosing structural heart disease, such as aortic stenosis or IHSS, which would be critically important to identify before a detailed rehabilitation program is begun. Its use in the diagnosis of coronary artery disease has previously been discussed in the section on stress echocardiography. Additionally, pericardial disease can be diagnosed by this modality.

HOLTER MONITORING

When there is concern that a patient may be having irregular heart beats (dysrhythmia), a Holter monitor allows recording of each heartbeat over the course of 24 hours. A similar test called a cardiac event monitor is a patient-activated EKG that the subject can wear for prolonged periods of time. These tests allow one to correlate any potential symptoms the patient may be having with a possible underlying heart rhythm disturbance.

CARDIAC CATHETERIZATION

The most complete test to fully evaluate coronary artery disease, or significant valvular dysfunction or to obtain other physiologic data is the heart catheterization. This is an invasive test that involves placing tubes or catheters directly in various heart chambers and coronary arteries. The angiographic study entails dye injection into the arteries, outlining their lumen so that one can accurately define any coronary stenosis. This test is the most definitive for evaluating coronary artery disease. The test is invasive, however, with a rate of 0.1% to 0.2% risk of untoward effect such as stroke, myocardial infarction, or death. Generally, this test is not performed unless there is a high degree of suspicion for a significant underlying cardiac problem.

VASCULAR STUDIES

A number of invasive and noninvasive tests are available to evaluate for vascular disease. The simplest test beyond physical examination is the ankle-brachial index. The test involves obtaining blood pressures both in the leg and arm and comparing them. An unfavorable ratio would suggest significant vascular disease in the lower extremities. Abdominal ultrasound and Doppler study allow one to image the abdominal aorta for atherosclerosis, abdominal aortic aneurysm, or dissection. Similarly, Doppler flow studies noninvasively measure blood flow. Identifying poor flow to a limb would lead one to suspect that a patient's leg pain may be of vascular origin rather than neuromuscular origin. There are other noninvasive tests that can similarly identify abdominal aortic disease, including computed axial tomogram (CAT) scan or magnetic resonance imaging (MRI) scan. Lastly an angiogram, although invasive, can definitively determine the anatomy of the abdominal aorta and lower extremity vasculature. All these invasive and noninvasive studies have a high degree of accuracy in making clinical diagnoses.

DIFFERENTIAL DIAGNOSIS FOR MUSCULOSKELETAL PRESENTATIONS

A major focus of this chapter has been to develop guidelines for health appraisal and risk stratification prior to initiation of an extensive spinal rehabilitation program. For every patient complaint, there is a differential diagnosis that should be entertained. The patient with unrecognized cardiovascular disease may initially present to a rehabilitation provider. It is important to determine the underlying cause of the patient's complaint so as not to embark on an incorrect therapeutic plan.

DISEASES ASSOCIATED WITH LOW BACK PAIN

Abdominal Aortic Disease

Low back pain associated with disease of the abdominal aorta may be due to aneurysmal dilatation, obstruction of the vasculature, or rupture. Abdominal aortic aneurysm is most commonly seen in men in the sixth and seventh decades of life. Such patients generally have a history of hypertension, generalized atherosclerosis, angina, or other peripheral vascular disease. Some studies have suggested a genetic predisposition for abdominal aortic aneurysm. On examination, palpation of the abdomen may reveal a pulsatile mass near the level of the umbilicus which may extend into the lower abdomen. Deep palpation may reproduce the patient's clinical pain syndrome. Auscultation often will reveal a bruit, and there may be decreased pulses in the femoral or dorsal pedal areas. Physical signs such as leg weakness or abnormal reflexes may be due to compromised blood flow to the spinal cord or impingement on the peripheral nerves.

Any of the tests listed previously to examine the abdominal vasculature can be quite useful in confirming the diagnosis. Because the symptoms of abdominal aortic disease may be myriad, the diagnosis should be considered in any patient at high-risk who presents with nondescript back pain that is exacerbated by activity.

Peripheral Vascular Disease

Vascular claudication generally is exacerbated by exertion and is relieved by rest, unlike nerve root impingement, which is more likely to be positional. Physical signs frequently noted include diminished or absent pulses, atrophic skin changes, and poorly healing wounds. The aforementioned vascular studies can help confirm the diagnosis.

Vesper's Curse

Vesper's curse is an interesting syndrome of concomitant neuropathic pain and cardiac disease in which patients present with symptoms of lumbar back pain with sciatic radiation associated with cardiac failure and lumbar spinal disease. The two components necessary are lumbar sacral disease, generally lumbar sacral stenosis (either complete or incomplete), or spondylolisthesis coupled with right-sided cardiac failure.[16,17]

Upon assumption of the supine position, there is redistribution of body fluids into the central cavity. With reduced right ventricular compliance as seen in congestive heart failure, the central venous pressures can be elevated and the pressure transmitted by collaterals into the paravertebral plexus of Batson, thus acutely exacerbating a chronic lumbar spinal stenosis. If the lumbar spinal stenosis itself is not complete, a restoration of normal hemodynamics results in a decrease in excessive venous distention and reduced lumbar root irritability, thus reducing the lumbar pain syndrome of Vesper's curse.

Pericarditis

Pericarditis on occasion can be confused with primary scapular or back pain. Pericarditis is an inflammatory condition of the pericardial sac surrounding the heart. A classic presentation is pain radiating to the back or scapula that is exacerbated in the supine position and relieved in the sitting position. Furthermore, deep inspiration may increase the pain intensity. On auscultation, a pericardial rub would confirm the diagnosis. Other tests that are useful include a sedimentation rate and echocardiogram.

Cardiac Angina

Cardiac ischemia from any source, be it atherosclerotic coronary artery narrowing, vasospastic angina, aortic stenosis, or IHSS, can cause referred pain to the back or shoulder. Evaluation of coronary disease has been discussed previously.

SUMMARY

Planning a rehabilitation protocol for the spinal patient is complex. The evaluation starts well before the patient enters the program. A health risk assessment should be performed to determine if there are special needs in a particular patient. This chapter has broadly reviewed guidelines for patients who may be at higher risk from cardiovascular complications. Methods to assess risk have been reviewed and specific cardiovascular diseases that may enter into the differential diagnosis have been summarized.

REFERENCES

1. Svensson HO, Vedan A, Wilhelmsson C. Low back pain in relation to other diseases and cardiovascular risk factors. *Spine*. 1983;8:277–285.
2. Cardus D, Ribas Cardus F, McTaggart WG. Coronary risk in spinal cord injury: Assessment following a multi-varied approach. *Arch Phys Med Rehabil*. 1992;73:930–933.
3. Gyntelberg F. One year incidence of low back pain among male residents of Copenhagen age 40–59. *Dan Med Bull*. 1974;21:30–36.
4. Westrin CG. Low back sick listing. *Acta Soc Med Scand*. 1970;2:127–134.
5. Yekutiel M, Brooks ME, Ohry A, Yoram J, Carel R. The prevalance of hypertension, ischemic heart disease and diabetes in traumatic spinal cord injured patients and amputees. *Paraplegia*. 1989;27:58–62.
6. Mittleman MA, Maclure M, Tofler GH. Triggering of acute myocardial infarction by heavy physical exertion. *N Engl J Med*. 1994;339(23):1677–1683.
7. Kestin AS, Ellis PA, Barnard MR. Effect of strenuous exercise on platelet activation state and reactivity. *Circulation*. 1993;88 (1):1502–1511.
8. Michael TH, Downing J. Screening for cardiovascular system disease. In: Boissonnault WG, ed. *Examination in Physical Therapy Practice: Screening for Medical Disease*. New York: Churchill Livingstone, 1991:33–73.
9. Cohen, M. *Cardiopulmonary Symptoms and Physical Therapy Practice*. New York: Churchill Livingstone, 1988.
10. Pate RR. ed. *Guidelines for Exercise Testing and Prescription*. Philadelphia: Lea & Febiger, 1991.
11. Stuart JR, Ellestad MH. National survey of exercise stress testing facilities. *Chest*. 1980;77:94.
12. Sheffield LT. Safety of exercise testing of volunteer subjects: The Lipid Research Clinic's prevalence study experience. *J Card Rehabil*. 1982;2:295–400.

13. Ellestad MH. ECG patterns and their significance. In: *Stress Testing—Principles and Practice*, 3rd ed. Philadelphia: FA Davis, 1986:223–276.
14. Beller GA. Myocardial perfusion imaging with thallium-201. In: Braunwald E, ed. *Cardiac Imaging*. Philadelphia: WB Saunders,1991:1047–1073.
15. Kiat H, Areeda J, Van Train K. Quantitative assessment of stress defect extent and reversibility on rest Tl 201/stress Tc 99m Sestamibi dual isotope myocardial perfusion SPECT: A prospective validation. *Circulation*. 1993;88(4):1–440.
16. LeBan MM, Wesolowski DP. Night pain associated with diminished cardiopulmonary compliance. *Am J Phys Med Rehabil*. 1988;67:155–160.
17. LeBan MM. Vespers curse night pain—The bane of Hypnos. *Arch Phys Med Rehabil*. 1984;65:501–504.

SECTION

III

Computer-Aided Performance Testing and Rehabilitation

Science without religion is lame, religion without science is blind.

—*Albert Einstein*
New York City, September 1940

Exercise is a unique intervention. Unlike some pharmacologic therapies, its impact on one risk factor or disease process is not offset by adverse effects or other risk factors. We are certain that if the effects of exercise could be bottled, it would be the most widely prescribed medication.

—*Linn Goldberg and Diane L. Elliot*
Exercise for Prevention and Treatment of Illness
F.A. Davis Co. (1994)

CHAPTER 14

Triaxial Dynamometry

David E. Stude, M.S. D.C. & Daryl Schapmire, M.S.

INTRODUCTION

Evaluation of the neuromusculoskeletal performance abilities of the trunk is of growing interest. The multifactorial nature of back pain poses a difficult diagnostic challenge for the clinician[1] and this is particularly alarming since the condition is so prevalent and so costly in industrial societies today, especially in the United States.[2–8] In spite of the extensive research attention that has been devoted to diagnosing and treating back pain, its prevalence is increasing.

The dynamic, multiplanar trunk performance dynamometer called the Isostation B-200 (Interlogics, Inc.; Hillsborough, NC) is described in this chapter (see Figure 14–1). This computer-aided dynamometer, which simultaneously measures several trunk performance parameters in all three primary planes of motion (sagittal, coronal, and transverse), has been the focus of a reasonable degree of research activity.[9–22]

ISOSTATION B-200

The instrument works by detecting and monitoring performance parameters (velocity of movement, torque, range of motion, etc.) with specialized devices (actuator, transducer, and potentiometer). It then transfers this information, by way of an electronic signal, to a computer capable of translating the signal to relevant measurement units (degrees per second, pound-feet, and degrees of motion).

One of the challenges faced in developing computer-aided spinal assessment equipment is creating a device that will functionally parallel human motion patterns or, in this case, at least measure parts of spinal performance reliably and with a degree of accurate predictability. There is no "gold standard" device that meets all the requirements of spinal human performance testing, but research studies using the B-200 suggest that, when used appropriately, it can be a useful tool in the spinal assessment process.[9–25]

PRACTICAL ADVANTAGES OF THE B-200

1. It is capable of measuring functional performance parameters in all three planes of motion simultaneously. This is an important consideration since the human body, when performing normal activities of daily living (ADLs), is not limited to uniplanar movements.
2. Testing can be performed with the subject in a seated or standing position. Many testing instruments used currently require that the subject be positioned in the seated position only, yet this does not reflect the functional position in which most injuries occur. Also, research studies demonstrate a relative increase in intervertebral disc pressure when assuming a seated position, compared to standing upright, suggesting the potential for increased likelihood of injury when the subject is asked to exert an effort in the seated posture. Therefore, use of the B-200 allows the clinician to choose which testing position is most appropriate, based on work-related ADLs, and which position is the safest, depending on the diagnosis.
3. It is capable of measuring trunk strength and trunk muscle endurance dynamically or isometrically. Sometimes a patient is in too much discomfort to be tested dynamically. Also, patients with significant intervertebral disc derangement may not be candidates for dynamic testing, but in some cases isometric strength and/or trunk muscle endurance can be useful. This device allows the clinician to

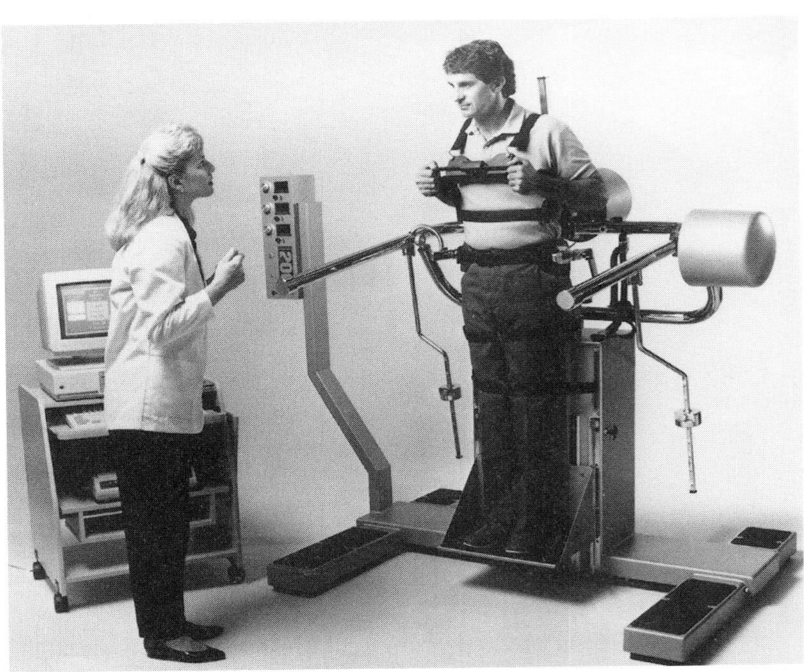

Figure 14–1. Isostation B-200 triaxial dynamometer.

choose a test protocol that is appropriate, informative, and safe.

4. The primary testing mode utilized for the B-200 is isoinertial (bilateral concentric). This means that the resistive force the subject works against is preset and fixed. It is usually established by the clinician and based on reported work-related demands, or is adjusted by the computer by using a percentage of the subject's maximum isometric strength. Testing in this isoinertial mode is potentially an advantage since it reflects similar types of functional movements that we all perform. Isokinetic testing, on the other hand, may have some benefits, but human activities do not occur with constant velocity and constantly changing resistive forces. Isometric testing can be used to reliably measure strength performance efforts (maximum voluntary contraction or muscle endurance) but may not be as helpful in measuring other performance parameters.

PRACTICAL DISADVANTAGES OF THE B-200

1. Although it claims to measure low back function, in reality it is measuring much more. The whole thoracolumbar spine, for example, is involved in trunk performance when testing is being conducted, and it is practically difficult to have the subject being tested completely avoid use of the upper extremities. In some ways this may be considered an advantage, since ADLs are performed in whole-body fashion, but these additional variables make computer-generated data more challenging to interpret.
2. The fact that the patient is restrained downward from the pelvis creates an opportunity to evaluate functional performance primarily of the thoracolumbar spine. This is an advantage if spinal function is a primary focus of the examination, but again, as mentioned previously, the body performs activities in a whole-body fashion. This means that the evalutor will be unable to address movement dysfunction throughout the entire kinetic chain and consequently will be unable to address functional compensations that may exist during complicated whole-body activities. This is certainly true generally for all objective testing instrumentation, and least of all, true for the B-200, since it evaluates trunk performance in all planes of motion simultaneously.
3. All objective instrumentation utilizes some sort of restraining system and this implies the potential for injury. There have been no published papers describing serious incidents with this kind of testing to date, and this is probably due to established absolute and relative contraindications to testing. These contraindications, when followed properly, will certainly reduce, if not avoid injury, but this means that individuals with serious conditions may not be able to be tested at all. These individuals may be part of the population that is difficult to diagnose and effectively treat, and part of that portion of the low back population in the chronic pain group, the most costly back pain population to society.

THE IMPORTANCE OF DYNAMIC TESTING AS ONE COMPONENT IN ASSESSING SPINAL FUNCTION

Our knowledge of strength performance is based on many studies that evaluated spinal and whole-body strength isometrically. Even though an attempt was made to evaluate dynamic, whole-body activities in the past through the use of isometric measurement devices, these measurements may not reflect real performance dysfunction and appear not to have strong predictive value. For example, Battie et al[26] demonstrated that isometric lifting strength had little predictive value in terms of identifying individuals at risk for incurring industrial back pain injuries. Furthermore, static biomechanical principles have been used[27] to help establish standards recommended by the National Institute for Occupational Safety and Health (NIOSH), yet these standards rest on circumstantial evidence that suggests lifting intensity may be related to the etiology of industrial low back injuries.[28–30] This was shown not to have a high practical value since in order for isometric strength tests to have predictive value, the job-related demands must require individual workers to exert an effort that reflects a high percentage of their maximum strength potential.[31–34]

The ability to evaluate spinal performance in a dynamic fashion is gaining more attention since there are studies that suggest we cannot use isometric measurement parameters to predict dynamic performance,[35–39] that static tests significantly underestimate the degree of dynamic, spinal axial loading, and that there is a poor correlation between lifting performance in individuals being tested isometrically and maximum acceptable lift performance ability determined through the use of psychophysical assessments.[40–45]

Even though microtrauma can potentially occur with the repetitive assumption of a poor posture or other prolonged or repetitive isometric activity, most injuries occur as a result of an individual performing a whole-body, three-dimensional, dynamic activity and most are associated with bending and/or twisting.[46–48] In addition, it has been demonstrated that rapid acceleration of the trunk can result in a significant increase in axial loading primarily at the lumbosacral junction,[49] and it is this region of the back that is most frequently involved in back injuries. The measurement of velocity with the use of the B-200 has been shown to be a sensitive measurement for back function in that it may be able to confirm subjective complaints of low back pain and it may have some predictive value in estimating the likelihood for back injury in asymptomatic individuals.[50] Furthermore, it is universally accepted that the spine moves in complex, coupled movement patterns[51–53] and so it seems logical that spinal performance assessment include a dynamic component.

In summary, there is evidence to suggest a lack of reliability in using the static strength model as a predictor of industrial back injuries or in accurately recommending safe, work-related, maximal lifting limits. Because it does not reflect dynamic trunk performance abilities, it is suggested that evaluation of the trunk include a dynamic component that is reliable for the measurement of performance parameters and that closely reflects those motions associated with activities of daily living.

RESEARCH CAVEATS

The B-200 evaluates trunk functional performance by simultaneously measuring torque, velocity, range of motion (total excursion in each plane of motion), and secondary coupled spinal movement patterns and testing inconsistencies in flexion, extension, rotation, and lateral flexion. It also provides several nonphysiological indicators that suggest the presence of testing inconsistencies.

RELIABILITY AND VALIDITY

When the decision to consider investing in a piece of evaluation equipment is appropriate, one of the most important considerations is that of reliability and validity. Table 14–1 suggests elements to consider prior to purchase of objective instrumentation. For example, inter- and intramachine reliability refer to a device that produces similar data when testing and retesting the same population. If your colleague was testing a patient and he asked you for another opinion, wouldn't it be important to know that you could evaluate this same individual and obtain similar performance data? Similarly, would it be nice to know that if you evaluated the same group of patients on 2 consecutive days (assume a theoretical model here) that you would obtain the same results for each individual (assume a nonremarkable interim history) and for the group as a whole? Then there is the question of inter- and intraexaminer reliability. If there are many technicians generating computer data from the same testing instrument, and from the same population of patients, are the data similar? Does one technician have the tendency to coach subjects more than others, and does this alter performance measurements? Is there a technician who has a tendency to restrain subjects more loosely than other

Table 14–1: Testing Instrumentation Selection Recommendations

1. Ability to reflect functional performance attributes
2. Reliability
3. Validity
4. Performance testing options:
   A. Mode(s)
   B. Testing position(s)
   C. Planes evaluated
5. Normative database and cost
6. Predictive value and long-term outcome success

technicians, and does this affect repeat performance measurements? Currently, there is no instrument that has been thoroughly and completely evaluated when it comes to all questions reflecting reliability. There are many measurement devices, however, that have been tested rigorously and this adds to the credibility of the instrument for use in a clinical setting. A valid instrument is one that measures what it purports to measure. For example, are data reflecting claimed measurements of torque actually measuring this performance parameter?

The B-200 has been the subject of a variety of testing protocols. Bench tests have been performed that show a reasonable degree of specificity.[54–56] Other studies have been conducted that have evaluated within-subject comparisons, and although the reproducibility of isometric torque and dynamic performance parameters was good, unresisted range of motion was not universally demonstrated to be reliable.[57–61] Total excursion within each plane of motion, however, was shown to be reproducible; therefore, some work may have to be done to more accurately identify the neutral position for instruments that allow subjects to move in multiple planes of motion. Since deviations in range of motion do not seem to have predictive value in estimating the prevalence of low back injuries, the clinical usefulness of reliably measuring small changes in flexibility may prove to be less critical than previously suspected by some investigators.

It is assumed that the presence of pain can impact performance parameters and therefore repeat measurements within groups of low back pain patients may be highly variable. Szpalski et al[62] showed excellent reproducibility for performance measurements taken within a group of chronic low back pain patients. In this study, and as demonstrated in studies mentioned above, range of motion from "neutral" position was the least reproducible measurement parameter. The authors in this study also suggest guidelines to help determine whether or not patient maximum effort is being exerted.

Another study was done to evaluate the presence of variance within four separate B-200 testing stations.[63] For isometric performance measurements, the between-machine variance was approximately 0% to 1.7%, and for dynamic measurements of velocity it was 0% to 3.8%. Once again range of motion, this time only in the sagittal plane, was demonstrated to be unreliable with between-machine variance measured at approximately 20%. The primary source of variation found within this study was that of between-subject differences, rather than between machine-variations. These differences, however, may be based on misinterpreted data and so may not be relevant conclusions.[64] In order to minimize the between-subject differences, it appears to be important that subjects be given instructions to perform movements at their preferred pace,[65–66] but in asymptomatic individuals, instructions to move at a preferred pace or to exert maximal effort do not appear to impact within-dynamic-trial performance measurements.[67] Some of the studies evaluating measurement variations, however, suffer from an insufficient number of subjects and this can influence statistical power and subsequent conclusions following data analysis.

TESTING PROTOCOLS

There is more than one evaluation protocol that can be utilized with the B-200. The first three protocols listed below represent commercially available testing protocols, and the last two are testing protocols that can be utilized by the testor, but results of which have to be recorded manually. These testing protocols include:

1. B-SCAN
2. B-SAFE
3. OOC
4. Isometric Trunk Muscle Endurance
5. Dynamic Trunk Muscle Endurance

B-SCAN Testing Protocol

The B-SCAN testing protocol allows the clinician to measure performance parameters by using preestablished, arbitrarily chosen resistance values that each patient works against. This means that all patients, regardless of age, gender, weight, fitness level, job description, and so forth, will be tested using these values. This software package, however, gives the clinician the option of changing resistance values and so it is particularly useful for special case considerations and especially useful in research studies that require careful control of this variable. This testing protocol is more specialized than the others.

B-SAFE Testing Protocol

This testing protocol allows the examiner to determine baseline performance characteristics of an individual when he or she is being compared to other individuals that perform similar work-related demands. It is used to screen individuals who are considering certain work-related activities or to screen a population of workers who are asymptomatic to determine if there are performance parameters that suggest the potential likelihood of future dysfunction and injury. Subject and population demographics help ensure the evaluator that relevant and applicable performance scores are obtained. Testing with the use of B-SAFE reveals performance scores that can be used to compare trunk performance of an individual to a normative database reflecting a mean score for that particular group. A performance score of 50 indicates an average score, when held against the comparison population. Scores below 50 indicate below average performance, and scores above 50 indicate above average performance. There are six performance scores obtained during B-SAFE testing, one for each of the primary planes of motion tested. These six scores are used to calculate a mean and this represents a composite score. A composite score reflects the overall performance ability of an individual, compared to the comparison population chosen. A composite score of 35 is one standard deviation below the mean composite score of 50 and a score of 65 is one standard deviation above the mean. Approximately 70% of all composite scores fall between a value of 35 and 65, assuming the population approximates a normal distribution. This information can be useful in job screening, in tailoring an exercise program, or in establishing baseline information so that repeat testing can determine progress made in a formal rehabilitation or work-hardening program.

OOC Testing Protocol

The OOC protocol was developed by Dr. Stephan Deutsch, MD, at the Occupational Orthopaedic Center (Pawtucket, RI) and is a widely used testing procedure for B-200 users. One advantage of this procedure is that the computer automatically programs dynamic resistance levels by using 25% and 50% of individual isometric trunk strength. Therefore, each person being tested is working against a percentage of his or her own maximal strength effort, rather than an arbitrarily assigned value. This adds a component of relative consistency within the testing process and is potentially a safer way to evaluate back pain patients. Since subjects in pain may behave and perform differently, and considering the multifactorial nature of back pain, dynamic resistance based on individual strength performance measurements may deserve more attention. Since this is frequently used, additional information will be provided about use of the OOC protocol, but the information applies to other testing protocols as well.

Figure 14–3. The lateral width of the lateral pelvic supports is adjusted and locked in place.

Prior to testing an individual on the B-200, regardless of the protocol selected, patients should be introduced to the testing principles and to the nature of the machine in a uniform fashion. Inconsistencies in patient orientation, patient instruction during testing, and restraining procedures and lack of expertise in operation of the B-200 Iso-

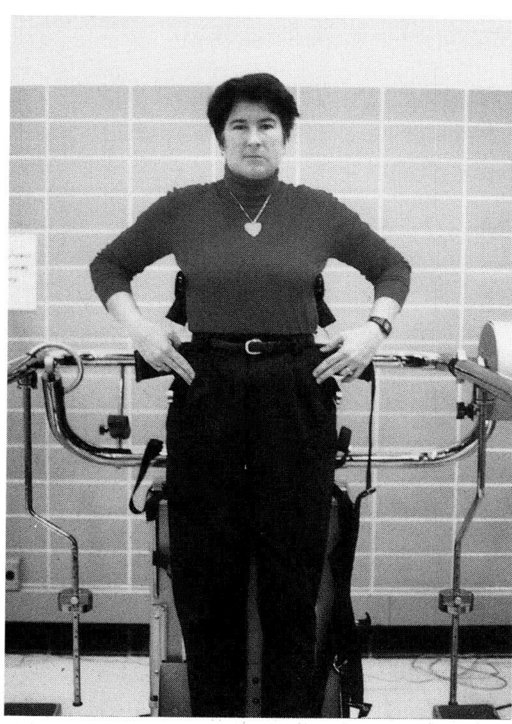

Figure 14–2. Once the patient is positioned properly, the vertical height is adjusted so that the anterosuperior iliac spine (ASIS) is in line with the holes in the lateral pelvic support.

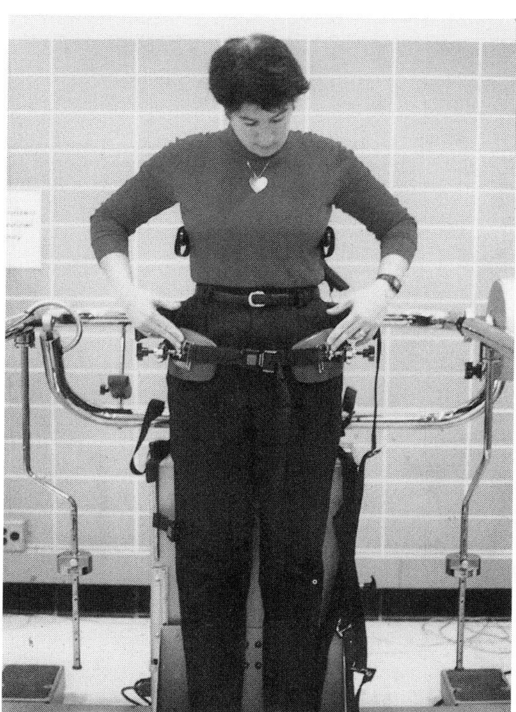

Figure 14–4. The hip pads are slid into the lateral pelvic supports and adjusted so that the pelvic movement is restrained and so that symmetry is observed.

station itself could all represent variables that could impact the reliability of performance data and so must be consistently addressed with every testing session.

It takes about 30 minutes to test an individual from start to finish, excluding time for initial data entry, paperwork, and data interpretation. The standard OOC testing protocol consists of the following:

1. Patient history and evaluation
2. Orientation of the patient to testing instrumentation
3. Moderate warmup
4. Range of motion—sequence 1
5. Isometric trunk strength (two trials in each plane of motion)
6. Dynamic exercise—sequence 1
7. Range of motion—sequence 2
8. Dynamic exercise—sequence 2

Since there are studies that demonstrate changes in subject performance with apprehension or learning, it is important to consistently introduce the testing instrumentation to each patient. The following are some suggested points that should be made with every individual being evaluated:

1. The B-200 test is part of an evaluation to help collect and record information about back performance. It is not "the test," but part of the evaluation process.
2. The B-200 is a passive device, which means that it will not move the patient, but rather the patient moves the machine. If the patient has to stop, the machine will stop also. The machine is programmed so that resistance will change automatically as a result of isometric strength performance and so it is very important that best effort be exerted, within the patient's own tolerance abilities.
3. Some tests will involve moving freely with no resistance at all (range of motion). Other tests will be performed with all the locks on the machine and so the machine will not move at all (isometric testing). This test will involve pushing as hard as possible in one direction at a time. Avoid exploding into the machine (ballistic movements), but best effort is necessary, within the patient's own tolerance abilities.
4. Coaching during the testing protocol is not recommended. Consistent instructions, prior to each testing sequence, however, are strongly recommended, in order to streamline testing procedures and to reduce intratesting variability. Instructing the patient to move as hard, as fast, and as far as possible, within his or her own tolerance abilities is appropriate prior to the dynamic sequence. Some studies, mentioned previously, however, suggest that for some individuals it may be most appropriate to allow them to exert at their preferred motion, in order to increase data reliability. It also may be a more appropriate measure (i.e., "What are you comfortable doing?"), as opposed to a measure of maximum capabilities. Use of videotapes to cover some of the introduction may be useful in conserving manpower resources, as well as helping to streamline a consistent approach to patient orientation.

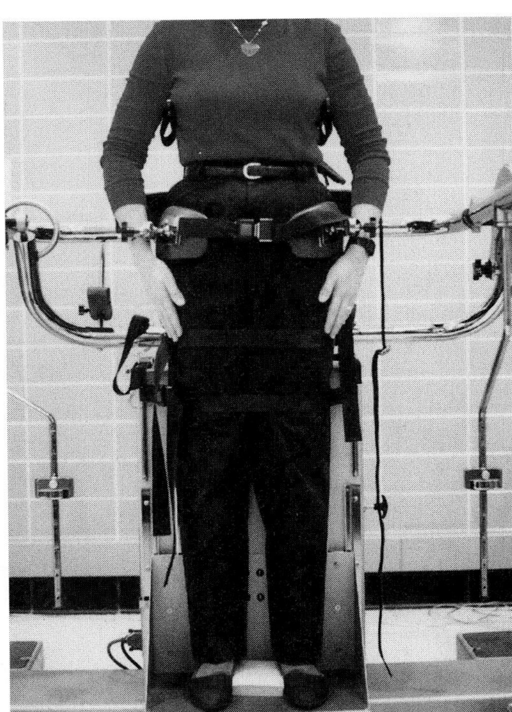

Figure 14–5. The lower extremity restraining straps are secured in place and tightened.

Figure 14–6. The sacral support piece is adjusted and secured in place.

The restraining procedure utilized when testing on the Isostation B-200 requires careful attention to detail. Testing on a machine that allows multiplanar movements can be considered an advantage in that it may more closely approximate real trunk performance, and a disadvantage in that it is associated with more variables that can be difficult to control. There have been no published studies that have directly addressed the restraining procedure in detail, but it has been the author's experience (Stude) that alterations in the chronology of the restraining method between testers can have a measurable impact on trunk performance data. It is suggested, until more information becomes available, that a consistent restraining protocol be utilized, and that the chronological order be followed as well.

RESTRAINING PROTOCOL

1. Place the patient on the footstand, without shoes (unless there are orthopedic requirements for orthotics, heel lifts, or required footwear), and adjust vertical height so that the anterosuperior iliac spine is inline with lateral pelvic supports (Figure 14–2).
2. Adjust and tighten lateral pelvic supports (Figure 14–3).
3. Secure hip pads (check for symmetrical depth of pads: "hole check") (Figure 14–4).
4. Apply and adjust tension on lower extremity straps at midthigh level and above the patella (Figure 14–5).
5. Adjust and secure sacral support (Figure 14–6).
6. Adjust the thoracic restraint device and associated components (Figure 14–7).
7. Adjust backpack height and counterweights (×2) so that machine is neutrally balanced prior to the initiation of the test (Figures 14–8 and 14–9).

Checklists can be used to monitor testing inconsistencies. A chronological list of restraining steps can be attached to a convenient place near the testing machine. A testing checklist (Table 14–2) should be used to track the course of the test progression, and an observation sheet (Table 14–3) can be used to monitor patient behavior and subjective pain reports.

Just prior to the initiation of a test and following or during the restraining process, each patient should be instructed consistently as follows:

1. "Keep your hands on the backpack but remember, your arms and hands are only along for the ride. Use your back to perform the required activities."
2. "Keep your feet back against the machine, keeping the feet flat during the test."
3. "Please breathe as comfortably as you can throughout the test and give your best effort, within your own tolerance abilities."

OOC Testing Advantages

The OOC testing protocol is widely used because of several practical advantages, including:

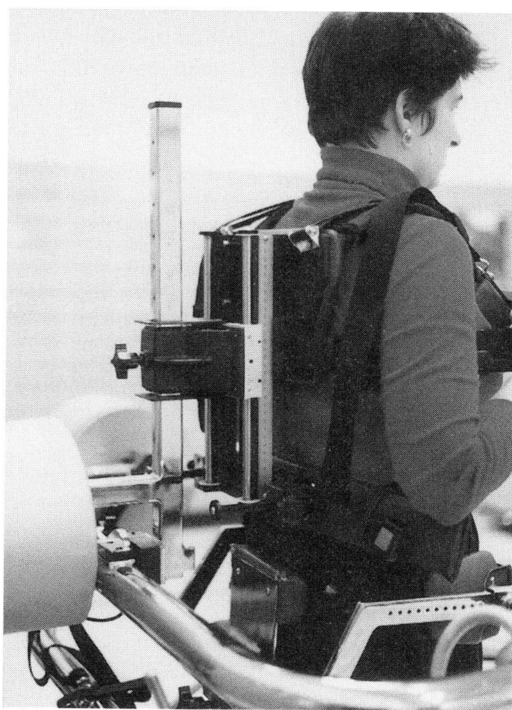

Figure 14–7. The thoracic restraining device and associated components are adjusted properly and locked into place.

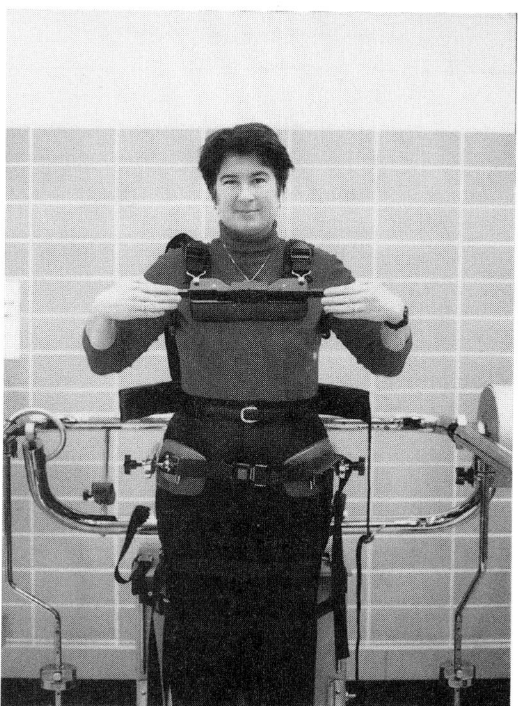

Figure 14–8. Backpack height should be adjusted to allow sufficient sagittal plane mobility and then locked into place.

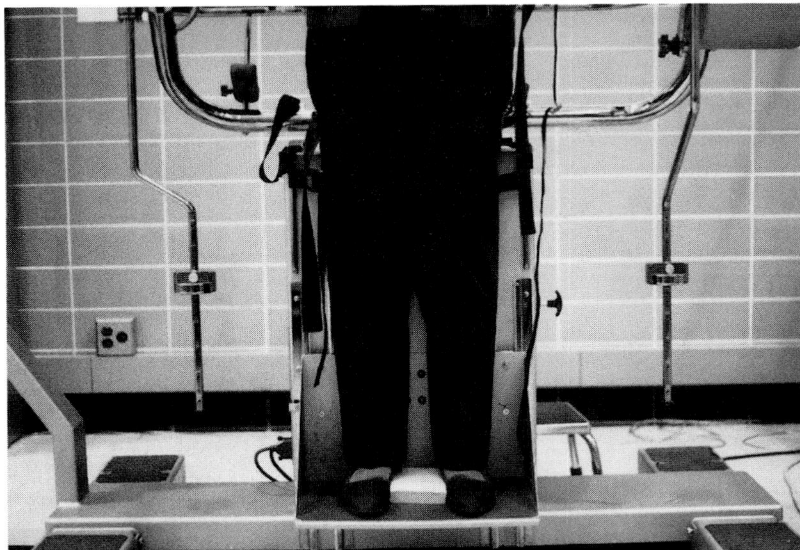

Figure 14–9. The counterweight height (×2) should be uniformly adjusted so that it corresponds to the setting on the thoracic restraining device, ensuring that the machine is neutrally balanced prior to test sequence initiation.

1. Patient safety is increased by introducing dynamic resistance levels that are calculated from each individual's isometric strength, rather than using arbitrarily chosen values.
2. Having patients work at 25% and 50% of their maximum isometric strength helps to accommodate the variability between patients.
3. A standardized testing procedure helps to reduce variability that is associated with patient behavior. There is evidence to suggest that instruction from the evaluator can impact patient effort[68] and that effort accommodation with changing resistance levels can be quantified.[69,70]
4. Actual measured parameters are used in conjunction with performance ratios, and this provides the clinician with information that can suggest the potential likelihood of testing inconsistencies, lack of best effort, or lack of motivation.
5. Performance data are compared to a normative database and this allows the clinician to classify the level of low back dysfunction as mild, moderate, or severe.
6. Parameters that characterize function are used to help evaluate normal patient testing behavior. For example, hesitancy, fatigue, and holdback are reflected in measured data and this assists in determining whether or not a patient has exhibited a consistent and maximal effort.
7. Baseline rehabilitation data help to compare patient performance data with other individuals of the same gender and within a similar age range. This information can be especially useful in establishing the principal focus of a rehabilitation program, or at least in assisting in the process of developing rehabilitation and/or work-hardening priorities. Repeat testing can help quantify changes in overall performance, especially in comparison to others in the same general class of gender and age.
8. Although not limited to this testing protocol, the OOC system helps to quantify low back dysfunction, so that objective information can be used to support a diagnosis for third-party payors, or for use in the legal arena.

ABSOLUTE CONTRAINDICATIONS TO B-200 TESTING

Clinical judgement by a qualified doctor will never be replaced by an algorithm, but a template of this kind can help direct a clinical decision. Absolute contraindications include, but are not necessarily limited to, the following:

1. Acute herniated intervertebral disc (nucleus pulposus prolapse) with distal extremity pain and/or neurological deficit.
2. Significant vertebral segmental dysfunction, for example, an unstable spondylolisthesis or vertebral fracture.
3. Pregnancy, unless a signed consent authorization form is obtained from the patient and her referring obstetrician.
4. Significant evidence to suggest the presence of osteoporosis or osteomalacia.

RELATIVE CONTRAINDICATIONS TO B-200 TESTING

1. Early postoperative laminectomy
2. Mild osteoporosis or osteomalacia
3. Rheumatoid arthritis in advanced stages
4. Relatively stable, but high-grade spondylolisthesis
5. Spinal internal fixation surgery (Harrington rod)

Table 14–2: OCC Back Evaluation Testing Checklist

OOC Back Evaluation System

Patient's name ____________________

ID # ____________________

____ **Evaluate the patient**

____ **Orientation to the B-200**

____ **Warmup**

____ **ROM sequence one** ____________________

Resist: 1/1/1. Test desc #: 1

____ **Isometric** ____________________

Resist: 63/118/63 (install mechanical locks). Test desc #: 2

Rotation	____ R	____ L	____ Max	____ 50%	____ 25%
Lateral flexion	____ R	____ L	____ Max	____ 50%	____ 25%
Flexion/ext (in flexion)	____ R	____ L	____ Max	____ 50%	____ 25%

____ **Dynamic sequence one** ____________________

Rotation	25%	Resist: ____ /118/63	Test desc #: 13
Rotation	50%	Resist: ____ /118/63	Test desc #: 27
Flexion/ext	25%	Resist: 63/ ____ /63	Test desc #: 14
Flexion/ext	50%	Resist: 63/ ____ /63	Test desc #: 28
Lateral flexion	25%	Resist: 63/118/____	Test desc #: 15
Lateral flexion	50%	Resist: 63/118/____	Test desc #: 29

____ **ROM sequence two** ____________________

Resist: 1/1/1. Test desc #: 1

____ **Dynamic sequence two** ____________________

Rotation	50%	Resist: ____ /118/63	Test desc #: 27
Rotation	25%	Resist: ____ /118/63	Test desc #: 13
Flexion/ext	50%	Resist: 63/____ /63	Test desc #: 28
Flexion/ext	25%	Resist: 63/____ /63	Test desc #: 14
Lateral flexion	50%	Resist: 63/118/____	Test desc #: 29
Lateral flexion	25%	Resist: 63/118/____	Test desc #: 15

____ **Observation Sheet**

Signature____________________

Date ____________

Table 14–3: OCC Evaluation Technician Observation Sheet

OOC Back Evaluation System

Before the Test

Patient's comments:

- ______ none
- ______ questions
- ______ safety concerns
- ______ pain concerns
- ______ doesn't understand
- ______ proves nothing
- ______ feels it will help
- ______ other ____________________

Reaction:

- ______ none
- ______ calm
- ______ cooperative
- ______ bored
- ______ fearful
- ______ nervous
- ______ timid
- ______ enthusiastic
- ______ other ____________________

During the test

Effort:

- ______ poor
- ______ fair
- ______ good
- ______ excellent
- ______ other ____________________

Reaction:

- ______ none
- ______ grimacing
- ______ pleasant
- ______ smiling
- ______ angry
- ______ reaching--leg
- ______ reaching--back
- ______ other ____________________

Movement:

test 1		test 2
______	slow	______
______	poor	______
______	hesitant	______
______	fair	______
______	good	______
______	fast	______

Changes:
Describe the patient's performance in test 2, compared to test 1:

- ______ slower
- ______ same
- ______ increased confidence
- ______ fatigue
- ______ faster

Pain

Before test:

- ______ none
- ______ slight
- ______ moderate
- ______ severe

During test:

- ______ none
- ______ slight
- ______ moderate
- ______ severe

After test:

- ______ none
- ______ slight
- ______ moderate
- ______ severe

After the test

Comments:

- ______ none
- ______ heavy backpack
- ______ claustrophobic
- ______ easier than expected
- ______ not too bad
- ______ worse than expected

Additional comments:

____
____
____
____
____
____
____
____
____

6. Acute phase of injury
7. Spinal infections
8. Congestive heart failure
9. Paget's disease
10. Stable angina
11. Claustrophobia
12. Past history of intracranial hemorrhage
13. Hypoparathyroidism
14. Abdominal aortic aneurysm
15. Respiratory insufficiency
16. Abdominal hernia
17. Status poststernotomy
18. History of use of anticoagulant therapy
19. Spinal tumors

RELATIVE INDICATIONS FOR TEST DISCONTINUATION

It may be necessary at times to discontinue a test after it has been in progress for a time. Reasons to discontinue a testing procedure include but are not necessarily limited to the following:

1. Dizziness
2. Shortness of breath
3. Chest, arm, or neck pain
4. Nausea
5. Sudden onset of rib pain that becomes worse with inspiration
6. Claustrophobia that severely impacts performance abilities
7. Reports of significantly worsening back pain and/or pain location that changes from central to peripheral

CLINICAL APPLICATIONS

The following are examples of B-200 trunk performance testing that have been used in the industrial setting and in the medicolegal arena. They do not demonstrate that the B-200 was, in and of itself, responsible for the outcomes that were reported. The B-200 may have served a key function, however, in providing a more comprehensive method for helping to reduce the costs associated with back injuries in industrial settings, and may assist in quantifying performance data that would be of assistance in directing judgements that reflect spinal dysfunction and permanent impairment. Further research will be necessary to delineate the specific role of testing instruments in the examples that follow, by controlling for all the variables that could have influenced reported outcomes.

Clinical Application 14–1

COCA-COLA ENTERPRISES

Coca-Cola Enterprises operates two bottling plants and 20 distribution centers in and around Atlanta, Georgia, employing nearly 1200 workers. Although the company's bottling and canning operations are highly automated, warehousing and delivery often require manual loading and unloading of heavy containers. Each day, for example, distribution center employees must move hundreds of soft-drink cases, weighing from 25 to more than 40 pounds each.

Of the worker compensation claims filed against the company each year, 65% involve injuries sustained while moving beverage containers. Back injuries account for 70% of compensation costs, according to Bill Grimes, Manager of Occupational and Environmental Safety.

To learn whether testing and physical training could help reduce injuries, lost productivity, and financial costs, Coca-Cola launched an experimental screening and exercise progam at one of its bottling plants. In conjunction with the Coca-Cola Healthworks Center, clinicians from Georgia Baptist Medical Center devised a 10-minute Isostation B-200 protocol for plant employees. Data from this baseline screening were used to evaluate back strength and function, to monitor each worker's function over time, and as comparison data in the event of an injury. The information was used to help design appropriate exercise regimens for employees, using Nautilus equipment.

The results of the program have been outstanding. During the first year, the plant experienced a 69% reduction in back injuries and an 87% drop in the average number of lost days. In addition, workers who do

continued

Clinical Application 14–1 *Continued*

suffer injury are now returning to work much faster than before.

Based on the success of this program, Coca-Cola recently launched an expanded program to obtain a more comprehensive profile of its work force. For this project, representative groups of employees of four Atlanta area distribution centers are being studied. The objectives are threefold:

1. To evaluate the effects of different exercise programs on injury rates and injury severity.
2. To develop more progressive therapies for rehabilitating injured workers.
3. To better weed out fraudulent or exaggerated claims.

By creating a profile of Coca-Cola's work force, Grimes also hopes to eventually establish a comprehensive screening program for new employees. This would be used to measure an applicant's strength, range of motion, and flexibility, so that prospective employees are not matched with jobs that exceed their physical capabilities.

Using the B-200 baseline test results, Grimes has already discovered that workers who score below average are more likely to suffer injury. Moreover, the size of their worker compensation claims tend to be significantly higher than the average. Thus, identifying and entering these "high-risk" employees in physical training programs is one of his major goals.

Although results of this latest project are not yet completed, Grimes believes that a screening/strengthening program for all workers will significantly reduce the number of job-related injuries. This should help the company, as a whole, to save millions of dollars annually.

For more information about this project, contact:
William H. Grimes, Safety Manager
Coca-Cola Enterprises
One Coca-Cola Plaza
Atlanta, GA 30313

Clinical Application 14–2

HASBRO, INC.

Making toy trucks, planes, and dolls may not seem especially hazardous, but employees who work the assembly lines and molding operations of Hasbro, Inc., in Pawtucket, Rhode Island, suffer the same sorts of injuries as workers in other types of factories. Repetitive bending and lifting have made back injuries Hasbro's No. 1 medical problem, followed by shoulder and wrist injuries, according to Kathleen Bryant, director of industrial nursing.

Before joining the nearby Occupational Orthopaedic Center in 1988, Hasbro employees required an average of 6 to 7 weeks to fully recover from back injuries. "What used to happen," says Bryant, "is that people would go to an orthopedic doctor or chiropractor. The old treatment was to prescribe medication—usually muscle relaxers—and bed rest."

In an effort to reduce the amount of time lost to injuries, Hasbro and the OOC launched an innovative "early intervention" program that involves same-day diagnosis and treatment.

The results? Workers suffering from back injuries are now returning to the job in 2 to 3 weeks, less than half the time it used to take. Overall, 68% of OOC patients are able to return to work the first day; 82% return within 2 weeks (the national average is 12 weeks).

Here's how Hasbro's program works: As soon as an employee is hurt, he or she reports the injury to a supervisor or to the medical department. A nurse or the attending supervisor then calls the OOC and schedules

Clinical Application 14–2 *Continued*

an appointment for the same day. With more serious back injuries, workers are tested using the Isostation B-200, which helps physicians evaluate the nature and severity of the injury. Based on the B-200 evaluation, doctors tailor a specific treatment for each patient. Rehabilitation usually begins on the date of injury.

"The OOC practices a new philosophy with back injuries," says Bryant. "They don't allow patients to lie in bed and do nothing: They get them up and they get them moving. The person begins mild exercises the very day of injury, or certainly the next day. We've found that this is really working: The muscles don't seem to tighten up, and people recover faster than those put on muscle relaxers."

Beside providing objective data to evaluate back muscle function after an injury, the B-200 is also used in the rehabilitation process to strengthen the injured muscles.

In addition to defining and treating the problem, says Bryant, the B-200 provides a reliable, objective determination of when the individual is ready to return to work. "In some cases, people can return to light duty. That's where companies can really save money. Under the physician's direction, people can often come back to work within 2 weeks, work fewer hours, perform lighter tasks, then return to normal duty in another 2 weeks."

Determining an individual's capabilites is a B-200 feature that may prove crucial to resolving some compensation cases.

Says Bryant: "There are doctors testifying in the courts day after day. You know that if you take your disability papers to them, they'll sign them and allow you to stay off the job, regardless of the truth. On the other hand, there are insurance doctors who'll say, "Yes, he can go back to work," when the poor person can't even stand up. Neither cares about the employee.

That's where the B-200 can come in. "A person cannot fake the machine out: You *do* receive an objective finding."

For more information, contact:
Dr. Stephen Deutsch
Occupational Orthopaedic Center
(401)722-2400
or
Kathleen Bryant
Director of Industrial Nursing
Hasbro Industries
(401)431-8397

Clinical Application 14–3

INGRAM BARGE COMPANY

The Ingram Barge Company is the third largest barge company in the United States, operating a fleet of tugboats on the Mississippi River and its tributaries. Employees live and work on these boats 24 hours a day for 30 days at a time. The pace of the work varies a lot. Workers are relatively idle for periods of time, and then perform tasks that are physically demanding—sometimes dangerous. Visibility is often poor, surfaces can be slippery; and arms and legs can get caught in the line. Furthermore, there is often a vertical displacement from boat to boat, depending on the weight of loads being carried.

The legal environment on the waterways is slightly different from that on land. Workers are protected by maritime laws and the Jones Act, which greatly favor the injured worker and provide no limit on the company's

continued

Clinical Application 14–3 *Continued*

liability. For workers covered under the Jones Act, the average award for lost time due to injury is $700,000.

The Ingram Barge Company's records showed that although the size of its work force was declining, both the injury rate and the related costs were on the rise. The company wondered whether some claims were truly job-related. It also questioned some of the medical and legal practices that were occurring.

To help deal with the increasing physical and financial costs of worker injuries—especially back cases—Ingram Barge approached Vanderbilt University's Ability Assessment Center. Under its direction, the company instituted three new procedures: (1) a more personalized interview process, (2) drug testing, and (3) a preemployment testing program.

Preemployment testing was based on an assessment of the tasks involved on the job. Tests included items such as a basic physical examination, and an Isostation B-200 evaluation. The B-200 documents trunk strength and function and provides baseline data used to determine whether an injured worker can return to full employment.

Clinicians at the Ability Assessment Center also implemented a 3-day training program for new workers, and worked with Ingram Barge Company to institute a transitional-duty program for partially rehabilitated workers. This program allows partially rehabilitated employees to be productive to the company. Transitional workers put in the same hours as those on normal duty, but are assigned less strenuous tasks.

The results of the first year of the preemployment assessment, screening, and education program have been impressive.

Although the number of lost-time nonback injuries remained constant (34 versus 32 per year), lost-time back injuries decreased by 43%. More importantly, the average number of days lost per back injury declined significantly. In the year before the program, the average number of days lost to nonback injury was 71; the number lost to back injury was 133. Within a year, these numbers were reduced to 46 days for nonback and 36 days for back injuries (note that the average number of days lost per back injury is now less than the rate for nonback injuries).

Through these programs, the Ingram Barge Company has reduced its cost by 75%—a savings of $1 million per year. As a result, the company has been able to increase the size of its workforce as it continues to improve the quality of life for its employees.

For more information about this program contact:
Dr. Dan Spengler
Vanderbilt Clinic
52430 Medical Center North
Nashville, TN 37232-5677
(615)322-4715

Clinical Application 14–4

B-200 USED IN COURT

CASE #11982
Verdict rendered November, 1988
DISTRICT COURT OF BOX BUTTE COUNTY, NEBRASKA
David L. Chalupa vs. Burlington Northern Railroad Company

B-200 Testimony provided by Priscilla Pope, PT, and Don McIntyre, PhD

Plantiff sued under the Federal Employer's Liability Act, seeking a disability settlement of approximately $600,000 for alleged shoulder and back injuries arising out of employment by defendant. Pretrial settlement offer by defendant of $90,000 was rejected by plaintiff.

Clinical Application 14–4 *Continued*

Plaintiff was evaluated with B-200 by Ms. Pope, who identified indicators of symptom magnification.

Ms. Pope's deposition on the B-200, as well as extensive courtroom testimony by Dr. McIntyre (V.P. of Research at Isotechnology) were admitted as evidence over objections of plaintiff's counsel. "The plaintiff's counsel did virtually everything they could to keep out the B-200 test results," according to defense attorney Tom Beam. "Fortunately . . . all the B-200 test results, came into evidence." During the trial, Dr. McIntyre was cross-examined at length on the B-200 design concepts, reliability, and applicability.

The jury awarded the plaintiff $121,000. According to defense attorney Beam, Burlington Northern Railroad considered this a major victory. One juror indicated to Mr. Beam after the trial that about half the jury was significantly influenced by the B-200 testimony. The plaintiff appealed the decision.

Clinical Application 14–5

B-200 USED IN COURT

CASE #87-01617CR
Verdict rendered May 1988
CIRCUIT COURT OF BROWARD COUNTY,
FT. LAUDERDALE, FLORIDA

Defendant's vehicle struck car in which plaintiff was riding causing injury to plaintiff's back. Plantiff sought $50,000 in damages, and rejected defendant's pretrial offer for $20,000 settlement.

Plaintiff was referred to Dr. Spievack for a B-200 evaluation shortly before the trial date. According to Dr. Spievack, the test revealed significant deficiencies in performance.

Dr. Spievack took his computer to the trial and actually reproduced the graphs on screen in front of the jury. "They were standing on top of each other to see the screen," Dr. Spievack said. "It was the only really objective information they saw."

The jury found for the plaintiff and awarded $200,000. The defense motion for appeal was denied.

TESTING VS. EXERCISE

The Isostation B-200 can be used for trunk performance testing and for rehabilitative exercise as well. There is software that provides the patient with visual biofeedback so that ranges of motion and resistance levels can be preset. It is the authors' opinion, however, that testing instruments are best suited to assist the clinician in the evaluation process and that rehabilitative exercise should be primarily based on nonmachine, low-technology, functional training methods (see Chapter 4). A study by Sachs et al[71] evaluated this premise more carefully. Patients with low back pain (nonsurgical candidates) were randomized into two groups: one that involved a comprehensive work-hardening program that involved non-computer-aided machine exercises and non-machine-based exercises and that lasted for 4 to 6 hours per session, and another group that underwent the same exercise protocol plus an additional 15 minutes of exercise on the Isostation B-200. There was no significant difference between these two groups, although both groups improved overall when compared to a third control group. The

B-200 was used to quantify changes in performance in all groups tested. A major weakness in this study was the significant difference in exercise duration between the work-hardening program (4 to 6 hours, 25 minutes per session) and exercise on the B-200 (15 minutes per session). This discrepancy would need to be normalized in order for conclusions to be meaningful. Also, the number of subjects participating in the study included 14 in the B-200 group and 18 in the non-B-200 group, introducing the potential for reduced statistical power. More research is necessary in this area. Presently, it may be appropriate that exercises be selected so that patients can be released to an at-home program (or local health club, if appropriate) and be capable of continuing recommended activities in order to enhance their self-sufficiency and long-term functional performance.

TRUNK MUSCLE ENDURANCE

Modern industrialized societies require individuals to perform repetitive tasks frequently, and many work-related demands involve assuming fixed and awkward postures. Therefore, it appears that trunk muscle endurance may play an important role in assisting an individual in meeting occupational demands safely, and that the measurement of trunk muscle endurance may assist in predicting the relative risk of individuals involved in demanding activities.

The NIOSH *Work Practices Guide for Manual Lifting*[72] summarizes, from other research studies, that the frequency and severity of back injuries increased significantly when the following criteria were met:

1. The objects that were lifted were heavy.
2. The objects that were lifted were bulky and therefore awkward to lift.
3. The objects involved were lifted from floor height.
4. The objects lifted were moved with high frequency.
5. The objects involved were lifted in an asymmetrical fashion (i.e. one-handed or along the lateral trunk with the torso twisted).

This suggests that work-related demands, and other activities of daily living, can involve complex movements that need to be accounted for accurately during the evaluation process when recommending rehabilitative exercises that parallel these challenging movements and postures. Genaidy et al[73] demonstrated that nonmachine, manual lifting tasks could be used to successfully increase endurance time by almost 250% in the group performing activities in a symmetrical fashion, and an almost 50% improvement in a group performing similar tasks in an asymmetrical fashion. The frequency of material handling increased in both groups as well.

The importance of trunk muscle strength compared to muscular endurance is still controversial. There are a number of studies that suggest that trunk muscle weakness may correlate with a higher incidence of low back dysfunction,[74–79] but there are other studies that demonstrate relatively little value in measuring trunk strength as a predictor of low back dysfunction. Nicolaisen and Jorgensen[80] showed a significant decrease in trunk muscle endurance within a group that suffered from low back pain to such a degree that they were incapable of performing work-related tasks successfully, compared to a group that was experiencing low back pain, but not enough to prevent them from working. They also could not find a correlation between trunk strength and history of back dysfunction, and others have supported this finding.[81]

In summary, trunk strength and muscular endurance both appear to play a role in directing safe activity, and at this point, neither can be minimized as a factor in rehabilitating

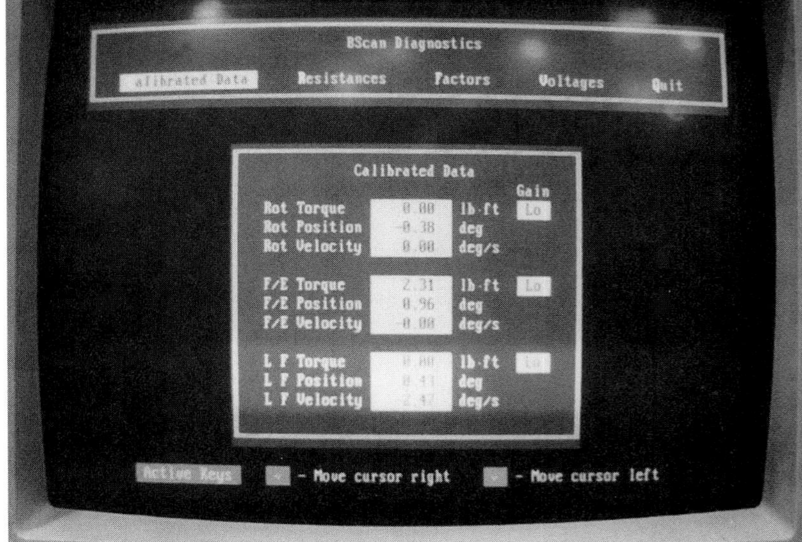

Figure 14–10. The computer screen demonstrates real-time values for use in trunk muscle endurance testing. The arrow indicates the number that the subject will be viewing when giving a maximum voluntary contraction (MVC) in the sagittal plane. The positive number will be visible when the subject is pushing back into extension.

Table 14–4: Standing B-200 Isometric Endurance Test Form

NAME: ID:

TEST 1 DATE: EXAMINER:

PLANE OF MOTION	MAX TORQUE MT (lbs-ft)	60% MT	HT[1]	LF[2]	PAIN GRADE[3] plus comments
	Trial 1 Trial 2 Trial 3				
EXTENSION					
FLEXION					

TEST 2 DATE: EXAMINER:

PLANE OF MOTION	MAX TORQUE MT (lbs-ft)	60% MT	HT[1]	LF[2]	PAIN GRADE[3] plus comments
	Trial 1 Trial 2 Trial 3				
EXTENSION					
FLEXION					

TEST 3 **Week 5** DATE: EXAMINER:

PLANE OF MOTION	MAX TORQUE MT (lbs-ft)	Avg of 60% MT of 1+2	HT[1]	LF[2]	PAIN GRADE[3] plus comments
	Trial 1 Trial 2 Trial 3				
EXTENSION					
FLEXION					

TEST 4 DATE: EXAMINER:

PLANE OF MOTION	MAX TORQUE MT (lbs-ft)	Avg of 60% MT of 1+2	HT[1]	LF[2]	PAIN GRADE[3] plus comments
	Trial 1 Trial 2 Trial 3				
EXTENSION					
FLEXION					

1 - **Holding time in seconds**

2 - **Limiting factors (P = Pain, F = Fatigue, A = Anticipation of Pain (apprehension))**

3 - **Standard Borg scale rating plus comments**

the spine successfully to promote long-term pain relief, patient self-sufficiency, and a suspected reduction in the likelihood of future back pain episodes. Appropriate physical activity is important for the long-term performance of demanding activities, and review articles describing the consequences of inactivity are available.[82]

Trunk muscular endurance can be measured on the B-200 by accessing the diagnostics portion of the B-200 utilities section, revealing real-time values for torque in all planes of motion including secondary planes of motion (Figure 14–10). The screen is then placed so it can be clearly viewed by the subject being tested, allowing him or her to "compete" against values on the screen as they generate a maximum voluntary contraction (MVC). The following is a summary of an endurance testing protocol that can be used with the Isostation B-200:

1. Introduce the patient to the instrument and testing procedure.
2. Restrain the patient as described previously.
3. Instruct the patient to push forward (assuming you are testing trunk flexor endurance) as hard as possible and hold briefly. The patient should be shown the area on the screen that reveals the number he or she is to compete against.
4. The testor records the maximum torque (pound-feet) value.
5. This process is repeated two more times, with a brief rest in between, and the average maximum torque value is calculated and recorded.
6. Sixty percent of the average maximum torque value is recorded. This value will be used to measure trunk endurance.
7. Instruct the patient, while he or she is looking at the screen, to generate enough force to reach the value calculated in item 6 above, minimally, and to hold this force for as long as possible.
8. Hold time is recorded in seconds. This can be repeated for all other planes (rotation, lateral flexion, and extension).

A copy of a trunk endurance measurement form is shown in Table 14–4. Note that there is a place for recording limiting factors and for helping to quantify the subjective level of exertion with use of the Borg rate of perceived exertion scale (Table 14–5).

Some research studies that evaluated trunk endurance used more than one subject posture when testing,[83] and this makes some of the data difficult to practically apply. It seems logical that the upright weight-bearing posture may recruit muscles for active work differently than when in a recumbent position, and therefore it seems logical to test trunk endurance in an upright posture in order to simulate muscle activation the way it would likely occur during normal activities of daily living. Exceptions to this premise may include individuals being tested who have severe low back dysfunction and are incapable of generating sufficient force in an upright position. The actual reasons for muscular fatique can be central or peripheral, as reviewed by Holder-Powell and Jones.[84]

Table 14–5: Borg Perceived Exertion Scale

RPE REVISED RATING	DESCRIPTION OF PERCEIVED EXERTION
0	None
1	Very light
2	Light (weak)
3	Moderate
4	Somewhat hard
5	Heavy (strong)
6	
7	Very heavy
8	
9	
10	Very, very heavy (almost maximum)

DATA INTERPRETATION

INTRODUCTION

The movement toward a managed health care model has increased the demand for providers of health care services to objectify test results. Some of the traditional methods of assessing patients during a musculoskeletal evaluation have been shown to lack the objectivity needed to make informed decisions regarding the need for treatment, degree of impairment,[85] or patient compliance with the evaluator's instructions. This third issue is extremely important in cases involving compensable injuries.

SOFTWARE PACKAGES AVAILABLE TO THE B-200 USER

As mentioned previously, Isotechnologies offers four primary software packages for use with the B-200. Each of the programs has a distinct application. BScan is a basic, raw data collection tool. The OOC Back Evaluation System[86] is the injury evaluation software. BSafe Industrial Screening System is a software package that compares performance to a user-selected population and is intended for use in healthy (asymptomatic) populations *only*. REHAB software allows the B-200 to be used as a therapeutic exercise device. An understanding of the capabilities of each package is necessary to maximize the use of the equipment in a clinical setting.

BSCAN DATA COLLECTION

BScan provides descriptive raw data regarding physical performance parameters, collecting triaxial measurements for velocities, torques, and position 50 times per second. BScan is the means by which information is collected and subsequently analyzed by two more advanced software packages, BSafe Industrial Screening and the OOC Back Evaluation System.

This software package provides several ways in which to analyze data, including tables displaying and/or comparing velocities, torques, and ranges of motion. Most of this information, however, is primarily of interest from a research perspective and will not be covered in these pages. Of more important clinical use are the custom graphs, which allow the user to view primary axis movement graphs or secondary (auxiliary) axis recruitment torque graphs, depending on the clinician's need. Custom graphs will be discussed later in this chapter.

BSAFE INDUSTRIAL SCREENING SYSTEM

Safe Industrial Screening is a software package that compares a subject's performance to a normative database of the clinician's choice. Because the statistical analysis provided by this software package merely describes a subject's performance relative to a user-selected population in terms of standardized test scores and percentile rankings, its use as a tool that can identify injured individuals is questionable. (For example, in a population of healthy, asymptomatic, elite athletes, one individual's test score does not necessarily indicate the need for treatment or provide meaningful information regarding functional status.)

BSafe software applies an "absolute" resistance level to all subjects. In other words, the workloads are the same for everyone tested on a given protocol. As a result of this approach, the workloads will be *too high* for some individuals, and they may be more likely to experience posttest soreness. For some individuals, the workloads are *too low*. This is also a potential cause for concern because the subjects are restrained securely at the pelvis. If these subjects easily overcome the applied resistance and move at high velocities, they too may experience a higher incidence of posttest soreness.

Additionally, there are valid concerns about the use of BSafe in light of the Americans with Disabilities Act and that legislation's requirement that preemployment testing be job-specific. Performance on the B-200 can in no way be considered as an "essential" function of any job (although some employers have misguidedly written "passing a B-200 test" into their job descriptions in the belief that scores below an arbitrarily set level can be used to exclude applicants from employment.

Employers have used BSafe Industrial Screening for years to set objective preemployment baselines for back function. For the most part, they have realized a reduction in losses as a result of their efforts. Historically, reductions in losses related to low back claims were *assumed* to have occurred because of the following factors:

1. Fraudulent claims are less likely to be filed, in the event of an injury. (No objective study has ever verified this to be true. Indeed, such a study would be difficult, if not impossible, to conduct. On the surface, this seems to be a reasonable assumption, although the author (Shapmire) is of the opinion that *most* patients have *some* organic basis for their claim.)
2. Comparisons of preinjury and postinjury BSafe performances will objectively determine the amount of lost function. There is an element of truth in this assumption, although the relationship between a BSafe test score and the ability to perform functional work tasks has never been demonstrated by clinical study. Also, the admissibility of such comparisons varies among court systems.)

In truth, the primary mechanism by which reductions in losses have been realized is probably the Hawthorn effect; i.e., *the act of testing performance changes behavior*. Concurrent with BSafe screening, employers and employees alike may become more keenly aware of the need for working safely and safety programs may also be instituted.

Regardless of the mechanism(s) which may be at work in helping reduce losses, the use of BSafe remains problematic for many clinicians because of the statistical analysis as well as the use of "absolute" resistances. If the Hawthorn effect is indeed at work with BSafe testing, it is reasonable to believe the phenomenon would also be manifested with another form of B-200 testing. The author suggests a modified OOC approach as an alternative to BSafe testing to set an objective, preinjury baseline. By using the first sequence of that protocol and the 50% "relative" resistance levels *only*, comparisons to asymptomatic subjects can be made. Therefore, the use of the OOC protocol is more helpful in identifying those individuals who are likely to have some degree of lumbar dysfunction. Because of what this author believes are obvious and substantial disadvantages to BSafe screening, no further discussion of the BSafe software package will be offered.

REHAB (EXERCISE) SOFTWARE

REHAB Software was Isotechnologies' (now Interlogics, Inc.) latest software package for the B-200. This is a very user-friendly package that allows the clinician almost endless choices in developing (and modifying) customized exercise protocols for patients. Virtually every parameter (repetitions, resistance, time for exercise, rest time, etc.) can be controlled by the clinician. The clinician can choose between multiaxial or uniplanar exercise modes, an option not available in the OOC and BSafe protocols.

Many back injuries have nonspecific diagnoses such as strain, sprain, or pain. Most of the time, all of the anatomical structures are intact but they fail to work together as a unit. Even in postsurgical patients or patients with resolving disc herniations, the tissue healing is complete, yet dysfunction remains because the spine fails to move in a fluid, synchronous manner. Remembering some basic physiology will help keep the patient comfortable during a rehabilitation program and facilitate a recovery.

In an injured patient, articulation of the joints is minimized if movement is avoided. For this reason, lubrication of the articular surfaces is also minimized. As a result of injury, normal neural transmission can be disrupted; for the back patient, this results in abnormal movement patterns of the spine. (Typically, this is referred to as *guarded* movement, during which the patient displays a preference for single-axis movement; however, *compensatory* movement can also be the result of injury. In such cases, patients tend to move awkwardly and recruit torque inappropriately from a secondary, or auxiliary, axis.) Injury can also disrupt the normal blood flow to tissue, which has immediate implications for the delivery of oxygen and other nutrients as well as the removal of the waste products of metabolism. Injured tissue frequently is dysfunctional, in part because of a buildup of scar tissue. Dysfunctional spines may also have joints that are disarticulated.

Given the factors cited above, it is reasonable to approach low back pain patients, particularly those with nonspecific diagnoses, as persons who have *movement disorders*. Clinical treatment options for these people will vary from one center to another, but taking into consideration the subtle, yet important microphysiology will affect your treatment approach with the B-200 as well as with manual therapies.

There is no *precise* agreement on how to use the B-200 for therapeutic exercise, just as there are no specific clinical methods on which there is universal agreement as to how to most effectively facilitate improvement of the back-injured patient. There are, however, some general guidelines to use when the B-200 is chosen as an adjunct to more traditional treatment protocols. An approach in which the patient performs a relatively high number of repetitions against light to moderate resistance levels is suggested. This avoids the soreness that could otherwise develop if a "maximum voluntary effort" protocol is chosen, particularly if the workloads are "high" relative to the patient's isometric strength. It is further suggested that patients work within pain-free ranges of motion and velocities.

To avoid applying inappropriate workloads, it is suggested the patient's isometric strength be measured (on an OOC test or in a customized REHAB software protocol) and used as a baseline. In using an endurance-type approach, workloads between 5% and 60% of maximum isometric torques are appropriate for rotation and lateral flexion. In the sagittal plane, the lesser of the two maximum torques (or, alternately, an average of flexion and extension torque) should be used as the baseline to determine the workload for this axis because there can be a difference in maximum flexion and extension torques. In all cases, high velocities while exercising against resistances below 25% of the maximum isometric torques should be discouraged to avoid excessive soreness following the rehabilitation session.

Some clinicians prefer to use multiaxial movement during rehabilitation exercise on the B-200. This approach, however, should be used with a great deal of caution. Circumduction or diagonal movement may be contraindicated for some patients. If multiaxial movement is chosen as a treatment option, the secondary axis resistances should be small and the velocities should be slow and controlled.

The author's preference is for uniplanar movement when using this software package. Theoretically, by allowing movement in only one axis at a time, while the patient is encouraged to recruit torque from the secondary axes, the patient can reestablish normal neural recruitment patterns. Lubrication of the joints is facilitated with movement, an increase in blood flow occurs during the exercise session, and adhesions can be broken down with movement when the patient is involved in unrestrained, dynamic activity outside of the B-200. B-200 exercise should be used as an *adjunct* to appropriate manual therapies and more traditional forms of exercise.

OOC Back Evaluation System

Injury evaluation on the B-200 is typically performed on the OOC system. Maximum voluntary effort is requested of the patient during the OOC evaluation. A test/retest protocol is used to record unresisted ranges of motion, isometric torques for each axis, and dynamic capabilities against work loads in uniplanar movement. The uniplanar movement on the B-200 during injury evaluation occurs because high workloads are placed on each of the two secondary (auxiliary) axes, thereby "channeling" all but the strongest subjects into single-axis movement. Uniplanar testing is felt to be safer and more comfortable for symptomatic subjects. Because of the intersubject differences inherent in multiaxial movement, the uniplanar approach also facilitates the establishment of normative comparisons.

Research supporting the use of the B-200 has come from a variety of sources independent of the manufacturer. Just a few of the more than 200 published articles and major presentations[87–92] are cited at the end of this chapter for the interested reader's futher investigation.

Comparison of physical performance parameters to a database of normal (asymptomatic) subjects classifies the level of dysfunction. Sensitivity and specificity for males and females is approximately 80%, using the number of abnormal indicators alone. Sensitivity and specificity should improve when all four categories of information are considered. Intrasubject comparisons are used to assess "effort" or "consistency."

In achieving the 80% rate of sensitivity and specificity, the OOC software system does not utilize thoraco-lumbar ranges of motion because of that parameter's inability to accurately identify either normal or symptomatic subjects. Additionally, factors totally unrelated to back dysfunction can affect ranges of motion. Some of those factors would include girth, hamstring or flexor tightness, and the volume of the bladder or gut contents. Velocities and secondary axis torques, however, do provide us with some good indication of lumbar function[93,94] and both play an important role in the OOC classification of performance.

The standard OOC protocol can be summarized as follows:

1. *Unresisted range of motion testing for all axes.* Patients are asked to move as far as possible in a slow, controlled manner against 1 lb · ft of resistance. This portion of the test is referred to as ROM 1 on the OOC report.
2. *Isometric testing of all axes.* The B-200 is mechanically locked into a machine-neutral position and the patient is asked to exert maximal torque against the equipment.
3. *Dynamic testing of all axes.* The patient is asked to move as far and fast as possible against the applied workload. Resistance levels for each of the dynamic activities is "relative" to the subject's isometric torque production in each axis. Workloads for rotation and lateral flexion are 25% and 50% of the maximum torques produced during isometric testing in the respective axes. In the sagittal plane, the lesser of the two maximums (of flexion and extension) is used as a baseline for calculating resistance. (As mentioned before, this is because there is frequently a large difference between torque production for each of the directions in this axis.)
4. *The unresisted range of motion testing is repeated in the same manner as ROM 1.* This step of the test is referred to as ROM 2 on the OOC report.
5. *Dynamic testing of all axes.* The portion of the test is conducted in the same manner as item 3 above. The only difference in this sequence of dynamic tests is that the order in which the workloads are applied has been reversed (50% followed by the 25% resistance level).

OOC data can be divided into four separate categories: abnormal indicators, baseline rehabilitation data, nonphysiological indicators, and BScan custom graphs. Additionally, some patients are believed to perform "consistently but submaximally." An attempt is made with the software analysis to identify when a submaximal effort occurs during an OOC evaluation. A discussion of each of the four data categories as well as the analysis for possible "consistent but submaximal effort" appears in the following pages. An additional section, "OOC Test Interpretation," is also included in the text that follows. That section uses actual test results and graphs to help integrate all of the information presented in the present section.

Abnormal Indicators

Abnormal indicators are maximum isometric torques, maximum velocities, or maximum secondary axis torques that fall below statistically important cutoff points. Maximum torques in either the primary or secondary axes that fall below the 2.5th percentiles and maximum velocities which fall below the 5th percentiles are considered to be *subnormal.* These cutoff points provide for an optimum balance in the sensitivity and specificity in classifying lumbar dysfunction.

The designations "Isometric Max Torque" and "Max Velocity" found on page 1 of the OOC report are self-explanatory. Arrows found under rotation or lateral flexion columns for "Isometric Max Torque" will be displayed in the middle of their respective boxes if *both sides* are subnormal. Because there may be large variations between flexion and extension torques, direction of the torque in the sagittal plane is differentiated.

The "Secondary Max Torque" designation on page 1 of the OOC report refers to recruitment torque from the auxiliary axes. Recall that dynamic testing on this equipment involves uniplanar movement. (Uniplanar movement is accomplished by the application of resistance levels in the auxiliary axes that essentially prevent movement in all but the axis being tested directly, referred to as the *primary axis.*) The presence of low or subnormal secondary axis torques in a *physiological* representation of movement is indicative of *guarded* movement. Low back pain patients will usually prefer uniplanar movement because the less complicated movement patterns tend to result in less discomfort. (Visualize the typical back patient's movement during any other kind of testing.)

There is a maximum possibility of 22 abnormal indicators in an OOC evaluation. The presence of 1 to 5 abnormal indicators would classify dysfunction as *mild*. If 6 to 10 abnormal indicators are registered, the dysfunction is *moderate*. Eleven or more subnormal scores reflect *severe* dysfunction.

Provided the test results are reflective of a consistent and maximal voluntary effort, subnormal scores are *usually* accompanied by functional deficits. Low scores can also occur if subjects are very small in stature or beyond the age of 55 (the oldest subjects in the OOC database). The entire clinical picture must, of course, be considered.

The absence of abnormal indicators *does not* mean the subject has normal *functional* abilities. Such a situation merely means the critical statistical thresholds have been surpassed. A maximum isometric torque which falls at the 2.6th percentile, for example, is not subnormal from a statistical standpoint. In clinical terms, however, there is no practical difference from the 2.6th and the 2.4th percentiles. Both measurements would indicate potential weakness. Therefore, the OOC software furnishes an additional method (baseline rehabilitation data) for classifying dysfunction.

Baseline Rehabilitation Data

Baseline rehabilitation data are bar graphs appearing at the bottom of the first page of an OOC report. These graphs answer the question, "How far above normal are the maximum primary axis isometric torques and the maximum velocities?" Test results are displayed according to the direction of isometric torque as well as maximum velocities at both workloads for each sequence of the test.

A line on the first page of the OOC report is drawn across the baseline rehabilitation data at the 20th percentile. Although the 20th percentile as a landmark for determining functional (as opposed to statistical) deficits has never been objectively demonstrated in a controlled study, clinicians who have used the B-200 in conjunction with functional capacity evaluations have found it to be a reasonably practical cutoff point. Anecdotally, they have found that the presence of several baseline graphs below the 20th percentile is often found concurrently with deficits during functional work activities. The entire clinical picture, including demographic information such as age and stature, should be considered.

Nonphysiological Indicators

There are six conditions (nonphysiological indicators) that the OOC software will flag as abnormal test behaviors. If only one of these conditions is recorded, the results of the test are considered to be *consistent*, or reflective of a maximum voluntary effort. If three or more nonphysiological indicators are recorded, the results are classified as *nonphysiological* and the reliability and validity of the physical performance parameters are highly suspect.

The presence of two nonphysiological indicators would classify the test results as *borderline* or *gray zone*, which is indicative of marginal consistency during the test. In such cases, it is left to the clinician to make an interpretation regarding consistency. If a well-rounded approach to testing has been taken, a pattern of behavior will often emerge and help the tester render an informed opinion. In the event a gray zone test is recorded, the clinician has three options: accept the results, reject the results, or withhold judgement until more information can be obtained. Sometimes a retest is a viable option.

The supernormal and subnormal ratios referenced in the six nonphysiological indicators (below) refer to large percentages of change (in the comparison of physical performance parameters). *Supernormal* ratios exceed the percentage of change that would be expected in 95% of a normal population and fall two standard deviations *above* the mean. *Subnormal* ratios also exceed the percentage of change that would be expected in 95% of a normal population; however, subnormal ratios fall more than two standard deviations *below* the mean. On the second page of the OOC report, all ratios followed by an arrow pointing downward are subnormal ratios. Upward-pointing arrows indicate a supernormal change. *All other values fall within two standard deviations of the mean.*

In trying to conceptualize how these ratios apply to patients, it is helpful to be aware of B-200 performance profiles one should expect in three, distinct populations of subjects: (1) normal, asymptomatic subjects; (2) elite athletes; and (3) patients (truly positive for dysfunction). Each of these population profiles are described as follows:

1. *Normal, asymptomatic subjects* tend to produce normal isometric torques. As a result, we can predict with some degree of accuracy the maximum ranges of motion that should be expected when a workload is applied. Ranges of motion tend to fall within normal limits and should be highly reproducible. As a result, we can predict with some degree of accuracy the maximum angular excursion (range of motion) that should be expected when the range of motion test is repeated, as well as when a workload is applied. Normal subjects also tend to produce normal velocities at both workloads (25% and 50%). As a consequence, when percentage changes in performance for average velocities at each of these workloads are calculated for a population of normals, the resulting ratios tend to be "normal" (fall within two standard deviations of the mean). The bottom line for normal subjects is that they tend to produce average values for ranges of motion, velocities, and torques. Their ratios also tend to be normal.
2. *Elite athletes* tend to produce high torque values and high velocities at both workloads. The percentage of change in average velocities tends to fall within normal limits (within two standard deviations of the mean). Ranges of motion for athletes are highly variable, dependent in part on the sport in which they participate. Their ranges of motion in any case would be highly reproducible and therefore comparisons between ranges of motions would fall within two standard deviations of the mean. The bottom line for elite athletes is that they tend to produce high torques and velocities. Ranges of motion, however, are quite variable. Their ratios, like the asymptomatic subjects, tend to be normal.
3. *Patients (truly positive for dysfunction)* tend to produce low ranges of motion, low isometric torques, and low velocities at both workloads. Unresisted range of motion ratios for this population tend to be normal, i.e., not much variation between trials. Because the applied workload is so low, unresisted ranges of motion should be highly reproducible. As such, these ratios tend to fall within two standard deviations of the mean. Resisted range of motion ratios, however, tend to be low normal or subnormal, an expression of the difficulty the patient experiences when trying to move a workload. As is the case with the resisted range of motion ratios, average velocity ratios in a patient population tend to be low normal or subnormal. These ratios are an expression of the difficulty the patient experiences when trying to move the 50% workload. The bottom line for patients (truly positive for dysfunction) is that they tend to produce low ranges of

motion, low isometric torques, and low velocities at both workloads. Unresisted range of motion ratios tend to be normal (within two standard deviations of the mean). However, resisted range of motion ratios and average velocity ratios are usually subnormal or low normal (approaching two standard deviations below the mean).

The six nonphysiological indicators and a brief explanation of each follows:

1. *Supernormal average velocity ratio in test sequence 2.* This is a comparison of the average velocity at the 50% workload to that at the 25% workload. The ratio is expressed as a percentage change. The presence of this condition indicates a ratio that exceeds those produced by 95% of the normative population. Furthermore, the measurements taken were in the last sequence of the test when fatigue would normally be expected, thereby producing a lower ratio. A supernormal ratio shows an unexpectedly good ability to move against the higher workload, based upon the average velocity at the 25% resistance level.
2. *Maximum velocity at 50% equal to or greater than maximum velocity at the 25% resistance in sequence 2 (of dynamic testing of all axes).* Sequence 1 violation of this condition is considered to be part of a learning curve and is, as such, not penalized. If maximum voluntary effort is offered throughout the test, this condition (a maximum velocity at a resistance which exceeds another by a factor of 2) theoretically should not occur.
3. *Subnormal isometric torque in the same axis with a secondary axis torque ratio greater than 1.0 in either test sequence.* Maximum voluntary effort should be measured in a primary axis during isometric testing. This nonphysiological indicator is registered if the primary isometric axis torque is below the 2.5th percentile but a measurement for that same axis subsequently reveals more torque when another axis is being tested in the dynamic mode. In other words, in the presence of statistically significant isometric weakness, higher torque should not be recorded while the same axis is serving as a secondary (auxiliary) axis.
4. *Subnormal isometric torque with a supernormal resisted range of motion ratio in the same axis, during both sequences.* This condition is flagged if the isometric measurements are subnormal and the range of motion during resisted movement greatly exceeds that which would be expected, based upon the unresisted range of motion measurement. In this instance, the percentage change is greater than would be seen in 95% of the normative database.
5. *Subnormal isometric torque with a supernormal average velocity ratio in the same axis during sequence 1.* This condition is similar to condition 4. It is registered if the isometric measurements are subnormal and the average velocity at the 50% resistance level is far more than would be expected, based upon the average velocity measurement at the 25% resistance. In this instance also, the percentage change exceeds that seen in 95% of the normative database.
6. *Subnormal range of motion 2/range of motion 1 when one other condition is present.* This ratio is expressed as a change in percentage. The presence of this condition represents a large decrease in performance during the second range of motion test. It is analogous to having extreme variations between goniometer measurements. The deterioration in range of motion against 1 lb · ft of resistance is greater than would be seen in 95% of the normative population when this condition is recorded.

Submaximal Effort During Consistent Tests

Some patients will perform consistently during a testing protocol, but ample evidence exists to indicate the test results reflect less than a maximum voluntary effort. For example, during functional testing, it is not uncommon for Jamar grip testing to produce low coefficients of variation (indicating a consistent effort), yet reveal an absence of variation between forces produced in each of the five positions (indicating a submaximal effort). A analogous situation can occur during B-200 dynamometry.

To identify possible consistent but submaximal test results, four initial criteria must be met. When these conditions have been recorded by the OOC software, a designation of "Results May Suggest Submaximal Effort" will appear on page 1 of the OOC test results. The clinician must then review each of six subsequent criteria to classify the test results.

If two of the subsequent criteria are met, the results continue to suggest a submaximal effort and, therefore, similar to a gray zone test. In these cases, the clinician is called upon to provide an informed opinion. The options are the same here as they are when two nonphysiological indicators are recorded. If three or more of the subsequent criteria are met, the results are believed to indicate a submaximal effort.

The initial criteria are listed and explained as follows:

1. *No more than one nonphysiological indicator.* In other words, these tests are consistent according to OOC criteria.
2. *Eleven or more abnormal indicators.* Ostensibly, the patient has severe lumbar dysfunction.
3. *All isometric maximum torques are subnormal in all planes.* In other words, no torques equal to or above the 2.5th percentile were recorded. The possible submaximal designation can never occur if just one torque in *any* direction falls at the 2.5th percentile.
4. *At least one abnormal maximum velocity parameter in each plane.* This is a statement of global, as op-

posed to specific, lumbar involvement and dysfunction.

The subsequent criteria are listed and explained as follows:

1. *Consistent range of motion 2/range of motion 1 ratios that are either subnormal, supernormal, or show zero change in all three planes*. Supernormal ratios would indicate extreme hesitancy in all three axes to move during the first range of motion test. Subnormal ratios would indicate extreme hesitancy to move in the second range of motion test. Zero change in all three axes (rare) could indicate a purposeful measuring of distance by the patient.
2. *At least three resisted range of motion/range of motion ratios subnormal in both test sequences*. This condition indicates substantially less range of motion during the resisted testing than would be expected, based upon the unresisted range of motion test. Based upon the range of motion during unresisted movement, movement with a workload when this condition is present is less than would be expected in 95% of a normal population.
3. *Subnormal average velocity ratio in test sequence 1 in all three planes*. This condition shows a hesitancy to move during the 50% resistance level in all three axes. Subnormal velocity ratios are less than would be seen in 95% of a normal population.
4. *All average velocity ratios normal in all three planes*. Patients with physiological dysfunction tend to produce low normal or subnormal average velocity ratios. The production of a supernormal ratio can be a nonphysiological indicator. Asymptomatic (normal) subjects usually produce average velocity ratios. It is not logical for patients with severe dysfunction to have normal average velocity ratios.
5. *At least five secondary axis maximum torques subnormal in both test sequences*. This condition shows a tendency to guard one's movements, which could be indicative of excessive hesitancy.
6. *No more than two baseline rehabilitation graphs at the 10th percentile or higher*. Even in patients with severe dysfunction, it is felt by the developers of the OOC system that a global statement of dysfunction may be representative of a submaximal effort. Research indicates that low torque production, low velocities, and limited ranges of motion may be part of an overall performance profile manifested by those exhibiting illness behaviors.[95–97]

BScan Custom Graphs

Prior to the development of the OOC software, the BScan graphs were the only tool by which clinicians made judgements regarding dysfunction and effort during B-200 testing. Interpreting B-200 test results solely on the basis of graphs depicting either movement in the primary axes or recruitment torques from the secondary axes was like trying to read tea leaves; there was considerable intertester variability in test interpretation. The graphs, however, do add an important dimension to test interpretation—with the caveat that they are not used as a substitute for understanding the two-page OOC report.

Although literally hundreds of graphs can be retrieved from theBScan software, there are only five custom graphs normally needed for test interpretation: All primary axis graphs (velocity versus position) and two graphs depicting secondary axis torque production (rotation torque during lateral flexion and lateral flexion torque during rotation) are of significance.

Graphs depicting movement against the 25% workload often appear normal—even in symptomatic subjects. Often, it is not until the workload is higher that movement pattern deviations become apparent. Thus, it is usually more illuminating to consider the high resistance graphs. Because second sequence graphs almost always very closely resemble first sequence graphs, it is usually not necessary to review second sequence graphs.

The reading of the graphs is facilitated by understanding the convention by which the designations of positive (+) and negative (−) are applied to the velocities, torques, and positions displayed on the graphs: All positive numbers indicate a velocity, torque, or position that involves movement to the right or flexion. All negative numbers indicate a velocity, torque, or position that involves movement to the left or extension.

It is generally improper to use the secondary axis torque graphs for consistency evaluation. There are larger differences in the secondary axis torque graphs between repetitions and between the patterns produced by individuals than between the primary axis graphs depicting velocity plotted against position. There is no definitive explanation for why this is the case; however, some possible reasons are:

1. The development of different strategies to accomplish physical work.
2. Neurological/physical differences between individuals.
3. Differences between work and recreational activities. (Activities requiring predominantly unilateral use of the trunk or extremities have been anecdotally linked to abnormal secondary axis torque graphs.)

There are large differences between individuals in the graph patterns when flexion/extension (torque) recruitment patterns are plotted against activity in the other axes. Recruitment of torque from rotation and lateral flexion during movement in the sagittal plane also varies greatly between subjects. No definitive statements can be made about expected secondary torque graph patterns when the sagittal plane values are plotted against parameters from another axis.

OOC TEST INTERPRETATION

Clinical Application 14–6

This test (Table 14–6) depicts a physiological or consistent performance. There were zero nonphysiological indicators recorded. The presence of eight abnormal indicators would classify the lumbar dysfunction as moderate. A review of the baseline rehabilitation data reveals that 17 of 18 parameters fell below the 20th percentile. Normally, this would be somewhat predictive of difficulty during functional work tasks (lifting, carrying, pushing, and pulling). Factors such as height, weight, and age may be important, however, in coming to any conclusions.

The second page of the OOC report in Table 14–6 provides the raw data from the test. The downward arrows indicate subnormal scores (below the 5th percentile). Upward arrows indicate supernormal scores (above the 95th percentile). The subnormal score for flexion torque (62.5 lb · ft) is listed on page 1 of the report as one of the eight abnormal indicators. The maximum velocities for rotation and flexion/extension (25% and 50% workloads) were subnormal for *both test sequences* and are also listed on page 1, being four of the abnormal indicators. Lateral flexion at the 25% workload was also subnormal in *both test sequences* and thus is also an abnormal indicator. The raw data for the final two abnormal indicators recorded during test 1 (shown at the bottom of page 2 of the OOC report under "Secondary Axes") are for flexion/extension as a secondary maximum torque during rotation and flexion/extension as a secondary maximum torque during lateral flexion. Because the torque production (recruitment) from the secondary axis was subnormal during *both test sequences,* abnormal indicators are highlighted on page 1 of the report.

The three ratios (percentage change) on page 2 are all normal, with the exception of the resisted range of motion ratios for rotation, both test sequences at the 25% resistance level. Physiological OOC tests generally have few ratios which are subnormal or supernormal.

Table 14–6: An OCC Computer Test Printout Demonstrating the Presence of a Physiological Testing Effort

OOC Evaluation Results for **•1209499**

Demographic Data

Age : 46
Height : 5 ft 7 in
Sex : M
Weight : 130 lbs

Diagnosis : Non-Symptomatic
Surgical Category : Non-Surgical
Activity Level Category : Heavy work

Resistance Settings

Rotation 25%	:	16 **lb-ft**
Rotation 50%	:	33 **lb-ft**
Flex/Ext 25%	:	16 **lb-ft**
Flex/Ext 50%	:	31 **lb-ft**
Lat Flex 25%	:	23 **lb-ft**
Lat Flex 50%	:	46 **lb-ft**

Abnormal Indicators [8]

	Rotation 25%	Rotation 50%	Flex/Ext 25%	Flex/Ext 50%	Lat Flex 25%	Lat Flex 50%
Isometric Max Torque			↓			
Max Velocity	↓	↓	↓	↓	↓	
Rotation Sec Max Torque						
Flex/Ext Sec Max Torque	↓					↓
Lat Flex Sec Max Torque						

Non-physiological Indicators [0]

1) not observed
2) not observed
3) not observed
4) not observed
5) not observed
6) not observed

Baseline Rehabilitation Data

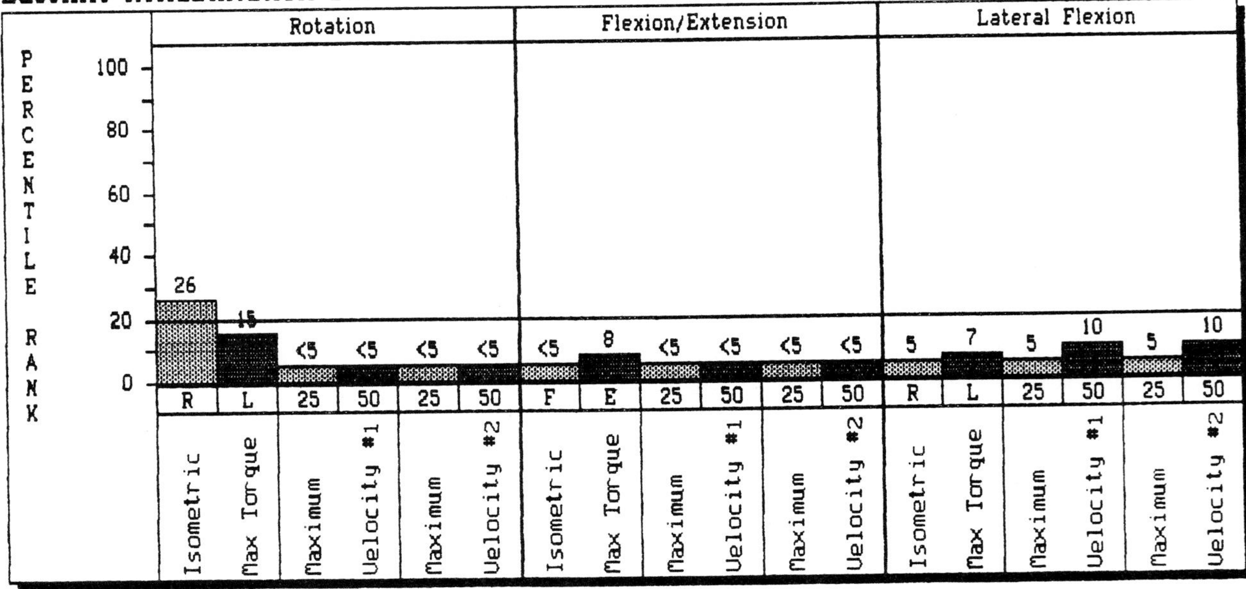

Continued on next page

Table 14–6: *Continued*

OOC Evaluation Results for #1209499

OOC Test	Rotation		Flex/Ext		Lat Flex	
Range of Motion						
ROM (deg) #1	47.5		79.3		66.2	
#2	62.9		82.7		67.9	
ROM #2 / ROM #1 (Δ%)	32.42		4.29		2.57	
Isometric						
Max Torque (lb-ft)	65.3		62.5↓ 125.1		92.5	
Dynamic	25%	50%	25%	50%	25%	50%
Resisted ROM / ROM (Δ%) #1	51.54↑	20.77	4.30	6.99	1.96	-10.46
#2	35.47↑	6.98	1.55	2.06	13.38	-6.37
Avg Vel 50% / Avg Vel 25% (Δ%) #1	-23.44		-13.49		-4.12	
#2	-33.33		-24.74		-47.84	
Max Velocity (deg/sec) #1	48.8↓	44.5↓	71.2↓	68.7↓	76.2↓	86.4
#2	65.7↓	59.4↓	78.8↓	66.1↓	99.1↓	78.8
Secondary Axes						
Rot Secondary Max Torq (lb-ft) #1	--	--	1.8↓	5.3↓	19.4	21.2
#2	--	--	8.8	14.1	33.5	24.7
F/E Secondary Max Torq (lb-ft) #1	16.2↓	27.8	--	--	23.2	27.8↓
#2	11.6↓	16.2↓	--	--	27.8	30.1↓
L F Secondary Max Torq (lb-ft) #1	25.2	38.7	3.4↓	3.4↓	--	--
#2	26.9↓	42.0	8.4	16.8	--	--

Key

↓ Subnormal, less than critical level

↑ Supernormal, greater than critical level

(see Statistical Review in OOC Back Evaluation System)

Clinical Application 14–7

This is a gray zone test (Table 14–7) (marginal for consistency), based upon the presence of two nonphysiological indicators. In tests such as these, the clinician must decide whether to accept or reject the test results or retest at a later time when more information is available. In this particular case, the test was classified as nonphysiological based upon the following factors:

1. Although the patient indicated extreme pain was occurring during the B-200 evaluation, particularly with any movement to the right, the BScan graphs showed normal movement patterns with symmetrical ranges of motion and velocities.
2. Waddell testing for nonphysical pain behaviors was positive in two of five categories (also gray zone).
3. The patient's decreased weight bearing during the evaluation was not consistent. She also bore weight equally on each foot while walking backwards and side to side bilaterally. The gait pattern was normal when leaving the clinic to enter her automobile.
4. Other components of the functional evaluation were also inconsistent.

It is not uncommon for persons producing gray zone tests to be absent from the workplace for extended periods of time. It is also not uncommon for them to perform consistently during a functional evaluation. *Giving the patient the benefit of the doubt whenever possible is recommended.* Look at the entire picture.

Clinical Application 14–8

Table 14–8 illustrates a nonphysiological effort by the patient. Notice the resistance settings in the upper-right hand corner of page 1. Five of six possible nonphysiological Indicators were recorded. Some of the nonphysiological conditions were recorded in more than one axis. Most of the ratios on page 2 are either supernormal or subnormal, with no obvious consistent pattern. Maximum velocities are well below the low end of normal (90 to 100 degrees per second). The BScan custom graph depicts minimal movement against very little resistance.

During functional testing of this patient, Waddell testing was positive in four of five categories and symptom magnification questionnaires were highly positive. Jamar grip testing was nonphysiological. Gait patterns were inconsistent. Upper extremity strength testing produced excessively high coefficients of variation. The addition of B-200 testing to the manual muscle evaluation and functional test completes the triad of testing protocols. Thus, in this evaluation of a patient (who had no objective medical findings), appropriate measures that are highly resistant to legal challenge were taken to move a problematic case to resolution.

Table 14–7: An OCC Computer Printout Demonstrating a Marginal Effort by the Subject

OOC Evaluation Results for #1098755

Demographic Data

Age : 32 **Sex** : F
Height : 5 ft 6 in **Weight** : 123 lbs

Diagnosis : Lumbar strain
Surgical Category : Non-Surgical
Activity Level Category : Medium work

Resistance Settings

Rotation 25%	:	6 lb-ft
Rotation 50%	:	12 lb-ft
Flex/Ext 25%	:	6 lb-ft
Flex/Ext 50%	:	12 lb-ft
Lat Flex 25%	:	7 lb-ft
Lat Flex 50%	:	15 lb-ft

Abnormal Indicators [16]

<table>
<tr><th></th><th colspan="2">Rotation</th><th colspan="2">Flex/Ext</th><th colspan="2">Lat Flex</th></tr>
<tr><th></th><th>25%</th><th>50%</th><th>25%</th><th>50%</th><th>25%</th><th>50%</th></tr>
<tr><td>Isometric Max Torque</td><td colspan="2">↓</td><td>↓</td><td>↓</td><td colspan="2">↓</td></tr>
<tr><td>Max Velocity</td><td>↓</td><td>↓</td><td>↓</td><td>↓</td><td>↓</td><td>↓</td></tr>
<tr><td>Rotation Sec Max Torque</td><td></td><td></td><td>↓</td><td>↓</td><td>↓</td><td>↓</td></tr>
<tr><td>Flex/Ext Sec Max Torque</td><td></td><td></td><td></td><td></td><td></td><td></td></tr>
<tr><td>Lat Flex Sec Max Torque</td><td>↓</td><td></td><td>↓</td><td></td><td></td><td></td></tr>
</table>

Non-physiological Indicators [2]

1) not observed
2) not observed
3) not observed
4) ↓ isometric torque with ↑ resisted ROM ratio : L F
5) ↓ isometric torque and ↑ avg velocity ratio, seq 1 : L F
6) not observed

Baseline Rehabilitation Data

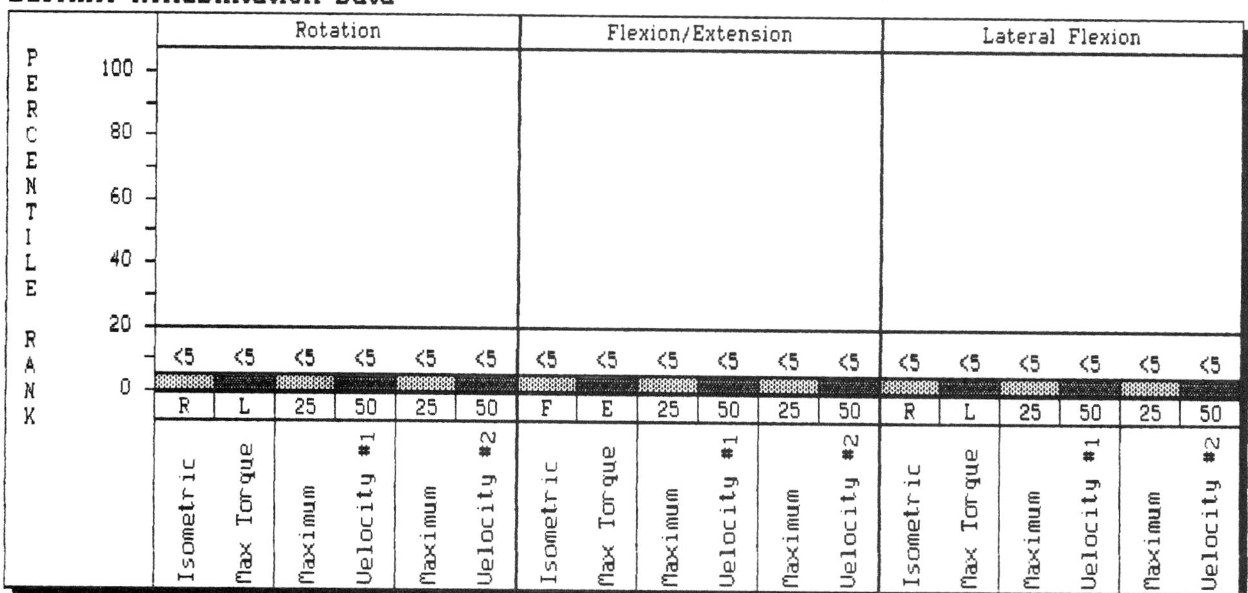

Continued on next page

Table 14–7: *Continued*

OOC Evaluation Results for

#1098755
30-NOV-92

OOC Test	Rotation	Flex/Ext	Lat Flex

Range of Motion

	Rotation	Flex/Ext	Lat Flex
ROM (deg) #1	61.6	44.4	50.3
ROM (deg) #2	70.3	48.6	47.6
ROM #2 / ROM #1 (Δ%)	14.12	9.46	-5.37

Isometric

	Rotation	Flex/Ext		Lat Flex
Max Torque (lb-ft)	24.6↓	23.7↓	37.9↓	29.8↓

Dynamic

		Rotation 25%	Rotation 50%	Flex/Ext 25%	Flex/Ext 50%	Lat Flex 25%	Lat Flex 50%
Resisted ROM / ROM (Δ%)	#1	28.22	31.29	20.00	28.57↑	13.91	23.48↑
	#2	14.52	-3.23	14.78	16.52	18.35	16.51↑
Avg Vel 50% / Avg Vel 25% (Δ%)	#1	0.57		0.00		4.17↑	
	#2	-15.45		-13.25		-16.50	
Max Velocity (deg/sec)	#1	43.1↓	45.4↓	31.2↓	25.5↓	38.6↓	41.2↓
	#2	43.1↓	40.8↓	34.0↓	28.3↓	38.6↓	36.0↓

Secondary Axes

		Rotation 25%	Rotation 50%	Flex/Ext 25%	Flex/Ext 50%	Lat Flex 25%	Lat Flex 50%
Rot Secondary Max Torq (lb-ft)	#1	--	--	1.6↓	1.6↓	3.3↓	9.8↓
	#2	--	--	1.6↓	1.6↓	3.3↓	8.2↓
F/E Secondary Max Torq (lb-ft)	#1	11.8	11.8↓	--	--	7.1	11.8
	#2	11.8↓	14.2	--	--	7.1↓	11.8
L F Secondary Max Torq (lb-ft)	#1	9.4↓	15.7↓	3.1↓	1.6↓	--	--
	#2	11.0↓	17.3	3.1↓	4.7	--	--

Key

↓ Subnormal, less than critical level

↑ Supernormal, greater than critical level
(see Statistical Review in <u>OOC Back Evaluation System</u>)

Table 14–8: OOC Computer Printout Demonstrating a Nonphysiological, and Therefore Unacceptable, Effort by the Subject

OOC Evaluation Results for #1097660

Demographic Data

Age	: 40	**Sex**	: F
Height	: 5 ft 10 in	**Weight**	: 140 lbs

Diagnosis : Lumbar strain
Surgical Category : Non-Surgical
Activity Level Category : Light work

Resistance Settings

Rotation 25%	: 1 **lb-ft**
Rotation 50%	: 2 **lb-ft**
Flex/Ext 25%	: 2 **lb-ft**
Flex/Ext 50%	: 4 **lb-ft**
Lat Flex 25%	: 2 **lb-ft**
Lat Flex 50%	: 4 **lb-ft**

Abnormal Indicators 16

	Rotation		Flex/Ext		Lat Flex	
	25%	**50%**	**25%**	**50%**	**25%**	**50%**
Isometric Max Torque	↓		↓	↓	↓	
Max Velocity	↓	↓	↓	↓	↓	↓
Rotation Sec Max Torque			↓		↓	↓
Flex/Ext Sec Max Torque						
Lat Flex Sec Max Torque	↓	↓		↓		

Non-physiological Indicators 5

1) ↑ avg velocity ratio, seq 2 : F/E
2) Max velocity 50% greater than or equal 25%, seq 2 : F/E, L F
3) Secondary axis torque higher than isometric torque : F/E
4) not observed
5) ↓ isometric torque and ↑ avg velocity ratio, seq 1 : F/E
6) ↓ range of motion ratio : F/E, L F

Baseline Rehabilitation Data

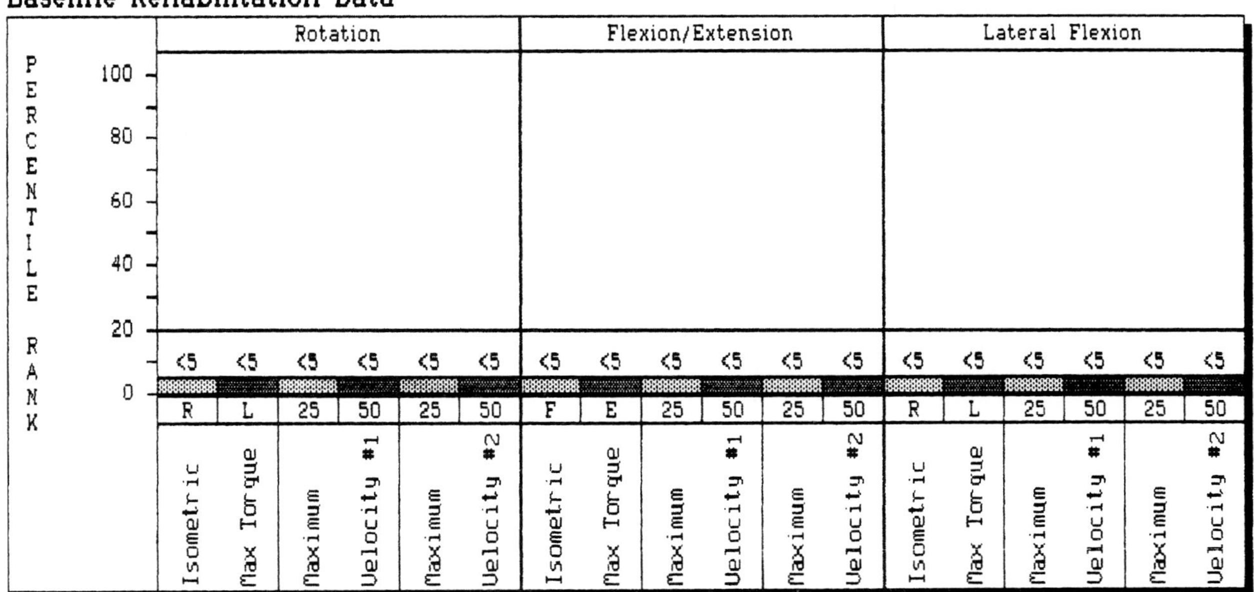

Continued on next page

Table 14–8: *Continued*

OOC Evaluation Results for *1097660

OOC Test	Rotation		Flex/Ext		Lat Flex	
Range of Motion						
ROM (deg) #1	6.0		2.5		13.5	
ROM (deg) #2	6.8		2.1		3.1	
ROM #2 / ROM #1 (Δ%)	13.33		-16.00↓		-77.04↓	
Isometric						
Max Torque (lb-ft)	4.9↓		9.5↓	7.1↓	7.8↓	
Dynamic	25%	50%	25%	50%	25%	50%
Resisted ROM / ROM (Δ%) #1	56.25↑	0.00	33.33↑	-100.00↓	-51.61↓	-74.19↓
Resisted ROM / ROM (Δ%) #2	-5.56	-27.78	20.00	20.00↑	57.14↑	0.00
Avg Vel 50% / Avg Vel 25% (Δ%) #1	-20.00		20.00↑		-44.44	
Avg Vel 50% / Avg Vel 25% (Δ%) #2	-26.32		0.00↑		-55.56	
Max Velocity (deg/sec) #1	9.1↓	6.8↓	2.8↓	2.8↓	7.7↓	2.6↓
Max Velocity (deg/sec) #2	9.1↓	4.5↓	5.7↓	5.7↓	5.1↓	5.1↓
Secondary Axes						
Rot Secondary Max Torq (lb-ft) #1	--	--	1.6↓	1.6↓	1.6↓	1.6↓
Rot Secondary Max Torq (lb-ft) #2	--	--	3.3↓	4.9	1.6↓	1.6↓
F/E Secondary Max Torq (lb-ft) #1	14.2	11.8↓	--	--	18.9	9.5↓
F/E Secondary Max Torq (lb-ft) #2	14.2	16.6	--	--	14.2	14.2
L F Secondary Max Torq (lb-ft) #1	6.3↓	4.7↓	4.7	3.1↓	--	--
L F Secondary Max Torq (lb-ft) #2	3.1↓	4.7↓	4.7	3.1↓	--	--

Key

↓ Subnormal, less than critical level

↑ Supernormal, greater than critical level

(see Statistical Review in OOC Back Evaluation System)

Clinical Application 14–9

In this test (Table 14–9), the following designation appears on page 1 of the OOC report: "Results may suggest submaximal effort." This means that all initial criteria have been met. Because only two of the subsequent criteria were met (conditions 5 and 6), the test is equivalent to a gray zone test and the clinician must classify the test with regard to consistency. This performance was classified as a valid by the evaluator.

Valid, reliable results were obtained during the functional assessment. Waddell testing was negative for nonphysical manifestations of pain. Questionnaires used to identify possible symptom magnification were negative. Functional testing was considered to be consistent. The patient, diagnosed as having a resolved disc herniation, completed a work-hardening program and returned to heavy work after 4 weeks of program participation.

Dr. Deutsch, the developer of the OOC system, recommends extensive psychological profiling for patients who produce tests such as the one shown in Table 14–9. It is the author's strongly held opinion that such an approach is not cost-effective and, furthermore, often discourages a positive relationship between patient and clinician. In the case of this particular patient, one must wonder what the rehabilitation results would have been had the patient been labeled as performing submaximally and subsequently had been administered an intrusive psychological evaluation. Additionally, legitimate questions regarding the reliability/validity of the Minnesota Multiphasic Personality Inventory (usually the instrument of choice by psychologists) have been brought to light by good clinical research.[98]

The possible submaximal designation is, without a doubt, the component of the OOC software analysis that is susceptible to challenge. In the author's experience, the factors that distinguish these patients from those who produce nonphysiological OOC tests include:

1. Longer time since injury.
2. Higher frequency of objective findings.
3. Better consistency during functional evaluations.
4. Higher return to work rate.

Test apprehension may account for some of these test results. Giving the patient the benefit of the doubt whenever possible is recommended. Concurrently addressing the patient's fear of physical activity while encouraging the patient's active involvement in the rehabilitation process and a resumption of normal nonwork activities will optimize the patient's chances for recovery.

Table 14–9: An OCC Computer Printout Demonstrating a "Grey Zone" Test, Indicating That the Consistency of Performance by the Subject was Borderline

OOC Evaluation Results for #1069772

Demographic Data

Age	: 49	**Sex**	: M
Height	: 5 ft 07 in	**Weight**	: 140 lbs
Diagnosis	: Hern. intervertebral disc		
Surgical Category	: Non-Surgical		
Activity Level Category	: Sedentary work		

Resistance Settings

Rotation 25%	: 7 **lb-ft**
Rotation 50%	: 15 **lb-ft**
Flex/Ext 25%	: 11 **lb-ft**
Flex/Ext 50%	: 23 **lb-ft**
Lat Flex 25%	: 13 **lb-ft**
Lat Flex 50%	: 26 **lb-ft**

Abnormal Indicators 20 **Results may suggest submaximal effort.**

	Rotation 25%	Rotation 50%	Flex/Ext 25%	Flex/Ext 50%	Lat Flex 25%	Lat Flex 50%
Isometric Max Torque	↓		↓	↓	↓	
Max Velocity	↓	↓	↓	↓	↓	↓
Rotation Sec Max Torque			↓	↓		↓
Flex/Ext Sec Max Torque	↓	↓			↓	↓
Lat Flex Sec Max Torque	↓	↓		↓		

Non-physiological Indicators 0

1) not observed
2) not observed
3) not observed
4) not observed
5) not observed
6) not observed

Baseline Rehabilitation Data

PERCENTILE RANK (0–100)

	Rotation						Flexion/Extension						Lateral Flexion					
Percentile rank	<5	<5	<5	<5	<5	<5	<5	<5	<5	<5	<5	<5	<5	<5	<5	<5	<5	<5
	R	L	25	50	25	50	F	E	25	50	25	50	R	L	25	50	25	50
	Isometric	Max Torque	Maximum	Velocity #1	Maximum	Velocity #2	Isometric	Max Torque	Maximum	Velocity #1	Maximum	Velocity #2	Isometric	Max Torque	Maximum	Velocity #1	Maximum	Velocity #2

Continued on next page

Table 14–9: *Continued*

OOC Evaluation Results for #1069772

OOC Test	Rotation	Flex/Ext	Lat Flex

Range of Motion

	Rotation	Flex/Ext	Lat Flex
ROM (deg) #1	52.5	53.3	48.5
#2	63.1	46.5	43.3
ROM #2 / ROM #1 (Δ%)	20.19	-12.76	-10.72

Isometric

	Rotation	Flex/Ext	Lat Flex
Max Torque (lb-ft)	29.5↓	45.0↓ 52.1↓	51.8↓

Dynamic

		Rotation 25%	Rotation 50%	Flex/Ext 25%	Flex/Ext 50%	Lat Flex 25%	Lat Flex 50%
Resisted ROM / ROM (Δ%)	#1	35.25	-1.44	30.16↑	35.71↑	-19.82	-9.01
	#2	-10.78↓	-23.35↓	20.00	2.73	10.10	-6.06
Avg Vel 50% / Avg Vel 25% (Δ%)	#1	-52.35↓		-12.96		-25.84	
	#2	-29.90		-20.81		-28.74	
Max Velocity (deg/sec)	#1	52.2↓	36.3↓	59.5↓	48.1↓	36.0↓	38.6↓
	#2	38.6↓	34.0↓	45.3↓	34.0↓	38.6↓	33.5↓

Secondary Axes

		Rotation 25%	Rotation 50%	Flex/Ext 25%	Flex/Ext 50%	Lat Flex 25%	Lat Flex 50%
Rot Secondary Max Torq (lb-ft)	#1	--	--	3.3↓	1.6↓	9.8↓	11.5↓
	#2	--	--	4.9↓	1.6↓	14.7	11.5↓
F/E Secondary Max Torq (lb-ft)	#1	7.1↓	11.8↓	--	--	4.7↓	11.8↓
	#2	9.5↓	14.2↓	--	--	9.5↓	11.8↓
L F Secondary Max Torq (lb-ft)	#1	14.1↓	17.3↓	6.3	4.7↓	--	--
	#2	7.8↓	11.0↓	4.7↓	6.3↓	--	--

Key

↓ Subnormal, less than critical level

↑ Supernormal, greater than critical level

(see Statistical Review in OOC Back Evaluation System)

SPECIALIZED TESTING PARAMETERS

Clinical Application 14–10

This graph (Figure 14–11) depicts movement that is symmetrical with regard to position and velocity. The graph seen here approximates the expected shape of all primary axis graphs of normal, asymptomatic individuals. Movement shown here was produced by a patient after rehabilitation for a nonsurgical disc herniation. Movement on the graph, following the sequence of the numbered arrows, occurs in the following order:

1. Neutral to right end range.
2. Right end range returning to neutral.
3. Neutral to left end range.
4. Left end range returning to neutral.

Normal, unimpaired movement is expected to be symmetrical in rotation and lateral flexion with the quadrants of the graph distributed equally. Although graphs in the sagittal plane should also be the shape depicted in Figure 14–11, the distribution of the quadrants will be somewhat different than during rotation and lateral flexion. Because we normally have more range of motion during flexion than extension and because it is usually possible to move at a higher velocity during extension than flexion, the *x* axis will usually be slightly above the center of the graph and the *y* axis will be a little to the left of center.

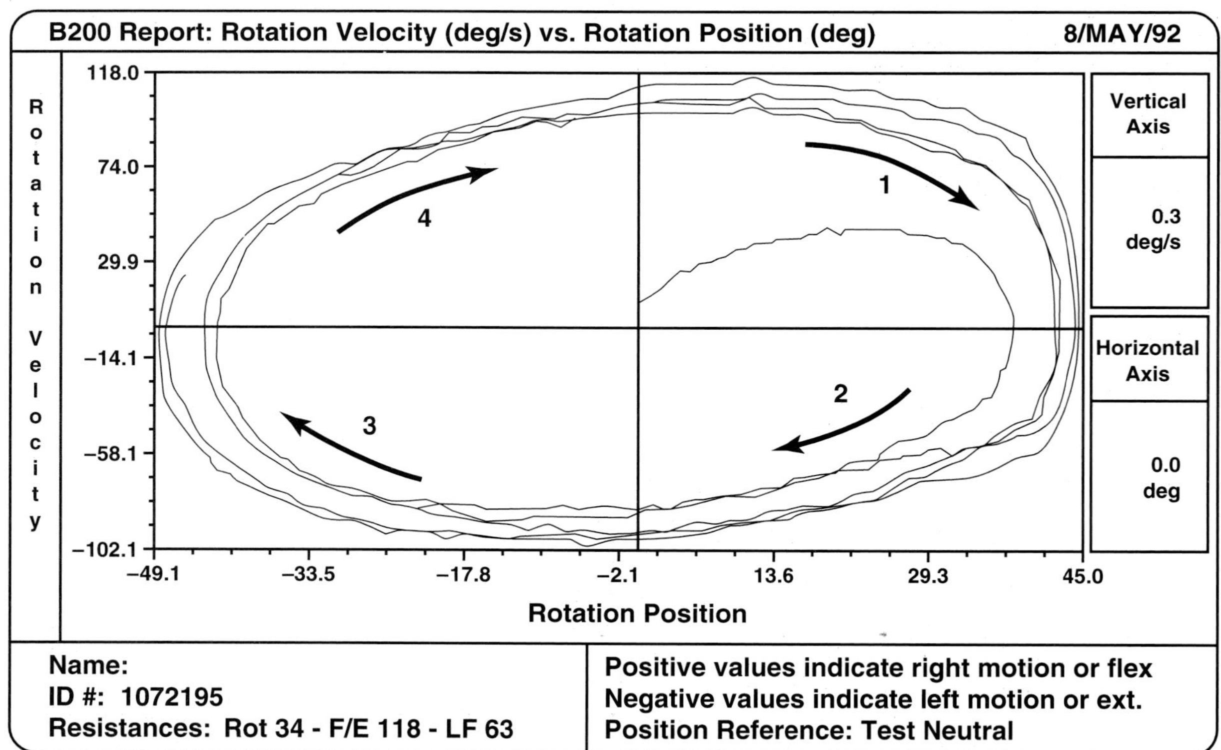

Figure 14–11. An Isostation B-200 computer printout demonstrating a repetition-by-repetition reflection of movement position and velocity.

Clinical Application 14–11

In this graph, (Figure 14–12), we see the normal pattern of recruitment torque from the secondary axis of lateral flexion, during movement in the primary axis of rotation. Notice the sequence of the application of the torques as indicated by the numbered arrows on the graph. Right lateral flexion torque (*y* axis, positive numbers) decreases as the end range of motion toward right rotation is approached (1). (This occurs because of the length-tension relationship.) Peak left lateral flexion torque occurs shortly after the return from far right rotation is initiated (2). Left lateral flexion torque then decreases as rotation to the left progresses (3). This cycle repeats itself in a synchronous pattern in normal movement.

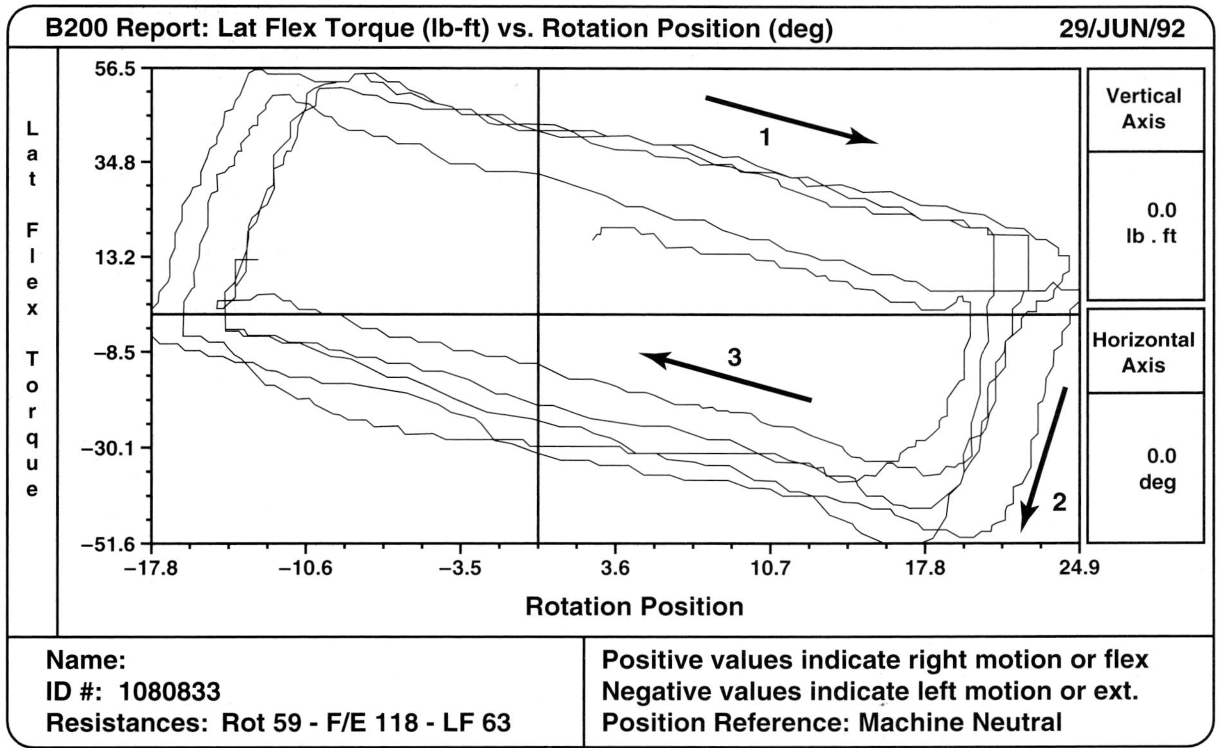

Figure 14–12. An Isostation B-200 computer printout demonstrating a repetition-by-repetition reflection of torque produced during movement along the primary axis and concomitant, secondary torque produced during movement in the secondary axis.

Clinical Application 14–12

Shown in this graph is the normal recruitment pattern of rotation torque during lateral flexion (Figure 14–13). Notice the sequence of the application of the torques as indicated by the numbered arrows. During lateral flexion, there is normally very little input from the axis of rotation (1) until the end range of motion is reached and a return in the opposite direction is initiated (2). Torque production then falls rapidly (3) and approaches zero when the subject is in the neutral position. When the end range of motion in the opposite direction is reached, a peak torque from rotation is generated (4). In conjunction with eccentric contraction in the primary axis (not seen on the graph), this auxiliary torque assists in reversing the direction of movement. As is the case with movement during rotation, a peak secondary axis torque is usually reached shortly after the initiation of movement away from the end range.

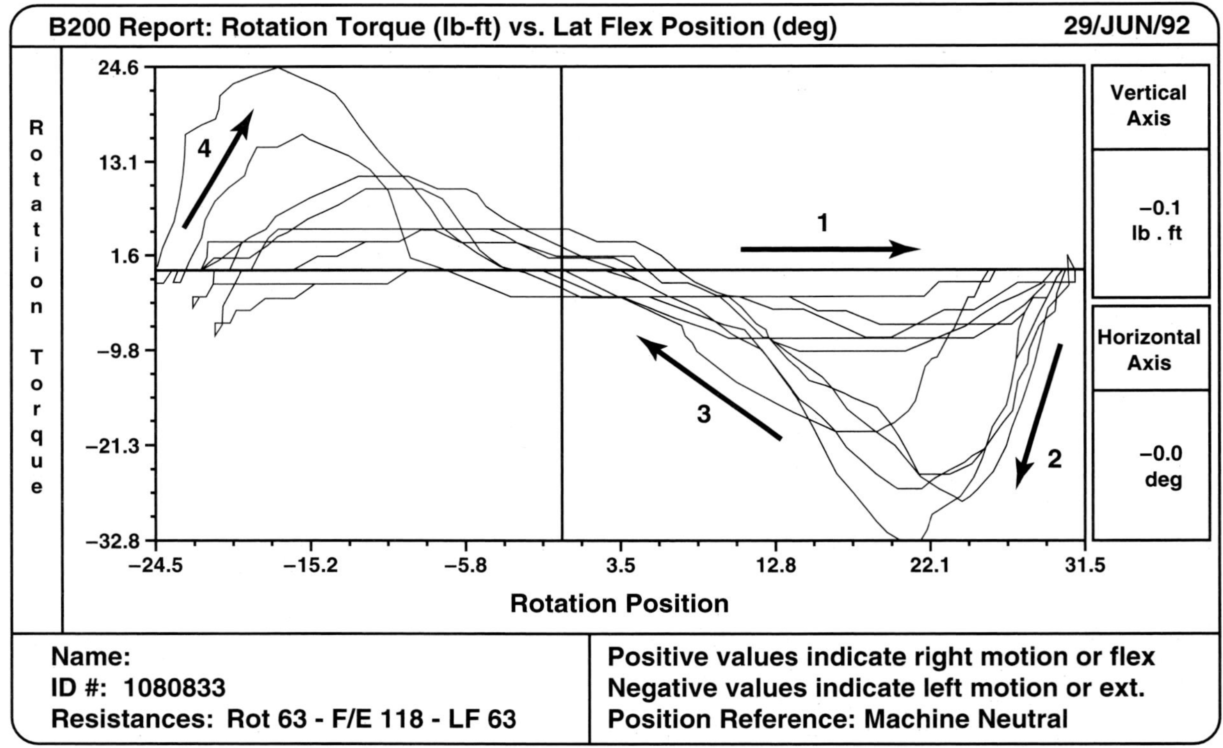

Figure 14–13. The spine moves in a coupled fashion and this Isostation B-200 computer printout demonstrates a repetition-by-repetition reflection of secondary rotational torque that is occurring while the trunk is laterally flexing.

Clinical Application 14–13

This graph (Figure 14–14) was taken from the test generated by the patient referenced earlier in Table 14–8. That test was classified as nonphysiological by the OOC software. The movement patterns show slow movement and a limited range of motion against a very light resistance level. Notice that even against a workload of 2 lb · ft (shown in the lower left-hand box on the graph), the patient is unable to move more than 1.5 degrees from a neutral position to the right. The spikes seen on this graph should not be interpreted as "uneven" or "jerky" movement. Rather, they are a result of the scale to which the graph is drawn. (The same graph enlarged to scale many times would appear much smoother.)

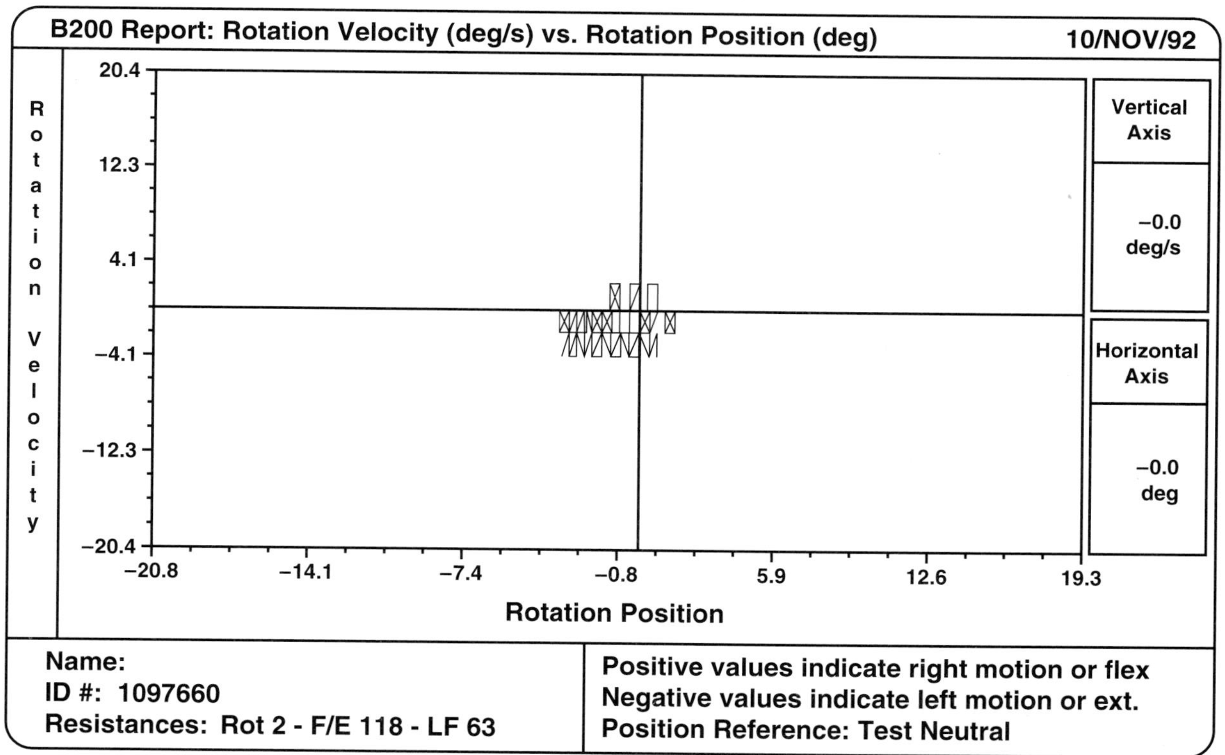

Figure 14–14. This Isostation B-200 computer printout demonstrates slow and limited movement by the subject being tested, against a very minimal resistance, strongly suggesting the presence of a nonphysiological testing outcome.

Clinical Application 14–14

Movement during lateral flexion is shown to be extremely asymmetrical in this patient with lumbar dysfunction (Figure 14–15). Right end range of motion is 6.1 degrees, and left end range of motion is 42.4 degrees. The movement pattern deviations are consistent in each repetition. Functional exercise could be prescribed that would help promote movement symmetry.

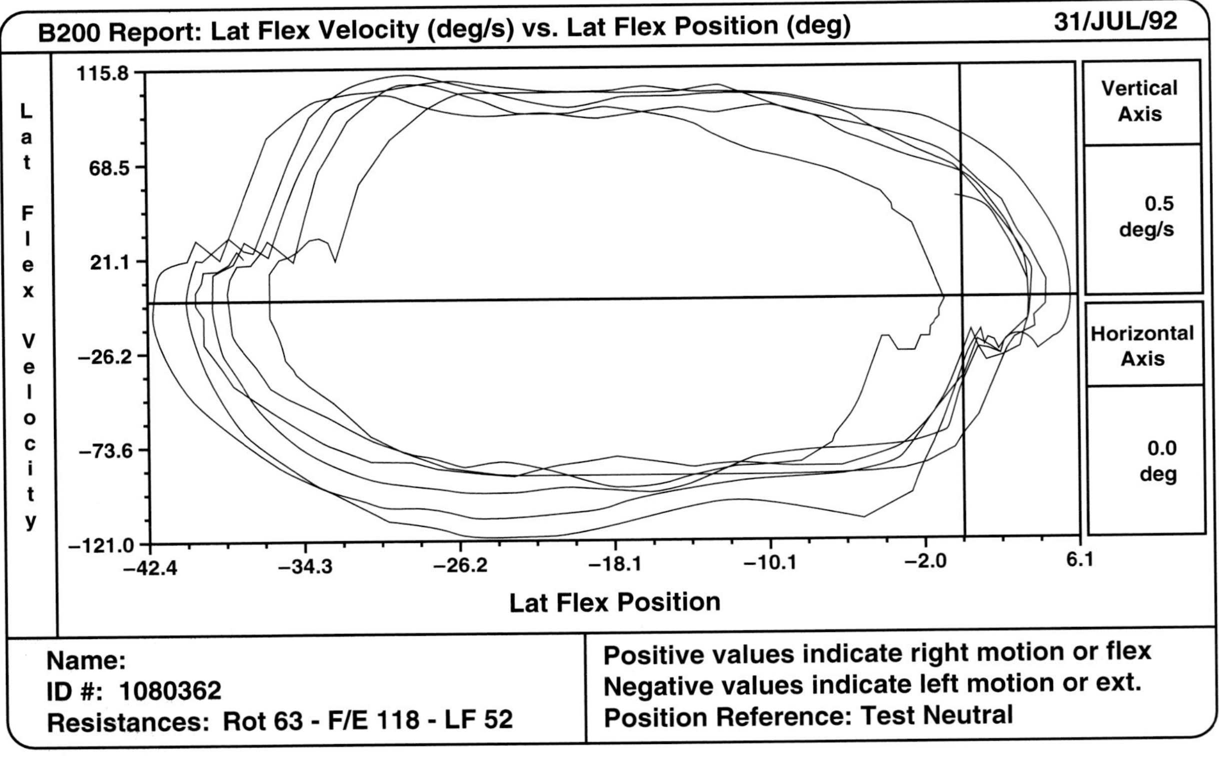

Figure 14–15. This Isostation B-200 computer printout demonstrates an asymmetrical range of motion deviation in lateral flexion, reduced to the right side of lateral flexion. The repetiton-by-repetition line signatures demonstrated consistency on the part of the subject being tested.

Clinical Application 14–15

This graph depicts the rotational torque generated during movement in the primary axis of lateral flexion (Figure 14–16). The greatest amounts of torque are produced as this subject initiates movement away from the right end range of motion. Movement away from the left end range toward the right is guarded, with significantly less rotational torque being generated than occurs when movement is from the right. As pain decreases and functional movement begins to return, it might be expected that retesting would demonstrate symmetrical and more consistent movement repetitions. Failure for this consistent pattern to return may suggest the need to reevaluate the exercise prescription, patient compliance, technique subtleties, or psychosocial elements that may be contributing to identified pattern dysfunction.

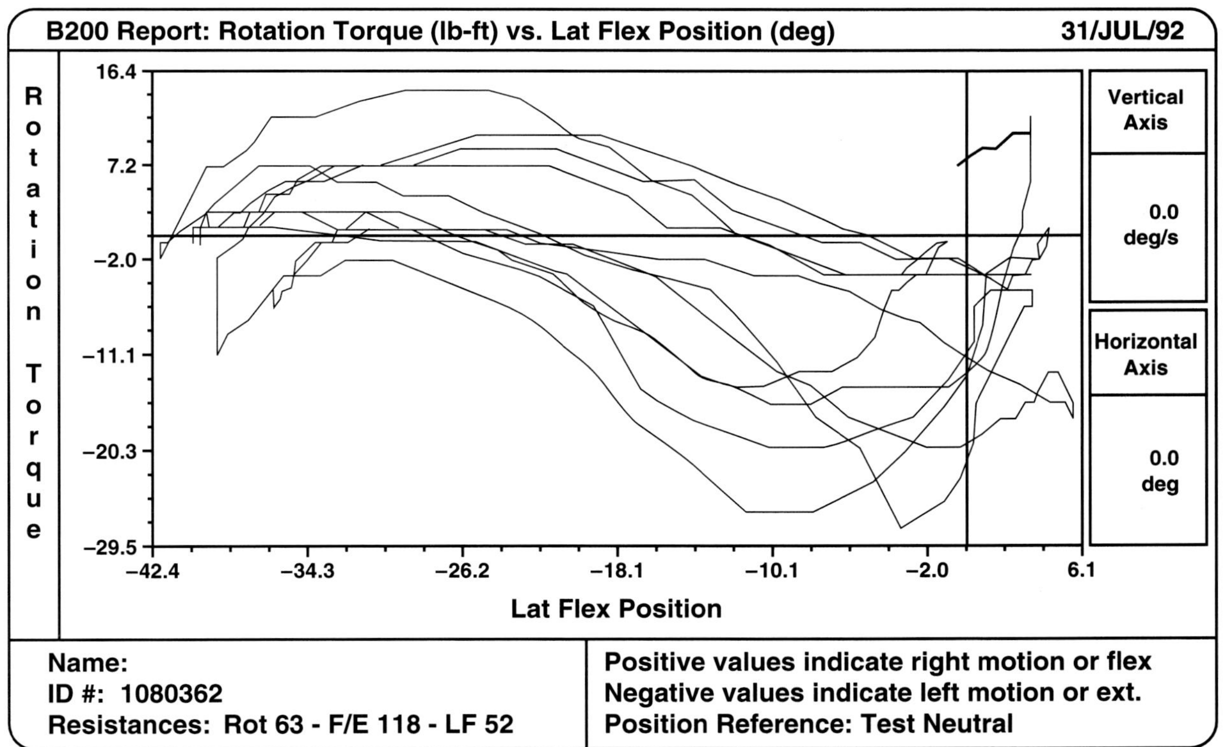

Figure 14–16. The Isostation B-200 computer printout reflects the relative degree of rotational torque generated during movement in the primary axis with lateral flexion. Notice the likely presence of subject guarding demonstrated by asymmetrical, but consistent, levels of torque produced, with movement away from the left side being much less when compared to the right side.

SUMMARY

Triaxial trunk dynamometry can be used to assist the health care provider in objectively evaluating trunk performance parameters. In addition to assessing clinical presentation, there are other potential uses for trunk performance testing, such as outcomes assessment in the research setting[99] and in the occupational health arena. For example, some work-related tasks and associated injuries may require objective, dynamic testing to better evaluate asymetrical handling maneuvers that have been shown to significantly influence loading of the spine.[100] In addition, using triaxial dynamometry may serve a specialized role in assisting to objectively evaluate, categorize, and predict human performance potential in the elite-level athlete. This was demonstrated by Muller et al[101] in elite-level rowers and for measuring sagittal back motion in college football athletes and nonathletes.[102]

The use of triaxial dynamometry was never intended to identify "malingerers," to be used punitively, or to identify "wrongdoers." These testing protocols, when used judiciously and accurately, can help identify those in need of treatment as well as assist in identifying those individuals for whom underperformance or inconsistent performance suggests a significant obstacle to successful rehabilitation. In this regard, even though the B-200 provides objective information regarding trunk performance, it also can suggest the presence of a nonphysiological test, which may reflect abnormal illness behavior.[103] The presence of a nonphysiological test outcome also has been found to correlate with a Waddell score reflective of those patients who exhibit excessive illness behavior.[104] Clinicians must realize that the presence of abnormal test behaviors during objective testing or any psychosocial test does not absolutely exclude the possibility of organic/functional impairment. The availability of functional psychosocial reflective data can be instrumental in the establishment of clinical case management recommendations that will improve the likelihood for successfully addressing those elements that are most responsible for the primary clinical presentation.

Triaxial dynamometry is an objective testing protocol that can be used to assist the clinician in the evaluation process for back pain patients.[105] This type of evaluation, like other computer-aided instrumentation protocols, may serve to provide specialized information for patients with difficult-to-manage cases, and so the establishment of selection criteria is essential during the initial screening process. The evidence, at this time, does not support the use of this instrument for routine clinical assessment, suggesting that selection criteria be established for challenging cases and that reevaluations be conducted prudently.[106] Furthermore, the evidence at this time also suggests that this instrument be reserved for assisting the clinician with trunk evaluation data collected during testing protocols, and not used routinely for rehabilitation training.[107]

LeClaire et al[108] showed that the Isostation B-200 had good diagnostic accuracy when compared to a single clinical evaluation. However, the presence of some inaccuracy for individual subjects suggests that clinicians should use this evaluation method as an assistive device when examining a patient with a difficult-to-manage back pain complaint, instead of relying on it for the only test that is performed on any one subject. Using the chronic category of back pain may serve as one excellent selection criteria for use of the Isostation B-200 lumbar triaxial dynamometer. Preliminary data strongly suggest that there are differences in isometric strength in flexion and rotation for chronic low back pain patients, when compared to normal, asymptomatic individuals, and when tested on the B-200 in a standing, weight-bearing position.[109] Movement velocity is also reduced in the chronic back pain population when subjects are moving against a resistance which is 50% of their maximum isometric strength. Since chronic back pain is costly, both in terms of direct and indirect costs, specialized testing and monitoring of trunk performance parameters may be appropriate.

Triaxial dynamometry was developed in an attempt to add a more precise, objective element to the evaluation of the back pain patient that meets preestablished selection criteria. This instrument is most appropriately used as an adjunct to the neuromusculoskeletal evaluation and functional capacity testing. It may at times need to be used in combination to provide enough data to successfully direct the case management recommendation(s) and, eventually, successful clinical outcomes. Use of objective testing protocols may also have strong potential in the occupational health and human performance, athletic, and geriatric populations when used prudently and with established selection criteria.

REFERENCES

1. Dillane JB, et al. Acute back syndrome: A study from general practice. *British Medical Journal*. 1966;2:82–84.
2. Deyo RA, Tsol-Wu YJ. Descriptive epidemiology of low-back pain and its related medical care in the United States. *Spine*. 1987;12:264–268.
3. National Center for Health Statistics. *Prevalance of Selected Impairments, United States—1977*. No. 134. (Hyattsville, MD: DHHS Publications(PHS), 1981:81–1562.
4. Frymoyer JW. et al. Risk factors in low-back pain: An epidemiological study. *Journal of Bone and Joint Surgery*. 1983;65A:213–218.

5. Andersson GBJ, et al. Epidemiology. In: *Occupational Low Back Pain*. Pope MH, et al, eds. New York: Praeger, 1984:101–114.
6. Spengler DM, et al. Back injuries in industry: A retrospective study. I. Overview and cost analysis. *Spine*. 1986;11:241–245.
7. Kelsey JL. *Epidemiology of Musculoskeletal Disorders*. New York: Oxford University Press, 1982:145–167.
8. Cassidy JD, Wedge JH. The epidemiology and natural history of low back pain and spinal degeneration. In: *Managing Low Back Pain*. WH Kirkaldy-Willis, ed. 2nd ed. New York: Churchill Livingstone, 1988:3–14.
9. Levene JA, et al. Trends in isodynamic and isometric trunk testing on the isostation B200. *Journal of Spinal Disorders*. 2, no. 1:20–34.
10. Parnianpour M, et al. The triaxial coupling of torque generation of trunk muscles during isometric exertions and the effect of fatiguing isoinertial movements on the motor output and movement patterns. *Spine*. 1988;13:982–992.
11. Gomez T, et al. Normative database for trunk range of motion, strength, velocity, and endurance with the isostation B-200 lumbar dynamometer. *Spine*. 1991;16(1):15–21.
12. Parnianpour M, et al. The relationship of torque, velocity, and power with constant resistive load during sagittal trunk movement. *Spine*. 1991;15(7):639–643.
13. Hirsch G, et al. Relationship between performance on lumbar dynamometry and Waddell score in a population with low-back pain. *Spine*. 1991;16(9):1039–1043.
14. Sachs BL, et al. Objective assessment for exercise treatment on the B-200 isostation as part of work tolerance rehabilitation. *Spine*. 1994;19(1):49–52.
15. Tan JC, et al. Isometric maximal and submaximal trunk extension at different flexed positions in standing. *Spine*. 1993;18(16):2480–2490.
16. Rytokoski U, et al. Measurement of low back mobility, isometric strength and isoinertial performance with isostation B-200 triaxial dynamometer: Reproducibility of measurement and development of functional indices. *Journal of Spinal Disorders*. 1994;7(1):54–61.
17. McIntyre DR. The stability of isometric trunk flexion measurements. *Journal of Spinal Disorders*. 1989;2 (2):80–86.
18. Parnianpour M, et al. Reproducibility of trunk isoinertial performances in the sagittal, coronal, and transverse planes. *Bulletin of the Hospital for Joint Diseases Orthopaedic Institute*. 1989;49(2):148–154.
19. Szpalski M, et al. Objective assessment of trunk function in patients with acute low back pain treated with tenoxicam. *Neuro-Orthopedics*. 1990;10:41–47.
20. Kerner M, Kurrant A. Relative isoinertial performance expressions for the isostation B-200. *Journal of Orthopaedic and Sports Physical Therapy*. 1990;12(2):60–65.
21. Parnianpour M, et al. A database of isoinertial trunk strength tests against three resistance levels in sagittal, frontal, and transverse planes in normal male subjects. *Spine*. 1989;14(4):409–411.
22. McIntyre D, et al. The characteristic of preferred low back motion. *Journal of Spinal Disorders*. 1990;3 (2):147–155.
23. Stricevic M, et al. Specificity of karate training: Comparative analysis of the isodynamic evaluation of abdominal and back muscles of beginner vs advanced karate athletes. *World Karate*. 1988;3–4:36–41.
24. Spengler D, Szpalski M. Newer assessment approaches for the patient with low back pain. *Contemporary Orthopaedics*. 1990;21(4):6–14.
25. Seeds R, et al. Abnormal patient data for the isostation B100. *Journal of Orthopaedic and Sports Physical Therapy*. 1988;10(4):121–133.
26. Battie M, et al. Isometric lifting strength as a predictor of industrial back pain reports. *Spine*. 1989;14(8): 851–856.
27. Ayoub M, et al. Determination and modeling of lifting capacity. Final report. HEW (NIOSH) Grant No. 5R010H–00545–02, 1989.
28. Troup J. Relation of lumbar spine disorders to heavy manual work and lifting. *Lancet*. 1965;1:857–861.
29. Andersson G. Epidemiologic aspects on low back pain in industry. *Spine*. 1981;6:53–60.
30. Chaffin D, Park K. A longitudinal study of low back pain as associated with occupational weight lifting factors. *American Industrial Hygiene Association Journal*. 1973;34:513–525.
31. Keyserling W, et al. Isometric strength testing as a means of controlling medical incidents on strenuous jobs. *Journal of Occupational Medicine*. 1980;22:332–336.
32. Liles D, et al. A job severity index for the evaluation and control of lifting injury. *Human Factors*. 1984;26:683–693.
33. Chaffin D. Human strength capability and low-back pain. *Journal of Occupational Medicine*. 1974;16:248–254.

34. Chaffin D, et al. Preemployment strength testing: An updated position. *Journal of Occupational Medicine*. 1978;20:403–408.
35. Marras W, Rangarajulu S. Trunk force development during static and dynamic lifts. *Human Factors*. 1987;29:19–29.
36. Wood G, Hayes K. A kinematic model of intervertebral stress during lifting. *British Journal of Sports Medicine*. 1974;8:74–79.
37. Foreman T, et al. Rating of acceptable load and maximal isometric lifting strengths: The effects of repetition. *Ergonomics*. 1984;27:1284–1288.
38. Freivalds A, et al. A dynamic biomechanical evaluation of lifting maximum acceptable loads. *Journal of Biomechanics*. 1984;17:251–264.
39. Smith J, et al. A biomechanical analysis of industrial manual material handlers. *Ergonomics*. 1982;25:299–308.
40. Garg A, et al. A comparison of isometric strength and dynamic lifting capability. *Ergonomics*. 1980;23:13–27.
41. Garg A, et al. Biomechanical stresses as related to motion trajectory of lifting. *Human Factors*. 1983;25:527–539.
42. Khalil T, et al. A comparative study of static and dynamic lifting tasks. Proceedings of the 28th annual Meeting of the Human Factors Society. 1984:595–599.
43. Kroemer K. An isoinertial technique to assess individual lifting capacity. *Human Factors*. 1983;25: 493–506.
44. Poulsen E. Prediction of maximum loads in lifting from measurement of back muscle strength. *Progressive Therapy*. 1970;1:146–149.
45. Kamon E, et al. Dynamic and static lifting capacity and muscular strength of steelmill workers. *American Industrial Hygiene Association Journal*. 1982;43:853–857.
46. Chaffin D, Parks K. A longitudinal study of low back pain as associated with occupational weight lifting factors. *American Industrial Hygiene Association Journal*. 1973;34:513–525.
47. Magova A. Investigation of the relation between low back pain and occupation: 4. Physical requirements. Bending, rotation, reaching and sudden maximal effort. *Scandinavian Journal of Rehabilitative Medicine*. 1973;5:186–190.
48. Berquist-Ulman M, Larsou V. Acute low back pain in industry: A controlled prospective study with special reference to therapy and confounding factors. *Acta Orthop Scandinavica*. 1970;170:1–117.
49. Freivalds A, et al. A dynamic biomechanical evaluation of lifting maximum acceptable loads. *Journal of Biomechanics*. 1984;17:251–262.
50. Marras W, Wongsam P. Flexibility and velocity of the normal and impaired lumbar spine. *Archives of Physical Medicine and Rehabilitation*. 1986;67:213–217.
51. Parnianpour M, et al. A non-invasive in vivo measurement technique for assessment of the six degrees of freedom of trunk motion. In: Lanta SA, King JA, eds. *Advances in Bioengineering*. New York: American Society of Mechanical Engineers, 1986:28–29.
52. Parnianpour M, et al. The triaxial coupling of torque generation of trunk muscles during isometric exertions and the effect of fatiguing isoinertial movements on the motor output and movement patterns. *Spine*. 1988;13:982–992.
53. Dumas G, et al. Quantitative anatomy of trunk muscles. *Proceedings of North American Congress on Biomechanics*. 1986:81–82.
54. Parnianpour M, et al. The triaxial coupling of torque generation of trunk muscles during isometric exertions and the effect of fatiguing isoinertial movements on the motor output and movement patterns. *Spine*. 1988;13:982–992.
55. Parnianpour M, et al. The validity and reliability of the B-200 isostation, a triaxial system for functional assessment of the trunk. Presented at BACKS, University of Texas, March 1987 and at AAOC, Dallas, TX, September 1987.
56. Parnianpour M. The effect of fatiguing isoinertial trunk flexion and extension movement and motor output. Dissertation. New York: New York University, 1987:120.
57. Dillard J, et al. Motion of the lumbar spine: Reliability of two measurement techniques. *Spine*. 1991;16:321–324.
58. Gomez T, et al. Normative database for trunk range of motion, strength, velocity, and endurance with the isostation B-200 lumbar dynamometer. *Spine*. 1991;16:15–21.
59. McIntyre D. The stability of isometric trunk flexion measurements. *Journal of Spinal Disorders*. 1989;2(2): 80–86.
60. Parnianpour M, et al. Reproducibility of trunk isoinertial performances in the sagittal, coronal and transverse planes. *Bulletin of the Joint Disease Orthopaedic Institute*. 1989;49:148–154.

61. Rondinelli R, et al. Estimation of normal lumbar flexion with surface inclinometry: A comparison of three methods. *American Journal of Physiological and Medical Rehabilitation*. 1992;71(4):219–224.
62. Szpalski M, et al. Reproducibility of trunk isoinertial dynamic performance in patients with low back pain. *Journal of Spinal Disorders*. 1992;5(1):78–85.
63. Szpalski M, Hayez J. Inter-test and inter-machine reliability of the isostation B-200 back testing dynamometer. *Journal of Orthopedic Sports and Physical Therapy*. *In press*.
64. McIntyre D. Letters to the Editor. *Spine*. 1994; 19(8):996–1000.
65. McIntyre D, et al. The characteristics of preferred low back motion. *Journal of Spinal Disorders*. 1990;3(2):147–155.
66. McIntyre D, et al. A comparison of the characteristics of preferred low back motion of normal subjects and low back pain patients. *Journal of Spinal Disorders*. 1991;4(1):90–95.
67. McIntyre D, et al. The relationships between preferred and maximum effort in low back motion. Accepted in *Clinical Biomechanics*. In press.
68. Johansson C, et al. Relationship between verbal command volume and magnitude of muscle contraction. *Physical Therapy*. 1983;63:1260–1265.
69. Milner-Brown H, et al. Quantifying human muscle strength, endurance and fatigue. *Archives of Physical Medicine and Rehabilitation*. 1986;67:530–535.
70. Smith S, et al. Quantification of lumbar function—part I: Isometric and multispeed isokinetic trunk strength measures in sagittal and axial planes in normal subjects. *Spine*. 1985;10:757–764.
71. Sachs BL, et al. Objective assessment for exercise treatment on the B-200 isostation as part of work tolerance rehabilitation. *Spine*. 1994;19(1):49–52.
72. National Institute for Occupational Safety and Health. *Work Practices Guide for Manual Lifting* (U.S. Department of Health and Human Services publication (NIOSH, 1981) 81–122.
73. Genaidy A, et al. A muscular endurance training program for symmetrical and asymmetrical manual lifting tasks. *Journal of Occupational Medicine*. 1990;32(3):226–233.
74. Addison R, Schults A. Trunk strengths in patients seeking hospitalization for chronic low-back disorders. *Spine*. 1980;5(6):539–544.
75. Alston W, et al. A quantitiative study of muscle factors in the chronic low back syndrome. *Journal of the American Geriatic Society*. 1966;14(19):1041–1047.
76. Berkson M, et al. Voluntary strengths of male adults with acute low back syndromes. *Clinical Orthopedics*. 1997;129:84–95.
77. Tucci J, et al. Effect of reduced frequency of training on lumbar extension strength. *Spine*. 1992;17(12):1497–1501.
78. Graves J, et al. Limited range-of-motion lumbar extension strength training. *Medicine and Science in Sports and Exercise*. 1992;24(1):128–133.
79. Suzuki N, Endo SA. A quantitative study of trunk muscle strength and fatigability in the low-back pain syndrome. *Spine*. 1983;8:211–219.
80. Nicolaisen T, Jorgensen K. Trunk strength, back muscle endurance and low-back trouble. *Scandinavian Journal of Rehabilitative Medicine*. 1985;17:121–127.
81. McNeill T, et al. Trunk strengths in attempted flexion, extension, and lateral bending in healthy subjects and patients with low-back disorders. *Spine*. 1980;5(6):529–538.
82. Bergel R. Disabling effects of inactivity and importance of physical condition: A historical perspective. *Exercise and Arthritis*. 1990;16(4):791–800.
83. Jorgensen K, Nicolaisen T. Two methods for determining trunk extensor endurance: A comparative study. *European Journal of Applied Physiology*. 1986;55:639–644.
84. Holder-Powell H, Jones D. Fatigue and muscular activity: A review. *Physiotherapy*. 1990;76(11):672–678.
85. Hayes B, Solyom C, Wing P, Berkowitz J. Use of psychometric measures and nonorganic signs testing in detecting nomogenic disorders in low back pain patients. *Spine*. 1993;18(10):1254–1262.
86. Deutsch S. *OOC Back Evaluation System*. Hillsborough, NC: Isotechnologies, Inc., 1992.
87. Hirsch G, Beach G, Cooke C, Menard M, Locke S. Relationship between performance on lumbar dynamometry and Waddell score in a population with low back pain. *Spine*. 1991;16(9):1039–1043.
88. McIntyre D, Glover L. Secondary axes activity of nnormal subjects and low back pain patients. *Journal of Spinal Disorders*. 1993;1(6):11–16.
89. Menard M, Cooke C, Locke S, Beach G, Butler T. Pattern of performance in low back pain during a comprehensive motor performance evaluation. *Spine*. 1994;19(12):1359–1366.
90. Parniapour M, Nordin M, Kahanovitz N, Frankel V. The triaxial coupling of torque generation on trunk muscles during isometric exertions and the effect of fatiguing isoinertial movements on the motor output and movement patterns. *Spine*. 1988;13(9):982–992.

91. Spengler D, Szpalski M. Newer assessment approaches for the patient with low back pain. *Contemporary Orthopaedics*. 1990;21(4).
92. Szpalski M, Fewrspiel C, Poty S, Hayes J, DeBaize J. Reproducibility of trunk isoinertial dynamic performances in patients with low back pain. *Spine*. 1992;5(1):79–85.
93. Marras W, Wongsam P. Flexibility and velocity for the normal and impaired lumbar spine. *Physical Medicine and Rehabilitation*. 1986;67:213–217.
94. McIntyre D, Glover L. Secondary axes activity of normal subjects and low back pain patients. *Journal of Spinal Disorders*. 1993;1(6):11–16.
95. Hirsch G, Beach G, Cooke C, Menard M, Locke S. Relationship between performance on lumbar dynamometry and Waddell score in a population with low back pain. *Spine*. 1991;16(9):1039–1043.
96. Menard M, Cooke C, Locke S, Beach G, Butler T. Pattern of performance in low back pain during a comprehensive motor performance evaluation. *Spine*. 1994;19(12):1359–1366.
97. Spengler D, Szpalski M. Newer assessment approaches for the patient with low back pain. *Contemporary Orthopedics*. 1990;21(4).
98. Hayes B, Solyom C, Wing P, Berkowitz J. Use of psychometric measures and nonorganic signs testing in detecting nomogenic disorders in low back pain patients. *Spine*. 1993;18(10):1254–1262.
99. Szpalski M, Hayes JP. Objective functional assessment of the efficacy of tenoxicam in the treatment of acute low back pain. A double-blind placebo controlled study. *British Journal of Rheumatology*. 1994;33(1):74–78.
100. Gagnon D, Gagnon M. The influence of dynamic factors on triaxial net muscular moments at the L5-S1 joint during asymmetrical lifting and lowering. *Journal of Biomechanics*. 1992;5(8):891–901.
101. Muller G, Hille E, Szpalski M. Function of the trunk musculature in elite rowers. *Sportverletzung Sportschaden*. 1994;8(3):134–142.
102. Strong LR, Titlow L. Sagittal back motion of college football athletes and non-athletes. *Spine*. 1997;22(15):1755–1759.
103. Nissan M, Bar-Ilan K. Physical three-dimensional testing of the lumbar spine using the Isostation B-200. *Harefuah*. 1996;131(7–8):222–227, 296.
104. Hirsch G, Beach G, Cooke C, Menard M, Locke S. Relationship between performance on lumbar dynamometry and Waddell score in a population with low back pain. *Spine*. 1991;16(9):1039–1043.
105. Bishop JB, Szpalski M, Ananthraman SK, McIntyre DR, Pope MH. Classification of low back pain from dynamic motion characteristics using an artificial neural network. *Spine*. 1997;22(24):2991–2998.
106. Newton M, Waddell G. Trunk strength testing with iso-machines. Part 1: Review of a decade of scientific evidence. *Spine*. 1993;18(7):801–811.
107. Sachs B, Ahmad S, Lacroix M, Olimpio D, Heath R, David J, Scala A. Objective assessment for exercise treatment on the B-200 isostation as part of work tolerance rehabilitation: A random prospective blind evaluation with comparison control. *Spine*. 1994;19(1):49–52.
108. LeClaire R, Esdaile J, Jequier J, Hanley J, Rossignol M, Bourdouxhe M. Diagnostic accuracy of technologies used in low back pain assessment: Thermography, triaxial dynamometry, spinoscopy and clinical examination. *Spine*. 1996;21(11):1325–1331.
109. Stude, D. Normative trunk performance characteristics in a chronic low back pain population measured with a triaxial dynamometer. Proceeding of the International Conference on Spinal Manipulation. 1993; A/M:99.

CHAPTER 15

ISOMETRIC DYNAMOMETRY

Suzan F. Ayers, MS & Michael L. Pollock, PhD (*deceased*)

INTRODUCTION

Traditional rehabilitation has employed primarily passive modalities (i.e., electrical stimulation, diathermy, ultrasound, injections, bed rest, mobilization, traction, massage, home exercises, hot/cold packs) that focus on symptoms, with generally unsuccessful results.[1] This lack of successful treatment outcomes prompted a more aggressive approach in the 1980s. A result of this more aggressive approach was the realization that weak lumbar musculature is often a risk factor for low back pain (LBP).[2,3] Strengthening these weak muscles is the logical route in aiding in the reduction of chronic (greater than 3 months' duration)[1] LBP. Research suggests that specific lumbar extension exercises serve to strengthen the lumbar extensor musculature, reduce pain and symptoms, and improve perceptions of physical and psychosocial functioning in chronic LBP patients.[4–11] These findings suggest outcomes that have the potential to reduce costs associated with this population.

Technological advances have allowed the development of means to assess and rehabilitate chronic LBP. These developments have also generated many tools with questionable reliability, safety, and application outcomes. The objective of this chapter is to address the merits of isometric (IM) dynamometry for the assessment of lumbar extension.

CURRENT STRENGTH TESTING METHODS

As with all strength tests, assessment of the lumbar extensors is critical for the evaluation of muscular integrity and is a key indicator of soft tissue weakness. Once a structural weakness is identified, the appropriate remedial steps can be introduced. The critical factor is reliably isolating the area of interest (i.e., erector spinae muscles) so that an accurate evaluation can be performed. In the past, most strength tests lacked adequate body stabilization and muscle isolation capabilities for this to be possible. Previous strength assessment research lacked standard testing protocols and little or no compensation for the effect of gravity on data generation. This chapter addresses these testing issues for different testing modes, especially those most commonly employed in active rehabilitation programs.

Over the years a wide variety of strength testing devices, both IM and dynamic (DYN), have been developed. Many have associated shortcomings that have been widely addressed in the literature.[1,3,5,7,12–22] These devices have been applied as one component of the evaluation process, but have been challenged as an effective means of active rehabilitation.

ISOMETRIC TESTING

By definition, an IM assessment involves a muscle (group) that contracts statically (without moving either concentrically or eccentrically). Historically, IM testing has been associated with limitations such as variations in the angle of pull when using cable tensiometers, difficulty in reproducing joint angles tested, lack of multiple joint angle tests, and the questionable relationship between IM tests and "function." This section outlines the details of using isolated lumbar extension isometric (LUMB EXT-IM) testing to achieve accurate assessment of the lumbar extensor muscles.

Graves et al[5,6] described a method of measuring maximum voluntary LUMB EXT-IM strength in a seated position through a 72° arc of lumbar range of motion (ROM) (72°, 60°, 48°, 36°, 24°, 12°, and 0° of trunk flexion). The movement arm of this testing device is attached to a strain gauge that is interfaced to an IBM computer. This allows the amount of torque being generated against the movement arm to be converted from ohms to foot-pounds (ft-lb).

Subjects are positioned so that the thighs are parallel to the seat, with feet resting on a footboard, and toes are angled slightly inward (to reduce pressure on the knees). Pressure is applied to the bottom of the feet with the lower legs positioned at approximately 45° of knee flexion. A femur restraint, positioned just above the knees, redirects the pressure from the tibias up the femurs. A lap belt (thigh restraint) is secured in place over the top of the thighs, just below the waist, and tightened to prevent any vertical movement of the thighs or pelvis (Figure 15–1). With the femur restraint acting as a fulcrum, the femurs are pushed down and back, forcing the pelvis against a specially designed lumbar pad (pelvic restraint). In this manner the femurs are used to anchor the pelvis against the pelvic restraint for stabilization. A headrest is adjusted to the level of the occipital bone for comfort, support, and positional standardization. Upper extremity standardization is achieved by two handlebars attached to the movement arm. Subjects are instructed to maintain a light grasp on the handles during the positioning and testing procedures.

After the pelvis is stabilized and the testing position standardized, subjects are checked for any limitations in their lumbar ROM between 0 and 72° of flexion. Subjects are then instructed to hold the upper body against the movement arm of the machine and assume a neutral, upright posture to establish the centerline of their torso mass (torso, head, and arms). A counterweight is locked to the movement arm at this position. This aligns the upper body, movement arm, and counterweight on the same frontal plane. The subject is then moved to 0° of lumbar flexion (full extension) and instructed to relax against the upper back and head pads attached to the movement arm. The height of the counterweight is then adjusted to neutralize the gravitational forces on the head, torso, and upper extremities. This counterweighting procedure is designed to offset the gravitational forces that have been found to introduce erroneous torque contributions during IM contractions.[12]

To begin each test, the movement arm is locked into place at 72° of flexion or to where the ROM is determined, if limited. Subjects are then instructed to extend their back against the upper back pad by gradually building tension over a 3- to 4-second period. The IM torque generated is displayed to the subjects as concurrent visual feedback on a video display terminal. Once maximal tension has been achieved, subjects are instructed to maintain the contraction for 1 additional second before relaxing over a 3- to 4-second period. After each IM contraction, a 10-second rest period is provided while the next testing angle is set. Testing is performed at the subject's most flexed position and every 12° through the subject's most extended position in the ROM (Figure 15–2). To ensure pelvic stabilization, the footboard and thigh restraints are tightened if lumbar-pelvic movement is noted during the test. This is easily checked by noticing any rotation of the pelvic restraint.

This method of IM testing has been developed to provide standardization of testing positions as well a measure of maximal torque production at each angle through an individual's full ROM. The application of IM contractions eliminates the impact forces and torque overshoot artifacts widely associated with dynamic testing.[13–15,23] These artifacts will be superficially addressed in the following section.

DYNAMIC TESTING

A DYN strength test involves some moving component, usually a weight stack or a movement arm. Typically, DYN strength tests have been limited by their less than optimal motor unit recruitment, the lack of safety and accuracy due

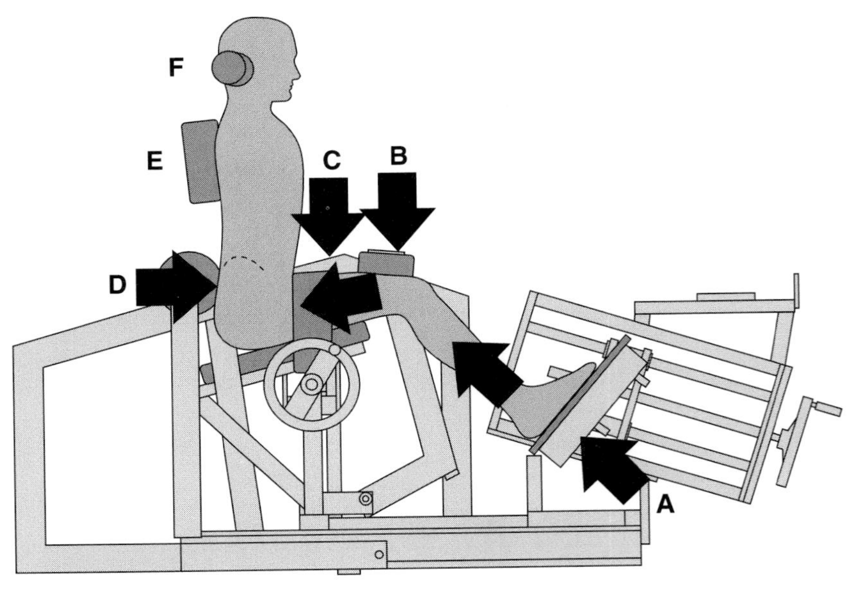

Figure 15–1. Restraining mechanisms for isolating the lumbar extensor muscles. A force that is imposed against the bottom of the feet **(A)** is transmitted by the lower parts of the legs to the femurs at an angle of approximately 45°. The femur **(B)** and thigh **(C)** restraints limit upward movement of the knees, upper aspect of the thighs, and pelvis. The pelvic restraint **(D)** prevents movement of the pelvis in the direction of extension. The upper back pad **(E)** is the point of torque production during LUMB EXT-IM testing. The head pad **(F)** provides for positional standardization of the head.

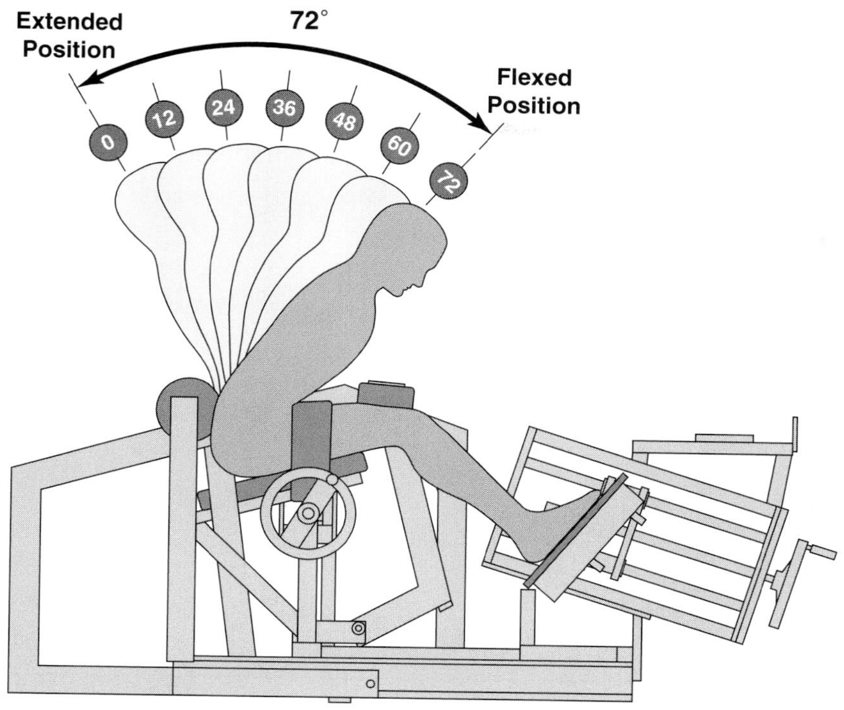

Figure 15–2. Standardized LUMB EXT-IM testing positions, throughout the full ROM, used to correlate position and torque.

to excessive forces introduced by momentum and inertia, and impact forces often associated with this method of testing. Dynamic testing devices differ according to the nature of resistance provided, with the majority falling into one of three categories: (1) constant load, (2) variable resistance, or (3) isokinetic resistance.

Constant load devices provide an unchanging resistance throughout all points in a given ROM. This can be achieved by using either free weights or a system of circular pulleys. The most widely used form of constant load resistance is barbells or free weights. This type of resistance is popular due to its relative ease of use, affordability, and diversity. It is limited, however, by the strength of the weakest joint angle in an ROM. This means that the maximum amount of resistance one is capable of moving is determined by the weakest joint angle, not the maximum amount of force the muscle itself can generate. Many constant load exercises also require the use of a spotter to be performed safely. These two factors, coupled with the lack of specificity provided by constant load exercises, make them less than optimal for evaluation purposes. Considering the vulnerability of the lumbar musculature and the lack of specificity, this method of resistance is inappropriate when evaluating LUMB EXT strength.

Variable resistance devices are designed to provide a resistance curve that matches a specific muscle's ideal strength curve. This is usually achieved through the use of cams or lever systems, which provide a mechanical advantage at certain points through a given ROM. Theoretically, by providing optimal overload throughout an ROM, maximum overload can be achieved. The dynamic nature of this type of activity, however, brings speed of movement into the equation. By moving under load at a high rate of speed through an ROM, momentum is created that can minimize the accuracy of a test. Additionally, these rapid movements introduce dangerously high impact forces that could create risk factors to an already weakened joint. This lack of specificity and unsafe testing methods make constant- and variable-resistance strength tests inappropriate for accurate assessment of LUMB EXT strength.

Theoretically, isokinetic (IK) dynamometers are designed to test "functional" strength. This is achieved by setting the device at a particular speed of movement and having the subject move the involved body part at that velocity. A major problem with this type of testing is that because of the associated acceleration and deceleration phases, a constant speed of movement cannot be maintained throughout an entire ROM. After overcoming inertia, the involved body part must accelerate to reach the preset velocity of the device. Once that speed is reached, the movement is immediately slowed by the sudden braking of the machine's movement arm. This deceleration phase is initiated by a potentially harmful impact force that can easily introduce injury to an already at-risk joint.[13] Such impact forces are associated with the IK testing artifact torque overshoot.[23] The accuracy of IK strength testing has been questioned, primarily because of the need for mathematical interpretation of the oscillations caused by this repeated braking and releasing of the velocity servomechanism.[13,16] Often, when the highest possible damp setting is used, the smoothest strength curve can be represented. However, using high speeds of movement during LUMB EXT testing increases

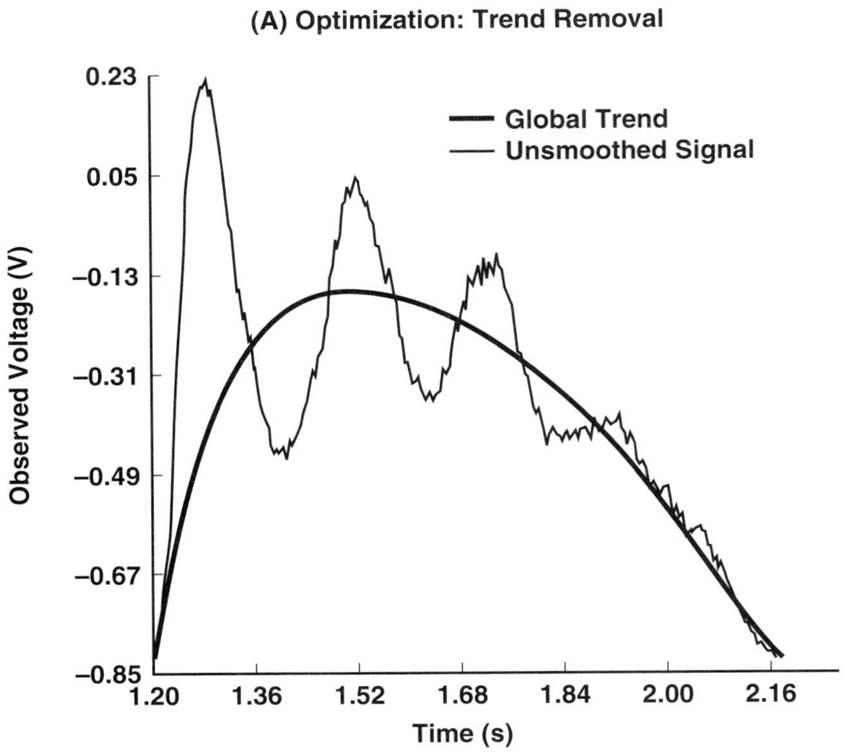

Figure 15–3. Global trend and unsmoothed signal during isokinetic dynamometry. This demonstrates the artificial shift of peak torque when dampened optimally.
(Data from Murray.[15])

impact forces and torque overshoot and creates more artifact.[14] An example of an isokinetic strength curve, with and without dampening, is depicted in Figure 15–3.[15]

Isokinetic device manufacturers have acknowledged the shortcomings of IK testing, and thus have incorporated a correction factor. This factor is called *dampening,* and it serves to smooth out the peaks and troughs created by the acceleration/deceleration phases and the torque overshoot created by the braking servomechanism. Depending on the damp setting used (0 to 4) when representing muscular strength, different torque levels will be depicted when representing the same raw data. Murray[15] depicted the shift that occurs when peak torque is represented as dampened instead of raw data. This testing artifact makes angle-specific measurements questionable, to say the least. As noted by Mayhew and Rothstein,[14] ". . . even the use of a single damp setting will have a variable effect when different speeds are being used for testing."

Finally, the most extreme shortcoming of IK strength tests is the failure to account for individual differences in strength curve shapes. All IK strength curves are represented as bell-shaped, regardless of the true curve shape generated by a muscle or muscle group.

By definition, IM testing does not have these same shortcomings when testing is done in a slow and controlled manner, using multiple joint angles. Because none of the aforementioned artifacts (limited ROM due to acceleration/deceleration, impact forces, torque overshoot, and dampening) are associated with IM testing, the prudence of IM testing is apparent.

REQUIREMENTS FOR ACCURATE ASSESSMENT OF THE LUMBAR EXTENSORS

By definition, the function of muscle is to produce force. This force production enables both movement and anatomic stabilization of body parts. Several components must be considered for lumbar strength to be accurately assessed: (1) it is essential to isolate the lumbar extensors via pelvic stabilization; (2) the influence of gravitational forces must be accounted for; (3) the effect of nonmuscular torques must be considered; and (4) reliable values must be obtained throughout a full ROM.[24]

PELVIC STABILIZATION

Typically, the lumbar extensors work in conjunction with the larger, more powerful hamstring and gluteal muscles to extend the trunk. Because of this cooperative effort, the relatively limited ROM the lumbar extensors can achieve (approximately 72°) is artificially enhanced by the greater ROM (approximately 180°) of the hip extensors.[24,25] If the pelvis is not stabilized, the gluteal and hamstring muscles are responsible for the majority of trunk extension movement and strength. This is due to their larger ROM, greater combined cross-sectional area, and longer movement arm compared to the extensors of the spine.[25] To assess only lumbar extension strength, the stronger hip extensors must be prevented from contributing to trunk extension.[17,18]

This can be achieved by testing in the manner described and depicted earlier, under isolated LUMB EXT-IM testing. Radiographic study has shown that when the legs and pelvis are adequately restrained, backward rotation of the pelvis is restricted to less than 3°.[26]

Three studies document the importance of pelvic stabilization in activating or training the paraspinal muscles.[6,27,28] Graves et al[6] compared LUMB EXT strength training with and without pelvic stabilization on the development of isolated lumbar extension strength. All subjects were tested for isolated LUMB EXT-IM through a 72° ROM before and after 12 weeks of variable resistance lumbar extension training. Subjects were randomly assigned to the stabilized training group, the nonstabilized training group, or the nontraining control group. The training groups both performed one set of 8 to 12 repetitions, one time per week, to volitional fatigue. These groups demonstrated significant and similar increases in the weight loads used for training. However, the post-training IM strength values revealed that only the stabilized training group demonstrated a significant improvement in isolated LUMB EXT-IM strength values relative to the control group. The authors proposed that the weight load increases demonstrated by the nonstabilized training groups was not directly attributable to the erector spinae (isolated LUMB EXT) muscles. They extrapolated that the demonstrated increases in weight loads were probably the result of the increased strength of the hamstring and gluteal muscles (trunk extension/rotation).

By placing electrodes on the paraspinal muscles, Udermann et al[27] performed an electromyographic analysis of the activation of the lumbar extensor muscles. Subjects were evaluated during rowing and dynamic LUMB EXT exercises, with and without pelvic stabilization. The researchers found that the activation of the paraspinal muscles during rowing exercise was minimal compared to the activation observed while exercising with the pelvis stabilized and to LUMB EXT DYN exercise without pelvic stabilization (Figure 15–4).

This was confirmed by Fujita et al[28] when they compared strength training using isolated LUMB EXT exercises, straight-leg dead lift, and Roman chair exercises (no pelvic restraints). After 12 weeks of training, their results showed significant hip/back strength gains specific to the modality used, and only isolated LUMB EXT training showed full ROM increases in isolated LUMB EXT-IM strength. Dead-lift training showed a partial effect of an increase in isolated LUMB EXT-IM strength. Although

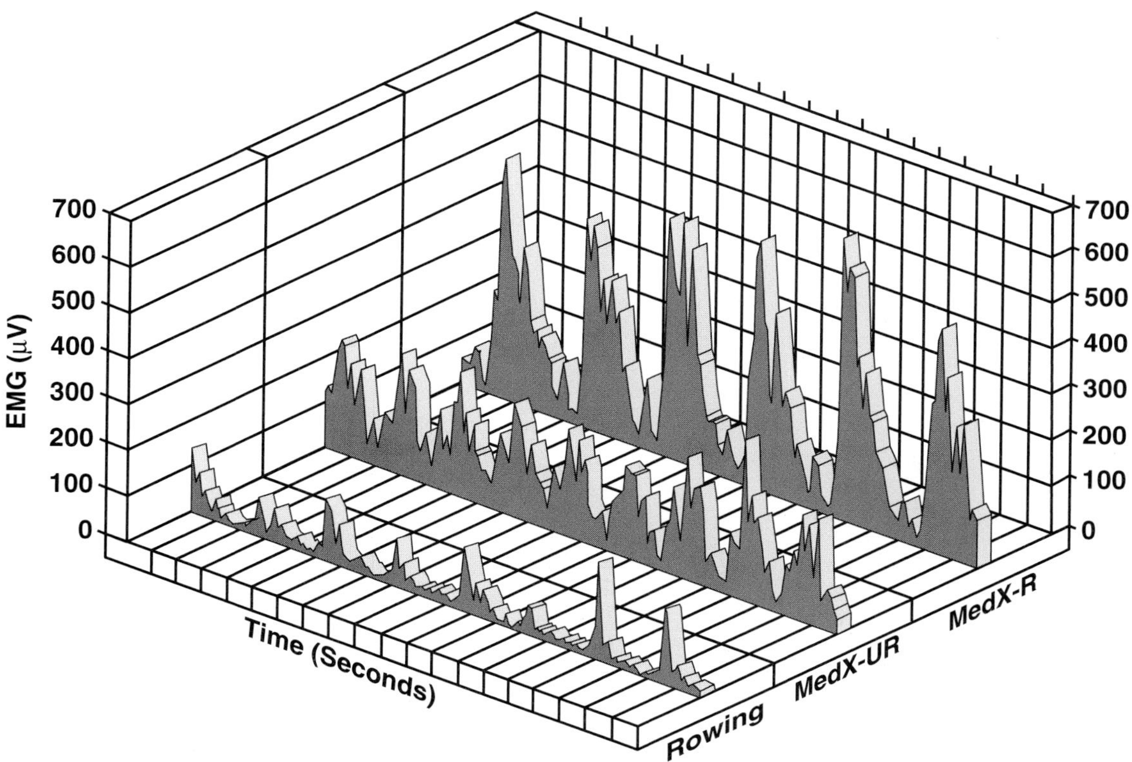

Figure 15–4. Surface EMG readings demonstrate the lack of activation of the paraspinal muscles during rowing exercise (Rowing) and unrestrained lumbar exercise (MedX-UR) compared to the activation observed while exercising on the MedX lumbar extension dynamometer (MedX-R).

(Data from Udermann et al.[27])

Roman chair training showed little or no effect on the isolated LUMB EXT muscles, strength gains were made in the gluteal and hamstring muscles.

Thus it is clear from these studies that in order to test or train the paraspinal muscles through a full ROM, the pelvis must be properly stabilized. Without stabilization, the stronger gluteal and hamstring muscles affect hip function (extension) and the lumbar muscles remain passive.

GRAVITY COMPENSATION

Winter et al[19] have reported that measurement errors in excess of 500% can occur when gravitational forces are not considered during muscular strength tests. This effect has been described by Fulton et al[29] as representing up to 25% of the mean torque values (Figure 15–5).

When assessing lumbar strength in the sagittal plane, as required for pelvic stabilization to occur, gravitational forces act upon the involved body parts and influence torque measurements.[7,14,19,20,30] According to Pollock et al,[12] gravity detracts from isolated LUMB EXT torque values in the flexed positions and adds to the torque values produced in the more extended positions. The authors used a prototype lumbar extension machine that allowed IM testing in both the sagittal and transverse (Figure 15–6) planes. During testing in the sagittal plane, a counterweight device was attached to the movement arm to account for the effects of gravity on isolated LUMB EXT torque production. This method of counterbalancing was described earlier, under isolated LUMB EXT-IM testing. During testing in the transverse plane, no counterweight was necessary because gravity no longer effects torque production in the direction of lumbar extension. The correlation between these tests ranged from r = 0.91 to 0.98 (0° to 72°, respectively) (Figure 15–7). Thus, the effectiveness of the counterweighting device in compensating for the effects of gravity during seated isolated LUMB EXT-IM strength testing was accurately assessed and validated (see Figure 15–6A).

ACCOUNTING FOR NONMUSCULAR TORQUE

Measured voluntary torque is a combination of the excitation-coupling process of skeletal muscle and the stored energy created by the stretching and compressing of soft tissues associated with a joint.[31] This stored energy has been observed during seated isolated LUMB EXT-IM testing, but has not been separated and quantified in the literature, with little exception.[32] The importance of this lies in the separation of all involuntary forces from the exclusively voluntary exertion generated by the lumbar extensor muscles. When using advanced technology for muscular assessment, it is possible to delineate and quantify these forces. To ignore this capacity is not only unwise, but yields inaccurate data.

Subtracting all involuntary forces (nonmuscular) that produce torque (gravity and stored energy) from a strength test leaves only those forces produced by the contractile elements of the muscle or muscle group (Figure 15–8). This has been termed *net muscular torque* (NMT), and is defined as the torque generated by volitional muscular contraction.[23] This value is unique in its exclusion of all non-muscular forces that have historically influenced muscular torque measurements. Because of the limitations associated with dynamic strength tests, NMT can only be quantified during IM strength tests. This quantification of NMT further enhances the clarity with which isolated LUMB EXT-IM strength can be evaluated.

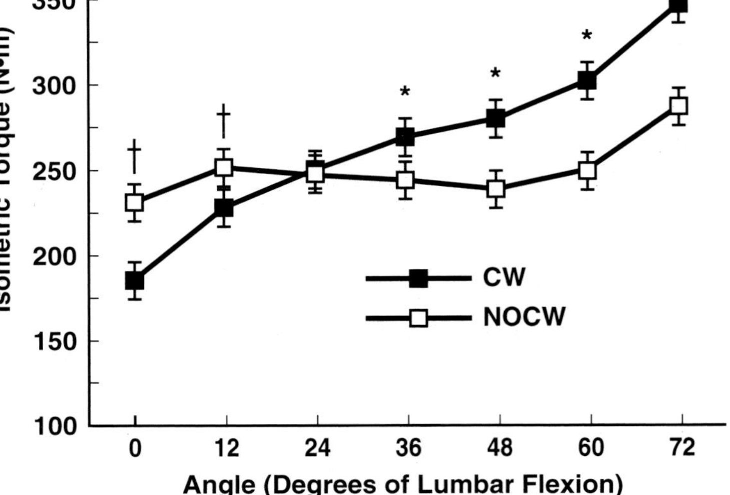

Figure 15–5. The influence of upper body mass during lumbar extension torque evaluation in the seated position. A group of 34 subjects was tested for isolated LUMB EXT-IM strength with a counterweight (CW) and again without a counterweight (NOCW). *The CW trial was significantly higher than the NOCW trial ($p \leq 0.05$). †The NOCW trial was significantly higher than the CW trial ($p \leq 0.05$).

(Data from Fulton et al.[29])

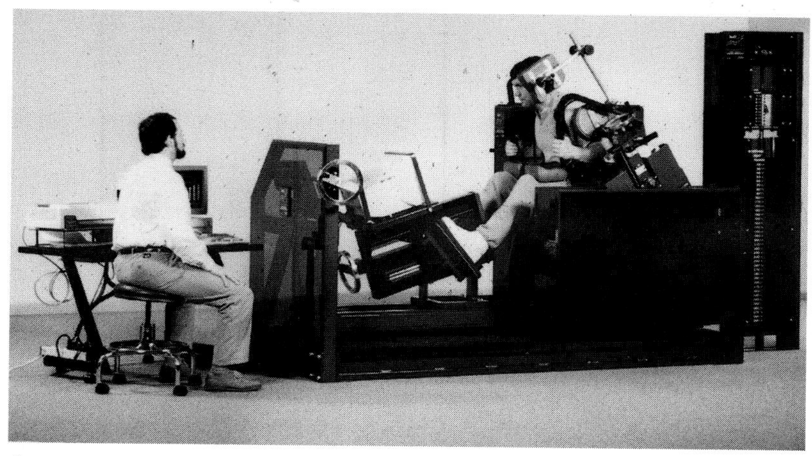

A

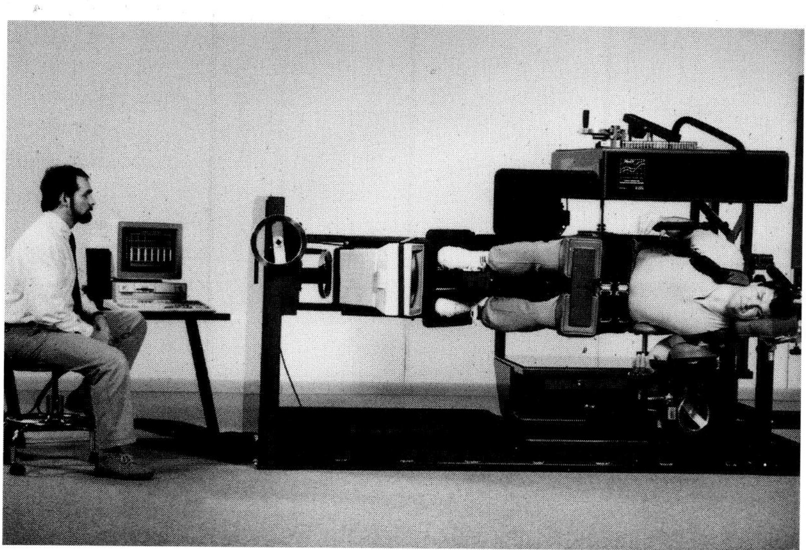

B

Figure 15–6. Prototype isolated lumbar extension strength testing tool, developed to assess the validity of the counterweighting mechanism. Testing was compared in the sagittal **(A)** and the transverse **(B)** planes.

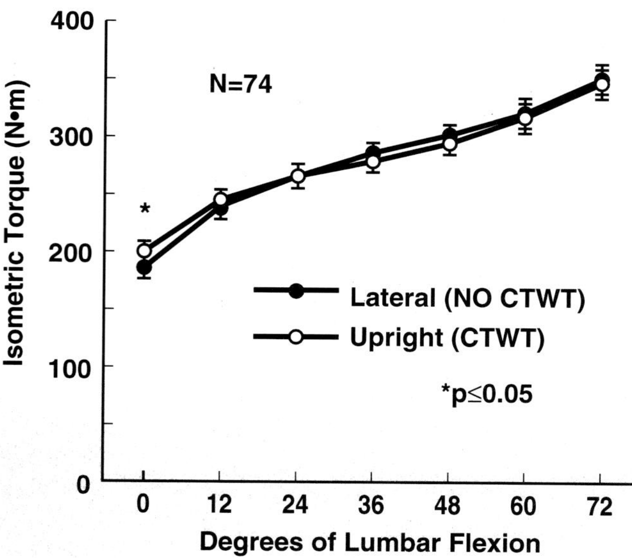

Figure 15–7. Isolated LUMB EXT-IM strength curves from testing in the sagittal and transverse planes. Correlations ranging from r = 0.91 to 0.98 (0° to 72°, respectively) were demonstrated.

(Data from Pollock et al.[12])

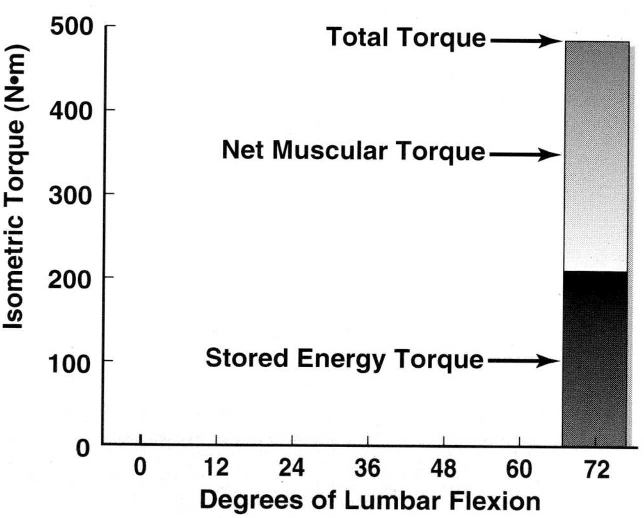

Figure 15–8. Resting involuntary torque is first recorded by the computer. The subject then performs a maximal isolated LUMB EXT-IM contraction, and the total torque is recorded. The difference between the total torque and the torque caused by involuntary factors represents the net muscular torque.

RELIABILITY OF FULL ROM ISOMETRIC TESTING

For a strength test to be meaningful, it must be reliable. To determine the reliability of isolated LUMB EXT-IM torque, Graves et al[5] evaluated 136 subjects who completed multiple joint angle tests through a 72° ROM (72°, 60°, 48°, 36°, 24°, 12°, and 0° of lumbar flexion) on 3 separate days. On days 1 and 2, subjects completed two isolated LUMB EXT-IM tests, separated by 20 to 30-minute rest intervals. On the third day, subjects completed one additional isolated LUMB EXT-IM test. The mean IM torque values, within-day reliability coefficients, and test variability improved from day 1 to 2. Mean strength values and variability statistics showed no additional improvement from day 2 to 3 [correlation coefficients ranged from 0.97 to 0.81 from full flexion (72°) to full extension (0°)]. Single test variability (standard error of the estimate) ranged from 6.7% to 11.0% of the mean torque values reported.[9] Because strength tests on humans typically vary between 5% and 10% due to normal human biovariations,[21] these values can be considered within the range of scientifically acceptable variation. Because of the improvements observed from day 1 to day 2, it was concluded that a practice test should be allowed before establishing baseline isolated LUMB EXT-IM extension strength values due to the learning effect.

Historically, IM testing has been limited by single joint angle testing, therefore falling under the same "limited ROM assessment" category as isokinetic strength tests. In work by Knapik and associates,[22] it was demonstrated that IM exercise resulted in a carryover of strength to approximately 20° on each side of the joint angle trained. This significant carryover of strength development on either side of the angle being tested was confirmed by Graves et al.[33] Thus, the measuring of isolated LUMB EXT-IM torque at 12° increments appears valid in the assessment of full ROM LUMB EXT strength.

The isolated LUMB EXT-IM strength testing model presented in this chapter accounts for this type of testing limitation by assessing maximal IM efforts through multiple joint angles in a pain-free ROM. The negative aspect of this type of test is the fatigue associated with multiple joint angle testing. Graves et al[33] identified the influence of testing order as affecting lumbar extension torque measurements. They concluded, however, that standardizing the testing order allows quantification of strength changes through a full ROM. When it is essential to obtain maximal IM torque values at multiple positions throughout a ROM, adequate recovery time between contractions must be allowed.

Clinical Application 15–1

ISOMETRIC STRENGTH TESTING IN CHRONIC LOW BACK PAIN REHABILITATION

The University of Florida's Center for Exercise Science research program has performed extensive isolated LUMB EXT-IM strength testing over the last decade. This testing has employed mainly the flexion to extension testing order, and has been used to establish normative data for both males and females (Figure 15–9). These normative values serve to quantify initial strength values and strength curves to identify weaknesses and curve abnormalities. They have also been used to evaluate strength gains and patient compliance over the course of an active rehabilitation program.

The isolated LUMB EXT-IM torque values generated during multiple joint angle testing are interfaced with a computer that automatically generates a strength curve. The initial strength curve gives the clinician an indication of baseline muscular weaknesses and serves as the basis for the rehabilitation protocol. The standard rehabilitation protocol uses monthly LUMB EXT-IM tests to document strength and ROM improvements. In this manner, clinicians can objectively quantify patient progress and determine the individual appropriateness and effectiveness of the exercise prescription. This isolated LUMB EXT-IM testing method is not designed to clinically diagnose specific spinal disorders, but is the basis of the initial evaluation and documentation of the patient's strength curve and ROM. This evaluation assists in the formulation of the treatment plan, which includes the exercise prescription. Generally, patients' strength curves fall approximately 1 to 2 standard deviations below the mean of the norms. As patients gain strength and approach normative strength values, pain is relieved or significantly reduced (approximately 80% of chronic LBP patients).[10,11] Also, daily activity levels increase and dysfunction is reduced.[4,10,11]

Clinical Application 15–1 continued

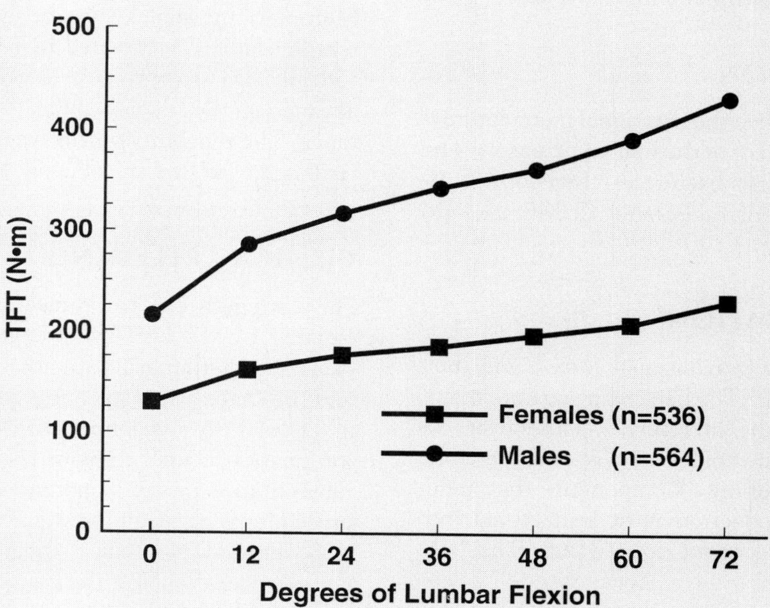

Figure 15–9. Isolated LUMB EXT-IM torque values for healthy, normal men and women.

Source: Unpublished data from the University of Florida, Center for Exercise Science Research Laboratory.

Since the focus of this chapter is IM dynamometry, the topic of active rehabilitation will not be exhaustively addressed. However, the importance of applying the isolated LUMB EXT-IM testing device in its concomitant role as a strengthening tool must be mentioned. The isolated LUMB EXT model used for IM testing also provides a means of variable resistance DYN exercise in both the concentric and eccentric phases of training. The same manner of isolating the pelvis is applied during the exercise training portion as during the isolated LUMB EXT-IM testing portion of the operation.

Because of the extreme weakness of the erector spinae muscles, large improvements in strength have been found within the first 8 to 12 weeks.[4,6,8,9,28,34] The recommended clinical protocol is 8 to 12 weeks long, with patients training two times per week for the first 4 weeks. Then training is reduced to one time per week for the remainder of the program. Graves et al[9] have also shown that one time per week of isolated LUMB EXT exercise is as effective as two or three times per week in increasing muscular strength and endurance. During each training session, subjects are encouraged to train for one set of 10 to 20 repetitions to volitional fatigue. As the ability to perform longer periods of exercise is achieved, the resistance is increased by approximately 5%. This overload provides the necessary stimulus for muscular hypertrophy and increased levels of strength. Once patients progress to the normative level and pain subsides, a reduced frequency of training to once every 4 weeks has been shown to maintain strength.[35] For more information concerning training results, see Risch et al,[4] Nelson et al,[10] and Holmes et al.[11]

SUMMARY

The use of isolated LUMB EXT-IM testing in the evaluation of chronic LBP patients has been widely studied, and has been shown to be accurate, reliable, safe, effective, and clinically relevant. The latest IM dynamometry has improved greatly over the years and includes many attributes that make it ideal for evaluating the lumbar spine.

PELVIC STABILIZATION

Stabilizing the pelvis to isolate the paraspinal musculature is critical for accurate assessment of the lumbar extensors. The role of pelvic stabilization has been researched and identified as a critical component of isolated LUMB EXT-IM strength assessments.[6,7,17,27,28]

GRAVITY COMPENSATION

The errors associated with gravitational forces, and their effect on isolated LUMB EXT-IM strength measurements, have been addressed in the literature.[19] This effect has been linked with inaccurate torque values, and therefore, inaccurate strength evaluations. Components that influence voluntary torque production must be factored into strength tests to determine accurate isolated LUMB EXT-IM strength.

ACCOUNTING FOR NONMUSCULAR TORQUE

Measured voluntary torque is also influenced by nonmuscular forces.[31] These forces, like gravitational forces, must be considered in isolated LUMB EXT-IM strength tests. Because of the artifacts associated with DYN strength tests, only isolated LUMB EXT-IM strength assessments can factor out this influence.

RELIABILITY OF FULL ROM ISOMETRIC TESTING

Multiple joint angles must be evaluated to accurately determine full ROM isolated LUMB EXT-IM strength. Historically, IM strength tests lacked this capability, so this advance in IM dynamometry is of great clinical importance. The reliability of this type of procedure has been determined,[33] so its clinical application is appropriate.

CLINICAL RELEVANCE

For a strength test to be meaningful, it must be reliable. Isolated LUMB EXT-IM strength tests are used by clinicians to determine a patient's baseline levels of strength and the shape and slope of his or her initial strength curve, and to identify any abnormalities that may be present. This information is used to assist the clinician in developing a rehabilitation protocol appropriate to each individual. This procedure is also employed across the course of an active rehabilitation protocol to quantify patient progress and compliance. Based on the research performed at the University of Florida, normative values have been established using subjects without chronic LBP. These values serve as a comparative value for patient progress. Research has shown that as chronic LBP patients normalize in strength values, pain decreases, and psychosocial function and daily activity levels improve.[4,10,11]

REFERENCES

1. Bigos S, Bowyer O, Braen G, et al. U.S. Department of Health and Human Services. *Acute Low Back Problems in Adults. Clinical Practice Guideline Number 14*. AHCPR Publication 95–0642. Rockville, MD: Agency for Health Care Policy and Research, Public Health Service, U.S. Department of Health and Human Services, December 1994.
2. *Back Injuries: Cost, Causes, Cases, and Prevention*. Washington DC: Bureau of National Affairs, 1988: 54–57.
3. Mayer T, Gatchel R, Kishino N, Keeley J, Mooney V. A prospective two-year study of functional restoration in industrial low back injury: An objective assessment procedure. *JAMA*. 1987;258:1763–1767.
4. Risch SV, Norvell NK, Pollock ML, et al. Lumbar strengthening in chronic low back pain patients. *Spine*. 1993;18:232–238.
5. Graves J, Pollock M, Carpenter D, et al. Quantitative assessment of full range-of-motion isometric lumbar extension strength. *Spine*. 1990;15:289–294.
6. Graves J, Webb D, Pollock M, et al. Pelvic stabilization during resistance training: Its effect on the development of lumbar extension strength. *Arch Phys Med Rehabil*. 1994;75:210–215.
7. Mayer T, Smith S, Keeley J, Mooney V. Quantification of lumbar function. Part 2: Sagittal plane trunk strength in chronic low-back pain patients. *Spine*. 1985;10:765–772.
8. Pollock M, Leggett S, Graves J, Jones A, Fulton M, Cirulli J. Effect of resistance training on lumbar extension strength. *Am J Sports Med*. 1989;17:624–629.

9. Graves JE, Pollock ML, Foster D, et al. Effect of training frequency and specificity on isometric lumbar extension strength. *Spine*. 1990;15:504–509.
10. Nelson B, O'Reilly E, Miller M, Hogan M, Wegner J, Kelly C. The clinical effects of intensive, specific exercise on chronic low back pain: A controlled study of 895 consecutive patients with 1-year follow up. *Orthopedics*. 1995;18:971–981.
11. Holmes B, Leggett S, Mooney V, Nichols J, Negri S, Hoeyberghs A. Comparison of female geriatric lumbar-extension strength: Asymptomatic versus chronic low back pain patients and their response to active rehabilitation. *J Spinal Disord*. 1996;9:17–22.
12. Pollock M, Graves J, Leggett S, et al. Accuracy of counterweighting to account for upper body mass in testing lumbar extension strength. *Med Sci Sports Exerc*. 1991;23:S66.
13. Murray D, Harrison E. Constant velocity dynamometer: An appraisal using mechanical loading. *Med Sci Sports Exerc*. 1986;18:612–624.
14. Mayhew T, Rothstein J. Measurement of muscle performance with instruments. In: Rothstein J, ed. *Measurement in Physical Therapy*. New York: Churchill Livingstone, 1985:57–102.
15. Murray D. Constant velocity torque. *Med Sci Sports Exerc*. 1986;18:603–611.
16. Bemben M, Grump K, Massey B. Assessment of technical accuracy of the Cybex II isokinetic dynamometer and analog recording system. *J Orthop Sports Phys Ther*. 1988;10:12–17.
17. Peterson CM, Amundsen LR, Schendel MJ. Comparison of the effectiveness of two pelvic stabilization systems on pelvic movement during maximal isometric trunk extension and flexion muscle contractions. *Phys Ther*. 1987;67:534–539.
18. Smidt G, Herring T, Amundsen L, Rogers M, Russell A, Lehmann T. Assessment of abdominal and back extensor function. *Spine*. 1983;8:211–219.
19. Winter D, Wells R, Orr G. Errors in the use of isokinetic dynamometers. *Eur J Appl Physiol*. 1981; 46: 397–408.
20. Fillyaw M, Bevins T, Fernandez L. Importance of correcting isokinetic peak torque for the effect of gravity when calculating knee flexor to extensor muscle ratios. *Phys Ther*. 1994;75:210–215.
21. Wakim K, Gersten J, Elkins E, Martin G. Objective recording of muscle strength. *Arch Phys Med*. 1950;31:90–100.
22. Knapik JJ, Mawdsley RH, Ramos NU. Angular specificity and test mode specificity of isometric and isokinetic strength training. *J Orthop Sports Phys Ther*. 1983;5:58–65.
23. Pollock M, Graves J, Carpenter D, Foster D, Leggett S, Fulton M. Muscle. In: Hochschuler S, Guyer R, Cotler H, eds. *Rehabilitation of the Spine: Science and Practice*. St. Louis: Mosby, 1993:263–284.
24. Jones A, Pollock M, Graves J, et al. *The Lumbar Spine*. Santa Barbara, CA: Sequoia Communications, 1988.
25. Farfan H. Muscular mechanism of the lumbar spine and the position of power and efficiency. *Orthop Clin N Am*. 1975;6:135–144.
26. Inanami H. Iwai Orthopaedic Hospital Rehabilitation Program. Presented at the International Spinal Rehabilitation Update '91 Symposium. Daytona, FL: September 12–14, 1991.
27. Udermann B, Iriso J, Graves J. Effect of pelvic restraint on hamstring, gluteal, and lumbar muscle EMG activation. *Med Sci Sports Exerc*. 1995;27:S210.
28. Fujita S, Brechue W, Kearns C, Pollock M. Effect of non-isolated lumbar extension resistance training on isolated lumbar extension strength. *Med Sci Sports Exerc*. 1997;29:S166.
29. Fulton M, Leggett S, Graves J, Pollock M, Carpenter D, Colding B. Effect of upper body mass on the measurement of isometric lumbar extension strength. Presented at the Orthopaedic Rehabilitation Association Conference. San Antonio, TX: 1990.
30. Herzog W. The relation between the resultant moments at a joint and the moments measured by an isokinetic dynamometer. *J Biomech*. 1988;21:5–12.
31. Chapman AE. The mechanical properties of human muscle. *Exerc Sport Sci Rev*. 1985;13:443–501.
32. Carpenter D, Leggett S, Pollock M, et al. Quantitative assessment of isometric lumbar extension net muscular torque. *Med Sci Sports Exerc*. 1991;23:S65.
33. Graves J, Pollock M, Leggett S, Carpenter D, Fix C, Fulton M. Limited range-of-motion isometric lumbar extension strength training. *Med Sci Sports Exerc*. 1992;24:128–133.
34. Carpenter D, Graves J, Pollock M, et al. Effect of 12 and 20 weeks of resistance training on lumbar extension torque production. *Phys Ther*. 1991;71:580–588.
35. Tucci J, Carpenter D, Pollock M, Graves J, Leggett S. Effect of reduced frequency of training and detraining on lumbar extension strength. *Spine*. 1992;17:1497–1501.

CHAPTER 16

Three-Dimensional Spinal Kinematics

PAUL ALLARD, PHD, P.ENG., NADER FARAHPOUR, MSC, HUBERT LABELLE, MD, CHARLES-HILAIRE RIVARD, MD, & MORRIS DUHAIME, MD

INTRODUCTION

The clinical aspects of low back problems have been well documented in a report by Spitzer.[41] These are closely associated with different types of industrial activities such as manual material handling, lifting, work intensity, static work posture, bending and twisting actions of the spine, pushing and pulling, to name but a few.[24] Frymoyer and Gordon[14] reported that at one time 13.8% of the American population suffered from a low back problem for more than 2 weeks and 5% had chronic symptoms. Furthermore, 2.5 million people had a temporary physical handicap, and a similar number of persons suffered at that time from a permanent handicap.

It appears that the incidence of back problems increases at a rate 14 times that of the population growth rate. In 1986, the cost associated with the loss of working hours and health services was estimated at over 11.1 billion for the United States.[6,45] In the province of Québec alone, low back pain accounts for 51% of all spinal injuries.[9]

NEED TO ASSESS SPINAL MOTION

Spinal mechanical dysfunction associated with low back pain has been investigated in many different ways, emphasizing its complexity. Gagnon and Smyth[15] have studied different material handling activities and their effect on muscle moments and the mechanical work of 13 body segments, including the L5/S1 level, by means of cinematography and force plate measurements. Shirazi-Adl et al[37] did some computer simulation using finite element modeling techniques to determine the effects of two direction-dependent representations of the annulus on the predicted state of stresses in the disc. Others[28,39] performed in vitro measurements on spinal segments, and Bryant et al[7] and Gracovetsky et al[17] studied in vivo back geometry and motion, respectively.

There is a need for quantitative measurements of the spine both fundamentally and clinically. The mechanical behavior of the functional spinal unit, or the smallest functional unit of the spine, consisting of two adjacent vertebrae and the contiguous soft tissues, is essential to our fundamental understanding of the whole spine. It is usually obtained by means of extensive laboratory work on spinal segments. This information is valuable in developing mathematical models of the spine. For example, Stokes and Gardner-Morse[42] used a finite element model, which represented an isolated ligamentous spine with realistic mechanical properties and idealized geometry, to analyze the interaction between vertebral deviation and axial rotation in scoliosis.

Clinical assessments provide incomplete information because of the inadequacy of the human eye. We are unable to visualize the spine and its muscular and ligamentous components. Radiographs, CT scans, and MRI images provide a clear image of the spine but in a static condition. Although some MRI systems are able to function at 30 Hz (30 images per second) with a limited field of vision covering a few vertebral bodies, the human eye cannot adequately detect the biomechanical intricacies of the spine in motion. The use of goniometers and video cameras allows for the quantification of trunk motion at rates reaching above 200 Hz.

Estimation of the spine and the back motions, in addition to other clinical measurements (radiographs, strength tests, etc.), can be a means to document the efficacy of therapeutic interventions. The effect of a body brace to correct a scoliotic spine cannot be solely assessed by a standing radiograph.

We are in continuous motion, and even in the sitting posture, our bodies cannot be maintained in a fixed position indefinitely.[8] Monitoring the movement of the back will document its flexibility. Improvement toward natural trunk motion after treatment for low back pain can be one of the return to work indicators. Indeed, the intensity and the duration of the rehabilitation program can be adapted to the needs of the patient. For some, the return to activity might be earlier, whereas for others the risk of additional spine injury could be reduced by prolonged treatment. This contributes to the optimization of treatment intervention strategies. Providing objective functional evaluations constitutes a supplement for the clinical team.

With recent advances in technology, motion can be assessed in all three directions. Bidimensional or planar analyses give only partial information relevant only to a specific plane of motion and neglect compensatory actions in the other planes that may occur simultaneously or be delayed in sequence. This chapter covers the current technology for assessing spine and back motion within a clinical setting, discusses the rationale of some kinematic models to describe spine motion, emphasizing combined or coupled trunk actions, and reports on their clinical applications.

KINEMATICS OF THE SPINE

Trunk kinematics or trunk motion is often assessed to determine the range of motion (ROM) of the spine following a back injury or before surgery. Patients with low back pain (LBP) disorders often display a limited ROM.[12,33] Understanding the underlying motions of the perturbed spine can provide a better understanding of the pathology, especially if a kinematic pattern can be established. Workplace factors and risks of occupationally related low back pain disorders experienced by the workers can also be correlated to different types of trunk motions. In another important orthopedic disorder, idiopathic scoliosis, restricted spinal motion can be associated with zones of rigidity attributed to the extent of the spinal deformity. Kinematic dysfunctions are addressed in a succinct review of the existing instrumentation. Because most systems are based on trunk motion measurements, their relationship to intervertebral movements is presented here and the need for clinically assessed intervetebral coupling mechanisms is discussed.

INSTRUMENTATION

There are several devices for assessing trunk motion, from the simple inclinometer to the use of positron emission tomography (PET). It should be noted that Steffen et al have used electromagnetic tracking sensors mounted on Kirschner wires inserted in the spinous process of L3 and L4 in able-bodied subjects to determine lumbar segmental motion in vivo.[41a] They reported dynamic recordings having a measurement error comparable with stereoradiographic methods. Although the amplitude for the segmental flexion-extension mean of 16.9° was similar to that reported previously, the measurement range was higher and the maximal ranges of motion were highly reproducible. This section limits itself to a few instruments and focuses on those contributing to three-dimensional (3-D) analysis of the trunk and spine, namely, radiography, goniometry, and videography.

RADIOGRAPHY

Radiographs of the spine in flexion, extension, and lateral bending are clinically useful but only provide two-dimensional (2-D) information. Intervertebral displacements calculated from any two radiographs represent the planar projection of the 3-D movement, and out-of-plane motions such as rotations are subject to large errors.[5] For example, a frontal plane radiograph of an able-bodied subject will show basically a straight spine. However, if the subject's pelvis or shoulders are slightly rotated forwards, part of the natural lumbar lordosis and thoracic kyphosis will show up on the radiograph. This will give the false impression of a small scoliosis. This can be further complicated in the case of idiopathic scoliosis, in which the shape of the spine assumes a twisted three-dimensional configuration.

The need to represent the spine as a 3-D structure has been considered for scoliotic assessment since the work of Koreska et al[21] on spinal deformities in Duchenne's muscular dystrophy. Others have studied spinal deformities in Friedreich's ataxia[2–4] and in idiopathic scoliosis,[43] as well as in low back pain.[33,44]

In the late 1970s and early 1980s, the vertebral bodies were modeled as a single point or centroid in space and the shape of the spine assumed that of the interconnecting centroids, as shown in Figure 16–1. Two orthogonal radiographs were taken, one posteroanterior and one sagittal. On the biplanar radiographs, the centroid of each vertebral body was identified and digitized. The 3-D coordinates were calculated from the referenced markers' images, the distance of the x-ray tube to the film plate, and similar triangle geometry. The centroids were linked together by means of a parametric cubic spline function. A spline function is basically a mathematical expression that enables us to fit a curve to a fixed set of data points. In this case, the data points were the 3-D coordinates of each vertebral body. From this line representation of the spine, Allard et al[2] were able to calculate the rotation and the torsion components of the scoliotic spine and their relative contributions to the progression of scoliosis in Friedreich's ataxia. This technique has since then evolved into a solid geometric representation of the spine and ribs.

Biplanar radiographs were also used to study intervertebral rotations in patients with LBP.[33] Patients with LBP alone had restricted flexion/extension movements at the lumbar levels and increased lateral bending and rotational motion.

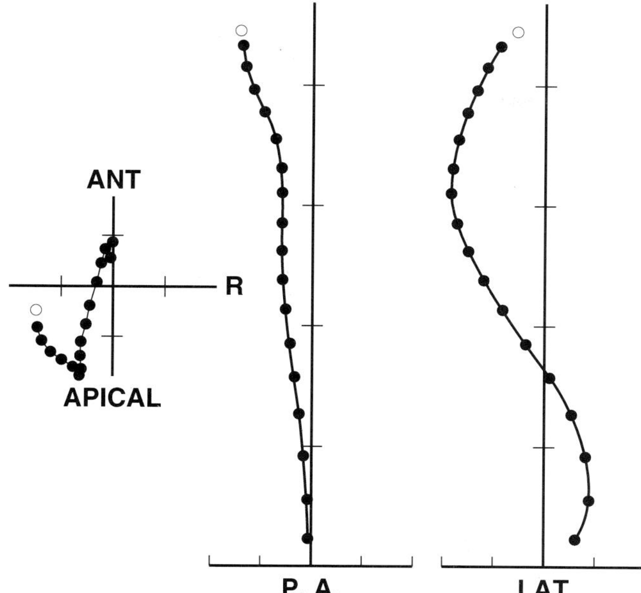

Figure 16–1. Three-dimensional shape of the spine. Note that the apical view is that of the spine as observed from above. This view was uniquely available through three-dimensional reconstruction of the spine.

From Allard et al.[2]

Not all radiographic studies were of the 3-D type nor were 3-D studies necessary. For example, Weitz[47] measured the relationship of the lateral bending sign to disc herniation in 300 patients who would normally be candidates for routine x-ray. He found that lateral bending radiographs can often pinpoint the level of disc herniation. Also, Weiler et al[46] analyzed the instability of the lumbar spine in the sagittal plane in 12 control subjects and 36 patients with chronic LBP. The patients were grouped according to the diagnosis of idiopathic LBP, lumbar disc prolapse, and degenerative disc disease. Although an instability factor based on the linear displacement of the vertebral body and its rotation was reported significant for the degenerative disc disease group, there was no significant difference between the other two patient groups.

From standard radiographs, clinical indices can be calculated, but, the results give inaccurate means to determine out-of-plane displacements or movements. Three-dimensional reconstruction techniques and advance modeling of the spine provide more accurate geometric information of the vertebral bodies and the spine. Nonetheless, radiography is an invasive technique and is essentially limited to static positions neglecting the effects of motion dynamics.

GONIOMETRY

Goniometry is related to the measurement of angles. These angles can give an indication of the curvature of a surface such as the back or the motion between two adjacent segments. Inclinometers are devices designed to measure the curvature of a surface. They usually consist of a fluid-filled disc in which a weighted needle is maintained vertically. The disc, graduated to cover the 360° range, is affixed to a straight-edge base. When the device rests on an oblique surface, the needle indicates the inclination of the surface.

Loebl[22] documents how inclinometers can be used to assess spinal posture and range of spinal movement. This technique was later improved by Mayer et al[26] using two inclinometers positioned over different spinal segments. The motion of a segment is obtained by subtracting the reading of one inclinometer from the other. The motion measured by the inclinometers was not significantly different from the radiographic range of motion.

Inclinometers are suited to quantify spinal curvatures in static postures and ranges of motion. They do not provide any information during the actual movement of the spine unless the readings are electronically sampled and stored. They provide useful clinical information for movements occurring only in a single plane at a time such as flexion/extension.

Goniometers are used to measure an angle about a joint, comparing one limb with respect to the other. In its simplest form the goniometer consists of two arms or levers held together at one end by a pin joint. The angle between two segments can be read off a scale fixed to one of the levers. By adding a battery-driven potentiometer at the joint of the goniometer, the variation in voltage provides a continuous measure of the angular motion. These devices, known as electrogoniometers, have been widely used in gait studies for the assessment of normal and pathological conditions. Since each potentiometer measures a single rotational movement at a joint, one would need three of them to carry out a planar analysis of the hip, the knee, and the ankle of a single lower limb. For a 3-D analysis, three potentiometers per joint are required, nine in all per limb! Essentially, electrogoniometers have been replaced by video cameras because the former (1) tend to constrain the limbs, (2) are cumbersome due to the weight and the cables, (3) are difficult to align with the anatomical joint center of rotation as well as to maintain their alignment during body movements, and (4) provide only kinematic data.

However, for some specific applications such as wrist and finger movements, in confined areas where an ergonomic analysis of the workplace is required and for measuring joint motion over several minutes or even hours,[40] electrogoniometers are extremely valuable. Furthermore, they are relatively inexpensive, and joint motion characteristics such as angular position, velocity, and acceleration are readily obtained at the worksite or clinic itself or shortly afterwards.

For these reasons, electrogoniometers have been adapted to monitor trunk motion. Paquet et al[31] used a potentiometer fixed to a plate at the sacral level connected by a curved flexible slat to another potentiometer at the thoracic level. The plates of the electrogoniometer are attached by straps to the trunk. During flexion and extension motions of the trunk, the slat decreases or increases its curvature, which is monitored at the ends by the potentiometers. The validity and reliability of these devices are comparable to those of the double-inclinometer method. This device and similar ones provide only sagittal information and are limited to dorsolumbar motion without identifying intersegmental movements.

Marras et al[24] also used a dorsolumbar electrogoniometer to study over 400 repetitive lifting jobs in 48 industries. It consists of a triaxial potentiometer capable of measuring the instantaneous position of the thoracolumbar spine about the three axes of rotation (flexion/extension, right and left bending, and clockwise and counterwise rotations). Three-dimensional trunk motions were assessed for different lifting tasks associated to jobs historically documented as either high- and low-risk and occupationally related to low back disorders. The major predictive biomechanical factors for high- and low-risk tasks were lifting frequency, load moment, trunk lateral velocity, trunk twisting velocity, and trunk sagittal angle.

The reliability of the goniometer has been assessed by Dopf et al[11] in a prospective study. A computerized goniometer (CA-6000 Spine Motion Analyzer) was found to be more reliable in measuring thoracolumbar motion than other previously tested techniques (Schoeber, Moll) including the double-inclinometer method. They concluded that females have more motion in left and right flexion, as well as in left rotation, than men. The dominant hand side did not affect spinal motion.

Although the Isostation B-200 is intended for other purposes, it can be used in assessing the range of motion of the trunk. It is an apparatus in which the subject stands on an adjustable platform. The pelvis is maintained in a fixed position by pads over the anterosuperior iliac spines while posterior pressure is applied through a pad on the ischial tuberosities or lower sacrum. The upper trunk, including the rib cage, is harnessed by shoulder straps with pressure pads over the sternum, scapulae, and thoracolumbar area. Trunk rotations in flexion and extension, lateral bending, and twisting are measured by potentiometers built into the device. As such, it behaves like a sophisticated electrogoniometer combined to a force measuring system.

In a study conducted by Dillard et al,[10] the reliability of the Isostation B-200 was compared to that of the two-goniometer technique. They found poor reproducibility in flexion and extension and somewhat better results in lateral bending and rotation. Poor performance of the B-200 was attributed in part to an inadequate pelvis fixation and to the malalignment of the mechanical axis of rotation of the device with that of the trunk. They concluded that an instrument such as the B-200 should not be used to solely measure the range of motion.

Electrogoniometers are useful tools for recording joint motion about a fixed axis of rotation. They can be used efficiently to record motion about several joints at a time. They have been applied successfully by Marras et al[24] in the evaluation of thoracolumbar movements associated with different industrial lifting tasks. In this study, significant large trunk motions occurred in all three planes. The major clinical limitation of electrogoniometers resides essentially in the number of joints that can be monitored; they are often restricted to the thoracolumbar junction to assess the relative motion between the thoracic and lumbar spine segments.

VIDEOGRAPHY

Video cameras make use of visible light or near-infrared light to track body movement. To facilitate data acquisition, markers are located on the body identifying anatomical landmarks and joints. In some video-based motion analysis systems, the markers are passive in the sense that they reflect unidirectional light back to the camera. The source can be fixed around the camera lens, as shown in Figure 16–2, for maximum efficacy. Other systems use battery powered light-emitting diodes (LEDs), which act as active markers. In this case, the marker sends the near-infrared light to the camera system. In all cases, specialized cameras digitize the video images and a video processor of some kind determines the planar coordinates of each marker. A 3-D reconstruction follows and the spatial position of each marker is known as a function of time or displacement.[1] Using methods developed in photogrammetry, the 3-D position or coordinate of an object can be determined from at a minimum of two different images of the same object. This procedure of transforming bidimensional image data points into 3-D coordinates is know as a reconstruction technique. The direct linear transformation technique developed by Marzan[25] is one of the best-known methods used in biomechanics.

Figure 16–2. A ring light mounted on a 60- to 200-Hz video camera.

Courtesy of the Motion Analysis Corporation, Santa Rosa, CA.

Passive markers can be tracked at a rate varying from 30 frames per second (Hz) to 200 Hz. They do not burden the subject and are visible from any directions within 360°. They usually consist of a spherical plastic support covered with reflective paper, paint, or dust. They are easily fixed on the subject by means of two-way adhesive tape. Since they are passive markers, they do not require any wiring or power of any sort, enabling maximum freedom of movement for the subject. Passive markers are simultaneously seen by the video camera and consequently, the number of markers to be tracked is unlimited. Some of the drawbacks that arise with these markers are related to their tracking and their labeling. During data acquisition markers may be masked by background illumination, resulting in poor contrast, or by themselves when crossing each other. This phenomena is known as occultation. Reflective surfaces other than those of the markers generate a spurious signal that interferes with marker identification or labeling. Special software is necessary to assign each marker to its particular anatomical or joint landmark.

Active markers are usually triggered independently, facilitating marker labeling and greater sampling rates, 300Hz or more. By increasing the number of active markers, the sampling rate is reduced accordingly. The external power supply and the connecting wires for control and synchronization can impede body movement. LEDs have a restricted light emission angle, making them more difficult to track whenever there is rotation.

There are a good number of commercial 3-D kinematic systems on the market, some of them having specialized software for trunk motion assessments. They can provide valuable information on compression and shear forces acting on the spine during different tasks corresponding to NIOSH guidelines. For kinematic assessment of the spine, they essentially give the same information as electrogoniometers: the trunk is considered as a solid unit articulated at the L5/S1 level (fifth lumbar and first sacrum level). Information can be of the planar or 3-D type.

Pearcy et al[32] were among the first to describe dynamic back movement using a camera-based system. Although they used six reflective markers, three on each of two rigs, they were able to show, on six subjects, consistent patterns of movement that were similar to previously reported data measured radiographically.

Later, Gracovetsky et al[17,18] developed a system consisting of 25 LEDs at the vertebral levels and on other parts of the body to study back motion. The markers are tracked by a 180-Hz optoelectronic system. A stick diagram of the spine is obtained by linking together the spatial coordinates of the markers representing the spinous processes. Planar and 3-D information is extracted from the three-dimensional representation of the whole spine. In other words, the position and orientation of the vertebrae are assumed to follow those of the general shape of the spine.

A similar approach was used by Allard et al[2] to describe the scoliotic spine in Friedreich's ataxia by means of intrinsic parameters related to the shape of the spine. Figure 16–3 illustrates schematically the 3-D orientation of a point lying on a spatially oriented curved path. The Frenet frame field is composed of a tangent unit vector T(s), a principal normal vector N(s), and a bionormal vector B(s) expressed in terms of the arc length. The Frenet formulas or mathematical equations are used to determine the curvature and the torsion of a curve. In this case, the curve is a line representation of the spine that passes the centroid of each vertebral body.

With their optoelectronic system, Gracovetsky et al[17,18] were able to show kinematic dysfunctions of the

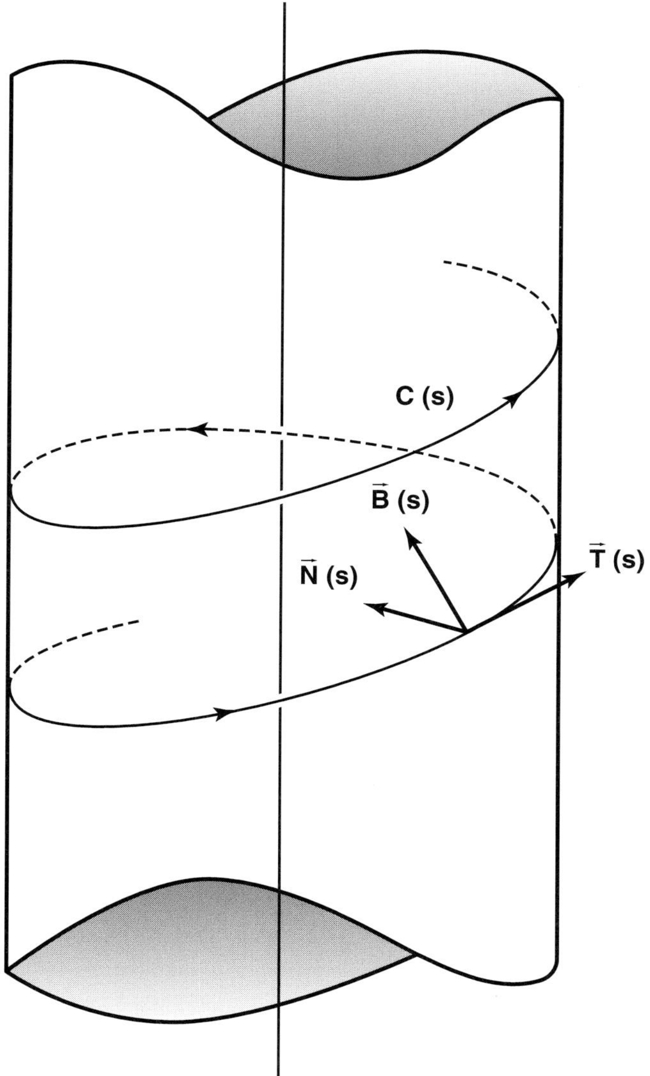

Figure 16–3. Three-dimensional representation of a curve following a helical path. Any point along the curve C(s) can be described in terms of its intrinsic parameters, namely, arc length s, curvature C,κ(s) and τ(s) in the Frenet frame field T(s), N(s) and B(s) where these stand for tangential, normal, and bionormal vectors located on the spatial curve C. *From Allard et al.*[2]

spine localized at specific vertebral levels. This is a novel idea for estimating pathological spinal movements. One can simulate trunk rigidity by limiting the amplitude of its range of motion but cannot willingly control intervertebral joint kinematics. This novel approach is a remarkable improvement over the traditional assessment methods in which basically only the thoracolumbar angular movements were quantified. Here, the whole spinal kinematics is analyzed and intervertebral joint motion estimated.

This technique is quite appealing but has some limitations. The spine is represented by known 3-D coordinates of point markers linked together. This is the simplest representation of a curve in space. The vertebrae are not kinematically modeled as such. To achieve such a goal, three markers per vertebra are required; thus 51 markers are needed to cover the 12 thoracic and 5 lumbar levels. Each vertebral body is not modeled as a centroid or point any more but rather as a solid body having six degrees of freedom with translation along the three axes and rotation about each axis.

Shirley et al[38] have compared the lumbar range of motion using three measurement devices. These were a video-based system (Spinetrak by Motion Analysis Corp.), a lumbar extension rehabilitation device (MedX), and a liquid inclinometer. The total range of motion was determined in 42 patients with low back pain. They reported that the lumbar sagittal range of motion was dependent on the device and the procedures used. Indeed, the video system was limited to a dynamic planar analysis whereas the other methods examined maximum static positions.

We have investigated the use of a 3-D video-based system in the assessment of normal and pathological trunk movements[13] and have also found kinematic dysfunctions in patients having idiopathic scoliosis. But before addressing this issue, several questions need to be answered. In using electrogoniometers and videographic techniques we assume that the trunk motions recorded by the potentiometers or the movements of the external markers are closely associated to those of the spine and even the vertebrae. Is this assumption justified? Can we relate trunk movements to the spine or the vertebrae? Is it necessary?

RELATIONSHIP BETWEEN EXTERNAL MARKERS AND SPINAL MOTION

Only invasive techniques such as radiography can really provide information on the position and orientation (attitude) of the vertebral bodies and the spine. All other biomechanical devices rely on one or more external devices to estimate spinal movements.

Few studies have addressed the problem of correlating surface measurements to vertebral motion. Bryant et al[7] investigated a noninvasive method by which the shape of the spine could be estimated in the sagittal plane. They first normalized the curve of the spine from T1 to L5 and then separated spline functions (by a mathematical curve-fitting technique) were developed to reproduce the curve of the spine from surface markers located over the spinous processes. Mapping functions enabled the transformation of skin profile to a vertebral centroid curve. Compared to the radiographic estimation, the vertebral centroid estimated from skin profiles had a standard error of estimate of 4 mm. They reported a lower value of 2 mm if the lumbar spine was considered separately. This approach is valuable in assessing kyphosis and lordosis in postural evaluations and for measuring spinal changes during growth, pregnancy, and aging, but not for postural changes involving axial rotation or curvatures in the frontal plane. Nonetheless, a direct relationship was found between the skin profiles and the vertebral locations in the sagittal plane.

An attempt was also performed by Sicard and Gagnon[39] to estimate the S1, T12, and the five lumbar vertebrae positions from skin profiles and five anthropometric measurements for postures assumed to be in the sagittal plane. The anthropometric measurements were stature, top of the head to chin insertion length, bicristal breadth, umbilical skin fold, and suprascapular skinfold. They reported an error varying between 1.68 cm to 1.82 cm in position and 2.6° to 6.7° in orientation. Their model appears to be sufficiently sensitive to evaluate the angular motion of the pelvis and the lumbar spine, but not intervertebral movements, except for the L4/L5 joint.

These two studies support the existence of a complex relationship between the external marker motion and spinal movements in the sagittal plane. Intervertebral motion estimations are difficult to determine since their displacement is smaller (less than 5 mm) than the present level of measurement error. To our knowledge, little if any work has been done to relate external marker motion to 3-D spinal or intervetebral movements. More research efforts are needed to determine the exact nature of this relationship.

On a relative basis, the movement of the external markers is tied to that of the spine. Factors such as different skin thicknesses in the thoracic and lumbar regions, the stretching of the skin during trunk flexion, the accurate identification of the spinous processes, and the changing height of the spine during the day, to name but a few, all have an effect on the amplitude of motion estimation either in translation or rotation. Nonetheless, the same underlying hypotheses relating trunk and spinal motion with the use of an electrogoniometer to assess thoracolumbar motion are applied when external markers located at different vertebral levels are used to quantify intervertebral joint motion. The smoothness in the shape of the skin profile (geometry) and in the kinematic parameters (displacement, speed, and acceleration) of the external markers are present in able-bodied subjects and perturbed in pathological cases.

Movements of the trunk and the spine have been well documented with respect to the anatomical planes.[48] The following section addresses the 3-D kinematics of the spine in which intervertebral motion occurs in more than a single plane, better known as coupling mechanisms in the spine.

COUPLING MECHANISMS

Primary motions of the spine and the trunk are those occurring in the anatomical planes, such as flexion, rotation, or bending. When the primary movement of the spine induces motion in another plane, the latter is considered as secondary. For example, Gracovetsky[16] reports significant axial rotation (secondary motion) in bending (primary motion). When this or any other combination of primary and secondary motions occurs, we are in the presence of a coupling mechanism.

Lovett[23] was among the first to identify coupling mechanisms in the spine. Since then, several authors have studied this coupling phenomena on both subjects and cadavers and have come up with different observations.[16] One of the difficulties in establishing a unified version of the facts lies in the different objectives of each report as well as in the methods used. Some addressed themselves to the lumbar spine only, neglecting the effect on the thoracic spine, whereas others looked at lateral bending and axial rotation effects between specific vertebral levels. For example, Pearcy and Tibrewal[34] found a different rotational direction (polarity) between the upper and lower lumbar levels.

Experimental protocols vary enormously. Some studied the whole spine from two radiographs taken in static position, whereas others focused on the spinal motion segment of cadaveric specimens. Nonetheless, the consensus agreed upon the presence of coupling patterns in the spine.

With the use of a mathematical model, Scholten and Veldhuizen[36] were able to analyze the influence of the facet joint orientation on the coupling pattern between lateral bending and axial rotation. For a lateral bend, the thoracic and lumbar vertebra, having a ventral inclination, will have a tendency to rotate toward the convexity of the spinal curve, whereas the dorsally inclined thoracic vertebra will rotate toward the concavity. They suggest that the kinematics of the spine be discussed in terms of the dorsally or ventrally inclined vertebrae rather than in terms of cervical, thoracic, and lumbar segments. These phenomena may explain in part the existing controversy on the direction of coupling between lateral bending and axial rotation in the thoracic and lumbar spines.

A systematic pattern in the coupling motion of the spine would be fundamental and essential in the understanding of spinal kinematics.[29] If such a pattern occurs, it may be perturbed in patients having low back pain. Following treatment, the coupling mechanism could return to normal, indicating the appropriate time to return to work, whereas in others the persistence of kinematic dysfunction even after treatment may be a contraindication to return to work. The treatment modality could be modulated in terms

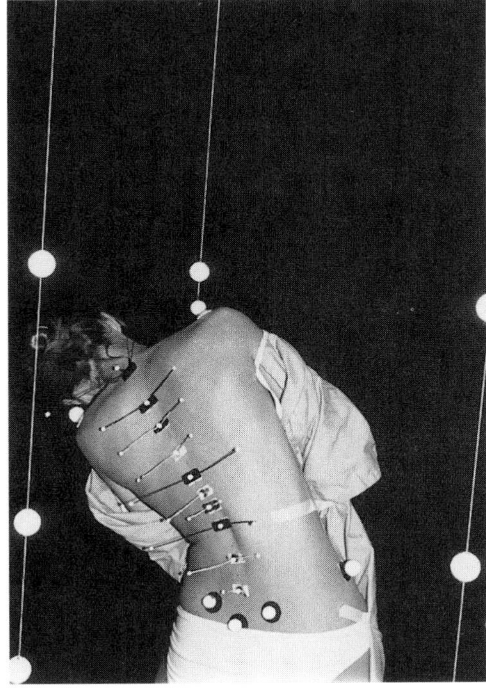

A

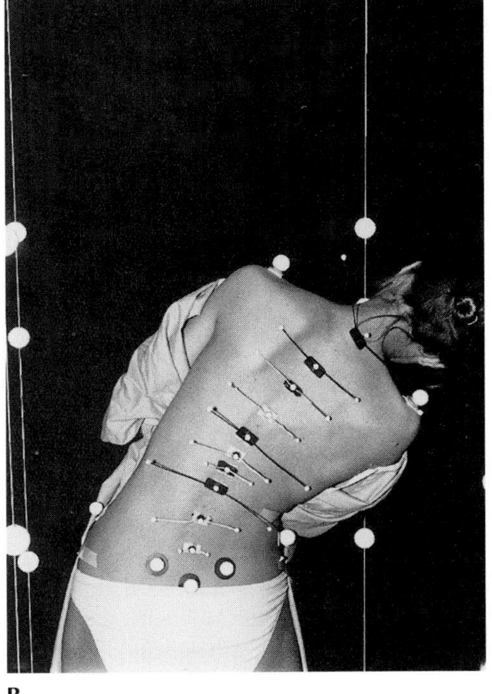

B

Figure 16–4. Triad markers are put over the spinous processes, and larger ones 25mm in diameter identify the pelvis and shoulders. To keep triad markers from hitting each other during trunk movements and to reduce the occultation problems during the tracking, the shorter rods are often placed in between the longer ones. The patient is shown in **(A)** left and **(B)** right bending.

of duration and intensity and be adapted to the patient's needs.

In scoliosis, abnormal coupling indicating zones of rigidity could be an indication of the extent of the deformed spine. This could be useful in assessing the progression of the scoliosis as well as evaluating the effect of bracing and estimating the vertebral levels to be surgically fused.

Kinematic assessment of the spine in able-bodied subjects shows very little coupling in the sagittal plane motion between axial rotation and trunk flexion,[20] whereas Weitz[47] has shown a perturbed axial rotation in a patient performing a lateral bend in the frontal plane. Thus, both plane of motion and pathology can affect trunk motion and coupling actions. This is in agreement with Pearcy et al[33] who reported compensatory axial rotation and bending in patients having low back injury during trunk flexion/extension movements.

The principal limitations of the in vitro studies are due to the small number of specimens, the few vertebral levels studied, and the absence of the natural lumbar lordosis and thoracic kyphosis. The in vivo experiments also have their limits. As mentioned earlier, radiography is an invasive technique restricted to static positions.[33,47] The use of Steinmann pins drilled into the spinous process[19] is also not recommended though very informative. Coupling mechanisms have also been identified by Hindle and Pearcy[20] and Marras et al[24] but only for the lumbar and thoracolumbar segments. Only Gracovetsky et al[17] were able to show kinematic dysfunctions at many levels but without measuring the coupling of the secondary spinal motions.

We have developed a novel technique based on a motion analysis system in which triads having three markers each are put on the skin over the spinous processes.[13] The position and the orientation of each triad are known with respect to the others. In a small number of subjects, axial rotation occurred during a lateral bend but very little as flexion or extension in the sagittal plane. Scoliotic spines behaved differently because of the levels of rigidity. This method is briefly presented here, and applications to normal spinal movements as well as to patients with scoliosis and low back injuries are given.

ESTIMATION OF THE INTERVERTEBRAL MOTION

Video-based systems are a noninvasive technique to obtain 3-D kinematics of the trunk. Although they provide an indirect measure of spinal kinematics, the behavior of the surface markers located on the trunk and pelvis is not totally unrelated to the intervetebral motion. Normal and pathological coupling actions have been documented using radiographic techniques and video-based systems. In the latter, several markers were used to study the 3-D movements of the lumbar and thoracic spine segments. Although intervertebral motion can be estimated using a single marker over each of the spinous processes, it does not fully represent the 3-D kinematics of each vertebra. This would require the use of three markers per vertebra.

A marker triad consists of a central (6 mm in diameter) reflective marker located on a flexible plastic base. On each side of the central marker, a thin, slender rod extends outwardly and is terminated by a marker. Those three markers form a single triad that uniquely identifies the vertebral level. The central marker is put over the spinous process with the rods pointing away from the spine, as shown in Figure 16–4 for right and left bending. The lengths of the rods vary from 20 to 50 mm to avoid a triad collision during trunk movements and to reduce the occultation problems in tracking the markers. Triads can cover the 12 thoracic and 5 lumbar levels or less according to the need. Other larger (25 mm in diameter) markers are used to identify the pelvis and shoulders.

An elaborate Motion Analysis Corporation eight-camera system is shown in Figure 16–5. Two cameras are fixed to the ceiling (1.4 m from the subject) to view the markers during trunk flexion. The other six are distributed in a semicircle at 1.5 m from and around the subject's back.

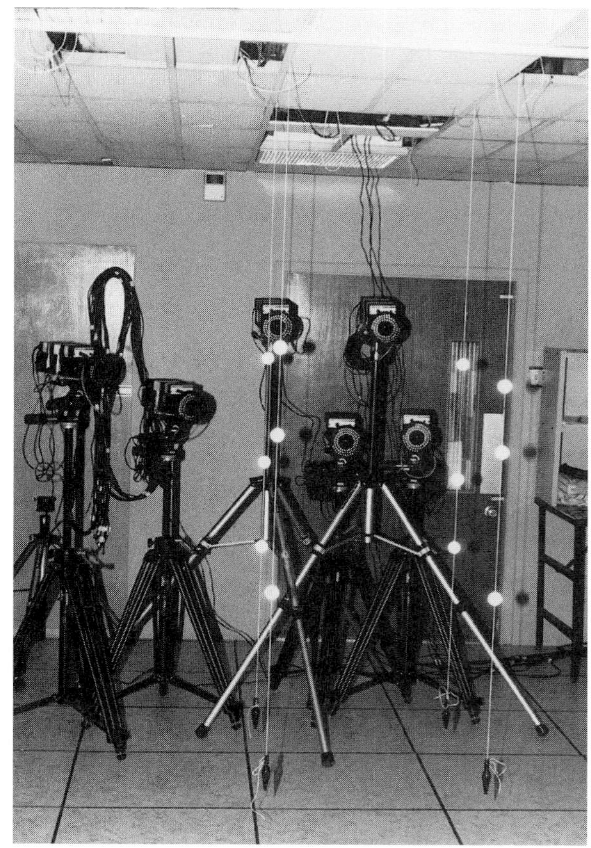

Figure 16–5. An eight–video camera system from Motion Analysis Corporation is shown. Two cameras are fixed to the ceiling to view the markers during trunk flexion. The other six are distributed in a semicircle around the subject's back. A calibration object consisting of twelve reference markers is located in the cameras' field of view.

Only four cameras are used at any one time. For example, the two central cameras and the two ceiling cameras are used for flexion movements, whereas for lateral bending, the two central cameras combined with the two most peripheral ones located on the same side of the lateral bend are used. With this particular camera layout, trunk flexion, rotation, and bending can be easily tracked without changing the camera configuration and recalibrating. Trunk extension is not quantified because the triad markers would interfere with each other and might come off.

Markers located on the trunk are filmed by the video cameras, which are synchronized by a video processor system controlled by a Sun IPX Sparc Station. This process is performed in real time; thus there is no need for videotapes. The direct linear reconstruction technique[25] is used to obtain the 3-D coordinates of all markers of each triad, as well as the shoulder and pelvis markers from the images of each marker taken by the cameras.

Although the following discussion is not essential, it provides technical information on the angular measurements taken between any two triad markers. This is provided because angular calculations are very much susceptible to error propagation. Thus, the last angle to be calculated will show the largest error. Consequently, the

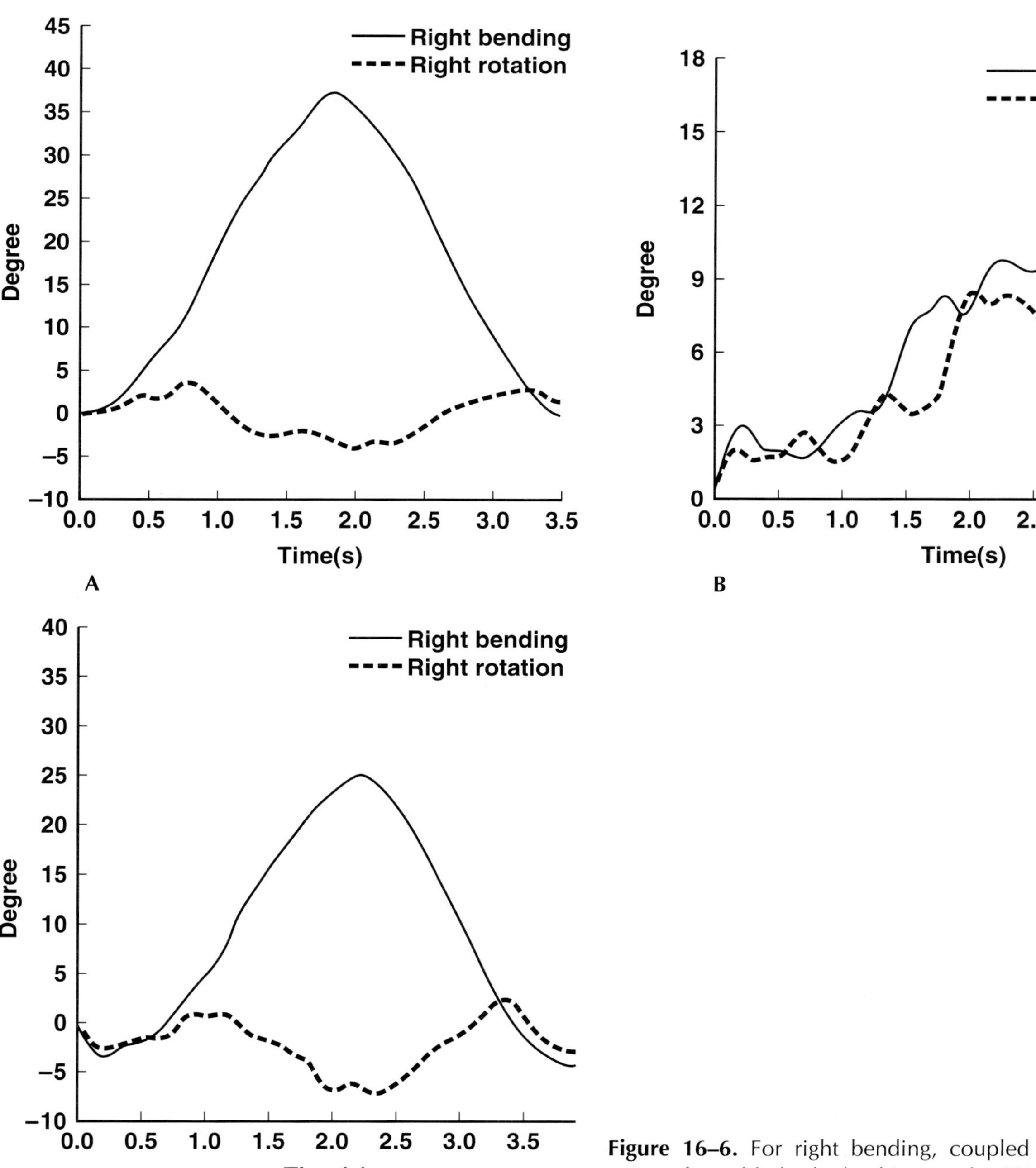

Figure 16–6. For right bending, coupled motion of the spine of an able-bodied subject at the **(A)** T1-S1, **(B)** T1-T12, and **(C)** T12-S1 levels.

primary movement is always calculated first. From the pelvis markers a body coordinate system is established. The X axis is positive toward the right, the Y axis is positively oriented in posteroanterior direction, and the Z axis is positive upward.

To estimate the rotations about those three axes, the Cardan angles are defined as follows: for flexion, the rotations are about Z, Y', and X"; for flexion/extension they are X, Z', and Y"; and for bending Y, Z', and X", where the prime and double prime correspond to the new coordinate system orientation after the first and second rotation, respectively. The Cardan angles are calculated for the standing neutral position and as a function of the trunk movements for any two vertebral levels from T1 to S1.

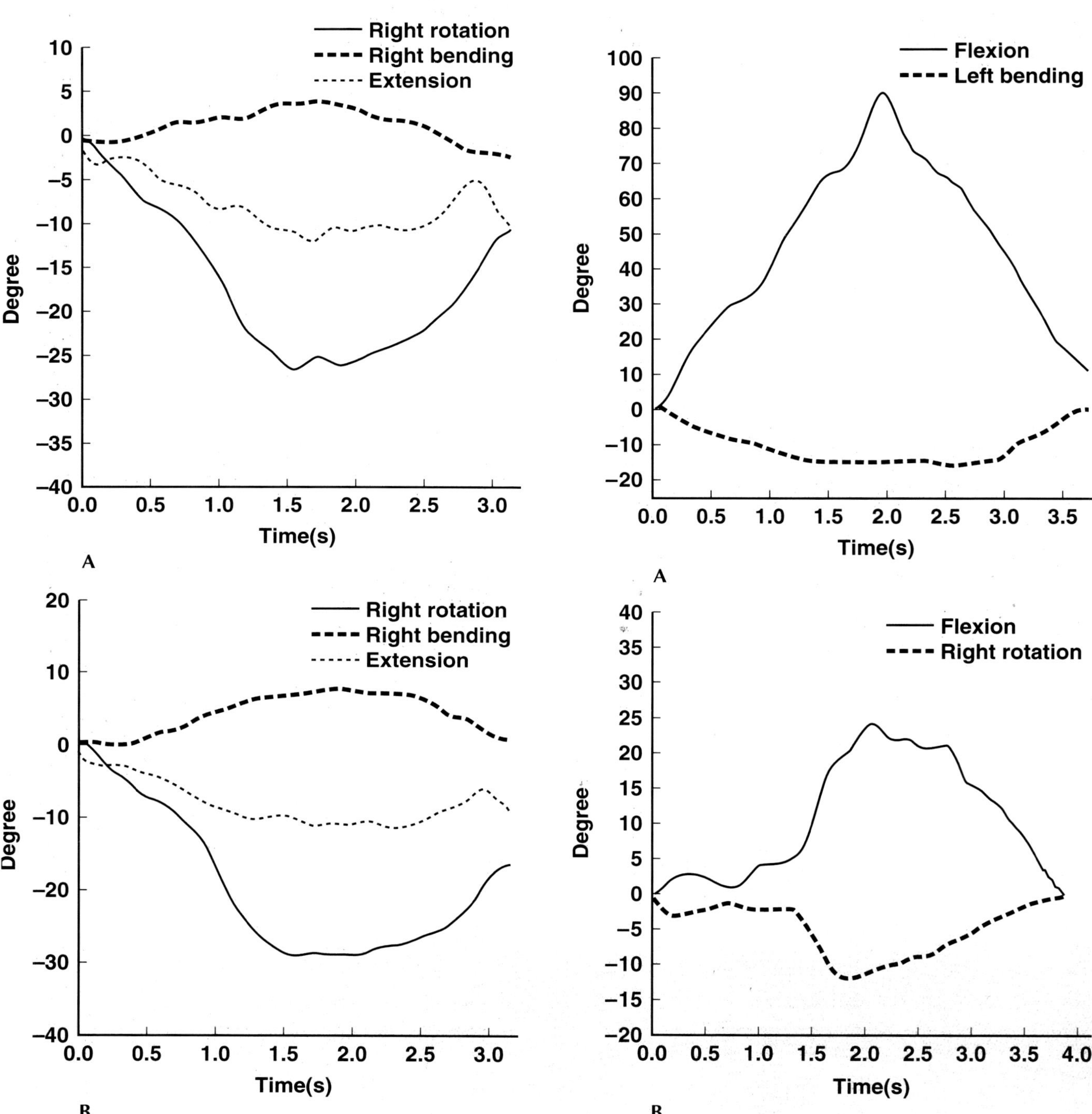

Figure 16–7. For right rotation, coupled motion of the spine of an able-bodied subject at the **(A)** T1-S1 and **(B)** T1-T12 levels.

Figure 16–8. For flexion, coupled motion of the spine of an able-bodied subject at the **(A)** T3-S1 and **(B)** T3-T12 levels.

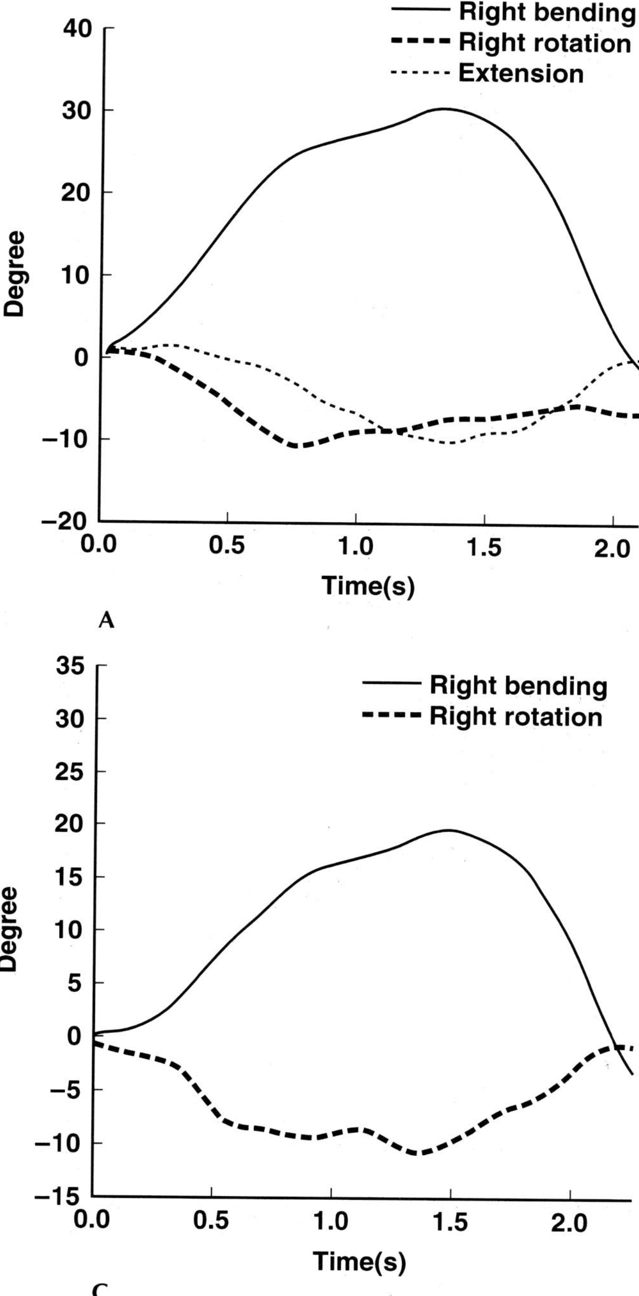

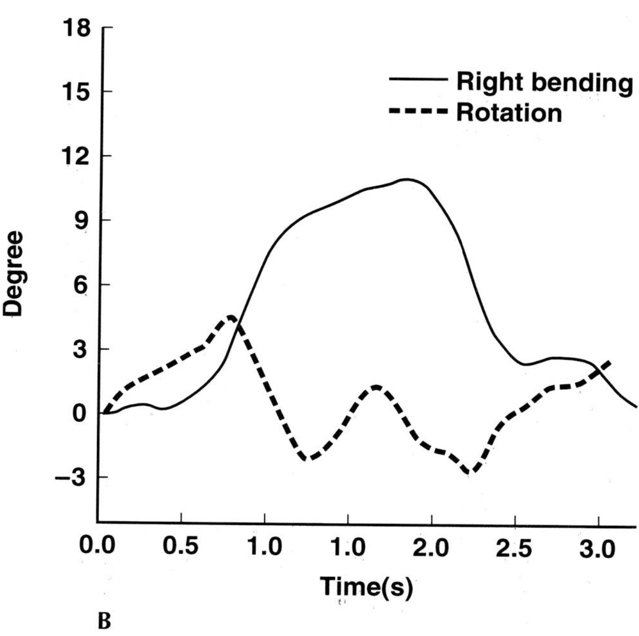

Figure 16–9. For right bending, coupled motion of the spine of an idiopathic scoliosis patient at the **(A)** T1-S1, **(B)** T1-T12 and **(C)** T12-S1 levels.

Figures 16–6 to 16–12 give an indication of the coupling mechanisms obtained from control, scoliotic, and low back pain subjects. All figures are presented in the same manner. The primary (bending) and compensatory (rotation or flexion) motions are given as a function of time for T1 to S1, thoracic, and lumbar segments. The exact spinal levels are indicated on each figure since they may vary according to the pathology.

A similar technique was used by Ployon et al[35] to study the motion of the scoliotic spine. Instead of triads, 14 reflective markers were located on bony prominences: 4 for the head, 2 for the shoulders, 3 for the pelvis, and 5 along the spine positioned in relation to the pathology. The researchers claimed the usefulness of video-based systems in helping clinicians to obtain 3-D data describing the evolution of posture and behavior of the scoliotic subjects.

KINEMATICS OF THE ABLE-BODIED SPINE

Data for a 21-year-old able-bodied subject are given in Figures 16–6 to 16–8. For a right bend (Figure 16–6A) of 40°,

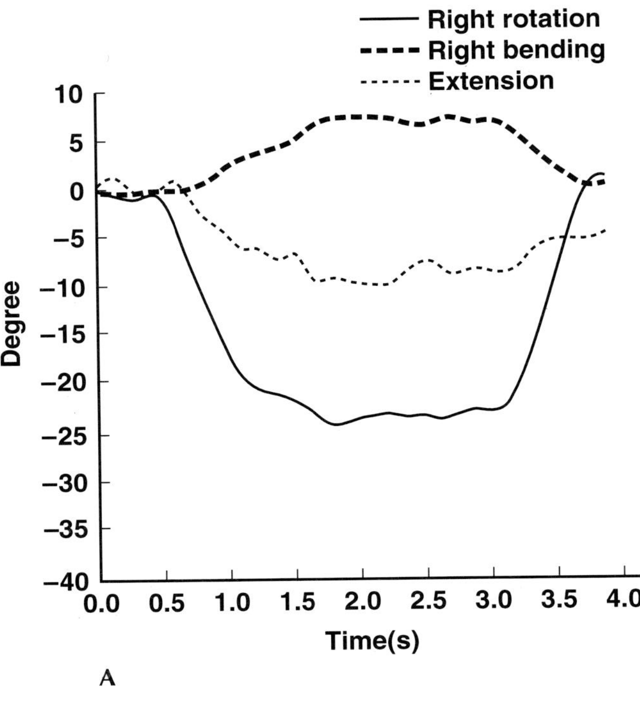

A

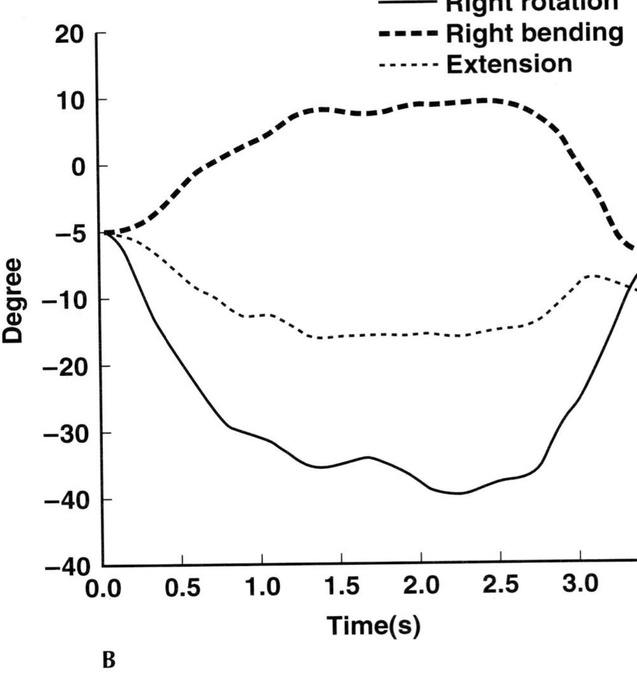

B

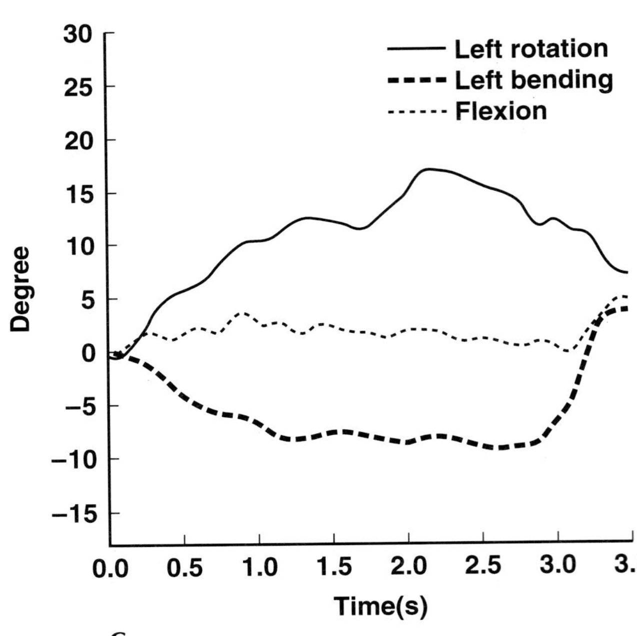

C

Figure 16–10. For right rotation, coupled motion of the spine of an idiopathic scoliosis patient at the **(A)** T1-S1, **(B)** T1-T12, and **(C)** T12-S1 levels.

there is no compensatory flexion and some but limited trunk rotation. Interestingly, the T1-T12 levels (Figure 16–6B) account for about 11° of bending and 8° of left rotation, whereas the T12-S1 levels (Figure 16–6C) show a greater range of bending (25°) and 7° of right rotation. The pattern for a left bend is similar to that of a right bend but with different polarities in the rotations.

A 25° rotation to the right, illustrated in Figure 16–7A, shows a 10° extension compensatory motion with some bending between T1 and S1. Besides motion of 2° to 4° in all three planes in the lumbar segment, the primary movements and their compensatory coupling essentially occurred in the thoracic segment (Figure 16–7B). The 28° rotation was coupled with an 8° right bend and 10° extension. For left rotation of the trunk, the thoracic segment responded similarly but with an opposite polarity for the bend.

For a 90° flexion between the T3 and S1 levels, there was a 12° right rotation (Figure 16–8A). Although most of the rotation occurred in the T3-T12 levels (12°), it accounted for only 25° of flexion (Figure 16–8B), whereas the lumbar spine displayed 60° of flexion with little rotation (5°).

In summary, the able-bodied spine kinematically behaved as expected. Bending was distributed along the tho-

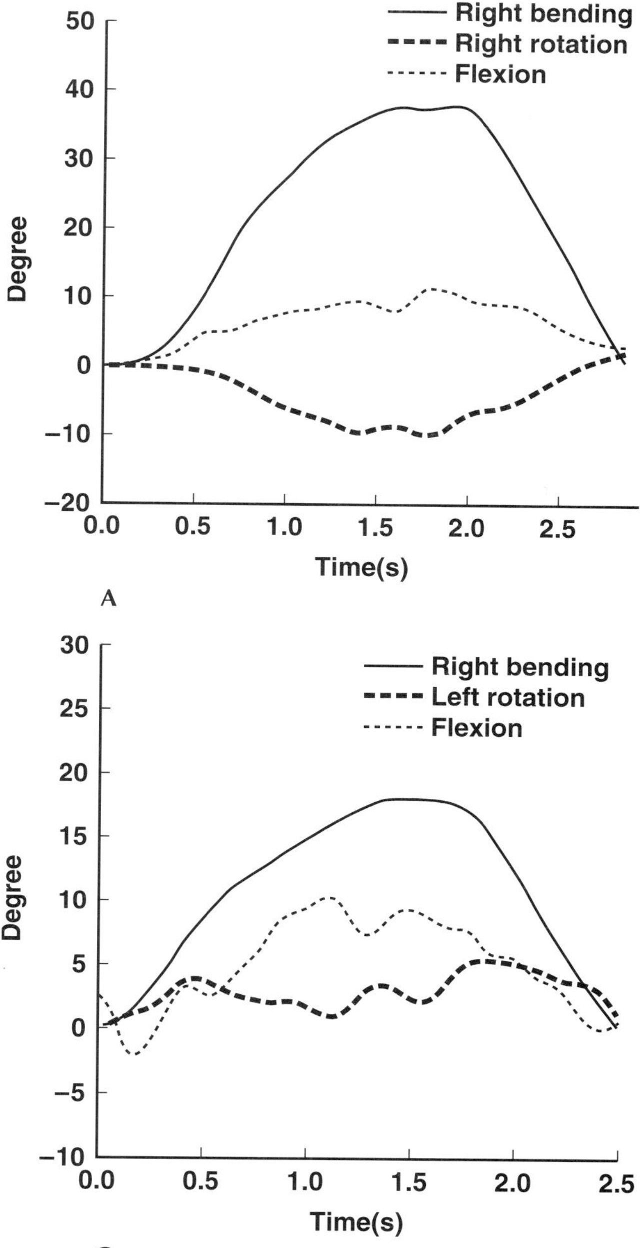

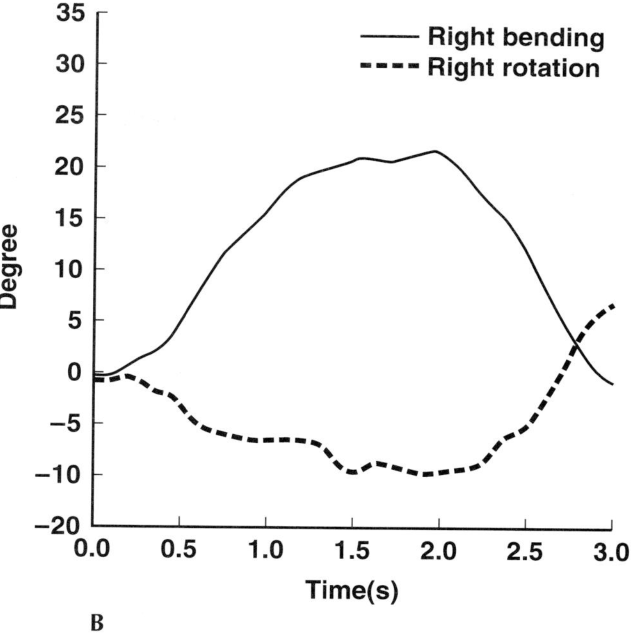

Figure 16–11. For right bending, coupled motion of the spine of low back pain patient at the **(A)** T1-S1, **(B)** T1-L1, and **(C)** L1-S1 levels.

racic and lumbar spines, flexion mostly occurred in the lumbar spine, and rotation was most important in the thoracic spine. Coupling manifested itself in different ways according to the primary movement. In bending, the accompanying lumbar rotation was in the opposite direction to that of the thoracic rotation. Rotation was combined by thoracic extension and ipsilateral bending. For right and left bending, as well as for rotation, a similar pattern was noticed but with different polarities. Another important observation is the smoothness of the curves except for small angles where there is more fluctuation. There is also a good timing in the coupling of the primary with the secondary movements. In other words, the compensatory effects in the other planes occurred and peaked at about the same time.

KINEMATICS OF THE SCOLIOTIC SPINE

Trunk movements of a 15-year-old girl having an idiopathic scoliosis are given in Figures 16–9 and 16–10. She had a double curve characterized by a right thoracic curve of 46° extending from T6 to T11 and a left lumbar curve of 35° from T11 to L4. Compared to the able-bodied subject of Figure 16–6, the pattern for a right bend is relatively similar when looking at the T1-S1 levels (Figure 16–9A). A 30° bend is coupled with a 10° right rotation. The lumbar segment (Figure 16–9C) behaves like its normal counterpart but with a smaller

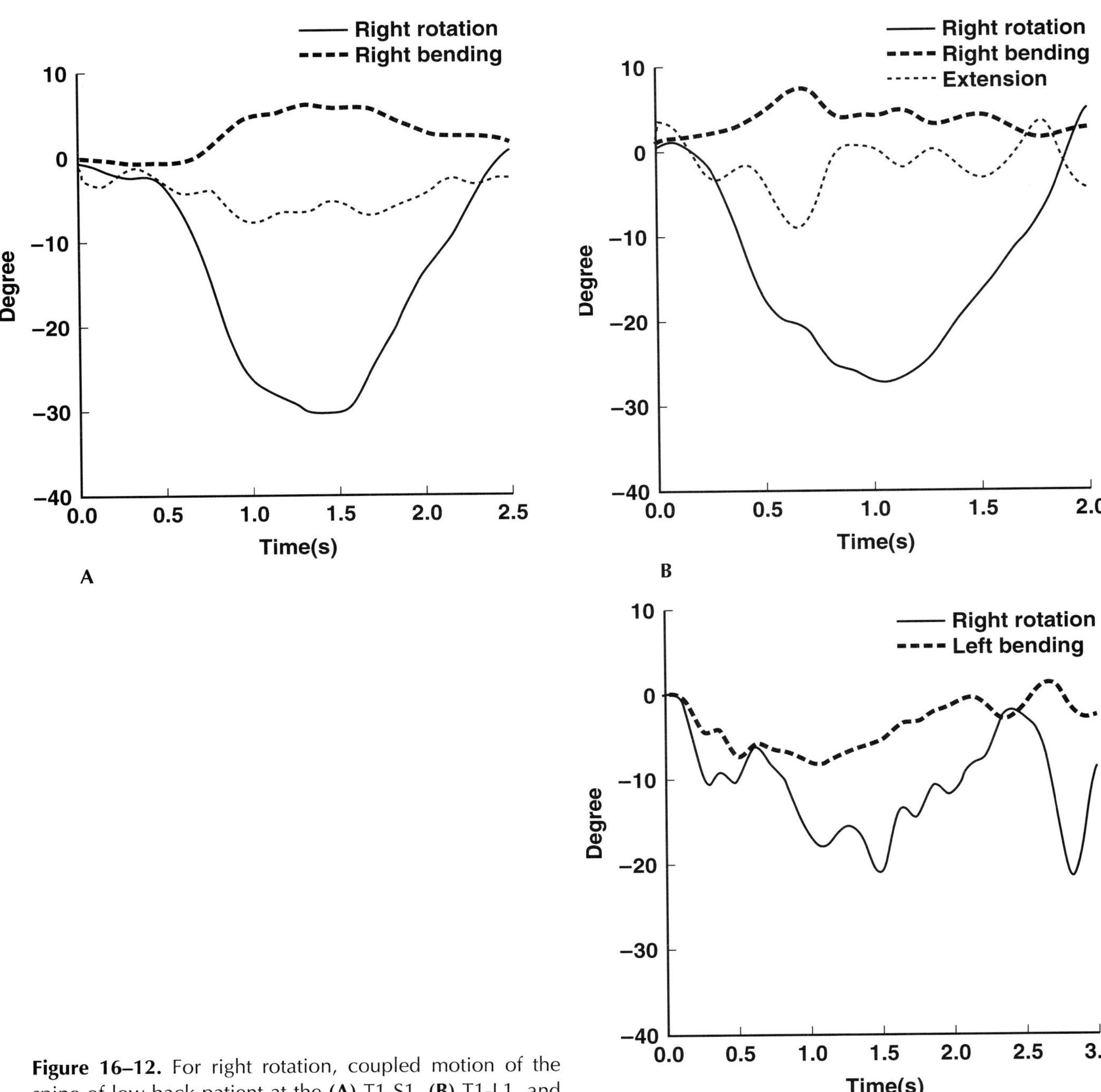

Figure 16–12. For right rotation, coupled motion of the spine of low back patient at the **(A)** T1-S1, **(B)** T1-L1, and **(C)** L1-S1 levels.

movement amplitude. Although the coupling is not affected, there is some limitation of motion. The main effect was noticed in the thoracic spinal (T1-T12) motion shown in Figure 16–9B, where there is essentially no secondary rotation. For this patient, the values for left bending were similar to those of the right bending motion. In both cases the peak amplitudes were less than those observed for the able-bodied subject.

We have documented the coupling mechanisms occurring in the trunk of the normal subjects and in idiopathic scoliosis for right bending.[13] The thoracic spine displayed opposite rotational polarities to the lumbar spine. Thus for a right bend, the thoracic spine had a left rotation that was coupled with spine extension, whereas the lumbar segment displayed a right rotation combined with some flexion. The ratio of thoracic over lumbar peak rotation was 0.80 +/−0.10 in controls. This was reduced to 0.45 +/−0.17 in the scoliosis group, indicating a thoracic rigidity regardless of the bending amplitude.

The right rotation of the T1-S1 level is coupled with 12° of extension and 20° of right bending. The thoracic markers followed a similar pattern but with a little less amplitude. In the able-bodied subject little was found to occur in the lumbar spine. In Figure 16–10C, there is an 18° left rotation although the primary movement was a right one. This is coupled with a 10° left bend and no extension. In other words, it appears that when the scoliotic thoracic spine is in flexion, there is no coupling movement either in bending or rotation.

KINEMATICS IN LOW BACK PAIN INJURY

The coupling mechanisms in a 40-year-old male subject having acute low back pain are shown in Figures 16–11 and 16–12. In lateral bending, trunk motion (T1-S1) has essentially a normal pattern and bending is combined with about 10° of rotation and an equivalent amount of flexion. Interestingly, the thoracic spine has about the same bending amplitude (22°) as the lumbar spine (18°), reflecting some form of rigidity in the latter. Right and left trunk (T1-S1) rotations were coupled with some limited bending and extension and behaved essentially normally. Although the thoracic spine displayed a similar behavior, little motion was observed in the lumbar spine.

A normal pattern was also noted for forward flexion. However, McClure et al[27] reported greater lumbar motion and velocity during the initial phase of extension in a group of asymptomatic patients having a history of low back pain. A video-based system was used to quantify the coupling mechanisms in able-bodied, scoliotic, and low back pain subjects. Kinematic dysfunctions were found to occur in different primary motions according to the pathology being assessed. It was important to relate the thoracic motion with the lumbar displacement to identify which segment was more affected.

SUMMARY

Three-dimensional kinematic analysis of the spine by either radiographic, electrogoniometric, or video techniques has shown promise and is now in clinical use. The questions that arise at this point in time are: Is this sufficient? What more do we need? Where should this lead?

Most clinical conclusions from 3-D studies have been challenged with a limited number of subjects and data variability. Although coupling motion in the spine appears to be accepted, it is still controversial. To deal with this controversy and establish distinctive normal kinematic patterns, a large number of able-bodied subjects must be assessed. It is unrealistic to expect that normative 3-D data on spinal kinematics should come from a single clinic or laboratory. Electronic mail (e-mail) makes it possible to consult and exchange information with different institutions at a very low cost. But before consulting data banks, accepted protocols for trunk and spinal kinematic assessments must be established.

Similarly, studies on well-defined clinical populations should be continued and encouraged. In this way, for example, data on patients with back pain, idiopathic scoliosis, and paralytic scoliosis should become available for clinical application.

With this type of basic knowledge of spinal kinematics arising from the normal and pathological spines, intervention studies can be carried out and outcome measures established. From these studies, rigid and flexible levels of the spine can be identified, coupling dysfunctions quantified, and treatment efficacy assessed.

By combining 3-D coordinates with a 3-D solid representation of the spine in motion, it may be foreseen that virtual reality could eventually be applied in helping the clinician in making a more accurate diagnosis and thus improve the prognosis. This would reflect the beginning of image-guided rehabilitation. Video information could be complemented by muscle activity patterns obtained by electromyographic techniques and force or strength data. Dynamic models of the trunk and spine could be used to estimate the outcome of the orthotic and surgical or therapeutic measures with the prediction displayed on the monitor. Spinal kinematics is an exciting and challenging field, and collaboration between clinicians and researchers will increase the utility of collected data for those in greatest need.

ACKNOWLEDGEMENTS

The authors wish to extend their gratitude to the people who have worked on the Orthobiom project at Sainte-Justine Hospital for their contribution in obtaining some of the experimental results presented in this chapter.

REFERENCES

1. Allard P, Stokes IAF, and Blanchi J-P. Three-dimensional analysis of human movement. *Hum Kinetics*. 1994;371.
2. Allard P, Dansereau J, Duhaime M, Geoffroy G. Scoliosis assessment in Friedreich's ataxia by means of intrinsic parameters. *Can J Neurol Sci*. 1984;11:582–587.
3. Allard P, Duhaime M, Raso JV, Thiry PS, Drouin G, Geoffroy G. Pathomechanics and management of scoliosis in Friedreich's ataxia patients: Preliminary report. *Can J Neuro Sci*. 1980;7:383–388.

4. Allard P, Dansereau J, Thiry PS, Raso JV, Geoffroy G, Duhaime M. Scoliosis in Friedreich's ataxia. *Can J Neurol Sci*. 1982;9:105–112.
5. Benson DR, Schultz AB, Dewald RL. Roentgenographic evaluation of vertebral rotation. *J Bone Joint Surg*. 1976;58A:1125–1129.
6. Boumphrey F. The difficult back patient. Presented at the AAOS-CME Update. Current concepts in lumbar disc disease. Cleveland, 1990.
7. Bryant JT, Reid G, Smith BL, Stevenson JM. Method for determining vertebral body positions in the sagittal plane using skin markers. *Spine*. 1989;14:258–265.
8. Chaffin DB, Andersson G. *Occupational Biomechanics*. New York: John Wiley, 1984:293.
9. CSST. Statisques sur les lésions musculo-squelettiques. Report from the Commission de la Santé et Sécurité au Travail du Québec, 1989.
10. Dillard J, Trafimov J, Anderson BJ, Cronin K. Motion of the lumbar spine. Reliability of two measurement techniques. *Spine*. 1991;16:321–324.
11. Dopf CA, Mandel SS, Geiger DF, Mayer PJ. Analysis of spine motion variability using a computerized goniometer compared to physical examination. *Spine*. 1994;19:586–595.
12. Dvorak J, Panjabi MM, Novotny JE, Chang DG, Grob D. Clinical validation of functional flexion/extension roentgenograms of the lumbar spine. *Spine*. 1991;16:943–950.
13. Farahpour N, Allard P, Labelle H, Duhaime M, Rivard C-H. Coupling mechanisms in the scoliotic spine. 2nd International Symposium on Three-Dimensional Scoliotic Deformities, Pescara, Italy, 1994.
14. Frymoyer JW, Gordon SL. Research perspectives in low-back pain. Report of a 1988 workshop. *Spine*. 1989;14:1384–1390.
15. Gagnon M, Smyth G. Muscular mechanical energy expenditure as a process for detecting potential risks in manual handling. *J Biomech*. 1991;24:191–203.
16. Gracovetsky S. *The Spinal Engine*. New York: Springer-Verlag, 1988.
17. Gracovetsky S, Kary M, Levy S, Said B, Pitchen I. Analysis of spinal and muscular activity during flexion/extension and free lifts. *Spine*. 1990;15:1333–1339.
18. Gracovetsky S, Kary M, Pitchen I, Levy S, Said B. The importance of pelvic tilt in reducing compressive stress in the spine during flexion-extension exercises. *Spine*. 1989;14:412–416.
19. Gregerson GG, Lucas DB. An in vivo study of axial rotation of the human thoracolumbar subjects. *J Bone Joint Surg*. 1967;49A:247–262.
20. Hindle RJ, Pearcy MJ. Rotational mobility of the human back in forward flexion. *J Biomed Eng*. 1989;11:213–219.
21. Koreska J, Robinson DE, Gibson DA. Three-dimensional analysis of spinal deformities. *J Eng Mechanics Div, ASCE*. 1978;104:239–253.
22. Loebl WY. Measurement of spinal posture and range of spinal movement. *Ann Phys Med*. 1967;9:103–110.
23. Lovett AW. A contribution to the study of the mechanics of the spine. *Am J Anat*. 1903;2:457–462.
24. Marras WS, Lavender SA, Leurgans SE, Rajulu SL, Allread WG, Fathallah FA, Ferguson SA. The role of dynamic three-dimensional trunk motion in occupationally-related low back disorders. *Spine*. 1993;18:617–628.
25. Marzan GT. Rational design for close-range photogrammetry. Doctoral dissertation, University of Illinois at Urbana-Champaign, 1975:219.
26. Mayer TG, Tencer AF, Kristoferson S, Mooney V. Use of noninvasive techniques for quantification of spinal range of motion in normal subjects and chronic low back dysfunction patients. *Spine*. 1984;9:588–595.
27. McClure PW, Esola M, Schreiner R, Seigler S. Kinematic analysis of the lumbar and hip motion while rising from a forward, flexed position in patients with and without a history of low back pain. *Spine*. 1997;22:552–558.
28. Panjabi M, Yamamoto I, Oxland T, Crisco J. How does posture affect coupling in the lumbar spine? *Spine*. 1989;14:1002–1011.
29. Panjabi MM. Experimental determination of spinal motion segment behavior. *Ortho Clin North Am*. 1977;8:169–180.
30. Panjabi MM. Experimental determination of spinal motion segment behavior. *Orthop Clin North Am*. 1978;8:169–180.
31. Paquet N, Malouin F, Richards CL, Dionne JP, Comeau F. Validity and reliability of a new electrogoniometer for the measurement of sagittal dorsolumbar movements. *Spine*. 1991;16:516–519.
32. Pearcy MJ, Gill JM, Whittle MW, Johnson GR. Dynamic back movement measured using a three-dimensional television system. *J Biomech*. 1987;20:943–949.

33. Pearcy MJ, Portek I, Shephard J. The effect of low-back pain on lumbar spinal movements measured by three-dimensional x-ray analysis. *Spine*. 1985;10:150–153.
34. Pearcy MJ, Tibrewal SB. Axial rotation and lateral bending in the normal spine measured by three-dimensional radiography. *Spine*. 1984;9:582–587.
35. Ployon A, Lavaste F, Maurel N, Skalli W, Roland-Gosselin A, Dubousset J, Zeller R. In-vivo experimental research into pre- and postoperative behavior of the scoliotic spine. *Hum Movement Sci*. 1997;16:299–308.
36. Scholten PJM, Veldhuizen AG. The influence of spine geometry on the coupling between lateral bending and axial rotation. *Eng Med*. 1985;14:167–171.
37. Shirazi-Adl A, Ahmed AM, Shrivastava SC. Mechanical response of a lumbar motion segment in axial torque alone and combined with compression. *Spine*. 1989;11:914–927.
38. Shirley FR, O'Connor P, Robinson ME, MacMillan M. Comparison of lumbar range of motion using three-dimensional measurement devices in patients with chronic low back pain. *Spine*. 1994;19:779–783.
39. Sicard C, Gagnon M. A geometric model of the lumbar spine in the sagittal plane. *Spine*. 1993;18:646–658.
40. Snijders CJ, Van Tiel MPJM, Nordin M. Continuous measurements of the spine movements in normal work situations over periods of 8 hours or more. *Ergonomics*. 1987;30:639–653.
41. Spitzer WO. Rapport du groupe de travail québécois sur les aspects cliniques des affectations vertébrales chez les travailleurs. Montreal: IRSST, 1986.

41a. Steffen T, Rubin RK, Baramki HG, Antoniou J, Marchese D. A new technique for measuring lumbar segmental motion in vivo. *Spine*. 1997;22:156–166.

42. Stokes IAF, Gardner-Morse M. Analysis of the interaction between vertebral lateral deviation and axial rotation in scoliosis. *J Biomech*. 1991;24:753–759.
43. Stokes IAF, Armstrong JG, Moreland MS. Spinal deformity and back surface asymmetry in idiopathic scoliotis. *J Orthop Res*. 1988;6:129–137.
44. Stokes IAF, Wilder DG, Frymoyer JW, Pope MH. Assessment of patients with low back pain by biplanar radiographic measurement of intervertebral motion. *Spine*. 1980;6:233–240.
45. Webster BS, Snook SH. The cost of compensable low-back pain. *J Occup Med*. 1990;32:13–15.
46. Weiler PJ, King GJ, Gertzbein SD. Analysis of sagittal instability of the lumbar spine in vivo. *Spine*. 1990;15:1300–1306.
47. Weitz E. The lateral bending sign. *Spine*. 1981;6:388–397.
48. White AA, Panjabi MM. *Clinical Biomechanics of the Spine*. Philadelphia: JB Lippincott, 1978

CHAPTER 17

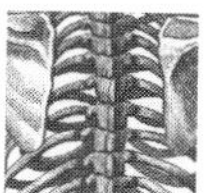

Isokinetic Dynamometry

DAVID ELTON, DC

INTRODUCTION

The isokinetic concept of exercise and first isokinetic dynamometer were developed in the mid- to late 1960s.[1–3] Due in part to the rapid incorporation of isokinetics into the practice of sports medicine, the first isokinetic testing and rehabilitation systems were primarily utilized in the management of extremity disorders, particularly the knees. As isokinetic systems evolved, they were found to be clinically useful due to their ability to objectively quantify patient function.

During the same time as the development and evolution of isokinetics, the problem of escalating costs associated with the management of spinal disorders has been and continues to be an area of intense research and debate. The acquisition of objective information regarding patient function is thought to be an integral part of the case management of the patient with a spinal disorder. As a result, isokinetic testing and rehabilitation systems have been adapted and developed for the specific requirements of trunk testing. Numerous studies using an isokinetic assessment of trunk function have demonstrated differences in mean test performance between back pain patients and healthy control subjects.[4–19] However, with large standard deviations leading to significant overlap between the groups, the ability to discriminate between patients and healthy subjects is limited.[20–23] What remains unclear is whether the differences in trunk function between back pain patients and healthy subjects are the cause or effect of back pain.[24–26]

The knowledge gained from the extensive research that has been performed on the utilization of isokinetics in the management of extremity conditions has not been easily extrapolated to spinal disorders. In the extremities the clinician is working with a one-joint complex with a single axis of rotation and, typically, a contralateral "healthy" joint for normative comparison. In the spine the clinician is faced with a multijoint complex and a variable axis of rotation, and, unlike the extremities, no contralateral counterpart for comparison.

Compiling normative data on the isokinetic assessment of trunk function has proven to be a challenging task. Several factors relating to differences in isokinetic testing systems, test protocols, and population characteristics have made the acquisition of normative trunk data difficult. Perhaps the most significant factor is the multifactorial nature of back pain coupled with contributing psychosocial issues frequently encountered in the back pain patient.

Objective measurements of impairment and disability are generally regarded as being valuable in the management of the back pain patient. As health care progresses through this era of cost containment, questions that remain to be answered regarding the costs and benefits of high-technology assessment tools include: How much objective data needs to be generated? Does the data enhance outcomes, and at what cost? High-technology assessment systems are capable of generating large amounts of data, but can this data be understood and applied, and is it clinically useful?

This chapter provides an introduction to isokinetic technology, presents the various isokinetic measurement parameters, and reviews the current status of isokinetic dynamometry in the management of the patient with a spinal disorder. To the extent possible, system-specific terminology has been avoided because in many instances the terms provide a less than accurate description of the actual phenomenon measured, which only serves to add confusion to an already complex technology.

ISOKINETIC CONCEPT OF TESTING AND EXERCISE

The isokinetic mode of testing and exercise has two unique characteristics: Accommodating resistance is provided to limit the speed of movement to a specific preselected angular velocity.[27–29] These unique attributes of isokinetic movement serve as the foundation for several of the proposed advantages of this mode of testing and exercise. Assessment systems utilizing other types of muscular contraction are the subject of other sections in this textbook and the reader is directed to those sections for a more in-depth discussion of the relative advantages and disadvantages of systems using each type of contraction. Table 17–1 presents a comparison of the four different contraction types, showing differences related to external resistance and angular velocity.

In an isometric contraction, muscle length remains constant when the muscle is activated. The amount of force generated by the musculoskeletal system is variable but is never sufficient to overcome the external resistance encountered, and as a result no movement occurs.

An isotonic contraction, more appropriately called a dynamic constant external resistance contraction,[30,31] occurs during a typical free-weight exercise. The external resistance, the weight to be moved, remains constant. The force generated by the musculoskeletal lever system to move the weight is variable depending on the changing muscle length and orientation of the lever arm system as movement occurs through the range of motion. The point in the range where the lowest amount of force can be generated determines the maximum weight that can be moved. This results in inefficient loading of the musculoskeletal lever system, making this type of contraction undesirable for the assessment of function. Both concentric (muscle shortens when activated) and eccentric (muscle lengthens when activated) movements can occur during an isotonic contraction.

Table 17–1: Characteristics of Contraction Types

	VELOCITY	EXTERNAL RESISTANCE
Isometric	No movement	Constant
Isotonic	Variable	Constant
Isodynamic	Variable	Constant
Isokinetic	Constant	Variable, accommodating

One high-technology trunk testing system uses an isodynamic (isoinertial) mode of assessment.[32–34] In order to initiate movement on this type of system, the subject must generate enough torque to overcome a preset level of resistance. If torque output remains below the preset resistance, no movement occurs, resulting in an isometric contraction. When torque output exceeds the preset resistance level, movement is initiated and torque output, range of motion, and velocity in the sagittal, frontal, and transverse planes are recorded. The system accommodates for acceleration and deceleration changes while the subject moves with a fixed level of resistance.

During an isokinetic contraction, accommodating resistance limits the speed of movement to a preselected angular velocity. Changes in force output from the musculoskeletal system that would accelerate or decelerate the body part above or below the preselected angular velocity are met with a corresponding increase or decrease in resistance, keeping angular velocity constant. This results in

Figure 17–1. Biodex isokinetic trunk testing system.
(Photo courtesy of Biodex.)

the musculoskeletal system being loaded maximally throughout the range of motion.[35] Although the angular velocity of the lever arm remains constant and is limited to the preselected speed, the velocity of muscular shortening is not constant because of the changing orientation of the musculoskeletal lever system as it progresses through the range of motion.[36]

Some isokinetic systems are able to provide accommodating resistance in both concentric and eccentric modes. There has been minimal research on the isokinetic assessment of eccentric trunk strength.[37] Figures 17–1 and 17–2 are pictures of two isokinetic trunk assessment systems.

The basic design principle of all isokinetic systems is a lever system rotating around a fixed axis of rotation that interfaces with the body part tested and provides resistance to limb movement. This accommodates the movement generated by the musculoskeletal lever system, limiting angular velocity to the preselected speed of movement.[38,39] The equipment lever system is attached to what is called a *dynamometer,* which houses either hydraulic or computer-controlled electronic servomotor mechanisms that provide accommodating resistance.[40,41]

A computer interface with the isokinetic dynamometer enables these systems to record the changing level of force produced by the musculoskeletal system and provide a graphic presentation of the force generating ability of the body part being evaluated. Through a software algorithm analysis, a variety of measurement parameters are derived from the torque curves recorded during an isokinetic assessment.

A passive, nonpowered, isokinetic dynamometer is able to provide accommodating resistance only. This type of system allows free limb acceleration. An active, powered, isokinetic dynamometer incorporates a controlled power source that enables the system to provide acceleration ramping and create an eccentric isokinetic contraction. An isokinetic system can be passive, active, or have the ability to operate in both modes.

A benefit of the accommodating resistance provided by isokinetic testing and rehabilitation systems is that the isokinetic assessment of trunk function has proven to be a safe testing modality. In extensive reviews of the literature a published report of back injury associated with isokinetic testing could not be found.[42,43]

With accommodating resistance, if the subject decreases force output or ceases to generate force, the resistance delivered by the test apparatus simultaneously decreases to the same level. The subject never encounters resistance that is greater than the subject's ability to generate force.

In deconditioned individuals, some muscular soreness is common following an isokinetic trunk test. Because the isokinetic assessment of trunk function typically does not involve an eccentric contraction, any soreness that does develop tends to be minimal and of short duration. However, the patient must be advised that this is a common occurrence and does not indicate reinjury, or a new injury.

ISOKINETIC MEASUREMENT PARAMETERS

This section presents a description of the most commonly reported isokinetic measurement parameters. The objective of this section is to introduce the basic measurement parameters using terminology that is as generic as possible.

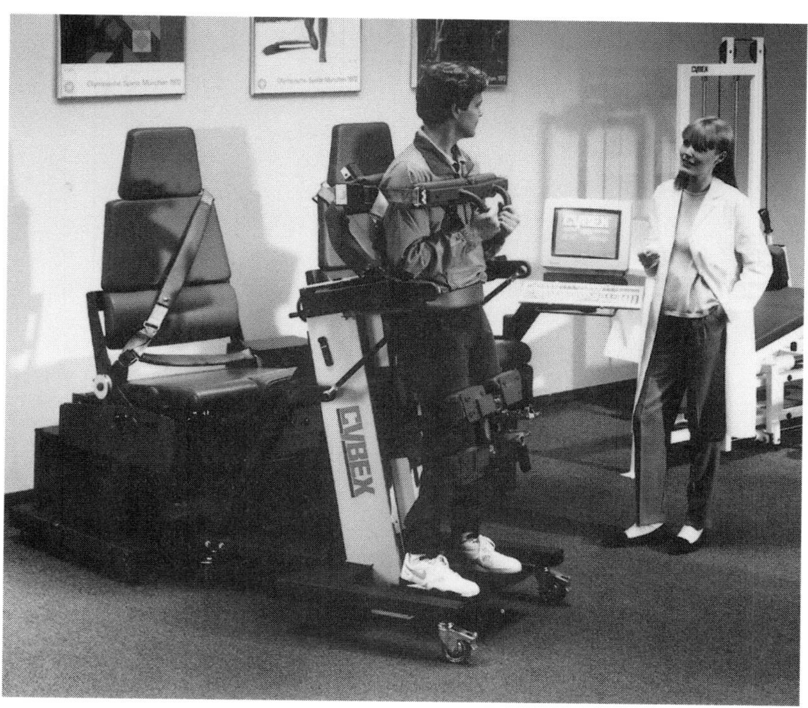

Figure 17–2. Cybex isokinetic trunk testing system.

(Photo courtesy of Cybex.)

Each manufacturer tends to develop its own terminology for specific measurement parameters, with the lack of uniformity leading to confusion and making comparison of data generated by different systems difficult. The computer interface with the test apparatus enables isokinetic testing systems to generate a large amount of data, much of which may be beyond the clinician's ability to meaningfully process and utilize.[44]

Although isokinetic systems quantify function through a variety of measurement parameters, there is a very high correlation between different isokinetic measures of force output, even at different test speeds, leading to the conclusion

		Speed #1	Speed #2	Speed #3	Speed #4
Number of Repititions:		6.0	6.0	6.0	18.0
		Extension			
Speed	*(deg/sec):*	60.0	120.0	60.0	120.0
Peak Torque	*(ft-lbs):*	263.8	232.4	245.3	214.9
Peak Torque Rep	*(rep #):*	4.0	2.0	1.0	2.0
Time to Peak Torque	*(msec):*	270.0	250.0	200.0	260.0
Angle of Peak Torque	*(deg):*	76.0	63.0	78.0	62.0
Coefficient of	*(%):*	4.6	6.5	7.9	4.7
Torque @ 30.0 deg	*(ft-lbs):*	158.0	138.2	170.3	108.4
Torque @ 0.2 sec	*(ft-lbs):*	182.8	178.2	245.3	152.4
Torque/Body Weight	*(%):*	202.9	178.8	188.7	165.3
Work/Body Weight	*(%):*	212.0	132.5	168.0	124.0
Max Rep Work	*(ft-lbs):*	275.5	172.2	218.3	161.2
Max Work "Rep"	*(rep #):*	4.0	2.0	2.0	4.0
Total Work	*(ft-lbs):*	1276.3	872.2	1119.0	2170.2
Work First Third	*(ft-lbs):*	460.7	309.2	417.5	831.9
Work Last Third	*(ft-lbs):*	341.3	278.5	362.6	646.9
Work Fatigue	*(%):*	25.9	10.1	13.1	22.2
Average Power	*(watts):*	270.8	317.1	234.2	260.9
		Flexion			
Speed	*(deg/sec):*	6.0	120.0	60.0	120.0
Peak Torque	*(ft-lbs):*	106.3	106.5	93.5	111.2
Peak Torque Rep	*(rep #):*	4.0	2.0	2.0	6.0
Time to Peak Torque	*(msec):*	210.0	170.0	310.0	330.0
Angle of Peak Torque	*(deg):*	43.0	49.0	48.0	66.0
Coefficient of	*(%):*	7.2	24.0	6.4	4.9
Torque @ 30.0 deg	*(ft-lbs):*	98.2	88.7	85.9	43.4
Torque @ 0.2 sec	*(ft-lbs):*	104.4	86.3	90.6	69.9
Torque/Body Weight	*(%):*	81.8	81.9	71.9	85.5
Work/Body Weight	*(%):*	55.7	53.8	58.7	57.9
Max Rep Work	*(ft-lbs):*	72.4	70.0	76.3	75.2
Max Work "Rep"	*(rep #):*	2.0	1.0	5.0	2.0
Total Work	*(ft-lbs):*	412.9	384.2	424.9	1098.4
Work First Third	*(ft-lbs):*	143.2	135.9	143.3	428.3
Work Last Third	*(ft-lbs):*	134.4	121.0	145.8	317.0
Work Fatigue	*(%):*	6.1	11.0	−1.7	26.0
Average Power	*(watts):*	86.9	130.6	89.0	121.0
Flex/Ext Ratio	*(%):*	40.3	45.8	38.1	51.7
Maximum ROM	*(deg):*	59.0	58.0	59.0	58.0
ROM-From	*(deg):*	32.0	32.0	32.0	32.0
ROM-To	*(deg):*	91.0	90.0	91.0	90.0

Figure 17–3. Sample isokinetic trunk test report.

that "All isokinetic measures are simply different measures of a single dimension of isokinetic performance."[45(p819)] In addition, "Investigators have found such strong relationships among simple measurements of peak torque and average torque, total work performed, initial torque acceleration energy and average power that little, if any, meaningful information was gained by calculating the latter parameters. Reduction of raw data to one number (peak torque) for each test movement is probably reasonable and may be a practical necessity for clinical use."[46(p1568)]

Figure 17–3 is a sample report from an isokinetic trunk test performed with a Biodex system. This demonstrates the large amount of data generated by an isokinetic trunk test. The clinician is advised to avoid being overwhelmed by the large quantity of data that may be contained in a report from an isokinetic assessment and evaluate those measurement parameters which have been shown to be the most reliable.

VELOCITY

One advantage of isokinetics is the ability to assess musculoskeletal function at a variety of angular velocities. Motion involves the exchange of kinetic energy, expressed by the formula:

$$\text{Kinetic Energy} = .05 \times \text{Mass} \times \text{Velocity}^2 \qquad (1)$$

According to Allen,[47] "The speed with which one moves a mass contributes more to the energy demands of motion than does the mass itself, yet in static isometric or isotonic tests only the mass is considered."

Doubling the mass moved while velocity remains constant will double the energy demands. Doubling the velocity of movement and keeping the mass constant will quadruple the energy required. As a result, devices that are able to take into consideration velocity, such as isokinetic testing systems, have a distinct advantage in the assessment of trunk function. Isokinetic testing systems are able to assess musculoskeletal function at a variety of angular velocities, from 0 degrees per second, an isometric contraction, up to approximately 450 degrees per second.

In the assessment of trunk function most test protocols utilize testing speeds of less than 240 degrees per second. Many patients with spinal disorders are unable to reach testing speeds of greater than 120 degrees per second, whereas healthy uninjured subjects can often reach speeds of 360 degrees per second or greater. The inability to generate force at high angular velocities has been reported to distinguish patients with low back pain from healthy test subjects.[48–50]

TORQUE

Torque refers to force acting around an axis of rotation. It is the product of the force generated times the length of the lever arm created by the subject interface with the isokinetic stabilization apparatus. Since isokinetic testing isolates the musculoskeletal system's action around an axis of rotation, force output is often quantified in terms of torque output.

Isokinetic testing systems produce a graph of the force output throughout the tested range of motion. Figure 17–4 provides an illustration of a torque curve produced during isokinetic trunk testing. At 0 seconds the subject is in a fully flexed starting position. As the subject exerts force, causing movement into extension, the system records the torque production causing the movement. At 1.0 seconds the subject has reached full extension, and torque production momentarily stops until the subject exerts a force causing movement into flexion. As the subject moves through the flexion phase of the movement, the system records torque production causing the flexion movement.

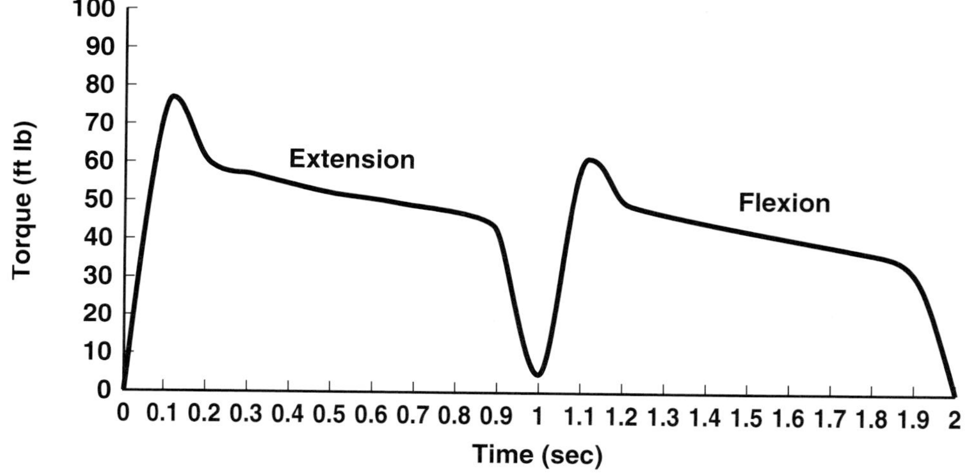

Figure 17–4. Torque curves produced during isokinetic trunk test.

TORQUE CURVES

Analysis of the torque curves produced during an isokinetic assessment yields a variety of information regarding the function of the musculoskeletal lever system tested. Torque curves from both limbs, in a knee test, for example, may be superimposed to provide a visual assessment of bilateral symmetry of muscle function. Using this same principle, torque curves produced during a reevaluation can be superimposed on the torque curves produced during an initial assessment to visually demonstrate changes in function.

There has been little research investigating whether particular spinal conditions present with a characteristic shape to the torque curve produced during isokinetic testing. There has been some work in this area regarding the isokinetic assessment of knee function. At this time no conclusions can be made regarding a patient's diagnosis simply from evaluating the shape of the torque produced during isokinetic testing.[51–53]

With a consistent, occasionally referred to as *maximal*, effort during isokinetic testing, a patient will produce a series of torque curves that are essentially identical in shape for each repetition performed.[54–57]

PEAK TORQUE

The peak torque is the greatest force developed for a particular movement during an isokinetic test and is illustrated in Figure 17–5. In this example peak torque is 80 ft·lbs.

Although frequently measured and reported, the peak torque produced is of limited value in that it conveys information regarding force production at only one point in the range of motion.[58] Two individuals may be able to generate identical peak torque yet have significantly different functional capabilities.

TIME TO PEAK TORQUE

The time to peak torque, as illustrated in Figure 17–5, is the length of time from the initiation of a muscular contraction to the point of peak torque production. In the example, the time it took to reach the peak torque of 80 ft·lbs. was 0.5 seconds.

This measurement parameter is also identified by a variety of similar terms such as *time rate of torque development*. Variation in time to peak torque has been reported to be associated with the following factors. Injury and/or pain leads to slow time to peak torque readings through the process of muscular inhibition.[59,60] This is a protective reflex response that is not under voluntary control. Slow time to peak torque readings can also be indicative of muscular deconditioning. Slow time to peak torque production has been reported to be due to poor motor unit synchronization and slow reflex potentiation.[61–63] With several factors (some of which are not related to subject performance) having the potential to influence this measurement, time to peak torque or similar measurements should not be heavily relied on as an indicator of the functional status of the patient.[64]

TORQUE TO BODY WEIGHT

In an effort to provide a comparison of function between individuals through normalizing for factors shown to have an influence on isokinetic test performance, a variety of ratios have been calculated and reported. Peak torque output is frequently reported relative to the patient's body weight. The resulting peak torque to body weight ratio (TBW) can typically be found in isokinetic reports. Body weight has been shown to account for some, but not all, variability in isokinetic trunk test performance.[65–68] As a result, the peak torque to body weight ratio may not be as useful for com-

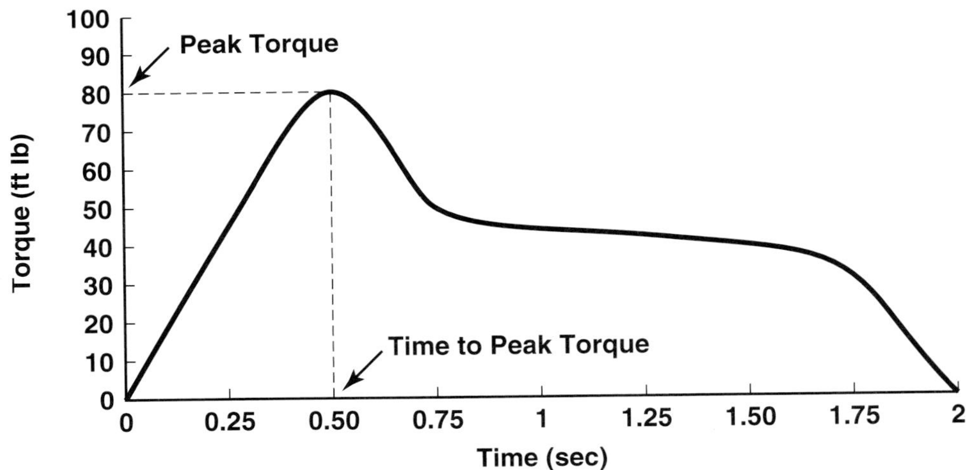

Figure 17–5. Peak torque and time to peak torque.

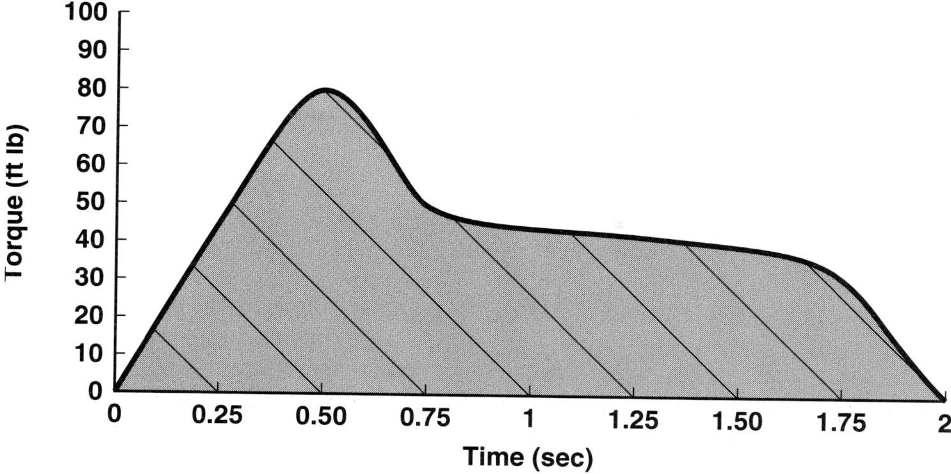

Figure 17–6. Work.

paring the capabilities of individual patients as is occasionally reported.

WORK

Work performed is a product of force multiplied by the distance the force acts through, or work = force × distance. In isokinetic testing, force is measured as torque, whereas distance is equal to the angular displacement of the movement. This results in the following formula for calculating work performed during an isokinetic test:

$$\text{Work} = \text{Torque} \times 6.28 \times \text{Range of motion (degrees)} \quad (2)$$

In isokinetic torque curve analysis, the work performed is equal to the area under the torque curve, as illustrated in Figure 17–6. Because range of motion is a critical component in the calculation of work performed, it must be known or controlled for when comparing work output during isokinetic trunk test performance.

The maximum work output for a single repetition of a multiple repetition test, *max rep work*, or the total work output for an entire test set, provides a more meaningful evaluation parameter than a peak torque measurement.[69,70] Although peak torque measures the maximum torque output at one point in the range of motion, work takes into consideration torque produced throughout the entire range of motion. When selecting one or two measurement parameters to evaluate, work would appear to be preferred to peak torque.

As Figure 17–7 illustrates, during isokinetic testing it is possible for two subjects to have identical peak torque and significantly different max rep work outputs. If only peak torque were compared, the subjects would appear to have

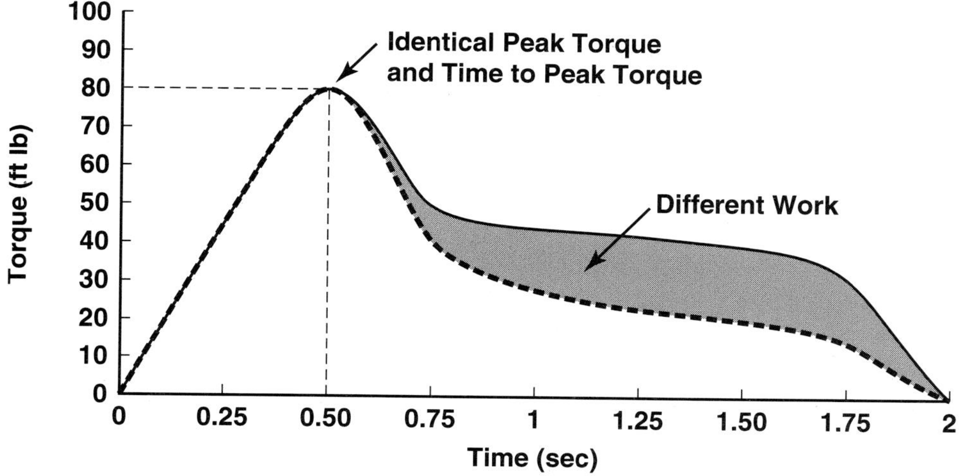

Figure 17–7. Difference between peak torque and work.

equal capabilities when in fact there is a significant difference in the abilities of the two subjects as measured by the work output.

WORK TO BODY WEIGHT

As was the case with the peak torque to body weight ratio, the effects of body weight can be controlled for when reporting the max rep work output. The resulting work to body weight ratio, (WBW) is then used to compare the performance of different subjects. As previously described, body weight may account for a small amount of the variability in isokinetic trunk testing; however, there are many other factors that influence test performance that limit the utility of this type of ratio.

POWER

Power is the rate of performing work. It is equal to the total work performed divided by the time taken to perform the work. Power is typically reported in watts. Either performing the same amount of work in less time or performing more work in the same amount of time increases power output. By incorporating three aspects of muscle function—torque, range of motion, and time—into a single measurement parameter, power is a frequently reported measurement parameter and is a better indicator of function than a peak torque measure.[71,72]

A source of confusion in isokinetic testing is the inaccurate reference to isokinetic tests performed at slow speeds, less than 60 degrees per second, as strength tests and tests performed at fast speeds, greater than 180 degrees per second, as tests of power. The fact is that strength is assessed by a variety of parameters, one of which is power, and both strength and power can be assessed at any test speed.[73]

FATIGUE

Fatigue is a multifactorial phenomenon that results in a reduction in a muscle's force-producing capability. As fatigue plays a critical role in the mechanism of many injuries, particularly activities involving repetitive motions or prolonged physical activity, a subject's endurance is frequently evaluated during isokinetic trunk testing.

Endurance or fatigue during isokinetic testing is generally assessed and reported in one of three formats.[74] The number of test repetitions performed before a 50% reduction in torque output is noted from the maximum level recorded, the total work performed in a predetermined number of repetitions, or the total work or number of repetitions performed in a predetermined amount of time. An additional method of assessing endurance is calculating a ratio of the total work performed in a predetermined number of repetitions performed at the end and the beginning of the test set,[75] as shown in Equation 17–3:

$$\text{Endurance Ratio} = \text{Work last 1/3 of test repetitions} \div \text{Work first 1/3 of test repetitions} \qquad (3)$$

The test-retest reliability of isokinetic assessment of endurance has been shown to be low, with little correlation to a patient's functional status.[76] However, studies have been performed that demonstrate the utility of incorporating an endurance measure in the isokinetic assessment of trunk function.[31,77] Further work needs to be done in improving the reliability of endurance measures obtained during isokinetic testing.

AGONIST/ANTAGONIST RATIO

There have been several studies that have examined the ratio of force production, termed the *agonist/antagonist ratio*, of the trunk extensor and flexor musculature.[78–85] This concept is derived from the knee joint, in which the hamstring/quadricep ratio is calculated for a variety of measurement parameters. An abnormal hamstring/quadricep ratio has been shown to be associated with knee dysfunction.[86]

Although it is generally accepted that the trunk extensors are stronger than the flexors, the specific extensor/flexor ratio has ranged from 1/1 to 2/1 depending on the study.[87] A trunk extensor/flexor ratio of 1.3/1 is the most commonly cited ratio, indicating that the extensors are 30% stronger than the flexors.[88–90] The variation in the extensor/flexor ratio is not surprising given the multitude of factors that can potentially influence the calculation of such a ratio. These factors are the topic of a subsequent section of this chapter.

Another problem with calculating ratios such as the trunk extensor/flexor ratio is that isokinetic torque measurements are interval-scaled.[91,92] The zero level on the torque curve from an isokinetic test does not represent an absence of torque generated by the musculoskeletal system. The torque curve provides a graph of the amount of resistive torque provided by the dynamometer to keep angular velocity at the preselected speed. The amount of torque generated to accelerate the body part to the test speed is omitted from all recordings. "Because both flexion and extension recordings are interval-scaled the ratio does not accurately reflect the relative strengths of the flexor and extensor muscles."[93(p805)] Although there has been some disagreement over the importance of using interval scaling or ratio scaling, the extensor/flexor ratio has been shown to be inaccurate.[94]

The trunk extensor/flexor ratio has been shown to be an unreliable measurement parameter at all testing speeds with test-retest errors approaching 50% of mean values and as a result this ratio has limited utility in clinical decision making.[95–98] With lack of agreement regarding what the normal trunk extensor/flexor ratio is, in addition to the inherent error in calculating such a ratio from an isokinetic test, making a determination about whether low back dysfunction is present based on a deviation in the extensor/flexor ratio is not possible given current knowledge.

This section has described a variety of isokinetic measurement parameters. Research has demonstrated that there is a high correlation between different isokinetic measures of force output. Clinicians should evaluate one or two measurement parameters when assessing performance on an isokinetic trunk test. The measurement parameters chosen should quantify force output throughout the range of motion, such as work or power. In this way the clinician can avoid being overwhelmed by the large quantity of data generated by an isokinetic trunk test.

VALIDITY AND RELIABILITY OF ISOKINETIC SYSTEMS

According to Sapega,[99(p1564)] "A number of seemingly minor technical factors can exert a major effect on the data from tests of muscular performance." The following paragraphs present some of the factors that influence the data generated during an isokinetic assessment of trunk function and that make data comparison between the isokinetic systems difficult if not impossible.

The validity of a test is the "ability of the test to accurately measure the specified function."[100(p1564)] Reliability is defined as "consistency of a measurement when all conditions are thought to be held constant."[101(p134)] A clinically useful assessment tool must be both valid and reliable.

The isokinetic dynamometer has generally been shown to be intrinsically accurate in the measurement of parameters such as velocity, torque, work, and power.[102–106] However, "Validity cannot be demonstrated for a device, but rather for the specific inferential use of a measurement."[107(p1843)] Inferential value indicates that test performance provides insight into the patient's ability to perform functional activities. Isokinetic testing, through the ability to test at a variety of angular velocities, is often described as being able to assess a patient's strength and endurance at "functional" speeds. Although some studies have indicated that isokinetic testing of the extremities has considerable inferential value with regard to the performance of functional activities,[108] there is not general agreement on this issue, nor has this been shown to be the case with isokinetic trunk testing.[109,110]

Although the inferential value of isokinetic testing remains questionable, the primary use of an isokinetic assessment system is as a tool capable of providing objective documentation of patient progress during therapy. It is for this use that isokinetic testing systems must be shown to be reliable assessment tools.

Dvir[111(p134)] states reliability must be established "in order to ensure that variation in the scores, over a period of time, reflect a true change rather than a measurement error." According to Sapega,[112(p1564)] "Attention to detail and standardization of techniques of testing are the most effective means of ensuring test and retest reliability."

Reliability consists of two components[113]: system reliability of the measurement instrument and repeatability of the measurements obtained. System reliability is far easier to demonstrate, and in this capacity most of the major isokinetic assessment systems have been shown to be reliable measurement tools.[114–121] The repeatability of measurement parameters obtained during isokinetic testing has proven to be the more difficult to demonstrate. Both examiner- and subject-dependent factors influence this aspect of reliability.[122–126]

Examiner-dependent factors affecting reliability include equipment calibration, subject positioning, stabilization, machine-subject axis of rotation alignment, and test protocol standardization.[127–130] Patient-dependent factors include motivation, pain sensitivity, skill learning ability, cooperation, and fatiguability.[131–134]

An important criterion for the performance of a reliability study is that the reliability of a testing device must be demonstrated "through the use of samples from populations with whom the device will be used clinically."[135(p800)] The majority of reliability studies that have been performed have used normal subjects.[136] Several of the previously described patient-dependent factors shown to adversely affect test reliability are associated with the back pain patient. As a result, the reliability of isokinetic testing tools in the assessment of the back pain patient may be less than that reported in the literature.[137]

Although there has been disagreement on the most appropriate materials and methods to be used in validity and reliability studies, the isokinetic dynamometer is generally regarded as a reliable and, depending on the application, valid testing tool. Although reliable and valid, each specific isokinetic system has a variety of features that make extrapolation of data from one isokinetic system to another difficult if not impossible.[138–143] This adds to the complexity of obtaining and utilizing normative data in the isokinetic assessment of trunk function.

This section presents the technical factors and system-dependent variables affecting the validity and reliability of isokinetic testing. Patient-dependent factors influencing test validity and reliability are presented in a subsequent section of the chapter.

Periods of acceleration and deceleration at the beginning and end of the tested range of motion, during which time angular velocity is less than the preselected test speed, introduce inertial artifacts that are controlled, corrected, or eliminated through ramp, damp, and windowing.[144–152] These data modification techniques are utilized by different isokinetic systems to varying degrees and are referred to by different names.

RAMP

Ramping is a means used by manufacturers of isokinetic equipment to provide resistance during periods in which the body part being tested is accelerating yet the angular

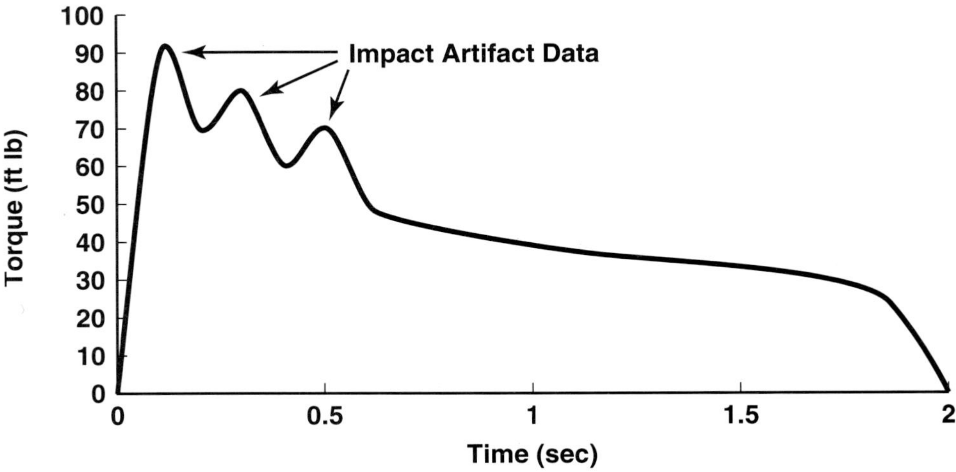

Figure 17–8. Impact artifact data.

velocity is less than the preselected speed of movement.[153] In essence ramping is controlled limb acceleration, as opposed to free limb acceleration. It can be thought of as an acceleration cushion. Ramping controls for inertial artifacts generated during acceleration by providing resistance at prescribed time or force intervals. Ramp is either controlled entirely by a computer-dynamometer feedback loop without clinician input, or is under control of the clinician, depending on the isokinetic system.

During a test utilizing ramping, resistance is provided and is recorded by the dynamometer and computer before the body part reaches the preselected angular velocity. During a test performed without ramping, free limb acceleration occurs and no resistance is encountered. Resistance is not recorded until the preselected angular velocity is reached. This difference between ramped and nonramped test environments is an important issue in comparing data among systems, or within the same system utilizing different ramp parameters.

In unramped systems, which allow free limb acceleration, an overshoot torque spike termed *impact artifact data*[154] occurs when the subject has accelerated to the preset test speed and the isokinetic system engages, causing an impulse load as the system provides resistance keeping the angular velocity at the preselected speed. This is illustrated in Figure 17–8. Impact artifact data typically occurs in the first 10 to 12 degrees of the tested range of motion and is characterized by a torque spike followed by a down-up oscillation on the torque curve. Impact artifact data leads to artificially elevated peak torque readings. Several factors determine the magnitude of the overshoot torque spike. Faster test speeds, heavier body parts, and more powerful

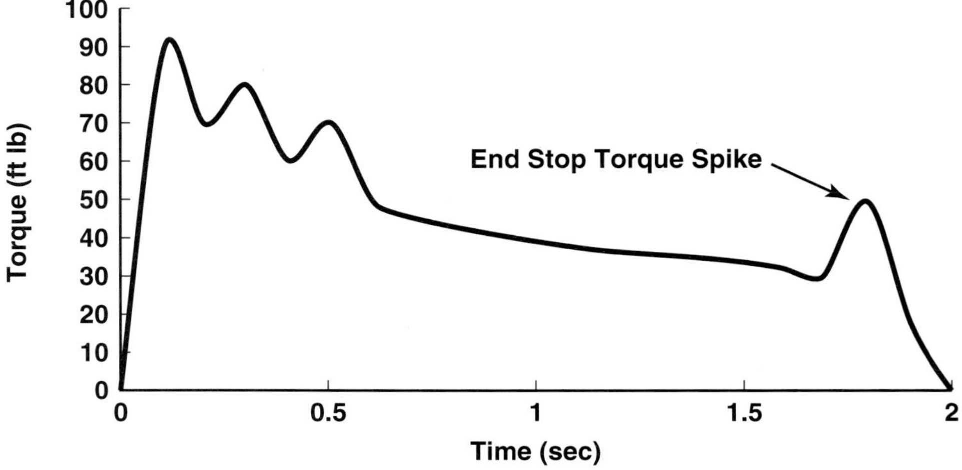

Figure 17–9. End stop torque spike.

muscle groups are associated with torque spikes of greater magnitudes. Both ramping and what is termed damp are utilized to control impact artifact data.

DAMP

Damp is a manipulation of the force output signal from the dynamometer. It is utilized to minimize impact artifact data, facilitating the acquisition of accurate torque measurements from an isokinetic test.[155–157] On computerized isokinetic systems, damp is provided automatically by the computer software. On noncomputerized analog systems, damp slows the speed of the stylus response. Different levels of damping are under the control of the examiner. The greater the degree of damping selected, the lower the torque measurement recorded. Studies have shown that the damp setting selected significantly affects the amount of torque reported.[158,159] As a result, the damp setting must be kept constant and must be known when comparing data generated by analog systems.

Similar, but not identical, to the impact artifact data is the "end stop torque spike,"[160] which is common to all isokinetic systems. This differs from the impact artifact data in that the end stop torque spike occurs at the end of the preselected range of motion. A torque spike is created as energy is dissipated to decelerate the body part from the preselected angular velocity. This is illustrated in Figure 17–9. As was the case with the impact artifact data, the end stop torque spike may lead to an artificially elevated peak torque measurement.

An important consideration regarding both impact artifact data and the end stop torque spike is that these forces occur and are dissipated at the input shaft of the dynamometer and at the interface between the body part and the stabilization apparatus. The musculoskeletal system of the individual being tested experiences only a small fraction of these forces.

CUSHION

The magnitude of the end stop torque spike depends on whether the system's range of motion end stop is mechanical or electric, and if electric, the amount of cushion used. The shorter the time or range over which energy must be dissipated to decelerate the body part, the more abrupt the change and the higher the recorded torque spike. Mechanical end stops decelerate the body part in approximately 5 degrees. Systems with electronic end stops enable the clinician to select a cushion setting. In effect this is deceleration ramping. With a hard cushion the subject is decelerated from the testing velocity to a stop in approximately the last 5 degrees of the tested range of motion. With a soft cushion this deceleration occurs more gradually, in approximately the last 15 to 20 degrees of the tested range of motion. Subjectively, patients are able to report a difference between the soft and hard cushion settings.

A soft cushion is desirable for improving the comfort of the individual being tested. However, the disadvantage associated with a soft cushion is that 20 degrees of the tested range of motion will not have occurred at the preselected test velocity and as a result will not be available for data analysis. Manufacturers of systems with a cushion setting recommend that the hardest possible cushion be used that remains compatible with patient comfort. This presents standardization challenges because the cushion setting significantly influences measurement parameters such as work and power and the cushion selection knob may be infinitely adjustable instead of having discrete settings.

DATA WINDOW

Isokinetic software packages enable the clinician to utilize an isokinetic window when analyzing and reporting data.[161] As illustrated by Figure 17–10, by windowing the data only

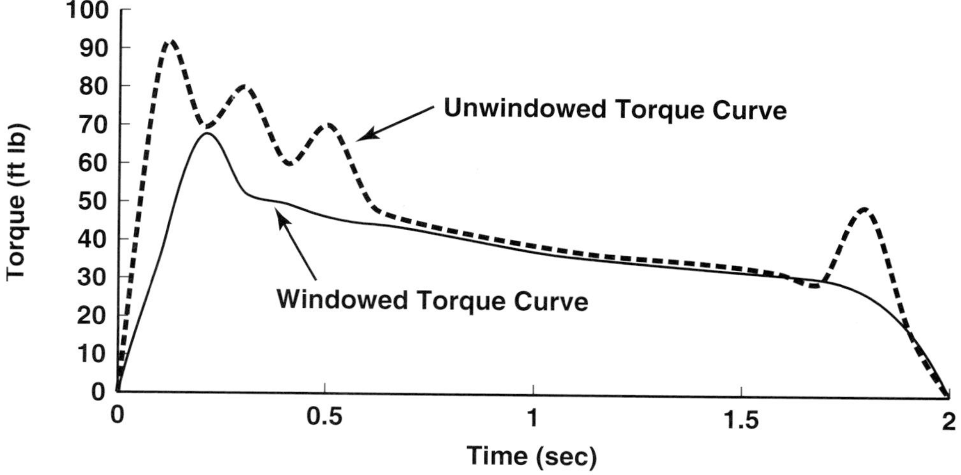

Figure 17–10. Difference between windowed and nonwindowed torque curves.

the torque produced at the preselected angular velocity is reported.

A soft cushion combined with windowed data leads to a significant reduction in the amount of data available for analysis. Research has shown that significant differences exist between windowed and nonwindowed data produced from the same isokinetic test.[162] Windowed data yields lower torque output. However, windowed data has been shown to improve intermachine reliability and is therefore desirable. When comparing isokinetic data, it is important to know whether or not the data was windowed.

In the development of the author's isokinetic trunk test protocol, performed on a system with electronic end stops, several trials were performed at the same test velocity using different cushion settings in both windowed and nonwindowed modes. Velocity curves throughout the tested range of motion and reports of comfort from test subjects were compared. A cushion selection of 75% of the hardest possible cushion was found to provide adequate comfort while maintaining the maximal possible range of motion at the preselected test velocity. The cushion setting is never varied from this setting.

POSITIONING/STABILIZATION

A large amount of research has been performed that demonstrates the importance of positioning and stabilization in obtaining reliable data during isokinetic testing.[163–180] The positioning and stabilization of the subject varies significantly between different isokinetic trunk testing systems. For example the Biodex Back Attachment system, pictured earlier in Figure 17–1, offers both semistanding and seated isolated lumbar positions with stabilization provided by Velcro straps and rotating thoracic and lumbar pads. A seated test posture is reported to provide better isolation of the abdominal and paraspinal musculature through minimizing the utilization of the lower extremity musculature during the test. One study found that a seated test position was tolerated better than a standing posture.[181] The Cybex TEF unit, pictured earlier in Figure 17–2, uses a standing position with a more rigid stabilization mechanism. A proposed benefit of standing test position is that this is a position that more closely approximates the posture the patient is likely to be in during the performance of daily activities and thus the test is more functional. A seated test position is believed to be associated with higher levels of intradiscal pressure than that produced during testing in a standing position. However, it must be recalled that there is not one published report of a back injury associated with isokinetic trunk testing.

Another issue related to subject positioning and stabilization during isokinetic trunk testing is the effect of the lower extremity kinetic chain state on test performance.[182] A closed lower extremity kinetic chain results in higher torque output in both trunk flexion and extension. A closed lower extremity kinetic chain results from a weight-bearing position with stabilization of the knees, hips, and pelvis. An open lower extremity kinetic chain results from a non-weight-bearing position and/or lack of stabilization of the knees, hips, and/or pelvis. Torque output has been shown to decrease as the lower extremity kinetic chain becomes more open.

The influence of the kinetic chain state of the lower extremities on isokinetic trunk test performance confirms the concept that function of the lumbar spine is related to the state of the lower extremities. This fact has important implications for both the assessment and rehabilitation of the back pain patient. Assessment procedures must take the entire kinetic chain into consideration. Dysfunction at any point in the chain can produce compensatory changes at other points in the chain. Rehabilitation of the back pain patient should address all components of the kinetic chain and include closed kinetic chain activities.

AXIS OF ROTATION

An important consideration in the positioning of the patient for an isokinetic test is the alignment of the axis of rotation of the test apparatus with that of the body part to be evaluated.[183–190] All currently available isokinetic systems share a common characteristic, a single fixed axis of rotation. The axis of rotation of the body part to be evaluated must be aligned with the axis of the test apparatus. In an isokinetic evaluation of knee function the determination of the correct axis of rotation is fairly simple. The axis of rotation of the isokinetic system and the axis of the knee joint are easily determined and aligned. The femur, tibia, and torso are stabilized, and all motion occurs at the knee joint.

Determining the proper axis of rotation for the lumbar spine is more difficult. Not only is a multijoint complex involved, but also stabilization of the pelvis, lower extremities, and torso is difficult. Most isokinetic trunk testing systems recommend aligning the axis of rotation at the anterior superior iliac spine (ASIS), a readily identified landmark that approximates the L5/S1 disc space. The greater trochanter, hip, and L2/3 junction have also been utilized as the axis of rotation for trunk testing. A computerized simulation of lumbar spine motion has demonstrated the L3 vertebral body as being the most appropriate axis of rotation for an isokinetic assessment of trunk function.[191] However, the L3 vertebral body has been shown to experience significant migration during trunk flexion and extension. The ASIS has been shown to be the most appropriate axis of rotation to be used during isokinetic assessment of trunk function using the Biodex system.[192]

LEVER ARM LENGTH

Related to subject positioning and stabilization is the length of the lever arm created by the equipment-subject interface. Given equal torque generating capabilities, a longer lever arm will yield higher torque, work, and power readings.[193–195] As a result of the different stabilization mechanisms used by the various isokinetic trunk testing systems, different lever arm lengths are created by the equipment-subject interface. This makes data comparison between systems difficult. In addition, a consistent positioning and stabilization protocol must be followed for tests performed on the same system in order to create identical or at least similar lever arm lengths in different subjects and during reevaluations.

GRAVITY

The effect of gravity acting on the coupled body part and lever arm during isokinetic testing has been demonstrated to significantly affect the data generated from a given isokinetic test.[196–201] As would be expected, the torque output measured for a body part moving with gravity is greater than the amount of torque produced due to musculoskeletal effort. When moving against gravity, lower than expected torque is recorded. In an effort to control for the effects of gravity, some isokinetic software packages have incorporated a gravity correction factor.

Gravity correction may be either dynamic or static. In a dynamically corrected system the influence of gravity on the body part–lever arm couple is assessed during performance of a pretest sample test effort. By contrast, in a statically corrected system, the body part–lever arm couple is placed in the position of maximum gravity influence, held there isometrically, and the resulting torque produced is measured. Whether one type of gravity correction or another offers an advantage or whether gravity correction is needed at all has not been determined through research. However, whether gravity correction was used or not is an important consideration in interpreting and comparing isokinetic trunk test performance.

The benefits of one isokinetic system over another may simply be a matter of marketing. To the clinician, the critical issue is whether the system provides valid and reliable data. The various isokinetic trunk testing systems have been proven to be safe, intrinsically valid, and reliable testing tools. However, significant differences exist between the systems, which makes comparison of data obtained on different systems difficult if not impossible. Within a system, issues such as damp, window, and cushion must be taken into consideration when comparing data. Extrinsic factors relating to the standardization of the test protocol utilized have a profound impact on reliability of data generated.

The issues presented in this section add to the complexity of the ongoing effort to gain a better understanding of spinal dysfunction. Isokinetic testing systems, through the production of valid and reliable data regarding patient strength and endurance, may be useful in documenting progress as a result of therapeutic intervention and/or the natural history of recovery from a back injury.

ASSESSMENT OF EFFORT

Accurate interpretation of the results of any objective assessment of physical performance requires that the evaluator take into consideration subject motivation and the degree to which the subject was able to put forth a maximum physical effort.[202]

Deficits in function from a test in which a "maximal" effort was put forth are attributed to deficits in the physical characteristics measured, for example trunk extensor strength, and serve as the foundation for a treatment plan. Deficits noted from a test in which less than a "less than maximal" effort was put forth can be attributed to physical and/or nonphysical sources.

The determination and labeling of the level of effort put forth during an isokinetic test receives a great deal of attention in the medicolegal arena in which high-technology assessment tools have been used as "spinal lie detectors."[203(p801)] In this setting the opinion that less than a maximal effort was put forth, occasionally inappropriately labeled as malingering, can have adverse consequences. It is because of this inappropriate use of isokinetic assessment instruments and the potential adverse impact on a patient's credibility that the use of high-technology testing devices in the assessment of patient effort requires a critical analysis.

The determination of the level of participation during isokinetic testing is based on the concept that during a maximal effort a consistent level of force will be generated at each point throughout the range of motion for each repetition performed in a multiple repetition test set. In isokinetic testing, a maximal effort will lead to a series of consecutive torque curves that are identical in shape. This is illustrated in Figure 17–11.

During a less than maximal effort it would be nearly impossible to produce an identical, but unknown, level of force, throughout the range of motion, or in other words, to produce consistently inconsistent torque curves. Figure 17–12 is an example of inconsistent torque curves produced during an isokinetic trunk flexion/extension assessment.

Torque curve consistency is quantified in several ways, from a simple visual assessment of curve consistency to a software-generated coefficient of variation measurement. To calculate the coefficient of variation, all the torque curves produced during a test set are sampled at identical points in the range of motion. Mean torque output and the standard deviations for each of these points are determined. The coefficient of variation is calculated according to the following formula:

$$\text{Coefficient of Variation} = \text{Standard deviation} \div \text{Mean torque output} \times 100 \quad (4)$$

The coefficient of variation from the trunk test in which a consistent effort was put forth, illustrated in Figure 17–11, was 9%. Figure 17–12, from a trunk test with an inconsistent effort, had a coefficient of variation of 23%.

The coefficient of variation is a well-accepted measurement parameter used in a variety of applications in addition to isokinetic testing. The threshold degree of variation separating a "maximal" from a "submaximal" effort is not clear. It has been suggested that a coefficient of variation of 15% or greater provides an indication that less than

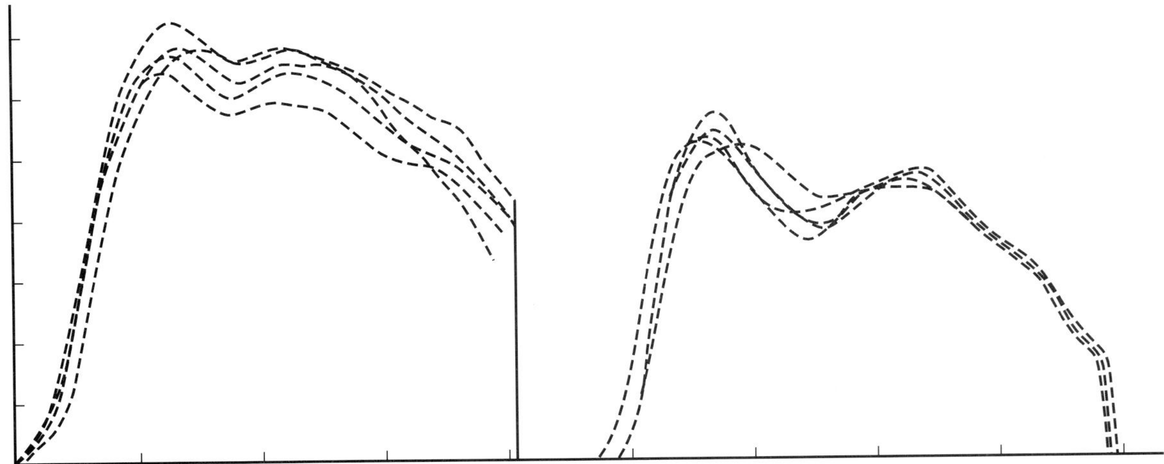

Figure 17–11. Consistent torque curves.

a maximal effort was put forth on the test. A thorough review of the subject reveals that there is no published information to support the 15% cutoff point.[204]

Figure 17–13 illustrates the distribution of coefficients of variation from the author's database of over 1800 isokinetic trunk tests performed on a population of back pain patients. This demonstrates that the majority of isokinetic trunk tests have a coefficient of variation of less than 15%. However, this can not be interpreted to mean that this degree of consistency of effort distinguishes maximal from submaximal efforts.

As the coefficient of variation increases, indicating less consistent performance, measurement parameters such as torque, work, power, and endurance decrease. Figure 17–14, from the authors database, demonstrates the relationship between average power output in trunk extension at 60 degrees per second and test coefficient of variation.

As the coefficient of variation during a test increases, power output decreases. This relationship exists for each isokinetic strength and endurance measurement parameter. As effort becomes less consistent, strength and endurance measures will decrease. In a test with a high coefficient of variation, performance deficits are not necessarily due to strength and endurance deficits. Other factors, such as pain and/or apprehension, may also play a role in limiting test performance.

The primary research on the differentiation between maximal and submaximal efforts has been performed on the assessment of grip strength with a hand-held dynamometer.[205–209] Extrapolating the results from this research, in which an isometric contraction is performed by the upper extremities, to the complex isokinetic assessment of trunk function has limitations.

There have been a number of studies performed that examine the relationship between test effort and the amount

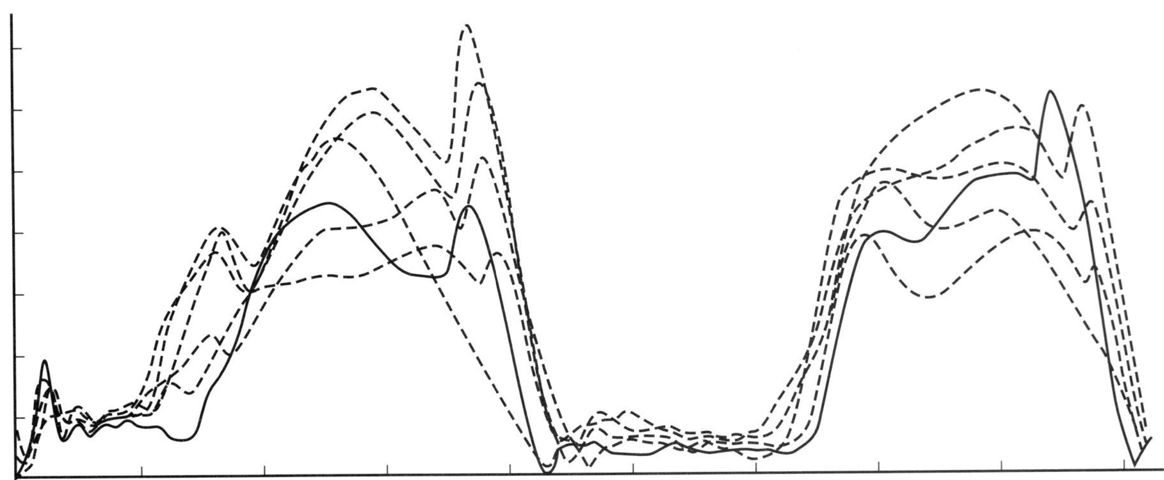

Figure 17–12. Inconsistent torque curves.

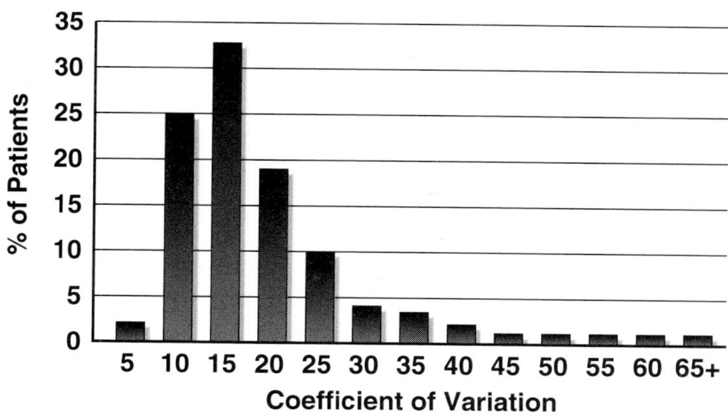

Figure 17–13. Distribution of coefficient of variation data

of variability in test performance during isokinetic testing.[210–212] The primary limitation in these studies is that healthy cooperative subjects are instructed to perform tests with both a maximal effort and a subjectively determined, for example 50% of maximum, level of submaximal effort. The coefficients of variation from both maximal and submaximal tests are then calculated and compared. This type of methodology results in a lower coefficient of variation for the maximal test. A threshold of between 10% and 20% is generally reported to distinguish between the maximal and submaximal efforts.

Extrapolation of data generated from a healthy population performing maximal and deliberate submaximal efforts to an injured population must be questioned. In an injured population, issues such as deconditioning, fear of increased pain, apprehension regarding the test environment, and poor understanding of test instructions present legitimate barriers to the performance of a consistent maximal effort during high-technology trunk testing. In the research setting the healthy subjects consciously "faked" a less than maximal effort. This label is then extrapolated to the injured patient who is legitimately performing an isokinetic test to the best of his or her abilities yet with less than the desired consistency.

In a study of effort during isokinetic testing, both healthy and low back pain patients were labeled as either consistent, slightly variable, or variable based on a visual assessment of torque curve consistency.[213] Tests in which torque curves were labeled either consistent or slightly variable were considered to represent maximal efforts, whereas those tests with variable torque curves were considered to represent submaximal efforts. In the low back patients, test performance from tests in which a submaximal effort was put forth was significantly lower than performance during tests in which a maximal effort was put forth. Performance for healthy controls was greater than that for low back patients putting forth a maximal effort. For all three groups—healthy controls, patients with maximal effort, and patients with submaximal effort—males were stronger than females. The authors conclude,[214] "People with low back pain frequently have factors such as depression, fear of reinjury and of pain, and a variety of other psychosocial factors that may influence their efforts in tests of strength."

Further clouding the issue of labeling effort based on torque curve consistency is the determination that normal subjects putting forth a maximal effort and low back pain patients using preferred submaximal effort, during a high-technology assessment of trunk function, produce output

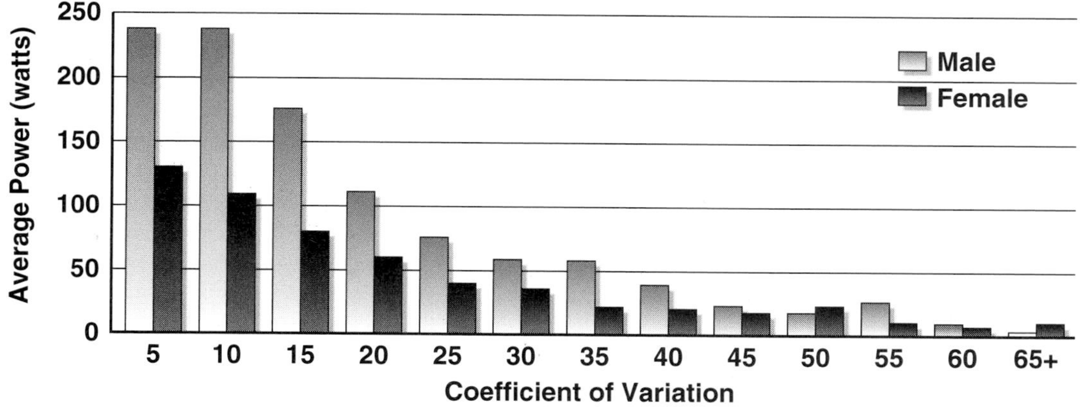

Figure 17–14. Relationship between coefficient of variation and power output.

which is equally consistent. Normal subjects and low back pain patients differ in preferred low back motion characteristics. Low back pain patients prefer motion that occurs at a slower velocity and through a smaller range of motion than healthy controls.[215]

When the low back pain patient is evaluated using a standardized isokinetic assessment protocol that requires that the patient move through a range of motion at velocities greater than the individual's preferred low back motion, inconsistent torque curve production is the result. If the patient was permitted to perform the test at the individual's preferred velocity and through the preferred range of motion, the consistency of torque curves produced would be improved.

In a study of the visual assessment of torque curves, mathematical measurement models and evaluators' subjective rating of effort were compared as methods of assessing the consistency of effort put forth during an isokinetic test performed by healthy cooperative controls instructed to put forth either maximal (100%) or submaximal (50%) efforts.[216] Visual assessment of torque curves was unable to distinguish maximal from submaximal efforts in 28% of subjects performing an isokinetic assessment of trunk flexion/extension strength. The mathematical measurement models were accurate in 90% to 92% of tests. The author concludes that "The correlation between curve variability and degree of effort is not perfect." In addition, "Clinical judgment is required in evaluating effort during tests of isokinetic trunk and lifting strength." Although the issue of labeling the level of effort put forth during an isokinetic test remains in need of further clarification, what is clear is that test performance as measured by any of a number of measurement parameters is related to consistency of torque output.

The presence of, or fear of, increased pain clearly has an influence on isokinetic test performance. The Acceptable Maximum Effort (AME) model[217] describes a method for working with a patient's pain in an attempt to obtain as consistent an effort possible during isokinetic testing. In this model the test subject progresses through stages of increasing effort until the maximum level of acceptable effort is reached. This is the degree of physical exertion that can be performed and that remains compatible with the patient's pain tolerance. The test is then carried out at this effort level. The development of a standardized isokinetic test protocol to be used with patients experiencing pain must in some fashion incorporate this concept through performance of pretest familiarization repetitions. These practice repetitions also serve to progress the patient along the learning curve associated with isokinetic test performance and facilitate patient warm-up.

Cooke et al[218] conclude, "Lumbar dynamometry should be regarded as an indicator of the level of performance at the time of testing, more as a psycho-physical test than as a valid measure of true muscle capacity." Cooke et al[219] go on to state that "Performance (during lumbar dynamometry) was enhanced after therapy primarily because of factors other than increases in muscle strength and range of motion. These factors might be psychological or behavioral in nature."

It is generally reported that conscious attempts to deceive, often labeled malingering, are rare in the isokinetic assessment of trunk function in the back-injured patient. Utilizing high-technology assessment tools for the detection of malingering is inappropriate based on the current literature. In addition, malingering is a legal concept, not a diagnosis. The clinician is not in a position to make such a determination.

The clinician can gain insight into the degree to which pain, apprehension, and severe deconditioning may be contributing individually or in combination to the patient's level of dysfunction by assessing the consistency of test performance during an isokinetic assessment of trunk function. This information can then be utilized in the formation of a treatment plan that is more specifically directed at those areas, physical and behavioral, that are contributing to the presenting dysfunction.

ISOKINETIC ASSESSMENT PROTOCOL DEVELOPMENT

The preceding sections have described several of the issues that have made the acquisition of normative data on the trunk function of normal subjects and patients with back injuries a complex and difficult task. In this section, the critical aspects of designing an isokinetic assessment protocol are explored.

Sapega states,[220] "The degree of attention and care that is necessary to conduct a well controlled test of muscular performance makes seemingly simple testing modalities as complex as some operative procedures. It is deceptively easy to measure something other than what one is actually attempting to measure, and it is surprisingly difficult to measure any parameter of muscular performance in a reproducible fashion. Obtaining valid and reliable results in a non-laboratory setting poses a considerable challenge to clinicians. Physicians must maintain strict quality control and consistent testing procedures if they conduct or supervise their own quantitative, in-house evaluation of muscular performance. When the results of a test that has been conducted at outside therapy facilities, especially multiple tests over time performed by different testers, are evaluated, great caution should be exercised when clinical judgements are based on small (less than 15 per cent) changes in performance. Outside facilities should have fully qualified staff and standardized test protocols that are available for review by physicians on request."

A review of the literature reveals that there are almost as many test protocols used as there are examiners. This makes extrapolation of data from one study to another difficult if not impossible. The end result is that beyond the following three general principles there is little agreement regarding what constitutes "normal" isokinetic trunk function:

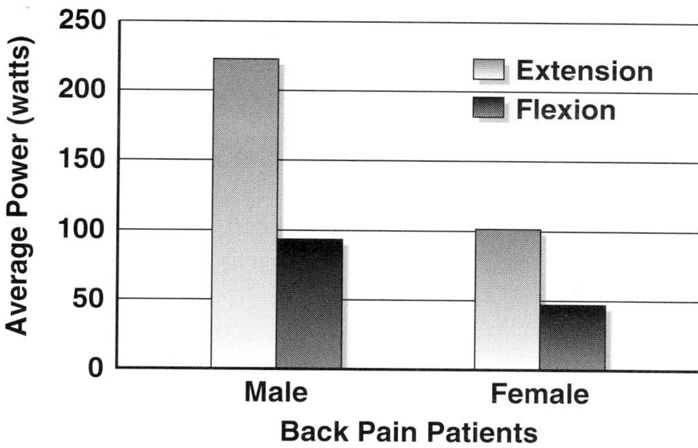

Figure 17–15. Power output in back pain patients.

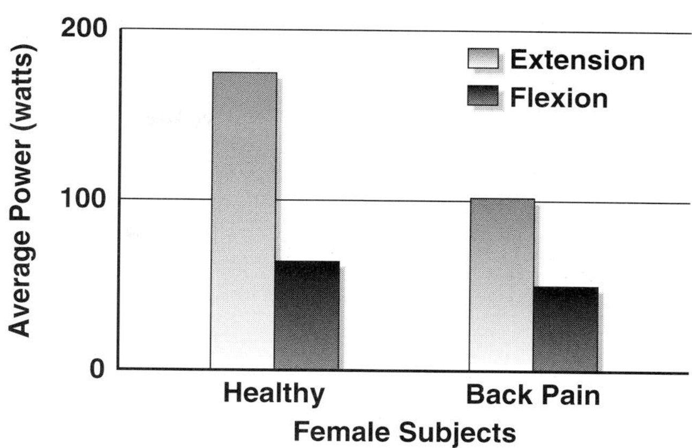

Figure 17–17. Comparison between healthy females and females with back pain

Extensors are stronger than flexors.
Males are stronger than females.
Although mean performance differs between healthy subjects and low back pain patients, standard deviations overlap, limiting the utility of isokinetic trunk testing in identifying the patient with low back pain.

Figure 17–15, from the author's database, demonstrates that for power output at 60 degrees per second in back pain patients, extensors are stronger than flexors in both males and females. In both flexion and extension males are stronger than females. When evaluating power output at 60 degrees per second in both male and female subjects, healthy controls are stronger than back pain patients in both extension and flexion. This is illustrated in Figures 17–16 and 17–17.

Human factors research has identified several issues related to the test environment that have been shown to influence human performance. These are presented in Table 17–2. To the extent possible these factors must be controlled and/or standardized to improve test reliability.[221]

For the clinician utilizing an isokinetic system, the development of an assessment protocol that will produce valid and reliable information is essential. However, what may be desirable in the research laboratory is not necessarily possible in the clinic environment, in which we are dealing with a variety of patients and reimbursement issues. These factors may place constraints on the assessment protocol that can be utilized in the clinic setting. To the extent possible the clinician must develop a protocol that provides an assessment that produces information of the highest possible validity and reliability. To follow are some of the issues to be considered when developing an assessment protocol, or when evaluating the protocol used by a clinic to which patients are referred.

Several studies have found a significant learning effect associated with the performance of isokinetic testing.[222–226] Performance during an initial test can be significantly less

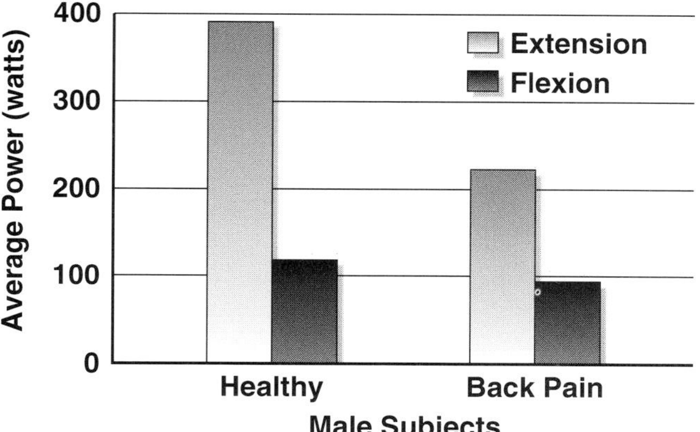

Figure 17–16. Comparison between healthy males and males with back pain.

Table 17–2: Environmental Influences on Test Performance

Man-machine interfaces	Knowledge of test results
Physical conditioning	Absent or negative reinforcement
Verbal or written communications	Pain or discomfort
Previous experience at task	Hunger or thirst
Motor requirements	Temperature, humidity, air quality
Task complexity	Distractions (noise, glare, movement)
Task speed and load	Degree of cleanliness
Consistency of cueing	Motivation and attitude
Knowledge of performance standards	Conflict of motive about performance

than performance on subsequent retests. This learning effect has been shown to be more pronounced in patients than in normal controls.

Most low back patients have never performed an isokinetic trunk test. The patient begins the test with a degree of apprehension about being asked to exert a maximal effort during an unfamiliar test, which the patient perceives may cause an increase in pain. The previously described Acceptable Maximum Effort (AME) model[227] is useful in gradually overcoming this initial apprehension. The number of repetitions and duration of this portion of the test protocol should be standardized as much as possible.

Once an acceptable maximum effort has been obtained, indicating the patient has become comfortable with the test environment, the actual test protocol can begin. It is generally accepted that a test-retest protocol yields results that most closely approximate a patient's maximal performance. In this type of assessment protocol the patient exerts a maximal effort during the standardized test protocol. The test is repeated after a standardized period of time. It has been shown that when the retest is performed on a subsequent day or when several retests are performed over a period of several days, test performance is maximized and variability is minimized. Without a test-retest protocol, isokinetic performance would likely be underestimated if based on the first test session, and subsequent progress evaluations would be likely to overestimate patient progress.

Although possible in the research laboratory, a test-retest protocol spanning 2 or more days is not practical in the clinic setting. Not only does this present unrealistic scheduling requirements, it is doubtful the clinician would receive reimbursement for each retest. Given these constraints, a test-retest protocol must be incorporated in a 1-day test session. By separating the test from the retest by a standardized period of time, a test protocol is created that provides the benefits previously described, while working within the scheduling and reimbursement constraints.

A standardized warm-up protocol serves as a means of preparing the patient for the physical demands of the test.[228] Most warm-up protocols will contain a series of stretches to be performed along with 5 to 10 minutes of submaximal aerobic activity such as stationary bicycling.

Newton et al[229] has found that isokinetic trunk testing during test speeds up to 120 degrees per second provides reliable measures of torque and force. However at speeds greater than 120 degrees per second, there is a lack of evidence indicating that isokinetic devices provide reliable measurements of these parameters. Several test protocols described in the literature utilize test speeds of 240 degrees per second or greater. Inability to generate force at faster speeds of movement has been reported to be a distinguishing feature of low back dysfunction.

Utilizing the concept of velocity spectrum testing, in which the patient is tested at several different speeds, most

Table 17–3: Example of Isokinetic Trunk Flexion-Extension Protocol

Equipment calibration	If the first test of week, calibrate system. If already calibrated, and first test of day, confirm calibration.
Informed consent	At time of the initial evaluation informed consent is obtained from patient. If consent is not given, test is not performed.
Equipment setup	Back attachment is attached and secured per manufacturer's recommendations. Prior to first test of day, or after several hours of down time, attach and secure back attachment, set range of motion to at least 60 degrees and run on passive mode at 60 degrees per second for several minutes to warm up system.
Cushion	Three-quarters of the way to the hardest possible setting.
Test sets, speeds, repetitions	Set 1–6 repetitions at 60 degrees per second Set 2–6 repetitions at 120 degrees per second Set 3–6 repetitions at 60 degrees per second Set 4–18 repetitions at 120 degrees per second
Patient warm-up	3-to-5-minute submaximal aerobic warm-up followed by standardized sequence of stretches.
Axis of rotation	L5/S1
Range of motion	Preset endpoints at 30 and 90 degrees on powerhead scale.
Positioning/stabilization	Knees at 20 to 25 degrees with feet supported by foot rest, both femur and pelvic straps secure, lumbar support to patient comfort, thoracic pad at midscapula, head rest to comfort.
Test instructions	Delivered in an encouraging but neutral tone. Number of repetitions performed is vocalized during test performance.
Report generation	Reports are generated in the windowed mode with curves smoothed. These functions minimize acceleration and deceleration artifacts, resulting in improved reliability.
Parameters evaluated	Work to body weight ratio (WBW), time to peak torque (TPT), power (POW), total work in the last 6 repetitions of the 18-repetition endurance set (END), coefficient of variation (CV), and range of motion (ROM).

Table 17–4: Mean Isokinetic Trunk Flexion-Extension Test Performance for Male Back Pain Patients (n = 590)

		EXTENSION							FLEXION						
		60			120				60			120			
	CV	WBW	TPT	POW	WBW	TPT	POW	END	WBW	TPT	POW	WBW	TPT	POW	END
AVG	**16**	**118**	**.42**	**225**	**65**	**.30**	**205**	**602**	**50**	**.36**	**97**	**36**	**.37**	**112**	**328**
%tile															
90	7	187	.21	342	113	.20	387	1026	70	.17	143	54	.19	207	525
80	8	158	.23	297	98	.22	313	894	63	.19	122	49	.22	168	448
70	10	140	.26	261	86	.24	267	773	59	.22	113	43	.26	146	405
60	11	128	.29	238	74	.25	227	669	54	.25	105	39	.30	131	364
50	13	115	.38	213	65	.27	197	586	51	.29	95	36	.34	112	333
40	14	101	.48	199	53	.29	155	516	46	.33	87	31	.41	92	297
30	17	92	.53	178	42	.32	123	288	42	.38	77	26	.47	77	249
20	20	76	.58	142	30	.36	86	291	36	.51	67	22	.52	57	197
10	26	55	.67	101	15	.52	42	166	28	.73	51	14	.56	32	141

Table 17–5: Mean Isokinetic Trunk Flexion-Extension Test Performance for Female Back Pain Patients (n = 629)

		EXTENSION							FLEXION						
		60			120				60			120			
	CV	WBW	TPT	POW	WBW	TPT	POW	END	WBW	TPT	POW	WBW	TPT	POW	END
AVG	**17**	**68**	**.53**	**100**	**33**	**.41**	**70**	**243**	**33**	**.61**	**47**	**20**	**.52**	**42**	**150**
%tile															
90	8	109	.23	171	63	.22	146	460	48	.21	71	35	.34	80	259
80	10	91	.28	136	50	.25	108	379	43	.28	63	30	.42	65	218
70	12	79	.39	120	40	.29	88	306	39	.34	55	26	.48	54	189
60	13	69	.50	106	34	.32	71	256	36	.43	50	22	.51	45	160
50	15	63	.55	95	27	.38	57	207	33	.53	45	18	.53	36	141
40	17	58	.58	82	23	.48	42	162	29	.72	40	15	.55	29	121
30	19	48	.63	73	18	.52	32	129	26	.84	36	12	.57	22	102
20	22	39	.70	60	12	.56	21	96	23	1.00	32	9	.60	16	78
10	30	32	.75	46	7	.62	11	54	18	1.08	25	6	.68	7	51

Key to Abbreviations in Mean Performance Tables

n =	Number of patients making up sample	END	Endurance, work in last one-third of 18-repetition set (ft·lb)
CV	Mean coefficient of variation from all test sets	60	60 degree per second test speed
WBW	Work to body weight ratio (%)	120	120 degree per second test speed
TPT	Time to peak torque (seconds)	Avg	Overall average performance for all patients
POW	Average power (watts)	%tile	Percentile rank from patient database

test protocols will perform multiple test sets, in a test-retest format, at speeds ranging from 30 to 360 degrees per second. The proposed benefit of using this type of protocol is that it enables the clinician to determine whether a deficit in function exists at a particular angular velocity. If a speed-specific deficit is present, the rehabilitative exercise regimen can be designed to specifically address the deficit in function.

The number of test repetitions utilized, as with several other factors in protocol development, varies greatly in the published literature. It has been shown that the minimum number of test repetitions that will yield reliable data is four. An isokinetic assessment of endurance must utilize a minimum of approximately 20 repetitions.

Patient positioning and stabilization are important considerations in obtaining valid and reliable test results. Each manufacturer will have specific positioning and stabilization recommendations. These must be utilized for each test performed. Any deviations from the manufacturer's recommendations must be shown to produce valid and reliable test results.

Each isokinetic assessment system will have a calibration function incorporated into the data reduction software package. Equipment should be calibrated according to the manufacturer's instructions, at or more frequently than recommended intervals. Ideally, equipment calibration will be confirmed before each test performed.

Standardization of test instructions is an important component of the test protocol that enhances reliability.[230–232] It is natural for the individual administering the test to vocalize enthusiastic encouragement during the performance of the test repetitions. However, this adversely effects test reliability. Prior to test performance a scripted description of the isokinetic system and components of the test should be performed. During test performance standardized instructions should be delivered in a encouraging, yet neutral tone. If the repetitions are counted during test performance, this should be performed using a neutral tone.

Several factors related to the testing environment and room in which an isokinetic test is performed should be controlled.[233] Distractions such as noise, radios, and glare should be eliminated. The testing room should be isolated from movements of staff and other patients as much as possible. Temperature and humidity should be maintained at comfortable levels. The isokinetic system should be kept clean and in good repair.

Table 17–3 summarizes the author's isokinetic trunk flexion-extension assessment protocol, which provides one example of how to control for the many factors which influence test reliability. All test instructions are scripted to ensure standardization. Before any staff member performs an isokinetic assessment with a patient, he or she must observe 10 isokinetic assessments. He or she must then perform 10 isokinetic assessments on fellow staff members. If he or she demonstrates the ability to successfully perform the isokinetic evaluation within the parameters described above, without error, the staff member is scheduled to perform isokinetic evaluations with patients. The first five isokinetic evaluations of patients are performed under the supervision of a fellow staff member. As a component of our quarterly quality assurance program, staff members must demonstrate the ability to perform an isokinetic assessment according to our clinic's protocol. If the staff member is unable to do so, he or she is restricted from performing further isokinetic evaluations until he or she is able to demonstrate competence in the evaluation procedure.

Tables 17–4 and 17–5 contain percentile rankings and mean test performance for female and male patients who have performed the author's isokinetic trunk flexion/extension protocol described above.

CONTRAINDICATIONS TO AND SELECTION CRITERIA FOR ISOKINETIC TESTING

Timm[234] describes four absolute contraindications and one relative contraindication to the performance of an isokinetic trunk test. Cardiovascular disease is the first absolute contraindication. Increases in heart rate, respiration rate, and blood pressure during isokinetic testing have the potential to adversely affect the patient with a cardiovascular disorder. A patient with a blood pressure of 150/195 or higher is to refrain from performance of an isokinetic trunk test according to Timm.

A second absolute contraindication for isokinetic trunk testing is when a patient is in the acute phase of rheumatoid arthritis, during which elevated blood flow and tissue temperature would increase joint inflammation. Cancer, systemic disease, or metastatic lesions that could be further advanced due to increased blood flow present the third absolute contraindication to isokinetic trunk testing. Pregnancy is the fourth absolute contraindication.

The one relative contraindication is professional judgement. An assessment procedure must in some way add to the clinical impression, facilitating the development of a treatment plan. If, in the judgement of the clinician, isokinetic testing will not change the course of treatment, or may potentially aggravate the patient's condition, the test should not be administered. Patients must be made aware of the risks associated with isokinetic through formal informed consent procedures.

Although the contraindications to isokinetic trunk testing are well defined, the selection criteria for performing an isokinetic trunk test are quite general.

Timm[235] describes the following indications for isokinetic testing. Isokinetic testing is appropriate for patients presenting with signs and symptoms of the deconditioning syndrome. Any patient with a spinal disorder accompanied by deficits in muscle strength and endurance is a candidate for isokinetic testing. A final indication for isokinetic trunk testing is a patient whose symptoms are not resolving in a reasonable period of time with appropriate treatment.

USES OF ISOKINETIC MEASUREMENT PARAMETERS

Information obtained from an isokinetic assessment is typically used as both an outcome measure and to assist with treatment planning. Outcomes assessment is defined as a procedure or method of measuring a change in patient status over time, primarily to evaluate the effect of treatment. Isokinetic assessment instruments are often described as being capable of providing objective outcomes data. Outcome measures are typically placed into one of four categories: impairment measures such as pain, range of motion, and strength; disability measures such as work and ADL status; direct and indirect costs associated with the patient's condition; and patient satisfaction with the various administrative and clinical processes involved in receiving care and recovering from his or her condition.

Isokinetic measurement parameters are categorized as impairment measures. Of the four types of outcome measures, impairment measures are the least important. Impairment measures generally, and isokinetic measurement parameters specifically, have not been demonstrated to correlate with a patient's functional abilities and limitations and as a result are of limited value beyond serving as a clinical indicator of progress or lack of progress. Incremental changes in impairment measures over time are of little value unless there is a corresponding significant change in a patient's disability level.

The most important outcome measures are those which report a patient's work and ADL status, and the direct and indirect costs associated with the patient's condition.

In addition to the lack of inferential value regarding a patient's ability to perform occupational activities, isokinetic measurement parameters suffer from an additional shortcoming as an outcome measure, the absence of a definite threshold level of improvement that must be demonstrated to indicate that treatment has been effective. There is a lack of consensus regarding how much improvement in an isokinetic measurement parameter must be documented before one can state that therapy has been effective in improving function.[236] From research on the evaluation of extremity function a bilateral difference of at least 10% is generally felt to indicate a significant, although not necessarily pathological, difference in function.[237] Sapega[238] concludes that a difference of 15% in a particular test parameter must be measured before a judgement is made regarding changes in performance. According to Byl[239(p129)] "The coefficient of variation indicates how much change is necessary before one can claim the change is statistically significant." If the coefficient of variation from an isokinetic trunk test was 10%, a 20% improvement in a strength measurement parameter would have to occur before one could state a significant strength gain had been achieved.

Although serving a limited role as an outcome measure, information obtained from an isokinetic assessment of trunk strength is beneficial in treatment planning. One of the most clinically relevant uses of the various isokinetic measurement parameters is for monitoring patient progress as a result of therapeutic intervention. Patient performance, during an appropriately designed and conducted isokinetic protocol, which is reported in the context of normative data produced by the identical isokinetic system and protocol, can provide insight into the relative abilities and limitations of the patient with respect to trunk flexor and extensor strength and endurance. These findings coupled with traditional examination procedures serve as the foundation for therapeutic exercise prescription. Subsequent isokinetic assessments provide an indication of whether the prescribed treatment program has been beneficial in reducing a patient's level of impairment.

The isokinetic assessment of trunk strength, although useful in a clinical setting, will remain of limited value as an outcome measure unless and until isokinetic measurement parameters can be demonstrated to correlate with a patient's functional status.

SUMMARY

Isokinetic assessment instruments are capable of providing a reliable baseline measurement parameter that may assist in treatment planning and from which patient progress can be documented. Although isokinetic instruments can provide information demonstrating that therapeutic intervention has been effective in reducing impairment, improvement in the isokinetic assessment of trunk function is not, in itself, an important outcome measure.

When referring a patient for an isokinetic assessment, or when considering the acquisition of an isokinetic system, the critical issue is not so much which type of system to use or acquire; rather, it is meticulous attention to the details that will produce reliable data from the assessment. Once reliable data is produced, pick one or two measurement parameters, such as work and/or power, to monitor changes in patient status.

To what extent high-technology assessment instruments enhance outcomes beyond what could be achieved through clinical judgement in conjunction with low-technology assessment instruments remains unclear.

With third-party payors requesting "objective information" as evidence of effectiveness of care, clinicians have increasingly utilized these instruments to facilitate reimbursement; it is perhaps in this use that the high-technology assessment systems have proven to be most beneficial.

What is certain is that cost containment and outcomes will remain important issues in the delivery of health care services, and as a result, the use of high-technology assessment instruments in the management of the patient with a spinal disorder will be the subject of ongoing cost-benefit analysis.

REFERENCES

1. Thistle HG, Hislop HJ, Moffroid M, Lawman EW. Isokinetic contraction: A new concept of resistive exercise. *Arch Phys Med Rehabil*. 1966;48:279–282.
2. Hislop HJ, Perrine JJ. The isokinetic concept of exercise. *Phys Ther*. 1967;47:114–117.
3. Moffroid M, Whipple R, Hofkosh J, Lowman E, Thistle H. A study of isokinetic exercise. *Phys Ther* 1969;49:735–746.
4. Newton M, Waddell G. Trunk strength testing with iso-machines: Part 1: Review of a decade of scientific evidence. *Spine*. 1994;18:801–811.
5. Newton M, Smerville D, Henderson I, Waddell G. Trunk strength testing with iso-machines: Part 2: Experimental evaluation of the Cybex II back testing system in normal subjects and patients with chronic low back pain. *Spine*. 1993;18:812–824.
6. Mayer TG, Gatchel RJ, Kishino N, Keeley J, Capra P, Mayer H, Barnett J, Mooney V. Objective assessment of spine function following industrial injury: A prospective study with comparison group and one year follow up. *Spine*. 1985;10:482–493.
7. Mayer TG, Smith SS, Keeley J, Mooney V. Quantification of lumbar function: Part 2: Sagittal plane trunk strength in chronic low back pain patients. *Spine*. 1985;10:765–772.
8. Mayer TG, Smith SS, Kondraske G, Gatchel RJ, Carmichael TW, Mooney V. Quantification of lumbar function: Part 3: Preliminary data on isokinetic torso rotation testing with myoelectric spectral analysis in normal and low back pain subjects. *Spine*. 1985;10:912–927.
9. Langrana NA, Lee CK, Alexander H, Mayott CW. Quantitative assessment of back strength using isokinetic testing. *Spine*. 1984;9:287–290.
10. Cooke D, Menard MR, Beach GN, Locke SR, Hirsch GH. Serial lumbar dynamometry in low back pain. *Spine*. 1992;17:653–662.
11. Reid S, Hazard RG, Fenwick JW. Isokinetic trunk strength deficits in people with and without low back pain: A comparison study with consideration of effort. *J Spinal Disord*. 1991;4:68–72.
12. Burdorf A, van Riel M, Snijders C. Trunk muscle strength measurements and prediction of low back pain among workers. *Clin Biomech*. 1992;7:55–58.
13. Nicholaisen T, Jorgensen K. Trunk strength, back muscle endurance and low back trouble. *Scand J Rehabil Med*. 1985;17:121–127.
14. Thorstensson A, Arvidson A. Trunk muscle strength and low back pain. *Scand J Rehabil Med*. 1982;13:69–75.
15. Hasue M, Fujiwara M, Kikuchi S. A new method of quantitive measurement of abdominal and back muscle strength. *Spine*. 1980;5:143–148.
16. McNeill T, Watwick D, Andersson G, Schultz A. Trunk strength in attempted flexion, extension, and lateral bending in healthy subjects and patients with low back disorders. *Spine*. 1980;5:529–537.
17. Addison R, Schultz A. Trunk strength in patients seeking hospitalization for chronic low-back disorders. *Spine*. 1980;5:539–544.
18. Berkson M, Schultz A, Nachemson A, Andersson G. Voluntary strength of male adults with acute low back syndromes. *Clin Orthop*. 1977;129:84–95.
19. Nachemson A, Lindh M. Measurement of abdominal and back muscle strength with and without low back pain. *Scand J Rehabil Med*. 1969;1:60–65.
20. Newton M, Waddell G. Trunk strength testing with iso-machines: Part 1: Review of a decade of scientific evidence. *Spine*. 1994,18:801–811.
21. Newton M, Smerville D, Henderson I, Waddell G. Trunk strength testing with iso-machines: Part 2: Experimental evaluation of the Cybex II back testing system in normal subjects and patients with chronic low back pain. *Spine*. 1993;18:812–824.
22. Langrana NA, Lee CK, Alexander H, Mayott CW. Quantitative assessment of back strength using isokinetic testing. *Spine*. 1984;9:287–290.
23. Reid S, Hazard RG, Fenwick JW. Isokinetic trunk strength deficits in people with and without low back pain: A comparison study with consideration of effort. *J Spinal Disord*. 1991;4:68–72.
24. Cooke D, Menard MR, Beach GN, Locke SR, Hirsch GH. Serial lumbar dynamometry in low back pain. *Spine*. 1992;17:653–662.
25. Hirsch G, Beach G, Cooke C, Menard M, Locke S. Relationship between performance on lumbar dynamometry and Waddell score in a population with low back pain. *Spine*. 1991;16:1039–1043.

26. McIntyre DR, Glover LH, Conino MC, Seeds RH, Levene JA. A comparison of the characteristics of referred low back motion of normal subjects and low back pain patients. *J Spinal Disord.* 1991;4:90–95.
27. Thistle HG, Hislop HJ, Moffroid M, Lawman EW. Isokinetic contraction: A new concept of resistive exercise. *Arch Phys Med Rehabil.* 1966;48:279–282.
28. Hislop HJ, Perrine JJ. The isokinetic concept of exercise. *Phys Ther.* 1967;47:114–117.
29. Moffroid M, Whipple R, Hofkosh J, Lowman E, Thistle H. A study of isokinetic exercise. *Phys Ther.* 1969;49:735–746.
30. Kraemer WJ, Fleck SJ, Deschenes M. A review: Factors in exercise prescription of resistance training. *NSCA J.* 1988;10:36–40.
31. Knuttgen HG, Kraemer WJ. Terminology and measurement in exercise performance. *J Appl Spt Sci Res.* 1987;1:1–10.
32. Levene JA, Seeds RH, Goldberg HM, Frazier M, Fuhrman GA. Trends in isodynamic and isometric trunk testing on the Isostation B200. *J Spinal Disord.* 1989;14:838–843.
33. Parnianpour M, Li F, Nordin M, Kahanovitz N. A database of isoinertial trunk strength tests against three resistance levels in sagittal, frontal, and transverse planes in normal male subjects. *Spine.* 1989;14:409–411.
34. Parnianpour M, Nordin M, Kahanovitz N, Frankel V. The triaxial coupling of torque generation of trunk muscles during isometric exertions and the effect of fatiguing isoinertial movements on the motor output and movement patterns. *Spine.* 1988;13:982–992.
35. Davies GJ. *A Compendium of Isokinetics in Clinical Usage and Rehabilitation Techniques.* 4th ed. Onalaska, WI: S & S Publishers, 1992.
36. Hinson MN, Smith WC, Funk S. Isokinetics: A clarification. *Res Q.* 1979;50:30–35.
37. Sapega AA. Muscle performance evaluation in orthopaedic practice. *J Bone Joint Surg.* 1990;72A:1562–1574.
38. Rothstein JM, Lamb RL, Mayhew TP. Clinical uses of isokinetic measurements: Critical issues. *Phys Ther.* 1987;67:1840–1844.
39. Dvir Z. Clinical applicability of isokinetics: A review. *Clin Biomech.* 1991;6:133–144.
40. Davies GJ. *A Compendium of Isokinetics in Clinical Usage and Rehabilitation Techniques.* 4th ed. Onalaska, WI: S & S Publishers, 1992.
41. Dvir Z. Clinical applicability of isokinetics: A review. *Clin Biomech.* 1991;6:133–144.
42. Newton M, Waddell G. Trunk strength testing with iso-machines: Part 1: Review of a decade of scientific evidence. *Spine.* 1994;18:801–811.

43–44. Sapega AA. Muscle performance evaluation in orthopaedic practice. *J Bone Joint Surg.* 1990;72A:1562–1574.

45. Newton M, Smerville D, Henderson I, Waddell G. Trunk strength testing with iso-machines: Part 2: Experimental evaluation of the Cybex II back testing system in normal subjects and patients with chronic low back pain. *Spine.* 1993;18:812–824.
46. Sapega AA. Muscle performance evaluation in orthopaedic practice. *J Bone Joint Surg.* 1990;72A:1562–1574.
47. Allen M, Pothier B. Isokinetic analysis of back injuries. 1992; unpublished manuscript.
48. Mayer TG, Smith SS, Keeley J, Mooney V. Quantification of lumbar function: Part 2: Sagittal plane trunk strength in chronic low back pain patients. *Spine.* 1985;10:765–772.
49. Allen M, Pothier B. Isokinetic analysis of back injuries. 1992; unpublished manuscript.
50. Parnianpour M, Nordin M, Sheikhzadeh A. The relationship of torque, velocity, and power with constant resistive load during sagittal trunk movement. *Spine.* 1990,15:639–643.
51. Davies GJ. *A Compendium of Isokinetics in Clinical Usage and Rehabilitation Techniques.* 4th ed. Onalaska, WI: S & S Publishers, 1992.
52. Sapega AA. Muscle performance evaluation in orthopaedic practice. *J Bone Joint Surg.* 1990;72A:1562–1574.
53. Nobbs LA, Rhodes EC. The effect of electrical stimulation and isokinetic exercise on muscular power of the quadriceps femoris. *J Orthop Sports Phys Ther.* 1986,8:260–268.
54. Mayer TG, Smith SS, Keeley J, Mooney V. Quantification of lumbar function: Part 2: Sagittal plane trunk strength in chronic low back pain patients. *Spine.* 1985;10:765–772.
55. Reid S, Hazard RG, Fenwick JW. Isokinetic trunk strength deficits in people with and without low back pain: A comparison study with consideration of effort. *J Spinal Disord.* 1991;4:68–72.
56. McIntyre DR, Glover LH, Conino MC, Seeds RH, Levene JA. A comparison of the characteristics of referred low back motion of normal subjects and low back pain patients. *J Spinal Disord.* 1991;4:90–95.

57. Hazard RG, Reid S, Fenwick J, Reeves V. Isokinetic trunk and lifting strength measurements: Variability as an indicator of effort. *Spine*. 1988;13:54–57.
58. Hinson MN, Smith WC, Funk S. Isokinetics: A clarification. *Res Q*. 1979;50:30–35.
59. Mayer TG, Smith SS, Keeley J, Mooney V. Quantification of lumbar function: Part 2: Sagittal plane trunk strength in chronic low back pain patients. *Spine*. 1985;10:765–772.
60–61. Davies GJ. *A Compendium of Isokinetics in Clinical Usage and Rehabilitation Techniques*. 4th ed. Onalaska, WI: S & S Publishers, 1992.
62. Nobbe LA, Rhodes EC. The effect of electrical stimulation and isokinetic exercise on muscular power of the quadriceps femoris. *J Orthop Sports Phys Ther*. 1986,8:260–268.
63. Watkins MP, Harris BA, Kozlowske BA. Isokinetic testing in patients with hemiparesis: A pilot study. *Phys Ther*. 1984;64:184–189.
64. Nobbe LA, Rhodes EC. The effect of electrical stimulation and isokinetic exercise on muscular power of the quadriceps femoris. *J Orthop Sports Phys Ther*. 1986;8:260–268.
65. Newton M, Waddell G. Trunk strength testing with iso-machines: Part 1: Review of a decade of scientific evidence. *Spine*. 1994;18:801–811.
66. Newton M, Smerville D, Henderson I, Waddell G. Trunk strength testing with iso-machines: Part 2: Expermental evaluation of the Cybex II back testing system in normal subjects and patients with chronic low back pain. *Spine*. 1993;18:812–824.
67. Delitto A, Crandell CE, Rose SJ. Peak torque to body weight ratios in the trunk: A critical analysis. *Phys Ther*. 1989;69:138–143.
68. Jerome JA, Hunter K, Gordon P, McKay N. A new robust index for measuring isokinetic trunk flexion and extension: Outcome from a regional study. *Spine* 1991;16:804–808.
69. Delitto A, Rose SJ, Crandell CE, Strube MJ. Reliability of isokinetic measurements of trunk muscle performance. *Spine*. 1991;16:800–803.
70. Rothstein JM, Delitto A, Sinacore DR, Rose SJ. Electromyographic, peak torque, and power relationships during isokinetic movement. *Phys Ther*. 1983;63:926–933.
71. Delitto A, Rose SJ, Crandell CE, Strube MJ. Reliability of isokinetic measurements of trunk muscle performance. *Spine*. 1991;16:800–803.
72. Rothstein JM, Delitto A, Sinacore DR, Rose SJ. Electromyographic, peak torque, and power relationships during isokinetic movement. *Phys Ther*. 1983;63:926–933.
73. Hinson MN, Smith WC, Funk S. Isokinetics: A clarification. *Res Q*. 1979;50:30–35.
74. Davies GJ. *A Compendium of Isokinetics in Clinical Usage and Rehabilitation Techniques*. 4th ed. Onalaska, WI: S & S Publishers, 1992.
75–76. Hinson MN, Smith WC, Funk S. Isokinetics: A clarification. *Res Q*. 1979;50:30–35.
77. Dvir Z. Clinical applicability of isokinetics: A review. *Clin Biomech*. 1991;6:133–144.
78. Newton M, Waddell G. Trunk strength testing with iso-machines: Part 1: Review of a decade of scientific evidence. *Spine*. 1994;18:801–811.
79. Newton M, Smerville D, Henderson I, Waddell G. Trunk strength testing with iso-machines: Part 2: Expermental evaluation of the Cybex II back testing system in normal subjects and patients with chronic low back pain. *Spine*. 1993;18:812–824.
80. Mayer TG, Smith SS, Keeley J, Mooney V. Quantification of lumbar function: Part 2: Sagittal plane trunk strength in chronic low back pain patients. *Spine*. 1985;10:765–772.
81. Rothstein JM, Lamb RL, Mayhew TP. Clinical uses of isokinetic measurements: Critical issues. *Phys Ther*. 1987;67:1840–1844.
82. Dvir Z. Clinical applicability of isokinetics: A review. *Clin Biomech*. 1991;6:133–144.
83. Delitto A, Rose SJ, Crandell CE, Strube MJ. Reliability of isokinetic measurements of trunk muscle performance. *Spine*. 1991;16:800–803.
84. Beimbom DS, Morrissey MC. A review of the literature related to trunk muscle performance. *Spine*. 1988;13:655–660.
85. Langrana NA, Lee CK. Isokinetic evaluation of trunk muscles. *Spine*. 1984;9:171–175.
86. Davies GJ. *A Compendium of Isokinetics in Clinical Usage and Rehabilitation Techniques*. 4th ed. Onalaska, WI: S & S Publishers, 1992.
87. Beimbom DS, Morrissey MC. A review of the literature related to trunk muscle performance. *Spine*. 1988;13:655–660.
88. Mayer TG, Smith SS, Kondraske G, Gatchel RJ, Carmichael TW, Mooney V. Quantification of lumbar function: Part 3: Preliminary data on isokinetic torso rotation testing with myoelectric spectral analysis in normal and low back pain subjects. *Spine*. 1985;10:912–927.

89. Beimbom DS, Morrissey MC. A review of the literature related to trunk muscle performance. *Spine*. 1988;1:655–660.
90. Reid JG, Costigan PA. Trunk muscle balance and muscular force. *Spine*. 1987;12:783–786.
91. Newton M, Waddell G. Trunk strength testing with iso-machines: Part 1: Review of a decade of scientific evidence. *Spine*. 1994;18:801–811.
92. Rothstein JM, Lamb RL, Mayhew TP. Clinical uses of isokinetic measurements: Critical issues. *Phys Ther*. 1987;67:1840–1844.
93. Newton M, Waddell G. Trunk strength testing with iso-machines: Part 1: Review of a decade of scientific evidence. *Spine*. 1994;18:801–811.
94. Delitto A, Crandell CE, Rose SJ. Peak torque to body weight ratios in the trunk: A critical analysis. *Phys Ther*. 1989;69:138–143.
95. Newton M, Waddell G. Trunk strength testing with iso-machines: Part 1: Review of a decade of scientific evidence. *Spine*. 1994;18:801–811.
96. Rothstein JM, Lamb RL, Mayhew TP. Clinical uses of isokinetic measurements: Critical issues. *Phys Ther*. 1987;67:1840–1844.
97. Jerome JA, Hunter K, Gordon P, McKay N. A new robust index for measuring isokinetic trunk flexion and extension: Outcome from a regional study. *Spine*. 1991;16:804–808.
98. Delitto A, Rose SJ, Crandell CE, Strube MJ. Reliability of isokinetic measurements of trunk muscle performance. *Spine*. 1991;16:800–803.

99–100. Sapega AA. Muscle performance evaluation in orthopaedic practice. *J Bone Joint Surg*. 1990;72A:1562–1574.

101. Dvir Z. Clinical applicability of isokinetics: A review. *Clin Biomech*. 1991;6:133–144.
102. Newton M, Waddell G. Trunk strength testing with iso-machines: Part 1: Review of a decade of scientific evidence. *Spine*. 1994;18:801–811.
103. Sapega AA. Muscle performance evaluation in orthopaedic practice. *J Bone Joint Surg*. 1990;72A:1562–1574.
104. Dvir Z. Clinical applicability of isokinetics: A review. *Clin Biomech*. 1991;6:133–144.
105. Bemben MG, Grump KJ, Massey BH. Assessment of technical accuracy of the Cybex II isokinetic dynamometer and analog recording system. *J Orthop Sports Phys Ther*. 1988;10:12 –17.
106. Patterson LA, Spivey WE. Validity and reliability of the Lido active isokinetic system. *J Orthop Sports Phys Ther*. 1992;15:32–36.
107. Rothstein JM, Lamb RL, Mayhew TP. Clinical uses of isokinetic measurements: Critical issues. *Phys Ther*. 1987;67:1840–1844.
108. Hinson MN, Smith WC, Funk S. Isokinetics: A clarification. *Res Q*. 1979;50:30–35.
109. Newton M, Waddell G. Trunk strength testing with iso-machines: Part 1: Review of a decade of scientific evidence. *Spine*. 1994;18:801–811.
110. Rothstein JM, Lamb RL, Mayhew TP. Clinical uses of isokinetic measurements: Critical issues. *Phys Ther*. 1987;67:1840–1844.
111. Dvir Z. Clinical applicability of isokinetics: A review. *Clin Biomech*. 1991;6:133–144.
112. Sapega AA. Muscle performance evaluation in orthopaedic practice. *J Bone Joint Surg*. 1990;72A:1562–1574.
113. Dvir Z. Clinical applicability of isokinetics: A review. *Clin Biomech*. 1991;6:133–144.
114. Bemben MG, Grump KJ, Massey BH. Assessment of technical accuracy of the Cybex II isokinetic dynamometer and analog recording system. *J Orthop Sports Phys Ther*. 1988;10:12–17.
115. Patterson LA, Spivey WE. Validity and reliability of the Lido active isokinetic system. *J Orthop Sports Phys Ther*. 1992;15:32–36.
116. Farrell M, Richards JG. Analysis of the reliability and validity of the kinetic communicator exercise device. *Med Sci Sports Exerc*. 1986;18:44–49.
117. Feiring DC, Ellenbecker TS, Derscheid GL. Test-retest reliability of the Biodex isokinetic dynamometer. *J Orthop Sports Phys Ther*. 1990;11:298–300.
118. Grabiner MD, Jeziorowski JJ, Divekar AD. Isokinetic measurements of trunk extension and flexion performance collected with the Biodex clinical data station. *J Orthop Sports Phys Ther*. 11:590–598.
119. Thigpen LD, Blanke D, Lang P. The reliability of two different Cybex isokinetic systems. *J Orthop Sports Phys Ther*. 1990;12:157–162.
120. Byl NN, Sadowsky HS. Intersite reliability of repeated isokinetic measurements: Cybex back systems including trunk rotation, trunk extension-flexion, and lift task. *Isok Ex Sci*. 1993;3:139–147.

121. Byl NN, Wells L, Grady D, Friedlander A, Sadowsky S. Consistency of repeated isokinetic testing: Effect of different examiners, sites, and protocols. *Isok Ex Sci*. 1991;1:122–130.
122. Newton M, Waddell G. Trunk strength testing with iso-machines: Part 1: Review of a decade of scientific evidence. *Spine*. 1994;18:801–811.
123. Sapega AA. Muscle performance evaluation in orthopaedic practice. *J Bone Joint Surg*. 1990;72A:1562–1574.
124. Dvir Z. Clinical applicability of isokinetics: A review. *Clin Biomech*. 1991;6:133–144.
125. Delitto A, Rose SJ, Crandell CE, Strube MJ. Reliability of isokinetic measurements of trunk muscle performance. *Spine*. 1991;16:800–803.
126. Smidt GL, Rogers MW. Factors contributing to the regulation and clinical assessment of muscular strength. *Phys Ther*. 1982,62:1283–1290.
127. Sapega AA. Muscle performance evaluation in orthopaedic practice. *J Bone Joint Surg*. 1990;72A:1562–1574.
128. Dvir Z. Clinical applicability of isokinetics: A review. *Clin Biomech*. 1991;6:133–144.
129. Delitto A, Rose SJ, Crandell CE, Strube MJ. Reliability of isokinetic measurements of trunk muscle performance. *Spine*. 1991;16:800–803.
130. Smidt GL, Rogers MW. Factors contributing to the regulation and clinical assessment of muscular strength. *Phys Ther*. 1982,62:1282–1290.
131. Sapega AA. Muscle performance evaluation in orthopaedic practice. *J Bone Joint Surg*. 1990;72A:1562–1574.
132. Dvir Z. Clinical applicability of isokinetics: A review. *Clin Biomech*. 1991;6:133–144.
133. Delitto A, Rose SJ, Crandell CE, Strube MJ. Reliability of isokinetic measurements of trunk muscle performance. *Spine*. 1991;16:800–803.
134. Smidt GL, Rogers MW. Factors contributing to the regulation and clinical assessment of muscular strength. *Phys Ther*. 1982,62:1283–1290.
135. Delitto A, Rose SJ, Crandell CE, Strube MJ. Reliability of isokinetic measurements of trunk muscle performance. *Spine*. 1991;16:800–803.
136–138. Newton M, Waddell G. Trunk strength testing with iso-machines: Part 1: Review of a decade of scientific evidence. *Spine*. 1994;18:801–811.
139. Sapega AA. Muscle performance evaluation in orthopaedic practice. *J Bone Joint Surg*. 1990;72A:1562–1574.
140. Dvir Z. Clinical applicability of isokinetics: A review. *Clin Biomech*. 1991;6:133–144.
141. Delitto A, Rose SJ, Crandell CE, Strube MJ. Reliability of isokinetic measurements of trunk muscle performance. *Spine*. 1991;16:800–803.
142. Francis K, Hoobler T. Comparison of peak torque values of the knee flexor and extensor muscle groups using the Cybex II and Lido 2.0 isokinetic dynamometers. *J Orthop Sports Phys Ther*. 1987;8:480–483.
143. Thompson MC, Shingleton LG, Kegerreis ST. Comparison of values generated during testing of the knee using the Cybex II plus and Biodex model B-2000 isokinetic dynamometers. *J Orthop Sports Phys Ther*. 1989;11:108–115.
144. Newton M, Waddell G. Trunk strength testing with iso-machines: Part 1: Review of a decade of scientific evidence. *Spine*. 1994;18:801–811.
145. Davies GJ. *A Compendium of Isokinetics in Clinical Usage and Rehabilitation Techniques*. 4th ed. Onalaska, WI: S & S Publishers, 1992.
146. Hinson MN, Smith WC, Funk S. Isokinetics: A clarification. *Res Q*. 1979;50:30–35.
147. Rothstein JM, Lamb RL, Mayhew TP. Clinical uses of isokinetic measurements: Critical issues. *Phys Ther*. 1987;67:1840–1844.
148. Dvir Z. Clinical applicability of isokinetics: A review. *Clin Biomech*. 1991;6:133–144.
149. Herzog W. The relation between the resultant moments at a joint and the moments measured by an isokinetic dynamometer. *J Biomech*. 1988;21:5–12.
150. Sinacore DR, Rothstein JM, Delitto A, Rose SJ. Effect of damp on isokinetic measurements. *Phys Ther*. 1983;1248–1250.
151. Wilk KE, Arrigo CA, Andrews JR. Isokinetic testing of the shoulder abductors and adductors: Windowed versus non-windowed data collection. *J Orthop Sports Phys Ther*. 1992;15:107–112.
152. Winter DA, Wells RP, Orr GW. Errors in the use of isokinetic dynamometers. *Eur J Appl Physiol*. 1981;397–408.
153. Davies GJ. *A Compendium of Isokinetics in Clinical Usage and Rehabilitation Techniques*. 4th ed. Onalaska, WI: S & S Publishers, 1992.

154. Sapega AA. Muscle performance evaluation in orthopaedic practice. *J Bone Joint Surg.* 1990;72A:1562–1574.
155. Hinson MN, Smith WC, Funk S. Isokinetics: A clarification. *Res Q.* 1979;50:30–35.
156. Rothstein JM, Lamb RL, Mayhew TP. Clinical uses of isokinetic measurements: Critical issues. *Phys Ther.* 1987;67:1840–1844.
157. Sinacore DR, Rothstein JM, Delitto A, Rose SJ. Effect of damp on isokinetic measurements. *Phys Ther.* 1983;1248–1250.
158. Rothstein JM, Lamb RL, Mayhew TP. Clinical uses of isokinetic measurements: Critical issues. *Phys Ther.* 1987;67:1840–1844.
159. Sinacore DR, Rothstein JM, Delitto A, Rose SJ. Effect of damp on isokinetic measurements. *Phys Ther.* 1983;1248–1250.
160–162. Wilk KE, Arrigo CA, Andrews JR. Isokinetic testing of the shoulder abductors and adductors: Windowed versus non-windowed data collection. *J Orthop Sports Phys Ther.* 1992;15:107–112.
163. Newton M, Waddell G. Trunk strength testing with iso-machines: Part 1: Review of a decade of scientific evidence. *Spine.* 1994;18:801–811.
164. Sapega AA. Muscle performance evaluation in orthopaedic practice. *J Bone Joint Surg.* 1990;72A:1562–1574.
165. Rothstein JM, Lamb RL, Mayhew TP. Clinical uses of isokinetic measurements: Critical issues. *Phys Ther.* 1987;67:1840–1844.
166. Dvir Z. Clinical applicability of isokinetics: A review. *Clin Biomech.* 1991;6:133–144.
167. Delitto A, Rose SJ, Crandell CE, Strube MJ. Reliability of isokinetic measurements of trunk muscle performance. *Spine.* 1991;16:800–803.
168. Byl NN, Sadowsky HS. Intersite reliability of repeated isokinetic measurements: Cybex back systems including trunk rotation, trunk extension-flexion, and lift task. *Isok Ex Sci.* 1993,3:139–147.
169. Byl NN, Wells L, Grady D, Friedlander A, Sadowsky S. Consistency of repeated isokinetic testing: Effect of different examiners, sites, and protocols. *Isok Ex Sci.* 1991;1:122–130.
170. Barr AE, Duncan PW. Influence of position on knee flexor peak torque. *J Orthop Sports Phys Ther.* 1988;9:279–283.
171. Davies GJ, Gould JA. Trunk testing using a prototype Cybex II isokinetic dynamometer stabilization system. *J Orthop Sports Phys Ther.* 1982;3:164–170.
172. Figoni SF, Christ CB, Massey BH. Effects of speed, hip and knee angle, and gravity on hamstring to quadriceps torque ratios. *J Orthop Sports Phys Ther.* 1988;9:287–291.
173. Graves JE, Fix CK, Pollock MML, Leggett SH, Foster DN, Carpenter DM. Comparison of two restraint systems for pelvic stabilization during isometric lumbar extension strength testing. *J Orthop Sports Phys Ther.* 1992;15:37–42.
174. Hanten WP, Ramberg CL. Effect of stabilization on maximal isokinetic torque of the quadriceps femoris muscle during concentric and eccentric contractions. *Phys Ther.* 1988;8:219–222.
175. Hart DL, Stobbe TJ, Till CW, Plummer RW. Effect of trunk stabilization on quadriceps femoris muscle torque. *Phys Ther.* 1984;64:1375–1380.
176. Stokes IAF. Axis of dynamic measurement of flexion and extension torques about the lumbar spine: A computer simulation. *Phys Ther.* 1987;67:1230–1233.
177. Stokes IAF, Gookin DM, Reid S, Hazard RG. Effects of axis placement on measurement of isokinetic flexion and extension torque in the lumbar spine. *J Spinal Disord.* 1990;3:114–118.
178. Thompson NN, Gould JA, Davies FJ, Ross DE, Price S. Descriptive measures of isokinetic trunk testing. *J Orthop Sports Phys Ther.* 1985;7:43–49.
179. Timm KE. Effect of different kinetic chain states on the isokinetic performance of the lumbar muscles. *Isok Ex Sci.* 1991;1:153–160.
180. Worrell TW, Denegar CR, Armstrong SL, Perrin DH. Effect of body position on hamstring muscle group average torque. *J Orthop Sports Phys Ther.* 1990;11:449–452.
181. Langrana NA, Lee CK. Isokinetic evaluation of trunk muscles. *Spine.* 1984;9:171–175.
182. Timm KE. Effect of different kinetic chain states on the isokinetic performance of the lumbar muscles. *Isok Ex Sci.* 1991;1:153–160.
183. Newton M, Waddell G. Trunk strength testing with iso-machines: Part 1: Review of a decade of scientific evidence. *Spine.* 1994;18:801–811.
184. Sapega AA. Muscle performance evaluation in orthopaedic practice. *J Bone Joint Surg.* 1990;72A:1562–1574.
185. Rothstein JM, Lamb RL, Mayhew TP. Clinical uses of isokinetic measurements: Critical issues. *Phys Ther.* 1987;67:1840–1844.

186. Dvir Z. Clinical applicability of isokinetics: A review. *Clin Biomech.* 1991;6:133–144.
187. Grabiner MD, Jeziorowski JJ, Divekar AD. Isokinetic measurements of trunk extension and flexion performance collected with the Biodex clinical data station. *J Orthop Sports Phys Ther.* 1990;11:590–598.
188. Herzog W. The relation between the resultant moments at a joint and the moments measured by an isokinetic dynamometer. *J Biomech.* 1988;21:5–12.
189. Stokes IAF. Axis of dynamic measurement of flexion and extension torques about the lumbar spine: A computer simulation. *Phys Ther.* 1987;67:1230–1233.
190. Stokes IAF, Gookin DM, Reid S, Hazard RG. Effects of axis placement on measurement of isokinetic flexion and extension torque in the lumbar spine. *J Spinal Disord.* 1990;3:114–118.
191. Stokes IAF. Axis of dynamic measurement of flexion and extension torques about the lumbar spine: A computer simulation. *Phys Ther.* 1987;67:1230–1233.
192. Grabiner MD, Jeziorowski JJ, Divekar AD. Isokinetic measurements of trunk extension and flexion performance collected with the Biodex clinical data station. *J Orthop Sports Phys Ther.* 1990;11: 590–598.
193. Smidt GL, Rogers MW. Factors contributing to the regulation and clinical assessment of muscular strength. *Phys Ther.* 1982;62:1283–1290.
194. Herzog W. The relation between the resultant moments at a joint and the moments measured by an isokinetic dynamometer. *J Biomech.* 1988;21:5–12.
195. Siewert MW, Ariki PK, Davies GJ, Rowinske MJ. Isokinetic torque changes based upon lever arm pad placement. *Phys Ther.* 1985;65:715.
196. Dvir Z. Clinical applicability of isokinetics: A review. *Clin Biomech.* 1991;6:133–144.
197. Barr AE, Duncan PW. Influence of position on knee flexor peak torque. *J Orthop Sports Phys Ther.* 1988;9:279–283.
198. Figoni SF, Christ CB, Massey BH. Effects of speed, hip and knee angle, and gravity on hamstring to quadriceps torque ratios. *J Orthop Sports Phys Ther.* 1988;9:287–291.
199. Worrell TW, Denegar CR, Armstrong SL, Perrin DH. Effect of body position on hamstring muscle group average torque. *J Orthop Sports Phys Ther.* 1990;11:449–452.
200. Fillyaw M, Bevins T, Fernandez L. Importance of correcting isokinetic peak torque for the effect of gravity when calculating knee flexor to extensor muscle ratios. *Phys Ther.* 1986;66:23–29.
201. Nelson SG, Duncan PW. Correction of isokinetic and isometric torque recordings for the effects of gravity: A clinical report. *Phys Ther.* 1983;63:674–676.
202. Sapega AA. Muscle performance evaluation in orthopaedic practice. *J Bone Joint Surg.* 1990;72A:1562–1574.
203–204. Newton M, Waddell G. Trunk strength testing with iso-machines: Part 1: Review of a decade of scientific evidence. *Spine.* 1994;18:801–811.
205. Bohannon RW. Differentiation of maximal from submaximal static elbow flexor efforts by measurement variability. *Am J Phys Med Rehabil.* 1987;66:213–217.
206. Assessing maximum effort in upper-extremity functional testing. *Work.* 1991;1:65–76.
207. Niebuhr BR, Marion R. Detecting sincerity of effort when measuring grip strength. *Am J Phys Med.* 1987;66:16–24.
208. Smith GA, Nelson RC, Sadoff SI, Sadoff AM. Assessing sincerity of effort in maximal grip strength tests. *Am J Phys Med Rehabil.* 1989;68:73–80.
209. Matheson LN, Bohr PC, Hart DL. Use of maximum voluntary effort grip strength testing to identify symptom magnification syndrome in persons with low back pain. *J Back Musculoskel Rehabil.* 1998;10:125–135.
210. Reid S, Hazard RG, Fenwick JW. Isokinetic trunk strength deficits in people with and without low back pain: A comparison study with consideration of effort. *J Spinal Disord.* 1991;4:68–72.
211. Hazard RG, Reid S, Fenwick J, Reeves V. Isokinetic trunk and lifting strength measurements: Variability as an indicator of effort. *Spine.* 1988;13:54–57.
212. Giles B, Henke P, Edmonds J, McNeil D. Reproducibility of isokinetic muscle strength measurements in normal and arthritic individuals. *Scand J Rehabil Med.* 1990;22:93–99.
213–214. Reid S, Hazard RG, Fenwick JW. Isokinetic trunk strength deficits in people with and without low back pain: A comparison study with consideration of effort. *J Spinal Disord.* 1991;4:68–72.
215. McIntyre DR, Glover LH, Conino MC, Seeds RH, Levene JA. A comparison of the characteristics of preferred low back motion of normal subjects and low back pain patients. *J Spinal Disord.* 1991;4:90–95.
216. Hazard RG, Reid S, Fenwick J, Reeves V. Isokinetic trunk and lifting strength measurements: Variability as an indicator of effort. *Spine.* 1988;13:54–57.

217. Khalil TM, Goldberg ML, Asfour SS, Moty EA, Rosomoff RS, Rosomoff HL. Acceptable maximum effort (AME): A psychophysical measure of strength in back pain patients. *Spine*. 1987;12:372–376.

218–219. Cooke D, Menard MR, Beach GN, Locke SR, Hirsch GH. Serial lumbar dynamometry in low back pain. *Spine*. 1992;17:653–662.

220. Sapega AA. Muscle performance evaluation in orthopaedic practice. *J Bone Joint Surg*. 1990;72A:1562–1574.

221. Swain AD. *Sandia Human Factors Program for Weapon Development*. SAND76-0326. Albuquerque, NM: Sandia Laboratories.

222. Newton M, Waddell G. Trunk strength testing with iso-machines: Part 1: Review of a decade of scientific evidence. *Spine*. 1994;18:801–811.

223. Newton M, Smerville D, Henderson I, Waddell G. Trunk strength testing with iso-machines: Part 2: Expermental evaluation of the Cybex II back testing system in normal subjects and patients with chronic low back pain. *Spine*. 1993;18:812–824.

224. Cooke D, Menard MR, Beach GN, Locke SR, Hirsch GH. Serial lumbar dynamometry in low back pain. *Spine*. 1992;17:653–662.

225. Davies GJ. *A Compendium of Isokinetics in Clinical Usage and Rehabilitation Techniques*. 4th ed. Onalaska, WI: S & S Publishers, 1992.

226. Sapega AA. Muscle performance evaluation in orthopaedic practice. *J Bone Joint Surg*. 1990;72A:1562–1574.

227. Khalil TM, Goldberg ML, Asfour SS, Moty EA, Rosomoff RS, Rosomoff HL. Acceptable maximum effort (AME): A psychophysical measure of strength in back pain patients. *Spine*. 1987;12:372–376.

228. Davies GJ. *A Compendium of Isokinetics in Clinical Usage and Rehabilitation Techniques*. 4th ed. Onalaska, WI: S & S Publishers, 1992.

229–230. Newton M, Waddell G. Trunk strength testing with iso-machines: Part 1: Review of a decade of scientific evidence. *Spine*. 1994;18:801–811.

231. Newton M, Smerville D, Henderson I, Waddell G. Trunk strength testing with iso-machines: Part 2: Expermental evaluation of the Cybex II back testing system in normal subjects and patients with chronic low back pain. *Spine*. 1993;18:812–824.

232. Davies GJ. *A Compendium of Isokinetics in Clinical Usage and Rehabilitation Techniques*. 4th ed. Onalaska, WI: S & S Publishers, 1992.

233. Swain AD. *Sandia Human Factors Program for Weapon Development*. SAND76-0326. Albuquerque, NM: Sandia Laboratories.

234–235. Davies GJ. *A Compendium of Isokinetics in Clinical Usage and Rehabilitation Techniques*. 4th ed. Onalaska, WI: S & S Publishers, 1992.

236. Delitto A, Rose SJ, Crandell CE, Strube MJ. Reliability of isokinetic measurements of trunk muscle performance. *Spine*. 1991;16:800–803.

237–238. Sapega AA. Muscle performance evaluation in orthopaedic practice. *J Bone Joint Surg*. 1990;72A:1562–1574.

239. Byl NN, Sadowsky HS. Intersite reliability of repeated isokinetic measurements: Cybex back systems including trunk rotation, trunk extension-flexion, and lift task. *Isok Ex Sci*. 1993,3:139–147.

SECTION

IV

Principles of Manual Treatment Methods in the Rehabilitation of Spinal Dysfunction

---

There is but one temple in the world and that is the body of man. Nothing is holier than this high form. We touch heaven when we lay our hand on a human body.

—*Novalis (Baron Friedrich von Hardenberg)*

It is the human touch after all that counts for most in our relation with our patients.

—*Robert Tuttle Morris*

CHAPTER 18

The Integration of Spinal Manual Adjustive Therapies with Exercise

Thomas F. Bergmann, DC, FICC

INTRODUCTION

Chiropractic health care focuses primarily on the evaluation and treatment of neuromusculoskeletal disorders. However, the multiple potential etiologies of ill health and the complex nature of health maintenance are not disregarded. Before any therapy can be employed, physicians must first ascertain whether there is a clinical basis for their specific form of treatment. The chiropractic physician considering manual or adjustive therapies must establish whether conditions exist that support this form of treatment or the need for other forms of treatment. Painful conditions affecting the locomotor system are very common disorders and are usually considered to originate from the joints and/or contiguous soft tissue structures. The question of whether the painful condition is due to impaired function of the particular joint or due to ischemic, metabolic, degenerative, or inflammatory changes is not of great importance, since all of these processes are generally considered part of a local disturbance.[1]

A working background knowledge of the causes of joint pain and dysfunction, as well as the clinical patterns, should allow the practitioner to develop a logical and confident approach to the treatment of the individual patient. However, treatment patterns tend to vary based on the training and philosophy of the practitioner, rather than being based on the specific clinical picture displayed by the patient. In this process the practitioner forces the patient to fit his or her treatment plan rather than designing treatment to address the specific needs of the patient (see Table 18–1).

Manual therapy has been proposed as a treatment for a wide variety of conditions, but it is most commonly associated with disorders that have their origins in pathomechanic or pathophysiologic alterations of the locomotor system and its synovial joints. The identification of the common functional components of the dysfunctional joint lesion is critical to the management of conditions affecting the neuromusculoskeletal system. This has, however, contributed to the misconception that all manipulative disorders have the same pathologic basis. Although many disorders that are apparently treated effectively with chiropractic manipulative procedures display joint and somatic functional alterations, there is a myriad of pathologic processes capable of inducing dysfunction of the locomotor system. When joint dysfunction is perceived as the sole cause of the disorder being considered for treatment, adjustive therapy may stand alone. However, when dysfunction is secondary to other disorders, then therapy directed to treat the source of the problem should be provided or made available to the patient.

It has long been a basic premise of chiropractic that a relationship exists between dysfunction of the nervous system and disease. It is also a fundamental historical premise that some aberration within the spinal column is capable of producing the neurologic dysfunction. To bring about this disturbance, a force of some kind must be applied to the vertebra or supporting structures. If the force is significant

Table 18–1: The Tie Between Evaluation and Treatment.

MY TREATMENT IS:	THEREFORE, 90% OF MY PATIENTS HAVE:
1. Disc surgery	1. Disc disease
2. Exercise	2. Weakness, stiffness
3. Muscle relaxants	3. Muscle spasm
4. Pain medication	4. Pain
5. NSAIDs	5. Inflammation
6. Manipulation	6. Fixations and subluxations

or allowed to continue over a period of time, the expected effect on the vertebral motion segment will be joint dysfunction. One of the proposals for a better understanding of locomotor dysfunction is an attempt to view joint pain not as a strictly local problem, but as a disorder which involves the locomotor system in general, thereby including both the osteoarticular and nervous components.[1]

It is for these reasons that a chapter on manipulative therapy is included in this work. The goal of manipulative therapy includes restoration of joint position and function to promote normal neurologic activity, allowing for the potential physiologic response of a homeostatic balance involving the osseous and soft tissues. When dysfunctional processes occur either directly through trauma or indirectly though repetitive or sustained stresses, the need for joint assessment procedures leading to the application of manipulative therapy is deemed appropriate. It must be understood that there are many forms of manual therapy and although the goals of treatment are similar, the applications and means of achieving the goals can be quite different. Historically, the most widely used form of manipulative therapy involves a high-velocity, low-amplitude (HVLA) thrust that causes a joint to go beyond its passive range of motion, entering its paraphysiologic range but without breeching the joint's limit of anatomic integrity. The focus here will be on the assessment for and application of the HVLA.

JOINT ASSESSMENT

The most specialized and significant therapy employed by the doctor of chiropractic involves the adjustment of the articulations of the human body. The use of manipulative therapy emphasizes the restoration of free movement between articular surfaces as well as affecting the contiguous soft tissues. Therefore, joint evaluation becomes the focal point of the patient examination. The chiropractic spinal examination is one major element that sets chiropractic apart from other health care professions. It is absolutely essential to have knowledge of anatomy, physiology, biomechanics, and kinesiology of the spine and extremities. The role of the chiropractic spinal examination is to detect and monitor joint dysfunction by noninvasive procedures. There is, however, no consensus at this time on the most valid, objective, and efficient means of detecting joint dysfunction. Knowing how complex the human body is, specifically the neuromusculoskeletal system, it is essential to employ a system that combines clinical indicators to decide on those joints in greatest need of intervention. Clinical experience suggests that doctors frequently employ an informal system of combining clinical indicators to make this decision.[2] Structural evaluation of the neuromusculoskeletal system should then be viewed in terms of a multidimensional index of segmental abnormality.[2,3]

The methods used in the joint assessment process are the same as utilized in other aspects of evaluation, that is, observation, palpation, percussion, and auscultation. However, palpatory procedures are emphasized significantly. Using the acronym PARTS, the five diagnostic criteria for spinal dysfunction are identified[4]:

P: *Pain/tenderness*. The perception of pain and tenderness may be evaluated in terms of location, quality, and intensity. The patient's description and location of pain is obtained through the history and a more precise localization and assessment of intensity of any tenderness is identified through palpation of osseous and soft tissue structures. Initial ratings and changes in pain intensity can be evaluated using visual analog scales, algometers, pain questionnaires, etc.

A: *Asymmetry/Alignment*. Asymmetrical qualities on a sectional (e.g., decreased cervical curve, lateral curve in the thoracic spine) or segmental level (relationship of one vertebra to another) are noted. This would include observation of posture and gait as well as palpation for misalignment of joint structures. Static x-ray evaluation may also be used to evaluate segmental or sectional asymmetry.

R: *Range of motion*. Changes in active, passive, and accessory joint motions are noted. These changes may be an increase or a decrease in mobility, though typically a decrease in motion is associated with the need for thrusting forms of manipulative therapy. Abnormalities of motion can be identified through motion palpation procedures, the use of range of motion measurement devices, and the use of functional x-rays.

T: *Tissue tone, texture, temperature*. Changes in the characteristics of contiguous and associated soft tissues including skin, fascia, muscles, and ligaments are noted. These changes are identified through observation, palpation, instrumentation, and tests for length and strength.

S: *Special tests*. Those testing procedures that are specific to a technique system are performed. Additionally, visceral relationships are considered as well as other testing procedures deemed necessary from data previously obtained.

The evaluation procedure must be an ongoing process. No matter how thorough the initial examination is, it cannot be expected to provide all of the answers. A treatment trial should be instituted with its effects assessed to determine whether it should be continued or a different plan devised. The detection of joint dysfunction is not an exact science, and any of the examination procedures used to detect joint dysfunction may produce false positives, false negatives, and equivocal results. Furthermore, few examination procedures used in the detection of joint dysfunction have been subjected to sufficient validity testing. None the less, chiropractic care and, in particular, the use of spinal manipulative therapy are growing in popularity and acceptance despite the inconsistencies that prevail in clinical practice and the lack of validation.

CLINICAL APPLICATION

Although over half of the body's mass comes from the musculoskeletal system, it remains the most clinically overlooked system in the body. However, the mechanical principles that determine what functions the body is able to perform are the same regardless of the activity, be it athletic, recreational, occupational, or daily living tasks.

Biomechanics is the application of mechanical laws to living structures, specifically to the locomotor system of the human body. Clinical biomechanics involves the study of the interrelationship between the bones, muscles, and joints. In mechanics, a lever is used to its advantage when a force moves it about a pivot point or fulcrum against a resistance. In the body, muscles provide the forces to move the bony levers around the joint, which forms a pivotal hinge. The efficiency of this musculoskeletal mechanical unit is dependent on the integrity of the joint and the surrounding soft tissues. Knowledge and understanding of how the joint movement, muscular action, and osseous lever systems work together to produce the composite activity in the joints of the spine and extremities are necessary to identify abnormalities and to apply corrective manipulative therapy.

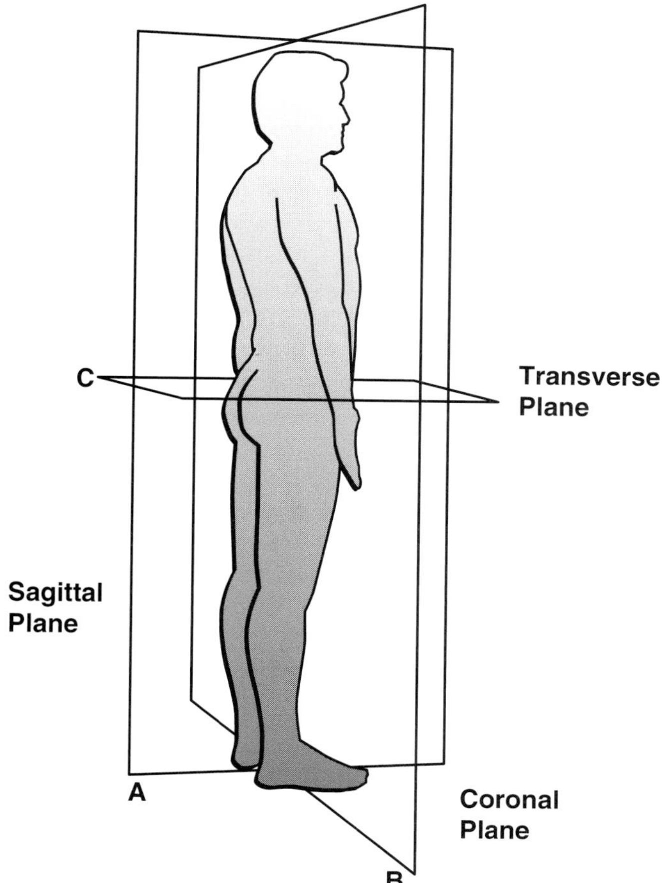

Figure 18–1. Specific body planes of reference: **(A)** midsagittal plane; **(B)** coronal plane; **(C)** transverse plane.

Among its many functions, the spine bears the important role of housing and protecting the spinal cord. In so doing, it must allow for the transmission of neural impulses to and from the periphery. Furthermore, the spine is the mechanism for maintaining erect posture while providing enough flexibility to permit movement within the body's three planes (Figure 18–1): the sagittal plane (flexion/extension movement), the transverse plane (axial rotation movement), and the coronal plane (lateral flexion movement) (Figure 18–2). The spinal motion segment, or functional unit, is the smallest component capable of performing the characteristic roles of the spine. It is composed of two vertebra and the contiguous soft tissues (Figure 18–3).

Understanding the overall function of the human spine has proved to be difficult and frustrating. It is important, however, to view the spine as an integrated unit that is capable of functioning as a single unit but also as a component of the locomotor system. There is a potential for clinical failure if consideration is not given to the whole being. An attempt to understand and correlate the pathomechanics of the spine with the clinical presentation is essential in developing rational and effective treatment.

Movement of the body's articulations occurs in three planes (Figure 18–1). The types of movement a joint can perform consist either of movement around an axis (rotation), motion along an axis, through a plane (translation), or a combination of the two. The rotational movements in the sagittal plane are flexion and extension, whereas translational movements in the sagittal plane consist of anterior to posterior and posterior to anterior glide. Rotational movement in the transverse plane is axial rotation, and translation movements in the transverse plane consist of axial compression and distraction. Rotational movements in the coronal plane are lateral flexion movements, and translational movements in the coronal plane consist of lateral glide (Figure 18–2).

A traditional cause of joint dysfunction has been explained in terms of structural changes. However, joint dysfunction can also occur through the phenomenon of movement restriction. The process may therefore be primarily related to muscle, the organ of active movement, rather than the joint, the structure associated with passive mobility. The role of shortened muscles in movement restriction has been described by Janda[1] with muscle relaxation techniques being used to purportedly mobilize the joints.

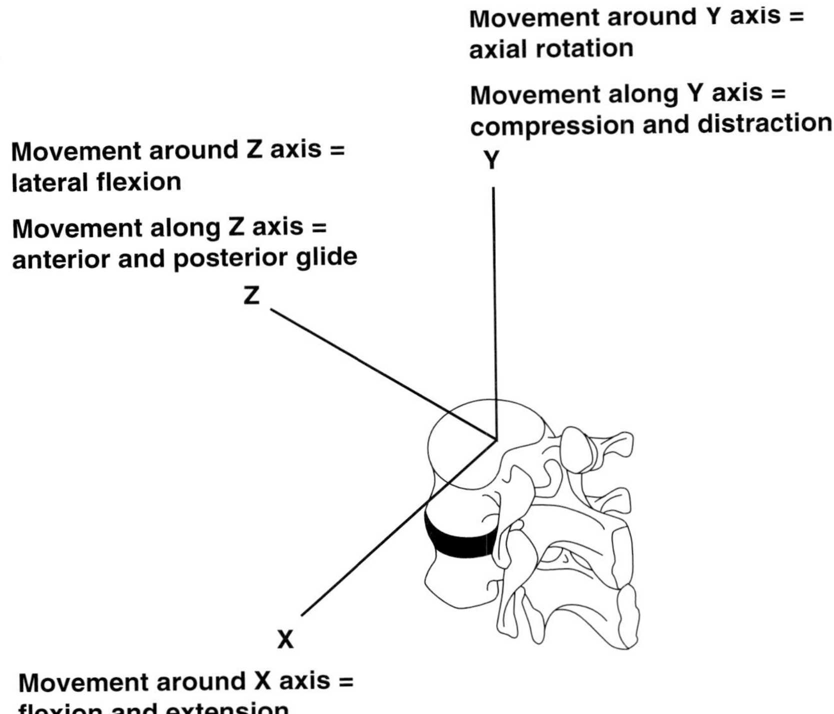

Figure 18–2. The three-dimensional coordinate system that delineates possible movements around (rotation) and/or along (translation) specific axes.

Articular dysfunction is identified by examining the joint for loss of normal mobility and range of motion, not only in its planes of voluntary motion, but also for the accessory movements of joint play and/or end feel. These accessory movements are not obtainable by voluntary muscular action.[5,5a] The need for joint manipulation is established by skilled examination of the joint specifically for loss of mobility in all of its planes of motion.

Manual therapy, with its emphasis on joint movement, has become increasingly important for the treatment of pain and dysfunction of the musculoskeletal system. The rationale used to explain the success of manual therapy has changed radically in recent years. Twomey[6] states that early explanations, which included concepts such as adjusting joint subluxations, restoring bony alignment, and reducing nuclear protrusion, have been shown to have no basis in

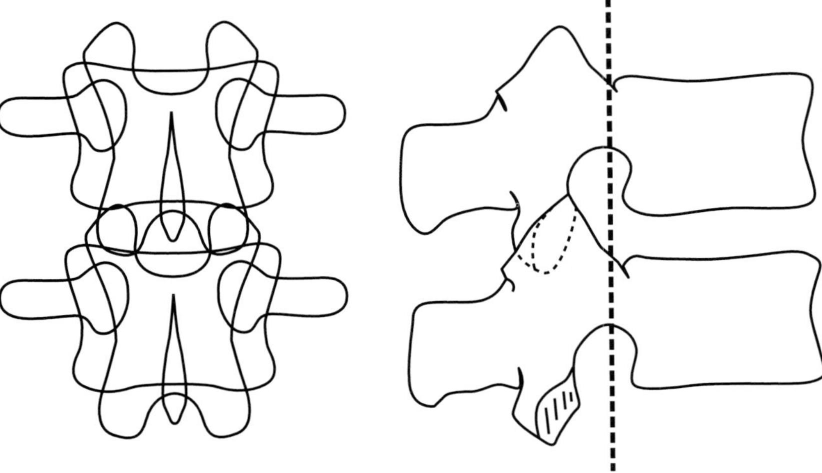

Figure 18–3. A spinal motion segment or functional unit composed of two vertebra and their contiguous soft tissues and forming a three-joint complex.

fact. Current biological research shows the value of movement in maintaining the health and strength of collagenous, muscular, and bony tissues and emphasizes the need for joint movement and for relatively high levels of activity throughout the life cycle. The musculoskeletal system thrives on stress and movement and reacts adversely to prolonged rest or immobilization.[6]

Sandoz[7,7a] defines the chiropractic adjustment as a passive manual maneuver during which the three-joint complex is suddenly carried beyond the normal physiologic range of movement without exceeding the boundaries of anatomic integrity. Various forms of manipulation exist affecting different aspects of joint function. The therapeutic emphasis is not on forcing a particular anatomic movement of a joint, but on restoring normal joint mechanics.

Manual therapy is applied in many forms, including massage, mobilization, muscle energy techniques, adjustment, and manipulation. The common characteristic in all of these methods is the application of external forces to the body to affect the flexibility and pain-free function of the spine and its contiguous tissues.[8] Moreover, all of these methods can act reflexively; that is, they act on sensory receptors—usually in the region where the pain is felt or where it originates—to produce a reflex response.[9(p1)] Pain warns us mainly against harmful functioning, and it is disturbance of function that is the most common cause of pain originating in the locomotor system.[10] Movement restriction at the segmental level and disturbed motor patterns at the central level may serve as examples.[10] The form of therapy used must vary according to the structures upon which it is to act. The optimal treatment for joint or spinal segment movement restriction is manipulation; the optimal treatment for disturbed motor patterns is remedial exercise.[9(p3)]

It is the great weakness of manipulative therapy, remedial exercise, etc.—methods concerned with improving the functioning of the motor system—that they have been, and for the most part still are, mainly concerned with therapy and far too little with clinical diagnosis of the conditions they are supposed to remedy.[9(p13)] It is generally difficult to determine whether any improvement in a patient's condition is due to the treatment offered,[10] especially if a specific diagnosis has not been established.

There are many controversies in the application of manipulative therapy. Of significance is the role of pain in deciding on the appropriateness of manipulation. Mitchell[11] states that if one treats the part where the patient experiences the pain, one will be treating the wrong part of the body most of the time. He goes on to quote Osler with "Pain is a liar." Mitchell bases this idea on the concept that in the musculoskeletal system, pain almost always develops and persists in the structures that are stressed the most by the adaptation to the dysfunction.

The opposite idea is extolled by Lewit, who states that if manipulative treatment is successful it will usually produce immediate relief of pain.[9(p11)] He adds that by far the most frequent cause of pain is disturbed function. This may involve passive joint mobility or active movement patterns. Manipulative treatment is directed to movement restriction of joints or motion segments of the spinal column. Pain in the locomotor system is, therefore, looked upon as a warning sign of harmful functioning that should be corrected in time before it causes permanent damage. Lewit also emphasizes that undiagnosed impairment of motor function is the most frequent cause of pain without a specific diagnosis, and treatment of the pain itself, without a thorough understanding of the functioning of the locomotor system, is courting failure.[9(p43)]

The main task of remedial exercise in disturbed function of the locomotor system is to correct faulty movement patterns (stereotypes) that are relevant to the patient's complaints. The most important pathogenic mechanism, to be treated first, is motor imbalance between muscle groups, manifested by faulty movement or posture.[9(p256)] Manipulative treatment is directed to movement restriction of joints or motion segments of the spinal column. The most important cause of the restriction is strain due to faulty movement patterns, trauma, or visceral disease. It is frequently found even in early childhood. Changes of mechanical function alone do not tend to cause clinical symptoms (pain). They constitute, however, the nociceptive stimulus that produces reflex changes in the segment (muscle spasm, hyperalgesic zones, etc.). If these are of sufficient intensity to pass the pain threshold, pain is felt. The most likely nociceptive stimulus is increased tension to the tissues in which they lie. Therefore, pain in the locomotor system is a warning sign of harmful functioning, which should be corrected in time before it causes permanent damage. It is probably the most frequent type of pain throughout the organism.[9(p43)]

Most thrusting forms of manipulative therapy will result in movement of joint surfaces either directly or indirectly. The purpose of these procedures is to restore normal articular relationship and function, restore neurologic integrity, and influence physiologic processes.

To apply an adjustive thrust, the specific characteristics of the dysfunctional joint must be known. The nature and extent of individual joint motion is determined by the joint structure and specifically by the shape and direction of the joint surfaces. No two opposing joint surfaces are perfectly matched, nor are they perfectly geometric. Because of the incongruence between joint surfaces, some joint space and "play" must be present to allow free movement and normal functioning of the joint.[12(p25–32)]

The joint demonstrates its characteristic joint play movements in the neutral or close-packed position, which is then followed by an active range of motion under the control of the musculature. A small degree of passive movement then occurs, followed by an elastic barrier of resistance called *end feel* or *end play*. A loss of either joint play or end feel can result in a restriction of motion, pain, or both. Active movements may be influenced by exercise, passive movement by traction and mobilization; but joint play and end feel movements are affected only when the joint is taken beyond the elastic barrier, creating a sudden yielding of the joint as it enters the paraphysiological space. This sudden separation of a joint, which produces the cracking sound, is termed *cavitation*. Movement of the joint beyond the paraphysiologic space would take the joint beyond its limit of anatomic integrity, causing joint trauma or pathology (Figure 18–4).

When joint dysfunction occurs, particularly in a vertebral motion segment, reflex changes may also occur in the same spinal segment. The effects may be evident in dermatomes, myotomes, and sclerotomes. The term *segmental facilitation* has been used to describe this phenomenon.[13] The restriction in movement of the joint may be caused by muscular tension or spasm. Indeed, the same contractile forces can either produce or oppose joint motion. However, although muscles have a strong and direct influence on functional movement of a joint, there are three joints that are not directly moved or opposed by muscles. These are the sacroiliac, the acromioclavicular, and the tibiofibular joints, all of which may demonstrate movement restrictions amenable to manipulative therapy. Furthermore, Lewit described an experiment in which 10 patients were examined for cervical spine joint dysfunction prior to abdominal surgery. They were reexamined while under anesthesia. The joint restrictions continued to be evident and in fact more easily recognizable under the anesthesia.[9(p17)]

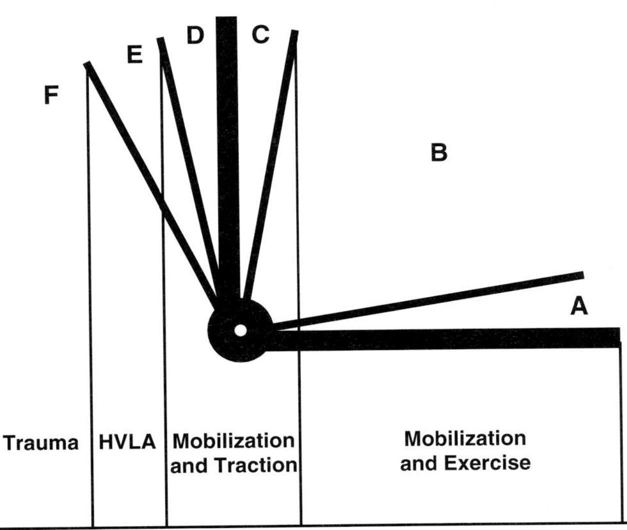

Figure 18–4. Joint motions: The diagram represents joint motion in one plane starting from a neutral position and the theraputic procedures that will specifically effect them. Joint play **(A)** occurs in the neutral position, followed by the active **(B)** and passive **(C)** ranges of motion. The passive range of motion goes beyond the active range from motion entering the joint's elastic limit **(D)** and encountering the elastic barrier. The paraphysiological space **(E)** is a potential space that becomes available to the joint after a cavitation. If the joint is carried beyond its anatomic limit **(F)**, joint disruption results.

Nevertheless, a significant factor in musculoskeletal function is the musculature and its nervous control. Each individual will have a "postural personality" that is an expression of the individual's muscular patterns and posture. Therefore, a frequent cause of joint dysfunction may be faulty neuromotor patterns caused by muscular imbalance and postural strain[9(p22)] or an inability on the part of the patient to consciously control musculoskeletal function. For academic purposes, the results of manipulation can include a combination of mechanical, soft tissue, neurologic, and psychologic effects. Although these will be discussed as separate entities, it is impossible for them to occur in isolation. Even when one effect has more emphasis, other effects will occur either directly or indirectly.

MECHANICAL EFFECTS

The mechanical effects of an adjustment include changes in joint alignment, dysfunctional joint motion, and spinal curvature dynamics. Generally the mechanical effects of an adjustment will be on derangements or disorders of the somatic structures of the body that have altered joint function. Causes of altered joint function may be acute injury, repetitive use injury, faulty posture or coordination, aging, congenital or developmental defects, or primary disease states.

There are several causes of acute and chronic mechanical joint dysfunction which include meniscoid entrapment or extrapment, muscle spasm, displaced disc fragments, and periarticular connective tissue adhesions. Gatterman[14] and Rahlmann[15] have reviewed these and concluded that more than one mechanism is likely to be involved in the development of joint dysfunction, although immobilization due to adhesions had the strongest literature support.

Intraarticular meniscoids are leaf-like, fibroadipose folds of synovium that are attached to the inner surface of the joint capsule and project into the joint cavity (Figure 18–5). These meniscoids have been found to be present in all of the posterior joints of the spine. Bogduk and Jull[16] have suggested that extrapment of these meniscoids may be the cause of restricted joint motion. Upon flexion, the inferior articular process of a zygapophyseal joint moves upward, taking the meniscoid with it. Upon attempted extension, the inferior articular process returns toward its neutral position, but the meniscoid, instead of reentering the joint cavity, impacts against the edge of the articular cartilage and buckles, representing a space-occupying lesion under the capsule. Pain occurs as a result of capsular tension, and extension motion is restricted. The application of an adjustive thrust will separate the articular surfaces and may release the extrapped meniscoid.[16]

Cyriax[17] continues to espouse the belief that displaced nuclear material along an incomplete radial fissure is the source of joint fixation. Postmortem dissection studies of degenerated discs have indeed identified radial fissures in the annulus fibrosus. Nuclear migration along these radial fissures has also been demonstrated by CT discography and

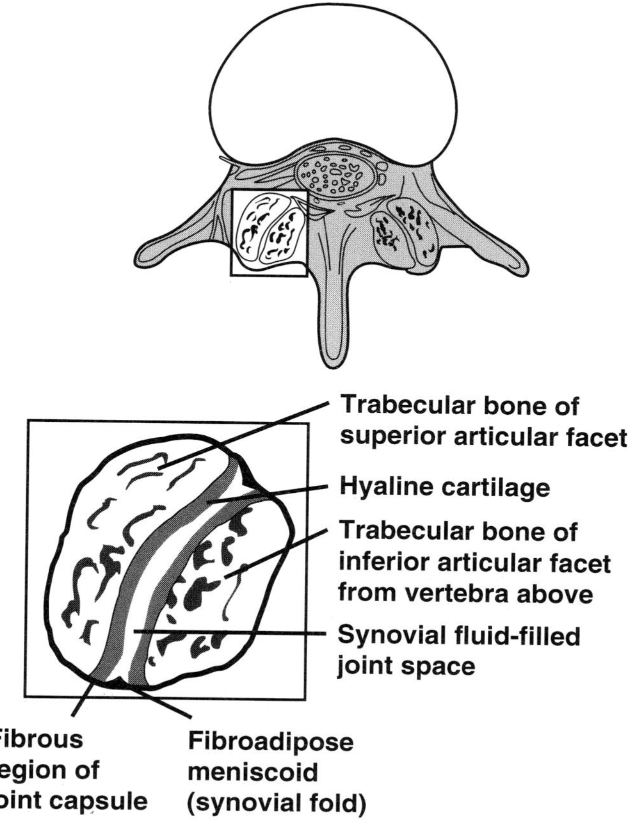

Figure 18–5. Fibroadipose meniscoid in a lumbar facet joint.

Table 18–2: Effects of Immobilization

Microscopic Effects:
Loss of parallelism of collagen fibers
Distorted cellular alignment
Increased randomness of matrix organization
Increased collagen cross-link formation
Periarticular Effects:
Thickening of joint capsule
Raised capsular tension
Connective tissue shrinking
Muscle atrophy
Bone demineralization
Intraarticular Effects:
Proliferation of fatty tissue
Obliteration of joint space
Pressure necrosis of the articular cartilage
Extension of marrow space into the subchondral plate
Cartilage erosion and ulceration in noncontact areas
Adhesions to articular cartilage
Articular cartilage tears at the site of adhesions
Biomechanical Effects:
Decreased ligament strength
Decreased lineal stiffness
Decreased energy absorbing capacity

Adapted from Akeson et al.[22]

correlated with the patient's pain.[18] However, a couple of questions remain unanswered regarding the disc's ability to restrict motion.

First, annular fissures are irreversible and do not mend with manipulation, yet manipulation can have an immediate and often lasting effect on joint fixation. Moreover, joint dysfunction and fixation can occur at segments in which there are no intervertebral discs, such as the atlantooccipital articulation and the sacroiliac articulations, to say nothing of the extremity joints. Finally, disc pathology can lead to spinal fixation through reflex muscle spasm. A painful and inflamed annular tear or disc herniation will cause reflex muscle spasm that will restrict motion.

Specific joint derangements are thought to create a mechanical blockage of movement and an unleveling of the motion segment, resulting in tension on the joint capsule and posterolateral annulus. Because the joint capsule and posterior annulus are pain-sensitive structures, tension on these elements may reflexively induce muscle splinting with further joint restriction. Therefore, mechanical joint dysfunction is considered to be a significant and frequent cause of spinal pain and a potential source of spinal degeneration.

SOFT TISSUE EFFECTS

The soft tissue effects of manipulation include changes in the tone and strength of supporting musculature and influence on the dynamics of supportive capsuloligamentous connective tissue (viscoelastic properties of collagen). Connective tissue elements lose their extensibility with immobilization.[19] With immobilization, water is released from the proteoglycan molecule, allowing connective tissue fibers to contact one another, encouraging abnormal cross-linking, and resulting in loss of extensibility.[20] It is hypothesized that manipulation can break the cross-linking and any intraarticular capsular fibroadipose adhesions, thereby providing free motion and allowing water imbibition to occur. Furthermore, the action of the adjustment can stretch segmental muscles, causing spindle reflexes that may decrease the state of hypertonicity.[21] The effects of immobilization are summarized in Table 18–2.[22]

After immobilization joints become stiff. Although some stiffness results from intraarticular adhesions to surfaces that normally glide past one another,[23] there is also evidence that ligamentous structures can shorten (contract) and hence limit joint motion.[24] It is likely that joint stiffness results from a combination of adhesion formation between normally gliding surfaces and active changes in ligament length. Manipulation of restricted joints will presumably tear the collagen cross-links and fibrous adhesions formed during joint immobilization. However, when articular or nonarticular soft tissue contractures are encountered, incorporation of procedures that minimize inflammation and maintain mobility should be considered. Viscoelastic structures are more amenable to elongation and deformation if they are first warmed and then stretched for sustained periods.[25] Therefore, the application of moist heat, ultrasound, and other warming therapies might be considered before applying sustained manual traction or home-care stretching exercises.[12(p150)]

NEUROLOGICAL EFFECTS

The neurologic effects of manipulation include reduction in pain, influencing spinal and peripheral nerve conduction and thereby altering motor and sensory function, and influencing autonomic nervous system regulation. Wyke[26] reported that manipulative procedures may stimulate the mechanoreceptors associated with synovial joints and thereby affect joint pain. He has identified four types of joint receptors. Types I to III are corpuscular mechanoreceptors that detect static position of the joint, acceleration and deceleration of the joint, direction of movement, and overdisplacement of the joint. The Type IV receptor is a network of free nerve endings that have nociceptive capabilities. Type IV receptors are inactive under normal conditions. However, in the presence of noxious mechanical or chemical stimulation, or if Types I to III receptors are not able to function, Type IV receptors become active and the sensation of pain is perceived. If manipulative therapy can restore normal function to the joint, allowing Types I to III receptors to function, the Type IV pain receptors should be inhibited, thereby decreasing the patient's pain. The structures most sensitive to noxious stimulation are the periosteum and joint capsule.

Additionally, there is evidence to support the concept that the spinal adjustment increases pain tolerance in the skin and deeper muscle structures, raises beta-endorphin levels in the blood plasma, and has an impact on the nerve pathways between the body wall and viscera that regulate general health.[27–32]

PSYCHOLOGICAL EFFECTS

The psychological effects of the laying on of the hands cannot be denied nor overlooked. Paris[33] states that with the addition of a skilled evaluation involving palpation for soft tissue changes and altered joint mechanics, the patient becomes convinced of the interest, concern, and manual skills of the clinician. If at the conclusion of the examination, manipulation is performed that results in an audible "pop" or "snap," the placebo factor will be undeniably high. Paris states that some patients report total relief within a second or two following a manipulation, which he considers far too short a time for any genuine benefit to be appreciated.[33] The astute clinician accepts and reinforces this phenomenon, recognizing that the patient is in need of all possible assistance. It should be noted, however, that the response rate to manipulative treatment cannot be totally accounted for by the placebo effect.

HIGH VELOCITY, LOW AMPLITUDE (HVLA) THRUST TECHNIQUE

Although *manipulation* is a term broadly used to define the therapeutic application of a manual force, chiropractors emphasize the application of specific adjustive techniques. It is necessary to understand that a wide variety of methods exist, so that the assumption that all forms of manual therapy are equivalent must be avoided.[34] Nearly 100 different named techniques have been identified within the chiropractic profession.[35] There are, however, factors that should influence the selection of manipulative procedures[36] (see Table 18–3). Through a consensus process, Gatterman[37] defined manual therapy, manipulation, mobilization, and adjustment (see Table 18–4).

A widely used form of chiropractic adjustment is characterized by a specific high-velocity and short amplitude thrust. This type of adjustive thrust is achieved by a transmission of force, using a combination of the muscular power and body weight of the practitioner. The force is delivered with controlled speed, depth, and magnitude through a specific contact on a particular structure such as the transverse or spinous process of a vertebra.[38] These same principles can also be applied to the extremity joints.

Haldeman implies that although there are a large variety of techniques within the entire field of spinal manipulation, that each has different therapeutic goals, and that each is administered according to different biomechanical or physiologic principles, the most commonly used manipulative technique is the short lever, high-velocity adjustment.[41] He characterizes this technique as a quick, small-amplitude, high-velocity thrust that is delivered to one of the small vertebral processes (specific short lever contact) in a specific direction.

Table 18–3: Factors Which Influence The Selection of Manipulative Procedures

1. Age of patient
2. Acuteness or chronicity of the problem
3. General physical condition of the patient
4. Clinician's size and ability
5. Effectiveness of previous and/or present therapy

Adapted from Greenman.[36]

Table 18–4: Manual Therapy Terminology

Manual Therapy:

Procedures by which the hands directly contact the body to treat the articulations and/or soft tissues.

Mobilization:

Movement applied singularly or repetitively within or at the physiological range of joint motion, without imparting a thrust or impulse, with the goal of restoring joint mobility.

Manipulation:

A manual procedure that involves a directed thrust to move a joint past the physiological range of motion, without exceeding the anatomical limit.

Adjustment:

Any chiropractic therapeutic procedure that utilizes controlled force, leverage, direction, amplitude, and velocity which is directed at specific joints or anatomical regions. Chiropractors commonly use such procedures to influence joint and neurophysiological function.

Adapted from Gatterman.[37]

Although technique applications may be highly variable, the underlying principles are fairly constant. Hoag et al state that a major subdivision of osteopathic manipulative therapy involves technique directed mainly to osseous structures and designed to restore normal joint mobility and weight distribution.[42] They describe the procedures used as positioning the patient in such a way that the force to be applied will cause motion between the affected segments and not be dissipated by the elasticity or mobility of other spinal or appendicular structures. After tension is taken up in muscles and ligaments from above and below the site to be mobilized, a force is delivered, usually to the upper of two segments, in a direction most likely to restore normal motion or apposition to the joint above or below the contact site. They add that frequently the procedure is accompanied by a cracking sound, which is regarded by patients and, unfortunately, by some physicians as well, as the indication of proper treatment. They further describe the thrust movement as rapid (high-velocity), of short distance (low-amplitude), and carefully calibrated according to the age and condition of the patient and the nature of the skeletal disorder.

Greenman[36] also writes that the high-velocity, low-amplitude thrust technique is one of the oldest and remains one of the most frequently used forms of manual medicine. He further states that such thrusts are usually applied as precisely as possible to a single joint level and for specific joint motion loss. It is his opinion that the high-velocity, low-amplitude thrust appears to be much more effective in subacute and chronic conditions than in acute somatic dysfunction, although he offers no support for these statements. Cremata et al[43] describe the Gonstead-type adjustment as a high-velocity, low-amplitude thrust applied to short lever arms such as a spinous process or transverse process. These authors feel that specificity is critical in the contacts taken as well as in the line of correction used, but offer no evidence or rationale as to why such specificity is important or even achievable.

The specific high-velocity, low-amplitude manipulation requires a sudden impulse thrust delivered to the joint. The delivery of this type of thrust occurs through the controlled extension of the clinician's elbows, requiring the isolated contraction of the triceps muscle at the elbow with a contraction of the pectoralis major muscle to stabilize the shoulder. A body-drop thrust may be incorporated with the impulse. Additionally, a mechanical drop section on the adjusting table may be used in conjunction with a thrust technique.

Another form of manual therapy is termed *joint mobilization*. It is applied within the physiologic passive range of joint motion and is characterized by a nonthrust, passive joint movement. By taking the joint to its barrier and repetitively moving along or beside it, it is thought that the barrier will be encouraged to recede.[44] Characteristics of a mobilization include a general contact on a number of bony structures with a single movement, a specific contact on a single bony structure with a multiple, repetitive movement action, or a general contact on a number of bony structures with multiple repetitive movement actions. Mobilization procedures are thought to help loosen and break adhesions and fixations, allowing the adjustment to be more effective.

Manual traction is yet another form of manual therapy in which joint surfaces are held in sustained separation for a period of time. Traction may be done solely through contacts made by the clinician or may be aided through the use of a mechanized table or other devices. These forces may be applied manually or mechanically. Traction techniques are thought to serve in aiding the application of an adjustment by first allowing physiologic rest to the area, relieving compressive pressure due to weight bearing (axial loading), applying an imbibing action to the synovial joints and discs, and opening the intervertebral foramina to allow a disruption of reflex neurologic cycles. Many of these procedures are also quite useful for elderly patients when a high-velocity, low-amplitude thrust may be nonindicated or contraindicated.

Manipulative procedures may also be specifically directed to the soft tissues. With all manual techniques, whether adjustment, mobilization, or traction is used, movements of the soft tissues take place. The justification for a separate classification is to draw attention to the prime importance of including techniques that have the specific purpose of improving the vascularity and extensibility of the soft tissues.[45] If one of the primary goals of manual therapy is the restoration of normal painless joint motion, then it would be essential that treatment should include measures to relax muscle and restore its normal vascularity, as well as extensibility to the other soft tissues. In addition to their use as primary therapies, soft tissue techniques are frequently

Table 18–5: Soft Tissue Manipulative Procedures

Massage:

The systematic therapeutic application of friction, stroking, percussion, and/or kneading to the body.

1. Effleurage
2. Petrissage
3. Friction
4. Pumping
5. Tapotement
6. Vibration

Therapeutic Muscle Stretching:

A manual therapy procedure designed to stretch myofascial tissue, using the principles of postisometric muscular reaction and reciprocal inhibition.

1. Proprioceptive neuromuscular facilitation (PNF)
2. Muscle energy
3. Rolfing
4. Connective tissue massage

Point Pressure Techniques:

Application of sustained or progressively stronger digital pressure; involves stationary contacts or small vibratory or circulatory movements.

1. Nimmo (receptor tonus technique)
2. Accupressure
3. Shiatsu
4. Reflexology
5. Body wall reflex techniques (Chapman and Bennett)

Positional Release Therapies:

Contends that improper neuromuscular mechanisms are responsible for establishing and/or maintaining joint motion abnormality.

1. Strain/counterstrain
2. Functional technique (active assisted motion therapy)
3. Visceral manipulation—a manual method for restoring mobility (movement of the viscera in response to voluntary movement or to movement of the diaphragm in respiration) or motility (inherent motion of the viscera themselves) of an organ, using specific gentle forces

Modified from Bergmann et al,[12] p. 129.

used as preparatory procedures for chiropractic adjustments.[12(p127–128)] A listing of soft tissue manipulative procedures is found in Table 18–5.

The skilled application of manual techniques may appear simple to the uniformed observer. However, control of the adjustive thrust necessitates lengthy practice sessions and skill development in order that the clinician be exact with respect to the magnitude, speed, and force of the thrust.[38] Learning the art of and application of manipulation demands a long training program and a professional commitment from those who undertake this lifework.[46] Many years of practice must be invested before any significant level of proficiency, clinical competence, or finesse is attained.[33] The chiropractic college curriculum is composed of 5 academic years that include basic science, clinical science, and clinical internship objectives. Over 500 hours are spent in developing and practicing the psychomotor skills necessary to deliver a HVLA thrust.

EVIDENCE OF EFFICACY

In spite of the fact that manipulation has been described clinically since the days of Hippocrates, there is a dearth of information about the scientific foundations of the indications for and the effects of manipulation in any form.[35] The chiropractic profession has remained dedicated to the use of manipulative therapy and, specifically, the adjustment, as a form of clinical intervention. Although manipulative therapy has been used for centuries and still occupies small niches in medical, osteopathic, and physical therapy practices, the chiropractic profession has done much to promote its use in the treatment of neuromusculoskeletal dysfunction.[39] However, the chiropractic profession has yet to experimentally substantiate the clinical value of any uniquely chiropractic method of health care.[40] Moreover, studies designed to compare the effectiveness of the many forms of chiropractic technique systems have not been done. It must also be emphasized that no technique system or evaluative procedure has been demonstrated or established as being more or less effective than any other for any condition. Studies comparing the effectiveness and efficiency of technique systems are long overdue.

The effectiveness of spinal manipulative therapy for the treatment of musculoskeletal dysfunction, particularly low back pain, can no longer be justifiably questioned.[47] Although the effectiveness of chiropractic adjustive therapy for treating back pain has been demonstrated[48–54] and patient satisfaction well established,[55–57] the reliability and validity of a number of the procedures used to detect joint subluxation/dysfunction has not been fully confirmed.[58–70] One difficulty in studying manipulative therapy is that the detection of joint dysfunction is not an exact science and any of the examination procedures utilized to detect subluxations may produce false positives, false negatives, and equivocal results. Based on the present data, it would seem prudent to refrain from drawing any firm conclusion on the independent reliability of many of the procedures commonly applied in the assessment of joint dysfunction. Definitive statements await further professional investigation.

Manipulative therapy needs validation in randomized, controlled clinical trials that would meet the skepticism of its critics. However, it is likely that even if such studies were done and manipulative therapy was found to be successful,

Table 18–6: A List of Studies on the Effectiveness of Spinal Manipulative Therapy: Descriptive Studies on Low Back Pain

AUTHOR AND YEAR	ENTRY CRITERIA	OUTCOMES	COMMENTS
Riches, 1930	LBP	75%.	33–92% depending on diagnosis, general anesthesia, SMT
Henderson, 1952	LBP disc protrusion	74%	20% in patients with root tension signs
Wilson and Ilfeld, 1952	Lumbar disc herniation	17%	17% had temporary relief, but no myelographic change
Mensor, 1955	LBP/disc protrusion	54%	General anesthesia, SMT-MD
Bremner, 1958	Lumbosacral strain	87%	General anesthesia, SMT + physiotherapy
Parsons and Cummings, 1958	LBP/disc syndrome	75%	Patients with root signs had half as good response
Bremner and Simpson, 1959	LBP	87%	1 SMT TX + physiotherapy + exercise
Bosshard, 1961	LBP/sciatica	90%	
Gray, 1967	Lumbar IVD syndrome	50%	General anesthesia. SMT + traction
Droz, 1969	Sciatica	53%	No relapse in 5y; 114% symptom free, 36% intermittent LBP
Warr et al, 1972	LBP	63%	No relapse in 6m, general anesthesia, SMT-MD + epidural injection
Tufvession et al, 1976	LBP/sciatica	76%	
Shanghai Institute et al, 1977	LBP/disc protrusion	85%	7% relapse, general anesthesia, SMT-MD
Breen, 1977	LBP	44%	44% had lasting results, 32% temporary improvement; randomly selected patients
Potter, 1977	LBP	71%	38-94% depending on duration and neurologic signs
Cassidy et al, 1978	LBP spondylolisthesis	82%	
Heyse-Moore, 1978	LBP/sciatica	50%	SMT-MD sciatic stretch under general anesthesia
Valentini, 1981	LBP disc syndrome	88%	Post-TX, 10% of patients had relapse within 6m
Hoehler and Tobis, 1982	LBP	73%	SLR post-TX increase; reliability of SLR reported
Banks, 1983	LBP facet + IVD syndrome		Post-TX lumbar disc angle change to values similar to 10 normal controls
Cox et al, 1983	LBP, leg pain	71%	Cox distraction + acupressure
Cox and Shreiner, 1984	LBP	75%	TX response of different types of LBP reported
Fonti and Lynch, 1984	LBP/sciatica	85%	
Salvi et al, 1984	LBP/sciatica	69%	
Kirkaldy-Willis and Cassidy, 1985	Severe LBP/leg pain	81% 48%	In referred pain syndromes In nerve root compression syndromes.
Sheladia and Johnston, 1986	LBP	79%	SMT-DC + physiotherapy + nutritional advice
Kuo and Loh, 1987	LBP/disc protrusion	84%	14% had relapses
Mierau et al, 1987	LBP/spondylolisthesis	80%	Observer-blinded study

Tables 18–6 and 18–7 are modified from Bronfort.[71]

Table 18–7: A List of Studies on the Effectiveness of Spinal Manipulative Therapy: Randomized Clinical Trials on Low Back Pain

AUTHOR AND YEAR	ENTRY CRITERIA	STUDY GROUPS	TX #/ RESULTS
Siehl et al, 1971	Disc herniation	G1: Conservative care + SMT, DO: G2: Conservative Care; G3: Disc surgery	? / 14% G1, 8% G2, & 47% G3 showed EMG improvement. Clinical improvement similar in G1 & G2 but inferior to G3
Glover et al, 1974	LBP unilateral hyperesthesia	G1: 1 SMT-MD + 4 daily sessions of detuned diathermy; G2. 5 daily sessions of detuned diathermy	1 / SMT superior immediately post-TX in patients with duration < 7d, Similar improvement in G1 & G2 after 3 d and 7d
Doran and Newell, 1975	LBP	G1: SMT-MD; G2. Physiotherapy; G3: Corset; G4: Analgesic + bed rest	6 / No difference at any time; Greenland et al.- SMT superior to corset at 3w, but not later
Bergquist-Ullman and Larsson, 1977	LBP	G1: SMT-PT; G2: Backschool 3h; G3: Low-intensity heat [placebo]	4 / G1 & G2: shorter symptom duration than G3. G2: shortest duration of sick leave. Equal numbers of relapses in ly in all three groups
Evans et al, 1978	LBP	G1: SMT-MD/analgesics; G2: Analgesics/SMT-MD.	3 / Temporary decrease in pain + increased lumbar flexion during SMT phase
Sims-Williams et al, 1978	LBP	G1: SMT-PT + mobilization + traction; G2: Heat [PT]	<14 / G1 patients rated improvements higher and physical disability lower than G2 at 1 m. and at 3m, increased SLR at lm in G1 No difference between groups at 12 m
Rasmussen, 1979	LBP	G1: SMT-MD/PT; G2: Shortwave diathermy.	6 / 92% of SMT group vs 25% of G2 were symptom-free after 2w, increased ROM only in SMT group
Sims-Williams et al, 1979	LBP	G1: SMT-PT + mobilization + traction; G2: Heat[PT]	<14 / No important clinical difference between groups at any time except at ly follow-up, where G2 had better back status than G1
Coxhead et al, 1981	LBP/sciatica	G1: Traction G2: SMT-PT G3: exercise G4: corset	? / At 4 w 78% of patients reported improvement and equal amount of time loss irrespective of TX; least pain in SMT group. Combining TXs superior to single treatment.
Hoehler et al, 1981	LBP	G1: SMT-MD; G2: Soft tissue massage	? / SMT less pain, disability, & more SLR than G2 after 1st TX, & less pain 3w after dis.
Zylbergold and Piper, 1981	LBP	G1: Heat + flexion exercise; G2: Heat + SMT-PT; G3: Ergonomic instruction	8 / More pain reduction, increased ROM, & functional activity in SMT group after 1m.
Farrell and Twomey, 1982	LBP	G1: Passive mobilization/SMT-PT; G2: Diathermy + exercise + ergonomic inst.	4 / SMT group fewer days & TXs to "symptom free" status, 91% recovered within 4w
Nwuga, 1982	LBP/disc herniation	G1: Heat + low-intensity exercise; G2: Oscillatory SMT	? / SMT superior to heat + exercise in increasing ROM and SLR at 6w
Godfrey et al, 1984	LBP	G1: soft tissue massage + SMT-MD/DC; G2. Min mass + low elec. stim	4 / No difference, both groups improved; Hoehler 1987: G1 superior to G2 at 3w.
Gibson et al, 1985	LBP	G1: SMT-DO; G2: Diathermy active; G3: Detuned diathermy	4 / Similar improvement (pain & ROM) in all three groups at 2w, 4w, and 12w
Waterworth and Hunter, 1985	LBP	G1: Anti-inflammatory drug; G2: Heat + exercise; G3: SMT-PT and/or McKenzie	<10 / all three groups showed similar improvement after 4d and 12d of therapy
Arkuszewski, 1986	LBP/sciatica	G1: Drugs, physiotherapy + SMT-MD; G2: Drugs, physiotherapy	6 / G1: Better global score than G2 at 1m and 6m
Waagen et al, 1986	LBP	G1: SMT-DC; G2: Sham SMT-DC	5 / The SMT group had more pain reduction post-TX & at 2w. Global index improved significantly at 2w compared to controls.
Hadler et al, 1987	LBP	G1: Mobilization-MD; G2: SMT-MD	1 / Patients with LBP for 2-4w at entry improved faster & to a greater degree with SMT than with mobilization.
Mathews et al, 1987	LBP + sciatica	G1: SMT-PT; G2: Heat	<10 / Faster + greater rate of recovery in SMT group at 2w in patients with decreased SLR.
Ongley et al, 1987	LBP without TX response	G1: Forceful SMT-MD + 6 injections; G2: Sham SMT-MD + 6 placebo injections	1 / G1 >40% better than G2 on both main outcomes at 1m, 3m and 6m
Postacchini et al, 1988	LBP with/without radiation	G1: SMT-DC?; G2: Drug; G3: Massage + diathermy; G4. Bed rest; G5 Back school; G6: Placebo ointment	11-17 / SMT superior at 3w in acute patients with/without radiation. Back school superior at 6 m in chronic patients without radiation
Kinalski et al, 1989	LBP	G1: SMT-MD; G2: Heat + traction + exercise?	? / Similar decrease in pain but shorter treatment time in G1
MacDonald and Bell, 1990	LBP	G1: SMT-DO + LBP prophylaxis; G2: LBP prophylaxis	5 / SMT superior 1-2w after TX start in patients with 14-28d of LBP duration. No difference at 4w
Meade et al, 1990	LBP	G1: Hospital SMT-PT; G2: SMT-DC	6-9 / 7% points lower disability in G2 at 6m, 12m, and 24m.

very little notice would be taken by the critics. Bronfort's[71] review of the literature relating to the effectiveness of spinal manipulation identifies numerous descriptive studies or clinical series, quasi-experimental trials, and more than 30 randomized clinical trials. The majority of these studies are on low back pain (65%) or cervical pain and headache (15%). The remainder report on a variety of other clinical conditions. These are summarized in Tables 18–6 and 18–7.

Controlled clinical trials are essential to determine which techniques are best used to treat which problems and under what circumstances. With this information, standards of care can be developed to best serve patients who suffer from problems of neuromusculoskeletal origin. The need is great and timely to begin the process of validating manual therapies, specifically those that are more unique to the chiropractic profession. The ultimate purpose of validating clinical procedures is to provide a means to examine and explain the process by which we can test and improve what we do, as health professionals, to and for our patients.

SUMMARY

Practitioners of manipulative therapy need to continue to develop skills and knowledge, not only in the area of therapeutics, but also in recognizing potential patients at risk. Studies to collect the facts should serve to quell fears in the minds of practitioners and disarm the opponents of manipulative therapy, who aim to denigrate by alarming the public with information that is distorted and overstated and implanting in the public mind a fear of a genuinely safe and effective form of health care.[72] Even in light of the fact that the disastrous complication of permanent neurologic damage is indeed so rare an event, the term *acceptable risk* is suitable when applied to manipulative therapies.[73]

In summary, this chapter has attempted to provide clarification to various aspects of manipulative therapy, including the definition of some terms, identification of a rationale for the use of manipulative therapy, criteria for application, and the role that manipulative therapy may play in rehabilitation of the locomotor system.

REFERENCES

1. Janda V. Pain in the locomotor system—A broad approach. In Grieve G, ed. *Modern Manual Therapy*. Melbourne: Churchill Livingstone, 1994:148–151.
2. Keating JC, Bergmann TF, Jacobs GE, Finer BA, Larson K. Interexaminer reliability of eight evaluative dimensions of lumbar segmental dysfunction. *J Manipulative Physiol Ther*. 1990;13(8):463–470.
3. Faucret B, Mao W, Nakagawa T, Spurgin D, Tran T. Determination of bony subluxations by clinical, neurological, and chiropractic procedures. *J Manipulative Physiol Ther*. 1980;3:165–176.
4. Bergmann TF. Chiropractic spinal examination. In Ferezy JS, ed. *The Chiropractic Neurological Examination*. Gaithersburg, MD: Aspen Publications, 1992:97–110.
5. Mennell JM. *Joint Pain*. Boston: Little, Brown, 1964.
5a. Maitland GD. *Peripheral Manipulation*. 2nd ed. London: Butterworths, 1977:1–29.
6. Twomey LT. A rationale for the treatment of back pain and joint pain by manual therapy. *Phys Ther*. 1992;72:885–892.
7. Sandoz R. Some physical mechanisms and affects of spinal adjustments. *Ann Swiss Chiro Assoc*. 1976;6:91.
7a. Sandoz R. Some reflex phenomena associated with spinal derangements and adjustments. *Ann Swiss Chiro Assoc*. 1981;7:45.
8. Triano JJ. Studies on the biomechanical effect of a spinal adjustment. *J Manipulative Physiol Ther*. 1992;15:71–75.
9. Lewit K. *Manipulative Therapy in Rehabilitation of the Motor System*. London: Butterworths, 1985:1–256.
10. Nachemson A. A critical look at the treatment for low back pain. *Scand J Rehabil Med*. 1979;11:143–147.
11. Mitchell FL. Elements of muscle energy technique. In: Basmajian JV, Nyberg R, eds. *Rational Manual Therapies*. Baltimore: Williams & Wilkins, 1993;318–319.
12. Bergmann TF, Peterson DH, Lawrence DJ. *Chiropractic Technique*. New York: Churchill Livingstone, 1993, 1–197.
13. Korr IM. Proprioceptors and somatic dysfunction. *J Am Osteopath Assoc*. 1975;74:638.
14. Gatterman MI. Indications for spinal manipulation in the treatment of back pain. *ACA J Chiro*. 1982;19(10):51–66.
15. Rahlmann JF. Mechanisms of intervertebral joint fixation: A literature review. *J Manipulative Physiol Ther*. 1987;10(4):177–187.
16. Bogduk N, Jull G. The theoretical pathology of acute locked back: A basis for manipulative therapy. *Manual Med*. 1985;1:78–82.
17. Cyriax J. *Textbook of Orthopedic Medicine*, Vol. 2. 9th ed. London: Ballier Tindall, 1974:57–66.

18. Vanharanta H, Sachs BL, Spivey MA, et al. The relationship of pain provocation to lumbar disc deterioration as seen by CT discography. *Spine*. 1987;12:295–298.
19. Akeson WH, Amiel D, Woo S. Immobility effects of synovial joints—The biomechanics of joint contracture. *Biorheology*. 1980;17:95.
20. Akeson WH, Amiel D, Mechanic GL, Woo S, Harwood FL, Hamer ML. Collagen cross-linking alterations in joint contractures: Changes in reducible cross-links in periarticular connective tissue collagen after nine weeks of immobilization. *Connect Tissue Res*. 1977;5:5.
21. Burger AA. Experimental neuromuscular models of spinal manual techniques. *Manual Med*. 1983;1:10.
22. Akeson WH, Amiel D, Woo S. Cartilage and ligament: Physiology and repair processes. In: Nicholas JA, Hershman EB, eds. *The Lower Extremity and Spine in Sports Medicine*. St. Louis: CV Mosby, 1986:3–41.
23. Evans EV, Eggers GWN, Butler JK, et al. Experimental immobilization and remobilization of rat knee joints. *J Bone Joint Surg*. 1960;42a:737–758.
24. Dahners LE. Ligament contraction—A correlation with cellularity and actin staining. *Trans Orthop Res Soc*. 1986;11:56.
25. White AA, Panjabi MM. *Clinical Biomechanics of the Spine*. 2nd ed. Philadelphia: JB Lippincott, 1990; 692–694.
26. Wyke BD. Articular neurology and manipulative therapy. In: Glasgow EF, Twomey LT, Schull ER, Kleynhans AM, eds. *Aspects of Manipulative Therapy*. New York: Churchill Livingstone, 1985;72–80.
27. Terrett ACJ, Vernon H. Manipulation and pain tolerance. *J Am Phys Med*. 1984;63(5):217–225.
28. Vernon HT, Dhami MSI, et al. Spinal manipulation and Beta-endorphin: A controlled study of the effect of a spinal manipulation on plasma Beta-endorphin levels in normal males. *J Manipulative Physiol Ther*. 1986;9(2):115–123.
29. Vernon HT. Pressure pain threshold evaluation of the effect of spinal manipulation on chronic neck pain: A single case study. *JCCA*. 1988;32(4):191–194.
30. Tran TA, Kirby JD. The effectiveness of upper cervical adjustment upon the normal physiology of the heart. *ACA J Chirop*. 1977;11:58–62.
31. Sato A, Swenson RS. Sympathetic nervous system response to mechanical stress of the spinal column in rats. *J Manipulative Physiol Ther*. 1984;7(3):141–147.
32. Briggs L, Boone WR. Effects of a chiropractic adjustment on changes in pupillary diameter: A model for evaluating somatovisceral response. *J Manipulative Physiol Ther*. 1988;11(3):181–189.
33. Paris SV. Spinal manipulative therapy. *Clin Orthop*. 1983;179:55–61.
34. Haldeman S. Spinal manipulative therapy and sports medicine. *Clin Sports Med*. 1986;5(2):277–293.
35. Bergmann TF. Various forms of chiropractic technique. *Chiro Technique*. 1993;5(2):53–55.
36. Greenman P. *Principles of Manual Medicine*. Baltimore: Williams & Wilkins, 1989: 94.
37. Gatterman MI, Hansen DT. Development of chiropractic nomenclature through consensus. *J Manipulative Physiol Ther*. 1994;17(5):302–309.
38. Grice AS. Biomechanical approach to cervical and dorsal adjusting. In Haldman S, ed. *Modern Developments in the Principles and Practice of Chiropractic*. New York: Appleton-Century-Croft, 1980;331–358.
39. Bergmann TF. Short lever, specific contact articular chiropractic technique. *J Manipulative Physiol Ther*. 1992;15:591–595.
40. Keating JC. Traditional barriers to standards of knowledge production in chiropractic. *Chiro Technique*. 1990;2(3):78–85.
41. Haldeman S. Spinal manipulative therapy: A status report. *Clin Orthop*. 1983;179:62–70.
42. Hoag JM, Cole WV, Bradford SG. *Osteopathic Medicine*. New York: McGraw-Hill, 1969:p.186.
43. Cremata EE, Plaugher G, Cox WA. Technique system application: The Gonstead approach. *Chiro Technique*. 1991;3:19–25.
44. Bourdillon JF, Day EA, Bookout MR. *Spinal Manipulation*. 5th ed. Stamford, CT: Appleton & Lange, 1987:126.
45. Grieve GP. *Common Vertebral Joint Problems*. 2nd ed. Edinburgh: Churchill Livingstone, 1988:535.
46. Lewit K. Manipulation—reflex therapy and/or restitution of impaired locomotor function. *Manual Med* 1986;2:99–100.
47. Byfield D. *Chiropractic Manipulative Skills*. Oxford, England: Butterworth-Heinemann, 1996.
48. Shekelle PG, Adams AH. *The Appropriateness of Spinal Manipulation for Low-Back Pain: Project Overview and Literature Review*. Palo Alto, CA: RAND Corp., 1991.
49. American Chiropractic Association. *Comparison of Chiropractic and Medical Treatment of Nonoperative Back and Neck Injuries 1976–77*. Des Moines, IA: American Chiropractic Association, 1978.

50. Brunarski DJ. Clinical trials of spinal manipulation: A critical appraisal and review of the literature. *J Manipulative Physiol Ther.* 1984; 7:243–249.
51. Nyiendo J. *Chiropractic Effectiveness*, Series No. 1. *Oregon Chiropractic Physicians Association Legislative Newsletter.* April 1991.
52. Anderson R, Meeker WC, Wirick BE, et al. A meta-analysis of clinical trials of spinal manipulation. *J Manipulative Physiol Ther.* 1992;15(3):181–194.
53. Waagen GN, Haldeman S, Cook G. Short term trial of chiropractic adjustments for the relief of chronic low back pain. *Manual Med.* 1986;2:63–67.
54. Meade TW, Dyer SD, Brown W. Low back pain of mechanical origin: Randomized comparison of chiropractic and hospital outpatient treatment. *Br Med J.* 1990;300:1431–1437.
55. Kane RL, et al. Manipulating the patient: A comparison of the effectiveness of physician and chiropractor care. *Lancet.* 1974;1:1333–1336.
56. Cherkin DC, MacCornack FA. Health care delivery. Patient evaluations of low back pain care from family physicians and chiropractors. *West J Med.* 1989; 150(3):351–355.
57. Cherkin DC, MacCornack FA, Berg AO. The management of low back pain—A comparison of the beliefs and behaviors of family physicians and chiropractors. *West J Med.* 1988; 149:475–480.
58. Russell R. Diagnostic palpation of the spine: A review of procedures and assessment of their reliability. *J Manipulative Physiol Ther.* 1983;6(4):181–183.
59. Keating J. Inter-examiner reliability of motion palpation of the lumbar spine: A review of quantitative literature. *Am J Chiro Med.* 1989;2(3):107–110.
60. Keating JC, Bergmann TF, Jacobs G, Finer B, Larson K. Interexaminer reliability of eight evaluative dimensions of lumbar segmental abnormality. *J Manipulative Physiol Ther.* 1990;13(8):463–470.
61. Brunarski DJ. Chiropractic biomechanical evaluations; Validity in myofascial low back pain. *J Manipulative Physiol Ther.* 1982; 7:243–249.
62. Addington ER. Reliability and objectivity of the anatometer, supine leg length test, thermoscribe ll, and the derm-therm-o-graph measurements. *Upper Cervical Monographs.* 1983;3:8–11.
63. Deyo R, McNiesh LM, Cone RD. Observer variability in the interpretation of lumbar spine radiography. *Arthritis Rheum.* 1985;28(9):1066–1070.
64. Antos JC, Robinson K, Keating JC, Jacobs GE. Interrater reliability of flouroscopic detection of fixation in the mid-cervical spine. *Chiro Technique.* 1990;2(2) 53–55.
65. Fuhr AW, Osterbauer PJ. Interexaminer reliability of relative leg-length evaluations in the prone, extended position. *Chiro Technique.* 1989;1:13–18.
66. Haas M. The reliability of reliability. *J Manipulative Physiol Ther.* 1991;14(3):199–208.
67. Keating J. Several strategies for evaluating the objectivity of measurements in clinical research and practice. *J Can Chiro Assoc.* 1988;32(3):133–138.
68. Boline P, Keating J, et al. Interexaminer reliability of palpatory evaluations of the lumbar spine. *Am J Chiro Med.* 1988;1(1):5–11.
69. Johnston W, Allan BR, et al. Interexaminer study of palpation in detecting location of spinal segmental dysfunction. *Am Osteopath Assoc.* 1983;82(11):839–845.
70. Panzer DM. The reliability of lumbar motion palpation. *J Manipulative Physiol Ther.* 1992;15(8):518–524.
71. Bronfort G. Effectiveness of spinal manipulation and adjustment. In: Haldeman S, ed. *Principles and Practice of Chiropractic*, 2nd ed. Stamford, CT, Appleton & Lange, 1992.
72. Terrett AGJ. Vascular accidents from cervical spine manipulation: Report on 107 cases. *Aust Chiro Assoc.* 1987;17(1):15–24.
73. Ferezy JS. Neural ischemia and cervical manipulation: An acceptable risk. ACA *J Chiro.* 1988;22:61–63.

CHAPTER 19

Mechanically Assisted Spinal Mobilization

Principles and Applications

James M. Cox, DC, DACBR

INTRODUCTION

Eighty to ninety percent of herniated lumbar disc cases are successfully handled with nonsurgical treatment,[1] and two factors are considered essential for a healthy low back:

1. Patent lumbar vertebral and osseoligamentous canal
2. Uncompromised cauda equina and nerve root within them

Degenerative disc disease increases weight bearing on the facet joints,[2,3] resulting in impaired facet joint function and degenerative osteoarthrosis of the zygapophyses. Hypertrophic vertebral end plate disc disease has the potential to stenose the vertebral and osseoligamentous canals (intervertebral foramen), compromising the cauda equina and its exiting nerve roots.

THE ROLE OF DISTRACTION ADJUSTMENTS IN SPINAL REHABILITATION

Distraction of the lumbar spine establishes patency of the vertebral and osseoligamentous canals by increasing the height of the intervertebral disc space, decreasing disc protrusion, and opening the lateral recesses of the vertebral canal while placing distension on the facet joints.[4] This author (JMC) feels that adjusting facet joints by placing them through their physiological ranges of motion while distraction is applied to the spine decreases the chance of inflicting foraminal stenosis while lateral flexion and rotation movements are employed.

Manipulating lumbar facet joints through their physiological ranges of motion, under distraction, may regain normal mobility for the motion segment. A healthy spine is strong and flexible; a painful back is weak and rigid. Regardless of the low back pain condition, distraction adjusting to increase spinal flexibility, coupled with strengthening the muscles of the abdomen, low back, and lower extremities, is desirable.[5] A vertebral motion segment (disc and facet articulations) that performs its physiological ranges of motion (flexion, extension, lateral flexion, circumduction, and rotation) is a healthy, normal articulation.

In the treatment of low back pain, the ultimate goal is to regain, to the maximum ability of the patient, these physiological ranges of joint movement. This is accomplished by chiropractic manipulative therapy and home exercise protocols performed by the patient as instructed by the treating physician. Low back wellness school training to teach the patient how to perform the activities of daily living with minimal spinal stress is added.

These attributes, as outlined in the following definition of Cox distraction manipulation, constitute the appropriate goals of back pain relief.

Cox distraction manipulation is a form of spinal manipulative therapy thought to have the following benefits[2,6–12]:

1. Increasing the intervertebral disc height to remove annular distortion in the pain-sensitive peripheral annular fibers.
2. Allowing the nucleus pulposus to assume its central position within the annulus and relieve irritation of the pain-sensitive annular peripheral fibers.
3. Restoring the vertebral zygapophyseal joints to their physiological relationships of motion.
4. Improving posture and locomotion while relieving pain, improving body functions, and creating a state of well-being.

CLASSIFICATION OF DISC DISEASE

Lumbar disc disease can be divided into two categories:

1. Internal disc disruption and herniation that have resulted in low back and sciatic nerve root compression to cause sciatic radiculopathy. In the case of sequestered free fragmentation of a disc, the patient may only have leg pain and no back pain. Fewer patients seen in general practice are in this classification.
2. Internal discal derangement resulting in low back pain with no sciatic nerve radiculopathy. Most pa-

Table 19–1: General Screening Considerations for Adult Patients With Low Back Pain

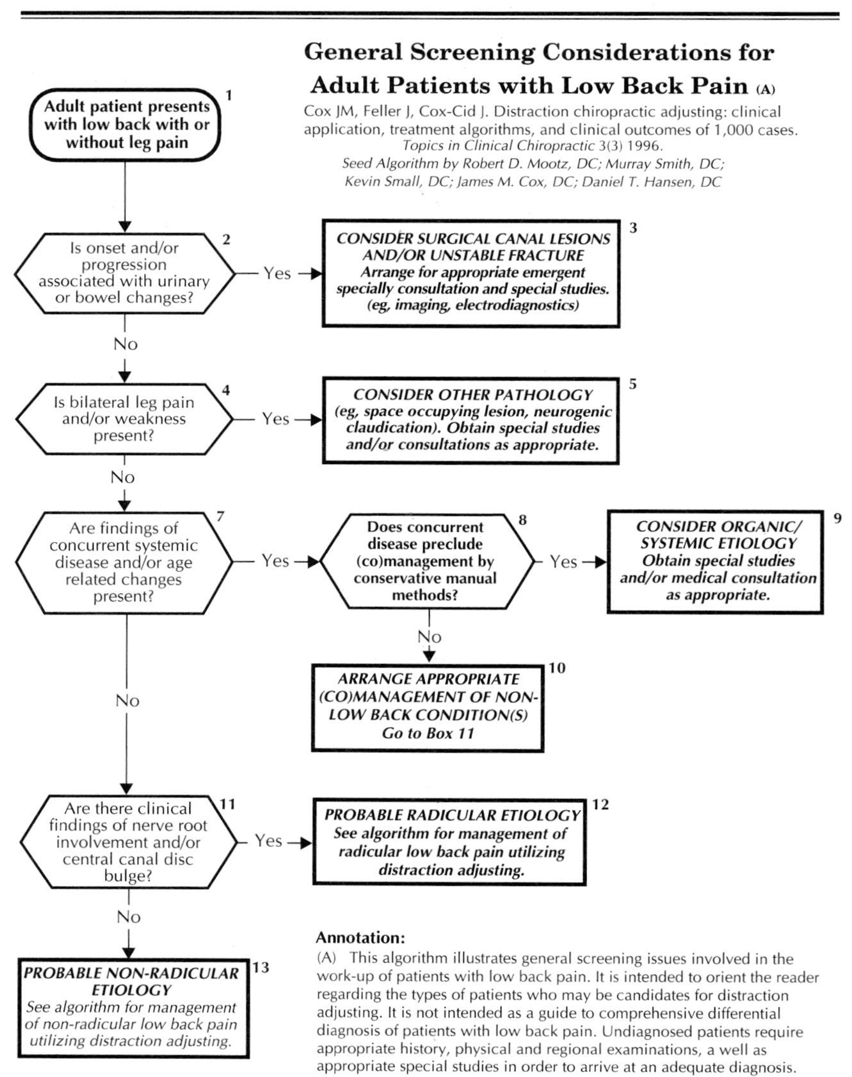

Reprinted with permission from: Distraction chiropractic adjusting: Clinical application and outcomes of 1,000 cases. Topics in Clinical Chiropractic. 1996;3(3):45–59, 79–81. Copyright Aspen Publishers, Inc.

tients with internal disc disruption termed *degenerative disc disease* are in this category.

DECISION-MAKING ALGORITHMS FOR THE DISTRACTION ADJUSTING PROTOCOL

Tables 19–1, 19–2, and 19–3 are algorithms for screening the patient to determine if manipulation is indicated, and to determine the treatment regime for radiculopathy and nonradiculopathy patients.

The suspected disc herniation patient is treated only with distraction and minimal flexion (Figure 19–9) (Table 19–2) until the sciatic pain is at least 50% relieved as measured subjectively by the Visual Analogue Scale and objectively by a 50% return of range of motion of the thoracolumbar spine and straight leg raise, and a 50% relief of pain on Kemp's sign and Dejerine's triad testing. The relief of leg pain with continuing low back pain is termed centralization of the pain.

At the point of 50% relief of the sciatic pain, the patient is treated with the same treatment applied to a patient without sciatica—placing the facet joints of the functional spinal units through their five physiological ranges of

Table 19–2: Management of Radicular Low Back Pain Utilizing Distraction Adjusting

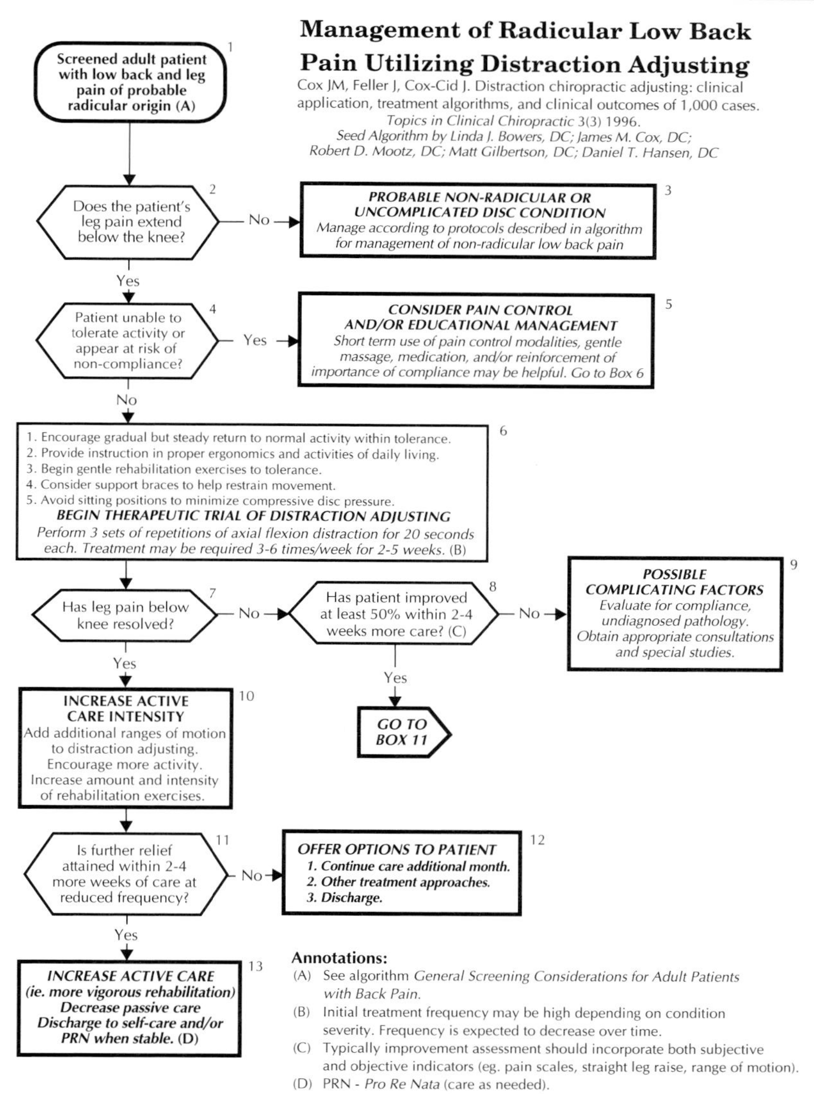

Reprinted with permission from: Distraction chiropractic adjusting: Clinical application and outcomes of 1,000 cases. Topics in Clinical Chiropractic. 1996;3(3):45–59, 79–81. Copyright Aspen Publishers, Inc.

Table 19–3: Management of Nonradicular Low Back Pain Utilizing Distraction Adjusting

Management of Nonradicular Low Back Pain Utilizing Distraction Adjusting

Cox JM, Feller J, Cox-Cid J. Distraction chiropractic adjusting: clinical application, treatment algorithms, and clinical outcomes of 1,000 cases. *Topics in Clinical Chiropractic* 3(3) 1996.
Seed Algorithm by James M. Cox, DC; Robert D. Mootz, DC; Linda J. Bowers, DC; Daniel T. Hansen, DC

1 **Screened adult patient with low back and/or leg pain of probable non-radicular origin** (A)

2 Does the patient have leg pain of radicular origin (below the knee)? — Yes → 3 ***CONSIDER POSSIBLE DISC INVOLVEMENT*** *See algorithm for management of radicular low back pain.*

No ↓

4 Patient unable to tolerate activity or appear at risk of non-compliance? — Yes → 5 ***CONSIDER PAIN CONTROL AND/OR EDUCATIONAL MANAGEMENT*** *Short term use of pain control modalities, medication, and/or reinforcement of importance of compliance may be helpful. Go to Box 6*

No ↓

6
1. Encourage rapid and steady return to normal activity.
2. Institute moderate rehabilitation exercises to tolerance.
3. Consider low back wellness education.

↓

7 Is a spondylolisthesis or transitional segment potentially contributing to pain? — Yes → 8 ***CONSIDER MODIFIED DISTRACTION ADJUSTING*** *Apply treatment above involved segment and monitor patient for tolerance. Follow remaining application protocols beginning in Box 9.*

No ↓

9 ***THERAPEUTIC TRIAL OF DISTRACTION ADJUSTING*** *Perform 1 set of 10 reps in all physiological ranges of motion. Aggressively institute rehabilitation exercises. Consider automated distraction adjusting at 2-3 visits/wk.*

↓

10 Has patient improved at least 50% within 2-4 weeks of care? (B) — Yes → 11 **Is further relief attained within 2-4 additional weeks of care at reduced frequency?** — Yes → 12 ***INCREASE ACTIVE CARE*** ***(ie, more vigorous rehabilitation) Decrease passive care. Discharge to self-care and/or PRN when stable.*** (C)

10 No ↓ 14 ***POSSIBLE COMPLICATING FACTORS*** ***Evaluate for compliance, undiagnosed pathology. Obtain appropriate consultations and special studies.***

11 No ↓ 13 ***OFFER OPTIONS TO PATIENT***
1. Continue care additional month.
2. Other treatment approaches.
3. Discharge.

Annotations:
(A) See algorithm *General Screening Considerations for Adult Patients with Back Pain.*
(B) Typically improvement assessment should incorporate both subjective and objective indicators (eg, anchored pain scales, range of motion, SLR).
(C) PRN - *Pro Re Nata* (care as needed).

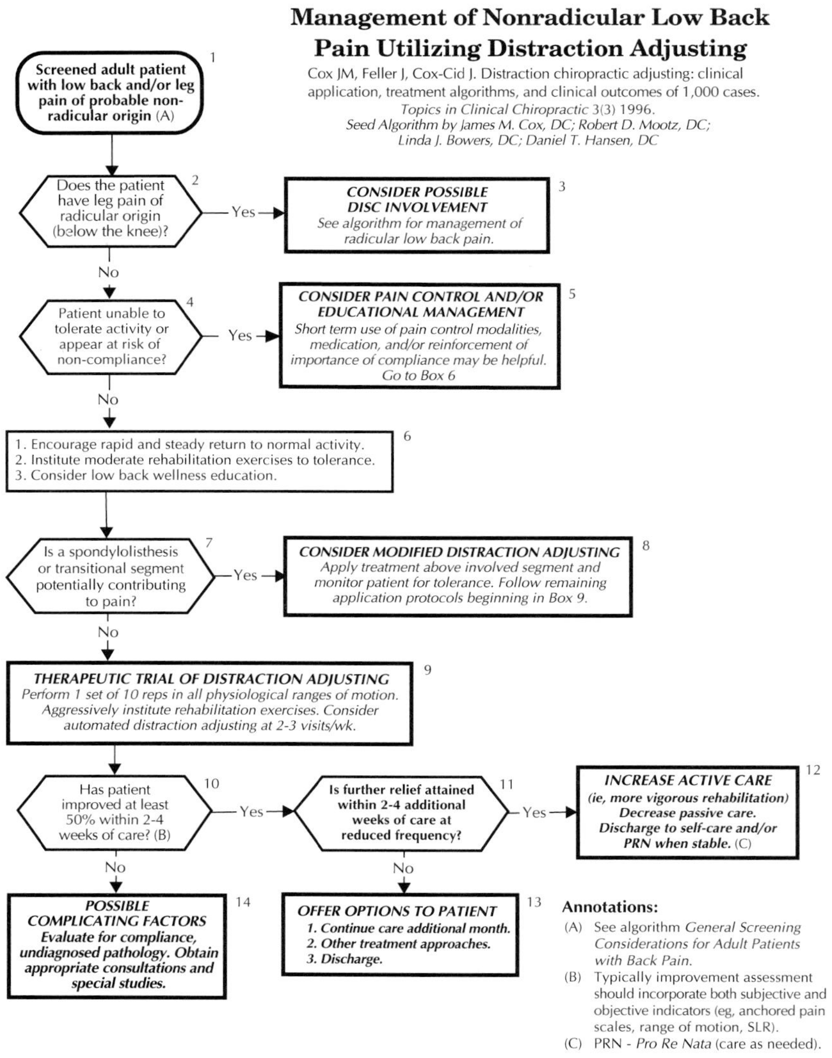

Reprinted with permission from: Distraction chiropractic adjusting: Clinical application and outcomes of 1,000 cases. Topics in Clinical Chiropractic. 1996;3(3):45–59, 79–81. Copyright Aspen Publishers, Inc.

motion (flexion, extension, lateral flexion, rotation, and circumduction) (see Table 19–3). Distraction is the first motion given because it allows opening of the intervertebral disc space, reduction of the disc protrusion, increase of the diameter of the osseoligamentous and vertebral canals, tautening of the ligamentum flavum, and zygapophyseal joint separation—all factors that reduce stenosis.[2,6–12]

RATIONALE FOR DISTRACTION ADJUSTING

Radiologic, clinical, and laboratory evidence[4–43] shows that disc herniation and other stenotic factors reduce during distraction. Under distraction, facet joint articulations can be manipulated with possibly much less chance of inducing stenosis due to further disc protrusion, facet imbrication subluxation, or buckling of the ligamentum flavum. Thus, potential pain infliction is reduced for the patient. Onel et al[4] explained the benefits of distraction of the lumbar spine, which are summarized in Figures 19–1, 19–2, and 19–3.

INTRADISCAL PRESSURE REDUCTION WITH DISTRACTION ADJUSTING

The following information is from data collected at the National College of Chiropractic from 1994 to 1997 with the collaboration of Loyola University Stritch School of

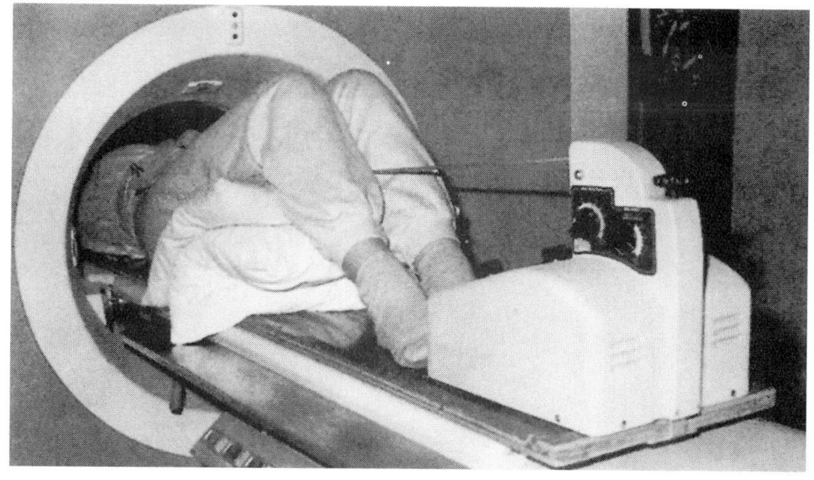

Figure 19–1. Computerized tomography is performed before and during 45 kg of distraction application. The position of the lumbar disc herniation patient during the CT investigation is shown; the traction device, with flexion of hips and knees to ensure the Williams position, is visible.

Reprinted with permission from: Onel D, Tuzlaci M, Sari H, Demir K. Computed tomographic investigation of the effect of traction on lumbar disc herniation. Spine. 1989;14(1):83, 86.

Medicine under a research grant from the Health Resources and Services Administration of the Department of Public Health of the Department of Health and Human Services.

Distraction adjustment of the lumbar spine of unembalmed whole cadavers (n=5) with pressure transducers in the nucleus pulposus of the lumbar discs showed that flexion distraction significantly reduced the intradiscal pressure at the distracted level of unpressurized discs from 39 to 192 mm Hg in the negative range, which was statistically significant ($p<0.01$). On pressurized discs, (which were pressurized with water), the intradiscal pressure dropped 117 to 720 mm Hg of negative pressure in the prone distracted position.[65]

Ramos[64] reported that disc pressures intraoperatively tested dropped during axial decompression to as low as −160 mmHg. Cyriax,[8] Quellette,[37] and Kramer[43] hypothesized that as the vertebrae in the spine are distracted, a negative pressure develops in the disc, which sucks back a protrusion.

In using distraction adjusting, it is necessary to remember that the intradiscal stress is not highest in the nucleus pulposus of the disc but rather within the inner and middle anulus fibrosus, especially posterior to the nucleus. Degenerative changes which affect intradiscal stress are not merely biochemical in origin but also structurally more important as a source of low back pain. Vertebral body end plate damage reduces the nuclear pressure by up to 57% and doubles the stress peaks within the posterior anulus.[66] When using distraction adjusting, it is necessary to realize that increasing intervertebral disc height and reducing intradiscal pressure seeks to normalize intradiscal pressure and reduce pressure on the pain-sensitive end plates of the vertebrae.

INTERVERTEBRAL DISC SPACE CHANGES UNDER DISTRACTION ADJUSTMENT

Radiographs taken of an unembalmed cadaver that was positioned in the prone position for distraction adjusting showed a 6 degree flexion angle between L5-S1 with an increased posterior disc height of 3 mm, and a 3.5 degree flexion angle between L4-L5 with a 1.87-mm increase of the posterior disc height. These results indicate motion between motion segments and an increase in the posterior neural element space; however, further research designs with computer modeling are needed to study these changes adequately.[65]

Ligament loads used in this adjusting procedure are well below failure loads when up to 6 degrees of flexion and 444 N of traction load is applied with the adjusting instrument table.[65] Future research papers will show the dimensional changes of height, width, and area within the intervertebral foramen when distraction adjustments are administered to the L4-L5 and L5-S1 levels.

Intradiscal pressure drops from 30 to 10 kg in the L3-L4 disc under the effect of a traction load of 30 kg.[36] Pelvic distraction in a flexion mode widens the posterior portion of the intervertebral disc spaces as follows: At L1-L2 the average distraction was 1.1 mm, L2-L3 was 2.0 mm, L3-L4 was 2.8 mm, L4-L5 was 2.3 mm., and L5-S1 was 0.8 mm.[32] Vertebral distraction is also credited for relief of back pain.[32]

HOW MUCH DISC REDUCTION IS NECESSARY FOR CLINICAL RELIEF?

Some patients, when treated nonsurgically, are relieved of sciatica, yet sometimes little or no disc herniation reduction on repeat CT or MRI is seen. Kramer[43] feels the most important factor in traction is the reduction of intradiscal pressure, which facilitates normalization of dislocated disc material.

Reports of total to no reduction in the size of the disc herniation in patients with posttreatment CT and MRI studies, who nevertheless had attained complete or partial relief of their low back and sciatic pain, are found.* No universally accepted premise to explain this phenomenon exists, but apparently only a few millimeters of reduced nerve root compression may suffice to relieve pain. The size of the vertebral canal housing the cauda equina is also very

*References 6,7,13,15,29,32,33,37,38,41,45.

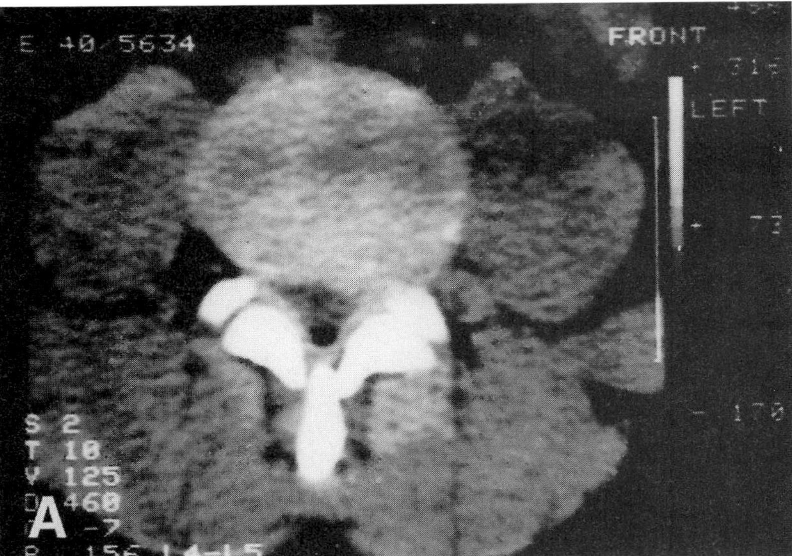

Figure 19–2. Prior to distraction, medial and left lateral disc prolapse at the L4–L5 level is seen invading the neural foramen. Note also the narrowing of the osseoligamentous canal by upward placement of the superior facet of L5, creating stenosis of the foramen.

Reprinted with permission from: Onel D, Tuzlaci M, Sari H, Demir K. Computed tomographic investigation of the effect of traction on lumbar disc herniation. Spine. 1989;14(1):83, 86.

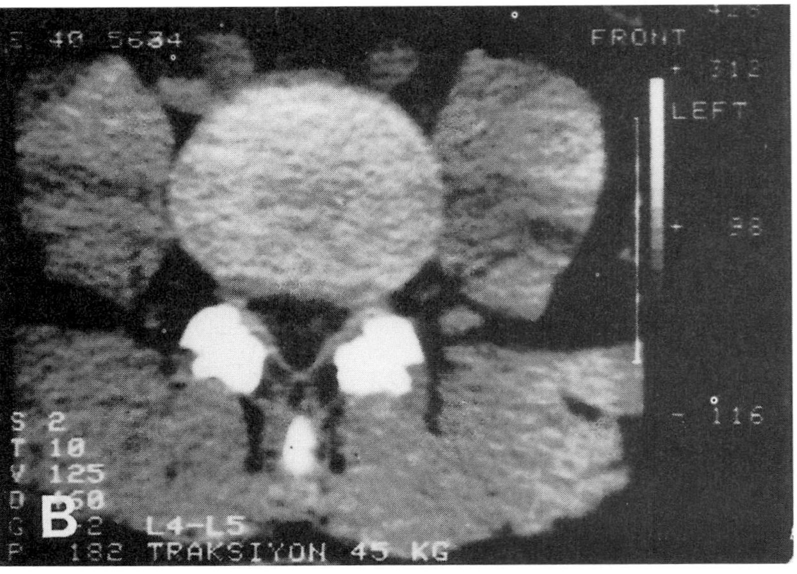

Figure 19–3. During distraction, regression of the herniated nucleus pulposus from the neural foramen is seen. The ligamentum flavum also appears to be tautened, allowing greater vertebral canal diameter. Also note how the osseoligamentous canal is opened as the superior facet of L5 is drawn downward under distraction.

Onel[4] states the following possible occurrences during distraction: The widened disc space drops intradiscal pressure and probably creates a negative intradiscal pressure that sucks the herniated disc back into place. The anterior and posterior longitudinal ligaments are stretched under distraction. The posterior longitudinal ligament is stretched and may "push back" the herniated disc towards the disc space. Therefore, the herniated nucleus pulposus seems to be reduced by the combination of the lowered intradiscal pressure sucking the nucleus pulposus back into the disc space as well as the pushing back of the disc by retraction of the posterior longitudinal ligament.

The interspinous spaces are seen to increase during distraction with the ligamentum flavum becoming thinner. It is felt that there is separation of the facet joints and stretching of the posterior longitudinal ligament.

Reprinted with permission from Onel D, Tuzlaci M, Sari H, Demir K. Computed tomographic investigation of the effect of traction on lumbar disc herniation. Spine. 1989;14(1):83–86.

important as a 2-mm difference in canal size has been seen to separate persons with and without back pain.[46] Narrowing of the vertebral canal can be due to stenosis introduced by abnormalities such as discal protrusion, facet hypertrophy, ligamentum flavum hypertrophy, or a combination of such forces. As shown by Onel,[4] these factors are reduced with distraction (Figures 19–1, 19–2, and 19–3).

CHEMICAL RADICULITIS

Degenerating nucleus pulposus material that leaks into the vertebral canal has been cited as a cause of sciatica because

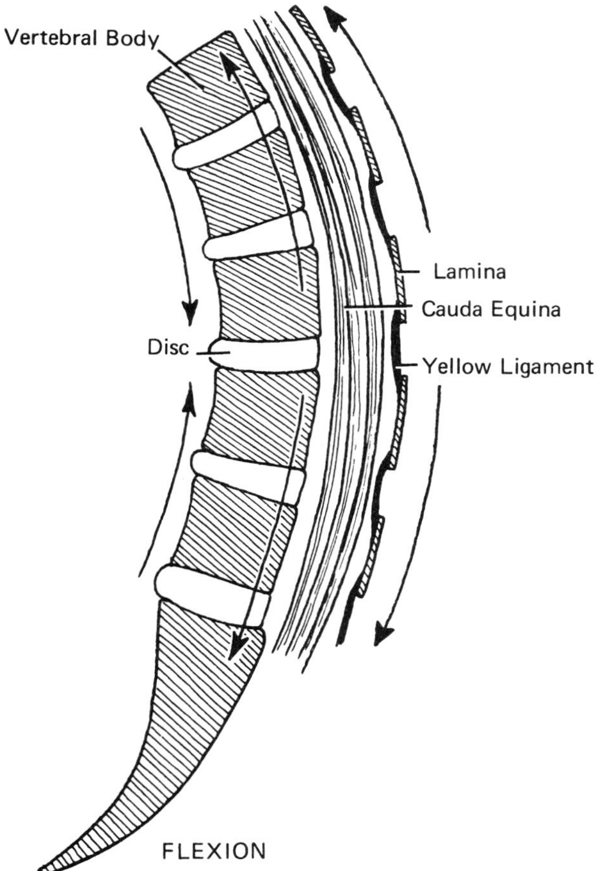

Figure 19–4. The effects of flexion on the lumbar spine are: (1) decrease in the intraspinal protrusion of the lumbar intervertebral disc; (2) slight increase in the length of the anterior wall of the spinal canal; (3) significant increase in the length of the posterior wall of the spinal canal; (4) stretching and a decreased bulge of the yellow ligaments within the spinal canal; (5) stretching and a decreased cross-sectional area of nerve roots; (6) an overall general increase in spinal canal volume and decreased nerve root bulk.

Reprinted from: Low Back Pain, *ed 1 (p. 259), by Finneson, BE with permission of J.B. Lippincott, copyright 1973.*

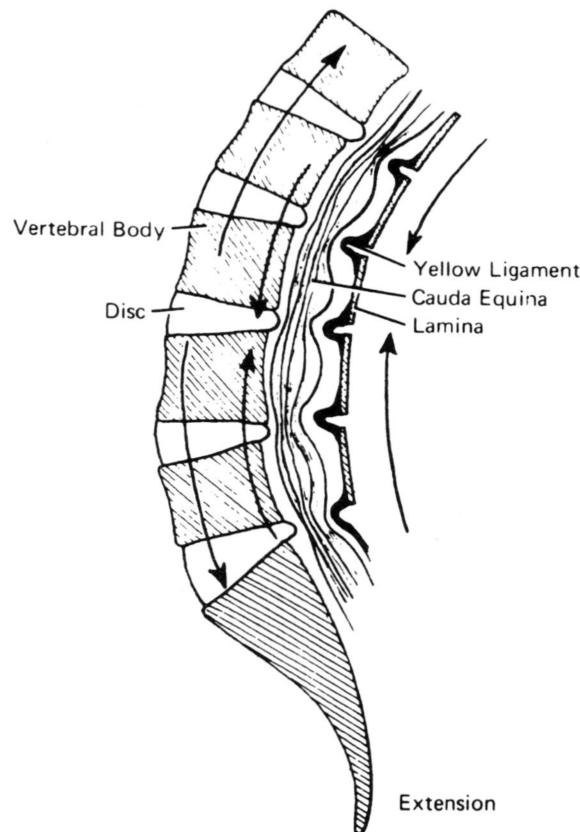

Figure 19–5. The effects of extension on the lumbar spine are: (1) bulging of the intervertebral discs into the spinal canal; (2) slight decrease in the anterior canal length; (3) moderate decrease in the posterior canal length; (4) enfolding and protrusion of the yellow ligaments into the spinal canal; (5) relaxation and an increase in the cross-sectional diameter of the nerve roots; (6) an overall decrease in the volume of the lumbar spinal canal and an increased nerve root bulk.

Reprinted from: Low Back Pain, *ed 1 (p. 259) by Finneson, BE with permission of J.B. Lippincott, copyright 1973.*

of the local nerve root edema and release of chemical irritant substances at the disc injury site.[47] Future research may find that the mechanical stimulation of circulation by distraction manipulation may help dissipate the biodegradation products of nuclear disc degeneration and thus form a basis of relief of chemical radiculitis.

USE OF EXTENSION AFTER ACUTE DISC LESION SYMPTOMS SUBSIDE

It is vital to not inflict further stenosis into the vertebral or osseoligamentous canal (intervertebral foramen) when disc protrusion is present; therefore, avoid extension movements until 50% percent relief of sciatic pain is obtained, which indicates the disc compression of the involved sciatic nerve root is decreasing. Disc herniation increases in size on extension motion and decreases under distraction alone, with or without the addition of flexion[48,49] (Figures 19–4, 19–5, and 19–6).

Schonstrom et al[50] showed that the spinal canal decreases its cross-sectional area by 16% (2 mm) in midsagittal diameter when moving from flexion to extension. Dai Liyang et al[51] showed that the sagittal diameter of the cadaver spinal canal increased 3.5 to 6.0 mm in flexion, making the increased space suitable to symptom relief.

NUCLEUS PULPOSUS MOVEMENT UNDER THE FORCES OF DISTRACTION, FLEXION, AND EXTENSION

The question of nucleus pulposus motion within the annulus fibrosus on flexion, distraction, and extension movements has been debated. Does intranuclear pressure increase on distraction and minimal flexion to cause further discal herniation? Several authors have proven, under CT/discography and MRI, that no nuclear movement on flexion or distraction occurs, but extension causes annular disc protrusion into the vertebral canal and induces stenosis.[52–54] Hydrostatic pressure within the nucleus pulposus can be higher in a lordotic, unsupported posture (such as anterior straight sitting) than in a flexed unsupported posture (posterior sitting). Therefore, any argument against flexed postures on the grounds that they increase hydrostatic pressure would appear to be unjustified.[55,56]

NUTRITIONAL BENEFITS OF FLEXION DISTRACTION

Flexion reduces compression on the posterior annular fibers of the disc, the facet joints are unloaded, and the transport of nutrients into the disc is stimulated.[55] Flexed postures favor diffusion of metabolites into the posterior half of the disc by improving fluid flow. Changes from lordotic to flexed postures aid the supply of nutrients to the disc. Impaired nutrient supply may lead to degenerative disc disease.[57]

COX TREATMENT OF DISC LESIONS WITH AND WITHOUT SCIATICA

Based on previously cited spinal mechanics studies in this chapter, controlled distraction of the spinal canal can reduce disc protrusion and stenosis. These are important as-

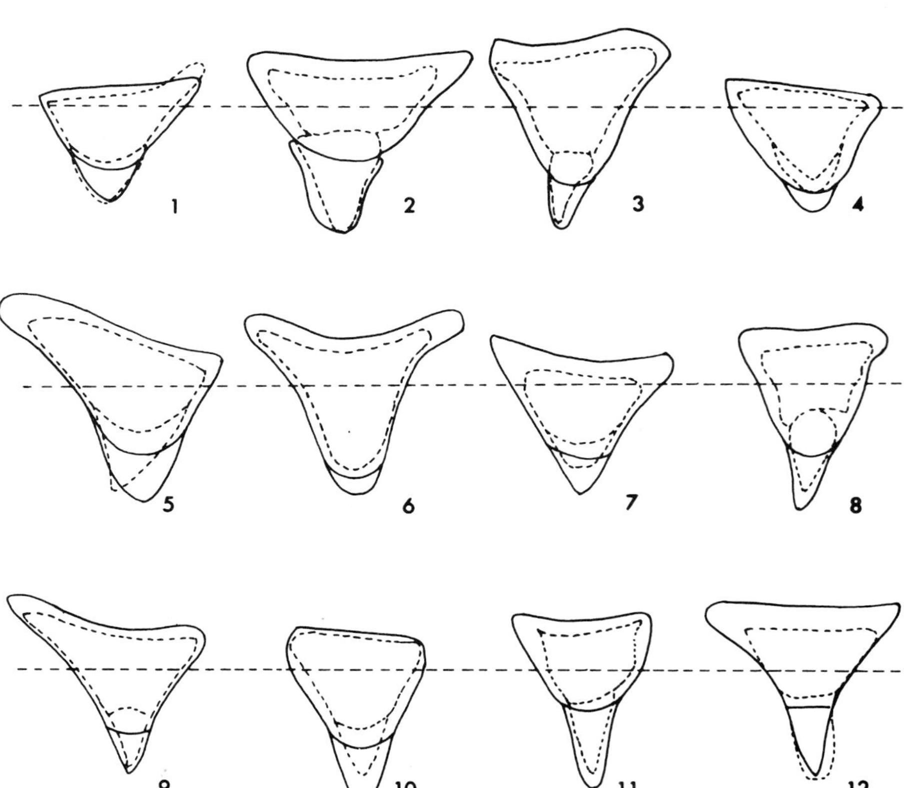

Figure 19–6. Drawings of the dural sac in flexion (solid line) and extension (broken line) in a study of 12 patients showing the reduced size of the vertebral canal in extension as compared with flexion. The horizontal line represents the interfacet line.

Reprinted with permission from Penning L, Wilmink JT. Posture-dependent bilateral compression of L4 on L5 nerve roots in facet hypertrophy: A dynamic CT-myelographic study. Spine. 1987; 12(5):495.

pects when applying manipulative or adjustive forces to the spine. Following is the protocol with distraction manipulation for the patient with a lumbar disc protrusion, and the subsequent therapy when 50% relief of sciatica is obtained.

CARE OF THE SCIATICA PATIENT

Special Note[58]: The following adjustment procedures performed under distraction are special forms of manipulative procedures. There is a certification course in the use of Cox flexion distraction procedures taught under the auspices of the National College of Chiropractic. This course includes 36 hours of instruction followed by a written and practical examination in the use of distraction manipulation. Successful passing of the test affords the doctor of chiropractic a listing in a book published by National College, so listing the designation of certification. Although it is not required for a doctor of chiropractic to have such a designation prior to using distraction procedures, the certification does attest to a degree of ability and competence in the use of these procedures. As author of this chapter, developer of flexion distraction manipulation procedures, and an instructor for the National College in these procedures, I recommend and endorse this certification course for the optimum use of these manipulation techniques.

The adjustments shown in this chapter are shown on equipment developed by Williams Healthcare Systems and named the Zenith-Cox table.

The sciatica patient receives only distraction adjustment with slight flexion added with the following protocol:

1. The patient is positioned prone on the Zenith-Cox distraction instrument. A flexion pillow may be placed under the abdomen for patient comfort by accommodating flexion posture (Figure 19–7).
2. Tolerance to distraction is determined as follows:
   - *Central distraction testing of the disc:* Apply specific palmar/thenar contact over the spinous process interspace of the level to be tested. Stabilize the spine with the contact hand and flex the caudad section of the table to patient tolerance, which will be a maximum of 2 inches of downward table movement or until the occiput of the patient is seen to move into extension. Hold for 4 seconds. If no pain in the back, buttock, or leg is produced, slowly return the pelvic section of the table to the horizontal (neutral) position and slowly remove the specific spinal contact. Move to the next lower spinous process and repeat the test procedure for pain elicitation. Continue testing to the lowest lumbar segment. Slowly return the pelvic section of the table to the horizontal (neutral) position and then slowly remove the specific spinal contact.
   - *Lateral distraction testing of the facet joint:* Hold the ankle of the uninvolved, nonpainful lower extremity, and apply traction of the facet joints. This is to determine pain production of the facet joint if distraction is applied. A specific thenar contact over the facet joint of the thoracic or lumbar region to be tested is made. Stabilize the spine with the thenar contact on the facet joint space and flex the caudad section of the table while holding the ankle. A maximum of 2 inches of downward table movement or until the occiput of the patient is seen to move into extension is

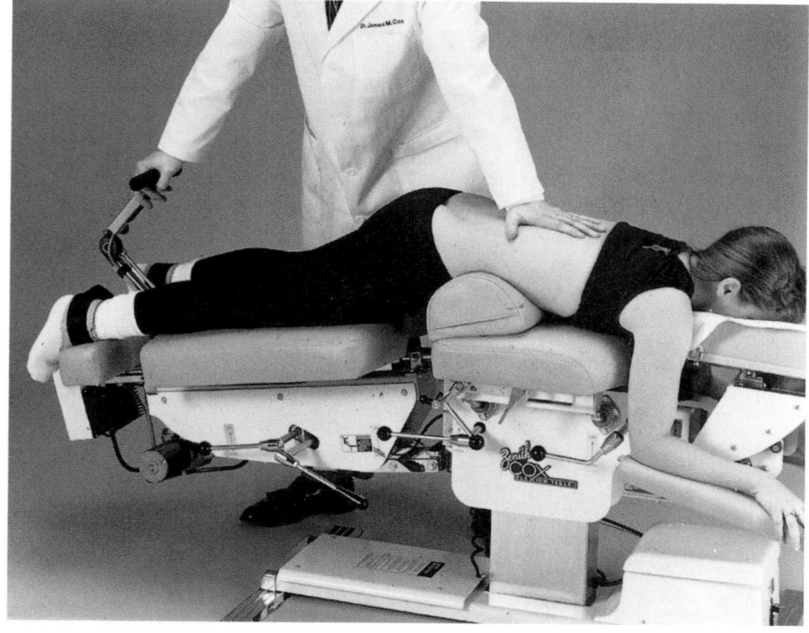

Figure 19–7. Patient placement over a flexion roll to accommodate slight flexion of the lumbar spine prior to distraction being carried out.

applied. Hold this contact for 4 seconds. If no pain in the back, buttock, or leg is produced, slowly return the pelvic section of the table to the horizontal (neutral) position and then slowly remove the specific spinal contact. Move to the next lower spinous process and repeat the test procedure for pain elicitation. Continue to the lowest lumbar segment. Slowly return the pelvic section of the table to the horizontal (neutral) position and then slowly remove the specific contact. Perform the test on the nonpainful side first and then repeat this lateral testing on the opposite or uninvolved side. *If pain is produced in the low back or extremities on tolerance testing, do not use distraction manipulation.*

3. If tolerant to distraction, ankle cuffs are placed on the patient.
4. The ankle extension section of the table is used to apply traction to the lower extremities in preparation for distraction of the spine.
5. Release the flexion lever.
6. Contact the spinous process above the disc to be distracted (Figure 19–8).
7. Bring the caudal section into gentle distraction with flexion of the caudal section until tautness is felt at the spinous process contact.
8. A 20-second distraction session is performed by bringing the caudal section of the table down 1 to 2 inches (shown as 2 degrees in Figure 19–9) while the spinous process contact lifts the vertebra cephalward. Another indicator of achieved distraction motion is extension of the patient's occiput, indicating sufficient traction is applied to the interspinous process. This point of occipital extension corresponds closely to the maximum 2 inches or 2 to 5 degrees of downward table flexion.
9. Five pumping actions are applied during the 20-second session. These are from the point of tautness to a 2-inch downward distractive distance with the caudal section of the table or until patient occipital extension occurs.
10. Three such 20-second sessions are applied. Between the 20-second distraction sessions, muscle massage or acupuncture point therapy may be applied, according to physician choice.
11. Following the three 20-second distraction sessions, the instrument is brought back to a slight flexion neutral position and the contact hand released. Then the cuffs are removed. Note: Apply distraction gently and increase the traction as patient relaxation and confidence occur. Some patients may feel weak or have discomfort in the low back after the treatment if application is too forceful.

If the patient has too much pain to lie on the abdomen, even with a flexion roll under the abdomen, the patient can be placed on his or her side, as shown in Figure 19–10, and the flexion distraction applied by utilizing the lateral flexion action of the instrument. Of interest is that pregnant females are comfortably manipulated while in this side-lying posture.

OTHER CARE OF THE DISC PATIENT WITH SCIATICA

It is not the scope of this chapter to cover the details of ancillary modes of treating spinal pain, but rather to concen-

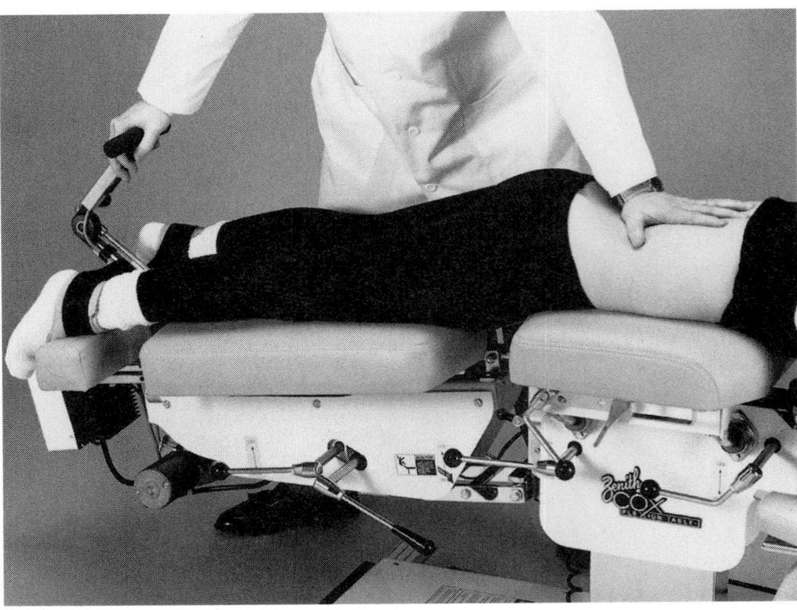

Figure 19–8. The doctor's thenar contact is on the spinous process directly above the disc space to be distracted.

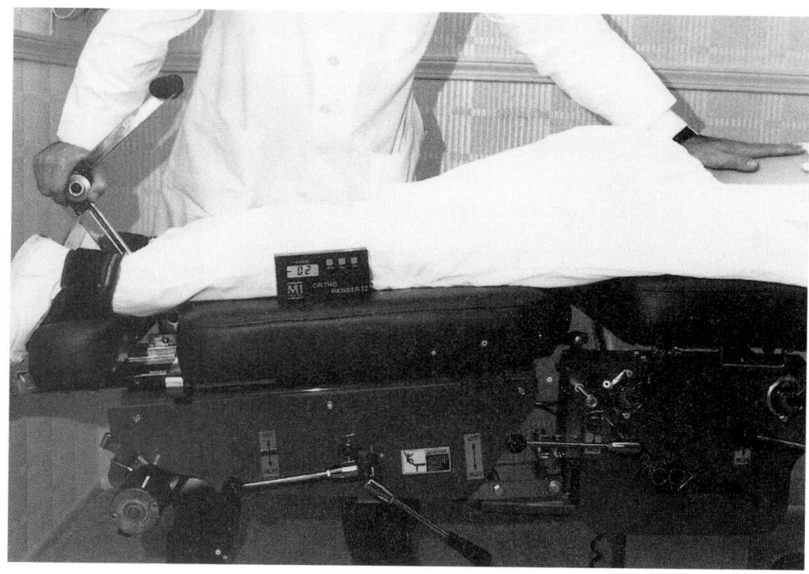

Figure 19–9. With the doctor's contact on the spinous process above the disc or facet joint to be distracted, the caudal section of the table slowly is brought into flexion distraction until a maximum of 2 inches or 5 degrees of downward motion is produced, or occipital extension of the patient is noted. The doctor's contact on the spinous process lifts cephalward with a steady and firm contact, applying one-third of the force under the spinous process and the remainder directed cephalward.

trate on distraction manipulation.[58] Therefore, the following treatment applications are only listed:

1. Physical therapy: Positive galvanism is applied over the disc.
2. Acupressure point therapy is given.
3. Alternating hot and cold fomentations.
4. Bracing.
5. Home care: exercises,[5] low back wellness school,[63] nutritional treatment.

PATIENT CARE OF THE DISC LESION IF NOT TOLERANT TO DISTRACTION

Naturally, distraction manipulation is not used if pain on tolerance testing is found. If pain is found on testing for tolerance, the care outlined in the previous section is used only until such time as the patient can tolerate distraction. This might be a matter of hours or days. If days, the patient goes home wearing a brace and performs the home instructions of not sitting, alternating hot and cold fomentations to the lumbar spine, and doing knee-chest and intraab-

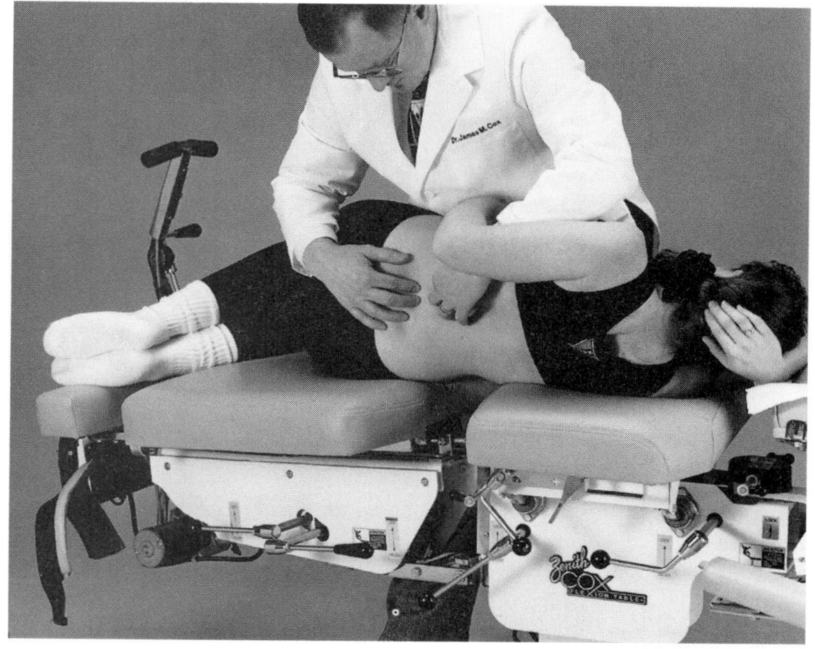

Figure 19–10. If pain is too great for the patient to lie on the abdomen, distraction is applied with the patient lying on the side and using the lateral flexion mode of the table to apply flexion. The doctor's right hand is controlling spinous process movement while the left thigh moves the caudal section of the table into lateral flexion.

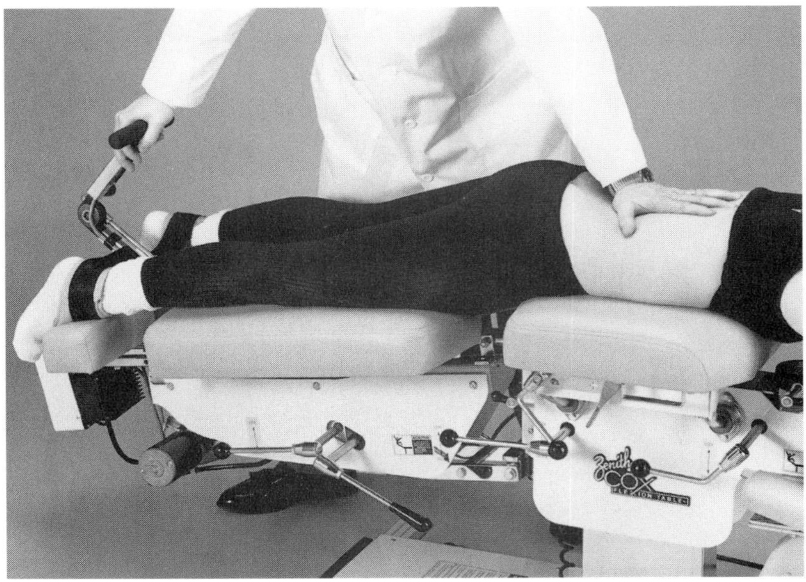

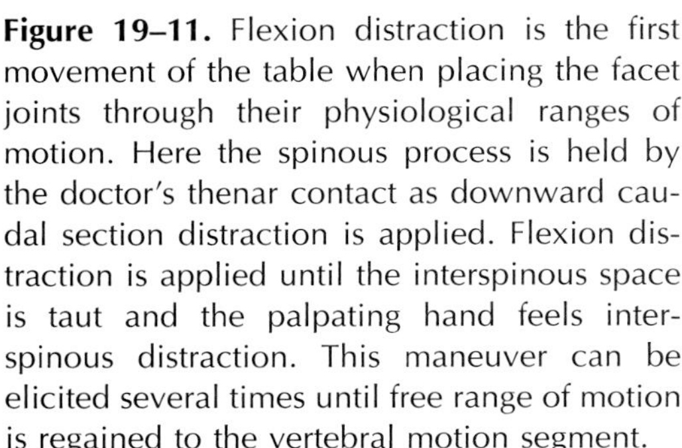
Figure 19–11. Flexion distraction is the first movement of the table when placing the facet joints through their physiological ranges of motion. Here the spinous process is held by the doctor's thenar contact as downward caudal section distraction is applied. Flexion distraction is applied until the interspinous space is taut and the palpating hand feels interspinous distraction. This maneuver can be elicited several times until free range of motion is regained to the vertebral motion segment.

dominal pressure increasing exercises. When distraction is tolerated, it is then implemented.

CARE OF THE PATIENT NOT RESPONDING TO DISTRACTION MANIPULATION

Tables 19–2 and 19–3 are the decision-making algorithms used to determine steps to be taken in a patient as response or failure to conservative distractive chiropractic adjusting occurs.

TREATMENT OF THE PATIENT WHO ATTAINS 50% RELIEF OF SCIATICA OR WHO ONLY HAS LOW BACK AND THIGH PAIN

A patient who only has low back or leg pain extending no lower than the knee, as well as the patient who has attained 50% relief of sciatic pain, is treated by placing the facet joints through normal physiological ranges of motion—flexion, extension, lateral flexion, circumduction, and rotation. Since different levels of the spine are capable of specific movements in preference to others, movement is patterned for the level of application; for example, rotation is not applied to the L4-L5 and L5-S1 levels because it is a restricted movement at those levels.

SPECIFIC MANIPULATIVE PROCEDURES

Flexion distraction (Figures 19–11 and 19–12) is the first movement used in any adjustment since it allows the intervertebral disc space to be increased, the facets to be separated into open relief, the ligamentum flavum to be tautened, and the vertebral canal diameters to be opened to maximum size (review Figures 19–1 through 19–6). In this

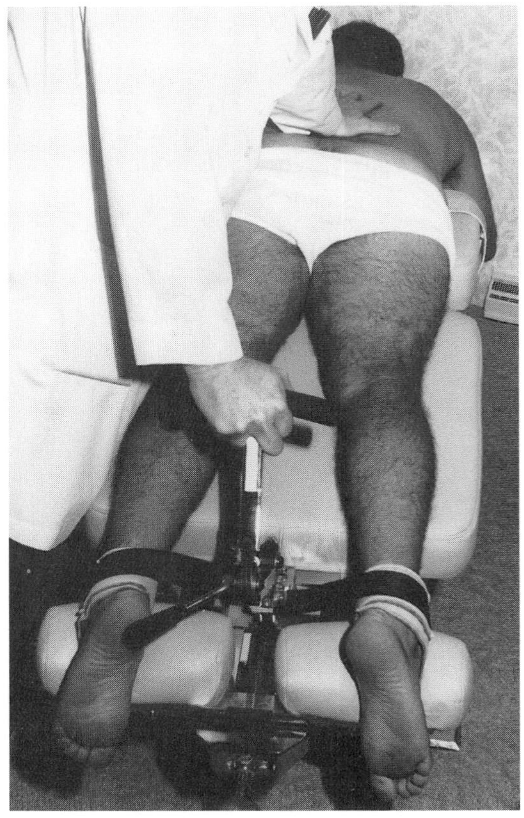

Figure 19–12. This shows another view of the application of flexion distraction as applied in Figure 19–11. The doctor's distracting arm is straight with the patient's spine, with one-third of the doctor's body weight applied under the spinous process and the other two-thirds directed cephalic under the spinous process contact.

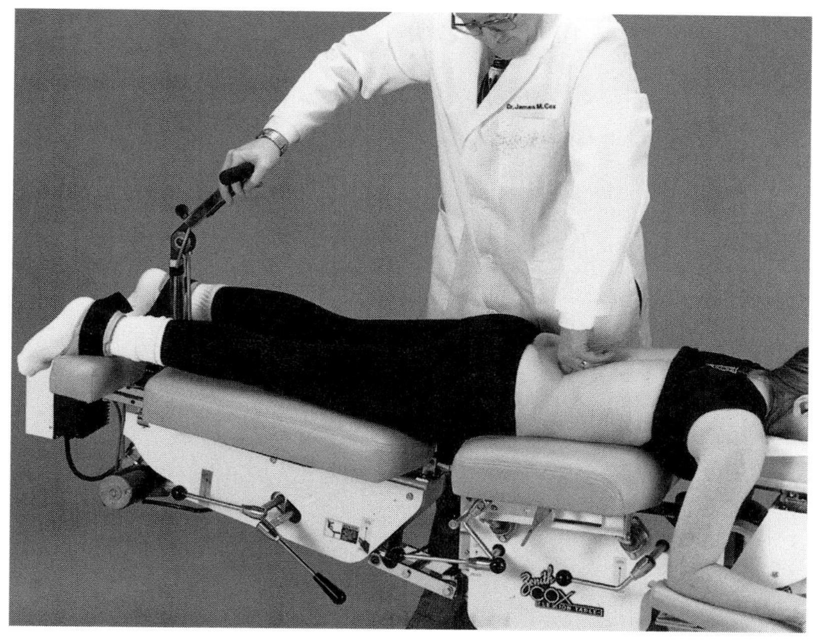

Figure 19–13. Extension is applied to the motion segment by placing an anterior force to the spinous process of the segment desired to be extended as the caudal section of the table is slowly brought into extension. Repeated attempts may be required to accomplish this movement, each attempting to increase both the downward motion with the contact hand and the extension motion of the table. Tolerance of the patient is monitored throughout this maneuver.

anatomical positioning, the facets can be placed into their other ranges of motion with less possibility of creating stenosis of the vertebral canal or intervertebral foramen.

Extension (Figure 19–13) is now used because it allows approximation of the posterior vertebral body surfaces. It has the potential to reduce annular strain and may help the healing of rents and tears in the annulus fibrosus. It also allows slack to the nerve roots since the cauda equina shortens during extension. At 50% relief of sciatic pain, the disc has likely healed sufficiently so it will not protrude on extension to compress the nerve root.

With the patient first under flexion distraction as shown in Figures 19–11 and 19–12, the caudal section of the instrument places the facet joints into *lateral flexion* (Figure 19–14).

In *circumduction* (Figure 19–15) the combined motion of flexion and lateral flexion is simultaneously applied to the facet joint. This procedure can provide return of range of motion to the subluxated facet demonstrating loss of mobility on motion palpation.

Rotation (Figures 19–16 and 19–17) is applied by placing the caudal or thoracic section of the instrument into rotation as flexion distraction is applied to the caudal end of the table. This is applied only from the L3-L4 segment cephalward into the thoracic spine since rotation is a limited motion in the lower lumbar segments. Figure 19–18 is a side view showing combined thoracic and lumbar spine section rotation as used in treating double scoliotic curves.

Before lateral flexion, extension, rotation, and circumduction of the facets are instituted, each motion is tested for tolerance by the patient. In addition to these manipulations, the patient is started on Nautilus extension exercises to strengthen the erector spinae muscles and the Cox home exercise program.[58]

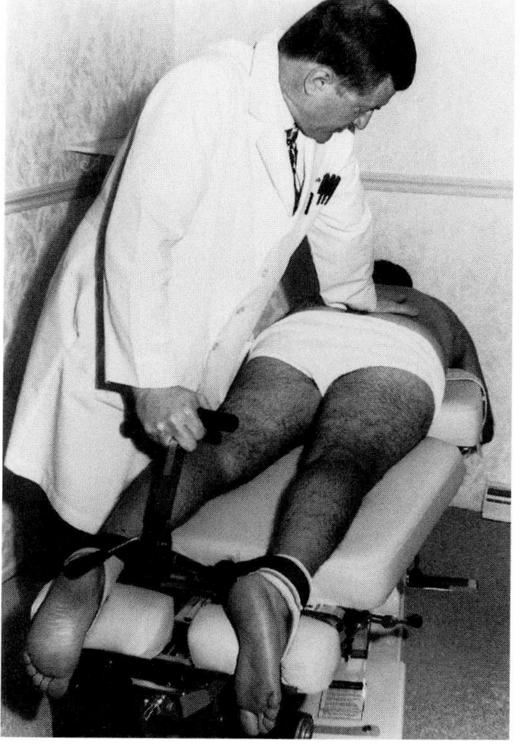

Figure 19–14. Lateral flexion of the facet joints is performed by contacting the spinous process above the facets to be manipulated. As the caudal section of the table moves into left lateral flexion, the doctor's contact hand will resist the spinous process on the left so as to accommodate left lateral flexion of the facets below the spinous process contact. The reverse is applied in right lateral flexion.

DISTRACTION MOTION-ASSISTED ADJUSTING

All of the techniques for nonradiculopathy patients shown in this chapter can be performed under automated axial distraction by pressing the switch on the handle or using the foot switch to apply axial distraction (see Figure 19–19). The switch on the handle allows the doctor to apply automated axial distraction as the facet joints are placed through their physiological ranges of motion. By using the foot switch, bilateral hand contact on the spine is possible for adjusting facet joint subluxations under distraction. This creates a continuous distraction of the spine which assists the adjustment of the facets by decreasing impaction pressure and increases the accommodation of cavitation.

In this mode of distraction adjusting, often the spinal contact during distraction application will produce cavitation of the facet joints. This is gentle without pain for the patient and often allows motion when vector thrust without traction would not yield cavitation. Automated axial distraction is never used to treat radiculopathy patients and is only used with a doctor in attendance.

SUMMARY OF STEPS IN TREATING ACUTE DISC SYNDROME

1. Patient positioning sequence on the Cox instrument: Locks secure with Dutchman roll in place if used.
2. If the patient seen within the first 4 days of injury or pain onset, apply ice for 10 minutes to lumbar spine before distraction manipulation.
3. Trigger point acupressure applied to:
   - Bladder meridian between spinous and transverse processes from L1 through sacrum (bladder points 22 to 35).
   - B49 in the belly of the gluteus maximus and piriformis muscles. Spend as much time on this point as needed to sedate or relax patients and their pain (very important point for sedation).
   - Posterior thigh to popliteal fossa (B54).
   - Lateral pelvis over the gluteus medius and minimus muscles
   - Posteriorly around hip joint, ischium, and upper hamstring muscles.
   - Posterior calf to plantar surface of foot and arch of foot.
4. Tolerance test before distraction applied: Decide whether to use ankle cuffs or not.
5. Apply distraction reduction:
   - Contact spinous process of vertebra above disc to be distracted with the thenar contact.
   - Release flexion lever, being careful that extension does not occur.
   - Apply thenar contact to spinous process by putting one-third of doctor pressure under spinous process and other two-thirds lifting cephalward. Use a broad hand contact so as to distribute doctor pressure over patient's lumbar spine.
   - Find taut point—all slack taken out of interspinous space contact. From here distraction is applied.
   - Apply three 20-second distraction sessions. The depth of distraction will be 2 inches or until occiput extension begins.
6. Postdistraction treatment:
   - Positive Myofasciatron galvanism is applied for 10 minutes to the involved disc, B49 in the belly of the gluteus maximus muscle, popliteal fossa B54, and any other points of strong pain and inflammation. Heat is applied while the positive galvanism is applied.
   - Following positive galvanism, tetanizing current is applied for 10 minutes to the paravertebral lumbar muscles, B49 in the belly of the gluteus maximus muscle, hamstring muscle origin at the ischium, gluteus minimus or medius muscle, calf muscles, or arch of foot. These locations of application are selected by the patient's subjective tenderness to palpation. It is very important to treat the lumbar paravertebral muscles and gluteus maximus. Other points are selective for individual patients. Cold packs are applied while the tetanizing current is applied.
   - Following tetanizing current, heat is again applied, alone, to the lumbar spine and pelvis.
   - Massage of the trigger points is repeated in acute disc cases.
   - A back brace is applied to acute disc cases or other severely painful backs.

HOME CARE GIVEN

1. Patient booklet of diagnosis explanation and homework for care of the back condition is supplied.
2. Discat (glycosaminoglycan, 100 mg) and glucosamine sulfate (500 mg) are prescribed at three or four tablets daily for 3 months and then reduced to two tablets daily. Calcium citrate is prescribed if osteoporosis or muscle spasm is present
3. Patient is given hot and cold packs to apply at home (10 minutes heat, 10 minutes cold, and 10 minutes heat) every 3 to 4 hours.
4. Cox exercises are given.
5. Liniment may be applied to the lumbar spine after applying alternating hot-cold-hot packs and performing the exercises.

6. A back brace is to be worn except when using heat, cold, or exercising. Wear it to bed while loosening the belt for comfort. This prevents excessive motion of the lumbar disc space and aids in healing. Decrease the use of the brace as healing occurs.
7. Low back wellness school date is given to patient and family to attend at next session.[63]
8. At the report of findings, this case management plan is outlined and explained to the patient.

STEPS IN TREATING NONSCIATICA OR SCIATICA PATIENT ATTAINING 50% RELIEF

1. Patient positioning as above.
2. Tolerance testing.
3. Flexion motion of facet:
   - Contact spinous process above vertebra to be flexed with doctor's thenar contact.
   - Table flexes for 10 one-second motions until interspinous tautening is felt, 2 inches of downward movement of the caudal section is attained, or the occiput moves into extension.
4. Lateral flexion of facet.
5. Circumduction of facet joints.
6. Rotation of facet joints.
7. Extension of facet joints.
8. Homework given as for acute disc case above. All homework is reduced by 50% as patient relief is attained until it is all stopped except for the exercises, discat, and training given in low back wellness school.

EFFECTIVENESS OF COX DISTRACTION ADJUSTMENT

Fluorographic study of the lumbar spine during flexion distraction adjustment showed that 75% of patients treated showed improved coupled motion, and such evidence of improved lumbar kinematics may explain the clinical effectiveness of this type of adjustment.[59]

Chronic low back pain was favorably affected by flexion distraction adjustment in a study of 67 patients in comparison to placebo care and a waiting list control.[60]

In another study, 576 low back and sciatica patients treated with flexion distraction showed excellent relief in 50% of the cases, very good in 14%, good in 12%, fair in 6%, poor in 4%, surgery in 3%, 10% stopped or didn't start treatment, and 1% were examined but not treated.[61]

CERVICAL AND THORACIC SPINE DISTRACTION MANIPULATIVE PROCEDURES

The distraction principles applied to the lumbar spine earlier can be adapted for use in the cervical and thoracic spines.[62] Figures 19–20 and 19–21 show the occipital and spinous process contacts by the doctor's hand when applying flexion distraction of the cervical or thoracic spines. Figures 19–22 through 19–25 illustrate the movements of the cervical headpiece unit.

Figure 19–26 shows tolerance testing prior to placing the occipital cup distraction unit on the patient. Distraction is only used if no adverse reaction to testing is shown. Figure 19–27 shows flexion distraction manipulation being applied to the cervical segments. Figure 19–28 shows lateral flexion being performed to the cervical and upper thoracic spine.

Figure 19–29 is circumduction motion directed to each facet. This is a coupled movement of flexion and lateral flexion administered to the facet joint. Figure 19–30 is rotation adjustment being applied to the lower cervical spine. Figure 19–31 shows extension adjustment being applied to the cervical segment. Figure 19–32 is flexion distraction adjusting applied to the mid- and lower thoracic spine with the use of a cervical cup flexion application.

In full spine distraction (Figure 19–33) the doctor contacts the occipital base with both hands while applying full spine distraction under axial automated distraction by the foramen magnum pump. This is an excellent stretch of the entire spine and is especially helpful for suboccipital tightness, headache, neck pain, scoliosis, thoracic spine myofascial pain, and preparation for vector thrust adjustment procedures.

Figure 19–34 shows combined spinal distraction by the foramen magnum pump technique with the occipital cups of the cervical headpiece and sacral base distraction by doctor hand contact.

SUMMARY

An abbreviated approach to treating lumbar, thoracic, and cervical spine manipulative problems under distraction, based on clinical and academic study, has been presented. It was not meant to be a complete treatise on the diagnostic and therapeutic considerations for low back pain but rather a presentation of the pertinent information upon which to consider distraction manipulative therapy. Fewer of our patients will typically have sciatica or upper extremity radiculopathy and clinical evidence of a herniated disc.

This small percentage will be treated with only distraction adjustment. The remaining majority of the low back, thigh, cervical or thoracic spine pain patients, to include the sciatica patient who has attained 50% relief of lower extremity pain, are given complete range of motion of their facet joints, always beginning with distraction and mild flexion so as to remove vertebral canal stenosis. This protocol is thought to minimize adverse manipulative reactions and maximize clinical relief for the most common patient complaint in chiropractic practice, namely low back, neck, shoulder, and thoracic spine pain.

No proven definitive answer, surgically or manipulatively, exists for the care of spinal pain. Onel[4] and others[5–43] have demonstrated positive effects on reducing disc protrusion, facet imbrication, and stenosis with application of flexion distraction principles. These studies, coupled with clinical outcome studies[5,7,15,17,60,61] suggest an important role for distraction adjustments in the management of cervical and lumbar spine pain syndromes, especially intervertebral disc dysfunction. More research studies are needed, with some presently being planned, to answer more definitively what this role is, how it is best implemented, and how its results are achieved.

FUTURE ONGOING RESEARCH IN DISTRACTION ADJUSTING PROCEDURES

The Health Resources and Services Administration of the Department of Health and Human Services has awarded a grant to the National College of Chiropractic, in concert with the Loyola School of Medicine, for comparing outcomes of low-back and/or leg-pain patients adjusted with distraction to outcomes of those under traditional medical treatment. The randomized patients will be treated at National College for distraction adjusting and at Loyola medical clinics for medical therapy. The principal investigator will be Ram Gudavalli, PhD, of the research department of the National College. James M. Cox, DC, DABCR, postgraduate faculty member of National College, and James Jedlicka, DC, clinical instructor at National College will be in charge of the chiropractic clinicians. A. G. Patwarden, PhD, chief of research at Loyola University will direct the medical protocol of the study. This is the second federal grant to have been awarded for chiropractic distraction research and will be run from 1997 to 2000.

As a final statement, for reasons of patient safety, it is strongly recommended that the procedures of distraction adjusting only be undertaken by a Doctor of Chiropractic trained in their application.

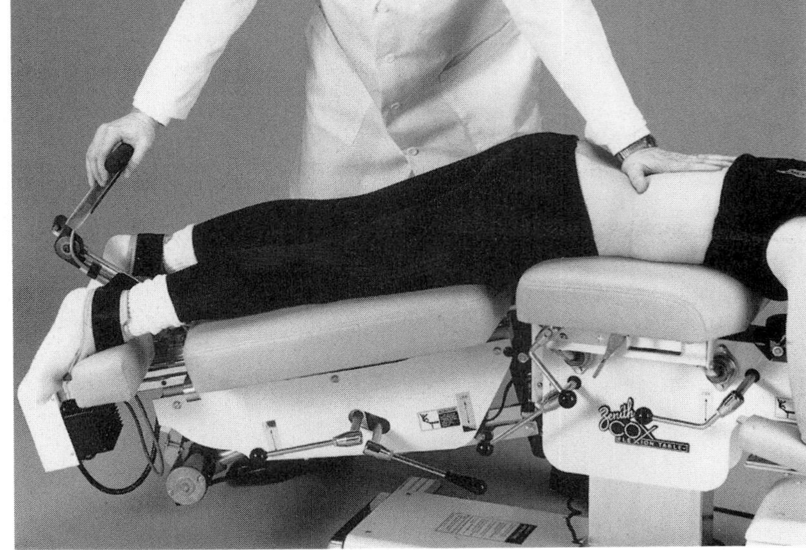

Figure 19–15. Circumduction is the coupled movement of the facet joints using both lateral flexion and flexion simultaneously. This is a strong manipulation for regaining physiological range of motion of a facet joint articulation. It is performed clockwise and counterclockwise.

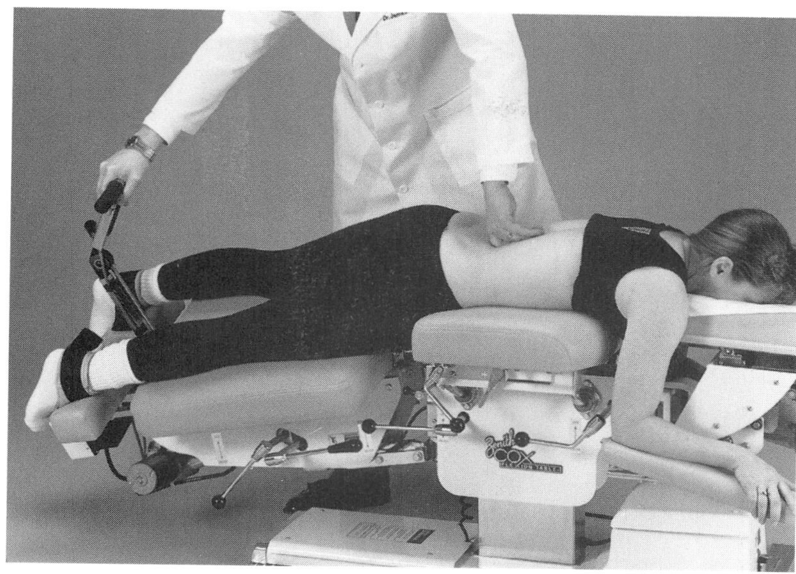

Figure 19–16. Rotation is applied by placing the caudal section of the instrument into rotation so as to accommodate subluxation reduction or merely to place joints through their normal motion of rotation. Remember rotation is only applied from the L3-L4 level cephalward. With rotation applied, flexion distraction or circumduction can be applied as shown.

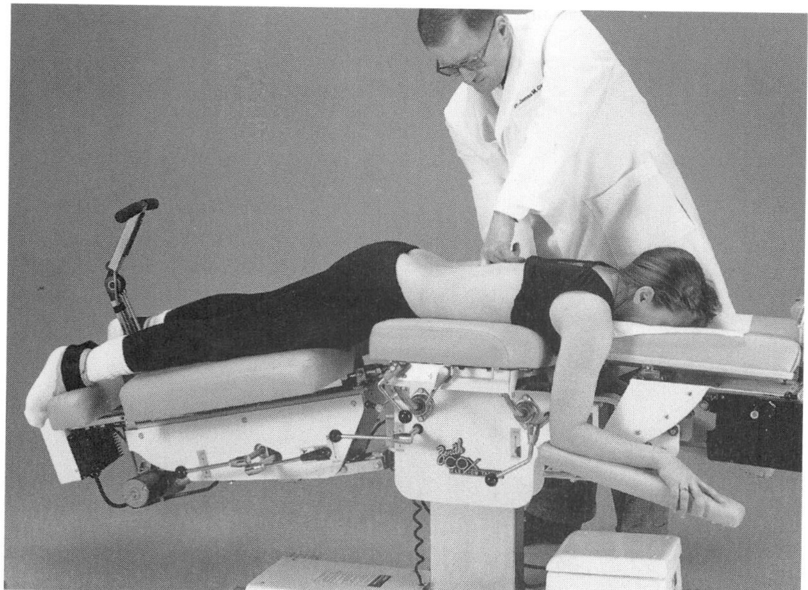

Figure 19–17. Rotation as described in Figure 19–16 can be applied to the thoracic spine by using the thoracic section of the table in a similar manner for rotation movement of the thoracic segments.

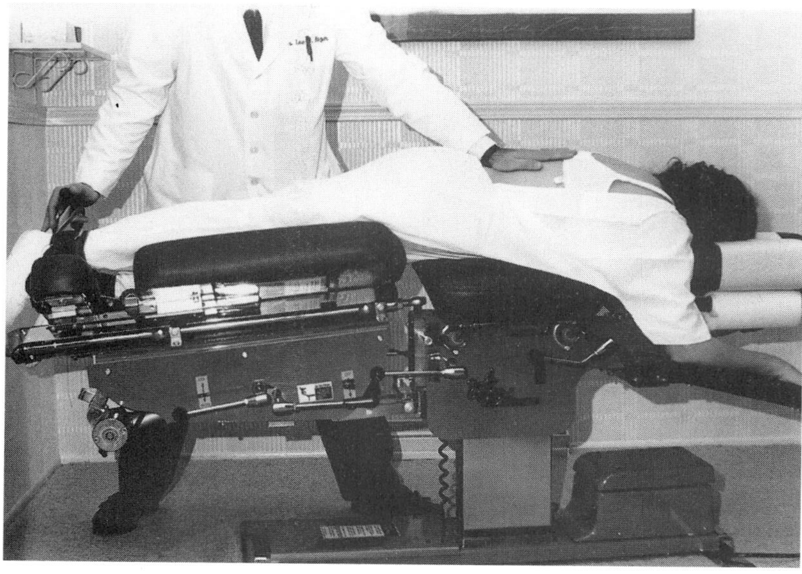

Figure 19–18. Shown is a combined rotation position of the thoracic and lumbar spines utilizing both the thoracic and lumbar sections of the table for rotation implementation and then applying flexion distraction and/or circumduction.

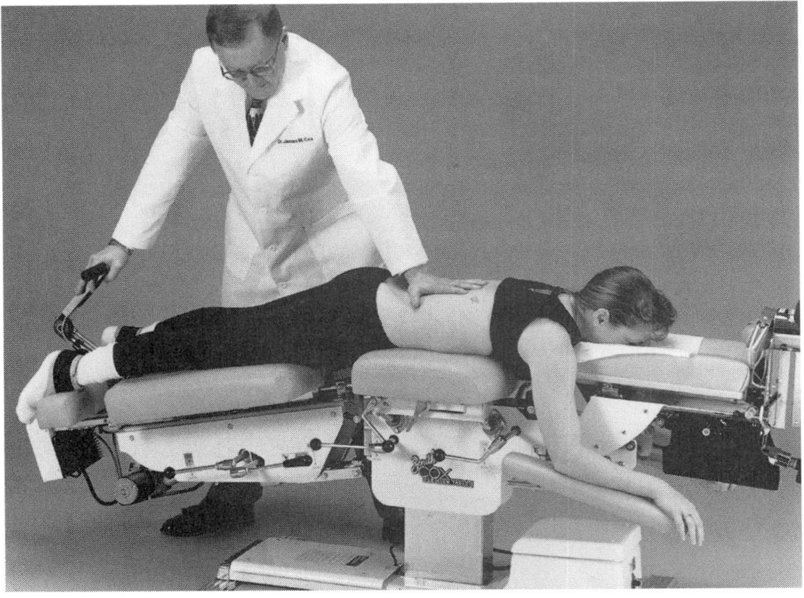

Figure 19–19. Here the doctor is shown pressing the switch on the tiller bar, which institutes automated axial distraction of the caudal section. All ranges of motion of the nonradiculopathy patient can be performed under this automated distraction, thus allowing the doctor to concentrate on treating the intervertebral and facet joint complex while using far less effort than manual distraction necessitates. This automated distraction is not used in patients with radiculopathy and disc herniations. It is also never used without a doctor present, thus the need for the doctor to press either the switch on the floor with the foot or on the handle with the thumb. Figure 19–33 also is an application of automated distraction of the full spine utilizing the foramen magnum pump.

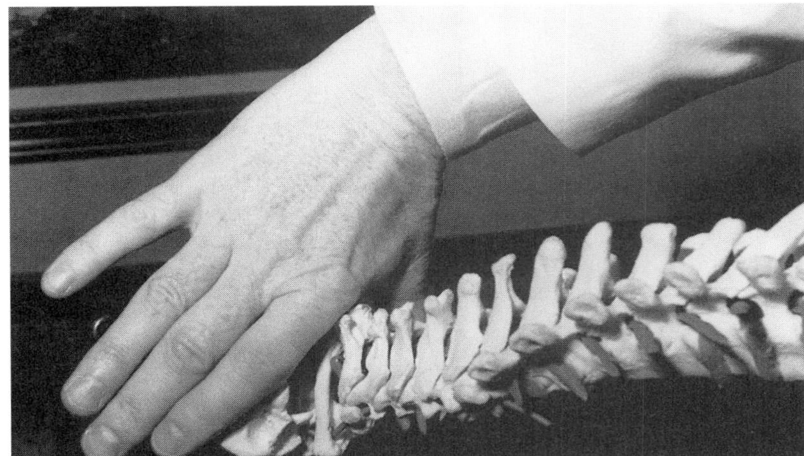

Figure 19–20. Anatomically, this shows how the doctor's contact hand cradles the patient's occiput when distraction manipulation is applied in a technique known as the foramen magnum pump, as shown in Figure 19–33.

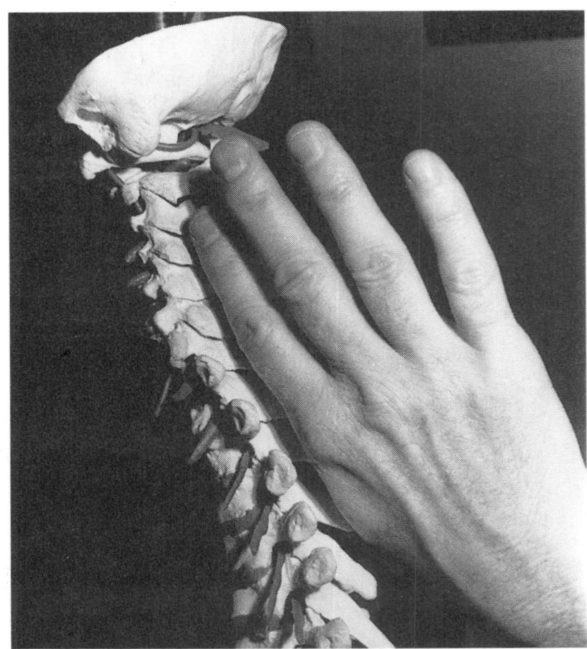

Figure 19–21. Contact of the patient's cervical or thoracic segment arch is demonstrated as applied when distraction manipulation is administered.

Figure 19–22. This is the position of the head-piece for applying flexion distraction manipulation of the cervical or thoracic spines.

Figure 19–23. This is the position of the head-piece for applying extension manipulation of the cervical or thoracic spines.

Figure 19–24. This is the position of the head-piece for applying lateral flexion manipulation of the cervical or thoracic spines.

Figure 19–25. This is the position of the headpiece for applying rotation manipulation of the cervical or thoracic spines.

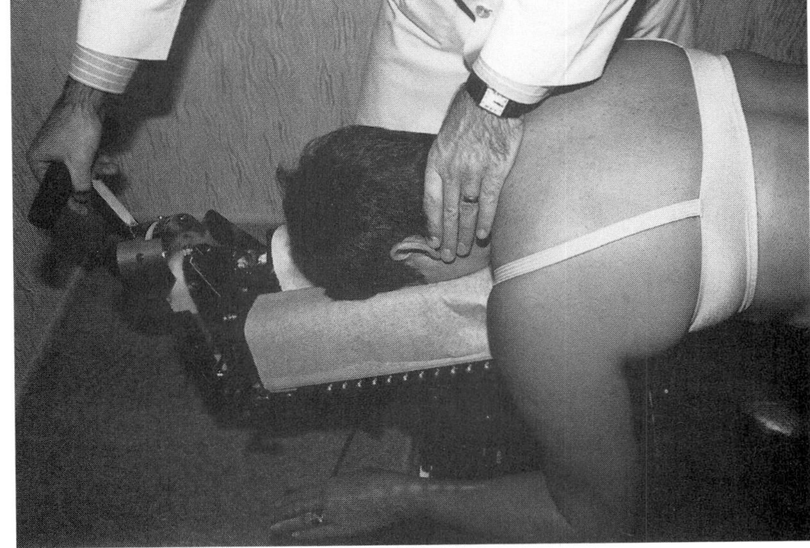

Figure 19–26. Tolerance to distraction of the cervical or thoracic spines is accomplished by grasping the occiput and cervical vertebral arches with the contact hand and applying a cephalward force as the headpiece is brought into flexion. Each segment, starting at the level to be manipulated, is tested, moving cephalward to test each segment above the primary level of care. Only after no pain or discomfort to the patient is noted is the occipital cup apparatus placed on the patient's occiput for further distraction manipulation.

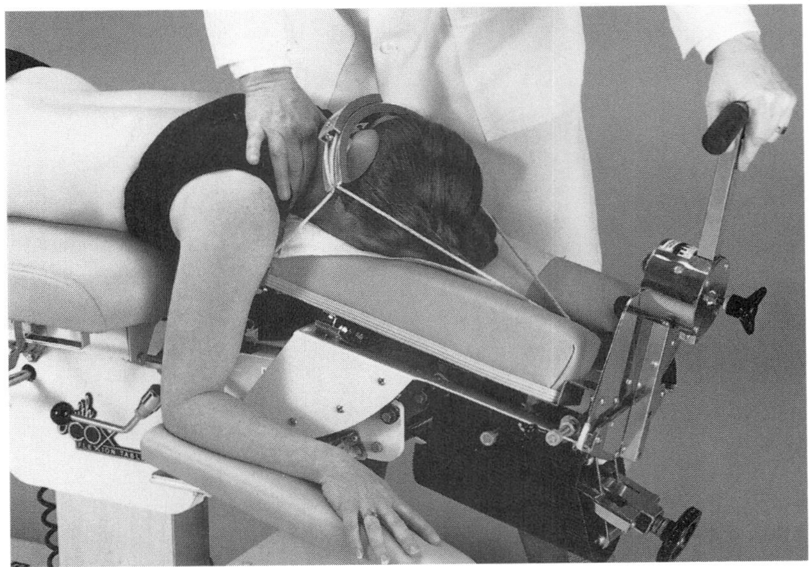

Figure 19–27. Flexion distraction is applied with the occipital cups in place. The doctor will contact the arch of the vertebra below the level of disc or facet to be distracted and manipulated while a caudad force is applied with the contact hand and the cervical headpiece is moved into flexion distraction motion.

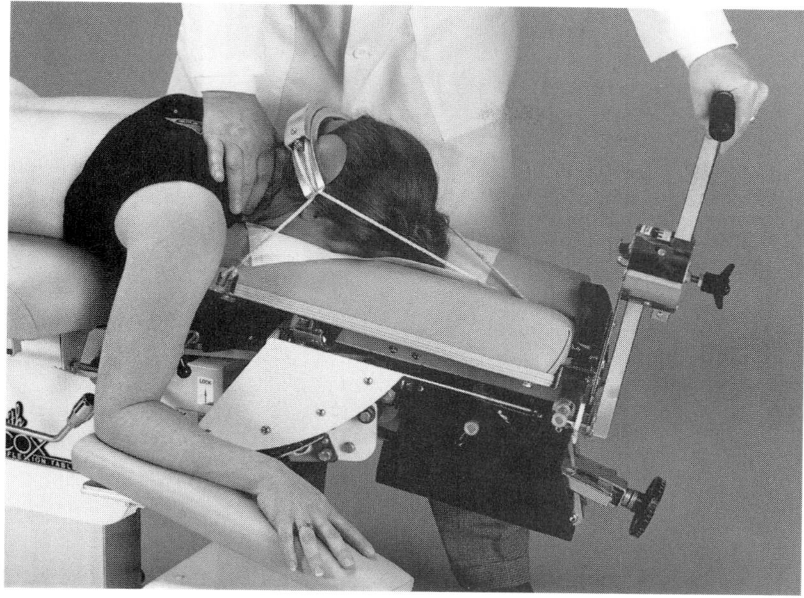

A

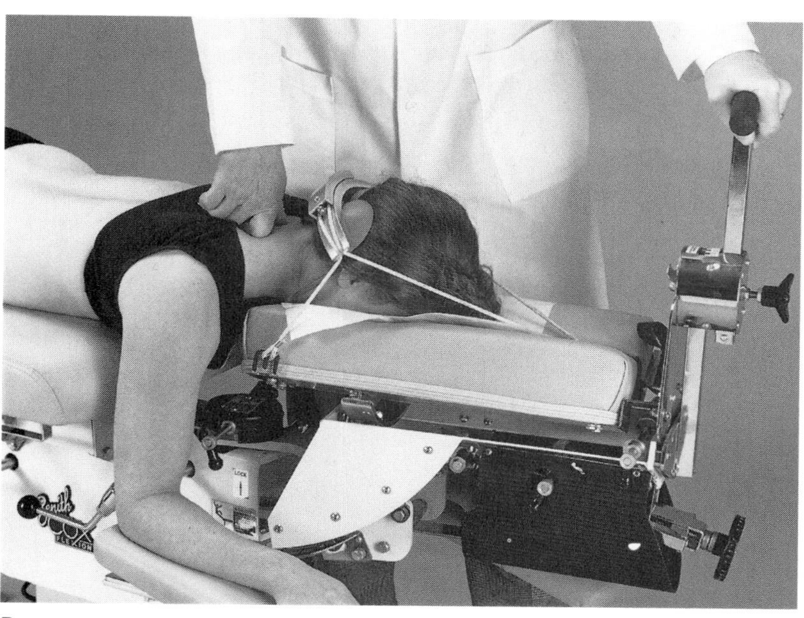

B

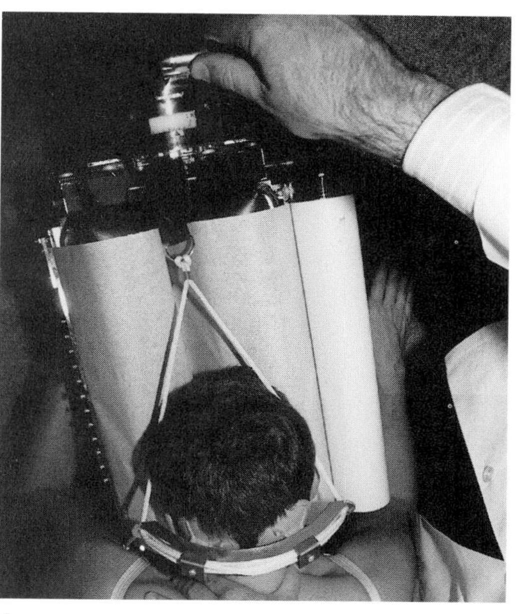

C

Figure 19–28. A. This figure demonstrates doctor contact and headpiece movement to produce left lateral flexion motion of a cervical segment. First, flexion distraction is created at the vertebral segment as shown in Figure 19–27; with left-sided resistance against the patient's vertebral arch by the doctor's hand contact, the headpiece is slowly brought into left lateral flexion. This maneuver is slowly administered and may need several attempts, always to patient tolerance, before increasing motion can be elicited. It may also require several sessions of care to accomplish the desired clinical result of maximum flexibility. **B.** The process applied to the left upper thoracic spine, an area which is often very resistant to movement with conventional high-velocity adjusting. This is an adjustment to regain free and reduced pain mobility of the often difficult to adjust upper thoracic spine. **C.** A view to show more closely the headpiece movement during left lateral flexion adjusting.

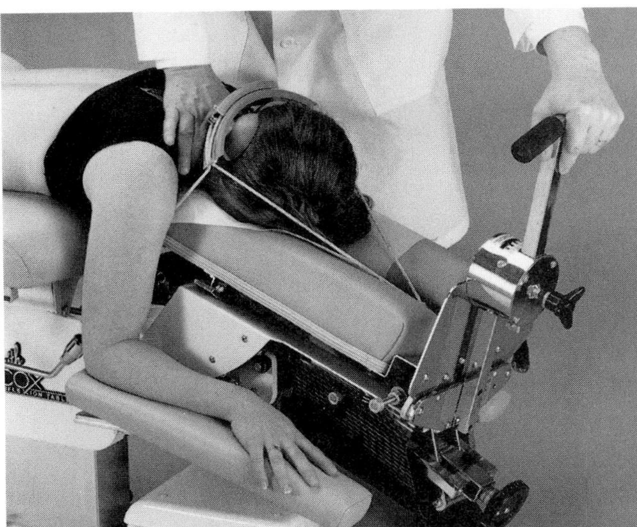

Figure 19–29. Circumduction adjustment of the cervical spine. Circumduction is a combination of flexion distraction and lateral flexion in a coupled motion and represents, in the author's opinion, the strongest force to regain physiological range of motion to any spinal motion segments.

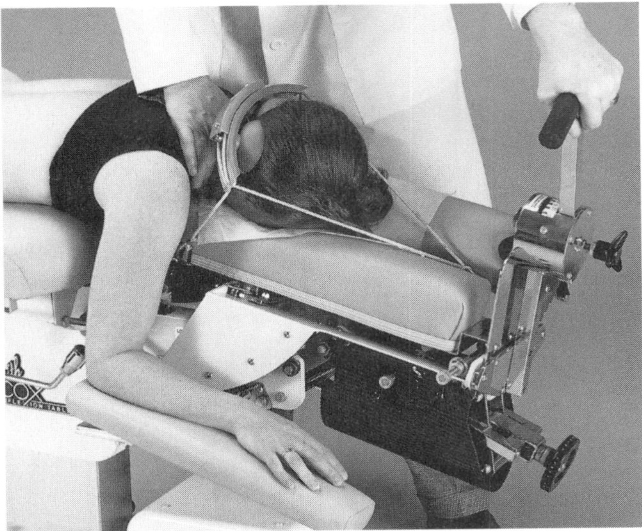

Figure 19–30. Rotation, as shown here, is applied by holding the patient's vertebral segment arch below the segment to be placed into rotation motion and then moving the headpiece into rotation movement to elicit rotation of the facet joints above the doctor's spinal contact.

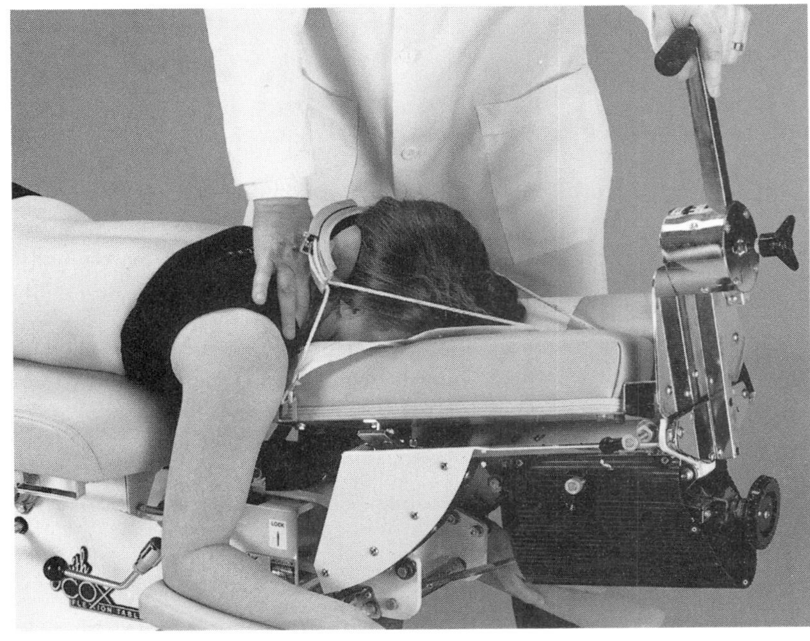

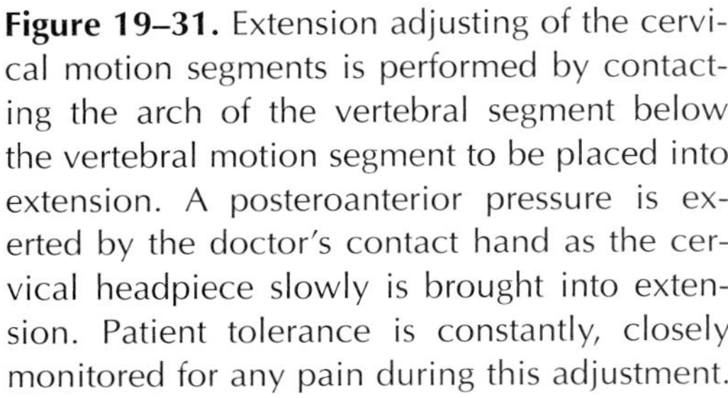

Figure 19–31. Extension adjusting of the cervical motion segments is performed by contacting the arch of the vertebral segment below the vertebral motion segment to be placed into extension. A posteroanterior pressure is exerted by the doctor's contact hand as the cervical headpiece slowly is brought into extension. Patient tolerance is constantly, closely monitored for any pain during this adjustment.

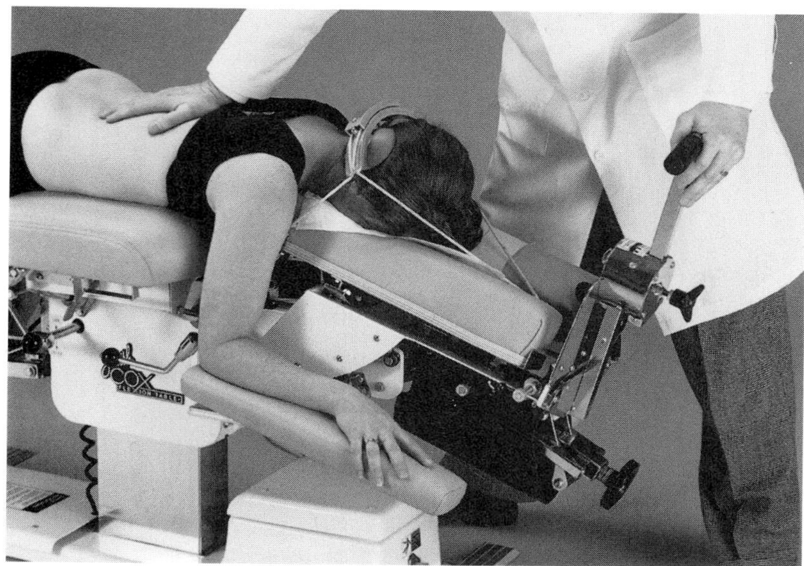

Figure 19–32. Thoracic spine distraction is given by contacting the spinous process below the segment to be distracted by the doctor's thenar contact. Distraction is accomplished by stabilizing the spinous process with a caudad pressure while the cervical headpiece applies distraction to the spine.

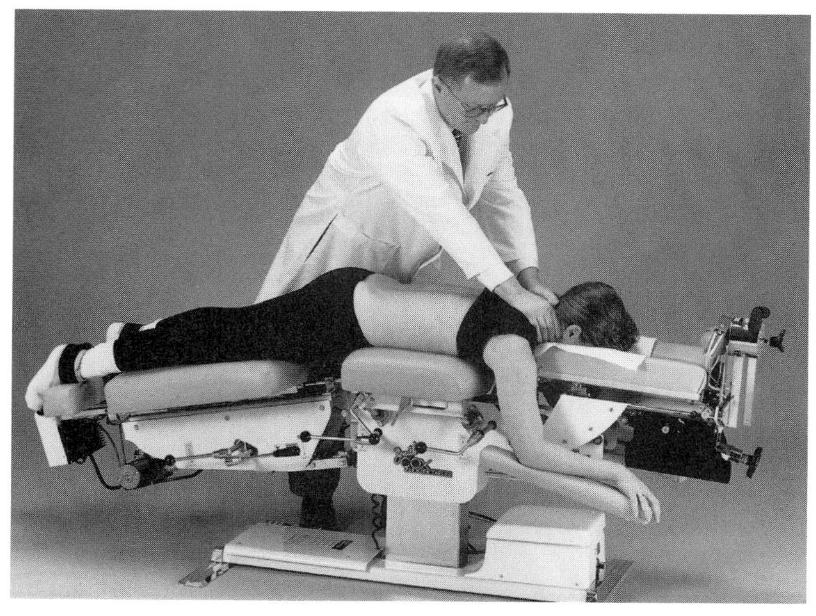

Figure 19–33. The foramen magnum pump is a full spine distraction applied by having the patient's ankles in the distraction cuffs, with the doctor cradling the occiput as shown and delivering full spine distraction by caudal section automated axial distraction administered by pressing the foot switch. This technique is excellent for relieving stress, neck pain and stiffness, midthoracic spine burning and scapular irritation, and generalized relaxation. Prior to any other manipulative moves, this process can sedate and relax most patients for further manipulative corrections.

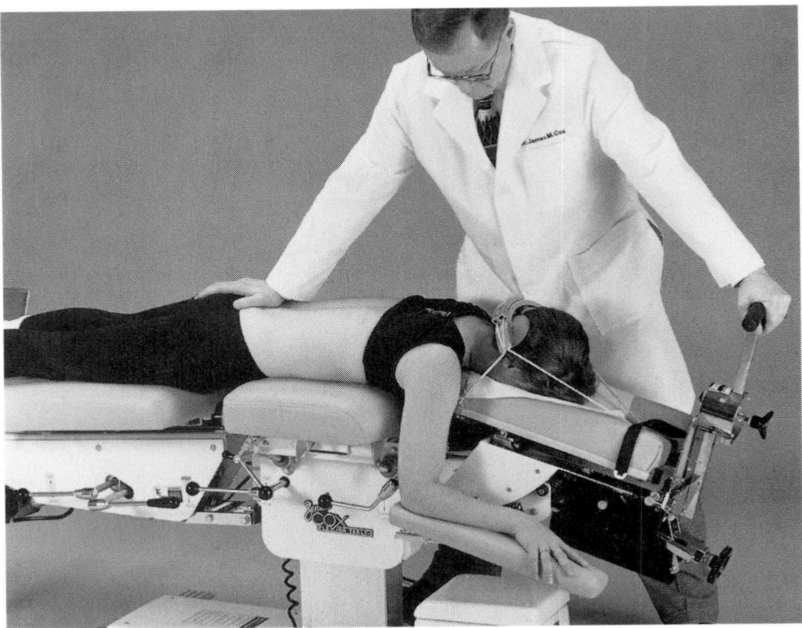

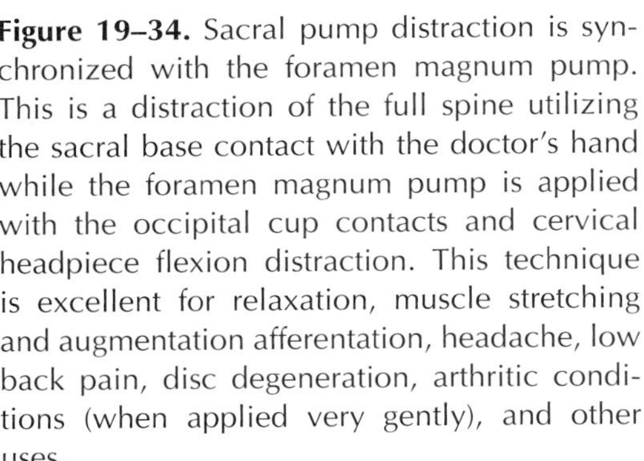

Figure 19–34. Sacral pump distraction is synchronized with the foramen magnum pump. This is a distraction of the full spine utilizing the sacral base contact with the doctor's hand while the foramen magnum pump is applied with the occipital cup contacts and cervical headpiece flexion distraction. This technique is excellent for relaxation, muscle stretching and augmentation afferentation, headache, low back pain, disc degeneration, arthritic conditions (when applied very gently), and other uses.

REFERENCES

1. Troup JDG. Straight-leg-raising (SLR) and the qualifying tests for increased root tension: Their predictive value after back and sciatic pain. *Spine*. 1981;6:526–527.
2. Adams MA, Hutton WC. The effect of posture on the role of the apophyseal joints resisting intervertebral compressive force. *J Bone Joint Surg*. 1980;62B:358–362.
3. Yang KH, King AI. Mechanism of facet load transmission as a hypothesis for low back pain. *Spine* 1984;9:557–565.
4. Onel D, Tuzlaci M, Sari H, Demir K. Computed tomographic investigation of the effect of traction on lumbar disc herniations. *Spine*. 1989;14(1):82–90.
5. White AA, Panjabi MM. *The Clinical Biomechanics of the Spine Pain from Clinical Biomechanics of the Spine*. Philadelphia: JB Lippincott, 1978;305–309.
6. Burton CV: Gravity lumbar reduction. In: Kirkaldy-Willis WH. *Managing Low Back Pain*. Edinburgh: Churchill Livingstone, 1983:196.
7. Neugebauer J. Re-establishing of the intervertebral disc by decompression. *Med Welt*. 1976;27:19.
8. Cyriax J. *Textbook of Orthopaedic Medicine*. *Diagnosis of Soft Tissue Lesions*, vol 1. 3rd ed. Baltimore: Williams & Wilkins, 1969:450–457.
9. Gupta RC, Ramarao SV. Epidurography in reduction of lumbar disc prolapse by traction. *Arch Phys Med Rehabil*. 1978;July:59.
10. Lind G. Auto-traction, treatment of low back pain and sciatica, an electromyographic, radiographic, and clinical study. Linköping, Sweden, 1974.
11. McElhannon JE. Council on Chiropractic Physiological Therapeutics: Traction, a protocol. ACA J. 1985;October:82.
12. Finneson BE. *Low Back Pain*. 2nd ed. 1980. Philadelphia: JB Lippincott, 1980:312.
13. Tien-You R. Lumbar intervertebral disc protrusion, new method of management and its theoretical basis. *Chin Med J(Engl)*. 1976;2:183–194.
14. Tsung-Min L, Tsung-Min Li, Chiang-hua W, Chen-Chung Y, Kuo-hsiu C, Kuei-fu T, et al. Vertical suspension traction with manipulation in lumbar intervertebral disc protrusion. *Chin Med J (Engl)*. 1977;3:407–412.
15. Burton C. The gravity lumbar reduction therapy program. *J. Musculoskel Med*. 1986;December;12–21.
16. Tkachenko SS. Closed one-stage reduction of acute prolapse of the intervertebral disc. *Orthop Travmatol Protez*. 1973;34:46–47.
17. Mathews JA, Yates DAH. Treatment of sciatica. *Lancet*. 1974;1:352.

18. Pomosov DV. Treatment of slipped discs by a closed reduction method. *Voen Med Zh*. 1976;7:76–77.
19. Edwards JP, et al. A comparison of chiropractic technics as they relate to the intervertebral disc syndrome. *Dig Chiro Econ*. 1977;November/December:92–101.
20. Potter GE. A study of 744 cases of neck and back pain treated with spinal manipulation. *J Can Chiro Assoc*. 1977;December:154–156.
21. Sharubina I. Effectiveness of using medical gymnastics together with traction in a swimming pool in the overall treatment of discogenic radiculitis. *Vopr Kurortol Fizioter Lech Fiz Kult*. 1973;38:536–557.
22. Kramer J. *Intervertebral Disc Diseases*. Chicago:Mosby-Year Book, 1981:166–167.
23. Mathews J. Dynamic discography: A study of lumbar traction. *Am Phys Med*. 1968;9:275–279.
24. Mathews J. The effects of spinal traction. *Physiotherapy*. 1972;58:64–66.
25. Godle IF, Reichmann S. The biomechanical influence of traction on the cervical spine. *Scand J Rehabil Med*. 1977;9:31–34.
26. Cox J. *Low Back Pain, Mechanism, Diagnosis, Treatment*. Baltimore: Williams & Wilkins, 1985:186–200.
27. Gargano FP, Jacobson RE. Transverse axial tomography of the spine. *Crit Rev Clin Radiol Nucl Med*. 1976;8:279–328.
28. Airaksinen O, Heikkinen A. Results of autotraction treatment for disc prolapse in a one year follow up study. Manual Med. 1989;3:129–131.
29. Cox JM. A hypothesis introducing a new calculation for discal reduction. *J Manipulative Physio Ther*. 1987;10(6):287–294.
30. Raney FL. The effects of flexion, extension Valsalva maneuver, and abdominal compression on the large volume myelographic column. International Society for the Study of the Lumbar Spine, San Francisco meeting, June 5–8, 1978.
31. Pilling JR. Water soluble radiculography in the erect posture: A clinico-radiological study. *Clin Radiol*. 1979;30:665–670.
32. DeSeze S, Levernieux J. Les tractions vertebrales. Premiers etude experimentales et resultats therapeutiques d'apres un experience de quatre annees. *Semaine de hospitales, Paris*. 1951;27:2085.
33. Larsson V, Choler V, Lindstrom A, et al. Autotraction for treatment of lumbago-sciatica: A multicenter controlled investigation. *Acta Orthop Scand*. 1980;51:791–798.
34. Cyriax J. *Textbook of Orthopaedic Medicine*. 7th ed. London: Bailliere Tindall, 1978.
35. Cyriax J. *Textbook of Orthopaedic Medicine*, vol. 1. 8th ed. London: Bailliere Tindall, 1983;315–316.
36. Lossing W. Low back pain and the Cottrell 90/90 Backtrac system. *Orthotics Prosthetics*. 1983;37:31–38.
37. Quellette JP. Low back pain: An orthopedic medicine approach. *Can Fam Physician*. 1987;33:693–694.
38. Stephens MM, O'Brien JP. The morphological changes in the lumbar intervertebral foramina in normal and abnormal motion segments after distraction. *Ann R Coll Surg Engl*. 1986;68:4.
39. Weatherell VF. Comparison of electromyographic activity in normal lumbar sacrospinalis musculature during static pelvic traction in two different positions. *J Sports Phys Ther*. 1987;February.
40. Awad EA. Effects of pelvic traction on the intervertebral disc. *Arch Phys Med Rehabil*. 1988;69:785.
41. Gillstrom P, Ericson K, Hindmarsh T: Computed tomography examination of the influence of autotraction on herniation of the lumbar disc. *Arch Orthop Trauma Surg*. 1985;104:289–293.
42. Yefu L, Jixiang F. Zuliang L, Zhenqian L. Traction and manipulative reduction for the treatment of protrusion of lumbar intervertebral disc—an analysis of 1,455 cases. *J Tradit Chin Med*. 1986;6:31–33.
43. Kramer J. *Intervertebral Disc Diseases: Causes, Diagnosis, Treatment, and Prophylaxis*. Chicago: Mosby-Year Book, 1981:164–166.
44. Nachemson A, Elfstrom G. Intradiscal dynamic pressure measurement in lumbar disc disease. *Scand J Rehabil Med* 1970;(Suppl)1:1–40.
45. Teplick JG, Haskin ME. Spontaneous regression of herniated nucleus pulposus. *AJNR*. 1985;6:331–335.
46. Clark GA, Panjabi MM, Wetzel FT. Can infant malnutrition cause adult vertebral stenosis? *Spine*. 1985;10:165–170.
47. Marshall LL, Trethewie ER. Chemical irritation of nerve root in disc prolapse. *Lancet*. 1973; August 11:320.
48. Finneson BE: *Low Back Pain*. Philadelphia: JB Lippincott, 1973:259.
49. Penning L, Wilmink JT. Posture-dependent bilateral compression of L4 on L5 nerve roots in facet hypertrophy: A dynamic CT-myelographic study. *Spine*. 1987;12(5):488.
50. Schonstrom N, Lindahl S, Willen J, Hansson T. Dynamic changes in the dimensions of the lumbar spinal canal: An experimental study in vitro. *J Orthop Res*. 1989;7:115–121.
51. Dai Liyang MD, Yinkan XU, Wenming Z, Zhihua Z. The effect of flexion-extension motion of the lumbar spine on the capacity of the spinal canal: An experimental study. *Spine*. 1989;14(5):523.

52. Vanharanta H, Ohnmeiss D, Stith W, Rashbaum R, Hochschuler S, Guyer R, Johnson R, Ritz S. Effect of repeated trunk extension and flexion movements as seen by CT/discography. North American Spine Society Third Annual Meeting, Colorado Springs, CO, July 24–27, 1988.
53. Gill K, Videman T, Shimizu T, Mooney V. The effect of repeated extension on the discographic dye patterns in cadaveric lumbar motion segments. *Clin Biomech.* 1987;2(4):205–210.
54. Epstein J. Dynamic MRI of the cervical spine. *Spine.* 1993.13(8):937–940.
55. Dolan P, Adams MA, Hutton WC. Commonly adopted postures and their effect on the lumbar spine. *Spine.* 13(2):197–201.
56. Adams MA, Hutton WC. Mechanics of the intervertebral disk. In: Ghosh P. *The Biology of the Intervertebral Disc,* vol. II. CRC Press, 1988:39–82.
57. Hutton WC, Adams MA. The biomechanics of disc degeneration. *Acta Orthop Belg.* 1987;53(2):143–147.
58. Cox JM: *Low Back Pain: Mechanism, Diagnosis and Treatment.* Williams & Wilkins, 1990:475–505.
59. Lawrence I, Mattioni S. A fluorographic study of lumbar spine biomechanics during passive motion in the prone position. Anglo-European College of Chiropractic, doctoral thesis, 1987.
60. Dutro CL, Meeker WC, Menke JM, Keene K. The efficacy of flexion-traction manipulation and inverted gravity traction for treatment of idiopathic low back pain. Pacific Consortium for Chiropractic Research, First Annual Conference on Research and Education, Sunnyvale, CA, June, 1986.
61. Cox JM, Shreiner S. Chiropractic manipulation in low back pain and sciatica: Statistical data on the diagnosis, treatment and response of 576 consecutive cases. *J Manipulative Physiol Ther.* 1984;7(1):1–11.
62. Cox JM. *Neck, Shoulder, and Arm Pain.* Private publication textbook, 1992.
63. Cox JM: Patient benefits of attending a chiropractic low back wellness clinic. *J Manipulative Physiol Ther.* 1994;17(1);25–28.
64. Ramos G, Martin W. Effects of vertebral axial decompression of intradiscal pressure. *J Neurosurg.* 1994;81:350–353.
65. Gudavalli MR, Cox JM, Baker JA, Cramer GD, Patwardhan AG. Intervertebral disc pressure changes during the flexion-distraction procedure for low back pain. International Society for the Study of the Lumbar Spine. Exhibit, June 1997.
66. Adams MA, McNally DS, Dolan P. Stress distributions inside intervertebral discs. *J Bone Joint Surg.* 1996;78B(6):965.

CHAPTER 20

Soft Tissue Assessment and Treatment Principles for Spinal Dysfunction

Active Release Techniques® Treatment for the Spine

P. Michael Leahy, DC, CCSP & Joe Pelino, DC, BSc, DACBSP

INTRODUCTION

The soft tissues of the spine are discussed in terms of alternations in performance and textures within a range between normal and abnormal. Variations of these will and ultimately do cause specific symptom patterns where certain stages of abnormal tissue alteration can often be predictable.

For example, when intramuscular fibrosis is present, the response to rehabilitation may be slower than optimum until this is reduced. Because the spinal soft tissues are subject to stresses and injuries their adaptive responses often become recurrent and chronic. This should lead one to consider cumulative trauma disorder (CTD) specifically in the search for more effective rehabilitative outcomes. CTDs include conditions described as myofascitis, neuro-myofascitis, tendonitis, mechanical dysfunction, sprain, and strain. The layperson, athlete, and healthcare provider might also experience CTD symptoms categorized by descriptive titles, such as golfer's elbow, tennis elbow, carpal tunnel syndrome, swimmer's shoulder, and sciatica. The language used with respect to a CTD may or may not limit the treatment outcomes. However, one must understand what changes are occurring to the tissues to ultimately provide treatment for resolving any and all limitations.

CTD is the result of acute injury, repetitive motion injury, or constant pressure or tension injury to the muscles, tendons, bones, blood vessels, fascia, and/or nerves. Clinically, CTD is the experience of symptoms and performance limitations initiated by these injuries and developed within the cumulative injury cycle (CIC). It is this presence of soft tissue alteration within this cycle that separates this disorder from other neuro-musculoskeletal system injuries.

INJURY TYPES

Acute Injury

Muscle and fascial tearing from an acute injury immediately results in inflammation. This attracts the white blood cell, fibrinogen, where the adhesion process easily sets in. If this is not treated correctly, the cumulative injury cycle may be initiated.[1]

Repetitive Motion Injury

Repetitive motion appears to be related to a specific physical factor.[2] In order to understand how repetitive motion injuries occur it is helpful to review a model of repetitive motion. This is a proportional model or guide and not an exact or linear equation.[3]

$$\text{Model of repetitive motion: } I \approx \frac{NF}{AR}$$

In this model the factors are:
I = insult to the tissues
N = number of repetitions
F = force or tension of each repetition as a percent of maximum available
A = amplitude of each repetition
R = relaxation time between repetitions (lack of pressure or tension on the tissue involved)

Using this model, one may better predict that the worst damage to tissues results from and is proportional to:

$$\frac{\text{(high repetitions) (high force)}}{\text{(small motions) (short relaxation time)}}$$

Vibration, for example, results in N that is very high, A that is very low, and R that is very low. The result is a total insult to the tissues that is very high. Poor and unchanging posture results in constant high forces in the musculature. F is high, A is near zero, and R is essentially zero. The total tissue insult is therefore high. A person who is very weak will use a higher percentage of maximum strength to accomplish a given task. F is high and total tissue insult is high.

Constant Pressure/Tension Injury

These factors will decrease circulation and compromise cell recovery. Cellular retention of calcium, poor repair, and altered function are but a few of the major results.[1,4] These factors by definition do not require a repetitive motion or any motion at all. An isometric contraction of a muscle or the muscle tension of poor posture are good examples of this potential injury scenario.

THE CUMULATIVE INJURY CYCLE

The cyclic nature of injury has been described for many years and is defined by the following factors and their relationships.[5] Each factor causes a subsequent factor to surface in the cycle (see Figure 20–1).

Weak and Tense Tissues

Repetitive effort, for example, tends to make the muscles tighten. When a muscle is chronically tight it tends to weaken and when a muscle is weak it tends to tighten.[6] The adjacent soft tissues may also become tight, adding to a negative cyclic progression.

Friction-Pressure-Tension

As a result of weak and tight tissues, the internal forces acting on the tissues rise. Friction, pressure, or tension can be present individually or in combination. If one or more of these factors is high enough, an acute injury and inflammation can result, even without external forces being applied (such as acute injury).

Decreased Circulation—Edema

The effect of increased forces on the tissues is a relative decrease in circulation. If a high pressure is applied over one of the vulnerable low pressure lymphatic channels, the result is edema. External forces in the form of constant pressure or tension may also have the effect of decreasing circulation or causing edema, contributing to negative cyclic progression.

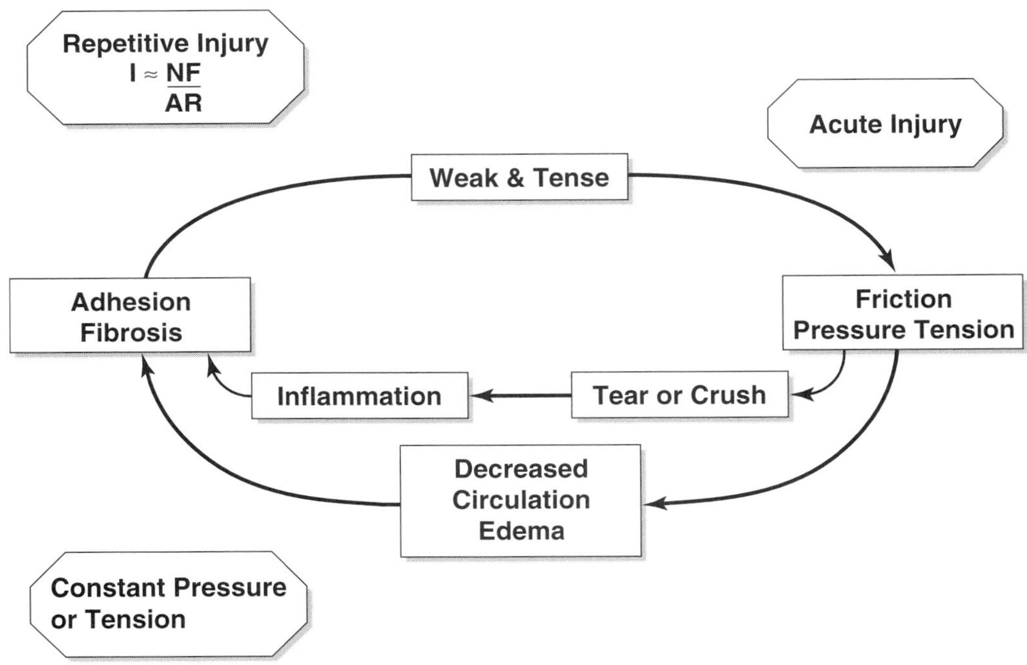

Figure 20–1. The Cumulative Injury Cycle

Adhesion-Fibrosis

Prolonged cellular hypoxia from restricted circulation may cause fibrosis and adhesions to occur in and between tissues.[7]

When the friction-pressure-tension factor is severe enough and/or when an acute injury occurs, these two additional factors can come into play.

Tear Or Crush

The physical disruption of the tissues (microscopic or macroscopic) can occur with sufficient force. This can be an external acute injury force, such as lifting, hyperflexion/extension, and surgery, or it can result from severely increased internal forces.

Inflammation

This results from the progressive accumulation of tissue injury and initiates the process of tissue adhesion, at which point the cycle continues to *weaken and tense tissues*.[1]

There are many extrinsic factors that affect the cycle in predictable ways. Smoking, for example, tends to make circulation less efficient and therefore contributes to perpetuating the cycle. Diabetes has a similar effect. Thyroid deficits tend to increase tension in the musculature and thereby influence the total insult to tissues as well as the "weak and tense" factor of the cumulative injury cycle. Hormonal changes associated with hysterectomy, excessive body weight, and pregnancy can all lead to predictable changes in the factors involved in this model of CTD.[2]

A diagram of the cumulative injury cycle is provided in Figure 20–1. The cycle is defined with two possible routes, the inflammatory cycle and the chronic cycle. These may occur exclusively or simultaneously to cause symptoms, alterations in movement performance and quality of texture of the soft tissues becoming the categorical CTD diagnosis.

Conditions

The cumulative injury cycle is self perpetuating. As this negative cycle progression continues, the symptoms and syndromes of cumulative trauma disorder surface. These may include poor response to rehabilitation, re-injury, nerve entrapment, and chronicity. When the cumulative injury cycle is not present, these syndromes are not defined as a CTD.

ACCURATE DIAGNOSIS

The diagnosis of soft tissue disorders has traditionally been inadequate and vague. The example of sciatica is inadequate for several reasons. It is not complete enough to indicate the exact tissue involved. More importantly, it does not convey the mechanism of injury. Sciatica is almost never the beginning or the end of the problem. Usually there is a biomechanical problem of the spine and soft tissues through the hip which leads to friction, pressure, or traction of a nerve root or peripheral nerve to at least one specific site. Another question therefore arises. What is the original injury and to which tissue may it be attributed? A three part diagnosis is therefore considered essential in order to establish a specific treatment intervention. It consists of the folowing:

1. Nature of the lesion, such as tear, adhesion, hypertension.
2. Exact tissue involved, such as gamelli, hamstrings, sciatic nerve.
3. Result of lesion, such as peripheral nerve entrapment, sciatica, facet syndrome, lymphatic edema.

In addition to the normal methods of examination, the clinician must add a much more detailed examination by way of palpation. The examination will be much more efficient with a thorough understanding of soft tissue biomechanical principles. For example, a runner presenting forward antalgia and hyperlordosis of the lumbar spine with paresthesias over the anterior thigh would suggest a psoas injury with femoral nerve entrapment.

The history of injury, sites of pain, strength of individual muscles, range of motion, soft tissue motion and relative motion, tissue texture, and tension will quickly lead to the cause of the problem. Learning soft tissue mechanics is a lengthy process but yields great dividends, specifically the delivery of a treatment system to eliminate symptoms without eliminating of the individual's choice to continue actions that might have caused the symptoms.

SOFT TISSUE CHANGES WITH INJURY

Soft tissues undergo a series of events after exposure to an injury. The inflammatory phase may last 24 to 72 hours and can be recognized by examination and recent history of trauma.[1] Muscle tension may exist as a result of pain and tissue irritation. The swelling associated with inflammation is very fluid like. The texture is more like a contained fluid and less like a firm mass with a palpable texture. The fluid is usually much more moveable than that of a lymphatic edema and is not confined to distinct borders like that of a cyst.

After inflammation, the muscles become altered in tension and texture. Hypertense fibers are palpable, and the overall texture seems to be "stringy" because of nonhomogeneous hypertension among the fascicles. This might be described as a "guitar string texture."

The actual tear or defect in a muscle or fascia is evident from the beginning, but after about three days the edges are more defined and palpable. After this period the edges become enlarged as the injury begins to heal with a fibrous process. Within a muscle this fibrous process leaves an adhesion that changes texture over time, from "guitar string" fibers to lumpy and then leathery. The defect in the tissue gets very firm, then spreads out into the surrounding tissue, leaving the ill-defined leathery area. All these changes typically occur in chronological order (see Table 20–1). The changes are most easily identified within muscle tissue and are similar in connective and neural tissues.

Table 20–1: Chronological soft tissue changes after an injury over time[3]

Inflamed	24 to 72 hours
"Stringy" muscles, lesions defined	2 days to 2 weeks
Lumpy tissue	2 weeks to 3 months
Leathery tissue, changes slowly	3 months and beyond

EXAMINATION

MANUAL EXAMINATION

In order to arrive at a proper diagnosis, the soft tissues must be examined for problems in the four major categories listed below. One must develop the experience to distinguish normal tissue status from altered or dysfunctional tissue status in each of these areas:

A. Tissue texture
B. Tissue tension
C. Tissue movement
   1. Joint motion and position
   2. Soft tissue motion and position
   3. Gliding of soft tissues over adjacent tissues
   4. Elasticity of muscle, fascia, ligament, and tendon range of motion for all tissue
D. Tissue function
   1. Strength and speed of muscle contraction
   2. Nerve conduction
   3. Circulation of blood and lymphatics

Normal tissue texture requires all adhesions to be released so that the resulting tissue is homogeneous with the surrounding tissue of the same type. All tissues have a texture that can be recognized as normal by palpation. Of course this means that some experience must be attained in order to differentiate between normal and altered tissues. Attaining normal texture does not mean that scar tissue must be completely eliminated, which would be an impossibility and actually undesirable as it serves a function in bringing a union of separated tissues. It does mean that the resulting tissue should resemble the original tissue as much as possible. When preinjury texture is not achieved, the modules of elasticity and damping coefficient are less than optimal. The otherwise normal negative feedback loop becomes altered, which leads to increased loads on the tissue to perform a task, altered biomechanics, agonist/antagonist muscle problems, and the likelihood of reinjury.

Normal tissue tension is important in all soft tissue. Muscle tissue should regain normal tonus throughout the structure. Fascia, ligaments, and tendons should all acquire a tension as close to preinjury status as possible. If normal tension is not achieved, proper biomechanics is unlikely and reinjury is likely. Peripheral nerve entrapment and vascular entrapment are prime examples of improper soft tissue tension causing pressure on adjacent structures.

Normal movement requires normal tension and function of the soft tissues. Proper joint position and motion are impossible without corresponding soft-tissue position, motion, and function. Voluntary effort can only compensate for some deficits in the soft tissues and it does so at the cost of added stresses. By properly addressing soft-tissue concerns, the speed at which joint manipulation and rehabilitation effect a change is improved. Conversely, if the soft tissue problems are not adequately addressed, the requirement for joint manipulation remains at a very high frequency and rehabilitative gains are slow.

Almost all soft tissue must glide over adjacent tissues. It is very common for this process to be limited by improper tension or an adhesion process. Once the adhesion process has set in, one tissue literally pulls on the other. Traction neurodesis is a prime example and is a common cause of peripheral nerve symptoms.[3] This may easily occur at the suboccipital muscles and the greater occipital nerve or the femoral nerve and genito-femoral nerve at the psoas muscle.

Elasticity of the soft tissues is often overlooked. In order to assess this, the tissue must be examined throughout its range of motion with appropriate loading performed at or near the maximum elongation of the tissue. Elasticity is important for function. If one looks at the equations of motion that apply to the musculoskeletal system, it is easy to see the extent of this influence.

Joint and soft tissue ranges of motion must be assessed together. For soft tissue motion, the examiner must be able to palpate the gliding of tissues over one another. This can be difficult to learn and frequently requires two or more years of practice. A good test of this skill is to find the median nerve as it courses posterior to or through the two bundles of the pronator teres. The nerve must slide by the muscle and not be significantly pulled by this structure. There are many other sites where a soft tissue must slide over another. It is the rule rather than the exception.

When joint range of motion is limited, the examiner must also establish whether this is due to joint limitation or restriction caused by the soft tissue. This can only be accomplished by palpating the soft tissues while moving the joint to its limits. If the soft tissue is the limiting factor, then the tension that develops in the soft tissue will be excessive, early, and palpable.

This brings us to the final factor, function. This includes proper strength, speed of contraction, and tonus of muscle, as well as proper nerve conduction and vascular function. Veinous and lymphatic drainage are the most susceptible to injurious insult because they are low pressure systems. It takes less pressure over them to cause a blockage. The lymphatic edema of the upper and lower extremity may recede over as short a time as 10 minutes after local blockage is treated. Improvements in other soft tissue functions such as strength, speed, and nerve function are rapid as well.

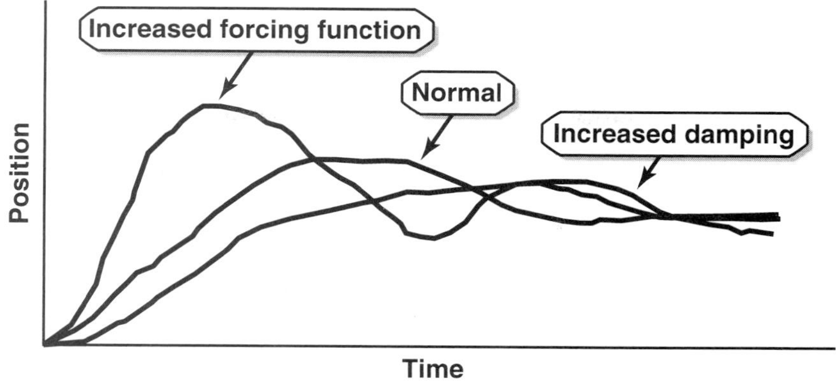

Figure 20–2. Soft-Tissue Changes After Injury

ALTERED BIOMECHANICS: JOINT AND SOFT TISSUE

When any of the factors are altered, the resulting function of the system is altered. The single loop negative feedback control system is the model of how the musculoskeletal system is controlled. Changes in the texture of tissues most often affect the damping coefficient of the system. This roughly resembles a car's shock absorber that is sticky and dampens too much.

The factors affecting the mechanism are:

- damping coefficient → adhesion, friction, moments of inertia
- forcing function → voluntary contraction

Changes in soft tissues after injury are considered in Figure 20–2. When the effort of muscle contraction is greater, the rate at which position approaches the desired result is faster, but more overshoots are a by-product. When an injury occurs that ultimately causes adhesions, the time necessary to achieve the result in position takes longer; adhesion is the result where the damping coefficient is increased and the time necessary to achieve the result is longer. The subject will usually increase effort to compensate for this. Peripheral nerve entrapment will alter the forcing function. By this method of analysis, the effects of soft tissue lesions are very predictable.

When the soft-tissue structures are injured, the sequel to the injury is one of altered biomechanics. For example, it is impossible for a muscle to undergo a significant tear, develop an adhesion, and then perform normally. Both function and movement are altered on a macroscopic scale.

ACTIVE RELEASE TECHNIQUES® TREATMENT

Active Release Techniques (ART®) treatment is a collection of soft tissue techniques for examination, diagnosis, and treatment of soft tissue disorders.[3] Much like any manipulation, it cannot be learned from the written word but must be learned in a practical setting, with hands-on instruction. A small portion of the information will be offered here in hopes of stimulating critical thought. It is also hoped that the availability of greatly improved clinical outcomes will become evident.

In ART® treatment, the tissue is placed in a shortened position. The lesion within or between structures is trapped with a specific contact as the tissue is drawn under the contact while the lesion is manipulated. The manipulation, tissue motion, and contact vary with the requirements of each tissue, each lesion, and the reaction of the tissue during the treatment. ART® treatment is a level 3 or level 4 soft-tissue manipulation of myofascial release.

- Level 1. Tissue positioned without tension, patient motion absent
- Level 2. Tissue positioned with tension, patient motion absent
- Level 3. Tissue is lengthened under contact, patient motion passive
- Level 4. Tissue is lengthened under contact, patient motion active

TREATMENT RULES OF APPLICATION

Certain guidelines must be followed in order to ensure maximum benefits with minimum complications. If these rules are not understood and followed, patient welfare is compromised.

- SOFT CONTACT: Use the specific contact taught hands on. It is impossible to learn the varied methods of contact without hands-on instruction experience.
- WORK LONGITUDINALLY: For many reasons, this method breaks the adhesions in and between tissues most effectively. For example, it is important to establish longitudinal freedom of motion within

a muscle. If passes are made across muscle fibers, the tissue will slide or roll under the contact before enough tension can be exerted on the fibrous tissue to reduce it.

- ACTIVE MOTION WHENEVER POSSIBLE: This provides the subject with a sense of control and also blocks pain at the lateral spinal-thalamic tract. More can be accomplished with less discomfort. The methods of active motion are very involved and are designed to maximize relative motion between tissues.
- SLOW MOTION: If any motions are fast or quick, the tolerance of the subject is reduced, and muscle tension is the reaction. This makes it difficult or impossible to achieve the desired results. The exact motions differ for each tissue and must be developed with extensive hands-on experience.
- PATIENT TOLERANCE: The pressure and number of passes are always limited to patient tolerance. There are several keys or indications of patient tolerance level that must be observed.
- TISSUE TOLERANCE: Each subject is different, and the tissues react to physical stimulation in a different manner. It is sometimes necessary to delay a treatment due to low tissue tolerance. This is indicated by physical as well as nonphysical indicators.
- WORK WITH LYMPHATIC AND VEINOUS FLOW: Bruising and lymphatic edema are almost completely avoided by employing accurate and specific methodologies.
- FREQUENCY OF ALTERNATE DAYS: Treatment frequency is never more often than alternate days. Greater frequency leads to tissue intolerance and protracted treatment plans. In some cases an even longer period between treatments is necessary.

Treatments should produce significant changes within two to three sessions. Three to five passes are made over any single area of tissue. Sometimes it is necessary to reduce treatment frequency to twice per week or even less when the tissue tolerance is low. If treatment is continued at nor-

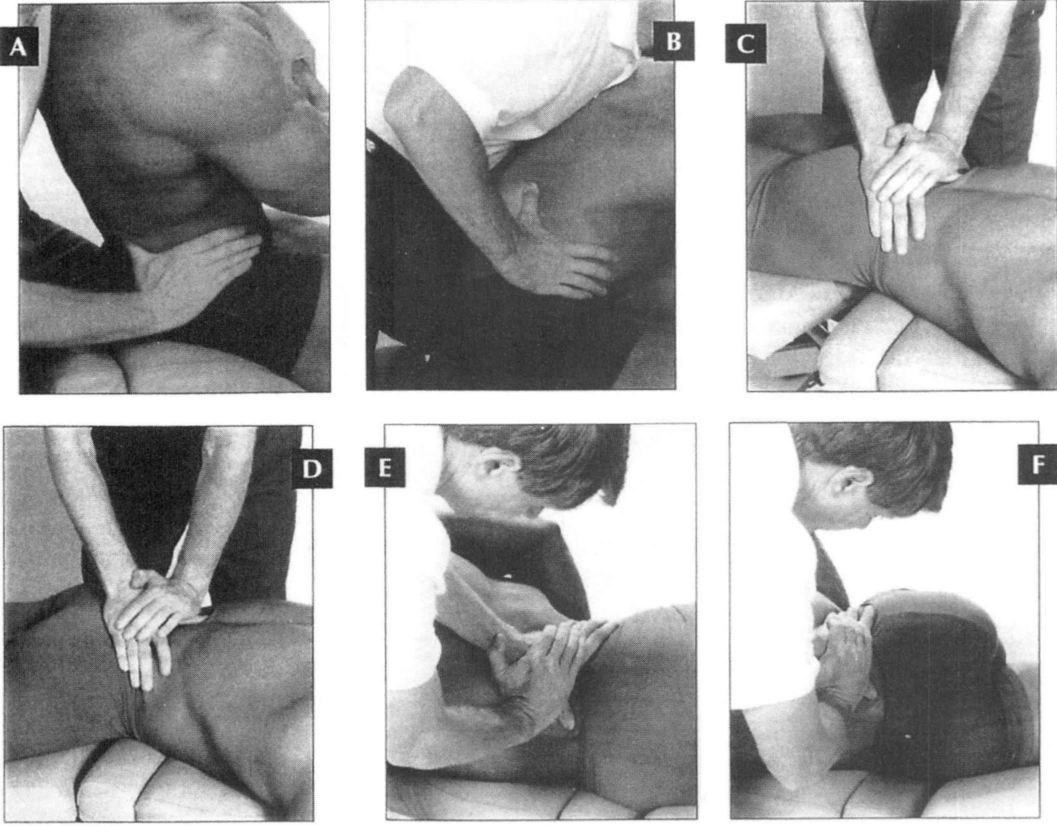

Figure 20–3. Treating the Erector Spinae. A. Patient is seated with lumbar spine in relative extension and lateral flexion toward the treated side. **B.** Contact tension is increased superiorly as patient is guided into flexion, rotation, and lateral flexion away from treated side. **C and D.** Patient is prone on the distraction table and is moved into flexion and opposite lateral flexion. **E and F.** Patient is lying on the side. Note provider's distal tension. The patient lengthens the muscle with knee flexion.

mal frequency in spite of low tissue tolerance, the number of visits required to resolve the problem goes up; sometimes resolution is impossible. Diminished muscle strength usually changes on the first or second visit. Treatment is not usually initiated during the inflammatory stage. When the injury is new (1 to 3 days), care must be taken to alter the directions of treatment to prevent increasing tension across a defect.

When trying to gauge progress it is important to realize that changes occur very quickly. After studying cases retrospectively, it has been found that the average number of treatments necessary to resolve peripheral nerve entrapment and chronic myofascial symptoms was less than six. If the provider finds many cases requiring more than 12 visits, a more careful re-evaluation will likely reveal other involved primary sites that were not identified initially.

APPLICATIONS OF ART® TREATMENT

ART® treatment requires accurate consideration of what the soft tissues are doing and what they feel like. Restoration of adequate and optimal soft tissue tension, texture, movement, and function requires that each case also consider proper patient history and complete physical examination, including appropriate diagnostic tools and imaging. Complete closure of cases is not achieved merely by how the structures are treated, but by the biomechanical relationships to movement, symptoms, and tissue textures. Use of the appropriate symptom pattern charts in the ART® *Manual*[8] will help the provider in complete and proper treatment of all the structures and their clinical relationships to other muscles and nerves.

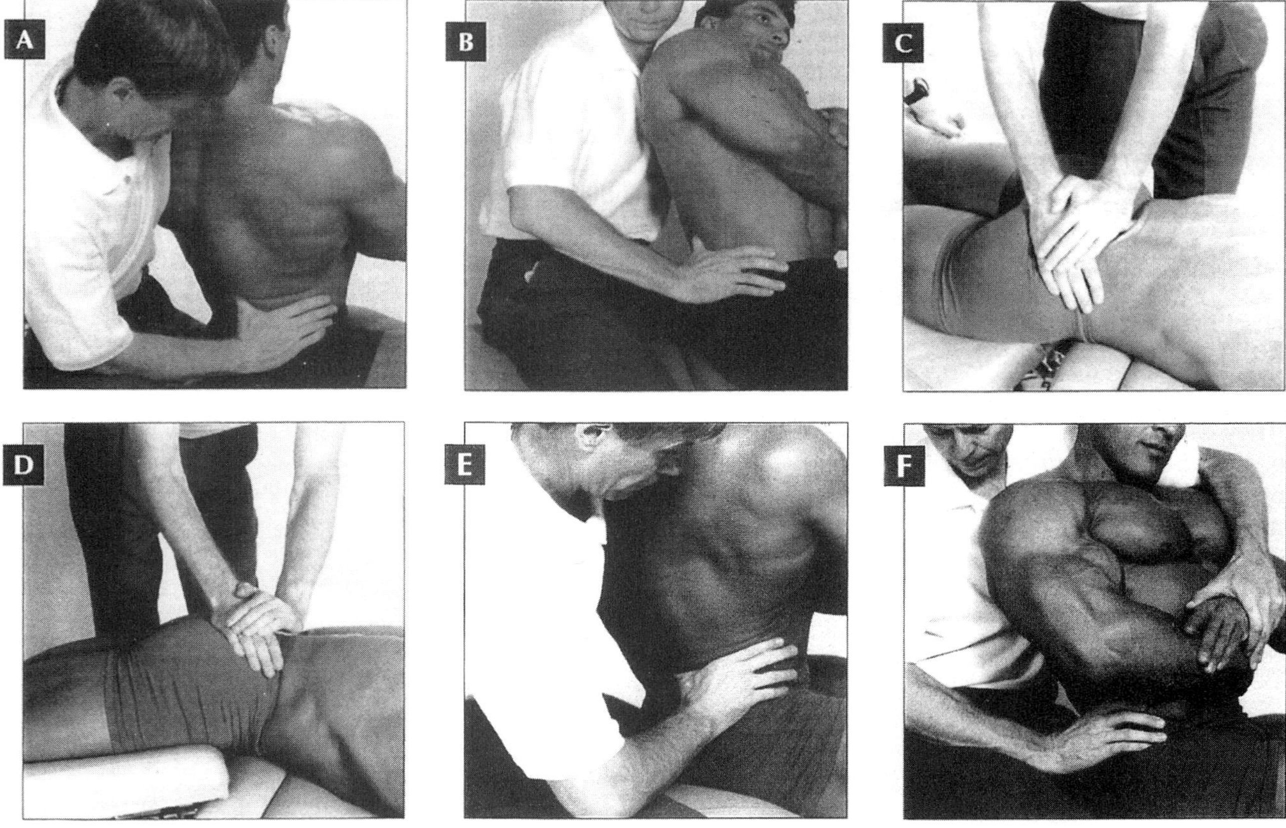

Figure 20–4. Treating the Multifidii and Rotatores. A. The right multifidus is shortened, with the patient in extension, ipsi lateral flexion, and spinous processes rotation toward the treated side. Contact tension is superior and medial from transverse to spinous process. **B.** Patient is being laterally flexed with spinous processes rotated away from the treated side. Note that the lumbar extension is maintained. **C.** Patient rests in ipsi lateral flexion and extension. **D.** Patient is laterally flexed away from the treated side, with lumbar flexion avoided. **E.** Right rotatores muscles are shortened, with the patient's spine in extension, lateral flexion, and spinous rotation to the treated side. **F.** Patient is maintained in relative extension, lateral flexion, and an emphasis of spinous rotation away from the treated side. The provider's contact tension remains from the transverse process, longitudinal, superior, and medial on the rotatores to the vertebral segment just superior.

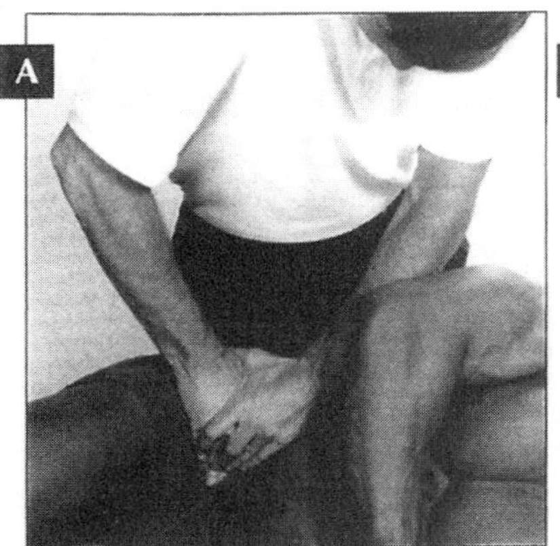

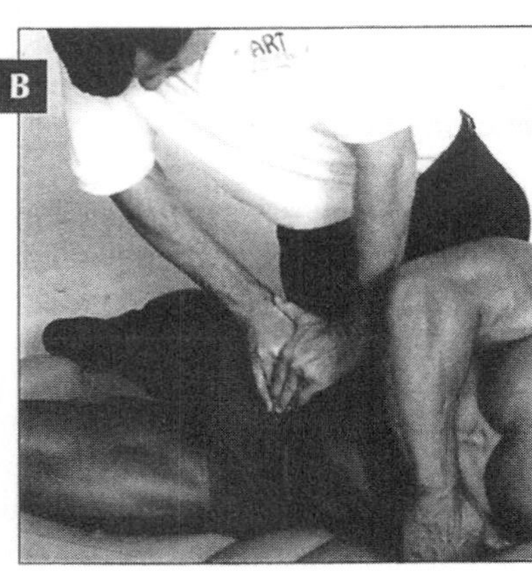

Figure 20–5. Treating the Psoas. A. Patient is lying on the side, hip and knee flexed, and psoas in the shortened position. Contact is worked from the anterior superior iliac spine medially onto the iliacus, and then the psoas, while moving the mesentary and abdominal contents medially. **B.** Tension is exerted superiorly on the psoas while the patient extends the hip.

Treating Erector Spinae

Erector spinae muscles are worked in the seated, side-lying, or prone position, with the aid of a distraction table. Because of the size and strength of these muscles, a considerable amount of pressure is used with a thumb or pisiform contact.

Begin with the patient in the seated position and the lumbar spine in as close to the anatomical position as possible (see Figure 20–3). Take up the tissue slack by contacting inferior to the area to be treated and tractioning into the lesion. Support the weight of the patient with the nontreating hand and have the patient begin to forward flex, laterally flex, and rotate away from the lesion. The sequence of these three motions will depend on which generates the most tension over the lesion. As the motion occurs, exert a superior tractioning force through the lesion while manipulating the lesion.

Treating the Multifidii and Rotatores

During ART® treatment of the multifidii and rotatores (see Figure 20–4), the provider palpates for increasing tension in the structure during its respective lengthening. When increasing tension is palpated during spinal segment rotation away from the treated side, the provider works the rotatores to the segment just superior. If, however, tension is palpated mostly during lateral flexion away from the treated side, the work is done to the multifidus, where tension direction is superior by more than one segment, to follow the longitudinal direction of the fibers towards the spinous process.

The patient is maintained in a relative neutral, nonflexion or minimal extension to keep the erector spinae muscles from becoming taut or engaged. Otherwise, adequate contact might not be achieved, and effective work to these spinotransversal muscles would decrease.

In treatment of back pain where successful outcomes are achieved by working the spinotransversal muscles, the provider must consider related treatment protocols for other structures, including psoas and suboccipital muscles.

Treating Psoas

The psoas muscles are almost always involved when treating the pelvis or lumbar spine. It is common to find extreme adhesion formation following surgical treatment to the lumbar spine. The basic methods used to treat this structure are no different from those used for others, but the art of their application is extremely difficult (see Figure 20–5). An improper method of contact will always make the condition worse, and for this reason the technique is only taught hands on. The muscle and fascia are usually treated from the distal end exterior to the pelvic cavity to the proximal end as superior as the most superior lumbar segment. Care must be taken to work the contact hand behind the abdominal contents as failure to do so will preclude effective

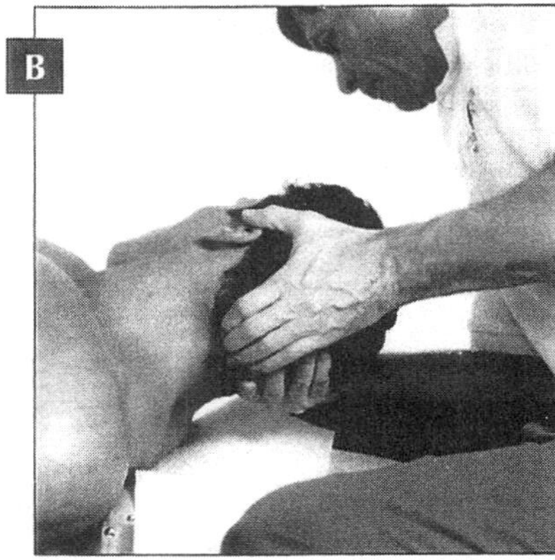

Figure 20–6. Treating the suboccipital muscles. A. Patient begins in cervical extension, with the contact in the inferior portion. **B.** Tension is drawn superiorly during patient flexion, especially in the upper segments.

treatment. It is common to see a femoral nerve entrapment resolved in 2 to 4 visits when performed correctly.

To work the femoral nerve free from tension causing symptom limitations, the expert ART® provider must treat psoas, iliacus, and quadratus lumborum at the site of the femoral nerve. To work the individual structure only will not completely resolve the insult of tension on the nerve.

Treating the Upper Spine

Treatment of the spine for symptom patterns of headache from the occipital to orbital regions would include soft-tissue consideration using the following specific protocols for various headache patterns (Table 20–2).

The suboccipital muscles are best treated in the supine position (Figure 20–6). These muscles often entrap the occipital nerves or cause tension at the base of the skull which if left untreated will exert a tension on the aponeurosis over the top of the skull to the occular muscles. This causes the headache that seems to be "somewhere behind the eye."

The patient's head and neck are placed in the extended position with lateral flexion and rotation toward the lesion in order to shorten the muscles and fascia as much as possible. With 3–4 fingers, the traction of the tissue is accomplished ending at the lesion. As the head and neck are flexed, rotated, and laterally flexed away from the lesion, the contact is moved through the lesion with specific manipulation. Care must be taken to avoid excessive pressure, which may duplicate the headache pain to an inordinate degree. Manipulation of the atlanto-occipital joint after treatment is usually easier to accomplish and necessary as part of the treatment protocol.

Table 20–2: ART® treatment protocols for symptoms related to headache[8]

Greater occipital nerve at semispinalis capitis
Greater occipital nerve at superior nuchal line
Third occipital nerve at trapezius/semispinalis capitis
Lesser occipital nerve and great auricular nerve at sternocleidomastoid
Dorsal ramus of C-2 at inferior oblique
Suboccipital nerve at superior oblique
Upper trapezius
Semispinalis capitis
Splenius capitis
Superior oblique
Inferior oblique
Rectus capitis posterior
Longissimus capitis
Vertebral artery tension test

SUMMARY

Expert knowledge of manual treatment of the anatomical structures of the spine allow for a vast differentiation of solutions to unlock the possible anatomical combinations that might present as a particular symptom limitation. Therefore, expert working knowledge of palpatory anatomy is paramount to provide the most effective treatment. Correcting biomechanical limitations requires an ability to affect these anatomical structures directly and safely. Once the tissues are free of adhesion restrictions, and restoration of texture, tension, movement and function is realized, then the necessary rehabilitation exercises become vital. In review of the law of repetitive motion, one can affect F, the percentage of muscular force necessary to perform the task, by specific exercises of resistance.

Appropriate stretches that are specific to the structures that had been treated might continue to prove invaluable. The individual is then capable to continue the lifestyle that might have caused the original problem. The integration of self-managed specific exercises to maintain optimal tissue texture, tension, movement, and function obligates the reader to read the other chapters of this text.

REFERENCES

1. Scarpelli DG, Chiga M. Cell injury and errors of metabolism. In: Anderson WAD, Kissane JM, eds. *Pathology*, 7th edition. St. Louis: C.V. Mosby, 1977;90–147.
2. Browne CD, Nolan MN, Faithful DK. *Occupational repetition strain injuries*. Occupational Repetition Strain Injuries Advisory Committee, Division of Occupational Health, New South Wales, 1984.
3. Leahy PM, Mock LE. Improved treatments for carpal tunnel. *Chiropractic Sports Medicine*. 1995;9:6–9.
4. Del Cacho E, Gallego M, Felices C, Bascuas JA. Myofibroblasts and myoepithelial cells in the chicken harderian gland. *Histology and Histopathology*. 1991;6(3):303–308.
5. Porterfield JA, DeRosa C. Mechanical neck pain. 6:176–179, Philadelphia: WB Saunders, 1995.
6. Gerr F, Letz R, Landrigan PJ. Upper-extremity musculoskeletal disorders of occupational origin. *Annual Review of Public Health*. 1991;12:543–566.
7. Dawes KE, Peacock AJ. Characterization of fibroblast mitogens and chemoattractants produced by endothelial cells exposed by hypoxia. *American Journal of Respiratory Cell & Molecular Biology*. 1994;10(5):552–559.
8. Leahy PM, Active Release Techniques® soft tissue management system for the spine manual. Active Release Techniques, Champion Health LLP; 1998.

SECTION

V

Exercise Methodology: Principles and Applications

We are under-exercised as a nation. We look instead of play. We ride instead of walk. Our existence deprives us of the minimum of physical activity essential for healthy living.

—John F. Kennedy

With your talents and industry, with science, and that steadfast honesty which eternally pursues right, regardless of consequences, you may promise yourself everything—but health, without which there is no happiness. An attention to health then should take place of every other object. The time necessary to secure this by active exercises, should be devoted to it in preference to every other pursuit.

—Thomas Jefferson
Letter to Thomas Mann Randolph, Jr., July 6, 1787

CHAPTER 21

Exercise Physiology

Application in Rehabilitation

Andrew S. Klein, MS, DC, DACBSP

INTRODUCTION

Principles of exercise physiology can be useful in the rehabilitation setting because knowledge of these principles can assist the clinician in addressing the regulation and integration of the different physiological systems. Just as researchers who work on the molecular and cellular level need to be aware of how their work can be integrated into the function of the whole system, clinicians need to keep abreast of advances that are being made on the cellular level. Knowledge of these advances will assist in the clinical decision-making process as it relates to patients who are being considered for entry into an active exercise program.

Successful outcomes in spinal rehabilitation may likely require knowledge of the intervertebral complex and its associated structures: nerves, blood vessels, ligaments, and muscles. Since global spinal motion requires the coordinated and synergistic involvement of many spinal segments, disease or dysfunction of one vertebral segment may likely affect the functional status of adjacent vertebral segments. One study examined the effects of exercise on patients with spinal dysfunction, but the researchers used only functional parameters as their primary outcome.[51] This has left many unanswered questions regarding the connection between mechanical stimuli and the functioning of cells, particularly as it relates to the healing process.

This chapter addresses the neuromuscular physiology of the spine as a functional unit and the integration of exercise physiology principles to assist in the clinical decision-making process.

SKELETAL MUSCLE STRUCTURE

Examination of the gross structure of the muscle reveals various layers of connective tissue. The muscle itself is a grouping of fasciculi surrounded by fibrous connective tissue known as the epimysium. It is the epimysium that blends the distal end of the muscle to help form the strong connective tissue that is the tendon. The fasciculus is a grouping of up to 150 muscle fibers. The connective tissue surrounding the fasciculi is the perimysium. The muscle fiber is surrounded by the endomysium. Beneath the endomysium is the sarcolemma, a thin membrane that envelops the cellular contents of the fiber. The protoplasm or sarcoplasm of the cell contains the contractile proteins, nuclei, fat and glycogen particles, enzymes, and cellular organelles.

Biopsy and examination of muscle fibers have been used to classify as many as eight fiber types.[70] The classification system that is based on the pH sensitivity of myofibrillar adenosine triphosphatase has been expanded to include "hybrid" types such as IIAB, IIAC, and IC.[78] It has become common practice to modify the histochemical procedures to differentiate only three fiber types.[28,67] Type I fibers are known as slow-twitch fibers and contain a high concentration of mitochondrial enzymes which are well suited for sustained aerobic metabolism.[27] These fibers have been labeled slow-oxidative (SO) fibers because of a slow speed of contraction and a notable reliance on oxidative metabolism. Type II fibers are known as fast-twitch fibers because of their ability to generate energy swiftly for a forceful muscle contraction. Type II fibers have been subdivided further based upon their rate of fatigue. Type IIA, which is known as fast-oxidative glycolytic

(FOG), is fatigue resistant. Type IIB, which is known as fast-glycolytic (FG), possesses the greatest anaerobic potential but is fatigable.[9]

Histochemical examination of skeletal muscle characteristics after 20 years of distance running training suggest that middle-aged runners had a significantly greater proportion of Type I fibers than when they were 20 years younger.[82] The subjects in this group who maintained their "highly trained" status did not show an increased percentage of Type I fibers. The increases seen in the percentage of Type I fibers may be a result of a decreased number of Type II fibers.

Although muscles may show a predominance of one fiber type as compared to another fiber type, there is still some intermingling of the different fiber types. More superficially located muscles tend to develop fiber type groupings which are dominated by fast-twitch fibers. Muscles that lie close to the bone generate secondary myotubes that apparently lead to a more balanced pattern of intermingled fiber types.[16]

Fiber type groupings have been assessed in men between the ages of 15 and 83 years.[45] Researchers found that (1) segregated fiber groups were common in young muscles; (2) random patterns of fibers existed in men between the ages of 30 and 50 years; and (3) an excess of enclosed fibers were found in men over the age of 60. These results imply that muscle fiber groupings are in some form of transition throughout life. These fiber type grouping results are similar to the resultant groupings found in a denervation-reinnervation model.[46]

It appears that there are decreases in muscle strength that are age-related,[29,68] and that Type I muscle fibers supply a greater percentage of the force generation as a person gets older.[71] Age-related weakness appears to be caused partially by the decreased cross-sectional area of Type II fibers[7,45] as well as the increased use of cellular space for noncontractile elements such as fat and connective tissue.[64]

One study demonstrates that, under normal conditions, muscle unit fibers were distributed in a mosaic pattern among fibers of other muscle units.[19] Experiments involving denervated muscles show that unit fibers tended to be grouped or "enclosed" together in the reinnervated muscle, and after a long period of reinnervation, the fiber types were all the same.[23,81] Do the similar fiber type grouping results that occur in men over the age of 60 and in muscle that has undergone reinnervation imply that a muscle denervation and reinnervation process is part of the normal aging of a muscle? It would be interesting to examine if a potential relationship exists between the resultant fiber type groupings of the denervation-reinnervation model, and the decreasing number of active motor units that is seen with an aging muscle.[8,58]

The information available to the health professional presents a clinical choice in treatment, when dealing with the older patient: Should one use a strength-oriented program to attempt to halt the loss of Type II fibers or a predominantly endurance-oriented program to keep the remaining Type I fibers innervated to their maximum potential?

The ultrastructure of the skeletal muscle is the subcellular organization within the muscle fiber. The subunits of the muscle fiber are myofibrils. There is a system of interconnecting tubular channels running parallel to the myofibrils known as the sarcoplasmic reticulum. The sarcoplasmic reticulum contains the vesicles that store calcium ions. The myofibrils are composed of even smaller subunits known as the myofilaments. The proteins actin and myosin account for about 80% of the myofibrillar complex. Actin and myosin, along with troponin and tropomyosin, are key proteins in the sliding filament theory.[55]

It is the sarcomere that is the functional unit of the muscle fiber or muscle cell. The sarcomere is the repeating unit between two Z-lines or discs. The Z-disc runs perpendicular to regions known as A bands and I bands. The bands are classified based on their appearance during microscopic magnification. The A band is darker in appearance, whereas the I band is lighter in appearance.

Parallel sarcomeres are thought to be bound to each other by a series of intermyofibrillar connections. This region of intermyofibrillar "bridges" is considered the exosarcomere, and it is thought that these bridges maintain the transverse integrity between sarcomeres.[44] These connections are known as "intermediate filaments" because they have a diameter of 10 nm, which is intermediate to actin (6 nm) and myosin (16 nm). A number of proteins have been identified in this class such as desmin, vimentin, and synemin.[30] Desmin appears to be the major intermediate filament in skeletal muscle[26] and may be very important in the regulation of myogenesis.[47] Vimentin is closely related to desmin,[75] and increases in these filaments usually indicate regeneration of muscle fibers. Nestin is the most recently discovered intermediate filament.[74] This filament appears to be an important component of the dynamic intermediate filament network necessary for muscular development and regeneration. These proteins along with the alpha-actinin wrap around the Z-discs and interconnect it to the neighboring discs in the plane.[89]

Exercise that damages the muscle tissue may cause a problem known as Z-disc streaming, defined as an ultrastructural change whereby the Z-discs of neighboring myofibrils lose their connection to each other.[22] The disruption of some of the intermediate fibers, but not all, may contribute to the addition of sarcomeres to the individual myofibrils.[86] Lynn and Morgan[49] measured the mean number of sarcomeres per fiber for different training protocols and found a clear increase in the number of sarcomeres after eccentric exercise. Exercise that could damage the intermediate fibers may damage the sarcoplasmic reticulum as well, which would result in increased intracellular calcium levels that would activate proteolytic enzymes leading to structural protein degradation.[88] Some of the proteins dissolved would be components of the Z-disc, and it is possible that new sarcomeres could then be inserted in the place of the dissolved Z-discs.

It has been seen that when sarcomeres were stretched, the overlap between actin and myosin filaments ended and a gap was present. Very thin filaments were noted to bridge this gap between nonoverlapped A bands and I bands.[76]

These filaments became known as gap filaments and have since been identified as titin[85] and nebulin.[87] These proteins are part of the elastic system of the sarcomere and appear to be important for the assembly of new sarcomeres. Titin appears to be attached to myosin and to help maintain the central location of the myosin filaments in the relaxed muscle.[33] There is an association between titin and longitudinally oriented stress fiber-like structures that play an important role in myofibrillogenesis.[84] Nebulin appears to act as a guide for actin to interact with myosin in instances when the sarcomere is stretched beyond the overlap of actin and myosin filaments;[52] however, it does not appear to significantly contribute to the elasticity of the actin filaments.[90]

There has been research showing the relationship between increases in muscle cross-sectional area (CSA) and increases in strength.[92] A relationship has also been demonstrated between increases in strength and increases in the CSA of muscle fibers while the total amount of fibers remained constant.[53,73] It is possible that among the benefits of exercise training are changes that are induced in the muscle fiber ultrastructure that allow an increased amount of sarcomeres within the existing population of muscle fibers.

Further work is needed to evaluate the connection between exercise and its effect on the endosarcomeric region. Horowits and Podolsky[33] have seen myosin filaments translocated to opposite halves of the sarcomere. This might indicate damage to the titin filaments that help anchor myosin to the Z-disc. This translocation of myosin might be the event that allows for the insertion of additional sarcomeres.

In order to follow a logical sequence of rehabilitation, a clinician should have information concerning ultrastructural and biochemical sequences regarding muscle repair. The insult to the tissue itself may result from overuse,[72] stretching,[25] eccentric exercise,[3] or trauma.[2]

There have been many research models set up to study muscle injuries. One study has used controlled forces to reproduce trauma that may be expected during collisions.[20] Another approach has been an effort to reproduce crush-type injuries.[79] It is important to remember the variability that typically presents with injuries. The nature of a lesion will vary with respect to external forces as well as the conformity of the tissue absorbing these forces. Best, McElhaney, Garrett, and Myers[5a] have shown that maximum strain of a stretched muscle occurs at the myotendinous junction. The stretch rate had an effect on the location of the rupture site in some of the muscles, but not all of the muscles. Some muscles were insensitive to the rate of tissue stretch. This confirms the need for an approach that allows for the individuality of every lesion encountered, regardless of the seeming familiarity of an injury.

MUSCLE RECEPTORS

Specialized sensory receptors can be found in the muscles that are sensitive to stretch, tension, and pressure. These receptors provide both conscious and unconscious afferent stimulation to help regulate movement. Often, injury to a structure will also lead to the disruption of these receptors. Therefore, rehabilitation needs to be directed at the retraining of these receptors. Three major groups of receptors have been recognized in muscles. These receptor groups are muscle spindles, Golgi tendon organs, and free nerve endings.[55]

Muscle spindles or intrafusal fibers provide afferent information concerning tension or length changes in the muscle. When stimulated by stretch, these receptors will provide a stronger contraction to reduce this stretch. The muscle spindle is anatomically in parallel with the other muscle fibers known as the extrafusal fibers. The muscle spindle can be further classified into nuclear chain fibers and nuclear bag fibers. The nuclear bag fiber, which is considered noncontractile, has annulospiral nerve fibers wrapped around its midregion. The annulospiral fibers act as receptors for the stretch reflex. The nuclear chain fiber is entwined with smaller, sensory fibers known as flower-spray endings. These flower-spray endings, which are myelinated and also responsive to stretch, are less sensitive to stretch than the annulospiral fibers. Activation of the flower-spray endings produces increased flexor and decreased extensor motor activity.[11]

Many clinicians forget that muscle spindles are a type of muscle fiber that can be fatigued just like the extrafusal fibers. Prolonged swimming of moderate intensity causes glycogen depletion to occur in the slow, then in the intermediate, and then in the fast intrafusal fibers.[91]

It would be interesting to examine fatigue effects on proprioceptors in a low-intensity exercise that mimics the work activities of low back pain patients. It appears that fatigue has no effect on the length of the muscle that needs to be reached before injury; however, fatigued muscles may reach the stretch position quicker because of the decreased ability to absorb energy.[50] The fatigue may be affecting the sensory intrafusal fibers as well as the extrafusal fibers. Generalized endurance training may increase the time to fatigue in these muscles.

Golgi tendon organs lie in series with the extrafusal muscle fibers and inhibit contractions caused by the intrafusal fibers. The Golgi tendon organs will bring about reflex inhibition when stimulated by tension of an excessive magnitude. These receptors are located in ligaments as well as muscles, and serve to protect both muscle and connective tissues.

The third group of receptors is the free nerve endings. They have been recognized in muscles and are associated with blood vessels. They are classified as both Group III and Group IV afferent fibers. These receptors are unmyelinated and have the slowest conduction velocity (Table 21–1).

Exercise will affect these specialized sensory receptors. The *exercise pressor reflex*[61] is a reflex neural mechanism that plays an important role in the regulation of cardiovascular response to exercise of varying intensities. Studies have evaluated the muscle afferents that trigger the cardiovascular response in a static muscle contraction. The responses

Table 21–1: Classification of Afferent Fibers

GROUP	DIAMETER (μM)	VELOCITY (M/S)	RECEPTOR
Ia	12–20	71–120	Muscle spindle, primary ending
Ib	12–20	71–120	Golgi tendon organ
II	4–12	31–70	Muscle spindle, secondary ending
III	<4	6–30	Unencapsulated nerve ending
IV	—	<2.5	Unencapsulated nerve ending

seen include increases in heart rate, cardiac output, and arterial pressure.[39] There is limited or no cardiovascular response when muscle spindles and Golgi tendon organs are stimulated.[56] It is generally agreed that muscle mechanoreceptors do not play a role in circulatory reflexes.[40] It is during stimulation of the free or unencapsulated nerve endings that the exercise pressor reflex is evoked.[62] It has become clear that it is the unencapsulated nerve endings, rather than the Group I and Group II afferents, that are responsible for the exercise neural reflex during a static contraction of the muscle.[57] Static contraction will also lead to a release of bradykinin from skeletal muscle[80] that contributes to the exercise pressor reflex.[65] The reflex may be partially attenuated by reactive oxygen species, such as hydrogen peroxide and the hydroxl radical, that are produced during muscular contraction.[6] A clinician must be cautious about increasing these parameters during an active inflammatory condition. If isometric exercises are started too early, the increased arterial pressure could compromise rehabilitative efforts by causing capillary leakage in tissue that is still damaged. This may partially explain why continuous passive movement has become one part of some rehabilitation programs.

NEUROMUSCULAR PHYSIOLOGY

One of the factors that influences muscle contraction is the neurological stimulus provided to the muscle fibers or motor units. The motor unit of the spinal cord consists of the anterior horn cell of the spinal cord and the muscle group that it innervates.[11] The intensity of muscle contraction is based on the ability to recruit available motor neurons and the ability to increase the firing rate of these motor neurons. The process by which the central nervous system controls the firing rate of motor neurons is known as rate coding.[60] Rate coding adjusts the firing rate of neural impulses moving down the motor neuron, which controls a specific motor unit.[43]

There is an indication that small muscles, which consist of deep muscles and axial segments of surface muscles (a high percentage of Type I fibers), initially rely on recruitment to increase muscular contraction.[17] As these muscles get close to 100% maximum voluntary contraction (MVC), the increase in muscular tension is due to increased rate coding in the activated motor units. At 30% MVC you can get 86% recruitment, and at 50% MVC you can get 100% recruitment. Excitation needs to increase to a threshold level to activate the motor unit, at which point the contribution of that motor unit changes from zero to approximately 10% to 50% of the maximum force capacity of that unit.[41] This shows that recruitment plays the dominant role initially, with rate coding taking over the dominant role as the muscle approaches MVC.[42] During active trunk exercise, this suggests that low-intensity exercises (50% MVC or less) could provide total motor unit recruitment of the deep muscles.

Larger muscles that tend to be more superficial, such as the trapezius and the latissimus dorsi, have a more mixed population of Type I and Type II fibers and therefore tend to operate in a different manner. Initial increases in muscle tension are due to rate coding of low-threshold motor units. As the muscle increases its level of tension, recruitment of higher-threshold motor units occur.[17] When the muscle nears MVC, increases in tension are due solely to rate coding. It appears that in large muscles with heterogenous populations of muscle fibers the increase in the muscle's tension is due to a combination of recruitment and rate coding except at the extremes of muscle tension. When the muscle is operating close to 0% or 100% MVC, rate coding plays the dominant role.[5] The use of a broad recruitment range shows that EMG measurements increase more rapidly at high force levels than at lower force levels.[24] Rehabilitation of these larger muscles would have to progress to a higher intensity of MVC to ensure maximal recruitment of motor neurons.

Much of the information on motor neuron recruitment patterns revolves around the principle known as the *size principle*.[32] Briefly, this principle states that the size of the motor neuron will ultimately determine its threshold or critical firing level. Smaller motor units, which are generally made up of Type I (slow-twitch) muscle fibers, have lower critical firing levels. Thus, smaller motor units will be recruited first in a muscle contraction.[13] Larger motor units, which are generally made up of type II (fast-twitch) muscle fibers, will be recruited later in the recruitment pattern. However, the linear relationship between local fiber twitch force and recruitment threshold does not translate into a constant increase in total muscular force due to recruitment over a large force range, as previously thought.[41,93] An abundance of research has supported the size principle,[12,18] but some scientists feel this principle only holds true when looking at unidirectional movements in which the muscle can be identified with a specific role. It is possible that a muscle can function as a primary mover in one task, but as a secondary mover in another task.

Person[66] states that recruitment patterns are task-specific and are regulated with respect to the nature of the task. With the muscle in a specific, fixed position the size principle would still apply. In a more complex movement that includes postural adjustments, the recruitment patterns can be as varied as the amount of postural adjustments needed to maintain a balanced position. The recruitment patterns would be modified at different cortical levels with respect to the constant flow of afferent feedback. If the clinician is working with a movement such as hip extension, there would have be to consideration for performing the movement in different postural positions (Figure 21–1).

Eccentric exercise also seems to effect the *Henneman size principle*.[33a] Eccentric contraction appears to shift activity toward the large motor units, which presumably contain fast-twitch muscle fibers. Along with this increased activity in large motor units was a selective decruitment in small motor units. Selective recruitment of large motor units with a concomitant decruitment of small motor units leads to a motor pattern in which muscle fibers that are not recruited during normal activities may be recruited first during an eccentric contraction. This could explain the increased damage to fast-twitch fibers with eccentric contractions as opposed to concentric contractions of equal intensity. The patient who comes in with paraspinal muscle pain from "just doing too much work," may actually be suffering from a motion that had a subtle eccentric component. Therefore, exercise therapy that includes an eccentric component may be very useful.

A

B

C

Figure 21–1. A. Hip extension from the prone position. **B.** Hip extension from the quadruped position. **C.** Hip extension from the standing position.

NEUROMUSCULAR JUNCTION

At the end of the myelinated motoneuron is an endplate, a specialized region called the neuromuscular junction. This end plate is a specialized structure of the sarcolemma, which receives the motor fiber, a highly arborized structure entering this junction.

Excitation occurs when an end plate potential spreads to the extrajunctional sarcolemma, stimulating the release of calcium. Inhibition of the fiber is due to an increase in the electrical potential in the membrane, creating an inhibitory postsynaptic potential (IPSP). The ability to activate all motoneurons is based on removing all inhibitory affects, which is known as *disinhibition*. Increased disinhibition may explain the strength increases noted in the early stages of strength and rehabilitation programs.[71a] These strength increases have been seen without accompanying increases in the size of the muscle.[80a]

There has been little research on neuromuscular junction adaptations with respect to exercise training. Recently, Deschenes et al[17a] studied the effects of both high-intensity training (HIT) and low-intensity training (LIT) on nerve terminal branching patterns of the neuromuscular junction. Both HIT and LIT caused conversions in nerve terminal branching. Total length of branching per terminal was significantly greater with HIT, but there were no differences in total number of branches per terminal. Both the length of secondary branches and the number of secondary branches were less with the LIT. The data suggests that exercise training leads to intensity-specific changes in nerve terminal branching patterns that were not attributable to muscle fiber type or hypertrophy.

During rehabilitation of patients it is accepted that strength gains will occur without a requisite gain in muscle size. Further research is also needed into strength gains made after accepted lengths of rehabilitation are completed. It might be possible that movement patterns practiced over a period of time may not lead to great increases of strength, but may lead to increased patterns of terminal branching, which could lead to more efficient motor patterns. It could be that the ability to disinhibit is related to increased branching patterns. These increased branching patterns could become one of the goals of the later stages of patient rehabilitation.

THE MUSCLE REPAIR PROCESS

Skeletal muscle tissue damage may arise from a number of causes. Research studies have analyzed skeletal muscle response to disease and physical insults such as muscular dystrophy,[21] crushing,[10] and traumatic injury.[3] Physical activity has been examined with respect to the relationship between muscle damage and overuse,[72] eccentric exercise,[15] and the tearing of fibers due to stretching.[25] Information with respect to biochemical and ultrastructural changes in the muscle after an injury could be fundamental to the application of rehabilitation procedures. Muscle responses to different types of damage may alter the clinical choice of procedures to be used.

There has been an attempt to determine the ultrastructural events occurring in skeletal muscle following acute blunt trauma.[20] Using a technique that had been previously reported on by Stratton et al,[79] a solid aluminum cylinder with a flat impact head was used to create an injury that resembled a muscle contusion of moderate severity. Inflammation was fully established at 1 to 2 days postinjury. This inflammation consisted of erythrocytes and polymorphonuclear leukocytes from the disruption of capillaries and small blood vessels at the 6-hour postinjury point. At 1 day postinjury, large amounts of mononuclear cells were observed in the endomysial connective tissue and the injured muscle cells. At 2 days postinjury, activated fibroblasts became very prevalent. It wasn't until 3 days postinjury that interstitial fibrosis was seen in association with the fibroblasts. At this point, an increasing proportion of muscle cells appeared normal. This contrasts with the muscle damage that appears following intense eccentric exercise.[22] With intense eccentric exercise, the focal disturbances of the striated band pattern indicating muscle damage were 32%, 52%, and 12% of the fibers 1 hour, 3 days, and 6 days postexercise, respectively. This may indicate that the inflammatory process is longer with eccentric exercise–induced damage and that the interstitial fibrosis associated with activated fibroblasts starts somewhere between days 3 and 6. From a clinical standpoint, antiinflammatory protocols may have to be a first priority for a longer period of time in an injury deemed to be caused by eccentric movements.

Fisher et al[20] showed that at 6 days postinjury, cellular observation indicated an abundance of fibroblasts actively synthesizing protein. Examination on day 14 postinjury showed the muscles to be histologically normal; however, complete repletion of muscle proteins did not catch up to the controls until day 21. Fisher et al[20] speculated that collagen deposition would impact the return of muscle function to previous capability levels due to the replacement of contractile tissue with noncontractile tissue. Rehabilitation might involve integrating procedures that would accelerate muscle cell regeneration while limiting scar formation at the same time.

Smith[77] proposed a sequence of events concerning muscle soreness that agrees with the process of inflammation put forth by other researchers.[1,34,69] The damage of muscle and/or connective tissue leads to an increase in circulating neutrophils, which migrate to the site of injury followed by monocytes. Monocytes synthesize large quantities of prostaglandins (PGE_2) that sensitize afferent nerve endings in muscle tissue, leading to the feeling of pain. The amount of monocytes peak at 48 hours, which is sometimes considered the time of maximum sorenesss in eccentric exercise–induced pain. In another study, however,[36] it was determined that peak mononuclear cell accumulation occurred as much as 1 week after peak soreness was experienced. It is not apparent that there is a relationship between macrophage accumulation and the sensation of soreness. Jones and Round[37] suggest that the soreness is due to an inflammation of connective tissue that sensitizes mechanoreceptors so that they can be easily activated when the muscle is palpated or moving. Fisher et al[20] noted that in a study on muscle damage in rats, there was a surprising lack of overt signs of pain or altered mobility in the rats despite a significant amount of muscle damage. Smith[77] noted that soreness only seemed apparent when the muscle was active or being palpated. It is possible that even with histologically observable inflammatory changes in an injured muscle, it is the change in connective tissue that may determine the sensations of pain and soreness.

Examination of the myotendinous junctions of patients with flaccid and spastic paralysis showed a decrease in the number of mechanoreceptors, and those that were found were degenerated, fibrotic, and atrophic. These mechanoreceptors were no longer connected to their muscle fibers and tendon bundles.[38] It would be interesting to see if these types of histological changes occur in chronic, musculoskeletal conditions. An important part of the protective feedback loop has been lost if myotendinous junctions can lose their mechanoreceptor input over a specified period of time.

Increases in serum enzymes have been observed in studies that have looked at possible muscle damage.[14,59] Creatine kinase (CK) activity has been targeted for research due to the increased CK levels associated with muscle soreness.[9a,83]

In the study by Triffletti et al,[83] muscle adaptation was examined with regard to changes in serum CK and muscle soreness after isometric exercise bouts. It was determined that performance of an isometric exercise results in an adaptation that lasts approximately 3 weeks, with the greatest adaptation occurring after one bout. The adaptations consisted of decreased serum CK, and decreased soreness as measured by a questionnaire. Byrnes et al previously used this questionnaire to establish a scale from 1 (normal) to 10 (very, very sore) that measured the perception of muscle soreness.[9a] Previous studies have also noted reduced CK levels after a program of exercise training.[22,54]

In a study that examined CK levels after repeated bouts of downhill running, Byrnes et al concluded that the performance of a single exercise bout had a prophylactic effect on muscle soreness and reduced CK serum levels for up to 6 weeks.[9a] Keeping in mind that downhill running involves a strong eccentric action of the quadriceps muscle group, this study appears to show that there is a prophylactic effect on muscle soreness in an eccentric training bout as well as in an isometric training bout.

Evidence has been presented by Grimby and Saltin[31] that there is a decrease in the total number of muscle fibers with increasing age due to the degeneration of a small percentage of the total muscle fiber population. It has also been suggested that there may be a pool of stress-susceptible muscle fibers that would be damaged by an initial bout of exercise.[4] It is the initial damage to these stress-susceptible fibers that would appear to cause the increased serum CK levels seen in the previously mentioned studies. Armstrong et al[4] suggested that these more fragile muscle fibers may be a result of disuse due to dysfunctional motor unit recruitment patterns. In studies examining muscle fibers following eccentric and exhaustive exercise,[4,22] only a small percentage of the total muscle fiber population showed signs of damage, and in subsequent training bouts there were less of the fragile fibers to be damaged leading to lower serum CK levels. These fragile fibers may be more likely to be Type II muscle fibers. Both in a low back pain study and denervated animal studies,[48] atrophy of Type II fibers appears to be more prominent than Type I fibers.

The research available indicates that there is a possibility that there is a pool of muscle fibers that are more vulnerable to damage. If these stress-susceptible fibers are part of the aging process, there may not be much to be done in the way of intervention. If these fibers are vulnerable to stress because of a disuse associated with dysfunctional motor unit recruitment patterns, however, then the clinician would need to address the dysfunctional motor patterns as well as the original injury that damaged the muscle fibers.

It has been suggested that the alteration of motor unit recruitment could not explain the lowered serum CK levels in repeated exercise bout training because it was believed that maximal eccentric contractions should recruit all motor units.[63] An eccentric muscle contraction, however, may recruit motor units at different times with different forces throughout the range of motion of a particular movement.[15] This would mean that the possibility of a neurological explanation must be considered. The long-lasting adaptation that is seen in muscle fibers with an initial exercise training bout may be a combination of decreasing the population of stress-susceptible fibers and increasing the efficiency of an exercise movement by "memorization" of a motor skill.

SUMMARY

Some basic principles of exercise physiology have been presented. These principles can be applied to help establish protocols for the rehabilitation of patients with musculoskeletal injuries. The information presented should be used to design a rehabilitation program that accomplishes specific rehabilitation goals. It is important to recognize the individuality of each patient's injury and to design a plan of care specific to that patient. Here is a summary of some of the principles that need to be addressed in the exercise program:

1. An older patient may need more general endurance programming. A set of exercises that calls for 10 repetitions in a 40-year-old patient would be adjusted to 15 repetitions at a lower intensity in a 60-year-old patient. These age categories are somewhat arbitrary because we do not know enough

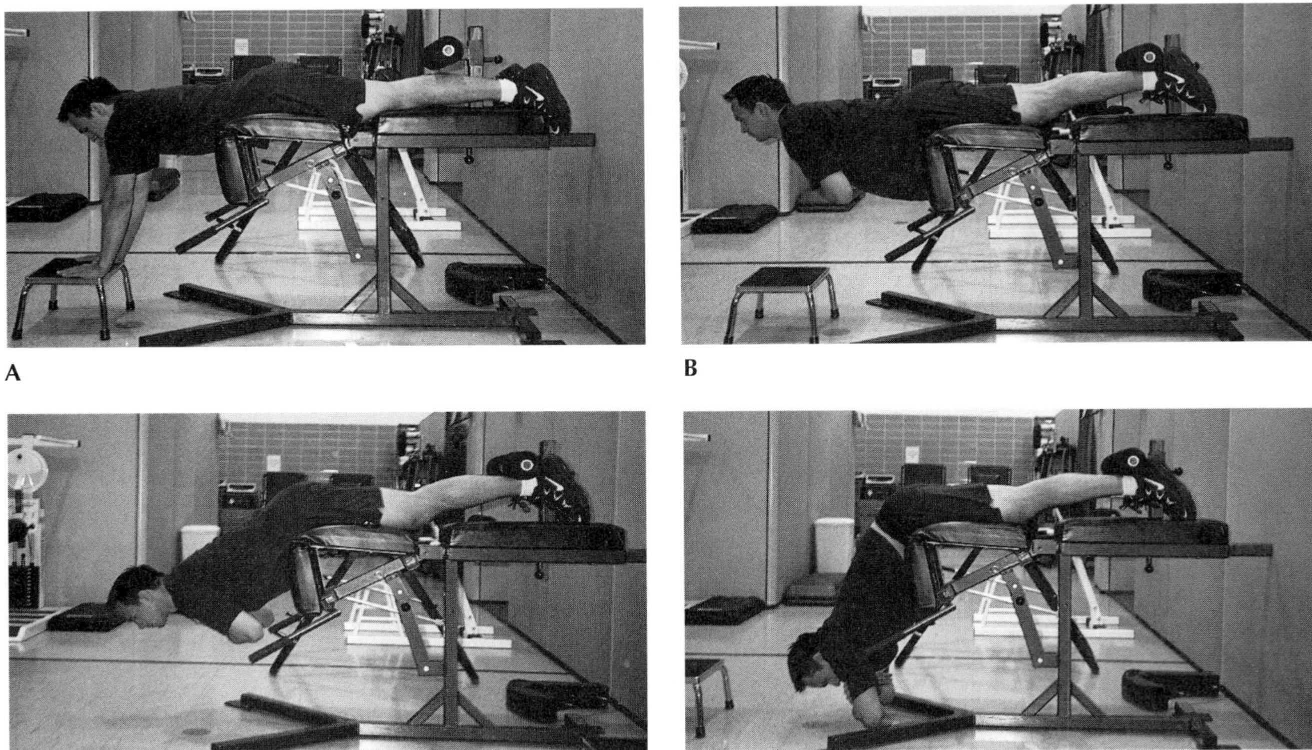

Figure 21–2. A. Starting position for eccentrically exercising the erector spinae; the patients may support themselves with a step stool in this position. **B.** The patients bring their arms across their chest and begin a slow descent into flexion; as an initial exercise, the patients may keep their hands on the step stool and exercise with partial weight bearing. **C.** The patients continue their slow, controlled descent. **D.** The finishing position; to begin the next repetition, the patients may use the step stool to push their body into the original starting position.

about biological age versus chronological age to have an exact delineation of clinical boundaries.

2. For flexibility, both passive, static stretch and a low-intensity dynamic stretch should be used to retrain the muscle proprioceptors.
3. In an acute muscle injury or acute exacerbation of a chronic injury, muscle contraction should be limited for 1 to 2 days to avoid the exercise pressor reflex in vulnerable tissue. This may be accomplished by bracing or restricted activity.
4. Eccentric exercises should be part of the rehabilitation program as soon as possible. The intensity of these exercises preclude them from being used in the first week, but after this initial period, these exercises should be incorporated into a program (Figure 21–2).
5. Along with exercise to stimulate the process of physical repair in the muscle, motor patterns should also be practiced to stimulate the neurological component of the muscle.

REFERENCES

1. Adams D, Hamilton TA. The cell biology of macrophage activation. *Annu Rev Immunol.* 1984;2:238–318.
2. Almekinders LC, Gilbert JA. Healing of experimental muscle strains and the effect of nonsteroidal anti-inflammatory medication. *Am J Sports Med.* 1986;14:303–308.
3. Armstrong RB. Muscle damage and endurance events. *Sports Med.* 1986;3:370–381.
4. Armstrong RB, Ogilvie RW, Schwane JA. Eccentric exercise-induced injury to rat skeletal muscle. *J Appl Physiol.* 1983;54:80–93.
5. Bellemare F, Woods JJ, Johansson R, Bigland-Ritchie B. Motor-unit discharge rates in maximal voluntary contractions of three human muscles. *J Neurophysiol.* 1983;50:1380–1392.

5a. Best TM, McElhaney J, Garrett WE Jr., Myers BS. Axial strain measurements in skeletal muscle at various strain rates. *J Biomech Eng.* 1995;117(3):262–265.

6. Bonigut S, Stebbins CL, Lonhurst JC. Reactive oxygen species modify reflex cardiovascular response to static contraction. *J Appl Physiol.* 1996;81(3):1207–1212.

7. Booth FW, Weeden SH, Tseng BS. Effect of aging on human skeletal muscle and motor function. *Med Sci Sports Exerc.* 1994;26:556–560.

8. Brown WFA. A method for estimating the number of motor units in thenar muscles and the changes in motor unit count with aging. *J Neurol Neurosurg Psychiatry.* 1972;35:845–852.

9. Burke RE, Edgerton VR. Motor unit properties and selective involvement in movement. *Exercise Sport Sci Rev.* 1975;3:31–81.

9a. Byrnes WC, Clarkson PM, White JS, Hsieh SS, Frykman PN, Maughan RJ. Delayed onset muscle soreness following repeated bouts of downhill running. *J Appl Physiol.* 1985;59(3):710–715.

10. Carlson BM. The regeneration of skeletal muscle: A review. *Am J Anat.* 1983;137:119–150.

11. Chusid JG. *Correlative Neuroanatomy and Functional Neurology.* Los Altos, CA: Lange Medical Publications, 1985.

12. Clamann HP, Gillies JD, Skinner RD, Henneman E. Quantitative measures of output of a motoneuron pool during monosynaptic reflexes. *J Neurophysiol.* 1974;37:1328–1336.

13. Clamann HP, Henneman E. Electrical measurement of axon diameter and its use in relating motoneuron size to critical firing level. 1976;39:844–851.

14. Clarkson PM, Litchfield P, Graves J, Kirwan J, Byrnes WC. Serum creatine kinase activity following forearm flexion isometric exercise. *Eur J Appl Physiol.* 1985;53:368–371.

15. Clarkson PM, Nosaka K, Braun B. Muscle function after exercise-induced muscle damage and rapid adaptation. *Med Sci Sports Exerc.* 1992;24(5):512–520.

16. Condon K, Silberstein L, Blau HM, Thompson WJ. Developement of muscle fiber types in the prenatal rat hindlimb. *Dev Biol.* 1990;138:256–274.

17. DeLuca CJ, Lefever RS, McCue MP, Xenakis AP. Behavior of human motor units in different muscles during linearly varying contractions. *J Physiol. 1982*;329:113–128.

17a. Deschenes MR, Maresh CM, Crivello JF, Armstrong LE, Karemer WJ, Covault J. The effects of exercise training of different intensities on neuromuscular junction morphology. *J Neurocytol.* 1993;22(8):603–615.

18. Desmedt JE, Godaux E. Ballistic contractions in fast or slow human muscles: Discharge patterns of single motor units. *J Physiol.* 1978;285:185–196.

19. Edstrom L, Kugelberg E. Histochemical composition, distribution of fibres and fatigability of single motor units. *J Neurol Neurosurg Psychiat.* 1968;31:424–433.

20. Fisher BD, Baracos VE, Shnitka TK, Mendryk SW, Reid DC. Ultrastructural events following acute muscle trauma. *Med Sci Sports Exerc.* 1990;22(2):185–193.

21. Foster AH, Carlson BM. Myotoxicity of local anesthetics and regeneration of the damaged muscle fibers. *Anaesth Analg.* 1980;58:727–736.

22. Friden J, Sjostrom M, Ekblom B. A morphological study of delayed muscle soreness. *Experentia.* 1981;37:506–507.

23. Fu S, Gordon T, Parry DJ, Tyreman N. Immunohistochemical analysis of fiber types within physiological typed motor units of rat tibialis anterior muscle after long-term cross-reinnervation. *Soc Neurosci.* 1992;18:1557.

24. Fuglevand AJ, Winter DA, Patla AE. Models of recruitment and rate coding organization in motor-unit pools. *J Neurophysiol.* 1993;70(6):2470–2488.

25. Garrett WE, Safran MR, Seaber AV, Glisson RR, Ribbeck BM. Biomechanical comparison of stimulated and nonstimulated skeletal muscle pulled to failure. *Am J Sports Med.* 1987;15:448–454.

26. Goebel HH. Desmin-related neuromuscular disorders (review). *Muscle Nerve.* 1995;18(11):1306–1320.

27. Gollnick PD. Effects on enzyme activity and fiber composition of human skeletal muscle. *J Appl Physiol.* 1973;34:107.

28. Gollnick PD, Hodgson DR. The identification of fiber types in skeletal muscle: A continual dilemma. *Exerc Sports Sci Rev.* 1986;14:81–104.

29. Grabiner MD, Enoka RM. Changes in movement capabilities with aging. *Ex Sports Sci Rev.* 1995;23:65–104.

30. Granger BL, Lazarides E. Desmin and vimentin coexist at the periphery of the myofibril Z-disc. *Cell.* 1979;18:1053–1063.

31. Grimby G, Saltin B. The ageing muscle. *Clin Physiol.* 1983;3:209–218.

32. Henneman E, Clamann HP, Gillies JD, Skinner RD. Rank order of motoneurons within a pool: Law of combination. *J Neurophysiol.* 1974;37:1338–1348.

33. Horowits R, Podolsky RJ. Transitional stability of thick filaments in activated skeletal muscle depends on sarcomere length: Evidence for the role of titin filaments. *J Cell Biol.* 1987;105:2217–2223.

33a. Howell JN, Chleboun G, Conatser R. Muscle stiffness, strength loss, swelling and soreness following exercise-induced injury in humans. *J Physiol.* 1993;464:183–196.

34. Jennische E, Skottner A, Hansson HA. Satellite cells express the trophic factor IGF-I in regenerating skeletal muscle. *Acta Physiol Scand.* 1987;129:9–15.

35. Jones DA, Newham DJ, Clarkson PM. Skeletal muscle stiffness and pain following eccentric exercise for the elbow flexors. *Pain.* 1987;30:233–242.

36. Jones DA, Newham DJ, Round JM, Tolfree EJ. Experimental human muscle damage: Morphological changes in relation to other indices of damage. *J Physiol.* 1986;375:435–448.

37. Jones DA, Round JM. *Skeletal Muscle in Health And Disease: A Textbook of Muscle Physiology.* New York: Manchester University Press, 1990:158–174.

38. Jozsa L, Kannus P, Jarvinen TA, Balint J, Jarvinen M. Number and morphology of mechanoreceptors in the myotendinous junction of paralysed human muscle. *J Pathol.* 1996;178(2):195–200.

39. Kaufman MP, Iwamoto GA, Longhurst JC, Mitchell JH. Effects of capsaicin and bradykinin on afferent fibers with endings in skeletal muscle. *Circ Res.* 1982;50:133–139.

40. Kaufman MP, Rybicki KJ, Waldrop TG, Ordway GA. Effect of ischemia on responses of group III and IV afferents to contraction. *J Appl Physiol.* 1985;51:644–650.

41. Kernell D. Organized variability in the neuromuscular system: A survey of task-related adaptations. *Arch Ital Biol.* 1992;130:19–66.

42. Kukulka CG, Clamann HP. Comparison of the recruitment and discharge properties of motor units in human brachial biceps and adductor pollicis during isometric contractions. *Brain Res.* 1981;291:44–55.

43. Lamb DR. *Physiology of Exercise: Responses and Adaptations.* New York: Macmillan, 1984.

44. Lazarides E, Granger BL, Gard DL. Desmin- and vimentin-containing filaments and their role in the assembly of the Z-disc in muscle cells. *Cold Spring Harb Symp Quant Biol.* 1981;46:351–378.

45. Lexell J, Downham DY. What is the effect of aging on type 2 muscle fibers? *J Neurol Sci.* 1992;107:250–251.

46. Lexell J, Taylor C, Sjostrom M. What is the cause of the aging atrophy? Total number, size and proportion of different fiber types studies in whole vastus lateralis muscle from 15 to 83-year-old-men. *J Neurol Sci.* 1988;84:275–294.

47. Li H, Choudhary SK, Milner DJ, Munir MI, Kuisk IR, Capetanaki Y. Inhibition of desmin expression blocks myoblast fusion and interferes with the myogenic regulators myoD and myogenin. *J Cell Biol.* 1994;124:827–841.

48. Lu DX, Huang SK, Carlson BM. Electron microscopic study of long-term denervated rat skeletal muscle. *Anat Rec.* 1997;248(3):355–365.

49. Lynn R, Morgan DL. Decline running produces more sarcomeres in rat vastus intermedius muscle fibers than does incline running. *J Appl Physiol.* 1994;77(3):1439–1444.

50. Mair SD, Seaber AV, Glisson RR, Garrett WE Jr. The role of fatigue in susceptibility to acute muscle strain injury. *Am J Sports Med.* 1996;24(2):137–143.

51. Manniche C, Asmussen K, Lauritsen B, Vinterberg H, Karbo H, Abildstrup S, Fischer-Nielson K, Krebs R, Ibsen K. Intensive dynamic back exercises with or without hyperextension in chronic back pain after surgery for lumbar disc protrusion. *Spine.* 1993;18:560–567.

52. Maruyama K, Matsuno A, Higuchi H, Shimaoka S, Kimura S, Shimizu T. Behavior of connectin (titin) and nebulin in skinned muscle fibers released after extreme stretch as revealed by immunoelectron microscopy. *J Muscle Res Cell Motil.* 1989; 10:350–359.

53. Maughan RJ, Watson JS, Weir J. Strength and cross-sectional area of human skeletal muscle. *J Physiol.* 1983;338:37–49.

54. Maxwell JH, Bloor CM. Effects of conditioning on exertional rhabdomyolysis and serum creatine kinase after severe exercise. *Enzyme.* 1981;26:177–181.

55. McArdle WD, Katch FI, Katch VL. *Exercise Physiology: Energy, Nutrition and Human Performance.* 3rd ed. Philadelphia: Lea & Febiger, 1991.

56. McCloskey DI, Matthews PBC, Mitchell JH. Absence of appreciable cardiovascular and respiratory responses to muscle vibration. *J Appl Physiol.* 1972;33:623–626.

57. McCloskey DI, Mitchell JH. Reflex cardiovascular and respiratory responses originating in exercising muscle. *J Physiol (Lond).* 1972;224:173–186.

58. McComas AJ, Upton RM, Sica REP. Motoneuron disease and aging. *Lancet.* 1973;II:1477–1480.

59. McCulley KK, Faulkner JA. Injury to skeletal muscle fibers of mice following lengthening contractions. *J Appl Physiol.* 1985;59:119–126.

60. Milner-Brown HS, Stein RB, Lee RG. Synchronization of human motor units: Possible roles of exercise and supraspinal reflexes. *Electroencephalogr Clin Neurophysiol.* 1978;38:245–254.
61. Mitchell JH, Kaufman MP, Iwamoto GA. The exercise pressor reflex: Its cardiovascular effects, afferent mechanisms, and central pathways. *Annu Rev Physiol.* 1983;45:229–242.
62. Mitchell JH, Mierzwiak DS, Wildenthal K, Willis WD Jr., Smith AM. Effects on left ventricular performance of stimulation of an afferent nerve from muscle. *Circ Res.* 1968;22:507–516.
63. Newham DJ, Jones DA, Clarkson PM. Repeated high-force eccentric exercise: Effects on muscle pain and damage. *J Appl Physiol.* 1987;63:1381–1386.
64. Overend TJ, Cunningham DA, Paterson DH, Lefcoe MS. Thigh composition in young and elderly men determined by computed tomography. *Clin Physiol.* 1992;12:629–640.
65. Pan HL, Stebbins CL, Longhurst JC. Bradykinin contributes to the exercise pressor reflex: Mechanism of action. *J Appl Physiol.* 1993;75(5):2061–2068.
66. Person RS. Rhythmic activity of a group of motoneurons during voluntary contraction of a muscle. *Electroencephalogr Clin Neurophysiol.* 1974;36:585–590.
67. Pette D, Staron RS. Cellular and molecular diversities of mammalian skeletal muscle fibers. *Rev Physiol Biochem Pharmacol.* 1990;1161–1176.
68. Porter MM, Vandervoort AA, Lexell J. Aging of human muscle: Structure, function and adaptability. *Scand J Med Sci Sports.* 1995;5:129–142.
69. Rodemann HP, Goldberg AL. Arachidonic acid, prostaglandin E2 and F2 alpha influences of protein turnover in skeletal and cardiac muscle. *J Biol Chem.* 1982;257:1632–1638.
70. Romanul FCA. Enzymes in muscle. I. Histochemical studies of enzymes in individual muscle fibers. *Arch Neurol.* 1964;11:355–368.
71. Roos MR, Rice CL, Vandervoort AA. Age-related changes in motor unit function. *Muscle Nerve.* 1997;20:679–690.

71a. Sale DG. Neural adaptation to resistance training (review). *Med Sci Sports Exerc* 20(5 Suppl):1988;135–145.

72. Salminin A, Kihlstrom M. Protective effects of indomethacin against exercise-induced effects of injury in mouse skeletal muscle fibers. *Int J Sports Med.* 1987;8:46–49.
73. Schantz P, Randall-Fox E, Hutchison W, Tyden A, Astrand PO. Muscle fiber type distribution, muscle cross-sectional area and maximal voluntary strength in humans. *Acta Physiol Scand.* 1983;117:219–226.
74. Sejersen T, Lendahl U. Transient expression of the intermediate filament nestin during skeletal muscle development. *J Cell Sci.* 1993;106(Pt 4):1291–1300.
75. Sjoberg G, Jiang WQ, Ringertz NR, Lendahl U, Sejersen T. Colocalization of nestin and vimentin'desmin in skeletal muscle cells demonstrated by three-dimensional fluorescence digital imaging microscopy. *Exp Cell Res.* 1994;214(2):447–458.
76. Sjostrand FS. The connections between A- and I-band filaments in striated frog muscle. *J Ultrastruct Res.* 1962;7:225–246.
77. Smith LL. Acute inflammation: The underlying mechanism in delayed onset muscle soreness? *Med Sci Sports Exerc.* 1991;23:542–551.
78. Staron RS, Johnson P. Myosin polymorphism and differential expression in adult human skeletal muscle. *Comp Biochem Physiol.* 1993;106B:463–475.
79. Stratton SA, Heckmann R, Francis RS. Therapeutic ultrasound, its effects on the integrity of a nonpenetrating wound. *J Orthop Sports Phys Ther.* 1984;5:278–281.
80. Symons JD, Theodossy SJ, Longhurst JC, Stebbins CL. Intramuscular accumulation of prostaglandins during static contraction of the cat triceps surae. *J Appl Physiol.* 1991;71:1837–1842.

80a. Tesch PA, Lindeberg S. Blood lactate accumulation during arm exercise in world class kayak paddlers and strength trained athletes. *Eur J Appl Physiol* 1984;52(4):441–445.

81. Totosy de Zepetnek J, Zung HV, Erdebil S, Gordon T. Innervation ratio is an important determinant of force in normal and reinnervated rat tibialis anterior muscle. *J Neurophysiol.* 1992;67:1385–1403.
82. Trappe SW, Costill DL, Fink WJ, Pearson DR. Skeletal muscle characteristics among distance runners: A 20-year follow-up study. *J Appl Physiol.* 1995;78(3):823–829.
83. Triffletti P, Litchfield PE, Clarkson PM, Byrnes WC. Creatine kinase and muscle soreness after repeated isometric exercise. *Med Sci Sports Exerc.* 1988;20:242–248.
84. van der Ven PF, Schaart G, Croes HJ, Jap PH, Ginsel LA, Ramaekers FC. Titin aggregates associated with intermediate filaments align along stress fiber-like structures during human skeletal muscle cell differentiation. *J Cell Sci.* 1993;106(Pt 3):749–759.
85. Wang K, McClure J, Tu A. Titin, a major myofibril component of striated muscle. *Proc Natl Acad Sci USA.* 1979;76:3698–3702.

86. Wang K, Ramirez-Mitchell R. A network of transverse and longitudinal intermediate filaments is associated with sarcomeres of adult vertebrate skeletal muscle. *J Cell Biol.* 1983;96:562–570.
87. Wang K, Williamson CL. Identification of an N2 line protein of striated muscle. *Proc Natl Acad Sci USA.* 1980;77:3254–3258.
88. Warhol MA, Siegel J, Evans WJ, Silverman LM. Skeletal muscle injury and repair in marathon runners after competition. *Am J Pathol.* 1985;118:331–339.
89. Waterman-Storer CM. The cytoskeleton of skeletal muscle: Is it affected by exercise? A brief review. *Med Sci Sports Exerc.* 1991;23:1240–1249.
90. Yasuda K, Anazawa T, Ishiwata S. Microscopic analysis of the elastic properties of nebulin in skeletal myofibrils. *Biophys J.* 1995;68(2):598–608.
91. Yoshimura A, Shimomura Y, Murakami T, Ichikawa M, Nakai N, Fujitsuka C, Kanematsu M, Fujitsuka N. Glycogen depletion of the intrafusal fibers in a mouse spindle during prolonged swimming. *Am J Physiol.* 1996;271 (Pt 2):R398–408.
92. Young A, Stokes M, Round JM, Edwards RHT. The effect of high-resistance training on the strength and cross-sectional area of the human quadriceps. *Eur J Appl Physiol.* 1983;13:411–417.
93. Zajac FE, Faden JS. Relationship among recruitment order, axonal conduction velocity, and muscle-unit properties of type-identified motor units in cat plantaris muscle. *J Neurophysiol.* 1985;53:1303–1322.

CHAPTER 22

Principles and Methods of Low Technology Exercise and Exercise Progression

Spinal Stabilization

David E. Stude, MS, DC, Richard A. Hills, PT, DC,
Pamela Snyder, PT, & Donald R. Murphy, DC

INTRODUCTION

The health care system continues to promote a competitive environment by requiring increased efficiency and effectiveness in clinical outcomes. Non-machine-dependent exercises, such as stabilization activities, provide the patient an opportunity for increased self-sufficiency in that these exercises can be performed at home without the need for more costly exercise equipment. There is strong evidence to suggest that an advantage exists for functional, three-dimensional training of patients in a less restricted environment.[1–3] Also, this type of exercise more closely reflects normal activities of daily living (ADLs). A focus on function, with an emphasis on maximizing education and self-management, will meet the goals of the individual, as well as enhance the effectiveness of the provider. This chapter emphasizes significant foundation material, which will establish a functionally effective basis for this type of exercise regime. Thorough literature support is not emphasized here, but rather a practical approach to spinal stabilization principles. Please refer to Chapter 1 for a more comprehensive review of the literature.

Stabilization exercise affects dynamic strengthening by incorporating three-dimensional activities into specific movement patterns. It addresses the keys to functional performance, which include:

- Coordination/proprioception
- Endurance
- Strength
- Flexibility
- Compliance

The capacity to perform work-related tasks, while simultaneously maintaining quality of movement over time, is not addressed by single-plane strengthening programs. Three-dimensional training assists in addressing substitution patterns, increases the overall strength profile, alters problems with balance or coordination, and improves overall endurance. These training activities are also called *functional training maneuvers*, since they require patients to perform movement patterns that more closely reflect real-life activity demands. This form of functional training is literature-supported, emphasizing early intervention, program individualization, and patient education.

EARLY INTERVENTION

The literature strongly supports the premise that early implementation of exercise is crucial in the treatment of low back pain.[2,4] This means that exercise is not an option, but a necessary intervention in the vast majority of case management programs. Clinical data and the judgment of an experienced health care professional will determine which types of exercise are most appropriate for each individual patient. Injured and fatigued muscles, for example, can produce compensatory patterns of movement and can further increase the susceptibility to end-range spinal loading. This further reinforces the premise that activity, not rest, will help to restore function. One key is to provide the patient with an understanding that pain is not necessarily harmful.

PROGRAM INDIVIDUALIZATION

The rehabilitation program is tailored to address identified deficiencies based on loss of function, and should progress from basic to advanced to functionally specific activities. Although exercises may overlap from patient to patient, individual differences must be accounted for in order to increase the likelihood for a successful outcome. Sensory-motor control protocols ensure that the functional quality of movement is maintained when the patient carries out an exercise maneuver in a specific range against a specific resistance. Primary objectives for this type of program include:

- Improving function of the neuromusculoskeletal system.
- Complimenting treatment in conjunction with manual therapy to address spinal mechanical and associated soft tissue dysfunction (i.e., neuromusculoskeletal dysfunction)[5,6]
- Establishing a method for assessing the treatment outcome.
- Providing patient motivation and guidance.

PATIENT EDUCATION

In order to successfully implement an exercise program, the following components must be observed:

- Provide patients with functional skills and knowledge regarding their problems in order to better cope with pain and return to a productive lifestyle.
- Establish realistic goals and expectations, with patients being included as members of the management team.
- Promote self-awareness and self-responsibility.

BACK TO THE BASICS

Early implementation of a functional exercise program is supported by current literature. Clinical outcomes are maximized by incorporating the basic principles of muscle physiology relative to spinal dysfunction. Functionally specific goals (occupational, recreational, or those related to ADLs) are then established. This section reviews the basics of muscle physiology and the spinal motion unit relative to function.

COORDINATION/PROPRIOCEPTION

Proper balance performance requires efficient coordination of muscle activity in response to postural perturbations and subtle postural deviations introduced by the external environment.[7,8] These perturbations are detected by the visual, vestibular, auditory, and somatosensory systems with the information transmitted to the motor system for the generation of appropriate postural responses.[9] This system is quite complex, with optimum function requiring coordinated communication between the sensory and motor systems.

MUSCLE FUNCTION

The mechanics of trunk function depend on the "interactive muscle performance" of spinal motion.[4,6,10] The abdominal muscles, for example, provide a balance of forces between the ligaments and the articular structures of the spine.[11] Contraction of the abdominal muscles can provide a corseting effect by tensing the midline ligaments and thoracolumbar fascia.[12] In addition, the obliques counteract torque and so can be protective during quick movements or during the reception of external forces, whereas the internal obliques protect against torsional stresses. The abdominals, especially the lower external obliques, tend to control lateral bending movements. Strengthening of the abdominal muscles, therefore, decreases the stress on the intervertebral joints while stabilizing the lumbar spine. Gracovetsky and Farfan[13] note that the abdominal mechanism works in conjunction with the thoracolumbar fascia and the midline ligaments of the spine, acting as a lumbar corset to stabilize against torque and sheer stresses. The erector spinae are integral in initiating and maintaining of spinal movements, reducing translational stress, and balancing anterior sheer forces. The trunk extensors need to be strong to maintain proper equilibrium, with the multifidi being most active. The latissimus dorsi, attaching to the lumbar vertebrae, provides a bracing effect for the spine, a concept called *muscle fusion*.[14]

The hip extensors are powerful muscles that assist in stabilizing the spine. Specifically, the gluteus maximus assists in controlling the lumbar spine during lifting activities. The gluteus medius is an important lateral hip stabilizer during the stance phase of gait.[7]

The psoas inserts onto the transverse processes of the lumbar vertebrae; therefore, its co-contraction can increase intradiscal pressure. The iliopsoas is a key muscle in controlling spinal position during rotational and sagittal plane movements. The contralateral muscle can derotate the spine when righting it from a lateral bending position.[15]

Strong quadriceps muscles are necessary to perform functional activities safely. This is especially important for the maintenance of a deep squat position, which would be required for lifting activities or sports such as tennis or racquetball.[16]

The hamstrings, if shortened, can influence lumbopelvic mobility and spinal range of motion. Thus, the hamstrings can have a strong impact on spinal function.[17,18]

Excessive lumbar spine torque can be reduced by moving the shoulders and hips together as a unit during activities involving the upper extremities, such as lifting or reaching. For example, a person with poor shoulder flexibility may compensate during such activities with increased spinal torsion at the thoracolumbar junction. If thoracolumbar segmental mobility is limited, the stresses may be transferred to the lower lumbar spine, which is susceptible to excessive secondary rotational stress.

The following hierarchy of trunk strength values is noted in the literature[19]:

- *Extension/flexion:* The agonist-antagonist ratio for trunk extension to flexion is approximately 1 : 3.
- *Side bending/rotation:* Rotation and side bending strength should be equal bilaterally, possibly allowing for a 10% asymmetry based on hand dominance.

Adequate trunk strength helps protect the spine from injury by providing support to joints and ligaments as well as preventing end-range spinal loading. Muscle may potentially reduce cartilage degeneration due to its shock absorbing quality.[20] This is the basis for functional training in a nonmachine-dependent environment. However, strength alone will not necessarily protect against repetitive injury. The key to functional training is to break activities down into component tasks while addressing the entire movement pattern from head to foot. For example, activities that involve a partial squat require adequate knee flexion, strong quadriceps and gluteus maximus, and maintenance of lumbopelvic neutral position. As a second example, trunk hyperextension, performed safely, should include co-contraction of the gluteal, hamstring, and paraspinal muscles, coupled with contraction of the lower abdominal muscles.

ANTERIOR MOTOR UNIT

Dura

The dura mater of the spine appears to be continuous with the epineurium of the peripheral nerves. This complex needs to be mobile and able to adapt to changes in spinal position. If fibrosis occurs, it can result in traction of the nerve root leading to ischemia and secondary neurological dysfunction. This can effect local blood flow, resulting in adverse tension affecting the dorsal root ganglion with subsequent hypoxia.

Disc

The anterior motor unit is stressed under high physical loads, with disc degeneration tending to occur following partial annulus fibrosus tears. Saal and Saal[15] noted a progressive lengthening of soft tissue structures caused by sustained loading as the day progresses. However, the disc itself tends to be more susceptible to physical stressors early in the day, resulting in an increased risk of injury. Sedentary occupations, for example, tend to facilitate degenerative disc disease. Injury to the disc can result in secondary changes in normal movement patterns, muscle substitution, and compensation. This chain of events can further increase the susceptibility of the disc to loading.

ENDURANCE

Rose and Rothstein[12] have provided an excellent framework regarding muscle mutability and adaptations to altered patterns of use. An understanding of muscle fiber types, mutability paradigms, and joint and muscle dysfunction will provide the basis for developing and implementing a successful treatment program.

Muscle disuse resulting from injury will affect total muscle function. The use of high repetitions and low loads in stabilization exercise has been studied by Salmons and Hendiksson.[21] The authors suggest that increased metabolic demands placed on muscle during endurance training result in adaptive changes in muscle properties that can be demonstrated by systematically changing the functional demand. This results in a consistent sequence of changes that occur in the muscle which is directly related to the muscle fiber type and duration of use. In fact, endurance training acts as a stimulus for muscular changes by increasing oxidative capacity. Increased oxidative capacity tends to occur in muscle fibers when intensity of the work is low and activity duration is high. These adaptations depend on the workload and effort. This supports the premise that exercise in both strengthening and endurance activities needs to be task-specific whether this is at work or home or is sports-oriented.

CASE MANAGEMENT COMPLICATIONS

In order to customize an exercise program to meet individual needs, it is important to address the biomechanics of the activity, the presence of pathomechanics, and the individual's functional profile. When making clinical decisions regarding spinal dysfunction, theoretical and research-based data suggest the following conclusions:

- The disc is weakened by excessive torsional stress.[22]
- Biomechanical changes can result from degenerative disc disease, surgery, and functional compensations.[23,24]
- Back and abdominal muscles may be weakened secondary to low back pain and surgery.[25–27]
- Psychosocial factors can play a role in recovery.[28–30]
- The reason for the recurrence rate of back pain is not clearly established.

Trunk muscle performance can be affected by spinal pathology.[19] Several authors have found that trunk extensors were affected to a greater degree than trunk flexors in patients with low back pain. Studies have shown a high correlation between individuals with chronic low back pain and those with muscular weakness.[25,26,31,32] Other evidence suggests that reduced strength of the abdominal and erector spinae muscles is associated with recurrence or persistence of low back pain.[31] Injury with resultant muscle spasm, a compensatory change in muscle function, muscle shortening, and additional fibrosis all produce a dysfunctional movement pattern. The optimal regeneration stimulus for low metabolic tissues is activity that promotes intermittent compression of associated structures. These structures can degenerate quickly when in a state of inactivity caused by pathological dysfunction. Thus, one goal of rehabilitation is to perform the exercise painlessly through specific functional ranges of motion, as soon as possible.

The deep spinal stabilizers, the multifidi, have been shown to be affected by acute and subacute low back pain. Hides et al[33] demonstrated multifidus muscle wasting ipsilateral to the side of pain in patients with acute and subacute low back pain. The site of muscle wasting also strongly correlated to the clinically determined segmental level of symptoms. In a follow-up study, Hides and Richardson[34] showed that multifidus muscle recovery does not occur spontaneously following resolution of acute low back pain. In this study those subjects who performed specific exercises designed to facilitate isometric contraction of the multifidus in co-contraction with the deep abdominal muscles demonstrated significant recovery of the multifidus when compared to those subjects who did not perform exercise therapy. O'Sullivan and Twomey[35] investigated the effects of these specific exercises in a population with spondylolysis or spondylolisthesis and chronic low back pain. The specific exercise group showed a significant reduction in pain levels and functional disability throughout the 30-month follow-up. The authors suggest a specific exercise approach, designed to facilitate the multifidi and deep abdominal musculature, appeared more effective than other conservative treatment programs in subjects with chronically symptomatic spondylolysis or spondylolisthesis.

Saal and Saal[15] reported on nonoperative treatment of herniated lumbar intervertebral discs with radiculopathy. They demonstrated that a herniated nucleus pulposus of a lumbar intervertebral disc with radiculopathy can be treated successfully with aggressive nonoperative care utilizing spinal stabilization exercises. Surgery should be reserved for those patients for whom function cannot be measurably improved, assuming secondary somatovisceral sequelae (i.e., loss of bladder or bowel function) can be avoided.

DISCECTOMY

A posterolateral disc injury that results in a discectomy can have biomechanical effects at that level. Goel et al[23] concluded that transitional neurorotational instability at the injury level is lessened after subtotal discectomy. Snyder[22] reported that removal of a 2-centimeter portion of the posterior annulus produced a 25% decrease in torque strength. Extension exercises are advised for treatment following subtotal discectomy, since extension appears to be the most stable spinal loading mechanism. Initially, lateral bending and rotation should be avoided.

OCCUPATIONAL FACTORS

Light versus Heavy Work

Hanson et al[36] did a study utilizing a randomized blinded trial of 150 men and women with chronic low back pain. They demonstrated that patients with lighter physical workloads or those less physically fit benefited from dynamic strengthening exercises, with an emphasis on trunk and leg strengthening. Those with harder workloads and those physically fit needed to improve their muscle coordination and control, as well as their static trunk endurance. This group incorporated isometric exercises for the abdomen and legs in conjunction with training of muscular coordination.

Blue Collar Workers

Lindstrom et al[37] evaluated whether graded activity restored occupational function in industrial blue collar workers who were sick-listed for 8 weeks due to subacute nonspecific mechanical back pain. The program was found to be successful in functional restoration of the patients as measured by return to work and a significant reduction in work loss. The following principles were included in developing the successful exercise programs:

- Individualized exercise programs were established.
- Performance records were developed and documented.
- Quotas performed in each trial were recorded.
- Program progression rates were determined prior to the quota phase.
- Positive reinforcement was frequently provided.
- Endurance, strengthening, and functional activities were included in all programs.
- Graded exercises were followed by something pleasant such as rest.
- Patient complaints of pain were recorded, but the program was not changed.
- Supervision and attention were decreased as the quota increased, emphasizing individual responsibility and self-management.

Material Handling

When prescribing an exercise program, it is critical to consider factors such as lifting technique, speed of lifting, and acceleration. Movement and load relationships are significantly influenced by lifting speed. Lifting increases the compressive force and the torque to the low back. Therefore, speed needs to be incorporated into these activities, making one aware of compressive forces and reactive torque. A greater force moment occurs at each load level when lifting at increasing velocity. Relative loads are less when lifting and handling of materials utilizing the legs and proper body mechanics as compared to poor lifting technique. Analysis of lifting style may determine whether specific strengthening or endurance issues may need to be addressed.

TRAINING CONCEPTS

An understanding of muscle fiber types, mutability paradigms, joint dysfunction, muscle atrophy, and fatiguability relative to the diagnosis will provide the foundation principles needed for developing and implementing a successful treatment program.[12]

Factors to be considered that have literature support include:

- Trunk extensors are more resistant to fatigue than flexors.[27]
- Males have less endurance than females.
- Local muscle fatigue predisposes individuals to injury.[27]
- Muscle is one of the most adaptable tissues of the body.[12]
- Knowledge of muscle mutability provides one basis for addressing movement pattern dysfunction and for prescribing a specific treatment program.[12]
- Multiple factors affect function, whether dealing with an acute or postsurgical patient or a well-trained athlete. These include components such as strength, endurance, coordination, flexibility, and psychosocial issues.[9,10,17,19,22,29,37]
- Muscle dysfunction can produce joint dysfunction which may make muscle fiber-predominance important.[12]

Sequential interaction of multiple muscle groups will stabilize and provide a protective mechanism to the spine. Functional activities incorporate movement in the sagittal, coronal, and transverse planes, or any combination of these. Repetition of normal movement patterns can lead to a "reflex status" of balanced muscle control.

Endurance versus Strengthening

It has been well documented that endurance activities increase muscle oxidative capacity with progressive strengthening primarily affecting ligaments and bone mass.[12] Increasing endurance may be more important than purely increasing strength in order to improve tolerance for daily activities that are highly repetitive in nature.[27]

Weight-Bearing versus Non-Weight-Bearing

The patient's responses in weight-bearing versus non-weight-bearing positions need to be taken into account when evaluating muscle function. For example, tension developed in the extensor muscles of the knee is greatest in the midrange when weight-bearing, but is greatest in full extension when seated. Biomechanically, function is reversed when extending the knee in a weight-bearing position compared with extending the knee in a seated position.

Different muscle contraction types elicit variable force profiles. The force-producing capabilities of a muscle are greatest when performing eccentric contractions, whereas concentric contractions produce less force. The force produced with a maximal isometric contraction lies between these two types of contractions.[38] Thus, consideration must be given to the type of muscle contraction utilized in the design of the rehabilitation program based on the patient's ability to tolerate the generated force and the desired training effect.

Operant conditioning is another factor to be considered in the rehabilitation program.[37] An effective way to change behavior is to change the consequences that follow that behavior. If a behavior or action is immediately and systematically followed by something pleasant, this positive reinforcement will increase or strengthen the desired response. However, if the consequence that follows the behavior is not pleasant, the behavior will probably be weakened.

STABILIZATION TRAINING PRINCIPLES

APPROPRIATE SUPERVISION

The exercises described in this chapter must be supervised initially by a trained health care professional with a "hands-on" approach throughout all phases of the rehabilitation program. Very subtle changes can take place in patient position and awareness that can only be corrected by careful observation and knowledge regarding optimal exercise technique. The goal is to emphasize patient awareness progressing to self-management through education. Consideration needs to be given regarding flexibility of the hamstrings, iliopsoas, rectus femoris, piriformis, and other hip rotators, the gastrosoleus group, and the upper thoracic region. One-on-one instruction emphasizes proper technique and control. Advancement is based on functional progression and pain reduction.

SENSORY-MOTOR RETRAINING

Sensory-motor retraining principles were initially developed by Janda.[17,39,40] It is a system of exercise designed to stimulate the proprioceptive system, allowing the central nervous system (CNS) to receive the appropriate afferent stimulation to effectively activate muscles that (due to dysfunction and injury) are being left out of movement patterns. Through the use of balance boards, rocker boards, wobble boards, balance shoes, balance beams, and minitrampolines, the patient can be lead through a series of exercises designed for maximum proprioceptive stimulation. Patients are also taught the proper use of body statics (posture) to prepare for establishing appropriate postural "sets" to be used during activities of daily living (ADLs).

Of utmost importance in the proper rehabilitation of individuals with pain syndromes of the locomotor system is the restoration of normal function followed by the functional optimization of the system as a whole. This should involve preparing the individual to interact with the environment in which he or she will be living and working. The proprioceptive system plays an important role in carrying out appropriate movement patterns that allow the individual to return to work or a recreational environment.

The CNS depends on normal afferent stimulation from the proprioceptive system for the efficient and chronological ordering of muscle activity when an individual is asked to perform a specific static or dynamic activity. Joint and/or muscle injury, sedentary lifestyle, and improper static posture can lead to the development of faulty movement patterns that can be learned, integrated on a subcortical level, and carried out during normal daily activities. It is hypothesized that this faulty movement pattern development can result from any one or combination of four factors.[18,40–42]

- Inappropriate afferent information being received by the CNS as a result of joint/muscle dysfunction following injury.
- Lack of proprioceptive stimulation resulting from a paucity of movement in a sedentary individual.
- Tightness and hyperactivity of certain key postural muscles, leading to inhibition of their antagonists.
- Inefficient postural "set" from which movement is derived.

Some combination of these four factors is often seen in the clinical setting, and all of the factors present must be assessed in order to achieve a successful long-term outcome. Thus, as with any skill-oriented exercise, the program starts with relatively easy tasks and progresses in difficulty as the patient becomes more adept and the locomotor system becomes more efficient at ordering the appropriate postural reactions in response to the unstable standing surface. The first skill that must be learned is the ability to contract the quadratus plantae (QP) muscle on the plantar aspect of the foot, a process that Janda describes as "making a short foot" (Figure 22–1). To "make a short foot," the patient is instructed to visualize the spine elongating and becoming wide. Special attention is paid to the position of the head relative to the rest of the body.[43]

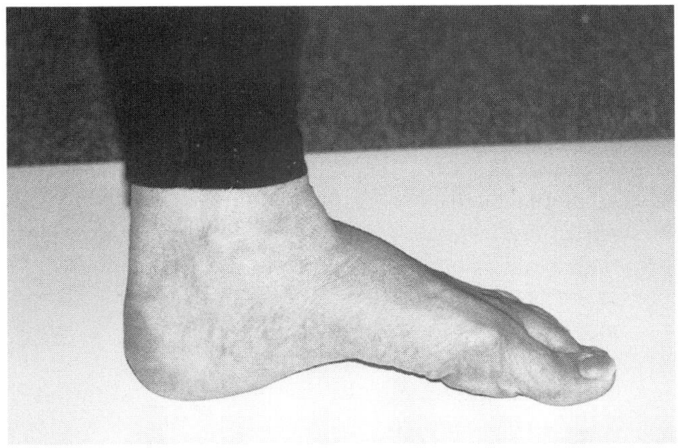

Figure 22–1. Making a short foot.

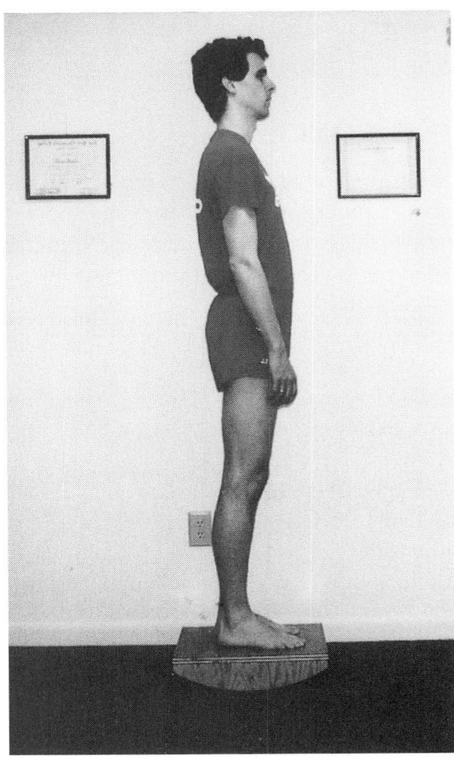

Figure 22–2. Patient balancing on a rocker board.

The QP is a muscle that is underutilized in our society today. The use of shoes with arch supports reduces the involvement of this muscle in the proper stabilization of the foot during gait. The QP muscle and the receptors in the skin on the bottom of the foot are important for the transmission of sensory feedback to the CNS for ordering efficient postural reactions.[44] Appropriate activation of the QP and stimulation of the skin receptors on the plantar surface of the foot are important factors in setting the stage for stimulation of the lower extremity proprioceptive system.

One foundation maneuver in the earlier stages of exercise progression is to have the patient stand on a stable rocker board (Figure 22–2). The patient is instructed to "make a short foot", then to establish a proper postural set. This decreases the habitual overactivation of certain muscles such as the sternocleidomastoid, upper trapezius, erector spinae, and iliopsoas, all of which are commonly overactive in individuals suffering from low back pain or other locomotor system disorders. Initially arms can be abducted to enhance the patient's ability to balance.

After the patient adapts to standing on a rocker board, he or she is progressed to a wobble board and the process of QP activation and establishment of correct postural set is repeated. The wobble board is unstable in all directions; therefore, it is not only more challenging but provides

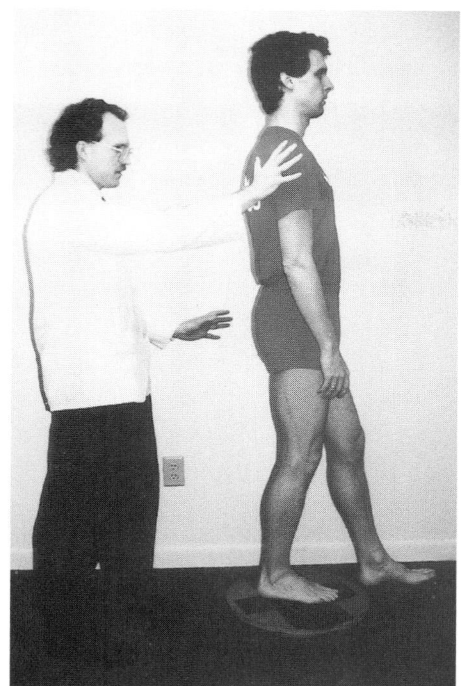

Figure 22–3. Challenging a patient's balance during maintenance of unilateral stance on a wobble board.

Figure 22–4. Patient walking on a balance beam with eyes closed.

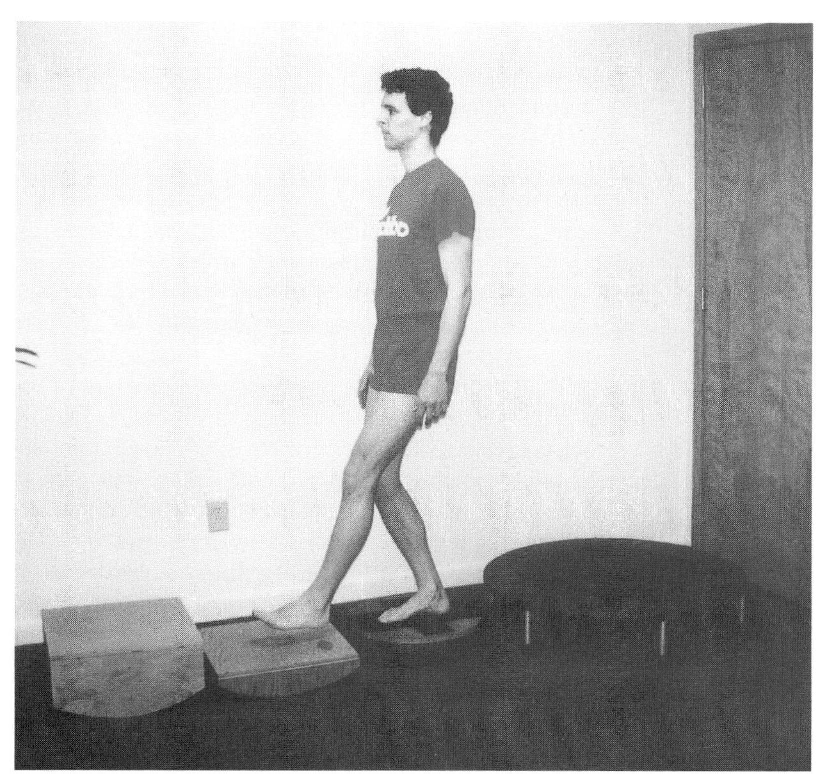

Figure 22–5. Patient maintaining an appropriate "postural set" while walking over surfaces of varying stability.

greater stimulation to the proprioceptive system. The patient begins on two feet, and then is progressed to standing on only one foot. One-legged standing is particularly important because it more accurately mimics the stance phase of gait. As the patient adapts to this, additional challenges can be provided, e.g., standing behind the patient and providing gentle pushes to various places on the body, thus forcing him or her to maintain balance while being subjected to perturbations (Figure 22–3).

The program can be made more dynamic by having the patient walk on difficult or unstable surfaces such as a balance beam (Figure 22–4) or a progression of several boards along with a mini-trampoline (Figure 22–5). It can also can be made sport-specific (Figure 22–6). This maximizes the program's effectiveness in training for ADLs (Figure 22–7).

Sensory-motor retraining allows the practitioner to introduce the essential proprioceptive signals on which the locomotor system depends for economical and efficient function. Most importantly, it facilitates muscles that often tend to become inhibited by stimulating inborn equilibrium reactions, i.e., those reactions essential to effective interaction with the environment.[39,41,45] Bullock-Saxton[41] demonstrated that sensory-motor retraining can be an effective method of improving the relative activation intensity and the activation timing of the gluteus maximus and medius muscles. These muscles tend to become inhibited easily in low back pain syndromes and become left out of the movement patterns in which they normally should be involved, thus placing increased stress on the other muscles involved in that pattern.[17] The most important pattern that involves the gluteus maximus and medius is gait; the gluteus maximus is the central focus of hip extension during the stance phase of gait, and the gluteus medius is an important lateral stabilizer of the pelvis during this phase.[10] Restoring normal harmony of activity to the muscles involved in any essential movement pattern is vital in the complete and successful rehabilitation of the individual.

Figure 22–7. Upper extremity resistive tubing exercises performed on a wobble board.

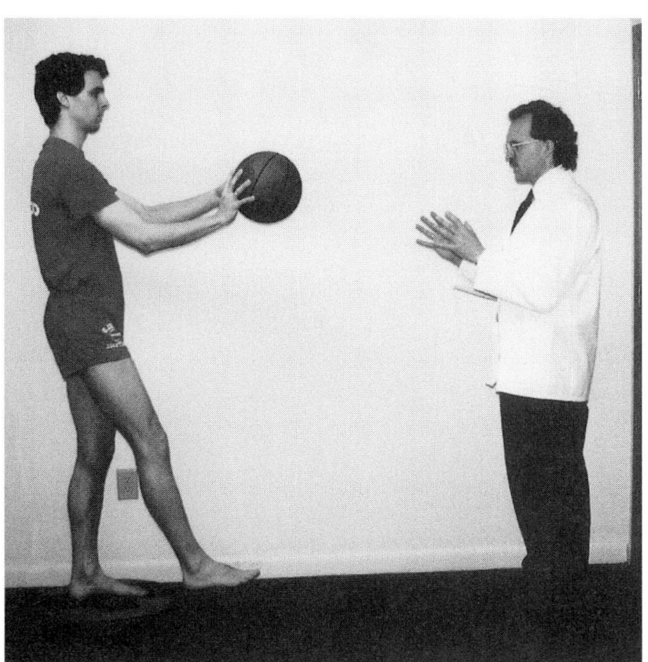

Figure 22–6. Patient playing catch with a basketball while maintaining a unilateral stance position on a wobble board.

Balogun et al[46] documented that gains in absolute strength are also made. They showed that increases in strength following a wobble board exercise program of the lower extremity muscles, particularly the tibialis anterior, were comparable to those typically seen following an isometric or isotonic exercise program. There was also an added benefit of time efficiency because the sensory-motor retraining exercises work muscles throughout the lower extremities and trunk at the same time; thus, there is decreased necessity for isolated or regional muscle group exercises.

Another benefit derived from sensory-motor retraining is in the often overlooked area of improved balance performance.[46] Byl and Sinnott[47] demonstrated that patients with low back pain were likely to have significantly greater postural sway and poorer performance on balance testing consisting of standing on one leg with eyes closed than were healthy controls. Whether this balance dysfunction resulted from the pain itself or is a predisposing factor to the development of back pain requires further investigation. Parkhurst and Burnett[24] showed that there was significant proprioceptive dysfunction of the lumbar spine in asymptomatic individuals who had a previous history of low back pain, when compared to controls. Improvement of balance performance may be a significant factor in the rehabilitation of these patients. Hoffman and Payne[48] showed that healthy subjects trained with sensory-motor principles had significantly improved balance performance, compared to controls. Balance performance can also be improved in patients suffering from disequilibrium and vertiginous syndromes by utilizing sensory-motor retraining.[49–51] It has been shown recently that progressive idiopathic scoliosis may be a primary disorder of processing of incoming proprioceptive and visuospatial impulses in the association cortex of the parietal lobe of the cerebrum.[52] Sensory-motor retraining may prove to be helpful in the rehabilitation of patients with this disorder. Balance performance is especially important in the elderly, because the risk of falling is very high in this age group and the consequences of falling (e.g., the development of hip fracture and other similar injuries) can be devastating. The quality of balance performance, and proximal lower extremity muscle activity and strength, each of which can be improved with sensory-motor retraining, have been shown to decrease with age and are particularly poor in those elderly individuals who have a propensity for falling.[49,53,54] A rehabilitation program that includes sensory-motor retraining can be essential in reducing the likelihood of falls in this population.

Practitioners who treat back pain patients have an appreciation for the importance of proper intersegmental function in a healthy back and the role that intersegmental dysfunction can play in the development of back pain syndromes. However, it appears that although many rehabilitation programs address the function of the large multisegmental muscles of the spine, they often neglect to address the function of the intrinsic spinal muscles. The segmental intrinsic spinal muscles, which include the intertransversarii, multifidi, interspinous, and suboccipital muscles, have an abundance of muscle spindles, the central connections of which are multisegmental, as opposed to the unisegmental reflex-arc function that most spindles and peripheral muscles have.[55,56] As such, rather than functioning primarily for the purpose of unisegmental stretch reflexes, the spindles of the intrinsic spinal muscles play an important role in the communication of the quality of intersegmental function to the nervous system. The majority of the motor neurons that connect to the intrinsic spinal muscles from the spinal cord are of the gamma variety, innervating the muscle spindles, rather than of the alpha variety, as is the case with most extrinsic muscles. The intrinsic muscles can therefore be thought of as functioning in a different capacity than the large multisegmental muscles of the spine. The approach to the rehabilitation of these muscles must be different than that to the larger muscles. Because of the high density of muscle spindles and gamma motor neurons in these muscles, they are best rehabilitated on a reflex basis, rather than on a voluntary contraction basis. This reflex activation of the intrinsic muscles is provided by sensory-motor retraining. This can be important in stabilizing an unstable segment as well as retraining optimal coordinated reflex activity of the intersegmental muscles, assisting in rehabilitating intersegmental spinal dysfunction.[4,10,50]

There are many benefits that can be derived from incorporating sensory retraining into the overall rehabilitation of the patient with a spinal injury. When indicated, it can enhance the coordinated function of the spine with the entire locomotor system optimizing the patient's ability to operate in a proprioceptive-oriented world.

REHABILITATION PROGRAM DESIGN

When designing a rehabilitation program, a number of factors must receive careful consideration. The stage of the disorder, whether acute, subacute, or chronic, will influence program design. The severity of the patient's condition, mild, moderate, or severe, will, of course, have a significant impact on when and how to start the rehabilitation process. The nature of the problem, e.g., the specific pathanatomic diagnosis, is another factor to be considered. For example, if the patient is suffering from central canal stenosis, exercises that might induce lumbar extension will need to be avoided. In addition to the factors previously mentioned, the patient's functional sensitivities (or functional loss), as described by Vollowitz,[57] can be key factors in rehabilitation program prescription.

Functional Sensitivities

The functional sensitivities are common patterns of physical limitation observed clinically. They are generally unrelated to a specific anatomic diagnosis in that the same diagnosis can present with varying physical limitations and require completely different rehabilitation approaches. However, there can be trends and common presentation observed clinically. The patient's functional sensitivities are determined by information gained during the case history and physical examination. Aggravating and easing activities and postures identified during the case history will give insight into the patient's functional loss. In addition, symptom-provoking positions observed during the physical examination will add further information. The functional sensitivities include load sensitivity, positional sensitivity, stasis (constrained posture) sensitivity, and pressure sensitivity.[57]

Load sensitivity is recognized as the inability of the spine to tolerate axial compression. A patient who exhibits this functional loss will be limited, because of symptom aggravation, in activities that increase spinal loading. For example, the patient may demonstrate a limitation in the amount of time he or she can tolerate upright (vertical) postures and must assume an unloaded (horizontal) position on a regular basis to reduce symptoms and/or avoid exacerbation. Of course, postures and/or activities that apply greater compressive forces to the spine, sitting versus standing for example, will be tolerated for shorter periods of time. The patient may be observed leaning on the arms to decrease the spinal compressive loads while standing or sitting. In this case, exercises that compress the spine must be avoided or limited. It may be appropriate to start the program in non-weight-bearing positions or utilize decompressive forces while the patient exercises. A common error is to introduce stationary cycling for the aerobic benefits in a sitting position without the means for the patient to decompress the spine, leading to symptom aggravation. Recumbent cycling, either partially or fully reclined, could help avoid this situation.

Positional sensitivity relates to symptom aggravation induced by assuming a specific spinal position, whereas other positions will have no effect or may actually relieve the symptoms. For example, during the case history it may be noted that low back pain is increased when the patient lays prone or while reaching overhead and is relieved when assuming a fetal position. During the physical examination low back pain is provoked during thoracolumbar extension whereas flexion is full and pain-free. This patient is demonstrating a pure extension sensitivity. Thus, exercises that induce thoracolumbar extension should be avoided or measures taken to limit the amount of extension. For example, the patient should limit or avoid extension during gymnastic ball sit-ups, and bridging activities may initially need to be completely avoided.

A patient with a stasis (constrained posture) sensitivity will not tolerate maintenance of a single position. The degree of sensitivity (or loss) can be graded as mild, moderate, or severe depending upon the amount of time the patient tolerates a static posture. The patient will relate increased symptoms when constrained to a single posture regardless of the position assumed. It may be impossible to find a comfortable position, whether lying down, standing, sitting, etc. During the physical examination, the patient is observed frequently weight shifting and changing position. He or she must eventually change position to find comfort. A rehabilitation program for the stasis-sensitive patient must include frequent changes in position. The number of exercises may be increased and performed in a circuit-type routine. A single exercise performed in a static position (constrained posture) would not be well tolerated.

Pressure sensitivity simply is a hypersensitivity to pressure applied directly over the spine. Skin sensitivity to direct contact is commonly seen in patients with low back pain in all stages of the condition, acute or chronic. In addition, spinous process and interspinous tenderness to palpation are frequently seen. This may represent supraspinous and/or interspinous ligament tenderness. The patient frequently notes that wearing tight clothing or sitting against hard surfaces will provoke pain. During exercise, any contact with the affected area will be painful. The patient may not tolerate the pressure of the gymnastic ball, a firm mat or table, or any form of low back support. The situation is easily resolved by choosing exercises that do not apply pressure to the involved area until the sensitivity has diminished or resolved.

Consideration of these functional sensitivities when designing a rehabilitation program can assist in understanding pain behavior and patterns observed when the patient does not tolerate the prescribed exercises. Frequently, patients will present with a combination of sensitivities. Identification of these functional loss patterns will assist in enhancing the likelihood for a positive clinical response to a tailored rehabilitation program.

EXERCISE WARM-UP AND POSTEXERCISE STRETCHING

Active stretching, also called dynamic range of motion training (D'ROM), can be useful as a warm-up prior to exercise or following an exercise session to improve range of motion. The technique is performed by the patient actively moving the joint(s) in the area to be stretched through a range of motion. As the patient contracts the agonist, the antagonist is lengthened and reciprocally inhibited. D'ROM can improve active control of a joint throughout the range of motion, therefore enhancing joint protection during performance of ADLs.[58]

INTRODUCTION TO STABILIZATION PRINCIPLES

Stabilization exercises develop isolated and coordinated muscle patterns that stabilize the spine in a neutral position, with the neutral position being defined as the most stable, least painful position of the spine for the task at hand, and preferably reflecting a lumbar lordosis within normal range.[9] Theoretically, the concept works by minimizing repetitive end-range loading and torsional stress of the spine. This can allow healing and potentially alter the spinal degenerative process.[15] The potential to slow the degenerative process is based upon the concept that repetitive end-range and/or torsional stresses can lead to degenerative changes. Utilizing these exercises minimizes the risk of exceeding physical stress limits. The length of the rehabilitation program is dependent upon the severity of pathology present, the degree of de-conditioning or weakness, mobility, and learning ability. Rehabilitation can potentially contribute to not only the obvious goal of increasing strength and improving function, but also to the less obvious goal of reducing reinjury. This stabilization exercise program initially requires conscious control of spinal position and facilitation of inhibited muscle groups through repetitive, well-controlled movements. The goal is to eventually establish a "subconscious" program known as *engram motor programming and kinesthetic awareness*. Engram motor programming is a physiological phenomenon that is best described as "muscle memory." Motor programming, necessary to perform a complex motion, is stored in the motor cortex as an engram from all the individual components of the motor act and is retrievable if conscious control is necessary.

Functional Range

The first step in stabilization training is to establish the patient's functional range (neutral position of the spine), in order to address muscular limitations and improve dysfunctional patterns. A substitution or dysfunctional pattern may occur in postoperative patients, acute patients, manual laborers, highly skilled athletes, or pregnant patients, for example. The stabilization activities require understanding of neutral position, how to attain and maintain appropriate posture, and how to progress into functional control-type maneuvers that eventually reflect ADL demands. A foundation for functional training and postural stabilization lies in teaching the patient to establish his or her own functional spinal positions. This can involve active and/or passive prepositioning of the spine in the functional range.[9] With passive prepositioning a painful or aggravating spinal position can be avoided by passively (i.e., without the patient's active assistance) positioning the spine away from the painful position. This can be accomplished with the use of supports such as towel rolls or foam back supports and/or positioning the limbs in such a way as to support the spine in the functional range. During active prepositioning the patient utilizes muscular control and conscious lumbopelvic awareness to maintain his or her functional position during exercise and ADLs. The patient is taught to utilize his or her own active muscle control ability to establish the range of pelvic movements, and therefore lumbar positions, that are most comfortable and least painful.

Figure 22–9. Maintenance of proper body mechanics while transitioning to lifting an object overhead.

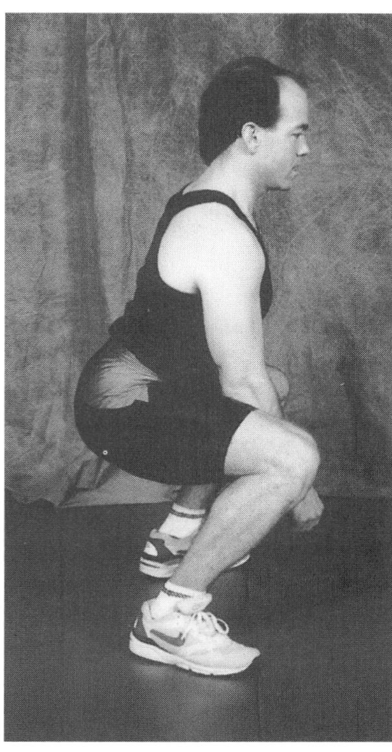

Figure 22–8. Lifting an object from the floor while maintaining proper squat position.

It is important to note that the functional position of the spine should not be looked upon as being a single, rigid position, but rather a range of positions that may change with variations in posture or activity.[9] Recognition of this will help the clinician avoid limiting the patient to a single position, thus decreasing range of motion and increasing avoidance behavior, which may lead to illness behavior.[28,29]

It is also important to teach the patient to appropriately maintain a stable functional range as he or she performs transitions from one body position to another. For example, if a patient is preparing to lift an object from the floor to overhead (Figure 22–8), the patient may be more comfortable and stable with the pelvis in a relatively anteriorly tilted position, but as the transition is made to lifting the object overhead (Figure 22–9), he or she may be more comfortable and stable with the pelvis in a relatively posteriorly tilted position. The establishment of the functional position of the spine allows the patient to find those lumbopelvic positions in which he or she can perform movements and exercises in which he or she may not ordinarily have been able to engage. This allows

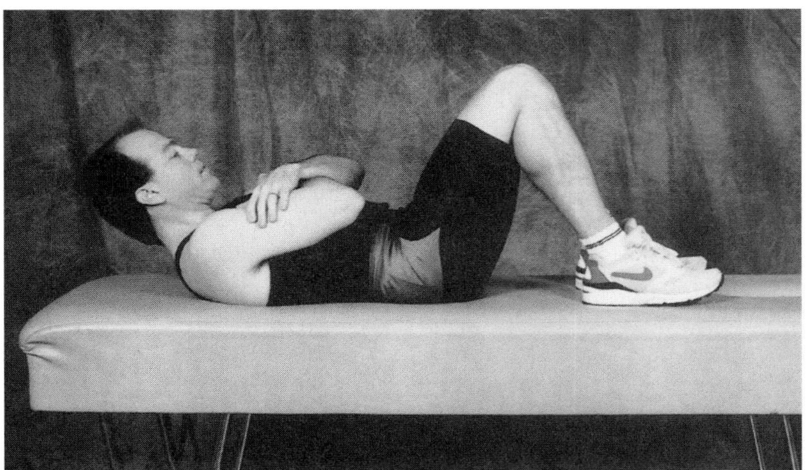

Figure 22–10. Modified sit-up performed with arms across the chest.

for early initiation of an exercise program, an essential ingredient for the proper rehabilitation of a low back disorder.[30,59]

Once the patient has been taught to establish and maintain a functional position in various postures, he or she is ready to be taught to maintain these positions while performing tasks with the extremities. This requires coordination and, in a more real fashion, simulates the situations of daily living in which one must perform various activities while maintaining stability of the spine, yet be focused on the task at hand.[9]

In patients with severe spinal dysfunction, isometric exercises are often necessary in order to train the patient to consciously activate the appropriate muscles in proper chronological sequence. Ultimately, one of the advantages of functional training, specifically spinal stabilization, is to enhance neuromotor control. Isometric activities must be carefully monitored and often sensory stimulation and palpation of specific muscle groups are necessary in order to provide patient biofeedback for inhibited and/or weakened muscle groups.

TRUNK STABILIZATION EXERCISE PROGRESSION AND TECHNIQUES

SUPINE PROGRESSION

Modified Sit-Ups

To train the anterior trunk musculature, it is often appropriate to have the patient assume a supine, hook-lying position, and then slowly raise the upper torso so that the shoulder blades become slightly elevated off the support surface. The arms are typically relaxed alongside the torso; but if the cervical spine is also being addressed, the arms and hands can be used to help support the head and neck. By placing the arms across the chest, modified sit-up activities can be performed with a relative increase in resistance to the lower trunk (Figure 22–10).

Sagittal plane modified sit-ups can be performed, or the abdominal oblique musculature can be emphasized as well. A modified sit-up flexing to 45 degrees causes the

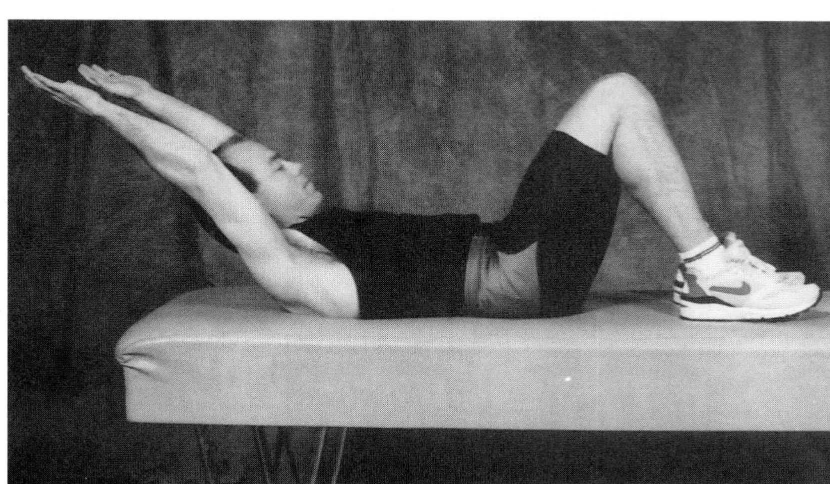

Figure 22–11. Modified sit-up performed with bilateral arm elevation.

Figure 22–12. When a patient is unable to perform a modified sit-up due to pain, another method of exercising the abdominal muscles is with manually resisted upper extremity activities.

greatest recruitment of the obliques and rectus abdominis with the knees bent to 45 degrees. For patients who have undergone laminectomy, trunk rotation during training should be avoided initially. It is recommended that the feet not be anchored when initiating these activities, as this would allow the hip flexor muscles to become the prime mover.

Another progression in increasing the demand level for performing modified sit-ups can be introduced by allowing the patient to elevate the arms partially. As a body part is moved farther from the patient's center of gravity, the relative resistance can be increased exponentially. For example, elevation of the arms overhead while performing modified sit-ups requires a significant increase in strength and control to perform properly (Figure 22–11). This activity can be performed with one arm overhead if the cervical spine needs to be supported and/or if the level of resistance provided by having both arms extended fully is too much for the patient to perform safely. Some patients may be unable to perform a modified sit-up that results in any significant upper torso movement without increasing pain. It is appropriate in this case to use upper extremity resistive exercises in order to isometrically train the abdominals (Figure 22–12). Hand-held devices to increase resistance can be added in a variety of ways (gymnastic ball, sandbag, or hand weights) and should be introduced as soon as the patient is able to safely tolerate an increase in activity demand (Figure 22–13).

Manually resisted activities can be introduced with the use of a wooden dowel utilizing proprioceptive neuromuscular facilitation (PNF) patterns, as illustrated in Figure 22–14. Resistance with this type of device can be provided in any direction with the level and direction of resistance manually altered simultaneously throughout the range of motion to meet the patient's ability.

At times, it is difficult to teach the patient to disassociate the hip flexors while performing a modified sit-up. In order to introduce the patient to this concept initially, it

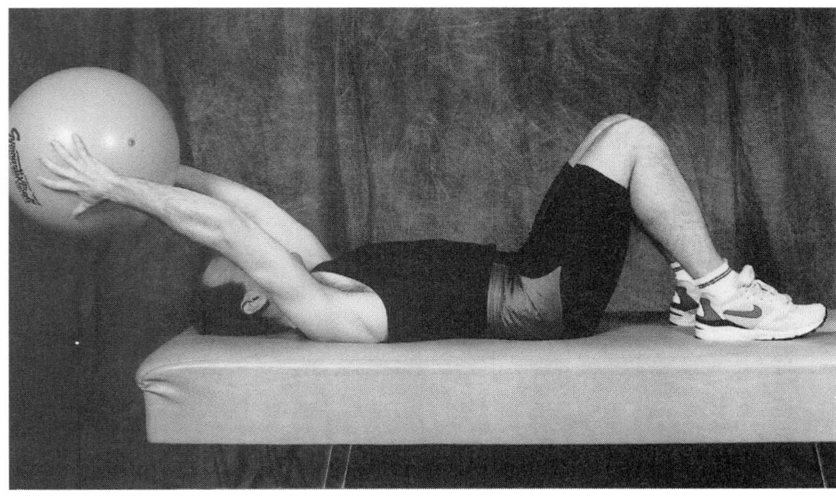

Figure 22–13. Isometric abdominal exercise utilizing upper extremity resistance with maintenance of neutral position.

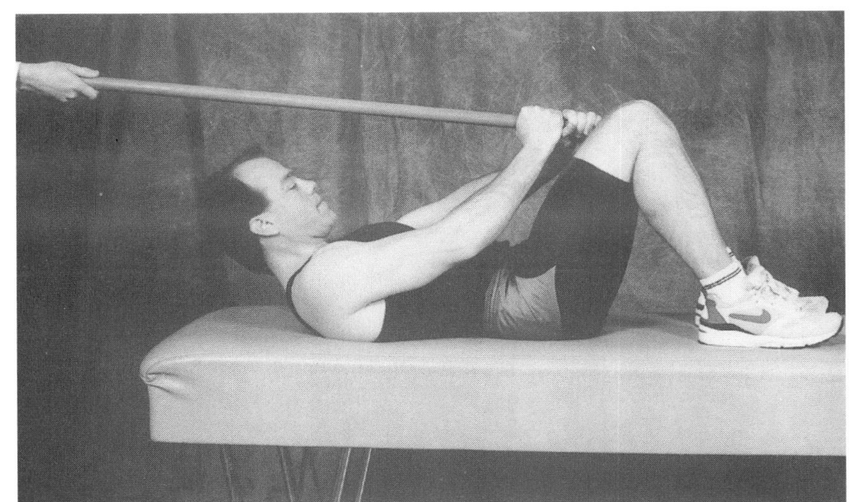

Figure 22–14. Manually resisted exercise and PNF patterns in conjunction with modified sit-ups.

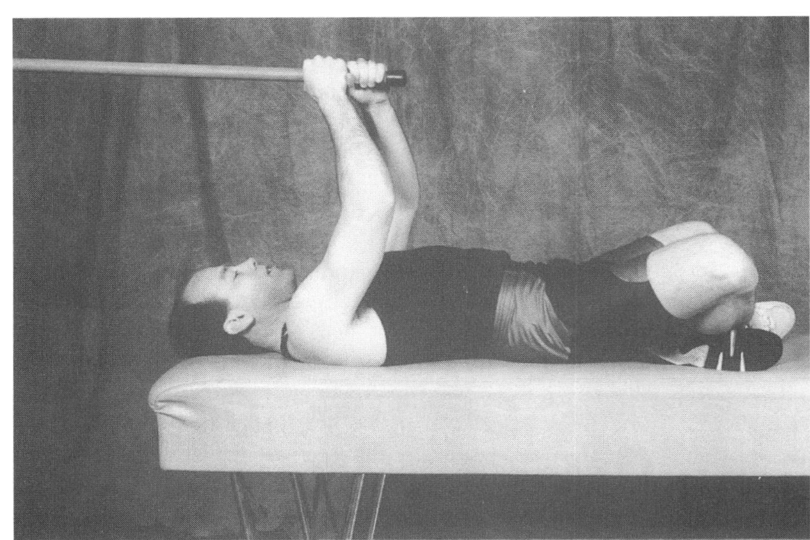

Figure 22–15. Cross-legged position during abdominal and upper extremity exercise.

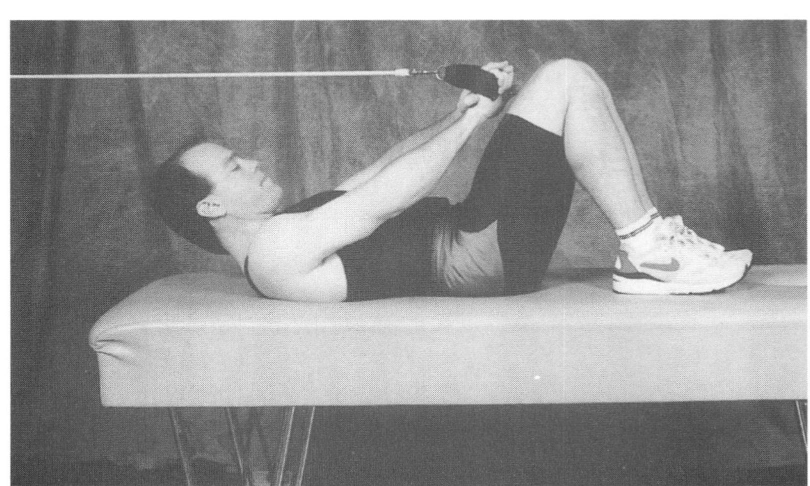

Figure 22–16. Modified sit-up performed with upper extremity resistive exercise.

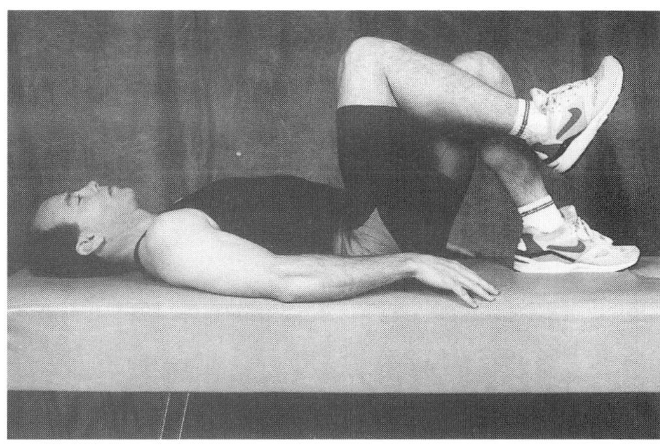

Figure 22–17. Dead-bug progression exercise lifting one knee to chest.

can be helpful to have the patient assume a cross-legged position (Figure 22–15). The patient is instructed to maintain lumbopelvic neutral position, yet to keep the legs relaxed as much as possible to avoid activation of the hip flexors. If the health care professional observing the patient notices that the adductors are beginning to contract, or that the knees are beginning to elevate, this is an indication of hip flexor activation providing the patient and the supervising professional feedback regarding this pattern of movement.

The use of resistive tubing is a higher-level progression and represents one way of providing progressive resistance as the upper extremities move through a range of motion. (Figure 22–16). Elevation of the head and upper torso and/or rotational maneuvers can also be introduced when appropriate with resistive tubing to activate oblique trunk musculature.

Dead-Bug Progression

The next step in increasing exercise demand for the abdominal musculature is introduction of the "dead-bug" progression activities. While maintaining lumbopelvic neutral position, the patient is instructed to begin the activity by flexing one knee toward the chest and then extending it fully, if tolerated safely (Figures 22–17 and 22–18). The range of motion frequently has to be adjusted to accommodate the patient's ability. For example, the leg may not be able to extend to 50% of full range of motion without the loss of lumbopelvic neutral position. This would simply be recorded on a daily basis and used as one outcome measure for documenting changes in functional performance abilities on a session-by-session basis. By bringing the arms from the sides and across the chest, the base of support becomes narrower, resulting in a relative increase in trunk resistance and three-dimensional balance demands.

The health care professional responsible for program supervision should closely observe the patient, avoiding even subtle changes in spinal position and subsequent loss of lumbopelvic control. Figure 22–19 demonstrates a more demanding dead-bug activity, with resistance increased by elevation of the arms bilaterally. This can be performed in unilateral fashion with the range of leg extension modified as is appropriate. Loss of lumbopelvic neutral position with migration into lumbar extension would indicate that this

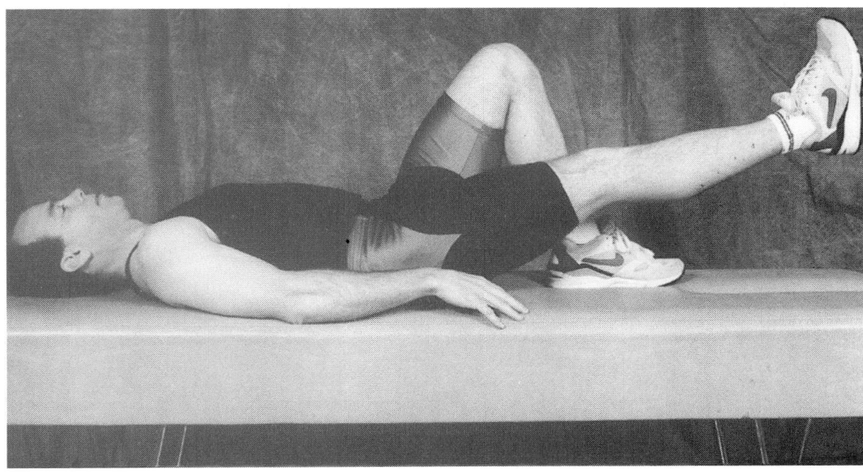

Figure 22–18. Dead-bug progression exercise extending the hip and knee.

Figure 22–19. Dead-bug progression exercise extending the hip and knee with bilateral arm elevation.

activity is too demanding for the patient or that the patient does not have the neuromotor control to perform this activity safely. Ultimately, it is necessary to develop higher-level exercise activities that require the patient to reflexively attain and maintain lumbopelvic neutral position. The use of torsional forces and manually applied resistance with a dowel applied by a health care professional will require that the patient is able to reflexively control lumbopelvic neutral position (Figure 22–20).

A significant increase in activity demand is introduced by having the patient assume a hook-lying position and elevate both lower limbs simultaneously. This will require enhanced lumbopelvic neuromotor control ability, and patients should be screened carefully before being introduced to these higher-level activities in order to avoid latent pain symptoms (Figure 22–21). Extension of one limb at a time can then be performed, as described previously, while isometrically maintaining lumbopelvic neutral position. Isometric head and neck flexion can be introduced if cervical strength is to be included in part of the exercise program and if this level of isometric resistance training can be tolerated safely by the patient. While in this position, the pa-

Figure 22–20. Dead-bug progression exercise utilizing upper extremity manually resisted exercise.

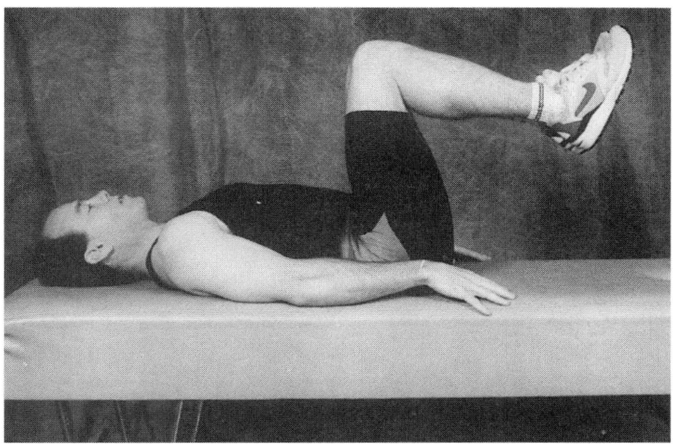

Figure 22–21. Higher-level dead-bug progression exercise elevating bilateral lower extremity.

tient should maintain upper cervical flexion by keeping the chin tucked in. Short neck flexor inhibition and weakness, with overactivation of the sternocleidomastoid and upper trapezius musculature, is a commonly seen pattern of dysfunction. In addition, cervical flexion can also assist in recruitment of anterior trunk muscles (Figure 22–22).

As described earlier, narrowing the base of support, by moving the arms from the table to an extended position above the upper torso, can be a way of significantly increasing trunk resistance. These positions can be held isometrically, or with partial to full dynamic range of motion activities performed with upper and lower extremities moving in an alternating fashion (Figure 22–23). Figure 22–24 demonstrates a patient performing high-level dead-bug progression activities with the upper and lower limbs moving simultaneously. The patient can also perform higher-level dead-bug activities with the lower extremities held stationary, as illustrated in Figure 22–25, while the upper extremities are resisted through a partial to full range of motion.

Placing objects in the hand and/or manually applied resistance activities can increase the energy level demand, with the direction, force, and velocity of resistance altered (Figure 22–26). Dowel resistance can be added as well, in oblique directions (Figures 22–27 and 22–28). The use of resistive tubing can be introduced as a form of progressive resistance with both legs elevated simultaneously, and this can be coupled with PNF patterns. It requires a significant increase in strength and neuromotor control in order to perform this type of activity safely. The direction of applied resistance should be based on clinically identified dysfunction (Figure 22–29). The recruitment of additional muscles, by involving the upper extremities, is an advantage in making activities more complex for those patients who are candidates for activities that will challenge them at a higher level. Asking the patient to perform isometric lower extremity activities (for example, isometric hip abduction utilizing a resistive band around the distal thighs), while maintaining lumbopelvic neutral position during upper extremity resistive exercise, will require a higher level of ability to stabilize the spine safely. These activities will help prepare the patient for weight-bearing activities that are complex and more specifically reflect normal ADLs.

Gymnastic Ball Exercises

Another method for training the anterior trunk musculature is with the use of the gymnastic ball. The gymnastic ball is very useful in that it helps facilitate the development of neuromotor control and hence three-dimensional balance and proprioception. It is a less stable environment than the performance of dead-bug progression activities on a mat or on a table, but the potential benefits are far greater if the patient can tolerate them safely. Most programs that utilize this functional training approach strongly consider the use of static/isometric exercise activities initially. This is done to provide a safety margin and to increase patient enthusiasm and decrease the presence of excessive postexercise soreness from improperly performed exercises or those that are prescribed in too advanced of a fashion initially.

Modified sit-up activities can be performed with the patient lying in a supine position, with the pelvis and thoracolumbar spine in contact with the ball and with lumbopelvic neutral position maintained (Figures 22–30 and 22–31). It is essential that patients emphasize their own conscious awareness of three-dimensional motor control and body position at all times. The patient can perform flexion and/or extension maneuvers with the upper trunk in order to train the abdominal musculature. Varying the patient position on the ball can easily change the level of resistance. For example, in a sit-up position, rolling the ball

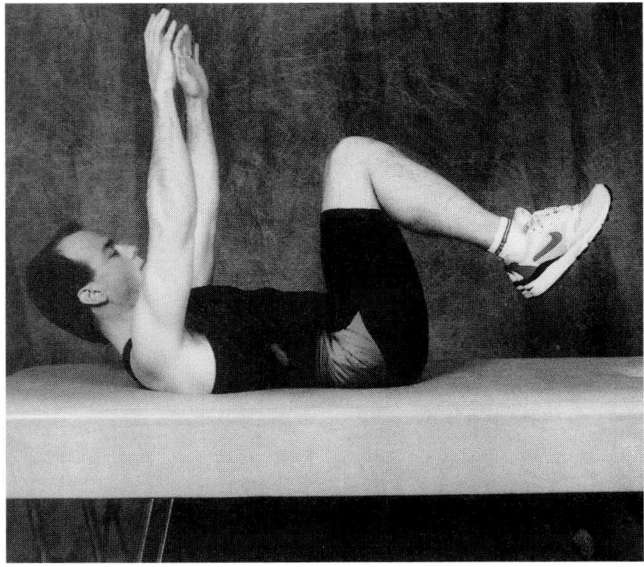

Figure 22–22. Dead-bug progression exercise with bilateral upper and lower extremities elevation and neck flexion.

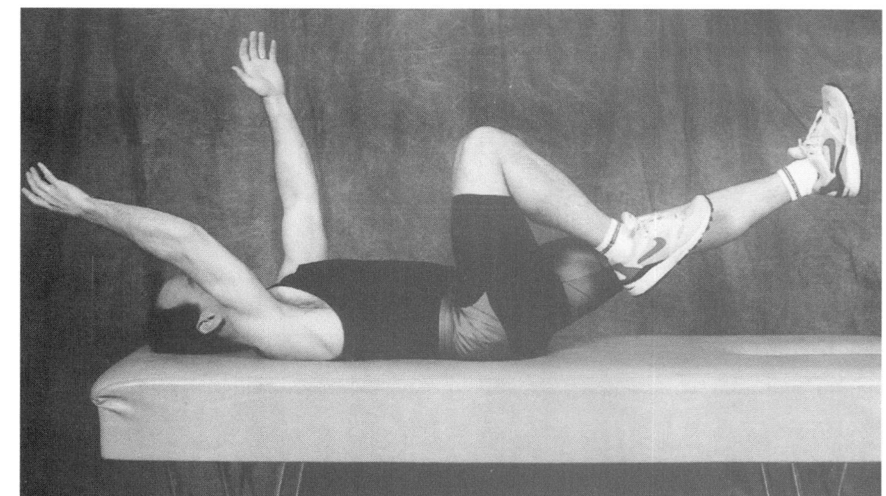

Figure 22–23. Dead-bug progression exercise with simultaneous movement of the opposite arm and leg.

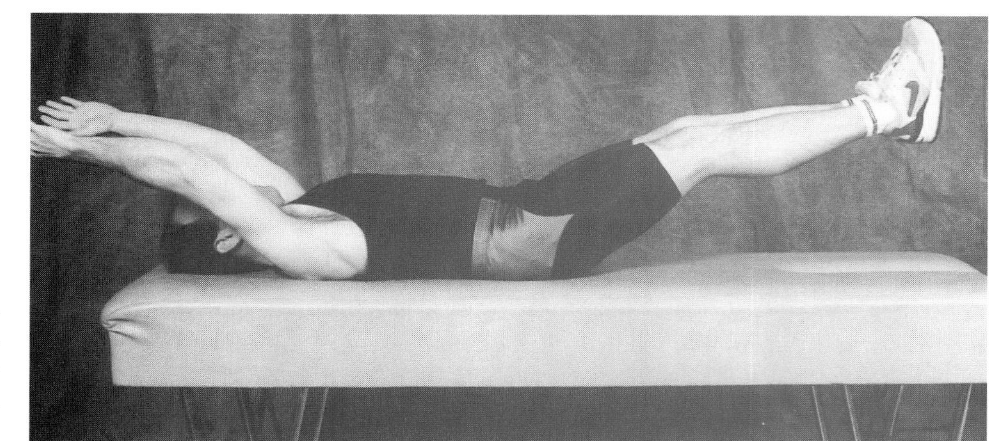

Figure 22–24. Dead-bug progression exercise with simultaneous movement of bilateral upper and lower extremities with maintenance of neutral position.

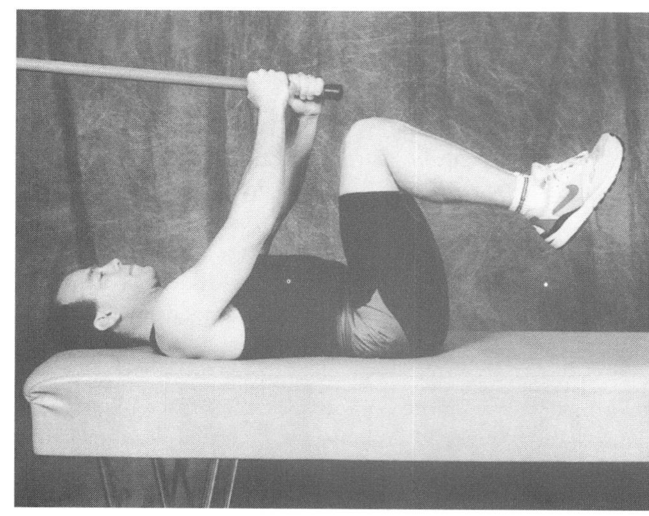

Figure 22–25. Dead-bug progression exercise with manually resisted upper extremities activity.

Figure 22–26. Dead-bug progression exercise with upper extremity resistance utilizing a small gymnastic ball and alternate lower extremity movement.

caudally will result in a relative increase in resistance to the anterior trunk musculature. Sit-ups on the gymnastic ball can be performed in a static or isometric mode if pain is experienced during dynamic sit-ups. The patient can progress to dynamic sit-ups once pain is no longer experienced during this exercise. Movement of the arms away from the center of gravity will increase the relative trunk resistance (Figure 22–32). Changes in the patient's position must be recognized initially so that the presence of latent symptoms can be avoided, as illustrated with this patient assuming a more extended position (Figure 22–33). For an extension sensitive patient this position may provoke pain; however, for a patient who is flexion sensitive this may be the starting position of choice.

Breathing technique should also be addressed. Patients commonly hold their breath during exercise and this should be avoided by reminding the patient to breathe during the exercise. If patients are performing modified sit-ups or abdominal exercise in a dynamic fashion, they should be instructed to exhale slightly during the exertion portion of the exercise activities, which typically occurs during the concentric contraction phase.

Extension of the arms away from the center of gravity, as illustrated in Figure 22–34, reflects a significant increase in lower trunk muscle activation. Loss of lumbopelvic neutral position during the exercise suggests that the patient is performing exercise activities that are too demanding at this time.

The use of PNF patterns and other variations with a wooden dowel or resistive tubing can be added to increase the complexity of the exercise activity and the relative level of resistance. The direction of the resistance provided can be modified to reflect identified dysfunction and weakness (Figures 22–35 and 22–36). Increasing the demand to the lower extremities and the complexity of the exercise can be accomplished with the use of an exercise band around the distal thighs (Figure 22–37). This exercise can significantly challenge the patient's control of lumbopelvic neutral position and can be useful in the facilitation of trunk musculature via the isometric hip abduction. This variation begins to more closely reflect the complexity of

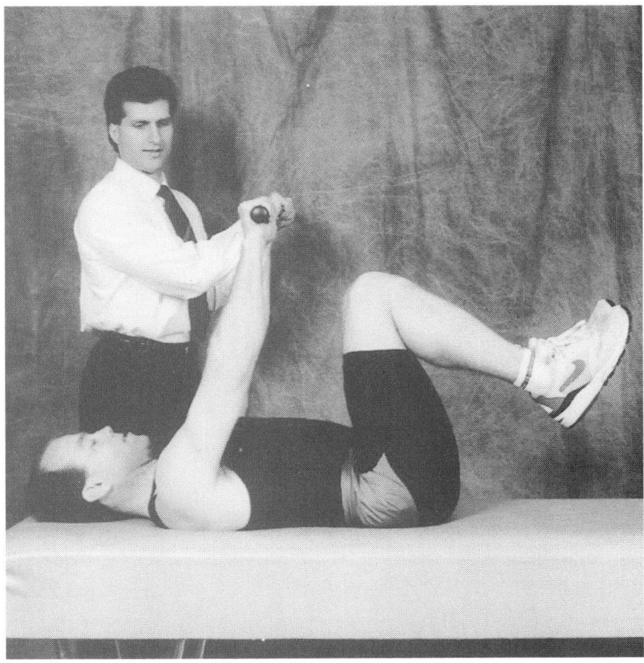

Figure 22–27. Dead-bug progression exercise with oblique patterns of applied upper extremity resistance.

Figure 22–28. Dead-bug progression exercise with isometric upper extremity manually resisted activities and alternate lower extremity extension.

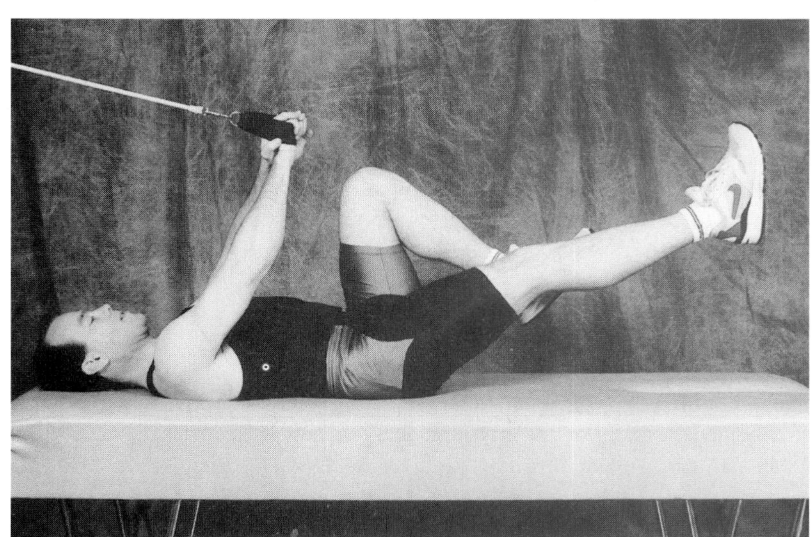

Figure 22–29. Dead-bug progression activity utilizing upper extremity activity with resistive tubing.

Figure 22–30. Starting position for gymnastic ball sit-up with arms across the chest.

Figure 22–31. Completion of gymnastic ball sit-up with arms across the chest.

Figure 22–32. Gymnastic ball sit-up with hands behind the head.

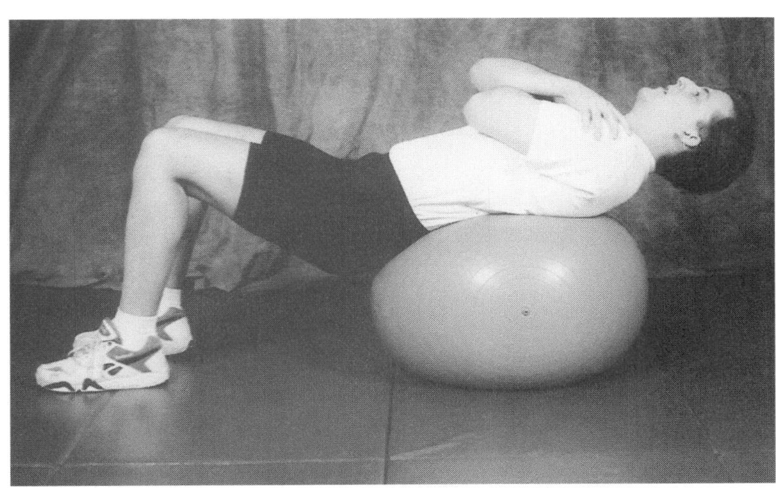

Figure 22–33. Gymnastic ball sit-up position with excessive lumbar lordosis.

Figure 22–34. Gymnastic ball sit-up performed with static bilateral arm elevation.

Figure 22–36. Gymnastic ball sit-up utilizing the wooden dowel varying the direction of upper extremity resistance.

ADLs in that the upper and lower extremities are involved in an activity while the trunk is stabilizing the spine. The opportunity for exercise variation with this kind of exercise methodology is unlimited and depends on the clinical expertise of the health care professional involved in program prescription and supervision (Figure 22–38).

Another exercise variation utilizing the gymnastic ball is that of bouncing on the ball while maintaining the spine in a neutral position. Bouncing on the ball forces the muscles of the spine to co-contract. This provides an endurance activity while maintaining proper spinal alignment. The quadriceps group and gluteal muscles contract while the trunk maintains a stable position. Moving from the feet by raising up on the toes initiates the use of the calf muscles. The arms can be incorporated into anaerobic and strengthening activities (i.e., shoulder rolls, repetitive abduction, or alternate shoulder swings). This exercise and variations can challenge all individuals whether acute, postsurgical, or a healthy trained athlete. Balance and coordination are stressed, in conjunction with strengthening.

Figure 22–35. Gymnastic ball sit-up with applied upper extremity manually resisted exercise utilizing the wooden dowel.

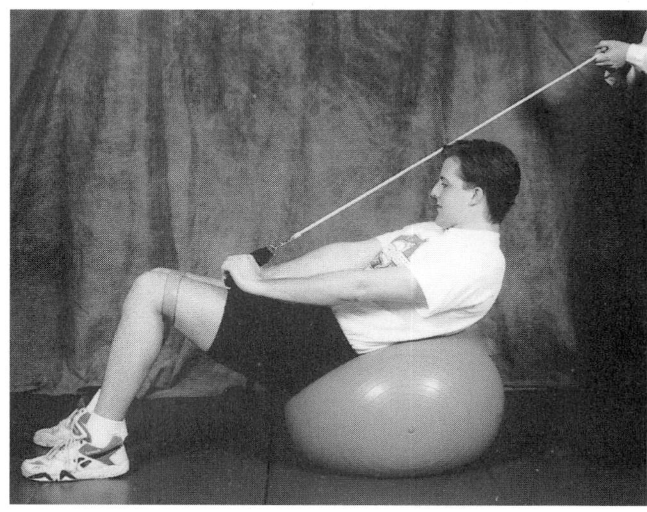

Figure 22–37. Gymnastic ball sit-up with resistive band around the distal thigh and upper extremity resistive tubing exercise.

Figure 22–38. Gymnastic ball sit-up variation utilizing upper and lower extremity resistive exercise.

Figure 22–40. Bilateral arm elevation during dynamic bridging activity.

The advantage of using the ball in this manner is that it facilitates three-dimensional balance activities. This exercise can be progressed in phases to challenge all fitness levels.

BRIDGING PROGRESSION

One way to exercise the posterior muscles of the trunk and lower extremities is to have the patient assume a supine static "bridge" position on a table or mat (Figure 22–39). This activates the quadratus lumborum, erector spinae, gluteal musculature, and the hamstrings. Arm positions can be changed to alter the lever arm length and hence the relative resistance (Figure 22–40), but one must be certain that the patient is assuming a relative neutral position, rather than allowing the spine to assume an extended position (Figure 22–41). This exercise can be performed statically and/or dynamically, and if the patient is incapable of performing full range of motion activities, partial range of motion static "holds" can be performed. It should be kept in mind that spinal loading maneuvers may also be appropriately combined with exercise regimens as described in Chapter 8, dealing with McKenzie principles.

The unilateral static bridge position can be assumed by the patient once it has been determined that the patient can safely control this level of exercise (Figure 22–42). This unilateral bridge can also be performed in a static or dynamic fashion with varying degrees of knee extension

Figure 22–39. Static bridging position with maintenance of lumbopelvic neutral position.

Figure 22–41. Bridging position with excessive lumbar extension.

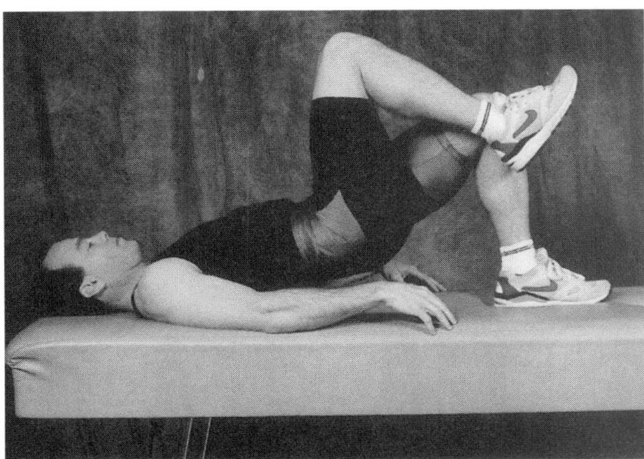

Figure 22–42. Unilateral static bridging with arms supported on the table.

Figure 22–44. Unilateral bridging position with bilateral upper extremity elevation.

(Figure 22–43). In addition, alteration of upper extremity position and the coordinated use of the upper and lower extremities can be utilized if appropriate (Figure 22–44).

The use of a sandbag over the mid to lower trunk can increase muscle demand. The use of hand-held devices while varying arm position can also significantly increase the level of difficulty (Figure 22–45). The use of a wooden dowel with resistance provided by a health care professional can be used in remarkable ways to specifically treat dysfunction and to train the patient to recruit appropriate musculature based on clinically identified dysfunction (Figure 22–46).

Applied resistance can be introduced with the patient assuming a bilateral or unilateral bridge position with the direction, force, velocity, and location of applied resistance altered to vary the demand level (Figure 22–47). Figure 22–48 illustrates a patient in a static bridge position with the arms extended and gripping resistive tubing. This activity can be modified and made more complex by having the patient dynamically move the hips and the arms simultaneously. The patient must use the whole foot rather than just the heel or forefoot, and maintenance of the lumbopelvic neutral position must be reflexive before program demand is increased significantly.

Figure 22–43. Unilateral bridging position with knee extension.

Figure 22–45. Unilateral static bridge with knee extension and applied upper extremity resistance utilizing a small gymnastic ball.

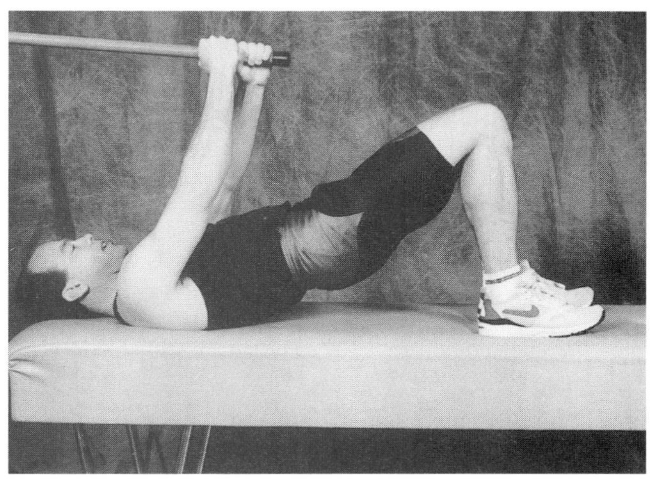

Figure 22–46. Manually applied resistance with a wooden dowel while maintaining a static bridging position.

Figure 22–47. Unilateral static bridge position while varying the direction of upper extremity resistance.

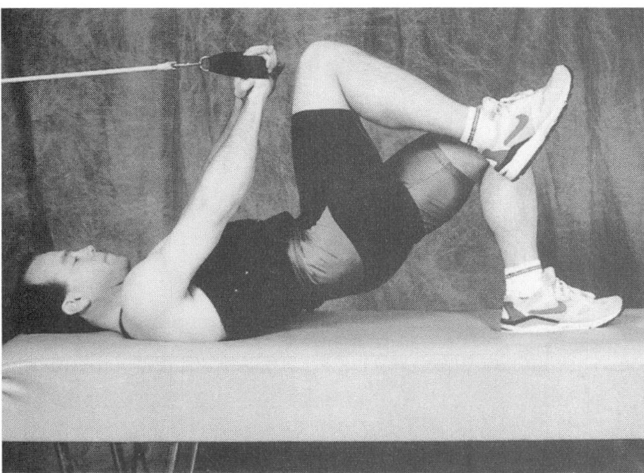

Figure 22–48. Isometric unilateral bridge position utilizing upper extremity resistive tubing exercises.

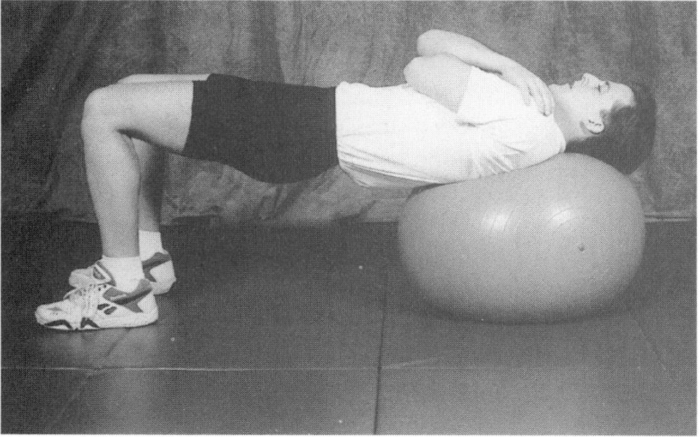

Figure 22–49. Gymnastic ball bridging position with arms across the chest.

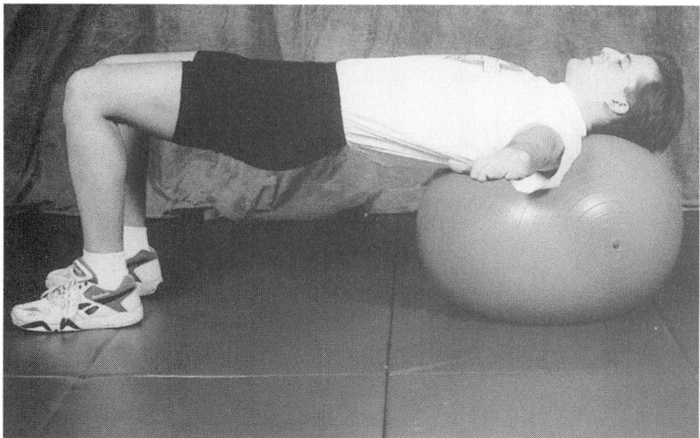

Figure 22–50. Gymnastic ball bridging with bilateral arm abduction.

Figure 22–51. Gymnastic ball bridging with upper extremity elevation.

Cervical flexion can be added if tolerated by the patient and if cervical strength and cervical neuromotor training are appropriate parts of the program prescription. The patient would be asked to exhale during the most exerting part of the movement. For this and all exercises, special attention should be given through observation and palpation to those muscles involved in the exercise. This will ensure complete contraction of the muscles involved and will provide a means of measuring progress for inhibited muscle groups. In addition, observe that symmetrical and controlled movement is maintained throughout the exercise.

Once patients reach a higher level of ability, they can proceed from static bridging activities to unilateral bridging performed dynamically using full and/or partial range of motion. When patients master exercise activities on a stationary surface, they can be advanced to a less stable environment such as the gymnastic ball (Figure 22–49). If based on clinical evaluation, varying degrees of hip extension can be introduced as a program modification.

Holding the arms alongside the trunk will create a wider and more stable base of support. This position can be used to increase the firing of the intrinsic muscles of the trunk. Figure 22–50 illustrates a patient assuming a position with the arms abducted, which is a more stable position. Holding the arms above the trunk in a vertical position (Figure 22–51) or with the arms fully extended will increase the recruitment of the abdominal musculature.

Exercises that require recruitment of multiple muscle groups make it necessary for the patient to have a higher skill level in order to attain and maintain lumbopelvic neutral position. Very complex activities require that this control ability become automatic (Figures 22–52 and 22–53),

Figure 22–52. Gymnastic ball bridging with bilateral upper extremity resistive tubing exercise.

or possible on a subconscious (subcortical) level. Having patients work against resistance applied by a health care professional can also require patients to automatically change their trunk stabilizers based on changing physical demands and adaptations in order to control their center of gravity. It should be a goal to train patients to the level where they are able to automatically activate static trunk stabilizers in order to enhance their ability to perform normal ADLs safely and efficiently.

Static unilateral gymnastic ball bridging activities can be performed, and this activity can be progressed to dynamic stabilization maneuvers when patients can be safely advanced (Figure 22–54). Another advanced exercise maneuver using the bridging position on the gymnastic ball is to ask the patient to perform a unilateral bridge while writing the alphabet with the extended lower limb, which will require automatic activation of the trunk stabilizing musculature. Manually applied resistance can be introduced as well to increase the level of difficulty (Figure 22–55). Changing the support surface can increase activation of different muscle groups, as illustrated in the performance of the gymnastic ball supine bilateral heel roll (Figure 22–56). Bridging with feet on the gymnastic ball can also be performed statically (Figure 22–57).

The use of the upper extremities in a static and/or dynamic fashion with added resistance can increase the challenge level dramatically and require automatic control of lumbopelvic neutral position (Figure 22–58). Weights can be held in an endless variety of positions in order to emphasize recruitment of muscles that are found to be dysfunctional.

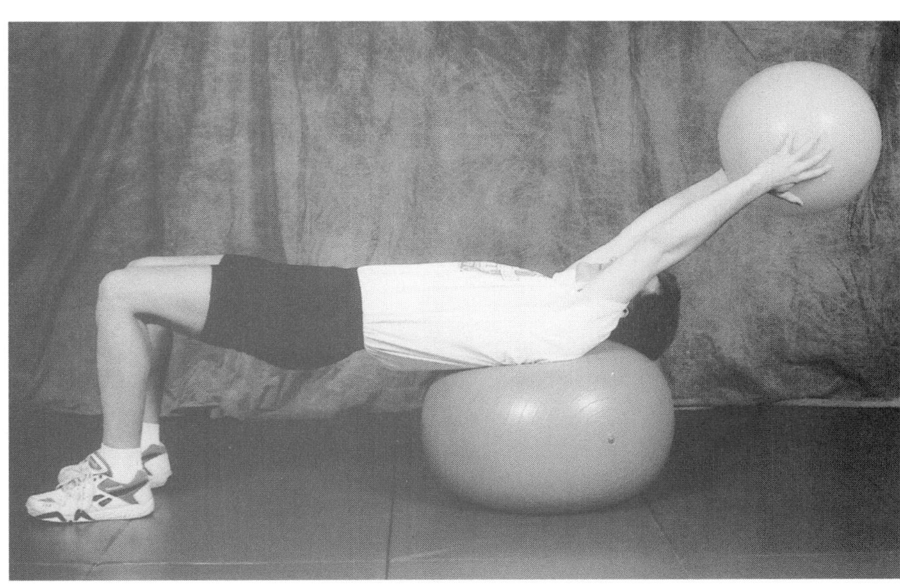

Figure 22–53. Gymnastic ball bridging position with upper extremity exercise utilizing a small gymnastic ball.

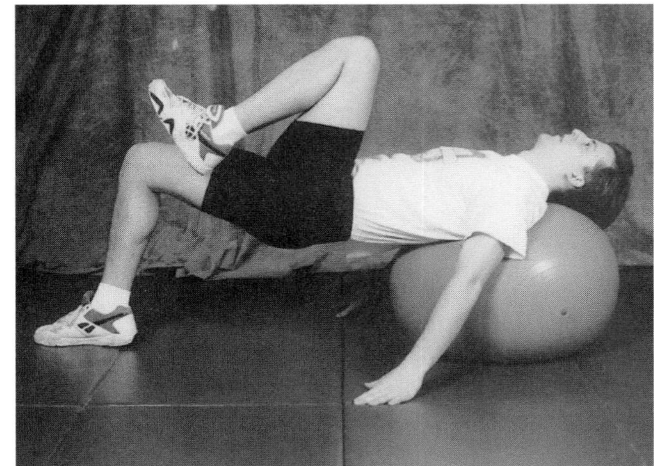

Figure 22–54. Static unilateral gymnastic ball bridging with hands on the floor.

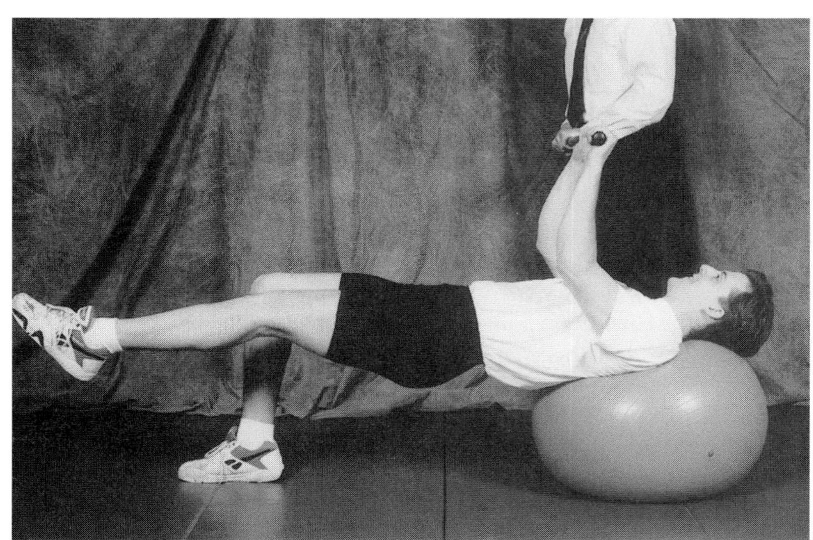

Figure 22–55. Unilateral gymnastic ball bridging with manually applied resistance.

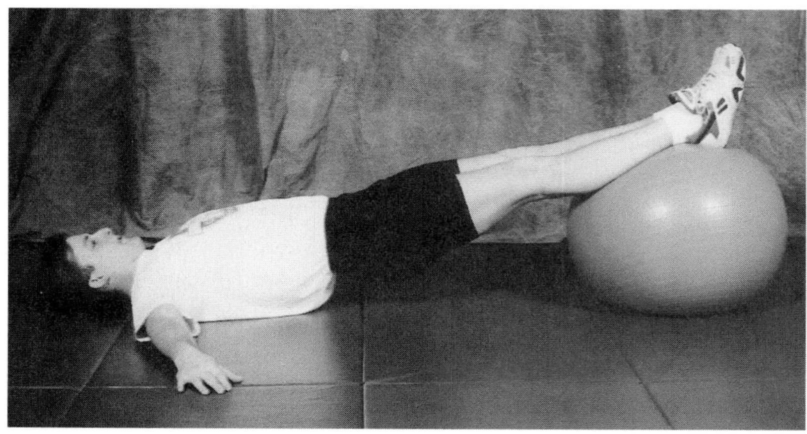

Figure 22–56. Gymnastic ball supine bilateral heel roll.

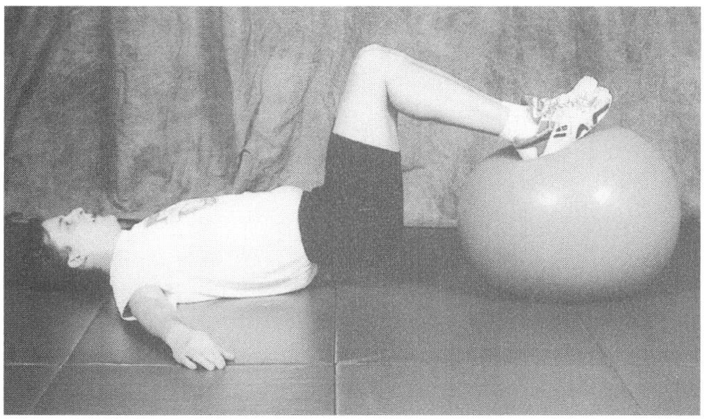

Figure 22–57. Static gymnastic ball bridging with feet on the exercise ball.

Figure 22–59. Starting quadruped position.

Quadruped Progression

Another more stable method for exercising the posterior muscles of the back involves having the patient assume a quadruped position (Figure 22–59). Initially a special emphasis should be placed on the patient attaining and maintaining cervical, thoracic, and lumbopelvic neutral positions. An alteration of extremity position, and therefore base of support, can increase or decrease relative resistance levels (Figure 22–60). Quadruped activities can initially be introduced by supporting the trunk anteriorly with the gymnastic ball if a greater degree of stability is required. If the upper back is being addressed in prescribing an exercise program, alternate arm extension can be performed in the quadruped position while the contralateral scapula is held stable (Figure 22–61). Leg extension can be performed to integrate the lower trunk and posterior leg muscle groups such as the quadratus lumborum, erector spinae, gluteal musculature, and hamstrings. Careful attention should be placed on being certain there is no significant pelvic rotation during this maneuver and that a neutral position can be maintained throughout full range of motion. If this is

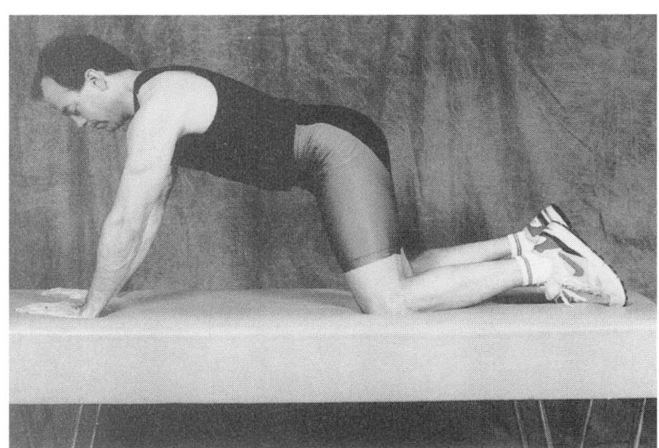

Figure 22–60. Quadruped position with a wider base of support.

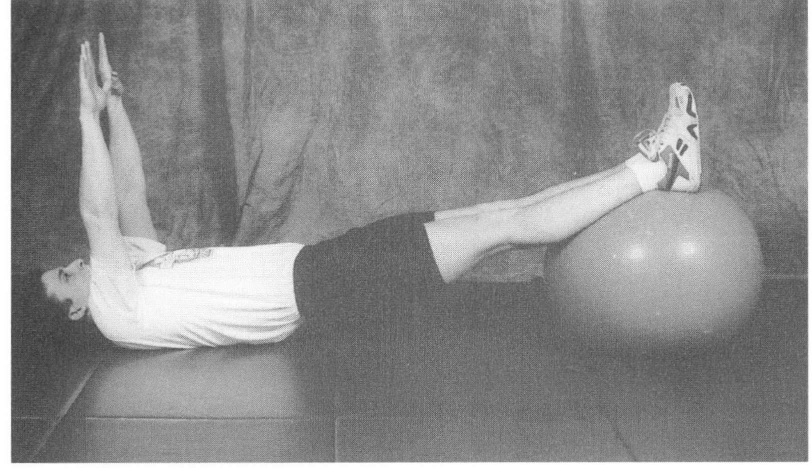

Figure 22–58. Gymnastic ball bridging with feet on the ball in conjunction with upper extremity activity.

Figure 22–61. Quadruped position with alternate upper extremity elevation.

not possible, lower-level activities can be introduced and/or partial range of motion exercises performed.

Arm and opposite leg extension can be performed simultaneously in the quadruped position as illustrated in Figure 22–62. Partial loss of lumbopelvic neutral position can be observed globally as illustrated in Figure 22–63. Changes in extremity position to alter the base of support and relative resistance levels can be easily introduced as appropriate. Quadruped positions can be modified to increase resistance to the upper back region in a way that reflects an identified dysfunction. Note the difference in position of the lower extremities and the degree of hip flexion between Figures 22–64 and 22–65 for introducing changes in the relative resistance to the lower trunk. Ankle weights, wrist weights, free-weight dumbbells, and manually resisted activities can be introduced in a variety of fashions to challenge the patient to develop appropriate neuromotor function.

Figure 22–62. Quadruped position with upper and lower extremity movement.

Figure 22–63. Loss of lumbopelvic neutral position during quadruped exercise.

Figure 22–64. Narrow base of support with upper extremity exercise.

Figure 22–65. Wide base of support with upper extremity exercise.

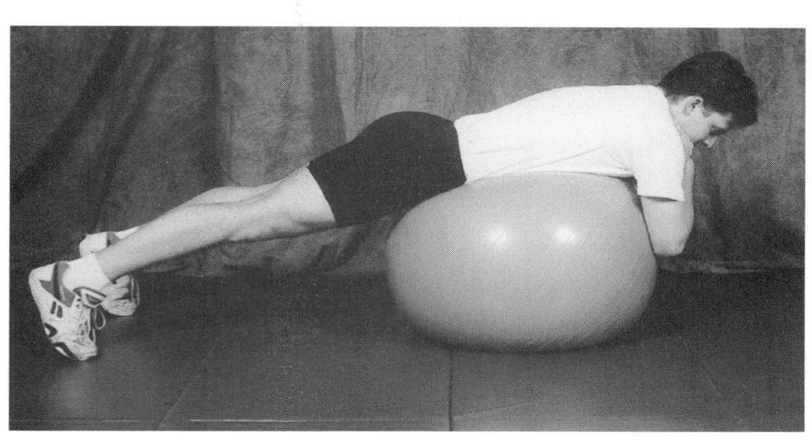

Figure 22–66. Basic starting position for prone gymnastic ball progression.

Prone Gymnastic Ball Progression

Prone gymnastic ball extension activities can be initially performed by having the patient assume a position with the torso placed on the gymnastic ball with the knees extended and the arms crossed in front of the exercise ball (Figure 22–66). Initially, the feet should be separated in order to provide a wide base of support and a higher level of stability. By bringing the feet closer together, the base of support becomes narrower and the level of stability decreases proportionally. Prone gymnastic ball upper extremity activities can be introduced to increase exercise demands (Figure 22–67). Extension of both arms and the use of resistive devices can increase activity of the lower trunk. However, maintaining proper technique for a significant period of time can be difficult (Figure 22–68). Although the low back muscles are significantly involved in these activities, the gluteal muscles are also involved, and this, by some health care professionals, is considered an advantage for protecting the back.

Manually applied resistance, in an infinite variety of directions and with variable force, can add to the level of demand in this prone position. The Morgan harness can be utilized in order to exercise the patient vigorously while simultaneously decompressing the spinal articular structures. This is an important advantage for those patients who are load-sensitive and/or who have intervertebral disc dysfunction with or without radicular symptoms. Multiple resistance vectors can be applied to challenge the neuromotor system yet prevent symptom exacerbation in this case by maintenance of lumbopelvic neutral position with simultaneous spinal decompression (Figures 22–69 and 22–70).

This activity, and others previously mentioned, do not specifically parallel ADLs. They are, however, closed-chain activities that require three-dimensional balance and coordination and in this way simulate daily activities that are of a moderate level of intensity. This "regional first step" to rehabilitating the patient with spinal dysfunction would eventually lead to work conditioning activities that would be upright and weight-bearing in nature.

Higher-level trunk extension exercises (gymnastic ball "in-and-outs") can be performed by having the patient hold the lower extremities parallel to the floor while using the upper extremities to move the trunk forward and backward on the gymnastic ball (Figure 22–71). As the ball moves toward the chest, the level of resistance to the lumbopelvic area increases dramatically so the range of motion will have to be adjusted to meet the patient's abilities. Subtle changes and alterations in lumbopelvic position can result in significant latent pain symptoms so the health care professional supervising the program must be very carefully attuned to these subtle changes.

Squatting Exercises

When it is appropriate to introduce weight-bearing activities, performance of the squat is an important functional ability that must be addressed. Principles mentioned previously can be applied in this exercise scenario such as partial versus full range of motion, static versus dynamic activity, foot position changes to alter the base of support, and resistance variation including speed of movement changes. Proper foot placement while performing the squat maneuver is essential. The feet should be placed slightly wider than shoulder width and the knees should track over the toes during dynamic squat activities. There is evidence to suggest that a wide stance will more effectively exercise the lateral quadriceps and the gluteal muscles, whereas a narrow base of support with the feet close together will emphasize the use of the quadriceps group as a whole. Special instruction must be given on appropriate postural stabilization. Patients also need to be reminded to consciously avoid ankle pronation and/or excessive valgus or varus stresses at the knee.

Patients can begin this activity by using the gymnastic ball as a stabilizer as illustrated in Figure 22–72. A partial and/or full squat, whichever is appropriate, can be maintained isometrically. While maintaining this static position, the difficulty can be increased by involving the upper extremities in manually resisted exercise (Figure 22–73).

Another way of significantly increasing the challenge level for patients who are candidates for static squat activities can be introduced by having them perform unilateral holds as illustrated in Figure 22–74.

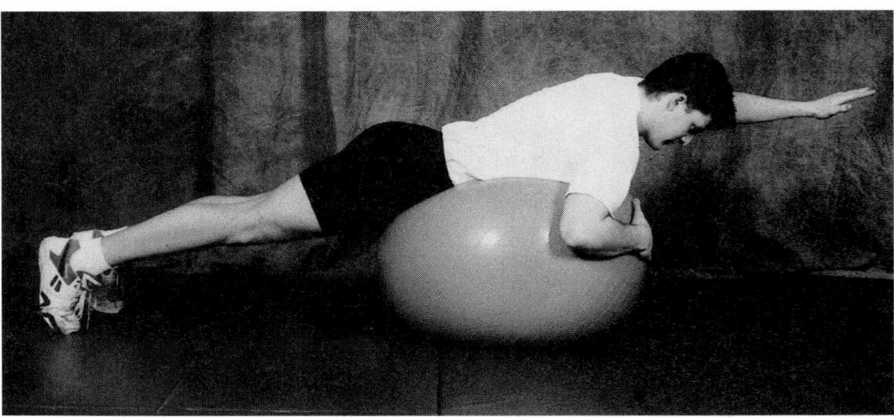

Figure 22–67. Prone gymnastic ball exercise with unilateral arm elevation.

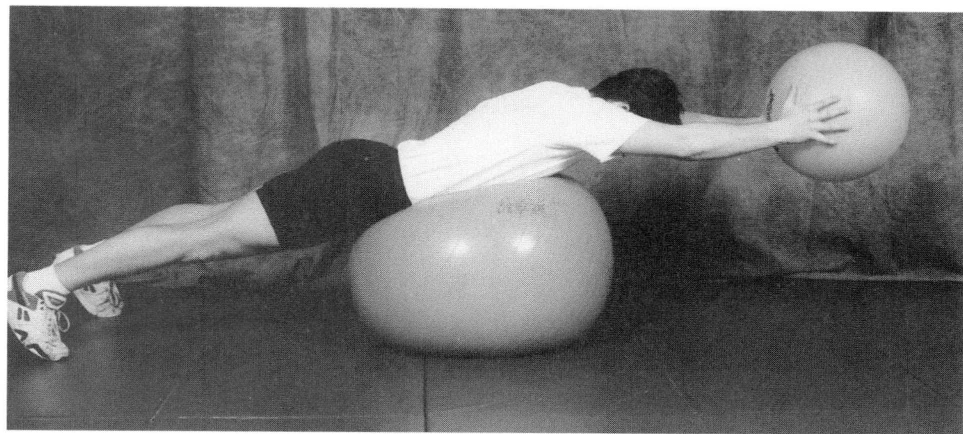

Figure 22–68. Bilateral arm elevation utilizing a small gymnastic ball.

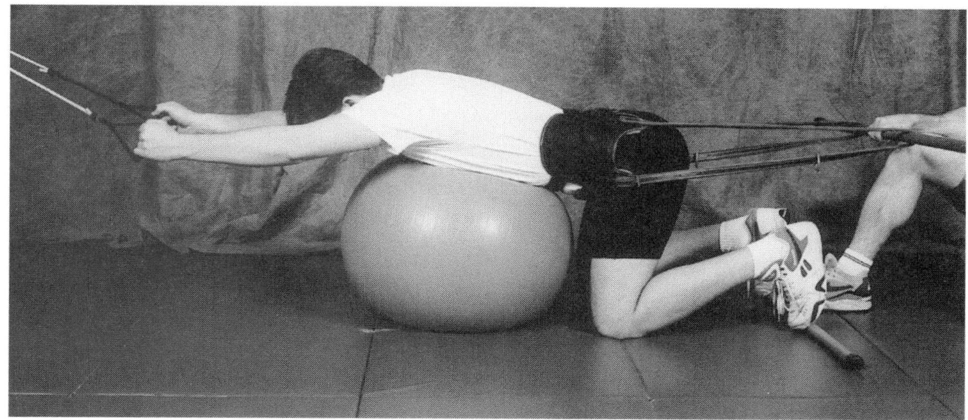

Figure 22–69. Use of the Morgan harness during prone gymnastic ball upper and lower extremity exercise (starting position).

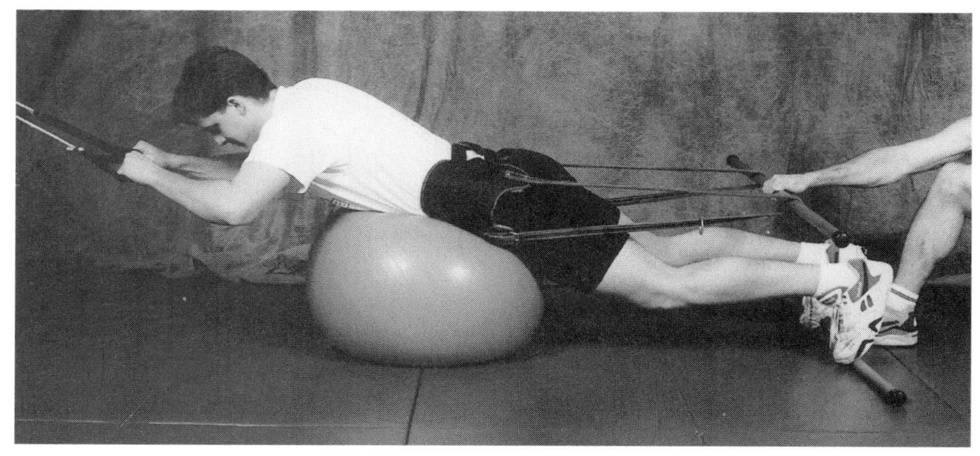

Figure 22–70. Prone gymnastic ball exercise utilizing the Morgan harness (exercise completed).

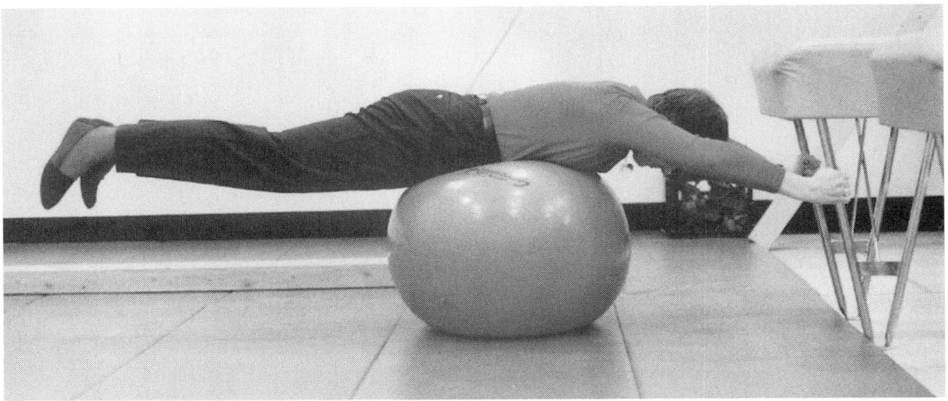

Figure 22–71. High-level trunk extension exercise (gymnastic ball "in-and-outs").

If trunk and leg strengthening is important to introduce early, and there is still a likelihood that the patient is load-sensitive and/or will benefit from spinal decompression, the Morgan harness system can be used as illustrated in Figure 22–75.

Once patients no longer need the support of the gymnastic ball, they should progress to unsupported squatting activities. Lumbopelvic neutral position must be maintained throughout the range of motion of this activity with an emphasis placed on proper body mechanics (Figure 22–76). A gymnastic ball, dumbbells, sandbags, or resistive tubing can be used for added resistance (Figure 22–77). In addition, varying the lever arm length can be used to modify the level of resistance.

The patients can also be asked to "play catch" with balls of varying weights and sizes (i.e., beach ball, medicine ball, etc.). This will simultaneously challenge multiple systems and may be necessary for patients who have complex, work-related tasks. Manually applied resistance can be utilized in a variety of directions, forces, and speeds in order to begin to mimic work-related demands (Figure 22–78).

Push-Up Progression

Push-ups can be performed to exercise the trunk and the upper and lower extremities simultaneously. One starting

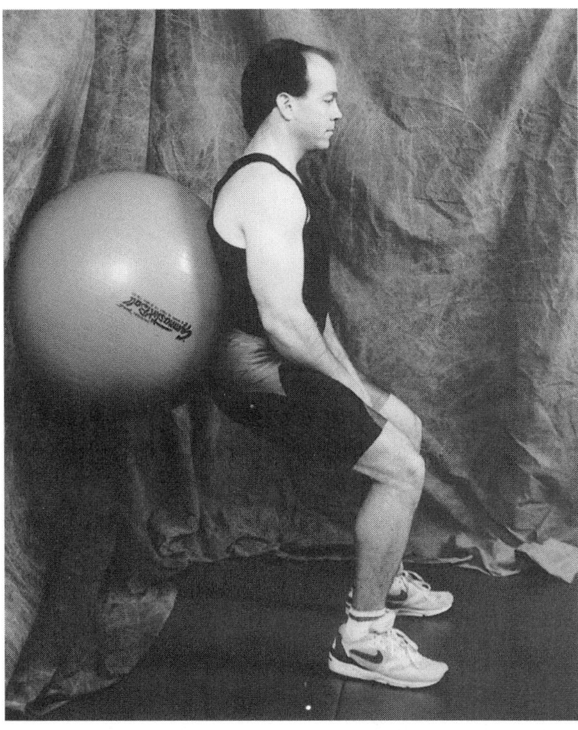

Figure 22–72. Wall squats with the lower back supported by the gymnastic ball.

Figure 22–73. Upper extremity manually resistive exercise during isometric wall squat position.

Figure 22–74. Unilateral isometric squat position with the gymnastic ball.

Figure 22–76. Static unsupported squat position with maintenance of lumbar lordosis.

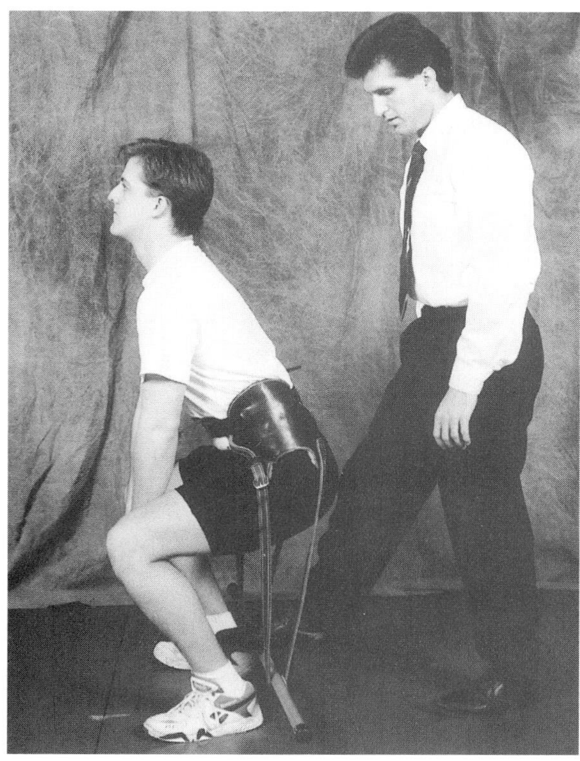

Figure 22–75. Use of the Morgan harness during dynamic squatting activities.

Figure 22–77. Squatting exercise utilizing upper extremity resistive tubing activities.

Figure 22–78. Isometric squat position with manually applied resistance utilizing a wooden dowel.

Figure 22–79. Entry-level push-up position on hands and knees.

and finishing position can be represented with the patient assuming a position on the hands and knees as illustrated in Figure 22–79. Alterations in the positions of the knees relative to the arms can result in significant increases in resistance loads and may be appropriate for some individuals. In addition, this position may simulate activities the patient may encounter during ADLs. Lumbopelvic neutral position must be controlled, as described earlier, so that spinal end-range loading can be avoided. To do this, the abdominal and gluteal musculature must be isometrically contracted to prevent lumbar extension. As the patient is required to repetitively control his or her lumbopelvic position during exercise, this control and awareness will occur automatically during ADLs and work-related activities. Figure 22–80 illustrates an example of the loss of lumbopelvic neutral position.

Push-ups can also be performed in the standard push-up position with maintenance of neutral position, as mentioned above, to increase the physical demands of the exercise. A more unstable environment can be created using the gymnastic ball to perform push-ups. This exercise can be performed in a variety of ways to change the resistance level and required proprioceptive awareness, as illustrated in Figures 22–81 and 22–82.

Balance Activities

There are a number of commercially available balance devices that can be used to assist in enhancing total body proprioception, functional ability, and strength development for the back and lower extremities. Balance activities will typically begin with patients placed in a position using the hands to stabilize themselves on a fixed object. When appropriate, they can begin to remove the support of the hands to increase balance demands. Initially, bilateral balance activities using both feet can be performed, and these can be complemented by adding manually applied resistance (Figure 22–83). For advanced programs, unilateral balance activities can be introduced for increasing functional demands. These sorts of enhanced activities can be particularly useful for the competitive athlete. Unilateral support activities can be performed statically and/or dynamically with the patient performing catching activities and/or with manually applied resistance. For sports rehabilitation it can be very valuable to have the person perform balance activities with the eyes closed to enhance three-dimensional proprioception. The key to increasing the level

Figure 22–80. Loss of lumbar lordosis during push-up position.

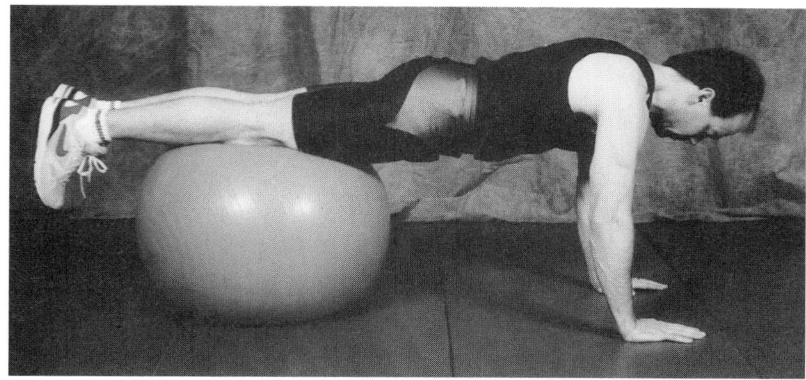

Figure 22–81. Push-up position utilizing the gymnastic ball.

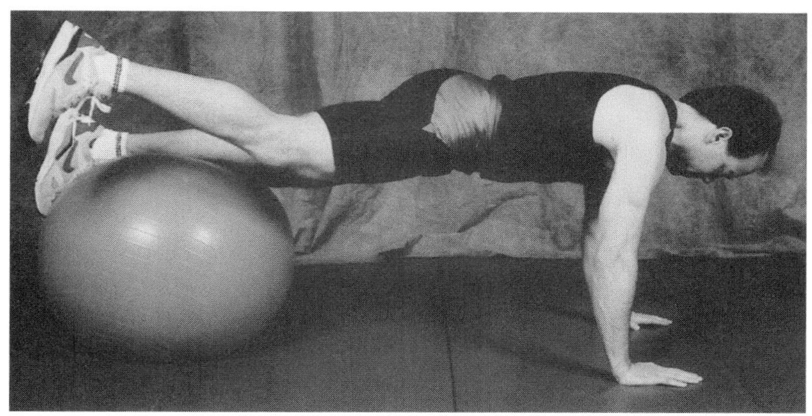

Figure 22–82. Higher-level push-up exercise with unilateral lower extremity support.

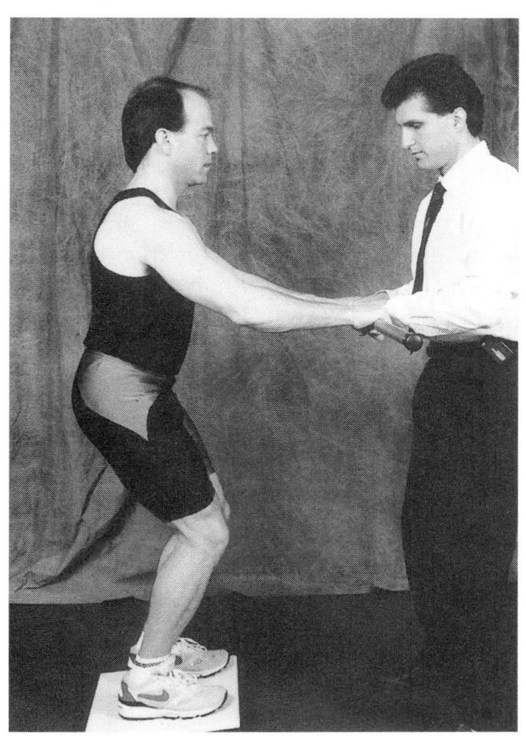

Figure 22–83. Balance training activities with manually applied resistance utilizing a wooden dowel.

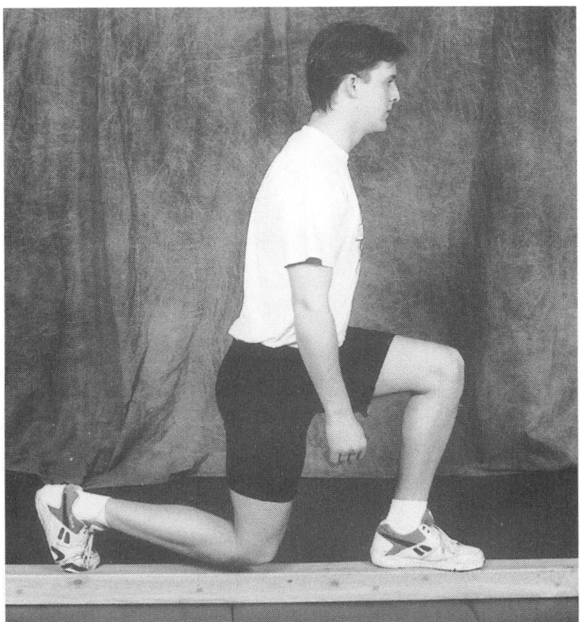

Figure 22–84. Lunges performed on a balance beam.

of difficulty with the use of these balance board devices is using progressively less stable surfaces.

Lunges can be performed on a flat stable or unstable surface with the eyes open and/or closed. These activities, again, may reflect more specific work-related demands and/or maneuvers typically employed during athletic competition (Figure 22–84).

Figure 22–85. Static squat performed on a balance beam.

Movement on a balance beam can be very effective for increasing neuromotor skills (balance and coordination activities). Normally when a patient is walking on the beam, the body processes millions of signals collected from the visual field to help identify his or her position in space and to make appropriate physical adjustments. By performing balance activities with the eyes closed, this visual information is removed and the patient is forced to rely on proprioceptive awareness to appropriately address three-dimensional balance and coordination. Examples of activities performed on the balance beam include walking side to side, front and backward walk, front and backward lunges, and dynamic and/or static squatting activities (Figure 22–85). Applied resistance with dowels, balls, or resistive tubing can be introduced. Playing catch with patients while they are walking on the beam is an excellent method of enhancing neuromotor skills.

SUMMARY

Current knowledge of spinal rehabilitation techniques, muscle and spinal pathophysiology, and psychosocial issues provides the foundation for functional restoration of patients with low back pain. The process starts with a proper diagnostic workup, followed by a functional examination identifying spinal and soft tissue dysfunction and possibly also an ergonomic and work demands assessment. Consideration should also be given to the presence of psychological factors and the social support system. An effective case management approach emphasizing individualized care can then be designed and implemented. A key component of the case management plan is the rehabilitation program. The rehabilitation program should be tailored to meet the unique needs of each patient, emphasizing a functional exercise approach, patient education, and self-management. Stabilization exercises and sensory-motor retraining provide the specificity required in functional training to optimize clinical outcomes. In addition, the non-machine-dependent approach to rehabilitation is a cost-effective means to patient independence.

Clinical Applications

CASE STUDY 1
REHABILITATION OF ACUTE LOW BACK PAIN PATIENT

This case illustrates the use of an active care model in a worker's compensation injury that was not resolving with chiropractic care alone.

HISTORY

The patient is a 48-year-old male manual laborer for a telecommunications company who injured his lower back while digging in wet clay soil. The mechanism of injury was a bending and twisting motion while lifting a full shovel out of a ditch. The patient experienced a sudden sharp pain in his low back, which lessened over the ensuing hour. He continued to work that day in some degree of pain. The next morning upon rising the patient was unable to get out of bed because of severe low back pain and right posterolateral lower extremity pain extending from his buttocks to the calf and lateral foot. He denied numbness or tingling into the lower extremity. The patient subsequently sought care at a chiropractic office that day. The patient's pain levels persisted but did lessen in severity over the next 3 weeks. At 6 weeks postinjury the patient's progress began to plateau, and the patient was referred for rehabilitation consultation at a multidisciplinary rehabilitation center. Habits included social drinking, and he was a nonsmoker. A temporary full disability was given, and the patient was off from work for a total of 15 weeks. Past medical history was remarkable for a previous low back injury 5 years previously that resolved following chiropractic care with no further episodes until this current injury. Systems review was unremarkable.

PHYSICAL EXAMINATION

The initial examination revealed a 5-foot 7-inch overweight male in obvious pain, demonstrating moderate guarding of low back motion during ADLs, an antalgic shift of the low back, hips shifted to the right, and a loss of lumbar lordosis. Thoracolumbar ROM was moderately limited by low back pain in flexion and extension, and mildly restricted in left lateral flexion. A severe limitation was present in right lateral flexion. Severe tenderness and hypertonicity of the lower lumbar paraverterbral musculature were present. Neurologically, lower extremity muscle stretch reflexes were graded as 2+ bilaterally, manual muscle testing was 5/5 bilaterally, the patient was able to heel and toe walk normally, and sharp/dull sensation was intact to the lower extremities. Straight leg raising was to 60 degrees and pain-free on the left and to 35 degrees on the right, reproducing the patient's lower extremity pain. Functional strength testing of the anterior and posterior trunk showed weakness of the abdominal musculature as evidenced by difficulty performing a partial sit-up maneuver (Figure 22–10) and low-level "dead bug" activities (Figures 22–17, 22–18, 22–19). Weakness of the right lumbar area was demonstrated during prone hip extension (with knee extension), as indicated by the presence of excessive lumbar lordosis occurring on the right during this maneuver when compared to the left. The patient was unable to voluntarily perform an isometric contraction of the right gluteal musculature in a prone position, demonstrating the presence of inhibition of that muscle group. The patient was not able to perform a squat maneuver beyond 45 degrees of knee flexion (one-third of a normal squat to the floor) without low back pain. Overall, the patient was in a fair to poor level of general fitness. Radiographic examination revealed moderate degenerative disc disease at L5-S1 with moderate spondylosis present at the same level.

REHABILITATION PROGRAM

A spinal rehabilitation program was initiated which included cardiovascular training of treadmill walking at a comfortable pace for 10 minutes and stationary bicycle riding for 5 minutes with the assistance of a standard walker placed behind the bike, which allowed decompression of the lower back by the patient's weight-bearing on his hands during the exercise. Non-weight-bearing (recumbent) floor and gymnastic ball (65-centimeters gymnastic ball) stabilization exercises were employed initially (Figures 22–16, 22–18, 22–31, 22–41, 22–56, and 22–66) and progressed to full weight-bearing, dynamic stabilization activities as progress was made in strength and tolerance for exercise (Figures 22–20, 22–23, 22–28, 22–32, 22–35, 22–38, 22–45, 22–53, 22–68,

continued

Clinical Applications (Continued)

22–73, and 22–78). The patient did not perform all of these exercises in a single session; rather these figures represent a progression of exercise over time. Static muscle stretching directed to the right gluteus medius and bilateral iliopsoas was given. Initially the rehabilitation program was 20 to 25 minutes in duration. Myofascial therapy techniques were performed to the hypertonic lumbar paraspinal musculature and right gluteus medius. Cryotherapy was applied following each treatment session. Spinal manipulative therapy continued in conjunction with the rehabilitation program. Within 3 to 4 weeks the program had progressed to a total time of 45 minutes, including aerobic training and the spinal stabilization exercises. At 8 weeks a work conditioning program was initiated in addition to the previously described program. The goal of the program was to return the patient to full, unrestricted duty at his prior position. Activities included instruction and active patient participation in neutral spine concepts related to ADLs and work activities of digging, lifting from numerous heights, bending, squatting, pushing, pulling, and carrying materials. The patient's previous job was graded as a heavy physical demands occupation; thus the program was progressed in a graded fashion to include work simulation of activities the patient would actually perform at realistic load levels.

From the initial stages of the rehabilitation program, an emphasis was placed on daily home exercises including walking, spinal stabilization exercises, and muscle stretching. In addition, self-care measures of cryotherapy and judicious use of a lumbar corset were given.

At 12 weeks, the patient was returned to light duty performing desk work, and within 2 weeks he returned to a field job of light to moderate physical demands level. In another 2 weeks, he was returned to his prior position performing heavy manual labor. His symptoms at that time had reduced to a mild ache with no limitations in daily activities due to the low back pain. Physical examination showed full and pain-free thoracolumbar ROM except for mild pain at the extreme of lumbar extension. Lumbar paravertebral tenderness persisted at a mild level. Strength assessment showed no remaining weakness of the low back, gluteal musculature, or abdominals. The patient's overall fitness level had improved to the point that the patient stated he had not been in this good of a physical conditioning for years. He had lost 10 pounds and demonstrated no limitations in physical ability during work-simulated activities. The patient was discharged with a home program of gymnastic ball exercises and muscle stretching to be performed three times per week (Figures 22–32, 22–54, 22–57, 22–68, 22–72, and 22–81).

DISCUSSION

This case illustrates the role of physical rehabilitation in the management of an acute low back pain patient who was not progressing prior to the initiation of the rehabilitation program. Could every case of acute low back pain benefit from a rehabilitation program? The literature indicates that in the case of worker's compensation low back injuries, the majority of dollars and resources spent are for a relatively small percentage of cases that become chronic and disabled due to the injury. Some form of rehabilitation appears to be indicated in all cases of low back pain. A formal program directed by a health care professional probably is not necessary or cost-effective. However, an independent home program of basic rehabilitation activities could benefit the majority of low back pain sufferers, with those that do not demonstrate progress toward resolution in a manner consistent with the natural history of LBP directed into a formal, supervised program. It is possible that such a case management strategy could positively impact the worker's compensation chronic LBP patient, reducing costs for caring for this population of patient.

CASE STUDY 2
POST-SURGERY REHABILITATION

This case illustrates the use of a spinal rehabilitation program in the management of the lumbar postsurgical patient who has a very active lifestyle.

HISTORY

The patient is a 25-year-old female triathlete and marathoner. She presented with an insidious onset of chronic bilateral LBP of 6 months' duration that was not resolving with conservative care, which included chiropractic care, self-directed exercise, activity modification,

Clinical Applications (Continued)

and rest. Prior history included three lumbar surgeries for spinal fusion of an unstable L5 spondylolisthesis. The patient was very active in sports from quite a young age, including gymnastics and volleyball. She experienced an initial onset of LBP at the age of 12 and following workup was found to have an L5 spondylolisthesis. A lumbar fusion with instrumentation was subsequently performed. Following the surgery, no formal rehabilitation was utilized, and the patient was told by the surgeon to slowly return to her prior level of activity with the only limitation being to avoid participation in gymnastics. She did return to competitive sports, however, and unfortunately experienced a fracture of the spinal instrumentation. A revision was necessary, with the patient experiencing an acute onset of cauda equina syndrome 2 days after the surgery while still hospitalized. A second surgery was performed to decompress the area. The patient recovered and was once again told to slowly resume normal activities, including sports, without the use of a formal rehabilitation program.

PHYSICAL EXAMINATION

The initial physical examination showed a very fit-appearing woman with an extremely well-developed and muscular build. Lumbar stiffness was apparent during ADLs, walking, or running. Lumbar ROM was not painful; however during active motion in all planes segmental mobility was noted to be very limited, with the patient primarily utilizing the hips during trunk movements. Palpation did not reveal tenderness of the lumbar or hip area. Hip extension ROM was moderately limited bilaterally. Neurologically, she was intact to muscle stretch reflexes of the lower extremities, muscle strength testing was graded 5/5, and sensation to sharp/dull was normal. Functional strength testing of the anterior and posterior trunk demonstrated good strength of the upper abdominal wall during a partial sit-up (Figure 22–10); weakness of the lower abdominals was evident with the patient being unable to perform a beginning level "dead-bug" (Figure 22–18) maneuver without loss of lumbar neutral position. Left lumbar paraspinal weakness was also noted during active prone hip extension with excessive lumbar lordosis occurring during this activity when performed on the left. The left gluteus medius was weak and graded as fair because of the presence of a positive Trendelenburg. Gluteal weakness was also demonstrated during floor and gymnastic ball bridging activities, with the patient having difficulty performing even low-level bridging maneuvers (Figures 22–39 and 22–49). The patient was unable to produce an isometric voluntary contraction of the left gluteal musculature in a prone position. This finding suggested the presence of reflex inhibition of the left gluteal area. Lumbar orthopedic tests were negative, and straight leg raise was to 60 degrees bilaterally and asymptomatic.

REHABILITATION PROGRAM

A spinal rehabilitation program was initiated consisting of daily home exercises in addition to a 3-day per week one-on-one program performed in a rehabilitation center. The program was initially directed at the hip extensors and abductors, low back extensors, and lower abdominals. Exercises included early progression floor and gymnastic ball bridging exercises (Figures 22–41, 22–43, 22–49, 22–50, and 22–56), prone gymnastic ball activities emphasizing voluntary gluteal contraction (Figures 22–66 and 22–67), standing gymnastic ball squats (Figure 22–72), and "dead-bug" exercises performed at a moderate level of difficulty (Figures 22–19 and 22–21). The patient was instructed to curtail running with biking and running in a pool utilized to maintain aerobic fitness. The pool running was performed both in deep water without the use of flotation assistance and in shallow water to minimize the effects of impact. The program also included flexibility training directed at the iliopsoas, rectus femoris, and hamstrings. Within two visits the patient had regained voluntary isometric control of the left gluteal musculature in a prone position. The program was progressed very rapidly as the patient gained strength and improved neuromotor control and proprioception. She progressed to high-level floor and gymnastic ball exercise and propriosensory training within 6 weeks (Figures 22–23, 22–25, 22–26, 22–53, 22–55, 22–57, 22–69, 22–71, 22–78, 22–81, and 22–84). Follow-up reexamination showed significant strength gains in all areas of previous weakness; however, the patient continued to demonstrate some degree of weakness of the left gluteal musculature during

continued

Clinical Applications (Continued)

higher-level gymnastic ball bridging exercise (Figure 22–54). The patient was instructed to return to running, slowly increasing her mileage and pace. She was able to do so without a return of symptoms and completed a marathon within the next few months, again without low back pain. The patient was placed on an independent home program of gymnastic ball exercises directed at resolving the remaining weakness of the left hip extensors and abductors (Figures 22–53, 22–54, and 22–57). Follow-up at 3 and 6 months indicated no return of low back pain during sports-related activity or ADL.

DISCUSSION

This case illustrates the importance of completing a rehabilitation program following spinal surgery, especially if one is to return to recreational or competitive athletics. Although the patient was very active, weakness and dysfunction remained resulting in activity-limiting low back pain. An individualized functional rehabilitation program was utilized in order to specifically address the long-term compensations, returning the patient to competitive running.

REFERENCES

1. Jordan A, Ostergard K. Rehabilitation of neck/shoulder patients in primary health care clinics. *Journal of Manipulative and Physiological Theraputics*. 1996;1:32–35.
2. Murphy DR. The passive/active care continuum: A model for the treatment of spine-related disorders. *Journal of the Neuromusculoskeletal System*. 1996;4:1:1–7.
3. Timm KE. A randomized-control study of active and passive treatments for chronic low back pain following L5 laminectomy. *Journal of Orthopedic and Sports Physical Therapy*. 1994; 20:276–286.
4. Sweeney T. Neck school: Cervicothoracic stabilization training. *Occupational Medicine*. 1992;7:1: 43–54.
5. Farfan H. Biomechanics of the lumbar spine. In: Kirkaldy-Willis WH, ed. *Managing Low Back Pain*. 2nd ed. New York: Churchill Livingstone, 1988:25–27.
6. Goel VK, Goyal S, Clark C, et al. Kinematics of the whole lumbar spine. *Spine*. 1985;10:543–554.
7. Bullock-Saxton JE, et al. Reflex activation of gluteal muscles in walking: An approach to restoration of muscle function for patients with low back pain. *Spine*. 1993;18(6):704–708.
8. Jones FP. Startle as a paradigm of malposture. *Perceptual and Motor Skills*. 1964;19: 21–22.
9. Morgan D. Concepts of functional training and postural stabilization for the low-back-injured. *Topics in Acute Care Trauma Rehabilitation*. 1988;2(4):8–17.
10. Hamdorf PA, et al. Physical training effects on the fitness and habitual activity patterns of elderly women. *Archives of Physical Medicine and Rehabilitation*. 1992;73:603–608.
11. Tesh KM, et al. The abdominal muscles and vertebral stability. *Spine*. 1986;12(5):501–508.
12. Rose SJ, Rothstein JM. Muscle mutability. *Physical Therapy*. 1982;62(12):1773–1787.
13. Gracovetsky S, Farfan H. The optimum spine. *Spine*. 1986;11:543–573.
14. Saal JA. Rehabilitation of football players with lumbar spine injury. *Physician and Sports Medicine*. 1988;16(10):117–125.
15. Saal JA, Saal JS. Nonoperative treatment of herniated lumbar intervertebral disc with radiculopathy. *Spine*. 1988;8(1):98–107.
16. Cappozzo A, et al. Lumbar spine loading during half-squat exercises. *Medicine and Science in Sports and Exercise*. 1985;17(5):613–620.
17. Janda V. Muscle weakness and inhibition (pseudoparesis) in back pain. In: Grieve GP, ed. *Modern Manual Therapy for the Vertebral Column*. New York: Churchill Livingstone, 1986;197–204.
18. Jones FP. The influence on postural set on pattern movement in man. *International Journal of Neurology*. 1963;4:60–71.

19. Beimborn DS, Morrissey C. A review of the literature related to trunk muscle performance. *Spine*. 1987;13(6):655–660.
20. Sinaki M, Grubbs NC. Back strengthening exercises: Quantitative evaluation of their efficacy for women aged 40 to 65 years. *Archives of Physical Medicine and Rehabilitation*. 1989;70(1):16–20.
21. Salmons S, Hendiksson J. The adapative response of skeletal muscle to increased use. *Muscle and Nerve*. 1981;4:94–105.
22. Snyder P. Rehabilitation after microdiscectomy. *Rehabilitation of the Lumbar Spine*.1993;46:609–614.
23. Goel VK, Nishiyama K, Weinstein J, et al. Mechanical properties of lumbar spinal motion segments as affected by partial disc removal. *Spine*. 1986;11:1008–1012.
24. Parkhurst TM, Burnett CN. Injury and proprioception in the lower back. *Journal of Orthopaedic and Sports Physical Therapy*. 1994;19(5):282–295.
25. Addison R, Schultz A. Trunk strength in patients seeking hospitalization for chronic low-back disorders. *Spine*. 1980;5:539–544.
26. Schmidt G, et al. Assessment of abdominal and back extensor function. A quantitative approach and results for chronic low-back patients. *Spine*. 1983;8:211–219.
27. Suzuki N, Endo S. A quantitative study of trunk muscle strength and fatigability in the low-back-pain syndrome. *Spine*. 1983;8:69–74.
28. Waddell G, et al. Chronic low back pain, psychologic distress and illness behavior. *Spine*. 1984;9(2):209–213.
29. Waddell G. A new clinical model for the treatment of low back pain. *Spine*. 1987;12(7):632–644.
30. Werneke MW, et al. Clinical effectiveness of behavioral signs for screening chronic low back pain patients in a work-oriented physical rehabilitation program. *Spine*. 1993;18(16):2412–2418.
31. Bergquist-Ullman J, Larsson U. Acute low back pain in industry: A controlled prospective study with special reference to therapy and confounding factors. *Acta Orthopaedica Scandinavica (Supplement)*. 1977;170:1–177.
32. Biering-Sorensen F. Physical measurements as risk indicators for low-back trouble over a one-year period. *Spine*. 1984;9:106–119.
33. Hides JA, Stokes MJ, Saide M, Jull GA, Cooper DH. Evidence of lumbar multifidus muscle wasting ipsilateral to symptoms in patients with acute/subacute low back pain. *Spine*. 1994;19(2):165–172.
34. Hides JA, Richardson CA, Jull GA. Multifidus muscle recovery is not automatic after resolution of acute, first-episode low back pain. *Spine*. 1996;21(23):2763–2769.
35. O'Sullivan PB, Phyty GD, Twomey LT, Allison GT. Evaluation of specific stabilizing exercise in the treatment of chronic low back pain with radiologic diagnosis of spondylolysis or spondylolisthesis. *Spine*. 1997;22(24):2959–2967.
36. Hansen FR, et al. Intensive dynamic back-muscle exercises, conventional physiotherapyy, or placebo-control treatment of low-back pain. *Spine*. 1992;18(1):98–107.
37. Lindstrom PT, et al. The effect of graded activity on patients with subacute low back pain: A randomized prospective clinical study with an operant-conditioning behavioral approach. *Physical Therapy*. 1992;72(4):279–290.
38. Sullivan JD, et al. The properties of skeletal muscle. *Orthopaedic Review*. 1986;15(6):17–31.
39. Janda V. 1988. Muscles and cervicogenic pain syndromes. In: Grant R, ed. *Physical Therapy of the Cervical and Thoracic Spine*. New York: Churchill Livingstone, 1988:153–166.
40. Janda V. Seminar notes. New York Chiropractic College, May 1989.
41. Bullock-Saxton JE. Local sensation changes and altered hip function following severe ankle sprain. *Physical Therapy*. 1992;74(1):17–31.
42. Murphy DR. The sternocleidomastoid muscle: Clinical considerations in the causation of head and face pain. *Chiropractic Technique*. 1995;7(1):12–16.
43. Gelb M. *Body Learning*. New York: Henry Holt, 1981.
44. O'Connell AL. Effect of sensory deprivation on postural reflexes. *Electromyography*. 1971;11(5):519–527.
45. Bobath K, Bobath B. The facilitation of normal postural reactions and movements in the treatment of cerebral palsy. *Physiotherapy*. 1964;50:246–262.
46. Balogun JA, et al. The effects of a wobble board exercise training program on static balance performance and strength of the lower extremity muscles. *Physiotherapy Canada*. 1992;44(4):23–30.
47. Byl NN, Sinnott PL. Variations in balance and body sway in middle aged adults: Subjects with healthy backs compared with subjects with low back dysfunction. *Spine*. 1991;16(3):325–330.
48. Hoffman M, Payne VG. The effects of proprioceptive ankle disc training on healthy subjects. *Journal of Orthopaedic Sports and Physical Therapy*. 1995;21(2):90–93.

49. Heitman DK, et al. Balance performance and step width in noninstitutionalized, elderly, female fallers and nonfallers. *Physical Therapy*. 1989;69(11):923–931.
50. Hubka MJ, Hubka MA. Conservative management of idiopathic hypermobility and early lumbar instability using proprioceptive rehabilitation. A report of two cases. *Chiropractic Technology*. 1989;1(3):88–93.
51. Mumenthaler M. *Neurologic Differential Diagnosis*. New York: Thieme-Stratton, 1985.
52. Herman R, et al. Idiopathic scoliosis and the central nervous system: A motor control problem. *Spine*. 1985;10(1):1–14.
53. Anacker SL, Di Fabio RP. Influence of sensory inputs on standing balance on community-dwelling elders with a recent history of falling. *Physical Therapy*. 1992;72(8):575–581.
54. Iverson BD, et al. Balance performance, force production and activity levels in noninstitutionalized men 60 to 90 years of age. *Physical Therapy*. 1990;70(6)348–355.
55. Bogduk N, Twomey LT. *Clinical Anatomy of the Lumbar Spine*. New York: Churchill Livingstone, 1987.
56. Nitz AJ, Peck D. Comparison of muscle spindle concentrations in large and small human epaxial muscles acting in parallel combinations. *American Surgery*. 1986;52:273–277.
57. Vollowitz, E. In: Goldberg L, Elliot D. *Exercises for Prevention and Treatment of Illness*. Philadelphia: FA Davis, 1994:18–37.
58. Murphy DR. Dynamic range of motion training: An alternative to static stretching. *Chiropractic Sports Medicine*. 1994;2:59–66.
59. Frymoyer JW. Predicting disability from low back pain. *Clinical Orthopaedics and Related Research*. 1992;279:103.

CHAPTER 23

Aquatic Rehabilitation for Low Back Dysfunction

CATHY MALONEY-HILLS, PT & MARY SANDERS, MS

INTRODUCTION

The physical, social, and economic consequences of spinal pain and dysfunction have been thoroughly documented and have provided a catalyst for an unprecedented expansion of land-based spinal rehabilitation programs. Numerous studies have confirmed the benefits of improving strength and fitness in spinal patients, including increased functional abilities, decreased pain, earlier return to former employment, and increased well-being.[50,52,73,89] Little, however, has been written regarding current concepts in spinal training in the aquatic environment. The purpose of this chapter is to demonstrate how current theories, techniques, and their practical applications in functional training and postural stabilization may be adapted from land to the aquatic environment.

HISTORY OF AQUATIC THERAPY

The therapeutic use of water for physical healing and spiritual renewal has been documented in numerous civilizations throughout history. Hot and cold water were employed for curative and recreational purposes by the Roman, Russian, Scandinavian, Turk, Greek, Native American, and Japanese cultures as early as 1000 B.C.[16,47] In the fourth century B.C., Hippocrates treated illness with contrast baths[16] and with hydrotherapy with friction.[47] Although use of public baths was widespread during the height of the Roman civilization, pools were neglected during the fall of the empire and by the fifth century A.D. were virtually in ruins.[47] The therapeutic use of water eventually resurfaced during the seventeenth and eighteenth centuries, and became considerably more prevalent in the nineteenth century. A center using cold water and strenuous exercise was started by Pressnitz in 1830.[16] This prompted the scientific community to study the effects of different water temperatures on tissues and ultimately disease processes, leading to the first "accepted physiological basis for hydrotherapy."[16(p2)]

In this century, health care practitioners have used the beneficial properties of water primarily for neuromuscular rehabilitation and orthopedic conditions, including arthritis (rheumatoid and osteoarthritis), ankylosing spondylitis, and extremity fractures or dislocation, as well as postsurgical rehabilitation. Pool therapy for spinal rehabilitation was examined by Duffield in the late 1960s. Exercises documented included range of motion, walking, swimming, spinal mobilization, and strengthening of the back extensors and abdominals.[16] Physiotherapists in Bad Ragaz, Switzerland, developed an aquatic therapy exercise technique incorporating proprioceptive neuromuscular facilitation (PNF) to treat patients with decreased joint range of motion, pain, and muscular weakness.[16] Buoyancy was used for both flotation and as a means of varying assistance or resistance. The Bad Ragaz method continues to be a popular technique employed by aquatic therapists today.

Traditional land-based exercise programs for low back pain have vacillated from an emphasis on flexion to extension with an instructional back class thrown in for prevention. In the 1980s, early pioneers of current "postural stabilization programs" instituted a new trend in back rehabilitation. Eileen Vollowitz applied principles from orthopedic manual therapy, PNF, neurodevelopmental treatment (NDT), and basic body mechanics into her spinal exercise programs. Vollowitz's patients demonstrated improved physical conditioning, safe body mechanics, and more efficient movement patterns.[89] Thus began the evolution of modern spinal stabilization. With demonstrated success and widespread popularity among physical therapists and patients alike, adaptation to the water soon followed. The techniques of aquatic spinal stabilization were first introduced by Rick Eagleston in 1987.[12] Aquatic exercise has now become a valuable tool used in rehabilitation of a vast population of patients, from elite athletes to the disabled.[12,16,26,30,35,46,57,67,71]

BENEFITS OF AQUATIC EXERCISE

Water provides unique opportunities for cardiovascular and muscular conditioning. Simply immersing a body in water decreases the effects of gravity on that body, and provides a supportive environment that can be used for resisted, active assisted, or passive exercise. A benefit of decreasing the effects of gravity is a reduction in compressive and shear forces on the joints. Patients experiencing sensitivity to weight-bearing or compressive spinal load can find relief of symptoms through the buoyant support of water.

Patients experience enhanced freedom of movement provided by the support of buoyancy. Water is an adaptable medium, providing variable degrees of resistance or assistance in any plane or pattern of movement or body position. Movements can be performed at a slower rate and with greater control because of the viscosity of water, which inherently reduces speed. Self-conscious patients are more comfortable in the privacy of water. Because the body is partially submerged, individuals can focus on their own skills without the pressure to 'keep up' with the group.

RESEARCH ON AQUATIC SPINAL REHABILITATION

A review of the literature documenting effects of aquatic spinal rehabilitation revealed very few studies of any sort. Langridge and Phillips[45] developed an aquatic back exercise program for 27 regular participants of a trial back pain association program in Australia. Each member completed a questionnaire regarding general history of injury, pain level, quality of life, and occupational limitations due to low back pain (LBP). Another questionnaire, completed 6 months later, included pain level, medical visits, use of medications since starting the program, quality of life, and occupational changes. Before and after each session, each member completed a visual analogue scale (VAS) indicating level of pain. All patients in this study had experienced chronic low back pain for a minimum of 6 months, with 81% suffering from back pain for over 3 years. Each participant performed eight aquatic exercises which were progressed through five levels of difficulty. The participant had to perform each exercise at a given level for three sessions without discomfort before advancing to the next level. After completing the final level in the pool, participants started the first of five levels of land exercises. Results indicated that 85% of participants reported decreased pain, 81% demonstrated improvements in pain level before and after each aquatic therapy session, 48% noted improvements in occupationally related LBP, and 96% experienced improvements in quality of life. In addition, 85% remained employed, 67% indicated decreased expenses for medication, and none of the participants increased their use of medication for LBP. Although the investigators were quick to indicate this study's limitations due to the low number of subjects, lack of controls, and unscientific collection of data, the apparent positive benefits of aquatic exercise for chronic back pain patients were evident. The authors also noted that exercising the participants in groups provided peer support and a means of directing patient management, further enhancing the perceived benefits and experience of enjoyment.

Woods[98] investigated the use of aquatic exercise and modified swimming strokes on muscular strength, range of motion (ROM), and pain levels in patients diagnosed with lumbosacral strain or laminectomy for intervertebral disc rupture. Eighteen patients were assessed before and after a 6-week treatment session with an original functional ability assessment checklist and the McGill Pain Questionnaire. Treatment included 18 one-hour sessions of isolated low back, abdominal, and lower extremity pool exercises as well as gradually increasing swimming distances. Results indicated 17 of the 18 patients (94%) demonstrated improvement in muscular strength and ROM, but only four patients (22%) noted diminished pain levels. The author supported these findings with earlier studies which found that subjective reports of pain were poor indicators of physical and occupational abilities. The methodology of this study contained some limitations, including a low number of patients and lack of control subjects. There was no information provided regarding chronicity or stability of the participants' back pain. Furthermore, no reference was made to modification of exercises for each individual's presenting signs and symptoms. The progression of activities appeared to be based on functional parameters, with symptomatology not a factor. Woods claimed that the functional ability assessment checklist was a simple, reliable, fast tool for assessing functional level. From a therapeutic standpoint, however, many of the activities on this checklist could be detrimental to patients with spinal disorders.[56,61,64,72]

Smit and Harrison[83] performed a pilot study involving 20 patients with a diagnosis of chronic spondylosis. Treatment was provided three times per week for 1 month with the goal of decreasing pain and increasing mobility and strength of the thoracolumbar spine. The duration of treatment sessions was progressed from 20 to 30 minutes and exercises were prescribed appropriately for each patient's current signs and symptoms. Pain levels were assessed via a

VAS 1 week prior to commencing treatment, the day of each treatment, 1 week after treatment ended, and through a questionnaire 3 months after treatment ended. Thoracolumbar mobility was measured during the first three examination sessions. Data regarding amount of pain medications taken, aggravating factors, previous treatments, and day and night pain patterns were collected 1 week prior to starting treatment and 3 months after treatment cessation. The final questionnaire also questioned participants about their overall status compared to prior to initiating the hydrotherapy program.

Results showed that 14 of the 19 patients who completed the study (74%) reported decreased pain levels the week following treatment cessation, with none of the participants reporting an increase in pain. Comparison of thoracolumbar ROM measurements taken the first day of hydrotherapy and those taken the week following cessation showed statistically significant improvement in all four directions (flexion, extension, right lateral flexion, and left lateral flexion). Four patients (21%) ceased taking medications, one changed drug treatment, and all others did not alter their usage of medications. The VAS at the 3-month follow-up demonstrated a statistically significant increase in pain when comparing the week following treatment cessation and the time the questionnaire was completed (3 months later). Fourteen patients (77%), however, still stated that they felt better or much better than they had prior to starting the hydrotherapy program. All but one patient, who reported no change, also noted improvements in activities of daily living (increased walking distance, increased sitting or standing tolerance, and greater ease of housecleaning).

Although lack of controls was the major limitation of this study, it strongly supports the findings by Langridge and Phillips that aquatic therapy can be effective in decreasing pain and improving function and quality of life for those suffering from chronic low back pain. When comparing the effects of aquatic exercise on pain levels, the results from the Woods study differ dramatically from the other two studies cited. The Woods study showed only 22% of participants reported diminished pain levels. The Langridge/Phillips and Smit/Harrison investigations found decreased pain levels in 85% and 74% of their participants, respectively. The primary difference in the Woods study was that the choice and progression of activities appeared to be based primarily on functional parameters, not daily presenting signs and symptoms. One could conclude from this contrast that the provision of exercises and their progression should be based on functional abilities, tolerance to the activities and positions used, and the dynamic nature of the symptoms.[7,12,57,60,73] Morgan[60] states that individuals involved in evaluation and treatment of patients with spinal pathology should have education in anatomy, physiology, and biomechanical application to movement disorders, and training and experience in evaluation and treatment of musculoskeletal disorders, with an emphasis on spinal conditions. The need for astute, skillful practitioners providing evaluation and appropriate treatment of individuals with spinal disorders is clearly evident.

PROPERTIES OF WATER

Understanding the benefits of aquatic exercise requires the knowledge and integration of exercise principles and their application to the properties of water. Water affects each body differently, and exercise prescriptions should address not only how a person responds to the water, but more importantly, how movements affect the action of water on the body. Many variables should be considered together when evaluating exercise design in water. Some of these variables, which differentiate exercise on land from exercise in water, include buoyancy, resistance, and balance. This section examines the properties of water and the predicted effects of the aquatic environment acting upon the body.

BUOYANCY

Archimedes' principle describes *buoyancy* as the upward force exerted on an immersed object at rest. This force is equal to the weight of fluid which is displaced.[16] Buoyancy acts on the body by pushing upward; each individual responds differently depending on body composition, height, bone density, and the overall surface area that is immersed. The interaction of these factors determines if a body will sink, float, or be neutrally buoyant (somewhere in between). Buoyancy of the entire body varies as the surface area immersed in the water changes. Simply lifting an arm overhead and out of the water decreases the buoyancy of the body. In deep water the body may submerge; in shallow water weight-bearing on the lower body may increase. Arms and legs have their own degree of buoyancy and must be considered separately when focusing on extremity training. A limb is assisted as it moves upward toward the surface of the water, and is resisted with movements down into the water.[23] The addition of buoyancy equipment or weights affects the entire body's response and may change the center of balance.

Optimal working buoyancy for regulating the amount of weight-bearing and resistance can vary according to the patient's needs and abilities. It is affected by water depth, the amount of body surface area immersed in the water, and body weight and composition. An optimal working depth in water assists in relieving symptoms by reducing weight-bearing, yet still affords stability and control of movement. When determining the optimal working depth in shallow water, buoyancy must be considered relative to the patient's ability to move with appropriate speed through the water using the feet for propulsion. Gravitational forces are decreased by 90% when the body is immersed in neck-deep water.[12] When working in water depth above the xiphoid process, with the lungs submerged, there is insufficient gravitational force to use the feet as a stable base of support. Maintaining stability is more difficult because the body must balance the center of buoyancy at the lungs with the center of gravity at the hips, where fat depositions may at times even negate the weight of the pelvic girdle. At this depth, each individual's body type and fat distribution will affect balance differently and must be considered during exercise design. Although joint compression may be reduced at this depth, consideration must be given to the patient's stability and ability to control movement. The use of 1- to 2-pound ankle weights can improve stability enough to enable the spinal patient to work with adequate control in greater water depth.

Considerations for buoyancy exercise design include the following[69]:

1. It is important to consider the effect of body type, equipment used, and surface area immersed in the water upon the degree of buoyancy affecting the entire body. Buoyancy is amplified as the body is submerged. When the lungs are submerged, patients can be evaluated for the ability to initiate movements and maintain control using the feet as a base of support and means of propulsion in shallow water (traveling move).
2. A person's ability to touch the bottom of the pool is not the criteria for establishing an optimal shallow water depth. The individual's ability to control balance and movement relative to the forces of buoyancy can be evaluated in relation to the development of speed and resistance in the water.
3. Buoyancy can be varied by changing depths. Aquatic activities performed without the feet touching the bottom of the pool (deep water exercise) can be mimicked in shallow water simply by lifting the feet off the bottom, working the exercise "suspended." The manipulation of buoyancy provides an opportunity for practitioners to develop progressive resistance programs. Equipment, such as a step, increases the effect of gravity and reduces buoyancy by decreasing water depth when the patient stands on the platform. The patient is still able to return to the more buoyant depth surrounding the step.
4. The addition of buoyancy equipment to the body or limb can be evaluated for its assistive or resistive effects. Exercises can be designed to work in opposition to buoyancy to add resistance or in the same direction for assistance of movements. For example, while a person is holding a foam dumbbell during elbow flexion, the biceps are assisted while the triceps contract eccentrically to resist the buoyant force toward the surface. Moving the foam dumbbell with elbow extension requires the triceps to contract concentrically. Holding buoyancy equipment should also be evaluated for potential systemic effects. The isometric activity of the upper extremities, even though light, may cause a dramatic elevation in blood pressure with normotensive individuals.

RESISTANCE

Water provides accommodating frictional *resistance* because of its viscosity.[23] When the body is submerged, resistance can be developed in any plane, pattern of movement, or body position. A number of variables should be considered in order to provide appropriate resistance in the water. These variables include turbulence, frontal resistance, speed, surface area, leverage, action/reaction, and inertia.

Duffield[16] states travel through water creates *turbulence*, which is defined as "a force differential created by movement."[12] Turbulence is a result of frontal resistance and laminar flow. *Frontal resistance* is defined as the resistance caused by an object's shape or profile during movement through fluid.[3] The tendency of the molecules of a fluid moving around an object (or body) to speed up or slow down in order to stay parallel to each other is called *laminar flow*.[3] Greater muscular work is required to continue movement against the increased forces of frontal resistance and laminar flow, especially as speed increases. Research shows oxygen consumption to be highest when individuals travel through water at their optimal working depth at maximum speed.[8,25,90] Kennedy et al.[41] found that running in nipple-deep water resulted in lower heart rates than waist-deep running. Additional findings revealed participants who exercised in bare feet reported having trouble gaining speed during traveling moves in nipple-deep water. The lack of traction, inability to overcome inertia, and floating effects of buoyancy most likely prevented participants from attaining the speeds necessary to produce the frontal resistance, drag, and turbulence required to develop optimal resistance against the body.

"Faster movement through the water results in greater drag and resistance, which increases the muscular work required for movement."[12(p391)] Heart rates increase with the speed of movements through water.[11,96] Lower body movements performed in water result in higher oxygen uptake (VO_2) than similar exercises performed on land.[11] *Speed* of exercise is considered differently in water, because movement of the body involves overcoming the additional force of the water working against it. Faster speed results in increased turbulence, frontal resistance, and laminar flow. Greater muscular work is required to maintain faster speed against these increased forces of resistance than with comparable movement on land. Research shows that only one-half to one-third the speed achieved during land walking and jogging was necessary for the same level of energy expenditure for walking and jogging in waist-deep water.[19] Because water completely surrounds the immersed body, exercises designed for strengthening any direction of motion will also require greater exertion than similar exercises performed on land.

The *surface area* of the body or limb moving through water will affect resistance during movement. Costill[12a] found exercise intensities were related to the level of muscular strength applied and were proportional to the surface area and speed of movement performed in the water. Resistance in the water is affected by surface area and leverage.

Techniques that increase surface area, such as wearing webbed gloves on the hands, increase the resistance to the arm as it moves through water. The longer the lever (such as the difference between a flexed and extended arm), the greater the resistance of movement through water. These factors should be considered together when determining the appropriate level of resistance. Small changes in resistance can have marked effects on patients whose symptoms are easily exacerbated.

Newton's third law states that for every action there is an equal and opposite reaction *(action/reaction)*.[93] In water this law can be used to increase or decrease resistance. If the arms push backward, the body is pushed forward. The speed of a body moving through water increases due to the reaction of the body to the backward thrust of the arms. Newton's law of action/reaction can also be used to oppose movement and localize work. For example, when the arms push backward assisting forward propulsion, the exercise can be designed so that, instead of yielding to the natural reaction, it can be opposed by jumping or kicking backwards. The level of difficulty increases because these forces work against each other. In evaluating exercise design, the direction of assistance should be determined and used to either assist or resist travel.

Inertia is the tendency of a body to remain in a state of rest or of uniform motion in a straight line until acted upon by a force to change that state.[93] Once the body has overcome the inertia of still water to begin movement, currents are created that can be used to assist movements in the same direction, or resist movements in the opposite direction. By repeating a pattern of movement back and forth quickly in the same area, currents resulting from overcoming the inertia in water can be used to create resistance. In some instances, it may be desirable to allow the currents to subside before working against them. For example, a body moving through water produces currents. A direction change creates opposing currents. Balance, stability, and control may be challenged as the body moves against the force of the currents. Stopping traveling, jogging in place, and sculling (figure-eight motion with the hands) will allow the currents to subside prior to changing direction. Currents can be very powerful and are especially important to consider during group exercise in which everyone is pushing the water in the same direction. People traveling in the center or back of a group, where the currents are greatest, can easily lose their balance.

Considerations for resistance exercise design include the following:

1. Speed and force of movement through water can be used in conjunction with surface area and lever (limb) length to regulate intensity.
2. Larger movements (one-half to one-third the speed of movements on land) can increase resistance by taking advantage of the effects of action/reaction and inertia.
3. Travel through water can be used to amplify the properties of water acting against the body and provide higher-intensity training.
4. Surface area and speed can be modified to provide appropriate resistance by changing lever arm length or by using equipment such as webbed gloves. The combination of surface area and speed of movement may overcome the assistive effects of buoyancy.
5. Resistance can also be provided manually by the clinician's hands, or by equipment such as resistive tubing.

BALANCE

Balance in water may be difficult to control because of the effects of buoyancy pushing upward. This is especially evident when excess adipose is deposited on the hips and thighs, and the effects of water currents and resistance are pushing and pulling against the body in many directions. When the lungs are submerged and the feet no longer provide a secure base of support, the body feels light and at the mercy of the action/reaction of movement and currents of the water. In response to this dynamic environment, sculling helps maintain balance. Taking advantage of the property of action/reaction, wearing webbed gloves on hands positioned flat in the water provides additional surface area for the upper body to lean on to assist with balance.

In waist-deep water the upper body moves through air with negligible resistance, while the lower body encounters varying amounts of resistance from the water. Webbed gloves on the hands can assist with balance, travel, or directional change. The increased surface area resulting from wearing webbed gloves slows the speed of the arms to more closely match the speed of the longer levers of the legs, assisting with balance and coordination. Pushing the hands backwards behind the hips in opposition to forward movement of the legs enhances balance. During deep water exercise synergistic arm and leg movements assist with balance as they work in opposition. Sculling is essential for balancing deep water activities, because the body is completely buoyant.

Thermoregulation is the ability to maintain a core body temperature by balancing metabolic heat production and heat loss.[75] Maintenance of thermal balance is important for optimal training. Oxygen consumption with swimming is greatest in colder water, primarily because of the energy cost of shivering to maintain core body temperature.[12] Craig and Dvorak[14] suggested a neutral temperature for shallow water vertical exercise in which heat loss is balanced by heat production. At 3.1 metabolic equivalents (METS), Craig and Dvorak recommended a water temperature of 34°C (93°F) and at 4.2 METS, which would correspond to vigorous travel work, the suggested temperature was 29°C (84°F). Even in water that was 32°C (90°F), Craig and Dvorak[14] reported an initial drop in core temperature which continued to decline with light work. Exercising with a reduced core temperature and reduced oxygen transport could affect oxygen consumption and central blood flow.[5,13,86]

Rennie[68] indicates that body fat may be a critical insulator in cold (25°C or 77°) water, especially during long immersions of 3 hours or more. Graham,[27] however, found that layers of muscle seem to be more effective insulators. Body mass and surface area can effect the body's responses to cold. Standing in water cooler than 32°C (90°F) will cause cooling that will affect exercise performance and comfort. Patients should continue moving their legs or arms to generate heat, or wear insulated clothing to slow heat loss.

Hydrostatic pressure is defined as the thrust of the molecules of a fluid upon the entire surface area of an immersed body.[16] Hydrostatic pressure against the body increases with depth. In a vertical position, the greatest pressure is at the feet. It is thought that the increase in pressure aids venous circulation and contributes to the reduction of edema, especially in the lower body. When designing exercises, the most important point to consider is that when the lungs are submerged, the increased hydrostatic pressure makes breathing more difficult; the lungs must be inflated against the resistance of the water. For this reason it is suggested that the patient practice breathing and inflating the lungs against the pressure. This will maximize lung volume and enable each patient to adjust to the new feeling of pressure against the chest.

AQUATIC CARDIOVASCULAR TRAINING

Current research studies show that aquatic cardiovascular training can be performed in both shallow and deep water.[6,11,31,33,36,58,71,75,84] Research by Thomas and Long[88] indicates that the blood pressure response to deep water running was comparable to the response to running on land. Systolic blood pressure, however, may increase initially upon immersion as a response to hydrostatic pressure on the body. In deep water exercise, heart rate decreased as stroke volume increased. Cassady and Nielson determined that aquatic exercises that emphasized lower extremity work produced higher cardiovascular intensities, even though heart rates may have been lower than comparable on-land predicted measures.[11] Travel through water resulted in higher oxygen consumption than stationary exercise and fell well within the American College of Sports Medicine (ACSM) recommended intensity range for aerobic exercise.[8,25,90,94] However, exercises in cool water (25 to 27°C or 77 to 81°F) that used extensive overhead arm movements above the surface of the water, in conjunction with stationary jogging, kicking, knee raises, bobbing, or jumping, demonstrated an exercise oxygen uptake below the minimum aerobic threshold even though the heart rate response was 82% of the maximal heart rate. The use of overhead and extensive upper extremity activities could explain the higher heart rate relative to the low oxygen uptake[4,82] and may indicate why this exercise design does not meet the criteria for aerobic training.[8]

Using heart rates to estimate exercise intensity in water may not be appropriate because research shows that the water depth, temperature, amount of armwork used, and use of hand-held equipment affect heart rates.[13,19,53,54] In addition, accurately counting heart rate on land has been proven to be difficult,[17] and in water is even more difficult. Cardiovascular intensities also varied with the skill level and motivation of the individuals, with highly skilled exercisers able to achieve higher heart rates than unskilled students.[70,71,95] The *rate of perceived exertion* (RPE or Borg scale) and the *talk test* give patients guidelines to target their own intensity. Although the accuracy of the talk test varies, Williams[97] feels that if a patient can only gasp out one to two words at a time, the exercise intensity is too great; patients should be able to say two- to three-word phrases. The talk test is most accurately used in conjunction with heart rate or RPE.

Considerations for cardiovascular exercise design include the following:

1. Travel through the water can be used to allow time and space for water to act against the body.
2. Patients can learn the exercise and compensate for balance when provided ample time for practice. Intensity can then be increased to achieve maximal training.
3. Cardiovascular intensity can be measured accurately if upper extremity activities are performed below shoulder level, requiring underwater work.
4. Cardiovascular conditioning can be enhanced by emphasizing leg movements.
5. Patients can be taught to use a combination of rate of perceived exertion (RPE), heart rate (if monitored), and the talk test to monitor intensity.
6. Exercising muscle groups can frequently be alternated to prevent local muscular fatigue so cardiovascular intensity can be maintained.

MUSCULAR STRENGTH AND ENDURANCE

A minimum level of muscular endurance may be necessary before patients can improve cardiovascular endurance.[75] Many training studies found that the resistance of water provided enough intensity to significantly improve muscular strength and endurance, especially for the upper body.[6,34,71,75] During an 8-week study by Sanders,[75] participants showed significant improvement in abdominal strength without performing conventional abdominal exercises. The significant improvement was attributed to frequent use of the abdominals required in the maintenance of functional position, through frequent cueing during a combined shallow and deep water program. Hoeger et al[33] showed that shallow water programs produced greater gains in upper body muscular strength than a low-impact aerobics program on land. During resistance exercises performed while standing in water, the muscles of the trunk and extensor muscles of the upper and lower extremities are the primary movers against resistance and buoyancy.[40] Strengthening these extensor muscles improves the efficiency with which activities of daily living are performed.

Considerations for muscular strength and endurance exercise design include the following:

1. Adequate repetitions and sets can be provided to target muscular conditioning, as the properties of water are applied.
2. Exercises can be designed so that the primary muscle group or pattern is worked. If the patient is able to control functional position during the activity, the other body movements (sculling or jogging) can be added for thermoregulation, if necessary.
3. Resistance can be increased by incorporating equipment that increases surface area (Sloggers, Aqua Chutes, hand buoys, webbed gloves) or increasing gravitational forces (a step), working more toward enhancing strength training.
4. When using resistive tubing, the thickness of the tube chosen can be determined by the patient's ability to move through the full range of motion prescribed without increasing symptoms, losing control of functional position, or sacrificing quality of movement.

EVALUATION AND GOALS OF TREATMENT

SUBJECTIVE EVALUATION

It is not within the scope of this chapter to provide a comprehensive review of the subjective examination, for it is covered in great detail elsewhere in the literature.[48,51,61,91] Specific subjective information relevant to aquatic exercise, however, is reviewed. Some of the primary goals of the subjective examination are to identify the type and extent of the patient's physical disorder(s), to gain insight into the patient's personality, and to determine the impact of the condition on the patient's life.[51] Information acquired from the subjective evaluation directs the course of the physical examination and treatment progression.[48] One of the primary objectives is to confirm that the referral is appropriate. Subjective findings that do not implicate musculoskeletal origins or correlate with the clinical picture could indicate more serious underlying pathology in which mechanical treatment would be inappropriate. In such cases the patient should be returned to the primary care referring practitioner for further workup. Important information about potential systemic involvement, effects of medication, or underlying causes of symptoms can be acquired through the following special questions[51]:

1. Is there a personal or family history of rheumatoid disease?
2. Has the patient had the "flu" recently?
3. Are there bilateral symptoms extending into feet or hands (cord compression)?
4. Has the patient noted recent unexplained weight loss?
5. Has the patient experienced dizziness, blurred vision, nausea and vomiting, or tinnitis (vertebral artery)?
6. Has the patient taken steroids or anticoagulants (especially recent or prolonged)?
7. Has the patient had problems with urinary control, genital and/or saddle numbness (cauda equina)?

Other relevant questions from the present history include those concerning symptom behavior, such as aggravating and alleviating factors: What is the length of time or number of repetitions needed to initiate symptoms? How quickly can symptoms be relieved? How long does the relief last? Common biomechanical patterns can be grouped and indicate if the patient is position-, load-, stasis- or pressure-sensitive.[61] Recording the time or number of repetitions an activity is tolerated and the symptoms resulting from exceeding the tolerable level provides a baseline for measuring progress. Information from the daily pattern of symptoms indicates optimal times of the day for treatment and exercise. Obtaining a clear picture of the patient's overall general health and fitness can help direct the starting level and rate of progression. A thorough social and occupational history is important in organizing an appropriate rehabilitation program. A mother with a spinal condition requires immediate instruction in proper body mechanics and compensatory ways to care for her child. A construction worker at home on disability, however, would benefit from initial instruction in activities of daily living (ADLs) with occupational training initiated later in the rehabilitation program.

The patient's past medical history also provides pertinent information regarding potential precautions and contraindications for aquatic rehabilitation, as noted in Table 23–1. Potential problems arising from fear of the water should not be overlooked. The patient should be informed

Table 23–1: Precautions and/or Contraindications for Aquatic Rehabilitation

Fever
Open wound
Contagious skin condition
Infectious disease
Severe/uncontrolled cardiovascular disease
Uncontrolled seizures
Bowel or bladder incontinence
Use of colostomy bag or catheter
Cognitive or functional impairment that would create a hazard to participation in the aquatic program
Severely limited endurance
Excessive fear of water
Sensitivities and/or allergic reactions to chemicals used in pools[12,16,29,57]

that experience in swimming is not a prerequisite to participation in an aquatic exercise program. Taking the time to inform the patient of what to expect the first few aquatic sessions would be an effective means of gaining trust and calming fears. The clinician can also use a preliminary land exercise session to educate the patient in the similarities or differences of exercising in the water. Finally, compiling a list and schedule of all medications the patient is currently taking may help to indicate optimal times for treatment and exercise.

Compiling the data from the subjective evaluation assists in identification of the individual's physical problem(s) and the severity, irritability, nature, and stage/stability (SINS) of the condition.[51] This information directs the course of the objective examination and subsequent treatment.

THE MUSCULOSKELETAL EVALUATION

As with the subjective evaluation, the major components of the musculoskeletal examination are well-documented.[10,15,18,28,37,39,48,56,61,85] Findings related to the aquatic exercise environment are addressed. Morgan, in his synopsis of Kaltenborn's work, provides a concise, thorough overview of the major components of the musculoskeletal examination (Table 23–2).

It is important to note any postural deviations exhibited by the patient. The patient presenting as flexed and laterally shifted may benefit from lateral shifting and extension in the supportive environment of the water. Likewise, a patient who adjusts lumbar position frequently while sitting in a chair, leans heavily on armrests, or needs to change position frequently during load-bearing activities may benefit from water's buoyant properties.[89,91] Observing the individual's general body type provides information about appropriate water depth and the possible use of buoyancy-enhancing devices versus weights to reduce symptoms (Figures 23–1 and 23–2). Circumferential measurements should be taken of body parts with swelling or atrophy. Healthy skin is a prerequisite for aquatic participation. If the patient has had recent surgery, the incision must be healed and free of infection. Assessing the patient's limitations in ADLs and use of assistive devices indicates the potential need for assistance in dressing, undressing, showering, or getting into or out of the pool.

Table 23–2: Major Components of the Musculoskeletal Examination

1. Inspection
   - Posture: habitual, antalgic, or compensatory body position
   - Shape: general body type, changes in normal contours, deformities, swelling, atrophy
   - Skin: color changes, scars, calluses, trophic and circulatory changes
   - Activities of daily living: gait, dressing and undressing, getting up and down from chair
   - Aids: use of cane, crutches, corsets, prostheses
2. Palpation
   - Temperature
   - Contour and shape
   - Moisture
   - Symmetry
   - Tenderness
   - Mobility and elasticity
   - Pulses
   - Crepitus
3. Neurologic examination
   - Deep tendon reflexes
   - Pathologic reflexes (i.e., Babinski's sign)
   - Sensory testing (light touch, pin prick, vibration, position sense)
   - Strength testing
   - Girth measurements
   - Tension signs (i.e., straight leg raising)
   - Special tests (i.e., coordination, balance, clonus, spasticity)
4. Tests of function (assess movement quantity and quality and symptom changes)
   - Active movements
   - Resisted movements
   - Manual muscle testing
   - Mechanical (isokinetic devices, strain gauges, dynamometers, tensiometers)
   - Specific functional maneuvers
   - Passive movements (also assess end feel)
   - Joints
     - Physiologic (rotations)
     - Accessory (translations)
   - Soft tissues
     - Length
     - Accessory movement
   - Standard movements in the cardinal planes
   - Functional movements around combined axes in multiple planes

Source: Kaltenborn F. *Mobilization of the Extremity Joints*. 4th ed. Oslo: Olaf Norlis Bokhandel, 1989: 39–43; and *The Spine*. 2nd ed. Oslo: Olaf Norlis Bokhandel, 1993:39–55. Adapted by Morgan D. The industrial patient: A physical therapist's perspective. *Topics in Acute Care and Trauma Rehabilitation*. 1988;2(4):41.

Neurologic examination with periodic reevaluation of abnormal findings is an important component of any spinal examination.[48] Patients exhibiting diminished proprioception benefit from the increased sensory input water provides.[12] Problems such as loss of balance and coordination are safely yet effectively challenged in the aquatic environment. The presence of abnormal neural tension signs will affect the prospective treatment plan. For example, a patient with a positive straight leg raise test at 35 degrees should initially avoid exercises involving hip flexion with full knee extension (especially hamstring stretching). The treatment plan would thus incorporate activities involving knee flexion with hip flexion until the straight leg raise normalizes.

Evaluating the functional behavior of the spine provides guidelines for appropriate exercise prescription, movements or activities that should be avoided, and a baseline from which to measure future progress.[61] Morgan also proposes that various movements, stresses, and positions be tested in determining the patient's asymptomatic range of movement, aggravating and alleviating factors, type of loading tolerated, and the length of time or number of repetitions these maneuvers are tolerated. For example, upon examination a patient reports a slight increase in low back pain with lumbar extension that increases with repetition and is eased with flexion. Appropriate exercises in the pool would avoid extension and facilitate the abdominals and gluteals, which assists the patient in maintaining a flexed lumbar position. It is important that the clinician perform regular reassessment of the patient's condition. Any changes, subtle or dramatic, in the patient's condition may require corresponding changes in the treatment program if treatment is to be effective.

Analysis of the tests of function (mobility, strength, endurance, and coordination) and the effects of these functional measures on the patient's symptoms provides relevant information for the clinical assessment and treatment plan. Hypomobile joints can be treated by mobilization or manipulation, whereas hypermoblile joints can be protected by stabilization exercises. Likewise, soft tissue mobilization and stretching can be performed in conjunction with the therapeutic pool program. The clinician should note results of testing muscle strength and length in relation to the patient's complaint and function. The clinician should not overlook assessing endurance and coordination through functional and occupationally related tasks because the quality of movement could be poor despite the presence of normal strength.[37,61]

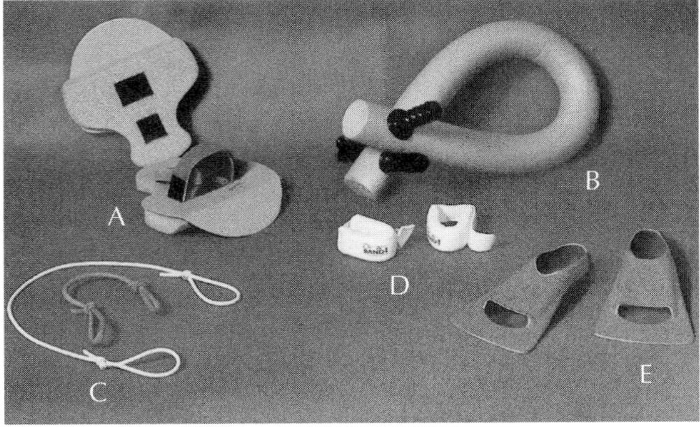

Figure 23–1. Equipment for aquatic rehabilitation. **A.** Sloggers.® **B.** Th'Horse.™ (Both A and B by AQUA-GYM, 813-960-9040.) **C.** Resistive tubing. **D.** 1 and 2-pound ankle weights. **E.** Zoomer's High Speed Training Fins (by Zoomer, 800-857-2909).

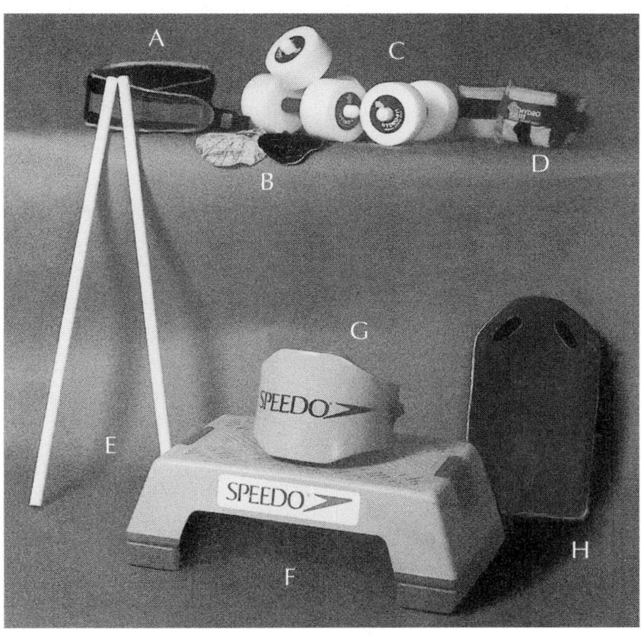

Figure 23–2. Equipment for aquatic rehabilitation. **A.** WAVE Belt.™ **B.** WAVE Webs.™ **C.** Hand Buoys.™ **D.** Buoyancy and Resistance Cuffs.™ (A to D by HYDROFIT, 800-346-7295.) **E.** PVC pipes. **F.** Aquatic Exercise Step.® **G.** Aquatic Fitness Belt. **H.** Aquatic Fitness Kickboard. (F to H by Speedo,® 213-726-1262 or 800-WET-STEP, ext. 4283.)

SCREENING AND EVALUATION OF PATIENTS FOR AQUATIC SPINAL TRAINING

The benefits of aquatic spinal training are available to a diverse patient population. Frail, deconditioned, and disabled individuals enjoy greater success and freedom of movement from using this enabling medium. Elite athletes are challenged in the water by high-intensity and sport-specific tasks that they otherwise would be unable to perform on land because of increasing joint compression and weight bearing caused by gravity.[46] Most individuals suffering from spinal pain and dysfunction, especially those sensitive to compressive spinal load and direct pressure, would be candidates for aquatic training provided they are motivated and comfortable with the aquatic environment.

Once information from the subjective and objective evaluations has been integrated and patient problems identified, the next step is to establish goals of treatment and a treatment plan. Morgan states, "Goal setting is related to, among other things, the severity of the injury, the chronicity of the problem and the functional level to which the patient must return."[61(p43)] Treatment should be aimed at correcting, compensating, or preventing the problem. Therapeutic goals for participants in an aquatic rehabilitation program include the following:[29,57,61]

Reduction of pain	Controlled weight bearing
Reduction of gait deviations	Increased relaxation
Improved mobility	Improved flexibility
Improved strength	Improved muscular and cardiovascular endurance
Improved posture	Skill simulation in a controlled environment
Improved functional activities	Increased patient responsibility for management of health care
Improved proprioceptive feedback and sensory stimulation	Control of excessive mobility (hypermobility)
Improved lumbopelvic coordination and control	
Improved coordination	

The long-term goal of aquatic rehabilitation is to progress the patient to a land-based spinal rehabilitation program. If the patient also desires to continue aquatic exercise training, the clinician can help with placement into a community-based program. Ideally, the clinician would help the patient transition to the community aquatics class by going to the class and providing modifications as needed to educate the lay instructor and the patient about safe exercises for the patient's condition.

BASIC PRINCIPLES OF AQUATIC SPINAL TRAINING

"Nothing discourages a patient faster than pain, frustration, and failure, so an overriding principle is to start with easy and painless exercises."[60(p13)] Maxims such as "No pain, no gain" can impede patient performance in spinal rehabilitation. Hislop[32] investigated the effect of pain on excitability of the central nervous system and concluded that pain can significantly interfere with muscular coordination, efficiency, and precision of activities. Furthermore, apprehension and fear could contribute to the tension, spasm, and pain that a patient experiences. Even the most effective exercise programs can fail in the absence of patient confidence, understanding, cooperation, and trust.

Some of the general considerations guiding the initial treatment plan include maintenance of lumbopelvic control, stability of the exercise, and awareness of functional sensitivities. Vollowitz[91] provides guidelines, based on functional sensitivities or functional loss, which assist in designing the exercise treatment plan for patients with low back pain. The four sensitivities include position, load, stasis, and pressure sensitivity.

Position sensitivity occurs when the patient's symptoms are worsened by specific postures and eased with other postures. Individuals who are extension-sensitive are more comfortable when the low back is positioned in flexion. They may prefer sitting to standing or walking, and may complain of increased symptoms with overhead activities or walking backward in the water. Those who are flexion-sensitive are more comfortable when the low back is positioned in extension. These individuals prefer to stand more than sit and may experience increased symptoms when they lean forward, walk forward in water, or perform activities with the arms reaching forward.

Load sensitivity occurs when symptoms are aggravated by the vertical compressive forces of gravity (standing, walking, running, sitting, coughing, and strong muscular contraction). Symptoms are eased by lying down, floating in water, applying traction to the low back, or wearing an elastic low back support. Individuals who are sensitive to load usually find relief of symptoms in the water; however, the clinician should take the time to find the patient's ideal water depth. The ideal water depth is that depth at which symptoms are eased and the patient is able to maintain balance and control of movements. Strapping 1- or 2-pound cuffs around the ankles can keep the feet in contact with the pool floor at nipple- or axillary-deep water depths. Buoyancy belts (deep water supports) can be used to decrease spinal load while exercising in shallow water. Deep water traction or exercises provide maximal unloading of the spine. Patients should be able to control their spinal position in deep water without experiencing any increase in symptoms with deep water work.

Stasis sensitivity occurs when positions or postures statically held for a period of time increase low back–related symptoms, whereas frequently changing the position provides relief. There is no position that consistently makes symptoms better or worse. The patient typically reports increased symptoms at night, upon awakening in the morning, or during any activities that involve static posture. These individuals typically find relief of symptoms while walking, running, or engaging in any dynamic, variable activity or task. Designing an exercise program for a patient who is stasis-sensitive should include frequent changes of position and activity.

Pressure sensitivity occurs when symptoms are increased by direct pressure to the low back and eased with removal of contact or pressure. Individuals with this sensitivity experience few problems with aquatic activities. A patient may complain of increased symptoms if wearing a buoyancy belt (deep water support) that encircles the waist or using equipment that causes direct pressure to the sensitive area.

The patient who demonstrates good lumbopelvic control is more stable, and the more stable the patient and the exercise, the greater the likelihood of success. Likewise, when load-sensitive patients demonstrate greater tolerance to weight bearing, exercises are performed in progressively shallower water to increase load. Exercises should start with pain-free movements in the cardinal planes, and progress to diagonal or torsional movements only after control is mastered in the cardinal planes,[60] since straight-plane movements are easier to stabilize and less likely to aggravate symptoms. Movements should also progress from gross, simple movement patterns to isolated, more complex patterns.[60] For example, a patient who is extension-sensitive would start with simple movements in the cardinal planes that would facilitate flexion via contraction of the abdominals and gluteals. Later progressions would challenge the patient to dynamically control the spine in flexion while performing more complex, independent extremity movements.

The principles and techniques of PNF can be readily adapted to exercising spinal pain patients in the aquatic environment. Janda[37] studied a group of 500 chronic low back pain patients and found that 80% showed slight but definite signs characteristic of mild cerebral dysfunction. He suggests that with low back pain there is a lack of proprioceptive stimulation from joints, muscles, skin, and other structures resulting in a poorly functioning sensorimotor system. Therefore, musculoskeletal dysfunction can impair motor regulation of the central nervous system. Janda strongly advocates the use of PNF techniques for patients suffering from low back pain and postural disorders.[37] Another study by Nelson et al[65] found PNF to be more effective than weight training in improving muscular strength and athletic performance. The superiority of PNF in improving athletic performance was felt to be due to greater specificity of training, irradiation, sensorimotor stimulation, and use of the stretch reflex. The investigators projected that athletes treated with PNF could return to preinjury levels of ability in approximately half the time it would take athletes using weight training.

Jull and Janda[37] emphasize the essential role muscles play in spinal pain. The authors propose that selective muscle tightness and weaknesses occur in predictable patterns and are related to their anatomical location and physiological function. Muscles that react to pain and pathology by overactivation and tightness are those that cross more than one joint and are postural in function. Those muscles that react by inhibition and weakening are one-joint muscles whose function involves rapid movement and that typically fatigue more quickly.[28,38] Jull and Janda stress that the initial goals of therapeutic treatment should be to regain normal length of tight muscles, which allows for a spontaneous disinhibition of the inhibited, weak muscles. This provides appropriate facilitation of weak muscles and optimal training of correct motor patterns. Table 23–3 depicts the functional division of muscle groups by tightness and weakness.

Table 23–3: Functional Division of Muscle Groups

MUSCLES PRONE TO TIGHTNESS	MUSCLES PRONE TO WEAKNESS
Gastrocsoleus	Peronei
Tibialis posterior	Tibialis anterior
Short hip adductors	Vastus medialis and lateralis
Hamstrings	Gluteus maximus, medius, and minimus
Rectus femoris	Rectus abdominis
Iliopsoas	Serratus anterior
Tensor fasciae latae	Rhomboids
Erector spinae (especially lumbar thoracolumbar, and cervical portions)	Lower portion of trapezius Short cervical flexors
Quadratus lumborum	Extensors of upper limb
Pectoralis major	
Upper portion of trapezius	
Levator scapulae	
Sternocleidomastoid	
Scalenes	
Flexors of the upper limb	

Source: Jull G, Janda V. *Muscles and motor control in low back pain.* In: Twomey L, Taylor J, eds. *Physical Therapy of the Low Back.* New York: Churchill Livingstone, 1987.

TREATMENT PLAN AND EXERCISES IN THE AQUATIC ENVIRONMENT

TREATMENT PLAN

If the patient is in the acute stage, that stage characterized by inflammation and pain, treatment is directed at reducing the inflammation and promoting healing. Immobilization is encouraged via short-term rest and supportive bracing using a lumbar corset, cervical collar, or taping of the lumbar spine if the patient is not stasis-sensitive.[61] Passive modalities such as ice, electrical stimulation, ultrasound, or various forms of heat including the warmer therapeutic pools can help relieve pain and spasm. The prudent use of manual therapy techniques such as manipulation and mobilization (accessory or physiologic passive movements) of the joints and soft tissues may accelerate healing by increasing segmental and general mobility and improving neural function.[24,44,55,63,99] Home self-treatment could include gentle isometrics of the abdominals, gluteals, and spinal extensors, use of heat and/or ice, and instruction in proper body mechanics for ADLs. If applicable, positioning, self-traction, lateral shifting, and extension exercises could also be included in the home program.[12,56,61] Morgan advocates early initiation of aerobic activity (walking, versaclimber, etc.) in order to relieve congestion of the inflamed area.[62] Water walking provides an ideal opportunity to minimize spinal load while exercising aerobically. Deep water aerobic activities such as the stepping motion with the Sloggers (similar to stair-climbing machines) provide almost complete unloading during aerobic exercise (Figure 23–3).

Figure 23–3. Use of Sloggers on the feet and wave webs on the hands creating a deep water aerobic activity similar to the stair climber or versa climber.

After the inflammation has subsided, treatment can be directed at the specific problems identified from the patient evaluation. Restrictions in joint or muscle mobility or hypermobility should continue to be addressed in conjunction with any water or land exercise therapy. If the problem involves hypermobility of the involved joint, excess movement could be controlled through passive supports such as braces, corsets, or taping. More effective treatment, however, would include instruction in the limits of the patient's functional range for posture and body mechanics and prescribing stabilization exercises.[61]

Prior to entering the pool, the patient should be taught and able to demonstrate isolated lumbopelvic ROM in various body postures including hook-lying, supine, prone, sitting, quadruped, standing, squatting against a wall, and squatting without wall support. Through exploring the range of positions of lumbar sagittal plane movement, one can find a patient's *functional position*, defined by Morgan as "the most stable and asymptomatic position of the spine for the task at hand."[60(p10)] This functional position may be a range of movement (functional range) or limited to a specific position and can vary according to body posture. For example, a patient squatting with the back against the pool wall may identify a functional range near the end range of extension, yet when walking in the pool find positions near the end range of flexion most comfortable. The patient should be capable of finding the functional range on a stable surface (on land) prior to doing so in an unstable environment (in water). It may require several land treatment sessions for the patient to demonstrate the ability to find a functional range in the various postures mentioned. It will, however, ease the transition to the wet environment, which makes lumbopelvic control more challenging because of decreased stability and limited visual feedback. Although the term *spinal stabilization* implies controlling the spine in a fixed position at all times, as it is sometimes taught, it is truly a dynamic concept requiring the clinician to constantly reassess changes in the patient's symptoms, tolerance to various activities and positions, and functional abilities.[61]

SAFETY CONSIDERATIONS

In order to provide an appropriate treatment program, the patient's initial psychological, physiological, and mechanical responses to the aquatic environment should be monitored. Potential difficulties with entering or exiting the pool would have been screened through the functional evaluation, but it is also important to note any difficulty with the task or if assistance is needed. Is there any response of fear to the water? Evaluate patient willingness to move one extremity at a time, to lift one or both legs, or to trust buoyancy. How does the patient respond to challenges to balance? The patient should demonstrate competency in recovering balance when falling forward, backwards, or sideways in shallow water. Activities in deep water require prior instruction in rolling techniques to resume desired positions and in breath control. Assessing the individual's thermal adaptation to the water is also important. With cooler temperatures of 28 to 30°C (82 to 86°F) note if the lips turn blue, the participant shivers, or other signs that more clothing or greater intensity of exercise will be required for comfort. With warmer temperatures of 31 to 37°C (87 to 98°F) observe physiological responses such as respiratory rate, skin color, sweat, and temperature for signs of heat intolerance. Heart rate, respiratory rate, and rate of perceived exertion responses should be taken for individuals with present or past history of cardiovascular or respiratory disease. Table 23–4 provides first aid procedures and prevention measures for various medical emergencies.

AQUATIC EXERCISES FOR LOW BACK DYSFUNCTION

Trial use of buoyancy enhancing devices such as deep water supports (DWS), kickboards, Th'Horse, hand buoys, etc., should be attempted to assess changes in patient symptoms and determine optimal water depth. Compressive spinal load can be reduced by hanging weights attached to a belt around the pelvis (the amount of weight depending on patient buoyancy, buoyancy-enhancing devices required, and tolerance to the traction). Strapping 1- or 2-pound weights around each ankle enhances stability and provides greater proprioceptive feedback for the less visible lower extremities. Figures 23–1 and 23–2 depict equipment and sources that can be used for aquatic spinal exercises. The optimal water depth for each patient will vary depending on patient height, body density, and distribution of adipose, amount of compressive spinal load desired, ability to control lumbopelvic position (the deeper the water, the greater the loss of stability), buoyancy-enhancing devices used, confidence, and changes in presenting signs and/or symptoms. After appropriate equipment and water depth for control of compressive spinal loading and comfort is determined, the patient is ready to explore his or her functional range while squatting against the pool wall, squatting without wall support and finally in standing with progressively increasing knee flexion (Figure 23–4). If the patient demonstrates the ability to actively preposition the spine into functional range in standing, the ability to maintain this position while walking forward, backward, and sideways can be evaluated. Progression of activities should always be preceded by assessment of the participant's ability to find and maintain his or her functional range throughout the exercise.

Aquatic programs can provide a private, supportive, low-impact environment where strength can be improved by adjusting resistance and buoyancy for optimal training levels. Repetitions and sets can be prescribed to work muscles to fatigue, and active rest (easy jogging with sculling or simply exercising the opposite muscle group) can be included to adjust intensity. Table 23–5 provides guidelines for increasing muscle strength and endurance. Upper body training includes the use of the lower body to assist in balance and thermoregulation and movement of primary upper body muscle groups targeted for muscular strengthening. Tables 23–6 and 23–7 provide intensity progressions, or variations of a movement to gradually change the level of difficulty by increasing or decreasing the workload. Table 23–6 depicts the intensity progression for upper body training. Standing in a staggered stance position (with resistance applied forward or backward) or standing in a slight squat (for resistance from side to side) helps maintain balance with resisted upper extremity activities. Table 23–7 presents the intensity progression for lower body training (Figures 23–5 to 23–7). The targeted muscle groups of the lower body act as the primary groups for muscular strengthening. Lower body training involves assistive movements of the upper body via sculling, pushing, and pulling for balance. These tables present a graduated progression of strengthening from low-intensity to high-intensity exercise.

Suggestions for exercises that can be used in aquatic rehabilitation for low back dysfunction are provided in Tables 23–8 and 23–9. Table 23–8 depicts exercises to be performed in shallow water (Figures 23–8 to 23–19), and Table 23–9 presents exercises to be performed in deep water. The exercises are presented in three levels of difficulty, with level 1 being the least difficult and level 3 being the most challenging.

Although some of these activities may also be beneficial for conditions involving the cervical and thoracic spine, the exercises presented are suggested for patients with disorders of the low back. Continued investigation of functional training and stabilization techniques involving the cervical and thoracic spine is greatly needed. With conditions involving cervical as well as lumbar dysfunction, special precautions should be taken to prevent stress on the cervical spine. Even the simple sculling movements of the upper extremities can irritate the smaller joints of the cervical spine. It is recommended that aquatic rehabilitation of individuals with cervical dysfunction be initiated carefully and progressed gradually, beginning with small-range upper extremity movements that are rhythmic and involve minimal resistance.

When necessary, various manual therapy techniques can be used in the pool. Lateral shifting and passive lumbar extension leaning into the pool wall can help correct antalgic postural deviations (Figures 23–20 and 23–21). Additional techniques for soft tissue and joint mobilization can be performed by the therapist while the patient is in the water. Figure 23–22 demonstrates the physical therapist performing a general mobilization to enhance lumbar extension with traction.

Stabilizing reversals (SR) is a PNF technique involving bidirectional static muscle contraction that can be safely used in the first level of aquatic rehabilitation.[1] The direction of force should start in cardinal planes and progress to include oblique or torsional forces as tolerated. SR can be performed while the patient squats with his or

Table 23–4: Emergency Checklist

MEDICAL CONDITION	CONCERN IN POOL VERSUS ON LAND	WHAT TO DO; HOW TO PREVENT
Insulin imbalance	In the event of insulin reaction or fainting condition, unconsciousness could lead to injury from fall or drowning.	Check for Medic Alert tags. Check on time and type of last food. Watch for signals of overexertion.
Diabetes	Feet become wet and soft; cuts are unnoticed and can become serious infections (feet are often numb).	Encourage participants to wear athletic shoes and to inspect their feet thoroughly when drying and before putting on street shoes.
Epilepsy	Reflections of the water can cause a seizure that could result in drowning. Dylantin, a drug for epileptic control, can increase the amount of water swallowed.	Check for tags. Keep an eye on individual and inform guard. Encourage individual to take medications regularly and wear sunglasses. Water is safe for a seizure if head can be supported.
Panic	Can create a startled reaction. Individual cannot move or speak because of panic. Patients may pick up feet even in standing depth, and may thrash about and exhaust themselves.	Educate participants to the environment. Know who are nonswimmers. Watch for those nearing "drop-offs." Teach balance recovery techniques.
Heart attack	Remove from the water to minimize shock. If no breathing or pulse, administer CPR.	Call EMS (911). Educate participants to recognize signs of overexertion. Encourage new participants to pace themselves. Use health release forms.
Alcohol/drugs	Temperature of the water can affect rate of absorption of some drugs. Impaired judgement may cause poor activity choices, i.e., diving into shallow end of pool.	Solicit information from participants on prescription/nonprescription drugs they are taking. Encourage abusive participants to abstain before class.
Hypothermia	Water at less than 86°F could cause some participants to become hypothermic. Watch for blue lips, shivering, and disorientation.	Encourage participants to wear T-shirt, thermal wear, and to keep hair dry (80% of heat loss is from the head). Have towels and warm clothing handy when leaving the pool. Encourage participants not to enter water until immediately before activity begins. Stretch following the exercise session.
Dehydration	Participants do not recognize sweating and loss of fluid in the water.	Encourage participants to have water containers at pool side that are accessible throughout the session.
Sunburn/blisters	Water will soften blisters, which can facilitate infections. Chorine is extremely drying to skin.	To prevent, wear T-shirt in the water. To treat, stay out of the water while blisters are large and full of fluid.
Heat exhaustion	Sunbathers and hot tub users can be victims if they stay too long and become dehydrated or overheated. They will appear sweaty, cold, and clammy.	Remove from heat source. Cool body with wet towels, etc., give sips of water as tolerated, and rest.
Heat stroke	Life-threatening emergency when body's heat releasing mechanism is overwhelmed. The patient is ill, red, hot to the touch, and not sweating.	Call 911 immediately; move to cool area, cool body quickly, using towels, water, and fans. Do not give anything to drink.
Asthma	Participant may panic with difficulty breathing. Attacks can be triggered by cold air, exercise, air pollution, and stress.	Asthmatics should warm up 15 to 30 minutes before engaging in vigorous exercise; cued to use nose breathing and keep their medication poolside. During an acute attack, call 911. The patients should be helped from the pool, positioned comfortably, reassured, and assisted in taking their medication.

Source: Adapted from Mary Sanders. *Aquatic Fitness System Instructor Training Manual.* London: Speedo International, 1993.

Figure 23–4. Exploring functional position while standing away from the pool wall. Th' Horse enhances buoyancy and traction to the the lumbar spine. The 1 and 2-pound ankle weights increase stability and LE proprioception.

Table 23–5: Guidelines for Increasing Muscle Strength and Endurance

Primary muscle groups:	Perform 8 to 25 repetitions, or until muscles begin to fatigue.
Active rest:	Easy jogging and sculling 15 to 30 seconds or work the opposite muscle group.
Repeat the sequence:	One to five sets.
Intensity:	Work at the highest level in the intensity progression (refer to Tables 23–6 and 23–7) at levels of moderate to somewhat hard. Active rest and repeat the sequence as needed.
Monitor intensity:	Perceived exertion for muscular fatigue.
Assisting muscle groups:	Enhance resistance by increasing speed and contributing to thermoregulation.

Table 23–6: Intensity Progression for Upper Body Training

INTENSITY	PROGRESSION VARIATIONS
Low	No equipment used; slowly slice hands through the water.
	No equipment used; fist or cup the hands during movements.
	Add webbed gloves and web the hands during movements to increase surface area.
	Maximize range of motion and speed with webbed gloves.
	Increase the speed of the lower body; add the step or travel through the water so resistance is increased using current forces, speed, inertia, and action/reaction for maximal resistance.
	Add other pieces of equipment to increase surface area and resistance such as hand buoys, aqua chute, or resistive tubing.
High	Increase the speed with the above equipment added.[76]

her back against the pool wall. Various pieces of equipment (hand buoys, Th' Horse, a kickboard, or dowels) can be used to help unload the spine and/or provide resistance for stabilization training. Force could be directed manually against equipment the patient holds or against the patient's shoulders, pelvis, knees, or head (if there are no cervical disorders). For example, the therapist pushes down on Th' Horse and tells the patient, "Don't let me push the horse down." The resistance provided should not overpower the patient and result in movement of Th' Horse. As the patient fully opposes the appropriate resistance, the therapist places the other hand on another area of Th' Horse and begins to build resistance in that direction. When the patient responds to the new force applied, the therapist moves a hand to apply resistance in a new direction (Figure 23–5). Smooth transition of resistance is necessary to prevent sudden movement and increasing symptoms. Although early pioneers of PNF[38,42] describe the proper resistance administered as maximal, current PNF instructors use the terms *optimal* or *appropriate* to more accurately describe the resistance provided.[1,49,74] Adler states, "The amount of resistance provided during an activity must be correct for the patient's condition and the goal of the activity."[1(p4)]

FUNCTIONAL TRAINING IN AQUATIC REHABILITATION

Aquatic rehabilitation for low back conditions should include training for functional activities. Simulating any land task can be accomplished in the water. This requires the clinician to appropriately apply the properties of water and know how to vary buoyancy and resistance in order to most effectively mimic land activities.[80]

Table 23–7: Intensity Progression for Lower Body Training

INTENSITY	PROGRESSION VARIATIONS
Low	Static partial squat position. Add stabilizing reversals or rhythmic stabilization (Figure 23–5). Add PNF patterns, exercises with dowels or tubing (Table 23–8).
	Water walk, cross-country ski, or jumping jacks with a small range of motion and slow speed.
	Neutral[a] working position with small range of motion of lower extremities and slow speed.
	Kicking using Th'Horse for support (Figure 23–6).
	Neutral working position; increase the speed and range of motion.
	Rebound[b] working position for cross-country ski, jog in place, or jumping jacks; start with small range of motion, and then gradually increase range of motion, force, and speed.
	Kicking sitting or prone on the kickboard. Add kickfins.
	Shallow water: add the step or chute. Deep water: add Sloggers.
	Slow down, and go to *suspended*[c] working position. Increase the range of motion, and then force and speed.
High	Slow down, and go to *rebound* working position. Increase the range of motion and travel through the water.[76]

[a]*Neutral position*: While still working in shallow water, the body is submerged to shoulder depth (so the lungs are submerged) and the feet lightly tap and slide along the pool bottom. As buoyancy supports the body, the range of motion of the legs is enlarged (Figure 23–7)
[b]*Rebound position*: Pressing forcefully off the bottom of the pool vertically, to increase the effects of gravity, laminar flow, water currents, turbulence, and impact.
[c]*Suspended position*: This position mimics deep water by working the completely buoyant body in a vertical position without touching the bottom. Buoyancy, speed, action/reaction, surface area, and leverage are affected differently during this working position. Sculling and synergistic arm and leg work are important for balance and coordination. Working in this position requires large increases in lower extremity range of motion and speed. It is generally recommended that patients with low back dysfunction not perform aquatic exercises in the suspended position without buoyancy equipment unless they can be performed successfully without sacrificing functional position and aggravating symptoms.[76]

Figure 23–5. Use of stabilizing reversals with the patient supported by Th'Horse while squatting against the pool wall. Resistance is provided by the physical therapist pushing against Th'Horse. The patient prevents Th'Horse from moving.

Figure 23–6. Kicking while supported by Th'Horse. The position can be varied from under the arms, handles facing forward or backward, or while sitting on Th'Horse.

Figure 23–7. Cross-country ski (LE movement only) with support of a kickboad.

Table 23–8: Aquatic Spinal Training Progression (Shallow)

EXERCISE	LEVEL 1	LEVEL 2	LEVEL 3
Squat	Against pool wall; manual stabilizing reversals (SRs): start with cardinal planes, and then add diagonal, torsional forces (Figure 23–8)	Away from pool wall; partner SR or rhythmic stabilization (RS) using elbow holds or dowel(s) (Figure 23–9)	Away from pool wall; Partner push-pull with dowel in multiple directions (Figures 23–10 and 23–11)

Figure 23–8. Stabilizing reversals through hand buoys while the patient squats against the side of the pool.

Figure 23–9. Partner rhythmic stabilization with bilateral elbow hold in staggered stance position.

Figures 23–10 and 23–11. Push-pull with dowels or PVC pipes in diagonal and straight-plane directions.

Table 23–8: (continued)

EXERCISE	LEVEL 1	LEVEL 2	LEVEL 3
Water Walk	Forward, backward, sideways; hands out of water	Increase speed; add upper extremity (UE) resistance (hands underwater)	Increase speed or run; progress UE resistance with wave webs, hand buoys, aqua chute, etc. (Figure 23–12)
Staggered stance UE exercises	Bilateral symmetrical UE movements; no equipment to add resistance to UEs	Bilateral, symmetrical UE PNF with tubing, aquatic exercise paddles, hand buoys, or wave webs (Figures 23–13 and 23–14)	Bilateral, asymmetrical PNF with tubing, aquatic exercise paddles, hand buoys, or wave webs (Figure 23–15)

Figure 23–12. Water walking or running with the Aqua Chute providing maximal resistance. Walking backward also provides a heavy workload for the abdominals, gluteals, and hamstrings.

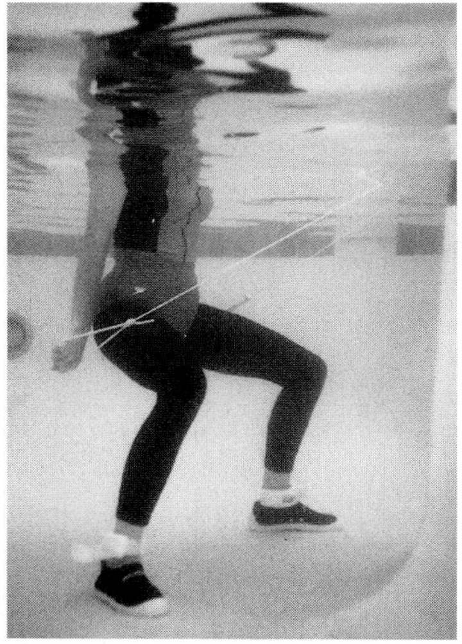

Figure 23–13. Bilateral shoulder extension, abduction, and internal rotation performed with resistive tubing. This can be performed in a static squat or staggered stance position depending on the stability required.

Figure 23–14. Bilateral shoulder extension and adduction with internal rotation using hand buoys. A staggered stance position is used for stability.

Figure 23–15. PNF chopping pattern while using hand buoy in a staggered stance position.

Table 23–8: (continued)

EXERCISE	LEVEL 1	LEVEL 2	LEVEL 3
Quadruped[12]	Prone, therapist assist mask & snorkel; alternating arm and leg movement; speed per tolerance	Prone; therapist assist mask and snorkel; simultaneous/ alternating arm and leg movement; moderate speed	Prone; no assist; mask and snorkel; deep water support (DWS); simultaneous/alternating arms and legs; moderate-fast speed or add equipment for resistance
Lower extremity PNF[a]	Standing; active hip ROM in the cardinal planes	Standing; active lower extremity (LE) patterns	Prone; manual resistance with LE patterns (Figure 23–16); standing: resistive tubing with LE patterns
Genuflexion[b]	Partial at tolerable depth	Full in shallow water or stepping down from a step (Figures 23–17 and 23–18)	Full on step and/or genuflexion in shallow water (rebound working position)

Figure 23–16. Manual resistance to right hip extension and abduction with internal rotation. The left foot pushing into the therapist's thigh is facilitating stability and irradiation. Note: Shoes are worn for photographic enhancement. PNF is optimally performed using direct manual contact with the skin.

Figure 23–17. Full genuflexion in shallow water.

Figure 23–18. Step down from the Aqua Step (pool step can be used) increases spinal load while working the quadriceps eccentrically.

Table 23–8: (continued)

EXERCISE	LEVEL 1	LEVEL 2	LEVEL 3
Squat-walk	Static squat: resisted shoulder adduction using resistive tubing with elbow fixed at 90 degrees	Squat-walk in diagonal directions; tubing stabilized against body	Squat-walk directly sideways, tubing stabilized against body (Figure 23–19)
Cross-country ski or jumping jacks[a]	Over kickboard, DWS or Th'horse; LE only (Figure 23–7)	Without buoyant support; feet sliding on pool floor; add UEs	Increase speed, rebound or jumping as tolerated; add wave webs or hand buoys

[a]Keep movements small and watch that movement occurs at the hip(s) and not the low back.
[b]Patients with a history of patellofemoral problems should limit the range of genuflexion or begin with static squats at tolerable depth. Treat patellofemoral joint and soft tissues as indicated.

Figure 23–19. Squat-walk directly sideways with resistive tubing stabilized against the body. Shoulders and hips remain parallel to the direction of movement to prevent rotation.

Figure 23–20. Lateral shift of the hips toward the pool wall to help self-correct lateral deviation.

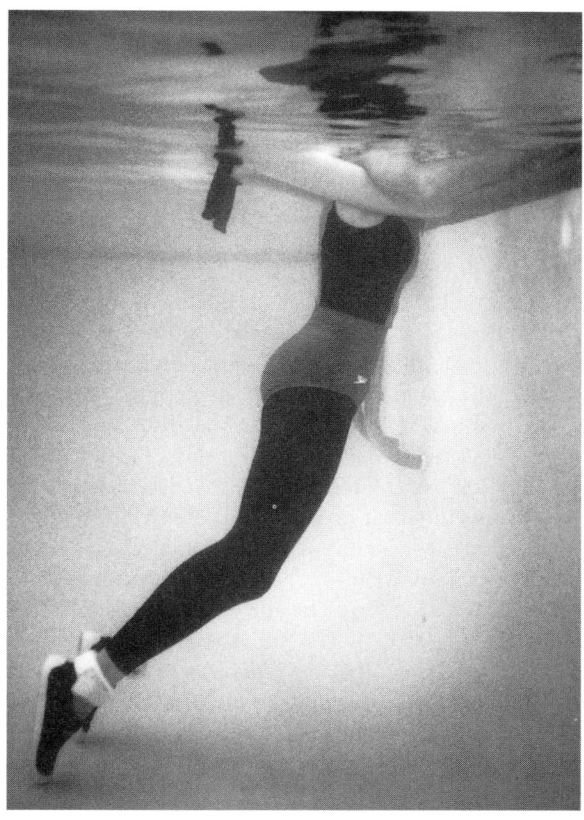

Figure 23–21. Passive lumbar extension while UEs are supported on the pool wall. Traction is enhanced by Th'Horse.

Several studies support the use of aquatic exercise to improve functional activities. Sanders et al[78] followed 61 sedentary women (mean age 75 years) through 16 weeks of water exercise. Results showed significant improvements in stride length, dynamic balance, agility, stair climbing, speed walking, sit to stand, and biceps curl for lifting. Templeton et al[87] studied 13 rheumatic disease patients as they participated in 8 weeks of aquatic therapy. Participants demonstrated significant gains in joint active range of motion and improvements in 18 activities of daily living.

The simplest functional task that can be performed in the pool is walking. Other basic ADLs such as sit-stand, balance activities, and stair climbing can safely be performed. More complex tasks, such as housecleaning, yardwork, lifting, pushing and pulling, occupational tasks and athletic activities are also effectively simulated in the water.[80] Emphasis should be placed on performing the task while maintaining functional position of the spine. The opportunity to perform these tasks in the water can also provide increased motivation, especially if pain restricts performance on land. Implementing functional training into aquatic rehabilitation programs can lead to improved body mechanics and efficiency of performing ADLs on land.

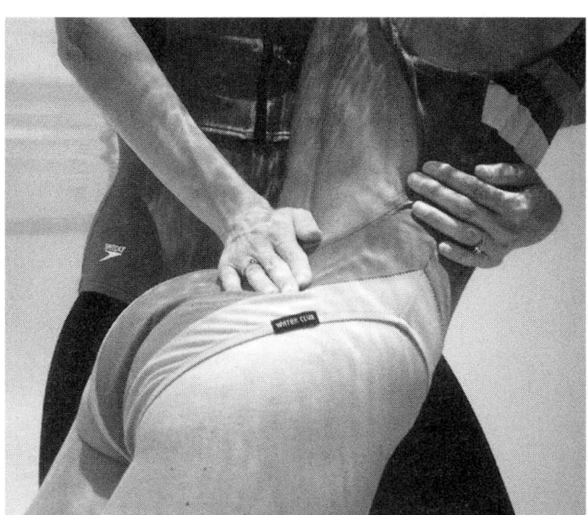

Figure 23–22. General mobilization technique to increase lumbar extension with traction. The patient can pull down with UEs against the pool wall (contract-relax), with the mobilization occurring during the relaxation phase.

DEEP WATER TRAINING

Deep water exercises (see Table 23–9) provide a non-weight-bearing environment and a vast range of levels of difficulty. There is complete loss of stability; thus spinal positional control is much more difficult. The clinician must be sure that the patient is successfully stabilizing the spine during deep water activities. With the exception of deep water traction (Figure 23–23) and level 1 kicking, it is recommended that the patient be proficient in similar level 2 shallow water exercises prior to attempting them in deep water. Any patient with limited functional range should be carefully monitored. Table 23–9 depicts some suggested deep water spinal training progressions. One special note of caution about buoyancy-enhancing devices: Not all deep water supports are created equally. It is recommended that therapists test different products and observe how they can change a patient's spinal position. The deep water support (DWS) with more foam in the back will most likely push the patient into flexion. The ideal DWS enables an individual to be supported in the functional position, allows for free UE movement, provides adequate buoyancy, can be adapted to passively position the lumbar spine into flexion or extension, and is comfortable to wear.

Figure 23–23. Passive lumbar extension while supported on Th'Horse in deep water.

Table 23–9: Aquatic Spinal Training Progression (Deep)

EXERCISE	LEVEL 1	LEVEL 2	LEVEL 3
Aerobics	DWS: water-jog or stair-climber movement	DWS: add wave webs or hand buoys	DWS: Add Sloggers Increase speed or time (Figure 23–3)
Kicking	On Aqua Gym in position of comfort; speed as tolerated (Figure 23–6)	Prone: on side of pool, mask and snorkel, staggered arm support or sitting on Aqua Gym or kickboard (Figure 23–24)	DWS: Sitting on kickboard or prone with kickboard straight below shoulders; add kickfins per tolerance (Figure 23–25)
UE Movements	DWS: legs jogging; arms sculling or doing straight-plane movements	DWS: Legs jogging; add UE PNF patterns	DWS: Legs jogging; add UE resistance via hand buoys, wave webs, or sloggers
LE Movements	DWS: arms sculling; LE active ROM in straight planes	DWS: Arms sculling; add LE PNF patterns, cross-country ski, or jumping jack leg movements	DWS: Arms sculling; add LE resistance via leg buoys or Sloggers
Marching	DWS: LE marching with hip and knee flexion to 90 degrees	DWS: prone with staggered arm support at side of pool; LE marching motion as previous	DWS: Prone with staggered arm support at side of pool; resistance to LEs added manually or via Sloggers (Figure 23–26)

Figure 23–24. Kicking with Zoomers (kickfins) while sitting on the kickboard.

Figure 23–25. Prone kicking using Zoomers (kickfins). The kickboard is positioned horizontally at 90 degrees; shoulder flexion facilitates the abdominal muscles. The neck should be in neutral position (mask and snorkel can be used).

Figure 23–26. Prone position while performing the "marching motion" with LEs. The hands hold the steps or are staggered at the side of the pool. Sloggers provide resistance for hip flexion and extension.

Athletes in training or in rehabilitation find that deep water activities provide tremendous challenges for cardiovascular, muscular, and sports-specific training.[12,26,35,46] Loss of motivation is frequently a problem with athletes during land rehabilitation because of inability to practice their sport. An athlete who is load-sensitive can still practice sport-specific skills in the water. The ability to train at higher levels in the water than on land is a major benefit of aquatic training. Levin, however, states that the motivational and psychological benefits might be the greatest advantages aquatic training provides athletes.[46]

STRETCHING

Although stretching is frequently performed in the aquatic environment, several factors make effective therapeutic stretching in water difficult, particularly with spinal patients. First of all, the lack of stability in the water presents a great challenge to patients attempting to maintain a functional spinal position. If the water temperature is cool, patients have to continue extremity movement in order to stay warm while maintaining spinal control and effectively stretching the appropriate muscle. This is a challenge for individuals *without* spinal disorders! Furthermore, many of the self-stretching techniques rely on gravity to increase the stretch. By diminishing the effects of gravity, the aquatic environment eliminates many of the safe self-stretching techniques used by patients with spinal disorders. Finally, Evjenth and Hamberg state that in order to achieve a therapeutic stretch, a stretch must be maintained for at least 15 seconds to 1 minute, or longer.[22] This is optimally accomplished on land with tables and belts stabilizing the spine and extremities so that effective stretching is accomplished without stress on the spine. With cooler water temperatures, self-stretching in the pool might be an appropriate activity for only level 3 patients with mild restrictions in muscle length. Stretching of mild restrictions in a warm, therapeutic pool is appropriate for level 2 or 3 patients. A viable option is to provide a home stretching program in which the patient is instructed to passively stabilize the spine while performing a prolonged stretch (5 to 10 minutes or longer).[59] Patients should be instructed in the PNF contract-relax technique for use in self-stretching.[1] Figures 23–27 to 23–35 depict self-stretching exercises performed in the pool by patients with minor restrictions in flexibility.

Figures 23–27 and 23–28. Two possible ways to stretch the hamstrings using the Aqua Step or Th' Horse. Use of the Aqua Step is most effective in shallow water because the greater weight bearing on the step provides greater stability.

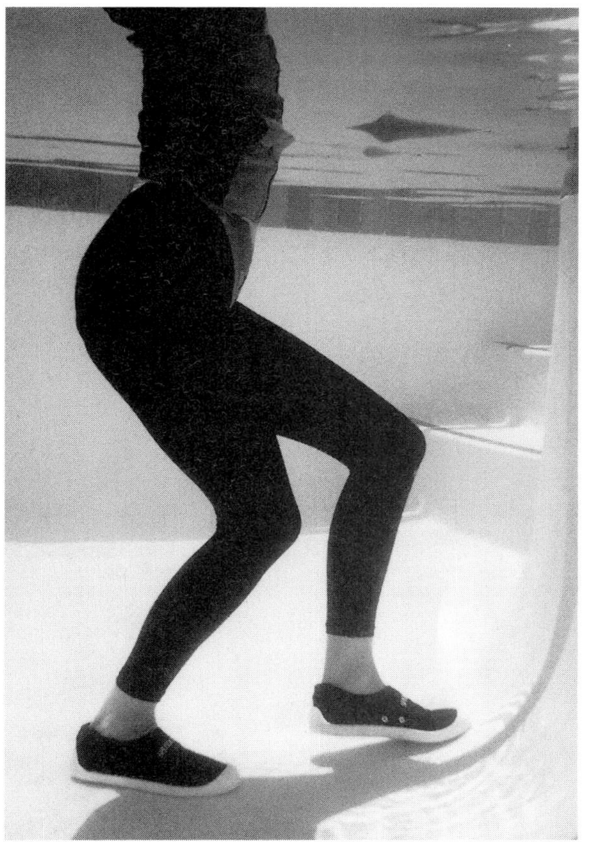

Figure 23–29. Soleus stretch using the pool wall for support.

Figure 23–30. Gastrocnemius stretch with the patient leaning into the pool wall.

Figure 23–31. Use of the buoyancy-enhancing properties of Th' Horse to increase the stretch of the quadriceps. Contract-relax can be performed by pushing the foot into Th' Horse, and then relaxing and letting Th' Horse increase the stretch. Holding onto the pool wall increases stability.

Figure 23–32. Use of the buoyancy-enhancing properties of Th' Horse to promote stretching of the adductors. Contract-relax can easily be performed in this position.

Figure 23–33. Hip flexor stretch on the pool step. The trunk is laterally flexed away from the side being stretched (not visible on photo).

Figure 23–34. Stretch for tensor fasciae latae. The hips are leaning into the pool wall to increase the stretch.

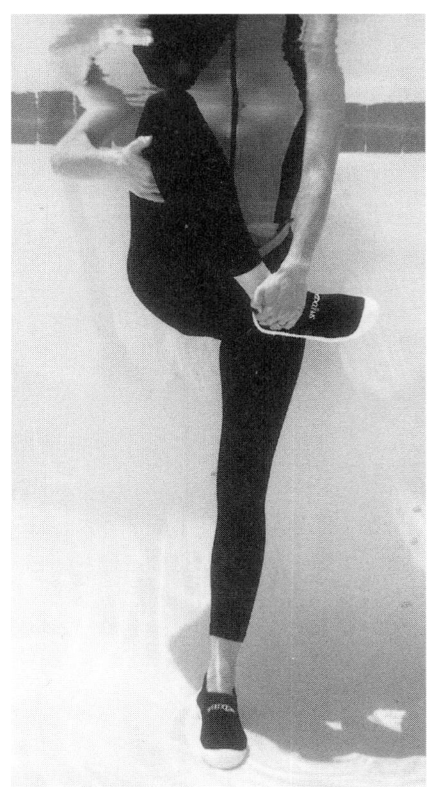

Figure 23–35. General stretch for the gluteal muscles. The right hand protects the knee joint and pulls into hip flexion. The left hand pulls on the ankle, increasing external rotation.

SUMMARY

The purpose of this chapter was to present the applications of functional training and spinal rehabilitation in the aquatic environment. The ultimate goal of spinal rehabilitation is to provide relief of symptoms, improve strength and conditioning, and motivate each patient to reach his or her physical potential. The exercises depicted in Tables 23–8 and 23–9 are suggested exercises, each to be chosen judiciously depending upon the patient's problems, goals, sensitivities, special treatment considerations, and tolerances. They are not meant to be definitive or all-inclusive, but can serve as guidelines and a catalyst for continued development in aquatic spinal rehabilitation.

REFERENCES

1. Adler S, et al. *PNF in Practice: An Illustrated Guide*. Berlin: Springer-Verlag, 1993.
2. American College of Sports Medicine. The recommended quantity and quality of exercise for developing and maintaining cardiorespiratory and muscular fitness in healthy adults. In: *The Official Position Papers of the American College of Sports Medicine*. 6th ed. Indianapolis:ACSM, 1991.
3. American Red Cross. *Swimming and Diving*. St. Louis: CV Mosby, 1992.
4. Astrand I, et al. Circulatory responses to arm exercise with different arm positions. *Journal of Applied Physiology*. 1968;25:528–532.
5. Avellini B, et al. Cardio-respiratory physical training in water and on land. *European Journal of Applied Physiology and Occupational Physiology*. 1983;53:255–263.
6. Barretta R. Physiological training adaptations to a 14 week deep water exercise program. Unpublished dissertation. University of New Mexico, Albuquerque, 1993.
7. Bates A, Hanson HH. *Aquatic Exercise Therapy*. Westbank, BC, Canada: A. Bates and N. Hanson, 1992.
8. Beasley B. Prescription pointers on aquatic exercise. *Sports Medicine Digest*. 1989;11(1):1–13.
9. Brennan B, et al. Gains in aquarunning peak oxygen consumption after eight weeks of aquarun training. *Medicine and Science in Sports and Exercise*. 1992;24(5):S23.
10. Butler D. *Mobilization of the Nervous System*. Melbourne: Churchill Livingstone, 1991.
11. Cassady S, Nielsen D. Cardiorespiratory responses of healthy subjects to calisthenics performed on land versus in water. *Physical Therapy*. 1992;72(7):62/532–68/538.
12. Cole A, et al. Lumbar spine aquatic rehabilitation: A sportsmedicine approach. In: *Handbook of Pain Management*. 2nd ed. Baltimore: Williams & Wilkins, 1994:386–400.
12a. Costill D. Energy requirements during exercise in the water. *Journal of Sports Medicine*. 1971;11:87–92.
13. Craig A, Dvorak M. Comparison of exercise in air and in water of different temperatures. *Medicine and Science in Sports and Exercise*. 1969;1(3):124–130.
14. Craig A, Dvorak M. Thermal regulation of man during water immersion. *Journal of Applied Physiology*. 1968;25:23–35.
15. Cyriax J. *Textbook of Orthopaedic Medicine*. 8th ed. London: Bailliere Tindall, 1982.
16. Duffield M. *Exercise in Water*. London: Bailliere Tindall, 1976.
17. Ebbeling C, et al. Comparison between palpated heart rates and the heart rates observed using the polar favor heart rate monitor during aerobics exercise class. Exercise Physiology and Nutrition Laboratory, University of Massachusetts Medical School (unpublished study), 1991.
18. Edwards B. Clinical assessment: The use of combined movements in assessment and treatment. In: Twomey L, Taylor J, *Physical Therapy of the Low Back*. New York: Churchill Livingstone, 1987:175–197.
19. Evans B, et al. Metabolic and circulatory responses to walking and jogging in water. *Research Quarterly*. 1978;49:442–449.
20. Evjenth O, Hamberg J. *Muscle Stretching in Manual Therapy*, vol. 1. Alfta, Sweden: Alfta Rehab Forlag, 1984.
21. Evjenth O, Hamberg J. *Muscle Stretching in Manual Therapy*, vol. 2. Alfta, Sweden: Alfta Rehab Forlag, 1984.
22. Evjenth O, Hamberg J. *Autostretching: The Complete Manual of Specific Stretching*. Alfta, Sweden: Alfta Rehab Forlag, 1989.
23. Fawcett C. Principles of aquatic rehabilitation: A new look at hydrotherapy. *Sports Medicine Update*. 1992;7(2):6–9.
24. Frank C, et al. Physiological and therapeutic value of passive joint motion. *Clinical Orthopedics and Related Research*. 1984;185:113–125.
25. Gleim G, Nicholas J. Metabolic costs and heart rate responses to treadmill walking in different depths and temperatures. *American Journal of Sports Medicine*. 1989;17:248–252.

26. Grace K. Hydrodynamics: Rehabilitation of running injuries. *Topics in Acute Care and Trauma Rehabilitation*. 1986;1(2):79–86.
27. Graham T. Thermal, metabolic, and cardiovascular changes in men and women during cold stress. *Medicine and Science in Sports and Exercise*. 1988;20(5):S185–S191.
28. Grieve G. *Common Vertebral Joint Problems*. New York: Churchill Livingstone, 1981.
29. Harralson K. Therapeutic pool programs. *Clinical Management*. 1985;5(2):10–12.
30. Harrison R. Tolerance of pool therapy by ankylosing spondylitis patients with low vital capacities. *Physiotherapy*. 1981;67(10):296–297.
31. Heberlein T, et al. The metabolic cost of high impact aerobics and hydro-aerobic exercise in middle aged females. *Medicine and Science in Sports and Exercise*. 1987;19:2.
32. Hislop H. Pain and exercise. *Physical Therapy Review*. 1960;40(2):98–106.
33. Hoeger W, et al. A comparison of selected training responses to water aerobics and low impact aerobic dance. *National Aquatics Journal*. Winter 1993;13–16.
34. Hoeger W, et al. Comparison of maximal VO2, HR and RPE between treadmill running and water aerobics. *Medicine and Science in Sports and Exercise*. 1992;24(5):S96.
35. Hughes D. Aquatic therapy in the management of low back dysfunction. *Sports Medicine Update*. 1992;7(2):10–15.
36. Johnson B, et al. Comparison of oxygen uptake and heart rate during exercises on land and in the water. *Physical Therapy*. 1977;57(3):273–278.
37. Jull G, Janda V. Muscles and motor control in low back pain: Assessment and management. In: Twomey L, Taylor J, eds. *Physical Therapy of the Low Back*. New York: Churchill Livingstone, 1987:253–278.
38. Kabat H. Central facilitation: The basis of treatment of paralysis. *Permanente Foundation Medical Bulletin* X 1952;(1–4):190–204.
39. Kaltenborn F, et al. *The Spine: Basic Evaluation and Mobilization Techniques*. 2nd ed. Oslo: Olaf Norlis Bokhandel., 1993.
40. Kennedy C. Water Fitness Research Forum. Presented at IDEA International Association of Fitness Professionals World Conference. Las Vegas, June 1994.
41. Kennedy C, et al. The influence of music tempo and water depth on heart rate response to aqua aerobics. Paper presented at IDEA Foundation International Symposium on the Medical and Scientific Aspects of Aerobic Dance. San Diego, October 1989.
42. Knott M, Voss D. *Proprioceptive Neuromuscular Facilitation*. 2nd ed. New York: Harper & Row, 1968.
43. Kolb M. Principles of underwater exercise. *Physical Therapy Review*. 1957;37(6):361–365.
44. Korr IM. Neurochemical and neurotrophic consequences of nerve deformation. In: Glasgow EF, et al, eds. *Aspects of Manipulative Therapy*. Melbourne: Churchill Livingstone, 1984:64–71.
45. Langridge J, Phillips D. Group hydrotherapy exercises for chronic back pain sufferers. *Physiotherapy*. 1988;74(6):269–273.
46. Levin S. Aquatic therapy: A splashing success for arthritis and injury rehabilitation. *The Physician and Sportsmedicine*. 1991;19(10):119–126.
47. Lowman C, Roen S. *Underwater Therapy*. Los Angeles: Los Angeles Orthopaedic Foundation, 1961.
48. Maitland G. *Vertebral Manipulation*. 5th ed. London: Butterworth, 1986.
49. Mangold M. Vallejo six-month clinical residency in proprioceptive neuromuscular facilitation (course notes). Kaiser Foundation Rehabilitation Center, Vallejo, CA. December–June, 1986.
50. Manniche C, et al. Clinical trial of intensive muscle training for chronic LBP. *Lancet*. 1988;12:1473–1476.
51. Matley K. The subjective evaluation. Paper presented at Kaiser Hospital inservice program. Sacramento, CA. 1988.
52. Mayer T, et al. A prospective two-year study of functional restoration in industrial low back injury: An objective assessment procedure. *Journal of the American Medical Association*. 1987;258(13):1763–1767.
53. McArdle W, et al. Metabolic and cardiovascular adjustment to work in air and water at 18, 25, and 33°C. *Journal of Applied Physiology*. 1976;40:85–90.
54. McArdle W, et al. *Exercise Physiology, Energy, Nutrition, and Human Performance*. 3rd ed. Philadelphia: Lea & Febiger, 1991.
55. McGonigle T, Matley K. Soft tissue treatment and muscle stretching. *Journal of Manual and Manipulative Therapy*. 1994;2(2):55–62.
56. McKenzie R. *The Lumbar Spine: Mechanical Diagnosis and Therapy*. Lower Hutt, Australia: Spinal Publications, 1981.
57. McNeal R. Aquatic therapy for patients with rheumatic disease. *Rheumatic Disease Clinics of North America*. 1990;16(4):915–929.

58. Michaud T. Aquarun training and changes in treadmill running, maximal oxygen consumption. *Medicine and Science in Sports and Exercise*. 1992;24(5):S23.
59. Moore M, et al. Course notes from the Folsom Physical Therapy Year-Long Orthopedic Manual Therapy Program. Folsom, CA, 1988.
60. Morgan D. Concepts in functional training and postural stabilization for the low-back-injured. *Topics in Acute Care and Trauma Rehabilitation*. 1988;2(4):8–17.
61. Morgan D. The industrial back patient: A physical therapist's perspective. *Topics in Acute Care and Trauma Rehabilitation*. 1988;2(4):38–46.
62. Morgan D. Balls, balances, cylinders, etc.: The use of unstable surfaces and other special rehabilitation techniques (course notes). Folsom Physical Therapy, Mill Valley, CA, February, 1994.
63. Morgan D. Principles of soft tissue treatment. *Journal of Manual and Manipulative Therapy*. 1994;2(2):63–65.
64. Nachemson A, Elfstrom G. Intravital dynamic pressure measurements in lumbar discs. *Scandinavian Journal of Rehabilitation Medicine*. 1970;2 (Suppl)(1):5–38.
65. Nelson A, et al. Proprioceptive neuromuscular facilitation vs. weight training for enhancement of muscular strength and athletic performance. *Journal of Orthopedic and Sports Physical Therapy*. 1986;7(5):250–253.
66. Paris S. Mobilization of the spine. *Physical Therapy*. 1979;59(8):988–994.
67. Prins J, et al. Effects of aquatic exercise training in persons with poliomyelitis disability. *Sports Medicine, Training and Rehabilitation*. 1994;5:1–11.
68. Rennie D. Tissue heat transfer in water: Lessons from the Korean diver. *Medicine and Science in Sports and Exercise*. 1988;20(5):S177–S183.
69. Rippee N, Sanders M. A clear view of water fitness research. *IDEA Today*. 1994;August:49–60.
70. Ritchie S, Hopkins W. The intensity of deep water running. *International Journal of Sports Medicine*. 1991;12:27–29.
71. Ruoti R, et al. The effects of nonswimming water exercise on older adults. *The Journal of Orthopedic and Sports Physical Therapy*. 1994;19(3):140–145.
72. Saal J. Rehabilitation of football players with lumbar spine injury (part 2 of 2). *Physician and Sportsmedicine*. 1988;16(10):117–125.
73. Saal, J, Saal J. Nonoperative treatment of herniated lumbar intervertebral disc with radiculopathy: An outcome study. *Spine*. 1989;14(4):431–437.
74. Saliba V, et al. Proprioceptive neuromuscular facilitation. In: *Rational Manual Therapies*, Basmajian J, Nyberg R. eds. Baltimore: Williams & Wilkins, 1994:243–284.
75. Sanders M. Selected physiological training adaptations during a water fitness program called Wave Aerobics. Master's thesis, University of Nevada, Reno, 1993.
76. Sanders M. *The Aquatic Fitness System Instructor Training Manual*. London: Speedo International, 1993.
77. Sanders M. *The Art and Science of Wave Aerobics*. Stow, Ohio: Fitness Wholesale, 1993.
78. Sanders M, Constantino N, Rippee N. A comparison of results of functional water training on field and laboratory measures in older women (Abstract). *Medicine and Science in Sports and Exercise*. 1997;29(5).
79. Sanders M, Feroah A. Biomechanical analysis of a water fitness movement using the Ariel Performance Computer System (unpublished data). University of Nevada, Reno, 1993.
80. Sanders M, Maloney-Hills S. Aquatic exercise for better living on land. *ACSM's Health and Fitness Journal*. 1998;2(3):16–23.
81. Sanders M, Rippee N. Specificity of training and deep water workout. In: *Speedo's Aquatic Fitness System Video Course*. London: Speedo International, 1994.
82. Shephard R. Tests of maximal oxygen uptake: A critical review. *Sports Medicine*. 1984;7:77–80.
83. Smit T, Harrison R. Hydrotherapy and chronic lower back pain: A pilot study. *Australian Journal of Physiotherapy*. 1991;37(4):229–234.
84. Stevenson T, et al. A comparison of land and water exercise programs for older individuals. *Medicine and Science in Sports and Exercise*. 1988;S 537.
85. Stoddard A. *Manual of Osteopathic Practice*. London: Hutchinson & Co, 1983.
86. Svedenhag J, Deger J. Running on land and in water: Comparative exercise physiology. *Medicine and Science in Sports and Exercise*. 1992;24:1155–1160.
87. Templeton M, et al. Effects of aquatic therapy on joint flexibility and functional ability in subjects with rheumatic disease. *Journal of Orthopedic and Sports Physical Therapy*. 1996;23(6):376–381.
88. Thomas D, Long K. Generalizability of deepwater exerciser blood pressure. *Research Quarterly for Exercise and Sport*. 1994;65S:A–30.
89. Torrey D, et al. Training the patient with low back dysfunction (course notes), Folsom Physical Therapy, Folsom, CA. April, 1988.

90. Town G, Bradley S. Maximal metabolic responses of deep and shallow water running in trained runners. *Medicine and Science in Sports and Exercise*. 1991;23(2):238–241.
91. Vollowitz E. Furniture prescription for the conservative management of low back pain. *Topics in Acute Care and Trauma Rehabilitation*. 1988;2(4):18–37.
92. Waddell G. A new clinical model for the treatment of low back pain. *Spine*. 1987;12(7):632–644.
93. White A, Panjabi M. *Clinical Biomechanics of the Spine*. Philadelphia: JB Lippincott, 1978.
94. Whitley J, Schoene L. Comparison of heart rate responses; Water walking versus treadmill walking. *Physical Therapy*. 1987;67(10):1501–1504.
95. Wilder R, Brennan D. Physiological responses to deep water running in athletes. *Sports Medicine*. 1993;16(6):374–380.
96. Wilder R, et al. A standard measure for exercise prescription for aqua running. *American Journal of Sports Medicine*. 1993;21(1):45–48.
97. Williams C. THR vs. RPE: The debate over monitoring exercise intensity. *IDEA Today*. 1991;April:36–42.
98. Woods D. Rehabilitation aquatics for low back injury: Functional gains or pain reduction? *Clinical Kinesiology*. 1989;43(4):96–103.
99. Wyke B, Polacek P. Articular neurology: The present position. *Journal of Bone and Joint Surgery*. 1975;57:401.

CHAPTER 24

Selecting Effective, Safe Exercise for Older Adults

Do's, Don'ts, and Maybe's Related to the Spine

ANN P. HOOKE, MA

INTRODUCTION

Although the basic principles of exercise (intensity, frequency, duration, overload, and specificity) apply to older adults as to younger adults, the goals of exercise change with age. The pragmatic functional needs of daily living increasingly dominate an older person's life as he or she strives to maintain social, emotional, and physical independence.[6] However, many of our common exercises have been developed to improve sport performance, physical fitness, or physical appearance—needs that are often of secondary importance to older people. To meet the needs of this population, selected exercises should pass the test of being functionally relevant, effective, and well tolerated by the client.

Exercises that are functionally relevant address the need of older adults to: (1) retain locomotor mobility; (2) retain the energy, strength, and joint mobility to perform activities of daily living; (3) reduce the incidence of incontinence; (4) reduce the incidence and severity of injuries related to falls; (5) reduce the severity of activity limitations related to chronic illness and disability; (6) retain the ability to function effectively in an emergency; and (7) maintain their positive self-concept through all the changes (of roles, income, self-image, and abilities) and losses that impact their lives.[10,14]

Coping with major changes and losses reduces one's ability to adapt to new situations; for example, requesting a person to regularly perform an unfamiliar exercise. Exercise compliance is increased when the exercise prescription is assimilated into the individual's total life experience by addressing functional, social, emotional, cognitive, and physical needs.[9] Because fluid and pain-free movements of the spine are essential for functional independence, relating preventive and rehabilitative forms of exercise to this independence is more effective than relating them simply to a specific physical outcome such as recovery from a specific injury or weight loss.[6]

INTEGRATION OF DATA FROM CLINICAL TRIALS AND PRACTICAL EXPERIENCE TO ADDRESS PROGRAM DESIGN

There is a growing body of research that supports the efficacy and effectiveness of increased levels of physical activity among the older adult population. For a review of the literature, the reader is referred to Shephard,[16] Smith and Gilligan,[18] Spirduso and Eckert,[19] and Chandler and Hadley.[2] Although there seems to be a growing consensus that increased levels of activity are beneficial, there is still widespread discussion regarding the appropriate mode, intensity, duration, and frequency of activity. Most of the clinical trials involve either a frail and very sedentary population in a managed care setting, or a healthy active population willing to come to a highly structured program in a hospital or university fitness setting. As a result, test programs are often very rigorous, or very modified. Meanwhile, the bulk of the older population falls between these two extremes of dependence and independence.

It should be assumed that in the general older population there are not only wide variations in levels of current physical activity participation and in physical health and function, but there is also a lifetime experience of activity or inactivity. In our highly competitive culture, the nonathlete (and silent majority) often chooses inactivity over failure. These are important factors to consider in developing exercise programs.[4] Many older adults have had little or no prior experience with even the most common activities and exercises. Patient, respectful, supportive education is critical. Opportunities to learn common recreational activities (such as swimming, bicycling, dancing, and games) or to learn common exercises and fitness activities through physical education programs were not available for some men and most women born before 1930. For these reasons, compliance to exercise programs is most successful when a program is informative, safe, effective, and enjoyable.[8] Program preference ranges from a very structured medically supervised program with quantitative goals (using METS, heart rates, rates of perceived exertion) to unstructured walking programs or to group physical activities that are primarily recreational and social in nature. As older adults often prefer water to land exercise, it is also important to provide water programs whenever possible.[17]

It may be most practical to provide this wide range of programs[3] through community agencies as YMCAs; senior centers; and community health, education, or recreation centers. Probably the largest single agency delivering land and water physical activity programs to older adults in the United States is the YMCA. In compiling a resource manual for administrators and leaders of older adult programs, the experience and editorial comments of teaching and administrative staff from many YMCAs was considered.[8] Although experience from clinical trials is useful, it is still quite limited. The practical experience of exercise instructors working with the general older population in these community settings is probably the best source of information about programs and specific exercises that are safe, effective, and enjoyable.

PREVENTIVE AND REHABILITATIVE EXERCISES FOR THE SPINE

Selecting exercises for older adults from the standard list of preventive and rehabilitative movements demands specific modifications of movement pace and movement range of motion. These modifications are unique to this population because their physical body shape and their age-related physical changes demand it. Older adults are wisely skeptical if the exercise prescription does not account for slower reaction and movement times, for increased difficulty with balance, for the reduced range of joint motion and reduced energy levels, and for the common increase in midsection size and decrease in length of the spine. The decline in body sense or perceptual awareness also dictates that exercises are more effective if positions are selected that assist the subject in isolating the requested movement from other movements.

The effectiveness of exercises can be improved if correct breathing patterns are included in exercise training. Exhalation should occur during any movement in which the spine is flexed, or in which there is a strong muscle contraction. Conversely, inhalation should occur during movements in which the spine is extended. Patterns of breath holding should be corrected. These patterns are most likely to occur while doing static stretches, balance exercises, movements involving strong contractions, spinal abduction exercises, or movements which challenge coordination. Help clients identify specific movements that trigger their individual breath-holding patterns so that the client can learn to cue himself or herself to breathe through the movement.

The following discussion of exercises is categorized according to purpose (joint mobility and muscle flexibility, and muscular strength and endurance) and by location (cervical, thoracic, and lumbar regions of the spine).

EXERCISES RELATED TO JOINT MOBILITY AND MUSCLE FLEXIBILITY

Exercises related to joint mobility and muscle flexibility are done with a slow tempo in controlled, consciously directed movements. Often the older adult will unconsciously introduce extraneous movements to these exercises. Simple, clear demonstrations, verbal instructions, corrective hands-on manipulation when appropriate, and mirrors are useful aids to correct these problems.

In American culture, there are strong inhibitions about many movements involving the spine. Yet, mechanically efficient movement demands strong, flexible back muscles and joints. Older adults are very happy to discover that basic conditioning exercises reduce their back pain and greatly improve their ability to perform demanding activities. They appreciate learning the following good movement practices. Injuries will be reduced if they eliminate ballistic movements. Stretching will be more effective if, initially, positions are not held longer than 15 seconds. When an older adult starts a stretching program, stretches held longer than 15 seconds often cause joint pain or muscle tiring with resultant compensatory movements that reduce the effectiveness of the particular stretch. With time and regular practice, stretching times should be increased to 30 seconds. Slower movement tempos will also give clients time to consciously feel the movement.[8(p122)]

Cervical Region

These exercises are most effectively done seated in a chair or in a standing position.

Cervical abduction-adduction

The subject is asked to draw the ear toward the shoulder and feel the stretch along the side of the neck. A common error is to add a rotational component such that the nose "points" diagonally downward toward the floor or upward toward the ceiling, instead of "pointing" straight ahead.

Cervical flexion-extension

The subject is asked to close the mouth, to tuck the chin in, to lengthen the back of the neck (flexion), and then to lift the chin slightly above horizontal while keeping a "long" neck (extension). Common errors are to drop the head forward without drawing the chin in (rotating around the horizontal axis), or to sag or drop the head back without extending through the neck. An extreme full neck extension may pinch the blood supply and cause dizziness, especially if the neck is sagging.

Cervical rotation

The subject is asked to turn the head to the right and then to the left, keeping the chin level. Dizziness is reduced if the subject is encouraged to pause and focus on a point at eye level straight ahead between the side-to-side turns. Both joint noise (sounding like sand or gravel in the neck joints) and pain at the outer limit of motion are common. Generally the noise is harmless and painless. However, the movement should be kept within a range that is comfortable. A common error is to add rotation of the shoulders and lower spine. Although this is harmless, the exercise is more effective if the movement is isolated to the cervical region.

Cervical horizontal flexion-extension

The subject is asked to keep the chin level and draw the head back (horizontal extension), and to return the head to the neutral position (horizontal flexion). This exercise counteracts the common postural problem of allowing the head to sag forward. The important part of this exercise is horizontal extension and not horizontal flexion.

Thoracic Region

These exercises are most effectively done seated in a chair or in a standing position near a wall or other vertical support.

Thoracic abduction-adduction

To perform abduction-adduction exercises, the weight of the upper body needs to be supported to reduce strain on the trunk muscles. Sitting in a chair, the subject is asked to place the feet and knees widely apart, and place hands on top of the thighs. In the standing position, the subject is asked to stand sideways to a vertical support such as a wall and place the inside hand on the wall at heart level. As an alternative, some short people may be able to use the back of a chair for support without being forced to lean forward as taller people must do, resulting in strain on the back. The subject is then asked to lift (abduct) one arm up and over the head with the palm facing the body midline and feel the stretch in the rib cage area. A common error is to add a rotational component, reducing the effectiveness of the isolated abduction movement. Hearing aide buzzing is reduced if the subject is asked to hold the arm slightly in front of or in back of the ear.

Thoracic extension

The subject is asked to sit or stand tall and to arch the upper spine by squeezing the elbows toward each other behind the back. A variation of this exercise is to ask the subject to hold the hips and lower spine in a stable position, and to gently press the chest forward and the shoulders and arms back in a slow controlled movement, feeling the extension in the thoracic spine.

Thoracic flexion

The subject is asked to sit or stand tall and round the upper spine by touching the elbows in front of the body. Many older adults will also feel a stretch in this region of the spine if they are asked to sit with feet and knees apart and to support the upper body weight by placing one hand on the thigh and by slowly reaching toward the floor with the other hand.

Thoracic rotation

This exercise is most effective if the subject is sitting in a chair holding the hips and lower spine in a stable position. The subject is asked to place the fingers on the shoulder tips, and then to slowly turn the shoulders and head to one side as far as comfortably possible.

Lumbar Region

These exercises have variations appropriate to different positions: standing, seated on the floor or in a chair, on hands and knees, and supine and prone lying.

Lumbar abduction-adduction

In a standing position, the subject is asked to place the feet apart, bend both the hips and knees slightly, and "wag" the hips from side to side. A variation of this exercise may be done in a "hands and knees" position (on a well-padded surface) and the subject is asked to slowly "wag the tail." A second abduction/adduction exercise is to crawl, slowly, on padded surface, taking "large steps" with the hands and knees and exaggerating the hip movements. A third abduction/adduction exercise is particularly suited to wheelchair subjects. Sitting deep in the chair, the subject is asked to lift and lower one "seat" and then the other "seat," without leaning the upper body side to side. Finally, supported side bends, as described above under the thoracic group, may also provide a moderate stretch to the lumbar spine and associated soft tissue structures.

Lumbar flexion-extension

These are standing exercises in which the leg and lumbar spine are flexed (high knee lifts) or extended (low leg extension lifts) (Figure 24–1) or in which flexion and extension are combined with abduction, as in slow controlled hip circles with the hip and knee joints slightly flexed. Hip circles may also be done effectively in the hands and knees position on a well-padded surface. Subjects may find it acceptable to do controlled "pelvic thrusts" in a standing position, if the movement is combined with arm movements completing the image of curling in (flexion) and arching or opening out (extension) (Figure 24–2).In the chair sitting version of this exercise, the subject is asked to first feel the "sitz" bones on the chair. Then by arching the low spine, the subject can feel the pelvis tipping forward. By rounding the low spine, the subject can feel the pelvis tipping backward, and feel the pressure on the sitz bones roll to a different position.

Sitting on the floor, lumbar flexion is achieved by first sitting tall with feet a bit apart, and toes pointing straight up, and then by folding the arms, leaning forward from the hips (not the shoulders), and holding this flexed position in a static stretch. This exercise is not recommended if a client is unable to start by sitting with the spine perpendicular to floor unaided by hand support (usually due to poor hamstring flexibility).

Lying supine on a padded surface, the standard pelvic tilt exercise is very effective (flexing and extending the lower spine). The subject should be trained to support the spine by deliberately contracting the low back and seat muscles as the pelvis is tipped and/or raised from the mat (lumbar extension), and to contract the abdominal muscles combined with forced exhalation as the spine is lowered and pressed into the mat (lumbar flexion).[15] These pelvic lifts are also a moderately effective stretching exercise for the quadriceps muscles in the lumbar extension position. The quadriceps are particularly difficult muscles for older adults to stretch safely without causing joint pain. Tight quadriceps muscles exaggerate hip flexion and reduce the ability of the subject to maintain a full upright posture. This postural deviation places excessive stress on the lum-

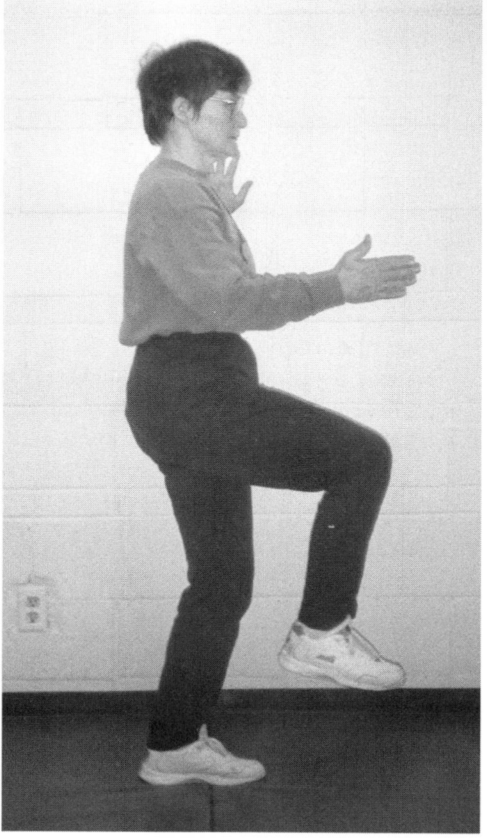

Figure 24–1. Lumbar flexion-extension exercise.

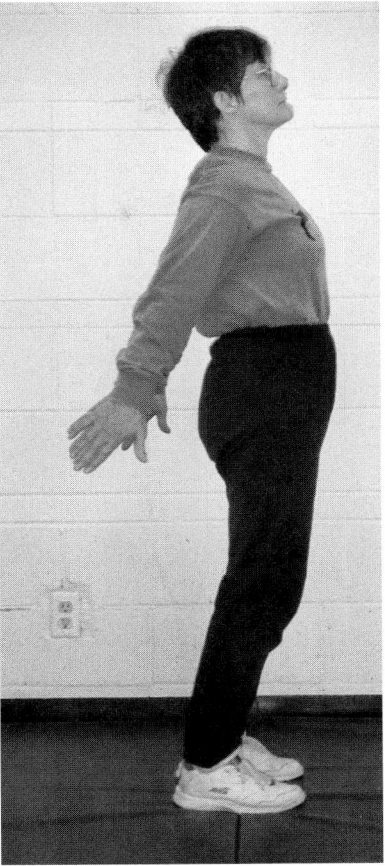

Figure 24–2. Lumbar flexion-extension exercise.

bar spine and makes standard quadriceps stretching exercises nearly impossible for many older adults.

A first alternative supine lumbar extension exercise starts from a bent knee position. The subject places his or her hands under one knee, draws the knee toward the shoulder, and slowing extends the opposite leg out along the floor pressing through the heel. As the stretch is held, the subject will be able to continuously draw the knee closer and closer toward the shoulder, increasing the stretch. To shift to the other side, the legs should be brought to the start position with knees bent and feet on floor to keep the pelvis in a neutral position.

A second alternative supine lumbar extension exercise starts with one leg (left) bent with the foot on the floor and the other leg (right) extended along the floor pressing through the heel, keeping the pelvis in a neutral position. The (left) arm lifts and reaches back over the head, keeping the hand turned so that the (left) thumb is pointing toward the floor. The subject is asked to consciously stretch from the (right) heel, through the pelvis and shoulder to the extended (left) arm. This exercise is particularly beneficial for subjects with scoliosis.

Lying prone on a padded surface, the subject is asked to perform a low chest lift by resting on the elbows (lower arms remain on mat) to support the upper body weight, keeping the head in line with the spine to avoid cervical hyperextension, and keeping the lift low, controlled, and in a comfortable range. Subjects with marked lumbar lordosis should not do this exercise.

Lumbar rotation

This exercise should be done by fixing the shoulder position and rotating the lumbar spine and hips or by fixing the hips and rotating the lumbar spine and shoulders. There are numerous possibilities using standing, chair, or floor sitting positions. Lying supine on a padded surface, the most effective lumbar rotation exercise is done by placing the legs together with the knees bent, and by supporting the spine by spreading the arms out to the side, palms down. From this start position, the subject is then asked to slowly lower the bent legs to one side, letting the legs and feet relax toward the floor, and to turn the head to look away from that side. To protect the back while shifting to the other side, the subject should be asked to bring one leg at a time back to the center start position, and to use abdominal muscles to support the movement.

Table 24–1 summarizes the exercises related to joint mobility and flexibility.

Table 24–1: Joint Mobility and Flexibility Exercises

LOCATION AND AXIS OF MOVEMENT	EXERCISE	COMMON ERRORS
Cervical Region		
Abduction/adduction	Draw ear toward shoulder	Add rotation
Flexion/extension	Tip head forward, tuck chin Tip head back, look up	Head and neck sag forward or backward
Rotation	Turn head to right and left	Chin drops; shoulder or spine rotation added
Horizontal flexion	Pull head back (chin level)	Lift or drop chin
Thoracic Region		
Abduction/adduction	Side bend (from low spine)	Bend from waist; rotation added; upper body weight unsupported
Extension	Arch upper back (inhale)	Hold breath
Flexion	Elbow touch in front of chest (exhale)	
Rotation	"Shoulder" turn	Add rotation of lower spine
Lumbar Region		
Abduction/adduction	Hip "wags", hip "circles", crawling; alternate "seat" lifts	Move from ankles in standing position
	Lateral legs lifts	Fail to abduct lumbar spine; outwardly rotate leg
Flexion/extension	Leg flexion/extension	Ballistic swing added
	Pelvic tilt/tuck	Cervical flexion added
	Sitting toe reach	Hold breath; add ballistic bounce; add thoracic and/or cervical flexion
	Prone chest lift	Lift too high; lock elbows; hyperextend cervical spine
Rotation	Supine bent knee drop to side	Extend leg(s) straining back
	Seated lumbar rotation	Low back rounded

EXERCISES RELATED TO MUSCLE STRENGTH AND ENDURANCE

The current American College of Sports Medicine (ACSM) guidelines for strength development among older adults is to perform dynamic, low-weight exercises 2 to 3 times per week, doing 8 to 12 repetitions of a given exercise in 2 or 3 sets. It is particularly important to train older adults to exhale on effort to prevent a marked increase in systemic arterial blood pressure and to avoid the Valsalva maneuver to prevent drops in venous blood return and resultant drops in blood flow to the heart and brain.[1,11]

Given that many older adults start an exercise program from a deconditioned state, the ACSM guidelines should be considered targets to strive toward rather than fixed rules in the initial stages. In consultation with the subject, set intensity, frequency, duration, and load goals that are acceptable to the subject. People quickly become discouraged if they experience excessive muscle fatigue, muscle or joint inflammation, exercise-induced osteoporotic fractures, or postexercise pain.[11]

Cervical Region

Muscular strength can be developed by using hand pressure on the head to add resistance to neck exercises listed above with one critical guideline: When resistance is added, the neck should be at or near the neutral position. Adding resistance when the neck is at or near the outer range of motion (in flexion, extension, abduction, adduction, or rotation) will place stress on associated anatomical structures and may invite injury. Building the strength of the spine extensor muscles is particularly important to counteract the common postural tendency toward forward flexion of the neck.

Thoracic Region

In the seated position, the extensors of the thoracic region may be strengthened by asking the subject to arch the upper spine, and to squeeze the elbows toward each behind the back and add a strong isometric contraction to the movement. Adding resistance (water, fixed resistance, weights, other hand equipment) to exercises in this position of shoulder extension may cause injury to the shoulder capsule.[7]

In the prone position, the extensor muscles can be effectively strengthened by doing low arm lifts with the arms stretched forward, sideward, or backward. Subjects are asked to lift the arm an inch or two from the mat. Do train subjects to keep their neck in neutral alignment avoiding the hyperextended position. Because of common postural problems, it is the thoracic extensor muscles that need to be strengthened. The flexors (pectorals) are normally overdeveloped relative to the strength of the back muscles.

Lumbar Region

Strength exercises for the lumbar region need to counteract the characteristically tight back muscles, the weak and overstretched antagonist muscles of the abdominal group, and the poor balance in the relative strength of the back and abdominal muscle groups. Because all of these muscles are often poorly conditioned, there is inadequate strength to control or counteract the pelvis tipping action of the iliopsoas group. Back pain is often caused by this uncontrolled "pulling" action on the lumbar spine. Exercise variations that incapacitate the action of the iliopsoas group are recommended. This can most commonly be achieved by selecting variations that maximize back support, and by reducing the load on the spine.[11]

Many of the lumbar flexibility exercises listed above, including flexion, extension, abduction, adduction, and rotation are also effective for building strength endurance by simply increasing the number of repetitions, or by slowing the movement so that the muscles are required to work against the pull of gravity.

Lumbar extensor muscles should be strengthened through the full range of motion. The various standing leg lifts are particularly effective for frailer populations who can only tolerate very low loads. Stronger individuals are able to do these exercises against resistance such as that provided by water, weights, or resistance bands. They are also able to perform low leg lifts in a prone-lying position on a padded surface. A combination exercise of a low (1 to 2 inches), prone, opposite arm and leg lift is also effective.

Lumbar flexor muscles, specifically the abdominal muscles, need particular attention. In standing positions, it helps to train older adults to consciously control their postural position using the abdominal muscles, tucking the pelvis under, and opening the hip to full extension. In chair seated positions, subjects should be asked to sit tall, keep the pelvis tucked under, and use their muscles (or if necessary, the chair back) to support the spine. It is also important for the comfort of the spine that the height of the chair seat allow the subject to place both feet comfortably flat on the floor and to have the backs of the thighs fully supported by the chair. From this position abdominal strength can be built by lifting one knee (unaided by arms) as close to the shoulder as possible while sitting tall, or by lifting a straight leg and holding it up off the chair seat. If the subject sits deep in the chair, leans forward, and places the hands under the thighs on the front edge of the chair, incapacitating the iliopsoas muscle, it is safe and effective to lift both legs from the floor, either bent or straight. The load to the abdominal muscles can be increased during many exercise movements if an isometric contraction is added.

Abdominal exercises can also be done in a supine position on a padded mat or firm bed if the subject is willing and able to rise from the floor. Having a wall or chair nearby to lean on while rising from the floor can be very helpful. In the supine hook-lying position both isometric and isotonic abdominal exercises are effective. Isotonic exercises may involve lifting the head and shoulders from the mat or they may involve lifting the hips from the floor with both hips and knees fully flexed.

Lumbar rotation

Do floor sitting rotation exercises as above, but use arm pressure against the leg to increase resistance.

Lumbar abduction

Do lateral leg lifts in a standing or side-lying position, being careful to keep the foot of the lifted leg from rotating outwards, to keep the lift low, and to consciously lift (abduct) the hip with each leg lift. In the side-lying position, train the subject to keep hips fully extended (open). To improve balance and comfort, bend the lower leg at the knee, place the hand of the upper arm on the floor in front of the chest, and rest the head on the lower arm.

Table 24–2 summarizes the exercises related to muscle strength and endurance.

CONTRAINDICATED MOVEMENTS RELATED TO THE SPINE

HOW CONTRAINDICATED MOVEMENTS ARE IDENTIFIED FOR INDIVIDUALS

There are some exercise movements that are less effective and may injure some people. These so-called contraindicated movements often cause injury or chronic pain.[12] The pain or injury is caused by exceeding the limit of tolerance of a joint or of the supporting musculature. These injuries are more common in untrained people and in older people particularly if they lack body experience of the movement or if they are in a weakened state following an accident, illness, or injury. We know that these exercises are often performed without problem by trained athletes or dancers, or as part of a habitual exercise regimen learned years ago. For example, there are frequent reports of older people doing standing ballistic toe touches as part of a daily exercise regimen for years without injury. The body seems to build adequate strength to support the movement despite the fact

Table 24–2: Muscle Strength and Endurance Exercises

LOCATION AND AXIS OF MOVEMENT	EXERCISE	ADDITIONAL COMMENTS
Cervical Region		
	Add isometric contraction or add resistance with hand pressure to flexion, extension, abduction, adduction exercises (Table 24–1)	Check that correct alignment is maintained if hand pressure is added.
Thoracic Region		
Flexion	Touch elbows in front of chest	Done in standing or seated positions
Extension	Draw elbows together behind back, add isometric contraction	Done in standing or seated positions
	Low arm and chest lifts	In prone position: larger women will find this position uncomfortable Keep neck in neutral alignment
Lumbar Region		
Flexion, especially abdominals	Many variations	Done in standing, seated in chair positions Keep pelvis tucked under; direct leg movement around belly (toward shoulder, not chest)
Extension	Standing leg extensions	Use controlled (versus ballistic) movement
	Prone, low single leg lifts	Weights or other resistance may be added
Abduction/adduction	Add isometric contraction, more repetitions, slower movement tempo to exercises listed in Table 24–1	
Rotation	Do seated on chair or floor; add resistance by using arm pressure against thigh	To eliminate flexion, sit tall without rounding back

that this movement has been considered contraindicated for many years. Yet, toe touches often cause injury in the untrained person who suddenly starts doing this movement, in the person experiencing high emotional stress, or in the person who has returned to a daily exercise routine following a break such as for health reasons.

For ethical reasons, the research on these movements is virtually nonexistent. The selection of high-risk movements has largely been based on the practical experience of exercise professionals working with young and middle-aged adults.[13] It is only recently that there has been discussion of these high-risk movements relevant to the older adult. It is safe to assume that these movements are more likely to cause injury among the older population because they are more likely to be less active, to be weakened by illness or disease, to have a variety of joint problems, to have proprioceptive deficiencies, or to have an increased imbalance in the relative strength of antagonistic muscle groups.

CONTRAINDICATED MOVEMENTS

In the present litigious climate, the subject of contraindicated movements has become a hotly debated issue in the fitness community. For several years, the list of specific contraindicated movements got longer and longer until exercise specialists wondered if the process had gone too far.[8] At present, the consensus has been to step back and list some general guidelines and to list a few specific exercise movements shown to have a repeatedly high incidence of injury. The general guidelines are to (1) avoid forced overflexing the knee or neck; (2) avoid overextending the knee, neck, or low back; (3) avoid applying a twisting force to the knee; (4) avoid applying lateral pressure to the knee; (5) avoid breath holding; (6) avoid stretching long weak muscles such as the abdominals; (7) avoid overdeveloping already stronger muscles such as the pectorals; (8) avoid aggravating common postural problems (forward head position, kyphosis, abdominal ptosis, medial rotation of the thigh, and foot pronation); (9) avoid overstretching ligaments around joints; (10) avoid passive stretching done by an untrained individual; (11) avoid movements which place marked compressive force on the spinal discs; and (12) avoid movements that cause subacromial impingement of the rotator cuff in the shoulder.[12] The following discussion covers some specific exercises associated with high rates of pain and injury.

Figure 24–3. Contraindicated yoga plough and inverted bicycle exercises.

The yoga "plough" and the inverted bicycle (Figure 24–3) exercise place high stress on the cervical spine because the inverted position of the body places a large amount of weight on the small joints and bones of the neck.[8,11–13]

The hyperextension phase of neck circling compresses the vertral arteries, reducing blood flow to the brain, and narrows the neural foramena, compressing nerves. The circling head movement across the back part of the circle often causes pain.[8,12,13] There are other situations in which neck hyperextension may also cause dizziness, nausea, discomfort, tingling, or numbness and appropriate modifications must be made. If the upper spine has become rounded, lying supine on a flat surface will cause uncomfortable neck hyperextension. Provide these people with a small pillow. When participants are doing exercises on their hands and knees, or are lying prone, they should turn sideways to the demonstrator so that they only need to turn their head to see the demonstration, rather than lift their head and hyperextend their neck.

Standing toe touches with straight legs are a risk to the lumbar spine, especially during the lift phase when the entire weight of the upper body is supported by a group of relatively small muscles in the low back.[8,12]

Supine double leg lifts are a risk to the low back because most older people are unable to counteract the strong pull of the iliopsoas muscles, which struggle to support the weight of the legs. This powerful (hyperextending) pull on the spine puts uneven pressure on the lumbar discs, often causing injury.[8,11–13] This exercise is safely modified by always keeping one knee bent with that foot flat on the floor while lifting the other leg.

Prone double leg and double arm lifts and the full "cobra" exercise are a risk to the low back (Figure 24–4). In these exercises, the low back is forcefully hyperextended, placing very uneven pressure on the lumbar discs.[8,12,13] Safe modifications are to keep an opposite arm and leg on the mat to support the body weight and prevent extreme hyperextension while doing prone arm and leg lifts; and to keep elbows on the mat while doing a modified "cobra" exercise.

Straight leg sit-ups may place high stress on the low back if the subject hyperextends the low back during the lift.[8,13] This is more likely to occur if the subject's feet are held down by a partner or other firm structure. Safe modifications are to do some form of curl-up as described above, or to do curl-downs from a sitting position (rolling to the side and up to repeat the exercise).

Uncontrolled back hyperextension as in "donkey kicks" can be a risk to the cervical, thoracic, or lumbar spine, particularly if both the leg and head are thrown into the hyperextended position.[8,12]

The hurdler stretch places a high torque pressure on the medial side of the knee and risks injury to the knee.[8,13]

Deep knee bends and the Burpee exercise place extreme stress on the knees because of the sudden forced overflexing of the knee joint. In addition, the extremely strong contraction of the quadriceps muscle during the lift phase may cause tearing at the distal attachment. The sudden shift in body position may cause dizziness from circulatory hypotension.[8–12]

Table 24–3 summarizes the exercises contraindicated for older adults.

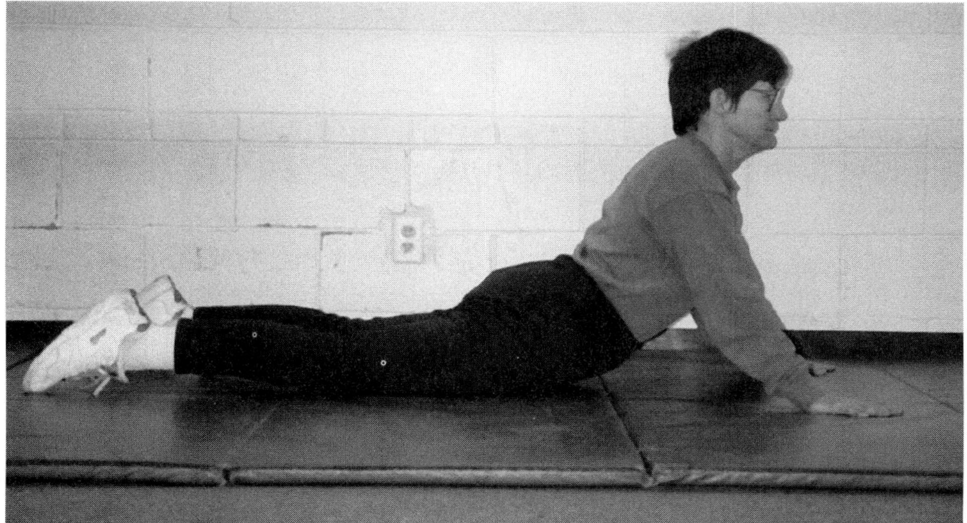

Figure 24–4. "Cobra" exercise in high-risk position.

Table 24–3: Contraindicated Exercises

In General Avoid:

- Forced overflexing of the knee or neck
- Overextending neck, knee, or low back
- Twisting the knee
- Pressing laterally on knee
- Holding breath
- Overstretching long weak muscles
- Creating imbalance by overdeveloping particular muscle groups
- Aggravating common postural problems
- Overstretching ligaments
- Passive stretching done by untrained individuals
- Marked even or uneven compressive force on spinal discs
- Subacromial impingement

In Particular Avoid:

- Yoga plough and inverted bicycle exercises
- Marked hyperextension of the neck (head circles)
- Standing, ballistic toe touching
- Supine double leg lifts
- Prone double leg and arm lifts
- Marked lumbar extension version of "cobra" exercise
- Straight leg sit-ups
- Uncontrolled back hyperextension ("donkey kicks")
- Hurdler stretch
- Deep knee bends (including the "Burpee" exercise)

QUESTIONABLE MOVEMENTS AS DEFINED BY THE AGING PROCESS AND INDIVIDUAL VARIATIONS IN THAT PROCESS

Many people might list certain additional exercises as contraindicated. It is probably more reasonable to consider them questionable and understand the situations that increase their risk.

An active-well trained older adult who is physically healthy and has a well-developed body sense is at lower injury risk. However, as the musculoskeletal system ages, there is a higher degree of injury risk with movement for a variety of reasons.

Joint deterioration creates situations in which mechanically efficient body alignment has been altered. For example, changes in the shoulder girdle and upper spine often result in a bony realignment, causing the chest to cave inwards and the shoulders to round. When this older adult tries to follow the direction "to stand tall and stretch the arm(s) above the head," the person compensates by hyperextending the lumbar spine, as the upper spine no longer permits the requested movement. Similar exercises in the supine position will also cause compensatory movements of lumbar hyperextension or neck hyperextension.[8] It is imperative that exercise instructors notice these compensatory movements and correct the position and action of the exercise to fit the body and joint alignment of that individual. Naturally, the skeletal system will age and deform in unique ways that need to be addressed by a trained exercise professional.

A second age-related change that increases injury risk is the uneven decline in strength of individual muscle groups, and the more general decline in overall muscle strength caused by less active lifestyles. The practical outcome of these changes is that movements that require muscles instead of bones to support the body weight may exceed the strength capabilities of the supporting muscles. Movement of the spine in any direction from the center line forces a proportion of the body weight to be supported by muscular contractions. If there is a marked difference or general decline in the relative strength of the muscle groups that stabilize the trunk, any marked bending movement involving the spine needs to accommodate these changes to reduce the risk of injury.

Finally, changes in body composition and body proportions alter the mechanics of any movement. As people age, there seems to be a predictable shortening of the spine due to disc degeneration. This shortening increases the difficulty of any forward flexion movement because the lower edges of the rib cage quickly run into the bones of the pelvic girdle. A secondary effect of this spine shortening is that it reduces the size of the body cavities. The internal organs are pressed forward against a frequently weakened abdominal musculature, creating the maligned "bulging belly!" As if to add insult to injury, the proportion of body fat increases with age and tends to be deposited in the midsection, and closer to the skin surface. The practical result is that the belly is often in the way when an older person is asked to do any of the common abdominal or hip flexion exercises. An instructor should select movements that allow the knees to be apart, allow the thigh to go "around" the belly, and allow the movement to be completed in a more open position.

Keeping these common age-related changes in mind, following are a group of specific exercises which should be avoided except in known and controlled situations.

The hydrant exercise (in which the knee and hip are held in a flexed position while the thigh is abducted and adducted) causes sudden hyperextension and places marked uneven compressional pressure on the discs of the lumbar spine. Traditionally this exercise is done on hands and knees. However, variations of the same movement are sometimes done standing or seated in chair, and are similarly problematic.[8,13]

Unsupported forward flexion of the spine, in which the knees are locked straight, obviously places the lumbar spine at risk for strain or injury. Despite the fact that this position is known to be mechanically inefficient, it is often included in exercise routines with the arms extended forward, often with hand weights adding even more unsupported upper body weight to the load on the low back. The risk can be greatly reduced if the feet are placed well apart and the knees are bent. It is still advisable to support the upper body weight by placing one hand on a thigh during the exercise and to train subjects to tighten the trunk muscles to give the back additional support.[8]

Spine bending (flexion) and twisting (rotation) exercises as in standing "windmills" and related movements done in seated or supine positions combine the risk of the unsupported spine with the risk of marked uneven compression on the lumbar discs due to combination of flexion and rotation.[8,13] Modifications that reduce the risk of injury are to support the upper body weight with a hand on a thigh, and to reduce or eliminate the rotational component.

Abdominal exercises in which the head is pulled forward by the hands (forced hyperflexion) encourage kyphosis and should be modified.[8,11,12] If it is desirable to do an abdominal exercise in which the head is lifted from the mat, the weight of the head may be supported by placing the hands on the low neck and upper back with the elbows held out to the side, eliminating the pulling action.

An unsupported spine during lateral trunk movements ("side-bends"), in seated or standing positions, encourages kyphosis because a rotational component is often inadvertently added. This movement also may put uneven stress on lumbar discs. If the center of weight (the midline bony structures) is also abducted to the point where it is no longer over the base of support, the spine becomes unsupported and is strained. Modifications to reduce the risk of injury are to broaden the base of support by placing the feet farther apart, to eliminate any rotational component, to support the spine by placing a hand on a wall or thigh (*not on the waist*), to tighten the trunk muscles, and to keep the center of weight over the support base.

Reaching through the legs with the arms in standing, chair seated, or supine positions places uneven and heavy compressional forces on the lumbar spine, particularly if the movement is done ballistically or with locked knees. There are also problems with dizziness because the head may drop below the level of the heart in the standing position. To reduce injury risk, train subjects to bend their knees, take their hands toward their toes, do the movement slowly, and keep the head above the level of the heart.

The supine double leg "L" position (lifting and holding both legs up) with legs in either straddle or vertical position may encourage lordosis and may cause uneven compression of the lumbar discs if the weight of the legs is not supported by being held over the hips. Most older adults lack the necessary abdominal strength or low back and hamstring flexibility to reach and maintain the necessary 90 degree position of legs with torso. It is easy to modify this position by placing one foot on the mat with the knee bent, supporting the weight of the lifted leg and eliminating the possible strong pull of the iliopsoas muscles on the lumbar spine.[8]

In chair seated positions, the L position (lifting and holding both legs up and straight forward, or doing a wide "scissors" movement from that position) may encourage lordosis and often causes lumbar pain. Double leg lifts may be done safely without stressing the lumbar spine if the subject sits to the back of the chair, giving the thighs full support, and leans the trunk forward, placing the hands on the front edge of chair. Another alternative is to simply keep one foot on the floor while the other leg is lifted.

Full arm flexion in standing, chair seated, or supine position, in which the subject is asked to attain a 180 degree flexion, may encourage lordosis if shoulder alignment restricts

Table 24–4: Questionable Exercise[a]

- Unsupported forward flexion, extension, or abduction of the spine
- Hydrant exercise (including standing and seated variations)
- Simultaneous flexion and rotation of the spine ("windmill" exercise)
- Forced flexion of the head and neck
- Hyperflexion of the lumbar spine by reaching arms through the legs
- Supine double leg "L" position
- Unsupported scissors or double leg "L" position seated in chair
- Forced full arm flexion
- Unmodified static stretches that ignore alignment and balance limitations

[a]These exercises place clients at higher risk of injury.

the movement and the subject does not maintain proper alignment of the lumbar spine.

Static stretching positions designed by and for younger joints may compromise the spine of an older adult. When a demonstrated position is physically not possible for an older adult to attain because of changes in joints and associated alignment of body segments, the older subject often compensates by unconsciously and improperly altering the alignment of other segments, often the spine. Stretches that commonly need to be modified are stretches of the triceps, spine rotators, hamstrings, quadriceps, leg adductors, and gastrocnemius muscle group. The leg stretches may also create balance problems and increase the risk of falling. Select positions to eliminate balance as a factor and to maintain optimal body alignment.

Table 24–4 summarizes these questionable exercises.

SUMMARY

Selecting safe and effective exercises for older adults must always accomodate the changes in body alignment; muscle strength, flexibility and contraction speed; joint range of motion; and body shape which are common among older adults. The free-standing and floor positions of many common exercises need to be modified to supported positions (standing by a wall, or seated in a chair). Due to common declines in balance, coordination, and overall muscle strength simpler versions of exercises are usually preferable. Obviously contraindicated exercises need to be avoided in all positions. Questionable exercises need to be considered with much caution as they often result in higher rates of irritation and injury in this population. Identifying effective modifications for a particular individual require keen observation and open communication between the client and exercise professional.

Clinical Applications

CASE STUDIES

Ginger, age 73, reports episodes of chronic low back pain with no identified pathology. Her lifestyle is moderately active. Her primary rehabilitative course in the past has been to rest and reduce activity. A daily walking exercise program wearing good shoes and walking on a softer surface (wood floor or even dirt path) was recommended. In addition, she was given lumbar flexion, extension, and abduction flexibility exercises and low-load lumbar strength exercises to do three times a week.[5]

Philip, age 68, reports impaired ability to dress himself and perform other activities of daily living because of stiffness. His lifestyle is moderately active. His overall strength is adequate. However, marked loss of muscle flexibility in the ankle extensors, knee flexors, hip extensors, and spinal rotators and loss of joint mobility in the shoulders and spine were noted. He was given a joint mobility and muscle flexibility program to be done most days of the week. Improved breathing patterns and slower movement tempos increased his ability to complete the exercise movements comfortably.

Don, age 75, reports limited spinal mobility following surgery for lumbar stenosis. Although movement of the lumbar and thoracic spine needs to be limited, an exercise program of daily walking was recommended. Further, an exercise program including muscle strength and flexibility of the limbs was strongly encouraged to provide compensatory capabilities for activities of daily living. All exercises were designed to place minimum stress on the spine itself. Exercise positions were limited to standing or supine positions because seated positions (on chair or floor) and other flat-lying positions caused pain. A small pillow is used to support the head in supine positions to maintain better alignment of the spine for this individual.

Brenda, age 64, reports frequent episodes of chronic back pain with a possible diagnosis of thoracic spinal stenosis. Her episodes of pain often occur during times of higher emotional stress. Her lifestyle is fairly inactive. A moderate daily walking exercise program was recommended with some exercises added to relax the mind and body. These included gentle supine lumbar flexion exercises in the hook-lying position with added breathing exercises.

Jennifer, age 81, reports chronic pain "under the right shoulder blade" which is apparently related to a mild scoliosis condition. Scoliosis involves a lateral curvature of the spine in a C-shaped misalignment. The muscles on the inside of the curve, in Jennifer's case on the right side, are overdeveloped and tight, lifting the right hip and pulling the (right) shoulder blade down out of alignment. These muscles need to be stretched. The muscles on the outside of the curve (left) are weaker and overstretched. These muscles need to be strengthened. A program was designed to address her strength and flexibility needs focusing on thoracic and lumbar flexion, extension, and abduction, including the scoliosis stretch noted above (alternative supine lumbar extension exercise). A program of walking with awareness of postural alignment was recommended. She was also asked to focus on keeping weight evenly supported by both feet while standing doing daily activities. It was suggested that objects being carried should be carried in the center, using both arms, or use the left hand primarily to carry handbags (lighter weight if possible).

REFERENCES

1. American College of Sports Medicine. *Guidelines for Exercise Testing and Prescription*. Philadelphia: Lea & Febiger, 1991:93–99.
2. Chandler JM, Hadley EC. Exercise to improve physiologic and functional performance in old age. *Clinics in Geriatric Medicine*. 1996;12(4):761–784.
3. Clark B. Principles of physical activity programming for the older adult. In: Leslie DK, ed. *Mature Stuff: Physical Activity for the Older Adult*. Reston, VA: American Alliance for Health, Physical Education, Recreation, and Dance, 1989:133–145.
4. Duda J. Motivating older adults. *Journal of Physical Education, Recreation, and Dance*. 1991;62(7):44–48.

5. Ferrell BA, Josephson KR, Pollan AM, Loy S, Ferrell BR. A randomized trial of walking versus physical methods for chronic pain management. *Aging*. 1997;9(1–2):99–105.
6. Guccione AA. Functional assessment of the elderly. In: Guccione AA, ed. *Geriatric Physical Therapy*. St. Louis: CV Mosby, 1993:113–123.
7. Harding WG. Keep your shoulders in the 'safe zone.' *Physician and Sportsmedicine*. 1993;21(12):93–94.
8. Hooke AP, Zoller M. *Active Older Adults in the YMCA: A Resource Manual*. Champaign, IL: Human Kinetics, 1992:115–154.
9. Jackson OL. Basic principles in rehabilitation: A conceptual model. In: Jackson OL, ed. *Therapeutic Considerations for the Elderly*. New York: Churchill Livingstone, 1987:1–22.
10. Jackson OL. Adapting physical therapy intervention in the elderly. In: Payton OD, ed. *Manual of Physical Therapy*. New York: Churchill Livingstone, 1989:723–724.
11. Kisner C, Colby LA. *Therapeutic Exercise: Foundations and Techniques*. Philadelphia: FA Davis, 1990:72–76, 145, 617–621.
12. Lindsay R, Corbin C. Questionable exercises—some safer alternatives. *Journal of Physical Education, Recreation, and Dance*. 1989;60(8):26–32.
13. Lubell A. Potentially dangerous exercises: Are they harmful to all? *Physician and Sportsmedicine*. 1989;17(1):187–192.
14. Means KM, Rodell DE, O'Sullivan PS, Cranford LA. Rehabilitation of elderly fallers: Pilot study of a low to moderate intensity exercise program. *Archives of Physical Medicine and Rehabilitation*. 1996;77(10):1030–1036.
15. Sarno JE. Therapeutic exercise for back pain. In: Basmajian JV, ed. *Therapeutic Exercise*. 4th ed. Baltimore: Williams & Wilkins, 1984:441–463.
16. Shephard RJ. *Physical Activity and Aging*. 2nd ed. Rockville, MD: Aspen, 1987.
17. Simmons V, Hansen PD. Effectiveness of water exercise on postural mobility in the well elderly: An experimental study on balance enhancement. *Journals of Gerontology, Series A, Biological Sciences & Medical Sciences*. 1996;51(5):M233–238.
18. Smith EL, Gilligan C. Biological aging and the benefits of physical activity. In: Leslie DK, ed. *Mature Stuff: Physical Activity for the Older Adult*. Reston, VA: American Alliance for Health, Physical Education, Recreation, and Dance, 1989:45–59.
19. Spirduso WW, Eckert HM. *Physical Activity and Aging*. Champaign, IL: Human Kinetics, 1989.

CHAPTER 25

Motivation and Exercise Compliance Among Older Adults

Ann P. Hooke, MA

INTRODUCTION

Motivation to comply is a key concern for the health care provider who works with older persons. Although the efficacy of exercise is generally well accepted by clients, the motivation to comply on a regular committed basis is often elusive. The comment, "I know the exercise would help, but I just can't get myself to do it," is all too familiar. This chapter looks at various aspects of motivation and provides a broader understanding of factors related to motivation, and thus enlarges the palette of motivators from which to draw incentives.

Motivation is a state of being impelled to action by the incentive of emotions, desires, or physiological needs.[2] This complex mechanism that drives behavior is multilayered. Its base, the will to survive, is the root of life itself. The first issue around compliance to an exercise program is the concern for survival, and then for safety from physical or emotional injury. At some level of consciousness every client is asking, "Is the benefit of exercise worth the risk of injury or death?" These primal issues may be deeply buried under more "adult" concerns. The challenge of the health provider is to determine which incentives will be most effective for a given individual: addressing their fears, appealing to other emotional needs, providing rewards, or emphasizing the physiological benefits.

As health providers, we can only "lead the horse to water." We cannot "make him drink." Our job is to define the task (the exercise prescription) and provide some form of external motivation. The client may act on our recommendations. With experiences of success, the behavior may become internally motivated. However, the progression from external to internal motivation is not guaranteed. For better results, our job must be more than merely prescribing exercise. We also need to determine effective motivators for a given client because long-term exercise compliance depends on experiences of success.

RELATIONSHIP OF PSYCHOSOCIAL, COGNITIVE, AND PHYSICAL FACTORS

Exercise prescriptions and programs that recognize and integrate the psychosocial, cognitive, and physical needs of the individual elderly client will be the most effective. Any change in physical or functional capacity of an older person provides a major challenge to living. Many authors have reported that improvement in physical capacity affects and is affected by cognitive factors, psychological well-being, and social functioning.[5,7,11,13] Therefore, it is important to consider the broader needs of these clients in planning intervention programs.

There are particular aspects of the physical factors which should be considered. As a group, aging clients show a wide variability in their neuromuscular capacities (reaction/ movement time, balance, coordination, agility), cardiorespiratory capacities, and their performance capabilities. There is a high incidence of chronic disease (heart, arthritis, hypertension, obesity, type II diabetes, cancer) in this population, which affects response to exercise. For these reasons, the functional ability to perform the activities of daily living may be limited and restrict the client's ability to participate in group or on-site programs outside the home. Exercise prescriptions need to account for all these possible physical limitations.

Cognitive factors that must be considered are perceptual abilities and comprehension. Providing basic knowledge about health and physical activity and specific knowledge about the particular situation are usually essential.

Finally, the success of an intervention program is usually affected by the client's psychosocial health. The status of social relationships, and of psychological and emotional health, strongly affects the client's motivation to follow an exercise prescription. Meanwhile, exercise compliance often results in improvements in mood and self-esteem and increased interest in social interaction. Reductions in stress, anxiety, and depression may occur. The complex interaction between social, physical, and psychological aspects is circular, with the possibility of spiraling upward or downward. A thorough review of the psychological benefits of physical activity may be found in Ostrow[19] and Stamford.[25]

This chapter discusses motivation from this broader perspective, considering cognitive and psychosocial factors in addition to the physical factors. Since all these factors are interrelated, the discussion is integrated. Further, additional emphasis is placed on the needs of the "hard to reach" client who is resistant to the potential benefits of exercise and is most difficult to motivate.

RELATIONSHIP OF EXERCISE PRESCRIPTION TO ATTITUDES

Attitudes of the older client toward the aging process, toward exercise, and toward the risks and benefits of physical activity can have a profound effect on motivation to comply with the exercise prescription. Health care providers often assume that others have equally positive attitudes toward exercise. This is not always the case! Because negative attitudes can put big stumbling blocks in the road to accepting the recommendations of the provider, it is very helpful to explore the client's attitudes.

Attitudes of health care providers toward aging can also have a marked positive or negative impact on recommendations. Providers are usually younger. The generally negative cultural attitude toward aging often infects the provider-client relationship. Before working with the older client, it helps to examine one's own attitudes toward aging, to break down the separating "we versus them" mentality. It helps to observe and listen to older members in one's own family, to imagine oneself at different ages, and to view one's own aging with compassion and acceptance.

ATTITUDES TOWARD THE AGING PROCESS

There is a wide range of attitudes toward the aging process by different individuals, and there is certainly a lot of variability in attitudes by an individual on any given day. Some days one feels very old; other days one feels ageless. Some days one accepts the aging process with good humor; other days one tries to fight or deny the aging process. Men view aging differently than women. People whose identity has been strongly based on physical attributes (be it beauty or physical or athletic ability) generally find aging more difficult. Aging does involve physical loss, but it involves gains in wisdom. Compassionate understanding by providers is most helpful.

Still, there are some attitudes that seem to be commonly expressed. Many people feel that after a certain age (maybe 40, 50, 60, or 70), they are "too old to exercise." Due to losses in coordination, balance, and agility, older people often feel awkward when they move. Their simple solution is to simply avoid exercise. The rationale commonly given is that daily activities provide adequate exercise, and that old age is synonymous with being frail.[14,22] This attitude toward aging can easily fuel a downward spiral in functional ability.

The question becomes, "Am I frail because I am old?" or "Am I (functionally) old because I am frail and in poor physical condition?" It appears that the lower the level of physical condition, the greater is the distortion in perception of performance ability. Less active individuals tend to be less aware of their potential capabilities, and they tend to be less aware of declines in muscle function (strength, speed, endurance), of increases in joint and tissue stiffness,[16] and of how limiting these changes are on functional ability. Regaining even minimal strength, flexibility, or stamina is often highly motivating. People learn that aging processes can indeed be slowed. To some, it even feels as if it has been reversed to some degree. Individuals who compete in any of the Masters athletic programs are average people who choose to challenge their physical capabilities.

ROLE OF PAST EXPERIENCE IN ATTITUDES TOWARD EXERCISE

It is useful to help a client assess his or her past experience and attitudes toward exercise. These positive or negative attitudes may be based on childhood sports experiences, on childhood rehabilitation experiences following an illness or injury, on recent rehabilitation experiences, on fitness or sports experiences, or merely on hearsay of other's experiences. Exercise instructors have known for a long time that there seems to be little relationship between attitudes toward exercise and any physical limits to activity. Some very physically limited individuals have very positive attitudes, and conversely physically able individuals can have negative attitudes.[14] Similarly, people who have had recent positive exercise experiences view rehabilitative exercise with optimism. It should be added that community exercise classes for older adults usually build positive attitudes toward the benefits of rehabilitative exercise,[5] and should therefore be actively supported by the health care community. Past experience helps to clearly define the similarities or dissimilarities of a current recommended exercise regimen from other experiences. It also helps to clarify the differences between rehabilitation exercise whose purpose is to restore functioning and which is usually less vigorous and conditioning exercises, which may be more intense.[1]

Positive attitudes toward exercise are associated with positive feelings and with minimal fear related to exercise. Past exercise experiences have provided these people with feelings of competence, success, pleasure, and healing, or a decrease in pain.[23] The provider will hear, "I must exercise because I enjoy __________; or I have, want, need __________," from the person with a positive attitude. Their self-talk is positive: "I will," "I can." They feel confident that the exercise goals are realistic and attainable, that they have a right to health and functional independence, and that their physical activity is supported by significant others.[7]

Conversely, attitudes may be negative with associated negative feelings. These feelings are often related to current depression and/or past experiences of failure, pain, injury, or overwhelming fear. The health provider may hear from the person with a negative attitude, "I can't exercise because I have, worry about, or feel __________." Self-talk is often framed in words of why one *should* exercise. The incentives usually come from external sources, such as authority figures (doctor), other health professionals, employers, family members, or the influence of the broader culture. When the incentives are based on internal fears of failure, it is still the judgment or punishment by others that often drives the behavior. In either case, the response is usually to exercise with a grudge, with less enthusiasm, interest, or commitment; and hoping to get it over with as soon as possible. Depending on the power of these figures over the client, exercise compliance may be good, but only for some limited amount of time.

If attitudes are negative, the first task is to help the client recognize and confront these negative attitudes. Dislodging negative beliefs and attitudes is possible, but not easy. However, it certainly is easier if both the client and provider are aware of the task at hand. The ultimate goal is to help the client become internally motivated. There are three broad steps to this process[5]:

1. Address the negative attitudes, fears, and experiences.
2. Use external rewards (awards, recognition, information on activity and health benefits) to encourage successful completion of goals.
3. Support internally motivated exercise by associating physical activity with the client's values, interests, and prior positive experiences and with the client's physical, social, and emotional needs.

ATTITUDES TOWARD THE RISKS AND BENEFITS OF PHYSICAL ACTIVITY

Obviously there are both risks and benefits of any prescribed physical activity. Compliance is governed by the client's perceptions of the risk-benefit equation.

Perceived Risks of Physical Activity

For older clients, there may be many perceived risks that the provider needs to address because these barriers or concerns may seem formidable to the older person.[7] These perceptions should be listened to and respected.

People hesitate to initiate participation for a variety of reasons. There may be practical concerns about cost, location, timing, conflicting commitments, weather, or logistics. Some clients think that they are too old, that their health or capability is not sufficient, or that the activity is not socially acceptable.[13]

The reasons given for dropping out of exercise are varied. The most common complaint is that the exercise is boring and not challenging, interesting, or enjoyable. The exercise may have been perceived as ineffective, too difficult, or too painful. Since exercise interventions are usually not instantly effective, support and encouragement are particularly important in the early phases to lessen these experiences of failure. If the client is in poor physical condition at the start of a program, overuse injuries are more likely to occur, often as a result of improper footwear or improper technique.[14]

In prescribing exercise, the assumption is that it will help cure a symptom. If the cause of a symptom is more psychosomatic and less physical, there is a high chance that the exercise will not be successful. The client may accept suggestions to look at potential psychological causes.[24]

Perceived Benefits of Physical Activity

Although there are wide variations among older adults of the perceived benefits of physical activity,[7] there is a consensus that the exercise must be safe, effective, and enjoyable.[13,14]

In a study of intrinsic motives for participation, Heitmann[13] evaluated 227 older subjects, age 60+. The motives of the male subjects, listed from most to least important, were: health, achievement, coping, social, appearance, and aesthetics. This order of motives is similar for younger males (below age 60). For female subjects, the order of priority was: health, social, coping, appearance, achievement, and aesthetics. By contrast, the motives of younger women are: health, appearance, achievement, coping, aesthetics, and social. In our culture, which places such emphasis on (youthful) physical appearance, emphasizing the benefits of physical activity on appearance may be counterproductive with people whose priorities have shifted! Emphasizing achievement, health, coping, and social benefits may be more productive.

In all these subjects, health is the top priority for motivation. Older adults, in particular, crave accurate information on reasonable expectations, on the rationale for a specific exercise, and on facts. Although they crave this information, they may hesitate to ask for it directly.

In summary, a list of practical tips to reduce the barriers to participation follow[20]:

- Shift the focus of exercise from negative aspects (time consumed, physical effort) to positive aspects (meeting and making friends, enjoying music, playfulness, scenery as part of the exercise experience).
- Support the participants in taking responsibility for healing, for choosing to take the time and make the effort to exercise instead of killing a similar amount of time with sedentary activities such as eating, TV viewing, compulsive reading, sleeping, etc.
- Openly discuss the possible outcomes of the exercise experience: initial muscle soreness, initial tiredness, subsequent decreases in pain, and gains in strength, functioning ability, energy, independence, and self-esteem.
- Suggest a variety of exercise modes and settings to accommodate different tastes. Limitations related to weather, to boring repetition, and to traditional fitness activities can all be erased by changing the modes and settings of physical activity.

RELATIONSHIP OF EXERCISE PRESCRIPTION TO FEARS

Attitudes are often stated openly: "I'm too old to exercise." Fears, whether perceived or underlying, are often silent powerful forces driving behavior. Although it is useful to understand attitudes, it is *essential* to be sensitive to fears. Each individual lives with different levels of fear. The fears of older adults are the same as fears of younger adults, but the imminence of death often gives fear more potency as we age. The strongest fears are related to fear of death and fear of loss of safety. After these fears are a host of other fears related to belonging, which are social issues.

Some people may be able to specifically name what it is they fear. These perceived fears may or may not be realistic fears. Other people may feel afraid, but not be able to name the cause of the fear. These are underlying fears. In either case, the end result is the same. Behavior is shaped by the fear.

As service providers, what should our practical response to client's fears be? To tell someone "not to be afraid," is not effective. We all remember that from our own childhood! On the other hand, it is effective when we acknowledge the reality of fears, as they relate to following the exercise prescription, and still provide caring support and encouragement. A professional, but calm, comfortable, familiar, and nonthreatening atmosphere is most helpful. Older adults will find the atmosphere most calming if activity is not rushed, and if people take the time to move slowly and speak slowly and clearly.[17] If fears are spoken of in an understanding and realistic manner, the power of fear can be greatly reduced.

FEARS RELATED TO SAFETY

1. The fear of death may be triggered by unfamiliar feelings of overexertion, or pain associated with movement.[6]
2. Injury with associated loss of body control may trigger fears of isolation or of dependence on others, which for some is worse than death. Although this fear is very real, it can lead to a new awareness that being vulnerable and in need of help permits others to express their care and love for the individual.
3. Fears of injury may be triggered by unfamiliar exercise positions or movements and by perceived high intensity, high resistance, or complexity of the exercises. Exercise equipment, itself, is often unfamiliar and frightening. Fears of injury can be greatly reduced if extra time is taken to slowly explain, demonstrate, and permit supervised practice of all aspects of the exercise prescription.
4. The fear of falling increases greatly with age because the incidence of falling does, in fact, increase with age. Injuries caused by falls often incapacitate individuals, further increasing fears. A vicious cycle is started in which declines in balance, agility, and coordination raise anxiety; movement becomes more cautious and restricted; real strength losses occur; and the chances of falling and being injured are increased. However, preventive exercises can build leg strength, balance, and coordination; walking, using stairs, and doing house and yard work have been shown to reduce the incidence of falls, the incidence of fall-related injuries, and the recovery time from injuries.[21] Further, regular practice in getting up and down from the floor safely helps to maintain balance and leg strength, and greatly reduces the anxiety around falling.[14] Teaching older adults useful tips related to getting up and down, such as using the arms to push against floor, knee, or solid object while rising from the floor, is helpful information. After an accidental fall, encourage older adults to stay on the floor (ground, sidewalk), if possible, until the shock (blood pressure drop) wears off. If they need help rising, assist them by providing firm support while rising with them. Avoid simply pulling them up.

FEARS RELATED TO BELONGING AND SOCIAL RELATIONSHIPS

1. The fear of being rejected may be triggered when the older adult's name is not known or is mispronounced, when personal contact is rushed and lacks eye contact, when it appears that inappropriate clothing has been worn, or when the older adult gets lost or becomes confused by procedures. In a group setting, these fears may be triggered if special attempts are not made to welcome new members into the group, to define procedures, and to help them get to know the other people. People whose physical shape is (or was) larger or smaller than the accepted norm (especially if this was true during childhood) often have strong fears of being noticed, and hence of being criticized and rejected. They are usually more comfortable if they are not the center of attention, at least until they feel accepted in a caring nonjudgmental way by both the exercise leader and others in a group. This type of relationship is supported if the leader sets the example by wearing comfortable, nonglamorous exercise clothing and if the leader sometimes selects exercise formations that allow people to see all the people in the room—not just the leader.
2. Ageism fears related to losing one's dignity are often triggered by disrespectful verbal and inappropriate printed communication. Hurried speech and demeaning word choice, tone, and volume are felt as disrespectful.[6] Small print size and non-age-adjusted content in printed materials feels insulting. Younger, trimmer, fitter exercise specialists can quickly make older adults feel very old if exercises are demonstrated in positions or ranges that are simply not possible for the joints of an older body. Always demonstrate movement in possible ways and ranges! A rule of thumb to follow is that the greater the difference in chronological age, in fitness level, in shape (height, width), or in body proportions (relative length of body segments), between the client and the exercise specialist, the greater the need for keen observation and modification by the specialist.[14]
3. Fears of failure can be very powerful.[13] Older adults may fear failing in the eyes of their family, themselves, or the health care provider. It helps to set easily attainable short-term goals and realistic long-term goals. In addition, environments that are sensitive to the visual, auditory, and physical comfort needs of the older adult also improve success.
4. Fears related to gender-related expectations and norms can inhibit participation. In many rural areas, and in more conservative regions of the country, there are wide differences in acceptable exercise movements between women and men. Consult local authorities before practicing in a new area.
5. Fears related to local sociocultural norms can inhibit participation. Exercise movements involving

Table 25–1: Common Exercise-Related Fears and Ways to Reduce Them

COMMON FEARS	WAYS TO REDUCE FEARS
Fear of death	Describe feelings of pain or overexertion which can be expected
Fear of loss of independence	Promote the realistic potential of preventive and rehabilitative exercise to assist in the maintenance of independence
Fear of dependence	Discuss client's choice between isolation or permitting necessary assistance from others or from mechanical aids
Fear of injury	Explain, demonstrate, and supervise all new aspects of the exercise prescription
Fear of falling	Use education and preventive exercises to reverse patterns of protective inactivity
Fear of being rejected	Establish a welcoming atmosphere to build feelings of belonging
Fear of being noticed as different	Select teaching methods which do not emphasize differences in shape or performance ability
Fear of ageism	Use language and printed materials and select exercises which do not exclude the older client
Fear of loss of dignity	Speak directly to the older client with respect and in an unhurried manner
Fear of failure	Select easily attainable short-term goals and realistic long-term goals
Fear of gender-related ostracism	Select movements and activities which meet local gender expectations of behavior
Fear of sociocultural-related ostracism	Select movements and activities which meet local sociocultural expectations of behavior
Fear of losing control	Express caring, compassion, and support for the expression of feelings
Fear of medical emergency	Openly review emergency procedures

the hips may not be acceptable. Older people may also be expected to be frail, inactive, and docile.

6. Fears related to "losing control," such as crying or expressing pain in front of others, for whatever reason, may inhibit participation.
7. Fears related to having a medical emergency in a public place may inhibit participation, particularly if the activity is to be done in a group.

Table 25–1 presents a summary of common exercise-related fears and suggestions for ways to reduce them. Fear can put major road blocks in the way of exercise compliance. Often fears seem to be triggered by what may appear to others to be relatively trivial issues. As experiences of success are the cornerstone of external motivation, attending to these common causes of fear will greatly enhance success rates. An effective way to address fear is to strive to meet the psychological needs of the client, which are discussed in the next section.

RELATIONSHIP OF PSYCHOLOGICAL NEEDS TO THE PRACTICAL APPLICATION OF THE EXERCISE PRESCRIPTION

Compliance with exercise prescriptions is greatly increased when the psychological needs of the individual are met. These needs range from needs for respect, acceptance, enjoyment, success, and understanding to needs for social support. Keeping in mind the fears discussed above, it is easy to see that psychological needs and fears are really two sides of one coin (Table 25–2). For example, the need for acceptance (positive aspect) is the other side of the fear of rejection (negative aspect). The motivation to comply with an exercise prescription is improved if these psychological needs are met, and in the process the related fears are allayed.

Older adults are often very practical. They do what they do for a reason. They want to know how and why a given exercise will benefit them. This pragmatic nature comes from having a clearer understanding of themselves and their psychological needs, and being willing to demand that their needs be met. They demand success, respect, acceptance, etc. However, the strength of a particular need varies from one individual to the next. In the client assessment process, it is important to include an assessment of these psychological needs, and to accommodate these needs and/or fears in forming the prescription.

1. *Need for respect*. Older adults, like all people, need to be patiently listened to, seen eye to eye, appropriately touched, and respectfully addressed in order not to feel diminished or discounted. Rehabilitation is often a new experience, which naturally raises questions and concerns. Yet, many people hesitate to ask questions or raise concerns. The older adult will feel supported and respected if providers ask, "What questions (or concerns) do you have?" instead of asking, "Do you have any questions?"
2. *Need for acceptance*. Acceptance includes being acknowledged as a person with specific unique needs, preferences, and personality by the professional provider. Jackson speaks of building a "bridge of trust"[16(p730)] between client and provider by speaking with a smile in supportive and encouraging ways, and providing suggestions for modifications as necessity dictates. It is important to speak in language that is easy to follow, using lay terminology and a relaxed pace of speech. Nonverbal techniques, such as active listening and attentive visual observation, also build trust as the client learns that he or she is worth being seen and heard. In short, the client needs to feel safe, and to feel accepted as a unique person.

Table 25–2: Relationship of Needs to Fears

NEEDS	RELATED FEARS
Need for respect	Fear of losing dignity, feeling worthless
Need for acceptance	Fear of rejection
Need to maintain independence	Fear of becoming dependent
Need to succeed and be competent	Fear of failure
Need for enjoyment	Fear of being bored
Need for understanding	Fear of being unable to cope (being seen as clumsy, emotional, or weak)
Need for social support	Fear of isolation, loneliness
Need for physical comfort	Fear of pain, discomfort
Need for safety	Fear of injury, death
Need for peaceful atmosphere	Fear of becoming confused, lost

3. *Need to maintain independence*. This need is often taken for granted by older adults until it is threatened. Then, it can become a strong motivator because we all prefer to be self-reliant, self-controlled, and capable of making our own decisions.[7] Hence, it is important for the client to clearly understand the relationship between successful rehabilitation and maintaining future independence. For the health provider, it is important to remember that it is the client who will make, during the execution phase, the final decision about the goals and pace of an exercise program.
4. *Need to experience competence and success*. Success and feeling competent mean feeling capable of meeting the demands of the moment, and seeing goals as individualized, reasonable and achievable.[7] It also means the provider must sense exercise-induced fears of failure, and take the initiative to stop the activity and choose an appropriate modification, which will then produce feelings of success. When these modifications are not made, the failure behaviors take over. The client gives up, loses the urge to speak or take action for oneself, and often quits.[16] The challenging task of the provider is to assist the client in setting reasonable expectations and goals for that individual to reduce the chances of experiencing failure. An additional benefit of successful exercise experiences is that the feelings of competence often seem to extend into other areas of life and family relationships.[8]

Table 25–3: Practices That Will Help Clients Meet Their Needs

NEEDS	PRACTICES
Need for respect	Listen to client.
	See client eye to eye.
	Use touch appropriately.
	Address client directly.
	Use unhurried speech and movement.
	Encourage client to ask questions.
	Give client honest assessments and realistic expectations.
Need for acceptance	Respect individual needs, preferences, personality to build trust.
	Use terms that are understandable.
	Speak with a smile in supportive ways.
	Provide an emotionally safe atmosphere.
Need to be independent	Use this powerful need to encourage compliance with rehabilitation program.
Need for success	Help client to set reasonable and achievable individualized goals.
	Support making exercise modifications before failure is experienced.
	Verbally reward success with positive affirmations.
Need for enjoyment	Focus on both the process and the product of achieving goals.
	Design activities to be enjoyable, rewarding, challenging, interesting.
Need for understanding	Show flexibility and compassion in helping client cope with losses.
Need for social support	Seek support of spouse, children, family.
	Facilitate socialization at program site.
Need for physical comfort	Modify temperature and humidity.
	Provide chairs at convenient locations.
	Provide information on appropriate clothing and shoes for activity.
	Provide cushioned equipment, mats.
Need for peaceful atmosphere	Modify music and voice volume.
	Eliminate other background noise.
	Keep exercise groups relatively small.
	Allow more space per client.
	Allow more time to respond to instructions.
	Allow for slower movement speed.

5. *Need for enjoyment*. In setting goals, the concern is with the end result, the product. It is also essential to be concerned about the process of achieving the goals. If the activity is not enjoyable, interesting, challenging, pleasurable, and immediately rewarding, there may be little motivation to maintain long-term compliance. For many clients the process is the most essential ingredient for success; the product is almost incidental, a mere bonus.
6. *Need for understanding*. Older adults experience a range of major losses: in physical and mental capabilities, of significant others, of living independence, and of social networks. Coping with loss, and with the resultant grieving process, may be overwhelming and requires our empathetic understanding. Situations requiring physical rehabilitation often occur during these higher stress times. Rehabilitation implies an additional significant loss, which often demands further adjustment to a new situation. In this crisis state, the client may not view the logic of rehabilitation as motivating in itself. It may be necessary to consider the larger picture of the client's physical and emotional needs and the social support system. An understanding provider may choose to modify standard procedures to maintain familiar daily habits and dress.[15]
7. *Need for social support*. Among older adults exercise compliance seems to be better in situations in which there is acceptance of the efficacy of exercise interventions by the community, by the doctor, by close friends, and by the family. Getting the support of a spouse, of children, or of other relatives is often an important additional external motivator.[7,26] Further, an exercise group in which friendly social interaction is facilitated can itself become an important form of social support.[4]
8. *Need for physical comfort*. Older bodies appreciate consideration! Both the temperature and humidity of pool and exercise areas should be modified. Chairs at convenient locations for resting, and for using while changing shoes, are helpful. Chairs used for exercise need to accommodate longer and shorter lower limb lengths. Information on comfortable shoes and clothing for the particular activity (which may be unfamiliar) is appreciated. Cushioned surfaces on equipment, on chairs, and on floor mats may be necessary for more sensitive joints.[14]
9. *Need for a peaceful atmosphere*. Compared to younger people, older adults are generally accustomed to less noise and activity at home. Increased levels of noise and confusion can be very distressing. In a rehabilitation setting older adults will feel more comfortable if music and voice volume are not loud, and if groups are small and separate from other activities in the facility. Small things like providing more space per participant, more time to change positions and activities, more time to respond to directions, and more time to move are all appreciated and improve performance and compliance because the experience is pleasant.

Table 25–3 summarizes the above needs and the practices that can satisfy them.

DESIGNING SUCCESSFUL EXERCISE PROGRAMS

Successful programs effect desired physiological change and gain motivated advocates for regular, long-term exercise participation. These programs, whether group or individual in nature, are safe, effective, and enjoyable. The safe and effective aspects of programs effect the actual physiological change, but it is the enjoyable aspect that produces the motivated response. There are a variety of ways to build enjoyment and motivation into programs. However, because many older clients have negative attitudes, fears, and concerns, they may seem to be "hard to reach." This population is by far the most challenging for the exercise program provider.

STRATEGIES TO COPE WITH THE HARD TO REACH

The hard to reach client needs a completely different approach from the already convinced client. The prior experience(s) of the hard to reach client with exercise or rehabilitation often involved shame, failure, or rejection. When these negative experiences date back to childhood, the client may lack any adult exercise experience. Setting short- or long-term goals is very hard because they have little basis for comparison. Goals are often set that are far too high: working too hard, too soon, too fast. Failure is common, and their self-fulfilling prophecy of failure is validated yet again.

Martin[18] reports that the hard to reach tend to be smokers, overweight, poorly motivated, and blue collar, and receive little social support from home. Their experience is "I tried it once, and it didn't work." Often they fall prey to commercial advertising, with hopes for easy, instant solutions, usually resulting in further failures.

For all these reasons, this population needs special, closely supervised treatment programs that focus on individual treatment, with primary emphasis on initial low duration of exercise, and only very gradual increases in exercise intensity. The lower intensity and duration within programs should be balanced with a higher frequency of participation opportunities. This high-frequency scheduling will also permit flexibility in meeting individual schedule needs. Select modes of exercise that are easy, adding complexity to the movements and/or activities very gradually.

During the early phases of the rehabilitation program, the primary goals must be to build feelings of confidence in self and in the body to heal; to build a social support system involving other clients, family, and employers; and to facilitate and reward regular participation. This population responds particularly well to appropriate attention and praise from leaders, fellow participants, and family for participation. During the early phases of rehabilitation, competence should not be emphasized.

For most of this population, group programs are preferable to individual programs. Small group programs are most effective because they permit the leader to see and interact with individual clients, addressing individual fears and psychological needs as noted above. Group programs should also encourage socializing between clients within the limits of safety. Enabling spouses to participate in group programs, if possible, will help develop family support for the client as well.

Making the program as easy and accessible as possible will reap long-term benefits. Select convenient locations within short travel distances with easy parking and few stairs. If possible, select times when the facility is less congested with people.

It has been found[23] that high levels of interaction between leader and client are very effective. During early phases, frequent positive reinforcement both during and after exercise builds self-confidence. Martin[18] also suggests shifting the focus of attention from feeling the physical effort to other visual images, games, or social interactions. During later phases, it is helpful to provide performance information in the form of immediate feedback to increase the level of perceived competence.

Table 25–4 gives a summary of motivational practices for hard to reach clients.

STRATEGIES TO PROMOTE TAKING RESPONSIBILITY FOR HEALING AND HEALTH

The fear of loss of independence is very strong. This fear can be used to advantage in developing strategies to promote clients' motivation to take responsibility for their healing and their health. There is a growing trend in the health care field to move this responsibility from health providers to the client by engaging the client from the very start in planning the rehabilitation process.

Include the client in the decision-making process as much as possible. During the assessment and planning phase, build in time to listen to the clients' attitudes, fears, needs, concerns, and expectations. Honestly inform them of the reasonable expectations of rehabilitation, particularly of the time and effort involved. Include them as equal and respected partners on their team. Engage them in the short- and long-term goal setting process. An injury involves some degree of loss of control of one's body, and a resultant loss of independence. Encouraging the client to maintain as much control as possible in other areas of functioning is very supportive and motivating. However, unless flexibility is built into the program, both short- and long-term goals can seem very rigid and invite failure. Older adults, in particular, have more up-and-down days because of variations in physical and emotional health, and in grieving processes. This variability needs understanding support and flexibility.

STRATEGIES FOR SETTING REASONABLE SHORT- AND LONG-TERM GOALS

Older adults are unique and pragmatic. They want to maintain functional independence as long as possible. Short-term goals will be most motivating if they are functionally

Table 25–4: Ways to Motivate Hard to Reach Clients

- Focus on very easily attainable short-term goals.
- Provide special closely supervised programs.
- Place focus on exercising in small groups.
- Select activities of lower intensity and duration, higher frequency.
- Select modes of exercise that are easy and enjoyable.
- Reward regular participation.
- Publicly recognize when individual goals are met.
- Focus more on building self-confidence, less on competence.
- Develop social support from employers and family, especially if client is female.
- Facilitate socialization among clients.
- Select accessible locations, with easy parking, short walks, few stairs.
- Provide immediate performance information only in later phases.

relevant to the client's ability to perform the activities of daily living (hygiene, self-care, mobility, house care) and to maintain contact with significant others.[12] Therefore, goal setting needs to include social aspects, cognitive aspects to associate relevancy with movement, and emotional aspects to build positive feelings, as well as the physical aspect of selecting exercise activities to achieve measurable results.

The physical aspect of goal setting involves two parts: the specific fitness goals and the preferred method of implementing these goals.[7] After the initial assessment, appropriate modes of fitness activity and methods of measurement are defined. Measurement that shows change in functional ability is more motivating than measurement that only shows changes in fitness measures.[3] The second part of the goal setting process relates to implementation (number and schedule of sessions, minutes per session, activity setting), and usually allows for a variety of choices on the part of the client.

The cognitive, social, and emotional aspects of goals enable the client to develop practical problem-solving strategies. If the client understands, cognitively, the connection between fitness and daily activities, motivation is increased because the client has the necessary information to develop new ways to perform daily activities. Similarly, if the social support of significant others is actively sought, motivation is increased. Significant others may be included in the assessment, goal-setting, and evaluation process; if appropriate, they may also be encouraged to become a part of the client's rehabilitation exercise group. Many rehabilitation programs also offer support groups, in addition to the physical rehabilitation program, which include significant others in some of the meetings. Finally, as the client builds emotional trust in the process, self-confidence and positive self-talk are developed, which provide an essential foundation for constructive real-life problem solving.

When the client sees the goal-setting and rehabilitation process as a collaborative effort between client, exercise leader, and significant others, trust, and emotional and physical safety are built into the process.[15] The client retains control of his or her healing process, which is very motivating.

STRATEGIES FOR SETTING LONG-TERM GOALS

The ultimate goal in the long term is to rehabilitate the client and to help the client develop and maintain consistent exercise habits.[3] There are several ways to support this process. The long-term rehabilitation goals need to be realistic.[21] The client needs to have as accurate an idea as possible of the time it will take to recover a definable degree of function. During the period of the rehabilitation, motivation for long-term exercise compliance is developed if there is frequent repetition of positive self-talk cues, and repetition of positive reinforcement. Self-talk cues are practical cues ("Remember to place the foot here," "Feel the muscle contract," etc.) that also build good exercise habits. It is also important to guide the client toward appropriate follow-up programs during the rehabilitation program, rather than at the end of the program.[18]

DESIGNING MOTIVATING PROGRAMMING

Each rehabilitation situation requires a specific set of individualized goals and an implementation process appropriate for the individual. However, in each case, the challenge is to make the rehabilitation as safe, as effective, and as enjoyable as possible if the client is to be motivated to reach his or her long-term goals. There are several ways to build motivation into programs, some of which are appropriate in all situations, and others of which are appropriate only in specific situations. It is important to consider the relationship of trust between the client and exercise leader, the atmosphere, the ways to build variety into the program, the risks and benefits of using music, and the ways to share information.

Trust Relationship

Building a relationship of trust between leader and client is essential. Much of the material in this chapter has emphasized ways to build compassionate and understanding relationships in which attitudes, fears, and needs are accepted and respected.

Atmosphere

The atmosphere of clinical settings and professional behaviors increase trust levels of participants. Yet, an atmosphere that is relaxed, personal, and friendly within the clinical setting is far more inviting than a cold, impersonal atmosphere. Successful programs encourage emotional expression and deliberately maintain an atmosphere of caring and support for the uniqueness of each individual. Creativity, individuality, spontaneity, and self-expression are welcomed.

When a "people come first" approach is used, programs are "people friendly" and are characterized by several distinct features. These programs provide consistency in scheduling, in personnel, and in procedures.[3] Appropriate social interaction (greeting, talking, eye contact, touching) is planned and facilitated. Appropriate polite methods are used to control socialization when it interferes with safe, effective exercise performance.[14]

The following methods can be used to increase socialization:

- In larger facilities, an open area with a welcome desk near the front door establishes an atmosphere of caring about people.
- Provide chairs near the exercise area where people can visit before and after the class.
- Encourage personnel to allow some free time before and after the class to visit with individual participants.

- Before activity starts, open the class with social activity for the whole group, which allows people to exchange names and see each other eye to eye.
- Build specific times into the program when people can exercise and talk simultaneously.
- Consider establishing a buddy system for use during class to provide physical and emotional support, if appropriate.
- Select some activities that are done in pairs, or small groups.
- Encourage socialization beyond the facility, if appropriate, by setting up a buddy system, by providing participant names and phone numbers to participants, or by planning other social activities.

The following methods can be used to control socialization:

- Talkers are often lonely people; converse with them before class.
- Limit the time when conversations might start: between exercise routines, during long explanations or demonstrations, or during long repetitious sequences.
- Increase the challenge (intensity, coordination) of the exercises.
- Change the order of activities.
- Change the exercise formation.

The atmosphere of successful programs encourages flexibility in adjusting exercise to meet individual needs. The individuals feel accepted as they are. In practical terms, this means that modifications for people with special needs (larger size, disease or disability limitations) are planned. Larger people feel accepted if exercise positions are selected that do not rely on marked hip flexion, provide an alternative to floor positions, and provide alternatives to larger-range leg and arm movements.[14] Similarly, the unique limitations of specific diseases and disabilities should be recognized and modifications provided by plan.

Variety

One of the most common complaints about exercise is that it is boring, lacking in imagination, playfulness, or pleasure. Yet, it is relatively easy to make exercise playful, imaginative, and fun by adding variety to the activities. Remember that long-term compliance is the most important goal; variety is preferable to perhaps more effective but less interesting patterns of movement.

It is desirable to give exercise variety by changing exercise positions, exercise formations, and specific muscle focus frequently. Mix stationary, moving, sitting, standing, and floor exercise positions. Vary exercise formations frequently (lines, circles, pairs, small groups, random spacing). Change muscle focus, such as alternating leg exercises with arm exercises. Avoid long repetitious sequences by doing fewer repetitions in a given set; shift to another exercise, and then return for another set of the original exercise. Alter the order of activities, and include some free activity time. Many exercises can seem quite new if small modifications are made in arm, hand, leg, or body positions.

Although many of these suggestions tend to draw attention away from the basic exercise movement itself, it is effective with some movements to focus total attention on the feeling of the movement. Muscle stretching and joint range of motion movements feel good, assuming there is no tissue injury, and the preferred slow, controlled movement tempo allows total attention to body sensations. Bringing full attention to the feel of muscle strengthening exercises can also be motivating. An extension of this total attention (or mindfulness) can be broadened to include larger parts of the body. For example, a shoulder exercise can be felt from the feet, the base of the spine, and out to the finger tips.

In some situations music and supplementary equipment are used to add variety to programs. Music is probably the most popular way to add enjoyment to a program. There are risks and benefits to using music, which will be considered below. There is also a wide range of attractive and affordable supplementary equipment available (balls, weights, resistance bands, wands, sticks, etc.). These add color and aesthetics and invite playfulness. Once the game box has been opened with supplementary equipment, leaders quickly discover the endless variety that games, simple dances, imagery, and group activities can add to a program.[9,10,14]

Risks and Benefits of Using Music

Music can be an important and motivating addition to an exercise program.[3,14,18] However, before including music the risks and benefits should be considered.

In some situations, music can increase injury risk. As hearing acuity declines with age, music interferes with the participant's ability to hear instructions. In situations in which visibility is an additional problem (as in floor and water exercises), music may need to be eliminated for safety reasons. The use of background music is not advisable in situations in which participants need to hear instructions because the music becomes a confusing addition to the total sound environment. Highly energetic music with strong rhythms can increase the risk of overdoing because the participant may be motivated to move at a higher intensity or longer duration than is safe.

It has become quite popular for exercise leaders to play music at a high volume (greater than 80 decibels), and to use a microphone to give instructions. High sound volume is often painful to older ears, and the loudness increases anxiety levels by triggering the fight or flight response. During an exercise class, participants should be able to speak to each other in normal conversational levels (60 to 80 decibels) and be heard by each other. The leader should also be able to hear participants.

On the other hand, there certainly are many benefits to using music. Music touches the soul. It adds pleasure and enjoyment to an activity. Therefore, it is very important to select styles of music that appeal to the older participant, and to utilize a variety of styles to appeal to the normal diversity of musical tastes among older adults. Besides older and contemporary popular music, show tunes, big-band, ragtime, Dixieland jazz, marches, traditional dance and folk music, country-western, semiclassical music, and some rock music are all suitable. It is also motivating to select music that evokes different emotional responses (joyfulness, assertiveness, peacefulness, playfulness, sensuality) and different movement responses (light, bold, carefree, precise, romantic, lilting, jazzy, powerful).

Music can also be used to increase the effectiveness of the exercise. By carefully selecting appropriate music tempos, the leader can encourage fuller, more complete movement. Further, neuromuscular coordination is challenged when a participant is asked to move in time with the music.

From a practical standpoint, the simple structural form of most exercise music allows it to be used as a timing and counting device. The leader can let the music do the counting as an alternative to providing verbal cues, which are more difficult to hear and follow. This also allows the leader to focus on nonverbal visual cues, which are easier to follow and more motivating.

Education

Sharing information has educational value, but it is also an important way to build self-esteem, respect, and trust. Successful program leaders recognize that they are both teachers and learners. The experience of every participant is unique and has the potential of providing useful information to the leader and to other participants. An atmosphere that supports this open dialogue needs to be planned into the program. Some participants will be very vocal even in a large group situation; others prefer sharing their wisdom in more private ways.

Peer comments can be very motivating because they often address common problems. Leading questions can help to draw out this information, such as: "What motivates you to exercise?" "Which way do you prefer to do (a particular) exercise?" "Which exercise do you find hard? painful? ineffective?" "When you do (a particular) exercise, where do you feel it?" "When you don't feel like exercising, how do you overcome that?" "How do you reward yourself for regular attendance?" "Which exercises or physical activities do you really enjoy?"

Obviously, as health professionals, we have important information to share with participants about health habits, appropriate exercise, correct performance patterns, and the benefits of exercise. Older adults also appreciate learning

Table 25–5: Characteristics of Motivating Exercise Programs

AREA OF CONCERN	CHARACTERISTICS
Building trust	Individual attitudes, fears, needs, and personalities are respected.
	Individuals are treated with compassion and understanding.
Atmosphere	A professional but friendly, relaxed, personal, and caring atmosphere is maintained.
	Emotional expression is supported.
	Creativity, spontaneity, individuality, and self-expression are welcomed.
	Programs provide consistency in scheduling, in personnel, and in procedures.
	Appropriate social interaction is facilitated.
	Social interaction is politely controlled when necessary.
	Program allows flexibility to modify activities for people with special needs.
Variety	Activities are planned which are safe, effective, and as playful, imaginative, and enjoyable as possible.
	A variety of exercise formations, exercise positions, and exercises are used.
	Long repetitious sequences are avoided.
	Supplementary equipment is used.
Music	Risks and benefits of music use are considered for each situation.
	Music is used when appropriate.
Education	Open dialogue between leader and clients is encouraged.
	Peer comments are solicited and respected.
	Current information related to health habits, appropriate exercise, and benefits of exercise is given to clients.
	Habitual, faulty movement patterns are corrected.
	Exercises which can effectively ameliorate common complaints are taught.
	Efficient body mechanics of the activities of daily living are reviewed.

about exercise movements that correct common complaints and exercise movements that, conversely, are likely to cause injury. Numerous authors[14,16,17] have observed that over a lifetime many habitual movement patterns may seem familiar and comfortable but are ineffective, and sometimes even cause pain or injury. Rehabilitation exercise should include observation and retraining of these faulty movement patterns. For example, teaching people how to breathe, sit, stand, rise from a chair or from the floor, walk, push, pull, lift, and carry objects, correcting faulty patterns, can all be very helpful. Older adults enjoy gaining information about basic body mechanics, and increasing their level of total body awareness.

Table 25–5 summarizes these five areas of concern for exercise programs and the motivational characteristics that address them.

Finally, older adults generally have a more wholistic view of themselves. Rehabilitation programs that treat more than the injured part are most successful. It is important to treat the injured part, its related uninjured part, both parts in relationship to the whole physical body, and the physical body in relationship with all the other aspects of self.

SUMMARY

Successful rehabilitation depends on a team effort of the client and the health provider. This effort starts with an exercise prescription and an assessment of the attitudes, fears, and the psychosocial, cognitive, and physical needs of the client. Because each client is unique, the motivational techniques a provider selects should be based on respectful listening to the client and keen observation of the client. Although including motivation as a part of the provider's responsibility makes the provider's task more challenging, the resulting successful outcomes reward both the client and provider.

REFERENCES

1. Allman JE. Exercise in sports medicine. In: Basmajian JV, ed. *Therapeutic Exercise*. 4th ed. Baltimore: Williams & Wilkins, 1984:485–518.
2. *American Heritage Dictionary of the English Language*. 3rd ed. Boston: Houghton Mifflin, 1992.
3. Chase V. Motivation and compliance in lifelong exercise programs. *CUPA Journal*. 1989;40(4):15–17.
4. Clark BA. Principles of physical activity programming for the older adult. In: Leslie DK, ed. *Mature Stuff: Physical Activity for the Older Adult*. Reston, VA: American Alliance for Health, Physical Education, Recreation, and Dance, 1989:133–145.
5. Daniel C, Kincaid J, Mendell R, Gray H. Leisure and recreation programming. In: Leslie DK, ed. *Mature Stuff: Physical Activity for the Older Adult*. Reston, VA: American Alliance for Health, Physical Education, Recreation, and Dance, 1989:159–177.
6. Demont ME, Peatman NL. Communicating values, and the quality of life. In: Guccione AA, ed. *Geriatric Physical Therapy*. St. Louis: CV Mosby, 1993:21–32.
7. Duda J. Motivating older adults. *Journal of Physical Education, Recreation, and Dance*. 1991;62(7):44–48.
8. Emery CF. Perceived change among participants in an exercise program for older adults. *Gerontologist*. 1990;30:516–521.
9. Ensign C. Dance for the older adult. In: Leslie DK, ed. *Mature Stuff: Physical Activity for the Older Adult*. Reston, VA: American Alliance for Health, Physical Education, Recreation, and Dance, 1989:221–240.
10. Fisher PP. *More Than Movement for Fit and Frail Older Adults: Creative Activities for the Body, Mind, and Spirit*. Baltimore: Health Professions, 1995.
11. Flynn M, Fash V. *Illinois White House Conference on Aging: Background Papers*. Springfield, IL: Illinois Department of Aging, 1981.
12. Guccione AA. Functional assessment of the elderly. In: Guccione AA, ed. *Geriatric Physical Therapy*. St. Louis: CV Mosby, 1993:113–123.
13. Heitmann HM. The learning environment and instructional considerations. In: Leslie DK, ed. *Mature Stuff: Physical Activity for the Older Adult*. Reston, VA: American Alliance for Health, Physical Education, Recreation, and Dance, 1989:119–130.
14. Hooke AP, Zoller M. *Active Older Adults in the YMCA: A Resource Manual*. Champaign, IL: Human Kinetics, 1992.
15. Jackson OL. Basic principles in rehabilitation: A conceptual model. In: Jackson OL, ed. *Therapeutic Considerations for the Elderly*. New York: Churchill Livingstone, 1987:1–22.
16. Jackson OL. Adapting physical therapy intervention in the elderly. In: Payton OD, ed. *Manual of Physical Therapy*. New York: Churchill Livingstone, 1989:723–734.

17. Johnson GW. *Progressive exercise program: A model approach for working with elderly patients*. In: Jackson OL, ed. *Therapeutic Considerations for the Elderly*. New York: Churchill Livingstone, 1987:197–210.
18. Martin JE. Strategies to enhance patient compliance. In: Franklin BA, Timmins GS, eds. *Exercise in Modern Medicine*. Baltimore: Williams & Wilkins, 1989:280–291.
19. Ostrow A. *Physical Activity and the Older Adult: Psychological Perspectives*. Princeton, NJ: Princeton Book Company, 1984.
20. Patrick K, Sallis JF, Long B, Calfas KJ, Wooten W, Heath G, Pratt M. A *new tool for encouraging activity*. *Physician And Sportsmedicine*. 1994;22(11):45–52.
21. Pollock CL. Breaking the risk of falls. *Physician and Sportsmedicine*. 1992;20(11):146–156.
22. Preisinger E, Alacamlioglu Y, Pils K, Saradeth T, Schneider B. Therapeutic exercise in the prevention of bone loss. A controlled trial with women after menopause. *American Journal of Physical Medicine and Rehabilitation*. 1995;74(2):120–123.
23. Rutherford WJ, Corbin CB, Chase LA. Factors influencing intrinsic motivation toward physical activity. *Health Values: Health Behavior, Education and Promotion*. 1992;16(5):19–24.
24. Sarno JE. Therapeutic exercise for back pain. In: Basmajian JV, ed. *Therapeutic Exercise*. 4th ed. Baltimore: Williams & Wilkins, 1984:441–463.
25. Stamford BA. Exercise and the elderly. In: Pandolf KB, ed. *Exercise and Sport Science Review*, vol 16. New York: Macmillan, 1988.
26. Wankel LM. Decision making and social support strategies for increasing exercise involvement. *Journal of Cardiac Rehabilitation*. 1984;4:143–152.

Index

A

Note: Page numbers followed by f or t refer to figures or tables, respectively.

B

C

D

G

H

I

J

K

L

P

Q

R

S

T